R. Gupta's®

Popular Master Guide

NATIONAL TESTING AGENCY (NTA)

CUET-UG

Common University Entrance Test for
Under Graduate Courses/Programmes

B.A. (Hons.)

ENGLISH

Entrance Exam

by

RPH Editorial Board

2027
EDITION

RAMESH PUBLISHING HOUSE, NEW DELHI

CUET Guidance Note For B.A. (Hons.) ENGLISH Aspirants

Dear students choosing the Right CUET paper combination is paramount for your chosen career. The distinction between a correct combination and a hasty choice can influence your chances of admission. This book specifically contains the CUET paper combination vital for your admission. But also note here that different Universities might have slightly different combinations and they might add one or more subject – papers requirement which need to be opted and studied by you from your own resources. So we advice you to refer the latest university notification mentioning the paper – combinations required for admission in your chosen university.

Published by
O.P. Gupta *for* Ramesh Publishing House

Admin. Office
12-H, New Daryaganj Road, Opp. Officers' Mess,
New Delhi-110002 ✆ 23275224, 23245124

E-mail: info@rameshpublishinghouse.com
For Online Shopping: www.rameshpublishinghouse.com

Showroom
• Balaji Market, Nai Sarak, Delhi-6 ✆ 23282525 📱 9354373464
• 4457, Nai Sarak, Delhi-110006

Book Code: R-2589

ISBN: 978-93-5477-444-7

Price: ₹ 695

Printed at: Deepak Offset, Delhi

CONTENTS

PREVIOUS YEARS' PAPERS (With explanatory answers)

ENGLISH

GENERAL TEST

★★★★★

Previous Years' Paper

Common University Entrance Test for UG Programmes

CUET-UG—ENGLISH LANGUAGE

Entrance Exam, 2026

(Exam held on 20-05-2026)

Subject Code : 101

1. Rearrange the following phrases to form a meaningful sentence:

A. to foreign universities is that only inferior
B. to make quick money by imparting sub-standard education
C. universities may enter into the Indian education system
D. the common objection to the opening up

Choose the ***correct*** answer from the options given below:

1. C, A, B, D
2. D, A, C, B
3. C, B, A, D
4. D, B, A, C

2. Complete the sentences given in List-I with the correct phrasal verbs given in List-II.

List-I (Sentence)	List-II (Phrasal verbs)
A. The police asked the people to _____ from the injured man.	I. stand by
B. Rahul always used to _____ for his younger brother in the playground.	II. stand down
C. The CEO of the company decided to _____ from his post because of the scandal.	III. stand back
D. I always knew that Juhi would _____ me, come what may.	IV. stand up

Choose the ***correct*** answer from the options given below:

1. A-I, B-II, C-III, D-IV
2. A-III, B-IV, C-II, D-I
3. A-II, B-III, C-IV, D-I
4. A-IV, B-I, C-III, D-II

3. Choose the grammatically correct sentences from the options below:

A. He reached the office when the manager spoke to the client.
B. He reached the office when the manager was speaking to the client.
C. He reached the office when the manager had been speaking to the client.
D. He reached the office when the manager had just finished speaking to the client.

Choose the ***correct*** answer from the option given below:

1. B and D only
2. A and D only
3. B and C only
4. A and C only

4. Fill in the blank with the correct option from the ones given below:

The scientist proposed _____ theory that challenged everything we knew.

1. an uppity
2. an upright
3. an uproarious
4. a groundbreaking

5. Select the correct word that best conveys the meaning of the following sentence from the options given below:

One who feeds on human flesh.

1. Cannibal
2. Carnivorous
3. Omnivorous
4. Herbivorous

6. Fill in the blanks given in List I with the appropriate words given in List-II:

List-I	List-II
A. She maintained a _____ attitude even in the face of repeated failures.	I. fragile
B. Her _____ tone conveyed genuine concern rather than mere formality.	II. resilient
C. She suffers as her _____ ego gets broken easily enough.	III. perfunctory
D. Their efforts for sustainable living were too _____ to make any difference	IV. heartfelt

Choose the ***correct*** answer from the options given below:

1. A-I, B-II, C-III, D-IV
2. A-IV, B-II, C-III, D-I
3. A-III, B-I, C-IV, D-II
4. A-II, B-IV, C-I, D-III

1. 2	**2.** 2	**3.** 1	**4.** 4	**5.** 1	**6.** 4

7. Choose the correct antonym of the underlined word in the following sentence from the given options:

The boy's illness **enervated** the whole community.

1. worried
2. enhanced
3. energised
4. weakened

8. Fill in the blank with the correctly spelled word from the options given below:

He dreams of becoming a successful ______ and starting his own venture.

1. entrepreneur 2. enterprenor
3. enterpreneur 4. entreprenior

9. Choose the correct reported construction of the given sentence:

It surprised us that he said, "I won't do it".

1. It surprised us that he said that he would not do it.
2. We were surprised that he said he will not do it.
3. He exclaimed with a surprise that he will not do it.
4. We looked with a surprise when he said he won't do it.

10. Fill in the blank with the most appropriate word from the options given below:

Despite the conflicting circumstances, she continued to speak _____, keeping her thoughts steady and grounded.

1. furtively 2. falteringly
3. composedly 4. conspicuously

11. Choose the correct word to complete the following sentence.

The doctor who particularly looks at ailing infants/children is referred to as _____.

1. Paediatrician 2. Pedantic
3. Philologist 4. Paedophile

12. Rearrange the following phrases to form a meaningful sentence:

A. valuable and timeless in our ancient tradition
B. with what is good and valuable in modern thought
C. one of the biggest responsibilities of the educated
D. women today is to synthesise what has been

Choose the ***correct*** answer from the options given below:

1. A, B, C, D 2. B, A, C, D
3. C, D, B, A 4. C, D, A, B

13. Rearrange the following phrases to make a meaningful sentence:

A. old ones, it also destroys some old truths and
B. the way of men's thinking and their lives
C. discovers new truths that thereby upsets
D. science does not merely add new truths to

Choose the ***correct*** answer from the options given below:

1. B, C, A, D 2. D, A, C, B
3. B, A, D, C 4. C, B, D, A

14. Fill in the blank with the most appropriate word from the options given below:

The council zeroed down on the _____ proposal after hours of serious deliberations.

1. most promising
2. promised
3. promise
4. most best

15. Match the phrases given in List-I with their meanings in List-II:

List-I	List-II
A. Pull up	I. to succeed
B. Pull through	II. to stop or scold someone
C. Pull off	III. to demolish
D. Pull down	IV. to recover from something

Choose the ***correct*** answer from the options given below:

1. A-II, B-IV, C-I, D-III
2. A-I, B-II, C-III, D-IV
3. A-IV, B-II, C-I, D-III
4. A-III, B-IV, C-I, D-II

16. Fill in the blank with the most appropriate option in the given sentence:

My sister _____ me only once or twice since the time she has been living in Cherapunji.

1. was messaging
2. has messaged
3. has been messaging
4. messages

17. Select the word from the given options that is most similar to the meaning of the underlined word.

We face the **arduous** days that lie before us in the warm courage of national unity.

1. promising
2. hopeful
3. difficult
4. smooth

7. 3	**8.** 1	**9.** 1	**10.** 3	**11.** 1	**12.** 4
13. 2	**14.** 1	**15.** 1	**16.** 2	**17.** 3	

18. Match the idioms/proverbs given in List-I with their meanings in List-II.

List-I	List-II
A. Lost in the clouds	I. Ruined
B. Go to the dogs	II. Confused
C. A fly in the ointment	III. Share the cost
D. To go Dutch	IV. Something trifling that mars the whole

Choose the ***correct*** answer from the options given below:

1. A-IV, B-II, C-I, D-III
2. A-III, B-IV, C-I, D-II
3. A-II, B-I, C-IV, D-III
4. A-I, B-III, C-II, D-IV

19. Select the word from the given options that is most similar in meaning to the word:

Gregarious

1. Introvert 2. Serious
3. Social 4. Sarcastic

20. Fill in the blank with the most appropriate word from the options given below:

_____ the task seemed daunting at first, the team managed to complete it within the stipulated time.

1. Although 2. Inspite of
3. Since 4. Nonetheless

21. Select the word that is the exact opposite of the word **Antagonism** in meaning from the given options:

1. Hostility 2. Cordiality
3. Animosity 4. Enmity

22. Match the expressions given in List-I with the correct figures of speech they illustrate given in List-II.

List-I	List-II
A. Visible darkness.	I. simile
B. She is the star of our family.	II. metaphor
C. I spent a sleepless night.	III. oxymoron
D. That baby boy is like a teddy bear.	IV. transferred epithet

Choose the ***correct*** answer from the options given below:

1. A-III, B-II, C-IV, D-I
2. A-I, B-II, C-III, D-IV
3. A-I, B-II, C-IV, D-III
4. A-III, B-IV, C-I, D-II

23. Fill in the blank with the most appropriate word from the options given below:

She agreed to mentor the team despite her _____ taxing schedule.

1. scantily 2. extremely
3. hardly 4. extravagantly

24. Select the word that best conveys the meaning of the following sentence:

A political or philosophical theory that advocates the elimination of all forms of government.

1. Existentialism 2. Totalitarianism
3. Anarchism 4. Utilitarianism

25. Choose the option that best describes the meaning of the underlined phrase from the options given below:

Though it was his maiden speech, he **brought down the house** with his dry humour.

1. received overwhelming applause
2. received criticism
3. was embarrassed
4. was thanked profusely

26. Select the grammatically correct sentences from the options given below:

A. Please stop making so much noise or I report you to the supervisor.
B. I work hard so that I may become financially independent.
C. An imminent event is one that will happen soon.
D. I'm not certain, but I guess it's raining later this afternoon.

Choose the ***correct*** answer from the options given below:

1. B and D only 2. A and C only
3. C and D only 4. B and C only

27. Fill in the blank with the most appropriate word from the options given below:

Did you meet your friends _____ the party in the clubhouse?

1. in 2. at
3. on 4. for

28. Choose the correctly spelled word from the options given below:

1. Mischivious 2. Mischeivious
3. Mischevious 4. Mischievous

29. Rearrange the following phrases to form a meaningful sentence:

A. the conclusion of the
B. we have not come to
C. immutability of this principle
D. simply through good motives

Choose the ***correct*** answer from the options given below:

1. A, C, B, D 2. D, B, A, C
3. B, A, C, D 4. C, B, D, A

18. 3	**19.** 3	**20.** 1	**21.** 2	**22.** 1	**23.** 2
24. 3	**25.** 1	**26.** 4	**27.** 2	**28.** 4	**29.** 3

30. Choose the correct options as the meaning of the given proverb:

Handsome is as handsome does.

1. Man's goodness lies in his good deeds and not in the good looks.
2. Handsome looks are good indeed.
3. Good looks are very important.
4. Good looks are as important as good work.

31. Match the same sounding words given in List-I with their meanings in List-II:

List-I (Words)	List-II (Meanings)
A. Wither	I. the condition of the atmosphere at a particular time
B. Whither	II. fade away
C. Weather	III. if
D. Whether	IV. direction

Choose the *correct* answer from the options given below:

1. A-I, B-II, C-III, D-IV
2. A-II, B-IV, C-I, D-III
3. A-I, B-III, C-IV, D-II
4. A-III, B-IV, C-I, D-II

32. Fill in the blank with the most appropriate word from the options given below:

When he alighted _____ the car, he was welcomed with open arms by his friends.

1. about
2. on
3. from
4. of

33. Choose the correct passive construction for the given sentence.

People were telling me all the time what to do and I didn't enjoy it.

1. All the time people were telling me what to do and I didn't like it.
2. I didn't enjoy being told all the time what to do.
3. I was told by people all the time what to do and I don't enjoy it.
4. I didn't enjoy people telling me what to do.

34. Identify the examples of the correct use of Metaphor from the following options:

A. He is the vulture of the state.
B. She behaved like a child.
C. To err is human, to forgive divine.
D. The waves thundered on the shore

Choose the *correct* answer from the options given below:

1. A and B only
2. C and D only
3. B and C only
4. A and D only

35. Choose the most appropriate option to complete the given sentence:

He is very able and proficient; _____ he works hard.

1. moreover
2. nevertheless
3. otherwise
4. however

36. Select the word from the given options that is most similar to the meaning of the word:

OFFSPRING

1. Forefather
2. Progenitor
3. Progeny
4. Ancestor

37. Fill in the blank with the most appropriate word from the options given below:

_____, there is a snake under the bush.

1. Look for
2. Look upto
3. Look out
4. Look into

38. Rearrange the following phrases to form a meaningful sentence:

A. next to our own in a gesture of expansive relaxation
B. in a motion that imitated exactly that way you or I
C. would bring out an arm and place it on the back of the chair
D. she turned and brought her arm onto the tarpaulin

Choose the *correct* answer from the options given below:

1. B, A, C, D
2. D, B, C, A
3. B, A, D, C
4. A, B, D, C

39. Fill in the blanks in given in List-I with the most appropriate words from List-II.

List-I	List-II
A. Ritu did not get involved in the scandal on account of her friend's _____.	I. suite
B. He filed a civil _____ against his siblings.	II. counsel
C. Some of the members of the _____ walked out in protest during the session.	III. suit
D. He surprised his wife by booking a special _____ on their anniversary.	IV. council

Choose the *correct* answer from the options given below:

1. A-II, B-III, C-IV, D-I
2. A-I, B-II, C-III, D-IV
3. A-III, B-II, C-IV, D-I
4. A-III, B-IV, C-I, D-II

30. 1	**31.** 2	**32.** 3	**33.** 2	**34.** 4	**35.** 1	**36.** 3	**37.** 3	**38.** 2	**39.** 1

40. Choose the option that is the opposite of the given word:

Rescind

1. Abrogate
2. Delimit
3. Continue
4. Reschedule

Direction (Qs. No. 41 to 45): *Read the passage and answer the questions that follow:*

In the ancient city of Varanasi, Arjun found his world transformed one monsoon afternoon. Born into a family of hardworking labourers, he was expected to follow in his father's footsteps, yet, Arjun harboured an unspoken passion for art that no one knew about. As dark clouds gathered and the first raindrops fell, he wandered through the narrow lanes of the old city, seeking solace from the predictable rhythm of life.

That day, as he took refuge under a vibrant awning in a bustling market, Arjun encountered an old painter named Raghav. With paint splattered hands and eyes that shimmered with decades of experience, Raghav noticed a spark in Arjun's eyes. He invited Arjun into his humble studio where canvases whispered stories of love, loss and hope. Inspired by Raghav's gentle mentorship, Arjun discovered his own unique style, blending tradition with innovation.

Over the time, his artwork became a mirror reflecting the emotions of the city and his reputation grew. Arjun's journey from a reluctant son to an emerging artist was not without hardship. Yet every challenge became a brushstroke in the masterpiece of his life. Eventually, his creations graced galleries beyond Varanasi, uniting cultures and hearts. In every piece, Arjun celebrated the resilience of the human spirit, proving that passion and perseverance can transform even the most ordinary life into a vibrant work of art.

His journey filled with unexpected lessons and creative breakthroughs taught him that every struggle offered a chance to begin anew, inspiring his art with hope and transformation.

41. Determine the primary theme illustrated in the narrative.

1. The inevitability of hardship for those who choose artistic paths for fulfilling their dreams.
2. The conflict between urban modernity and ancient traditions in daily life that acts as a hindrance in one's path.
3. The fleeting beauty of monsoon afternoons in ancient cities encourage people to follow their passion.
4. The transformative influence of mentorship and following one's passion despite adversity.

42. Which word in the passage means: lively

1. Resilience
2. Shimmer
3. Humble
4. Vibrant

43. Interpret the change in Arjun's outlook on life through the passage:

1. He learned to view every hardship as an essential element in his personal masterpiece.
2. He became indifferent to challenges and avoided confronting any obstacles whatsoever.
3. He rejected the essential idea of change and chose to adhere strictly to his old routine.
4. He focussed solely on attaining commercial success, disregarding personal growth and art.

44. Deduce the message the author conveys about overcoming obstacles:

1. Struggles are insurmountable barriers that only worsen one's chance of success.
2. Every challenge offers an opportunity to grow and transform one's life with resilience.
3. Only those with privileged background can successfully overcome life's obstacles.
4. Obstacles invariably lead to failure, regardless of personal determination or passion.

45. Evaluate the impact of Arjun's artwork as described in the passage:

1. His art remained confined within the narrow lanes of Varanasi with little recognition.
2. His work was not received well leading to further isolation from society.
3. His creations resonated deeply, uniting diverse cultures and inspiring many people.
4. His art was solely a personal hobby that never gained any public attention though it gave him a lot of satisfaction.

Direction (Qs. No. 46 to 50): *Read the given passage carefully and answer the questions that follow:*

An excerpt from 'Life of Pi'

I wept like a child. It was not because I was overcome at having survived my ordeal, though I was. Nor was it the presence of my brothers and sisters, though that too was very moving. I was weeping because Richard Parker had left me so unceremoniously. What a terrible thing it is to botch a farewell. I am a person who believes in form, in the harmony of order. Where we can, we must give a meaningful shape. For example—I wonder—could you tell my jumbled story in exactly one hundred chapters, not one more, not one less? I'll tell you, that's one thing I hate about my nickname, the way that number runs on forever. It's important in life to conclude things

40. 3	**41.** 4	**42.** 4	**43.** 1	**44.** 2	**45.** 3

properly. Only then you can let go. Otherwise you are left with words you should have said but never did, and your heart is heavy with remorse. That bungled goodbye hurts me to this day. I wish so much that I'd had one last look at him in the lifeboat, that I'd provoked him a little, so that I was on his mind. I wish I had said to him then— yes, I know, to a tiger, but still— I wish I had said, "Richard Parker, it's over. We have survived. Can you believe it? I owe you more gratitude than I can express. I couldn't have done it without you. I would like to say it formally: Richard Parker, thank you. Thank you for saving my life. And now go where you must. You have known the confined freedom of a zoo most of your life; now you will know the free confinement of a jungle. I wish you all the best with it. Watch out for Man. He is not your friend. But I hope you remember me as a friend."

(An excerpt from 'Life of Pi')

46. Who do you think Richard Parker is in the passage?
1. A celebrity
2. An elder brother
3. An imaginary friend
4. A wild animal

47. According to the passage, the nararator's pain for the 'bungled goodbye' is symbolic of the universal human tendency to:
1. overthink the past relationships
2. seek validation from others even from animals
3. attach deep meaning to goodbyes
4. avoid confronting difficult situations

48. The protagonist broke into tears:
1. as he had accomplished his goal
2. when he saw his siblings
3. when Richard Parker left abruptly
4. as Richard Parker wanted a ceremonial exit

49. What does the narrator dislike about his nickname?
1. It's difficult to pronounce
2. His friends bullied him for this
3. The number in it goes on forever
4. Richard Parker didn't like it

50. The narrator experiences _____ when he recalls how Richard Parker was instrumental in saving his life multiple times in that arduous adventure.
1. pain 2. gratitude
3. revitality 4. enervation

EXPLANATORY ANSWERS

1. "The common objection to the opening up to foreign universities is that only inferior universities may enter into the Indian education system to make quick money by imparting sub-standard education." The arrangement starts logically with the subject in phrase D, followed by phrase A which introduces the objection. Phrase C completes the main idea by stating that inferior universities may enter the Indian education system, and phrase B concludes the sentence by explaining their motive. Thus, the sequence D, A, C, B forms a grammatically correct and meaningful sentence.

2. **A. The police asked the people to stand back from the injured man – III. stand back – "Stand back"** means to move away or keep a safe distance. It correctly fits the situation where people are asked to stay away from the injured man.

B. Rahul always used to stand up for his younger brother in the playground – IV. stand up – "Stand up for" means to defend or support someone. It correctly describes Rahul protecting and supporting his younger brother.

C. The CEO of the company decided to stand down from his post because of the scandal – II. stand down – "Stand down" means to resign or step down from a position. It appropriately completes the sentence.

D. I always knew that Juhi would stand by me, come what may – I. stand by – "Stand by" means to remain loyal and support someone in every situation. It best suits the given context.

3. **B. He reached the office when the manager was speaking to the client** – This sentence is grammatically correct because the **past continuous tense** ("was speaking") shows that the manager's conversation was in progress when he reached the office.

D. He reached the office when the manager had just finished speaking to the client – This sentence is also correct because the **past perfect tense** ("had just finished") indicates that the manager completed the conversation immediately before his arrival.

A. He reached the office when the manager spoke to the client – This sentence does not clearly express the intended sequence of the two past actions, making it less appropriate in the given context.

C. He reached the office when the manager had been speaking to the client – The **past perfect continuous tense** is not suitable here because it emphasizes the duration of an action rather than the simple sequence of events.

Therefore, only sentences B and D are grammatically correct, making Option 1 the correct answer.

46. 4	**47.** 3	**48.** 3	**49.** 3	**50.** 2

4. The adjective **"groundbreaking"** means innovative, original, or introducing completely new ideas. Since the sentence refers to a scientific theory that challenged existing knowledge, **"a groundbreaking theory"** is the most appropriate and meaningful expression. The other options—**uppity** (arrogant), **upright** (honest or vertical), and **uproarious** (very funny or noisy)—do not fit the context of a scientific theory. Therefore, **Option 4** is the correct answer.

5. A **cannibal** is a person or animal that eats the flesh of other human beings. The term specifically refers to feeding on **human flesh**, which exactly matches the meaning given in the question. The other options are incorrect because **carnivorous** refers to flesh-eating animals in general, **omnivorous** refers to organisms that eat both plants and animals, and **herbivorous** refers to organisms that feed only on plants. Therefore, **Option 1** is the correct answer.

6. **A. She maintained a resilient attitude even in the face of repeated failures – II. resilient** – The word **resilient** means able to recover quickly from difficulties or setbacks. It correctly describes a person who remains strong and positive despite repeated failures.

   B. Her heartfelt tone conveyed genuine concern rather than mere formality – IV. heartfelt – The word **heartfelt** means sincere and deeply felt. It appropriately describes a tone that expresses genuine concern and emotion.

   C. She suffers as her fragile ego gets broken easily enough – I. fragile – The word **fragile** means easily damaged or hurt. It correctly describes an ego that is easily affected by criticism or disappointment.

   D. Their efforts for sustainable living were too perfunctory to make any difference – III. perfunctory – The word **perfunctory** means carried out with little interest, care, or effort. It suitably describes efforts that are superficial and ineffective.

   Therefore, the correct matching is A-II, B-IV, C-I, D-III, making Option 4 the correct answer.

7. The word **"enervated"** means weakened, exhausted, or deprived of physical or mental strength. Therefore, its opposite or antonym is **"energised",** which means filled with energy, strength, enthusiasm, or vitality. In the given sentence, the boy's illness **enervated** the whole community, implying that it made everyone feel weak and discouraged. The other options are incorrect because **worried** expresses anxiety, **enhanced** means improved or increased, and **weakened** is actually a synonym of **enervated**, not its antonym. Therefore, **Option 3** is the correct answer.

8. The word **"entrepreneur"** is the correct spelling and refers to a person who establishes, manages, and takes the financial risks of a business or enterprise. It fits the sentence perfectly because the person dreams of becoming successful and starting his own venture. The other options are incorrect as they are misspelled forms of the word and are not accepted in standard English usage. Therefore, **Option 1** is the correct answer.

9. This is the correct reported form of the given sentence because the reporting verb **"said"** is in the past tense, requiring the future form **"won't"** to change to **"would not."** The pronoun **"I"** is correctly changed to **"he"** to match the speaker, while the rest of the sentence remains grammatically accurate. The other options either fail to follow the rules of tense change, use incorrect reporting structures, or contain grammatical errors. Therefore, **Option 1** is the correct answer.

10. The word **"composedly"** means calmly, confidently, and with self-control, especially in difficult or stressful situations. In the sentence, despite conflicting circumstances, she continued to speak in a steady and balanced manner, making **"composedly"** the most suitable choice. The other options are incorrect because **furtively** means secretly, **falteringly** means hesitantly or with uncertainty, and **conspicuously** means in a way that attracts attention. Therefore, **Option 3** is the correct answer.

11. A **paediatrician** is a medical doctor who specializes in the diagnosis, treatment, and care of infants, children, and adolescents. Since the sentence refers to a doctor who particularly treats ailing infants and children, this is the most appropriate term. The other options are incorrect because **pedantic** refers to someone excessively concerned with minor details, **philologist** is a scholar of language, and **paedophile** refers to a person with a criminal sexual interest in children. Therefore, **Option 1** is the correct answer.

12. The meaningful sentence is: **"One of the biggest responsibilities of the educated women today is to synthesise what has been valuable and timeless in our ancient tradition with what is good and valuable in modern thought"**. The sentence begins with **C**, which introduces the subject, and **D** completes it by identifying **educated women today** and introducing the verb phrase **"is to synthesise what has been"**. Phrase **A** correctly completes **"what has been"** by adding **"valuable and timeless in our ancient tradition"**, while phrase **B** completes the comparison with **"what is good and valuable in modern thought"**. This arrangement is grammatically accurate, logically connected, and conveys the intended meaning completely. Therefore, **Option 4** is the correct answer.

13. The meaningful sentence is: **"Science does not merely add new truths to old ones, it also destroys some old truths and discovers new truths that thereby upsets the way of men's thinking and their lives"**. The sentence begins with **D**, introducing the subject **"Science"**. Phrase **A** naturally follows by completing the contrast with **"old ones"**. Phrase **C** continues the

idea by explaining that science destroys old truths and discovers new ones, while **B** completes the sentence by stating their effect on people's thinking and lives. Therefore, **Option 2** is the correct answer.

14. The adjective **"most promising"** means showing the greatest potential for success or producing the best results. Since the council selected one proposal after careful discussion, this phrase best fits the context. The other options are incorrect because **"promised"** is a verb form, **"promise"** is a noun or verb, and **"most best"** is grammatically incorrect due to double comparison. Therefore, **Option 1** is the correct answer.

15. **A. Pull up – II. to stop or scold someone** – The phrasal verb **"pull up"** commonly means to stop someone or rebuke them for improper behaviour. It is often used when correcting or warning a person.

B. Pull through – IV. to recover from something – **"Pull through"** means to recover successfully from an illness, difficulty, or dangerous situation. It indicates overcoming a serious problem.

C. Pull off – I. to succeed – **"Pull off"** means to achieve or accomplish something difficult successfully. It is used when a challenging task is completed with success.

D. Pull down – III. to demolish – **"Pull down"** means to knock down or demolish a building or structure. It also refers to bringing something down physically.

Therefore, the correct matching is A-II, B-IV, C-I, D-III, making Option 1 the correct answer.

16. The **present perfect tense** ("has messaged") is the most appropriate because it refers to an action that has occurred a limited number of times during a period that began in the past and continues to the present. The clause **"since the time she has been living in Cherapunji"** indicates an ongoing time period, while **"only once or twice"** shows the frequency of the completed action within that period. The other options do not correctly express this relationship between the past and the present. Therefore, **Option 2** is the correct answer.

17. The word **"arduous"** means **difficult, strenuous, or requiring great effort and perseverance**. In the given sentence, it describes the challenging days that lie ahead and emphasizes that they will require courage and determination to face. The other options—**promising**, **hopeful**, and **smooth**—do not convey the idea of hardship or demanding circumstances. Therefore, the word **"difficult"** is the closest in meaning, making **Option 3** the correct answer.

18. **A. Lost in the clouds – II. Confused** – The idiom **"lost in the clouds"** refers to someone who is absent-minded, confused, or lost in thought. It describes a person who is not paying attention to reality.

B. Go to the dogs – I. Ruined – The idiom **"go to the dogs"** means to deteriorate, decline, or become ruined over time. It is commonly used for a person, institution, or situation that has greatly worsened.

C. A fly in the ointment – IV. Something trifling that mars the whole – This idiom refers to a small defect or minor problem that spoils an otherwise good situation. Even a tiny flaw can reduce the overall value or enjoyment.

D. To go Dutch – III. Share the cost – The expression **"go Dutch"** means that each person pays for their own expenses or everyone shares the bill equally instead of one person paying for all.

Therefore, the correct matching is A-II, B-I, C-IV, D-III, making Option 3 the correct answer.

19. The word **"gregarious"** means sociable, friendly, and enjoying the company of other people. A gregarious person likes interacting with others and is comfortable in social situations. Among the given options, **"social"** is the closest in meaning. The other options are incorrect because **introvert** is the opposite of gregarious, **serious** refers to one's attitude, and **sarcastic** describes a style of speaking. Therefore, **Option 3** is the correct answer.

20. The conjunction **"although"** is used to introduce a contrast between two ideas. In the sentence, it contrasts the task appearing difficult at first with the team's successful completion of it within the stipulated time. The other options are incorrect because **"in spite of"** must be followed by a noun or gerund, **"since"** indicates reason rather than contrast, and **"nonetheless"** is an adverb that does not fit grammatically at the beginning of this sentence. Therefore, **Option 1** is the correct answer.

21. The word **"antagonism"** means hostility, opposition, or active dislike towards someone. Its exact opposite is **"cordiality"**, which means warmth, friendliness, and sincere goodwill in relationships. The other options—**hostility**, **animosity**, and **enmity**—are all synonyms of antagonism rather than antonyms. Therefore, **Option 2** is the correct answer.

22. **A. Visible darkness – III. Oxymoron** – An **oxymoron** is a figure of speech in which two contradictory or opposite words are placed together to create a striking effect. The expression **"visible darkness"** combines opposite ideas, making it an oxymoron.

B. She is the star of our family – II. Metaphor – A **metaphor** makes an implied comparison without using words such as *like* or *as*. Here, the person is directly compared to a **star**, suggesting that she is the most admired or outstanding member of the family.

C. I spent a sleepless night – IV. Transferred epithet – A **transferred epithet** transfers an adjective from the person it actually describes to another noun. In this expression, **"sleepless"** logically describes the person, but it is used with **"night"**.

D. That baby boy is like a teddy bear – I. Simile – A **simile** is a comparison using the words **"like"** or **"as"**. The baby boy is compared to a teddy bear using **"like"**, making it a simile.

Therefore, the correct matching is A-III, B-II, C-IV, D-I, making Option 1 the correct answer.

23. The adverb **"extremely"** means *to a very great degree* and correctly modifies the adjective **"taxing"**, which means demanding or exhausting. The sentence conveys that she agreed to mentor the team despite having a very demanding schedule. The other options do not fit the context because **scantily** means insufficiently, **hardly** means scarcely, and **extravagantly** means excessively in an unnecessary or lavish manner. Therefore, **Option 2** is the correct answer.

24. **Anarchism** is a political and philosophical theory that advocates the abolition of all forms of government and believes that society should function through voluntary cooperation without centralized authority. The other options are incorrect because **existentialism** deals with individual existence and freedom, **totalitarianism** supports absolute government control, and **utilitarianism** is an ethical theory based on the greatest good for the greatest number. Therefore, **Option 3** is the correct answer.

25. The idiom **"brought down the house"** means to receive an extremely enthusiastic response from the audience, especially through an outstanding speech, performance, or act. In the given sentence, although it was his **maiden speech**, his dry humour impressed the audience so much that they responded with loud applause and appreciation. The other options are incorrect because the idiom does not refer to criticism, embarrassment, or being formally thanked. Therefore, **Option 1** is the correct answer.

26. **B. I work hard so that I may become financially independent** – This sentence is grammatically correct because **"so that"** properly introduces the purpose of working hard, and **"may become"** correctly expresses the intended result.

C. An imminent event is one that will happen soon – This sentence is also grammatically correct. The adjective **"imminent"** means something that is about to happen in the near future, making the definition accurate.

A. Please stop making so much noise or I report you to the supervisor – This sentence is incorrect because the verb should be **"will report"** instead of **"report"** to express a future consequence.

D. I'm not certain, but I guess it's raining later this afternoon – This sentence is incorrect because **"it's raining"** should be **"it will rain"** or **"it's going to rain"** when referring to a future event.

Therefore, only sentences B and C are grammatically correct, making Option 4 the correct answer.

27. The preposition **"at"** is correctly used to refer to a specific event or occasion, such as **a party, a meeting,** or **a function**. Therefore, the sentence **"Did you meet your friends at the party in the clubhouse?"** is grammatically correct and natural. The other prepositions—**in, on,** and **for**—do not fit this context. Therefore, **Option 2** is the correct answer.

28. **"Mischievous"** is the correct spelling of the adjective that describes a person who is playful, naughty, or inclined to cause harmless trouble. It is commonly used for children or someone with a teasing nature. The other options are incorrect because they contain spelling errors and are not accepted in standard English. Therefore, **Option 4** is the correct answer.

29. The meaningful sentence is: **"We have not come to the conclusion of the immutability of this principle simply through good motives."** The sentence begins with **B**, introducing the subject and verb. Phrase **A** follows naturally to form **"the conclusion of the,"** while **C** completes the object as **"immutability of this principle."** Finally, **D** completes the sentence by explaining that the conclusion was not reached **simply through good motives.** Therefore, **Option 3** is the correct answer.

30. The proverb **"Handsome is as handsome does"** teaches that a person's true worth is judged by **actions and character rather than physical appearance**. It emphasizes that good behaviour, kindness, and noble deeds are more important than outward beauty. The other options incorrectly give importance to physical appearance, which is contrary to the meaning of the proverb. Therefore, **Option 1** is the correct answer.

31. **A. Wither – II. fade away** – **"Wither"** means to become dry, weak, or shrivel up due to loss of freshness or moisture. It is commonly used for plant[illegible] and can also describe gradual decline.

B. Whither – IV. direction – **"Whithe[illegible]** *what place* or *in which direction*. It [illegible] indicate the destination or dire[illegible]

C. Weather – I. the co[illegible] at a particular tim[illegible] atmospheric condi[illegible] such as temp[illegible]

D. Wheth[illegible] to ex[illegible]

[illegible]

T[illegible]

D-[illegible]

32. The [illegible] a veh[illegible] **"from"** [illegible] Thus, **"a** [illegible] correct exp[illegible] **of**—are inco[illegible] is the correct [illegible]

33. This is the correct passive construction because the active expression **"People were telling me"** changes to **"being told"**, shifting the focus from the doer of the action to the receiver. The sentence retains the original meaning while correctly using the passive voice. The other options either remain in the active voice, use incorrect tense, or fail to convert the sentence into proper passive construction. Therefore, **Option 2** is the correct answer.

34. A. He is the vulture of the state – This is a **metaphor** because a direct comparison is made between **"he"** and **"a vulture"** without using words such as *like* or *as*. It implies that the person is cruel, greedy, or exploits others.

D. The waves thundered on the shore – This expression uses **metaphorical language** by comparing the loud sound of the waves to **thunder**, creating a vivid image of their force and intensity. It is therefore treated as a metaphorical expression in this context.

B. She behaved like a child – This is a **simile** because the comparison is made using the word **"like"**.

C. To err is human, to forgive divine – This is a **proverb/epigrammatic statement** expressing a general truth and does not contain a metaphor.

Therefore, the correct answer is Option 4: A and D only.

35. The adverb **"moreover"** is used to add further information that strengthens the previous statement. In the sentence, **"He is very able and proficient; moreover, he works hard,"** the second clause adds another positive quality, making the statement more emphatic. The other options are incorrect because **nevertheless** and **however** indicate contrast, while **otherwise** expresses an alternative consequence. Therefore, **Option 1** is the correct answer.

36. The word **"offspring"** means a person's children or descendants. **"Progeny"** has the same meaning and refers to one's descendants or children. The other options—**forefather**, **progenitor**, and **ancestor**—refer to predecessors or earlier generations rather than descendants. Therefore, **Option 3** is the correct answer.

37. The phrasal verb **"look out"** is used to warn someone about an immediate danger or to ask them to be careful. In the sentence, **"Look out, there is a snake under** **he bush,"** it serves as a warning to avoid possible rm. The other options are incorrect because **look** means to search, **look up to** means to admire or t, and **look into** means to investigate. Therefore, 3 is the correct answer.

ngful sentence is: **"She turned and brought** **to the tarpaulin in a motion that imitated** **way you or I would bring out an arm and place it on the back of the chair next to our own in a gesture of expansive relaxation."** The sentence begins with **D**, introducing the action. Phrase **B** explains how the action was performed, **C** completes the comparison, and **A** concludes the sentence by describing the position and gesture. Therefore, **Option 2** is the correct answer.

39. A. Ritu did not get involved in the scandal on account of her friend's counsel – II. counsel – The word **"counsel"** means advice or guidance. It correctly fits the sentence, indicating that Ritu stayed away from the scandal because of her friend's wise advice.

B. He filed a civil suit against his siblings – III. suit – A **"suit"** is a legal case brought before a court of law. Hence, **"civil suit"** is the correct legal expression.

C. Some of the members of the council walked out in protest during the session – IV. council – A **"council"** is a body of elected or appointed members who meet to discuss and make decisions on public or organizational matters. It correctly fits the context.

D. He surprised his wife by booking a special suite on their anniversary – I. suite – A **"suite"** is a set of luxurious rooms, especially in a hotel. It appropriately completes the sentence describing an anniversary celebration.

Therefore, the correct matching is A-II, B-III, C-IV, D-I, making Option 1 the correct answer.

40. The word **"rescind"** means to revoke, cancel, withdraw, or officially repeal a law, agreement, order, or decision. Its opposite is **"continue"**, which means to keep something in force, remain effective, or carry on without cancelling it. The other options are incorrect because **abrogate** is a synonym of *rescind*, **delimit** means to fix or define boundaries, and **reschedule** means to arrange for a different time. Therefore, **Option 3** is the correct answer.

41. The passage mainly highlights how Arjun's life changes through **Raghav's guidance** and his determination to pursue his passion for art despite social expectations and hardships. His perseverance, combined with the support of a mentor, enables him to overcome challenges and achieve recognition. Thus, the central theme is the power of mentorship, passion, and resilience to transform an ordinary life into an extraordinary one. Therefore, **Option 4** is the correct answer.

42. The word **"vibrant"** means **lively, energetic, colourful, and full of life**. In the passage, it describes the bustling market and later symbolizes the richness and liveliness associated with Arjun's artistic journey. The other options are incorrect because **resilience** means the ability to recover from difficulties, **shimmer** means to shine with a soft light, and **humble** means modest or simple. Therefore, **Option 4** is the correct answer.

43. The passage clearly states that **"every challenge became a brushstroke in the masterpiece of his life"**, showing that Arjun gradually began to see difficulties as valuable experiences that contributed to his growth. Instead of being discouraged, he used every struggle to strengthen his character and inspire his art. Therefore, **Option 1** is the correct answer.

44. The author emphasizes that hardships should not be viewed as obstacles to success but as opportunities for learning, growth, and self-transformation. Arjun's determination, perseverance, and positive attitude enabled him to overcome difficulties and achieve success. The passage concludes that resilience and passion can turn struggles into stepping stones for a better future. Therefore, **Option 2** is the correct answer.

45. The passage states that Arjun's artwork was displayed in galleries beyond Varanasi and that his creations **"united cultures and hearts"**. His paintings reflected human emotions and inspired hope, making his work widely appreciated. Thus, his art achieved recognition beyond his hometown and had a meaningful impact on many people. Therefore, **Option 3** is the correct answer.

46. Richard Parker is a **wild animal**, specifically a tiger, as indicated by the narrator's words, **"yes, I know, to a tiger, but still."** Throughout the passage, the narrator speaks to Richard Parker with affection and gratitude, acknowledging that the animal played a vital role in his survival. Therefore, **Option 4** is the correct answer.

47. The narrator regrets that he could not bid a proper farewell to Richard Parker. He believes that endings should be meaningful because they help people find closure and move on without regret. This reflects the universal human tendency to value heartfelt goodbyes and attach emotional significance to parting moments. Therefore, **Option 3** is the correct answer.

48. The narrator clearly states that he was **not weeping merely because he survived or because he met his family**, but because **Richard Parker left him without any farewell.** The sudden and unceremonious departure left him with lasting sadness and regret. Therefore, **Option 3** is the correct answer.

49. The narrator mentions that one thing he dislikes about his nickname is **"the way that number runs on forever"**. This reflects his preference for order, structure, and proper conclusions, in contrast to something that appears endless. Therefore, **Option 3** is the correct answer.

50. The narrator repeatedly expresses his sincere **gratitude** towards Richard Parker for saving his life during the difficult journey. He wishes he had been able to thank him properly before they parted, showing deep appreciation and respect. Although the farewell caused him pain, the dominant emotion while recalling Richard Parker's role is one of thankfulness. Therefore, **Option 2** is the correct answer.

YOUR SPACE

Previous Years' Paper

Common University Entrance Test for UG Programmes

CUET–UG—GENERAL TEST

Entrance Exam, 2026

(Exam held on 20-05-2026)

1. One morning after sunrise, Rashi and Neelam were talking to each other face to face at Tilak Chowk. If Neelam's shadow was exactly to the right of Rashi. Which direction Neelam was facing?

1. West 2. North
3. South 4. East

2. In the following question, a set of five figures A, B, C, D and E are given. Find the correct answer by combining some of these figures which would form a complete square.

A. 

B. 

C. 

D. 

E. 

Choose the *correct* answer from the options given below:

1. B, D and E only 2. A, C and E only
3. A, B and E only 4. A, C and D only

3. Which plateau is known as the 'Roof of the world'?

1. Deccan Plateau 2. Tibetan Plateau
3. Patagonian Plateau 4. Bolivian Plateau

4. Arrange the sequence of events in the order of their occurence:

A. With the merger of Hyderabad State and Andhra State, Andhra Pradesh came into being.
B. The Andhra Pradesh Reorganization Act, bifurcated the state into two - Telangana and Andhra Pradesh.
C. Jharkhand became a full-fledged state after its bifurcation from Bihar.
D. The enactment of Uttaranachal (Alternation of Name) Act, the state was renamed as Uttarakhand.

Choose the *correct* answer from the options given below:

1. A, B, C, D 2. A, D, C, B
3. A, C, D, B 4. B, C, D, A

5. Which series of Indian satellites is used for telecommunications, broadcasting and meteorology?

1. GSAT series
2. INSAT series
3. IRS series
4. RISAT series

6. In a row of 40 girls when Kavita was shifted to her left by 4 places her numbers from left end of the row becomes 12. What was the number of Suman from the right end of the row if the Suman was three places to the right of Kavita's original position?

1. 20 2. 24
3. 22 4. 26

7. Identify the festival held annually in December that showcases the rich culture of Nagaland.

1. Hornbill Festival
2. Bihu Festival
3. Wangala Festival
4. Chakpchar Kut Festival

1. 2	**2.** 1	**3.** 2	**4.** 3	**5.** 2	**6.** 3	**7.** 1

8. Raj, Mayank and Neer, can complete a work in 30, 35 and 28 days, respectively. Consider the following statements:

A. Raj and Mayank, together will complete the work in $\frac{210}{13}$ days.

B. Mayank and Neer, together will complete the work in $\frac{140}{3}$ days.

C. Raj and Neer, together will complete the work in $\frac{420}{29}$ days.

D. Raj, Neer and Mayank, together will complete the work in $\frac{420}{41}$ days.

Choose the ***correct*** answer from the options given below:

1. A, B and D only
2. B, C and D only
3. A, B, C and D
4. A, C and D only

9. In how many different ways, can the letters of words OPTICAL be arranged so that the vowels are never together?

1. 720 2. 1440
3. 4320 4. 5040

10. Match List-I with List-II.

List-I (Books)	List-II (Authors)
A. Hind Swaraj	I. J.L. Nehru
B. Glimpses of World History	II. Amartya Sen
C. The Argumentative Indian	III. A.P.J. Abdul Kalam
D. Wings of Fire	IV. M.K. Gandhi

Choose the ***correct*** answer from the options given below:

1. A-I, B-II, C-III, D-IV
2. A-IV, B-I, C-II, D-III
3. A-II, B-III, C-IV, D-I
4. A-III, B-IV, C-II, D-I

11. The value of y for which the distance between the points P(10, y) and Q(2, 2) is 10 unit.

1. –4 and 8
2. 4 and –8
3. –6 and 8
4. 6 and –8

12. Match List-I with List-II.

List-I (Study)	List-II (Topic)
A. Pedology	I. Viruses
B. Taxonomy	II. Soil
C. Mycology	III. Classification
D. Virology	IV. Fungi

Choose the ***correct*** answer from the options given below:

1. A-II, B-III, C-IV, D-I
2. A-II, B-I, C-III, D-IV
3. A-II, B-IV, C-III, D-I
4. A-III, B-II, C-I, D-IV

13. In which year did India celebrate the 150th anniversary of the national song?

1. 2020 2. 2025
3. 2024 4. 2023

14. In given of the following, find out the which of the figures (1), (2), (3) and (4) complete the figure matrix.

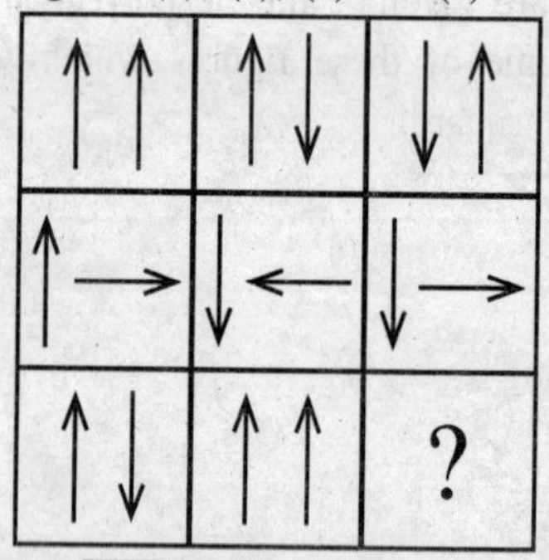

1. 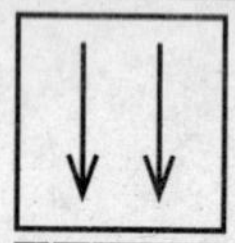
2. 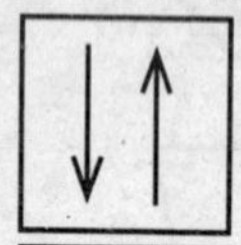
3. 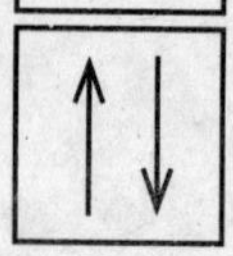
4. 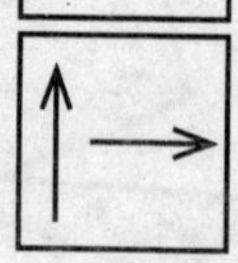

15. Where should an object be placed in front of the same convex lens to obtain the same real image the same size the same object?

1. At infinity
2. At the principal focus of the lens.
3. Between the optical center of the lens and its principal focal point
4. At twice the focal length.

16. The current time is 10 minutes past 3 in the afternoon. What will the be angle between the hour hand and the minute hand of the clock, 4 hours and 30 minutes from now?

1. 40° 2. 10°
3. 25° 4. 15°

8. 4 **9.** 3 **10.** 2 **11.** 1 **12.** 1 **13.** 2 **14.** 1 **15.** 4 **16.** 2

17. Which apex public policy think tank of the Government of India acts as the nodal agency tasked with catalyzing economic development?

1. NITI Aayog 2. Reserve Bank of India
3. IRDAI 4. NABARD

18. According to a certain code language.

(*i*) 'min fin bin gin' means 'trains are always late'.
(*ii*) 'gin din cin hin' means 'drivers were always punished'.
(*iii*) 'bin cin vin rin' means 'drivers stopped all trains'.
(*iv*) 'din kin fin vin' means 'all passengers were late'.

Which word is represented by 'fin'?

1. trains 2. late
3. drivers 4. always

19. Match List-I with List-II.

List-I	List-II
A. The number π is a/an	I. whole number
B. 0 is a/an	II. complex number
C. $\sqrt{-1}$ is a/an	III. composite number
D. 6 is a/an	IV. irrational number

Choose the ***correct*** answer from the options given below:

1. A-I, B-II, C-III, D-IV
2. A-IV, B-I, C-II, D-III
3. A-IV, B-II, C-I, D-III
4. A-IV, B-III, C-II, D-I

20. The number of iron balls, each 1 cm in radius, that can be made from an iron sphere of diameter 12 cm is:

1. 36 2. 216
3. 864 4. 1728

21. Which of the following is a leguminous crop?

1. Jawar 2. Millets
3. Sesamum 4. Pulses

22. In given of the following question, choose the correct mirror image of the fig. (X) from amongst the four alternatives (1), (2), (3) and (4) given along with it?

R E A S O N I N G

1. ЯƎAƧOИIИG 2. ꓘEꓯƧOИIИG
3. ӘИIИOƧAƎЯ 4. ӘИIИOSAƎЯ

23. From the top of the tower of 24 meter height, a man observes a child playing on the ground at an angle of depression of 30°. After sometimes, he observed that the angle of depression is 60°. Find the distance covered by kid.

1. $8\sqrt{3}$ meter 2. $16\sqrt{3}$ meter
3. $24\sqrt{3}$ meter 4. $32\sqrt{3}$ meter

24. If the mode of any data is 36.8 and the mean is 35.37, then the value of median is:

1. 34.85 (approx.) 2. 35.85 (approx.)
3. 35.65 (approx.) 4. 36.85 (approx.)

25. Match List-I with List-II.

List-I (Inventors)	List-II (Inventions)
A. Homi J. Bhabha	I. White Revolution
B. Verghese Kurien	II. Raman Effect
C. C.V. Raman	III. Surgery
D. Sushruta	IV. Indian Nuclear Programme

Choose the ***correct*** answer from the options given below:

1. A-I, B-III, C-II, D-IV
2. A-IV, B-I, C-II, D-III
3. A-III, B-I, C-II, D-IV
4. A-I, B-IV, C-II, D-III

26. Which country exite the World Health Organization in January 2025?

1. United State of America
2. China
3. Brazil
4. Russia

27. The calendar for the year 2019 will be the same for the year:

1. 2030 2. 2024
3. 2042 4. 2028

28. Which of the following committees were part of the Constituent Assembly?

A. Drafting Committee
B. Flag Committee
C. Union Constitution Committee
D. Provincial Constitution Committee

Choose the ***correct*** answer from the options given below:

1. A, C and D 2. A, B and C
3. A, B, C and D 4. B, C and D

29. Which pair of countries shares a maritime boundary with India?

1. Pakistan and Myanmar
2. Sri Lanka and Nepal
3. Maldives and Sri Lanka
4. China and Bhutan

17. 1	**18.** 2	**19.** 2	**20.** 2	**21.** 4	**22.** 3	**23.** 2
24. 2	**25.** 2	**26.** 1	**27.** 1	**28.** 3	**29.** 3	

30. Consider the following statements:
Which is/are true?
A. The sum of any two sides of a triangle is greater than the third side.
B. The median of a triangle divides it into two triangles of equal area.
C. The diagonals of a parallelogram bisect each other.
D. The diagonals of rhombus are equal and bisect each other.
Choose the ***correct*** answer from the options given below:
1. A, B and C only
2. A, B and D only
3. B, C and D only
4. A, B, C and D

31. In given of the following question a letter-number series is given with one or more terms missing as shown by (?). Choose the missing term out of the given alternative.
GBL, JFN, MJP, ?
1. PRM 2. PNR
3. ONQ 4. PMS

32. The probability that a card drawn from a pack of 52 cards will be a spade or a queen is:
1. $\frac{2}{13}$ 2. $\frac{4}{13}$
3. $\frac{1}{13}$ 4. $\frac{1}{52}$

33. One says, "Give me a hundred rupees, friend! I shall then become twice as rich as you". The other replies, "If you give me ten rupees, I shall be six times as rich as you". What is the amount of their (respective) capital?
1. ₹ 40, ₹ 170
2. ₹ 50, ₹ 175
3. ₹ 50, ₹ 150
4. ₹ 40, ₹ 180

34. Arrange the following events as they occurred in history.
A. The Partition of Bengal
B. The First Anglo-Carnatic War
C. The Transfer of Capital from Calcutta to Delhi
D. The Ilbert Bill Controversy
Choose the ***correct*** answer from the options given below:
1. B, D, A, C 2. A, B, C, D
3. D, A, B, C 4. C, B, D, A

35. Consider the following statements regarding resource classification based on origin:
A. Biotic resources are obtained from the biosphere and have life.
B. Abiotic resources are composed of non-living things.
C. Human beings, flora and fauna are examples of abiotic resources.
D. Rocks and metals are examples of biotic resources.
Choose the ***correct*** answer from the options given below:
1. A, B and D only
2. A, B and C only
3. A, B, C and D
4. A and B only

36. Six members of a family, namely P, Q, R, S, T, U are travelling together, Q is the son of R but R is not the mother of Q. P and R are a married couple. T is the brother of R. S is the daughter of P. U is the brother of Q. How many male members are there in the family?
1. 3 2. 5
3. 4 4. 6

37. Ibn Batuta, an African traveller, visited India during the reign of the following ruler.
1. Balban
2. Ala-ud-din Khalji
3. Iltutmish
4. Mohammad bin Tughlaq

38. The kidneys in humans are part of system that performs one of the following functions.
1. Nutrition
2. Excretion
3. Transportation
4. Respiration

39. Study the following information carefully and answer the questions.
Six people P, Q, R, S, T and U are sitting on the ground in a hexagonal shape (not necessarily in the same order). All the sides of hexagon so formed, are of same length, P is not adjacent to Q or R; S is not adjacent to R or T : Q and R are adjacent: U is the middle of S and R. If one neighbour of P is S, who is the other one?
1. Q 2. T
3. U 4. R

30. 1	**31.** 2	**32.** 2	**33.** 1	**34.** 1	**35.** 4	**36.** 3	**37.** 4	**38.** 2	**39.** 2

40. In given of the following question, you are given figure (X) followed by four alternative figures (1), (2), (3) and (4), such that figure (X) is embedded in one of them. Trace out the alternative figure which contains figure (X) as its part.

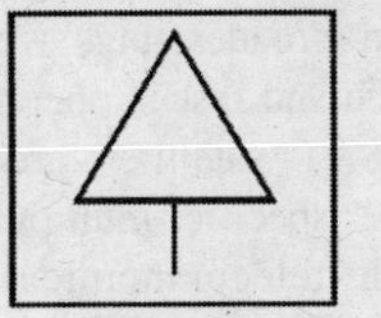

Figure (X)

1. 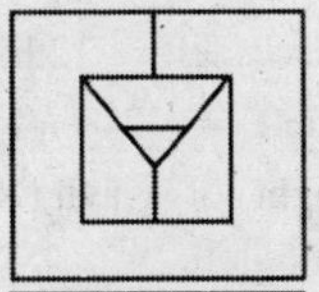
2. 
3. 
4. 

41. In a row of students, there are 27 students in first row, 24 in the second, 21 in the third, and so on. There are 6 students in last row. How many students are there in all row?

1. 120 2. 123
3. 132 4. 135

42. Find the missing character from among the given alternatives.

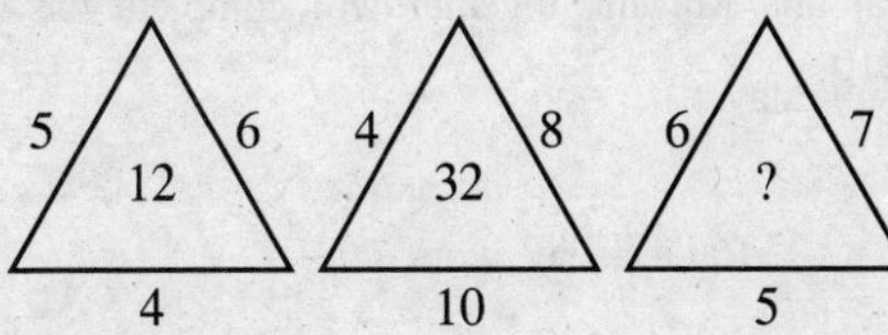

1. 47 2. 21
3. 210 4. 41

43. A shopkeeper marks up the worth of his product by 60%. If he increases the discount from 15% to 20%, his profit will be decreased by ₹ 32. How much profit/loss would he get, if he offered a 25% discount on the marked price?

1. 40 2. 60
3. 80 4. 120

44. Rig Veda is a:

1. Book of Sacrifices
2. Book of Melodies and Charts
3. Book of Magical and Technical Formulae
4. Book of Hymns

45. Which river is common to Budapest, Belgrade and Vienna?

1. Danube 2. Nile
3. Thames 4. Mississippi

46. Which of the following can be understood when a bottom of a vessel blackens on a outside during cooking?

1. The food is not fully cooked.
2. The fuel has a high moisture content.
3. Combustion is incomplete.
4. The fuel is combusting completely.

47. The speed of a 90 meter long train is 45 km/h. A man is standing right next to the railway line. How much time will the train take to cross the speed increases by 20%?

1. 4.8 second 2. 5.0 second
3. 6.0 second 4. 7.2 second

48. A bag contains five-rupee, one-rupee, 50-paise and 25-paise coins in the ratio 3 : 5 : 6 : 8. If the total amount of money in the bag ₹ 225. The number of coins of each kind in ascending order:

A. No. of coins of 25 paise
B. No. of coins of one rupee
C. No. of coins of 50 paise
D. No. of coins of five rupee

Choose the ***correct*** answer from the options given below:

1. A, C, B, D 2. B, A, D, C
3. D, A, C, B 4. D, B, C, A

49. The difference between compound interest and simple interest on a sum for 2 years at 20% per annum, when the interest is compounded annually is ₹ 32. If the interest were compounded half-yearly, the difference in two interests would be:

1. ₹ 25.64 2. ₹ 38.46
3. ₹ 51.28 4. ₹ 64.10

50. In given of the following question consists of four problem figure marked (A), (B), (C), (D) and four answer figure marked (1), (2), (3) and (4). Select a figure among the answer figure which will continue the series established by the four problem figure.

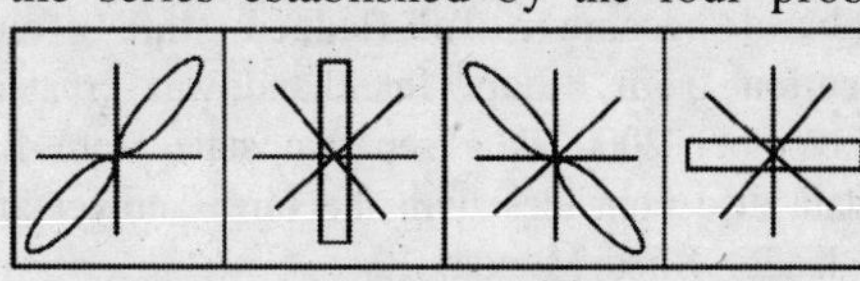

(A) (B) (C) (D)

1. 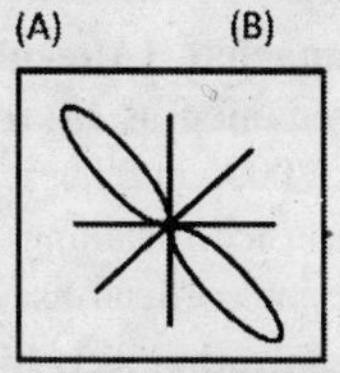
2. 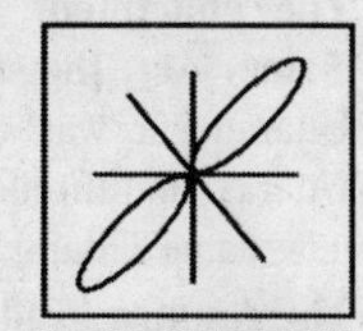
3. 
4. 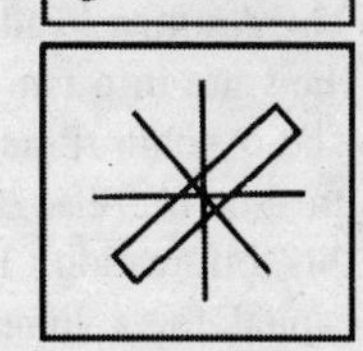

40. 3 **41.** 3 **42.** 2 **43.** 3 **44.** 4 **45.** 1 **46.** 3 **47.** 3 **48.** 4 **49.** 3 **50.** 3

EXPLANATORY ANSWERS

1. One morning after sunrise, the Sun is in the east, so Neelam's shadow must fall towards the west. Since Neelam's shadow was exactly to the right of Rashi, Rashi's right side must be towards the west. A person whose right side is towards the west is facing south. As Rashi and Neelam were talking face to face, Neelam must be facing the direction opposite to Rashi. Therefore, Neelam was facing north.

2. Figure E supplies a straight left side and bottom side of the square, so it works as one corner-forming piece of the final figure. Figure D is a right-angled triangular piece, and after suitable rotation, its two perpendicular sides can form another corner of the square while its slanting side becomes an internal joining edge. Figure B has a straight outer side and an angular projection which fits into the remaining space between D and E, completing the square without leaving a gap or causing overlap. Figures A and C do not fit in the same complete-square arrangement because their projections disturb the regular outer boundary. Therefore, the correct combination is B, D and E only.

3. The Tibetan Plateau is known as the 'Roof of the World' because it is the highest and largest plateau on Earth. It lies mainly in Tibet and parts of China, India, Nepal and Bhutan, and its average elevation is about 4,500 metres above sea level. The plateau is surrounded by major mountain systems including the Himalayas, Kunlun and Karakoram ranges. Many important Asian rivers such as the Indus, Brahmaputra, Mekong and Yangtze originate from this high plateau region.

4. A. **With the merger of Hyderabad State and Andhra State, Andhra Pradesh came into being:** Andhra Pradesh was formed on 1 November 1956 under the reorganisation of states on linguistic basis. It united Andhra State with the Telugu-speaking areas of the former Hyderabad State.

   C. **Jharkhand became a full-fledged state after its bifurcation from Bihar:** Jharkhand was created on 15 November 2000 as a separate state from Bihar. The date also coincides with the birth anniversary of tribal leader Birsa Munda.

   D. **The enactment of Uttaranachal (Alternation of Name) Act, the state was renamed as Uttarakhand:** Uttaranchal was created in 2000 and later renamed Uttarakhand through the concerned renaming law. The new name Uttarakhand came into official use in 2007.

   B. **The Andhra Pradesh Reorganization Act, bifurcated the state into two - Telangana and Andhra Pradesh:** The Andhra Pradesh Reorganisation Act led to the creation of Telangana as a separate state in 2014. After this bifurcation, Hyderabad was made the common capital for a limited period.

5. The INSAT series of Indian satellites is used for telecommunications, broadcasting and meteorology. INSAT stands for Indian National Satellite System and it is one of India's major multipurpose satellite systems. These satellites support television broadcasting, weather forecasting, disaster warning, search and rescue operations, and communication services. GSAT satellites are also communication satellites, but the specific multipurpose series traditionally linked with telecommunications, broadcasting and meteorology is INSAT.

6. Kavita's position after shifting 4 places left = 12th from left.
   Kavita's original position from left = 12 + 4 = 16th.
   Suman was 3 places to the right of Kavita's original position = 16 + 3 = 19th from left.
   Total girls = 40.
   Suman's position from right = 40 - 19 + 1 = 22.
   Therefore, Suman was 22nd from the right end of the row.

7. The Hornbill Festival is held annually in December and showcases the rich culture of Nagaland. It is celebrated mainly at Kisama Heritage Village near Kohima and is often called the "Festival of Festivals" of Nagaland. The festival presents Naga tribal dances, folk songs, traditional food, handicrafts, indigenous games and cultural performances. It is an important event for promoting tourism and preserving the cultural identity of various Naga tribes.

8. A. Raj and Mayank together will complete the work in $\frac{210}{13}$ days:

   Raj's 1-day work = $\frac{1}{30}$,

   Mayank's 1-day work = $\frac{1}{35}$.

   Together, $\frac{1}{30}+\frac{1}{35} = \frac{7+6}{210}=\frac{13}{210}$,

   so time taken = $\frac{210}{13}$ days. Hence, A is correct.

   B. Mayank and Neer together will complete the work in $\frac{140}{3}$ days:

   Mayank's 1-day work = $\frac{1}{35}$,

   Neer's 1-day work = $\frac{1}{28}$.

   Together, $\frac{1}{35}+\frac{1}{28} = \frac{4+5}{140}=\frac{9}{140}$,

   so time taken $\frac{140}{9}$ days, not $\frac{140}{3}$ days.

   Hence, B is incorrect.

C. Raj and Neer together will complete the work in $\frac{420}{29}$ days:

$$\text{Raj's 1-day work} = \frac{1}{30},$$

$$\text{Neer's 1-day work} = \frac{1}{28}.$$

$$\text{Together,} \quad \frac{1}{30}+\frac{1}{28} = \frac{14+15}{420} = \frac{29}{420},$$

so time taken $= \frac{420}{29}$ days. Hence, C is correct.

D. Raj, Neer and Mayank together will complete the work in $\frac{420}{41}$ days:

$$\text{Together, their 1-day work} = \frac{1}{30}+\frac{1}{35}+\frac{1}{28}.$$

$$\frac{1}{30}+\frac{1}{35}+\frac{1}{28} = \frac{14+12+15}{420} = \frac{41}{420},$$

so time taken $= \frac{420}{41}$ days. Hence, D is correct.

9. Here the condition is "all the three vowels are never together", which means the three vowels O, I and A should not come together as one complete block. Total arrangements of the 7 distinct letters of OPTICAL are 7! = 5040. If all three vowels are together, then OIA can be treated as one block, so there are 5 units: one vowel block and four consonants P, T, C, L. These 5 units can be arranged in 5! = 120 ways, and the 3 vowels inside the block can be arranged in 3! = 6 ways. Thus, arrangements with all three vowels together

$$= 5! \times 3! = 120 \times 6 = 720.$$

Therefore, arrangements in which all the three vowels are never together = 7! – (5! × 3!) = 5040 – 720 = 4320.

10. **A. Hind Swaraj — IV. M.K. Gandhi:** Hind Swaraj was written by Mahatma Gandhi in 1909. It presents his views on civilisation, self-rule, non-violence and criticism of modern materialistic life.

B. Glimpses of World History — I. J.L. Nehru: Glimpses of World History was written by Jawaharlal Nehru in the form of letters to his daughter Indira. It covers major events and civilisations of world history in a simple explanatory style.

C. The Argumentative Indian — II. Amartya Sen: The Argumentative Indian is written by economist and Nobel laureate Amartya Sen. The book discusses India's intellectual traditions, public reasoning, democracy, identity and cultural debates.

D. Wings of Fire — III. A.P.J. Abdul Kalam: Wings of Fire is the autobiography of Dr. A.P.J. Abdul Kalam, written with Arun Tiwari. It describes Kalam's early life, scientific career, work in India's missile programme and his inspirational journey.

11. Using distance formula,

$$PQ = \sqrt{(10-2)^2+(y-2)^2}.$$

$$\text{Given distance} = 10,$$

$$10 = \sqrt{8^2+(y-2)^2}$$

$$100 = 64 + (y-2)^2$$

$$(y-2)^2 = 36$$

$$y-2 = \pm 6$$

$$y = 8 \text{ or } y = -4$$

Therefore, the value of y is –4 and 8.

12. **A. Pedology — II. Soil:** Pedology is the scientific study of soil, including its formation, classification, physical properties and distribution. It is important in agriculture, geography and environmental studies because soil type affects fertility, vegetation and land use.

B. Taxonomy — III. Classification: Taxonomy deals with the classification, naming and identification of living organisms. It helps arrange organisms into groups such as kingdom, phylum, class, order, family, genus and species on the basis of similarities and differences.

C. Mycology — IV. Fungi: Mycology is the branch of biology that studies fungi. It includes the study of mushrooms, moulds, yeasts and fungal diseases, and is important in medicine, agriculture, food processing and biotechnology.

D. Virology — I. Viruses: Virology is the scientific study of viruses and virus-like agents. It deals with their structure, replication, diseases caused by them, vaccines and methods of prevention and control.

13. India celebrated the 150th anniversary of the national song "Vande Mataram" in 2025. The song was composed by Bankim Chandra Chattopadhyay and later included in his famous novel *Anandamath*. "Vande Mataram" played an important role in India's freedom movement because it became a patriotic slogan and inspired nationalist feeling. It was adopted as the national song of India, while "Jana Gana Mana" is the national anthem.

14. In the figure matrix, the movement of the arrows follows a fixed directional pattern. In the third column, the left-side arrow remains downward in the first two boxes, so it should remain downward in the missing box also. The right-side arrow in the third column changes step by step from upward to rightward, and then to downward. Therefore, the missing figure must contain two downward arrows. Hence, figure 1 correctly completes the matrix.

15. To obtain a real image of the same size as the object using a convex lens, the object should be placed at twice the focal length, that is, at 2F. In this position, the image is also formed at 2F on the other side of the lens. The image formed is real, inverted and equal in size to the object. This is a standard image formation case of a convex lens and is frequently used in ray-diagram based questions.

16. Current time = 3:10 p.m.

After 4 hours 30 minutes, time = 7:40 p.m.

At 7:40, minute hand position = 40 × 6 = 240°.

Hour hand position = $7 \times 30 + 40 \times \frac{1}{2}$.

$= 210 + 20 = 230°$.

Angle between hands = 240° - 230° = 10°.

Therefore, the correct mathematical answer is 10°, which corresponds to option 2, not option 1.

17. NITI Aayog is the apex public policy think tank of the Government of India and acts as a nodal agency for promoting cooperative federalism and catalysing economic development. It replaced the Planning Commission in 2015. NITI Aayog advises the government on policy matters, supports long-term developmental planning and encourages innovation-based governance. It also works with States and Union Territories for inclusive and sustainable development.

18. From statement (*i*), 'min fin bin gin' means 'trains are always late'.

From statement (*ii*), 'gin din cin hin' means 'drivers were always punished'.

Common code in (*i*) and (*ii*) is 'gin', and common word is 'always', so 'gin' = always.

From statement (*iii*), 'bin cin vin rin' means 'drivers stopped all trains'.

Common code in (*i*) and (*iii*) is 'bin', and common word is 'trains', so 'bin' = trains.

In statement (*i*), the remaining codes are 'min' and 'fin', and the remaining words are 'are' and 'late'.

From statement (*iv*), 'din kin fin vin' means 'all passengers were late'.

Common code between (*i*) and (*iv*) is 'fin', and common word is 'late'.

Therefore, 'fin' represents 'late'.

19. **A. The number π — IV. irrational number:** π is an irrational number because it cannot be written exactly in the form $\frac{p}{q}$, where pand qare integers and $q \neq 0$. Its decimal expansion is non-terminating and non-recurring, which is a key property of irrational numbers.

B. 0 — I. whole number: 0 is a whole number because the set of whole numbers begins with 0 and continues as 0, 1, 2, 3,.... Whole numbers are non-negative integers, so 0 is included in this category.

C. $\sqrt{-1}$ — II. complex number: $\sqrt{-1}$ is represented by *i*, the imaginary unit. Since complex numbers are expressed in the form $a + ib$, where aand bare real numbers, $\sqrt{-1}$ belongs to complex numbers.

D. 6 — III. composite number: 6 is a composite number because it is a positive integer greater than 1 and has more than two factors. Its factors are 1, 2, 3, and 6, so it is not a prime number.

20. Radius of bigger sphere = $\frac{12}{2}$ = 6 cm.

Radius of each smaller iron ball = 1 cm.

Number of balls = $\frac{\text{Volume of bigger sphere}}{\text{Volume of one smaller sphere}}$

$$= \frac{\frac{4}{3}\pi(6)^3}{\frac{4}{3}\pi(1)^3} = \frac{216}{1} = 216$$

Therefore, 216 iron balls can be made from the iron sphere.

21. Pulses are leguminous crops because they belong to the family Fabaceae or Leguminosae. These crops include gram, pea, lentil, arhar, moong and urad, and they generally produce seeds in pods. Leguminous crops are important in agriculture because many of them fix atmospheric nitrogen in the soil through root nodules containing Rhizobium bacteria. Jowar and millets are cereal crops, while sesamum is an oilseed crop, so the correct answer is pulses.

22. In a vertical mirror image of the word REASONING, the order of letters is reversed and every letter is laterally inverted. Therefore, the image must begin with the mirror form of G and end with the mirror form of R. The correct mirror image sequence is the reversed form of G,N,I,N,O,S,A,E,R. Option 3 correctly shows the laterally inverted shapes of the letters, including the reversed form of S, while option 4 does not show the correct mirror form of S. Therefore, option 3 is correct.

23. Height of tower = 24 m.

Initial angle of depression = 30°, so initial horizontal distance

$$= \frac{24}{\tan 30°} = 24\sqrt{3}$$

Later angle of depression = 60°, so later horizontal distance

$$= \frac{24}{\tan 60°} = \frac{24}{\sqrt{3}} = 8\sqrt{3}$$

Distance covered by the kid

$$= 24\sqrt{3} - 8\sqrt{3} = 16\sqrt{3}$$

Therefore, the distance covered by the kid is $16\sqrt{3}$ metre.

24. Using empirical relation,

$$\text{Mode} = 3\text{ Median} - 2\text{ Mean}$$
$$36.8 = 3\text{ Median} - 2(35.37)$$
$$36.8 = 3\text{ Median} - 70.74$$
$$3\text{ Median} = 36.8 + 70.74 = 107.54$$
$$\text{Median} = \frac{107.54}{3} = 35.8466 \approx 35.85$$

Therefore, the value of median is approximately 35.85.

25. **A. Homi J. Bhabha — IV. Indian Nuclear Programme:** Homi Jehangir Bhabha is regarded as the father of the Indian nuclear programme. He played a major role in establishing institutions like the Tata Institute of Fundamental Research and strengthening India's atomic energy research.

B. Verghese Kurien — I. White Revolution: Verghese Kurien is known as the father of the White Revolution in India. His work through Operation Flood and the Amul cooperative model made India one of the world's largest milk-producing countries.

C. C.V. Raman — II. Raman Effect: C.V. Raman discovered the Raman Effect, which explains the scattering of light by molecules. For this discovery, he received the Nobel Prize in Physics in 1930, becoming the first Asian Nobel laureate in science.

D. Sushruta — III. Surgery: Sushruta is known as an ancient Indian pioneer of surgery. His work, the Sushruta Samhita, describes surgical instruments, procedures and methods, including early forms of plastic surgery.

26. The United States of America initiated its withdrawal from the World Health Organization in January 2025. The decision was linked with an executive order issued after Donald Trump returned to office, and the formal process required notice before the withdrawal could take full effect. Among the given options, China, Brazil and Russia did not match this January 2025 WHO withdrawal context. Therefore, the intended correct answer is United State of America.

27. The year 2019 was an ordinary year, and its calendar will repeat in another ordinary year having the same first day of the year. From 2019 to 2030, the total shift in days is 11ordinary-year shifts plus 3leap-year shifts for 2020, 2024 and 2028.

$$11 + 3 = 14$$
$$14 \div 7 = 0 \text{ remainder}$$

So the weekdays repeat exactly. Since 2030 is also an ordinary year, the calendar for 2019 will be the same for 2030.

28. A. Drafting Committee: The Drafting Committee was one of the most important committees of the Constituent Assembly. Dr. B.R. Ambedkar was its Chairman, and it prepared the draft text of the Constitution.

B. Flag Committee: A committee connected with the national flag was also part of the Constituent Assembly's work. It helped in finalising the design and adoption of the national flag of India.

C. Union Constitution Committee: The Union Constitution Committee was headed by Jawaharlal Nehru. It dealt with the structure and powers of the Union government under the future Constitution.

D. Provincial Constitution Committee: The Provincial Constitution Committee was headed by Sardar Vallabhbhai Patel. It dealt with the constitutional framework and governance of provinces in independent India.

29. Maldives and Sri Lanka both share maritime boundaries with India. India and Sri Lanka are separated by the Palk Strait and the Gulf of Mannar, while India and Maldives have a maritime boundary in the Indian Ocean region. Nepal and Bhutan are landlocked countries and do not share maritime boundaries with India. China also does not share a maritime boundary with India. Therefore, the correct pair is Maldives and Sri Lanka.

30. A. The sum of any two sides of a triangle is greater than the third side: This is the triangle inequality property. It is a basic condition for forming a valid triangle and applies to all types of triangles.

B. The median of a triangle divides it into two triangles of equal area: A median joins a vertex to the midpoint of the opposite side. Since both smaller triangles have equal bases on the same line and the same height, their areas are equal.

C. The diagonals of a parallelogram bisect each other: This is a standard property of every parallelogram. Each diagonal cuts the other into two equal parts, though the diagonals need not be equal in length.

D. The diagonals of rhombus are equal and bisect each other: This statement is incorrect because the diagonals of a rhombus bisect each other but are not generally equal. Equal diagonals occur in a square, which is a special type of rhombus.

31. In the series GBL, JFN, MJP, the first letters are G, J, M, which move by +3, so the next first letter is P. The second letters are B, F, J, which move by +4, so the next second letter is N. The third letters are L, N, P, which move by +2, so the next third letter is R. Therefore, the missing term is PNR.

32. Total cards in a pack = 52.
Number of spade cards = 13.
Number of queen cards = 4.
Queen of spades is common to both groups, so it should be counted only once.

$$\text{Favourable cards} = 13 + 4 - 1 = 16$$
$$\text{Probability} = \frac{16}{52} = \frac{4}{13}$$

Therefore, the probability that the card drawn is a spade or a queen is $\frac{4}{13}$.

33. Let the first person have \(x\) and the second person have y.

$$x + 100 = 2(y - 100)$$
$$x - 2y = -300$$
$$y + 10 = 6(x - 10)$$
$$y - 6x = -70$$

Putting $y = 6x - 70$ in the first equation:

$$x - 2(6x - 70) = -300$$
$$x - 12x + 140 = -300$$
$$-11x = -440$$
$$x = 40$$
$$y = 6(40) - 70 = 170$$

Therefore, their respective capitals are 40 and 170.

34. B. The First Anglo-Carnatic War: The First Anglo-Carnatic War was fought during 1746–1748 between the British and the French in South India. It was connected with the wider Anglo-French rivalry and marked the beginning of European military competition in the Carnatic region.

D. **The Ilbert Bill Controversy:** The Ilbert Bill Controversy took place in 1883 during Lord Ripon's viceroyalty. The issue concerned the power of Indian judges to try European offenders, and it exposed racial discrimination under colonial rule.

A. **The Partition of Bengal:** The Partition of Bengal was carried out in 1905 by Lord Curzon. It divided Bengal into Eastern Bengal and Assam on one side and the remaining Bengal on the other, leading to the Swadeshi Movement.

C. **The Transfer of Capital from Calcutta to Delhi:** The transfer of the capital from Calcutta to Delhi was announced in 1911 at the Delhi Durbar. Delhi became the new imperial capital because of its historical and political significance.

35. A. **Biotic resources are obtained from the biosphere and have life:** This statement is correct because biotic resources include living or once-living components of the environment. Examples include human beings, plants, animals, forests and fisheries.

B. **Abiotic resources are composed of non-living things:** This statement is correct because abiotic resources are non-living physical and chemical resources. Examples include rocks, metals, minerals, water, air and sunlight.

C. **Human beings, flora and fauna are examples of abiotic resources:** This statement is incorrect because human beings, flora and fauna are living components. Therefore, they are classified as biotic resources, not abiotic resources.

D. **Rocks and metals are examples of biotic resources:** This statement is incorrect because rocks and metals are non-living natural resources. Therefore, they are examples of abiotic resources, not biotic resources.

36. Q is the son of R, and R is not the mother of Q, so R is the father and therefore male. P and R are a married couple, so P is female. T is the brother of R, so T is male. S is the daughter of P, so S is female. U is the brother of Q, so U is male, and Q is already male as the son of R. Thus, the male members are R, Q, T and U, making the total number of male members 4.

37. Ibn Batuta visited India during the reign of Mohammad bin Tughlaq. He was a Moroccan traveller from Africa and came to India in the 14th century. Mohammad bin Tughlaq appointed him as a Qazi in Delhi, which shows the ruler's patronage of learned foreigners. Ibn Batuta's travel account, *Rihla*, gives useful details about the administration, society and life of that period.

38. The kidneys in humans are part of the excretory system. Their main function is to filter blood and remove nitrogenous wastes such as urea from the body in the form of urine. Kidneys also help regulate water balance, salt concentration and acid-base balance in the body. Nutrition is mainly related to the digestive system, transportation to the circulatory system and respiration to the respiratory system.

39. Six persons are arranged around a hexagon, and Q and R are adjacent while U lies between S and R. Since P is not adjacent to Q or R and one neighbour of P is S, the remaining valid placement makes T the other neighbour of P. S cannot be adjacent to T according to the given condition, so T cannot be on the side of S; it must be on the other side of P. Therefore, the other neighbour of P is T.

40. In embedded-figure questions, the outer square box is generally treated as the boundary of the answer option and not necessarily as a part to be matched, because every alternative figure is already placed inside a square box. Therefore, the required figure to be traced is the upright triangle with a vertical line extending downward from the centre of its base. In option 3, the inner triangle and the short vertical line below its base correctly reproduce figure (X) in the same orientation. The extra triangular outline around it does not affect the answer because the required figure is clearly embedded inside the larger figure. Therefore, option 3 correctly contains figure (X) as its part.

41. Number of students in rows forms an arithmetic progression:

$$27, 24, 21, ..., 6$$

Here, first term $a = 27$, common difference $d = -3$, last term $l = 6$.

$$l = a + (n - 1)d$$
$$6 = 27 + (n - 1)(-3)$$
$$6 = 27 - 3n + 3$$
$$3n = 24$$
$$n = 8$$

Total students:

$$S_n = \frac{n}{2}(a+l) = \frac{8}{2}(27+6)$$
$$= 4 \times 33 = 132$$

Therefore, there are 132 students in all rows.

42. In each triangle, the number inside is obtained by multiplying the three outside numbers and then dividing by 10.

For the first triangle:

$$\frac{5\times6\times4}{10} = \frac{120}{10} = 12$$

For the second triangle:

$$\frac{4\times8\times10}{10} = \frac{320}{10} = 32$$

For the third triangle:

$$\frac{6\times7\times5}{10} = \frac{210}{10} = 21$$

Therefore, the missing character is 21.

43. Let cost price = ₹ x.

Marked price after 60% markup:

$$MP = 160\% \text{ of } x = \frac{160x}{100} = 1.6x$$

Increase in discount from 15% to 20% means extra discount = 5% of marked price.

Given decrease in profit = ₹ 32,

so $5\% \text{ of } 1.6x = 32$

$$\frac{5}{100}\times 1.6x = 32$$

$$0.08x = 32$$

$$x = 400$$

If discount is 25%, selling price:

$$SP = 75\% \text{ of } 1.6 \times 400$$

$$SP = \frac{75}{100}\times 640 = 480$$

Profit: 480 − 400 = 80

Therefore, he would get a profit of 80.

44. Rig Veda is a book of hymns and is the oldest of the four Vedas. It contains hymns dedicated to various deities such as Agni, Indra, Varuna, Soma and Ushas. These hymns reflect early Vedic religious ideas, prayers, nature worship and social life of the Vedic people. The Yajur Veda is mainly connected with sacrificial formulae, the Sama Veda with melodies, and the Atharva Veda with magical and ritual formulae.

45. The Danube River is common to Budapest, Belgrade and Vienna. Vienna is the capital of Austria, Budapest is the capital of Hungary, and Belgrade is the capital of Serbia. The Danube is one of Europe's most important rivers and flows through or along the borders of several European countries. It has historically been significant for transport, trade, culture and settlement in Central and Eastern Europe.

46. When the bottom of a vessel blackens on the outside during cooking, it indicates incomplete combustion of the fuel. In incomplete combustion, there is insufficient oxygen supply, due to which carbon particles or soot are produced. These soot particles get deposited on the outer surface of the vessel and make it black. Complete combustion generally produces a cleaner flame and does not normally leave such black deposits.

47. Original speed of train = 45 km/h.

Speed increased by 20%:

$$45+\frac{20}{100}\times 45 = 45 + 9 = 54 \text{ km/h}$$

Convert into m/s:

$$54\times\frac{5}{18} = 15 \text{ m/s}$$

Length of train = 90 m.

Time taken to cross a man standing near the railway line:

$$\text{Time} = \frac{\text{Length}}{\text{Speed}} = \frac{90}{15} \text{ seconds}$$

Therefore, the train will take 6.0 seconds.

48. Let the number of five-rupee, one-rupee, 50-paise and 25-paise coins be $3x$, $5x$, $6x$ and $8x$.

Total value:

$$5(3x) + 1(5x) + 0.50(6x) + 0.25(8x) = 225$$

$$15x + 5x + 3x + 2x = 225$$

$$25x = 225$$

$$x = 9$$

A. No. of coins of 25 paise:

$$8x = 8 \times 9 = 72$$

This is the highest number of coins because 25-paise coins have the smallest denomination but the largest ratio share.

B. No. of coins of one rupee:

$$5x = 5 \times 9 = 45$$

This number is more than the five-rupee coins but less than the 50-paise and 25-paise coins.

C. No. of coins of 50 paise:

$$6x = 6 \times 9 = 54$$

This comes after one-rupee coins in ascending order because $54 > 45$.

D. No. of coins of five rupee:

$$3x = 3 \times 9 = 27$$

This is the smallest number of coins because five-rupee coins have the highest denomination and the smallest ratio share.

Ascending order of number of coins: 27, 45, 54, 72

Therefore, the correct order is D, B, C, A.

49. For 2 years, difference between compound interest and simple interest when compounded annually:

$$\text{Difference} = P\left(\frac{r}{100}\right)^2$$

$$32 = P\left(\frac{20}{100}\right)^2 \Rightarrow 32 = P\times\frac{400}{10000}$$

$$32 = 0.04P$$

$$P = 800$$

Simple interest for 2 years:

$$SI = \frac{800\times 20\times 2}{100} = 320$$

If compounded half-yearly, rate per half-year = 10%, number of half-years = 4.

$$CI = 800\left[\left(1+\frac{0}{100}\right)^4 - 1\right]$$

$$CI = 800[(1.1)^4 - 1]$$

$$= 800(1.4641 - 1)$$

$$CI = 800 \times 0.4641 = 371.28$$

Difference: 371.28 − 320 = 51.28

Therefore, the required difference is ₹ 51.28.

50. In the series, the main figure is formed on the same central 8-spoke line pattern, while the thick added shape changes alternately between a curved petal-like loop and a rectangular bar. Figures A and C contain the curved loop, while figures B and D contain the rectangular bar, so the next figure must again contain the curved loop. The position of the thick shape also rotates step by step by 45°: from the diagonal position in A, to vertical in B, to the opposite diagonal in C, and then to horizontal in D. Therefore, the next curved loop should appear again on the bottom-left to top-right diagonal axis. Among the given options, figure 3 correctly continues both the shape alternation and the rotation pattern.

YOUR SPACE

Previous Years' Paper

Common University Entrance Test for UG Programmes

CUET-UG—ENGLISH LANGUAGE

Entrance Exam, 2025

(Exam held on 27-05-2025)

Subject Code: 101

Directions (Qs. No. 1-4): *Read the given passage and answer the questions that follow:*

Virtues are the result of repeated actions, as habits lay the foundation of moral excellence. Right from the beginning of their lives, children are taught good habits by their parents and teachers. Magnanimity, helpfulness and sacrifice are great virtues which need to be well cultivated in human beings. Trees give shade for the benefit of others, while they themselves stand enduring the scorching heat of the sun. They selflessly bear the fruit which is consumed by birds, animals and human beings. Rivers travel hundreds of kilometers, irrigating the land and providing water for all living beings. Flowers spread their scent to make the environment pleasant. Nature teaches us to tolerate pain for the sake of service to others. Henna yields its reddish hue when ground into a paste. Sugarcane yields sweet juice when it is pressed. Flowers get pierced through with a needle to embellish us with garlands.

The character of virtuous men and women is also like the above things and elements of Nature. What is the use of this perishable and mortal frame if it is not used for the benefit of others? To live our life only for ourselves is to live like cats and dogs. People who are noble at heart do not abandon human virtues even if they have to lose their lives. A Sanskrit couplet says—"Whether men praise them or no, whether they get riches or no, whether they live long or soon die, the virtuous will never waver from the path of righteousness."

1. Which of the following is NOT mentioned in the passage?

1. Being truthful is the most important sign of virtuosity.
2. Nature teaches us to endure pain and serve others.
3. A self-centred existence is a bestial existence.
4. Not abandoning the right path even in the face of death.

2. In the passage, what is meant by "mortal frame"?

1. Nature
2. Animals
3. Land
4. Human body

3. According to the passage, which of the following is NOT true?

1. Parents and teachers inculcate good habits in children from the early stages.
2. There are parallels between the character of virtuous human beings and Nature.
3. Ethical behaviour is not dependent upon praise or reward.
4. The virtuous deviate from their path, if they aren't duly acknowledged.

4. Which of the following does not exemplify 'endurance', according to the passage?

1. Trees enduring the scorching heat of the Sun.
2. Sugarcane getting pressed to yield juice.
3. Trees bearing fruit and flowers spreading fragrance.
4. Henna being ground and turned into a paste.

Directions (Qs. No. 5-8): *Read the given passage and answer the questions that follow:*

Uma could not sing; but since learning to write, she had developed the habit of writing down any song she heard, to lessen the pain of not being able to sing it. Today the beggar woman was singing…

Resentful anguish welled up in Uma's heart. She called the singer secretly to her room, shut the door and began to write down the song in her eccentric spelling.

Tilakmanjari, Kanakmanjari and Anangamanjari observed everything through the crack in the door, and burst out, clapping their hands, "Boudidi, we've seen what you're doing!"

Uma quickly unfastened the door and began to plead with them, "Darling sisters, please don't tell anybody. I beg you, please don't. I'll never do it again. I'll never write again…"

1. 1 **2.** 4 **3.** 4 **4.** 3

At length, Uma noticed that Tilakmanjari was eyeing her exercise-book. She ran and clutched the book to her chest. Her sisters-in-law tried to take it away from her by force, but when they did not succeed, Anangamanjari went to summon her brother.

Pyarimohan arrived and sat down grimly on the bed. He said in a voice like thunder, "Give me the exercise-book."

The little girl clasped the exercise-book to her chest and directed a glance of utter supplication at her husband's face. But when she saw Pyarimohan was getting up to snatch the book from her, she flung it down, covered her face with her hands and collapsed on the floor.

5. Pyarimohan is bound to Uma by ....
1. paternal-ties
2. the bond of friendship
3. marital-ties
4. fraternal-ties

6. What is meant by "eccentric" in the passage?
1. neat and beautiful
2. strange and incorrect
3. written in the upper case
4. written in European languages

7. Why did Uma develop the habit of writing down any song she heard?
1. To alleviate her anguish at her lack of skill at singing.
2. To work upon and enhance her recently acquired skill at writing.
3. To compile all the songs in her exercise book.
4. To be able to learn to sing the song later.

8. What does the phrase 'a glance of utter supplication' mean in the passage?
1. an extremely angry and irritated look
2. a look of total excitement
3. a look showing celebration
4. a look of request and prayer

Directions (Qs. No. 9-12): *Read the given passage and answer the questions that follow:*

Solace. He turned the roll of paper between his fingers and wondered if that had not been his error—to search always for solace when there was other game to hunt in the forest. Had he had more spirit, more nerve, more desire and ambition, then perhaps he would have instead hunted for success, distinction, magic. Perhaps he would have followed in pursuit of an art, published a book of poetry, earned a name for himself, a little fame, even gold bangles for Sarla...

But the thought was puerile that it was made him spit out a bitter shred of tobacco. Every effort he had made had ended in defeat: most of the poems he had written and sent to Murad had been rejected, his monograph never published; his wife and son eyed him with blatant disappointment; nor had he won the regard of his colleagues or students. The inherent weakness in his father that had made him an ineffectual, if harmless, teacher and householder, had been passed on to him. He felt it inside him like an empty hole, one he had been staring at all his years, intimidated by its blackness and blankness. Even his attempt to fill it with a genuine and heartfelt homage to a true poet, a man who had distinguished himself as he would have liked to do, had been defeated by all the obstacles that sprang up in his life like shards and pebbles sent up at every step. It was one more blow, and perhaps the bitterest of all.

9. Choose a word similar in meaning to the word-Puerile

1. childish	2. melancholy
3. cosmopolitan	4. precocious

10. What does the word 'game' in the given phrase symbolise, 'other games to hunt in the forest'
1. Wild animals in the forest
2. Desires or goals being pursued
3. Playful activities
4. Rules of a competition.

11. On the basis of your reading identify the tone of the passage.

1. Contemptuous	2. Mournful
3. Satarical	4. Disillusioned

12. Who does Deven blame for his failure in life?
1. His wife and son
2. His lack of creativity
3. His father's submissive and timid nature
4. His inherited activism and assertiveness

13. Arrange the parts in the correct sequence to form a meaningful sentence:

(A) peeps into the dark abyss of human consciousness,
(B) Neruda conceives poetry not as something which has
(C) its deliberate relation with things of beauty, but rather as an art which
(D) something which has the ability to perceive suffering

Choose the **correct** answer from the options given below:

1. (B), (C), (A), (D)	2. (A), (D), (C), (B)
3. (C), (A), (B), (D)	4. (D), (B), (C), (A)

5. 3 **6.** 2 **7.** 1 **8.** 4 **9.** 1 **10.** 2 **11.** 2, 4 **12.** 3 **13.** 1

14. Select the correct antonym for the word: HEGEMONY

1. Supremacy 2. Leadership
3. Prosperity 4. Independence

15. Arrange the following parts in the correct sequence to form a meaningful sentence:

(A) the three best hypotheses
(B) ask them to get together
(C) the group has come up with
(D) in fours and decide on

Choose the **correct** answer from the options given below:

1. (A), (D), (C), (B) 2. (C), (B), (D), (A)
3. (B), (D), (A), (C) 4. (D), (B), (C), (A)

16. Complete the idioms given in List-I with their second part given in List-II:

List-I (Idiom's first part)	List-II (Idiom's second part)
(A) To hit the nail	(I) to injury
(B) To add insult	(II) before the horse
(C) To put the cart	(III) in the air
(D) To build castles	(IV) on the head

Choose the **correct** answer from the options given below:

1. (A) - (I), (B) - (III), (C) - (II), (D) - (IV)
2. (A) - (II), (B) - (IV), (C) - (III), (D) - (I)
3. (A) - (IV), (B) - (I), (C) - (II), (D) - (III)
4. (A) - (III), (B) - (IV), (C) - (I), (D) - (II)

17. Select the correct synonym for the word: DISCONCERTING

1. Embarrasing 2. Comfortable
3. Suave 4. Adroit

18. Select the correct antonym for the word: Valiant

1. Nervous 2. Kind
3. Coward 4. Brave

19. Arrange the following parts in the correct sequence to form a meaningful sentence:

(A) tell a lie to the teacher
(B) he is between the devil
(C) neither betray his friend nor
(D) and the deep sea as he can

Choose the **correct** answer from the options given below:

1. (A), (C), (B). (D) 2. (B), (D), (C), (A)
3. (C), (B), (D), (A) 4. (D), (A), (B), (C)

20. Rearrange the following parts in the correct sequence to form a meaningful sentence

(A) better known as the shifting cultivation
(B) garia is a folk dance performed in
(C) Tripura revolves around the Jhum culture,
(D) Tripura where the life and culture of the people of

Choose the **correct** answer from the options given below:

1. (C), (A), (B), (D) 2. (D), (C), (B), (A)
3. (A), (B), (D), (C) 4. (B), (D), (C), (A)

21. Fill in the blank in the given sentence with the correct option:

The person who studies the structure and composition of the earth to know about its history and antiquity is called a ....

1. Botanist 2. Geologist
3. Cartographer 4. Geographer

22. The little priest was not an interesting man to look at, having stubby brown hair and a round and stolid face which did not give away anything.

The word STOLID in the above sentence means:

1. Frowning 2. Darkish
3. Emotionless 4. Hateful

23. Fill in the blanks in the sentences given in List-I with the appropriate words given in List-II.

List-I (Sentences)	List-II (Words)
(A) The .... silence in the courtroom was broken only by the sound of a pen tapping.	(I) eccentric
(B) Her .... behaviour raised eyebrows at the otherwise formal event.	(II) penetrating
(C) The .... weather made the trek arduous for the beginners.	(III) oppressive
(D) The professor gave a .... analysis of the painting, revealing hidden layers of meaning.	(IV) inclement

Choose the **correct** answer from the options given below:

1. (A) - (I), (B) - (III), (C) - (II), (D) - (IV)
2. (A) - (III), (B) - (I), (C) - (IV), (D) - (II)
3. (A) - (II), (B) - (IV), (C) - (I), (D) - (III)
4. (A) - (IV), (B) - (II), (C) - (III), (D) - (I)

24. Which of the following words does not refer to one of the movements of a horse?

1. Trotting 2. Cantering
3. Galloping 4. Spinning

14. 4	**15.** 3	**16.** 3	**17.** 1	**18.** 3	**19.** 2	**20.** 4	**21.** 2	**22.** 3	**23.** 2	**24.** 4

25. Match the words given in List-I with the appropriate definitions in List-II.

List-I (Words)	List-II (Definitions)
(A) Neurologist	(I) one who treats heart diseases
(B) Orthodontist	(II) one who studies causes and diagnosis of diseases
(C) Cardiologist	(III) one who corrects and straightens irregular teeth
(D) Pathologist	(IV) one who cures nerve-related diseases

Choose the **correct** answer from the options given below:

1. (A) - (I), (B) - (III), (C) - (IV), (D) - (II)
2. (A) - (IV), (B) - (III), (C) - (I), (D) - (II)
3. (A) - (II), (B) - (IV), (C) - (I), (D) - (III)
4. (A) - (III), (B) - (I), (C) - (II), (D) - (IV)

26. Rearrange the following parts in the correct sequence to form a meaningful sentence

(A) the lives of labourers
(B) *Pahala Pandhav* is
(C) Shrilal Shukla's
(D) a realistic portrayal of

Choose the **correct** answer from the options given below:-

1. (A), (B), (C), (D) 2. (A), (B), (D), (C)
3. (B), (A), (D), (C) 4. (C), (B), (D), (A)

27. Arrange the following parts in the correct sequence to form a meaningful sentence:

(A) who is a doctor, (B) for his higher studies
(C) has gone to America (D) my brother Jagan,

Choose the **correct** answer from the options given below:

1. (A), (D), (B), (C) 2. (B), (C), (D), (A)
3. (D), (A), (C), (B) 4. (C), (A), (D), (B)

28. Select the word closest in meaning to the word 'ARDUOUS' from the options given below:

1. Mysterious 2. Continuous
3. Supportive 4. Difficult

29. Match the words given in List-I with their corresponding definitions in List-II.

List-I (Words)	List-II (Definitions)
(A) Meteorologist	(I) One who studies election and trends in voting
(B) Cosmologist	(II) One who studies fossils and the history of life forms on the earth
(C) Psephology	(III) One who studies and predicts atmospheric phenomena
(D) Paleontologist	(IV) One who studies the universe, its origin, expanse etc.

Choose the **correct** answer from the options given below:

1. (A) - (II), (B) - (I), (C) - (IV), (D) - (III)
2. (A) - (IV), (B) - (II), (C) - (III), (D) - (I)
3. (A) - (I), (B) - (III), (C) - (II), (D) - (IV)
4. (A) - (III), (B) - (IV), (C) - (I), (D) - (II)

30. Rearrange the following parts in the correct sequence to form a meaningful sentence:

(A) technology, political opinions, military capacities, education, lifestyle,. inter alia
(B) there has been growing awareness and rise in urge to be at par with
(C) with increasing purchasing power and larger disposable incomes
(D) current trends in different countries across the world in terms of science,

Choose the **correct** answer from the options given below:-

1. (D), (B), (C), (A) 2. (A), (B), (C), (D)
3. (C), (B), (D), (A) 4. (C), (A), (B), (D)

31. Select the correct antonym for the word: PLACATE

1. Provoke 2. Appease
3. Hate 4. Nullify

32. Select the correct antonym for the word: PURGE

1. Contaminate 2. Truncate
3. Conceal 4. Complicate

33. Choose the correct synonym for the word: DISDAIN

1. Astonish 2. Contempt
3. Destruction 4. Exhaustion

34. Select the correct expression to complete the sentence: It .... since morning.

1. has been raining 2. has raining
3. will raining 4. rain

35. Rearrange the following parts in the correct sequence to form a meaningful sentence:

(A) culture is a characteristic
(B) the vision
(C) way of life inspired by
(D) and values of life.

Choose the **correct** answer from the options given below:

1. (A), (C), (B), (D) 2. (A), (B), (C), (D)
3. (B), (A), (D), (C) 4. (C), (B), (D), (A)

25. 2 **26.** 4 **27.** 3 **28.** 4 **29.** 4 **30.** 3 **31.** 1 **32.** 1 **33.** 2 **34.** 1 **35.** 1

36. Select the correct antonym for the word: BELLIGERENT

1. Brave
2. Friendly
3. Hostile
4. Bemused

37. Match the words given in List-I with the appropriate definitions in List-II.

List-I (Words)	List-II (Definitions)
(A) Aviator	(I) controls and operates the flight of an aircraft
(B) Jurist	(II) knows several languages, mainly foreign
(C) Lexicographer	(III) an expert in the legal field
(D) Linguist	(IV) writer of a dictionary

Choose the **correct** answer from the options given below:

1. (A) - (I), (B) - (II), (C) - (IV), (D) - (III)
2. (A) - (II), (B) - (IV), (C) - (III), (D) - (I)
3. (A) - (I), (B) - (III), (C) - (IV), (D) - (II)
4. (A) - (III), (B) - (I), (C) - (II), (D) - (IV)

38. Select the correct antonym for the word: Zenith

1. Horizon
2. Nadir
3. Savage
4. Sober

39. Select the correct expression to complete the sentence What is the time .... ?

1. for your watch
2. at your watch
3. by your watch
4. from your watch

40. Choose the appropriate word to fill in the blank in the given sentence:
.... they had been waiting in line all night, I was sure they'd get the tickets for the show.

1. As though
2. Because of
3. Since
4. Until

41. Select the correct antonym for the word: INIQUITOUS

1. Unfair
2. Wicked
3. Virtuous
4. Hilarious

42. Choose the correct word from the given options to fill the blank in the sentence given below:
"Pakhom .... with him and the deal was closed at one thousand Rupees."

1. played
2. negotiated
3. disagreed
4. fought

43. Match the words given in List-I with their definitions in List-II.

List-I (Words)	List-II (Definitions)
(A) Theology	(I) A branch of philosophy that deals with the nature of existence
(B) Epistemology	(II) The study of the origin of the human race, its customs, beliefs and development
(C) Ontology	(III) A part of philosophy that deals with knowledge
(D) Anthropology	(IV) The study of religion and beliefs

Choose the **correct** answer from the options given below:

1. (A) - (I), (B) - (II), (C) - (III), (D) - (IV)
2. (A) - (I), (B) - (III), (C) - (II), (D) - (IV)
3. (A) - (IV), (B) - (III), (C) - (I), (D) - (II)
4. (A) - (III), (B) - (IV), (C) - (I), (D) - (II)

44. Match the idioms given in List-I with the underlined part of the sentences given in List-II.

List-I (Idioms)	List-II (Sentences)
(A) turned over a new leaf	(I) This unexpected new difficulty roused me to do my best.
(B) set his face against	(II) It is a matter of gratification that he changed for the better.
(C) put me on my mettle	(III) It is pointless to worry about the result before it's declared.
(D) to meet trouble half-way	(IV) As a social reformer, he sternly opposed child labour.

Choose the **correct** answer from the options given below:-

1. (A) - (I), (B) - (II), (C) - (III), (D) - (IV)
2. (A) - (II), (B) - (IV), (C) - (I), (D) - (III)
3. (A) - (II), (B) - (I), (C) - (IV), (D) - (III)
4. (A) - (III), (B) - (IV), (C) - (I), (D) - (II)

45. Select the correct synonym for the word: BENEDICTION

1. benefit
2. forgiveness
3. blessing
4. calmness

46. Select the correct synonym for the word: EPHEMERAL

1. Putrid
2. Invisible
3. Temporary
4. Permanent

36. 2	**37.** 3	**38.** 2	**39.** 3	**40.** 3	**41.** 3	**42.** 2	**43.** 3	**44.** 2	**45.** 3	**46.** 3

47. Rearrange the following parts in the correct sequence to form a meaningful sentence

(A) producing harmones, proteins lend satiety, prevent

(B) hunger pangs at bay, managing both weight and calories

(C) apart from building muscle, repair tissues and

(D) quick breakdown of sugar in the blood and keep

Choose the **correct** answer from the options given below:

1. (C), (A), (D), (B)
2. (A), (B), (C), (D)
3. (D), (C), (A), (B)
4. (D), (B), (C), (A)

48. Select the correct meaning of the underlined word in the sentence given below:

His desultory efforts at studying made it clear that he was not serious about passing the exam.

1. cautious
2. impetuous
3. guileful
4. unenthusiastic

49. Match the sentences given in List-I with the correct figures of speech given in List-II:

List-I (Sentences)	List-II (Figures of speech)
(A) The wind whispered through the trees.	(I) Alliteration
(B) A plumber's house always has a leaking tap.	(II) Oxymoron
(C) She opened her eyes to the deafening silence	(III) Irony
(D) The buzzing bees drew attention.	(IV) Personification

Choose the **correct** answer from the options given below:

1. (A) - (IV), (B) - (III), (C) - (II), (D) - (I)
2. (A) - (III), (B) - (I), (C) - (II), (D) - (IV)
3. (A) - (I), (B) - (IV), (C) - (III), (D) - (II)
4. (A) - (II), (B) - (III), (C) - (IV), (D) - (I)

50. Rearrange the following parts in the correct sequence to form a meaningful sentence:

(A) had left before Namita

(B) the large group

(C) reached the venue for her performance

(D) of Sattriya dancers

Choose the **correct** answer from the options given below:

1. (B), (C), (A), (D)
2. (B), (A), (D), (C)
3. (B), (D), (A), (C)
4. (C), (B), (D), (A)

EXPLANATORY ANSWERS

1. (1): Being truthful is the most important sign of virtuosity: This point is not found in the passage. The author emphasizes virtues like magnanimity, helpfulness, sacrifice, and righteousness, but never mentions truthfulness as a key virtue. Therefore, this option is correctly identified as not mentioned.

2. (4): The term "mortal frame" refers to the human body, which is described as perishable. The passage suggests that if the body is not used for the benefit of others, it serves no noble purpose. Thus, using one's life selflessly is seen as true virtue.

3. (4): The virtuous deviate from their path, if they aren't duly acknowledged: This is not true as per the passage. It clearly states that virtuous people stay committed to righteousness, regardless of praise, wealth, or life span. The Sanskrit couplet confirms this idea strongly.

4. (3): Trees bearing fruit and flowers spreading fragrance: These acts are beneficial but do not show "endurance" or suffering. The passage defines endurance through actions like facing the sun's heat or being pressed or pierced. Hence, this option does not truly reflect endurance.

5. (3): The passage identifies Pyarimohan as Uma's husband, especially when it says "a glance of utter supplication at her husband's face." This clearly establishes that the bond between them is marital, not paternal or fraternal. His commanding tone and her pleading reaction further indicate a traditional husband-wife relationship.

6. (2): The word "eccentric" in "eccentric spelling" means that Uma wrote words in a peculiar and incorrect manner. Since she was newly literate, her spellings were likely unconventional. The passage implies she spelled words phonetically or in her own unique way, not neatly or correctly.

7. (1): Uma couldn't sing and felt deep pain because of it. She started writing songs she heard as a way to reduce this sorrow. The passage clearly states she developed this habit "to lessen the pain of not being able to sing," which makes option 1 the accurate reason.

8. (4): "Utter supplication" means a deep and humble plea. Uma looks at her husband with such a pleading expression, silently begging him not to take away her book. The tone is one of desperation and emotional appeal, fitting the meaning of request and prayer.

9. (1): The word "puerile" means childish or immature. In the passage, the thought that achieving fame and success could still be possible is called "puerile," indicating that Deven himself sees it as naive or juvenile, not grounded in reality.

10. (2): The phrase "other game to hunt in the forest" is metaphorical. Here, "game" symbolizes ambitions or goals like success, art, poetry, and fame that Deven feels he failed to pursue due to his constant search for solace or comfort.

47. 1	**48.** 4	**49.** 1	**50.** 3

11. (2, 4): Both "mournful" and "disillusioned" tones are present in the passage. The narrator expresses mournful regret over missed opportunities and failed ambitions. At the same time, there is a clear sense of disillusionment—he once hoped for recognition, poetry, success, and meaning, but now sees all those dreams shattered. He even calls his hope "puerile," showing that he no longer believes in it. Therefore, the combined tone is rightly described as mournful and disillusioned, and 2 & 4 is the correct answer.

12. (3): Deven blames his father's weakness, which he believes was passed on to him. He feels this inherited trait made both of them ineffectual in life. He sees it as a black hole inside him that prevented him from achieving anything meaningful.

13. (1): The correct sequence is: Neruda conceives poetry not as something which has (B), its deliberate relation with things of beauty, but rather as an art which (C), peeps into the dark abyss of human consciousness, (A), something which has the ability to perceive suffering (D). This order forms a logical and grammatically correct sentence describing Neruda's view of poetry.

14. (4): Hegemony means dominance or leadership, especially by one state or group over others. The opposite of dominance is independence, where no control or influence is exerted by another power. Hence, Independence is the correct antonym.

15. (3): The meaningful sentence is: Ask them to get together (B), in fours and decide on (D), the three best hypotheses (A), the group has come up with (C). This sequence maintains proper structure and meaning in a collaborative task context.

16. (3): (A) - (IV), (B) - (I), (C) - (II), (D) - (III)

(A) To hit the nail on the head (IV) – means to describe exactly what is causing a situation.

(B) To add insult to injury (I) – means to make a bad situation worse.

(C) To put the cart before the horse (II) – means to do things in the wrong order.

(D) To build castles in the air (III) – means to make unrealistic plans or dreams.

17. (1): The word "disconcerting" refers to something that causes discomfort, confusion, or embarrassment. It unsettles a person and makes them feel uneasy or awkward. Among the given options, "embarrassing" is the closest synonym in both tone and meaning.

18. (3): "Valiant" means showing courage, bravery, or heroism. Its direct opposite would be someone who lacks courage, i.e., a "coward." A coward avoids danger or challenge due to fear, which is the antonym of being valiant.

19. (2): The correct sentence is: He is between the devil (B), and the deep sea as he can (D), neither betray his friend nor (C), tell a lie to the teacher (A). This describes a dilemma with no good outcome.

20. (4): The meaningful sentence is: Garia is a folk dance performed in (B), Tripura where the life and culture of the people of (D), Tripura revolves around the Jhum culture, (C), better known as the shifting cultivation (A). This forms a coherent and informative statement.

21. (2): A geologist studies the Earth's structure, materials, and processes to understand its history and formation. The question mentions learning about the Earth's structure and antiquity, which directly relates to the work of a geologist, not a geographer or cartographer.

22. (3): The term "stolid" means showing little or no emotion. In the sentence, the priest's face "did not give away anything," which supports the meaning of being unexpressive or emotionless.

23. (2): (A) - (III), (B) - (I), (C) - (IV), (D) - (II)

(A) **Oppressive silence:** Refers to a tense, heavy quietness, often making people feel uncomfortable or pressured—common in intense places like courtrooms.

(B) **Eccentric behaviour:** Means odd or unusual conduct; at a formal event, such behaviour would naturally draw attention.

(C) **Inclement weather:** Describes harsh or severe weather—like rain, storms, or cold—making physical activity like trekking difficult.

(D) **Penetrating analysis:** Means a deep and insightful examination that uncovers hidden details or meanings, often used in intellectual or academic contexts.

24. (4): Trotting, cantering, and galloping are standard horse gaits, each indicating a specific speed or movement pattern. Spinning, however, is not a recognized horse gait and does not describe movement used in equestrian contexts.

25. (2): (A) - (IV), (B) - (III), (C) - (I), (D) - (II)

(A) **Neurologist:** treats nervous system disorders (IV)

(B) **Orthodontist:** specializes in correcting teeth alignment (III)

(C) **Cardiologist:** deals with heart-related issues (I)

(D) **Pathologist:** studies disease causes and diagnosis (II)

26. (4): The correct sequence is: Shrilal Shukla's (C), *Pahala Pandhav* is (B), a realistic portrayal of (D), the lives of labourers (A). This forms a clear and meaningful sentence introducing the author and theme of the work.

27. (3): The sentence becomes: My brother Jagan, (D) who is a doctor, (A) has gone to America (C) for his higher studies (B). This flows smoothly and logically describes the subject and his action.

28. (4): The word "arduous" means something that is difficult, strenuous, or requiring great effort. It does not relate to mystery, supportiveness, or continuity, making "difficult" the correct synonym.

29. (4): (A) - (III), (B) - (IV), (C) - (I), (D) - (II)

(A) Meteorologist – (III): A meteorologist studies and predicts weather and atmospheric conditions such as rainfall, storms, and temperature changes.

(B) Cosmologist – (IV): A cosmologist is concerned with the study of the universe, including its origin, structure, and overall dynamics like the Big Bang theory.

(C) Psephology – (I): Psephology is the branch of political science that deals with the study of elections and voting trends.

(D) Paleontologist – (II): A paleontologist examines fossils and ancient life forms to understand Earth's biological history.

Each word is matched with its correct scientific field, making Option 4 the correct answer.

30. **(3):** The sentence reads: With increasing purchasing power and larger disposable incomes (C), there has been growing awareness and rise in urge to be at par with (B), current trends in different countries across the world in terms of science, (D), technology, political opinions, military capacities, education, lifestyle, inter alia (A).
This sequence builds logically from cause to effect and covers all aspects clearly.

31. **(1):** Placate means to calm, pacify, or soothe someone who is angry. The opposite of calming is to provoke, which means to stir up anger or annoyance. Therefore, provoke is the correct antonym.

32. **(1):** Purge means to cleanse or remove impurities. The opposite would be to make something impure or dirty, which is contaminate. So, contaminate is the correct antonym.

33. **(2):** Disdain means a strong feeling of dislike or contempt for someone or something considered unworthy. It does not relate to astonishment or exhaustion. Hence, contempt is the correct synonym.

34. **(1):** The sentence refers to a continuous action starting in the past and still ongoing, which calls for the present perfect continuous tense. So, "It has been raining since morning" is grammatically correct.

35. **(1):** The sentence reads: Culture is a characteristic (A), way of life inspired by (C), the vision (B), and values of life (D). This sequence is grammatically logical and meaningful.

36. **(2):** Belligerent means hostile or aggressive, especially in a confrontational way. The opposite of being aggressive is friendly, which indicates a peaceful and kind attitude. Hence, friendly is the correct antonym.

37. **(3):** (A) - (I), (B) - (III), (C) - (IV), (D) - (II)
(A) **Aviator – (I):** One who operates or flies aircraft.
(B) **Jurist – (III):** A legal expert or authority in law.
(C) **Lexicographer – (IV):** A person who writes or compiles dictionaries.
(D) **Linguist – (II):** Someone who knows or studies multiple languages, especially foreign ones.

38. **(2):** Zenith means the highest point or peak. Its antonym is nadir, which means the lowest point. The two are direct opposites in figurative and literal usage, making nadir the correct answer.

39. **(3):** The correct phrase is "What is the time by your watch?", which is the standard and idiomatic way of asking someone the time based on their watch. Other options are grammatically or idiomatically incorrect.

40. **(3):** The sentence is giving a reason for the speaker's certainty that the people would get the tickets. "Since" means because, which fits perfectly: "Since they had been waiting in line all night..." conveys both cause and context.

41. **(3):** Iniquitous means extremely wicked, immoral, or unjust. The correct antonym is virtuous, which refers to someone who is morally good, righteous, or ethical. Hence, virtuous is the correct opposite.

42. **(2):** The sentence "Pakhom .... with him and the deal was closed at one thousand Rupees" refers to reaching a deal. The word negotiated best fits here, as it means discussing terms to arrive at an agreement. Other options do not suit the context of closing a deal.

43. **(3):** (A) - (IV), (B) - (III), (C) - (I), (D) - (II)
(A) **Theology – (IV):** Theology is the study of religion and beliefs, focusing on divine concepts, scriptures, and spiritual matters.
(B) **Epistemology – (III):** Epistemology is a branch of philosophy that deals with knowledge—its nature, sources, and limits.
(C) **Ontology – (I):** Ontology studies the nature of existence and being, examining what entities exist and how they relate.
(D) **Anthropology – (II):** Anthropology is the study of human beings, including their origins, development, cultural customs, and evolution.

44. **(2):** (A) - (II), (B) - (IV), (C) - (I), (D) - (III)
(A) **Turned over a new leaf – (II):** This idiom means to reform or start afresh, which matches the sentence where someone changed for the better.
(B) **Set his face against – (IV):** This means to firmly oppose something, matching the context of sternly opposing child labour.
(C) **Put me on my mettle – (I):** Means to test someone's strength or ability, as in the sentence about a difficulty that made someone do their best.
(D) **To meet trouble half-way – (III):** Refers to anticipating or worrying about trouble before it happens, matching the idea of worrying before results are declared.

45. **(3):** Benediction means a blessing or expression of good wishes, especially at the end of a religious service. Among the options, blessing is the most accurate synonym.

46. **(3):** Ephemeral means lasting for a very short time. The best synonym among the options is temporary, which also refers to something not permanent or enduring.

47. **(1):** The sentence becomes:
(C) Apart from building muscle, repair tissues and
(A) producing hormones, proteins lend satiety, prevent
(D) quick breakdown of sugar in the blood and keep
(B) hunger pangs at bay, managing both weight and calories.
This arrangement logically explains the multiple roles of proteins in the body.

48. **(4):** Desultory means lacking a plan, purpose, or enthusiasm. In the sentence, it reflects that his studying was aimless and showed no real effort, making unenthusiastic the correct meaning.

49. **(1):** (A) - (IV), (B) - (III), (C) - (II), (D) - (I)
(A) The wind whispered... – Personification (IV): giving human traits to wind
(B) A plumber's house always has a leaking tap – Irony (III): unexpected contradiction
(C) Deafening silence – Oxymoron (II): two opposite terms used together
(D) Buzzing bees... – Alliteration (I): repetition of initial consonant sounds

50. **(3):** The correct sequence is:
(B) The large group
(D) of Sattriya dancers
(A) had left before Namita
(C) reached the venue for her performance.
This order forms a clear, grammatically correct sentence.

Previous Years' Paper

Common University Entrance Test for UG Programmes

CUET-UG—GENERAL TEST

Entrance Exam, 2025

(Exam held on 27-05-2025)

Subject Code: 501

1. Jatin is ninth from the front in a column of boys. There were thrice as many behind him as there were in front. How many boys are there between Jatin and the fifth boy from the end of the column?

1. 33
2. 20
3. 21
4. 19

2. Earth Hour, the voluntary one hour blackout observed by 187 countries on 23rd day of March every year, to mark a battle against global warming, was first organized by which organization of the following:

1. Green Peace
2. World Health Organization
3. World Wildlife Fund for Nature
4. People for Ethical Treatment of Animals

3. Which one of the following is credited as the 'pioneer of rocket technology' in India?

1. Haider Ali
2. Sher Shah Suri
3. Tipu Sultan
4. Alauddin Khilji

4. C is to the East of B, which is to the North of D. If A is to the South of D, then in which general direction of C is A?

1. South
2. South-West
3. North
4. North-East

5. Earthquake refers to the vibration on the earth's surface caused by catastrophic endogenetic forces.

(A) The magnitude or intensity of energy released by an earthquake is not measured by the modified Mercalli Intensity Scale.

(B) The place on the ground surface which is perpendicular to the focus is called the epicenter.

(C) Seismology is the special branch of geology that deals with the study of earthquakes.

(D) Shadow zones are some specific areas where earthquake waves do not occur or occur rarely.

Choose the **correct** answer from the options given below:

1. (A), (B) and (D) only
2. (A), (C) and (D) only
3. (A), (B) and (C) only
4. (B), (C) and (D) only

6. A, B, C, D, E, F and G are sitting around a circular table facing the center. E is second to the right of F, who is sitting on the immediate right of C. A & D are the only persons sitting between G & E.

(A) B is third to the right of G.

(B) C is the immediate right of G.

(C) D is the immediate right of B.

(D) G is second to the left of F.

Choose the **correct** answer from the options given below:

1. (C) and (D) only
2. (A), (B) and (D) only
3. (A), (B) and (C) only
4. (A), (B), (C) and (D)

7. Arrange the sequence of national events in the order of their occurrence.

(A) Inauguration of Prerna Sthal.

(B) Droupadi Murmu takes oath as the 15th President of India.

(C) Karpoori Thakur, referred to as 'Jan Nayak', became the 49th recipient of the Bharat Ratna.

(D) India became the first country to prepare a full list of fauna, called 'Fauna of India'.

Choose the **correct** answer from the options given below:

1. (A), (B), (C), (D)
2. (B), (A), (D), (C)
3. (B), (C), (A), (D)
4. (C), (B), (D), (A)

1. 4	**2.** 3	**3.** 3	**4.** 2	**5.** 4	**6.** 2	**7.** 3

8. A trader sells wheat at 10% profit and uses weight 10% less than the actual measure. What is his actual percentage gain?

1. 18.18% 2. 20%
3. 22.22% 4. 10%

9. Choose the number which is different from the others.

1. 295 2. 552
3. 729 4. 906

10. Which of the following is called the 'Tiger of the Ganges' along with the distinction of being the 'National Aquatic Animal'?

1. Ghariyal 2. Dolphin
3. Royal Bengal Tiger 4. Hippopotamus

11. How many degrees will the hour hand move, in the time within which the minute hand moves 240°?

1. 20° 2. 18°
3. 24° 4. 22°

12. 'Amar Sonar Bangla', the national anthem of present day Bangladesh was written by which of the following poets?

1. Bankim Das Chatterjee
2. Rabindra Nath Tagore
3. Ashfaq Ullah Khan
4. Sarojini Naidu

13. Who among the following emperors fought the 'First Battle of Panipat'?

1. Babur and Sikandar Lodhi
2. Akbar and Hemu
3. Humayun and Sher Shah Suri
4. Babur and Ibrahim Lodhi

14. When seen through a mirror, an analog clock shows quarter to four. The correct time shows by the clock:

1. 9:15 2. 9:45
3. 8:15 4. 8:45

15. If the slant height of a cone is decreased by 15 per cent and the radius of its base is increased by 20 per cent, then by what per cent will its curved surface area change?

1. 2 per cent decrease
2. 2.5 per cent decrease
3. 2.5 per cent increase
4. 2 per cent increase

16. Match the following missions to their respective purposes:

List-I (Mission)	List-II (Purpose)
(A) Chandrayaan-3	(I) Development and launch of a dual-frequency synthetic aperture radar satellite
(B) Gaganyaan-3	(II) Attempt for soft landing on moon
(C) NISAR	(III) Solar Observatory Mission
(D) Aditya-L1	(IV) India's first crewed (human) space mission

Choose the **correct** answer from the options given below:

1. (A) - (II), (B) - (IV), (C) - (I), (D) - (III)
2. (A) - (I), (B) - (III), (C) - (II), (D) - (IV)
3. (A) - (IV), (B) - (I), (C) - (III), (D) - (II)
4. (A) - (III), (B) - (IV), (C) - (I), (D) - (II)

17. Manish is eighteenth from the right end and Rahul is fifth from the left end in a row of boys. If there are seven boys between Manish and Rahul, how many boys are there in the row?

1. 29 2. 30
3. 31 4. 41

18. The partition of Bengal in 1905 was realized during the Viceroyship of:

1. Lord Mountbatten
2. Lord Dalhousie
3. Lord Irwin
4. Lord Curzon

19. Trace out the figure, from among the following options, in which the figure (X) is embedded:

(X)

1.  2. 

3.  4. 

8. 3	**9.** 1 & 3	**10.** 2	**11.** 1	**12.** 2	**13.** 4
14. 3	**15.** 4	**16.** 1	**17.** 2	**18.** 4	**19.** 4

20. A bag contains 3 red, 2 blue, 5 green and 4 yellow balls. If two balls are picked at random, what is the probability that either both are red or both are blue?

1. 1/7 2. 3/91
3. 4/91 4. 5/91

21. The sum of n terms of the series

$$1+\frac{3}{2}+2+\frac{5}{2}+3+\frac{7}{2}+......$$

1. $\frac{n(n+1)}{2}$ 2. $\frac{n(n+3)}{4}$
3. $\frac{(n+1)(n+2)}{4}$ 4. $\frac{n(n+3)}{2}$

22. The component of the blood which helps to fight infections is:

1. Erythrocytes 2. Plasma
3. Platelets 4. Leukocytes

23. A boy travels between point A and point B at a speed of 6 km/h and returns at a speed of 9 km/h. If the total time taken by him is 1 hour 15 min, the distance between A and B is:

1. 6.5 km 2. 5.5 km
3. 4.5 km 4. 9 km

24. In the given question, a statement is followed by two assumptions. You have to decide which of the assumptions is implicit in the statement and choose your answer accordingly.

Statement: Over The Top (OTT) platform has become indispensable for the entertainment of people.

Assumptions:

I. People enjoy watching content on OTT.
II. OTT is the only medium of entertainment.

1. Only assumption II is implicit.
2. Only assumption I is implicit.
3. Both I and II are implicit.
4. Neither I nor II is implicit.

25. In the letter series, some of the letters are missing, which are given in the alternatives (A), (B), (C) and (D).

m n o n o p q o p q r _ _ _ _ s t u

(A) r (B) s
(C) q (D) p

Choose the **correct** sequence from the options given below:

1. (C), (B), (D), (A) 2. (A), (B), (C), (D)
3. (B), (A), (D), (C) (B), (D), (C), (A)

26. The value of gravity (g) on the Moon is .... of that on the earth's surface.

1. 1/2 2. 1/3
3. 1/6 4. 1/9

27. In the given question, find out which of the following answer figures completes the figure matrix?

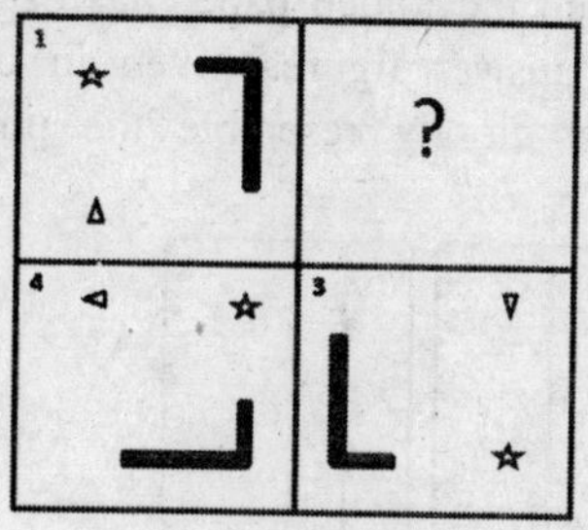

1. 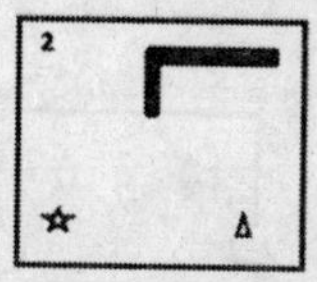
2. 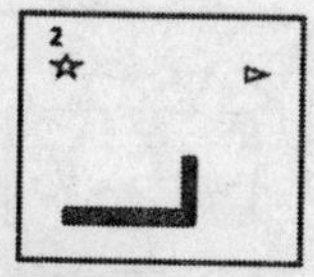
3. 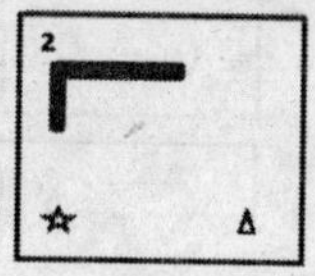
4. 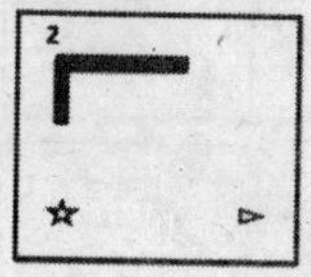

28. P and Q together can do a piece of work in 60 days. Q and R together can do it in 120 days. P and R together can do it in 90 days. In what time can Q alone do the same work?

1. 144 days 2. 720 days
3. 360 days 4. 720/7 days

29. Soap consists of:

1. Alkali salts of higher fatty acids
2. Calcium carbonate, aluminum silicate and gypsum
3. Sodium silicate and silicate of a base, like calcium or lead
4. Sodium silicate and ammonium nitrate

30. Match List-I with List-II.

List-I	List-II
(A) Remainder when 17^{35234} is divided by 8	(I) 0
(B) Remainder when 4444 is divided by 9	(II) 1
(C) Unit's digit of $(34)^{15}+(34)^{16}$	(III) 2
(D) Unit digit of 7^4-9^3	(IV) 7

Choose the **correct** answer from the options given below:

1. (A) - (II), (B) - (IV), (C) - (I), (D) - (III)
2. (A) - (I), (B) - (II), (C) - (III), (D) - (IV)
3. (A) - (II), (B) - (IV), (C) - (III), (D) - (I)
4. (A) - (IV), (B) - (II), (C) - (I), (D) - (III)

20. 3 **21.** 4 **22.** 4 **23.** 3 **24.** 2 **25.** 4 **26.** 3 **27.** 4 **28.** 1 **29.** 1 **30.** 1

31. The number of diagonals in a Hexagon is:

1. 6
2. 7
3. 8
4. 9

32. The figures X, Y and Z given below show a sequence of folding of paper. The fig. (Z) shows the manner in which the folded paper has been cut. Choose from the answer figures given in options which would most closely resemble the unfolded form of fig. (Z).

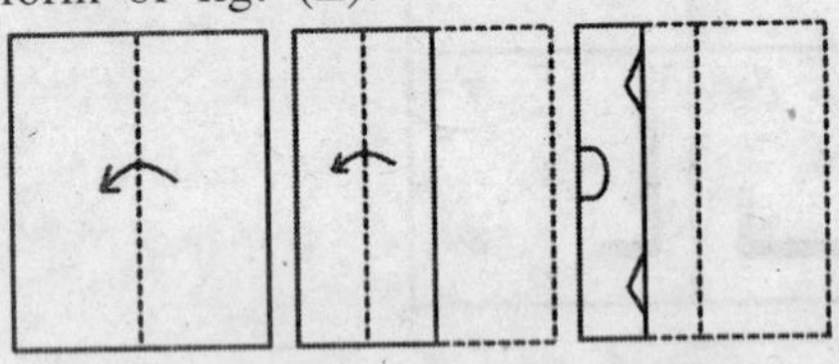

X Y Z

1. 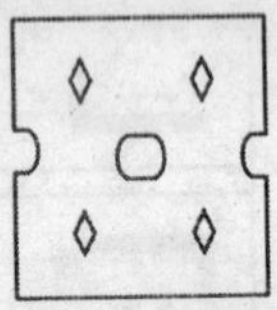
2. 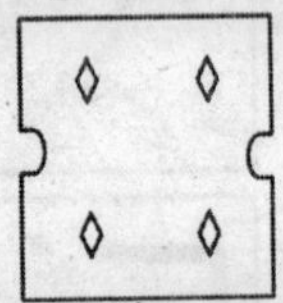
3. 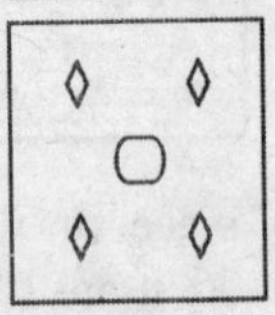
4. 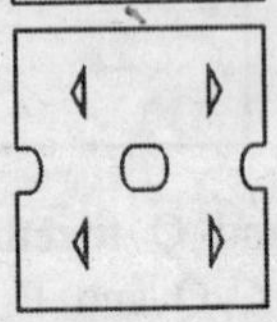

33. If the area of an equilateral triangle is $36\sqrt{3}$ cm^2, then the length of the side is:

1. 12 cm
2. 9 cm
3. 6 cm
4. 3 cm

34. Arrange the sequence of the stages of human progress in order of their occurrence.

(A) The Palaeolithic Age
(B) The Chalcolithic Age
(C) The Neolithic Age
(D) The Mesolithic Age

Choose the **correct** answer from the options given below:

1. (A), (B), (C), (D)
2. (B), (A), (D), (C)
3. (D), (A), (B), (C)
4. (A), (D), (C), (B)

35. Select a suitable figure from the answer figures which will substitute this question mark so that a series is formed in order.

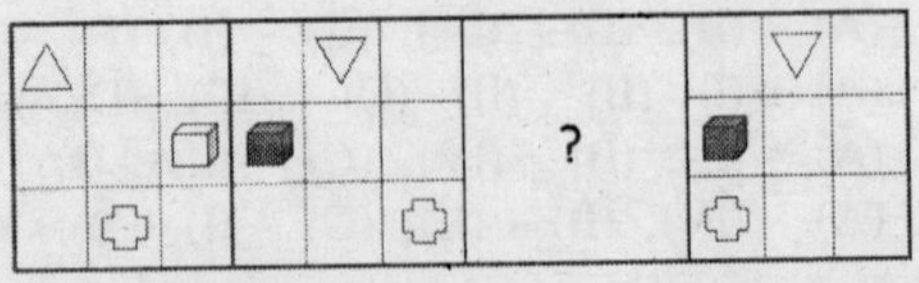

1. 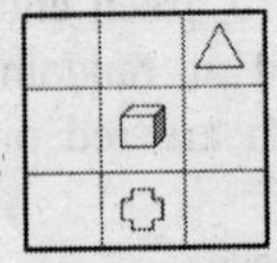
2. 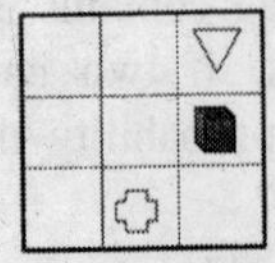
3. 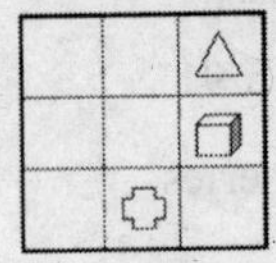
4. 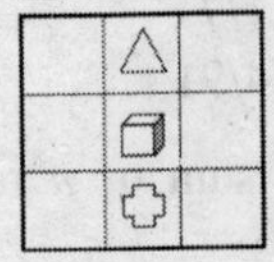

36. The sum of the digits of a 4-digit number is subtracted from the number. The resulting number is always:

1. divisible by 6
2. divisible by 9
3. divisible by 4
4. divisible by 8

37. Trace out the alternative figure from among the following options in which the figure (X) is embedded (rotation is not allowed):

(X)

1. 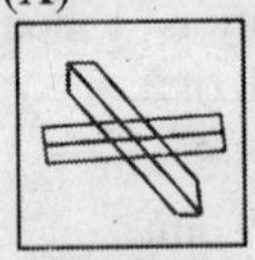
2. 
3. 
4. 

38. 3 men or 15 boys can do a piece of work in 3 days. In how many days will 2 men and 5 boys do this work?

1. 15 days
2. 25 days
3. 30 days
4. 40 days

39. The nearest integer to 6650 which is exactly divisib by 429 is:

1. 6864
2. 6435
3. 6436
4. 6535

40. Which of the following nicknames would you mo likely relate to Thailand?

1. Land of Thousand Elephants
2. Land of Morning Calm
3. Land of White Elephants
4. Land of Tigers

41. If 10% of X = 15% of Y = 1/5 of Z, th X : Y : Z is:

1. 6 : 3 : 4
2. 10 : 15 : 18
3. 15 : 10 : 18
4. 6 : 4 : 3

31. 4 **32.** 1 **33.** 1 **34.** 4 **35.** 3 **36.** 2 **37.** 2 **38.** 3 **39.** 1 **40.** 3 **41.** 4

42. In the given question, a statement is followed by two conclusions numbered I and II. You have to assume everything in the statement to be true, then consider the two conclusions together and decide which of them logically follows beyond a reasonable doubt from the information given in the statement.

Statement: Birds of same feather flock together.

Conclusions:

I. Similar people tend to associate with each other.

II. A group of birds have beautiful feathers.

1. Only conclusion I follows
2. Only conclusion II follows
3. Both I and II follow
4. Neither I nor II follows

43. Choose the correct water image of the given figure, amongst the following answer figures:

1. 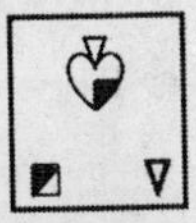
2. 
3. 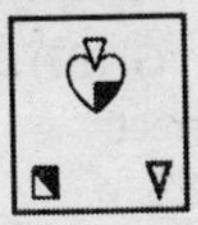
4. 

44. The relation between Mean, Median and Mode for symmetrical distribution is:

1. Mode = 2 Median – 5 Mean
2. Mode = 4 Median – Mean
3. Mean = Median = Mode
4. Mode = 2 Median = Mean

45. Which one of the following answer figures completes the figure matrix given below:

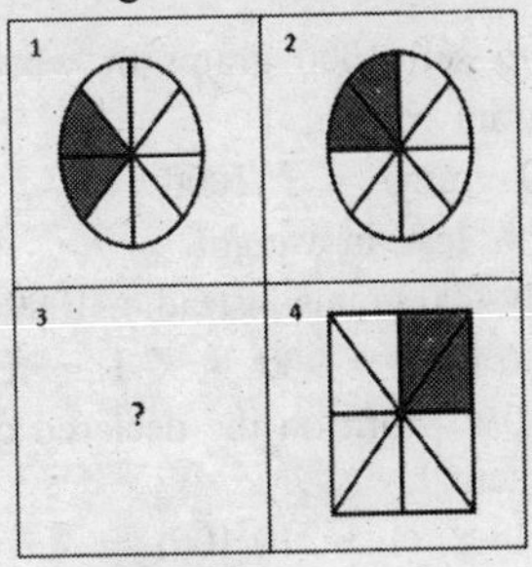

1. 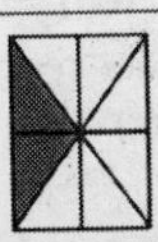
2. 
3. 
4. 

46. Mohiniyattam is a solo female dance form known for its rhythmic and unbroken flow of body movements.

(A) The love and devotion to god Vishnu is usually the theme of this dance form.

(B) This dance form belongs to the state of Andhra Pradesh.

(C) Mohiniyattam has the grace and elegance of Bharatanatyam and the vigor of Kathakali.

(D) The dancers attire in a beautiful white and gold bordered Kasavu sari with distinctive white jasmine flowers around a French bun at the side of her head.

Choose the **correct** answer from the options given below:

1. (A), (B) and (C) only
2. (A), (B) and (D) only
3. (A), (C) and (D) only
4. (B), (C) and (D) only

47. The question below consists of a question and two statements numbered I and II given below it. You have to decide whether the data provided in the statements is sufficient to answer the question.

The last Tuesday of February 2024 fell on which date?

I. The first Tuesday of that month fell on 6th.

II. The last day of that month was Thursday.

1. The data in the statement I alone is sufficient to answer the question.
2. The data in the statement II alone is sufficient to answer the question.
3. The data in both statements I and II together are necessary to answer the question.
4. The data either in statement I alone or in statement II alone are sufficient to answer the question.

48. By looking in a mirror, it appears that it is 6:05 on an analog clock. What is the actual time?

1. 11:30   2. 5:50
3. 5:55   4. 11:28

49. For what value of k, the system of equations $3x - ky - 3 = 0$ and $2x - 3y - 4 = 0$ has no solution?

1. 6   2. 9
3. 5   4. 9/2

50. Paris Olympics 2024 was held in the vicinity of which river?

1. Seine   2. Thames
3. Colorado   4. Nile

42. 1	**43.** 3	**44.** 3	**45.** 2	**46.** 3	**47.** 4	**48.** 3	**49.** 4	**50.** 1

EXPLANATORY ANSWERS

1. Jatin is 9th from the front, so there are 8 boys ahead of him. According to the question, the number of boys behind him is three times the number in front:
$8 \times 3 = 24$ boys behind Jatin.
Therefore, total number of boys
$= 8$ (in front) $+ 1$ (Jatin himself) $+ 24$ (behind)
$= 33$ boys.
The fifth boy from the end will be at position number
$= 33 - 5 + 1 = 29$ from the front.
Jatin is 9th from the front.
The number of boys between Jatin (9th) and the fifth from end (29th) $= 29 - 9 - 1 = 19$ boys.

2. Earth Hour was first initiated by the World Wide Fund for Nature (WWF) in 2007 in Sydney, Australia. It is observed annually on the 23rd of March in over 180 countries, encouraging individuals, communities, and businesses to turn off non-essential lights for one hour to raise awareness about global warming and environmental conservation.

3. Tipu Sultan is regarded as the pioneer of rocket technology in India. He and his father Haider Ali developed iron-cased rockets which were used effectively during wars against the British, especially in the Anglo-Mysore wars. These Mysorean rockets influenced later European military rocket designs.

4. C is to the east of B, and B is to the north of D, so C is northeast of D. A is to the south of D.
Thus, from C's position (northeast of D), A would lie toward the southwest.
Hence, A is in the south-west direction from C.

5. (B), (C) and (D) only

(A) is incorrect because the Modified Mercalli Intensity Scale does measure the intensity of shaking, not magnitude, so the statement is factually wrong.

(B) is correct: the epicenter is the point on the earth's surface directly above the earthquake's focus.

(C) is correct: seismology is the branch of geology that studies earthquakes.

(D) is correct: shadow zones are regions where seismic waves are not recorded due to the wave refraction and absorption patterns inside Earth.

6. We are given:
- E is second to the right of F,
- F is sitting on the immediate right of C,
- A and D are the only persons sitting between G and E.

Let's fix positions clockwise using the given information.
Start by placing C at position P1, then:
- F is to the immediate right of C $\Rightarrow$ F at P2
- E is second to the right of F $\Rightarrow$ E at P4

So far:
P1 – C   P2 – F
P3 – (unknown)   P4 – E

Now use the clue: A and D are the only persons sitting between G and E.
So G _ A D _ E (clockwise), placing A and D between G and E.
Try placing:
- E at P4
- Then P5 = A, P6 = D, P7 = G

Now filled:
P1 – C   P2 – F
P3 – B (only person left)   P4 – E
P5 – A   P6 – D
P7 – G

Complete clockwise arrangement:
C – F – B – E – A – D – G
Now check each option:
(A) B is third to the right of G
From G (P7), count clockwise:
1st = C (P1), 2nd = F (P2), 3rd = B (P3) $\Rightarrow$ True
(B) C is immediate right of G
From G (P7), immediate right is P1 = C $\Rightarrow$ True
(C) D is immediate right of B
From B (P3), immediate right is P4 = E $\Rightarrow$ False
(D) G is second to the left of F
From F (P2), moving left:
1st left = C (P1), 2nd left = G (P7) $\Rightarrow$ True
So, only (A), (B), and (D) are correct.
Answer: 2: (A), (B) and (D) only.

7. Let's arrange the events with year:
(B) Droupadi Murmu became President in July 2022
(C) Karpoori Thakur awarded Bharat Ratna in January 2024
(A) Prerna Sthal inaugurated in February 2024
(D) 'Fauna of India' list launched in March 2024
Correct sequence of occurrence:
(B) → (C) → (A) → (D)
Answer: 3: (B), (C), (A), (D).

8. Let the trader claims to sell 1000 grams of wheat.
Cost Price (CP) per gram = Re. 1
So, actual CP of 1000 grams = ₹ 1000
However, he gives 10% less in weight.
That means he gives only 900 grams instead of 1000 grams.
So, actual cost to the trader = 900 × ₹ 1 = ₹ 900
He sells the wheat at 10% profit on the declared quantity (1000 grams), not on actual.
So, SP = 1000 × ₹ 1 × (1 + 10/100) = ₹ 1100
Thus, for 900 grams of wheat, the trader receives ₹ 1100.
His gain = ₹ 1100 – ₹ 900 = ₹ 200
Now calculate percentage gain:

$$\text{Percentage gain} = \frac{\text{Gain}}{\text{Actual CP}} \times 100 = \frac{200}{900} \times 100$$
$$= 22.22\%.$$

9. This question allows for two valid interpretations, each highlighting a different number as the odd one out based on distinct logical reasoning:

Logic 1 – Perfect Power Logic:

- 729 is a perfect cube (9^3) and also a perfect sixth power (3^6), making it unique among the given numbers.
- 295, 552, and 906 are not perfect squares, cubes, or higher powers.

So, 729 stands out due to its special mathematical structure.

Logic 2 – Divisibility by 5:

- 295 ends in 5 ⇒ divisible by 5.
- 552, 729, and 906 do not end in 0 or 5, so they are not divisible by 5.

Thus, 295 is the only number in the group divisible by 5.

Since both logics are equally valid and highlight different numbers, both 295 and 729 are correct answers, depending on the reasoning applied.

Answer: 1 and 3: 295 and 729.

10. The Ganges River Dolphin is referred to as the 'Tiger of the Ganges' due to its importance in the river ecosystem. It is also officially declared as the National Aquatic Animal of India by the Government.

11. The minute hand of a clock moves 6° per minute (360° in 60 minutes).

To move 240°, time taken = 240 ÷ 6 = 40 minutes.

The hour hand moves 0.5° per minute (360° in 12 hours = 0.5° per minute).

So, in 40 minutes, hour hand moves = 0.5 × 40 = 20°.

12. 'Amar Sonar Bangla' is the national anthem of Bangladesh. It was written by Rabindra Nath Tagore in 1905 during the Swadeshi movement, as a protest against the partition of Bengal by the British. The first ten lines of this song were adopted as the national anthem by Bangladesh in 1971.

13. The First Battle of Panipat took place in 1526 between Babur, the founder of the Mughal Empire, and Ibrahim Lodhi, the last ruler of the Delhi Sultanate.

Babur's victory marked the beginning of Mughal rule in India and the end of the Lodhi dynasty.

14. When a clock shows 3:45 in the mirror, the actual time is calculated by subtracting from 12:00.

12:00 – 3:45 = 8:15

Therefore, the actual time shown by the clock is 8:15.

15. Curved Surface Area (CSA) of a cone

$$= \pi \times r \times l$$

Let original radius = 100, slant height = 100

$$\text{Original CSA} = \pi \times 100 \times 100 = 10000\pi$$

$$\text{New radius} = 100 + 20\% = 120$$

$$\text{New slant height} = 100 - 15\% = 85$$

$$\text{New CSA} = \pi \times 120 \times 85 = 10200\pi$$

$$\%\text{ change} = \frac{10200 - 10000}{10000} \times 100 = 2\%$$

So, the curved surface area increases by 2%.

16. Let's match the missions correctly:

(A) Chandrayaan-3 → (II) Attempt for soft landing on the moon: Chandrayaan-3 was ISRO's mission to achieve a successful soft landing on the Moon. It succeeded in August 2023.

(B) Gaganyaan-3 → (IV) India's first crewed (human) space mission: Gaganyaan aims to send Indian astronauts (Gagannauts) into space. Gaganyaan-3 is part of this human spaceflight programme.

(C) NISAR → (I) Development and launch of a dual-frequency synthetic aperture radar satellite: NISAR (NASA-ISRO Synthetic Aperture Radar) is a joint Earth observation mission with a dual-frequency radar for climate and disaster monitoring.

(D) Aditya-L1 → (III) Solar Observatory Mission: Aditya-L1 is India's first solar mission, launched to study the Sun's outer atmosphere (corona and solar wind).

Answer: 1: (A) – (II), (B) – (IV), (C) – (I), (D) – (III).

17. Given:

- Manish is 18th from the right end
- Rahul is 5th from the left end
- 7 boys are between them

So, total boys = (Position of Manish from right) + (Position of Rahul from left) + (Number of boys between them) = 18 + 5 + 7 = 30.

18. The Partition of Bengal was carried out in 1905 during the viceroyalty of Lord Curzon. The stated purpose was administrative efficiency, but it was widely seen as an attempt to divide and weaken nationalist sentiments in Bengal. The partition was strongly opposed and later annulled in 1911.

19. The given figure (X) is a "Y" shaped structure — it consists of a vertical line with two diverging arms at the top, forming a symmetric "Y".

Now let's carefully examine each option:

- **Option 1:** Contains a combination of hexagonal lines and verticals, but the structure does not form a Y shape. *(Incorrect)*
- **Option 2:** Has intersecting triangles forming an hourglass or "X" shape, which is not similar to figure (X). *(Incorrect)*
- **Option 3:** Shows a triangle with internal divisions but does not clearly form a Y-shaped structure. The lines do not match the alignment of figure (X). *(Incorrect)*
- **Option 4:** If you closely observe the center, you can clearly identify the "Y" shape embedded within. It consists of a vertical line with two lines diverging upwards, exactly as in figure (X). *(Correct)*

Therefore, figure (X) is correctly embedded in Option 4.

20. Total number of balls in the bag

= 3 red + 2 blue + 5 green + 4 yellow = 14 balls

We are required to find the probability that either both balls are red or both are blue when two balls are drawn at random.

Total number of ways to choose 2 balls out of 14

$$= {}^{14}C_2 = \frac{14 \times 13}{2} = 91$$

Now, Number of ways to choose 2 red balls = ${}^3C_2 = 3$

Number of ways to choose 2 blue balls = ${}^2C_2 = 1$

So, favourable outcomes = 3 + 1 = 4

Therefore, required probability = 4/91.

21. The given series is: $1+\frac{3}{2}+2+\frac{5}{2}+3+\frac{7}{2}+...$

Observe the pattern:

- Odd-positioned terms: 1, 2, 3, ... form an arithmetic sequence of natural numbers
- Even-positioned terms: $\frac{3}{2}, \frac{5}{2}, \frac{7}{2}$, ... also form an arithmetic sequence

Let's calculate the sum of first few terms and test the formulas:

For $n = 1$: $1 \rightarrow$ Sum $= 1$

Check Option 2:

$$1\times\frac{1+3}{2} = \frac{4}{2} = 2 \rightarrow \textit{(Incorrect)}$$

$$n = 2: \quad 1+\frac{3}{2} = \frac{5}{2}$$

$$\text{Option 2:} \quad 2\times\frac{2+3}{2} = 2\times\frac{5}{2} = 5 \rightarrow \textit{(Incorrect)}$$

$$n = 4: \quad 1+\frac{3}{2}+2+\frac{5}{2} = \left(\frac{1}{2}\right)+\left(\frac{3}{2}+\frac{5}{2}\right)$$

$$= 3 + 4 = 7$$

$$\text{Option 2:} \quad 4\times\frac{4+3}{2} = 4\times\frac{7}{2} = 14 = 14 \rightarrow \textit{(Correct)}$$

$$n = 5: \quad 1+\frac{3}{2}+2+\frac{5}{2}+3 = (1+2+3)+\frac{3}{2}+\frac{5}{2}$$

$$= 6 + 4 = 10$$

$$\text{Option 2:} \quad 5\times\frac{5+3}{2} = 5\times\frac{8}{2} = 20 \rightarrow \textit{(Correct)}$$

Hence, the formula that correctly represents the sum of n terms of the series is: $\frac{n(n+3)}{2}$.

22. The component of blood that helps in fighting infections is known as Leukocytes, or white blood cells (WBCs). They are part of the immune system and function to identify and destroy harmful pathogens like bacteria, viruses, and other foreign invaders.

Other options:

- **Erythrocytes (RBCs):** Carry oxygen
- **Plasma:** Transport medium for cells and nutrients
- **Platelets:** Help in blood clotting

Only leukocytes have the defensive role against infections.

23. Let the distance between A and B be x km.

Time taken to go from A to B at 6 km/h $= \frac{x}{6}$ hours

Time taken to return from B to A at 9 km/h $= \frac{x}{9}$ hours

$$\text{Total time} = 1 \text{ hour } 15 \text{ minutes}$$
$$= 1.25 \text{ hours}$$

$$\text{So,} \quad \frac{x}{6}+\frac{x}{9} = 1.25$$

Take LCM of 6 and 9 = 18

$$\frac{3x+2x}{18} = 1.25 \Rightarrow \frac{5x}{18} = 1.25$$

$$\Rightarrow \quad x = \frac{1.25\times18}{5} = \frac{22.5}{5} = 4.5$$

Therefore, the distance between A and B is 4.5 km.

24. Statement: "Over The Top (OTT) platform has become indispensable for the entertainment of people."

- **Assumption I:** People enjoy watching content on OTT — Implicit, because unless people find OTT entertaining, it wouldn't be considered indispensable.
- **Assumption II:** OTT is the only medium of entertainment — Not implicit, as the statement says OTT is indispensable, not exclusive.

Only the first assumption logically follows from the statement. Answer: 2: Only assumption I is implicit.

25. Given sequence:

m n o | n o p | q o p | q r _ _ _ _ s t u

Break the series into overlapping trios:

- m n o
- n o p
- o p q
- p q r
- q r s
- r s t
- s t u

So, missing letters after "q r" must be:

s, t, p, q ⇒ But needs to fit full letter structure.

However, based on the pattern, after "q r", the correct 4-letter gap to reach "s t u" should be:

s, t, u, v, but that conflicts.

Let's look again:

From "m n o", next trio = shift one forward each time:

n o p
o p q
p q r
q r s
r s t
s t u

So the missing letters are: s, t, u, v — but since the sequence given already ends at "s t u", the missing 4 letters just before that are: r, s, t, u

Therefore: The missing letters are: (B) s, (D) p, (C) q, (A) r.

But reordered correctly, matching pattern: (B), (D), (C), (A).

26. The gravitational acceleration on the Moon is approximately 1/6th of that on Earth.

- Earth's gravity ≈ 9.8 m/s^2
- Moon's gravity ≈ 1.63 m/s^2

$$\frac{1.63}{9.8} \approx \frac{1}{6}.$$

27. To solve this figure matrix, let's analyze both shapes and symbols row-wise and column-wise.

Step 1: Analyze arrow shapes (thick L-shapes):

- In the first row, images (1) and (2) both have an L-shape rotated differently.
- In the second row, images (4) and (3) also have L-shapes in different orientations.

Now observe the positions of the thick L-shapes:

- From left to right in the top row: shape rotates 90° clockwise from 1 to 2.

- From left to right in the bottom row: shape rotates 90° clockwise from 4 to 3.

So, following the same logic, the L-shape in the missing figure (top right) must be a 90° clockwise rotation of the shape in cell (2).

Looking at cell (2), the shape is a vertical L. Its 90° clockwise rotation is the horizontal L found in option 4.

Step 2: Analyze the small symbols (triangle, star, etc.):

Each box contains a triangle and a star, and their positions also follow a consistent diagonal symmetry or shifting across rows/columns.

Following the same position trend of symbols (as seen in cells 1, 2, 3, and 4), the triangle and star in the missing cell match the placement seen in option 4.

Thus, both the thick L-shape and the symbol positions match in option 4.

28. Let the total work be 1 unit.

We are given:

- P and Q together can complete the work in 60 days $\Rightarrow$ (P + Q)'s 1-day work = 1/60
- Q and R together can complete the work in 120 days $\Rightarrow$ (Q + R)'s 1-day work = 1/120
- P and R together can complete the work in 90 days $\Rightarrow$ (P + R)'s 1-day work = 1/90

Now, add all three equations:

$$(P + Q) + (Q + R) + (P + R) = \frac{1}{60}+\frac{1}{120}+\frac{1}{90}$$

$$\Rightarrow \quad 2(P + Q + R) = \text{LCM of } 60, 120, 90 = 360$$

Convert each to a common denominator:

$$\frac{1}{60} = \frac{6}{360}; \frac{1}{120} = \frac{3}{360}; \frac{1}{90} = \frac{4}{360}$$

$$\Rightarrow \quad \text{Sum} = \frac{6+3+4}{360} = \frac{13}{360}$$

$$\text{So,} \quad 2(P + Q + R) = \frac{13}{360}$$

$$\Rightarrow \quad P + Q + R = \frac{13}{720}$$

Now subtract (P + R)'s work to get Q's work:

$$Q = (P + Q + R) - (P + R)$$

$$= \frac{13}{720}-\frac{1}{90}$$

Convert 1/90 to denominator 720:

$$\frac{1}{90} = \frac{8}{720} \Rightarrow Q = \frac{13-8}{720} = \frac{5}{720}$$

Therefore, Q alone can complete the work in:

$$= \frac{720}{5} = 144 \text{ days.}$$

29. Soap is formed by saponification, where alkali (such as NaOH or KOH) reacts with fatty acids or triglycerides. This forms alkali salts of higher fatty acids, which we commonly call soap.

Other options refer to ingredients used in glass, ceramics, or fertilizers.

30. Let's solve each part of List-I and match with the correct element from List-II:

(A) Remainder when $17^{(35234)}$ is divided by 8:

Use modulo patterns.

Since $17 \equiv 1 \pmod 8$, then $17^n \equiv 1^n \equiv 1 \pmod 8$ for any n.

$\Rightarrow$ Remainder = 1 $\to$ Matches with (II)

(B) Remainder when 4^{4444} is divided by 9:

Powers of 4 modulo 9 cycle as:

$$4^1 \equiv 4 \pmod 9$$
$$4^2 \equiv 7 \pmod 9$$
$$4^3 \equiv 1 \pmod 9$$

Cycle: 4, 7, 1 (length 3)

Now, 4444 ÷ 3 gives remainder 1

$\Rightarrow$ So, $4^{4444} \equiv 4^1 \equiv 4 \pmod 9$ $\to$ Matches with (IV)

(C) Unit digit of $(34)^{15} + (34)^{16}$:

Look at unit digit pattern of 4:

$$4^1 = 4$$
$$4^2 = 16 \to \text{unit digit } 6$$

Cycle: 4, 6 (length 2)

For 4^{15} $\to$ odd $\Rightarrow$ unit digit = 4

For 4^{16} $\to$ even $\Rightarrow$ unit digit = 6

Sum = 4 + 6 = 10 $\Rightarrow$ Unit digit = 0 $\to$ Matches with (I)

(D) Unit digit of $7^4 - 9^3$:

7^4: powers cycle $\to$ 7, 9, 3, 1 $\Rightarrow$ 7^4 $\Rightarrow$ unit digit = 1

9^3: powers cycle $\to$ 9, 1 $\Rightarrow$ 9^3 $\Rightarrow$ unit digit = 9

Now 1 − 9 = -8 $\Rightarrow$ take unit digit = 2

$\to$ Matches with (III)

Correct matching: (1): (A)-II), (B)-(IV), (C)-(I), (D)-(III).

31. Formula for number of diagonals in an n-sided polygon $= \dfrac{n(n-3)}{2}$

For a hexagon ($n = 6$): $= \dfrac{6(6-3)}{2} = 6 \times \dfrac{3}{2} = 9$.

32. Let's analyze the folding and cutting step by step:

- **Figure X:** The paper is first folded vertically in half, from left to right.
- **Figure Y:** Then the paper is again folded vertically from right to left, making a total of two vertical folds. So, the paper is folded into quarters (1/4th of its original width).
- **Figure Z:** Shows cuts made on the folded paper: One semicircular cut on the vertical edge (middle of the folded sheet)

  Two diamond-shaped cuts at the top and bottom

Now, when the paper is unfolded, the cuts will mirror along both fold lines.

- The semicircular cut, made at the center fold, will mirror to form two symmetrical semicircles on either side, resulting in two full circular notches on the middle of left and right edges.
- The diamond cuts on the folded sheet will replicate four times upon full unfolding (mirroring across both folds).

Among the options:

- Option 1 shows:
  4 diamond shapes — correctly placed due to mirroring
  2 semicircular edge notches — correct as per the central vertical cut

Thus, the unfolded paper must look like Option 1.

33. We are given that the area of an equilateral triangle is: $36\sqrt{3}\ \text{cm}^2$

The formula for the area of an equilateral triangle with side length aaa is:

$$\text{Area} = \frac{\sqrt{3}}{4}a^2$$

Substitute the given area into the formula:

$$\frac{\sqrt{3}}{4}a^2 = 36\sqrt{3}$$

Divide both sides by $\sqrt{3}$:

$$\frac{1}{4}a^2 = 36$$

Multiply both sides by 4: $a^2 = 144$

Take the square root of both sides: $a = \sqrt{144} = 12$

Therefore, the length of each side of the equilateral triangle is 12 cm.

34. The correct chronological order of the prehistoric ages of human progress is:

(A) Palaeolithic Age – Old Stone Age: beginning of human tools and hunting

(D) Mesolithic Age – Middle Stone Age: transition phase, microliths used

(C) Neolithic Age – New Stone Age: agriculture, domestication begins

(B) Chalcolithic Age – Copper-Stone Age: early use of metal tools

Therefore, the correct sequence is:

Palaeolithic → Mesolithic → Neolithic → Chalcolithic.

35. Let's analyze the movement and transformation of the three elements in the figure across the series from left to right:

Top row (Triangle) – 1st Item:

Pattern:

- It moves one step forward in each frame (left to right)
- It also alternates its orientation (inverted every time)

Sequence:

1. ▲ in column 1
2. ▼ in column 2
3. ▲ in column 3
4. ? → should be in column 4 and inverted ⇒ ▼
5. ▼ in column 5
6. ?

So, triangle in column 4, facing downward (▼)

Middle row (Cube) – 2nd Item:

Pattern:

- Moves 2 steps at a time, alternating forward and backward
- Also alternates color between white and black

Sequence (position and colour):

1. White cube in column 2
2. Black cube in column 3 (→ moved forward 1 step, and changed colour)
3. ? → Now should move 2 steps back, from column 3 → column 1, and colour switches to white
4. Then black cube reappears in column 2 in the next image

So, cube should be white, placed in column 1

Bottom row (Plus symbol) – 3rd Item:

Pattern:

- Remains in same shape and colour, and moves 1 step forward each time

Sequence:

1. **Column 3**
2. **Column 4**
3. **Column 5**

So, in the missing frame, it should be in column 6

But we are to find the missing figure before that — so before it reaches column 5, it was in column 4

→ It must be in column 4 in the missing image

Final Expected Configuration:

- Top row: ▼ in column 4
- Middle row: White cube in column 1
- Bottom row: White plus in column 4

Check which option matches:

Option 3 shows:

- ▼ (triangle) in column 4
- White cube in column 1
- White cross in column 4

Perfect match.

36. Let the 4-digit number be represented as N.

Let the sum of its digits be S.

We are given: The number N – S is always divisible by a certain number.

General Rule: For any number, if you subtract the sum of its digits from the number itself, the result is always divisible by 9.

Why? Let's prove it algebraically:

Let the number be:

N = $1000a + 100b + 10c + d$ where a, b, c, d are the digits of the number

Sum of digits $= a + b + c + d =$ S

Then,

$N - S = (1000a + 100b + 10c + d) - (a + b + c + d)$

$= 999a + 99b + 9c$

Each term on the right-hand side is divisible by 9:

$999a = 9 \times 111a$, $99b = 9 \times 11b$, $9c = 9 \times c$

Hence, N – S is divisible by 9

This is a known divisibility property for all whole numbers.

37. We are given a base figure (X), which consists of two intersecting thin lines forming an 'X' shape, where each line has a small outward bend at its ends. The figure is formed by two clean, curved strokes crossing each other. The task is to identify which of the given options contain this exact figure embedded without rotation.

Let's analyze each option carefully:

Option 1:

- Contains thick, straight overlapping bands.
- The structure is geometrically rigid and lacks the distinctive outward curves found in figure (X).
- No accurate embedding of (X) is observed.

Not a match.

Option 2:

- Among all the lines in the structure, the inner intersecting lines are thin and angled, matching the curved outward strokes of figure (X).
- These lines exactly replicate the direction, style, and bending of figure (X) without rotation.

Perfect match

Option 3:

- Composed of thick, diagonal strips with squared ends.
- The distinctive curving ends of figure (X) are not present.
- The lines do not replicate the gentle bend seen in (X).

Not a match

Option 4:

- Similar to Option 3, features wide angular bands.
- No visible trace of the specific curve-ended X shape from figure (X).

Not a match

Hence, only Option 2 correctly embeds figure (X) without rotation and preserves the exact style, shape, and orientation of the curved intersecting lines.

38. We are given:

3 men or 15 boys can complete the work in 30 days.

From this, we calculate total work:

Work = 3 men × 30 days = 90 men-days

This is the same as 15 boys × 30 days = 450 boys-days

We are asked: In how many days will 2 men and 5 boys complete the same work?

Let's convert all workers into a common unit, say man-days:

From the given, 3 men = 15 boys ⇒ 1 man = 5 boys

So, 1 boy = 1/5 man

Now, 2 men = 2 man

5 boys = 5 × (1/5) = 1 man

Total workforce = 2 + 1 = 3 men

Therefore, 2 men and 5 boys together are equivalent to 3 men, and since 3 men can do the work in 30 days, 2 men and 5 boys will also complete the work in 30 days.

39. We are asked to find the nearest integer to 6650 that is exactly divisible by 429.

Step 1: Divide 6650 by 429

$$6650 \div 429 \approx 15.5$$

So, the two closest multiples of 429 are:

- 429 × 15 = 6435
- 429 × 16 = 6864

Step 2: Compare both with 6650:

- $|6650 - 6435| = 215$
- $|6864 - 6650| = 214$

Since 6864 is only 214 away and 6435 is 215 away, 6864 is numerically closer to 6650.

Also, both 6435 and 6864 are divisible by 429, but the question specifically asks for the nearest such number. Among the options, Option 1 is 6864, which is the correct choice.

40. Thailand is commonly referred to as the "Land of White Elephants." This nickname comes from the cultural and historical reverence for white elephants in Thai royal traditions.

Other options:

- Land of Thousand Elephants = Laos
- Land of Morning Calm = South Korea
- Land of Tigers = India (also used loosely for Southeast Asia)

Answer: 3: Land of White Elephants.

41. Given: 10% of X = 15% of Y = 1/5 of Z

Let the common value be k

Then, $10X/100 = k \Rightarrow X = 10k$

$15Y/100 = k \Rightarrow Y = (20k)/3$

$(1/5)Z = k \Rightarrow Z = 5k$

Now find the ratio X : Y : Z

$$X = 10k,\ Y = 20k/3,\ Z = 5k$$

Now take LCM of denominators (1 and 3): Multiply all by 3:

$$X : Y : Z = 30k : 20k : 15k$$

Now divide all by 5: = 6 : 4 : 3.

42. Statement: "Birds of same feather flock together."

Meaning: People who are similar in nature or interests stick together.

- Conclusion I: Similar people tend to associate with each other → *True*
- Conclusion II: A group of birds have beautiful feathers → *This is not implied*

Only the first conclusion logically follows.

43. We are asked to find the water image of the given figure — this is a vertical reflection over a horizontal axis. In a water image:

- The top and bottom elements swap places.
- The left and right sides remain unchanged.
- All shapes are also inverted vertically.

Let's break down the original figure (from top to bottom):

- **Top-left:** Small black square
- **Top-right:** White triangle pointing upwards
- **Center:** Spade pointing upwards with a downward-pointing triangle inside it
- **Bottom-center:** (None visible in original, triangle is at the base of the spade)

Applying the water image transformation:

1. Black square (top-left) → moves to bottom-left, remains black square
2. White triangle (top-right, pointing up) → moves to bottom-right, becomes downward-pointing
3. Spade with triangle:
   Spade inverts → now points downward
   Internal triangle (was pointing down) → now becomes pointing up
4. No new elements appear at the top

Now check the options:

- Option 1: Spade triangle is still downward → *(Incorrect)*
- Option 2: White triangle on bottom-right is pointing up →. *(Incorrect)*
- Option 3: Spade is correctly inverted
  Internal triangle is now upward — *(Correct)*
  Black square is at bottom-left — *(Correct)*
  White triangle is at bottom-right, pointing downward — *(Correct)*

Matches all water image rules

- Option 4: Black square is misplaced, triangle is on the wrong side — *(Incorrect)*.

44. In a symmetrical distribution, particularly a normal distribution (bell-shaped curve), the values of Mean, Median, and Mode are all equal and located at the center of the distribution. This is a fundamental property of symmetric distributions, where the data is evenly distributed around a central value.

So, Mean = Median = Mode

This condition does not hold for skewed distributions, but for symmetrical ones, it is always true.

45. We are given a 2 × 2 matrix of figures, where the top row contains circular figures and the bottom row contains square figures, all divided into 8 equal sectors.

Our task is to identify the logical relationship between the figures and determine which figure correctly completes the missing position (Box 3).

Step 1: Analyze the top row (Figures 1 and 2)

- **Figure 1 (Top-Left Circle):** Two adjacent sectors are shaded – they occupy the top-left and bottom-left positions (forming a vertical block on the left side).
- **Figure 2 (Top-Right Circle):** The shaded block has moved one sector clockwise. Now the shaded sectors are in the top-right and bottom-right.

So, the rule in the top row is: "Two adjacent sectors are shaded, and in the next figure, the pair shifts one position clockwise."

Step 2: Analyze Figure 4 (Bottom-Right Square)

- Figure 4 has two adjacent shaded sectors in the square – they are in the top-left and top-right.

To follow the same rule as the top row but in reverse, we should now move one sector backward (counter-clockwise) to determine the shading in Figure 3 (the missing figure).

So, if in Figure 4 the shaded sectors are:

- Top-left and top-right (adjacent on the top side), then in the previous step (Figure 3), the shaded sectors must have been:
- Left and top-left, which is one step back counter-clockwise.

Step 3: Find the matching option

Look for the option where the square has two adjacent shaded sectors in the left and top-left positions.

Option 2 matches this exactly.

46. Let's evaluate each statement:

(A) "The love and devotion to god Vishnu is usually the theme of this dance form."
Correct. Mohiniyattam is based on themes of love and devotion, often associated with Lord Vishnu, especially his female form Mohini, making this statement accurate.

(B) "This dance form belongs to the state of Andhra Pradesh."
Incorrect. Mohiniyattam is a classical dance form of Kerala, not Andhra Pradesh.

(C) "Mohiniyattam has the grace and elegance of Bharatanatyam and the vigor of Kathakali."
Correct. It blends the elegance and lasya (grace) of Bharatanatyam with the drama and energy of Kathakali, both of which are classical dance forms of South India.

(D) "The dancer's attire in a beautiful white and gold bordered Kasavu sari with jasmine flowers..."
Correct. This description accurately reflects the traditional costume worn in Mohiniyattam performances.

Hence, only statements (A), (C), and (D) are correct.

47. The data either in statement I alone or in statement II alone are sufficient to answer the question.

Question: What was the date of the last Tuesday in February 2024?

Statement I: The first Tuesday was on 6th February 2024.

If 6th is Tuesday, then subsequent Tuesdays are:

13th, 20th, and 27th ⇒ So, last Tuesday = 27th February

Statement I alone is sufficient.

Statement II: The last day of February 2024 was Thursday.

2024 is a leap year, so February has 29 days.

If 29th is Thursday, then 27th was Tuesday ⇒ Last Tuesday = 27th February

Statement II alone is also sufficient.

Thus, either statement alone is enough to answer the question.

48. To find the actual time from a mirror image of an analog clock, subtract the given time from 11:60.

Given mirror time = 6:05

Real time = 11:60 – 6:05 = 5:55

So, the actual time is 5:55.

49. We are given two equations:

1. $3x - ky = 3$ 2. $2x - 3y = 4$

The condition for no solution in a system of linear equations is:

$$\frac{a_1}{a_2} = \frac{b_1}{b_2} \neq \frac{c_1}{c_2}$$

Let's apply: $\frac{3}{2} = \frac{k}{3} \Rightarrow k = \frac{3 \times 3}{2} = \frac{9}{2}$

Now check: $\frac{3}{2} = \frac{9/2}{3} = \frac{3}{2}$ But $\frac{-3}{-4} = \frac{3}{4} \neq \frac{3}{2}$

So, the condition is satisfied when $k = 9/2$.

50. The Paris Olympics 2024 are being held in venues located along and near the River Seine, which flows through the heart of Paris, France. Major events and even the opening ceremony are planned along this river.

Previous Years' Paper

Common University Entrance Test for UG Programmes

CUET (UG) B.A. (Hons.) English Entrance Exam, 2024*

ENGLISH

1. Re-arrange the following phrases in the right sequence to form a meaningful sentence.

(*a*) for seven hours but was hardly
(*b*) because of the absence of any motivation
(*c*) able to decide who the murderer was
(*d*) she worked on the case

Choose the **correct** answer from the options given below

A. (*a*), (*c*), (*d*), (*b*) B. (*d*), (*a*), (*c*), (*b*)
C. (*d*), (*c*), (*b*), (*a*) D. (*a*), (*b*), (*c*), (*d*)

2. Fill in the blank with the **correct** option.

The candidate assured the interviewers that the dip in her grades during her second semester was an ____ since she had always been a top scorer in the first semester.

A. anomaly B. allay
C. adage D. abatement

3. Match the words in List-I with their definitions in List-II.

List-I (Words)	List-II (Definitions)
(*a*) Theocracy	I. One who keeps drugs for sale and puts up prescriptions
(*b*) Megalomania	II. One who collects and studies objects or artistic works from the distant past
(*c*) Apothecary	III. A government by divine guidance or religious leaders
(*d*) Antiquarian	IV. A morbid delusion of one's power, importance or godliness

Choose the **correct** answer from the options given below:

	(*a*)	(*b*)	(*c*)	(*d*)
A.	III	IV	I	II
B.	IV	III	II	I
C.	I	III	IV	II
D.	III	IV	II	I

4. Fill in the blank with the **correct** option.

A small ______ between two children ended up as a group fight.

A. altercation B. match
C. contest D. race

5. Replace the underlined word with the most appropriate SYNONYM.

For sometime now, we've been <u>toying</u> with the idea of transferring all our business from physical to online sales only.

A. launch
B. showing
C. considering
D. careful

6. Select the word opposite in meaning to the underlined word.

At first the workers were agreeable to the proposals of their Manager, but later they were <u>reconciled</u> to the new proposals.

A. resistant B. estranged
C. cooperate D. agreed

1. B **2.** A **3.** A **4.** A **5.** C **6.** A, B

*** This Previous Year Paper has been given here as a Combination of CUET (UG) 2024 different exams for the Subjects 'English and General Test', which have been mapped to this course.**

7. Complete the sentences given in List-I with the appropriate words given in List-II:

List-I (Sentences)	List-II (Words)
(*a*) She was able to give a ______ explanation in the court for her presence near the crime scene.	I. collaborate/d
(*b*) The Rockland Hospital ______ with AIIMS to conduct a free cancer screening camp.	II. corroborate/ing
(*c*) Though she has shown only 4% improvement in achieving her target yet her efforts are ______.	III. credible
(*d*) The doctors give the prognosis by ______ their diagnosis with several tests.	IV. creditable

Choose the **correct** answer from the options given below:

	(*a*)	(*b*)	(*c*)	(*d*)
A.	I	II	III	IV
B.	I	III	II	IV
C.	III	I	IV	II
D.	II	IV	I	III

8. Fill in the blank with the **correct** option.

Most of the guests arrived for the concert ______ bus.

A. by B. with
C. from D. through

9. Choose the word closest in meaning to the underlined word.

Why did you make that flippant remark about her choice of clothes?

A. sarcastic
B. disrespectful
C. casual
D. indifferent

10. Select the word OPPOSITE in meaning to the underlined word.

The thief showed his disbelief when informed that his partner had been arrested.

A. displayed B. concealed
C. battled D. marked

11. Fill in the blank with the **correct** option.

The President finally had to ______ the demands of the public for his resignation.

A. ignore B. initiate
C. accede to D. condone

12. Re-arrange the following parts of a sentence in their correct sequence to form a meaningful sentence.

(*a*) for organizations which provide
(*b*) services to customers on a face-to-face basis
(*c*) employees with whom they deal is very important
(*d*) the quality of the relationship between customers and

Choose the **correct** answer from the options given below:

A. (*a*), (*b*), (*d*), (*c*) B. (*c*), (*a*), (*b*), (*d*)
C. (*b*), (*d*), (*a*), (*c*) D. (*d*), (*a*), (*c*), (*b*)

13. Re-arrange the following parts of a sentence in their correct sequence to form a meaningful sentence.

(*a*) as a concept fundamental to
(*b*) especially with the injunction to treat equals equally
(*c*) justice is associated with the notion of equity and equality,
(*d*) ethical theory and political philosophy,

Choose the **correct** answer from the options given below:

A. (*d*), (*b*), (*c*), (*a*) B. (*c*), (*a*), (*b*), (*d*)
C. (*b*), (*a*), (*d*), (*c*) D. (*a*), (*d*), (*c*), (*b*)

14. Match the idioms in List-I with their meanings in List-II:

List-I (Idioms)	List-II (Meanings)
(*a*) blow the gaff	I. feel unable to deal with something
(*b*) at the end of your tether	II. feel terribly ashamed and embarrassed
(*c*) be full of beans	III. divulge a secret
(*d*) want to curl up and die	IV. be full of energy

Choose the **correct** answer from the options given below:

	(*a*)	(*b*)	(*c*)	(*d*)
A.	III	I	IV	II
B.	II	IV	I	III
C.	IV	I	II	III
D.	III	IV	I	II

7. C **8.** A **9.** B, C **10.** B **11.** C **12.** A **13.** D **14.** A

15. Match the blanks in List-I with the Preposition in List-II:

List-I (Sentences)	List-II (Prepositions)
(*a*) The edited version of her article is indistinguishable _______ her first version.	I. with
(*b*) I just don't feel any affinity _______ his prose style. It's too caustic.	II. to
(*c*) Her ideas are not all that dissimilar _____ mine.	III. for
(*d*) It would be wrong to mistake his diffidence _______ his arrogance or coldness.	IV. from

Choose the **correct** answer from the options given below:

	(*a*)	(*b*)	(*c*)	(*d*)
A.	IV	I	II	III
B.	I	III	II	IV
C.	IV	II	I	III
D.	III	IV	I	II

16. Re-arrange the parts in their correct sequence to form a meaningful sentence:

(*a*) students with tools for critical thinking
(*b*) cooperative learning is an
(*c*) that enhances creativity and provides
(*d*) eclectic and unique teaching method

Choose the **correct** answer from the options given below:

A. (*a*), (*c*), (*b*), (*d*) B. (*b*), (*d*), (*c*), (*a*)
C. (*b*), (*a*), (*d*), (*c*) D. (*c*), (*b*), (*d*), (*a*)

Directions (Qs. No. 17-22): *Read the given passage and answer the six questions that follow.*

When I was in my late teens and still undecided about which language I should write in, he told me that the language one is born into, one's mother tongue, can be the only possible medium of creative expression.

For most of his life, my father, Sripat Rai, had been a Hindi editor and critic. Off and on, he translated writings into English from Hindi. He was fond of saying that a failed writer becomes a critic. The weight of his literary expectation came, eventually, to rest on me. He seemed happy that I was showing an inclination for writing. "She will go far," he told my mother after reading the first story that I sent him from Melbourne.

My father's pronouncement on the mother tongue stayed with me when I later started writing fiction in Hindi. Another thing that I barely acknowledged even to myself was that I felt something like shame whenever I thought of writing in English. It seemed wrong for a granddaughter of Premchand even to be thinking so. Our family had a certain linguistic pride. I knew that Premchand was famous, but I had not at that time realised the extent of his popularity.

The fact that I was the granddaughter of Premchand, followed me everywhere. Everyone had a story to tell about their personal engagement with his fiction—the shopkeeper, the long time cook in my father's Delhi house, a tea vendor, etc. The list was long, for there was practically no one who had not read something by him that had moved them. However, it was this very ubiquity, the reverence and love that he inspired in people, that made of him something too large for me to comprehend in the early years of my life. It led also to the strange feeling that, without having read him and just by being related to him, I had somehow inhaled his writing. The reading happened much later.

17. The author grew up with the expectation that she would take up _______.

Fill in the blank with the **correct** option to complete the sentence.

A. editorship of a magazine.
B. translation of literary pieces.
C. creative writing.
D. the job of a critic.

18. When her father said, "She will go far", he meant that _______.

Fill in the blank with the **correct** option to complete the sentence.

A. she will travel widely.
B. she will achieve great heights in life.
C. she will go too far, one of these days.
D. she will settle in a far-off place.

19. Choose a Statement which is **not** true with respect to the passage:

A. The author felt pressurized to write in Hindi because of her father.
B. She felt obligated to carry on the legacy of Premchand.
C. Her family was chauvinistic about the English language.
D. She was in awe of the extensive reach of her grandfather's writings.

15. A **16.** B **17.** C **18.** B **19.** C

20. Premchand became too large for her to understand mainly because of ______ .

(*a*) his ability to connect with people from all walks of life.
(*b*) the fact that she feared him.
(*c*) the kind of love and reverence that he inspired in people.
(*d*) her constant anxiety of failing him.

Choose the **correct** answer from the options given below:

A. (*a*) and (*d*) only
B. (*a*) and (*c*) only
C. (*b*) and (*c*) only
D. (*c*) and (*d*) only

21. 'Inhaled his writing' refers to:

Choose the **correct** option from the following:

A. imbibing his style subconsciously.
B. being compelled to write like him.
C. being influenced by what people said about him.
D. her father's expectation from her.

22. Choose the correct meaning of the word "Ubiquity" as it appears in the passage:

A. Occasional
B. Restricted
C. Omnipresence
D. Unwanted

Directions (Qs. No. 23-28): *Read the given passage and answer the six questions that follow.*

Free will is the ability to decide and act free from any influence of past events or environment. It implies complete freedom to make any choice absolutely. We clearly don't have free will. Our decisions and actions are never divorced from our past.

We have a conditioned mind. Our memories, past impressions and experiences bias and shape our thoughts and actions in the present. It is our karmic imprint. Not just what we are born with, but also what we accumulate while living. We can consider it as the result of our genetic code, upbringing and environment. It's our backstory.

The only way to experience free will is to get rid of all such conditioning; to neutralise our karmic imprint; to be independent of our psychological coding. That's possible only if we can purify our mind by letting go of all our ego, attachments and fixed beliefs. Then we can reside in the truth of our being.

The above is an exacting definition of free will. What we commonly mean by free will is that we have a choice in most situations like, who you choose to marry, what profession you pursue or how you react to someone's aggression. Sounds reasonable, But here's the catch. Our ability to make that choice too is significantly restricted, dictated by our predispositions.

This applies even to our ability to bring about change within ourselves. Despite a strong resolve to be calmer, kinder or less anxious, our ability to manifest that change depends, partly on our emotional and mental wiring. That's why some people succeed in such efforts more than the others.

If you wish to expand the scope of your agency, explore ways to engage in sustained inner work, deepen your self-awareness, examine and reform your conditioned beliefs. But then, I wonder if your inclination to embark on that journey too depends on your current karmic coding.

23. The author argues that humans don't have "free will" because ______ .

Fill in the blank with the **correct** option to complete the sentence.

A. our decisions are shaped by past events and environmental influences.
B. we are born with pre-determined choices that we are forced to make.
C. we are always dictated by our mind to make irrational choices.
D. human beings are born slaves of social constructs and expectations.

24. "Karmic imprint" referred to in the passage implies ______ .

Fill in the blank with the **correct** option to complete the sentence.

A. the ability to bring about change in oneself.
B. our genetic code, upbringing and environment
C. the truth of our being, our individuality.
D. the wrong doings and vices of our past lives.

25. "Free will" can be experienced if ______ .

Fill in the blank with the **correct** option to complete the sentence.

A. we embrace our past experiences and conditioning
B. we make choices without considering the consequences.
C. we let go of our ego, attachments and fixed beliefs.
D. we accumulate more and more karmic imprints

20. B	21. A	22. C	23. A	24. B	25. C

26. The author proves that the idea of "free will" is a myth by suggesting that ______.

Fill in the blank with the **correct** option to complete the sentence.

A. our ability to make a choice is restricted by our predispositions.
B. we are unable to bring a change in ourselves.
C. our choices are solely guided by the current environment.
D. our choices are completely independent of past events and our genetic code.

27. What does the author propose as a means to expand the scope of one's agency?

Choose the **correct** option.

A. Making choices frequently and impulsively.
B. Engaging in sustained inner work and self-awareness.
C. Holding on to fixed beliefs and stringent mindsets.
D. Ignoring one's past experiences and dispositions.

28. What do you think could be a suitable title for this passage?

Choose the **most appropriate** option.

A. Definition of "Free Will".
B. Our backstory—key to a successful life.
C. Do human beings really have "Free Will"?
D. Making Choices—Every Man's Prerogative!

Directions (Qs. No. 29-34): *Read the given passage and answer the six questions that follow.*

On a chilly winter evening, nothing warms you up better than a cup of hot cocoa. Chocolate was first consumed in liquid form by the Olmec people of northwestern Central America around 1500 BCE. It was even enjoyed by the Aztec Emperor Montezuma, and the Aztec word for it (*xocolatl*, pronounced *shoh-kwah-tl*) evolved into the English word Chocolate.

But the Aztecs didn't serve their cocoa hot. And since sugar had not yet arrived from Europe, back then, the drink was often flavoured with peppers and spices. It may not have been quite as indulgent as today's version, but it was more palatable if you believed, as the Aztecs did, that chocolate was a gift from the Gods and had healing properties.

After the Spanish arrived in the Americas in the 1500s, liquid chocolate made its way across the pond, where wealthy Europeans added sugar and drank it warm. In *Chocolate : History, Culture and Heritage,* author Bertram Gordon says hot chocolate became "the beverage of the aristocracy," as sugar was still a luxury.

Soon enough, though, hot chocolate caught on with the masses. Chocolate houses—a cross between cafes and casinos—started popping up around 17th-century Europe. In these lively places, hot chocolate was poured from gilded pots into elegant cups (for a posh experience, one can still find it today at the famed Parisian tearoom Angelina's, which is also in New York City). But by the end of the 18th century, chocolate houses had mostly died off, partly because the cost of chocolate was much higher than that of coffee or tea.

Taking a tour of international cups of cocoa, Italians serve it like a thick pudding. Colombians serve it with a dollop of soft cheese while Mexicans punch it up with vanilla, chilli powder and cinnamon. And Filipinos serve it with mango chunks.

29. Cocoa was first introduced by the:

A. American people B. Olmec people
C. Aztec people D. Spanish people

30. The Aztec people made their cocoa palatable by:

A. serving it cold
B. adding sugar to the drink
C. spiking it with spices
D. drinking it as a medicine

31. Why did hot chocolate become "the beverage of the aristocracy" in Europe?

A. The essential ingredient was out of reach of the commoners.
B. The Queen had a marked chocolate maker.
C. Only wealthy Europeans could buy it.
D. It was being consumed by the pharma companies.

32. The Chocolate Houses didn't survive past the 18th century as:

A. people preferred tea/coffee to hot chocolate.
B. it catered to the not so elite of the society.
C. chocolate was costlier than tea or coffee.
D. the supply of cocoa dwindled over the years.

33. Choose the correct statement from the following:

A. Italians serve hot chocolate flavoured with spices.
B. Mexicans serve hot chocolate topped with a dollop of cream.
C. Colombians serve hot chocolate topped with a dollop of cheese.
D. Filipinos served hot chocolate flavoured with peppers.

26. A **27.** B **28.** A, C **29.** B **30.** C, D **31.** A, C **32.** C **33.** C

34. Choose the correct meaning of the underlined expression in the following sentence:

Soon enough, though, hot chocolate caught on with the masses.

A. was readily available in cafes.
B. became popular among the commoners.
C. hot chocolate did not appeal to people.
D. masses got attracted to the rich experience of drinking hot chocolate.

Directions (Qs. No. 35-40): *Read the given passage and answer the six questions that follow.*

Coffee's genetic make-up is no trivial concern; 10 million tonnes of the crop were grown and sold in 2022-23. The coffee that we drink comes from two species: Coffea Canephora, which is also known as Robusta and Coffea Arabica, known as Arabica. In many cases, beans from the two species are blended to make a brew. But the beans of single species are also roasted and sold. Overall, Arabica beans represent around 56% of all coffee sold.

Most genetic variation in living organisms comes from hybridization with other species. However, this is a relatively rare event for Coffea Arabica because it has more than two copies of each chromosome - a phenomenon called polyploidy. Coffea Canephora has two copies of each chromosome, but Coffea Arabica contains multiple copies. This makes it much more difficult for Arabica to interbreed with other species.

As a result, Coffea Arabica's main source of single nucleotide variation is mutation, which occurs at a steady rate over time. However, the species is also relatively young, having formed as a hybrid of Robusta and Coffea Eugenioides - another coffee species that is not widely cultivated - within the past 50,000 years. From that single plant, which has basically no variation, you create the whole species, and then the variation is only the novel mutations that have occurred since that event.

Despite this, there is substantial variation in the physical characteristics of the Arabica coffee plant, including different flavour profiles in the beans and variations in disease resistance, says emeritus geneticist Juan Medrano at the UC Davis Coffee Center at the University of California, Davis. "We're always talking about low variability fat the DNA level, but there is variability at the structural level, at the chromosomal level, at the level of deletions... and insertions," Medrano says.

35. Which of the following varieties of coffee is the most sold in the world?

A. Coffea Canephora
B. Coffea Arabica
C. Coffea Eugenioides
D. A blend of Coffea Canephora and Coffea Arabica

36. Which of the following species of coffee has more than two copies of each chromosome?

A. Arabica
B. Robusta
C. Coffea Eugenioides
D. A blend of Arabica and Robusta

37. Which of the following statements is true about coffea Arabica?

A. Hybridization is the main source of its genetic variation.
B. It has only two copies of each chromosome.
C. It displays the phenomenon of polyploidy.
D. It is easily interbred with other species.

38. Which of the following species of coffee developed only in the last 50,000 years?

A. Coffea Canephora B. Coffea Eugenioides
C. Arabica D. Robusta

39. Which of the following types of variability is not very high for Coffea Arabica?

A. Variability at the structural level.
B. Variability at the chromosomal level.
C. Variability at the level of deletions and insertions.
D. Variability at the DNA level.

40. Choose the statement that is factually **incorrect** from the options given below.

A. It is possible to roast the beans of a single species of coffee.
B. Two species of coffee can be blended to make a brew.
C. Due to its genetic make-up, novel mutations do not occur in the species Coffea Arabica.
D. Variations in disease resistance can be seen in the Arabica coffee plant.

41. Re-arrange the following phrases in correct sequence to form a meaningful sentence.

(*a*) created by human
(*b*) collective cultural heritage
(*c*) all languages
(*d*) communities are our

Choose the **correct** answer from the options given below:

A. (*a*), (*b*), (*d*), (*c*) B. (*b*), (*a*), (*d*), (*c*)
C. (*c*), (*a*), (*d*), (*b*) D. (*d*), (*b*), (*c*), (*a*)

34. B, D **35.** B **36.** A **37.** C **38.** * **39.** D **40.** C **41.** C

42. Fill in the blank with the **correct** option, to form a meaningful sentence.

The Principal addressed us in the assembly and ______ the rumours of an early summer break.

A. defended B. quashed
C. cleared D. rebuked

43. Complete the sentences given in List-I with the appropriate phrasal verbs given in List-II.

List-I (Sentences)	List-II (Phrasal verbs)
(*a*) She was very ______ with him for his offensive remarks on women in politics.	I. give away
(*b*) I have plenty of interesting books to ______ to book lovers.	II. cut down
(*c*) Strange that people easily ______ to temptation and ruin their reputation!	III. cut up
(*d*) Rahul is trying to ______ on his smoking.	IV. give in

Choose the **correct** answer from the options given below:

	(*a*)	(*b*)	(*c*)	(*d*)
A.	I	II	III	IV
B.	II	IV	I	III
C.	I	II	IV	III
D.	III	I	IV	II

44. Complete the sentences given in List-I with the appropriate adverbs given in List-II:

List-I (Sentences)	List-II (Adverbs)
(*a*) I thought the restaurant would be expensive but it was ______ affordable.	I. badly
(*b*) It was a serious accident. But the car was ______ damaged.	II. reasonably
(*c*) The meeting was a disaster as it was very ______ organized.	III. quickly
(*d*) Mira is gifted, she has the ability to learn any language ______.	IV. hardly

Choose the **correct** answer from the options given below:

	(*a*)	(*b*)	(*c*)	(*d*)
A.	II	IV	I	III
B.	IV	II	III	I
C.	I	II	IV	III
D.	III	IV	I	II

45. Choose the appropriate word pair to complete the sentence:

I didn't know Rahul was in the hospital. If I ______, I would ______ him.

A. knew, go
B. had known, have visited
C. have known, be going
D. know, had gone

46. Identify the option closest in meaning to the underlined word:

The movie star's biography is a glossy, <u>sycophantic</u> portrayal.

A. cowardly
B. domineering
C. flattering
D. insolent

47. Choose the correct ANTONYM of the underlined word:

The Minister unleashed a <u>compliment</u> against the newspaper for its biased editorial on illiteracy among women in his constituency.

A. denunciation
B. endorsement
C. regulation
D. speculation

48. Choose the correct SYNONYM for <u>redoubtable</u> from the options given below.

A. flimsy B. perplexing
C. formidable D. voluble

49. Choose the correct ANTONYM for <u>sullen</u> from the options given below.

A. morose B. reticent
C. timid D. genial

50. Rearrange the following parts in the correct sequence to make a meaningful sentence:

(*a*) are inborn but our
(*b*) constituents of flavour, are learned
(*c*) our responses to basic tastes
(*d*) perceptions of smells, the main

Choose the **correct** answer from the options given below:

A. (*b*), (*d*), (*a*), (*c*)
B. (*a*), (*c*), (*b*), (*d*)
C. (*c*), (*a*), (*d*), (*b*)
D. (*c*), (*b*), (*d*), (*a*)

42. B	43. D	44. A	45. B	46. C	47. A	48. C	49. D	50. C

EXPLANATORY ANSWERS

1. **(B):**

(*d*) She worked on the case – introduces the subject and the action.

(*a*) for seven hours – specifies the duration of the action.

(*c*) but was hardly able to decide who the murderer was – describes the result of her effort, indicating difficulty in solving the case.

(*b*) because of the absence of any motivation – provides the reason behind the difficulty faced.

The complete sentence would be: "She worked on the case for seven hours but was hardly able to decide who the murderer was because of the absence of any motivation."

2. **(A):** In the sentence, "anomaly" is the most suitable word because it refers to an irregularity or deviation from what is expected or usual. The candidate is explaining that the drop in her grades during the second semester was unusual compared to her consistent top performance in the first semester.

3. **(A):**

(*a*) **Theocracy:** (*iii*) A theocracy is a system of government where religious leaders control the state, or where the state's policies are governed by divine principles or religious doctrines.

The term reflects a political system where religious authority is central.

(*b*) **Megalomania:** (*iv*) Megalomania is a psychological condition where an individual has an exaggerated sense of their own power, importance, or godliness.

This delusion of grandeur is often marked by a belief in one's supreme abilities or dominance.

(*c*) **Apothecary:** (*i*) An apothecary is a historical term for someone who prepares and sells medicines.

This role is akin to that of a modern pharmacist, who manages prescriptions and medicinal products.

(*d*) **Antiquarian:** (*ii*) An antiquarian is a person who studies, collects, or deals in antiques and historical artifacts.

This term is used to describe someone who has a deep interest in historical objects or artistic works from the past.

4. **(A):** The sentence describes a situation that escalated from a small issue to a bigger conflict. "Altercation" means a noisy argument or disagreement, especially in public. Therefore, the sentence should read: "A small altercation between two children ended up as a group fight."

5. **(C):** The word "toying" in this context means considering or thinking about an idea in a casual or preliminary way. The most appropriate synonym for "toying" is "considering."

6. **(A, B):**

(A) **Resistant:** This term means opposed to or unwilling to accept something. It is opposite to reconciled, which means to become resigned or accepting of a situation.

(B) **Estranged:** This term refers to being alienated or disconnected, which is also opposite to reconciled, as it implies a lack of acceptance or harmony with the situation.

7. **(C):**

(*a*) She was able to give a credible explanation in the court for her presence near the crime scene.

(*iii*) "Credible" means believable or convincing, which fits the context of providing a reliable explanation.

(*b*) The Rockland Hospital collaborated with AIIMS to conduct a free cancer screening camp.

(*i*) "Collaborated" means worked together, which is appropriate for describing joint efforts between organizations.

(*c*) Though she has shown only 4% improvement in achieving her target yet her efforts are creditable.

(*iv*) "Creditable" means deserving praise or recognition, fitting for acknowledging her efforts despite modest improvement.

(*d*) The doctors give the prognosis by corroborating their diagnosis with several tests.

(*ii*) "Corroborating" means confirming or supporting with additional evidence, which is suitable for describing the process of validating a diagnosis.

8. **(A):** The preposition "by" is used to indicate the means or method of transport. Therefore, the sentence should read: "Most of the guests arrived for the concert by bus."

9. (B & C): The word "flippant" means not showing a serious or respectful attitude. "Disrespectful" is the closest in meaning as it directly indicates a lack of respect. "Casual" also fits because a flippant remark can be considered overly casual or not serious. Therefore, both "disrespectful" and "casual" are correct.

10. (B): The word "showed" means to display or exhibit something. The opposite of showing would be to conceal or hide. Therefore, the correct word is "concealed."

11. (C): The phrase needed must indicate yielding to demands. "Accede to" means to agree to a request or demand. Therefore, the correct sentence is: "The President finally had to accede to the demands of the public for his resignation."

12. (A):

(*a*) introduces the context: "For organizations which provide."

(*b*) specifies the type of service provided: "services to customers on a face-to-face basis."

(*d*) continues with the main point: "the quality of the relationship between customers and."

(*c*) concludes the thought: "employees with whom they deal is very important."

The sentence is "For organizations which provide services to customers on a face-to-face basis, the quality of the relationship between customers and employees with whom they deal is very important."

13. (D):

(*a*) introduces the topic: "as a concept fundamental to."

(*d*) specifies the field: "ethical theory and political philosophy."

(*c*) links the topic with the main point: "justice is associated with the notion of equity and equality."

(*b*) adds detail about the application: "especially with the injunction to treat equals equally."

The sentence is "Justice is associated with the notion of equity and equality, as a concept fundamental to ethical theory and political philosophy, especially with the injunction to treat equals equally."

14. (A):

(*a*) blow the gaff - III. divulge a secret: To reveal or disclose something that was supposed to be kept secret.

(*b*) at the end of your tether - I. feel unable to deal with something: To reach the limit of one's patience or endurance.

(*c*) be full of beans - IV. be full of energy: To be very lively, energetic, or enthusiastic.

(*d*) want to curl up and die - II. feel terribly ashamed and embarrassed: To feel extremely embarrassed or ashamed, often wanting to disappear or hide.

15. (A):

(*a*) The edited version of her article is indistinguishable from her first version. IV. from: Used to indicate that two things are not distinguishable from each other.

(*b*) I just don't feel any affinity with his prose style. I. with: Used to express a lack of connection or relationship with something.

(*c*) Her ideas are not all that dissimilar to mine. II. to: Used to show similarity or comparison between two things.

(*d*) It would be wrong to mistake his diffidence for his arrogance or coldness. III. for: Used to indicate a misunderstanding or misinterpretation of something.

16. (B):

(*b*) "Cooperative learning is an": This introduces the subject of the sentence, which is cooperative learning.

(*d*) "eclectic and unique teaching method": This describes what cooperative learning is—an eclectic and unique teaching method.

(*c*) "that enhances creativity and provides": This clause explains what the teaching method does, namely enhancing creativity and providing something.

(*a*) "students with tools for critical thinking": This completes the explanation by specifying what the teaching method provides—tools for critical thinking for students.

The Sentence is "Cooperative learning is an eclectic and unique teaching method that enhances creativity and provides students with tools for critical thinking."

17. (C): The passage indicates that the author grew up with the weight of her father's literary expectations, particularly in creative writing. Her father, a Hindi editor and critic, was happy that she showed an inclination for writing. Therefore, the author grew up with the expectation that she would take up creative writing.

18. (B): When her father said, "She will go far," he meant that she would achieve great heights in life. This interpretation aligns with the context of the father's pride in her writing abilities and his expectations for her future success.

19. (C): The statement "Her family was chauvinistic about the English language" is not true with respect to the passage. The passage mentions that her father had translated writings into English from Hindi and felt that the mother tongue should be the medium of creative expression, which indicates a preference for Hindi rather than chauvinism against English.

20. (B): Premchand became too large for her to understand mainly because of his ability to connect with people from all walks of life (*a*) and the kind of love and reverence that he inspired in people (*c*). The passage describes how everyone had a personal engagement with his fiction and how the reverence he inspired made him difficult for her to comprehend.

21. (A): 'Inhaled his writing' refers to imbibing his style subconsciously. The author felt that just by being related to Premchand, she had somehow absorbed his writing, even before she read his works.

22. (C): The word "ubiquity" in the passage means omnipresence. It refers to the widespread presence and influence of Premchand's writings, as practically everyone the author encountered had read something by him.

23. (A): The author argues that humans don't have "free will" because our decisions are shaped by past events and environmental influences. The passage explains that our memories, past impressions, and experiences bias and shape our thoughts and actions in the present.

24. (B): "Karmic imprint" referred to in the passage implies our genetic code, upbringing, and environment. The passage describes karmic imprint as the result of what we are born with and what we accumulate while living, influenced by our genetic code, upbringing, and environment.

25. (C): "Free will" can be experienced if we let go of our ego, attachments, and fixed beliefs. The passage states that to experience free will, one must get rid of all conditioning and be independent of psychological coding by letting go of ego, attachments, and fixed beliefs.

26. (A): The author proves that the idea of "free will" is a myth by suggesting that our ability to make a choice is restricted by our predispositions. The passage explains that even our ability to bring about change within ourselves is significantly restricted by our emotional and mental wiring.

27. (B): The author proposes engaging in sustained inner work and self-awareness as a means to expand the scope of one's agency. The passage suggests that to expand one's agency, one should engage in inner work, deepen self-awareness, and examine and reform conditioned beliefs.

28. (A & C): The most suitable title for this passage is "Do human beings really have 'Free Will'?" The passage questions the existence of free will and explores how our choices are influenced by past events, conditioning, and predispositions. The title "Definition of 'Free Will'" also fits as the passage provides a detailed explanation of what free will means and its constraints. Therefore, both options A and C are suitable titles.

29. (B): Cocoa was first introduced by the Olmec people. The passage mentions that chocolate was first consumed in liquid form by the Olmec people of northwestern Central America around 1500 BCE.

30. (C & D): The Aztec people made their cocoa palatable by spiking it with spices and believed that chocolate had healing properties. The passage notes that since sugar had not yet arrived from Europe, the Aztecs often flavored their drink with peppers and spices and believed that chocolate was a gift from the Gods with healing properties. Therefore, both options C and D are correct.

31. (A & C): Hot chocolate became "the beverage of the aristocracy" in Europe because the essential ingredient was out of reach of the commoners and only wealthy Europeans could buy it. The passage explains that after the Spanish arrived in the Americas, liquid chocolate made its way to Europe where wealthy Europeans added sugar and drank it warm, as sugar was still a luxury. Therefore, both options A and C are correct.

32. (C): The Chocolate Houses didn't survive past the 18th century as chocolate was costlier than tea or coffee. The passage states that by the end of the 18th century, chocolate houses had mostly died off partly because the cost of chocolate was much higher than that of coffee or tea.

33. (C): Colombians serve hot chocolate topped with a dollop of cheese. The passage describes that Colombians serve hot chocolate with a dollop of soft cheese.

34. (B & D): The underlined expression "caught on with the masses" means became popular among the commoners and masses got attracted to the rich experience of drinking hot chocolate. The passage mentions that soon enough, hot chocolate became popular and chocolate houses started popping up around 17th-century Europe, suggesting it appealed to a wider audience. Therefore, both options B and D are correct.

35. (B): The passage states that Arabica beans represent around 56% of all coffee sold, making Coffea Arabica the most sold variety of coffee in the world.

36. (A): The passage mentions that Coffea Arabica contains multiple copies of each chromosome, a phenomenon called polyploidy, indicating that Arabica has more than two copies of each chromosome.

37. (C): The passage states that Coffea Arabica displays the phenomenon of polyploidy, meaning it has more than two copies of each chromosome, making option C the true statement about Coffea Arabica.

39. (D): The passage highlights that Coffea Arabica has low variability at the DNA level compared to structural and chromosomal levels, as well as levels of deletions and insertions.

40. (C): The passage mentions that novel mutations do occur in the species Coffea Arabica since it has a steady rate of mutation over time.

Therefore, the statement that due to its genetic make-up, novel mutations do not occur in Coffea Arabica is factually incorrect.

41. (C):

(*c*) "All languages" introduces the subject of the sentence.

(*a*) "created by human" provides more detail about the subject, describing what all languages are.

(*d*) "communities are our" explains the relationship between the languages and human communities.

(*b*) "collective cultural heritage" concludes by defining what the languages represent.

The sentence is "All languages created by human communities are our collective cultural heritage."

42. (B): The Principal addressed us in the assembly and quashed the rumours of an early summer break. "Quashed" means to put an end to or suppress, which fits the context of addressing and ending rumours.

43. (D):

(*a*) - (*iii*) Correct phrasal verb: "cut up" (means to be very critical or upset).

So, the sentence should be: "She was very cut up with him for his offensive remarks on women in politics."

(*b*) - (*i*) Correct phrasal verb: "give away" (means to distribute something for free).

So, the sentence should be: "I have plenty of interesting books to give away to book lovers."

(*c*) - (*iv*) Correct phrasal verb: "give in" (means to surrender or yield).

So, the sentence should be: "Strange that people easily give in to temptation and ruin their reputation!"

(*d*) - (*ii*) Rahul is trying to ____________ on his smoking.

Correct phrasal verb: "cut down" (means to reduce or decrease).

So, the sentence should be: "Rahul is trying to cut down on his smoking."

44. (A):

(*a*) - (*ii*) Correct adverb: "reasonably" (means moderately or fairly).

So, the sentence should be: "I thought the restaurant would be expensive but it was reasonably affordable."

(*b*) - (*iv*) Correct adverb: "hardly" (means barely or not significantly).

So, the sentence should be: "It was a serious accident. But the car was hardly damaged."

(*c*) - (*i*) Correct adverb: "badly" (means poorly or ineffectively).

So, the sentence should be: "The meeting was a disaster as it was very badly organized."

(*d*) - (*iii*) Correct adverb: "quickly" (means at a fast pace).

So, the sentence should be: "Mira is gifted, she has the ability to learn any language quickly."

45. (B): "Had known" is the past perfect tense, which indicates that the knowledge of Rahul being in the hospital would have been relevant in the past.

"Have visited" is the past perfect conditional form of the verb, meaning that if the condition (knowing Rahul was in the hospital) had been met, the action of visiting him would have occurred.

So, the complete sentence would be: "I didn't know Rahul was in the hospital. If I had known, I would have visited him."

46. (C): Sycophantic means behaving or done in an obsequious way to gain advantage; essentially, it refers to excessively flattering or ingratiating oneself to someone in power. Flattering also means showing excessive praise or admiration, this aligns with the meaning of sycophantic.

47. (A): Compliment refers to an expression of praise or admiration. Denunciation is the action of publicly condemning or criticizing someone or something, which is the opposite of giving praise or admiration.

48. (C): Redoubtable means inspiring fear or awe; having a formidable presence. Formidable similarly means inspiring fear or respect through being impressively large, powerful, intense, or capable.

49. (D): Sullen describes a gloomy, sulky, or brooding mood or demeanor. Genial means friendly and cheerful, which is the opposite of being gloomy or sulky.

50. (C):

(*c*) "Our responses to basic tastes" introduces the subject of the sentence.

(*a*) "are inborn but our" follows logically, describing the nature of these responses.

(*d*) "perceptions of smells, the main" continues by shifting focus to another aspect related to the main constituents of flavour.

(*b*) "constituents of flavour, are learned" completes the thought by contrasting the inborn responses to learned perceptions.

So, the rearranged sentence is: "Our responses to basic tastes are inborn but our perceptions of smells, the main constituents of flavour, are learned."

GENERAL TEST

1. From the given options, which pass connects Jammu with Srinagar?
   A. Banihal Pass
   B. Nathu La Pass
   C. Niti Pass
   D. Rohtang Pass

2. Which of the following is not correctly matched regarding Padma Awards-2024?
   A. Padma Vibhushan Award → Shri Konidela Chiranjeevi
   B. Padma Shri Award → Mithun Chakraborty
   C. Padma Bhushan Award → M. Fathima Beevi
   D. Padma Bhushan Award → Sitaram Jindal

3. Match List-I with List-II.

List-I (Person)	List-II (Area of Work)
(*a*) Vishakhadatta	I. Medicine
(*b*) Kartikeya Sarabhai	II. Poet
(*c*) Charaka	III. Environmentalist
(*d*) Satyendra Nath Bose	IV. Mathematics

Choose the **correct** answer from the options given below:

	(*a*)	(*b*)	(*c*)	(*d*)
A.	I	III	IV	II
B.	II	III	I	IV
C.	II	I	III	IV
D.	III	IV	I	II

4. If $\sin A = \frac{4}{5}$, then $(3 - \tan A)(2 + \cos A) = ?$
   A. $\frac{12}{5}$
   B. $\frac{13}{3}$
   C. $\frac{13}{5}$
   D. 3

5. A man can row a boat at 8 km/h in still water. If the speed of the water current is 2 km/h and it takes him 2 hours to row to a place and come back, then how far off (in km) is the place?
   A. 7.5
   B. 6
   C. 9.5
   D. 10

6. The following states were formed after 1960. What was the correct sequence of their formation?
   (*a*) Haryana (*b*) Sikkim
   (*c*) Nagaland (*d*) Goa

Choose the **correct** answer from the options given below:
   A. (*c*), (*b*), (*a*), (*d*)
   B. (*c*), (*a*), (*b*), (*d*)
   C. (*c*), (*d*), (*a*), (*b*)
   D. (*d*), (*c*), (*a*), (*b*)

7. Out of the given options, which scheme's objective is to conduct an annual survey at the gram panchayat level to monitor the progress in the development process of the rural areas?
   A. Mission Antyodaya (2022-23)
   B. Mission Karmayogi (2022-23)
   C. Mission Rashtriya Gokul (2022-23)
   D. Mission Atmanirbhar Bharat (2022-23)

8. Which one of the following countries is **not** a member of the "Quadrilateral Security Dialogue", also known as "QUAD"?
   A. China
   B. Japan
   C. India
   D. Australia

9. Who has become the first woman chairperson of the Railway Board of India Railways in 2023?
   A. Jaya Verma Sinha
   B. Mita Vashishth
   C. Ravneet Kaur
   D. Vasudha Gupta

10. Match List-I with List-II.

List-I (Country)	List-II (Currency)
(*a*) Myanmar	I. Ruble
(*b*) Russia	II. Ngultrum
(*c*) Malaysia	III. Kyat
(*d*) Bhutan	IV. Ringgit

Choose the **correct** answer from the options given below:

	(*a*)	(*b*)	(*c*)	(*d*)
A.	III	I	II	IV
B.	III	I	IV	II
C.	IV	I	III	II
D.	II	I	IV	III

1. A **2.** B **3.** B **4.** B **5.** A **6.** B **7.** A **8.** A **9.** A **10.** B

11. "Jhulaghat Suspension Bridge" between India and which country has become fully operational now?

A. Bhutan B. Nepal
C. China D. Myanmar

12. Due to ocean acidification when the ocean becomes more acidic, what happens to the pH level of the ocean?

A. The pH level goes down.
B. The pH level stays the same.
C. The pH level goes up.
D. The pH level becomes zero.

13. Who is the first para-athlete to receive the Padma Bhushan award in India?

A. Bhavina Patel
B. Devendra Jhajharia
C. Avani Lekhara
D. Mariyappan Thangavelu

14. Zemu Glacier is located in which state of India?

A. Uttarakhand
B. Himachal Pradesh
C. Sikkim
D. Arunachal Pradesh

15. Who among the following is Chile's first woman President?

A. Mary Robinson
B. Michelle Bachelet
C. Kim Campbell
D. Jennifer Shipley

16. Which organisation developed and launched 'Ugram' Indigenous Assault Rifle for the armed forces?

A. ISRO B. BEL
C. HAL D. DRDO

17. Which of the following substances is a bad conductor of electricity?

A. Diamond
B. Gold
C. Silver
D. Graphite

18. Which of the following disease is caused due to the deficiency of proteins?

A. Arthritis
B. Kwashiorkor
C. Goitre
D. Night Blindness

19. Match List-I with List-II

List-I (Navy–Institution)	List-II (Place)
(*a*) INS Chilka	I. Goa
(*b*) INS Hansa	II. Andhra Pradesh
(*c*) INS Satavahana	III. Kerala
(*d*) INS Garuda	IV. Odisha

Choose the **correct** answer from the options given below:

	(*a*)	(*b*)	(*c*)	(*d*)
A.	III	I	II	IV
B.	I	IV	II	III
C.	IV	I	III	II
D.	IV	I	II	III

20. DRDO has conducted the first successful flight test of Agni-5 missile equipped with MIRV technology. What is the full form of MIRV?

A. Multiple Independently Targetable Re-Entry Vehicle
B. Mission India Target Re-Entry Vehicle
C. Multiple Independently Technology Re-Entry Vehicle
D. Multiple Indirect Targetable Re-Entry Vehicle

21. Which Indian has won the "Ramon Magsaysay Award-2023"?

A. Korvi Rakshand
B. Ashwini Kumar
C. Dipti Ranjan Sahoo
D. Dr. Ravi Kannan R.

22. Who has been appointed the Chairman of the 16th Finance Commission of India?

A. Ajay Narayan Jha
B. Smt. Annie George Mathew
C. Pradip Kumar Mohanty
D. Dr. Arvind Panagariya

23. Sri Ranganathswamy Temple which is situated in Tamil Nadu, is dedicated to which deity?

A. Lord Shiva B. Lord Vishnu
C. Goddess Durga D. Goddess Lakshmi

24. The Election Commission of India gets the power to conduct elections from which of the following articles?

A. Article 324 B. Article 280
C. Article 264 D. Article 26

11. B	**12.** A	**13.** B	**14.** C	**15.** B	**16.** D	**17.** A	**18.** B
19. D	**20.** A	**21.** D	**22.** D	**23.** B	**24.** A		

25. Match List-I with List-II.

List-I (Centre of Handicraft)	List-II (State)
(*a*) Mon	I. Arunachal Pradesh
(*b*) Nalbari	II. Assam
(*c*) Pasighat	III. Meghalaya
(*d*) Tura	IV. Nagaland

Choose the **correct** answer from the options given below:

	(*a*)	(*b*)	(*c*)	(*d*)
A.	IV	II	I	III
B.	I	III	IV	II
C.	IV	III	I	II
D.	I	II	IV	III

26. In which state is "Amchang Wildlife Sanctuary" located?

A. Assam B. Rajasthan
C. Odisha D. Manipur

27. India's first 3-D printed Post Office has been inaugurated in:

A. Guwahati B. Kolkata
C. Mumbai D. Bengaluru

28. What should come in the place of the questions mark (?) in the following alphanumeric series?

A1X, B4P, E25J, J100F, ?

A. O289D B. O225E
C. Q289D D. Q225E

29. In the given analogy, choose the word which will replace the question mark :

NEGI : MVTR :: SING : ?

A. TRNS B. TRNT
C. FRMT D. HRMT

30. In a certain code language 'ki ru pi' means 'nobody like cruel', 'ki mi cha' means 'king was cruel' and 'ru pi cha' means 'nobody like king'. What is the code for 'was' in the given code language?

A. ki B. mi
C. cha D. ru

31. Read the following information carefully to choose the best option for the question:

'P % Q' means that 'P is the sister of Q'
'P + Q' means that 'P is the son of Q'
'P × Q' means that 'P is the husband of Q'
'P – Q' means that 'P is the brother of Q'

Which of the following means 'A is the son-in-law of G'?

A. A × U + S × G
B. A + S % U × G
C. A – S + U × G
D. A × U % S + G

32. If 26th January, 2020 was a Sunday, then what day of the week was it on 16th March of that year?

A. Sunday B. Monday
C. Tuesday D. Wednesday

33. What will be the measurement of the angle made by the hour and minute hands of a clock when the time is 'quarter past 3'?

A. $6\frac{1}{2}^\circ$ B. 10°
C. $7\frac{1}{2}^\circ$ D. $8\frac{1}{2}^\circ$

34. If in a certain code language, 'MERCURY' is coded as 'NGUGZXF', then how will 'ENTANGLE' be coded in the same code language?

A. FPXFSMSM B. FPWESMSM
C. FPWESNSN D. FPWFTNSM

35. The problem given below consists of a question and two statements numbered I and II. You have to decide whether the data provided in the statements are sufficient to answer the question.

How many sisters does Sunny have?

I. Sunny is the only son of his parents.
II. Sunny's parents have three children.

A. Only statement I alone is sufficient to answer the question.
B. Only statement II alone is sufficient to answer the question.
C. Statements I and II together are sufficient to answer the question.
D. Either statement I or II alone is sufficient to answer the questions.

36. A boy leaves his house. He travels 6 km towards South, then travels 8 km towards West and further travels 9 km towards South. How far and in which direction is he from his house now?

A. 13 km, South West
B. 17 km, South West
C. 17 km, North West
D. 13 km, West

25. A **26.** A **27.** D **28.** C **29.** D **30.** B **31.** D **32.** B **33.** C **34.** B **35.** C **36.** B

37. Find out which of the answer figures completes the figure matrix:

Problem figure:

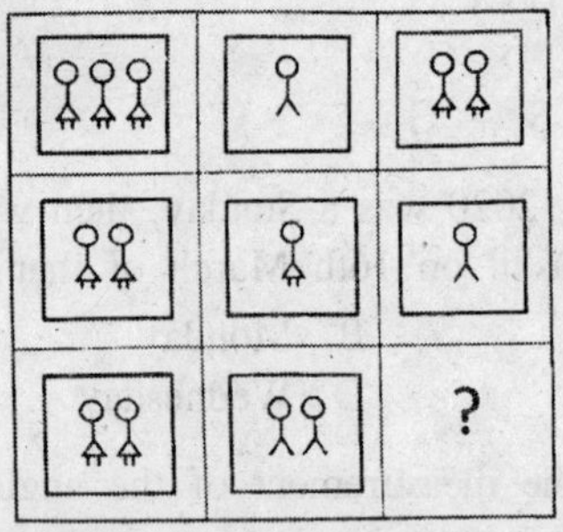

A. 
B. 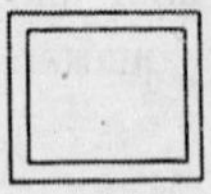
C. 
D. 

38. A clock seen through a mirror shows 'quarter to seven'. What is the correct time shown by the clock?

A. 6:15 B. 6:17
C. 5:17 D. 5:15

39. The sequence of folding a piece of paper and the manner in which the folded paper has been cut is shown in the following figures. How would this paper look when unfolded?

A. 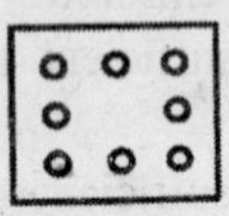
B. 
C. 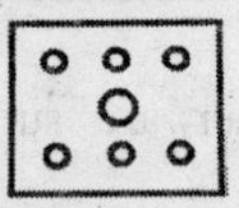
D. 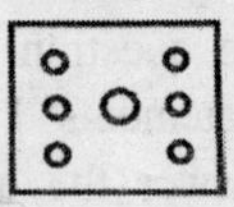

40. Find out the missing (?) number and letter.

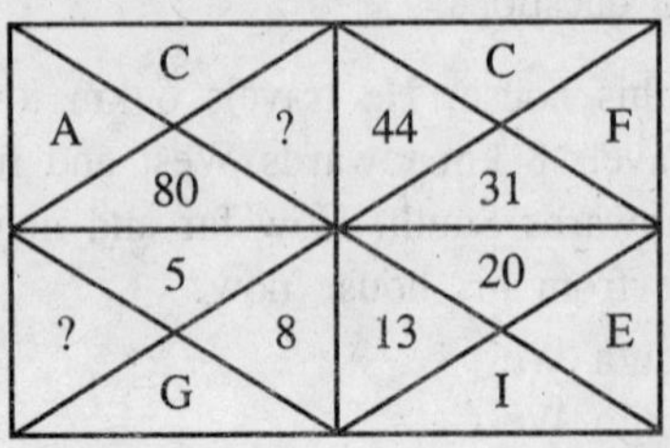

A. 59 and K B. 61 and L
C. 61 and K D. 59 and L

41. What will be the next number of the series

3, 6, 10.5, 17, 26, ?

A. 31 B. 38
C. 40 D. 41

42. In a class of 40 students, Anjali's rank is thrice that of Anita. There are 4 students who have ranks worse than that of Anjali. Anita's rank in the class is:

A. 9th B. 10th
C. 18th D. 12th

43. Six people E, H, K, M, S and U are seated in a circle facing the centre. U and H are immediate neighbours of M. E is the only person sitting between K and S. H is to the immediate right of S. Who is to the immediate right of U?

A. M B. E
C. K D. S

44. Find out which of the answer figures from the options can be formed using all the pieces given in the problem figure.

Problem figure

A. 
B. 
C. 
D. 

45. Read the given statements and conclusions carefully assuming that the information given in the statements is true, even if it appears to be at variance with commonly known facts. Decide which of the given conclusion(s) logically follows from the statements.

Statements:

No keyboard is a mouse
All mouses are computers.
All computers are laptops.

Conclusions:

I. All mouses are laptops.
II. All computers can never be keyboards.

A. Only conclusion I follows
B. Only conclusion II follows
C. Neither conclusion I nor II follows
D. Both conclusions I and II follow

37. B **38.** D **39.** B **40.** B **41.** B **42.** D **43.** C **44.** C **45.** D

46. Simplify: $24 \div 4 \times 2 + 8 - 4 = ?$

A. 1 B. 7
C. 16 D. 56

47. The difference of the greatest and the smallest of the fractions $\frac{1}{2}, \frac{8}{11}, \frac{7}{8}, \frac{7}{9}, \frac{5}{6}$ is:

A. $\frac{3}{8}$ B. $\frac{6}{7}$
C. $\frac{7}{9}$ D. $\frac{1}{3}$

48. The sum of LCM and HCF of two numbers is 854. If the LCM is 60 times the HCF and one of the numbers is 70, then the other number is:

A. 160 B. 164
C. 168 D. 172

49. The present age of Harish is 8 times the sum of the ages of his two sons at present. After 8 years, his age will be 2 times the sum of the ages of his two sons. The present age of Harish (in years) is:

A. 31 B. 32
C. 33 D. 34

50. In an examination, it is required to get 300 marks to pass. A student gets 225 marks and is declared fail by 10% marks. What are the maximum marks of the examinations?

A. 700 B. 750
C. 800 D. 850

51. In a class of 40 students, ratio of boys and girls is 3 : 2 and the average marks scored by boys is 42 and that by girls is 46. Then the average marks scored by the whole class is:

A. 43.4
B. 43.6
C. 43.8
D. 44

52. The sum of three numbers is 136. If the ratio between the first number and the second number is 2 : 3 and that between the second and third number is 5 : 3, then the first number is:

A. 42 B. 40
C. 36 D. 32

53. An item is sold for ₹ 504 after allowing 20% discount and still a profit of 5% has been earned. The marked price is how much more than the cost price?

A. ₹ 120 B. ₹ 135
C. ₹ 150 D. ₹ 160

54. A certain sum becomes ₹ 2,356 in 3 years and ₹ 2,660 in 5 years on simple interest. The value of sum is:

A. ₹ 1800 B. ₹ 1880
C. ₹ 1900 D. ₹ 1980

55. In a square, lengths of the diagonals are $(4k + 6)$ cm and $(7k - 3)$ cm. The area of the square (in cm^2) is:

A. 144 B. 162
C. 169 D. 172

56. The volume of a cylinder having base radius 3 cm is 396 cm^3. Find its curved surface area (in cm^2). (Use $\pi = 22/7$)

A. 280 B. 301.5
C. 264 D. 320.6

57. A tap can fill a tank in 6 hours. After half the tank is filled, three more similar taps are opened. What is the total time taken to fill the tank completely?

A. 4 hours
B. 5 hours
C. 3 hours 30 minutes
D. 3 hours 45 minutes

58. A train running at the speed of 80 km/h crosses a 350 m long tunnel in 36 seconds. The length of the train (in m) is:

A. 350 B. 380
C. 420 D. 450

59. If the mean of 3, 4, 9, $2k$, 10, 8, 6 and $(k + 6)$ is 8, and mode of 2, 2, 3, $2p$, $(2p + 1)$, 4, 4, 5 and 6 (p is a natural number) is 4, then the value of $(k - 2p)$ is :

A. 0 B. 1
C. 2 D. 3

60. In a triangle ABC, points D and E are on AB and AC respectively such that DE is parallel to BC. If AD = 6 cm, DB = 4 cm, AE = 9 cm, then the length of EC (in cm) is:

A. 7 B. 6.4
C. 6 D. 5.5

46. C	**47.** A	**48.** C	**49.** B	**50.** B	**51.** B	**52.** B	**53.** C
54. C	**55.** B	**56.** C	**57.** D	**58.** D	**59.** C	**60.** C	

EXPLANATORY ANSWERS

1. **(A):** The Banihal Pass connects Jammu with Srinagar, playing a crucial role in linking the Jammu region with the Kashmir Valley. Located in the Pir Panjal range at an elevation of about 2,832 meters (9,291 feet), it is traversed by the Banihal-Qazigund road tunnel, also known as the Jawahar Tunnel, which ensures all-weather connectivity between the two regions.

2. **(B):** Padma Shri Award — Mithun Chakraborty
The incorrect match regarding the Padma Awards-2024 is Mithun Chakraborty listed as a Padma Shri awardee. In reality, Mithun Chakraborty was honored with the Padma Bhushan for his significant contributions to Indian cinema.

3. **(B):**

   (*a*) **Vishakhadatta - Poet (II):** Vishakhadatta was an ancient Indian poet and playwright, known for his work "Mudrarakshasa."

   (*b*) **Kartikeya Sarabhai - Environmentalist (III):** Kartikeya Sarabhai is a renowned Indian environmentalist and founder of the Centre for Environment Education (CEE).

   (*c*) **Charaka - Medicine (I):** Charaka was an ancient Indian physician, known as the author of the "Charaka Samhita," a seminal text on Ayurveda.

   (*d*) **Satyendra Nath Bose - Mathematics (IV):** Satyendra Nath Bose was an Indian physicist and mathematician, best known for his work on quantum mechanics and the Bose-Einstein statistics.

4. **(B):** Given, $\sin A = \frac{4}{5}$

$$\therefore \quad \cos A = \sqrt{1-\sin^2 A} = \sqrt{1-\left(\frac{4}{5}\right)^2}$$

$$= \sqrt{1-\frac{16}{25}} = \sqrt{\frac{9}{25}} = \frac{3}{5}$$

$$\therefore \quad \tan A = \frac{\sin A}{\cos A} = \frac{\frac{4}{5}}{\frac{3}{5}} = \frac{4}{3}$$

$$\therefore (3 - \tan A)(2 + \cos A)$$

$$= \left(3-\frac{4}{3}\right)\left(2+\frac{3}{5}\right)$$

$$= \left(\frac{5}{3}\right)\left(\frac{13}{5}\right) = \frac{13}{3}.$$

5. **(A):** Given, speed of boat in still water = 8 km/h and speed of current = 2 km/h

$\therefore$ Speed upward = 8 − 2 = 6 km/h

and speed downward = 8 + 2 = 10 km/h

Let, distance = d

$$\text{Then,} \quad \frac{d}{6}+\frac{d}{10} = 2$$

$$\Rightarrow \quad d\left(\frac{1}{6}+\frac{1}{10}\right) = 2$$

$$\Rightarrow \quad d\left(\frac{5+3}{30}\right) = 2$$

$$\Rightarrow \quad d = \frac{2\times 30}{8}$$

$$\Rightarrow \quad d = \frac{15}{2} = 7.5 \text{ km}$$

Hence, required distance = d = 7.5 km.

6. **(B):**

   (*c*) **Nagaland:** Formed on December 1, 1963, becoming the 16th state of India. It was created to recognize the distinct identity and culture of the Naga people.

   (*a*) **Haryana:** Formed on November 1, 1966, when it was separated from Punjab. This reorganization was based on linguistic lines to cater to the Hindi-speaking population.

   (*b*) **Sikkim:** Became the 22nd state of India on May 16, 1975. Before this, Sikkim was a protectorate and then a kingdom under Indian suzerainty.

   (*d*) **Goa:** Became the 25th state of India on May 30, 1987, through the 56th Amendment of the Constitution of India. The day is celebrated annually as Goa Statehood Day.

7. **(A):** Mission Antyodaya (2022-23) aims to enhance the living conditions of rural areas by conducting an annual survey at the gram panchayat level. This initiative monitors the progress in the development process, ensuring that various governmental schemes and programs are effectively implemented and yielding the desired outcomes.

8. **(A):** The "Quadrilateral Security Dialogue" (QUAD) is a strategic alliance comprising Japan, India, Australia, and the United States, aimed at enhancing cooperation on security and regional stability in the Indo-Pacific region. China is not a member of this dialogue.

9. (A): Jaya Verma Sinha made history in 2023 by becoming the first woman chairperson of the Railway Board of Indian Railways. Her appointment marks a significant milestone in the history of Indian Railways, reflecting progress towards gender equality in top administrative positions.

10. (B):

(*a*) **Myanmar - The Kyat (III)** is the official currency of Myanmar. It is used for all financial transactions within the country and is represented by the symbol "Ks." The Kyat is subdivided into 100 pyas, though smaller denominations are rarely used.

(*b*) **Russia - The Ruble (I)** is the currency of Russia, symbolized as "₽" or "RUB." It is one of the oldest currencies in the world and has been in use since the 13th century. The Ruble is subdivided into 100 kopecks and is crucial for everyday transactions within Russia.

(*c*) **Malaysia - The Ringgit (IV),** often abbreviated as MYR, is the currency of Malaysia. It is symbolized by "RM" and is subdivided into 100 sen. The Ringgit is used throughout Malaysia and is essential for domestic commerce and trade.

(*d*) **Bhutan - The Ngultrum (II)** is Bhutan's currency, represented by the symbol "Nu." It is pegged to the Indian Rupee and is used in all financial transactions within Bhutan. The Ngultrum is subdivided into 100 chetrum.

11. (B): The "Jhulaghat Suspension Bridge," connecting India and Nepal, has recently become fully operational, enhancing cross-border connectivity and facilitating easier movement of people and goods between the two countries. Located in the Uttarakhand region of India, this bridge is a significant infrastructure development aimed at strengthening bilateral ties and improving access to remote areas on both sides of the border.

12. (A): Ocean acidification occurs when excess carbon dioxide (CO_2) from the atmosphere dissolves in seawater, forming carbonic acid. This process decreases the pH level of the ocean, making it more acidic. As a result, the pH level goes down, which can negatively impact marine life, particularly organisms with calcium carbonate shells or skeletons, such as corals and shellfish, by affecting their ability to form and maintain these structures.

13. (B): Devendra Jhajharia is the first para-athlete to be honored with the Padma Bhushan, one of India's highest civilian awards. Known for his exceptional achievements in para-athletics, Jhajharia is a javelin thrower who has won multiple gold medals at the Paralympic Games, including in 2004 and 2016.

14. (C): The Zemu Glacier is located in Sikkim, India, within the Kanchenjunga range of the Himalayas. It is one of the largest glaciers in the eastern Himalayas and feeds several important rivers in the region. The glacier is renowned for its stunning natural beauty and is a crucial source of water for the surrounding ecosystems.

15. (B): Michelle Bachelet made history as Chile's first woman President, serving two non-consecutive terms from 2006 to 2010 and again from 2014 to 2018. Her presidency marked a significant milestone for gender equality in Chilean politics.

16. (D): The 'Ugram' Indigenous Assault Rifle was developed and launched by the Defence Research and Development Organisation (DRDO), which is India's premier defense research agency. This advanced assault rifle is designed to enhance the capabilities of the Indian armed forces with its modern features and improved performance.

17. (A): While diamond is a form of carbon and has a strong covalent bonding structure, it does not have free electrons or ions to conduct electricity, making it an insulator. In contrast, gold, silver, and graphite are good conductors of electricity.

18. (B): Kwashiorkor is a serious nutritional disorder caused by a deficiency in dietary protein, despite adequate caloric intake. It primarily affects young children and is characterized by symptoms such as swelling of the abdomen and legs (edema), irritability, liver damage, and skin changes. The condition arises when there is not enough protein in the diet to meet the body's needs for growth and repair, leading to severe physical and metabolic disturbances.

19. (D):

(*a*) **INS Chilka - Odisha (IV):** INS Chilka is the premier naval training establishment for the Indian Navy, located near Chilika Lake in Odisha.

(*b*) **INS Hansa - Goa (I):** INS Hansa is a significant naval air station located in Dabolim, Goa, serving as the base for the Indian Navy's aviation operations.

(*c*) **INS Satavahana - Andhra Pradesh (II):** INS Satavahana is a naval submarine training base located in Visakhapatnam, Andhra Pradesh, focusing on training submariners.

(*d*) **INS Garuda - Kerala (III):** INS Garuda is a naval air station situated in Kochi, Kerala, and plays a crucial role in naval aviation operations.

20. (A): MIRV, or Multiple Independently Targetable Re-Entry Vehicle, is a missile technology that enables a single missile to carry multiple warheads, each capable of being directed to a different target independently. This enhances the missile's effectiveness and strategic value, as it allows for a single launch to potentially strike several targets simultaneously, increasing the chances of mission success and complicating defense measures for adversaries.

21. (D): Dr. Ravi Kannan R. was awarded the Ramon Magsaysay Award in 2023 for his exemplary work in delivering quality healthcare to underserved communities in India. As a prominent oncologist, Dr. Kannan has dedicated his career to providing medical services to patients in remote and economically disadvantaged regions.

22. (D): Dr. Arvind Panagariya has been appointed the Chairman of the 16th Finance Commission of India. He is an esteemed economist and former Vice Chairman of NITI Aayog, known for his expertise in economic policy and development.

23. (B): The Sri Ranganathswamy Temple in Tamil Nadu is dedicated to Lord Vishnu, one of the principal deities in Hinduism. Located in Srirangam, it is one of the most significant Vaishnavite temples in India and is renowned for its grandeur and architectural excellence.

24. (A): Article 324 of the Indian Constitution provides for the establishment and powers of the Election Commission of India, empowering it to supervise, direct, and control the entire process of elections to the Parliament and State Legislatures, as well as the office of the President and Vice President of India.

25. (A):

(*a*) **Mon - Nagaland (IV):** Mon is a district in Nagaland known for its rich tradition of tribal crafts, including traditional weaving and basketry, reflecting the diverse cultural heritage of the Naga tribes.

(*b*) **Nalbari - Assam (II):** Nalbari in Assam is renowned for its traditional Assamese handicrafts, particularly handloom products like muga silk and traditional weaving techniques.

(*c*) **Pasighat - Arunachal Pradesh (I):** Pasighat in Arunachal Pradesh is noted for its indigenous crafts, including intricate woodwork and weaving, showcasing the craftsmanship of the local tribes.

(*d*) **Tura - Meghalaya (III):** Tura in Meghalaya is recognized for its traditional handicrafts, including weaving and bamboo crafts, which are integral to the cultural expressions of the Garo tribe.

26. (A): The Amchang Wildlife Sanctuary is located in Assam, near the city of Guwahati. This sanctuary is renowned for its rich biodiversity, including a variety of wildlife such as elephants, tigers, and several species of birds and reptiles. It serves as an important conservation area, protecting the natural habitat and promoting ecological balance in the region.

27. (D): India's first 3-D printed Post Office was inaugurated in Bengaluru, showcasing a groundbreaking approach in construction technology. The building, created using 3-D printing techniques, exemplifies innovation in architectural design and efficiency. This project reflects a move towards modernizing infrastructure and highlights India's commitment to adopting cutting-edge technology in various sectors.

28. (C):

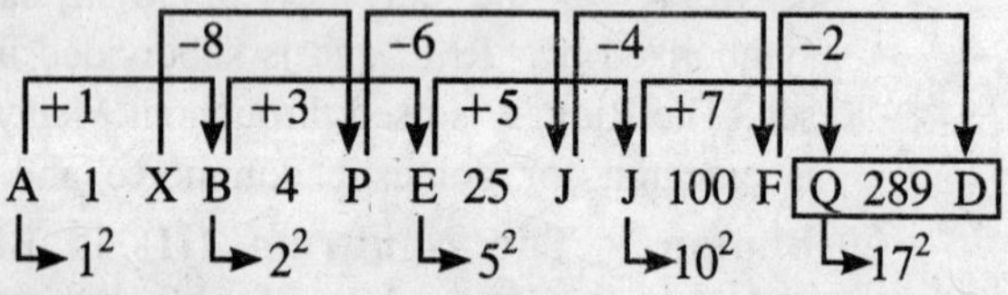

∴ Q289D should come in the place of the question mark in the series.

29. (D): Alphabets in natural series and reverse series

A = Z, B = Y, C = X, ... X = C, Y = B, Z = A

Given, NEGI : MVTR

⇒ N E G I → M V T R

Similarly, S I N G → H R M T

So, NEGI : MVTR :: SING : **HRMT**

30. (B): Given, 'ki ru pi' = 'nobody like cruel' ...(*i*)

'ki mi cha' = 'king was cruel' ...(*ii*)

'ru pi cha' = 'nobody like king' ...(*iii*)

From (*i*) and (*ii*),

'cruel' = 'ki'

From (*ii*) and (*iii*),

king = cha

From (*ii*), mi = was

So, 'mi' is the code for 'was' in the given code language.

31. (D): (D) A × U % S + G

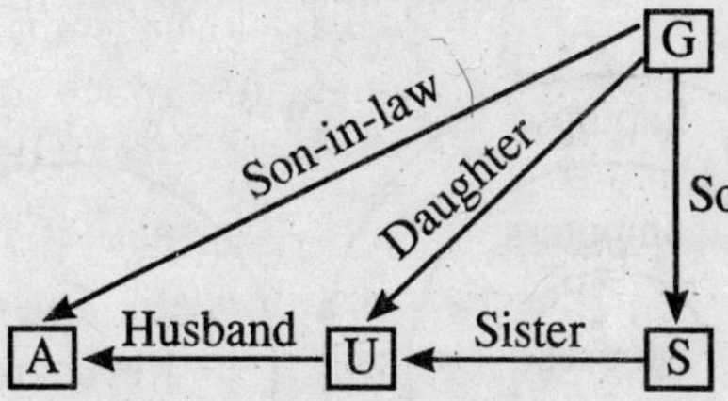

So, option (D) means 'A' is the son-in-law of 'G'.

32. (B): Given, 26 January, 2020 = Sunday

∴ 25 January, 2020 = Saturday

Number of day from 26 January, 2020 to 16 March, 2020

= 6 + 29 + 16 = 51 days

= 7 × 7 + 2 = 2 odd days

∴ 16 March, 2020 = Saturday + 2 days

= Monday.

33. (C): Here, 'quarter past 3' = 3 hours 15 minutes

Angles traced by the hour hand in 12 hours = 360°

Angled traced by hour hand in 3 hours 15 minutes

i.e., $= \frac{13}{4}$ hours

$$= \frac{360°}{12} \times \frac{13}{4} = \frac{195}{2} = 97\frac{1}{2}^{\circ}$$

Angled traced by minute hand in 60 minutes = 360°

∴ Angle traced by it in 15 minutes

$$= \left(\frac{360°}{60} \times 15\right) = 90°$$

Hence, required angle $= \left(97\frac{1}{2}^{\circ} - 90°\right) = 7\frac{1}{7}^{\circ}$.

34. (B): Given,

M E R C U R Y
+1 +2 +3 +4 +5 +6 +7
N G U G Z X F

Similarly,

E N T A N G L E
+1 +2 +3 +4 +5 +6 +7 +8
F P W E S M S M

So, 'ENTANGLE' will be coded as 'FPWESMSM'.

35. (C): From given statements (I) and (II).

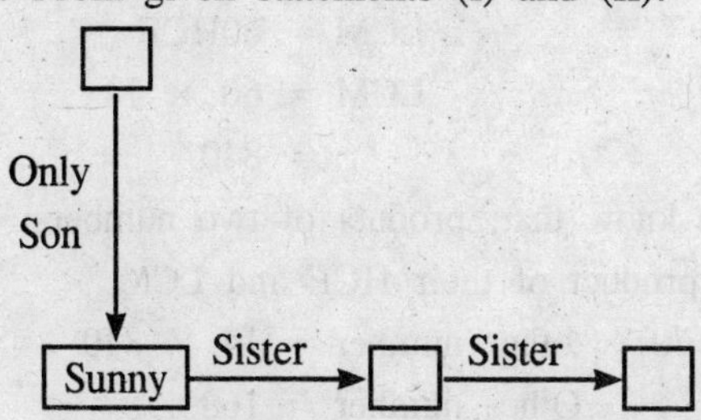

Sunny has 2 sisters.

So, Statements (I) and (II) together are sufficient to answer the question.

36. (B): Here, Starting point = A = house

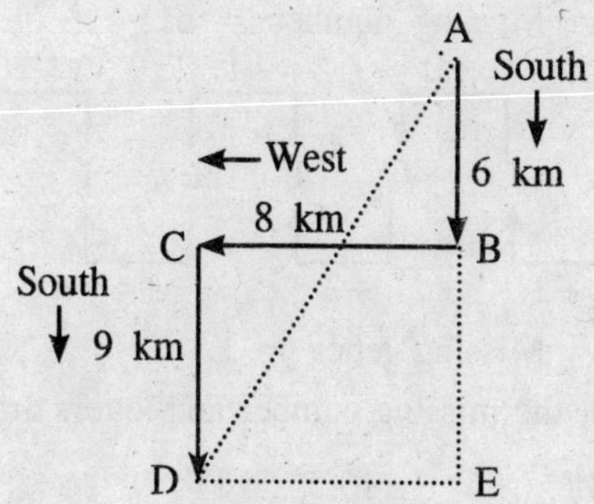

AB = 6 km

BC = 8 km

CD = 9 km

∵ AB + CD = 6 + 9

= 15 km = AE

and BC = ED

= 8 km

$$\therefore \quad AD = \sqrt{AE^2 + ED^2}$$

$$= \sqrt{(15)^2 + (8)^2}$$

$$= \sqrt{225 + 64} = \sqrt{289}$$

= 17 km

He (D) is 17 km far and in South-West direction from his house now.

38. (D): A clock seen through a mirror show quarter to seven = 6:45

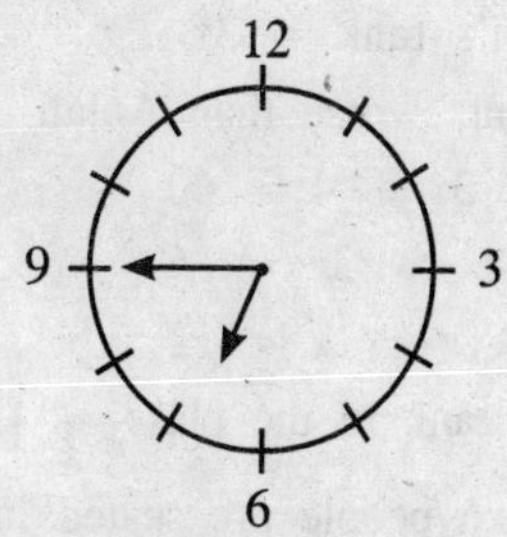

Now, correct time

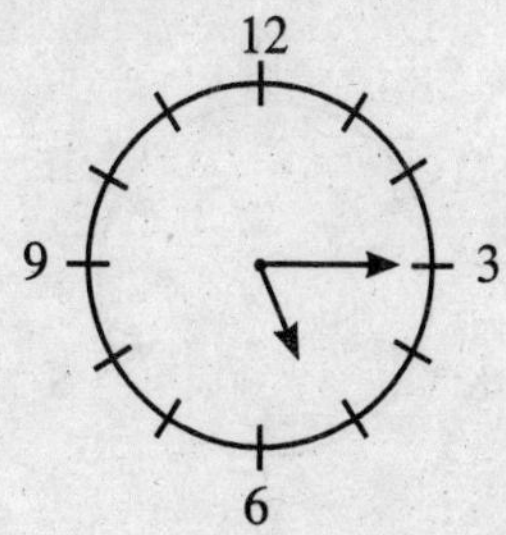

Hence, correct time show by the clock = 5:15.

40. (B):

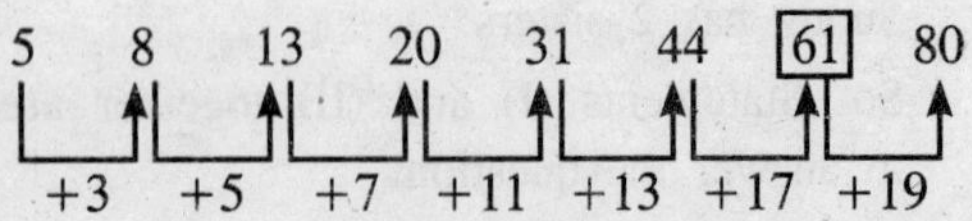

Here, 3, 5, 7, 11, 13, 17 and 19 are prime numbers.

∴ ? = Missing number = 61.

and

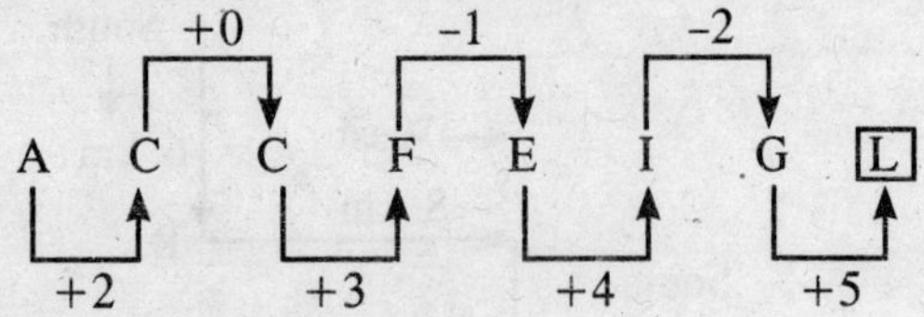

∴ ? = Missing letter = L

Hence, the missing number and letters are 61 and L.

41. (B):

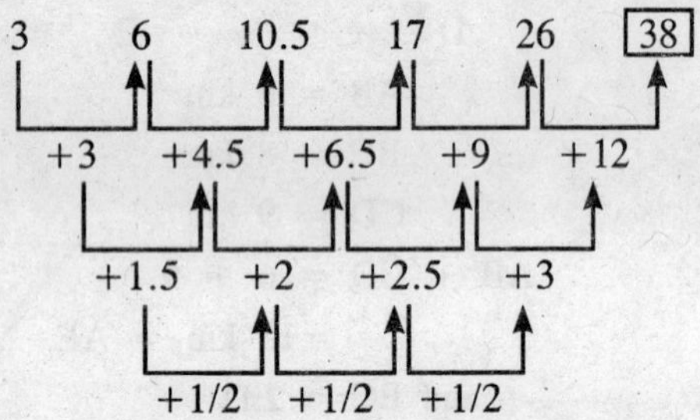

? = the next number of the series = 38.

42. (D): Given, Number of students in a class = 40

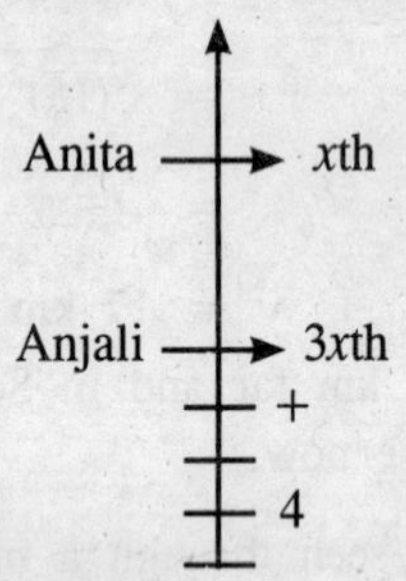

Let Anita's rank = x

Then, Anjali's rank = $3x$

and 4 students worse than Anjali

So, $3x + 4 = 40$

⇒ $3x = 36$

⇒ $x = 12$

So, Anita's rank in the class = 12th.

43. (C): Given, 6 people are seated in a circle facing the centre

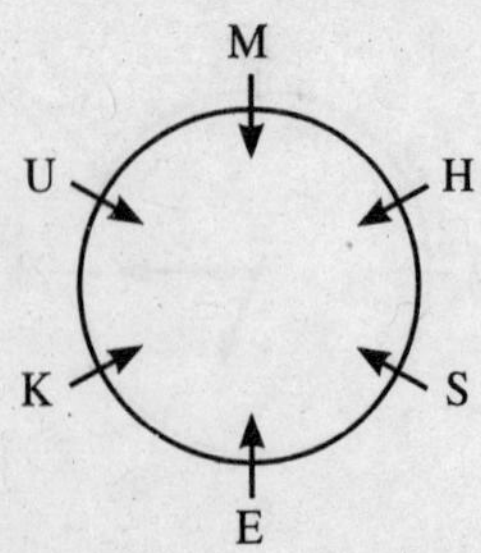

Here, K is the immediate right of U.

45. (D): From given statements:

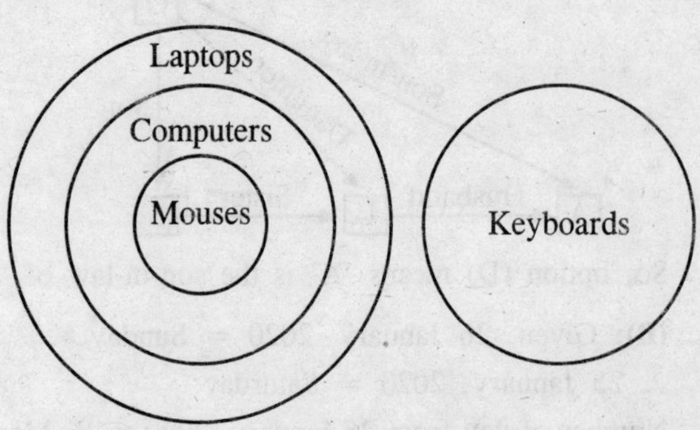

Conclusion:

I. All Mouses are laptops. (True)

II. All Computers can never be keyboards. (True)

Here, Both conclusions I and II follow.

46. (C): $24 \div 4 \times 2 + 8 - 4$

$= 6 \times 2 + 8 - 4$

$= 12 + 8 - 4$

$= 20 - 4 = 16.$

47. (A): ∵ $\frac{1}{2} = 0.5 \quad \frac{8}{11} = 0.72$

$\frac{7}{8} = 0.85 \quad \frac{7}{9} = 0.77$

$\frac{5}{6} = 0.83$

∴ Greatest fraction $= \frac{7}{8}$

and smallest fraction $= \frac{1}{2}$

∴ Required difference $= \frac{7}{8} - \frac{1}{2} = \frac{7-4}{8} = \frac{3}{8}$

48. (C): Given LCM + HCF = 854

and LCM = 60 HCF

∴ 60HCF + HCF = 854

⇒ 61HCF = 854

⇒ $\text{HCF} = \frac{854}{61} = 14$

⇒ HCF = 14

∴ LCM = 60HCF

⇒ LCM = 60×14

= 840

We know that, product of two numbers = product of their HCF and LCM

⇒ $70 \times$ other number $= 14 \times 840$

⇒ Other number = 168.

49. (B): Let present age of Harish be z years and present ages of his two sons be x years and y years

Then, $z = 8(x + y)$ ...(i)

After 8 years,

$z + 8 = 2(x + y + 8 + 8)$

$\Rightarrow z + 8 = 2(x + y) + 32$ ...(ii)

From (i) and (ii),

$$z + 8 = 2\times\frac{z}{8}+32$$

$$\Rightarrow z + 8 = \frac{z}{4}+32$$

$$\Rightarrow z-\frac{z}{4} = 32 - 8$$

$$\Rightarrow \frac{4z-z}{4} = 24$$

$$\Rightarrow \frac{3}{4}z = 24 \Rightarrow z = 32 \text{ years}$$

Hence, the present age of Harish is 32 years.

50. (B): Let the maximum marks of the examination $= x$

Then, $$300 - 225 = x\times\frac{10}{100}$$

$$\Rightarrow 75 = \frac{x}{10}$$

$$\Rightarrow x = 750.$$

51. (B): Given, number of students in a class = 40

Boys : Girls = 3 : 2

$$\therefore \text{Number of boys} = 40\times\frac{3}{5} = 24$$

$$\text{and number of girls} = 40\times\frac{2}{5} = 16$$

Now, Total marks scored by boys

$= 24 \times 42 = 1008$

and total marks scored by girls

$= 16 \times 46 = 736$

Hence, the average marks scored by the whole class

$$= \frac{1008+736}{40} = \frac{1744}{40} = 43.6.$$

52. (B): Given, the sum of 3 numbers = 136

First : Second = 2 : 3 = 10 : 15

Second : Third = 5 : 3 = 15 : 9

∴ First : Second : Third = 10 : 15 : 9

Then, the first number $= 136\times\frac{10}{10+15+9}$

$$= 136\times\frac{10}{34} = 4 \times 10 = 40.$$

53. (C): Marked price $\times \frac{100-20}{100}$ = ₹ 504

$$\Rightarrow \text{M.P.} \times \frac{4}{5} = ₹\ 504$$

$$\Rightarrow \text{M.P.} = 504\times\frac{5}{4}$$

$$\Rightarrow \text{M.P.} = 126 \times 5 = ₹\ 630$$

and cost price $\times \frac{105}{100}$ = ₹ 504

$$\Rightarrow \text{C.P.} = 504\times\frac{100}{105} = 504\times\frac{20}{21}$$

$$\Rightarrow \text{C.P.} = 24 \times 20 = 480$$

So, M.P. – C.P. = 630 – 480 = ₹ 150

Hence, the marked price is ₹ 150 more than the cost price.

54. (C): Given, sum become ₹ 2356 in 3 years and sum become ₹ 2660 in 5 years.

∴ Simple interest in 5 – 3 = 2 years

= 2660 – 2356 = ₹ 304

$\Rightarrow$ Simple interest in 3 years $= \frac{304}{2}\times 3$

= 152 × 3 = ₹ 456

∴ The value of sum = 2356 – 456 = ₹ 1900.

55. (B): In a square, length of diagonals are equal

$$\therefore 4k + 6 = 7k - 3$$

$$\Rightarrow 7k - 6k = 6 + 3$$

$$\Rightarrow k = 9$$

$$\therefore \text{Diagonal} = 4k + 6$$

$$= 12 + 6 = 18 \text{ cm}$$

$$\text{and diagonal} = \text{Side}\sqrt{2}$$

$$\Rightarrow 18 = \text{Side}\sqrt{2} \Rightarrow \text{Side} = 9\sqrt{2}$$

$$\therefore \text{Area of the square} = (\text{Side})^2 = \left(9\sqrt{2}\right)^2$$

$$= 162 \text{ cm}^2.$$

56. (C): The volume of a cylinder = 396

$$\Rightarrow \pi r^2h = 396$$

$$\Rightarrow \pi(3)^2h = 396$$

$$\Rightarrow \pi h = \frac{396}{9} = 44$$

$\Rightarrow \quad \pi h = 44$

Its curved surface area $= 2\pi rh$

$= 2\pi h \times 3 \quad [\because \pi h = 44]$

$= 2 \times 44 \times 3$

$= 264 \text{ cm}^2.$

57. (D): A tap can fill a tank in 6 hours

$\Rightarrow$ A tap can fill $\frac{1}{2}$ tank in 3 hours

and remaining part of tank fill in $\frac{\frac{1}{2}}{\frac{4}{6}}$ hours

$= \frac{1}{2} \times \frac{6}{4} = \frac{3}{4}$ hours

$= \frac{3}{4} \times 60 = 45$ minutes

$\therefore$ The total time taken to fill the tank completely

$= 3$ hours $+ 45$ minutes

$= 3$ hours 45 minutes.

58. (D): Let the length of the train $= x$ m

Then, $\quad \frac{x + 350}{80 \times \frac{5}{18}} = 36$

$\Rightarrow \quad x + 350 = 36 \times 80 \times \frac{5}{18}$

$= 2 \times 80 \times 5$

$\Rightarrow \quad x + 350 = 160 \times 5 = 800$

$\Rightarrow \quad x = 800 - 350$

$\Rightarrow \quad x = 450$ m.

59. (C): Given, mean $= 8$

$\therefore \quad \frac{3 + 4 + 9 + 2k + 10 + 8 + 6 + (k + 6)}{8} = 8$

$\Rightarrow \quad 46 + 3k = 8 \times 8$

$\Rightarrow \quad 3k = 64 - 46 = 18$

$\Rightarrow \quad k = 6$

and 2, 2, 3, $2p$, $(2p + 1)$, 4, 4, 5 (p is a natural number)

$\Rightarrow 2, 2, 3, 2 \times 2, (2 \times 2 + 1), 4, 4, 5$

$\Rightarrow 2, 2, 3, 4, 5, 4, 4, 5$

Given, $\quad$ Mode $= 4$

$\Rightarrow \quad 2p = 4$

$\Rightarrow \quad p = 2$

Henec, $\quad (k - 2p) = 6 - 2 \times 2$

$= 6 - 4 = 2.$

60. (C): Given, in ΔABC,

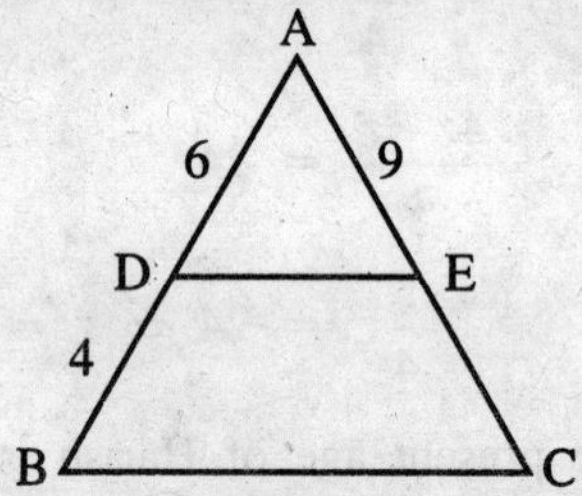

DE || BC

AD = 6 cm

DB = 4 cm

AE = 9 cm

From Thales theorem,

In ΔABC, $\quad \frac{AD}{DB} = \frac{AE}{EC}$

$\Rightarrow \quad \frac{6}{4} = \frac{9}{EC}$

$\Rightarrow \quad 6EC = 9 \times 4$

$\Rightarrow \quad EC = \frac{9 \times 4}{6} = \frac{36}{6} = 6$

$\Rightarrow \quad EC = 6$ cm.

Previous Years' Paper (Solved)

(Common University Entrance Test for UG Programmes)

CUET (UG)–B.A. (Hons.) English Entrance Exam, 2023*

ENGLISH

Directions (Qs. No. 1-5): *Read the following passage to answer question:*

The village school was located in a prominent place where apart from the school, there were a few shops, a small temple and a government dispensary. The headmaster of the school was a learned and scholarly man loved by all. The dispensary was looked after by a doctor and a male nurse. The doctor attended the dispensary very punctually and used to retire to his residence after the duty hours and never allowed anyone to visit his residence after the duty hours.

The school was housed in dilapidated building and very often the headmaster used to take the children out to the nearby garden where they could play and take part in various sports and games under the able supervision of the headmaster.

One day a stray dog entered the garden when the children were playing. One of them pelted a stone at the dog and it started barking and all of a sudden became boisterous and bit a child in the leg. The boy was very badly hurt and his leg started bleeding. The children who by this time became panicky rushed to the headmaster who together with a few students, took the child to the nearby dispensary and then to the doctors residence.

The headmaster knocked at the door of the doctor for help. But the doctor refused to open the door and made it clear that he would not attend to anyone howsoever serious he may be, during his leisure hours. However the headmaster continued to knock at the door and finally the doctor opened the door when he saw the headmaster trembling with fear and the student in agony and pain.

The doctor mellowed down now and took the child to the dispensary for bandaging and giving necessary injections and medicines. The doctor was impressed by the dedication and sincerity of the headmaster. He realized his folly and decided to attend to the needy and sick even during his leisure hours.

1. The village school was located near the:

A. Forest B. Market
C. Library D. Pond

2. After the duty hours the government dispensary doctor normally:

A. Slept and dreamt
B. Spent time with his family
C. went to his private clinic
D. Rested at home and never allowed visitors

3. All of a sudden a dog became boisterous and it bit a child in the leg. The dog got angry mainly because:

A. One boy did mischief
B. Dog was feeling hungry
C. Dog saw another dog
D. Boy did not give food to the dog

4. The head master was trembling with fear at the doctor's residence along with the injured boy. The doctor was:

A. afraid of higher officials
B. afraid of student's parents
C. not opening the door
D. impressed with the dedication of the headmaster

5. Find the synonym from a passage which means "To become less extreme in behaviour".

A. Stray B. boisterous
C. mellowed D. Folly

Directions (Qs. No. 6-10): *Read the following passage to answer question:*

The needs of a nations people are bigger and much more important than any other considerations. The mission of parliament is that it has to be alive and dynamic over issues vital to the existence of our very nationhood. Our freedom did not come as a gift. The whole country struggled for decades to achieve the first vision of independence, so

*** This Previous Year Paper has been given here as a Combination of CUET (UG) 2023 different exams for the Subjects 'English and General Test', which have been mapped to this course.**

we have to protect it. There were excellent leaders in all walks of life-science, education and industry. To preserve this freedom from intruders and others who would compromise it is our bounden duty and not a matter of choice and convenience. No ideology is above the security and prosperity of our country. No agenda is more important than harmony among the people. Students should get ready to transform India into a developed nation. Ignite your minds and think big.

A teacher once said, 'Give me a five-year-old child. After seven years, no God or Devil will be able to change the chiid.' Will all teachers be such gurus? The administrators have a great opportunity to link the people and political leaders. They should always take decisions that are good for the people I believe it is only executives like empowered district collectors who can assist transformation. The state-Central integrated fund has to be deployed in mission mode programmes.

6. We have to protect our nations Independence as we got it after:
A. excellent leader
B. War and Fight
C. Struggle for decades
D. Help from foreign country

7. To transform India into a Developed Nation Dr. A.P.J. Abdul Kalam expects his students to:
A. Ignite the minds B. Fire the mind
C. Use the mind D. Clean the mind

8. The one who can link the people and political leaders even to assist for transformation. They are known as:
A. Leader B. Administrators
C. Manager D. Major

9. The existence of Nation hood is maintained by:
A. Country B. Office
C. Collectorate D. Parliament

10. Find the synonym from the passage which means:
'Trespasser'
Choose the correct option:
A. Leader B. Teacher
C. Intruder D. Collector

Directions (Qs. No. 11-15): *Read the following passage to answer question:*

Village Resource Centres (VRCs) were established by the Indian Space Research Organisation (ISRO) as part of its societal mission of bringing space-based services emanating from Satellite Communication (SatCom) and Earth Observation (EO) to rural society. While SatCom provides the method for an effective delivery of information and services across vast regions, EO provides community-centric information regarding geo-referenced land records; natural resources; the environment; sites for exploiting ground water for potable use and recharging: wasteland and reclamation; watershed profile; and cropping patterns. It can also provide customized local area information. These systems are very useful for predicting disaster, giving early warning and vulnerability-related information.

ISRO has undertaken the mission of assisting the VRC programme with a portfolio of services which are being established in collaboration with forty partner agencies across twenty-two states. A total of 473 VRCs have been set up with plans for rapid expansion in the future. Each VRC essentially has digital connectivity; specialty health care providers enabled via the Indian National Satellite System (INSAT); Spatial information on natural resources facilities for primary health care and distance education.

11. Village resource centres were set up by the ______ to bring space based centres to rural society:
A. Sat com
B. Indian Space Research Organisation
C. Earth observation
D. Indian National Satellite system

12. ISRO has undertaken the mission of assisting the village Resource Centres Programme with forty partner agencies across ______ states.
A. Twenty One B. Twenty Two
C. Twenty Three D. Twenty Five

13. Match List-I with List-II:

List-I	*List-II*
(*a*) SatCom	(*i*) Village Resource Centres
(*b*) VRCs	(*ii*) Indian National Satellite System
(*c*) ISRO	(*iii*) Satellite Communication
(*d*) INSAT	(*iv*) Indian Space Research Organisation

Choose the correct answer from the options given below:

	(*a*)	(*b*)	(*c*)	(*d*)
A.	(*iii*)	(*iv*)	(*i*)	(*ii*)
B.	(*iv*)	(*ii*)	(*iii*)	(*i*)
C.	(*ii*)	(*iv*)	(*i*)	(*iii*)
D.	(*iii*)	(*i*)	(*iv*)	(*ii*)

14. Find a word from the passage that means the same as 'to assume things before it happens'.
A. Communications B. Observations
C. Information D. Prediction

15. Find a word from the passage that is an antonym of the word 'safe/secure'.
A. Exploitation B. Expansion
C. Vulnerable D. Collaboration

16. Fill in the blank with the correct determiner:
The teacher asked him ______ questions.
A. much B. a few
C. any D. every

17. Change the following into direct speech:

He requested me to shut the door.

A. He told, "The door should be shut."

B. He said, "Please shut the door."

C. He said, "Shut the door."

D. He ordered, "Close the door."

18. Fill in the blank with the correct adverb:

I ______ met him at the conference on Sunday but discussed a lot of things.

A. Always B. Never

C. Briefly D. Finally

19. Which of the following sentences does ***not*** use the correct modals.

(*a*) I swim across the river when I was young.

(*b*) It may rain next Friday

(*c*) I expected that I would get a first class

(*d*) One ought to respect the environmental laws

(*e*) This used to be a dense jungle.

Choose the ***correct answer*** from the options given below:

A. (*a*) and (*d*) only B. (*a*) only

C. (*e*) only D. (*c*) and (*d*) only

20. Complete the sentence by choosing the appropriate options:

He gave ______ European ______ one-rupee coin.

A. the, an B. a, a

C. an, an D. the, a

21. Complete the sentence by choosing the appropriate set of prepositions:

He is notoriously mean ______ his treatment ______ his servants.

A. in, of B. with, of

C. of, with D. for, of

22. Synonym of the word "alleviate".

(*a*) worsen (*b*) grow

(*c*) lessen (*d*) increase

(*e*) reduce

Choose the ***correct answer*** from the options given below:

A. (*a*) and (*e*) only B. (*c*) and (*e*) only

C. (*b*) and (*d*) only D. (*a*) only

23. Choose the correct Exclamatory sentence of the given sentence:

The Night is very beautiful.

A. How beautiful is the night!

B. Night is so beautiful!

C. What beautiful night!

D. Night is too beautiful!

24. Choose the option that has been correctly changed from Direct to Indirect speech.

Adesh said, "Please shut the door behind you."

(*a*) Adesh requested me to please shut the door behind me.

(*b*) Adesh said that I request you to shut the door behind you.

(*c*) Adesh said to shut the door behind you.

(*d*) Adesh said to me that I request to shut the door behind you.

Choose the ***correct answer*** from the options given below:

A. (*a*) only B. (*b*) only

C. (*c*) only D. (*d*) only

25. Match the underline phrases with their meanings:

List-I (Phrases)	***List-II (Meanings)***
(*a*) I had so much work to do but the fever got the best of me	(*i*) Peaceful time
(*b*) They spent their halcyon days in a village	(*ii*) Vulnerable/Weak spot
(*c*) He earned really well but ended up penniless. Gambling was his achilles heel	(*iii*) Competent for a work
(*d*) A doctor worth his salt will advise people for healthy eating	(*iv*) Take advantage of something

Choose the ***correct answer*** from the options given below:

	(*a*)	(*b*)	(*c*)	(*d*)
A.	(*iv*)	(*i*)	(*ii*)	(*iii*)
B.	(*iv*)	(*ii*)	(*i*)	(*iii*)
C.	(*i*)	(*iii*)	(*ii*)	(*iv*)
D.	(*iv*)	(*iii*)	(*ii*)	(*i*)

26. Choose the correct meaning of the underlined word from the following sentence:

The minister entered the hall with his entourage.

A. cars B. belongings

C. following subordinates D. police

27. Find out the adverbs from the given sentence and tick the correct option given below:

People often complain about foolish things and easily try to escape from the reality.

A. complain, reality B. often, easily

C. easily, complain D. often, escape

28. Choose the option with the same meaning:

Camouflage

(*a*) disguise (*b*) cover

(*c*) demonstrate (*d*) fabric

Choose the ***correct answer*** from the options given below:

A. (*a*) only B. (*b*) only

C. (*c*) only D. (*d*) only

29. Complete the sentence using the correct options:

When I reached the station, the train

A. been leaving

B. had been already leaving
C. had already left
D. has left

30. State the kind of clause for the underlined part of the given sentence:

The Children whom I teach in standard 8 are very disciplined.

A. Adverb clause B. Adjective clause
C. Noun clause D. Adverb clause of time

31. Match List-I with List-II to complete the idioms:

List-I	*List-II*
(*a*) At one's	(*i*) tongue
(*b*) Hold one's	(*ii*) fingertips
(*c*) Lose one's	(*iii*) head
(*d*) Win	(*iv*) hands down

Choose the correct answer from the options given below:

	(*a*)	(*b*)	(*c*)	(*d*)
A.	(*ii*)	(*i*)	(*iii*)	(*iv*)
B.	(*i*)	(*ii*)	(*iii*)	(*iv*)
C.	(*iv*)	(*iii*)	(*ii*)	(*i*)
D.	(*ii*)	(*i*)	(*iv*)	(*iii*)

32. Find the correct Antonym of the word 'Terrible':

A. scaring B. soothing
C. horrible D. frightening

33. Match List-I with List-II for suitable antonyms:

List-I (*Word*)	*List-II* (*Antonym*)
(*a*) Charming	(*i*) Hide
(*b*) Occasional	(*ii*) Miser
(*c*) Generous	(*iii*) Hideous
(*d*) Exhibit	(*iv*) Regular

Choose the correct answer from the options given below:

	(*a*)	(*b*)	(*c*)	(*d*)
A.	(*iii*)	(*iv*)	(*ii*)	(*i*)
B.	(*iv*)	(*ii*)	(*iii*)	(*i*)
C.	(*iii*)	(*ii*)	(*i*)	(*iv*)
D.	(*ii*)	(*i*)	(*iv*)	(*iii*)

34. Arrange the following in the correct sequence:

(*a*) With telling us about
(*b*) has been mainly occupied
(*c*) the finite world has been analysed
(*d*) the elements into which
(*e*) The language of man

Choose the correct answer from the options given below:

A. (*e*), (*b*), (*a*), (*d*), (*c*) B. (*a*), (*e*), (*b*), (*d*), (*c*)
C. (*e*), (*a*), (*b*), (*d*), (*c*) D. (*e*), (*d*), (*a*), (*b*), (*c*)

35. Match the phrases with their meaning:

List-I	*List-II*
(*a*) Set in	(*i*) to treat with contempt
(*b*) Wind up	(*ii*) extinguished
(*c*) look down upon	(*iii*) begin
(*d*) put out	(*iv*) bring to an end

Choose the correct answer from the options given below:

	(*a*)	(*b*)	(*c*)	(*d*)
A.	(*ii*)	(*iii*)	(*iv*)	(*i*)
B.	(*iv*)	(*ii*)	(*iii*)	(*i*)
C.	(*iii*)	(*i*)	(*iv*)	(*ii*)
D.	(*iii*)	(*iv*)	(*i*)	(*ii*)

36. Choose the option that gives the correct meaning of the foreign word:

'animus'

A. good intention B. bad intention
C. mean while D. self love

37. Identify the correct passive voice form of the following sentence:

One should keep one's promises.

A. Promises need to be kept.
B. Promises should be kept.
C. Nobody keeps promises.
D. One has kept one's promises.

38. Complete the sentence with suitable option:

You ______ stood by your friends in their bad times.

A. ought to have B. should
C. must D. can have

39. Choose the correct question tag for the given sentence:

She doesn't really know how to get out of the problem?

A. Isn't she? B. doesn't she
C. does she? D. Is it?

40. Choose the correct option to change the following sentence into passive voice.

Your behaviour astonished me.

A. I was astonished by you with your behaviour.
B. You are astonished by me with behaviour.
C. I was astonished by your behaviour.
D. With your behaviour you were astonished

41. Choose one word which can be substituted for the given sentence:

'One who acts against religion'.

A. Egoist B. Heretic
C. Optimist D. Stoic

42. Fill in the blank with the suitable homonym

Choose the correct one from the following.

Ravi writes in his note book today.

The marriage is performed as per Hindu ______.

A. Rites B. Wrights
C. Rights D. Raight

43. Parts of a sentence are given in a jumbled order. Arrange the parts in the correct sequence to form a meaningful sentence.

(*a*) the resistance (*b*) of
(*c*) depend on (*d*) what does
(*e*) a conductor

Choose the correct answer from the options given below:
A. (*d*), (*a*), (*e*), (*c*), (*b*) B. (*d*), (*a*), (*b*), (*e*), (*c*)
C. (*b*), (*a*), (*d*), (*e*), (*c*) D. (*d*), (*a*), (*c*), (*b*), (*e*)

44. Choose the correct idiomatic expression.
The staff agreed to execute the plans.
A. Carry away B. Lay out
C. Turn down D. Carry out

45. Complete the omitted/grammatically correct sentence:
"Asoka two lives, one as ruthless conqueror and the as a compassionate ruler"
(*a*) Asoka led two lives one as the most ruthless conqueror and the as a compassionate ruler.
(*b*) Asoka led two various lives, one ruthless conqueror and the as a compassionate ruler.
(*c*) Asoka led two live one as ruthless conqueror and the as a famous compassionate ruler.
(*d*) Asoka led two lives one as ruthless conqueror and the other as a compassionate ruler.
(*e*) Asoka led two lives one as ruthless conqueror so and the as a compassionate ruler.

Choose the correct answer from the options given below:
A. (*a*) only B. (*b*) only
C. (*e*) only D. (*d*) only

46. Choose the correct subject for a letter of enquiry for a course in Choreography:
A. Enquiry for choreography
B. Course in choreography
C. Enquiry regarding course in choreography
D. Enquiry in course of choreography

47. Choose the correct Assertive sentence of the given sentence:
Alas that youth should pass away!
A. It is sad that youth has passed away
B. It is sad to think that youth should pass away
C. It is sad that youth shall pass away
D. It is sad that youth passes away

48. Complete the sentence in List-I with the correct preposition from List-II:

	List-I	*List-II*
(*a*)	____ the street the piper slept	(*i*) in
(*b*)	Little Jack Horner sat ____ a corner	(*ii*) into
(*c*)	Old mother Hubbard went ____ the cupboard	(*iii*) over
(*d*)	The cow jumped ____ the moon	(*iv*) to

Choose the correct answer from the options given below:

	(*a*)	(*b*)	(*c*)	(*d*)
A.	(*ii*)	(*i*)	(*iv*)	(*iii*)
B.	(*i*)	(*ii*)	(*iv*)	(*iii*)
C.	(*iii*)	(*ii*)	(*i*)	(*iv*)
D.	(*ii*)	(*iii*)	(*iv*)	(*i*)

49. Find out which part of the sentence has an error.
The captain along with his team are practicing very hard for the forthcoming matches.
A. The Captain along with his team
B. are practicing very hard
C. for the
D. forthcoming matches

50. Spot the Error
(*a*) Copernicus proved (*b*) that Earth
(*c*) moves (*d*) round
(*e*) the sun

Choose the correct answer from the options given below:
A. (*b*) only B. (*c*) only
C. (*d*) only D. (*e*) only

ANSWERS

1. (B): The village school's location is mentioned in the passage as being in a prominent place surrounded by some shops, a tempie, and a government dispensary. There's no direct mention of the school being near a forest, library, or pond. However, the presence of shops suggests a market-like setting, which makes option B the most likely answer.

2. (D): The doctor's routine after his duty hours is clearly stated in the passage. It says that the doctor "used to retire to his residence after the duty hours and never allowed anyone to visit his residence after the duty hours." This directly indicates that he rested at his home and was strict about not entertaining visitors during that time.

3. (A): The primary reason the dog became aggressive and bit a child is directly linked to a particular action from one of the children. The passage mentions, "One of them pelted a stone at the dog." This act of mischief from the child triggered the dog's aggressive behavior. In this scenario, pelting a stone can be seen as a direct threat, leading to the dog's defensive reaction.

4. (D): The doctor's initial refusal to help was overridden when he saw the headmaster's state of extreme worry and the injured student's pain. The passage says, "the doctor opened the door when he saw the headmaster trembling with fear and the student in agony and pain." Following this, the doctor's subsequent actions and feelings were influenced by the headmaster's dedication. The doctor was "impressed by the dedication and sincerity of the headmaster." The headmaster's commitment to the well-being of his student is evident here, showcasing the strong bond and sense of responsibility educators often feel towards their students.

5. (C): The term "mellowed" in the passage refers to the doctor's change in behavior from strict and unyielding to more understanding and compassionate. The phrase "The doctor mellowed down now" indicates a reduction in his earlier stern behavior. In this context, "to mellow" means to become gentler or more lenient, which aligns with the definition of "to become less extreme in behavior."

6. (C): India's hard-won independence came after a prolonged "struggle for decades," as stated in the passage. This wasn't a result of wars or direct fights, nor was it a gift from excellent leaders or foreign aid. The mention of the prolonged struggle underscores the sacrifices, non-violent protests, negotiations, and relentless efforts made by the entire nation to free itself from colonial rule.

7. (A): Dr. A.P.J. Abdul Kalam, a visionary leader and former President of India, always emphasized on the power of the youth. In the passage, he inspires students to "ignite your minds" as a means to transform India into a developed nation. Igniting the mind symbolizes invoking curiosity, passion, and a thirst for knowledge and innovation.

8. (B): "Administrators" are pinpointed in the passage as having a significant role in bridging the gap between the people and political leaders, subsequently aiding in transformation. Administrators, in this context, likely refer to government officials and civil servants who are responsible for implementing policies and ensuring governance at the grassroots level.

9. (D): The "existence of our very nationhood" is closely tied to the mission of the "parliament," as highlighted in the passage. A nation's parliament is its supreme legislative body and represents the collective will of its people. It enacts laws, discusses national issues, and holds the government accountable.

10. (C): The term "intruder" is synonymous with 'trespasser'. An intruder is someone who enters a place without permission or authorization, often with malicious intent. In the context of the passage, the term is used to emphasize the importance of safeguarding India's hard-won freedom from those who might seek to harm or compromise it. The reference to intruders can be seen as a broader metaphor for any force or ideology that might threaten India's sovereignty, harmony, or security.

11. (B): The **Indian Space Research Organisation (ISRO)** is credited with setting up Village Resource Centres (VRCs) to extend space-based services to the rural populace. ISRO, established in 1969, has been instrumental in utilizing space technology for India's development, especially focusing on rural and remote areas.

12. (B): The passage clearly mentions that ISRO has collaborated with forty partner agencies spread out across **twenty-two states** for the VRC program. India, with its diverse geography and vast area, has always faced challenges in ensuring that the benefits of technology and development reach even the most remote corners. The initiative to span across twenty-two states shows the program's expansive reach, attempting to bring the advantages of space technology to a broader spectrum of the Indian population.

13. (D): Matching the terms with their respective meanings or representations, we get:

- SatCom (*a*) aligns with Satellite Communication (*iii*), which is a technology for relaying and broadcasting information using satellites.
- VRCs (*b*) stands for Village Resource Centres (*i*), which are centers established in rural regions to provide space-based services.
- ISRO (*c*) is the acronym for Indian Space Research Organisation (*iv*), the space agency of the Government of India.
- INSAT (*d*) matches with Indian National Satellite System (*ii*), a series of multipurpose geostationary satellites commissioned by ISRO to cater to telecommunications, broadcasting, meteorology, and search and rescue operations.

14. (D): The word **'Prediction'** means to foresee or anticipate an event before it takes place. In the realm of space technology and observation, prediction plays a pivotal role, especially in forecasting natural calamities, weather patterns, or any other potential events that could have significant societal implications.

15. (C): The term **'Vulnerable'** denotes a state of susceptibility or being prone to harm, danger, or risk. In contrast to being 'safe' or 'secure,' a vulnerable state means that there's potential exposure to harm. In the context of space-based observations, understanding vulnerabilities becomes vital. By identifying areas, populations, or resources that are vulnerable - be it to natural disasters, climate change, or any other threats - proactive measures can be adopted to mitigate adverse impacts. (B) The correct option is "a few." In this context, "questions" is a countable noun. The determiner "much" is used with uncountable nouns, "any" usually appears in negative or interrogative contexts, and "every" doesn't fit grammatically. "A few" is used to indicate a small number of countable nouns. Therefore, "The teacher asked him a few questions." is the appropriate construction.

16. (B): Direct speech is a direct quotation of what someone else said. The phrase "He requested me to shut the door." can be changed to direct speech as "He said, 'Please shut the door". The word "please" implies a request. The other options do not convey the sense of a request as directly and politely as option B does.

17. (B) **18. (C)** **19. (B)**

20. (B): The correct answer is "a European a one-rupee coin." In this case, "European" is used as a noun referring to a person from Europe. When we refer to a singular, unspecified entity, we use the indefinite article "a" before consonant sounds and "an" before vowel sounds. "European" starts with a "y" sound (a consonant sound) and "one-rupee coin" starts with a "w" sound (also a consonant sound). Therefore, "a" is the appropriate article for both nouns.

21. (A): The correct set of prepositions is "in" and "of." We use "in" to describe a manner or way in which something is done, and "of" to show possession or relation. Therefore, "He is notoriously mean in his treatment of his servants" implies that he treats his servants in a mean manner.

22. (B): The word "alleviate" means to make a situation or a pain less severe. Out of the given options, "lessen" and "reduce" are synonyms to "alleviate" as they both convey the idea of diminishing or decreasing something in intensity, degree, or amount.

23. (A): An exclamatory sentence is one that expresses strong emotion. In this context, "How beautiful is the night!" is the correct exclamatory form of "The night is very beautiful." This structure ("How [adjective] is [subject]!") is a common form of expressing admiration or surprise in English exclamatory sentences.

24. (A): When converting direct speech to indirect speech, the exact words of the speaker are paraphrased and certain changes are made to pronouns, tense, and words showing place and time. The correct conversion of "Adesh said, 'Please shut the door behind you.'" is "Adesh requested me to please shut the door behind me." This captures the essence of the request made by Adesh without directly quoting him.

25. (A): Matching the phrases with their meanings:

- (*a*) "I had so much work to do but the fever got the best of me" corresponds to (*iv*) "Take advantage of something." This phrase implies that the fever overcame or overwhelmed the person, preventing them from working.
- (*b*) "They spent their halcyon days in a village" matches with (*i*) "Peaceful time." "Halcyon days" is an idiom that means a calm, peaceful, or happy period in the past.
- (*c*) "He earned really well but ended up penniless. Gambling was his Achilles heel" aligns with (*ii*) "Vulnerable/Weak spot." An "Achilles heel" refers to a person's main weakness or vulnerability.
- (*d*) "A doctor worth his salt will advise people for healthy eating" pairs with (*iii*) "Competent for a work." The idiom "worth one's salt" means to be competent or deserving of one's salary or position.

26. (C): The word "entourage" refers to a group of people attending or surrounding an important person. In this context, it pertains to the minister's accompanying group, which can be his aides, assistants, or any other group of followers. Hence, the most accurate meaning among the given options is "following subordinates."

27. (B): An adverb is a word that modifies a verb, an adjective, or another adverb. In the given sentence, "often" modifies the verb "complain" and "easily" modifies the verb "try." Therefore, the correct adverbs from the sentence are "often" and "easily."

28. (A): The term "camouflage" means to disguise something, usually to make it blend in with its surroundings. Out of the given options, "disguise" directly captures the essence of "camouflage." Thus, the word "disguise" is synonymous with "camouflage."

29. (C): The sentence indicates a completed action in the past relative to another past action or event. The train had already departed by the time the speaker reached the station. The correct tense to denote this sequence of past events is the past perfect tense, which is formed using "had" + past participle. Therefore, "had already left" is the appropriate completion for the sentence.

30. (B): Clauses in English can function as different parts of speech and can be classified based on their function. In the sentence "The Children whom I teach in standard 8 are very disciplined," the underlined clause "whom I teach in standard 8" provides additional information about "The Children," making it an adjective clause. An adjective clause modifies a noun (in this case, "The Children") and often starts with relative pronouns like "who," "whom," "whose," "which," or "that."

31. (A): Idioms are fixed expressions with meanings not directly deducible from the individual words. For the given idioms: (*a*) "At one's fingertips" means having information or a skill readily available. (*b*) "Hold one's tongue" means to refrain from speaking. (*c*) "Lose one's head" suggests panicking or acting without thinking. (*d*) "Win hands down" means to win easily. Thus, the correct matches are (*ii*), (*i*), (*iii*), and (*iv*) respectively.

32. (B): Antonyms are words that have opposite meanings. The word 'Terrible' denotes something causing fear or dread. Among the given options, "soothing" suggests calmness and comfort, making it the opposite of "terrible."

33. (A): Matching words with their antonyms: (*a*) The opposite of "Charming," which means attractive, is "Hideous" implying ugly. (*b*) "Occasional" means happening from time to time, while "Regular" implies happening frequently. (*c*) "Generous" means giving more than is necessary or usual, while its opposite "Miser" denotes a person who hoards money and avoids spending. (*d*) "Exhibit" means to display or show, while "Hide" means to conceal. So, the correct antonyms are (*iii*), (*iv*), (*ii*), and (*i*).

34. (A): Arranging sentences in a logical order is essential for coherence. The correct sequence forms a comprehensible statement about human language: "The language of man (*e*) has been mainly occupied (*b*) with telling us about (*a*) the elements into which (*d*) the finite world has been analysed (*c*)."

35. (D): Understanding the meaning of phrases is essential for comprehension: (*a*) "Set in" means to begin or commence. (*b*) "Wind up" denotes bringing something to a conclusion or end. (*c*) "Look down upon" signifies treating someone with contempt or considering them inferior. (*d*) "Put out" means extinguished, usually in the context of a light or fire. The correct matches are (*iii*), (*iv*), (*i*), and (*ii*).

36. (B): The Latin word "animus" refers to a feeling of ill will, animosity, or hostility. Thus, the correct meaning of 'animus' in the given context is "bad intention."

37. (B): Changing a sentence to passive voice involves shifting the focus from the doer of the action to the receiver of the action. The sentence "One should keep one's promises" focuses on the act of keeping promises, so in passive form, it becomes "Promises should be kept," which emphasizes the promises themselves.

38. (A): The given sentence implies a sense of obligation or duty in the past that wasn't met. The phrase "ought to have" suggests a missed obligation or something that should have been done in the past but wasn't. Thus, "You ought to have stood by your friends in their bad times" indicates that it was expected or would have been right for the person to stand by their friends, but they didn't.

39. (C): Question tags are short questions at the end of statements. They're used mainly in speech. When the main part of the sentence is negative, the question tag is positive. "She doesn't really know" is negative, so the tag should be positive: "does she?"

40. (C): To form the passive, you use the appropriate form of verb "to be" + the past participle of the main verb. The given sentence, "Your behaviour astonished me," is in the active voice where "me" is the object. In its passive form, "me" becomes the subject and the focus shifts to the feeling, making it "I was astonished by your behaviour."

41. (B): A "heretic" is someone who holds beliefs that are contrary to the accepted beliefs of a particular religion. The definition provided "One who acts against religion" aligns closely with this term. An egoist is someone centered on their own needs, an optimist is someone who looks at the positive side of things, and a stoic is someone who endures pain without showing feelings.

42. (A): Homonyms are words that are pronounced the same but differ in meaning, derivation, or spelling. In this context, the word "Rites" (religious practices or ceremonies) is suitable. "Wrights" refers to makers or builders (like "wheelwright"), "Rights" are entitlements or freedoms, and "Raight" is not a standard English word.

43. (B)

44. (D): Idiomatic expressions are phrases that have a figurative meaning different from their literal meaning. The phrase "carry out" means to execute or perform an action, which aligns with the given statement about executing plans. "Carry away" means to become overly enthusiastic, "Lay out" is to present or explain something in detail, and "Turn down" means to reject or decline.

45. (D): Constructing the sentence, we need to establish a comparison between two types of lives led by Asoka. The sentence "Asoka led two lives one as ruthless conqueror and the other as a compassionate ruler" correctly juxtaposes the two contrasting phases of his life. It also uses correct parallel structure, using "one as" and "the other as" to introduce the two lives.

46. (C): "Enquiry regarding course in choreography" is the most comprehensive and clear subject for a letter of inquiry. It explicitly states that the inquiry is about a course specifically in choreography. While the other options also imply an inquiry about choreography, option C provides the most direct and clear phrasing for the context.

47. (B): An assertive sentence is a declarative statement. The original sentence, "Alas that youth should pass away!", is an exclamatory sentence that conveys a feeling of sadness about the passing of youth. The closest option that captures this sentiment in a declarative way is "It is sad to think that youth should pass away."

48. (A)

49. (B): The phrase "The captain along with his team" requires a singular verb because "along with" doesn't make the noun plural. So, the verb "are" should be changed to "is". The correct statement should be "The captain along with his team is practicing very hard for the forthcoming matches."

50. (A): Copernicus did not just prove "that Earth" but rather "that the Earth." Proper nouns like Earth, when referred to as the planet we live on, often take the definite article "the." The rest of the statement, "moves round the sun," is accurate, as it accurately captures the heliocentric theory that Copernicus is known for.

GENERAL TEST

1. Ministry of Health and Family Welfare has launched 'Nikshay Poshan Yojana' related to eradication of which of the following disease?

A. Dengue B. Malaria
C. Tuberculosis D. Kala-Azar

2. Match List-I with List-II.

List-I (Important Days)	List-II (Date)
(*a*) National Youth Day	I. 28th February
(*b*) Army Day	II. 12th January
(*c*) National Science Day	III. 15th January
(*d*) National Safety Day	IV. 4th March

Choose the ***correct*** answer from the options given below:

	(*a*)	(*b*)	(*c*)	(*d*)
A.	II	III	IV	I
B.	II	III	I	IV
C.	III	II	I	IV
D.	IV	III	I	II

3. If P(E) = 0.05, what is the probability of 'not E'?

A. 0.05 B. 0.45
C. 0.95 D. 0.55

4. Find the next term in the alpha-numeric series:

Z1A, W8C, T27E, Q64G, N125I, __?__

A. K216L B. K216K
C. L343K D. L343L

5. Which of the following statements are incorrect?

(*a*) Volume of a cone = $\frac{1}{3}\pi r^3 h$

(*b*) Volume of a cone = $\frac{1}{3}\pi r^2 h$

(*c*) Volume of a hemispere = $\frac{2}{3}\pi r^2$

(*d*) Volume of a hemispere = $\frac{2}{3}\pi r^3$

(*e*) Volume of a cylinder = $\frac{1}{3}\pi r^3 h$

Choose the ***correct*** answer from the options given below:

A. (*a*), (*b*) and (*d*) only
B. (*a*), (*b*) and (*c*) only
C. (*a*), (*c*) and (*e*) only
D. (*c*), (*d*) and (*e*) only

6. Five children Arun, Bhuvi, Charu, Deepak and Emmy are sitting along the corners of a pentagonal table facing the centre. Bhuvi is between Emmy and Charu. Deepak is to the right of Emmy. Who is to the left of Charu?

A. Bhuvi B. Arun
C. Charu D. Deepak

7. A man standing on the bank of a river observes that the angle subtended by a tree standing on the opposite bank is 60° on his side of Bank. When he moved away 24 m from the bank, he finds the angle to be 30°. Find the breadth of the river:

A. 12 B. 18
C. 26 D. 20

8. The first satellite in space was launched by:

A. U.S.A.
B. United Kingdom
C. U.S.S.R.
D. France

9. Given below are two statements: one is labelled as Assertion (A) and the other is labelled as Reason (R).

Assertion (A): Polar areas have high atmospheric pressure.

Reason (R): These areas receive minimum sunshine throughout the year.

In the light of the above statements, choose the ***most appropriate*** answer from the options given below:

A. Both (A) and (R) are correct and (R) is the correct explanation of (A)
B. Both (A) and (R) are true, but (R) is not the correct explanation of (A)
C. (A) is true, but (R) is false
D. (A) is false, but (R) is true

10. Which one of the following numbers is not a prime number?

A. 241 B. 337
C. 391 D. 571

11. If the mean of 5 observations x, $x + 2$, $x + 4$, $x + 6$ and $x + 8$ is 11, then value of x:

A. 7 B. 43
C. 51 D. 8

12. Amar is 16th from the left end in a row of boys and Vishal is 18th from the right end. Satish is 11th towards the right of Amar and 3rd towards the right of Vishal side end. How many boys are there is a row?

A. 45 B. 26
C. 39 D. 41

13. Following question is based on the information given below:

(*i*) 'R × S' means 'R is father of S'
(*ii*) 'R – S' means 'R is sister of S'
(*iii*) 'R + S' means 'R is mother of S'
(*iv*) 'R ÷ S' means 'R is brother of S'

In the expression A + B × C ÷ D how is C related to A?

A. Son
B. Grandson
C. Granddaughter
D. Grandmother

14. Given below are two statements:

Statement (I): Right to information has been granted to every citizen of India under Right to information Act, 2005 which came into force on 12th October, 2005.

Statement (II): Right to information is a fundamental Right.

In the light of the above statements, choose the ***most appropriate*** answer from the options given below:

A. Both Statement I and Statement II are true
B. Both Statement I and Statement II are false
C. Statement I is true, but Statement II is false
D. Statement I is false, but Statement II is true

15. Given below are two statements: one is labelled as Assertion (A) and the other is labelled as Reason (R).

Assertion (A): The 73rd Amendment granted constitutional states to the Gram Sabha.

Reason (R): The Balawant Rai Mehta committee mentioned the Gram Sabha.

In the light of the above statements, choose the ***most appropriate*** answer from the options given below:

A. Both (A) and (R) are correct and (R) is the correct explanation of (A)
B. Both (A) and (R) are correct, but (R) is not the correct explanation of (A)
C. (A) is true, but (R) is not false
D. (A) is false, but (R) is true

16. Select the figure from the options which will continue the series established by the problem figure:

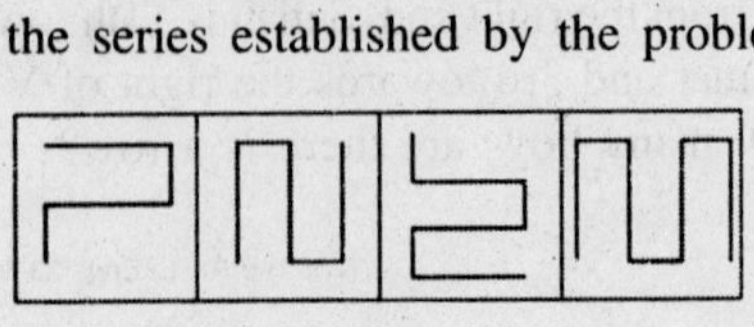

A. 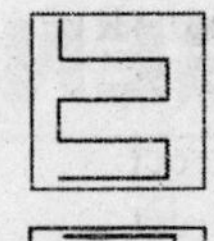 B. 

C.  D. 

17. The sum of an Infinite geometric series is 4 and the sum of the cubes of the terms of the same GP is 192. The Common Ratio of the original geometric series is:

A. $\frac{1}{2}$ B. $-\frac{1}{2}$
C. $\frac{1}{4}$ D. $-\frac{1}{4}$

18. A clock is started at noon. By 20 minutes part 6, the hand had has turned through:

A. 175° B. 180°
C. 185° D. 190°

19. Match List-I with List-II.

List-I (World Organization)	List-II (Headquarters)
(*a*) BRICS	I. Geneva (Switzerland)
(*b*) NATO	II. Shanghai (China)
(*c*) WTO	III. Kathmandu (Nepal)
(*d*) SAARC	IV. Brussels (Belgium)

Choose the ***correct*** answer from the options given below:

	(*a*)	(*b*)	(*c*)	(*d*)
A.	III	IV	I	II
B.	IV	II	I	III
C.	II	IV	I	III
D.	II	IV	III	I

20. The Credit of inventing soap by using Mustard oil and some alkalies goes to which of the following scientist?

A. Chakrapani
B. Sushruta
C. Nagarjuna
D. Patayjali

21. Given below are two statements, one is labelled as Assertion (A) and the other is labelled as Reason (R).

Assertion (A): Clothes are not washed properly in hard water.

Reason (R): Hard water contains many minerals.

In the light of the above statements, choose the ***most appropriate*** answer from the options given below:

A. Both (A) and (R) are correct and (R) is the correct explanation of (A)

B. Both (A) and (R) are correct, but (R) is not the correct explanation of (A)
C. (A) is correct, but (R) is not correct
D. (A) is not correct, but (R) is correct

22. How many 3 digit even numbers can be formed from the digits (0-9) if repetition of digits are allowed?

A. 350 B. 400
C. 450 D. 1000

23. Which of the planet have no satellite?
(*a*) Mercury
(*b*) Neptune
(*c*) Satrun
(*d*) Venus

Choose the ***correct*** answer from the options given below:
A. (*b*) and (*d*) only
B. (*a*) and (*b*) only
C. (*b*), (*c*) and (*d*) only
D. (*a*) and (*d*) only

24. If CE || DB, what is the value of x:

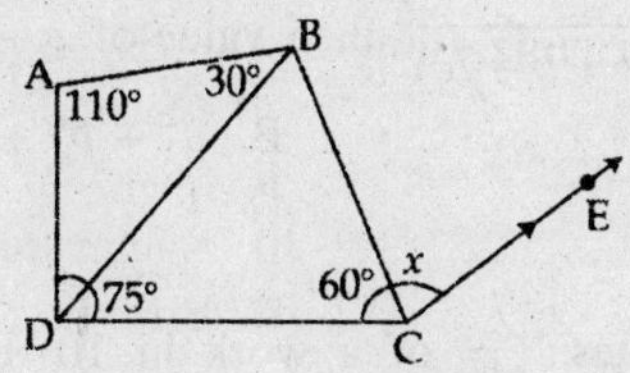

A. 45° B. 30°
C. 75° D. 85°

25. Who was the Chief Justice of India when public interest litigation (PIL) was introduced to the Indian Judicial system?
A. M. Hidayatullah
B. A.M. Ahmadi
C. P.N. Bhagwati
D. A.S. Anand

26. How many cubes are there in a group?

A. 10 B. 16
C. 18 D. 20

27. The only continent through which Tropic of Cancer, Equator and Tropic of Capricorn passes?
A. Asia B. Australia
C. Antarctica D. Africa

28. Facing towards North, Ravi walks 30 m. He then turns left and walks 50 m. He again turns left and walks 30 m. How far is he from his original position and towards which direction?
A. 30 m, North
B. 20 m, East
C. 20 m, South
D. 50 m, West

29. Find out the figure that can be formed from the piece given below:

A.  B. 

C.  D. 

30. Complete the picture series:

A.  B. 

C.  D. 

31. Find from amongst the figure, the one which resembles the pattern formed when the transparent sheet is folded along the dotted line.

A.  B. 

C.  D. 

32. Who among the following gave the popular slogan "Home Rule is my birthright and I will have it"?
A. Annie Besant
B. Lokamanya Tilak
C. Dadabhai Naoroji
D. Aurobindo Ghose

33. ₹ 800 becomes ₹ 956 in 3 years at a certain rate of simple interest. If the rate of interest is increased by 4%, what will ₹ 800 amount to in 3 years:

A. ₹ 1,020.80 B. ₹ 1,025
C. ₹ 1,052 D. ₹ 1,050

34. Two statements in the following questions, followed by two conclusions I and II. Read the conclusion and decide most suitable answer.

Statements : All horses are goats.
No goat is a donkey.

Conclusions : I. No horse is a donkey.
II. Atleast some goats are horses.

A. If only conclusion I follows.
B. If only conclusion II follows.
C. If both conclusion I and II follows.
D. If none of the conclusion follows.

35. ISRO Launched "GSAT-6A" satellites on:

A. 31 August, 2017 B. 29 March, 2018
C. 05 June, 2017 D. 12 January, 2018

36. A trader sold half of his articles at 60% profit, half of the remaining at 20% loss and the rest was sold at the cost price. In total transaction his gain % or loss % will be:

A. Gain 20% B. Loss 5%
C. Gain 40% D. Gain 25%

37. Match List-I with List-II.

List-I (Name of City)	**List-II** (Famous for production of)
(*a*) Ahmedabad	I. Machine tools
(*b*) Bangalore	II. Aluminium
(*c*) Bhilai	III. Textiles
(*d*) Renukoot	IV. Steel

Choose the ***correct*** answer from the options given below:

	(*a*)	(*b*)	(*c*)	(*d*)
A.	I	II	III	IV
B.	II	III	IV	I
C.	III	I	IV	II
D.	IV	III	II	I

38. The 36th National Games 2022 was held in which of the following state?

A. Goa B. Gujarat
C. Haryana D. Karnataka

39. Find out the wrong number in the sequence:

40960, 10240, 2560, 640, 200, 40, 10

A. 40 B. 640
C. 200 D. 2560

40. The constitution authorises the president to make provisions for discharge of duties of Governor in extraordinary circumstances under the ______.

A. Article 160 B. Article 162
C. Article 165 D. Article 310

41. The fibre crop which is known as the Golden Fibre?

A. Cotton B. Hump
C. Natural Silk D. Jute

42. The first person to use crystal for radio wave detection was:

A. J.C. Bose B. H.C. Verma
C. S.N. Bose D. C.V. Raman

43. The surface area (in m^2) of a sphere of radius 7 cm is: (Use $\pi = 22/7$)

A. 0.0616 B. 6.16
C. 61.6 D. 0.616

44. By selling on book for ₹ 250, loss percentage is 10%. What is the cost price?

A. ₹ 277.7 B. ₹ 250
C. ₹ 285 D. ₹ 315

45. If $\frac{x}{(b-c)(b+c-2a)} = \frac{y}{(c-a)(c+a-2b)}$

$= \frac{z}{(a-b)(a+b-2c)}$ then value of $x + y + z$ is:

A. $a + b + c$ B. $a^2 + b^2 + c^2$
C. 0 D. 1

46. A completes $\frac{7}{20}$ of a work in 10 days. Then he completes the remaining work with the help of B in 5 days. The time required for A and B together to complete the entire work is:

A. $\frac{100}{29}$ days B. $\frac{100}{13}$ days
C. $\frac{100}{17}$ days D. $\frac{200}{13}$ days

47. Look at the statement and mark the correct answer on the conclusions that follows:

Statements : (*a*) Shubham is my cousin.
(*b*) A cousin may be a aunt's son, uncle's son or son of parent's step-siblings.

Conclusions : I. Shubham is my sisters son.
II. Shubham is my uncle's son.

A. Only conclusion I follows.
B. Only conclusion II follows.
C. Both conclusion I and II follows.
D. Neither conclusion I nor II follows.

48. If Today is Monday, After 62 it will be:

A. Wednesday B. Saturday
C. Sunday D. Thursday

49. The price of rice increases by 30%. A family reduced its consumption so that the expenditure of the rice is up only by 10%. If the total consumption of the rice before the price rise was 10 kg per month, then the consumption of rice per month at present (in kg) is:

A. $7\frac{6}{15}$ B. $8\frac{1}{15}$

C. $8\frac{6}{13}$ D. $8\frac{5}{13}$

50. The volume of a sphere of radius r is obtained by multiplying its surface area with:

A. $\frac{4}{3}$ B. $\frac{r}{3}$

C. $\frac{4r}{3}$ D. $3r$

51. If EFFECTIVE is coded as FEGDDSJUF, then how RELATIVE can be written in that code?

A. TDNZVHXD   B. TCNAVGXC

C. SDMZUHWD   D. SCMAUGXD

52. A bag contains 6 red, 4 blue and 10 white balls. A ball is picked from the bag at random. What is the probability that it is neither white nor blue?

A. $\frac{20}{6}$ B. $\frac{3}{10}$

C. $\frac{2}{5}$ D. $\frac{1}{2}$

53. Find the area of an equilateral triangle each of whose sides measures 4 cm:

A. $4\sqrt{3}$ cm^2 B. $4\sqrt{3}$ m^2

C. $3\sqrt{3}$ cm^2 D. $3\sqrt{3}$ m^2

54. The difference between two numbers is 24. If one number is 2 times the second, then the two numbers will be:

A. 36, 12   B. 48, 24

C. 32, 8   D. 12, 6

55. Choose the correct mirror image:

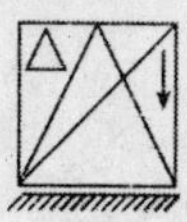

A.    B. 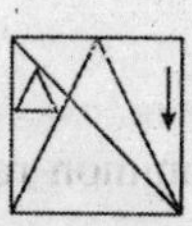

C.    D. 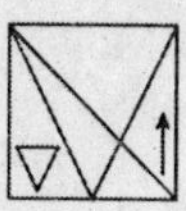

56. Match List-I with List-II.

List-I	List-II
(*a*) First speaker of Lok Sabha	I. Dr. Amartya Sen
(*b*) First Indian to get Bharat Ratna Award	II. G.V. Mavalankar
(*c*) First Indian recipient of Nobel Prize in Economics	III. Dr. S. Radhakrishnan
(*d*) First Indian Nobel Laureate	IV. Rabindra Nath Tagore

Choose the ***correct*** answer from the options given below:

	(*a*)	(*b*)	(*c*)	(*d*)
A.	II	III	I	IV
B.	II	III	IV	I
C.	III	II	I	IV
D.	IV	III	I	II

57. Who has been honoured with the Golden ball award in the FIFA World Cup 2022?

A. Kylian Mbappe   B. Luka Modric

C. Lionel Messi   D. Enzo Fernandez

58. A boy is running at a speed of p km/h to cover a distance of 1 km but due to slippery ground his speed is reduced by q km/h ($p > q$). If he takes r hours to cover the distance, which of the following condition is true:

A. $\frac{1}{r} = (p - q)$ B. $r = (p - q)$

C. $r = \frac{1}{p+q}$ D. $r = p + q$

59. What can be placed at '?' if both side of ': :' have same relationship between numbers:

85 : 42 :: 139 : ?

A. 68   B. 69

C. 70   D. 67

60. Commemoration of national days should always be encouraged in schools and colleges. Which of the following statement given below is a strong argument:

(*a*) This type of commemoration gives opportunity to children and youth to value to contribution of people who built our nation.

(*b*) There is nothing wrong in celebrating a day and enjoy once is a while.

(*c*) These events hamper the focus of students from regular study.

A. Argument (*a*) and (*b*) are strong

B. Only argument (*a*) is strong

C. Argument (*b*) and (*c*) are strong

D. Only argument (*c*) is strong

ANSWERS

1. (C) **2. (B)**

3. (C): Required Probability of 'not E'.

$$= 1 - 0.05$$

$$= 1 - \frac{5}{100} = \frac{100-5}{100}$$

$$= \frac{95}{100} = 0.95.$$

4. (B) **5. (C)**

6. (B):

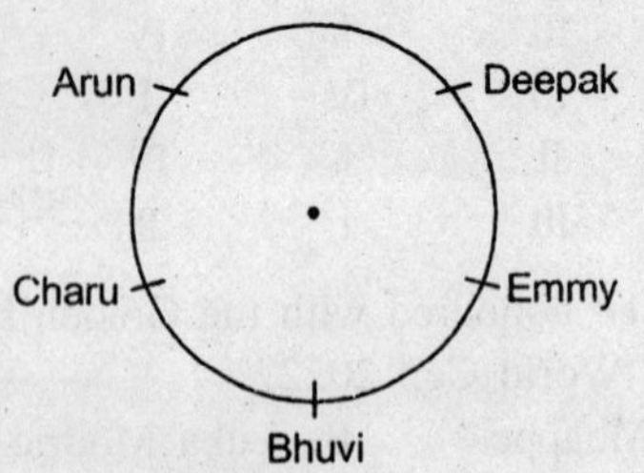

Clearly, Arun is left of Charu.

7. (A):

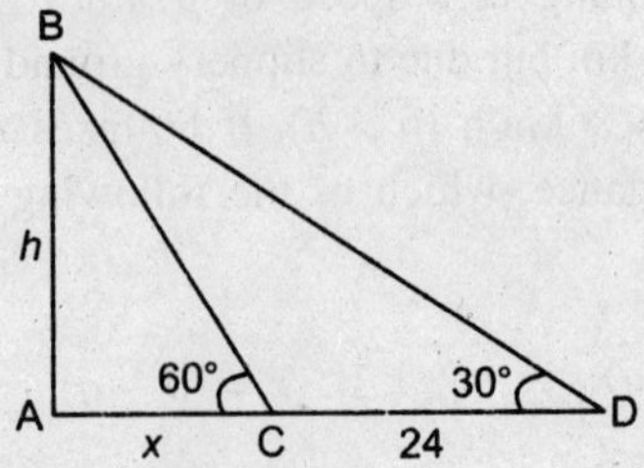

$$\tan 60° = \frac{h}{x}$$

$$\Rightarrow \quad \sqrt{3} = \frac{h}{x}$$

$$\Rightarrow \quad h = \sqrt{3}x$$

$$\tan 30° = \frac{h}{x+24}$$

$$\Rightarrow \quad \frac{1}{\sqrt{3}} = \frac{h}{x+24}$$

$$\Rightarrow \quad \sqrt{3}h = x + 24$$

$$\Rightarrow \quad 3x = x + 24$$

$$\Rightarrow \quad 2x = 24$$

$$\Rightarrow \quad x = 12$$

Hence, breadth of the river = 12 m.

8. (C) **9. (B)**

10. (C): 391 is not a prime number because 391 is divided by 17 and 23.

11. (A): Total of 5 observations = 11 × 5 = 55

$$\therefore x + x + 2 + x + 4 + x + 6 + x + 8 = 55$$

$$\Rightarrow \quad 5x + 20 = 55$$

$$\Rightarrow \quad 5x = 35$$

$$\Rightarrow \quad x = 7$$

Hence, the value of x = 7.

12. (D) **13. (B)** **14. (C)**

15. (B) **16. (C)**

17. (B):

$$S_\infty = \frac{a}{1-r}$$

$$\Rightarrow \quad 4 = \frac{a}{1-r}$$

$$\Rightarrow \quad \frac{a}{1-r} = 4 \qquad ...(i)$$

$$(a)^3 + a^3r^3 + a^3r^6 + ... = 192$$

$$\Rightarrow \quad \frac{a^3}{1-r^3} = 192 \qquad ...(ii)$$

Divide the cube of (*i*) by (*ii*), we get,

$$\frac{a^3}{(1-r)^3} \times \frac{(1-r^3)}{a^3} = \frac{(4)^3}{192} = \frac{64}{192} = \frac{1}{3}$$

$$\Rightarrow \quad \frac{1-r^3}{(1-r)^3} = \frac{1}{3}$$

$$\Rightarrow \quad \frac{1^2 + r + r^2}{1 + r^2 - 2r} = \frac{1}{3}$$

$$\Rightarrow \quad r^2 - 2r + 1 = 3(1 + r + r^2)$$

$$\Rightarrow r^2 - 2r + 1 - 3 - 3r - 3r^2 = 0$$

$$-2r^2 - 5r - 2 = 0$$

$$\Rightarrow \quad 2r^2 + 5r + 2 = 0$$

$$\Rightarrow \quad 2r^2 + 4r + r + 2 = 0$$

$$2r(r + 2) + 1(r + 2) = 0$$

$$(2r + 1)(r + 2) = 0$$

$$r = -\frac{1}{2}$$

or

$$r = -2$$

Hence, common ratio = $-\frac{1}{2}$.

18. (D) **19. (C)** **20. (A)**

21. (B)

22. (C): For a number to be even, we must have 2, 4, 6, 8, 0 at the unit's place.

Since, digits can be repeated.

Hence, required number of numbers

$$= 5 \times 10 \times 9 = 450.$$

23. (D)

24. (D):

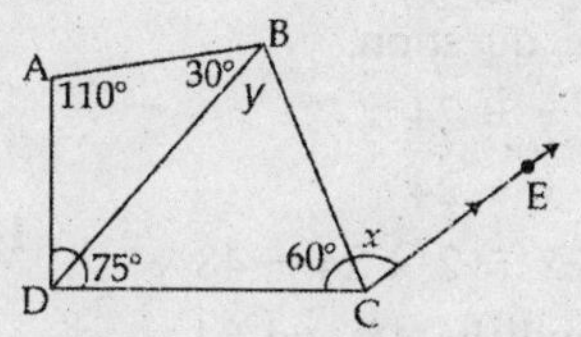

$\because$ CE || DB

$$\angle A + \angle B + \angle C + \angle D = 360°$$

$$\Rightarrow 110° + y + 30° + 60° + 75° = 360°$$

$$\Rightarrow y + 275° = 360°$$

$$\Rightarrow y = 360° - 275° = 85°$$

($\because$ CE || DB $\Rightarrow \angle x = \angle y$)

Hence, $x = y = 85°$.

25. (C) **26. (D)** **27. (D)**

28. (D):

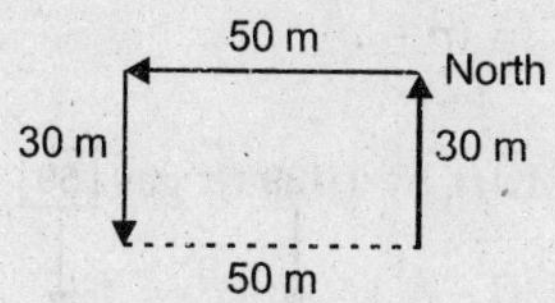

Ravi is 50 m away from his original position and towards west direction.

29. (C) **30. (D)** **31. (C)**

32. (B) **33. (C)** **34. (C)**

35. (B)

36. (D): Let total articles = 100

C.P. of each article = ₹ 100

Total C.P. = 100 × 100 = ₹ 10000

S.P. of half articles = $5000 \times \frac{160}{100}$ = ₹ 8000

S.P. of half of remaining articles

= $2500 \times \frac{80}{100}$ = ₹ 2000

S.P. of rest articles = ₹ 2500

Total S.P. = ₹ 8000 + 2000 + 2500

= ₹ 12500

Profit = 12500 − 10000

= ₹ 2500

Profit % = $\frac{2500}{10000} \times 100 = 25\%$.

37. (C) **38. (B)**

39. (C): 40960 10240 2560 640 [160] 40 10

÷4 ÷4 ÷4 ÷4 ÷4 ÷4

Hence, wrong number = 200.

40. (A) **41. (D)** **42. (A)**

43. (A) Surface area of sphere = $4\pi r^2$

$$= 4 \times \frac{22}{7} \times 7 \times 7 = 616 \text{ cm}^2$$

$$= \frac{616}{10000} \text{ m}^2 = 0.0616 \text{ m}^2.$$

44. (A): Selling price = ₹ 250

Loss = 10%

Then, Cost price = $\frac{100}{90} \times 250$

= ₹ $\frac{2500}{9}$ = ₹ 277.7

45. (C): Let $\frac{x}{(b-c)(b+c-2a)} = \frac{y}{(c-a)(c+a-2b)}$

$$= \frac{z}{(a-b)(a+b-2c)} = k$$

$\therefore$
$$x = k(b - c)(b + c - 2a)$$
$$y = k(c - a)(c + a - 2b)$$
$$z = k(a - b)(a + b - 2c)$$

Now, $x + y + z = k[(b - c)(b + c - 2a) + (c - a)(c + a - 2b) + (a - b)(a + b - 2c)]$

$= k[b^2 + bc - 2ab - bc - c^2 + 2ac + c^2 + ac - 2bc - ac - a^2 + 2ab + a^2 + ab - 2ac - ab - b^2 + 2bc]$

$= k[0] = 0.$

46. (B): $\because \frac{7}{20}$ part of a work A can do in 10 days

Remaining part = $1 - \frac{7}{20} = \frac{13}{20}$ part of work

$\because$ (A + B)'s 5 days work = $\frac{13}{20}$ part

$\therefore$ (A + B)'s 1 day work = $\frac{13}{20 \times 5} = \frac{13}{100}$

Hence, (A + B) can do whole work in $\frac{100}{13}$ days.

47. (D)

48. (C): Today is Monday. After 63 days (7 × 9) it will be Monday.

Hence, after 62 days it will be Sunday.

49. (C)

50. (B): The Volume of sphere $= \frac{4}{3}\pi r^3$

Surface area of sphere $= 4\pi r^2$

Hence, the volume of sphere of radius r is obtained by multiplying its surface area with $\frac{r}{3}$.

51. (C): As,

E	F	F	E	C	T	I	V	E
+1	–1	+1	–1	+1	–1	+1	–1	+1
F	E	G	D	D	S	J	U	F

Similarly,

R	E	L	A	T	I	V	E
+1	–1	+1	–1	+1	–1	+1	–1
S	D	M	Z	U	H	W	D

52. (B): Red ball = 6

Blue ball = 4

White ball = 10

Required probability $= \frac{6}{20} = \frac{3}{10}$

53. (A): Area of an equilateral triangle

$$= \frac{\sqrt{3}}{4}(\text{Side})^2$$

$$= \frac{\sqrt{3}}{4}\times(4)^2 = \frac{\sqrt{3}}{4}\times 16$$

$$= 4\sqrt{3}\ \text{cm}^2.$$

54. (B): Let second number = x

∴ One number = $2x$

According to the question,

$$2x - x = 24$$

$$\Rightarrow x = 24$$

$$\therefore 2x = 2 \times 24 = 48$$

Hence, number will be 48 and 24.

55. (D) **56. (A)** **57. (C)**

58. (A): Relative speed = $(p - q)$ km/hr

Distance = 1 km

Time = r hours

$$\therefore \text{Speed} = \frac{\text{Distance}}{\text{Time}} = \frac{1}{r}$$

$$\Rightarrow (p - q) = \frac{1}{r}$$

Hence, $\frac{1}{r} = (p - q)$.

59. (B): 85 : 42 :: 139 : [69]

$$85 = \frac{85-1}{2} = \frac{84}{2} = 42 \qquad 139 = \frac{139-1}{2} = \frac{138}{2} = 69$$

Hence, 69 will come at the place of question mark.

60. (B)

Previous Years' Paper (Solved)

(Common University Entrance Test for UG Programmes)

CUET (UG)–B.A. (Hons.) English Entrance Exam, 2022*

ENGLISH

Directions (Qs. No. 1-6): *Read the following passage to answer question:*

The first form did not really see very much of Erica because she did not have lessons with them. But even if they met her in a passage or in the art room or gym they looked the other way. In the common-room at night Erica had a miserable time. Not one of the second form girls also would have anything to do with her. Loud remarks about sneaks and cowards were made in her hearing. The only person who ever threw her a word at all was the bad-tempered Margery Fenworthy. Erica did not like Margery any more than the other girls did but she was so grateful to be spoken to even, by the surly first former that she almost began to like the girl.

'I'm surprised you speak to Erica, Margery,' said Pat, when she had heard Margery ask to borrow Erica's stationery said Margery, in her usual rude way. 'You're none of you friendly to me, and I know what it is to have people being beastly to you.' 'But Margery, it's your own fault,' said Pat in surprise. 'You're so rude and sullen. You never smile and joke.' Margery, 'you don't give me a chance.' 'Oh, Margery, what a fib'! Cried Pat. 'It's you who never give us a chance to be decent to you. You scowl and glower and frown all the time.' 'If you're going to pick me to pieces you can save yourself the trouble', said Margery, fiercely. 'I don't care tuppence for any of you. And if I want to speak to that wretched Erica, I shall. Who cares for a pack of silly girls, and a crowd of stuck-up teachers? I don't Pat was astonished. What a strange girl Margery was! Did she really want a chance of being friends with the others? Was she terribly shy? What was behind that funny manner of hers? Pat talked about it with her twin. 'Margery is always making enemies she said.' 'I spoke to her today about it and she accused us of never giving her a chance! Do you think we ought to do something about it?'

1. Match List-I with List-II.

List-I *(Part A)*	*List-II* *(Part B)*
(*a*) Loud remarks about sneaks and cowards were made	(*i*) in the presence of Erica
(*b*) Margery Fenworthy	(*ii*) was very unpopular
(*c*) "Oh Margery ... it's you who never give us a chance to be decent"	(*iii*) said Pat
(*d*) The girl with a twin sister named	(*iv*) Pat

Choose the correct answer from the options given below:

	(*a*)	(*b*)	(*c*)	(*d*)
A.	(*i*)	(*ii*)	(*iv*)	(*iii*)
B.	(*i*)	(*ii*)	(*iii*)	(*iv*)
C.	(*ii*)	(*iv*)	(*iii*)	(*i*)
D.	(*iv*)	(*iii*)	(*i*)	(*ii*)

2. From the given options, choose the one which is correct according to the passage.

The girls mentioned in the passage are:

(*a*) Erica, Margery and Pat

(*b*) Erica and Pat only

(*c*) Only Patricia

(*d*) Joan, Erica and Patricia

A. (*b*) B. (*a*)

C. (*c*) D. (*d*)

3. From the given options, select the one which is right and correct according to the passage:

A. "I am surprised you speak to Margery, Erica" said Pat

B. "I am surprised you speak to Erica, Pat" said Margery

*** This Previous Year Paper has been given here as a Combination of CUET (UG) 2022 different exams for the Subjects 'English and General Test', which have been mapped to this course.**

C. "I am surprised you speak to Margery, Pat" said Erica

D. "I am surprised you speak to Erica, Margery" said Pat

4. From the passage Margaret fenworthy comes across as ______. Select the option which is correct according to the passage.

A. A bad tempered, unpopular girl
B. Heroic and a strong mountaineer
C. Saintly and a recluse
D. A cynical middle aged woman

5. From the passage it may be concluded that Erica was very.

Select the option which is correct according to the passage.

A. Lonely, friendless and timid
B. Dominating and Arrogant
C. Cunning and stupid
D. Brilliant and very popular

6. From the passage it becomes clear that: (choose the correct option).

Not one of the First Form girls would have anything to do with Erica because:

A. She did not have any lessons with them
B. She used to mind her own business
C. She was unfriendly, rude and selfish
D. Erica was away on a holiday in Paris with her family

Directions (Qs. No. 7-12): *Read the following passage to answer question.*

She took me by the hand walked me into the lobby like a five-year old child. Didn't she know I was pushing 15? This was the third home Nancy was placing me in-in a span of eight months! I guess she felt a little sorry for me. The bright fluorescent lights threatened to burn my skin as I walked towards a bouncy-looking lady with curly hair and a sweetly-smiling man. They called themselves Allie and Alex. Cute, I thought.

After they exchanged the usual reams of paperwork, it was off in their Chevy Suburban to get situated into another new home. This time, there were no other foster children and nor another biological child. Anything could happen.

Over the next few weeks, Allie, Alex and I fell into quite a nice routine. She'd make pancakes for breakfast, or he'd fry up some sausage and eggs. They sang a lot, even danced as they cooked. They must have just bought the house because, most weekends, we were either painting a living room butter yellow or staining a coffee table mocha brown.

I kept waiting for the other shoe to drop. When would they start threatening a loss of pancakes if I didn't mow the lawn? When would the sausage and eggs be replaced with unidentifiable slosh because he didn't feel like cooking in the morning? But, it never happened. They kept cooking, singing and dancing like a couple of happy fools.

It was a Saturday afternoon when Allie decided it was time to paint the brick fireplace white. As we crawled closer to the dirty old firepit, we pulled out the petrified wood and noticed a teeny-tiny treasure box! We looked at each other in wonder and excitement. She actually said, "I wonder if the Leprechauns left it!"

7. Over the next few weeks who all fell into a nice comfortable routine?

Select the correct option.

A. Nancy
B. Allie and Nancy
C. The narrator, Allie and Alex
D. Only Alex

8. "She took me by the hand and walked me into the lobby...". The 'me' refers to the:

A. Narrator and the protagonist of the passage
B. Narrator and the footballer
C. A filmstar and a villain
D. The headmaster of an English school

9. On a Sunday afternoon, what did Allie decide to do?

Select the correct option.

(*a*) Crawl towards the dirty old garage
(*b*) Paint the brick firepit white
(*c*) Sing a song
(*d*) Write a letter to the President

Choose the correct answer from the options given below:

A. (*a*) B. (*b*)
C. (*c*) D. (*d*)

10. It appears from the passage that over the next few days the narrator and the other two characters were:

Select the correct option.

A. Relaxed and comfortable
B. Stressed and anxious
C. Depressed and gloomy
D. Plotting revenge

11. Match List-I with List-II:

List-I	*List-II*
(*a*) Nancy	(*i*) Treated the narrator as if he was a 5 year old child
(*b*) Allie	(*ii*) Made pancakes for breakfast
(*c*) Alex	(*iii*) Fried sausages and eggs
(*d*) Narrator	(*iv*) Was placed in the 3rd home

Choose the correct answer from the options given below:

	(*a*)	(*b*)	(*c*)	(*d*)
A.	(*i*)	(*ii*)	(*iii*)	(*iv*)
B.	(*iv*)	(*iii*)	(*ii*)	(*i*)
C.	(*iv*)	(*i*)	(*iii*)	(*ii*)
D.	(*ii*)	(*iv*)	(*i*)	(*iii*)

12. From the passage it may be assumed that the narrator was a 15 year old teenager without parents because the passage talks about.

Select the correct option.

A. Foster home for the narrator and other foster children
B. Cleaning firepits
C. Church and Chapels of Great Britain
D. Malls of a Metropolitan city

Directions (Qs. No. 13-18): *Read the following passage to answer question.*

Workers and Slaves

The Pharaohs may have believed that it was their links with the Gods that kept Egypt going, but really it was the hard work of the ordinary people. It was they who dug the soil, worked in the mines and quarries, sailed the boats on the river Nile, marched with the army into Syria or Nubia, cooked food and raised children. Slavery was not very important in ancient Egypt, but it did exist. Most of the slaves were prisoners who had been captured during the many wars Egypt fought with their neighbours in the Near East. Slaves were usually treated well and were allowed to own property. Many Egyptian workers were serfs. This meant that their freedom was limited. They could be bought and sold along with the estates where they worked. Farmers had to be registered with the government. They had to sell crops at a fixed price and pay taxes in the form of produce. During the season of the Nile floods, when the fields lay under water, many workers were recruited into public building projects. Punishment for those who ran away was harsh.

13. From the passage we get to know that a distinct quality of ancient Egypt under the Pharaohs was the fact that.

Select the correct option.

A. Though slavery existed slaves were not treated harshly at all
B. The Pharaohs were very democratic and handsome
C. No Egyptian working in ancient Egypt worked as a serf
D. The river Nile would stop No flowing during the rains in Egypt

14. From the passage we get to know that in ancient Egypt many workers were known as serfs. These were people with:

Select the correct answer.

A. Workers with limited freedom in ancient Egypt
B. Students with limited Intelligence in modern Egypt
C. Nobility with limited power in medieval Egypt
D. Pharaohs with limited connection with the gods of Egyptian Gods

15. What according to the passage was the reason of ancient Egyptian progress and prosperity.

(*a*) The link the Pharaohs claimed they had with the Gods
(*b*) The labour and hard work of the ordinary men in ancient Egypt
(*c*) The mines and quarries full of germs armed with rockets and missiles and jewals in ancient Egypt
(*d*) The modern smart Egyptian army

Choose the correct answer from the options given below:

A. (*a*) B. (*b*)
C. (*c*) D. (*d*)

16. From the given passage options, select the one which is true according to the passage.

(*a*) Pharaohs believed that it was their link with the Gods that favoured Egypt
(*b*) The ordinary people worked overtime to destroy Egypt
(*c*) The Pharaohs did not believe they were connected to the Gods
(*d*) The Pharaohs were the hard working slaves of ancient Egypt

Choose the correct answer from the options given below:

A. (*c*) B. (*b*)
C. (*a*) D. (*d*)

17. Select the option that is **incorrect** according to the passage.

A. In the Egypt under the Pharaohs, slaves were allowed to own property
B. Most of the slaves were prisoners captured in the many wars Egypt fought with its neighbours in the NEAR EAST
C. Slaves were well treated in ancient Egypt
D. Slavery was extremely important in ancient Egypt

18. Match List-I with List-II.

List-I	*List-II*
(*a*) Serfs could be	(*i*) Farmers
(*b*) Registered with the government	(*ii*) Recruited workers during the rainy season
(*c*) Public building projects	(*iii*) Bought and sold along with the estates were they worked
(*d*) Harsh punishment	(*iv*) For those who ran away

Choose the correct answer from the options given below:

	(a)	(b)	(c)	(d)
A.	(i)	(ii)	(iii)	(iv)
B.	(iv)	(iii)	(ii)	(i)
C.	(iii)	(i)	(ii)	(iv)
D.	(ii)	(iii)	(iv)	(i)

Directions (Qs. No. 19-22): *From the given options select the one that is opposite in meaning to the given word:*

19. ACQUITTED
A. Promoted B. Burdened
C. Convicted D. Development

20. RELINQUISH
A. Garbage B. Harmonize
C. Beautify D. Possess

21. CAPACIOUS
A. Limited B. Charming
C. Foolish D. Colourful

22. FRAUDULENT
A. Candid B. Direct
C. Forthright D. Genuine

Directions (Qs. No. 23-26): *From the given options select the figure of speech of the poetic device used in expression.*

23. Both wry with the laboured ease of loss.
A. Simile B. Personification
C. Oxymoron D. Metaphor

24. Far Far from gusty waves.
A. Oxymoron B. Alliteration
C. Simile D. Personification

25. The smiling young trees provided a strange comfort.
A. Personification B. Metaphor
C. Simile D. Oxymoron

26. Like angels from heaven the paratrooper landed on earth.
A. Personification B. Oxymoron
C. Simile D. Pun

Directions (Qs. No. 27-30): *From the given options, select the one which correctly explains the expression.*

27. To be at sixes and sevens.
A. To be a primary school student
B. A state of total confusion and disorder
C. To be certain of batting well in a cricket match
D. To give away secrets

28. Once in a blue moon.
A. Most regularly B. Very often
C. Very rarely D. Once in a fortnight

29. A wild goose chase.
A. A Foolish and useless enterprises
B. To hunt wild life
C. A violent chase of criminals
D. To speak harshly

30. To burn a hole in the pocket.
A. To steal from someone's pocket
B. To destroy someone else's belongings
C. To burn address accidentally
D. To spend money very quickly

Directions (Qs. No. 31-34): *Choose the word from the given options that is closest in meaning to the given word.*

31. PUGNACIOUS
A. Rebellious B. Amusing
C. Quarrelsome D. Desirable

32. CLING
A. Attach B. Detach
C. Release D. Forward

33. ENCHANTING
A. Witty B. Pleasant
C. Comical D. Harmful

34. GIGANTIC
A. Miniature B. Monstrous
C. Diligent D. Awkward

Directions (Qs. No. 35-38): *From the given options, select the one that will rightly substitute the given expression.*

35. Period of 10 years.
A. Decade B. Fortnight
C. Annuity D. Millennium

36. One who loves and collects books.
A. Rockstar B. Bibliophile
C. Bellicose D. Bohemian

37. The killing of a new-born child.
A. Homicide B. Suicide
C. Massacre D. Infanticide

38. Detailed plan of a journey.
A. Passport B. Travelogue
C. Itinerary D. Timetable

Directions (Qs. No. 39-42): *From the given options, select the one that carries the same relation as.*

39. Attach : Detach
A. Barren : Fertile B. Timid : Coward
C. Ridiculous : Funny D. Jealous : Envious

40. Medley : Mixture
A. Iterate : Repeat B. Coarse : Fine
C. Abundance : Scarcity D. Triumph : Failure

41. Retreat : Advance
A. Garrulous : Talkative
B. Oblivion : Forgetfulness
C. Savage : Civilised
D. Obstinate : Stubborn

42. Meek : Modest

A. Blunt : Sharp B. Finally : Eventually

C. Clever : Stupid D. Condemn : Approve

Directions (Qs. No. 43-46): *From the given options, select the rightly spelt word:*

43. A. Katastrophic B. Catestrefic

C. Catastrophic D. Catostrofik

44. A. Kamunism B. Communism

C. Cummonism D. Cumunism

45. A. Cooperative B. Cauperative

C. Koperative D. Coperative

46. A. Pnemonia B. Pneumonia

C. Newmonia D. Nemonia

Directions (Qs. No. 47-50): *Rearrange the following jumbled group of words to make a meaningful sentence.*

47. (*a*) Penetrate the biological tissues

(*b*) Will produce unprecedented amount

(*c*) A large scale exchange of nuclear weapons

(*d*) Of radiation that can

Choose the correct answer from the options given below:

A. (*a*), (*b*), (*d*), (*c*) B. (*c*), (*d*), (*a*), (*b*)

C. (*c*), (*b*), (*d*), (*a*) D. (*a*), (*b*), (*c*), (*d*)

48. (*a*) During the last few years

(*b*) People in this area

(*c*) The mission has provided

(*d*) Able service to all the needy

Choose the correct answer from the options given below:

A. (*b*), (*d*), (*c*), (*a*) B. (*c*), (*d*), (*b*), (*a*)

C. (*a*), (*b*), (*d*), (*c*) D. (*c*), (*b*), (*a*), (*d*)

49. (*a*) Him tu rush to his village immediately

(*b*) An urgent telegram asking

(*c*) He has received

(*d*) No other message other than

Choose the correct answer from the options given below:

A. (*c*), (*d*), (*b*), (*a*) B. (*b*), (*c*), (*a*), (*d*)

C. (*c*), (*d*), (*a*), (*b*) D. (*a*), (*b*), (*c*), (*d*)

50. (*a*) He managed to make sense

(*b*) It was the first time when

(*c*) Of the book even though

(*d*) He read anything on the subject

Choose the correct answer from the options given below:

A. (*d*), (*c*), (*a*), (*b*) B. (*b*), (*a*), (*d*), (*c*)

C. (*a*), (*c*), (*b*), (*d*) D. (*a*), (*b*), (*c*), (*d*)

ANSWERS

1. (B): The question requires matching statements from List-I with appropriate statements from List-II. (*a*) "Loud remarks about sneaks and cowards were made" can be matched with (*i*) "in the presence of Erica" as the passage mentions that such remarks were made in Erica's hearing. (*b*) "Margery Fenworthy" matches with (*ii*) "was very unpopular" since the passage describes that nobody liked Margery except Erica, which indicates her unpopularity. (*c*) "Oh Margery ... it's you who never give us a chance to be decent" is a statement made by Pat as mentioned in the passage, so it matches with (*iii*) "said Pat". (*d*) The girl with a twin sister is named Pat, so this matches with (*iv*) "Pat".

2. (B): According to the passage, the girls mentioned are Erica, Margery, and Pat. Thus, option (*a*) is the correct answer.

3. (D): In the passage, the exact line reads, "'I'm surprised you speak to Erica, Margery,' said Pat," which directly matches with option (D).

4. (A): Margery Fenworthy is described in the passage as someone with a bad temper. It's mentioned that she is the only one who spoke to Erica and that she is not liked by the other girls. Hence, she comes across as "A bad tempered, unpopular girl".

5. (A): Erica is described as having a miserable time in the common room and no one from the second form girls wanted to have anything to do with her. This suggests that she was lonely and friendless. The fact that she was grateful to Margery, who was known to be bad-tempered, indicates her timidity. Hence, she comes across as "Lonely, friendless, and timid".

6. (A): The passage directly mentions "The first form did not really see very much of Erica because she did not have lessons with them". This indicates that the reason for the First Form girls not interacting with Erica was that she didn't have lessons with them. Therefore, the correct option is "She did not have any lessons with them".

7. (C): The passage mentions that "Over the next few weeks, Allie, Alex, and I fell into quite a nice routine." This clearly indicates that the narrator, along with Allie and Alex, settled into a comfortable daily pattern. This routine involved cooking breakfast together, singing, dancing, and doing house chores.

8. (A): The pronoun "me" in the line "She took me by the hand and walked me into the lobby..." refers to the individual narrating the events of the story. As the passage progresses, the experiences and emotions of this individual are described in the first person. The narrator is the protagonist, or the central character, of this passage.

9. (B): The passage states, "It was a Saturday afternoon when Allie decided it was time to paint the brick fireplace white." This clearly indicates that on that particular day, Allie's plan was to paint the fireplace. Thus, the correct answer is that she decided to "paint the brick firepit white."

10. (A): The characters' interactions, as depicted in the passage, showcase a harmonious environment. They engage in collaborative activities like cooking and house chores, enjoying music and dance. There's no indication of stress or discomfort, making the atmosphere appear "relaxed and comfortable."

11. (A): From the passage, we gather the following: (*a*) Nancy - "She took me by the hand walked me into the lobby like a five-year old child." Thus, Nancy treated the narrator as if he was very young, which matches with (*i*). (*b*) Allie - "She'd make pancakes for breakfast..." clearly aligns with Allie making pancakes or option (*ii*). (*c*) Alex - "or he'd fry up some sausage and eggs". This line directly refers to Alex's cooking activities, indicating (*iii*). (*d*) Narrator - "This was the third home Nancy was placing me in..." which means the narrator was being placed in multiple homes, corresponding with (*iv*).

12. (A): The passage's narrative revolves around the experiences of a teenager, presumably without parents, as indicated by mentions of foster care and multiple placements in different homes. The theme of the story underscores the trials and tribulations, as well as the moments of warmth, faced by children in foster care. The recurrent mention of "foster home" and the transition between them makes it evident that the narrator was in the care system, making the option about "foster home for the narrator and other foster children" the most logical inference from the story.

13. (A): Slavery existed in ancient Egypt but what set it apart from many other ancient civilizations was the treatment of slaves. The passage specifically states that "Slavery was not very important in ancient Egypt, but it did exist." It further clarifies that slaves were usually treated well and even had the right to own property. Tnis contrasts with many ancient societies where slaves were often treated poorly and had very limited rights, if any at all.

14. (A): The term 'serfs' in the context of the passage refers to workers whose freedom was limited. They were tied to the land or estates where they worked, and they could be bought and sold along with these estates. This feudal-like system bound the serfs to the land, making their economic and personal freedoms restricted. In essence, while they weren't slaves, they lacked many of the rights associated with free citizens.

15. (B): While the Pharaohs believed that their connections with the Gods were responsible for Egypt's prosperity, it was, in reality, the hard work and labor of ordinary people that drove the nation forward. They worked in various sectors, from agriculture to mining, which contributed to the overall development and sustenance of the ancient Egyptian civilization. The strength of a civilization often rests on the shoulders of its everyday workers, and in ancient Egypt, this was no different.

16. (C): The passage clearly mentions that the Pharaohs had a strong belief that their connections with the Gods were what favored Egypt. This belief, however, contrasts with the reality, which was that the ordinary people's hard work and contributions were the actual foundation of Egypt's success.

17. (D): The passage explicitly states that "Slavery was not very important in ancient Egypt," which directly contradicts the statement "Slavery was extremely important in ancient Egypt." Thus, the latter statement is incorrect based on the information provided.

18. (C): By matching the provided lists: (*a*) "Serfs could be bought and sold along with the estates where they worked," which corresponds to (*iii*). (*b*) The passage says, "Farmers had to be registered with the government," aligning with (*i*). (*c*) During the season of the Nile floods, when fields lay underwater, "many workers were recruited into public building projects," matching with (*ii*). (*d*) The passage mentions a "harsh punishment for those who ran away," which correlates with (*iv*). Therefore, the correct match is (*a*)-(*iii*), (*b*)-(*i*), (*c*)-(*ii*) and (*d*)-(*iv*).

19. (C): Acquitted refers to the formal and legal declaration that someone is not guilty of a criminal charge. It is the conclusion of a judicial process that finds the accused innocent. On the other hand, "Convicted" means that a person has been found guilty of a criminal charge. Therefore, it stands as the direct opposite of "Acquitted".

20. (D): "Relinquish" means to voluntarily give up or let go of something, especially some rights, title, or possession. It signifies the act of releasing or parting with something one holds. Contrarily, "Possess" implies owning, holding, or having control over something. If you relinquish your right to something, you're giving up your claim or control over it. But if you possess something, it's in your ownership or control. This dynamic displays the contrasting nature of the two terms.

21. (A): "Capacious" is an adjective used to describe something that has the ability to contain a lot, often used in the context of a space or container being large in size or volume. Think of a capacious room or a capacious bag—they can hold much. The term "Limited" points towards something being confined, restricted, or not expansive. In the context of space or volume, "Limited" would mean that there's a lack of abundance or room. Thus, it serves as the antonym to "Capacious".

22. (D): The term "Fraudulent" relates to deceit, trickery, or wrongful deception with the intention to gain something (often monetary) or deceive someone. It's associated with acts that are not genuine or honest. "Genuine", conversely, denotes authenticity, realness, or being free from pretense, affectation, or deceit. A genuine item is real and not a counterfeit, and a genuine person is sincere and not trying to deceive. Given this contrast in their inherent meanings, "Genuine" stands opposite to "Fraudulent".

23. (C): The expression "laboured ease" stands out as a juxtaposition of contradictory terms. "Laboured" typically denotes something that requires effort or hard work, whereas "ease" signifies comfort or lack of difficulty. When combined, these words create an oxymoron, which is a figure of speech that merges contrasting ideas to portray complex emotions or situations. In this case, the oxymoron "laboured ease" conveys the paradoxical feeling of finding comfort or acceptance in loss, even though the process is painful.

24. (B): The phrase "Far Far from gusty waves" prominently displays the repetition of the initial sound "f" in both "Far" and "from". This deliberate use of the same initial consonant sound in closely positioned or consecutive words is called alliteration. Alliteration is employed in both prose and poetry to create rhythm, catch the reader's attention, and emphasize particular sections of the text.

25. (A): In the statement "The smiling young trees provided a strange comfort," trees are ascribed the human-like quality of "smiling." Trees, in reality, do not smile, but this attribution of a human trait to a non-human entity is called personification. Personification is a figurative device that endows animals, objects, or abstract ideas with human characteristics or behaviors, making them more relatable and allowing writers to create vivid imagery and emotional resonance.

26. (C): The phrase "Like angels from heaven the paratrooper landed on earth" draws a direct comparison between the paratrooper and angels using the word "like." This comparative statement that uses "like" or "as" to draw parallels between two dissimilar entities is known as a simile. Similes are a staple of poetic language, enabling poets to conjure imaginative visuals and evoke deeper emotions by juxtaposing familiar concepts with unfamiliar or unexpected ones. Here, the comparison magnifies the gracefulness and perhaps the surprise of the paratrooper's landing.

27. (B): The idiom "to be at sixes and sevens" signifies being in a state of confusion or disarray. It traces its origins to a dispute between two London guilds about their precedence in the 14th century. The guilds, the Merchant Taylors and the Skinners, were both founded in close succession, leading to the debate. In various processions, they rotated their positions annually between the sixth and seventh spots, hence the phrase. Over time, the term became more generalized, referring to any state of confusion or disorder, and not just about specific rankings.

28. (C): The expression "once in a blue moon" denotes an event that happens very infrequently. A blue moon refers to the rare occurrence when there are two full moons in one calendar month. Traditionally, each month has one full moon, but occasionally, the lunar cycle's timing aligns such that a second full moon, termed a "blue moon," appears. Although blue moons are not technically blue, the rarity of the phenomenon has led to the popularization of this phrase in English language, symbolizing something that doesn't happen often.

29. (A): To go on "a wild goose chase" means to pursue something that is unattainable or is a fruitless endeavor. Historically, a "wild goose chase" was a type of horse race in which the lead rider pursued a course of his choosing and others followed at set intervals, much like wild geese flying in formation. Over time, the phrase's meaning shifted, and it began to refer to a pointless or unattainable pursuit, mirroring the futility of chasing after a wild goose.

30. (D): The idiom "to burn a hole in the pocket" refers to the urge to spend money rapidly, especially when one has disposable income or newfound wealth. The visual imagery suggests money being so hot or uncomfortable that it "burns" its way out of one's pocket, emphasizing the impulsive nature of the spending. This expression underlines the human tendency to sometimes act irresponsibly with money, especially when one feels they have more than they're used to.

31. (C): The word "PUGNACIOUS" is derived from the Latin word "pugnare", which means "to fight". It refers to a person who is eager or quick to argue, quarrel, or fight. Thus, the word "Quarrelsome" best captures its essence. Pugnacious individuals are often confrontational and can be challenging to engage with in discussions because of their aggressive nature. Their readiness to dispute can make collaborations difficult, as they may often challenge perspectives aggressively, even if the situation doesn't warrant such a reaction.

32. (A): To "CLING" is to hold on tightly to something or someone. It can also refer to objects that stick closely to surfaces, like wet clothes that cling to the body. The word "Attach" closely resonates with this meaning. In a more abstract sense, people might cling to ideas, memories, or feelings, indicating a reluctance to let go or move on. Attachment can be both physical, like sticking or adhering to a surface, and emotional, like being closely bound or connected to a thought, feeling, or another person.

33. (B): The term "ENCHANTING" is used to describe something that is charming or captivating, often in a delightful or magical way. Something enchanting draws you in and holds your attention because of its beauty or charm. The word "Pleasant" is closely aligned with this sentiment. Enchanting experiences or sights can often evoke feelings of wonder and amazement. They often stand out in memory because of the strong positive emotions they generate. Such moments or things leave a lasting impact, making us want to relive or revisit them.

34. (B): "GIGANTIC" describes something that is very large or enormous in size. It emphasizes an extreme scale or magnitude that often surpasses ordinary standards or expectations. "Monstrous" in this context aligns closely with this meaning, emphasizing the vastness or enormity of something. When we refer to something as gigantic, we often compare it with regular-sized counterparts to underscore its impressive or overwhelming size. The term has its roots in the word "gigant", which historically referred to the Giants of Greek mythology, legendary beings renowned for their immense size and strength.

35. (A): A "Decade" specifically refers to a period of 10 years. Originating from the Greek word 'dekas', which means 'ten', it is commonly used to categorize historical, technological, cultural, or personal events and advancements. For instance, the 1960s is referred to as a decade, and it's often associated with cultural revolutions, civil rights movements, and significant shifts in music and fashion. It's a convenient way to encapsulate years that share common characteristics.

36. (B): A "Bibliophile" is an individual who has a great appreciation for or collects books. The term is derived from the Greek words 'biblion' (book) and 'philos' (loving). A bibliophile often possesses a deep reverence for books, not just for their content, but sometimes also for their physical form, binding, history, and even the art of bookmaking. While all bibliophiles love books, not all of them are collectors. Some might just enjoy reading and surrounding themselves with books without the intent of collecting rare or antique editions.

37. (D): "Infanticide" is the act of killing an infant, usually by a parent. The term comes from Latin 'infans', meaning unable to speak, and 'caedere', which means to kill. Historically and in some cultures, infanticide was practiced for various reasons, including economic distress, the undesirability of the child due to gender or deformities, or societal pressures. Modern societies largely condemn and criminalize infanticide, viewing it as a heinous act. However, it's essential to understand the underlying causes, such as postpartum depression or societal pressures, that might drive someone to commit such an act.

38. (C): An "Itinerary" is a detailed plan or route of a journey. It can be as basic as a list of places one intends to visit or as detailed as specifying dates, times, modes of transportation, and lodging details. People often use itineraries when planning trips to ensure they maximize their time and experiences. Travel agents, tour operators, or even individuals planning their vacations often draft itineraries. In a broader sense, an itinerary can also refer to a planned route or journey for business trips, political campaigns, or any event that requires traveling between multiple locations.

39. (A): "Attach" and "Detach" are antonyms. While "attach" means to fasten or join something to something else, "detach" refers to the act of separating or removing something. Similarly, "Barren" and "Fertile" are antonyms. A barren land is one that cannot produce or is too poor to produce vegetation, while fertile land is rich in nutrients and is conducive for the growth of plants. These terms often describe soil quality in agriculture. Fertile soils are sought after for farming because they can support a diverse range of crops and result in better yields.

40. (A): "Medley" and "Mixture" are synonymous. Both words refer to a combination of different things. For instance, in music, a medley is a blend of several tunes played one after another. Likewise, a mixture refers to a substance made by combining two or more different materials. Similarly, "Iterate" and "Repeat" convey the same idea. To iterate is to say or perform again, often used in the context of computer programming or design processes. Repeat, a more general term, simply implies doing something again.

41. (C): "Retreat" and "Advance" are antonyms. Retreat means to withdraw or move back, often used in military contexts when referring to troops moving away from enemy forces. On the other hand, advance means to move forward or make progress. Similarly, "Savage" and "Civilised" are opposites. A society described as savage is viewed as primitive or lacking the cultural and social refinements of a civilized society. It's essential to approach these terms with caution, as labeling a society "savage" can be ethnocentric and disrespectful. It's always crucial to respect cultural differences without imposing judgments based on one's own cultural standards.

42. (B): "Meek" and "Modest" are similar in their connotations. While meek implies a mild nature or submissive character, modest means having or showing a moderate estimation of one's abilities or achievements. It's about not being boastful or arrogant. Similarly, "Finally" and "Eventually" are synonymous. Both terms denote an outcome that follows a series of events or a period. For instance, "She finally/ eventually arrived at the party" means she arrived after some delay or events. Both words indicate the culmination of waiting or anticipation.

43. (C): The correct spelling is "Catastrophic." The term "catastrophic" refers to something that causes or involves a catastrophe, which is a sudden and widespread disaster. The root word "catastrophe" comes from the Greek "katastrophç," meaning an overturning or a sudden end. In contemporary usage, the word can describe natural disasters like earthquakes or human-made disasters like wars. It's also frequently used in casual speech to refer to significant failures or blunders.

44. (B): The rightly spelt word is "Communism." Communism is a sociopolitical and economic ideology and movement whose ultimate goal is the establishment of a communist society, which is a socioeconomic order structured upon the ideas of common ownership of the means of production and the absence of social classes, money, and the state.

45. (A): "Cooperative" is the correct spelling. A cooperative is a business organization owned and operated by a group of individuals for their mutual benefit. It can also describe a willingness to cooperate with others.

46. (B): "Pneumonia" is the correctly spelt term. Pneumonia is a type of infection that inflames the air sacs in one or both lungs. The air sacs may fill with fluid or pus, causing cough, fever, chills, and difficulty breathing. The "p" at the beginning of the word is silent, which can make the pronunciation and spelling tricky for some.

47. (C): The correct sequence is "(*c*) A large scale exchange of nuclear weapons (*b*) Will produce an unprecedented amount (*d*) Of radiation that can (*a*) Penetrate the biological tissues." From a grammatical perspective, this arrangement forms a subject-predicate-object construction, which is standard in English grammar. Here, "(*c*) A large scale exchange of nuclear weapons" acts as the subject, "(*b*) Will produce" is the verb phrase, and the remaining parts "(*d*) Of radiation" and "(*a*) Penetrate the biological tissues" work as the object and modifier, respectively, providing more details about the consequences of the action.

48. (B): The coherent arrangement is "(*c*) The mission has provided (*d*) Able service to all the needy (*b*) People in this area (*a*) During the last few years." This sequence begins with the main clause "(*c*) The mission has provided (*d*) Able service" which provides the core information. Following this, "(*b*) People in this area" acts as the qualifier, giving specifics about the recipients. Finally, "(*a*) During the last few years" serves as a temporal adverbial phrase, situating the action in time.

49. (A): The proper order is "(*c*) He has received (*d*) No other message other than (*b*) An urgent telegram asking (*a*) Him to rush to his village immediately." Starting with "(*c*) He has received" introduces the subject and the verb. The clause "(*d*) No other message other than" acts as a restrictive modifier, emphasizing the uniqueness of the message. The phrases "(*b*) An urgent telegram asking" and "(*a*) Him to rush to his village immediately" provide further details, functioning as object and purpose clause respectively.

50. (C): The correct sequence is "(*a*) He managed to make sense (*c*) Of the book even though (*b*) It was the first time when (*d*) He read anything on the subject." The main clause is "(*a*) He managed to make sense (*c*) Of the book," where "He" is the subject, "managed" is the verb, and "Of the book" is the prepositional phrase acting as an object. The clause "(*b*) It was the first time when (*d*) He read anything on the subject" is a subordinate clause providing a reason or condition for the main clause, with "It" referring to the act of understanding the book.

GENERAL TEST

1. Who got the Major Dhyan Chand Khel Ratna Award 2021 for his excellent performance in cricket?

A. Mithali Raj B. Shikhar Dhawan
C. Virat Kohli D. M.S. Dhoni

2. UNESCO has added this festival to its 2021 list of Intangible Cultural Heritage:

A. Durga Puja B. Diwali
C. Holi D. Kali Puja

3. Which mission has been renamed as Pradhan Mantri Digital health Mission (PM-DHM)?

A. Ayushman Bharat
B. Awaz Health Insurance Scheme
C. Aam Aadmi Bima Yojna
D. National Digital Health Mission (NDHM)

4. The theme of 'Shikshak' Parv-2021 was:

A. Quality and Sustainable Schools: Learning from schools in India
B. Learning Outcomes
C. Quality Teachers for Quality Education
D. Holistic Development

5. Light Combat Helicopters (LCH) are developed by:

A. Bharat Electronics
B. Defence Research and Development Organisation
C. Hindustan Aeronautics Limited
D. Bharat Dynamics

6. Out of the alternatives choose the most appropriate description about the three given words.

Bangle : Anklet : Necklace

A. These are Games product
B. These are jewellery
C. These are metals
D. These are Stationery items

7. From the following pairs select the combination of right pair from the following options.

(*a*) Kuwait : Taka (*b*) Greece : Dinnar
(*c*) Argentina : Peso (*d*) Bangladesh : Taka
(*e*) Sweden : Krona

Choose the correct answer from the options given below.

A. (*c*), (*d*), (*e*) B. (*a*), (*b*), (*c*)
C. (*b*), (*c*), (*d*) D. (*a*), (*d*), (*e*)

8. Arrange the given words in the sequence in which they occur in the dictionary.

(*a*) Firmament (*b*) Finish
(*c*) First (*d*) Fissure
(*e*) Fiscal

Choose the correct answer from the options given below:

A. (*b*), (*c*), (*d*), (*a*), (*e*) B. (*a*), (*b*), (*c*), (*d*), (*e*)
C. (*b*), (*a*), (*c*), (*e*), (*d*) D. (*e*), (*a*), (*b*), (*c*), (*d*)

9. Match List-I with List-II:

List-I	*List-II*
(*a*) Ellora caves	(*i*) Jaipur
(*b*) Amer Fort	(*ii*) Agra
(*c*) Golden Temple	(*iii*) Aurangabad
(*d*) Taj Mahal	(*iv*) Amritsar

Choose the correct answer from the options given below:

	(*a*)	(*b*)	(*c*)	(*d*)
A.	(*i*)	(*iii*)	(*iv*)	(*ii*)
B.	(*iii*)	(*i*)	(*iv*)	(*ii*)
C.	(*iv*)	(*iii*)	(*i*)	(*ii*)
D.	(*iii*)	(*iv*)	(*i*)	(*ii*)

10. Match List-I with List-II.

List-I (*River*)	*List-II* (*Continents*)
(*a*) Nile	(*i*) North America
(*b*) Mississippi	(*ii*) South America
(*c*) Ganga	(*iii*) Africa
(*d*) Amazon	(*iv*) India

Choose the correct answer from the options given below:

	(*a*)	(*b*)	(*c*)	(*d*)
A.	(*iii*)	(*i*)	(*iv*)	(*ii*)
B.	(*iii*)	(*ii*)	(*iv*)	(*i*)
C.	(*i*)	(*iii*)	(*iv*)	(*ii*)
D.	(*iii*)	(*iv*)	(*ii*)	(*i*)

11. Among the four options given below three have similarities find the odd one out.

A. Scurvy B. Influenza
C. Beri Beri D. Rickets

12. Match List-I with List-II.

List-I	*List-II*
(*a*) Saina Nehwal	(*i*) Boxing
(*b*) Mary Kom	(*ii*) Wrestling
(*c*) Mithali Raj	(*iii*) Badminton
(*d*) Geeta Phogat	(*iv*) Cricket

Choose the correct answer from the options given below:

	(*a*)	(*b*)	(*c*)	(*d*)
A.	(*iii*)	(*i*)	(*iv*)	(*ii*)
B.	(*iii*)	(*i*)	(*ii*)	(*iv*)
C.	(*iv*)	(*i*)	(*ii*)	(*iii*)
D.	(*iii*)	(*ii*)	(*iv*)	(*i*)

13. Match List-I with List-II.

List-I	*List-II*
(*a*) Hepatitis	(*i*) Blood
(*b*) Pneumonia	(*ii*) Joints
(*c*) Arthritis	(*iii*) Liver
(*d*) Thalassemia	(*iv*) Lungs

Choose the correct answer from the options given below:

	(*a*)	(*b*)	(*c*)	(*d*)
A.	(*iii*)	(*iv*)	(*ii*)	(*i*)
B.	(*iii*)	(*i*)	(*ii*)	(*iv*)
C.	(*iv*)	(*iii*)	(*i*)	(*ii*)
D.	(*ii*)	(*iii*)	(*iv*)	(*i*)

14. In the following questions arrange the given words in the sequence that occur in the dictionary.

(*a*) Whiter (*b*) Wound
(*c*) Writer (*d*) Worked
(*e*) Worst

Choose the correct answer from the options given below:

A. (*a*), (*d*), (*b*), (*e*), (*c*) B. (*a*), (*d*), (*e*), (*b*), (*c*)
C. (*d*), (*a*), (*b*), (*e*), (*c*) D. (*d*), (*a*), (*e*), (*b*), (*c*)

15. Among the four options, three have the same property. Find the odd one out.

A. Mole Hills B. Nilgiri Hills
C. Aravali Hills D. Shivalik Hills

16. Which of the following is a leap year?

A. 1500 B. 700
C. 1300 D. 2000

17. Which one of the following diagram represents Automobile, Cars, Motorcycle?

A. 
B. 
C. 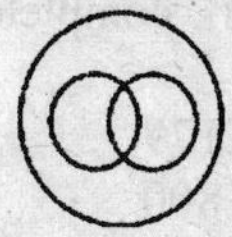
D. 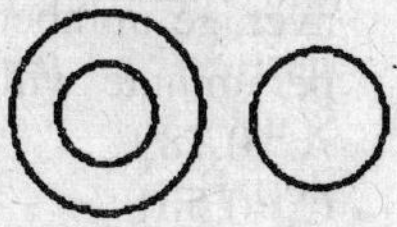

18. In the given questions select the related word from the alternatives.

Horse : Jockey : Car ______

A. Brake B. Chauffeur
C. Seatbelt D. Steering

19. Among the four options given below three have similar properties. Find the odd one out:

A. Ginger B. Beetroot
C. Carrot D. Cabbage

20. Monu rides his bicycle north wards, then turned left and rides one km and again turned left and rides 2 km. Monu found himself exactly one km west of his starting point. How far did he ride north wards initially?

A. 5 km B. 2 km
C. 3 km D. 4 km

21. Which among the following is the biggest planet of our solar system?

A. Saturn B. Jupiter
C. Mars D. Venus

22. From the given option which word can't be formed from the letters given in:

"PERMANENT"

A. MENTOR B. TRAMP
C. AMPERE D. REMANT

23. Arrange the following words as they occur in the english.

(*a*) Explosive (*b*) Explicit
(*c*) Exponent (*d*) Exposition
(*e*) Explore

Choose the correct answer from the options given below:

A. (*b*), (*e*), (*c*), (*a*), (*d*) B. (*e*), (*b*), (*c*), (*a*), (*d*)
C. (*e*), (*b*), (*a*), (*c*), (*d*) D. (*b*), (*e*), (*a*), (*c*), (*d*)

24. What is meaningful/logical order of the words given below?

(*a*) Type (*b*) Save
(*c*) Open (*d*) Print
(*e*) Close

Choose the correct answer from the options given below:

A. (*c*), (*a*), (*d*), (*b*), (*e*) B. (*a*), (*c*), (*b*), (*d*), (*e*)
C. (*c*), (*a*), (*b*), (*d*), (*e*) D. (*a*), (*c*), (*d*), (*b*), (*e*)

25. The pH value of human's urine in human is about:

A. 2.5 B. 4.0
C. 6.0 D. 9.0

26. HEAVY can be coded as 8, 5, 1, 22, 25, then LIGHT will be coded as.

A. 12, 7, 9, 8, 20 B. 12, 9, 7, 8, 20
C. 7, 8, 9, 12, 20 D. 9, 7, 8, 12, 20

27. Who is known as the 'Father of Green Revolution' in India?

A. Verghese Kurien B. M.S. Swaminathan
C. Dr. Lalji Singh D. Dr. Balram Jakhad

28. Justice is always related to ______.

A. Deceit B. Just
C. Generosity D. Nobility

29. In Rigveda, the river Jhelum is known as:

A. Sutridri B. Parushini
C. Vitasta D. Asikni

30. A person is going towards north in the night and he sees Dhruv tara and sees it on his left side. Which of the following statements justify the fact?

A. Always B. Sometimes
C. Generally D. Never

31. The first Indian women Fighter Pilot to fly a fighter jet is:
A. Avani Chaturvedi B. Gunjan Saxena
C. Shubhangi Swaroop D. Bhawana Kanth

32. Match List-I with List-II.

List-I	*List-II*
(*a*) Pedology	(*i*) Study of muscles
(*b*) Pisciculture	(*ii*) Study of growing old
(*c*) Myology	(*iii*) Study of soils
(*d*) Gerontology	(*iv*) Study of fish

Choose the correct answer from the options given below:

	(*a*)	(*b*)	(*c*)	(*d*)
A.	(*ii*)	(*iv*)	(*iii*)	(*i*)
B.	(*ii*)	(*iii*)	(*i*)	(*iv*)
C.	(*iv*)	(*ii*)	(*i*)	(*iii*)
D.	(*iii*)	(*iv*)	(*i*)	(*ii*)

33. The interest earned on ₹ 25000 in 5 years at simple interest is ₹ 1500. What is the rate of interest?
A. 1.1% B. 1.2%
C. 1.4% D. 1.6%

34. Given that $a : b = 5 : 3$ and $b : c = 2 : 5$
Which of the following is true?
A. $a < b < c$ B. $b < c < a$
C. $b < a < c$ D. $a < c < b$

35. Arrange the given ratios in descending order.
(*a*) 7 : 15 (*b*) 15 : 23
(*c*) 17 : 25 (*d*) 21 : 39

Choose the correct answer from the options given below:
A. (*c*) > (*a*) > (*b*) > (*d*) B. (*a*) > (*d*) > (*c*) > (*b*)
C. (*c*) > (*b*) > (*d*) > (*a*) D. (*d*) > (*a*) > (*b*) > (*c*)

36. A is younger than B by 7 years. If their ages are in the respective ratio of 7 : 9 then how old is A?
A. 31.5 years B. 16.5 years
C. 24.5 years D. 18.5 years

37. Match List-I with List-II.

List-I	*List-II*
(*a*) First country to use Glass	(*i*) New Zealand
(*b*) First country to make Written Constitution	(*ii*) Russia
(*c*) First country to do Artificial Satellite Experiment	(*iii*) USA
(*d*) First Country to impose Carbon Tax	(*iv*) Egypt

Choose the correct answer from the options given below:

	(*a*)	(*b*)	(*c*)	(*d*)
A.	(*iv*)	(*iii*)	(*ii*)	(*i*)
B.	(*iii*)	(*iv*)	(*i*)	(*ii*)
C.	(*ii*)	(*i*)	(*iii*)	(*iv*)
D.	(*i*)	(*ii*)	(*iv*)	(*iii*)

38. The average of 3 odd consecutive numbers is 15. What is the sum of first and last numbers?
A. 30 B. 20
C. 40 D. 35

39. In the formula "W = Fs cos θ", the angle between force and displacement (θ) is equal to 90°, the net work done will be:
A. Double B. Positive but not double
C. Negative D. Zero

40. What is the value of 70% of 420 + 30% of 280?
A. 284 B. 268
C. 368 D. 378

41. 2.56 expressed as a per cent of 1.6 is:
A. 16% B. 25%
C. 160% D. 90%

42. P can do a work in 12 days. Q can do the same work in 10 days. If P and Q come together, both of them can complete the same work in how many days?
A. $2\frac{2}{11}$ days B. $3\frac{3}{11}$ days
C. $5\frac{5}{11}$ days D. $4\frac{4}{11}$ days

43. $\frac{3}{4}$ part of tank is filled by a motor pump in 15 minutes, then the rest part of the tank will be filled in.
A. 3.5 minutes B. 5 minutes.
C. 8 minutes D. 20 minutes

44. The ratio of two numbers is 5 : 6 and their HCF is 8. What is the LCM of these numbers?
A. 180 B. 240
C. 280 D. 140

45. A can complete a work in 4 minutes. B in 5 minutes, C in 6 minutes and D in 10 minutes respectively. The average number of units of work completed by them per minute will be:
A. 0.789 B. 0.179
C. 0.501 D. 0.800

46. The value of 2 ÷ 2 – 2.
A. 1 B. –1
C. 0 D. $\frac{1}{2}$

47. The network in the graphical area spread over countries, is known as:
A. LAN B. VAN
C. MAN D. WAN

48. A chair is sold for ₹ 96 at 20% loss. The cost price of the chair is:
A. ₹ 120 B. ₹ 80
C. ₹ 115.20 D. ₹ 76.80

49. The value of $\dfrac{(8.9)^2-(2.1)^2}{8.9-2.1}$.

A. 8.6 B. 6.8
C. 10.0 D. 11.0

50. The value of $\left(\dfrac{x}{y}\right)^{2a-3b}\times\left(\dfrac{x}{y}\right)^{3b-4c}\times\left(\dfrac{x}{y}\right)^{4c-2a}$.

A. $\dfrac{x}{y}$ B. 1
C. 0 D. $\left(\dfrac{x}{y}\right)^{2a+3b+4c}$

51. In parallelogram ABCD, angle A is greater than angle B by 10°, the measure of angle D is:

A. 95° B. 75°
C. 85° D. 65°

52. If the length of diagonals of a rhombus are 10 cm and 24 cm then the side of the rhombus is:

A. 26 cm B. 24 cm
C. 13 cm D. 12 cm

53. In the figure AOB is a straight line then the value of x is:

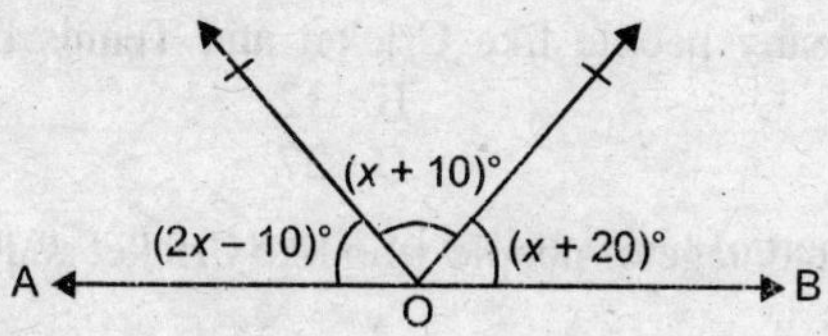

A. 60 B. 50
C. 40 D. 70

54. How much time, the Constituent Assembly took to complete the Constitution?

A. 02 years, 11 months and 18 days
B. 02 years, 18 months and 11 days
C. 03 years, 11 months and 18 days
D. 03 years, 18 months and 11 days

Directions (Qs. No. 55-57): *In the given figure ABCD is a square and radius of semi circle is 7 cm.*

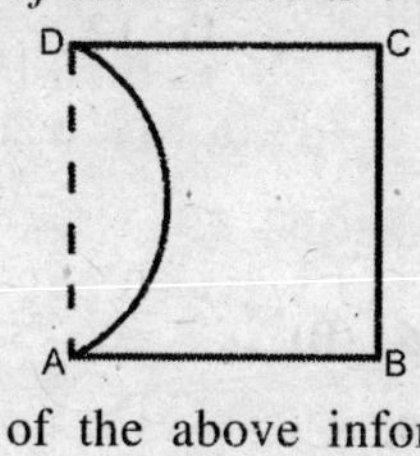

On the basis of the above information answer the questions.

55. The side of the square is:

A. $\dfrac{7}{2}$ cm B. 7 cm
C. 14 cm D. 12 cm

56. The perimeter of the figure is:

A. 42 cm B. 20 cm
C. 86 cm D. 64 cm

57. Area of the figure is:

A. 119 cm^2 B. 273 cm^2
C. 350 cm^2 D. 42 cm^2

Directions (Qs. No. 58-60): *The marks of 5 students in a unit test are given below:*

$x-1,\ 2x+1,\ 2x-2,\ x-1,\ 2x+3$ where $x=5$.

On the basis of above information answer the questions.

58. The mode of data in numerals is:

A. 11 B. 13
C. 4 D. 8

59. The median of data in numerals is:

A. 11 B. 4
C. 8 D. 13

60. The mean of the data in numerals is:

A. 4 B. 8
C. 13 D. 11

61. Some dens are rooms. All rooms are walls. Some walls are bricks. All bricks are plates.

(*a*) Some plates are walls
(*b*) Some walls are dens
(*c*) Some bricks are rooms
(*d*) Some plates are rooms

Choose the correct answer from the options given below:

A. (*a*) and (*c*) only B. (*b*) and (*c*) only
C. (*a*) and (*b*) only D. (*c*) and (*d*) only

62. If A means '–', B means '÷', C means '+' and D means '×', then 45B3C18A4D6 = ?

A. 179 B. 9
C. 18 D. 152

63. What will be next figure of the series?

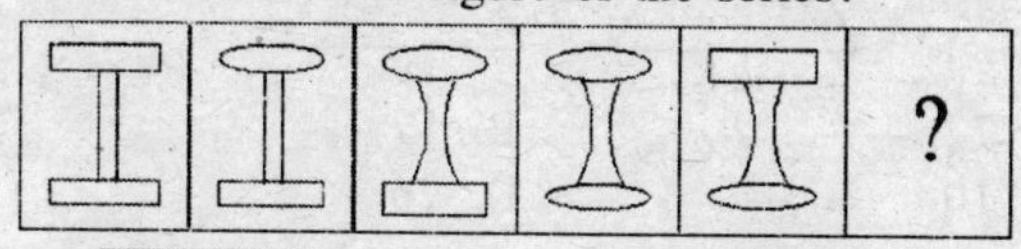

A. 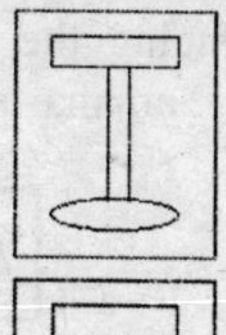
B. 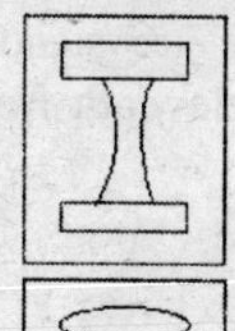
C. 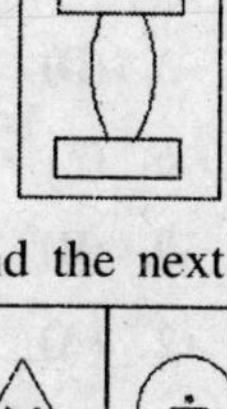
D. 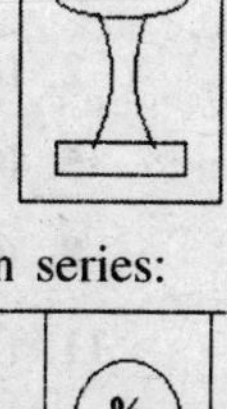

64. Find the next figure of given series:

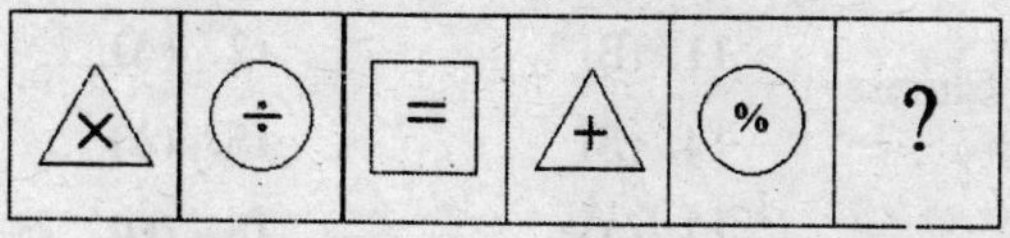

A. 

B. 

C. 

D. 

65. Find the next item of given series.

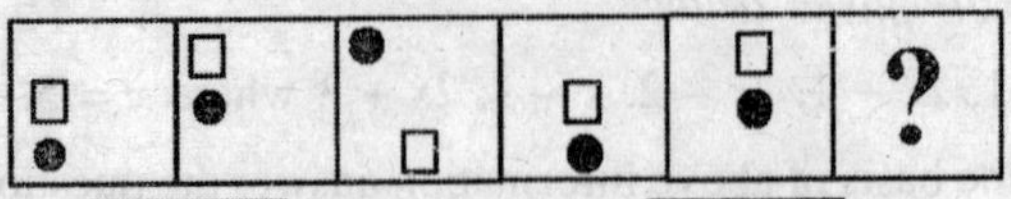

A. 

B. 

C. 

D. 

66. Out of the four alternatives choose the most appropriate description about the given words.

Sarnath : Kapilvastu : Sanchi

A. There are places having massive pillars
B. These are linked with lord Buddha
C. These are famous for stone caves
D. These have ancient Universities

67. A meaningful word starting with A is made from the first, the second, the fourth, the fifth and the sixth letters of the word 'CONTRACT'. Which of the following is the middle letter of the word?

A. T B. O
C. C D. R

68. Find the missing number from the following given option:

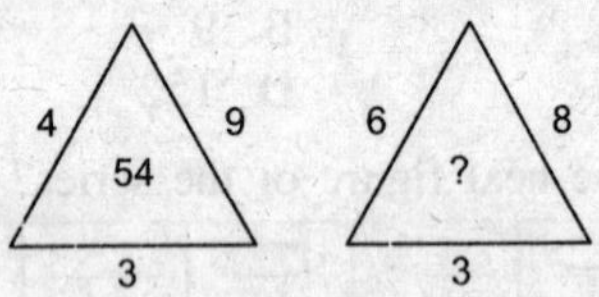

A. 72 B. 17
C. 10 D. 26

69. Forty girls are standing in a row facing the North. Amita is eleventh from left end and Sanjana is thirty first from the right end of the row. How for will Smita, who is third to the right to Amita in the row, be from Sanjana?

A. 3rd B. 4th
C. 2nd D. 5th

70. Find the missing number from the following given options.

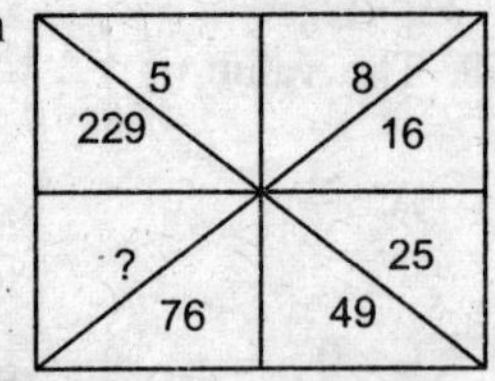

A. 150
B. 53
C. 125
D. 148

71. Among the options given below three have similarities. Find the odd one out.

A. Rice B. Wheat
C. Chick peas D. Corn

Directions (Qs. No. 72-75): *Read details carefully for questions.*

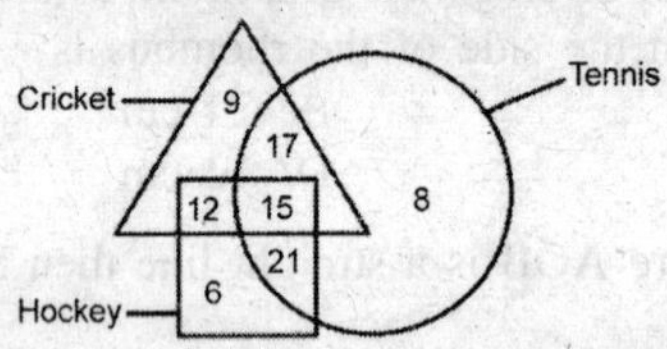

72. How many people like Cricket and Tennis both?

A. 17 B. 32
C. 15 D. 27

73. The percentage of people who like Cricket and Hockey both is ______.

A. 36.36% B. 30.68%
C. 33.3% D. 42.04%

74. Let C, H and T represents number of people who likes Cricket, Hockey and Tennis respectively. The ratio of C : H : T is:

A. 53 : 54 : 61 B. 61 : 54 : 53
C. 54 : 53 : 61 D. 54 : 61 : 53

75. How many people like Cricket, Tennis and Hockey games all together.

A. 21 B. 17
C. 15 D. 12

ANSWERS

1. (A) **2.** (A) **3.** (D)
4. (A) **5.** (C) **6.** (*)
7. (A) **8.** (C) **9.** (B)
10. (A) **11.** (B) **12.** (A)
13. (A) **14.** (B) **15.** (A)
16. (D) **17.** (A) **18.** (D)
19. (D) **20.** (B) **21.** (B)
22. (A) **23.** (D) **24.** (C)
25. (C) **26.** (B) **27.** (B)
28. (*) **29.** (C) **30.** (*)
31. (A) **32.** (D)

33. **(B):** Rate of interest $= \dfrac{SI \times 100}{P \times t}$

$$= \frac{1500 \times 100}{25000 \times 5}$$

$$= \frac{6}{5} = 1.2\%.$$

34. (C): $a : b = 5 : 3$ and $b : c = 2 : 5$

$$a : b : c = 5 \times 2 : 3 \times 2 : 3 \times 5 = 10 : 6 : 15$$

$\therefore$ $b < a < c$ is true.

35. (C): $\frac{7}{15} = 0.466$

$\frac{15}{23} = 0.652$

$\frac{17}{25} = 0.68$

$\frac{21}{39} = 0.538$

$\therefore$ $\frac{17}{25}, \frac{15}{23}, \frac{21}{39}, \frac{7}{15}$ are is descending order.

Hence, $(c) > (b) > (d) > (a)$.

36. (C): Let B's age $= x$ years

$\therefore$ A's age $= x - 7$ years

$$\frac{x-7}{x} = \frac{7}{9}$$

$\Rightarrow$ $9x - 63 = 7x$

$\Rightarrow$ $2x = 63$

$\Rightarrow$ $x = \frac{63}{2} = 31.5$

$\therefore$ A's age $= 31.5 - 7 = 24.5$ years.

37. (A)

38. (A): Let three odd consecutive numbers are x, $x + 2$ and $x + 4$

$x + x + 2 + x + 4 = 15 \times 3$

$\Rightarrow$ $3x + 6 = 45$

$\Rightarrow$ $3x = 39 \Rightarrow x = 13$

$\therefore$ first no. = 13, last number = 13 + 4 = 17

$\therefore$ Sum of first no. and last no. = 13 + 17 = 30.

39. (D): $W = Fs \cos 90°$

$W = 0$

$\therefore$ The net work done will be zero.

40. (D): 70% of 420 + 30% of 280

$$= \frac{70}{100} \times 420 + \frac{30}{100} \times 280$$

$$= 294 + 84 = 378.$$

41. (C): 2.56 = 1.6% of x

$\Rightarrow$ $\frac{256}{100} = \frac{16x}{1000}$

$\Rightarrow$ $x = \frac{256 \times 10}{16} = 160\%$.

42. (C): P's 1 day work $= \frac{1}{12}$

Q's 1 day work $= \frac{1}{10}$

(P + Q)'s 1 day work $= \frac{1}{12} + \frac{1}{10} = \frac{5+6}{60} = \frac{11}{60}$

$\therefore$ (P + Q) can do whole work $= \frac{60}{11} = 5\frac{5}{11}$ days.

43. (B): $\frac{3}{4}$ part of tank is filled in 15 minutes

$\therefore$ $\frac{1}{4}$ part of tank is filled in $\frac{15 \times 4}{3} \times \frac{1}{4} = 5$ minutes.

44. (B): Let numbers are $5x$ and $6x$

HCF of $5x$ and $6x = x$

$\therefore$ $x = 8$ [HCF = 8 given]

$\therefore$ Numbers are 40 and 48

$$\text{LCM} = \frac{40 \times 48}{8} = 40 \times 6 = 240.$$

45. (B): (A + B + C + D)'s 1 minute work

$$= \frac{1}{4} + \frac{1}{5} + \frac{1}{6} + \frac{1}{10}$$

$$= \frac{15+12+10+6}{60} = \frac{43}{60}$$

$\therefore$ The average no. of units of work

$$= \frac{43}{60 \times 4} = \frac{43}{240} = 0.179.$$

46. (B): $2 \div 2 - 2 = 1 - 2 = -1$.

47. (*)

48. (A): Let C.P. = ₹ 100

Loss $= \frac{20}{100} \times 100 =$ ₹ 20

S.P. = 100 – 20 = ₹ 80

When S.P. ₹ 80 then C.P. = ₹ 100

When S.P. ₹ 96 then C.P. = ₹ $\frac{100}{80} \times 96$

$\therefore$ CP = ₹ 120.

49. (D): $\frac{(8.9)^2 - (2.1)^2}{8.9 - 2.1} = \frac{(8.9 + 2.1)(8.9 - 2.1)}{(8.9 - 2.1)}$

$= 8.9 + 2.1 = 11.0.$

50. (B): $\left(\frac{x}{y}\right)^{2a-3b} \times \left(\frac{x}{y}\right)^{3b-4c} \times \left(\frac{x}{y}\right)^{4c-2a}$

$$= \left(\frac{x}{y}\right)^{2a-3b+3b-4c+4c-2a} = \left(\frac{x}{y}\right)^0 = 1.$$

51. (C):

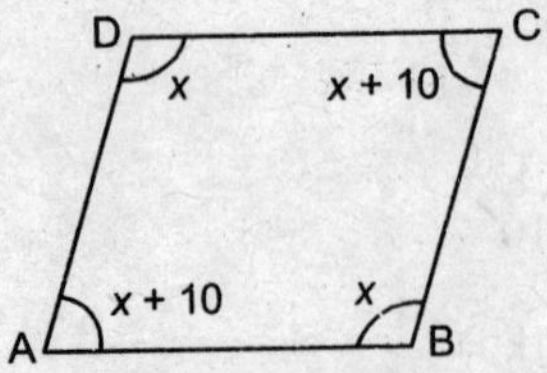

$\because$ ABCD is a ||gm

Let $\angle B = x°$

$\therefore$ $\angle A = (x + 10)°$

$\angle A + \angle B + \angle C + \angle D = 360°$

$\Rightarrow x + 10° + x + x + 10 + x = 360°$

$\Rightarrow$ $4x + 20° = 360°$

$\Rightarrow$ $4x = 340°$

$\Rightarrow$ $x = 85°$

$\therefore$ $\angle D = 85°$.

52. (C):

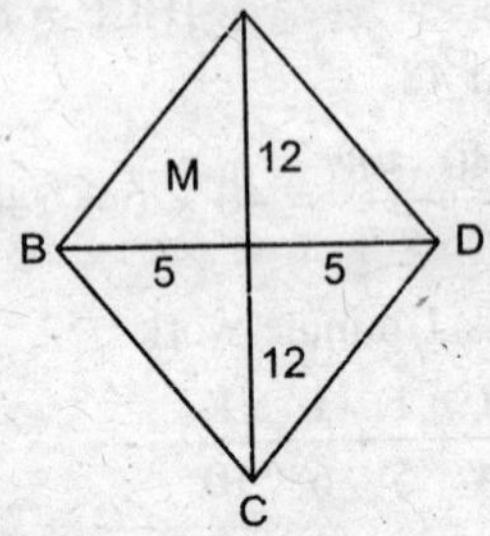

ABCD is a rhombus

In ΔABM,

$(AB)^2 = (12)^2 + (5)^2 = 144 + 25 = 169$

$\Rightarrow$ AB = 13 cm

Hence, the side of rhombus = 13 cm.

53. (C):

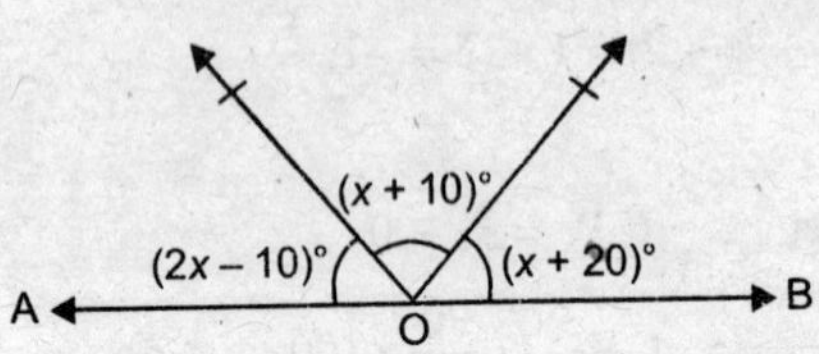

In the given figure, AOB is a straight line

$\therefore (2x - 10)° + (x + 10)° + (x + 20)° = 180°$

$\Rightarrow$ $4x + 20° = 180°$

$\Rightarrow$ $4x = 180° - 20° = 160°$

$\Rightarrow$ $x = 40°$.

54. (A)

55. (C): $\because$ Radius of semi circle = 7 cm

$\therefore$ Side of the square = 7 × 2 = 14 cm.

56. (D)

57. (A): Area of the figure = 119 cm^2.

58. (C): $x - 1, 2x - 1, 2x - 2, x - 1, 2x + 3$

$\because$ $x = 5$, then obtained marks are,

4, 9, 8, 4, 13

Mode of data = 4.

59. (C): First write the data in ascending order,

4, 4, 8, 9, 13

Here $n = 5$ which is odd

$\therefore$ median = $\frac{n+1}{2}$ th term

$= \frac{5}{2}$ th term

= 3rd term = 8

Hence, median = 8.

60. (B): Mean = $\frac{4+4+8+9+13}{5} = \frac{38}{5} = 7.6 = 8.$

61. (C)

62. (B): 'A' means –, 'B' means ÷, 'C' means +, 'D' means ×

$45 \div 3 + 18 - 4 \times 6$

$= 15 + 18 - 24 = 33 - 24 = 9.$

63. (A) **64. (C)** **65. (B)**

66. (B) **67. (A)**

68. (A):

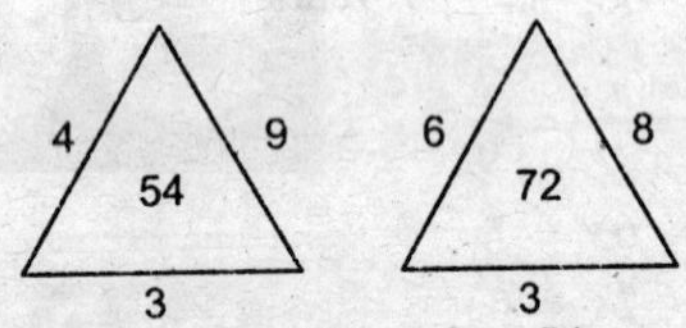

$4 \times 3 \times 9 \div 2 = 108 \div 2 = 54$

$6 \times 3 \times 8 \div 2 = 144 \div 2 = 72$

Hence, 72 will come at the place of question mark.

69. (B)

70. (D):

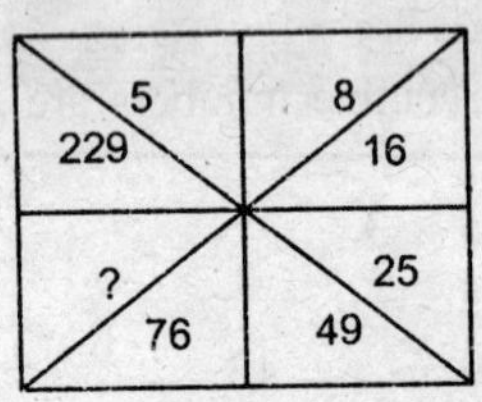

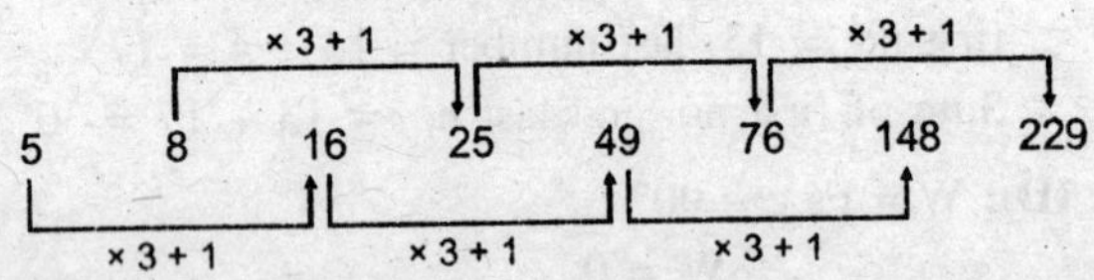

Hence, 148 will come at the place of question mark.

71. (C)

72. (B): 32 people like Cricket and Tennis both.

73. (B): Required % = 30.68%

74. (A): No. of people who likes Cricket

= 27 + 26 = 53

No. of people who likes Hockey = 27 + 27 = 54

No. of people who likes Tennis = 32 + 29 = 61

The ratio of C : H : T = 53 : 54 : 61.

75. (C): No. of people who likes Cricket, Tennis and Hockey all together = 15 which is common in all.

CUET-UG

SECTION-IA

ENGLISH LANGUAGE

Comprehension

Comprehension is a very important part of English paper. The questions on comprehension lay particular stress on understanding a given passage. You are required to read a passage or poem and answer a few questions based on it. Various comprehension questions are set solely with the objectives named below:

1. To test your ability to detect the central idea or the focal point in the given passage.
2. To test your ability to understand and interpret the given passage or poem.
3. To judge your capability to pick out the various arguments put forward by the writer for or against something.
4. To test your accuracy and richness of vocabulary.
5. To test your academic ability to understand the implied and the clearly and fully expressed ideas of the writer of the passage or poem.
6. To test, occasionally, your power of appreciating critically the views contained in the given passage or poem.

While answering comprehension questions, you must comply with the following important points:

1. First, read the whole passage or poem attentively, carefully and quickly.
2. Read it for the second time, slowly but steadily.
3. Work out the probable meaning of new words, from the context in which they have been used.
4. Underline and look for transitional words and phrases as an aid to comprehension.
5. The process of elimination should be used while selecting the correct answer.
6. Your answers should be brief and to the point, where-ever required.

I. CLOZE TEST

A cloze test is a procedure in which a person is asked to supply words that have been removed from a passage as a test of his ability to comprehend text. Practise it regularly to score well.

Directions: *In each of the following passages some numbered blank spaces are given. For each numbered blank space answer choices are given. Pick out the one which is the most appropriate for that blank space. Keep the trend of the passage in mind.*

PASSAGE-1

A drug which has been ....(1).... promoted here for fever and pain ....(2).... has invited medical ....(3).... over its ....(4).... side-effects following adverse reactions and its ....(5).... withdrawal in certain European countries. The scientific advisory committee has issued a ....(6).... advice on the ....(7).... of the drug ....(8).... some serious ....(9).... in the liver. While most doctors in India ....(10).... there is not need to ....(11).... yet, they also admit that they ....(12).... ....(13).... about it as most studies on the drug are industry ....(14).... .

QUESTIONS

1. A. aggressively B. astonishingly
C. surprisingly D. immensely

2. A. treatment B. relief
C. cure D. removal

3. A. concern B. criticism
C. discussion D. debate

4. A. probable B. probably
C. possible D. possibly

5. A. unconditional B. immediate
C. consequent D. subsequent

6. A. precautionary B. preliminary
C. formal D. informal

7. A. sell B. purchase
C. recommendation D. marketing

8. A. reminding B. following
C. thinking D. caring

9. A. complications B. problem
C. complexity D. consequences

10. A. suggest B. insist
C. lay D. say

11. A. worry B. react
C. panic D. exorbitant

12. A. think B. know
C. knew D. known

13. A. a bit B. a little
C. a few D. little

14. A. based B. sponsored
C. surveyed D. experimented

PASSAGE-2

I believe the biggest challenge ....(1).... the world is that of ....(2).... poverty across a large ....(3).... of the ....(4).... population and the continued ....(5).... between the rich and poor nations. The globalisation ....(6).... of the Nineties was ....(7).... to change all that and it has not made a significant impact as yet. Indeed, poverty today is the single biggest ....(8).... of place and democracy. It is high time that even the most ....(9).... rich citizen or indeed all of us ....(10).... people, realise that the only way to ....(11).... prosperity is to defeat poverty.

QUESTIONS

1. A. confronting B. facing
C. spoiling D. destroying

2. A. acute B. continued
C. general D. common

3. A. proportion B. share
C. portion D. fraction

4. A. universal B. en bloc
C. entire D. global

5. A. disputation B. disparity
C. discrimination D. tensile

6. A. struggle B. efforts
C. wave D. air

7. A. considered B. perpetually
C. supposed D. perhaps

8. A. curse B. enemy
C. hurdle D. obstruction

9. A. complacent B. compliant
C. fatuous D. inconsiderate

10. A. well-to-do B. cultured
C. privileged D. developed

11. A. defend B. debilitate
C. protect D. save

PASSAGE-3

What the daily newspapers nowadays ....(1).... carry are the reports of ...(2).... murders, killings, genocides and ....(3).... cleansing all over the world. India is not an exception ...(4).... For a moment one is sure ....(5).... the principle of religious tolerance, peace and ....(6)...., which were the ....(7).... of Indian society, that are now slowly but steadily ....(8).... hatred, anger, distrust and religious intolerance. Making things worse are the divisive practices being ....(9).... by some ....(10).... minds that have led to the rise of religious fundamentalism. And this is a ....(11)...., which is ....(12)..... in the form of hundreds of innocent lives being lost in all corners of the country.

QUESTIONS

1. A. usually B. generally
C. regularly D. casually

2. A. huge B. massive
C. brutal D. mass

3. A. ethnic B. ethical
C. evasive D. eventual

4. A. to it B. in it
C. for it D. on it

5. A. of thinking
B. to think about
C. to think of
D. thinking about

6. A. conscientious B. compassion
C. rapacity D. sagacity

7. A. heart B. core
C. cornerstones D. milestones

8. A. are replaced with
B. replaced by
C. being replaced by
D. being replaced with

9. A. precluded B. precipitated
C. predisposed D. fabricated

10. A. perverted B. scrupulous
C. nefarious D. ruthless

11. A. calumny B. bane
C. crass D. denouncement

12. A. visible B. coming
C. taking its toll D. resulting its toll.

PASSAGE-4

The outstanding ....(1)... of the development of science and technology can neither be realised nor enriched in an atmosphere with disturbed ....(2).... balance, ...(3).... to pollution hazards. The ....(4).... of pollution and conservation of the natural ecosystems in all the development efforts are ....(5).... not merely for the growth of our ....(6).... but for our very existence on this earth. It demands the ....(7)... that it deserves. Although ....(8).... is expressed in various circles for ....(9).... the environmental balance and ....(10).... of forests, but at the same time there is a large scale ....(11).... of forests, as ....(12).... evidenced in several river valley projects ....(13).... at the national level.

QUESTIONS

1. A. capacity B. potential C. possibility D. advancement
2. A. economical B. natural C. ecological D. polluting
3. A. susceptible B. adversely C. salubrious D. pernicious
4. A. removal B. eradication C. discarding D. evolution
5. A. imperil B. imminent C. impulsive D. imperative
6. A. status B. sociability C. economy D. environment
7. A. importance B. attention C. value D. care
8. A. interest B. enthusiasm C. deep concern D. anxiety
9. A. maintaining B. evolving C. developing D. rising
10. A. growing B. maintaining C. maintenance D. regeneration
11. A. degeneration B. degradation C. deprivation D. dereliction
12. A. blatantly B. vitally C. vividly D. indiscreetly
13. A. executed B. planned C. organised D. undertaken

PASSAGE-5

India is a country where women ....(1).... worshipped and ....(2).... at the same time. If mantras have been chanted to ....(3)... the Goddesses, ...(4).... have also been hurled at a domestic wife questioning her devotion and ....(5).... . Their position has remained more or less the same ....(6).... . Though women have taken ....(7).... since the country achieved independence, they still are a ....(8).... of political, socio-economic and legal neglect. The current year has seen a number of government ....(9).... to empower women. Though these are ....(10)...., much will depend on the ....(11).... implementation of these schemes or else they ....(12).... achieve the targets, they have set for themselves.

QUESTIONS

1. A. are B. were C. has been D. have been
2. A. cursed B. blamed C. crucified D. insulted
3. A. placate B. please C. plead D. respect
4. A. curses B. expletives C. obscenity D. objurgation
5. A. virginity B. purity C. chastity D. fecundity
6. A. till date B. over time C. till now D. until now.
7. A. remarkable progress B. advancement C. rapid strides D. important steps
8. A. object B. subject C. matter D. victim
9. A. machinery B. initiatives C. project D. plannings
10. A. laudable B. languor C. lascivious D. lassitude
11. A. efficient B. thorough C. appropriate D. effective
12. A. would not B. should not C. will not D. cannot

PASSAGE-6

We are ....(1).... about our success and failure in every field. No doubt, we start our actions with ....(2).... but still in a corner of our mind ....(3).... about success and failure and ....(4).... makes us tense. And this tension sometimes ....(5).... that it effects our efficiency and performance. So, we ....(6).... remember that the mind is efficient ....(7).... it is cool, not hot or tense. The tease or excited mind ....(8).... produce rational concepts or ....(9).... thought processes. A calm person has his senses fully ....(10).... with the environment ....(11).... he places himself. A restless person ....(12).... notice anything, consequently he gets into trouble with himself and others and ....(13).... everything.

QUESTIONS

1. A. always worried B. anxious always
C. curious always D. in doubt-always

2. A. over-confidence B. full confidence
C. full enthusiasm D. full effort

3. A. a doubt remains still
B. remains a doubt
C. still remians a doubt
D. a doubt still remains

4. A. intentionally B. unnecessarily
C. necessarily D. unconsciously

5. A. become so intense
B. grow so much
C. become so intensive
D. become so serious

6. A. must B. have to
C. will have to D. shall have to

7. A. when B. when only
C. only then when D. only when

8. A. can never B. could not
C. connot D. possibly

9. A. obnoxious B. obligatory
C. objective D. orderly

10. A. engrossed B. paralleled
C. identified D. sunk

11. A. on which B. in which
C. at which D. where

12. A. do not B. does not
C. did not D. cannot

PASSAGE-7

Great books do not spring from something ....(1).... in the great men who wrote them. They are the ....(2).... of their very core, the ....(3).... of the life itself of the authors. And literature cannot be said to ....(4).... its true purpose. Until it ....(5).... translated into the actual life of him who reads. Literature is the ....(6).... of true ideas and high emotions and life is ....(7).... of ideas and emotions. In a world ....(8).... of literature, the intellectual and emotional activity of all ....(9)... exceptionally gifted men would quickly sink and ....(10).... to a narrow circle. The broad, the noble, the generous would tend to disappear ....(11).... accessible storage. And life would be ....(12).... degraded, because the ....(13).... idea and the pretty emotion would never feel the upward pull of the ideas and emotions of genius.

QUESTIONS

1. A. accidental B. remarkable
C. strange D. superficial

2. A. affluence B. effluence
C. excellence D. magnificence

3. A. outcome B. offspring
C. flow D. expression

4. A. have served B. done
C. achieve D. accomplished

5. A. is B. has been
C. gets D. has

6. A. store B. stock
C. vast reservoir D. huge collection

7. A. expression B. expansion
C. storage D. constituted

8. A. devout B. devolve
C. deterrent D. deprived

9. A. but few B. except
C. but a few D. people

10. A. die B. spoil
C. dissolve D. retract

11. A. for want of B. desiring
C. searching D. for

12. A. altogether B. correspondingly
C. contrarily D. actually

13. A. beautiful B. ornamental
C. stupid D. fallacious

PASSAGE-8

Patriotism is one of the qualities that touches the heart of the ....(1).... countrymen. When a soldier fights and dies in saving his country from the enemy, his sacrifice in this way is termed as ....(2).... and attains the ....(3).... worthy of worship. Thus in a war the soldier gets ....(4).... without surrendering, by which he ....(5).... saved his life, ...(6).... the hearts of his fellow being. This situation is true not only in ....(7).... an enemy but anyone who struggles to acheive a ....(8).... aim without surrendering and ....(9).... his life. He ....(10).... succeeded but he leaves a ....(11).... for others to follow who will definitely win and attain the victory ....(12).... the adversaries..

QUESTIONS

1. A. humble B. rustic
C. fellow D. sophisticated

2. A. intelligent B. virtuous
C. supreme D. courageous

3. A. death B. martyrdom
C. end D. goal

4. A. vanquished B. vanguard
C. reward D. award

5. A. would have had B. would be able to
C. would have D. could have

6. A. attracting B. winning
C. taking D. getting

7. A. struggling B. killing
C. winning D. fighting

8. A. esteemed B. high
C. patriotic D. laudable

9. A. offers B. sacrifices
C. lays D. present

10. A. could have B. could not have
C. may have D. may not have

11. A. trail B. trial
C. goal D. situation

12. A. upon B. over
C. on D. against

PASSAGE-9

Our beautiful sunbright ....(1).... is being systematically damaged by industrial pollution ....(2).... into rivers like the Ganga and Jamuna, ...(3).... wastes from atomic plants ....(4).... into-the world's oceans, and poisonous gases ....(5).... with the ozonosphere. ....(6)...., tropical rain forests and green pastures are ....(7).... under the pressure of a ....(8).... population. Rivers like the Narmada are being dammed to change nature's ....(9).... surface ....(10).... between flora and fauna, and sloping mountain terrain is being ....(11).... into mini oceans to supply electricity to the ....(12).... industrial stomach of our age.

QUESTIONS

1. A. ecology
B. ecosystem
C. environment
D. physical phenomena

2. A. directed B. channelled
C. scattered D. accumulated

3. A. atomic B. scientific
C. nuclear D. bumptious

4. A. diverted B. routed
C. outstretched D. overflown

5. A. channelled B. routed
C. scattered D. mixed

6. A. Besides B. Instead
C. Addition to D. Above all

7. A. diminishing B. reducing
C. minimising D. disappearing

8. A. proliferating B. profiting
C. projecting D. pronounceable

9. A. smooth B. well balanced
C. rough D. unequal

10. A. equilibrium B. equality
C. equation D. equity

11. A. contracted B. convulsed
C. conjured D. converted

12. A. hungry B. greedy
C. vacant D. ever starving

PASSAGE-10

Only ....(1)...., people find a long journey by motor-car ....(2).... . Mostly a long journey by train is much more comfortable and ....(3).... . The tracks, the coaches and the smooth though swift motion ....(4).... the pleasantness of the train journey. ....(5).... at the beautiful countryside from a window seat in a fast moving train has a ....(6).... of its own. A night journey ....(7).... its pleasures too. One can experience a sense of adventure ....(8).... a restful sleep. Modern railway travel being ....(9)... comfortable than in the past, ...(10).... the childhood excitement of ....(11).... the train and its engine as ....(12).... of visual and imaginative delight.

QUESTIONS

1. A. exceptionally B. ordinarily
C. unusually D. abnormally

2. A. disagreeable B. unenjoyable
C. strange D. agreeable

3. A. enjoyable B. suitable
C. appropriate D. enjoying

4. A. hike B. jolt
C. contribute D. all add to

5. A. Observing B. Enjoying
C. To look D. Looking

6. A. comfort B. complacence
C. delight D. satisfaction

7. A. had B. has
C. have D. has have

8. A. alongwith B. together with
C. addition to D. adding to

9. A. highly B. extensively
C. exceptionally D. so much more

10. A. revives B. vibrates
C. regenerates D. enliven

11. A. fancying B. enjoying
C. feeling D. dreaming

12. A. subjects B. objects
C. centre D. focus

PASSAGE-11

Women were earlier considered as the kitchen keepers and house keepers – that was ....(1).... as their ....(2)... field of activity. ....(3)... women began to get educated and came out ....(4)... the social and potitical field and today they are there in all fields and are ....(5)... equal emloyment as the menfolk. Not only this they are ....(6)... themselves in those fields. Two important reasons behind the changed ....(7)... are : firstly, Womens are ....(8)... themselves duly qualified and want to use-their talents to seek an employment; and secondly, with the price-index ....(9).... everyday it is found necessary for the middle class families that the wife having ....(10).... academic qualifications working and ....(11).... the family income. This while giving them a social status, also helps the family to have a better standard of living, which everyone ....(12).... for and rightly too.

QUESTIONS

1. A. recognised B. realized
C. regarded D. looked

2. A. exclusive B. only
C. working D. one

3. A. Day by day B. Slowly
C. Later D. Gradually

4. A. on B. in
C. at D. to

5. A. finding B. seeking
C. enjoying D. sharing

6. A. distinguishing B. proving
C. mastering D. struggling

7. A. scenario B. circumstances
C. society D. culture

8. A. thinking B. finding
C. educating D. proving

9. A. excelating B. intensifying
C. changing D. escalating

10. A. registered B. recognised
C. requisite D. minimum

11. A. substituting B. segment
C. influencing D. suplement

12. A. do crave B. does crave
C. starve D. do starve

PASSAGE-12

Importance of music especially in today's hum drum life cannot be ....(1).... Today man is surrounded by ....(2).... worries and listening to music ....(3).... his nerves. Music acts as a ....(4).... and soothes the nerves. It is a fine art and groups of all ages ....(5).... to its sweet sound. A person gifted with aesthetic ....(6).... finds music as a food for his soul. Some of the great musicians of the world ....(7).... in high esteem ....(8).... of the kind of they produce western, oriental, classical, pop or light. These musicians ....(9).... concerts which attract people from all walks of life. If people are ....(10).... to balming music, they will definitely find life a rich and healthy ....(11)..... In this way, the importance of music is really ....(12).... .

QUESTIONS

1. A. overstated B. understated
C. irrelevant D. relevant

2. A. varied B. innumerable
C. different D. variegated

3. A. calm B. cure
C. soothe D. please

4. A. stimulant B. catalyst
C. machinery D. device

5. A. are attracted B. get attracted
C. are pleased D. feel pleasure

6. A. beauty B. blessing
C. capabilities D. knowledge

7. A. were held B. are held
C. are taken D. are received

8. A. no matter B. considering
C. respectively D. irrespective

9. A. popularize B. organize
C. form D. propagate

10. A. forced B. brought
C. introduced D. exposed

11. A. stage B. experience
C. achievement D. thing

12. A. considerable B. unavoidable
C. imimense D. recognisable

PASSAGE-13

There are groups of people in ....(1).... developing countries who are in poverty line and who became the victims and ....(2).... in a self-fulfilling vicious of poverty. ....(3).... of the parents in the society ....(4).... afford to send their children to school. ....(5)...., the children often go to the labour force ....(6).... in order to ....(7).... the family income and to help the economic ....(8).... of the family. The Indian Government and educational ....(9).... are taking adequate steps for their standard of living and ....(10).... opportunities for schooling with full day food and other required ...(11)... .

QUESTIONS

1. A. each B. all C. whole D. every
2. A. engulfed B. surrounded C. trapped D. fall
3. A. line B. circle C. frame D. structure
4. A. can't B. couldn't C. cannot D. can never
5. A. Though B. Despite C. Instead D. Even so
6. A. at an early age B. in his growing stage C. in his childhood D. at his childhood
7. A. add B. supplement C. hike D. improve
8. A. servility B. survivality C. conditon D. situation
9. A. activist B. executives C. planners D. propagonist
10. A. approving B. alloting C. distributing D. providing
11. A. privileges B. facilities C. necessities D. factors

PASSAGE-14

What is urgently, ...(1).... in our country is a proper survey and a planned assessment of what sort of jobs ....(2).... demand both in the public as well as in the private sector and there ....(3).... a controlled enrolment in institutes and institutions which should be training young men in such needed jobs. It is a ....(4).... task, no doubt, but when the government and the private agencies ....(5).... make large scale survey for so many other problems of the country why cannot this grave problem of unemployment be ....(6).... at a priority basis and money and manpower be invested and ....(7).... to make an assessment of the requirements and then the process of their fulmilment ....(8).... . What is actually needed is not only scheming and planning but actually to have a ....(9)... to find the root of the ....(10).... . Only then can the ....(11).... be found out.

QUESTIONS

1. A. demanded B. needed C. prevalent D. lacking
2. A. are of B. are at C. are most in D. currently
3. A. needs to be B. is C. are D. shall be
4. A. labourious B. Herculean C. time taking D. stupendous
5. A. can B. could C. are out to D. readily
6. A. noticed B. surveyed C. treated D. observed
7. A. used B. employed C. organised D. treated
8. A. be worked out B. be taken up C. be decided D. be developed
9. A. spirit B. will C. motive D. strength
10. A. malady B. grievances C. curse D. paradox
11. A. treatment B. cure C. remedy D. solution

PASSAGE-15

A sudden flood of ....(1).... dangerous toys like swords and bow and arrow make their ....(2).... in the market during the Dussehra festival. ....(3)...., eyes can and do get injured ....(4).... by these toys and ....(5)...., the victims aare innocent children. ....(6).... by the Ram Lila and similar television serials, children ....(7).... swords at each other or fire arrows from bows which ....(8).... to permanent blindness if ....(9).... to hit the eye. This happens ....(10).... if the injury is servere and not managed properly. Any injury in and around the eye ....(11).... taken seriously land managed on an emergency basis.

QUESTIONS

1. A. potentially B. instantly C. constantly D. inevitably
2. A. arrival B. appearance C. place D. position
3. A. unknowingly B. undoubtedly C. undauntedly D. unfortunately
4. A. advertently B. inadvertently C. unfortunately D. unknowingly
5. A. almost B. almost always C. all the time D. very often

6. A. Motivated B. Inspired
C. Encouraged D. Taught

7. A. attack B. take out
C. brandish D. home

8. A. can lead B. could lead
C. would lead D. lead

9. A. it targets B. it comes
C. they happen D. they are

10. A. usually B. generally
C. commonly D. more often

11. A. are to be B. is to be
C. shall be D. may be

PASSAGE-16

The scientist of today is a man of ....(1).... ambition. He is not contented with ....(2).... he has achieved, but wants to be a creator of new and surprising things so that the common people may ....(3).... at the marvels of his ....(4)...., feel thrilled and go away ....(5).... by his superior wisdom and his ....(6).... inventiveness. The new and challenging scientific forces now ....(7).... by him in the universe will continue to work ....(8).... in ever increasing numbers, to lead mankind to ....(9).... material progress, and to ....(10).... in its hand unlimited power for conquering ....(11).... territories of knowledge and experience.

QUESTIONS

1. A. increasing B. elevating
C. soaring D. diversing

2. A. what B. whatever
C. those D. that

3. A. broad B. work
C. gape D. deride

4. A. invention B. genius
C. life D. achievement

5. A. impressed B. dejected
C. attracted D. motivated

6. A. enviable B. reliable
C. unavoidable D. considerable

7. A. brought B. given
C. let loose D. realised

8. A. fruitfully B. miracles
C. magic D. wonders

9. A. unscathed B. unrelenting
C. unmitigated D. unprecedented

10. A. keep B. allot
C. load D. place

11. A. greater B. varied
C. unknown D. more and more

PASSAGE-17

Education of the future has to ....(1).... human values and see that the human factor is not neglected. The task of education is to help the individual to know himself. ....(2).... as the individual is ignorant of his ....(3)...., his potentialites and his mission of life, he ....(4).... contribute in a creative manner ....(5).... his own growth and development of the society. It is often said that, as education is the ....(6).... of the thinking elite of the nation, ...(7).... the nation's future depends on its system of education. This is true to some ....(8).... .But ....(9)...., the general outlook of society has also a strong ....(10).... on education itself so that education can only be reformed when a ....(11).... change has already begun in society.

QUESTIONS

1. A. consider B. protect
C. care D. preserve

2. A. Till then B. So long
C. Uptill then D. Till that time

3. A. own B. credibilities
C. nature D. real self

4. A. can't B. could not
C. could never D. cannot

5. A. in B. throughout
C. to D. towards

6. A. developing process B. development
C. building up D. guidance

7. A. much of B. many of
C. mostly D. mainly

8. A. limit B. horizon
C. context D. extent

9. A. conversely B. alternately
C. actually D. outwardly

10. A. hearing B. relation
C. opposition D. affinity

11. A. consequent B. corresponding
C. subsequent D. similar

PASSAGE-18

Every action we perform ....(1).... a result. And, naturally, we lay claim ....(2).... the results or fruits ....(3).... from that action in the ....(4).... that it is we who perform the action. This is .....(5).... ignorance because ....(6).... is it the Lord who ....(7).... the result of any action, it is by His will ....(8).... that even the action is accomplished. The will of the Lord ....(9).... whether we cooperate with His will or strive ....(10).... If God wills that an action takes place, he arranges for the ....(11).... for it to happen. It is ....(12).... experience that sometimes despite our best efforts we ....(13).... achieve the results we desire, and at other times the seemingly most ....(14).... situations mysteriously get ....(15).... . ....(16).... way man chooses to act, both the act and the outcome of the cost are dependent ....(17).... on the will of the Lord.

QUESTIONS

1. A. produce B. produces C. causes D. undergoes
2. A. on B. at C. to D. for
3. A. occuring B. obtaining C. deriving D falling
4. A. belief B. hope C. fantasy D. folly
5. A. sheen B. keen C. sheer D. sheathe
6. A. alone B. only that C. not only D. for only
7. A. declares B. decides C. ordains D. ornate
8. A. completely B. entirely C. only D. alone
9. A. prevails always B. prevails everywhere C. is prevalent D. always prevails
10. A. alone B. always C. constantly D. independently
11. A. wherewithal B. whereabouts C. whatsoever D. wherefore
12. A. usual B. general C. universal D. common
13. A. does not B. may not C. do not D. might not
14. A. intractable B. intangible C. internecine D. intricate
15. A. subsided B. resolved C. solved D. converted
16. A. Whatever B. All the C. All those D. Whichever
17. A. mainly B. actually C. entirely D. generally

PASSAGE-19

For centuries, women not only in India but all over the world ....(1).... treated as ....(2).... secondary position to men. ....(3).... human history men ....(4).... far greater power then women to name, classify, and order the worlds in which they both live. ....(5).... studies in various parts of the world point out to a wide ....(6).... in male and female roles ....(7).... cultures and demonstrate the possibility of change in these sex-determined roles. The 20th century in particular ....(8).... the cause of gender justice by internationalizing struggles for equality ....(9).... women and other oppressed people. Women's struggles against their ....(10).... were interwined in ....(11).... degrees with ideologies and movements based on the values of freedom, self-determination, equality, democracy and justice.

QUESTIONS

1. A. has been B. have been C. had been D. were
2. A. occupying B. taking C. possessing D. serving
3. A. All through B. Throughout C. Since D. From
4. A. have B. had C. have had D. enjoy
5. A. Sociological B. Anthropological C. General D. Practical
6. A. concord B. repulsion C. disagreement D. variation
7. A. among B. across C. between D. of
8. A. developed B. envolved C. promoted D. entertained
9. A. for B. to C. among D. by
10. A. subsidiary B. subsequent C. subservience D. subordination
11. A. various B. varying C changing D. differeing

PASSAGE-20

What is required today in our country is ....(1).... of a new political culture based on full respect for human liberty, on pluralism and on a better social deal for all. The major ....(2).... facing us today is to carry out democratic transformation in all the ....(3)...., social, cultural, economic and political. The events of the 20th century ....(4).... one thing absolutely clear that human ....(5)...., everywhere, specially in countries whose political structures were ....(6).... to reflect the revolutionary aspirations of the people ....(7).... not only under stress and strain but are ....(8).... vast upheavals because of the ....(9).... of democracy. At the same time it has also to be understood that democracy cannot be ....(10).... into a static mould.

QUESTIONS

1. A. growing B. developing
   C. creating D. creation
2. A. development B. crisis
   C. challenge D. drawback
3. A. corners B. context
   C. realm D. spheres
4. A. have made B. has made
   C. had made D. made
5. A. travails B. traverse
   C. trapse D. transverse
6. A. supposed B. meant
   C. caused D. forced
7. A. were B. was
   C. are D. have been
8. A. developing B. evolving
   C. experiencing D. faced with
9. A. denial B. rebuff
   C. rebuttal D. absence
10. A. shaped B. flex
    C. frozen D. caused

PASSAGE-21

We are living in very exciting ....(1).... . The ....(2).... change is dizzying and the impact this progress is having on our present and – more importantly – on our future is difficult to ....(3).... in its ...(4).... . This is the age of ....(5).... micro processors, sophisticated software, new hardware technology and high bandwith, high-speed networks. The PC gave us a new way to work, play and ....(6).... . In fact, it brought ....(7).... our desktops computing power, which until a few years ....(8).... had only been available to corporates. With the ....(9).... of the internet, the PC ....(10).... us the most convenient and flexible way to head on to the Net.

QUESTIONS

1. A. periods B. days
   C. phase D. times
2. A. phase B. pace
   C. sphere D. drastic
3. A. guess B. forecast
   C. comprehend D. approximate
4. A. whole B. entirety
   C. fruition D. fullness
5. A. strong B. changing
   C. powerful D. sonorous
6. A. convey B. communicate
   C. entertain D. enjoy
7. A. onto B. to
   C. on D. at
8. A. back B. earlier
   C. behind D. before
9. A. addendum B. adherence
   C. afoot D. advent
10. A. allowed B. privileged
    C. brought D. offered

PASSAGE-22

Visualisation is a strong ....(1).... to memory. Those persons who ...... (2) ..... a powerful memory cannot do so without taking the help of visualisaton. Such persons have developed the .o ....(3).... visualisation even in such ....(4).... tasks as remembering names and numbers. These persons have the names and numbers ....(5).... in their brain even after hearing those names and figues only once. On the other hand those who take the help of revising to memorise ....(6).... to forget it once they have ....(7).... the practice of revising ....(8).... the ones who have applied visualisation to memorise. Psychologists ....(9).... in visualisation a powerful tool for personality development. The more you visualise, the more you are ....(10).... your attitude and behaviour to the blue prints of your vision and ....(11).... more you are inching towards success.

QUESTIONS

1. A. way B. path
   C. aid D. symptom
2. A. command B. master
   C. rule D. enjoy
3. A. use B. apply
   C. put D. place
4. A. trivial B. difficult
   C. mundane D. unscrupulous
5. A. impress B. imprinted
   C. impinge D. store
6. A. bent B. incline
   C. prone d. tend
7. A. dropped B. left
   C. gave up D. given up
8. A. unlike B. opposite
   C. contrary D. not like
9. A. found B. have found
   C. sees D. finds
10. A. shaping B. moulding
    C. making D. attuning
11. A. actually B. factually
    C. subsequently D. consequently

PASSAGE-23

....(1).... people today remember the war that was fought after China invaded India in 1962. Not because the war was never really ....(2).... . Nor because it was ....(3).... almost before it began. The reason is ....(4).... that most of us were yet to be born. The main reason for the Chinese attack seems to ....(5).... to establish the ....(6).... order, expose our ....(7)...., put us in our place. The official reason, ...(8)...., was the territorial dispute, ...(9).... more than 100,000 square kilometres. ....(10).... speaking, India borders Tibet, not China. The McMohan Line ....(11).... the border with Tibet in what is now Arunachal Pradesh was the result of a 1914 treaty ....(12).... British India and Tibet. This was not ....(13).... to the Chinese the result was a .....(14)..... nose. The Chinese attack was ....(15).... fast and furious. ....(16).... brave soldiers ....(17).... down their lives, but India was simply unable to halt the ....(17).... . Panic quickly ....(18)....

QUESTIONS

1. A. A few B. Few
C. Fewer D. A little

2. A. joined B. combined
C. acted D. approved

3. A. finished B. ceased
C. over D. stopped

4. A. simple B. simply
C. common D. commonly

5. A. had been B. have
C. had D. have been

6. A. pecking B. unavoiding
C. powerful D. selfish

7. A. projections B. pretensions
C. presumption D. pretending

8. A. more over B. probably
C. perhaps D. however

9. A. effecting B. causing
C. affecting D. influencing

10. A. Formally B. Informally
C. Broadly D. Technically

11. A. relating B. dividing
C. defining D. laying

12. A. among B. between
C. of D. by

13. A. favourable B. favoured
C. acceptable D. accepting

14. A. angry B. bloody
C. honed D. blitz

15. A. quick B. prick
C. sudden D. unassuming

16. A. Some B. Few
C. Many D. A lot of

17. A. onrush B. onset
C. omnipotence D. omen

18. A. come in B. gone in
C. set in D. set out

PASSAGE-24

Man has always been ....(1).... with flying because it ....(2).... a sense of freedom, of romance and thrill-something too ....(3).... to resist. It is the task of the ....(4).... of the skies to safeguard Indian air-space from unwelcome ....(5)..... . The Indian Air Force ....(6).... a chequered and glorious history. From its ....(7).... days of single-engine aeroplanes like Tempests and Spitfires to the state of the art multi-engine, supersonic MIG and Sukhoi fighters, the Indian Air Force ....(8).... a long way. In addition to the already existing ....(9).... of aircraft and weapon systems, plans are ....(10).... to enhance its air defence power and ....(11).... capability through upgradation and ....(12).... .

QUESTIONS

1. A. fascinated B. moved
C. inspired D. fancied

2. A. generates B. cultivates
C. reaps D. evokes

3. A. envisaging B. impressing
C. enchanting D. laudable

4. A. sentiness B. sedulous
C. venturous D. fervid

5. A. emigrants B. intruders
C. foreigners D. tourists

6. A. had B. have
C. have had D. has had

7. A. early B. undeveloped
C. growing D. embryonic

8. A. had come B. has come
C. have come D. came

9. A. invention B. inventory
C. mechanism D. technique

10. A. progressive B. afresh
C. afoot D. affluent

11. A. combat B. increase
C. intensify D. ensure

12. A. acquistion
B. acknowledgement
C. acquiescence
D. accumulation

PASSAGE-25

Libraries were never ....(1).... the place to ....(2).... They never will be. But those who've visited libraries for the ....(3).... pleasure of it will testify to the feeling of ....(4).... on entering the labyrinth ....(5).... high with books. Suddenly, a ....(6).... spent reading seems the ideal. It's a similar experience to ....(7).... in a bookshop. The difference : in the second situation, despair ....(8).... you as your eyes zoom ....(9).... on the price; in the first there is the ....(10).... that all these books are yours for the asking. Today, ...(11)...., liberary use is almost ....(12).... necessity-based. The reading room is ....(13).... full with students poring ....(14).... their books..

QUESTIONS

1. A. realised B. seen
C. recognised D. considered

2. A. hung out B. hang out
C. hang out in D. hung out in

3. A. mere B. sheer
C. trivial D. trifle

4. A. exhilaration B. exhaustion
C. expedition D. extrapolation

5. A. going B. moving
C. pik D. towering

6. A. long time B. whole life
C. life time D. life long

7. A. browsing B. move about
C. move D. stroll

8. A. swamps B. swab
C. swoon D. swoop

9. A. at B. on
C. in D. upon

10. A. idea B. surity
C. certainty D. knowledge

11. A. although B. however
C. in fact D. moreover

12. A. wholly B. partially
C. outwardly D. purely

13. A. tight B. completely
C. over crowded D. cramped

14. A. into B. onto
C. over D. upon

PASSAGE-26

The ....(1).... of a country does not depend on the abundance of its revenue but more ....(2).... by its citizens; its men of education, enlightenment and character. It is for the ....(3).... of higher learning to ....(4).... an academic environment of equity, justice and fair play where those ....(5).... in the ....(6).... task of nation building can ....(7).... their responsibilities in a spirit of sincerity, dedication and commitment. Higher education in India ....(8).... great strides after independence. The ideal of education is to ....(9).... for self-preservation but which also prepares us to recognise and ....(10).... the rights of others and to shoulder our ....(11).... as responsible citizens.

QUESTIONS

1. A. prospects B. fortune
C. protrusion D. gaiety

2. A. illustrated B. emancipated
C. defined D. apprehended

3. A. institute B. centre
C. college D. university

4. A. encourage B. embark
C. promote D. polish

5. A. employed B. recruited
C. held D. engaged

6. A. paramount B. ardous
C. lucrative D. laudable

7. A. dispense B. disburse
C. carry D. discharge

8. A. have taken B. had taken
C. has taken D. is taking

9. A. evoke B. prepare
C. encourage D. cultivate

10. A. concede B. preserve
C. coddle D. clung

11. A. obligations B. obduracy
C. obsequiousness D. portfolio

PASSAGE-27

Observation is one of the key ....(1).... of modern corporate behaviour. Indeed it has long been the ....(2).... for humans and animals generally. It is essential for every corporate citizen to be able to taste the ....(3).... of what is happening around him all the time, not merely to survive but to ....(4).... . ....(5).... the corporate corridors to check which way the wind is blowing ! Know when it is appropriate to get your ....(6).... in and when it is ....(7).... to maintain a low profile. To ....(8).... a career with the ease and ....(9).... of a winner, you need to be able to ....(10).... a disaster before it happens ! You need to take an advantage before someone else ....(11).... . You need to be at the right place before someone else ....(12).... there. Observation or paying attention to what's happening around us is essential ....(13).... . We need to take the time to ....(14).... the habit of paying attention so that we can make our work ....(15).... and so that we can stand at ease! Career ,...(16).... will be the happy outcome!

QUESTIONS

1. A. approach B. method C. tactics D. means
2. A. rule B. norm C. convention D. technique
3. A. presence B. essence C. events D. problem
4. A. thrive B. throb C. fare D. blow
5. A. Sniff B. Snuffle C. Spin-off D. Splutter
6. A. shore B. oar C. objective D. ogle
7. A. correct B. right C. prudent D. prudish
8. A. carry B. initiate C. continue D. conduct
9. A. caprice B. comfort C. over-confidence D. aplomb
10. A. forecast B. apprehend C. guess D. foretell
11. A. do B. does C. takes D. gets
12. A. come B. comes C. get D. gets
13. A. everytime B. alltime C. everywhere D. forever
14. A. reap B. sow C. cultivate D. grow
15. A. easy B. easier C. easiest D. simple
16. A. advancement B. progression C. achievement D. cultivation

PASSAGE-28

The ....(1).... Euphoria over the ....(2).... fall in the cost of domestic air travel has ....(3).... to a more realistic appraisal of what is on offer. The aggressive ....(4).... schemes offered since the beginning of July have certainly been good news for certain categories of passengers who probably value .....(5).... above anything else. For them, the heavily discounted fare ....(6).... enables them to afford air travel for the first time. In fact, the ....(7).... of the fare cut ....(8).... such that in specific instances air travel compares ....(9).... to the fares charged by the Railways for upper class travel. Obviously, it ....(10).... for a change in mindset to switch to air travel in ....(11).... to, say, rail transport in India. Economy and affordability will certainly be key ....(12).... but they must be made available ....(13).... a fairly long period. To put it differently, cheaper air travel or at least a ....(14).... fare structure ....(15).... institutionalised in the country.

QUESTIONS

1. A. embryonic B. early C. ending D. initial
2. A. casual B. sudden C. surprising D. dramatic
3. A. raised B. caused C. given way D. gave way
4. A. lucrative B. lofty C. laudable D. promotional
5. A. expenses B. affordability C. comfort D. time
6. A. scheme B. structure C. system D. circular
7. A. portion B. ratio C. magnitude D. proportion
8. A. are B. is C. has been D. have been
9. A. very slightly B. very favourably C. specifially D. generally
10. A. causes B. calls C. invites D. lures
11. A. choice B. favour C. preference D. alternative
12. A. determinants B. detrimenetals C. performers D. issues
13. A. over B. for C. to D. through
14. A. different B. distinctive C. reducing D. differential
15. A. must be B. has to be C. ought to be D. have to be

PASSAGE-29

"I need a break" is a common ..... (1) ..... among the ....(2).... middle and elite classes – under ....(3).... pressure to perform, to live up to their own artificial standards, to earn, and earn some more and ....(4).... some more. But in this vortex, time is at a ....(5)...., and the much needed break ....(6).... materialises because harried professionals are unable to stay away from work long enough ....(7).... from the city and breathe in some fresh air—metaphorically and literally. And weekends? They are ....(8).... lazing at home, ...(9).... on chores, or may be watching some mind numbing television programme. Because it would be hard to think of a place you ....(10).... escape to that was far enough from the city to be ....(11).... and yet close enough to ....(12).... as a weekend break.

QUESTIONS

1. A. restrain B. refrain
C. remark D. saying
2. A. hurried B. harried
C. worried D. busy
3. A. continuous B. consequent
C. constant D. stable
4. A. even B. add
C. farther D. then
5. A. premium B. minimum
C. limitation D. restriction
6. A. never often B. often never
C. although never D. sometimes do not
7. A. to stay away B. to escape
C. to go away D. to get moved
8. A. there B. for
C. those D. some
9. A. getting B. catching
C. catching up D. catching down
10. A. can B. ever
C. would D. could
11. A. refreshed B. refreshing
C. resting D. rejoining
12. A. consider B. anticipate
C. contemplate D. meditate

PASSAGE-30

Every monsoon I'm reminded of an incident that ....(1).... many years ago when I was a young man ....(2).... my first job in Mumbai. I was staying with my sister in those days. On one wet and windy night I ....(3).... with friends, and as it happens when you are in pleasant company, the ....(4).... . It was past ten when I finally bid goodby to my companions and moved towards my sister's house. It had rained the whole day, and it ....(5).... to drizzle again. The rain had ....(6).... people indoors earlier than usual and the dimly-lit street I was walking along was ....(7).... . I had heard that the road was ....(8).... . They said one could hear a woman calling for help on some nights. As I proceeded, I suddenly saw a figure walking ....(9).... me. A bandicoot chose to ....(10).... across my path, just then she seemed to have ....(11).... into thin air. Then I heard a faint ....(12).... for help. This frightened me and as such I turned and fled. The next morning I came to know from my sister that the bandicoot was no other but her friend who had mistakenly thought she was being ....(13).... . Out of fear she was looking behind and walking when she ....(14).... into a ditch. Now every monsoon, I'm reminded of my ....(15).... on that wet night.

QUESTIONS

1. A. happened B. occured
C. took place D. had taken place
2. A. in B. on
C. working at D. working with
3. A. had been out B. went for outing
C. had gone D. was out
4. A. time passes B. time runs
C. time flies D. time files
5. A. has B. was
C. began D. had begun
6. A. pushed B. sent
C. send D. driven
7. A. calm B. peace
C. lonely D. deserted
8. A. mysterious B. ghostly
C. haunted D. devilish
9. A. before B. in front of
C. a head D. near
10. A. scuttle B. scurry
C. scuff D. scrouge
11. A. faded B. vanished
C. vaporised D. melted
12. A. sound B. voice
C. cry D. whisper
13. A. followed B. chased
C. pursued D. caught
14. A. fall B. stumbled
C. threw D. jumped
15. A. foolishness B. ignorance
C. confusion D. cowardice

PASSAGE-31

Most of India's educational institutions, ...(1).... by hiring people who are ....(2).... qualified to be teachers. They are ....(3).... an unhappy group, which is ill-paid and which commands ....(4).... respect. Sadly, it is these men and women who have the enormous duty of ...(5).... tomorrow's society, a responsibility that remains ...(6)... . Children are ....(7).... in this terrifying circle : they are ....(8).... into submission, their innocence is destroyed and their lives become ....(9).... joyless. What follows is still ....(10).... . A violent childhood ....(11).... a violent adulthood. A child who faces the ....(12).... of an adult grows up ....(13).... that violence is the answer to all problems. They become ....(14).... individuals and often their intellectual development ....(15).... in the absence of congenial peace.

QUESTIONS

1. A. get away B. manage
C. run D. go away

2. A. not really B. really not
C. virtually not D. not actually

3. A. commonly B. mainly
C. specifically D. usually

4. A. scant B. scanty
C. scarce D. rare

5. A. forming B. moulding
C. framing D. making

6. A. unsatisfied B. unprecedented
C. unfulfilled D. unrequited

7. A. taught B. caught
C. captured D. chained

8. A. battered B. split
C. squeezed D. shaped

9. A. universally B. utterly
C. wholly D. complete

10. A. unfavourable B. bad
C. not good D. worse

11. A. may lead to
B. may grow to
C. may reach to
D. would develop to

12. A. consequences B. wrath
C. grief D. wretch

13. A. thinking B. supposing
C. infering D. believing

14. A. complex B. complicated
C. rough D. sanguine

15. A. slows down B. moves slowly
C. hampers D. brakes

PASSAGE-32

Men ....(1).... the maker of their own destinies and they ....(2).... make the destiny of the society and the nation. Life is a great gift of God to men and man ....(3).... making constant efforts to live a ....(4).... life right from the stone age to the modern one. But it is man who ....(5).... to think out how to live well. The ....(6).... before mankind today is between self-preservation and self-destruction. Science has given men all the powers that they need but the new millennium ....(7).... new challenges. We are ....(8).... what nature has given us—forests are being cut down, slums are being ....(9)...., rivers are being polluted. Medical science has made great ....(10)....; but the population is growing in a geometrical ....(11).... . Our natural resources like coal and oil are being ....(12).... . Atomic energy is our only hope. The ....(13).... welcome of the new millennium lies in our determination and hope for self-preservation ....(14).... self-destruction.

QUESTIONS

1. A. are B. have been
C. being D. had been

2. A. unitedly B. ultimately
C. conjointly D. co-exist to

3. A. have been
B. are
C. has been
D. have had been

4. A. congenial
B. cordial
C. congregational
D. congruent

5. A. have B. is
C. are D. has

6. A. optional B. choice
C. possibilities D. probabilities

7. A. presents B. places
C. offers D. puts forth

8. A. destroying B. ignoring
C. neglecting D. wasting

9. A. developed B. constructed
C. created D. manufactured

10. A. advancement B. advances
C. achievement D. inventions

11. A. dimension B. angle
C. index D. proportion

12. A. deported B. deplored
C. depleted D. disposed

13. A. actual B. real
C. warm D. innate

14. A. upon B. over
C. on D. above

II. PASSAGES

Directions: *Read each of the following passages carefully and choose the best answer to each question out of the four alternatives and mark it in the Answer Sheet.*

PASSAGE-1

Cyber crime is the branded stigma defacing the culture and magnanimity of computer technology. It is up keeping the flag with indomitable triumph against developing computer technology worldwide.

Modern age is striding with marching steps of technology revolution beating the past decade of ancestral belief with ultimate care. Computer invention has unfolded the mystery of quick access with the objective of minimum manpower and cutting the time consumption parameters.

As each coin has dual face of its portrait, likewise computer technology is sick of creeping virus. Synthetic manmade dilemma of site hackers activation is causing setback to the expanding anchor of revolutionary device with great loss of time, economy and data profile as suffered by consumers. A recent report from Internet security firm Websense estimates that 85.6 per cent of all the unwanted e-mails contained links to spam sites. The company's data suggests that the number of malicious sites grew 233 per cent in the last six months and saw 671 per cent growth in the number of malicious sites during the last year. In June alone, the total number of e-mails detected as containing viruses increased by 600 per cent compared to May.

Chat rooms, blogs and message boards where the users post comments have been identified as the top targets of hackers and spammers due to the high traffic these attract. According to Websense, 95 per cent of user-generated comments to blogs, chat rooms and message boards during the first half of 2009 were malicious.

It is advisable not to click on spurious links and stay away from keying in passwords at unknown sites as they are most likely to be spammed. Hackers can steal your passwords and log in to your account and access critical information like account numbers and contact details among other things.

QUESTIONS

1. The above passage is:
A. an advisory for the computer users.
B. an advisory for the Internet users.
C. a warning against possible threat to the Internet users.
D. related to chat rooms, blogs and message boards.

2. People who use chat rooms and blogs,
A. are safe and have no threats from spam.
B. are more prone to malicious e-mails.
C. create virus and hack the accounts of others.
D. are unsafe.

3. According to the writer, it is not safe to:
A. log on to spurious links.
B. access one's own account frequently.
C. have essential information stored in a computer.
D. include data-stealing code.

4. Hackers and spammers, according to the writer, are:
A. a new threat to the Internet users and the economy.
B. only pranksters and not serious threat to the system.
C. trained, professional technocrats who are an asset.
D. not expert professionals.

5. Which word in the passage is synonym of *weblog*?
A. blog B. password
C. site D. e-mail

6. Which agency has assessed the data record with spam sites?
A. Microsoft
B. Internet security from Google
C. Websense
D. Spammers

7. Which month dominates the e-mails detection data record?
A. May B. June
C. Last six months D. Last year

PASSAGE-2

South Asian tropical weather reels valuable geographical aesthetic beauty surrounded by wildlife, mountains, steep elevations with dense forest. Human sapiens has been old and innocent victim of natural calamities branded as flood, hurricane, storm, earthquake and tsunami since ages.

Biological data depicts the loss of valuable men and material suffered by mankind owing to the chain reaction by such fatal natural incidents. Global warming has turned an eyesore to the rapid glory of rising civilsation with great mystery yet to be unfolded. UNO data reveals the rate of mortality owned due to natural disaster with great sway of cruel time factor.

Of the 245 natural disasters in the first 11 months of 2009, 224 or 91.4 per cent were due to weather, a UN study has found.

Of the 58 million people affected, 55 million were affected by weather-related disasters, which accounted for $15 billion (₹ 7,05,000 crore) spent in coping with these disasters.

A study has found that half of these disasters, mainly storms and floods, have taken place in Asia, Debarati Guha Sapir of Brussels-based CRED said.

And this data does not include the loss due to drought because that takes longer to account for. Guha Sapir said, "We have found that this is due to global warming, weak political systems, urbanisation, weak infrastructure, population increase and deforestation."

"We have to cap the emissions of greenhouse gases because they produce greater risk of disasters," WMO head Michel Jerraud said. Greenhouse gases, mainly carbon dioxide, are causing the climate change that is already affecting farm output, making droughts, floods and storms more frequent and more severe, and raising the sea level.

QUESTIONS

1. Mark the correct statement(s).

1. Weather is responsible for most of the natural disasters.
2. There is no need to worry about the climatic changes.
3. All the nations are trying to have a common pact to tackle natural disasters.

A. 1 is correct B. Only 2 is correct
C. Only 3 is correct D. 1 and 2 are correct

2. Which one of the following statements is not true?
A. More than 58 million people have been affected by natural disasters.
B. $15 billion have been spent in coping with these disasters.
C. Most of the natural disasters have taken place in Asia.
D. The report does not include the loss caused by droughts.

3. The main cause of natural disasters is :
A. global warming
B. weak political system
C. deforestation
D. all of these

4. The first priority before the nations and the scientists across the world is :
A. to cap the emission of greenhouse gases.
B. to reach an agreement on the nuclear weapons.
C. to help one another when natural disasters occur.
D. to find out the causes of natural disasters.

5. Which word in the passage means the same as *serious*?
A. Reduce B. Severe
C. Underlined D. Underscore

6. Which region is mainly affected by these disasters?
A. United Nation B. Africa
C. Asia D. Brussels

7. Which statement is true?
A. Sea level rise is an alarming incident.
B. Rapid urbanisation is a curse to the global warming.
C. Deforestation with climatic change is responsible for green house gaseous effect.
D. All of these.

PASSAGE-3

Time has brought forth different classical and instrumental range of device that serves healing element to the aweful and mentally distressed state of affair. Temperament compatibility matching is a reasonable trend of motion adhered with the concept of body movement termed as dance therapy.

Dance has mobilised different acknowledgement of its noted culture proclaimed by experts and sensational aspirants. Vedas describe the dance origin from aryan culture to the creeping span of modern India. Archaeological Survey of India has claimed the civilsation existence issue owing to excavation of past events traced in the stone idols displayed in dance "mudra".

Dance is an art form that generally refers to movement of the body, usually rhythmic and to music, used as a form of expression, social interaction or presented in a spiritual or performance setting. Gymnastics, figure skating and synchronised swimming are sports that incorporate dance, while martial arts Kata are often compared to dances. Motion in ordinarily inanimate objects may also be described as dances (the leaves dance in the wind). Every dance, no matter what style, has something in common. It not only involves flexibility and body movement, but also physics. If the proper physics is not taken into consideration, injuries may occur. Choreography is the art of creating dances. The person who creates (*i.e.* choreographs) a dance, is known as the choreographer. Dance has certainly been an important part of ceremony, rituals, celebrations and entertainment since the birth of the earliest human civilisations. Archaeology delivers trace of dance from prehistoric times such as the 9,000 years old Rock Shelters of Bhimbetka painting in India and Egyptian tomb painting depicting dancing figures from circa 3300 BC. One of the earliest structured uses of dance may have been in the performance and in the telling of myths. Before the production of written languages, dance was one of the methods of passing these stories down from generation to generation.

QUESTIONS

1. Dance does not necessarily involve:
   A. movement of the body.
   B. face expression.
   C. rhythmic movements.
   D. costumes.
2. According to the passage, which one of the following sports does not incorporate dance?
   A. Figure skating B. Gymnastics
   C. Chess D. Swimming
3. Which one, according to the passage, is not common in all the dances?
   A. Flexibility B. Body movement
   C. Music D. Physics
4. Physics in every dance is an important element to:
   A. master the art of dance.
   B. to perform it scientifically.
   C. to save oneself from injury.
   D. to get an award.
5. In prehistoric times dance was:
   A. a substitute of written language.
   B. a source of entertainment.
   C. a necessary ritual.
   D. not allowed in royal palaces.
6. Choreographer is a term addressed to:
   A. a sports trainer B. a gym coach
   C. a painting teacher D. a dance teacher
7. What does the term 'the telling of myths' refer to?
   A. Telling the beads B. Vedic convention
   C. Spiritual recitation D. Protest march

PASSAGE-4

Personal sentiments exposure portray in sober class of distinct feature with fair and pleasant expression. As the cruelty can be overpowered by the amicable terms likewise, impossible review let with expression can be publically announced by either electronic device or diary writing habit. On line conversation such as chattering, message convey are the rampant tool of the time to manage in communication congestion.

Blogs, online versions of personal diaries, have been a craze for quite some time now. Some of us, before the Internet age, used to maintain a small diary to jot down random thoughts, reflections, sayings, poems and other such stuff. Their online versions, however, are much more than that. The biggest difference between a blog and a personal diary is while the latter was a very private affair accessible not even to family members, a blog is a public account. In fact the whole world connected to the internet gets to read its contents if they come across it.

What a blogger should keep in mind while blogging is that by displaying our thoughts, emotions, opinions and personal life in full public glory, we are revealing a part of our private life. We are giving outsiders, strangers, friends, colleagues and relatives a full view of what's happening inside us and without lives, something we would hesitate to do in real life. Once blogging begins, it's difficult to control, and we end up sharing our personal thoughts and emotions that we would otherwise have kept to ourselves. The blog entices us, and we fall to be bait.

Blogs don't preserve our anonymity. They let us publish our pictures, professional and personal details, physical address and locations, etc. The biggest precaution to be observed therefore is to think twice before publishing anything, and ask oneself if one would like to make such matters public. The blog readers try to judge us, understand us, get information about us and take pleasure while peeping into our private lives without realising it.

QUESTIONS

1. Blogs are __________.
   A. diaries B. personal diaries
   C. online diaries D. official diaries
2. Earlier the personal diaries were not available even to family members but blog can be read by:
   A. family and friends
   B. friends only
   C. anyone who connects to the Internet
   D. relatives
3. Which one of the following statements is not true?
   A. Blogging does not affect our privacy.
   B. Blogging displays our private life in public.
   C. Blogging cannot be controlled easily.
   D. Blogging allows outsiders to peep into our personal life.
4. The writer in the above passage:
   A. favours blogging.
   B. criticises the practices.
   C. does not want the reader to become a victim of blogging.
   D. favours blogging but with some precautions.
5. Which word in the passage stands for *an account from on point of view*?
   A. version B. block
   C. affair D. account
6. The word Anonymity in the passage refers to:
   A. hostility B. friendship
   C. unacknowledged D. differences
7. What precaution is stressed by the narrator while releasing personal information?

A. Suggest Comprehensive issue only
B. Reader friendly blog appreciation
C. Hiding personal facts
D. Diary maintenance

PASSAGE-5

Pleasure and sorrow being twin face of a coin suffers the sign of commend and condemn since long before the historic ages. Warriors outcry with victory decorated with deep throat laugh has marked the sentimental coverage of battle filed victory. Baffled war victims, war widows, dependents are the oppressed classes. They seek relief against those causing sabotage to their established settlement.

The history of literature really began long before man learned to write. Dancing was the earliest of the arts. Man danced for joy round his primitive camp fire after the defeat and slaughter of his enemy. He yelled and shouted as he danced and gradually the yells and shouts became coherent and caught the measure of the dance and thus the first war song was sung. As the idea of God developed, prayers were framed. The song and prayers became traditional and were repeated from one generation to another, each generation adding something of its own. As man slowly grew more civilsed, he was compelled to invent some method of writing by three urgent necessities. There were certain things that were dangerous to forget and which, therefore, had to be recorded.

It was often necessary to communicate with persons who were some distance away and it was necessary to protect one's property by making tools and so on, in some distinctive manner. So man taught himself to write and having learned to write purely for utilitarian reasons, he used this new method for preserving his songs and his prayers. Of course, among these ancient people, there were only a very few individuals who learned to write, and only a few could read what was written.

QUESTIONS

1. Liguistic comment and condemn refers to:
A. physical grudge against sorrows
B. a temporary verbal communication
C. slip of tongue with praise and denounce
D. a communal fury against the joys

2. Which one of the following statements is true?
A. Study reveals the historic onslaught with cruelty only.
B. Suffers pledge to reform the existing tyranny.
C. A permanent code of sympathetic temper is sought by the suffers.
D. Language dominates with great passion during mental aggression.

3. Before man invented writing, ______.
A. literature was passed on by word of mouth
B. prayres were considered literature
C. literature was just singing and dancing
D. all of the above

4. According to the passage, dance originated from
A. literature B. yelling and shouting
C. prayers D. war

5. Writing was invented because
A. there were certain things which had to be remembered.
B. there were certain things which had to be communicated to the people who were away.
C. there were certain rituals which had to be preserved.
D. all of the above

6. Which one of the following statements is not true?
A. Since only a few individuals had learnt to write and a few could read what was written.
B. Prayers were developed after the idea of god developed.
C. People learned writing for utilitarian reasons.
D. Dancing was the earliest form of art.

7. Which one of the following words in the passage stands for *ancient*?
A. primitive B. traditional
C. coherent D. utilitarian

PASSAGE-6

Quality dominates the world ahead of its spherical, classical, racial or any undue discrimination ever exercised by any individual. Physical characteristics of a produce differs its structural attribution in quality from substandard produce with richness of prolong usage features declared by the claimant. Talent Hunt initiated by quality seekers have turned the table of established brand on account of innovative additions presented by their hardships.

The simple message that quality matters because it is cheaper to do things right the first time is yet to sink into the thinking of Indian managers and workers who seem quite content to live in their cloistered world where mediocrity reigns supreme. It is only the ignorant who believe that quality consciousness is a cultural trait. Barely half a century back no one associated Japan with high quality, but today 'Made in Japan' is a symbol of assured quality. The daily drill at school is far more important than the seasonal seminar and an obsession with quality at home is the best way of convincing the world that we value good quality. Indian exports will never be recognised for quality unless Indians are known to insist on good quality at home.

Global appreciation surrounds the exceptional brand by keeping up the physical standard neatly and efficiently. It is designed to meet the international standards' numerous logos and certificates to upkeep the label of quality consciousness. It has prime motto of swaying clean chit observation to the sanctioned produce without any objection. Modern age has been proved a turning point to the old established traditional belief. They are using tiring house hold produce to industrial device responsible to deface the status of rapid development. We breath into the cool and fresh air of healthy surrounding devised by mankind monitored by quality management with rigorous span or struggle tackled with due care.

QUESTIONS

1. The theme of the passage is:
A. quality consciousness
B. export promotion
C. quality management
D. promoting Indian culture

2. According to the passage, the Indian exports will never be recognised for quality:
A. unless there is technical advancement.
B. unless there is competition.
C. unless the Indians are known to insist on good quality.
D. unless government supports the exporters.

3. Which one of the following statements is true?
A. Indians are known for their insistence on quality.
B. Indians are not quality conscious.
C. Japan is not known for its quality product.
D. 'Made in Japan' is not a symbol of assured quality.

4. The best way to convince the world about quality is:
A. to conduct seminars on quality control.
B. to advertise the products.
C. to value for quality products at home.
D. all of the above

5. According to the passage, the main fault with the Indian managers is that:
A. they are not hard-working.
B. they are not quality conscious.
C. they are not well trained in quality control.
D. they lack technical knowledge.

6. How quality consciousness is termed as a cultural trait with the ignorant?
A. The mature opinion of quality.
B. Quality dominates ahead of traditional belief.
C. Cultural trait justifies any quality standard.
D. Quality consciousness leads to management growth.

7. Why 'Made in Japan' is a symbol of assured quality?
A. Traditional belief
B. Quality consciousness
C. Age old negligence suffering
D. High export offer

PASSAGE-7

Creamy outlook with soft speech presentation is a prima facie attraction that brings joy on the withering faces with a mixture of sensational touch. Smile with grace is the ultimate boon to the mankind keeping away any melancholy at bay. Old age is often miscalculated as liability with little attention paid to them. Their talents and learned potential is buried alive with undue care by oblivious approach due to disfigured or deformed physical structure taken over by aged talents of the society.

It happens to us all, however hard we may try to delay the process. We grow old. Cosmetic surgery may remove the wrinkles, skin which has sagged may be tightened by means of a facelift and hair dresser may dye grey hair a more youthful colour, but we cannot remain young forever.

However, what is important is the quality of life. Some people are lucky to be taken care of at home whereas others may have to move to residential homes. The worst part of ageing is that often the mind becomes less alert. As people grow older, they experience short term memory. Later some may suffer from dementia, often in the form of Alzheimer's disease.

By no means all people are in this category. Many senior citizens are in the possession of all their faculties and see retirement as a time of freedom. Not only that if they have a generous retirement pension, they are likely to be quite well off with money to be spent on a holiday and other luxuries. Because of this, both businesses and government have a new respect for what is known as grey power.

It is unfortunate that many people regard old people as geriatrics who have one foot in the grave. Someone should remind them that they too would be old one day!

They are honoured with senior citizen label granted by the authority with due regard paid from distinct possession of living cadres. One should always bear in mind the old saying "Tit for Tat". Which denotes its symbolic regulation of periodical sufferings. The aforesaid misdoings of emotional disparity, done by striding steps is a curse to the mankind.

QUESTIONS

1. Cosmetic surgery :
A. helps in the retention of youth forever.
B. cannot stop the natural process of ageing.

C. is the solution to ageing.
D. is the fancy of the rich.

2. While ageing man's greatest worry is :
A. his growing wrinkles.
B. his short term memory.
C. his quality of life.
D. moving to a residential home.

3. The government considers grey power as :
A. a liability
B. an asset
C. neither an asset nor a liability
D. a spent force

4. Retirement is seen as a time of freedom because people :
A. no longer have to go to office.
B. can enjoy their earnings.
C. can spend time with their families.
D. finally move into residential homes.

5. *geriatrics* in the passage refers to :
A. handicapped people
B. doctors for the aged
C. a branch of medicine
D. aged people

6. What is the theme of the passage?
A. Old is gold
B. The grey power
C. Youth domination in the society
D. Aged suffering

7. What does the phrase 'suffer from dementia' refer to?
A. Harmful
B. Short term memory loss
C. Lunacy
D. Paralysis

PASSAGE-8

1. The world is teemed with different continents and oceans surrounded with settled and manless island as declared by the geographical experts of the world.
2. Pacific island dominates amongst the oceans escorted with wildlife, ecosphere and manageable resources with identified culture of scientific explorations. Man hunt for unseen spheres remains a landmark occasion yearning for lavish search with instrumental approach. Galapagos Islands remind us of such human efforts noted for spherical search with wildhunt.
3. The Galapagos Islands in the Pacific Ocean are a rocky, lonely spot, but they are also one of the most unusual places in the world. The reason is that they are the home of some of the last giant tortoises left on earth.
4. Weighing hundreds of pounds, these tortoises wander slowly around the rocks and sand of the islands. Each of these islands has its own particular kind of tortoise. There are seven different kinds of tortoises on the eight islands.
5. Hundreds of years ago, thousands of tortoises wandered around these islands. All that changed when people started landing there. When people first arrived, their ships had no refrigerators. This meant that fresh food was always a problem for the sailors on board. The giant tortoises provided a solution to his problem.
6. Ships would anchor off the islands, and crew would seize as many tortoises as they could. Once the animals were aboard the ship, the crew would roll the tortoises onto their backs and use them for soups and stews.
7. Human search never ends with seeking variable resources sustainable to their growth-oriented programme. Man hunt with crew supported by voyage turns the pages of historical map to best transformation regions discovered by his hardcore practice. How long 'wants' arrest his peace of mind with the dream of next destination is yet to know with.

QUESTIONS

1. The author calls the Galapagos Islands an unusual place because :
A. they are in the Pacific Ocean.
B. the endangered giant tortoises are found there.
C. they are rocky and lonely spots.
D. they are located off the western coast of South America.

2. Which statement is correct?
A. There is one kind of tortoise found on the seven islands.
B. There are eight kinds of tortoises found on the eight islands.
C. There are seven kinds of tortoises found on the eight islands.
D. All the tortoises are on one island.

3. The giant tortoises provided a solution to the problem of not having refrigerators because :
A. the sailors went looking for refrigerators as they were starving.
B. fresh food was available in plenty as the sea was vast.
C. the fresh giant tortoise could be killed and eaten whenever the sailors were hungry.
D. the sailors seized the tortoise to store in refrigerators.

4. *Ships would anchor off the islands* means that Ships:
   A. would go off
   B. would be near the shore
   C. would be off to another land
   D. would go to another island
5. In paragraph 6 the word crew means:
   A. the new settlers.
   B. the men arriving on Galapagos Islands.
   C. the men working on the ships.
   D. the men catching the tortoises.
6. Mark the True statement which best suits the passage.
   A. Galapagos is the unusual island due to regular plains.
   B. People landed at Island duely in search of tortoises.
   C. Lack of refrigerators made crew turn to tortoises.
   D. Tortoises numbered more than crews on the Island.
7. Soups and stews refers to :
   A. soup apart with flesh.
   B. soup extracted out of tortoise cooking.
   C. tortoise fat.
   D. a synthetic process of vegetation.

PASSAGE-9

The goal of the fair, to be held at the Cervantes Institute in the Indian capital, is to attract the largest number of students in order to present them with information on the educational programmes Spain has to offer, primarily postgraduate. Studying in Spain gives students an added advantage of living and studying in one of the world's most important economies that also aims for an internationalisation of its university system, which plays a decisive role in knowledge-based economy.

In this context, the Spanish universities, both private and public, numbering 77 in total, offer Master degrees and PhD programmes adapted to the European Higher Education Area; a harmonised space between all European countries that have opted to participate in this model. This implies that any student that obtains a postgraduate degree in a Spanish university will automatically have their studies recognised in any participating country and may continue their doctoral studies without needing to validate their degree. In addition, Spanish universities are offering more and more postgraduate degrees in English in order to attract international students. Nevertheless, it is also very common for students to come to Spain intending to complete postgraduate studies in Spanish as well. Students are offered a double advantage from, first, studying in high quality university programmes, and second, studying in a rapidly growing language, that will soon reach 500 million speakers. Spanish is also the official language in more than 20 countries and a second language in important economies such as the United States and Brazil, which gives graduates and edge when entering the workforce.

These are just a few reasons why studying in Spain is such a unique opportunity. On February 19 and 20th, Indian students are invited to visit the Cervantes Institute where they can directly ask the universities any and all questions about studying in Spain as well as get information about programmes that the universities offer.

Another incentive for students to attend will be the prize drawing for six intensive Spanish courses at Spanish universities in summer 2011. The six big winners will have air fare, accommodations, and tuition paid for while attending the month-long course.

QUESTIONS

1. The objective of the fair is ________.
   A. to tell about Spain
   B. to tell about the courses being started in India
   C. to impart information about education in Spain
   D. none of the above
2. Decisive role means ________.
   A. taking decisions   B. important role
   C. key role   D. minor role
3. Spanish Universities are offering programmes in English because ________.
   A. English is a global language
   B. it wants to get students from all over the world
   C. English is easy to understand
   D. it is easy to get professors to teach in English
4. One of the advantages of studying in Spain is that ________.
   A. it is a beautiful country
   B. education there is cheap
   C. courses are easy
   D. Spanish is the second language in some important countries
5. Those who attend the fair ________.
   A. will get to participate in a prize draw
   B. will be given free air ticket to Spain
   C. will get fee waiver for one term
   D. none of the above

PASSAGE-10

An incandescent bulb lights up when electrical power heats a metal filament wire to a high temperature until it glows. You usually get them rated between 15 and 100 watts. Meanwhile, fluorescent lamps (tubes and their newer compact versions, known as CFLs) use inert gases inside to fluoresce and produce light. There are also lamps that use an array of light-emitting diodes (LEDs) working in the way electrons behave, a phenomenon called electro luminescence. Because LED lamps are costly, very few homes use them—and it's best to wait a while before buying for their prices to come down, just as you did with CFLs over the past years.

At about ₹ 20 a piece, incandescent bulbs may look cheap, but they are not. They waste some 90 per cent of the power consumed—as heat. Consumers preferred them to energy-efficient fluorescent tubes not just because they are cheaper, but also because you may place them in choice lamp shades. Or because the bluish-white illumination from tubes can seem harsh and unnatural, and may contribute to glare and eyestrain.

If you don't like the way tube lights look in the hall or bedroom, use them only in passages, verandas and the kitchen.

QUESTIONS

1. Bulbs light up when ______.
A. metal filament burns
B. electricity heats up metal filament
C. electric current is in excess
D. metal comes in contact with heat

2. CFLs use ______.
A. gases like Argon, Krypton, etc.
B. mercury
C. thin metal strips
D. any of the above

3. Electro luminescence is the process where ______.
A. electrons and protons react to emit light
B. diodes function as electrons and emit light
C. light is generated by water
D. light is generated by sun

4. Incandescent bulbs are costly because ______.
A. they cost ₹ 20 a piece
B. they break easily
C. their power consumption is high
D. none of the above

5. Bulbs are used because they ______.
A. are cheap
B. conserve energy
C. you can place them in choice lamp shades
D. none of the above

PASSAGE-11

Conservation of water in the agricultural sector is essential since water is necessary for the growth of plants and crops. A depleting watertable and a rise in salinity due to overuse of chemical fertilisers and pesticides have made matters serious. Various methods of water harvesting and recharging have been and are being applied all over the world to tackle the problem. In areas where rainfall is low and water is scarce, the local people have used simple techniques that are suited to their region and reduce the demand for water. In India's arid and semi-arid areas, the 'tank' system is traditionally the backbone of agricultural production. Tanks are constructed either by bunding or by excavating the ground and collecting rainwater.

Rajasthan, located in the Great Indian Desert, receives hardly any rainfall, but people have adapted to the harsh conditions by collecting whatever rain falls. Large bunds to create reservoirs known as khadin, dams called johads, tanks and other methods were applied to check water flow and accumulate run-off. At the end of the monsoon season, water from these structures was used to cultivate crops. Similar systems were developed in other parts of the country. These are known by various local names *jal talais* in Uttar Pradesh, the *haveli* system in Madhya Pradesh, *ahar* in Bihar, and so on.

QUESTIONS

1. There is an increase in water salinity due to ______.
A. conservation of water
B. depletion of water
C. overuse of chemical fertilisers and pesticides
D. water harvesting

2. 'Depleting watertable' means ______.
A. reduction in the groundwater level
B. measurement of water level
C. recharging of water level
D. usage of fertilisers and pesticides

3. In arid and semi-arid regions, rainwater is collected by ______.
A. using industrial methods
B. constructing tanks
C. harvesting of water
D. adapting to the harsh conditions

4. How much rainfall does Rajasthan, the state in the Great Indian Desert, receive?
A. plenty of rainfall B. no rainfall
C. moderate rainfall D. scanty rainfall

5. Where do farmers of Rajasthan get water from to cultivate their crops after the monsoon season?
A. from tanks, bunds, dams and reservoirs
B. from whatever rain that falls
C. from excess rainwater
D. from the rivers

PASSAGE-12

Every family with two or more children often experiences sibling rivalry at one time or the other. Childrer in general, fight with each other for their parents' attention. They fight among themselves mostly on trivial issues. If it does not get excessive, this kind of rivalry can, in fact, be a healthy competition that trains children to share, respect one another. They will learn to deal with frustration and displeasures in the maturing process.

The firstborns generally feel that they don't have to share their parents' love and attention. But when the next baby or siblings come along, they feel neglected and that changes everything. The first child starts to feel that he/she is no longer the centre of attraction and that he/she is being sidelined because of the new one. Some children might develop negative feelings and emotional imbalance, which may lead to regressive behaviour.

Such problems could be averted if right moves are taken. One way is to explain the firstborns about the arrival of a new child. They need to establish a connection with the new baby before it is born. Older children should be trained to show a positive attitude towards their siblings. They should be involved, along with their parents, in teaching their siblings social and manual skills, which in turn, helps them to accept them. Sometimes personality differences and parental conflicts too have an impact on the children. Parents have to show patience, understand these issues and should openly communicate with their children to resolve them.

QUESTIONS

1. Sibling rivalry means fight between ______.
A. firstborn and second child
B. children of same parents
C. children born to different parents
D. cousins and relatives

2. 'Why do firstborns feel neglected by the arrival of a new child in the family?
A. because they have to share their parents' love and attention
B. because of their negative attitude
C. because they hate their siblings
D. because parents do not love them

3. What does the word 'regressive' in para 2 mean?
A. emotional imbalance
B. withdraw or shy away
C. negative feeling
D. harsh or rude

4. How can older children develop a positive attitude towards their siblings?
A. by developing sibling rivalry
B. by keeping away from their siblings
C. by their involvement in matters related to the young ones
D. by dominating their siblings

5. What should parents do to control sibling rivalry?
A. allow children to fight among themselves
B. do not allow any communication between children
C. punish the children
D. openly communicate with children to resolve issues

PASSAGE-13

Music can have strong consequences on our feelings. One should try to gain benefits from the power of music. Music, in general, helps one to calm down and feel revitalized. It helps to beat a bad mood or to continue a good state of mind. To cheer up or to enhance vitality, one should listen to music with beats, lots of drumming and a fast tempo. When one wants to relax after a busy day, instrumental music with less percussion and a slower rhythm can help. Listening to soothing music before stressful activities has a lot of benefits and so is always advised. A collection of preferred relaxing tunes help to combat stress at work. One can change one's frame of mind by switching from one kind of music to another. To feel refreshed, it is better to start with something tranquil and soothing and to slowly pick up the pace and the beat. But when one prefers to settle down after a busy schedule, follow the reverse style.

Music is an incredible means that people can use to communicate things, especially their feelings and emotions. When added to speech in a song, it becomes a powerful device of communication. Music generally needs special aptitude, inborn talent and rigorous practice. Also, a person needs to have fine muscular strength in order to sing in tune or play a musical instrument. Recollection of the notes demands good memory power. Besides, many people feel that music and love are connected to each other. A person tries to make an impression on his/her love by way of selecting appropriate music.

QUESTIONS

1. Music with fast beats and lots of drumming __________.
A. boosts up one's energy
B. calms down one's mind
C. is less beneficial
D. leads to stress

2. What does 'percussion' mean?
A. stressful condition
B. tranquil mood

C. thumping or fast beat
D. inborn talent

3. What kind of music is preferred when a person wants to settle down?
A. music with lots of percussion
B. first upbeat music and then soothing music
C. music of string instruments
D. first gentle music and then fast music

4. Why is music considered to be a powerful means of communication?
A. because it helps people to express their emotions
B. because it is an incredible tool
C. because it reduces stress at work
D. because it enhances energy in people

5. What qualities are needed for a person to sing or play a musical instrument?
A. love, talent, speech and memory
B. aptitude, emotion, strength and love
C. knowledge, emotion, love and talent
D. aptitude, talent, practice and strength

PASSAGE-14

In order to heal your emotional baggage and prevent it from possibly costing you yet another relationship, you must recognise the roots of your emotional pain or fears and acknolwedge your accountability in them.

According to psychologists, one should review the event or experience that you think caused you to be hurt and identify your role in the experience. "Allow yourself to learn from that and forgive yourself—often misplaced guilt can be the cause for fear. Acknowledge that your past does not have to dictate your future. Release all the emotional hurt and fears that were weighing you down and standing in the way of your seeing each individual relationship for its own merit and potential. It can be difficult to let go of the security blanket of past behaviours but assure yourself that you no longer need them. Sometimes one may require professional help to be able to identify, draw links, acknowledge, accept and forgive themselves. In the end, it all comes down to trust. Want to leave that baggage behind? Allow yourself to trust again," concludes a psychologist.

QUESTIONS

1. It is important to understand _________.
A. pain
B. emotions
C. cause of emotional pain
D. effect of emotional pain

2. It is advised that we should _________.
A. stop feeling the pain
B. review the event
C. take rest
D. all of the above

3. We should not allow the past _________.
A. to guide our future
B. to bother us
C. actions to make today's decision
D. to affect our present

4. We should learn to let go _________.
A. pain
B. negative emotion
C. fear
D. the security of the past

5. The most important thing in life is _________.
A. trust B. love
C. compassion D. fear

PASSAGE-15

Maintaining work-life balance is necessary because imbalance wreaks chaos in life. Increased pressure on one side will affect the other side too.

After all, the two cannot be completely disconnected! The first step towards this is finding the cause for the imbalance.

Some of the potential causes are—you are genuinely overloaded with work, you are incompetent, your time management skills are poor or you chase conflicting goals.

Once you identify the problem, you should admit it and work towards overcoming it. When you are better organised, your efficiency increases. Make a list of activities and prioritise them. This should be done on daily, weekly and monthly basis.

Plan in advance how you will deal with impending additional responsibilities. If you have to spend extra time at the office, inform your family about it and seek their support. If you have to take leave, inform your boss.

When your organisation is going through a change, there is a crisis or you are vying for a promotion, it can be inevitable to spend more time at work. So explore alternative ways to show your loved ones that you care. When you are with your family and friends, make the most of the time. Do not think about work at least during the 'special' time you allotted for them.

Pay attention to your health. Sleep well. Spend time on activities that can help beat fatigue. Allot time for physical exercises, yoga or sports.

QUESTIONS

1. Chaos here means __________.
   A. disturbance B. confusion
   C. happiness D. calmness
2. As soon as we identify the problem we should __________.
   A. work towards overcoming it
   B. forget it
   C. overcome it
   D. none of the above
3. When there is extra work one should _______.
   A. stay up at night B. work from home
   C. plan in advance D. all of the above
4. When one is spending time with family _________.
   A. one should carry work also
   B. one should relax and sleep
   C. one should keep thinking about work
   D. one should not think about work
5. It is important to take care of one's health because __________.
   A. it helps to be positive and chargeable
   B. one can do more work
   C. work is worship
   D. none of the above

PASSAGE-16

You are at a party and want to watch your weight and health. However when the appetisers are served you notice nothing looks healthy. The next thing you know, you go ahead and eat those decorative little morsels and blow your eating plan. Stop!

Those little delicious nuts in that bowl are chock-full of nutrition. They will improve your cardiovascular health; hold cancer prevention properties and help you lose weight. It's hard to believe but it's true!

The idea that something from nuts may actually help weight control seems a little counter-intuitive at first; bearing in mind the reputation nuts have for being both fatty and fattening. Nuts are nutrient-packed, healthy 'primal' food, and something that experience shows satisfy the appetite and prevent overeating at meal time. High in proteins, unsaturated fats may aid in weight loss and other disease-fighting properties.

What do nuts have that is heart-healthy? Nuts are an intensely fatty food, with about 80 per cent of the calories they offer coming from fat. But bear in mind that the type of oils found in nuts such as almonds, cashews, walnuts is predominantly the healthy monounsaturated and polyunsaturated type.

Researchers found that people who eat nuts regularly have lower risk of heart disease. In 1998, a study conducted by the Harvard School of Public Health found that women who ate nuts less than four times a week were 40 per cent less likely to die of heart disease. Further, potential heart health benefits of nuts were also found among men. In 2002, the Physician's Health Study found that men who consumed nuts two or more times per week had reduced risk of sudden cardiac death.

QUESTIONS

1. Nuts possess _________.
   A. nutritive value
   B. fattening properties
   C. oil
   D. all of the above
2. During meal time nuts _________.
   A. add taste to the food
   B. satisfy appetite
   C. should not be consumed
   D. create an urge for water
3. Nuts contain _________.
   A. unhealthy oils B. cholesterol
   C. healthy oils D. none of the above
4. People who consume nuts regularly ______.
   A. are not prone to heart attacks
   B. are prone to heart attacks
   C. are not prone to kidney failure
   D. are prone to kidney failure
5. Sudden cardiac death means death due to __________.
   A. kidney failure
   B. sudden heart failure
   C. sudden brain malfunction
   D. increase in lung pressure

PASSAGE-17

Acupuncture is an ancient form of healing that dates back to Stone Age. It is a technique of inserting and manipulating fine needles into specific points on the body to relieve pain or for therapeutic purposes. Acupuncture originated in China and is most commonly associated with traditional Chinese medicine. As per the traditional Chinese medical theory, acupuncture points are situated on meridians along which 'Qi' (pronounced as 'chee'), the vital energy, flows. Apparently, there is no known histological basis for the existence of acupuncture meridians. Different types of acupuncture such as Classical Chinese, Japanese, Tibetan, Vietnamese and Korean are practised throughout the world.

The practice of acupuncture is based on the understanding that a vital energy flows along channels or meridians throughout our bodies. When this energy becomes blocked or does not flow freely, it causes disharmony or disease. In order to correct this disharmony, the vital force must be stimulated so that it moves freely again. A set of very fine needles are used to stimulate peculiar points located on the flow of energy and the actions of the various acupuncture points to treat diseases and disharmonies in the body. Quite significantly, acupuncture is not usually painful. Acupuncture needles are tiny and are quickly inserted through the skin, where the nerves that transmit pain are located. The sensation of the insertion is like a "quick pinch". In general, there is an agreement that acupuncture is safe when administered by well-trained practitioners using sterile needles and that further research is appropriate.

QUESTIONS

1. Where does vital energy flow through in human bodies?
A. through muscle cells
B. through blood cells
C. through meridians
D. through sense organs

2. How are acupuncture points stimulated?
A. by inserting find needles into specific points on the body
B. by knowing the histological basis
C. by flow of vital energy
D. by going to China

3. A person specialising in the technique of Acupuncture is called ________.
A. a practitioner
B. an acupuncturist
C. a classical Chinese
D. a medical doctor

4. How is a disease caused as per the traditional Chinese medical theory?
A. when one feels a quick pinch
B. when blood does not flow through the vessels
C. when needles are inserted into specific points
D. when vital energy does not flow freely through meridians

5. Where are the acupuncture needles inserted?
A. in the nerve cells where vital energy flows
B. on the upper part of the right or left hand
C. in the skin where the nerves transmitting pain are found
D. in the muscular part of the hip region

PASSAGE-18

While many of India's parks have been developed from the hunting preserves of princely India, Keoladeo, popularly known as Bharatpur Wildlife Sanctuary, is perhaps the only case where the habitat has been created by a maharaja. In earlier times, Bharatpur town used to be flooded regularly every monsoon. In 1760, an earthen dam, called the Ajam Dam, was constructed, to save the town from this annual vagary of nature. The depression created by extraction of soil for the dam was cleared and this became the Bharatpur Lake.

At the beginning of this century, this lake was developed and divided into several portions. A system of small dams, dykes, sluice gates, etc., was created to control the water level in different sections. This became the hunting preserve of the Bharatpur royalty and also one of the best duck-shooting wetlands in the world. But hunting was prohibited by mid-60s and the area was then declared a national park on 10 March 1982. This was later accepted as a World Heritage site in December 1985.

The major attractions of tourists visiting this park are the numerous migratory birds, which come from as far away as Siberia and Central Asia to spend their winters in Bharatpur, before returning to their breeding grounds. The migratory birds at this bird sanctuary include several species of Cranes, Pelicans, Geese, Ducks, Eagles, Hawks, Shanks, Stints, Wagtails, Warblers, Wheatears, Fly catchers, Buntings, Larks and Pipits, etc.

QUESTIONS

1. Bharatpur Wildlife Sanctuary was developed ________.
A. from the hunting preserves of princely India
B. by constructing Ajam dam
C. by the Maharaja of Bharatpur Royalty
D. from the floods of every monsoon

2. What is the reason behind the construction of Ajam dam?
A. to develop a hunting preserve
B. to develop a wildlife sanctuary
C. to bring an end to floods
D. to save the town from being flooded

3. One of the best duck-shooting wetlands of the world is ________.
A. Princely India B. Bharatpur lake
C. Ajam dam D. Bharatpur royalty

4. When was Bharatpur Lake given the status of a national park?
A. 10 March 1982 B. 10 January 1982
C. 10 December 1985 D. 10 October 1985

5. What are migratory birds?
   A. birds from Siberia and Central Asia
   B. birds that travel long distances during some seasons
   C. birds from Bharatpur Wildlife Sanctuary
   D. birds from the hunting preserves of India

PASSAGE-19

Lexicographer : a writer of dictionaries, a harmless drudge, that busies himself in tracing the original, and detailing the signification of words. Thus said Samuel Johnson in his Dictionary, with an ironic swipe at his own work. It wasn't the first dictionary of the English language, but it continued to be regarded as an authoritative if quirky icon of language for more than two centuries. In two volumes and 2,300 pages, Johnson tried to tidy up a notoriously untidy and promiscuous language, though he knew at the same time that it was futile to attempt to straitjacket it. We tend to think of dictionaries as "anonymous" productions, but Johnson's personality is all over the work. In his bitter definition of a patron, "commonly a wretch who supports with insolence, and is paid by flattery", Johnson took care of his own patron, Lord Chesterfield, who had promised to help financially but had not delivered till too late. Since Johnson's Dictionary, which has been reprinted, abridged, and is still written about, there have been books too numerous to count on the English language: Melvyn Bragg's The Adventure of English: The Biography of a Language, the most recent (2004), Raymond Williams' Keywords: A Vocabulary of Culture and Society (1985), one of the most respected. But there are hundreds of others.

QUESTIONS

1. Samuel Johnson made an ironic remark at his own work by calling a lexicographer __________.
   A. a harmless drudge
   B. a writer of dictionaries
   C. one who is busy in tracing the original
   D. all the above
2. Johnson's Dictionary __________.
   A. continues to be regarded as an authority on icons
   B. was one of the first dictionaries of English language
   C. was regarded a quirky icon of language
   D. has been printed for more than two centuries
3. Tick the correct statement.
   A. Since Johnson's dictionary many have been reprinted.
   B. Johnson's dictionary has been reprinted and abridged.
   C. Johnson abridged his dictionary many times.
   D. Johnson abridged Melvyn Bragg's 'The Adventure of English'.
4. Which of the following statements are true?
   (1) Johnson's dictionary has two volumes.
   (2) His dictionary defines 'patron' as commonly a wretch who supports with insolence, and is paid by flattery.
   (3) Lord Chesterfield was Johnson's patron.
   (4) Lord Chesterfield did not help Johnson financially.
   A. (1) and (3) are True, (2) and (4) are False.
   B. All are True.
   C. (1), (2) and (3) are True and (4) is False.
   D. (2), (3) and (4) are True and (1) is False.
5. Find a word in the passage that means the same as 'unsuccessful'.
   A. swipe B. insolence
   C. straitjacket D. futile

PASSAGE-20

Swaminathan went to school feeling that he was the worst perjurer on earth. His conscience bothered him : he wasn't at all sure if he had been accurate in his description of Samuel. He could not decide how much of what he had said was imagined and how much of it was real. He stopped for a moment on the roadside to make up his mind about Samuel.... His cane skinned people's hands. Swaminathan cast his mind about for an instance on this. There was none within his knowledge. Years and years ago he was reputed to have skinned the knuckles of a boy in the First Standard and made him smear the blood on his face. No one had actualy seen it. But year after year the story persisted among the boys.... Swaminathan's head was dizzy with confusion in regard to Samuel's character—whether he was good or bad, whether he deserved the allegations in the letter or not.... he felt an impulse to run home and beg his father to take back the letter. But Father was an obstinate man.

As he approached the yellow building he realised that he was perjuring himself and was ruining his teacher. Probably the Headmaster would dismiss Samuel and then the police would chain him and put him in jail. For all this disgrace, humiliation and suffering who would be responsible? Swaminathan shuddered. The more he thought of Samuel, the more he grieved for him. As he felt the bulge of the letter in his pocket, he felt like an executioner.

As he entered the school gate an idea occurred to him, a sort of solution. He wouldn't deliver the letter to the Headmaster immediately, but at the end of the day—to that extent he would disobey his father and exercise his independence. There was nothing wrong in it, and Father would not know it anyway. If the letter was given at the end of the day there was a chance that Samuel might do something to justify the letter.

Swaminathan stood at the entrance to his class. Samuel was teaching arithmetic. He looked at Swaminathan for a moment, Swaminathan stood hoping that Samuel would fall on him and tear his skin off. But Samuel merely asked, 'Are you just coming to the class?'

QUESTIONS

1. Swami was not comfortable going to school that day because __________.
   A. he was not well
   B. he had lied about his teacher Samuel
   C. he had not done his home work
   D. his friend was not there
2. He was not sure about Samuel's character because __________.
   A. what he knew was all hearsay
   B. what he knew was his imagination
   C. other teachers had told him so
   D. none of the above
3. Swami's father was not likely to take back the letter because __________.
   A. he believed that Samuel was a good teacher
   B. his father wanted to help Swami and other children
   C. he was a very stubborn man
   D. all of the above
4. Swami decided to __________.
   A. give the letter to the Headmaster
   B. give the letter directly to Mr. Samuel
   C. tear off the letter
   D. give it to the Headmaster at the end of the school
5. As Swami was late to the school he expected __________.
   A. Mr. Samuel to hit him
   B. Mr. Samuel will allow him into the class
   C. to be shouted at by Mr. Samuel
   D. none of the above

PASSAGE-21

Leadership does not exist without followership. A leader has to be accepted by the group which the former is supposed to lead. To gain acceptability the leader should cause an emotive impact on the group members. The character exhibited by leaders make them dear to their followers. A leader is one who effectively inspires employees to achieve worthwhile goals. What character of the leader motivates the followers? It is not pomp and show or flattery or sanctioning more incentives.

Pomp and show creates a sense of awe and the leader is defied rather than emulated. Flattery is unrealistic and cannot serve as a long-term motivational tool.

A leader's style should be one that can be emulated by all irrespective of cadre, class or calibre. Simplicity in one's day-to-day conduct is the only thing that can be adopted by all. When the leader is simple, he is counted as one belonging to the group of which he is the leader. That's to motivate the people. Motivation is the innate quality that enables an individual or group to contribute unlimitedly with limited means. It is the proud prerogative of enlightened human beings.

QUESTIONS

1. Leadership co-exists with __________.
   A. obedience B. followership
   C. discipline D. incentives
2. The pre-requisite for the success of a leader is __________.
   A. obedience by the group
   B. simplicity of the leader
   C. acceptability by the group he is supposed to lead
   D. strict discipline of the group
3. The leader should cause an emotive impact on the group members as __________.
   A. to ensure obedience
   B. to enforce discipline
   C. to control the group
   D. to gain acceptability
4. To inspire employees to achieve long term goals, a leader should not use __________.
   A. sanctioning more incentives
   B. flattery
   C. pomp and show
   D. all of the above
5. Find a word having the same meaning as 'emotive' from the words given below:
   A. Prerogative B. Enlightened
   C. Sensitive D. Proud

PASSAGE-22

We first became aware that something unusual was happening when one of the ship's officers came up to the Chief Engineer, who sat at one table and spoke to him on a low voice. The Chief Engineer at once stood up and with a brief excuse which told us nothing, left the dining room. At first we thought that there had been an accident or that a fire had broken out on board ship, but soon the word went round that a man had been floating in the sea. Then we noticed that the ship had slowed down and was beginning to turn round, with a rather violent motion. Some of the passengers did not wait to finish their meal, but at once rushed upon deck. Others crowded round the portholes, making it impossible for us to eat in comfort. There was such confusion in the dining room that we decided to join those who had come up on deck.

There we learnt that one of the crew had seen a man in the sea some distance from the ship. He had informed the captain who at once ordered the ship to be turned round. We were now only two hundred yards or so from the man and a life boat had already been lowered into the sea. In it there were four sailors, who were sitting ready at the oars, an officer and the ship's doctor. The officer shouted an order and the sailors began to row away the ship. But looking in the same direction as the boat was going, we were able to make out the position of the man in the water. He was clinging to a large piece of wood. At last, after what seemed to us an age the life boat reached the man and two of the sailors pulled him on the boat. This was not at all easy for the sea was rather rough. Then the sailors began to row back to the ship again. The life boat was raised out of the water and the rescued man, wrapped in a blanket was helped out on the deck. Leaning on the arm of the ship's doctor, but still able to walk, in spite of his terrible experience he was led off to the ship's hospital. As he passed along the deck everyone cheered loudly.

QUESTIONS

1. 'We' here refers to __________.
   A. the crew members
   B. the sailors
   C. the passengers of the ship
   D. all of the above

2. The Passengers rushed to the back of the ship because __________.
   A. the ship was drowning
   B. a fire had broken out on board ship
   C. a fight had broken up
   D. the crew was trying to save a drowning man

3. It was tough for the crew to save the drowning man as __________.
   A. the weather was rough
   B. the sea was rough
   C. the man was unwilling to come along with the sailors
   D. the ship had moved ahead

4. Everyone cheered the man loudly as ______.
   A. he had saved the drowning man
   B. he had informed about the drowning man
   C. he had survived a terrible experience
   D. he was the doctor who treated the drowning man

5. The words or the phrase in the passage that means 'it came into knowledge' is _________.
   A. seem to us an age
   B. with a rather violent motion
   C. in comfort
   D. the word went round

PASSAGE-23

In this world there is no worse nuisance than a boy at the age of fourteen. He is neither ornamental nor useful. It is impossible to shower affection on him as a smaller boy; and he is always getting in the way. If he talks with a childish lisp he is called a baby, and if in a grown-up way he is called impertinent. In fact, talk of any kind from him is resented. Then he is at the unattractive, growing age. He grows out of his clothes with indecent haste: His voice grows hoars and breaks and quivers; His face grows suddenly angular and unsightly. It is easy to excuse the shortcomings of early childhood, but it is hard to tolerate even unavoidable lapses in a boy of fourteen. He becomes painfully self-conscious, and when he talks with elderly people is either unduly forward, or else so unduly shy that he appears ashamed of his own existence.

Yet, it is at this age that in his heart of hearts, a young lad most craves recognition and love; and he becomes the devoted slave of any one who shows him consideration. But none dare openly love him, for that would be regarded as undue indulgence and therefore bad for the boy. So, what with scolding and chiding, he becomes very much like a stray dog that has lost its master.

His own name is the only paradise that a boy of fourteen can know. To live in a strange house with strange people is little short of fortune; while it is height of bliss to receive the kind looks of women and never to suffer their slights.

QUESTIONS

1. The expression 'he is always getting in the way' means that he is __________.
   A. found/seen everywhere you go
   B. behaving in a different way from expected/desired
   C. always troubling others with his undesired ways
   D. he goes where he is asked to

2. A lad of fourteen years of age is resented because __________.
   A. he behaves too childishly
   B. he acts like a grown-up
   C. his behaviour becomes neither of a child nor of a grown-up
   D. he looks troublesome

3. A fourteen-year-old boy becomes self-conscious when __________.

A. when he is regarded neither as a young nor a grown-up
B. when he is slighted by elders
C. when he is not appreciated for his good actions
D. none of the above

4. The great bliss for such a boy is ________.
A. to be rewarded for his achievements
B. to receive the kind glances of women
C. to have the company of jolly friends
D. to do what he likes to do

5. The writer's own attitude towards the fourteen-year-old boy is ________.
A. satirical B. sympathetic
C. indifferent D. none of the above

PASSAGE-24

For years, Fukuoka was widely known as the closest city that Japan had to Venice. It might not have enjoyed the splendid architecture, piazzas or the Basilica San Marco of the Italian city, but the people of the largest metropolis on Kyushu, Japan's most southerly main island, prided themselves on the carefully maintained network of rivers that emptied into the graceful curve of Hakata Bay and gave Fukuoka its blue credentials. Today, however, the capital of Kyushu is forging a new identity for itself as green complements the blue.

Not satisfied with pioneering a method of semi-aerobic landfill known the world over as "The Fukuoka Method", the city has gone on to implement some highly exacting rubbish-segregating standards for both homes and businesses. And it has ambitious plans to turn itself into the world's first city to be powered by hydrogen, a project that is under way and will eventually evolve into a "corridor" of homes and businesses linking Fukuoka with the larger cities of Osaka, Nagoya and eventually, the mammoth Tokyo, some 900 kilometres to the rest.

All that and yet Fukuoka is still regarded as the most pleasant place to live in Japan and among the best in the world. In its annual quality of life survey in July 2010, Britain's *Monocle* magazine ranked Fukuoka the 14th "most liveable" city on the planet, thanks in part to its air connections with the rest of Asia, its low crime rate, sub-tropical climate, excellent public transport services and cultural opportunities.

City authorities also received high marks for subsidising local residents who want to install solar-energy systems in their homes to the tune US$1.2 million. Elsewhere, funds have been invested in the creation of green spaces.

QUESTIONS

1. The city of Fukuoka is considered ________.
A. closest to Venice B. different from Venice
C. Peaceful city D. close to Rome

2. Green complements the blue means ________.
A. green and blue do not go together
B. green and blue go well with each other
C. If we have green in a place, it is auspicious to have blue there
D. none of these

3. Fukuoka has set very high standards for
A. cleanliness
B. keeping city green
C. separating bash at home as well as work place
D. maintaining clean air

4. Fukuoka is high on the list of the most liveable cities in the world because ________.
A. there is less crime
B. environment is clean
C. excellent connectivity, within and outside the city
D. all of the above

5. Residents of Fukuoka who wish to install solar powered system ________.
A. Know the advantages of the same
B. will be subsidised by the state
C. are encouraged by the government
D. none of these

PASSAGE-25

A tiger relies on stealth to catch its prey. It has excellent eyesight and hearing, which help it track animals in the dark. Tigers hunt large animals such as deer and wild pigs, which will provide food for a few days. They slink up on their prey unseen, only charging when they are within about 20m (65 ft). Tigers kill their prey by biting the back, its neck or throat, then dragging it away into thick cover to feed. When they have eaten enough, they conceal the carcass with leaves so they can return to it later on. Male tigers can eat up to 40 kg (85 lb) of meat in one meal.

Tigers love water and often bathe or cool off in rivers and pools during the heat of the day. They usually hunt at night and rest during the day. Most tigers live alone, although mothers with cubs or young siblings sometimes hunt together. A male tiger roams a territory of up to 100 sq km (60 sq. miles) in area, defining its boundaries with scent markings, droppings and scratch marks on boulders or trees. These signals tell other tigers about its sex and size as well as its territory. Tigers also communicate by roaring and moaning. They defend their territory fiercely against rival males, but will tolerate some overlap with the smaller territories of females.

QUESTIONS

1. Stealth means ________.
A. by cheating

B. secret way
C. attacking from front
D. jumping at the prey

2. Tigers hunt big animals because ______.
A. it is easy to hunt them
B. their meat is tasty
C. the meat will last them a few days
D. they are easily available

3. Tigers drag their prey into the bush ______.
A. so that nobody can disturb them
B. it is cool under a bush
C. other animals may snatch their prey
D. to conceal it

4. During the hot summer season ______.
A. tigers like to cool by staying in water
B. tigers go off to sleep
C. tigers stay under the bush
D. tigers move to cooler areas

5. Tigers prefer to ______.
A. stay in small groups
B. stay alone
C. stay as a family
D. take care of their young one

PASSAGE-26

The Kidneys of nearly five per cent of people under the age of 20 are not functioning normally, a study shows. The youngsters have albumin in the urine, which indicates that they could develop a serious kidney disease later in their lives. Doctors say that more youngsters today are at a risk of kidney malfunction due to lifestyle changes, which includes smoking, consumption of junk food and less physical activity from desk-bound jobs. On the eve of World Kidney Day, doctors are stressing on the early detection of Kidney malfunction as the only way to reduce serious complications and chronic kidney disease.

For the pilot study, the institute of nephrology at a hospital used a home detection kit that is dipped in urine to show presence of protein in the sample. During the study, 1,000 people were given the kits. A total of 265 returned them with feedback. Of this, 5% of the young population had urinary protein.

Doctors say that the main issue with kidney disease is the lack of early detection. If detected early, patients can avoid reaching the stage of dialysis, which indicates irreversible and serious kidney damage. "Simple health screening test comprising urine tests, blood test and ultrasounds are important. Early diagonsis and treatment for kidney disease can significantly delay and even prevent kidney failure and need for dialysis." said doctors. One doctor said home detection kits would help in early detection, and added that they were targeting young people in colleges and IT firms to use this kit.

QUESTIONS

1. As many as ______ of youngsters have kidney problem.
A. 20% B. 5%
C. 22% D. 12%

2. This problem is mainly due to ______.
A. obesity in youngsters
B. change in lifestyle
C. poor intake of water
D. none of the above

3. The main problem with kidney related disease is ______.
A. it is fatal
B. it cannot be treated
C. it cannot be detected early
D. it is painful

4. Simple tests will help in ______.
A. preventing and delaying kidney failure
B. giving treatment
C. relieving pain
D. all of the above

5. Hospitals are targeting colleges and IT firms because ______.
A. youngsters need it the most
B. these places have only youngsters
C. they want to bring down kidney issue among youngsters
D. all of the above

PASSAGE-27

Global warming this century could trigger a run away thaw of Greenland's ice sheet and other abrupt shifts such as a dieback of the Amazon rainforest, scientists say.

They urged governments to be more aware of "tripping points" in nature, tiny shifts that can bring big and almost always damaging changes such as a melt of Arctic summer sea ice or a collapse of the Indian monsoon.

"Society may be lulled into a false sense of security by smooth projections of global change," the scientists at British, German and American institutes wrote in a report saying there were many little-understood thresholds in nature.

"The greatest and clearest threat is to the Arctic with summer sea ice loss likely to occur long before, and potentially contribute to, Greenland ice sheet melt", they wrote in the journal "Proceedings" of the National Academy of Sciences. "Tipping elements in the tropics, the boreal zone, and west Antarctica are surrounded by large uncertainty", they wrote, pointing to more potential abrupt shifts than seen in a 2007 report by the UN Climate Panel.

A projected drying of the Amazon basin, linked both to logging and to global warming, could set off a dieback of the rainforest. Many of these tipping points could be closer.

Other sudden changes linked to climate change, stoked by human use of fossil fuels, included a dieback of northern pine forests, or a stronger warming of the Pacific under El Nino weather events that can disrupt weather world-wide, they wrote.

A possible greening of parts of the Sahel and the Sahara, if monsoon rains in West Africa were disrupted, was one of the few positive abrupt shifts identified by the scientists.

Even a moderate warming could set off a thaw of Greenland's ice sheet that could then vanish in 300 years—raising sea levels by 20 ft, or 2 meters a century and threatening coasts, Pacific islands and cities from Bangkok to Buenos Aires. The UN Climate Panel foresees a rise in world sea level ranging up to about 80 cms this century and reckons that a thaw of Greenland would take hundreds of years longer.

The new study said a disappearance of Arctic sea ice in summer time could happen in coming decades—earlier than projected by the UN panel. That could stoke further global warming as dark water soaks up more heat than ice and snow.

QUESTIONS

1. Global warming can cause ______.
A. thawing of green land
B. excess rain
C. severe draught
D. a green earth

2. Nations should be sensitive to small changes that can cause ______.
A. famine
B. melting of Arctic ice
C. decrease in sea level
D. chill in polar regions

3. There could be a die-back of the rainforest because of ______.
A. drying of Amazon Basin.
B. water level
C. ses level
D. melting glaciers

4. As a result of rains in West Africa ______.
A. Sahara will turn into desert
B. Sahara will turn green
C. flood will come
D. none of these

5. According to a UN panel report _____ in this century.
A. sea level will decrease
B. sea level will remain same
C. sea level will rise
D. none of these

PASSAGE-28

From time immemorial drugs have been used by humans for medical purposes. But never before had the abuse ... (A) ... narcotics caused such unprecedented worldwide concern and posed an alarming menace to the society. According to recent World Health Organization estimates, there are millions of ... (B) ... addicts and abusers of cocaine, opium, barbiturates, sedatives and tranquilizers all over the world. It is now an international problem that ... (C) ... the Indian government. Recent movies like Udta Punjab have highlighted that the consumption of drugs has affected the youth in the state of Punjab adversely. Taking a drug other than for medical reason in amount, strength, frequency or manner that ... (D) ... the physical and mental functioning is drug abuse. Drug abuse is a painful problem for the addict, for the family and for all those who touch their lives. It is mostly the youngsters that fall prey to drugs. At this stage, the youngsters are especially vulnerable to pressure from friends. The future generation is virtually being crippled under the impact of drugs. Due to intake of drugs, the person may lose will power, concentration, memory and judgement capacity. There is a need to create awareness amongst the youth as well as work towards rehabilitation of those trapped in ...(E)... abuse.

QUESTIONS

1. Choose the most appropriate option for (B):
A. heroin B. heroine
C. medicine D. work

2. Choose the most appropriate option for (D):
A. mends B. damages
C. invigorates D. augments

3. Choose the most appropriate option for (E):
A. object B. environment
C. substance D. habitat

4. Choose the most appropriate option for (C):
A. surprises B. pleases
C. bothers D. amuses

5. Choose the most appropriate option for (A):
A. by B. of
C. from D. through

PASSAGE-29

Once upon a time there was a bird. It was ignorant. It sang all right, but never recited scriptures. It hopped pretty frequently, but lacked manners. Said the Raja to himself: "Ignorance is costly at the long run. For fools consume as much food as others, and yet give nothing in return."

He called his nephews to his presence and told them that the bird must have a sound schooling. The pundits were summoned, and at once went to the root of the matter. They decided that the ignorance of the bird was due to their natural habit of living in poor nest. Therefore, according to pundits, the first thing necessary for this bird's education was a suitable cage. The pundits had their rewards and went home happily. A golden cage was built with gorgeous decorations. Crowds came to see it from all parts of the world. "Culture, captured and caged" exclaimed some, in a rapture of ecstasy and burst into tears. Others remarked: "even if culture be missed, the cage will remain, to the end, a substantial fact. How fortunate for the bird." The goldsmith filled his bag with money and lost no time in sailing homewards.

The pundits sat down to educate the bird. With proper deliberation they took their pinch of snuff, as one of them said: "Text-books can never be too many for our purpose!" The nephews brought together an enormous crowd of scribes. They copied from books, and copied from copies, till the manuscripts were piled up to an uncatchable height. Men murmured in amazement. "Oh, the tower of culture, egregiously high! The end of it lost in the clouds!" The scribes, with light hearts, hurried home, their pockets heavily laden. The nephews were furiously busy keeping the cage in proper trim. As their constant scrubbing and polishing went on, the people said with satisfaction: "This is progress indeed!" Men were employed in large numbers, and supervisors were still more numerous. These, with their cousins of all different degrees of distance, built a palace for themselves and lived there happily ever after. Whatever may be its other deficiencies, the world is never in want of fault-finders; and they went about saying that every creature remotely connected with the cage flourished beyond words, excepting only the bird.

When this remark reached the Raja's ears, he summoned his nephews before him and said: "My dear nephews, what is this that we hear?" The nephews said in answer: "Sire, let the testimony of the goldsmiths and the pundits, the scribes and the supervisors, be taken, if the truth is to be known. Food is scarce with the fault-finders, and that is why their tongues have gained in sharpness." The explanation was so luminously satisfactory that the Raja decorated each one of his nephews with his own rare jewels.

The Raja at length being desirous of seeing with his own eyes how his education department engaged itself with the little bird, made his appearance one day at the great hall of learning. From the gate rose the sounds of conch-shells and gongs, horns, bugles and trumpets, cymbals, drums and kettle drums, tom-toms, tambourines, flutes, fifes, barrel-organs and bagpipes. The pundits began chanting mantras with their topmost voices, while the goldsmiths, scribes, supervisors, and their numberless cousins of all different degrees of distance, loudly raised a round of cheers.

The nephews pleased, the Raja was about to remount his elephant, when the fault-finder from behind some bush, cried out: "Maharaja, have you seen the bird?"

"Indeed, I have not!" exclaimed the Raja. "I completely forgot about the bird. Turning back, he asked the pundits about the method they followed in instructing the bird. It was shown to him. He was immensely impressed. The method was so stupendous that the bird looked ridiculously unimportant in comparison. The Raja was satisfied that there was no flaw in the arrangements. As for any complaint from the bird itself, that simply could not be expected. Its throat was so completely choked with the leaves from the books that it could neither whistle nor whisper. It sent a thrill through one's body to watch the process.

This time, while remounting his elephant, the Raja ordered his state ear-puller to give a thorough good pull at both the ears of the fault-finder. The bird thus crawled on, duly and properly, to the verge of inanity. In fact, its proper was satisfactory in the extreme. Nevertheless, nature occasionally triumphed overt training, and when the morning light peeped into the bird's cage it sometimes fluttered its wings in a reprehensible manner. And, though it is hard to believe, it pitifully packed at its bars with its feeble break. "What impertinence!" growled the Kotwal.

The blacksmith, with his forge and hammer took his place in the Raja's Department of Education: Oh, what resounding blows! The iron chain was soon completed, and the bird's wings were clipped. The Raja's brother-in-law looked back, and shook their heads, saying: "This bird not only lacks good sense, but also gratitude!" With text-book in hand and baton in the other, the pundits gave the poor bird what may fitly be called lessons!

The Kotwal was honoured with a title for his watchfulness, and the blacksmith for skill in forging chains. The bird died.

(A Parrot's story by Rabindra Nath Tagore)

QUESTIONS

1. The Raja wanted the bird to have sound schooling because

A. the bird was consuming the resources of the state but giving nothing in return.

B. he wanted to eventually kill the bird.

C. he wanted to show his gratitude towards the bird.

D. he wished to set before his subjects an example of love towards nature.

2. 'The tower of culture' symbolizes
A. money B. raja
C. manuscripts D. cage

3. The word 'impertinence' refers to
A. disrespect B. stupid
C. loyalty D. civility

4. The status of the 'bird' in this story can be compared today with that of a
A. head of the school
B. student
C. teacher educator
D. teacher

5. The bird died in the end because
A. it lacked good sense
B. its cage was dirty
C. Its natural instincts were suppressed
D. it was brutally beaten up by the Raja

PASSAGE-30

Rakesh was on his way home from school when he bought the cherries. He paid fifty paise for the bunch. It took him about half-an-hour to walk home, and by the time he reached the cottage there were only three cherries left. 'Have a cherry, Grandfather,' he said, as soon as he saw his grandfather in the garden. Grandfather took one cherry and Rakesh promptly ate the other two. He kept the last seed in his mouth for some time, rolling it round and round on his tongue until all the tang had gone. Then he placed the seed on the palm of his hand and studied it. 'Are cherry seeds lucky?' asked Rakesh.

'Of course.'

'Then I'll keep it.'

'Nothing is lucky if you put it away. If you want luck, you must put it to some use.'

'What can I do with a seed?'

'Plant it.'

So, Rakesh found a small space and began to dig up a flowerbed. 'Hey, not there,' said Grandfather, 'I've sown mustard in that bed. Plant it in that shady corner, where it won't be disturbed.' Rakesh went to a corner of the garden where the earth was soft and yielding. He did not have to dig. He pressed the seed into the soil with his thumb and it went right in. Then he had his lunch, and ran off to play cricket with his friends, and forgot all about the cherry seed.

When it was winter in the hills, a cold wind blew down from the snows and went whoo-whoo-whoo in the deodar trees, and the garden was dry and bare. In the evenings Grandfather and Rakesh sat over a charcoal fire, and Grandfather told Rakesh stories and in turn Rakesh would read to him from the newspaper, Grandfather's eyesight being rather weak. Rakesh found the newspaper very dull – especially after the stories – but Grandfather wanted all the news.

One morning in the garden he bent to pick up what he thought was a small twig and found to his surprise that it was well rooted. He stared at it for a moment, then ran to fetch Grandfather, calling, 'Dada, come and look, the cherry tree has come up!' 'What cherry tree?' asked Grandfather, who had forgotten about it. 'The seed we planted last year –look, it's come up!' Rakesh went down on his haunches, while Grandfather bent almost double and peered down at the tiny tree. It was about four inches high. 'Yes, it's a cherry tree,' said Grandfather. 'You should water it now and then.' Rakesh ran indoors and came back with a bucket of water. 'Don't drown it!' said Grandfather. Rakesh gave it a sprinkling and circled it with pebbles. 'What are the pebbles for?' asked Grandfather. 'For privacy,' said Rakesh. He looked at the tree every morning, but it did not seem to be growing very fast, so he stopped looking at it except quickly, out of the corner of his eye. And, after a week or two, when he allowed himself to look at it properly, he found that it had grown – at least an inch!

The cherry tree grew quickly during monsoon. It was about two feet high when a goat entered the garden and ate all the leaves. Only the main stem and two thin branches remained. 'Never mind,' said Grandfather, seeing that Rakesh was upset. 'It will grow again; cherry trees are tough.' Towards the end of the rainy season new leaves appeared on the tree. Then a woman cutting grass scrambled down the hillside, her scythe swishing through the heavy monsoon foliage. She did not try to avoid the tree: one sweep, and the cherry tree was cut in two. When Grandfather saw what had happened, he went after the woman and scolded her; but the damage could not be repaired. 'Maybe it will die now,' said Rakesh. 'Maybe,' said Grandfather. But the cherry tree had no intention of dying. By the time summer came again, it had sent out several new shoots with tender green leaves.

One day he found a bright green praying-mantis perched on a branch, peering at him with bulging eyes. Rakesh let it remain there; it was the cherry tree's first visitor. The next visitor was a hairy caterpillar, who started making a meal of the leaves. Rakesh removed it quickly and dropped it on a heap of dry leaves. Come back when you're a butterfly,' he said.

Winter came early. The cherry tree bent low with the weight of snow. In February it was Rakesh's birthday. He was nine – and the tree was four, but almost as tall as Rakesh. One morning, when the Sun came out, Grandfather came into the garden to 'let some warmth get into my bones,' as he put it. He stopped in front of the cherry tree, stared at it for a few moments, and then called out,

'Rakesh! Come and look! Come quickly before it falls!' Rakesh and Grandfather gazed at the tree as though it had performed a miracle. There was a pale pink blossom at the end of a branch. 'There are so many trees in the forest,' said Rakesh. 'What's so special about this tree? Why do we like it so much?' 'We planted it ourselves,' said Grandfather. That's why it's special. 'Just one small seed,' said Rakesh, and he touched the smooth bark of the tree that he had grown. He ran his hand along the trunk of the tree and put his finger to the tip of a leaf. 'I wonder,' he whispered. 'Is this what it feels to be God?'

QUESTIONS

1. The plot of the story revolves around the concept(s) of:
   A. relation between grandfather and Rakesh
   B. hope, responsibility, perseverance and pride
   C. how to plant trees
   D. how to feel like God
2. The author is an ardent lover of:
   A. cherries B. grandfather stories
   C. nature and animals D. reading newspaper
3. Why does Rakesh circle the plant with some pebbles?
   A. His grandfather asked him
   B. He likes to play with pebbles
   C. To beautify his garden
   D. For privacy
4. In the story, the Cherry tree symbolises:
   A. beauty B. innocence
   C. birth D. survival
5. The status of 'the cherry tree' in this story can be compared today with that of a:
   A. birds B. trees
   C. animals D. humans

III. POETRY

Directions: *Read the following poems carefully and choose the best answer to each question out of the four alternatives and mark it in the Answer Sheet.*

POEM-1

It is an ancient Mariner,
And he stoppeth one of three.
'By thy long grey beard and glittering eye,
Now wherefore stopp'st thou me?
The Bridegroom's doors are opened wide,
And I am next of kin;
The guests are met, the feast is set:
May'st hear the merry din.'
He holds him with his skinny hand,
'There was a ship,' quoth he.
'Hold off! unhand me, grey-beard loon!'
Eftsoons his hand dropt he.
He holds him with his glittering eye —
The Wedding-Guest stood still,
And listens like a three years' child:
The Mariner hath his will.

— ST Coleridge

QUESTIONS

1. What is the most potent factor with the Ancient Mariner that enables him to hold the wedding guest?
   A. His glittering eye B. His skinny hand
   C. His long grey-beard D. His starting words.
2. What is the significance of comparing the wedding guest to a three years' child?
   A. A three years' child is innocent.
   B. He is afraid of a strange man.
   C. He is fond of listening to stories.
   D. He cannot run away from a grown-up man.
3. Which among the following is not an argument presented by the wedding-guest?
   A. The wedding-guest is a close relative of the Bridegroom.
   B. His participation in some ceremonies is essential.
   C. Merry-making is already going on.
   D. Other guests have already arrived.
4. The Ancient Mariner is:
   A. A young man
   B. A middle-aged man
   C. An old man
   D. It is not clear from the text
5. The Mariner's story is related to:
   A. A ship B. Giants
   C. Fairies D. A forest

POEM-2

Shall I hear the lament of the nightingale, submissively lending my ear?
Am I the rose to suffer its cry in silence year after year?
The fire of verse gives me courage and bids me no more to be faint.

With dust in my mouth, I am abject: to God I make my complaint.

Sometimes You favour our rivals then sometimes with us You are free,

I am sorry to say it so boldly. You are no less fickle than we.

(Iqbal: 'Complaint to God')

QUESTIONS

1. What fault does the poet find in God?
   A. God causes misery to people.
   B. He opposes the poet and his companions and favours their opponents.
   C. He is fickle.
   D. He does not care for the poor.

2. What gives courage to the poet?
   A. The song of the nightingale.
   B. The power of poetry.
   C. The sweet smell of the rose.
   D. God's mercy.

3. What is the present mood of the poet?
   A. He is distraught.
   B. He is in a happy mood.
   C. He is in a contemplating mood.
   D. He is talking only frivolously.

4. Why does the poet use the word "lament" for the song of the nightingale?
   A. The nightingale is sad at poet's miserable condition.
   B. It is only teasing the poet.
   C. It seems sad to the poet only.
   D. Proverbially, the nightingale is said to sing sweet but sad songs.

5. In what situation is the rose placed in the poem?
   A. Very advantageous situation.
   B. Helpless situation.
   C. Confusing situation.
   D. Situation of expectation.

POEM-3

'In vain to me the smiling mornings shine,
And reddening Phoebus lifts his golden fire;
The birds in vain and amorous descant join,
Or cheerful fields resume their green attire.
These ears, alas! for other notes repine;
"A different object do these eyes require;
My lonely anguish melts no heart but mine;
And in my breast the imperfect joys expire;"
Yet morning smiles the busy race to cheer,
And new-born pleasure brings to happier men;
The fields to all their wanted tribute bear;
To warm their little loves the birds complain.
"I fruitless mourn to him that cannot hear,
And weep the more because I weep in vain."

— Thomas Gray

QUESTIONS

1. The poet's object in the given poem cannot hear him because:
   A. He has gone deaf.
   B. He does not care for him.
   C. He is awfully busy.
   D. He is dead.

2. What does nature bring to the poet?
   A. A sense of loss
   B. A feeling of joy
   C. A sense of satisfaction
   D. A feeling of charm

3. Why does the poet use the phrase "in vain" so many times?
   A. To tell about the uselessness of his existence.
   B. To tell about the uselessness of beauties of nature and his wails.
   C. To tell about the uselessness of birds' love.
   D. To tell about waste of morning time.

4. What feeling can a keenly observant reader get from a study of the first twelve lines and the last two lines?
   A. A feeling of harmony.
   B. A feeling of amplitude.
   C. A feeling of dichotomy of sense.
   D. A sense of overall satisfaction.

5. What does the morning bring to the "happier men"?
   A. A sense of loss.
   B. A new joy.
   C. A feeling of sorrow.
   D. A feeling of sympathy.

POEM-4

'Turn on the prudent Ant thy heedless eyes,
Observe her labours, Sluggard, and be wise;
No stern command, no monitory voice,
Prescribes her duties, or directs her choice;
Yet, timely provident, she hastes away
To snatch the blessings of a plenteous day;
When fruitful Summer loads the teeming plain,
She crops the harvest, and she stores the grain.

How long shall sloth usurp thy useless hours,
Unnerve thy vigour, and enchain thy powers?
While artful shades thy downy couch enclose,
And soft solicitation courts repose,
Amidst the drowsy charms of dull delight,
Year chases year with unremitted flight,
Till Want now following, fraudulent and slow,
Shall spring to seize thee, like an ambush'd foe.

— Dr Samuel Johnson

QUESTIONS

1. What can be said to be the overwhelming quality of an ant?
A. Industriousness
B. Dutifulness
C. Time-consciousness
D. Regular routine

2. What will finally overtake a sluggard?
A. Sloth B. Waste of time
C. Loss of energy D. Want

3. What does the Ant do in summer?
A. It enjoys the beauties of nature.
B. It sits in the shade of trees.
C. It fills its stores with grain.
D. It spends time eating summer fruits.

4. Which among the following is not the characteristic of Want?
A. Fraudulence
B. Ambush
C. Springing over the enemy.
D. Abusing the enemy.

5. What is the main characteristic of summer?
A. It is a very hot season.
B. It is a fruitful season.
C. It expects all to do their duties.
D. It always comes on time.

POEM-5

On their own feet they came, or on shipboard,
Camel-back, horse-back, ass-back, mule-back,
Old civilisations put to the sword.
Then they and their wisdom went to rack;
No handiwork of Callimachus,
Who handled marble as if it were bronze,
Made draperies that seemed to rise
When sea-wind swept the corner stands:
His long lamp-chimney shaped like the stem
Of a slender palm, stood but a day;
All things fall and are built again,
And those that build them again are gay.

— WB Yeats

QUESTIONS

1. Which of the following means of transport was not used by the destroyers of old civilizations?
A. By sea
B. By air
C. On the backs of animals
D. On foot

2. What is the eternal law of life?
A. Destruction and recreation
B. Destruction
C. Creation
D. Failure of art

3. Which of the following could Callimachus do?
A. Make a long thin lamp-chimney last long.
B. Engrave in bronze.
C. Make metallic artefacts.
D. Work with marble without breaking it.

4. Is there no hope for civilizations?
A. Yes, there is.
B. No, there's none.
C. The poet gives no clue to it.
D. There is only a little hope.

5. Who get real happiness from their activity?
A. The destroyers. B. The builders.
C. The observers. D. The sea-creatures.

POEM-6

I lay in sorrow, deep *distressed*:
My *grief* a proud man heard;
His looks were cold, he gave me gold
But not a kindly word,
My sorrow passed—I paid him back
The gold he gave to me;
Then stood *erect* and spoke my thanks
And blessed his *Charity.*
I *lay* in *want,* in grief and pain:
A poor man passed my way;
He bound my head, he gave me *bread*
He watched me night and day.
How shall I pay him back again,
For all he did to me?

Oh, gold is great, but greater far
    Is *heavenly* Sympathy!

—Charles Mackey

QUESTIONS

1. The proud man heard the poet
   A. crying in sorrow B. sing in joy
   C. lying in misery D. crying due to pain
2. The proud man helped the poet by
   A. giving him comfort
   B. assisting him to lie down
   C. his cold looks
   D. giving him gold
3. The poet thanked the proud man by
   A. speaking nicely to him
   B. giving him money
   C. praising him
   D. blessing his large-heartedness
4. The poor man helped the poet by
   A. giving him comfort
   B. binding his body
   C. giving him food
   D. serving him like his own
5. The word 'heavenly' means
   A. relating to paradise
   B. like that of heaven
   C. like angels
   D. like gods

POEM-7

The earth was green, the sky was blue;
    I saw and heard one sunny *morn*
A *skylark hang* between the two,
    A singing *speck* above the corn.
A stage below in gay *accord*,
    White butterflies danced on wing,
And still the singing skylark *soared*,
    And silent sank and soared to sing.
The *cornfield stretched* a *tender* green
    To right and left beside my walks;
I knew he had a nest unseen
    Somewhere among the million *stalks*.
And as I *paused* to hear his song
    While swift the sunny moments *slid*,
Perhaps his *mate* sat listening long,
    And listened longer than I did.

—Christina Rossetti

QUESTIONS

1. The skylark sang when
   A. it rained
   B. the sun shone
   C. the earth was green and the sky without clouds
   D. there were clouds
2. The skylark while singing looked like
   A. a star B. an insect
   C. an eagle D. a small dot
3. The skylark rose upwards and upwards
   A. while flying B. while singing
   C. as it sang D. as it flew
4. The nest of the skylark was
   A. in the fields below
   B. among the numberless stems of corn
   C. beside other nests
   D. among trees
5. The word 'paused' means
   A. stopped B. stood erect
   C. flew across D. went straight

POEM-8

The Forst *performs* its secret *ministry*,
Unhelped by any wind. The owlet's cry
Came loud—and *hark*, again! loud as before.
The *inmates* of my cottage, all at rest,
Have left me to that *solitude*, which suits
Abstruser musings : save that at my side
My *cradled infant slumbers* peacefully.
Tis calm indeed! so calm, that it disturbs
And *vexes meditation* with its strange
And extreme silentness ......

—S.T. Coleridge

QUESTIONS

1. The 'secret ministry' of the frost is that
   A. it is falling on the ground
   B. it ministers the earth
   C. it has a secret deal with the nature
   D. it deals with the air
2. There is silence all round. This is seen in the phrase
   A. and hark, again
   B. all at rest
   C. that solitude
   D. Abstruser musings
3. Who is sleeping in the cradle?
   A. the poet's son B. the poet's child
   C. the poet's nephew D. a stranger baby

4. What disturb(s) the calm?
A. the surroundings B. nature
C. weather D. calmness

5. The word 'meditation' means
A. prayers B. thought
C. deep thought D. deep ideas

POEM-9

She *dwelt* among the *untrodden* ways
Beside the springs of Dove,
A Maid whom there were none to praise
And very few to love :
A *violet* by a *mossy* stone
Half hidden from the eye!
—*Fair* as a star, when one
Is shining in the sky.
She lived unknown, and few could know
When Lucy *ceased* to be;
But she is in *grave,* and, oh,
The difference to me!

—William Wordsworth

QUESTIONS

1. Lucy lived a lonely life because
A. no person loved her
B. no one praised her
C. there was no human population
D. she was born in nature

2. Lucy was like a
A. rose flower B. a star
C. a violet flower D. a daffodil

3. She died on unknown death because
A. no one knew her
B. no one could tell where she died
C. she was never known
D. no one knew when she died

4. That the poet is sad over Lucy's death is clear in the words :
A. she is in grave
B. oh
C. the difference to me
D. Lucy ceased to be

5. The word 'untrodden' means
A. not covered
B. unwalkable
C. not walked over
D. hard to walk

POEM-10

I wandered lonely as cloud
That *floats* on high o'er *vales* and hills,
When all at once I saw a crowd,
A *host* of golden daffodils ;
Beside the lake, beneath the trees,
Fluttering and dancing in the breeze.
Continuous as the stars that shine
And *twinkle* in the milky way,
They *stretched* in never-ending line
Along the *margin* of a *bay* :
Ten thousasnd saw I at a *glance,*
Tossing their head in *sprightly* dance.
The waves beside them danced; but they
Outdid the *sparkling* waves in *glee* :
A poet could not but be gay,
In such a *jocund* company;
I *gazed*—and gazed—but little thought
What wealth the show to me had brought.
For oft, when on my couch I lie
In vacant or in *pensive* mood,
They *flash* upon that inward eye
Which is the bliss of *solitude*;
And then my heart with pleasure fills
And dances with the daffodils.

—William Wordsworth

QUESTIONS

1. The poet compares himself with
A. a cloud that is rainy
B. a cloud
C. a floating cloud
D. a daffodil

2. The daffodils danced
A. like stars
B. beside the lake
C. like twinkling stars
D. in lake water

3. The daffodils made the waves shy in their
A. dancing B. shining
C. sparkling D. shaking

4. The poet's wealth from daffodils is
A. the bliss of solitude
B. their dancing
C. their bright colour
D. his joyful heart

5. The word 'sprightly' means
A. happy B. blissful
C. joyful D. playing

POEM-11

Is this a holy thing to see
In a rich and fruitful land,
Babes reduc'd to *misery,*
Fed with cold and *usurous* hand?
Is that *trembling* cry a song?
Can it be a song of joy?
And so many children poor?
It is a land of poverty?
And their sun does never shine,
And their fields are *bleak and bare,*
And their ways are fill'd with thorns :
It is *eternal* winter there.
For where'er the sun does shine,
And where'er the rain does fall,
Babes can never hunger there,
Nor poverty the mind *appall.*

—William Blake

QUESTIONS

1. 'Rich and fruitful land' stands for
A. U.S.A. B. England
C. India D. China

2. Babies there sing a song with
A. joy B. trembling hands
C. a trembling cry D. sadness

3. If the babies live a miserable life, that country is indeed a country of
A. sick children B. happy children
C. poor children D. hungry children

4. 'It is eternal winter there' means
A. children's life is not happy
B. children's future is bleak
C. winter is all the year around
D. winter is at the peak

5. The word 'usurous' means
A. of zamindar
B. very cruel
C. of money lender
D. of trader

POEM-12

There was a family of rabbits
who lived near a *pack* of wolves.
The wolves *announced* that they did
not like the way the rabbits were
living. One night several wolves were
killed in an earthquake and this was
blamed on the rabbits, for it
is well known that rabbits *pound*
on the ground with their *hind*
legs and cause earthquakes. On
another night one of the wolves was
killed by a bolt of *lightning*
and this also was blamed on the
rabbits. The wolves *threatened* to *civilise* the
rabbits if they didn't behave, and
the rabbits decided to run away
to a desert island. But the other
animals, who lived at a great distance,
shamed then saying, "You must stay where
you are and be brave. This is no world
for escapists. If the wolves attack you,
we will come to your aid, in all
probability." So the rabbits continued
to live near the wolves. And one day
there was a *terrible* flood which
drowned a great many wolves. This was
blamed on the rabbits, for it is
well known that they with long
ears cause floods. The wolves *descended* on
the rabbits for their own good,
and imprisoned them in a dark *cave,*
for their own protection.
When nothing was heard about
the rabbits for some weeks, the other
animals demanded to know what
had happened to them. The wolves
replied that the rabbits had been
eaten and since they had been
eaten the affair was a purely
internal matter.
"They were trying to escape" said
the wolves, "and, as you know, this
is no world for escapists."

—James Thurber

QUESTIONS

1. Rabbits do an activity that is similar to earthquakes. It is
A. moving the soil
B. causing earthquakes
C. shaking their hind legs
D. striking the ground

2. The second time wolves died due to
A. electricity B. lightning
C. floods D. earthquakes

3. The other animals advised the rabbits not to go away because
A. they shouldn't be affraid of wolves
B. there was no fear
C. they must be brave
D. they should oppose the wolves

4. The lesson of the incident is that those who escape
A. can't live
B. can't progress
C. shall be free from danger
D. shall lag behind

5. The word 'announced' means
A. went away B. spoke
C. whistled D. declared

POEM-13

The countryside must *preserved*
(Preferably miles away from me.)
Neat hectares of the *stuff* reserved
For those in need of flower or tree.
I'll make do with *landscape* painting
Film *documentaries* on TV
And when I need to escape, *panting,*
Then open-mouthed I'll head for the sea.
Let others *stroll* and take their *leisure,*
In grasses wade upto their knees.
For I *derive* no earthly pleasure
From the green green *rash* that makes me *sneeze.*

—Roger McGough

QUESTIONS

1. The poet feels that the countryside should look
A. green
B. covered with vegetation
C. full of flowers
D. good with trees

2. The poet would like to satisfy himself of his desire to see nature from
A. films B. documentaries
C. TV D. cable TV

3. The poet gets immense pleasure when he is far from
A. natural beauty
B. countryside
C. villageside
D. film documentaries

4. The poet hates the greenery because it makes him
A. sick B. dissatisified
C. a nature lover D. sneeze

5. The word 'landscape' means
A. a scene of nature
B. physical scene of a place
C. nature beauty
D. vegetation

POEM-14

One infant grows up and becomes a *jockey;*
Another plays basketball or hockey,
This one the prize ring hates to enter
That one becomes a *tackle or center,*
I am just as glad as glad can be
That I'm not them, that they're not me.
With all my heart do I admire
Athletes who *sweat* for fun or hire,
Who take the field in *gaudy pomp,*
And *maim* each other as they *romp,*
My *limp and bashful spirit* feeds
On other people's *heroic deeds.*
Now A runs ninety yards to score,
B knocks the champion to the floor.
C risking *vertebrae and spine,*
Lashes his steed across the line,
You'd think my *ego* it would please
To *swap* positions with one of these.
Well, ego might be pleased enough,
But zealous athletes play so rough,
They do not ever, in their dealings
Consider one another's feelings.
I'm glad that when my struggle begins
Twixt prudence and ego, prudence wins.
Athletes, I'll drink to you
Or eat with you,

Or anything except compete with you,
Buy tickets worth their weight in *radium,*
To watch you *gambol* in a stadium.
And reassure myself anew
That you're not me and I'm not you.

—Ogden Nash

QUESTIONS

1. The poet admires the sportspersons who
   A. win the game
   B. perspire for goals
   C. beat other participants
   D. enjoy playing

2. The poet's spirit enjoys
   A. the great sport feats of the players
   B. seeing them getting injured
   C. knocking one another of sportspersons
   D. their fighting for the goal

3. What makes the poet not to be a sportsperson?
   A. hatred to be a player
   B. wisdom to avoid playing
   C. fear of injuries
   D. careless playing leading to injuries

4. The poet will do anything
   A. to see the players playing
   B. to go to the stadium
   C. for the sportspersons
   D. for the well-being of the players

5. The word 'prudence' means
   A. athletics   B. wisdom
   C. skill   D. bravery

POEM-15

The *fair breeze* blew, the white foam flew,
The *furrow* followed free;
We were the first that ever burst
Into that silent sea.
Down dropt the breeze, the sails *dropt* down,
T was sad as sad could be;
And we did speak only to break
The silence of the sea!
All in a hot and copper sky,
The bloody Sun, at noon,
Right up above the mast did stand,
No bigger than the Moon.
Day after day, day after day,
We *struck,* nor breath nor motion;
As *idle* as a painted ship
Upon a painted ocean.

—S.T. Coleridge

QUESTIONS

1. The weather became fine and this is clear from
   A. the wind blowing very fast
   B. the wind blowing leisurely
   C. the furrow being free
   D. the white foam

2. But soon the weather became very bad as
   A. the ship couldn't move
   B. the sails couldn't gather wind
   C. they became sad
   D. they couldn't speak

3. The sky became
   A. very hot
   B. bloody
   C. hot and copper like
   D. very perspiring

4. The ship looked like a painted one because it
   A. couldn't run   B. couldn't move
   C. got fully aground   D. got anchored

5. The word 'mast' means
   A. a pillar
   B. sailing prop
   C. upright post in a ship
   D. upright post of wood in a ship

POEM-16

The old priest Peter Gilligan
Was *weary* night and day;
For half his *flock* were in their beds,
Or under green *sods* lay.
Once while he *nodded* on a chair,
At the *moth-hour* of *eve,*
Another poor man sent for him,
And he began to *grieve.*
"I have no rest, nor joy, nor peace,
For people die and die";
And after cried he, "God forgive!
My body *spake,* not I!"
He knelt, and *leaning* on the chair
He prayed and fell asleep;
And the moth-hour went from the fields,
And stars began to *peep.*

"*Mavrone,* mavrone! The man has died
While I slept on the chair";
He *roused* his horse out of its sleep,
And rode with little care.
He rode now as he never rode,
By rocky *lane and fern*;
The sick man's wife opened the door :
"Father! You come again!"
"And is the poor man dead?" he cried.
"He died an hour ago."
The old priest Peter Gilligan
In grief *swayed to and fro.*
"When you were gone, he turned and died
As merry as a bird."
The old priest Peter Gilligan
He knelt at that word.

—W.B. Yeats

QUESTIONS

1. Peter Gilligan was very tired because he
A. had not slept for long
B. had been serving the people day and night
C. nursed the sick
D. cared much for his own people

2. He worried much because
A. his people were dying
B. he had had no sleep
C. his own people were sad
D. the poor man came to him

3. He regretted that the man died
A. when he had slept
B. when it was midnight
C. when no one was near him
D. when he slept

4. Father Gilligan found when he visited the poor man's house that
A. God nad visited in his place
B. God had excused him
C. he was not wanted
D. he couldn't do anything

5. The word 'moth-hour' means
A. late evening B. midnight
C. morning D. mid-day

POEM-17

It takes much time to kill a tree,
Not a simple *job* of the knife
Will do it. It has grown
Slowly *consuming* the earth,
Rising out of it, feeding
Upon its *crust, absorbing*
Years of sunlight, air, water,
And out of its *leprous hide*
Sprouting leaves.
So *hack and chop*
But this alone won't do it.
Not so much pain will do it.
The bleeding *bark* will heal
And from close to the ground
Will rise *curled green twigs,*
Miniature boughs
Which if unchecked will expand again
To former size.
No,
The root is to be pulled out
Out of the *anchoring* earth;
It is to be roped, tied,
And pulled out—*snapped out*
Or pulled out *entirely,*
Out from the earth-cave,
And the strength of the tree *exposed,*
The source, white and wet,
The most sensitive, hidden
For years inside the earth.
Then the matter
Of *scorching* and *choking*
In sun and air,
Browning, hardening,
Twisting, withering,
And then it is done.

—Gieve Patel

QUESTIONS

1. The tree has come out of the earth after
A. taking breath in the atmosphere
B. using the soil
C. feeling the heat of the sun
D. absorbing the crust.

2. If the tree is chopped, it will still
A. live B. wither
C. stand D. heal

3. If the tree is chopped, its leaves will
A. glisten
B. grow to their former size

C. will rise from the ground
D. shine beautifully

4. The 'white and wet' part of a tree when uprooted is its
A. source
B. sensitive part
C. life
D. important part

5. The word 'hidden' means
A. clear B. obscure
C. safe D. concealed

POEM-18

The quality of mercy is not *strain'd*;
It droppeth as the gentle rain from heaven
Upon the place beneath. It is twice blest.
It blesseth him that gives and him that takes.
T is *mightiest* in the mightiest; it *becomes*
The *throned monarch* better than his *crown*;
His *sceptre* shows the force of *temporal* power,
The *attribute* to *awe* and *majesty,*
Wherein doth sit the *dread* and fear of kings;
But mercy is above this sceptred *sway,*
It is enthroned in the hearts of kings,
It is an attribute to God himself;
And earthly power doth then show likest God's
When mercy *seasons* justice.

QUESTIONS

1. Mercy is compared with
A. rain
B. king
C. monarch
D. gentle rain

2. Mercy adds more glory to a
A. king
B. monarch
C. monarch's crown
D. monarch sitting in his throne

3. When does mercy becoem God-like?
A. when it enters a king's heart
B. when it mixes with the king's grace
C. when it is seasoned with justice
D. when mercy seasons a king's justice

4. What shows the temporal power of a monarch?
A. his throne B. his mercy
C. sceptre D. his crown

5. The word 'attribute' means
A. quantity B. quality
C. absolute D. feature

POEM-19

Whose *woods* these are I think I know,
His house is in the village thought,
He will not see me stopping here
To watch his woods fill up with snow.
My little horse must think it *queer*
To stop without a farmhouse near
Between the woods and frozen lake
The darkest evening of the year.
He gives his *harness bells* a shake
To ask if there is some mistake.
The only other sound's the sweep
Of easy wind and *downy flake.*
The woods are lovely; dark and deep,
But I have promises to keep,
And miles to go before I sleep,
And miles to go before I sleep.

QUESTIONS

1. The poet is standing
A. in a village
B. on the bank of a river
C. in a forest
D. by the side of a lake

2. When the poet stands, the horse
A. shakes its harness bells
B. shakes the bells
C. stands silently
D. asks a question

3. What kind of a weather is it?
A. wet and cloudy
B. cold and snowy
C. very cold and windy
D. cold and windy

4. '... before I sleep' means here
A. before I sleep on my bed
B. before I die
C. before I go home and sleep
D. before I 'sleep' at one level and **before I 'die'** at another

5. The words 'downy flake' mean
A. soft particles of snow
B. soft snow
C. fluffy snow
D. soft and fluffy

POEM-20

The little creature
with a hundred feet
was on its journey
to where
only it knew.
My civilised foot
dressed in polished leather
came down upon it
even so gently
there was only a soft sound
signifying
the end
of a creature of God
my Maker
I looked to see
if my *sole* was *spoiled*
and walked away

QUESTIONS

1. '... with a hundred feet' actually means
A. a hundred feet
B. many feet
C. about a hundred feet
D. near about a hundred feet

2. The poet calls his foot 'civilised' because he
A. means it otherwise
B. is civilised
C. is wearing polished shoes
D. looks civilised

3. This poem can be classified as
A. humorous B. religious
C. satirical D. romantic

4. The poet walked away. It means he
A. didn't bother about the death of the centipede
B. remained indifferent towards the centipede's death
C. regetted the centipede's death
D. felt pity for the insect

5. The word 'signifying' here means
A. displacing B. indicating
C. making it important D. proving

ANSWERS

I. Cloze Test

PASSAGE-1

1	2	3	4	5	6
A	B	A	C	D	A
7	**8**	**9**	**10**	**11**	**12**
A	B	A	B	C	B
13	**14**				
D	B				

PASSAGE-2

1	2	3	4	5	6
B	B	A	D	B	C
7	**8**	**9**	**10**	**11**	
C	B	A	C	A	

PASSAGE-3

1	2	3	4	5	6
C	D	A	A	B	B
7	**8**	**9**	**10**	**11**	**12**
C	D	B	A	B	C

PASSAGE-4

1	2	3	4	5	6
B	C	A	B	D	C
7	**8**	**9**	**10**	**11**	**12**
B	C	A	D	B	A
13					
D					

PASSAGE-5

1	2	3	4	5	6
D	C	A	B	C	B
7	**8**	**9**	**10**	**11**	**12**
C	D	B	A	D	C

PASSAGE-6

1	2	3	4	5	6
A	B	D	B	A	B
7	**8**	**9**	**10**	**11**	**12**
D	C	D	C	B	B

PASSAGE-7

1	2	3	4	5	6
A	B	D	A	B	C
7	**8**	**9**	**10**	**11**	**12**
D	D	C	D	A	B
13					
D					

PASSAGE-8

1	2	3	4	5	6
C	C	B	A	D	B
7	**8**	**9**	**10**	**11**	**12**
D	D	C	D	A	B

PASSAGE-9

1	2	3	4	5	6
B	B	C	B	D	A
7	**8**	**9**	**10**	**11**	**12**
D	A	B	C	D	D

PASSAGE-10

1	2	3	4	5	6
A	D	A	D	D	C
7	**8**	**9**	**10**	**11**	**12**
B	B	D	A	A	B

PASSAGE-11

1	2	3	4	5	6
C	B	D	A	B	A
7	**8**	**9**	**10**	**11**	**12**
A	B	D	C	A	B

PASSAGE-12

1	2	3	4	5	6
A	B	C	A	B	C
7	**8**	**9**	**10**	**11**	**12**
B	D	B	D	B	C

PASSAGE-13

1	2	3	4	5	6
D	C	B	C	C	A
7	**8**	**9**	**10**	**11**	
B	B	C	D	B	

PASSAGE-14

1	2	3	4	5	6
B	C	A	D	C	C
7	**8**	**9**	**10**	**11**	
D	A	B	A	C	

PASSAGE-15

1	2	3	4	5	6
A	B	D	B	D	B
7	**8**	**9**	**10**	**11**	
C	A	C	D	B	

PASSAGE-16

1	2	3	4	5	6
C	A	C	B	A	A
7	**8**	**9**	**10**	**11**	
C	B	D	D	D	

PASSAGE-17

1	2	3	4	5	6
D	B	D	D	D	C
7	**8**	**9**	**10**	**11**	
A	D	A	A	B	

PASSAGE-18

1	2	3	4	5	6
B	C	B	A	C	C
7	**8**	**9**	**10**	**11**	**12**
C	D	D	D	A	D
13	**14**	**15**	**16**	**17**	
C	A	B	D	C	

PASSAGE-19

1	2	3	4	5	6
B	A	B	C	B	D
7	**8**	**9**	**10**	**11**	
B	C	D	D	B	

PASSAGE-20

1	2	3	4	5	6
D	C	D	A	A	B
7	**8**	**9**	**10**		
C	C	A	C		

PASSAGE-21

1	2	3	4	5	6
D	B	C	B	C	B
7	**8**	**9**	**10**		
A	D	D	D		

PASSAGE-22

1	2	3	4	5	6
C	A	B	C	B	D
7	**8**	**9**	**10**	**11**	
A	A	B	D	D	

PASSAGE-23

1	2	3	4	5	6
B	A	C	B	A	A
7	**8**	**9**	**10**	**11**	**12**
B	D	C	A	C	B
13	**14**	**15**	**16**	**17**	**18**
C	B	C	C	A	C

PASSAGE-24

1	2	3	4	5	6
A	D	C	A	B	D
7	**8**	**9**	**10**	**11**	**12**
D	B	B	C	A	A

PASSAGE-25

1	2	3	4	5	6
D	C	B	A	D	C

7	8	9	10	11	12
A	A	C	D	B	D
13	14				
D	A				

PASSAGE-26

1	2	3	4	5	6
A	C	B	C	D	B
7	8	9	10	11	
D	C	B	A	A	

PASSAGE-27

1	2	3	4	5	6
C	B	B	A	A	B
7	8	9	10	11	12
C	A	D	D	B	D
13	14	15	16		
C	C	B	B		

PASSAGE-28

1	2	3	4	5	6
D	D	C	D	B	B
7	8	9	10	11	12
C	C	B	B	C	A
13	14	15			
A	D	C			

PASSAGE-29

1	2	3	4	5	6
B	B	C	D	A	B
7	8	9	10	11	12
A	B	C	D	B	C

PASSAGE-30

1	2	3	4	5	6
B	C	A	A	D	D
7	8	9	10	11	12
D	C	C	B	B	C
13	14	15			
A	B	D			

PASSAGE-31

1	2	3	4	5	6
A	B	D	A	B	C
7	8	9	10	11	12
B	A	B	D	A	B
13	14	15			
D	A	A			

PASSAGE-32

1	2	3	4	5	6
B	C	C	A	D	B
7	8	9	10	11	12
C	A	C	B	D	C
13	14				
B	B				

II. Passages

PASSAGE-1

1	2	3	4	5	6
A	D	A	A	A	C
7					
B					

PASSAGE-2

1	2	3	4	5	6
A	A	D	A	B	C
7					
D					

PASSAGE-3

1	2	3	4	5	6
D	C	D	C	A	D
7					
B					

PASSAGE-4

1	2	3	4	5	6
C	C	A	D	A	D
7					
C					

PASSAGE-5

1	2	3	4	5	6
B	D	D	B	D	C
7					
A					

PASSAGE-6

1	2	3	4	5	6
A	C	B	C	B	C
7					
B					

PASSAGE-7

1	2	3	4	5	6
B	C	C	B	D	B
7					
C					

PASSAGE-8

1	2	3	4	5	6
B	C	C	B	B	C
7					
A					

PASSAGE-9

1	2	3	4	5
C	C	B	D	A

PASSAGE-10

1	2	3	4	5
B	A	B	C	C

PASSAGE-11

1	2	3	4	5
C	A	B	D	A

PASSAGE-12

1	2	3	4	5
A	A	B	C	D

PASSAGE-13

1	2	3	4	5
A	C	B	A	D

PASSAGE-14

1	2	3	4	5
C	B	A	D	A

PASSAGE-15

1	2	3	4	5
B	A	C	D	A

PASSAGE-16

1	2	3	4	5
A	B	C	A	B

PASSAGE-17

1	2	3	4	5
C	A	B	D	C

PASSAGE-18

1	2	3	4	5
B	D	B	A	B

PASSAGE-19

1	2	3	4	5
D	C	B	C	D

PASSAGE-20

1	2	3	4	5
B	A	C	D	A

PASSAGE-21

1	2	3	4	5
B	C	D	D	C

PASSAGE-22

1	2	3	4	5
C	D	B	C	D

PASSAGE-23

1	2	3	4	5
A	C	D	B	A

PASSAGE-24

1	2	3	4	5
A	D	A	D	B

PASSAGE-25

1	2	3	4	5
B	C	D	A	B

PASSAGE-26

1	2	3	4	5
B	B	C	A	D

PASSAGE-27

1	2	3	4	5
A	B	A	B	C

PASSAGE-28

1	2	3	4	5
A	B	C	C	B

PASSAGE-29

1	2	3	4	5
A	C	A	B	C

PASSAGE-30

1	2	3	4	5
B	C	D	D	D

III. Poetry

POEM-1

1	2	3	4	5
A	C	B	C	A

POEM-2

1	2	3	4	5
C	B	A	D	B

POEM-3

1	2	3	4	5
D	A	B	C	B

POEM-4

1	2	3	4	5
B	D	C	D	B

POEM-5

1	2	3	4	5
B	A	D	A	B

POEM-6

1	2	3	4	5
C	D	D	D	B

POEM-7

1	2	3	4	5
C	D	B	B	A

POEM-8

1	2	3	4	5
A	B	A	D	C

POEM-9

1	2	3	4	5
A	C	D	B	C

POEM-10

1	2	3	4	5
C	B	A	A	C

POEM-11

1	2	3	4	5
B	C	C	B	C

POEM-12

1	2	3	4	5
D	B	C	B	D

POEM-13

1	2	3	4	5
B	B	A	D	B

POEM-14

1	2	3	4	5
A	A	D	A	B

POEM-15

1	2	3	4	5
B	B	C	C	D

POEM-16

1	2	3	4	5
B	A	D	A	A

POEM-17

1	2	3	4	5
B	A	B	A	D

POEM-18

1	2	3	4	5
D	D	C	C	B

POEM-19

1	2	3	4	5
C	A	C	D	A

POEM-20

1	2	3	4	5
B	A	C	B	B

English Literature : At a Glance

THE OLD ENGLISH PERIOD (I) (ANGLO-SAXON PERIOD) (450-1050)

Beowulf is probably the oldest epic of the Teutonic world. It is believed to be belonging to the first half of the sixth century.

Some important works of the Anglo-Saxon period (Pre-Christian Era)

Some important works of the Anglo-Saxon period are: *The Ruined Burg, The Lover's Message. The Maiden's Complaint, The Wanderer* and *the Seafarer.*

'The Wanderer is also known as *'Widsith'*. The work is based on the wandering life of the gleeman.

Belonging to this period, we also have *"Deor's Lament"*, which, according to Long is, "much more poetic than *'Widsith,'* and is the one perfect lyric of the Anglo-Saxon period.

In the *Seafarer*, we have glimpses of hard sea life along with the call of the sea, which we, in our times, find more pronouncedly, but perhaps less picturesquely, in Masefield's *"Sea-Fever"*.

Some Christian writers of the Anglo-Saxon period

Whereas the pagan literature of the Anglo-Saxon period was chiefly in the form of oral legends which they had brought with them from the foreign lands which they previously inhabited, the Christian writing mainly came into existence as a result of the teachings of the monks who had come under the influence of two schools—the Augustinian School (from Rome) and Northumbrian School (from Ireland).

While the former, did not produce much lasting works, the latter produced a number of good and great writers, *e.g.*, **The Venerable Bede (673-735), Caedmon (seventh century)** and **Cynewulf (eighth century)**.

Besides the poets mentioned above, we have **Alfred (848-90)** who is chiefly known as a translator.

ANGLO-NORMAN PERIOD (1066-1350)

Some important works of the Anglo-Norman period

One important work of this period is *Geoffrey's "Historic Regum Britanniae"* (1137) commonly known as *"History"*. Geoffrey is believed to have died in 1154.

Geoffrey's work which became immensely popular in his own life, is a mixture of pagan and Christian legends and is based more on lies than on real historical events.

However, the said work has its literary value for its poetry and romance pertaining to king Arthur and his Knights, and hence, it became a source of inspiration and scintillating subject matter for such illustrious authors as Malory, Shakespeare and Tennyson.

Geoffrey's work was in Latin verse. Thereafter appeared *"Layman's Brut"* (c. 1200) which has its main interest in giving Arthur's legends in (Anglo-Saxon) English itself.

Then there appeared what are known as *"Metrical Romances"* which were based on the "matter" of France, Rome and Britain.

While in the *Matter of France,* **Charlemagne's** exploits dominated and in the *Matter of Rome* Alexander's adventures and the war of Troy were the main subjects, in the *Matter of Britain*, exploits of Arthur and his knights of the Round Table were chief subject matter. There were a number of cycles pertaining to the knights of Arthur, among them being **Sir Gawain (1350)** *Quest of the Holy Grail, Death of Arthur, Merlin, etc.*

Besides the above, other works of the period included ballads, lyrics and such poems as the *Owl and the Nightingale, Ormulum, Cursor Mundi (1320), The Pearl, Patience, Cleanness, etc.* Also **Roger Bacon's** *"Opus Majus"* appeared in 1267.

THE AGE OF CHAUCER (1340-1400)

The Hundred years war between England and France had already started in 1338 when **Chaucer** was born in **1340**.

In the earlier years of the war, England was all-powerful and under Edward III it won victories over France at Sluys in 1340 and Crecy in 1346, culminating in the capture of Calais in 1347.

Another thumping victory was won by the Black Prince, Edward III's son in 1356 by defeating the French at Poitiers.

As a result of the English victories, the English foreign trade began to flourish, particularly in the export of wool to Flanders, which filled the coffers of the English king and the people also became richer, as we notice conspicuously in **Chaucer's** *Canterbury Tales* when we consider the lot of so many characters, particularly those belonging to landed aristocracy.

This picture is also graphically depicted in **Trevelyan's** *British History of Six Centuries.*

It was unfortunate for England that in the moment of its glory it was overtaken by plague, the Black Death which took a heavy toll of life all over Europe in 1348-49.

As a result of the Black Death, most of the labourers who escaped death, left the country, and this caused an intense scarcity of the availability of essential commodities at cheap rates. To meet this menace, the Parliament tried to force the labourers to accept the same wages as they were getting before the Black Death, and it all finally precipitated into the well-known Peasants' Revolt during the reign of Richard II.

In spite of the passage of certain statutes purported to safeguard the English clergy against the undue domination of the Pope, the low simmering of wrath among the clergymen for several reasons, there emerged in the "Lollards Movement" under the leadership of the redoubtable Wyclif.

Another prominent feature, this one in the literary world, was the slow advent of the spirit of New Learning from Italy and drastic changes in the structure of the English language which had already been continuing as the inevitable outcome of the Norman conquest at Hastings in 1066.

These were the general conditions in which the most significant writers of the age—**Chaucer, Langland, Dunbar,** etc. lived and flourished, thus heralding a new age slowly, but boldly and surely.

MAJOR AUTHORS AND THEIR WORKS OF CHAUCER'S AGE

Sir Thomas More (1478-1535)

Utopia (English Version)

William Tyndale (1485-1536)

New Testament

Geoffrey Chaucer (1340-1400)

The Boke of the Duchesse

The Romaunt of the Rose

The House of Fame

Troylus Cryseyde

The Canterbury Tales

Legends of Good Women

The Parliament of Fouls

Wyclif (1320-1384)

The Bible

John Heywood (1564-1627)

Four P's

Thomas Sackville and Thomas Norton : (1536-1608) (1532-1584)

Gorboduc

The Seventeenth Century

THE RENAISSANCE (1578-1625)

The Renaissance of English Literature coincides with the Age of Queen Elizabeth I. Hence, in the history of English literature, this period is also called as the *Elizabethan Age*. The inspiration for the great works of this period came from the prolific translations into English of works of ancient Rome and Greece. Thus, Plutarch's *Lives* was translated by **Sir Thomas North (1579)** from the French version. Montaigne's Essays was translated by **John Florio (1603)**. In verse, Ovid's *Metamorphoses* was translated by **Arthur Golding (1565, 1567)**. Among other works of foreign origin translated into English were Ariosto's *Orlando Furioso* by **Harrington (1591)**, and Homer's *Iliad* by **George Chapman (1598)**.

The rising English stage and the English novel borrowed from Boccaccio, Cinthio, Bandello and Straparola — the Italians. Attracted though England was to Italian art, it resisted the evil influences of debauchery, crime and passions that the Italian spirit represented. Yet, the time was ripe in England for the full development of every art and literary form. Renaissance means *a flowering again of art and culture.* It inculcated a sense of wonder in things. England also wanted to rival Spain, France and Portugal in her navigational triumphs. Thus in 1578, Sir Francis Drake circumnavigated the world, and in 1588, the English navy destroyed the Armada. The same spirit of adventure moved literature. In *Apologie for Poetrie*, Sidney described the poet — of all sciences 'the monarch'. Poets were encouraged to innovate new styles and rhythms.

Poetry

Three great men of letters led the Renaissance in England — Spenser, Sidney and Lyly.

Edmund Spenser (1552-1599) wrote the *Shepheardes Calendar* (1579)—an allegory. The union of line and metre is varied and rich. In *Hymnes In honour of Love and Beautie*, he sets forth his philosophy, the conflict in his mind between paganism and Christianity. He also wrote a satire named, *Mother Hubberd's Tale* to denounce the neglect of arts and letters. His pastoral, *Colin Clout's Come Home Again* describes his stay in London in 1589. His *Amoretti* (1595) are sonnets on love and his *Epithalamion* is an ode, But his masterpiece is the *Faerie Queene* (1589, 1595), an allegory in which characters represent virtues and vices. In it his lyrical quality and colour-effects are at their best. The *Faerie Queene* is Queen Elizabeth. The nine-line stanza he used is now called the *Spenserian stanza*.

Sir Philip Sidney (1554-1586) was a scholar, knight and courtier. In 1580 he wrote *Arcadia* which has a blend of pastoral and heroic elements It is a romance of chivalry and love. The language is characterized by *pathetic fallacy* — endowing inanimate objects with feelings and sensations. William Shakespeare borrowed from this style. His other poem, *Astrophel and Stella* (1591) describes his lost love for the daughter of an Earl. His *Apologie for Poetrie* (1595) written in an unaffected prose, is a plea for poetry.

John Lyly (1554-1606) invented an artistic, flowery style called *euphuism* through his famous romance, *Euphues, the Anatomy of Wit* (1579). This style was adopted by the refined people of the Court. The style is characterized by the use of alliteration and antithesis, fantastic metaphors and similes based on mythology, and natural history of flora and fauna.

The works of these three trail-blazed many poets and sonneteers like Samuel Daniel, Michael Drayton, Thomas Watson, Henry Constable and Thomas Lodge. Notable works from 1590 to 1603 were **Samuel Daniel's (1562-1619)** *The Civil Wars* (1595) describing the *War of the Roses*, **Michael Drayton's (1563-1631)** *Id^a, the Shepherd's Garland, The Baron's Wars, England's Heroicall Epistles* (1603) and *Poly-Olbion*, a long description of England in 15,000 alexandrines or lines of twelve syllables. England came to be known as *"a nest of singing birds"* because of the great number of lyrics and poems written in this period. **Thomas Campion (1567-1620)** published an anthology called *Two Books of Ayres* (1612). Many of the best poems are found in plays by Ben Jonson, Thomas Dekker, Beaumont and Fletcher, and Webster. But those of William Shakespeare are probably the most beautiful. In his *Sonnets*, he describes his love for a married woman who betrays him. Other poems of this period are Marlowe's Hero and Leander (1598), Shakespeare's *Venus and Adonis* (1593) and *The Rape of Lucrece* (1594).

After Elizabeth's reign, in James I rule, poetry became religious and didactic. The Protestant spirit dominated the literary works. The poems of George Wither, William Browne, the Fletcher brothers and William Drummond show the influence of Spenser still.

Ben Jonson (1573-1637) was the greatest humanist of the time. He was mainly a playwright but wrote poems also. His poetry is found in collections like Epigrams and The Forest (1616) and The Underwoods (1640). He was a satirist and neo-classicist being influenced by the Latin classics.

John Donne's (1573-1631) poetry is revolut-ionary. He disobeys the laws of rhythm and uses a device called the metaphysical conceit in which strangely opposite ideas are juxtaposed.

Prose

Much of the prose of the period is poetical, influenced by euphuism. Robert Greene, Thomas Lodge, Thomas Nashe, Thomas Deloney, and Thomas Dekker are the major writers. **Robert Greene's (1558-1592)** works include *Mamilia* and *Menaphon* and **Thomas Lodge's (1558-1625)** include *Rosalynde: Euphues Golden Legacie* (1590). **Thomas Nashe (1567-1601)** wrote pamphlets like The *Anatomie of Absurdities* and *The Terrors of the Night*. **Thomas Dekker's (1572-1632)** *The Gils Horne booke* is famous for its picturesque prose. Most of the poets and prose writers of this period were also dramatists. Shakespeare used prose for homely and humorous scenes and verse for tragic ones.

Many writers of the English Renaissance were inspired by the literary criticism of the Continent to write some themselves. Stephen Gosson's *The Schoole of Abuse* (1579) and *Sidney's Apologie for Poetrie* are good examples. Sidney eulogizes the poet as a law-giver. The period also saw works of religious prose. **Richard Hooker's (1554-1600)** pamphlet on the Marlin Marprelate controversy is a famous one. Hooker's *Of the Laws of Ecclesiastical Polity* (1594) is a masterpiece of English prose. The most seminal work of the period is the authorized version of the Bible published in 1611. The work was commissioned by James 1. A beautiful prose minus archaism is used by the revisers. The diction was to influence the English language very deeply. It is the language of daily speech, yet fresh and lofty.

Side by side with religious literature, secular and philosophical literature, mostly written by **Francis Bacon (1561-1626)**, came out. He had taken all knowledge as his province and elaborated his doctrines in his *Novum*

Organum (1620). His ideas influenced the formation of *The Royal Society for Improving Natural Knowledge* in 1645. His most popular work is his *Essays* written on diverse topics in a terse, epigrammatic style. The English writers quote copiously from Bacon today. His sentences are household terms. Take for example, "*He that hath wife and children hath given hostages to fortune*". "*Some books are to be tasted, others to be swallowed and some few to be chewed and digested*".

Another great prose-writer of the period was **Robert Burton (1577-1640)** whose *The Anatomy of Melancholy* (1621) is full of pedantry. He borrowed from numerous sources and is full of melancholy and jests; his style abounds in synonyms and epithets.

Drama

Drama thrived in the Renaissance. Foreign influence, especially of Italy, predominated. Plays were written so that the public would enjoy them and applaud the stage. There was a great variety of plays written — pure tragedy, tragi-comedy, historical drama, romantic comedy, comedy of errors, farce, pastoral, etc. The stage was a simple structure, circular in form with a courtyard open to the sky. A platform projected into the courtyard. Boys played the female roles. The public consisted of groundlings and courtiers on galleries. The unities of time, place and action were disregarded. Farce and tragedy were found in succession.

Several mythological allegories were acted before the court. **John Lyly's** euphuistic romances like *Campaspe* (1584), *Sapho and Phao, Endymion* (1592), *Midas* were praises of the queen. **George Peele (1558-1598)** wrote *The Araygnement of Paris* (1584) and *The Old Wives' Tale*. There were violent plays like **Thomas Kyd's (1558-1594)** The *Spanish Tragedie* (1585) and **Christopher Marlowe's (1564-1593)** *Tamburlaine, the Great* (1587) and *Doctor Faustus* (1592). *Doctor Faustus* is an allegory on the Renaissance love of power. It shows how Doctor Faustus, the scientist, sells his soul to the devil for twenty-four years of full power to satisfy every desire. In the end his agony increases as the devil approaches to claim his soul. Marlowe also wrote *The Jew of Malta*, which shows the unbridled love for wealth, and the historical play Edward II. Marlowe crafted the blank verse (mighty line as Shakespeare called it and used). This was suited to the fiery speeches of his characters.

The towering genius of the age was certainly **William Shakespeare (1564-1616)**. He was versatile and wrote about 36 plays and 144 sonnets. "Shakespeare was not of an age but for all times" and "Poets are born not made", wrote Ben Jonson about him. He created a gallery of nearly 800 characters who typify personalities found through human history. Julius Caesar's pride and ambition, Macbeth's unbridled ambition, King Lear's dotedness, and Othello's susceptibility to suspicion against his wife — are tragic flaws that govern men even today.

Shakespeare was not educated except for a few years at a grammar school. He had 'little Latin and less Greek' and read books in translation from Latin and Greek. He adapted the stories into a World entirely his own, instinct with life and vibrancy. Shakespeare began his career by acting for the stage. Then he wrote plays and staged them, mainly to seek court patronage. His great success made him the envy of his contemporaries like Robert Greene. In his tragedies he depicts the fall of great men owing to a tragic flaw in their character. Although they had the will to change their destiny, a fate controlled them. He used the beliefs of his time like the supernatural powers and phenomena to capture the interest of his audience. Some of his historical plays are *Richard II* (1596) and *King John* (1595). Among the romantic comedies *As You Like It* (1600), *The Merchant of Venice* (1596) and *Twelfth Night* (1601) are popular. *A Midsummer Night's Dream* (1595) is a fairy play. *Romeo and Juliet* (1594) is a tragicomedy. He used prose and blank verse.

His *Henry IV* (I & 2) (1597, 1598) contain much more blank verse than his other plays. In depth of psychological insight, and power of style *Hamlet* (1601), one of Shakespeare's great tragedies, stands supreme. *The Tempest* (161I) is one of his last plays which shows the dramatist's mellowed maturity.

Even after 400 years, Shakespeare's plays are very popular, being translated into almost every important language. *"Age cannot wither her nor custom stale her infinite variety"*; Shakespeare described Cleopatra in these words. The same may be said about his plays also.

Ben Jonson was Shakespeare's antithesis. He borrowed the style of the classics and was very erudite. He carefully studied society and wrote about it. He took the different 'humours' or dominating characteristics of men and satirized them in *Every Man in his Humour* (1598) and *Every Man out of his Humour* (1599), *Volpone, or the Fox* (1605) and *The Alchemist* (1605). He also wrote the historical tragedies, *Sejanus His Fall* (1603)' and *Catiline His Conspiracy* (1611). The plays are very true to history. John Marston, Thomas Dekker, Thomas Heywood and Middleton were other playwrights of the age. John Webster (1580-1625) is famous for horror plays like *The White Devil* (1609-1612) and *The Duchess of Malfi* (1613-1614).

MAJOR AUTHORS AND THEIR WORKS

Edmund Spenser (1552-1599)

The Faerie Queene
The Shepheardes Calendar
Amoretti

Epithalamion
Prothalamion
Mother Hubberd's Tale
The Ruins of Time
The Tears of the Muses
Astrophel

Phillip Sidney (1554-1586)

Arcadia
Astrophel and Stella
An Apologie for Poetrie

Ben Jonson (1573-1637)

Every Man in His Humour
Every Man Out of His Humour
Volpone Or the Fox
Cynthia's Revels
The Alchemist
Bartholomew Fayre
Epicaene or the Silent Women
Sejanus His Fall
Catline His Conspiracy
The Poetaster
The Devil as an Ass
The Masque of Beauty

Samuel Daniel (1562-1619)

Delia
Civil Wars between the Two Houses of Lancaster and York

Michael Drayton (1563-1631)

The Battle of Agincourt
England's heroic Epistles
The Barons' Wars
Polyolbion

William Shakespeare (1564-1616)

The Two Gentlement of Verona
The Merry Wives of Windsor
Measure for Measure
The Comedy of Errors
Love's Labour's Lost
The Taming of the Shrew
All's Well that Ends Well
A Midsummer Night's Dream
The Merchant of Venice
Much Ado About Nothing
As You Like it
Twelfth Night
Romeo and Juliet
Macbeth
Hamlet
King Lear
Othello
Antony and Cleopatra
Julius Caesar
Timon of Athens
Coriolanus
Titus Andronicus
Troilus and Cressida
King John
King Richard the Second
King Henry the Fourth-Part First
King Henry the Fourth-Second Part
King Henry the Fifth
King Henry the Sixth-First Part
King Henry the Sixth-Second Part
King Henry the Sixth-Third Part
King Richard the Third
King Henry the Eighth
Cymbeline
Pericles
The Winter's Tale
The Tempest
Venus and Adonis and Rape of Lucrece (Narrative Poems)
Sonnets (154 in number).

Christopher Marlowe (1564-1593)

Tamburlaine the Great
Edward II
Doctor Faustus
The Jew of Malta
The Tragedy of Dido, Queen of Carthage.

George Peele (1558-1597)

The Araygnement of Paris
The Famous Chronicle of King Edward I

Robert Greene (1560-1592)

Frier Bacon and Frier Bungey
Orlando Furioso
Pandosto

Thomas Nashe (1567-1601)

The Unfortunate Traveller Or The Life of Jack Wilton

Thomas Lodge (1558-1625)

The Wounds of Civil War
Rosalynde

Thomas Kyd (1557-1595)

The Spanish Tragedy

John Lyly (1554-1606)
Euphues, The Anatomy of Wit
Euphues and His England
Endymion

Francis Bacon (1561-1626)
Essays
The Advancement of Learning
The New Atlantis
Novum Organum

John Webster (1580-1625)
The White Devil
The Duchess of Malfi
The Devil's Law Case.

Thomas Heywood (1575-1650)
A Woman Killed with Kindness
The English Traveller
The Captives

Robert Burton (1577-1640)
The Anatomy of Melancholy

Sir Thomas Browne (1605-1682)
Religio Medici
Vulgar Errors
Hydrotaphia or Urne Burriale
Christian Morals

Thomas Hobbes (1588-1679)
Leviathan

Jeremy Taylor (1613-1667)
The Liberty of Prophesying
Holy Living
Holy Dying

END OF THE RENAISSANCE (1625-1660)

Prose

Puritanism set the trend for the literature during the reign of Charles 1. The Bible was the guiding spirit which may be best seen in Milton's works. The zealous Calvinists enforced Presbyterianism. The passionate curiosity for life which characterized the Renaissance gave place to a search for salvation. **Sir Thomas Browne (1605-1682)** was a scientist, but in his *Pseudodoxia Epidemica or Vulgar Errors* (1646), we see his belief in miracles. His *Religio Medici* (1642) speaks of the vanity of earthly life. **George Herbert's (1596-1633)** *The Country Parson* and **Jeremy Taylor's (1613-1667)** *Holy Living* (1650) and *Holy Dying* (1651) are sermons championing religious freedom. **John Milton (1608-1674)**, who is famous as a poet, wrote numerous pamphlets in favour of divorce which are models of beautiful prose. His *Areopagitica* (1644) is a speech for the liberty of unlicensed writing.

Another great prose-writer was **Thomas Hobbes (1588-1679)** whose *Leviathan* (1651) is a famous work. He was an empiricist and realist and believed that sensations and ideas are caused by physical reasons. Numerous works of ethics, sociology and history were written. *The History of the Rebellion and Civil Wars in England* was written by **Edward Hyde (1609-1674). Izaac Walton (1593-1683)** wrote the biographies of John Donne and George Herbert. *The Compleat Angler* (1653) is his famous work on the post-Civil War scene and contains descnptions of the English countryside.

Poetry

Two types of poets existed then — the Cavaliers, who were the Royalists, and the religious or Metaphysical poets. Thomas Carew, Sir John Suckling, John Cleveland, Robert Herrick were Cavalier poets who displayed epicurean tastes. Imagination and sensuous imagery predominate their poems. Among the religious poets, Herbert, Crashaw, Vaughan and Marvell stand out. They were mystics. **George Herbert's (1593-1633)** style is simple and expresses Christian piety in his anthology The Temple (1633). His poems *The Pulley and Love* are very popular. **Richard Crashaw (1613-1649)** used fantastic conceits; e.g. he describes the maudlin St. Mary Magdalene's eyes as "walking baths, compedious oceans", **Henry Vaughan (1622-1695)** was a mystic and his poem The Retreat is a nostalgic longing for the blissful heavenly state of childhood.

John Milton's greatest achievement was his *Paradise Lost* (1667). In theme it deals with the fall of man. In form, it follows the strict unity of the classical epic. His other poems are *L'Allegro* (1632), *Il Penseroso* (1632), *Comus* (1634), *Lycidas* (1637), *Samson Agonistes* (1671), etc.

RESTORATION LITERATURE (1620-1734)

Prose

In 1660, Charles II returned to the throne and the Puritan republic ended. The year is also marked as the beginning of the modem literature. **John Bunyan's (1628-1688)** works, *Grace Abounding* (1666) and *The Pilgrim's Progress* (1678) are the last surviving works of Puritan faith. The Pilgrim's Progress is an allegory describing the trials and tribulations on the way to salvation as faced by a Christian. Bunyan's prose is a blend of common speech and the grandeur of the revised Bible.

The scientific spirit took over the reign. The Royal Society of London for the Improvement of Natural

Knowledge, to which Bacon and William Harvey (who discovered the circulation of blood) had contributed, now had many learned men. **Sir Isaac Newton** published Principia in 1687. He discovered the laws of gravity, of the diffraction of white light and the theory of fluxions.

John Locke (1632-1704) propounded a new philosophy of commonsense and intelligent reasoning in his *An Essay Concerning Human Understanding* (1690). It lays stress on development of character. It was to influence the English thought. Voltaire was one of his French disciples.

Poetry

Restoration literature was derived from pre-Commonwealth national literature and was a reaction against Puritan oppression. It rejected severe moral codes of conduct and was chiefly satiric in nature. **Samuel Butler's (1612-1680)** poem, *Hudibras* published in three parts (1663, 1664 & 1678), is a typical work of this period. It is inspired by *Don Quixote*. He satirizes Sir Hudibras as a grotesque Presbyterian with a squire called Ralpho. It lays bare all the human follies in octosyllabic couplets. Many court poets like **Andrew Marvell (1621-1678)** and **John Oldham (1653-1683)** were veterans of the Republican era and satirize the follies of the new age.

The great poet of the period was **John Dryden (1631-1700)**. He excelled in almost every kind of composition. He wrote a series of heroic stanzas in honour of Cromwell on his death. He was a disciple of the metaphysical poets displaying their far-fetched images and conceits. In *Astraea Redux* (1660), he celebrated the return of Charles II and in *Annus Mirabilis* (1667) he commemorated the Great Fire of London and the war with Holland. He was a staunch Tory and his famous satires are *Absalom and Achitophel* (1681), *The Medal and Mac-Flecknoe*. In this last work he satirizes Shadwell, the Whig poet. *The Hind and the Panther* (1687) is an allegory on Catholicism and Anglicanism. Dryden also translated the classics, chiefly Persuis and Juvenal. He turned Virgil's *Aeneid* into brilliant couplets. His *Alexander's Feast* is an ode in honour of St. Cecilia.

Drama

The dramatic works of the Restoration were licentious and full of cynicism. They regarded the moral code of the Puritans as a matter of ridicule. Scenery now played an important part on the stage and actresses, not boys, played the female roles. The theatre was regarded as a place of vice and evil. Shakespeare's plays were rewritten and his tragedies like *Romeo and Juliet* given happy endings. French influence dominated and extraordinary superhuman feats were described. Heroes were presented as ideals and were made to give pompous speeches.

Dryden wrote many plays like *Aurengzebe* or *The Great Mogul* (1675) and The Conquest of Granada (1669, 1670) which abound in rhetoric.

The tragedians were **Thomas Otway (1651-1685)**, Nathaniel Lee (1653-1692) and **Nicholas Rowe (1674-1718)**. The comedy of this period reflects the gay intrigues of the society. Caricature and farce were used and obscenity also touched it. The main aim was to amuse. **Sir George Etheredge (1635-1691)** was an innovator and **William Wycherley (1640-1715)** was a moralist playwright. **William Congreve (1670-1729)** wrote a series of masterpieces including *The Way of the World* (1700). **John Vanbrugh** (1664-1726) and **George Farquhar (1678-1707)** were other comedy writers of the period.

Criticism

Dryden was the first English critic. *The Essay of Dramatick Poesie* (1668) is his longest single prose work and a major piece of English literary criticism. It is in the form of a discussion between four characters, one of whom is Dryden himself. It deals with topics related to theatre and evaluates the works of the Elizabethan dramatists, especially of Shakespeare.

The Diarists of the Restoration Period

One of the sources of information and genres of prose writing during the Restoration were diaries. The important names are those of John Evelyn, Samuel Pepys and Roger North. **John Evelyn (1620-1706)** was a rich man who had cultured tastes. He was a member of the Royal Society and had wide interests in diverse fields like gardening, forestry, navigation and architecture. His *Diary* which was written almost throughout his lifetime throws a floodlight on the major social and national events of the time like the Galley Slaves and the Great Fire. It is written in a plain, graphic style. **Samuel Pepys (1633-1703)** had a chequered career. Coming from the middle classes, he joined the civil services and rose to be the secretary of the Admiralty. He also became the President of the Royal Society and a member of Parliament. His famous *Diary*, covering a period of ten years, is in the form of confessions. It was written in laconic sentences like the messages of a telegram and was in a sort of code which was deciphered only in 1825. The diary shows him to be a man of versatile interests like music, science and literature. But the most controversial aspect is the detailed confessions of his life. Nobody seemed to guess he was a libertine, a morally debauched character who could stoop to low means. When we read the diary, it seems he is writing of another person. **Roger North** belonged to an elite family. He was a Tory gentleman and was engaged in the politics of the times. His famous work is *North's Lives of the Norths* containing biographies of three relatives and an autobiography. His pen pictures and anecdotes are in colloquial style.

MAJOR AUTHORS AND THEIR WORKS

Robert Herrick (1591-1574)
Noble Numbers
Hesperides

Thomas Carew (1598-1639)
Poems
'He that loves a rosy cheek'

Sir John Suckling (1660-1642)
'Ballad upon a Wedding'
'Why so pale and wan, Fond Lover'?

Andrew Marvell (1621-1678)
'To His Coy Mistress'
'The Rehearsal Transprosed'
'Ode upon Cromwell's Return from Ireland'
New Letters (a Prose Work)

George Herbert (1593-1633)
The Temple
Affliction
Easter Wings
The Collar
Man

Richard Crashaw (1613-1649)
Carmen Deo Nostro
The Infant Morturs
Steps to the Temple

John Milton (1608-1674)
Paradise Lost (in twelve Books)
Paradise Regained
Comus
Lycidas
Samson Agonistes
L'Allegro
Ill Penseroso
Areopagitica (Prose Work)
Ode on the Morning of Christ's Nativity
Sonnets (including) :
'On His Blindness'
'On the Late Massacre in Piedmont'
'When the Assault was Intended to the City'
'On His Having Arrived at the Age of Twenty-three'
A large number of Tracts and Pamphlets in support of the Parliament

John Donne (1573-1631)
Songs and Sonnets
Aires and Angels
A Nocturnall upon Lucies Day
A Valediction : Forbidding Mourning
The Extasie
Devotions (Sermon in Prose)
Ignatius His Enclave (a Prose Work)
Of the Progress of the Soul
Death's Duell

Abraham Cowley (1618-1667)
Pyramus and Thisbe
The Mistress
The Davideis
Pindarique Odes
Constantia and Philetus
Discourse by Way of Vision
Concerning the Government of Cromwell (a Prose Work)

Henry Vaughan (1622-1695)
Poems
Regeneration
The Retreat
Olor Iscanus
Thalia Redivia
Silex Scintillans

John Dryden (1631-1700)
(i) *Heroic Stanzas on the Death of Oliver Cromwell*
Astraea Redux (on the Restoration of Charles II)
Absalom and Achitophel
Religio Laici
The Hind and the Panther
The Fables
Annus Mirabilis
The Medal
Mac Flecknoe
Alexander's Feast
Prefaces to His Plays (in Prose)
An Essay of Dramatic Poesy
(ii) *Dryden's Plays*
Tyrannic Love
Conquest of Granada
All for love
The Rival Ladies
The Indian Emperor
Aureng-Zeb
Don Sebastian
Cleomenes
Love Triumphant

John Vanbrugh (1664-1726)
The Relapse
The Provoked Wife
The Confederacy

George Farquhar (1678-1707)
The Recruiting Officer
The Beaux Stratagem

Thomas Otway (1652-1685)
Orphan
Venice Preserved
Don Carlos
Alcibiades

Nathaniel Lee (1653-1692)
Nero
The Rival Queens
Sophonisba

John Bunyan (1628-1688)
The Pilgrim's Progress
Grace Abounding
The Life and Death of Mr. Badman
The Holy War

John Locke (1632-1704)
Essay on the Human Understanding
Treatise on Government
Thoughts on Education

John Evelyn (1620-1706)
Diary

Samuel Pepys (1633-1703)
Diary

The Eighteenth Century

THE AUGUSTAN AGE (1700-1740)

In general, the eighteenth century was the age of understanding and enlightenment. The emphasis was on the advancement of the human mind. Sensibility was the guiding principle. This age borrowed the humour and poetic technique of the previous century.

This age is generally called *The Augustan Age* or *The Age of Queen Anne* because the queen patronized the men of letters. The period is also known as the Classical Age. It Was an age of tolerance and harmony and was guided by reason. Dryden still wrote and was a contemporary of French authors Corneille, Racine and Moliere. Many English works were translated by the French. Poetry was still for aristocrats and the courts, but prose spread among the common public. People demanded instructions and information and practical hints for living. This led writers to use a simple style to be comprehensible to all.

Poetry

Matthew Prior (1664-1721) began by writing a parody of The Hind and the Panther in which he expounded his opinions on politics. **Sir Samuel Garth (1661-1791)** and **Joseph Addison (1672-1719)** used the heroic couplet of Dryden. Addison described Marlborough's victory at Blenheim in his poem *The Campaign* (1704). But the poetical luminary of the period was **Alexander Pope (1688-1744)**. He polished Dryden's couplet and used it as a weapon of satire, like in the famous *An Essay on Man* (1732-1734). His *An Essay on Criticism* (1711) and *The Rape of the Lock* (1712, 1714) are other great works. The latter is in mock-heroic style and describes the anger of a lady whose lock of hair had been cut off. Pope also translated the Iliad. He wrote *The Dunciad* (1728) to castigate bad poets. His *Imitations of Horace* (1733-1737) is highly admired even today.

Jonathan Swift, usually known as a prose writer, also showed a gift or versification like in his poem *On the Death of Dr. Swift*. **John Gay (1685-1732)** was popular for his fables like *The Hare with Many Friends* and his songs in *The Beggar's Opera*. **Edward Young's (1683-1765)** *The Commaint, or Night Thoughts on Life, Death, and Immortality* (1742), is a poet's delight in meditation underlining the vanity of all earthly glory.

Prose

This period saw an increasing demand for the circulation of facts and ideas among the public. **Daniel Defoe (1659-1731)** was a trail-blazer as a Journalist and his popular works are *The True-Born Englishman* (1701) and *The Shortest way with the Dissenters* (1702). Defoe wrote the first English nove! Robinson Crusoe (1719), which is a children's classic or collection of adventure stories. He cultivated the art of reporting and presented his stories as historical narratives which are precise and practical.

Steele, Addison, Swift, Arbuthnot were the other great prose-writers of the time. They introduced a style adorned by figures of speech. The periodicals of Steele and Addison contain essays which deal with practical moral questions and reflect the morals of the time.

Richard Steele (1672-1729) led a dissipated life and was full of remorse for it. He extols the **Bible as a guide** in life in his work *The Christian Hero*. **He launched the** journal *The Tatler* in 1709. **Joseph Addison** propagated rational and moderate ideas He collaborated with Steele on *The Tatler*. Steele then founded *The Spectator* in 1711 and

Addison again collaborated. Here they were merely the spectators of the society and its foibles. It epitomizes the whole nation. The character of Sir Roger de Coverley is a masterpiece, a comic personality with eccentricities. Other characters, Sir Andrew Freeport. Will Honeycomb, Captain Sentry capture the imagination of the readers.

Jonathan Swift (1667-1745) enjoyed ridicule rather than correction. He lays bare all the vices of man as something that are beyond correction. He ridiculed the modern authors in his The *Battle of the Books* (1704) and attacked the Papists and Presbyterians in *The Tale of a Tub* (1704). His most popular work is a children's classic, *Gulliver's Travels* (1726), which is also a satire on politics, religions, science and nature of man.

John Arbuthnot (1667-1735) was another humanist and man of wit and is known for his *The History of John Bull* (1712), an amusing allegory on the politics of the time.

During this period a number of deists like Locke, Collins and Tindal propounded a philosophy advocating reasoning rather than superstitious beliefs as advocated by orthodox Christians. Earl of Shaftesbury (1671-1713), Lord Bolingbroke (1678-1751) and Mandeville were other rationalists of the time who wrote many prose works.

THE AGE OF TRANSITION (1740-1800)

Like all other periods of transition, this age was also disturbed and confused. Two movements can be clearly observed in the writings of the time: (*i*) the allegiance to the old order of classicism, and (*ii*) the search after the new order of Romanticism. The period was marked by new learning, new philosophy, growth of historical research and new realism.

This period is also known as the *Age of Johnson* because **Samuel Johnson (1709-1784)**, the greatest English man of letters, flourished during this period. Samuel Johnson was a versatile man of letters translator, journalist, commentator, critic, novelist, biographer and poet. He created two satirical poems, *London* (1738) and *The Vanity of Human Wishes* (1749). He had a supple style and describes his personal reflections in his essays *The Rambler* (1750-1752) and *The Idler* (1758-1760). His *Dictionary of English Language* (1747-1755) shows remarkable precision in definition and a feeling for the correct use of words. Besides the novel *Rasselas, Prince of Abyssinia* (1759) his best works are biographical and literary studies and his edition of *Shakespeare* (1765). His *Lives of the Poets* (1777-1781) is a biographical work. His admirer James Boswell's famous biography of Johnson has made him immortal. He is described here in candid details. His prejudices, excellences and demerits are all laid bare.

Poetry

Poetry showed the influence of Dryden and Pope. It was mainly didactic and satirical and the couplet still was the major form.

Oliver Goldsmith's (1728-1774) *Deserted Village* (1770) is a masterpiece of the period. **James Thomson's (1700-1748)** *The Seasons* (1730) is a praise of the beauties of Nature in all her diversity. Other noteworthy poems of the period are **William Collins' (1721-1759)** *Ode to Evening*, a delightful lyric, and **Thomas Gray's (1716-1771)** *Elegy Written in a Country Churchyard* (1751).

A general belief in human liberty was seen as the French Revolution proceeded. **William Cowper** (1731-1800) who wrote *The Ballad of John Gilpin,* **George Crabbe (1754-1832)**, the Scotsman **Robert Burns (1759-1796)** and the mystic **William Blake (1757-1827)** echoed the sentiments of the period. Burns was a farmer and wrote in original racy dialect thus causing a break from convention. Blake was a visionary and his poems are collected in *Songs of Innocence* (1789) and *Songs of Experience* (1794). In *The Tyger,* he uses the Lamb as a symbol of innocence and of Jesus, and the Tiger as the symbol of evil in the world, of the evil seen in the French Revolution where thousands were sent to the guillotine.

Novel

The period saw the development of the novel. A series of masterpieces came out. In the novel, the author could describe events in detail. Defoe's novels so far were based on strange subjects. Now they concentrated on commonplace events of family life and society. Adventure of earlier novels gave place to character portrayal. The novels were very long and filled with minute details. **Samuel Richardson (1689-1761)** wrote *Pamela, or Virtue Rewarded* (1740) and *Clarissa Harlowe* (1747-1748). **Henry Fielding (1707-1754)** is famous for *Joseph Andrews* (1742) and *Tom Jones* (1749), **Tobias Smollet (1721-1771)** wrote *The Adventures of Roderick Random* (1748) and *The Expedition of Humphry Clinker* (1771), **Laurence Sterne (1713-1768)** wrote *Tristram Shandy* (1760), and **Oliver Goldsmith** *The Vicar of Wakefield* (1766).

Letter

There were famous letter writers also, like **Lord Chesterfield (1694-1773). Horace Walpole (1719-1797), Thomas Gray and Richardson**. Frequently, a series of letters was bound into book-form. Collections of this kind were the letters of **Lady Mary Wortley Montagu (1689-1762)**, written to Pope from Constantinople, and of Thomas Gray, from the Lake District. Chesterfield's letters to his son contain comments on political and social matters. Richardson's *Pamela* is entirely in letter-form.

Drama

The century was the age of the great novels. Drama lost originality and talent. People saw Shakespeare's plays enacted, but what attracted them was the genius of the actors. However, there were a few good plays written. For instance, Johnson's *Irene* (1749), Fielding's *The Miser*, Goldsmith's anti-sentimental comedy *She Stoops to Conquer* (1773), and Sheridan's *The School for Scandal* (1777) and *The Rivals* (1775).

Historical Work

Towards the last part of the century the history of England was rocked by many revolutionary changes the impact of which were felt in English literature. Till the mid-18th century Victorian England reigned supreme. She was mistress of the seas and her imperial rule covered many colonies. In 1776, America declared her independence and the British Parliament was divided on the issue. Many Britishers favoured the American claims. In 1789, the French Revolution broke out and here too the Britishers were divided into two camps. Inspired by the writings of Rousseau, many believed the Revolution was being fought for the right causes. The Parliament resounded with the speeches of the famous. Some even accused Warren Hastings for his extortion policies in India and some others were against slave-trade.

Treatises on philosophy by **David Hume (1711-1776)** and histories by **William Robertson (1721-1793)** and political economy (*Wealth of Nations*) by **Adam Smith (1723-1790)** came out.

Edmund Burke (1729-1797) read law and began writing to propound his views on human feelings and emotions. His language is as oratorical in Parliament at the trial of Warren Hastings as in his famous writing *A Philosophical Inquiry into the Origin of our Ideas of the Sublime and the Beautiful* (1756).

Other orators who expressed themselves in writing were Tom Paine, Godwin and Jeremy Bentham. **William Godwin (1756-1836)** advocated the elimination of government in *Enquiry Concerning Political Justice* (1793). He proscribed law, marriage, gratitude, everything that limited liberty. His monumental work is *The Decline and Fall of the Roman Empire* (1776-1788) in which he describes the growth of Christianity and his belief in reason rather than the divine. At the same time **William Paley (1743-1805)** wrote *A View of the Evidences of Christianity* (1794) to prove the existence of miracles by logic.

MAJOR AUTHORS AND THEIR WORKS

Alexander Pope (1688-1744)

Pastorals
An Essay on Criticism
Windsor Forest
The Rape of the Lock
Dunciad
Translation of Iliad and Odyssey
To Lord Bathrust
On the Use of the Riches
An Essay on Man
Epistle to Dr. Arbuthnot
Of the Knowledge and Characters of Men
Of the Characters of Women
The Messiah
Satires and Epistles of Horace Imitated

Matthew Prior (1664-1721)

Solomon on the Vanity of the World
Alma : or the Progress of the Mind
The Town and Country Mouse

John Gay (1685-1732)

Fables
The Shepherd's Week
The Rural Sports
Trivia
The Beggar's Opera
The Streets of London

Edward Young (1683-1765)

Night Thoughts

Dr. Samuel Johnson (1709-1784)

The Vanity of Human Wishes
London
The Lives of the Poets
Preface to Shakespeare
Dictionary of the English Language
A journey to the Western Islands of Scotland
The Rambler
Rasselas
Prince of Abyssinia
The Life of Savage
The Adventurer
The Idler

Daniel Defoe (1661-1731)

Robinson Crusoe
Mall Flanders

Colonel Jack
The Memoirs of a Cavalier
Captain Singleton
Journal of the Plague Year
Roxana

Jonathan Swift (1667-1745)
The Battle of the Books
A Tale of a Tub
Gulliver's Travels
Journal to Stella
The Drapier's Letters
Cadenus and Vanessa

Joseph Addison (1672-1719)
The Spectator
The Campaign
Public Credit
The Vision of Mirza
Cato
Rosamond
The Drummer

Richard Steele (1672-1729)
The Tatler
The Guardian
The Funeral
The Lying Lover
The Tender Husband
The Conscious Lover

Thomas Gray (1716-1771)
Elegy Written in a Country Churchyard
On a Distant Prospect of Eton College
On the Death of a Favourite Cat
The Bard
The Progress of Poesy
The Fatal Sisters
The Descent of Odin

The Nineteenth Century

THE ROMANTIC AGE (1798-1830)

The eighteenth century literature of England was inspired by reason, but the nineteenth century was the age of imagination. The Preface to the *Lyrical Ballads* by William Wordsworth and Samuel Taylor Coleridge in 1798, heralds the period of English Romanticism. The authors of this work were disgusted with the excesses of the French Revolution, they condemned the Rationalist Movement. England turned away from the literature of France and transferred her sympathies to Germany. The philosophical doctrine of Romanticism was inspired by Germany. Romanticism was essentially poetic. Although poles apart in their political beliefs, Wordsworth and Shelley both considered the poet as the guide, prophet and seer of mankind.

Poetry

For the great Romantics — Wordsworth, Shelley, Keats, Byron — the study of the wondrous world of feelings, senses, instincts, of Man' relation to Nature, were of prime importance. Romanticism is shot with *metaphysics*. As M. Lanson puts it, *tout traverse de frissons metaphysique* Alexander Pope had used poetry to depict the thoughts of the philosophers in his *Essay on Man*. The Romantics, dedicated to Romantic imagination — *the esemplastic imagination* as Coleridge called it — were convinced that what was revealed to their poetic intuitions, was right, the Truth. Mysterious forces divine in origin moved the earth, not cold rationalist cause and effect. Pope's couplet was dull and too precise governed by convention. The Romantics sought a lyrical form using unusual images and association of words. They found models for these in the Renaissance and the old popular poetry.

William Wordsworth (1770-1850) is aptly called the "High Priest of Nature". He saw Nature as the *'Stern Daughter of the voice of God'*, man's conscience whose balmy presence never disappointed. He was born in 1770 in the picturesque Lake District of England. Here he spent happy years of his childhood in communion with God and Nature. After study at Cambridge, he went to France in 1791 and was enthused by the cause of the Revolution. But when the Reign of Terror came and thousands died at the guillotine, his fine sensibilities, his search for human equality and peace received a rude shock. He engaged himself in the philosophy of William Godwin for sometime. Finding no solution to the problem of human pain, he finally turned to the study of Nature. In the poems of the Lyrical Ballads he describes the mundane happenings of country life, the activities of humble people. He used their common dialect with its flawed grammar as his style. He decries the coming of the industrial era which mechanized English life. With no ornament, his poetry draws its power from the intensity of his feelings and imagination, In The Prelude (1805), a long poem, Wordsworth set out to look back and retrospect on his life. He follows the growth, the turnings of his poetic genius since childhood, ruminates on his errors and recalls the corrective lessons of Nature. In his great moral poem, The Excursion (1814), he uses a philosophy to refute the pessimism that the Revolution had brought.

Samuel Taylor Coleridge (1772-1834) was Wordsworth's "Spirits Brother". He was guided by the same philosophy of the imagination. While Wordsworth's imagination gave him a special vision of the common things of rustic life, Coleridge stirred up the supernatural. To appredіate his poetry peopled with strange, translunary beings like the Ancient Mariner, one needs *'that willing suspension of disbelief that constitutes poetic faith'*, In *The Rime of the Ancient Mariner*, Coleridge describes tne strange adventures of a sailor in a ship. Having killed an albatross, the mariner suffers from hallucinations. The poem, with strange rhythm and cadences, creates a wondrous world. Coleridge was a master of lyrical style. His other famous poems are *Christabel* (1816), and *Kubla Khan* (1816). *Kubia Khan* was written as a result of an opium dream and described the wonderful, strange palace of the Chinese king, Kubla Khan. Coleridge certainly fulfils the meaning of *'Renaissance'* as *'a renascence of wonder'*.

Robert Southey (1774-1843) wrote poetry based on outlandish settings and myths like *Thalaba, the Destroyer* (1801), *The Curse of Kehama* (1810), and *Roderick, the Last of the Goths* (1814). His descriptions are rich and graphic and he uses a great variety of verse forms. He wrote a number of poems in ballad form.

Walter Scott (1771-1832) also had an interest in ballad poetry. He translated the *Lenore* from German (1796). His *The Minstrelsy of the Scottish Border* (1802) shows a great romantic interest in the Middle Ages and the days of chivalry.

The second generation of great Romantic poets include Shelley, Keats and Byron.

Percy Bysshe Shelley (1792-1822) gave up his title and wealth to write poetry. His aim was to awaken mankind to the millenium, the coming future, which would remove human anguish and sorrow. His famous ode, *Ode to the West Wind* is an impassioned exhortation — *Make me thy lyre eu'n as the forest is ...... If Winter comes, can Spring be far behind?* He came under the influence of William Godwin, the philosopher. He proclaimed himself an atheist at the age of 21. His works include *Queen Mab* (1813), *Prometheus Unbound* (1818-1819), which shows human revolt against false gods, *To a Skylark, Adonais* (1821), which is an elegy to Keats, and The Cenci (1819). Shelley's style is a mixture of abstractions and visual images.

John Keats (1795-1821) was the most sensuous of the great Romantic poets. As we read his poems, richly laden with imagery and associations, all the senses are stirred up the visual, olfactory, auditory and tactile. It is said he tasted pepper in wine to describe certain lines. His famous odes are *To a Nightingale, To Autumn* and *On a Grecian Urn.*

Lord George Gordon Byron (1788-1824) was a wealthy nobleman who shunned the popular beliefs of his times. He was notorious as a dilletante. At the age of 19, he wrote Hours of Idleness (1807). With the publication of *Childe Harold's Pilgrimage* (1812) he became famous. Childe Harold was Byron himself, the figure of the disillusioned man, the hero fed up of pleasures and debauches. He lives an outlawed life and is rebellious in spirit. He took on more incarnations in his poems, *The Giaour* (1813), *The Corsair* (1814), *The Siege of Corinth* (1815). In these he displayed his own passions and eccentricities. In 1816, divorced from his wife, he retired to Switzerland and then to Italy. He wrote a number of plays — *Manfred* (1817), *Cain* (1821) and *The Deformed Transformed* (1824). The crowning work was his lyrical, satirical *Don Juan* (1819-1823). He went to Greece to fight for its independence, but died of illness. His satire is political, against England and also against English hypocrisy and cant. His licentious descriptions caused scandals. Don Juan, his magnum opus, is written in ottava rima or eight-line stanzas and is full of wit and mockery.

Thomas Moore (1779-1852), Thomas Campbell (1777-1844), Samuel Rogers (1763-1855), Jamess Hogg (1770-1835), Walter Savage Landor (1775-1864) and **Leigh Hunt (1784-1859)** were other poets of the time.

Novel

Novels of terror and mystery prospered from 1800 to 1830. **Matthew Gregory Lewis** (1775-1818) wrote *Tales of Terror* (1800) and *Tales of Wonder* (1801). **Charles Lamb's (1775-1834)** *Tales from Shakespeare* (1807) is very popular even today. *Mrs Shelley,* the poet's wife, wrote the classic *Frankenstein* in which a scientist creates a monster that turns on its creator and destroys his most beloved ones. It is a novel of prophetic fear. **Miss Mary Mitford** wrote on country life and **Maria Edgeworth (1767-1849)** brought out educational novels like Belinda (1801) and *Tales of Fashionable Life* — novels for children.

Jane Austen (1775-1817) produced half a dozen novels which are drawing-room comedies of life. They study the passion and distress of young ladies and the life of country-folk. The novels — *Pride and Prejudice* (1813), *Sense and Sensibility* (1811), *Emma* (1816), *Persuasion* (1818), *Mansfield Park* (1814), *Northanger Abbey* (1818) — are realistic and witty, full of bracing dialogue.

Walter Scott was Scotland's greatest novelist recreating the past of his country's myths and ballads with rich humour. *Waverly* (1814), *Guy Mannering* (1815), *The Heart of Midlothian* (1818) contain history and direct observation. In *Ivanhoe* (1820), he describes the history of England in the days of the legendary Richard, the Lion Heart. *Kenilworth* (1821), *Quentin Dunward* (1823) were his other famous historical novels. He imbued the Romantic era with a love for the Middle Ages.

Prose/Criticism

The Romantic Age saw a number of reviewers and critics like **Jeremy Bentham (1748-1832)**, who expounded utilitarian doctrines, **Sydney Smith (1771-1845)**, and **William Cobbett (1762-1835)**. Coleridge, the poet, interpreted the doctrines of Kant and Schelling which show the distinction between pure reason and practical reason.

Lamb, Hazlitt, De Quincey and Leigh Hunt were Romantic critics of literature. **Charles Lamb's** essays on Shakespeare's tragedies state that we cannot do justice to them by staging them since the passions which are to be felt in their intensity are torn to tatters by the gimmickry of the actors. **William Hazlitt's (1778-1830)** criticism of some of Shakespeare's characters like Falstaff — *he laughs three inches below the flesh* — is a masterpiece. Coleridge's famous work of criticism, *Biographia Literaria* (1817), marvellously analyses Wordsworth's poetry. The Romantics believed that Shakespeare's art was organic like a work of Nature and *"esemplastic"* — able to blend different elements by imagination. **Thomas De Quincey's (1785-1859)** style is penetrating and incisive when criticizing the poets in *The Confessions of an English Opium Eater* (1821).

MAJOR AUTHORS AND THEIR WORKS

William Wordsworth (1770-1850)

The Lyrical Ballads
The Prelude
The Excursion
Tintern Abbey
Ode on Intimations of Immortality
Michael
The Solitary Reaper
Loadamia
Ode to Duty
To Milton
The Leech-Gatherer
Upon Westminster Abbey
The Rainbow
We Are Seven
The World Is Too Much with Us
To the Cuckoo
The Daffodils
Lucy Gray
Simon Lee
Early Spring
Strange Fits of Passion Have I Known

Walter Scott (1771-1832)

The Bride of Lammermoor
Ivanhoe
Quentin Durward
The Heart of midlothian
Old Mortality
The Antiquity
Guy Mannering
Waverly
Rob Roy
Kenilworth
Red Gauntlet
The Black Dwarf
The Monastery
The Abbot
The Pirate
The Fortunes of Night
The Betrothed
The Talisman
Woodstock
Lives of the Novelists
Life of Napoleon
Tales of Grandfather
The Lay of the Last Minstrel
The Minstrelsy of the Scottish Border
Marmion
The Lady of the Lake
Rockeby

Robert Southey (1774-1843)

Joan of Arc
Wat Tyler
After Blenheim
The Holly Tree
The Scholar
A Vision of Judgement
Madoc
Life of Nelson
Thalaba the Destroyer
Roderick
The Curse of Kehama

S.T. Coleridge (1772-1834)
Biographia Literaria
Table Talk
Aids to Reflection
Christabel
Kubla Khan
The Rime of the Ancient Mariner
France : An Ode
Destiny of Nations
Frost at Midnight
Dejection : An Ode
Youth and Age
Religious Musings

Lord Byron (1788-1824)
Childe Harold's Pilgrimage
Don Juan
The Bride of Abydos
Manfred
The Giaour
Hours of Idleness
The Vision of Judgement
The Prisoner of Chillon
Lara
Marino Faliero
English Bards and Scotch Reviewers
The Siege of Corinth
The Corsair
Cain

P.B. Shelley (1792-1822)
On the Necessity of Atheism
The Revolt of Islam
Prometheus Unbound
The Mask of Anarchy
Hellas
The Cenci
The Witch of Atlas
The Indian Serenade
Ozymandias of Egypt
Epipsychidion
Alaster
Queen Mab
Adonais
Ode to the West Wind
The Cloud
Ode to a Skylark
O World! O Life! O Time!
Defence of Poetry (a Prose Work)
To Night
The Sensitive Plant
A Lament

John Keats (1795-1821)
Endymion
Lamia
Hyperion
The Eve of St. Agnes
Isabella
The Eve of St. Mark
La Belle Dame Sans Merci
Ode to a Nightingale
Ode to Autumn
Ode On a Grecian Urn
Ode to Psyche
On Melancholy
On First Looking into Chapman's Homer
Bright Star

Jane Austen (1775-1871)
Sense and Sensibility
Pride and Prejudice
Mansfield Park
Emma
Persuasion
Northanger Abbey

Charles Lamb (1775-1834)
Essays of Elia
The Last Essays of Elia
John Woodvil
Tales from Shakespeare
Specimens of English Dramatic Poets
The English Comic Writers
The Old Familiar Faces

William Hazlitt (1778-1830)
Characters of Shakespeare's Plays
The English Poets
The English Comic Writers
The Dramatic Literature of the Age of Elizabeth
The Round Table : A Collection of Essays
Table Talk on Men and Manners
The Spirit of the Age

Thomas De Quincey (1785-1859)
Confessions of an English Opium Eater
Joan of Arc
English Mail Coach
Dream Fugue
Murder Considered as One of the Fine Arts
Suspiria de Profundis

Samuel Rogers (1763-1855)

Pleasures of Memory

Italy

James Hogg (1770-1835)

Kilmeny

The Queen's Wake

Thomas Campbell

Pleasures of Hope

Theodoric

Gertrude of Wyoming

Lachiel

Lord Ullin's Daughter

The Last Man

Ye Mariners of England

Hohenlinden

The Battle of Baltic

Thomas Moore (1779-1852)

Lalla Rookh

Irish Melodies

Leigh Hunt (1784-1859)

Story of Rimini

Autobiography

Walter Savage Landor (1775-1864)

Gebir

Hellenics

Imaginary Conversations

The Citations of William Shakespeare

Pericles and Aspasia

THE VICTORIAN ERA (1830-1880)

During this era, the conflict between religion and science, mysticism and rationalism, became intense. There were those who, influenced by Darwin's theory of evolution as expounded in his *On the Origin of Species,* lost their faith in the biblical explanation of man's descent from Adam and Eve. They wanted to shun dogma and accept the scientific spirit. Others lamented the loss of faith and the rising consumer values. Mat thew Arnold in his poem *Dover Beach* writes:

"The Sea of Faith was once too at the full.....

But now I only hear its long withdrawing melancholy roar......"

Prose

Carlyle and Ruskin echoed the prophecies of the Romantic era in their prose works. **Thomas Carlyle (1795-1881)**, the Scotsman, abandoned orthodoxy and came under the influence of the German writers Schiller, Novalis, Richter and Goethe. His work *Sartor Resartus* (1833-1834) is a sort of allegory based on a German professor who has written a treatise on clothes. He penetrates through the clothes to the essence of the man's being. Carlyle was also a historian. His historical works are *The French Revolution* (1837) and *The History of Frederich II of Prussia, called frederik the Great* (1858-1865). These are satirical and prophetic, expounding how man and society are organized. He was against materialism and praised the Magi and prophets of the past. He advocates strength and power.

John Ruskin (1819-1900) was indignant about the ugliness of existence brought in by industrialism and the machine. *Unto This Last* (1860), which influenced Gandhiji's economic theories, describes his disgust for soulless labour. He was a student of arts. *Modern Painters* (1843, 1860) is about landscape painters like Turner. He also wrote *The Seven Lamps of Architecture* (1849) and *The Stones of Venice* (1851-1853), praising Gothic art.

Matthew Arnold (1822-1888), the poet, wanted his countrymen to inculcate classical qualities to become harmonious in morals and in ereative works. The English must break away from their insular moorings by imbibing the teachings of Greece and the French. He is *the detector-general of the intellectual failings of his own nation*. Poetry, according to him, is important in character formation, and culture is *"the minister of the sweetness and light essential to the perfect character"*. His works include *On translating Homer, The Study of Celtic Literature and Essays in Criticism* (1865, 1889). He wrote St. Paul and Protestantism advocating that dogma should be removed from Christianity and it should adjust itself to the findings of science.

A number of philosophers, historians and scholars wrote in this period. Charles Darwin's theory of evolution dramatically affected human thought. **John Stuart Mill (1806-1873)** expounded the processes of logic and political economy. **Herbert Spencer (1820-1903)** and **Thomas Henry Huxley (1825-1895)** were scientists. **Thomas Babington Macaulay (1800-1859)** was a poet, essayist and historian who advocated English education in India. The Oxford Movement gave rise to religious writers like **John Keble (1792-1866)** and **John Henry Newman (1801-1890)**. Newman's famous work is *Apologia pro Vita Sua* (1864) in which he explains why he had converted to the Roman Church.

Novel

The transition from Walter Scott's novels to Charles Dicken's first novel in 1836 is a great one. When Queen Victoria ascended the throne, **Frederick Marryat (1792-1848)** produced sea-stories; **Edward Bulwer Lytton (1803-1873)** wrote about Byronic heroes, attractive criminals and historical novels like *The Last Days of Pompeii* (1834); **Benjamin Disraeli** (1804-1881), the Prime Minister of England, wrote *Coningsby: or The New Generation* (1844) and *Sybil: or The Two Nations* (1845) to show that the aristocrats of the society had a duty towards the unfortunate ones. In Disraeli's novels, one finds the politics of Queen Victoria's reign.

Perhaps the greatest Victorian novelist is **Charles Dickens (1812-1870)**, whose identification with the underdog in society was unmatched by any writer. One reason for this is his own troubled childhood led in penury under the shadow of a father who was in debtor's prison. The part of his life comes through vividly in his novel *David Copperfield* (1849-1850) which is also an indictment of the cruel, unimaginative schools of his times. He was a master craftsman in character delineation. A host of characters and their dialogues have become household in the English-speaking world. Thus the incorrigible optimist Micawber, Geakle, Pickwick, Fagin and others are types of characters that may be seen all around us anywhere. Dickens had a forgiving sense of humour. He never let bitterness creep into his recreations of painful events of the past. Among his famous novels are: *Pickwick Papers* (1836; in the picaresque style), *Barnaby Rudge* (1841) and *A Tale of Two Cities* (1859; based on the French Revolution), *Oliver Twist* (1837) and *Hard Times* (1854); novels exposing social conditions. He has a picturesque style and concrete imagination.

William Makepeace Thackeray (1811-1863) made a penetrating analysis of upper middle class and aristocratic society. He was a master of irony. In *The Book of Snobs* (1849), he ridicules the tendency to fawn on nobility and to imitate their manners. *Vanity Fair* (1847-1848), *History of Pendennis* (1848-1850), *The Newcomes* (1853-1855), *The History of Henry Esmond* (1852) and *The Virginians* (1857-1859) are pictures of contemporary life in which he depicts human eccentricities and follies. He was adept at reproducing jargon and idiolects.

The Romantic spirit was still alive in the works of the Bronte sisters. **Charlotte Bronte (1816-1855)** wrote *Jane Eyre* (1847), the story of a governess in a terrifying house. Her sister **Emily Bronte (1818-1848)** wrote *The Wuthering Heights* (1847), set in a wild landscape. Powerful passions and characters have made this one of the greatest novels of all times.

George Eliot (1819-1880), a pen-name for Mary Ann Evans, wrote Adam Bede (1859), the story of a girl who was forced to murder her own baby. *The Mill on the Floss* (1860) and *Romola* (1863) are other novels by her. In *Middlemarch, a Study of Provincial Life* (1871-1872), the novelist builds up, from the lives of a great number of deeply studied characters, the complex picture of the life of a small town.

Poetry

The poetry of this period still shows the influence of the Romantic Era. **Alfred, Lord Tennyson (1809-1892)** was an eclectic, selecting the best of his forerunners. He was first interested in style and metre, but later on ideas started interesting him. A great many poems by him are flawlessly beautiful. If *The Lotus Eaters* is softly languourous, *Ulysses* has a striking severity. Tennyson also experienced the intellectual crisis of his times and shared its anxieties. For instance, *The Princess* (1847) is occupied with the question of feminism. *In Memoriam* (1850) is one of his most beautiful poems. It is an elegy on the premature death of his friend Arthur Hallam. It concerns itself with the belief in immortality, the conflict between the hopes of Christianity and the rationalism of science. It is composed of octosyllabic quatrains. He shows a type of Byronic revolt in Locksley Hall (1886) and Maud (1855). In *Idylls of the King* (1859, 1869, 1889) he took Arthurian legends as his theme.

Robert Browning (1812-1889) was famous for using the technique of dramatic monologue in his poems. Through the protagonists of his poems he gives vent to his feelings, passions and aspirations. Thus in *Paracelsus* (1835), he describes the highly ambitious hero who wanted to transform man's life. We find here Browning's views on truth and philosophy. His other poems include *Sordello* (1840), *Pippa Passes* (1841), *My Last Duchess, Porphyria's Lover* and his masterpiece, *The Ring and the Book* (1868-1869). In his works we find an excess of thought and a rare vocabulary. He uses blank verse dexterously. His brusque speech, broken syntax and uneven rhythm are in contrast to Tennyson's. As Pound and Eliot have said, Browning brought verse nearer to modem colloquial speech. Browning's characters are remote in time and culture. Some of these are Rabbi Ben Ezra, Fra Lippo Lippi and Andrea del Sarto. In *The Ring and the Book* he takes as his subject an Italian crime and explores the minds of all his characters. He strikes a note of hope in his poems. The lines *"God's in his heaven/And all's well with the world"* lay bare his beliefs. But in general, Browning is considered a difficult poet.

Matthew Arnold (1822-1888) was a reflective poet with a melancholic bent. A deep brooding pensiveness informs his poetry. Dover Beach shows his concern with the loss of faith in a world of science. His epic poem *Sohrab and Rustum, Tristram and Iseult, The Scholar Gypsy* are other famous works.

Dante Gabriel Rossetti, William Morris and Algernon Charles Swinburne together are known as the Pre-Raphaelite poets. They affected Raphael, the Renaissance painter, in their desire to paint sonorous wordpictures which may not have much content to conveyor any philosophy to reveal. It was in accordance with the aestheticism of Ruskin. In fact Rossetti and Morris were painters as well as poets. They worshipped beauty like John Keats did. Robert Buchanan attacked these poets as belonging to *the fleshly school of poetry.*

Dante Gabriel Rossetti (1828-1882) translated the Italian poet Dante's *Vita Nuova*. His *The Blessed Damozel* is an exquisite poem and his best sonnets are contained in *The House of Life* in which he extols his young and beautiful wife. They are full of rich sounds and images and mystic symbols. Rossetti was inspired by the ballads of the Middle Ages. Like the primitive Italian painters, he uses rich colours and depicts warm sensuous feelings.

William Morris (1834-1896) was enchanted by Gothic art of the Middle Ages. His poems drew inspiration from those of Froissart, Chaucer and Malory. He borrowed stories from Scandinavia and Iceland. His poems are like frescoes and are very lyrical in quality. The famous ones are *The Earthly Paradise* (1868-1870) and *The Life and Death of Jason* (1867). These works show rhythm and use of archaism. He strove to bring civilization back to art from the utilitarian industrialization.

Algernon Charles Swinburne (1837-1909) was a prodigy. He was a musician, and a sonority of rhymes filled his poetry. He took romantic themes like revolt against society, hatred of monarchy and struggle against traditional morality. His *Atalanta in Calydon* (1865) is his masterpiece and is known for its choral passages.

To these poets of the Victorian Age must be added the name of **Edward Fitzgerald (1809-1883)** whose **The Rubaiyat of Omar Khayyam (1859)** is a classic.

MAJOR AUTHORS AND THEIR WORKS

Alfred Lord Tennyson (1809-1892)

The Princess
In Memoriam
Maud
Enoch Arden
Idylls of the King
Queen Mary
Harold
Backet
Akbar's Tomb
Crossing the Bar
Locksley Hall
Locksley Hall Sixty Years After
Dora
Poems by Two Brothers
The Falcon
The Cup
Poems Chiefly Lyrical
Ulysses
Poems Chiefly Lyrical
Ulysses
The Lotos-Eaters
The Death of Oenone and Other Poems

Robert Browning (1812-1889)

Pauline
Paracelsus
Strafford
Sordello
Bells and Pomegranates
Christmas Eve and Easter Day
Men and Women
Dramatis Personae
The King and the Book
Asolando
Pippa Passes
Fra Lippo Lippi
Andrea del Sarto
King Victor and King Charles
Dramatic Lyrics
Dramatic Romances and Lyrics

Matthew Arnold (1822-1888)

Sohrab and Rustum
Tristram and Iseult
Balder Dead
Empedocles on Etna
Stanzas from the Grande Chartreuse
The Strayed Reveller and Other Poems
Dover Beach
Thyrsis
Scholar Gypsy
On Translating Homer
New Poems
On the Study of Celtic Literature
Essays in Criticism

Culture and Anarchy
Literature and Dogma
Mixed Essays
Friendship's Garland
God and the Bible

D.G. Rossetti (1828-1882)
The Blessed Damozel
World's Worth
Ave
The White Ship
Sister Helen
Eden Bower
The House of Life
Ballads and Sonnets

Christina Georgina Rossetti (1830-1894)
The Goblin Market
The Prince's Market
A Pageant and Other Poems

William Morris (1834-1896)
The Defence of Guenevere
The Life and Death of Jason
The Earthly Paradise
A Dream of John Bull
News from Nowhere
A Tale of the House of the Wolfings
The Roots of the Mountains
The Story of the Glittering Plain
The Sundering Flood
Hope and Fears for Art
Signs of Change

A.C. Swinburne (1837-1909)
Atalanta in Calydon
Erechtheus
Tristram of Lyonesse
Chasteland
Bathwell
Mary Stuart
William Blake : A Critique
A Study of Shakespeare
A Study of Ben Jonson
Songs Before Sunrise

Edward Fitzgerald (1809-1883)
Euphranor : A Dialogue on Youth
Translation of Rubaiat

Thomas Carlyle (1795-1881)
Sartor Resartus
The French Revolution
Heroes and Hero-Worship
Past and Present
The Letters and Speeches of Oliver Cromwell
Latter-day Pamphlets
Life of John Sterling
History of Frederick the Great
Chartism

John Ruskin (1819-1900)
The Modern Painters
Salsette and Elephanta
The Seven Lamps of Architectur
The Stones of Venice
The Two Paths
Unto This Last
Munera Pulveris
Time and Tide by Wear and Tyne
Fors Clavigera
Sesame and Lilies
The Crown of Wild Olive

T.B. Macaulay (1800-1859)
History of England from the Accession of James II
Lays of Ancient Rome

Charles Dickens (1812-1870)
Pickwick Papers
Nicholas Nickleby
Martin Chuzzlewit
Dombey and Son
David Copperfield
Bleak House
A Tale of Two Cities
Great Expectations
Our Mutual Friend
Edwin Drood
Oliver Twist
Little Dorrit
Baraby Rudge
The Uncommercial Traveller
A Christmas Carol
Hard Times
Old Curiosity Shop

William Makepeace Thackeray (1811-1863)
Vanity Fair

Barry Lyndon
Pendennis
Henry Esmond
The New Comes
The Virginians
Adventures of Philip
The Book of Snobs
The History of Pendennis
Lovel the Widower
The Round about Papers
The English Humorists of the Eighteenth Century
The Four Georges
Rebecca and Rowena
The Rose and The Ring
Ivanhoe—the Legend of the Rhine

George Meredith (1828-1909)

The Ordeal of Richard Feveral
Evan Harrington
Emilia in England
Rhoda Fleming
Vittoria
The Adventures of Harry Richmond
Diana of the Crossways
One of Our Conquerous
The Amazing Marriage
The Egoist
Beauchamp's Career
The Tragic Comedians

Charlotte Bronte (1816-1855)

Jane Eyre
Shirley
The Professor
Villette

Emily Bronte (1818-1848)

Wuthering Heights

George Eliot (1810-1880)
(Mary Ann Evans)

Adam Bede
The Mill on the Floss
Silas Marner
Scenes of Clerical Life
Life of Jesus
Romola
Fleix Holt the Radical
Daniel Deronda
Middlemarch

Benjamin Disraeli (1804-1881)

Vivian Gray
Sybil : Or the Two Nations
The Voyage of Captain Popavilla
Henrietta Temple
Coningsby : or the New Generation
Tancred : or the New Crusade
The Wondrous Tale of Alroy and the Rise of Iskander
Contarini Fleming : A Psychological Auto-biography

R.L. Stevenson (1850-1894)

Travels with a Donkey in the Cevennes
An Inland Voyage
Virginibus Pueresque
New Arabian Nights
Treasure Island
The Strange Case of Dr. Jackyll and Mr. Hyde
Kidnapped
The Black Arrow
The Master of Ballantrae
Catriona
Underwords
A Child's Garden of Verses

Thomas Hardy (1840-1828)

Under the Greenwood Tree
Desperate Remedies
A Pair of Blue Eyes
Two on a Tower
Far From the Madding Crowd
The Return of the Native
The Mayor of Casterbridge
Tess of the D'Urbervilles
Jude the Obscure
The Hand of Ethelberta
The Trumpet Major
The Woodlanders
The Well-beloved
A Laodicean
A Group of Noble Dames
Life's LIttle Ironies
Wessex Poems
The Dynasts
A Changed Man
Winter Words
The Waiting Supper and Other Tales

The Modern Age (1880 Onwards)

As the 20th century dawned, new values replaced the old ones and shaped the literature of Great Britain. England fast lost its imperial image as her colonies revolted and fought for independence. Industrialization progressed by leaps and bounds and the two World Wars brought economic depression. All this affected the content of literature. Writers sought new vehicles of expression. The findings of **Sigmund Freud** in the realms of psychology took novelists to the subconscious mind. A great number of writers who became famous men of letters in English came from Ireland (**G.B. Shaw, W.B. Yeats, James Joyce and Samuel Beckett**) and from America (**T.S. Eliot and Ezra Pound**). Socialism became a practising creed and feminism raised her head. Dogmatic Christianity was more or less ignored. Although great strides were made in scientific inventions, science could not provide suitable answers to the deep questioning of the human mind resulting in ethical philosophy. The age saw the end of feudalism. Victorian reticence and prudery gave way to decadence in literature. English writers came under the influence of the French Parnassians and Symbolists. Scandinavia and Russia represented by **Ibsen** and **Tolstoy** also influenced the British men of letters. Many a poet wished to fight free from the fixed rules of versification and wrote in free verse. Many imitated the American poet **Walt Whitman**. English literature became more expansive in its concerns. The life and culture of foreign lands were depicted. Although **Kipling** was an imperialist, his works go beyond England. Being born in India, his works give a graphic view of the country. The great Celtic Revival under Yeats brought a new strain to English literature. Finally, the theatre, lying dormant for a century, now woke up with renewed vigour.

Criticism

The Age began with scholarly works in literary history. **Leslie Stephen (1832-1904)** wrote biographical and critical essays. He produced *The English Utilitarians and the Dictionary of National Biography*. He was an agnostic and rationalist. **A.C. Bradley (1851-1935), H.J.C. Grierson (1866-1960)** and **Edward Dowden (1843-1913)** were other famous critics. Bradley is famous for his critical work on Shakespeare's tragedies.

Walter Horatio Pater (1839-1894) propounded the literary doctrine *Art for Art's Sake* which was a quest for the most refined pleasure. The exquisite in art came from a reflection of the past. He eulogized the accomplishments of the Renaissance. His prose style was rich, musical and classical. His works include *Studies in the History of the Renaissance* (1873) and *Marius the Epicurean* (1885).

John Addington Symonds (1840-1893) was another admirer of the Renaissance. **Oscar Wilde (1856-1900)**, more known as a novelist and dramatist, gave a wider dimension to the theory of Art for Art's Sake by spicing it with wit and paradox. **George Saintsbury (1845-1933)** and **Sir Walter Raleigh (1861-1922)** were other famous critics.

Poetry

Most of the poetry written in this period are the works of those more renowned as novelists: Robert Louis Stevenson, Rudyard Kipling and Thomas Hardy. William Butler Yeats, who pioneered the Celtic Revival, Thomas Steams Eliot, whose *Wasteland* is a watershed leading to modern poetry, Gerard Manley Hopkins, the Catholic poet, are the famous poets of this period.

Rudyard Kipling (1865-1936) wrote on imperialist themes in *Barrack Room Ballads* (1892), *The Seven Seas* (1896) and *Five Nations* (1903). These poems were aimed by their rugged music to rouse people to protest. He combined folk-music with music-hall chorus. It had the sound of drum beats and bugle-calls and even the refinements of chamber music. The poetry of imperialism, heroism of national policy, contained slang and even biblical allusions. In fact, his popularity was that of Walt Whitman, the national poet of America. Many of his subjects were from India, like the poem *Gunga Din*.

W.E. Henley (1849-1903) also wrote poetry which praised Britain's colonial power. *The Song of the Sword, For England's Sake* and *London Voluntaries* are some of his better-known poems.

There were also a group of poets called the Decadents. They were aesthetes and their doctrine was 'Art for Art's Sake'. **Oscar Wilde** was the leading poet of the group. *The Ballad of Reading Gaol* (1898) is his famous work inspired by his crime and imprisonment.

A group of poets had a pessimistic view of life. **John Davidson (1857-1909), Ernest Dawson (1867-1900)** and **A.E. Housman (1859-1936)** are some of these poets. But the leading pessimist of the age was **Thomas Hardy (1840-1928)**, better known as a novelist. He published *Wessex Poems* (1898) after the novel *Jude the Obscure* failed to receive public acclaim. His poetry was musical and highly individual. He had a disillusioned view of life. From 1903 to 1908, he produced the vast poetical work *The Dynasts*, written under the background of Napoleon's struggle against Europe combining real history with symbolic flashes. His poem, *To an Unborn Pauper Child,* reveals his utter dejection with life: *'Breathe : hid heart'*, it begins.

Francis Thompson (1859-1907) and **Gerard Manley Hopkins (1844-1889)** were religious poets of the beginning of the twentieth century. Thompson's poem, *The Hound of Heaven* is a masterpiece. It describes God as a Heavenly Hound chasing man to capture his soul and man fleeing Him in the pleasures of life. The Jesuit, Hopkins invented a new type of verse called *'sprung rhythm'*. It was filled with strange word coinages and is difficult for the ordinary reader to understand. His poetry reflects the conflirt within him between his attraction to Roman Catholicism and his joy tor the beautiful creation. He wrote a number of religious poems of which *The Wreck of the "Deutschland"* is one of the best. It describes the death of five Franciscan nuns on board the ship, *Deutschland.*

Irish, English and Continental influences met in **W.B. Yeats (1865-1939)**. He Was born in Ireland but came to live in London. He was influenced by the strange mystical visions of William Blake, by pre-Raphaelite refinement and even the mysticism and occultism of the Orient, especially of India. His poetry is an attempt to revive Celtic mysticism and Irish mythology. Apparently it Was Yeats who introduced Rabindra Nath Tagore to the West. He also came under the influence of Verlaine, a French symbolist poet. His best poetry is in *The Wild Swans at Coole* (1919), *The Tower* (1928) and *The Winding Stair* (1933). Some of his well-known poems are: *Easter* (1916), *The Second Coming, Byzantium, A Prayer for my Daughter, Leda and Swan, Sailing to Byzantium, Meru, Lapis Lazudili, Among School Children,* etc. His progress as a poet can be assessed by comparing the beautiful but simple *Lake Isle of Innisfree* with the beautiful and profound *Byzantium.*

The towering poet of the 20th century is **Thomas Steams Eliot (1888-1965)**. Eliot came on to the scene when the West was passing through tremendous upheavals — belief in religion, especially of the Church was fading, democracy was the new experiment in politics, and many modernist trends were noticeable in literature. Eliot proclaimed himself "a royalist in politics, an Anglo-Catholic in religion and a classicist in literature". Tradition, according to him, was not the dead past but the past living in the present. In his essay *Tradition and the Individual Talent,* he states that "the talent of an artist shows itself not where he differs from the ancients but where, in his work, they assert their immortality". Eliot's poetry shows metaphysical, symbolist and imagist strains, but his individual talent shines forth unmistakeably. An eclectic philosophy, borrowed from his own Christianity and Buddhism and the Upanishads informs his poetry. His poetry, especially *The Wasteland* (1922) is a poem that describes the zeitgeist (spirit of the times) and the *angoisse metaphysique* (metaphysical anguish) of life in post-World War Europe. It begins with the sentence *"April is a cruel month"* and this sets the strain lor the whole poem. A brooding sense of futility and human inanity pervades modern life. Eliot achieves this effect by a combination of literary allusions to the past which stirs associations, and by what is called as the *objective correlative.* This last technique means that images are described which call up an emotion or a feeling. His other poems are *The Lave Song of J. Alfred Prufrock* and *Four Quartets* (1944). These lines from the *Four Quartets* may sum up the disillusionment of the times: *"Footfalls echo in the memory/Down the passage one could not take / To the door one could not open".* Eliot was a poet of spiritual regeneration.

As the century proceeds, a host of poets make their mark **Stephen Spender (1909-1995), W.H. Auden (1907-1973), C. Day Lewis (1904-1972), Louis MacNeice (1907-1963)** — all of them wrote with a Social awareness, exposing the horror of the bourgeois culture and capitalist exploitation and the terror of totalitarianism.

We cannot end this section of the early modern twentieth century without a reference to **Rupert Brooke (1887-1915), Wilfred Owen (1893-1918)** and **Siegfried Sassoon (1886-1967)** popularly known as the "War poets". They had served the Armed Forces in the First World War, and after 1918, disillusioned by the horrors they had witnessed took their pens to write against the war. The poem *The Soldier* is one of the finest lyrics in the English language. It describes the poet's sense of impending death in battle and his love for his country: *"If I should die/Think only this of me/That there is a part of England/Buried in some foreign land".* Another poem is Sassoon's *Everyone Sang,* which describes the exultation felt by the soldiers returning home after the General Armistice was signed. They are described as *freed birds.*

Novel

Just like poetry, the novel of this century reflects the great passions and strivings of the age. The discoveries of **Sigmund Freud (1856-1939)** revealed the relationship of man's behaviour to his subconscious mind. The subconscious contains impressions of past experiences which influence a person's attitudes and behaviour. These discoveries led not only to new methods of psychiatric treatment but also to new dramatic techniques in the art of the novel. The stream-of-consciousness method used by James Joyce and Virginia Woolf spring from these discoveries. The modem novel is more and more concerned with an analysis of human behaviour. The focus shifts from a description of the external atmosphere to the thoughts of the characters.

Thomas Hardy's works are tinged with a gloomy pessimism reminiscent of Schopenhauer, and an analogy may be found in his works to Flaubert and Zola from

France. Hardy's country Dorsetshire and the surroundings become the 'Wessex' of his novels. His work is full of realistic descriptions of the countryside. The places, full of pre-historic and Roman remains, heaths, have a character, and influence the people living there. The pre-historic past presses on the life of today. He is adept at delineating rustic characters. Man is a puppet of fate and an uncontrollable destiny drives him along life. A bitter helplessness pervades his novels *Far from the Madding Crowd* (1874), *The Return of the Native* (1878), *The Mayor of Casterbridge* (1886), and *Jude the Obscure* (1895). His success reached a climax with *Tess of the d'Urbervilles* (1891). His *Tess of the D'UrberviUes* and *Jude the Obscure,* because of their frank handling of sex and religion, aroused the hostility of the reading public. These two books, however, present Hardy's most moving indictments of the human situation.

The works of George Robert Gissing (1857-1903) produce a sense of absolute dejection. He worked as an ill-paid hack in the poor districts of London and described these places vividly in his books. Although impressed by Charles Dickens, his writings show none of Dickens' humour. One bitter, wretched world, a miserable London, exists in his works. Thus *Demos, a Story of English Socialism* (1886) describes the futility of socialist agitation, *The Nether World* (1889), the wretchedness of the London slums, *New Grub Street* (1891), the hopeless lot of a penniless writer, and *The Odd Women* (1893), the plight of unmarried women. His style is as bare and unaffected as his ideas.

Robert Louis Stevenson (1850-1894) stands in contrast to Hardy and Gissing in his recreation of the life of action and adventure. Although he suffered from an incurable malady, he did not lose faith in himself. He brought out *An Inland Voyage* (1878), *Travels with a Donkey in the Cevennes* (1879), *The Silverado Squatters, Treasure Island* (1833), *Kidnapped* and *The Master of Ballantrae* (1889) among others. The last three are very popular among children the world over. He also wrote children's adventure classics like *The Treasure Island* (1883), *Dr Jekyll and Mr. Hyde* (1886) and *Kidnapped* (1886). In *Dr. Jekyll and Mr Hyde* he touches upon the dual nature of man his good and evil aspects. His style is vivid and full of interesting details.

Another great novelist was the Pole, **Joseph Conrad (1857-1924)**, who perfected his knowledge of English and wrote in a vivid style with a strong foreign accent. His experience of sailing life and work in the English merchant service gave him the ideas to write masterpieces like *The Nigger of the Narcissus* (1897), and *Lord Jim: A Tale* (1900). Like the Slavs he was preoccupied with the problem of human misery. *Lord Jim* and *The Heart of Darkness* (1902) show his anger at what the white man had done to exploit Africa and other nations. A trait of his narrative technique is the gradual picture of his character formed from fragmentary descriptions of witnesses. He has a rich, sensuous prose style full of striking imagery.

Rudyard Kipling wrote stories about Indian life: *Plain Tales from the Hills* (1888) and *Soldiers Three* (1888). *Plain Tales from the Hills* depicts an Englishman's encounter with the strange East. Kipling was born in Bombay and spent his early life in India. He knew the land and its customs, its people and languages. His best book is *Kim* (1901), the story of a half-Irish boy, who speaks the language of the rustics of India and accompanies a Buddhist Lama on his search for "Nirvana" or Salvation. Kipling is adept at describing the sights and smells of India and its colourful people with their racy dialects. He also wrote two animal epics entitled, *The Jungle Book* (1894) and a series of short stories for children like *Captains Courageous* (1897), just *So Stories* (1902) and *Puck of Pook's Hill* (1906). Kipling was influenced by Carlyle's doctrine of energy. As a spokesman of the Imperialist theme he believed that it was ideal for a person to sacrifice himself for his tribe. He believed that especially the white man was ordained to rule and lead nations. His works praise Britain's hegemony over her colonies.

Shortly after Kipling, came H. G. Wells and John Galsworthy who were Socialists and criticized the English society. **H.G. Wells** (1866-1946) began by writing stories with a semi-scientific flavour like *The Time Machine* (1895), *The Island of Dr Moreau* (1896), *The Invisible Man* (1897) and *The War of the Worlds* (1898). The stories are ingenuously plotted and thrill and disturb the readers. Later on Wells' interest shifted to social problems. He became a member of the Fabian Society. He wrote *Mankind in the Making* (1903) describing how society would look like when reformed by socialism. He also satirized the society in *Love and Mr Lewisham* (1900), *Kipps* (1905). *Tono-Bungay* (1909) and *Marriage* (1912). He does not glorify Britain's past and he scorns the existing institutions of his country. He wrote a number of remarkable books after the outbreak of World War I in 1914. These show his restless self-examining spirit. Some of these are *Mr Britling Sees it through* (1916) and *The Undying Fire* (1919).

In the works of **John Galsworthy (1867-1933)** we find an artistic conscience. Like Wells, he also attacked the concept of property and commercialism in his novels. He too exposed and criticized national prejudices, especially those existing among his own class, the landed gentry. He was widely read in Continental Literature and was especially influenced by France and Russia. Turgenev with his noble realism was his ideal. He is a detached and impartial observer of his country's decadent values. He advocates a fearless search for truth. *In The Island Pharisees* (1904) he exposes the stagnation of thought among English privileged classes. A similar theme is touched in other novels like *The Country House* (1907), *The Patrician* (1911) and *The Dark Flower* (1913) where country squires, aristocracy and artists are critically studied. *The Forsyte Saga* (1922) is his masterpiece. It is a natural history of the rich upper-middle class family. He describes their attitude to events like the Great War, the growth of socialism, unemployment and the coal strike.

Enoch Arnold Bennett (1867-1931) wrote a number of different types of novels presenting a detailed picture of an industrial district in the provinces. He is a realist like the French nationalists. His masterpiece is *The Old Wives' Tale* (1908).

G.K. Chesterton (1874-1936) was a champion of tradition and he refuted and opposed the attacks of his contemporaries against English society in *Orthodoxy* (1908), *The Napoleon of Notting Hill* (1904). He believed in tradition sanctified by ages of experience and even in the religious bond between men. His style is effective with the use of imagery and comparison and he spices it with plenty of humour.

James Joyce (1882-1941) pioneered a new type of novel with the *stream-of-consciousness* technique. Characters in *Ulysses* (1922) unreel themselves by a sort of interior monologue. Speech is mimicked and styles are parodied. *Ulysses* is modelled on the *Odyssey* of Homer and set in the slums of Dublin. The thousand pages of this novel cover just one day in the life of Leopold Bloom and Stephen Dedalus. Joyce coined words from several languages and was a master craftsman with wit and conceits. His other famous work is the autobiographical *A Portrait of the Artist as a Young Man* (1916) which describes his adolescence and sensuous tendencies.

Virginia Woolf (1882-1941) continued the stream-of-consciousness technique. Her works *To the Lighthouse* (1927) and *Mrs Dallaway* (1925) reveal the hidden inner life of her characters.

E.M. Forster (1879-1970) was the novelist of cultural relations. In **A Passage to India** (1924) he studies the conflict between the west and the east and takes a favourable stand for the latter. *Where Angels Fear to Tread* (1905) studies how the cultural divide between an Italian girl and her English husband leads to the ruination of their marriage and life.

D.H. Lawrence (1885-1930) was a prolific writer. His outspoken views on sexual relations raised much hue and cry. He considered sex the religion of the blood. His novels were dubbed pornographic. He believed in the free expression of human personality, in being guided by unrestrained primitive instincts. In *Sons and Lovers* (1913) he studies the relationship of son and mother and the social disparity of a father, a coalminer and a mother, a teacher. The novel is autobiographical. Other works by him are *The Rainbow* (1915), *Women in Love* (1921), and *The Plumed Serpent* (1926). *The Rainbow,* suppressed as obscene, treats the conflict between man and woman. *Lady Chatterley's Lover* (1928) was canned for being obscene.

George Orwell (1903-1950) wrote novels which were an indictment of totalitarian government: *Animal Farm* (1945) and *Nineteen Eighty-Four* (1949). **Aldous Huxley's** *Brave New World* (1932) is a prophetic book about the future of civilization in the context of scientific advancement.

Drama

After Shakespeare, **George Bernard Shaw (1856-1950)** is the great playwright whose works enlivened the British stage. Shaw, like Ibsen, believed in drama as a vehicle for ideas. He had a rich Irish sense of humour and his plays are satires on various social and philosophical themes. His general technique was to discuss the problem of his play first in its preface. Often this preface is longer than the play itself. *Widowers' Houses* (1892) was his first play. In this he discusses the problem of Housing. In *Mrs Warren's Profession* (1894) he lays bare the profession of a prostitute. In *Arms and the Man* (1894) the theme is the chocolate-cream soldier. Shaw was an iconoclast breaking well-established idols or myths. Thus this play disillusions us of the romantic image of a soldier. He is not one who is willing to die for his country, but one who loves his life. When the enemy is weak, he attacks, but withdraws and takes to his heels if the enemy is strong. George Bernard Shaw had a keen interest in the English language and formulated a standard pronunciation for it. He studies the theme of how language can influence one's rise in the social ladder. Professor Higgins succeeds in teaching a flower-girl to rid herself of a cockney accent and to speak well enough to pass for royalty! In *Man and Superman* we see Shaw as a master conversationalist. Ideas are discussed without much action taking place in the play. *The Apple Cart* (1929) shows the weaknesses of democracy. Although an Irish man, Shaw did not write on Irish themes as such.

Oscar Wilde reminds one of the Restoration playwrights Sheridan and Congreve in his comedy of manners. His style is full of paradox and verbal wit. Some of his famous plays are *Lady Windermere's Fan* (1892), *A Woman of No Importance* (1893) and *The Importance of Being Ernest* (1895).

John Galsworthy's plays *Sfrife* (1909), *Justice* (1910) and *Loyalties* (1922) were based on the theme of class exploitation.

W.B. Yeats contributed to the Irish drama. His Celtic theme comes through in *The Countess Cathleen* (1892) and *The Land of Heart's Desire* (1894). **Sean O'Casey** (1884-1964) and **J. M. Synge** (1871-1909) were other noted Irish playwrights. The latter's plays, *The Playboy of the Western World* (1907) and *Riders to the Sea* (1904) are famous.

T.S. Eliot's contribution to the modern theatre were religious and moral plays. He uses the Greek "chorus" style in *Murder in the Cathedral* (1935) to heighten the dramatic effect of the murder of Thomas Becket by the Archbishop of Canterbury's men. *The Family Reunion* (1939) is a play about sin and expiation. Eliot pruned verse to sound like prose. This is done dexterously in *The Cocktail Party* (1949) and *The Confidential Clerk* (1953) where characters speak verse which sounds like prose.

A group of playwrights came to be known as the "Angry Young Men". **John Osborne (1929-1994)** was the most prominent of them. His play *Look Back in Anger* (1956) catches the mood of the frustrated youth in post-War England. In his plays, he exposes the wretchedness of the working class.

Harold Pinter (1930-2008) mixes comedy and horror in his plays like *The Birthday Party* (1958).

Another group of dramatists drew their inspiration from France. *The Absurd Theatre*, as it was called, began in France with Albert Camus, Jean Genet anJ Ionesco as its pioneers. In England, **Samuel Beckett (1906-1989)** was the Irish dramatist of this school. His plays *Endgame* (1955), *Krapp's Last Tape* (1958) and *Waiting For Godot* (1906) show the meaninglessness of human action and the unrelieved gloom of existence.

MAJOR AUTHORS AND THEIR WORKS

George Bernard Shaw (1856-1950)

Widowers' Houses
Candida
You Never Can Tell
Man and Superman
Back to Methuselah
Saint Joan
Heartbreak House
The Philanderer
Mrs. Warren's Profession
Caesar and Cleopatra
John Bull's Other Island
Major Barbara
The Doctor's Dilemma
Getting Married
The Apple Cart
Pygmalion
The Dark Lady of the Sonnets
Plays Pleasant and Unpleasant
The Millionaire
The Intelligent Woman's Guide to Socialism
Everybody's Political What is What
Cashel Byron's Profession
Love Among the Artists
Androcles and the Lion
The Devil's Disciple
The Man of Destiny

W.B. Yeats (1865-1939)

The Land of Heart's Desire
The Countess Cathleen
The Shadowy Waters
The Hour-glass
The Resurrection
The King's Threshold
On Baile's Strand
The Cat and the Moon
Ideas of Good and Evil
Discoveries
The Wind among the Reeds
The Wanderings of Oisin
The Tower
The Winding Stair and Other Poems
Lake Isle of Innisfree
Byzantium

John Galsworthy (1867-1933)

The Silver Box
Strife
The Skin Game
The Man of Property
Justice
Loyalties
Escape
The Inn of Tranquility
The Forsyte Saga
The Country House
Fraternity
The Patrician
The Dark Flower
Saint's Progress
Maid in Waiting
Flower Wilderness

Rudyard Kipling (1865-1936)

Kim

The Jungle Book
Barrack-room Ballads
Departmental Ditties
The Seven Seas
The Five Nations
Tales from the Hills
Soldiers Three
Life's Handicap
The Phantom Rickshaw
Many Inventions
The Day's Work
Just-so Stories for Little Children
Rewards and Fairies
Debits and Credits

H.G. Wells (1866-1946)

The Time Machine
Love and Mr. Levisham
Kipps
The History of Mr. Polly
Mr. Britling Sees It Through
Christina Albertas Father
The Wonderful Visit
The Island of Dr. Moreau
The Invisible Man
The War of the Worlds
The First Men in the Moon
The Food of the Goas
Marriage
Experiment in Autobiography
The Contemporary Novel

Joseph Conrad (1857-1924)

The Nigger of the 'Narcissus'
Typhoon
Lord Jim
Victory
Almayer's Folly
An Outcast of the Islands
Youth
Heart of Darkness
The Secret Agent
The Shadow of Line
Suspense-A Napoleonic Novel

Arnold Bennett (1867-1931)

The Old Wives' Tale
Clayhanger
Riceyman Steps
Buried Alive
Hilda Lessways
These Twain
Sacred and Profane Love
The Pretty Lady
The Love Match
The Author's Craft

Walter de la Mare (1873-1956)

Peacock Pie
Memoirs of a Midget
Songs of Childhood
Bells and Grass
The Traveller
Early the Morning
Love

T.S. Eliot (1888-1965)

The Waste Land
Prufrock and Other Observations
Gerontion
The Hollow Men
Ash Wednesday
Four Quartets
Sweeney Agonistes
Murder in the Cathedral
The Rock
The Family Reunion
The Cocktail Party
The Confidential Clerk
The Sacred Wood
After Strange Gods
The Elder Statesman
The Idea of a Christian Society
What is a Classic?
For Lancelot Andrews
The Use of Poetry and the Use of Criticism
Elizabethan Essays
Points of View

Virginia Woolf (1882-1941)

The Voyage Out
Jacob's Room
Mrs. Dalloway
To The Light House
The Waves
Flush
Orlando : A Biography
The Common Reader
Roger Fry
The Death of the Moth
Mr. Bennett and Mrs. Brown

A Room of One's Own
Between the Acts (Unfinished)

E.M. Forster (1879-1970)

Abinger Harvest
Two Cheers for Democracy
A Passage to India
Howard's End
The Hill of Devi
The Celestial Omnibus
Collected Short Stories
Where Angels Fear to Tread
The Longest Journey
The Story of the Siren
A Room with a View
The Eternal Moment

James Joyce (1882-1941)

Ulysses
Portrait of the Artist as a Young Man
Finnegans Wake
Dubliners

D.H. Lawrence (1885-1930)

Sons and Lovers
Woman in Love
Lady Chatterly's Lover
The Rainbow
The White Peacock
Kangaroo
The Plumed Serpent

Aldous Huxley (1894-1963)

Point Counter Point
The Burning Wheel
Those Barren Leaves
Brave New World
After Many a Summer
Eyeless in Gaza
Antic Hay
Time Must Have a Stop
Crome Yellow
The Defeat of Youth
The Perennial Philosophy
The Devils of Loudun

George Orwell (1903-1950)

The Animal Farm
The Road to Wigan Pier
Nineteen Eighty-Four
Burmese Days
Keep the Aspidistra Flying

Oscar Wilde (1854-1900)

The Sphinx
The Ballad of Reeding Gaol
The Canterville Ghost
De Profundis
The Duchess of Padua
The Importance of Being Earnest
An Ideal Husband
Lady Windermere's Fan
Salome
The Picture of Dorian Gray
The Happy Prince and the Other Tales

Harold Pinter (1930-2008)

The Birthday Party
The Dumb Waiter
The Care Taker
A Night Out
The Home Coming
Old Times
Silence

Indian Writing in English

ANAND, MULKRAJ (1905-2004)

He was greatly influenced by Premchand on the one hand and Tagore on the other.

Works

Some of his famous novels are :

1. The Village (1939)
2. Across the Black waters (1940)
3. The Sword and the sickle (1942)
4. Untouchable (1933) (his first novel)
5. Seven summers (1951)
6. Private Life of an Indian Prince (1953)
7. The Big Heart (1945)
8. Coolie (1936) (It was recast in seventies)
9. Two Leaves and a Bud (1937)
10. The Old Woman and the Cow (1960)
11. The Road (1961)
12. Death of a Hero (1963)
13. Confession of a Lover (1976)
14. Morning Face (1968)

AUROBINDO, GHOSE (1872-1950)

- He was known as the "firebrand" of India.
- He was a poet, a saint, a philosopher, statesman, yogi and a prophet.
- He is one of the pre-Independence Titanic trio of Indian poets—Tagore, Aurobindo and Sarojini Naidu.
- He is chiefly known for his
  - *(i)* Savitri (1953) a poetic epic on a grand scale.
  - *(ii)* The Life Divine (1939-40)
  - *(iii)* Essays on Gita
- He is a great exponent and proponent of ancient Indian thought.
- According to R. K. Singh, "Aurobindo is sympathetic to the modernist trends in writing and study of poetry and, in fact, himself adopts some of the methods followed by the modern poets."
- To quote Mr. Singh again, "In Aurobindo's literary order, poetry is a means of spiritual expression that helps to open the consciousness..."

CHATTERJEE, BANKIM CHANDRA (1838-94)

- He is generally called 'The Father of Bengali fiction.'
- Today he is most known for his patriotic bent of mind.
- In all he wrote 14 novels.
  - *(i)* Some of them are historical.
  - *(ii)* Others are social.
  - *(iii)* Still others are philosophical with stress on renunciation and non-attachment.
- Some of his novels are :
  - *(i)* *The Poison Tree (1884):* It is a story of Hindu life in Bengal of the period
  - *(ii)* Kapalkundala (1885)
  - *(iii)* Durgeshnandini (1890)
  - *(iv)* Krishnakanta's Will (1895)
  - *(v)* The Two Rings (1897)
  - *(vi)* Rajmohan's Wife (1904) (published posthumously)
  - *(vii)* Anand Math (1884)

CHAUDHURI, NIRAD, C. (1897-1999)

- He came into limelight with the publication of his "The Autobiography of an Unknown Indian." (1951).
- His other important works are:
  - *(i)* A Passage to India (1959)
  - *(ii)* Continent of Circe (1966)
    (He received the Duff Cooper Memorial Prize).
  - *(iii)* The Intellectual in India (1967)
  - *(iv)* To Live or Not to Live (1970)
- He is known for his most correct and chaste prose for which he has earned much acclaim from the scholars and critics, including Khushwant Singh.

DESAI, ANITA (Born-1937)

- She is a renowned novelist and short story writer.
- Some of her famous novels are :
  - *(i)* Cry, the Peacock (1963)
  - *(ii)* Voices in the City (1965)
  - *(iii)* Bye-Bye, Blackbird (1971)
  - *(iv)* Fire on the Mountain (1977)
  - *(v)* Clear Light of Day (1980)
- Her collection of short stories is captioned "Games at Twilight" (1978)

GANDHI, M.K. (1869-1948)

1. His famous work in English is "My Experiments with Truth."
2. The work is an important autobiographical writing which is held in high esteem for its truthfulness, frankness, simplicity and directness of expression in non-ornamental effective English.

MARKANDAYA, KAMALA (1924-2004)

1. She is one of the modern novelists and is known for her:
   - *(i)* Nectar in a Sieve (her first novel) (It is a novel on miserable rural life).
   - *(ii)* Some Inner Fury (1955)
     (It is a novel of violence and destruction)
   - *(iii)* A Silence of Desire (1960)
     (It is a novel urging the readers to speak out frankly to unburden their hearts).
   - *(iv)* Possession (1963)
     (The problem of possession is discussed in this novel).
   - *(v)* A Handful of Rice (1966)
     (It depicts the life of the poor classes in Madras).
   - *(vi)* The Coffer Danus (1969)
   - *(vii)* The Nowhere Man (1972)
   - *(viii)* Two Virgins (1973)
   - *(ix)* The Golden Honeycomb (1977)
   - *(x)* Pleasure City (1982).

KHUSHWANT SINGH (Born-1915)

- He is known for his novels :
  - *(i)* Train to Pakistan (his masterpiece)
  - *(ii)* I Shall Not Hear the Nightingale (1959). (It describes the social life of a Sikh family during the pre-Independence period).
- "The Mark of Vishnu" is another of his well-known works.
- Some of his known stories
  - *(a)* Karma
  - *(b)* When Sikh Meets Sikh
  - *(c)* The Rape, etc.
- He is also known for his:
  - *(i)* A History of the Sikhs
  - *(ii)* Translation of Japji Sahib, etc.
- His regular columns appear weekly in some dailies, *e.g.* :
  - *(i)* 'With Malice Towards One And All'—The Hindustan Times.
  - *(ii)* 'This Above All'—The Tribune.
- Mulk Raj Anand is stated to have said that Khushwant Singh's "Train to Pakistan" is likely to last, while about his other creative literary work, one may have some doubts.
- Among his latest work is "Truth, Love and Little Malice."

MULLER, MAX (1823-1900)

- He was a famous Indologist, German orientalist and linguist, who unearthed a lot of ancient Indian history and Sanskrit scriptures, the Rig Veda, in particular, of which he published six colossal volumes, for which he had got an assignment from the East India Company in 1847.
- Actually he was a student of Sanskrit, who started comparative study of languages and "Avesta" (in 1845) which is the renowned sacred book of the Zoroastrians.
- He gave seven lectures on Indian and ancient Indian philosophy at Cambridge University, which have now been published by Rupa & Co. under the caption: "India: What Can it Teach Us?"
- He distinguishes the highest wisdom of Greece and India by using the terms "to know ourselves" and "to know our self", respectively.
- Muller makes very appreciative comments on the Rig Veda and the Vedic Religion.

NAIDU, SAROJINI (1879-1949)

- She is a well-known Indian English poet who started writing poetry at a very early age and she was inspired by Edmund Gosse to choose Indian themes and scenery rather than imitating the English classics.
- She is now known as 'The Nightingale of India.'
- She took a keen interest in India's struggle for freedom.

Some of her works are :

1. The Golden Threshold (1905)
2. The Bird of Time (1912)
3. The Broken Wing (1917)
4. The Sceptred Flute (1946)
5. The Feather of the Dawn (1961)
   (It appeared posthumously)

Some of her famous poems are :

1. The Queen's Rival
2. Palanquin Bearers
3. To My Fairy Fancies
4. The Pardah Nashin
5. Awake
6. Village Song
7. The Soul's Prayer
8. Fishermen of Coromondel
9. It You Call Me
10. Caprice
11. Summer Woods
12. Songs of Radha
13. The Bird Sanctuary, etc.

NANDY, PRITISH (Born-1951)

- He was the editor of the 'Illustrated Weekly of India' and has now Telecast a T.V. serial over the Doordarshan: "Hungama Unlimited."
  - *(i)* He is a prolific poet, though he is still not considered one of the best.
  - *(ii)* Most of his poetry has been dismissed by critics as mere experimental gimmickry. Such was Saleem Peeradina.
  - *(iii)* Even Nissim Ezekiel dubbed him to be a poetaster.
- Some of his works are :
  - *(i)* Gods and Olives (1967)
  - *(ii)* On Either Side of Arrogance (1968)
  - *(iii)* From the Outer Bank of the Brahmputra (1969)
  - *(iv)* Riding the Midnight River (1975)
  - *(v)* In secret Anarchy (1979), etc.
- He has written a number of anthologies and translated a number of poets including Agyeya, Amrita Pritam, Kaifi Azmi etc.
- He has also written some short stories and a verse play.

NARAYAN, R.K. (1906-2001)

- Of the three great novelists, Narayan, Anand and Rao, it is Narayan who has won the maximum accolade both in India and abroad.
- One of his great achievements is his creation of the famous town of Malgudi like Hardy's Wessex.
- Narayan is the true master of humour, irony, realism, romance and artistry.
- Most of his novels and stories depict the life of people of South India.
- It is sometimes held that Narayan lacks true pathos, genuine depth of feeling, realistic description of poverty and misery, the elements which go in for making a novelist a great one.
- However, he has earned much popularity as a novelist, and within the range of his own art, he cannot be taken except with due regard and attention.

Some of his famous novels are :

1. Swami and Friends (1935)
2. Bachelor of Arts
3. The English Teacher
4. The Financial Expert
5. Mr. Sampath (1949)
6. The Guide (1958)
7. The Man-eater of Malgudi
8. The Dark Room (1939)
9. Waiting for the Mahatma
10. The Vendor of Sweets
11. The Painter of Signs (1976)

(He won the Sahitya Akademi Award for 'Guide' in 1961)

R.K. NARAYAN (as a short story writer)

- Some of his stories have appeared in the following collections:
  - *(i)* Malgudi Days
  - *(ii)* Dodu and Other Stories
  - *(iii)* Cyclone and Other Stories
  - *(iv)* Gods, Demons and Others

Narayan has written a few hundred stories, most of them quite interesting and highly readable:

Some of his famous short stories are :

1. The Golden
2. A Career
3. The Snake Song
4. Man Hunt
5. A Willing Slave
6. An Astrologer's Day
7. The Doctor's word
8. God of Troubles, etc.

NEHRU, JAWAHARLAL (1889-1964)

- He needs no introduction as a freedom fighter, statesman and first Prime Minister of India.
- Some of his literary works are :
  - *(i)* An Autobiography (1936)
  - *(ii)* Glimpses of World History (1939)
  - *(iii)* Discovery of India (1946)
- Children enjoy reading his "Letters from Father to His Daughter."
- He is known for his simple, chaste, poetic English which is a model of natural style.

PRITAM, AMRITA (1919-2005)

- She is the most famous Punjabi Author.
- She won the Jnanpith Award for her "Kagaj Te Kenvas" in 1981.
- Her best known autobiographical work which appeared in the seventies is "Rasidi Ticket."
- *(i)* Her "Shadows of words : An Auto-biography" (a transcreation of the Hindi original by Jyoti Sabharwal) has been published by Macmillan in 2002.

  (ii) The book presents "an inner journey down the memory lane" presented by the author, who considers old age the best part of her life, like the last sips of tea, which are "usually the sweetest."

RADHAKRISHAN, SARVAPALLI (1888-1975)

- He is known as an outstanding educationist and a philosopher who presented the Hindu/Indian viewpoint to the world.
- His works include
  - *(i)* An Idealist View of Life (Lectures)
  - *(ii)* Indian Philosophy (1923,1927)
  - *(iii)* The Hindu View of Life (1932)
  - *(iv)* An Idealist View of Life (1932)
  - *(v)* Eastern Religious and Western Thought (1939)
- He wrote in a very simple, intelligible prose-style.

RAO, RAJA (1908-2006)

- His famous works are:
  - *(i)* The Serpent and the Rope (1960)
  - *(ii)* Kanthapura (1938)
  - *(iii)* The Cat and Shakespeare (1965-66)
- *(i)* He was awarded the Sahitya Akademi Award for his 'The Serpent and the Rope' in 1964.

  (ii) He was also decorated with Padma Bhushan in 1969.

Raja Rao as a short story writer

- He is also a well-known short story writer.
- His first collection of short stories was "Jauni" which was published in France in 1930.
- The collection: "The Cow of the Barricades" was published in 1947

Some of his famous short stories are :

1. Akkayya
2. The Little Gram-shop
3. Kanaka Pal
4. Narsiga

ROY, ARUNDHATI (Born-1961)

She made her debut with her novel: "The God of Small Things" which won her the Booker Prize in 1997, besides a handful amount running into crores as royalty for less than four hundred pages which comprise the said novel.

DE, SHOBHA (Born-1948)

- She is a renowned contemporary Indian English novelist and T.V. serial script writer.
- Some of her novels are prescribed in universities in England and Australias.
- Her T.V. serial "Swabhiman" which ran into numerous episodes was telecast over the Doordarshan.
- *(i)* She has become even more popular with her serial "Kittie Party" telecast over the Zee T.V.

  (ii) According to the Tribune, it "is a clever insight into the mind of today's urban Indian women poised at the crossroads of modernity and tradition."

TAGORE, RABINDRANATH (1861-1941)

Tagore was a versatile genius. He was a :

(i) poet
(ii) novelist
(iii) short story writer
(iv) dramatist
(v) musician
(vi) actor (in dramas)
(vii) painter
(viii) statesman and a host of other things.

Some of his famous novels are :

1. The House and the World (1919)
2. The Wreck (1921)
3. Gora (1923)

VIVEKANANDA, SWAMI (1863-1902)

He is a well-known Indian seer, prophet, recluse preacher, lecturer and poet, who:

(i) made the ancient Indian philosophy known to the whole world at the Parliament of Religious in Chicago, USA.

(ii) Brought about a wave of resurgence among the Indian masses through his stirring spiritually inspired speeches which were also full of:

(a) patriotic fervour

(b) love for universal brotherhood.

(c) spirit of social uplight, etc.

Glossary of Literary Terms

Abridged edition

Condensed or shortened version of a work.

Absence

1. It is a modern term which is used to explain a work of art on the basis of aspects which are absent rather than those which are manifestly present in the work.

Acronym

1. A word formed from the initial letters of other words, *e.g.*

   NOIDA for New Okhla Industrial Development Authority.
2. The word may be considered synonymous to 'acrostic'.

Acrostic

1. It is a form of literary exercise in which the first letters of each line in a poem form a word as we read downwards.
2. Here are two Acrostics by H.S. Bhatia :

   (i) "Wait, O little child, wait!
   In the wind lies thy message,
   Not in the hubbub of the worldly;
   Else you may repent, says the sage."
   (The word formed is "WINE"

Act

Major division in a dramatic work.

Adage

Maxim or proverb.

Addendum

Addition or appendix to a book.

Aesthetic Realism

1. *(i)* According to Hudson, "Esther Waters" by George Moore was a landmark in this movement toward aesthetic realism.
   (ii) This movement was the vehicle of the new realists of which Moore and Gossing were representatives.
   (iii) According to Hudson, "they mistook mere ugliness for frankness and "seeing life steadily and seeing it whole."

Alexandrine

1. It is a line of six iambic feet instead of five.
2. It is not known for certain how this line originated.
3. It appears that it was evolved by Spenser by adding the Alexandrine to the eight-line stave (a b a b b c b c) of Chaucer that he used in the Monkeys Tale.

Alienation Effect

It was a term devised by the famous German playwright, Bartolt Brecht, who wanted to bring home the need, for realization of a kind of 'alienation' of the audience and the actors from the stage during the performance of a play, as the play being a play and not a part of real life.

Allegory

1. When the abstract or spiritual ideas are presented through living images, the result is the allegory.

Examples of Allegorical Works

1. The Pilgrim Progress
2. The Scarlet Letter
3. The Faery Queene
4. Morality Plays, such as "Everyman".
5. Seven Deadly Sins in Dr. Faustus, etc.

Alliteration

1. It signifies the repetition of initial consonant sounds, *e.g.*

   The furrow followed free.

Almanac

Book or table comprising a calendar of days, weeks and months indicating special occasions or events.

Anagnorisis

It means Discovery or Reversal in a Tragedy.

Anagram

Letters or word or phrase which, when re-arranged, form a new word.

Anapaest

It comprises two unaccented syllables followed by an accented one:

(i) Redeploy

(ii) Introduce

(iii) Camouflage

Androcentrism

The term implies the predominance of man in all social and intellectual activities.

Anecdote

Brief account or story about an individual.

'Angry Young Men'

It was a movement which came into existence in the second half of the twentieth century, mainly as a result of Osborn's play: "Look Back In Anger."

Annotation

Textual comment on a book.

Anthology

Collection of poetry or prose from diverse sources.

Anticipated Future

See 'Prosopopaeia'

Antithesis

1. It signifies the setting of one thing against another, often of opposite sense *e.g.*

   'A *friend never* betrays, an *enemy always* does.
2. 'Antithesis' can be expressed in literature also by presenting two aspects (of life) side by side, *e.g.* the real and the marvellous.

Aphorism

Short statement of a truth or dogma couched in memorable terms.

Apostrophe

It implies an exclamatory address to a person. (usually a dead one), some inanimate object or an abstract idea, *e.g.*

"Milton! thou shouldst be living with us at this hour..."

Archaism

It is a word or phrase which is no longer in use, *e.g.* loon, quoth, yclept, eftsoon(s), etc.

Archetypal Approach to Criticism

1. This Approach is also called Mythological, Ritualistic or Totemic Approach.
2. It endeavours to study literature on the basis of myth.

Areopagitica

This is the name of Milton's famous prose pamphlet, pleading for freedom, freedom of the press, in particular.

Argot

Slang or coarse vernacular language.

Aside

1. It is a kind of device similar to "soliloquy" (being probably comparatively brief) when a character speaks to himself.
2. The best example of an "aside" may be Shylock's words : "How like a fawning publican he looks" in Act. I sc. 3 of The Merchant of Venice.

Assonance

Unlike the alliteration (which signifies the repetition of consonant sounds), it signifies the repetition of vowel sounds, *e.g.*

1. I *hear* him *bear* the mark of a *seer* on his head.

Autobiography

An account of a person's life by himself or herself.

Avant-garde

Without going into historical aspects of the word, one can say that it implies those (persons) who support or create the newest ideas, fashions (generally literary or artistic), techniques, styles, etc. in an art, piece of literature, etc.

Ballad

1. Broadly-speaking, there are two kinds of ballads:
   (i) Traditional Ballads such as those pertaining to Robin Hood, Chevy Chase, etc.
   (ii) Modern Ballads, such as The Rime of Ancient Mariner, etc.

Bathos

1. It is a term to denote anticlimax.
2. It is generally used when there is sudden descent or fall from the sublime to the trite or ridiculous, *e.g.*

   Delay not thine departure hence,

   For thou mightst have a hot pudding, Awaiting thee.

Belles lettres

Essays on literary studies and the aesthetics of literature.

Bibliography

List of works on a particular subject or author.

Biography

An account of a person's life.

Blank verse

Poetry with unrhymed line endings (usually written in iambic pentameters).

Blurb

These are the words of praise or description of a book in a nutshell, inserted usually by the publisher on the cover page or jacket of the book, to attract the reader's eye.

Bound verse

Verse based on metrical pattern.

Burlesque

It is a way of writing which generates irony, humour and satire, *e.g.* Cervantes' Don Quixote, Samuel Butler's Hudibras, etc.

Bowdlerize

To 'cleanse' a work by omitting or cutting out indecent passages, phrases or words.

Cacophony

When the excessive use of high sounding words is made such that the meaning is lost or diminished in value in the sound, the result is cacophony instead of euphony.

Cadence

Rhythm and phrasing of language.

Caesura

1. In classical prosody, 'Caesura' means "break between words within a metrical foot." (Concise Oxford).
2. In English prosody, it means "pause about middle of line." (ibid.).
3. A Caesura "which does not immediately follow the ictus" is known as 'Feminine Caesura" (Chambers 20th century).

   (**Note :** In modern connotation, Caesura implies natural pause in a line of verse and not an unnatural or forced one)

Canon

Collection of works established as genuine.

Canto

Division of an epic or narrative poem.

Caption

Short description accompanying an illustration.

Caricature

The chief characteristics of characters are sometimes so exaggerated by the author that the characters look like some humorous or even funny creatures. The result is the creation of caricatures. This is what Dickens (more than any other author) has done.

Catalogue

List of books or works.

Catastrophe

1. It signifies the complete (often sudden) devastation of the fortunes of a character (often the hero and/or the heroine) in a play or piece of fiction.

Catharsis

This is the term used for the ousting of the emotions of pity and fear in the tragedy.

Chronicle Plays

1. These are the plays based on (English) History.
2. Such plays became very popular among the people in the sixteenth century.
3. These plays contain almost every important character, real or legendary, in the period of the times concerned.

Cipher

Writing that employs sub-stitution or transposition of letters.

Classic

(i) A classic (in reality, any book) is "the expression of man" as an individual.

(ii) It is also the expression of his mindset and the stance taken by him.

Cliche

Any word, phrase or expression that has lost its real effect for having been too frequently used by authors or laymen is called a cliche which may otherwise be quite lovable, *e.g.*

(i) The news is too good to be true.

(ii) The sorrow was too deep for tears.

(iii) Thanking you in anticipation, etc.

Climax

1. It is the main point of interest in a play or novel which is reached usually in the third act (or sometimes 4th of a 5 act of a play) or towards the end.
2. The resolution often takes place after the Climax or the forces for it start working or increase their intensity after it.

Colloquial

1. In speech, we sometimes make use of certain words and phrases which are not acceptable in standard speech
2. Such colloquial expressions should be avoided in all formal speech or writing.

Colonialism

1. The term differs from 'colonization' as the term may imply political or economic control of policies in a political unit without real annexation of land.

Colonisation

Literarily, the most significant modernist theories in the matter of

(i) colonisation

(ii) post colonisation

(iii) decolonisation, and

(iv) neo-colonisation have been provided and practised by—

(a) Ngugiwa Thiong'o

(b) Soyinka

(c) Achebe Chinua, etc.

Comedy

Humorous dramatic piece; *high comedy* has welldrawn characterization and witty dialogue; *low comedy*, or *slapstick* has absurd situations and boisterous action; *farce* is exaggerated comedy; *tragi-comedy* is a blend of the tragic and comic; *satire* uses sarcasm and wit to ridicule people's follies and vices (originally in verse).

Comic Relief

1. It is the name given to the brief light or comic dramatic action within the performance of a regular serious play to bring about a relief to the spectators to regain their real selves, for a short while to relax their strained nerves and prepare for further action, often more serious and culminating into breath-taking, gasping climax before denouement.

Conceit

1. A conceit is a far-fetched or highly complex and even obscure or unintelligible comparison between two, often dissimilar, persons or objects.
2. It was commonly used by the Elizabethans particularly the Metaphysical poets, especially Donne.

Concordance

Alphabetical index of words in a work, or works by a single author.

Confidant/Confidante

1. In a play when a character takes upon himself/herself the task of some secret or information characteristic about a character to another, the character indulging in such an activity is known as a "confidant" (mas.) or "confidante" (fem.)
2. Such information or secret is generally in the matter of love.
3. A good example of a 'confidante' is Nerissa in the Merchant of Venice.

Connotation

1. It signifies the suggested or implied meaning of word as against the transparent or literary meaning.
2. Connotative devices are brought into play by the artists, poets in particular to enhance pleasure and acceptability conveyed by words and other expressions.
3. Poets like Keats and T.S. Eliot frequently resort to the device of suggestiveness which is akin to connotation.

Consummation

1. When a work achieves complete satisfaction on all counts-literary as well as artistic, it is consummation that results.
2. An artist who has the knack, calibre or skill to make this achievement, is a consummate artist.

Copyright

Protective law to prevent pirating or plagiarism of an author's work.

Couplet

Two successive rhyming lines in poetry.

Court Comedy

1. It is opposed to the Domestic Comedy in the sense that instead of domestic scenes it contains other elements which attract a different kind of audience, *e.g.*
   (i) endless play of words
   (ii) elaborate dialogues
   (iii) repartees, jests, retorts, etc.

Cycle

Group of works united by an overall theme.

Dactyl

1. Dactyl means one accented syllable followed by two unaccented ones, e.g.
   (i) Lazily
   (ii) Separate
   (iii) Unspoken.

Decayed (or Constant) Metaphor

See Metaphor

Deism

1. A "deist" is a theist who believes in the existence of God but rejects the idea of a revealed religion.

Denouement

1. It is the final resolution of the problem in a piece of dramatic performance.
2. The best document comes about when it arises naturally out of the action of the play and not through the 'Deus ex machina'.

Detonation

When a word refers to its literal meaning independent of the meaning which the author may intend to convey, it is the device of "Detonation" which is at play.

Diabolus Ex Machina

1. The term literally means "devil out of the machine".
2. When all of a sudden a person or an event spoils the whole good game, causing unmitigated misery, it is the work of "Diabolus Ex Machina".
3. Thus, the term signifies sudden, unexpected turn of events for a plightful situation.

Dialect

Manner of speaking pertaining to a particular class or geographical region.

Dialectic

1. It was used originally to refer to the nature of a logical argument.
2. Later, it began to be linked to Kant, Hegel and Marx in varying forms.
3. The three generally accepted aspects of 'dialectic' are:
   (i) Thesis: It is akin to the (original) idea.
   (ii) Antithesis: It implies the inherent opposition in the thesis, which may operate after some time.
   (iii) Synthesis: It implies the resolution of the conflict to evolve a higher (or final) truth.

Dialogue

1. Dialogue is something very important in any poetic or prose play or a piece of prose fictions.
2. *(i)* The nature of the dialogue, including its language depends upon the kind of the play—a tragedy, comedy, romance, etc. or the kind of the scene prevailing there at the time and place of the dialogue.

(ii) Much also depends upon the taste of the spectators or audience which again is related to the spirit of the age :

A Dialogical Novel

1. It is a kind of novel in which a number of voices, interactive in the scheme, operate in work, resulting in a kind of dialogue (or series of dialogues) as against the Monologic Presentation.

Diary

Sequential private record of personal and other events kept by an individual.

Diction

1. It refers to the selection, arrangement and order of words.
2. The term which has become more popular in literary world is "Poetic Diction" to which a lot of space has been devoted by Wordsworth in his "Preface to Lyrical Ballads."

Dictionary

Book containing the words of a language, and their definitions, alphabetically; two-language dictionaries contain the corresponding words of both languages and their meanings, also alphabetically; any book that gives words and phrases about a particular subject, arranged alphabetically.

Didactic

A work is didactic in nature when it undertakes to teach a moral, *e.g.* much of Wordsworth's poetry.

Digest

Publication where works are abridged.

Digression

1. When a writer, instead of carrying on the main plot or incident, starts indulging in a side story, dialogue or descriptive narration, it is digression that results.
2. Digression gives extraneous pleasure which is not inherent in or indispensable to the main story.
3. Digression can sometimes enhance the value of a work but more often it mars its spirit.

Documentary

Form of fiction or drama based on documentary evidence provided by newspapers, recent historical reports or other contemporary or recent factual evidence.

Doggerel

Rough, ill-constructed verse.

Domestic Comedy

1. One of the earliest examples of the Domestic Comedies is "Gammer Gurton's Needle" (Cir. 1562)
2. It presents realistic life of the peasant class of its times.
3. It is full of fun and coarse humour.

Double entendre

Ambiguity in a word or expression, one of whose meanings is usually bawdy or frivolous.

Drama

Work to be performed on a stage by actors.

Dramatic Irony

It is a device occurring in a drama when a character on the stage is unaware of a fact which the audience know and understand.

Dramatic Monologue

1. It is a kind of drama or piece of dramatic poetry in which only one character speaks out throughout the performance and script.

Dramatis Personae

Characters in a play.

Duologue

Conversation between two characters in a play, story or poem.

Edition

Total number of copies of a book printed from unchanged set of type.

Electicism

The term implies the gleaning of facts or ideas from different sources instead of depending on just one source (or a few sources).

Elegy

Serious meditative poem; often lamenting death.

Empathy

In a play or novel, when the reader or spectator begins to feel like the hero/heroine or some particular character as if he/she were that character, it is "empathy" which is at play.

Empiricism

Empiricism implies the importance of experiment and experience in the matter of gaining knowledge.

Encyclopedia

Comprehensive work encompassing and describing many aspects of knowledge; specialist work covering comprehensively a subject or discipline.

Epic

Long narrative poem incorporating myth, legend, folklore and history, about the deeds of heroes, warriors, important people: a grandiose treatment of an individual's or nation's story.

Epic Style

1. It is a style which is dignified and exalted (as grand style is), as:
   (i) Paradise Lost by Milton
   (ii) Aeneid by Virgil
   (iii) Iliad by Homer
   (iv) Hyperion by Keats, etc.
2. Sometimes, it is, also referred to as 'heroic' style.'

Epigram

1. It signifies some brief, witty word, saying or piece of writing.
2. Pope's work, for instance, is a model of "Epigrammatic" style.
3. Bacon's essays are a bundle of Epigrams.

Epilogue

It is the last item in a work of art (as in a drama) which often declares or comments upon the conclusion of the work.

Epistle

Direct address to another person, a 'letter' in the form of verse.

Epitaph

Valediction to dead person or persons; inscription on a tomb or grave.

Epithet

1. It comprises a word or group of words to describe the chief characteristics of a person, *e.g.*
   (i) Alexander the Great
   (ii) The Holy Bible.

Eponymous

Person whose name becomes the title of the work.

Erastianism

1. It implies the doctrine that the state should have supremacy over the church in ecclesiastical matters.
2. Erastianism was one of the doctrines which was vehemently opposed by the followers of the Oxford Movement
3. The doctrine is probably wrongly ascribed to Erastus.

Essay

Short composition, usually in prose, discussing a topic or variety of topics.

Euphemism

1. When an unpleasant expression has to be made in a comparatively pleasant or less harsh way, the mellowed or toned down words which are used express euphemism, *e.g.*
   (i) Instead of saying about a person "He acted foolishly, we can say, "He should have acted more wisely."
   (ii) Instead of saying about a person that he has died, we sometimes say, "God Almighty has called him" or "He has left for his heavenly abode."

Euphony

1. It signifies the pleasant combination of words which create desirable rhythms and tonal effects without interfering with the intended meaning.
2. An excessive use of such devices can lead to tautology or bombasticism and sound superficial or facile.
3. The generally accepted antonym of euphony is "Cacophony".

Euphuism

1. An ornate, floral style of writing popularized by Lyly.

Exposition

It signifies a way of writing where explanations are not withheld or suppressed but manifestly made clear to the reader for immediate response based on clarity.

Fable

A short narrative in prose or verse, often with animals, that points a moral.

Fiction

General term for an imaginative work, usually in prose.

Figure of Speech (or of Rhetoric)

It signifies the unusual use of words to heighten their effect.

First person

Style of novel, etc., in which narrator is a character.

Flashback

1. When a writer while presenting a situation suddenly refers to a past situation or event, it is the device of "flashback" that he exploits.
2. Browning, T.S, Eliot and Stream of consciousness novelists, in particular, take advantage of this device.

Folk tale

Story handed down by word of mouth from generation to generation.

Foot

In poetry, rhythmic unit of two or three syllables.

Foreshadowing

1. It is a device in which the author himself prepares the spectators (or readers) for the catastrophe or some important event which may be on the cards.
2. Such a device checks the readers, etc. from suffering from the malady of disbelief.
3. Shakespeare is probably one of the greatest masters of this device, and it is sometimes believed that one of the main reasons of Shakespeare's grand success was his convincing mastery over the technique of foreshadowing.

Foreword

Short introduction to a work.

Free verse (vers libre)

Poetry free from mechanical restrictions such as metre and rhyme, cadenced according to meaningful stress.

Fustian

It means the use of pompous, ornate, Euphuist or bombastic language.

Gazetteer

Geographical dictionary or index.

Ghost writer

Person who undertakes literary work for another who takes the credit.

Glossary

Alphabetical list of unfamiliar or uncommon words, usually appended to work in which they appear.

Haiku

According to Oxford Dictionary, "A Haiku is a Japanese poem of seventeen syllables, in three lines of five, seven and fine traditionally evoking images of the natural world."

Haplology

"Omission in utterance of a sound resembling a neighbouring sounds (as 'idolatry' for 'idololatry') (ibid.)

Haplography

"The inadvertent writing once of what should have been written twice." (Chambers 20th Century Dictionary)

Heroic Couplet

1. A couplet written in iambic pentametre is known as a 'heroic couplet'.

Heroic verse

1. A poem written in heroic couplets is known as 'heroic verse,' *e.g.* Pope's poems such as:
   (i) Essay Man
   (ii) Essay in Criticism
   (iii) The Rape of the Lock, etc.

Homily

1. It is a term pertaining to a work which instead of laying stress on artistic or aesthetic standards, undertakes to urge the readers on to a high moral life.
2. It is just like a sermon in a church.
3. Such are the most of the poems of Longfellow.

Homograph

1. It implies a word which has the same spelling and pronunciation as another, but is different in meaning and origin from the other, *e.g.* :
   (i) bear (*n*) an animal
   (ii) bear (*v*) (to) tolerate
   (iii) bear (*v*) (to) carry

Homonym

1. *(i)* It is "a word having the same sound and perhaps the same spelling as another, but a different meaning and origin" (Chambers.....)
   (ii) Hence, *Homonymous* means: " having the same name : having different *significations* and origin but the same sound." (ibid.)

Hurd, Bishop

1. He aroused great interest in the Gothic and imaginative literature with his "Letters on Chivalry and Romance" (1762)

Hyperbole

1. It is a figure of speech which expresses an exaggerated statement to heighten the effect of a rhetorical statement, *e.g.*
   (i) O child, may you never die!
   (ii) Child is Father of the Man

Idiom

Form of expression of phrase peculiar to its language and possessing a meaning other than its literal one.

Idolatry

1. It means the worship of an image which is believed to be the abode of a superhuman being.

Idyll

Short pastoral poem conveying mood of happy innocence.

Imagism

School of poetry (early 1900s) concerned with precise language, direct treatment, and freedom of form.

Imperialism

1. It means the state policy for a country (as of England and certain other European countries, in particular during certain periods of history) to expands its area by annexing foreign lands and sub-during the natives.

Impersonality

1. It means that the author himself should not be palpably visible in a piece of literature, in other words, the work should be done on highly objective lines.

Indianism

When an expression is commonly used in India but is not used by the English, it is called an "Indianism," *e.g.*

(i) 'demise' instead of 'death'

(ii) 'bearer' instead of 'waiter'

(iii) 'left for his heavenly abode' instead of 'died,' etc.

Interior Monologue

1. It is a device, as used by James Joyce in Ulysses, to express the thoughts, feelings and emotions of a character on usually more than one levels of consciousness.
2. It is a sort of inner debate which may or may not be conflict in essence.

Interludes

1. Just as Miracles passed into Moralities, the latter gradually passed into Interludes, as the people wanted entertainment along with instruction.

Introduction

Essay stating author's intention to reader.

Inversion

It is the figure of speech (much used by Milton but ridiculed by many modern critics) in which words are presented in their unnatural order, *e.g.*

O God's glory I sing,

And to His Mercy I pray.

Irony

1. It is a device used to convey a meaning which is the opposite of the apparent meaning, *e.g.* What a brave son of India Jai Chand was!

Jingle

Verse or verses with strong rhyme and rhythm.

Journal

Paper, periodical or magazine.

Judicial Criticism

1. It is the kind of criticism which is a sort of judgement on a writer or his work of art.
2. Such kind of best example is Pope's "Essay on Criticism".

Legend

Story about a particular person containing myth and historical fact; explanation of symbols on a map or chart.

Lexicon

Dictionary, especially for Classical and Middle Eastern languages.

Limerick

1. It is a kind of humorous verse written in five jingling lines.
2. The form seems to have derived "from a refrain formerly used, referring to 'Limerick' in Ireland." (Chambers 20th Century Dictionary)

Linguistics

The scientific study of language.

Litotes

1. It is akin to "understatement" which is sometimes used by writers to emphasise the desired meaning, *e.g.* India is not lagging in Information Technology.
2. However, more often it is an "understatement used ironically, especially using a negative to express the category as :

   'I shan't be sorry when it's over' meaning 'I shall be very glad', or 'It was no easy matter' for 'It was very difficult.'"

   (Advanced Learner's Dictionary)

Lyric

Usually short, song-like poem in which the poet expresses personal feelings.

Manuscript

Book or work written by hand.

Maxim

Short statement or even sentence containing a general truth about human conduct and human nature.

Melodrama

1. It was a crude form of drama which appealed to the groundings who were not much interested in the artistic minuteness such as the plot, characterization, etc.
2. They wanted only entertainment through striking scenes and absorbing movement of incidents and situations.

Metaphor

1. It is a kind of simile when a comparison is suggested rather than explicitly stated, such that 'as' or 'like' is not used in such a case, *e.g.*
   (i) Lala Lajpat Rai was the Lion of Punjab.
   (ii) I see a lily on thy face.

Meter

Patterns of stressed and unstressed syllables in verse.

Metonymy

1. It implies the use of the name of some person or thing for another person or thing, *e.g.*
   (i) Have you studied 'Milton'?
   (Milton here means Milton's works).
   (ii) In the 'light' of these remarks:
   ('light' here means in view of....)
   (iii) Sceptre and Crown (i.e. monarchy)
   Must tumble down.

Metre

It may not be possible or even necessary to describe it here in full detail, but we can have a cursory look at the following :

1. *Monometre :* It means a line (or verse) with a single iamb (foot)
2. *Dimetre:* It means a line with two iambs.
3. *Trimetre:* It means a line with three iambs.
4. *Tetrametre:* It means a line with four iambs.
5. *Penta metre:* It means a line with five iambs.
6. *Hexta metre:* It means a line with six iambs.
7. *Hepta metre:* It means a line with seven iambs.

Miracle and Mystery Plays

1. These plays were sponsored by the church and were originally held within the premises of the church, but later, as the number of audience swelled, the boundaries of the church seemed too limited and the plays began of be held outside the church.
2. *(i)* The Miracle plays represented the lives of saints, and later for any biblical theme.
   (ii) The Mystery plays represented scenes from the life of Jesus Christ.

Mock Heroic

When an apparent epic is presented in a light vein, it is known as a "mock heroic" poem piece of fiction, etc., *e.g.*

(i) The Rape of the Lock

Modernism

1. Towards the close of the 20th century, a movement against such modes as realism and naturalism started in all forms of literature and art such as poetry, drama, novel, music, painting, architecture, sculpture, etc. which continued unabated during the first world war period and partly upto the middle of the century.

Modulation

1. Of necessity poetry is musical.
2. As in music, to avoid poetry from falling into "monotony," there is the system of "modulation" which here means, changing the key or tone, to introduce the element of variety to give or enhance pleasure.

Monologue

Single person addressing an audience alone, in drama, verse or prose. *Interior monologue*: unspoken but thought speech in verse or prose.

Moralities or Morality Play

1. They were basically allegories on the same lines as Miracles, or Mysteries but without direct represent of scriptural or Christ-concerned events or personages.
2. In Moralities abstract virtues and vices like Wisdom, Goodness, Justice, Evil, Vice, Greed, Lethargy, Lust, etc. were personified and presented on stage as persons.

Myth

Non-factual story that embodies explanation of how something comes to exist, usually involving supernatural or superhuman creatures.

Narrative

Story or tale in prose or verse.

Narratology

1. It means the study of different forms and structures of a narrative work in the matter of its various syntactical, literary and grammatical frameworks.

Neoclassicism

Movement of late 17th and 18th century reviving classical values in English literature, emphasizing discipline, reason and clarity.

Neologism

Newly-coined word.

New Wave (la Nouvelle Vague)

Movement in literature and cinema originating in France in late 1950s that attempted to eschew fixed values, revealing a character by the way he experienced objects and events, which were often meticulously described.

Nom de plume

Term used to indicate a fictitious name used by a writer to represent his work.

Novel

Extended piece of prose fiction.

Novelette

Long short story of some 15,000 words.

Novella

Prose fiction longer than a short story, shorter than a novel (about 30,000 words), concentrating upon a single event.

Obscurity

1. When a writer's language is not (or not easily) intelligible to the reader, the work concerned is termed as obscure.

Ode

Lyric poem describing an event or feelings about a person, object or event *Pindaric Ode* (Greece) written for choral recitation in units of three stanzas; *Horatian Ode* (Rome) consisted of succession of stanzas following pattern of first one.

Omniscient Author

It is a device used by some outstanding modern novelists to move freely from the objective narrative to the internal or subjective psyche of a character or characters and then comment freely and apparently unattached on the significance, possibility or outcome of any or some events.

Onomatopoeia

When the very sound (pronunciation) of a word conveys the sense of the object producing such sound, the use of onomatopoeia becomes clear *e.g.*,

(*i*) The *lashing* of waves on the sea-shore

(*ii*) The *rustle* of leaves

(*iii*) The *hissing* of the snake

(*iv*) The *jungle* of coins

(*v*) The *clanging* of arms.

Oxymoron

1. It is a figure of speech in which two apparently contradictory words or terms are used to convey, a paradoxical sense, e.g.

   (*i*) 'busy-idle days' (Lamb in Dream children)

   (*ii*) Life in Death (Coleridge in 'Rime.....').

Pantomime

1. Pantomimes became popular in England particularly in the first quarter of the 18th century.
2. A Pantomime is a dramatic representation pertaining to some myth, legend or traditional tale (or it may have some fairy element in it).

Parable

A story which conveys a moral lesson is known as a parable, as for instance, the biblical parables.

Paradox

It is a figure of speech in which a truth is brought home through the use of self-contradictory statement, *e.g.*

(*i*) Cowards die many a time before their death.

(*ii*) Discretion is the better part of valour.

(*iii*) After death, we awake into an eternal life.

Parallelism

1. It is a rhetorical device where balancing sentences, phrases or words are used to enhance effect, e.g.

   What is important is not what you say, but what is important is what you mean.
2. Excessive use of this device leads to monotony and superficiality.

Parody

Comic imitation of serious words, style, sense, subject of a writer to make them appear ridiculous.

Pastoral

Literature depicting idealized rural life.

Pathetic Fallacy

When nature is shown as sympathising with human lot, the device used is called "pathetic fallacy," *e.g.*

(*i*) Byron's description of the battle of Waterloo in Childe Harold's Pilgrimage.

(*ii*) The behaviour of slow-moving nature in Tennyson's "Lotos-eaters".

Pedantry

1. The term refers to the excessive display of knowledge such as:

   (*i*) Foreign words and phrases

(ii) Allusions
(iii) Archaic words
(iv) high sounding and sesquipedalian words
(v) cataloguing, etc.

when these are not strictly needed within the context of the work.

Periodic Sentence

A sentence in which the Principal clause occurs at the end when it is preceded by one or more subordinate clauses, such that the sense is clear only when the whole sentence is read, is known as a 'periodic sentence'.

Periodical

Magazine or journal published regularly.

Periphrasis

1. It means a round about way of saying a thing, *e.g.* An idle singer of an empty day, etc.
2. The term is close to circumlocution and euphemism in sense and effect.

Personification

1. It is a device where inanimate objects are shown as those having life and behaving likewise, *e.g.*

"But yonder comes the powerful *king* of day."

—*Thomson*

Pessimists

Although in English literature, we have a number of pessimist poets or a good number of poets expressing at times pessimistic ideas or writing sometimes in a pessimistic mood, yet two of the poets are known in particular, as "Pessimists." They are:

(i) Thomas Hardy
(ii) A.E. Housman

Philology

Study of literature. language and linguistics.

Picaresque

Chronicle of adventures of a rogue; originated in 16-century Spain.

Plagiarism

Wrongful appropriation and publication of another's work as one's own.

Platitude

It means a truth or generalization which is too well-known mainly because of its overuse, *e.g.*

Truth is evergreen.

Pleonasm

(a) It means the use of words more than those which are absolutely necessary, *e.g.*

1. He sat *down* on the ground.
2. He looked up *high* towards the sky.
3. He has got *sole* monopoly over such kind of business.

(b) In essence, it is akin to Tautology or circumlocution.

Plot

Plan or organization of events and characters in a play, work of fiction or poem as to induce curiosity and suspense in the audience or reader.

Poem

Literary work which may be in rhyme, blank verse or a combination of the two.

Poetic Diction

1. Diction stands chiefly for choice of words.
2. In poetry, poetic diction is unavoidable as mere metre is not enough to make a poem a literary piece of work.
3. In other words, mere versification or combination of words in rhyme or any other verse form does not make poetry.
4. The poets resort to several devices in this regard, some of which are :
   (i) Use of similes, metaphors, symbols, inversions, and other figures of speech as such as hyperbole, irony, antithesis, personification, etc.
   (ii) Omission of some parts of speech or grammatical rules.
   (iii) Use of archaic or uncommon words.
   (iv) Change in order of words, etc.
   (v) Use of picturesque phrases and expressions
   (vi) Use of other ornamental devices such as epithets
   (vii) Use of highly musical lies, fanciful flights etc.

Poetic Justice

1. It means the reward or punishment handed down to the characters at the end of a work of art according to their deeds.

Poetry

Any kind of metrical composition in a literary work.

Pornography

Work in which there is a deliberate emphasis on the sexual behaviour of characters, in order to arouse sexual excitement.

Potboiler

Work written essentially to gain the author a livelihood.

Precis

Concise statement; short summary of a work.

Preface

Introduction to a work.

Prologue

It is often the original statement by the writer (as in a drama) which highlights the chief aim of the work which is going to be unfolded or staged.

Propaganda

Work devoted to the dissemination of an idea or belief, usually biased.

Prose

Writings not in verse.

(Modern) Prose Style

1. The English prose style started by Bacon, flourished in the hands of Addison and Steele and numerous essayists and prose stylists that followed.
2. As a fine example of the latest modern prose style, Naipaul who won the Nobel Prize for Literature in 2001 deserves to be mentioned.

Prosody

Study of the handling of language in poetry.

Prosopopaeia

1. This figure of speech is used when:
   (i) The past (called the Historic Present) is written in the present tense:
   Sohrab and Rustam clash with their full might.
   (ii) The (anticipated) future is written in the present tense:
   Here, we go to our new house tomorrow with all our belongings carried in a lorry and then tucked in elegant mahogany almirahs.

Pseudonym

Name other than the true one used by an author to represent his work.

Psychological Process

It is the process applied to the study of a piece of literature to penetrate another's mind and to study the activities, utterances, etc. of various characters, as, for instance, to arrive at the exact nature of Hamlet's madness whether there was "method" in it or not.

Pun

1. When a word gives several meanings (often for fun) as in a play, it is the "pun" that is used.
2. Shakespeare is a great master of this device.
3. **Example :**
   (i) This is the *book*.
   (ii) It means
   (a) any book
   (b) a holy book, often the Bible.

Realism

Literature that attempts to depict life objectively and faithfully.

Refrain

Phrase, line or lines repeated at intervals or at the end of a stanza in poetry.

Review

Notice or critical article on musical, artistic or literary work.

Revue

Theatrical entertainment made up of sketches, dances, songs, recitals and improvised pieces, usually humorous, satirical or topical.

Rhetoric

Art of using language, in speaking or writing, to persuade. The persuasive style (rather than the content) of a work.

Rhythm

1. It signifies the measured regular beat or movement of sounded words in language.
2. Rhythm is a must in poetry as well as prose, as it introduces or enhances the element of pleasure, interest and curiosity.

Rhyme

Echoing sound or audible similarity in two or more words, especially at endings. Device used to construct much poetry.

Riddle

Puzzle, question or enigma; conundrum.

Roman a clef

Novel based upon actual people under disguised names.

Romance

Tale of chivalry, originally written in verse (Medieval times); term applied now to any wonderful or mysterious tale far removed from reality.

Romance Languages

1. Languages which have emerged straightaway from Latin and/or Greek, are called Romance Languages.

Romanticism

Movement originating in late 18th century as revolt against neoclassicism, emphasizing imaginative style.

Saga

Lengthy prose work, sometimes in several parts, describing the history and events surrounding medieval kings, warrriors and, recently, fictitious families.

Satire

Any work in which wickedness, folly, vice and corruption in individuals and society is exposed by ridicule and scorn.

Science fiction

Literature based on scientific fact or fantasy, on earth or on other worlds in space, often set in periods in the distant future.

Semantics

Branch of linguistics dealing with meaning, and the change of meaning, in words.

Semiology

General study or science of signs with which humans communicate with each other (including words and their use in every context).

Sermon

Verbal instruction of some length, usually religious.

Short story

Work of fiction usually revolving around single event.

Sic

Included in brackets after a printed word or quoted passage to indicate that it is quoted accurately, however actually incorrect.

Simile

1. When we draw comparison between two persons by using (usually 'like', as-so or as) it is the 'simile' that we make use of, *e.g.*
   (i) As red as a rose
   (ii) As happy as a lark
   (iii) She looked like a violet, half-hidden behind the rock.
2. *An Exaggerated Simile:* It is a simile in which the sense is clearly exaggerated, *e.g.*
   (i) He ran as fast as lightning
   (ii) He has in himself the force as much as there is in ten horses.

Slang

Colourful and vernacular language of the street, marketplace, barrackroorn, workplace, sportsplace and playground.

Soliloquy

Kind of monologue in which a stage character expresses his thoughts and feelings.

Song

Poem or verse set to music.

Sonnet

14-line poem of set rhyme-scheme; Elizabethan (Shakespearean) *ababcdcdefefgg*, Italian *abbaabba cdcdcd* (or *cdecde*).

Stanza

Group of lines of verse in definite pattern, usually repeated in a poem.

Strophe and Anti Strophe

1. Strophe is "the song sung by the chorus (in a Greek play) as it moved towards one side, answered by an exact counterpart." (Chambers 20th Century Dictionary)
2. Anti-Strophe is the term for the Strophe, "as it returned: part of any ode thus answered..." (*ibid.*)

Style

Characteristic manner of expression in prose or verse; the way in which a thing is written by an author.

Stock Material

Material necessary for a writer to write.

Stock Characters

Characters that are commonly found in most of pieces of dramas or fiction.

Stock Situations

Situations which are frequently presented byauthors in their works.

Synthesis, Poetry of

The term "Poetry of Synthesis" is referred to by I.A. Richards, and it has been thus explained by Cleanth Brooks—

"... a poetry which does not leave out what is apparently hostile to its dominant tone, and which, because it is able to fuse the irrelevant and disordant, has come to terms with itself and invulnerable to irony."

Structure

"The structure meant is a structure of meaning, evaluations and interpretations : and the principle of unity which informs it seems to one of balancing and harmonizing connotations, attitudes and meanings."

Tragedy of Blood (And Thunder)

1. It was basically a melodramatic presentation of horrible, gory scenes.
2. The first famous tragedy of this kind is Kyd's "Spanish Tragedy".

Sublimity

1. It is a term which is used to describe inexplicable beauty which is beyond any rules to describe or measure.

Symbolism

French poetic movement of late 19th century that developed as revolt against realism, concentrating on evoking emotions by use of indirect suggestion (symbol and metaphor); flourished in Russia at turn of century as literary movement, and later in British novel.

Synecdoche

1. This figure of speech is used when the understanding of one thing by means of another is employed.
2. This can be done in several ways, some of which are mentioned below :
   (i) When a part stands for a whole or genus, e.g. We have fifty *hands* in our factory. (hands = workers)
   (ii) When a whole or genus stands for a part, e.g. He belongs to a different *world* from yors (world = category, social set-up, economic status, etc.)
   (iii) When an individual represents a class, *e.g.*
   He is the *Nestor* of our village.
   (Nestor = the oldest man)

Syntax

It means :

(i) The way a sentence is constructed
(ii) Arrangement of words in writing (or in speech) according to the rules of grammar
(iii) Rules pertaining to this system or arrangement.

Synonym

A word similar in meaning to another.

Synopsis

Outline of the main points of a work; a summary.

Tale

Spoken or written narrative.

Tautology

Overuse of synonyms or repetition of ideas in sentence.

Theme

Central idea of a work, rather than its subject.

Thesis

Long essay or treatise on a subject, usually expository; work presented to examiners for academic qualification.

Third person

Style of novel, etc., in which narrator is outside action.

Tract

Short printed treatise on religious or political subject.

Tragedy

It is "a drama in which the principal characters are involved in desperate circumstances or led by overwhelming passions. It is invariably serious and dignified. The movement is always stately, but grows more and more rapid as it approaches the climax ; and the end is always calamitous, resulting in death or dire misfortune of the principals."

Tragic Flaw

1. In Shakespeare's tragedies, in particular, we often find a particular flaw in the character of the hero which ultimately leads to the fall of his destiny, along with the fall of his state or estate.

Transferred Epithet

When an epithet is transferred from a person to a thing, it is known as a 'transferred epithet', *e.g.*

(i) It is a *foolish* idea
(ii) Let *happy* days come.

Translation

Rendering of a work into another language.

Treatise

Formal work examining a subject and the principles underlying it.

Trochaic Line Metre

1. A line in verse is known as a *"trochaic" line* when the first, third and other odd syllables in it are accented (as in the 'Iambic metre') irrespective of the length of the line.
2. A poem comprising such lines is known as having been written in the "Trochaic" metre.

Understatement

1. It is practically the opposite of hyperbole and is sometimes used by the writers to emphasise indirectly the desired meaning.

Vade mecum

Manual or handbook carried for frequent reference.

Verisimilitude

It is the likeness of truth presented in a work of art that makes it similar to the characteristics or situation in real life and that enables the readers to accept it ungrudgingly as truth (and may be, sometimes, more than real happening in life).

Vernacular

Domestic or native language.

Versification

Study of how traditional verse is constructed.

Wit

(*i*) Dryden defines (in "Annus Mirabilis") wit as "delightful imagining of persons, actions, passions or things."

Yarn

Story or tale, sometimes improbable and far-fetched.

Literary and Media Knowledge

NOBEL PRIZE FOR LITERATURE 2000–2021

Year	Laureate	Country	Language	Genre(s)
2000	Gao Xingjian	China, France	Chinese	novel, drama, literary criticism
2001	V. S. Naipaul Trinidad & Tobago	United Kingdom	English	novel, essay
2002	Imre Kertesz	Hungary	Hungarian	novel
2003	J. M. Coetzee	South Africa	English	novel, essay, translation
2004	Elfriede Jelinek	Austria	German	novel, drama
2005	Harold Pinter	United Kingdom	English	drama
2006	Orhan Pamuk	Turkey	Turkish	novel, screenplay, essay
2007	Doris Lessing	United Kingdom	English	novel, drama, poetry, short story, memoirs
2008	J. M. G. Le Clezio	France Mauritius	French translation	novel, short story, essay
2009	Herta Muller	Germany Romania	German	novel, poetry
2010	Mario Vargas Llosa	Peru Spain	Spanish drama	novel, short story, essay
2011	Tomas Transtromer	Sweden	Swedish	poetry, translation
2012	Mo Yan	China	Chinese	novel, short story
2013	Alice Munro	Canada	English	short story
2014	Patrick Modiano	France	French	novel
2015	Svetlana Alexievich	Belarus (Born in Ukrainian SSR)	Russian	history, essay
2016	Bob Dylan	United States	English	poetry, songwriting
2017	Kazuo Ishiguro	United Kingdom (born in Japan)	English	novel
2018	Olga Tokarczuk	Poland	Polish	novel

Year	Laureate	Country	Language	Genre(s)
2019	Peter Handke	Austria	German	novel
2020	Louise Gluck	United States	English	poetry
2021	Abdulrazak Gurnah	United Kingdom (born in Tanzania)	English	novel

MAN BOOKER PRIZE (2000–2021)

Year	Winner	Book	Genre	Country
2000	Margaret Atwood	The Blind Assassin	Novel	Canada
2001	Peter Carey	True History of the Kelly Gang	Historical novel	Australia
2002	Yann Martel	Life of Pi	Fantasy novel	Canada
2003	DBC Pierre	Vernon God Little	Novel	Australia, Mexico
2004	Alan Hollinghurst	The Line of Beauty	Historical novel	United Kingdom
2005	John Banville	The Sea	Novel	Ireland
2006	Kiran Desai	The Inheritance of Loss	Novel	India
2007	Anne Enright	The Gathering	Novel	Ireland
2008	Aravind Adiga	The White Tiger	Novel	India
2009	Hilary Mantel	Wolf Hall	Historical novel	United Kingdom
2010	Howard Jacobson	The Finkler Question	Novel	United Kingdom
2011	Julian Barnes	The Sense of an Ending	Novel	United Kingdom
2012	Hilary Mantel	Bring Up the Bodies	Historical novel	United Kingdom
2013	Eleanor Catton	The Luminaries	Historical novel	New Zealand
2014	Richard Flanagan	The Narrow Road to the Deep North	Historical novel	Australia
2015	Marlon James	A Brief History of Seven Killings	Historical/ experimental novel	United Kingdom
2016	Paul Beatty	The Sellout	Satirical novel	United States of America
2017	George Saunders	Lincoln in the Bardo	Historical/ experimental novel	United States of America
2018	Anna Burns	Milkman	Novel	United Kingdom
2019	Margaret Atwood	The Testaments	Novel	United Kingdom
2019	Bernardine Evaristo	Girl, Woman, Other	Experimental Novel	United Kingdom
2020	Douglas Stuart	Shuggie Bain	Novel	United Kingdom & United States
2021	Domon Galgut	The Promise	Novel	South Africa

SAHITYA AKADEMI AWARDS–2021

Name	Language	Name	Language
Anuradha Sarma Pujari	Assamese	Namita Gokhale	English
Bratya Basu	Bengali	Daya Prakash Sinha	Hindi
Mwdai Gahai	Bodo	DS Nagabhushana	Kannada
Raj Rahi	Dogri	Wali Mohd Aseer Kashtawari	Kashmiri

Name	Language	Name	Language
Sanjiv Verenkar	Konkani	Meethesh Nirmohi	Rajasthani
George Onakkoor	Malayalam	Vindeshwariprasad Mishr "Vinay"	Sanskrit
Kiran Gurav	Marathi	Niranjan Hansda	Santali
Chhabilal Upadhyaya	Nepali	Arjun Chawla	Sindhi
Hrushikesh Mallick	Odia	Ambai	Tamil
Khalid Hussain	Punjabi	Gorati Venkanna	Telugu

JNANPITH AWARD WINNERS (2000-2021)

Award Winners	Year	Award Winners	Year
Dr. Indira Goswami (Assamese)	2000	Pratibha Ray (Odiya)	2011
Rajendra Keshav Lal Shah (Gujarati)	2001	Ravuri Bharadhwaja (Telugu)	2012
D. Jayakanthan	2002	Kedarnath Singh (Hindi)	2013
Vinda Karandikar (Marathi)	2003	Bhalchandra Nemade (Marathi)	2014
Rehman Rahi (Kashmiri)	2004	Raghuveer Chaudhari (Gujarati)	2015
Kunwar Narain (Hindi)	2005	Shankha Ghosh (Bengali)	2016
Ravindra Kelekar (Konkani) and		Krishna Sobti (Hindi)	2017
Satyavrat Shastri (Sanskrit)	2006	Amitav Ghosh (English)	2018
O.N.V. Kurup (Malayalam)	2007	Akkitham Achuthan Namboothiri (Malayalam)	2019
Akhlaq Khan Shahryar (Urdu)	2008	Nilamani Phookan (Assamese)	2020
Amar Kant & Shrilal Shukla (Hindi)	2009	Damodar Mauzo (Konkani)	2021
Chandrasekhar Kambar (Kannada)	2010		

Famous Books and Authors

Book	Author
A Secular Agenda	Arun Shourie
A Suitable Boy	Vikram Seth
Accession of Extinction	D.R. Mankekar
Adam Beda	George Eliot
Adhe Adhure	Mohan Rakesh
Adonis	P.B. Shelley
Adventures of Huckleberry Finn	Mark Twain
Adventures of Sherlock Holmes	Arthur Conan Doyle
Adventures of Tom Sawyer	Mark Twain
Advise and Consent	Allen Drury
Affluent Society	J.K. Galbraith
After the Dark Night	S.M. Ali
Age of Reason	Jean Paul Sartre
Agni Pariksha	Acharya Tulsi
Agni Veena	Kazi Nazrul Islam
The Agony and the Ecstasy	Irving Stone
Ain-i-Akbari	Abul Fazal
Ajat Shatru	Jai Shankar Prasad

Book	Author
Akbarnama	Abul Fazal
Alchemist, The	Ben Jonson
Alice in Wonderland	Lewis Carroll
All is Well that Ends Well	William Shakespeare
All things Bright and Beautiful	James Herroit
Amar Kosh	Amar Singh
Ambassador's Journal	J.K. Galbraith
Ambassador's Report	Chester Bowles
An American Tragedy	Theodore Drieser
An Autobiography	Jawaharlal Nehru
An Eye to China	David Selboume
An Idealist View of Life	Dr. S. Radhakrishnan
An Unknown Indian	Nirad C. Choudhury
Anandmath	Bankim Chandra Chatterjee
Ancient Mariner	Samuel Taylor Coleridge
And Quiet Flows the Don	Mikhail Sholokhov
Androcles and the Lion	George Bernard Shaw
Animal Farm, The	George Orwell

Book	Author
Anna Karenina	Count Leo Tolstoy
Another Life	Derek Walcott
Answer of History	Mohammed Raza Pahlavi
Antony and Cleopatra	William Shakespeare
Ape and Essence	A. Huxley
Apple Cart	George Bernard Shaw
Arabian Nights	Sir Richard Burton
Area of Darkness	V.S. Naipaul
Arms and the Man	George Bernard Shaw
Around the World in Eighty days	Jules Verne
Arrangement, The	Elia Kazan
Arrival and Departure	Arthur Koestler
Arrowsmith	Sinclair Lewis
Arthashastra	Kautilya
As You Like It	William Shakespeare
Ascent of the Everest	Sir John Hunt
Ashtadhyayi	Panini
Asian Drama	Gunnar Myrdal
Asia and Western Dominance	K.M. Panikkar
Atoms of Hope	Mohan Sundara Rajan
August 1914	Alexander Solzhenitsyn
August Coup, The	Mikhail S. Gorbachev
Autumn Leaves	O. Pulla Reddi
Avanti Sundari	Dandi
Babur Nama	Zaheeruddin Mohammed Babur
Babbit	Sinclair Lewis
Back of Methuselah	George Bernard Shaw
Backward Place, A	Ruth P. Jhabwala
Bandicoot Run	Manohar Malgonkar
Bang-i-Dara	Mohammed Iqbal
Bangla Desh The Unfinished Revolution	Lawrence Liftschultz
Banyan Tree, The	Hugh Tinker
Beast and Man	Murry Midgely
Beginning of the Beginning	Acharya Rajneesh
Betrayal of Pearl Harbour	James Rusbridge and Eric Nave
Bend in the Ganges, A	Manohar Malgonkar
Ben Hur	Lewis Wallace
Bermuda Triangle	Charles Berlitz
Berry Patches	Yevgeny Yevtushenko
Best and the Brightest, The	David Halberstan
Between the Lines	Kuldip Nayar
Beyond Modernisation, Beyond Self	Sisir Kumar Ghose
Bharat Bharati	Maithili Sharan Gupta
Bharatiya Parampara Ke Mool Swar	Govind Chandra Pande
Big Breach, The	Richard Tomlinson
Big Fisherman, The	Lloyd C. Douglas

Book	Author
Biopgraphia Literaria	Samuel Taylor Coleridge
Bisarjan	Rabindra Nath Tagore
Birth and Death of Sun	George Gamow
Bitter Sweet	Noel Coward
Black Arrow, The	Robert Louis Stevenson
Blind Ambitions	John Dean
Blind Beauty	Boris Pasternak
Blind Men of Hindustan ! Indo-Pak Nuclear War	General K.S. Sundarji
Bliss was it in that Dawn	Minoo Masani
Bloodline	Sidney Sheldon
Blue Bird	Maurice Macterlink
Bone People, The	Kerl Hulme
Born Free	Joy Adamson
Bread, Beauty and Revolution	Khwaja Ahmed Abbas
Breakthrough	Gen. Moshe Dayan
Bride for the Sahib and other Stories, A	Khushwant Singh
Bride's Book of Beauty, The	Mulk Raj Anand
Broken Wings	Sarojini Naidu
Brothers Karamazhov	Fyodor Dostoevsky
Bubble, The	Mulk Raj Anand
Bhudha Charitam	Ashvaghosha
Bunch of Old Letters, A	Jawaharlal Nehru
Butterfield-8	John O' Hara
By Love Possessed	James Cozzens
Caesar and Cleopatra	George Bernard Shaw
Cancer Ward	Alexander Solzhenitsyn
Candida	George Bernard Shaw
Candide	Voltaire
Canterbury Tales	Geoffery Chaucer
Cardinal, The	Henry M. Robinson
Centennial	James Michener
Chandalika	Rabindra Nath Tagore
Chemmeen	Thakazhi Sivasankar Pillai
Cherry Orchard	Anton Chekov
Chesaplake	James A. Michener
Chidambara	Sumitra Nandan Pant
Chikaveera Rajendra	Masti Venkatesh Iyengar
Children of Gebelawi	Naguib Mahfouz
Childe Herolds Pilgrimage	Lord Byron
China Passage, A	J.K. Galbraith
China's Watergate	Leo Goodstadt
Chinese Betrayal	B.N. Mullick
Chitra	Rabindra Nath Tagore
Chittirappaval	P.V. Akilandam
Chomas Drum	K. Shivaram Karnath
Chronicle of a Death Foretold	Gabrel Garcia Marquez
Class, The	Eric Segal
Climate of Treason	Andrew Boyle

Book	Author
Comedy of Errors	William Shakespeare
Common Sense	Thomas Paine
Comus	John Milton
Communist Manifesto	Karl Marx
Confessions	J.J. Rousseau
Confessions of a Lover	Mulk Raj Anand
Confessions of an Opium Eater, The	Thomas Dequicey
Confidential Clerk	T.S. Eliot
Conquest of Self	M.K. Gandhi
Conservationist, The	Ms. Nadine Gordimer
Continent of Circle	Nirad C. Choudhury
Coolie	Mulk Raj Anand
Coup, The	John Updike
Count of Monte Cristo	Alexander Dumas
Court Dancer	Rabindra Nath Tagore
Covertly Papers	Joseph Addison
Cresent Moon	Rabindra Nath Tagore
Crescent over Kashmir	Anil Maheshwari
Crime and Punishment	Fyodor Dostoevsky
Crisis into Chaos	E..M.S. Namboodiripad
Crisis in India, The	Ronald Segal
Critique of Pure Reason, A	Immanuel Kant
Crown and the Loincloth, The	Chaman Nahal
Crown of Wild Olive, The	John Ruskin
Cry My Beloved Country	Alan Patan
Culture in the Vanity Bag	Nirad C. Choudhury.
Curtain Raisers	K. Natwar Singh
Dangerous Summer, The	Ernest Hemingway
Darkness at Noon	Arthur Keostler
Dark Room, The	R.K. Narayan
Dashkumar Charitam	Dandi
Das Kapital	Karl Marx
Daughter of the East	Benazir Bhutto
David Copperfield	Charles Dickens
Day in Shadow, The	Nayantara Sehgal
Days of His Grace	Eyvind Johnson
Dean's December	Saul Below
Death of a City	Amrita Pritam
Death of a Patriot	R.E. Harrington
Death of a President	William Manchester
Death, The Supreme Friend	Kakasaheb Kalelkar
Debacle	Emile Zola
Decameron	Giovanni Boccaccio
Decline and Fall of the Roman Empire	Edward Gibbon
Decline and Fall of Indira Gandhi	D.R. Mankekar and Kamala Mankekar
Decline of the West	O Spengier
Deewan-i-Ghalib	Mirza Ghalib
Delhi	Khushwant Singh
Democracy Means Bread and Freedom	Piloo Mody
Democracy Redeemed	V.K. Narsimhan
Descent of Man	Charles Darwin
Deserted Village	Oliver Goldsmith
Devdas	Sharat Chandra Chatterjee
Die Blendung	Elias Canetti
Dilemma of our Time	Harold Joseph Laski
Diplomacy in Peace and War	J.N. Kaul
Discovery of India	Jawaharlal Nehru
Distant Drums	Manohar Malgonkar
Distant Neighbours	Kuldip Nayar
Divine Comedy	A. Dante
Divine Life	Swami Sivananda
Doctor's Dilemma	George Bernard Shaw
Dolls's House, A	Ibsen
Don Juan	Lord Byron
Don Quixote	Saavedra Miguel de Cervantes
Double Helix, The	J.D. Watson
Dragon's Teeth	U.B. Sinclair
Dream in Hawaii, A	Bhabani Bhattacharya
Dream of Fair to Middling Women	Samuel Beckett
Dreams Roses and Fire	Eyvind Johnson
Dr. Jekyll and Mr. Hyde	Robert Louis Stevenson
Durgesh Nandini	Bankim Chandra Chatterjee
Dynamics of Social Change	Chandra Shekhar
Earth	Emile Zola
Earth Mother, The	Pupul Jayakar
Economic Planning of India	Ashok Mehta
Economics of the Third World	S.K. Ray
Eduction of Public Man	Hubert Humphery
Eight Lives	Raj Mohan Gandhi
Elegy Written in a Country Church Yard	Thomas Grey
Emile	J.J. Rousseau
Emma	Jane Austen
End of Era	C.S. Pandit
Ends and Means	Aldous Huxley
Envoy to Nehru	Escott Reid
Essays for Poor to the Rich	John Kenneth Galbraith
Essays of Elia	Charles Lamb
Essays on Gita	Sri Aurobindo Ghosh
Eternal Himalayas	Major H.P.S. Ahluwalia
Eternal India	Indira Gandhi
Executioner's Song	Norman Mailer
Expanding Universe	Arthur Stanley Eddington
Eye of the Storm, The	Patric White
Face to Face	Lasse & Mrs. Lisa Berg
Faces of Everest	Maj. H.P.S. Ahluwalia
Facts are Facts	Khan Abdul Wali Khan

Book	Author
Fall of a Sparrow, The	Salim Ali
Family Reunion	T.S. Eliot
Far From the Madding Crowd	Thomas Hardy
Far Pavilions, The	M.M. Kaye
Faraway Music, The	Svetlana Allilueva
Farewell the Trumpets	James Morris
Farewell to Arms, A	Ernest Hemingway
Farm House	George Orwell
Father and Sons	Ivan Turgenev
Faust	J.W. Von Goethe
Fidelio	L. Beethoven
Fifth Horseman, The	Larry Collins and Dominique Lapierre
Final Days, The	Bob Woodward and Carl Bernstein
Finding a Voice-Asian Women in Britain	Amrit Wilson
Fire Next Time, The	James Balbwin
First Circle	Alexander Solzhenitsyn
Flames form the Ashes	P.D. Tandon
Flounder, The	Gunter Grass
Food Nutrition and Poverty in India	V.K.R.V. Rao
For Whom the Bell Tolls	Ernest Hemingway
Forbidden Sea, The	Tar Ali Baig
Forsyte Saga	John Galsworthy
Forty Nine Days	Amrita Pritam
Freedom At Midnight	Larry Collins and Dominique Lapierre
French Revolution	Thomas Carlyle
Friends and Foes	Sheikh Mujibur Rehman
Friends not Masters	Ayyub Khan
From Here to Eternity	James Jones
From India to America	L. S. Chandrashekhar
From Raj to Rajiv	Mark Tully & Zaheer Masani
Ganadevata	Tara Shanker Bando-padhyay
Gandhi and Stalin	Louis Fisher
Gardener	Rabindra Nath Tagore
Gathering Storm	Winston Churchill
Geeta Govinda	Jaya Dev
Ghasiram Kotwal	Vijay Tendulkar
Gita Rahasya	Bal Gangadhar Tilak
Glimpses of World History	Jawaharlal Nehru
Godan	Munshi Prem Chand
Godfather, The	Mario Puzzo
God of Small Things, The	Arundhati Roy
Gold Bat, The	P.G. Wodehouse
Golden Gate	Vikram Seth
Golden Threshold, The	Sarojini Naidu
Gone with the Wind	Margaret Mitchel
Good Earth	Pearl S. Buck

Book	Author
Gora	Rabindra Nath Tagore
Grammar of Politics	Harold Joseph Laski
Grapes of Wrath	John Steinbeck
Great Challenge, The	Louis Fishcer
Great Depression of 1990, The	Ravi Batra
Great Expectations	Charles Dickens
Great Gatsby	F. Scott Fitzgerald
Great Illusion	Norman Angel
Great Tragedy	Z.A. Bhutto
Guide, The	R.K. Narayan
Gulag Archipelago	Alexander Solzhenitsyn
Gul-i-Naghma	Raghupati Sahai (Firaq) Gorakhpuri
Gulistan and Bostan	Sheikh Saadi
Gulliver's Travels	Jonathan Swift
Gurusagaram	O.P. Vijayan
Hamlet	William Shakespeare
Handful of Dust, A	Evelyn Waugh
Harry Potter*	J.K. Rowling
Harsha Charita	Ban Bhatt
Heat and Dust	Ruth P. Jhabwala
Heir Apparent	Dr. Karan Singh
Henderson, the Rain King	Saul Below
Henry Esmond	William Thackeray
Hero of our Times	Richard Hough
Heroes and Hero Worship	Thomas Carlyle
Higher than Hope	Fatima Meer
Himalayan Blunder	Brigadier J.P. Dalvi
Hindu Civilization	J.M. Barrier
Hinduism	Nirad C. Choudhury
Hindu View of Life	Dr. S. Radhakrishnan
Hounds of Baskervilles, The	Arthur Conan Doyle
House Divided	Pearl S. Buck
House for Mr. Biswas, A	V.S. Naipaul
Huckieberry Finn	Mark Twain
Human Factor	Graham Greene
Humboldt's Gift, The	Saul Bellow
Humour	Ben Johnson
Hunchback of Notre Dame	Victor Hugo
Hungary Stones	Rabindra Nath Tagore
I Am Not an Island	K.A. Abbas
I Follow the Mahatma	K.M. Munshi
Idiot, The	Fyodor Dostoevsky
Idols	Sunil Gavaskar
Idylls of the King	Alfred Teennyson
If I am Assassinated	Z.A. Bhutto
Illiad	Homer
Importance of Being Earnest	Oscar Wilde
In Afghanistan's Shadow	Salig S. Harrison
In Evil Hour	Gabriel Garcia Marquez

Book	Author
In a Free State	V.S. Naipaul
In Memorium	Alfred Lord Tennyson
In Search of Gandhi	Richard Attenbrough
In Search of Identity	Anwar-al-Sadat
India A Wounded Civilization	V.S. Naipaul
India Changes	Taya Zinkin
India Discovered	John Keay
India Divided	Rajendra Prasad
India from Curzon to Nehru and After	Durga Das
India Remembered	Percival and Margaret Spear
India of Our Dreams	M.V. Kamath
India, The Critical Years	Kuldip Nayar
India Today	Rajni Palme Dutt
India We Left	Humphry Trevelyan
India Wins Freedom	Maulana Abul Kalam Azad
Indian Home Rule	M.K. Gandhi
Indian Muslims	Mohammed Mujeeb
Indian Muslims The Need For a Positive Outlook	Wahiduddin Khan
Indian Philosophy	Dr. S. Radhakrishnan
Indian War of Independence	V.D. Savarkar
India's China War	Neville Maxwell
India's Priceless Heritage	N.A. Palkhivala
India	Magasthenes
Indira's India	S. Nihal Singh
Indira Gandhi's Emergence and Style	Nayantara Sehgal
Inheritance of Loss, The	Kiran Desai
Inner Circle, The	Jonathan Frost
Inside Asia (also, Inside Europe and Inside Africa)	John Gunter
Inside Third Reich	Albert Spencer
Intimacy	Jean Paul Sartre
Invisible Man	H.G. Wells
Iron in the Soul	Jean Paul Sartre
Isabella	John Keats
Islamic Bomb	Stev Weissman and Herbert Krounsney
Island in the Steams	Ernest Hemingway
Is Paris Burning	Larry Collins And Dominique Lapierre
Ivanhoe	Sir Walter Scott
Jane Eyre	Charlotte Bronte
Jazz	Toni Morison
Jean Christopher	Roman Rolland
Jinnah-India-Partition Independence	Jaswant Singh
Jobs for Millions	V.V. Giri
Judgement, The	Kuldip Nayar

Book	Author
Judge's Miscellany, A	M. Hidayatullah
Jullius Caesar	William Shakespeare
Jungel Book	Rudyard Kipling
Justice of Peace Ke Aansu	Janardan Prasad Singh
Kadambari	Bana Bhatt
Kagaz te Kanwas	Amrita Pritam
Kali Aandhi	Kamleshwar
Kamayani	Jai Shanker Prasad
Kamasutra	S.J. Vatsyayan
Kanthapura	Raja Rao
Kapal Kundala	Bankim Chandra Chatterjee
Kashmir-Behind the Vale	M.J. Akbar
Kaya Kalp	Munshi Prem Chand
Kayar	Thakazhi Sivasankara Pillai
Ken Attendant Godot	Samuel Backett
Kenilworth	Sir Walter Scott
Khak-i-Dil	Jan Nissar Akhtar
Kidnapped	Robert Louis Stevenson
Killer Angels	Michael Shaara
Kim	Rudyard Kipling
King of Dark Chamber	Rabindra Nath Tagore
King Lear	William Shakespeare
Kipps	H. G. Wells
Kissinger Years, The	T.N. Kaul
Kitni Navon Main Kitni Bar	S.H. Vatsyayan
Kore Kagaz	Amrita Pritam
Kublai Khan	Samuel Taylor Coleridge
Kulliyat-i-Iqbal	M. Iqbal
Kumar Sambhava	Kalidas
L'Allegro	John Milton
La Divine Comedia	A. Dante
Lady Chatterley's Lover	D.H. Lawrence
Lady of the Lake	Sir Walter Scott
Lajja	Ms. Taslima Nasreen
Last Days of Pompeii	Edward George Lytton
Last Maharaja, The	Jean Louis Nou and Jacques Pouchepadass
Last Thing	C.P. Snow
Laws Versus Justice	V.R. Krishna Iyer
Lead Kindly Light	Vincent Shean
Le Contract Social (The Social Contract)	J.J. Rousseau
Leaders	Richard Nixon
Leaves of Grass	Walt Whiteman
Letters from the Field	Margaret Mead
Les Miserables	Victor Hugo
Leviathan	Thomas Hobbes
Life Divine	Aurbindo Ghosh
Life of Dr. Johnson	James Boswell
Light that Failed	Rudyard Kipling

Book	Author
Lines of Fate	Marek Kharitonov
Lipika	Rabindra Nath Tagore
Living Room	Graham Greene
Lolita	V. Nabokov
Long Walk to Freedom	Nelson Mandela
Look Back in Anger	John Osborne
Lord of the Files	William Golding
Lost Child	Mulk Raj Anand
Lost Honour	John Dena
Lotus Eaters	A Tennyson
Love Story	Eric Segal
Lycidas	John Milton
Macbeth	William Shakespeare
Magic Mountain	Maharishi Ved Vyas
Main Street	Sinclair Lewis
Major Barbara	George Bernard Shaw
Making of a Midsummer Night's Dream, The	David Selbourne
Malgudi Days	R.K. Narayan
Malti Madhav	Bhavabhuti
Malavikagnimitra	Kalidas
Man and Superman	George Bernard Shaw
Man Eaters of Kumaon	Jim Corbett
Man of Destiny	George Bernard Shaw
Mankind and Mother Earth	Arnold Toynbee
Man, The Unknown	Lewis Carroll
Man for All Seasons, A	Robert Bolt
Man for Moscow	G. Wynne
Many Worlds	K.P.S. Menon
Marriage and Morals	Bertrand Russel
Masters, The	C.P. Snow
Mati Matal	Gopinath Mohanty
Maurice	E.M. Forster
Mayor of Casterbridge	Thomas Hardy
Meghdoot	Kalidas
Mein Kampf	Adolf Hitler
Memories of Hope	Charles de Gaulle
Memories of Malgudi	R.K. Narayan
Men who Kept the Secrets	Thomas Powers
Men who Killed Gandhi, The	Manohar Malgonkar
Merchant of Venice	William Shakespeare
Middle Ground, The	Margaret Drabble
Middle March	George Eliot
Midnight's Children*	Salman Rushdie
Midsummer Night's Dream, A	William Shakespeare
Mill on the Floss	George Eliot
Miser, The	Moliere
Mistaken Identify	Nayantara Sehgal
Moby Dick	Hermann Melville
Modern Painters	John Ruskin
Moon and Six Pence	W. Somerset Maugham

Book	Author
Moonlight Sonata	L Beethoven
Mookhajiva Kanasugalu	K. Shivram Karnath
Mother	Maxim Gorky
Mother India	Katherine Mayo
Mountbatten and Independent India	Larry Collins & Dominique Lapierre
Mountbatten and The Partition of India	Larry Collins & Dominique Lapierre
Mrinalini	Bankim Chandra Chatterjee
Mrs. Gandhi's Second Reign	Arun Shourie
Much Ado About Nothing	William Shakespeare
Mudra Rakshasa	Vishakhadatta
Murder in the Cathedral	V.S. Eliot
Muslim Dilemma in India	M. K. A. Baig
My Days	R.K. Narayana
My Early Life	M.K. Gandhi
My Experiments with Truth	M.K. Gandhi
My India	S. Nihal Singh
My Life and Times	V.V. Giri
My Music, My Love	Ravi Shankar
My Own Boswell	M. Hidayatullah
My Presidential Years	R.Venkata Raman
My Struggles	E.K. Nayanar
My Truth	Indira Gandhi
Mysterious Universe	James Jens
Naked Came the Stranger	Penelope Ashe
Naked Face, The	Sidney Sheldon
Naked Triangle, The	Balwant Gargi
Naku Thanthi	D.R. Bendre
Nana	Emile Zola
Nature of Mass Poverty, The	J.K. Galbraith
Natya Shastra	Bharat Muni
Neela Chand	Shiv Prasad Singh
Nehru Family and Sikhs	Harbans Singh
Netaji Dead or Alive	Samar Guha
New Dimensions of India's Foreign Policy	Atal Behari Vajpayee
Nine Days' Wonder	John Mansfield
Nineteen Eighty-four	George Orwell
1999-Victory Without War	Richard Nixon
Nisheeth	Uma Shanker Joshi
Niti-Sataka	Bharatrihari
Nixon in White House	Seymour M. Hersh
Non-Violence in Peace and War	M.K. Gandhi
Nuclear India	G.G. Mirchandani and P.K.S. Namboodari
O'Jerusalem	Larry Collins and Dominique Lapierre
Occasion for Loving	Nadine Gordimer
Oddakkuzal	G. Shankara Kurup
Odyssey	Homer

Book	Author
Of Human Bondage	W. Somerset Maugham
Old Man and the Sea	Ernest Hemingway
Oliver Twist	Charles Dickens
Omeros	Derek Walcott
One Day on the Life of Ivan Denisovich	Alexander Solzhenitsyn
One Hundred Years of Solitude	Gabriel Marquez
One World	Wendell Wilkie
One World to Share	Sridath Ramphal
Origin of Species	Charles Darwin
Oru Desattinte Katha	S.K. Pottekkatt
Oscar and Lucinda	Peter Carey
Othello	William Shakespeare
Other Side of Midnight, The	Sidney Sheldon
Our Films, Their Films	Satyajit Ray
Paddy Clarke Ha Ha Ha	Roddy Doyle
Pakistan Papers	Mani Shankar Aiyer
Painted Veil	W. Somerset Maugham
Painter of Signs	R.K. Narayan
Pair of Blue Eyes, A	Thomas Hardy
Pakistan Crisis	David Loshak
Pakistan Cut to Size	D.R. Mankekar
Pakistan, The Gathering Storm	Benazir Bhutto
Panchatantra	Vishnu Sharma
Paradise Lost	John Milton
Paradise Regained	John Milton
Passge to England, A	Nirad C. Choudhury
Passage to India, A	E.M. Forster
Past and Present	Thomas Carlyle
Pather Panchali	Bibhuti Bhushan Bandhopadhayaya
Patriot, The	Pearl S. Buck
Personal Adventure, A	Theodore H. White
Peter Pan	J. M. Berrie
Pickwick Papers	Charles Dickens
Pilgrim's Progress	John Bunyan
Pinjar	Amrita Pritam
Plans for Departure	Nayantara Sehgal
Portrait of India	Ved Mehta
Post Office	Rabindra Nath Tagore
Power and Glory	Graham Greene
Power That Be	David Halberstan
Pratham Pratishruti	Ashapurna Devi
Prelude	William Wordsworth
Prem Pachisi	Munshi Prem Chand
Premonitions	P.N. Haksar
Price of Power	Kissinger
Pride and Prejudice	Jane Austen
Prince	Nicolo Machiaveli

Book	Author
Principla	Issac Newton
Prison and Chocolate Cake	Nayantara Sehgal
Prison Diary	Jaya Prakash Narayan
Prisoner of Zenda	Anthony Hope
Prisoner's Scrapbook, A	L.K. Advani
Prithviraj Raso	Chanda Bardai
Professor, The	Charlotte Bronte
Promises to Keep	Chester Bowels
Pygmalion	George Bernard Shaw
Pyramids of Sacrifice	Peter L. Berger
Radharani	Bankim Chandra Chatterjee
Rage of Angels	Sidney Sheldon
Raghuvansha	Kalidas
Ragtime	E.L. Doctorow
Rainbow, The	Pearl S. Buck
Rains Came	Louis Bromefield
Rajtarangini	Kalhana
Ram Charita Manas	Tulsidas
Ramayana	Maharishi Valmiki
Rangbhoomi	Munshi Prem Chand
Rang-i-Shairi	Raghupati Sahai (Firaq Gorakhpuri)
Rape of Bangladesh	Anthony Mascarenhas
Rape of the Lock	Alexander Pope
Ratnavali	Harsh Vardhan
Razor's Edge	W. Somerset Maugham
Rebel, The	Albert Camus
Rebirth	Leonid Brezhnev
Red and Black, The	Stendhal
Red Badge of Courage	Stephan Crane
Red Star over China	Edgar Snow
Reflections of the French Revolution	Edmund Burke
Reminiscences of the Nehru Age	M.O. Mathai
Reprieve	Jean Paul Sartre
Republic	Plato
Resurrection	Count Leo Tolstoy
Return of the Native, The	Thomas Hardy
Returning to the Source	Acharya Shree Rajneesh
Revenue Stamps, The	Amrita Pritam
Rich Like Us	Nayantara Sehgal
Riding the Storm	Harold MacMillan
Rights of Man	Thomas Paine
Rise and Fall of the Great Powers	Paul Kennedy
Ritu Samhara	Kalidas
Rivals, The	R.B. Shridan
Road to Folly	Leslie Ford
Robe, The	Lloyd C. Douglas
Robinson Crusoe	Daniel Defoe

Book	Author
Romeo and Julliet	William Shakespeare
Rubaiyat	Omar Khayyam
Rubaiyat-i-Omar Khayyam	Edward Fitzgerald
Sadar-i-Riyasat	Karan Singh
Saket	Maithili Sharan Gupta
Sakha Ram Binder	Vijay Tendulkar
Samler's Planet	Saul Bellow
Sands of Time	Sidney Sheldon
Satanic Verses	Salman Rushdie
Sanctuary	William Faulkner
Satyartha Prakash	Swami Dayanand
Savitri	Sri Aurobindo Ghosh
Scarlet Letter	Nathaniel Hawthorne
Scarlet Pimpernal	Baroness Orczy
Sceptred Flute	Sarojini Naidu
Scholar Extraordinary	Nirad C. Choudhury
School for Scandal, The	R.B. Sheridan
Scope of Happiness, The	Vijayalakshmi Pandit
Search for Home, A	Sasthi Brata
Sense and Sensibility	Jane Austen
Sense of Time, A	H.S. Vatsyayan
Sesame and Lilies	John Ruskin
Seven Lamps of Architecture	John Ruskin
Seven Summers	Mulk Raj Anand
Shadow from Ladakh	Bhabani Bhattacharya
Shahnama	Firdausi
Shakuntala	Kalidas
Shalimar	Manohar Malgonkar
Shall We Tell the President	Jeffrey Archer
Shape of Things to Come	H.G Wells
Shame	Salman Rushdie
She Stoops to Conquer	Oliver Goldsmith
Ship of Fools	Katherine Anne Porter
Shivaji, The Great Patriot	Lala Lajpat Rai
Shoes of the Fisherman, The	Morris West
Silas Marner	George Eliot
Six Characters in Search of an Author	Lugi Pirandello
Slave, The	Issac Bashevis Singer
Small Land	Leonid Brezhnev
Sohrab and Rustam	Matthew Arnold
Song of India, The	Sarojini Naidu
Sonnets, The	William Shakespeare
Sons and Lovers	D.H. Lawrence
Sound and the Fury, The	William Faulkner
Soz-i-Watan	Munshi Prem Chand
Spaniard in the Works, A	John Lennon
Spirit of the Age	William Hazlitt
Spy Catcher	Peter Wright
St. John	George Bernard Shaw
Story of My Life	Moshe Dayan
Story of Real Man	Nikolayev Polevol
Strangers and Brothers Omnibus	C.P. Snow
Sunny Days	Sunil Gavaskar
Study of History, A	Arnold Toynbee
Swami and Friends	R.K. Narayan
Swapnavasvadatta	Bhasa
Sword and the Sickle	Mulk Raj Anand
Tale of a Tub, A	Jonathan Swift
Tale of Two Cities, A	Charles Dickens
Tales from Shakespeare	Charles Lamb
Talisman	Sir Walter Scott
Tamas	Bhisham Sahni
Tarzan of the Apes	Edger Rice Burroughs
Tears of D'Urbervlles	Thoms Huardy
Tempest, The	William Shakespeare
Thank You, Jeeves	P.G. Wodehouse
The Garden of Life	Naveen Patnaik
The White Tiger*	Arvind Adiga
Thieves in the Night	Arthur Koestler
Thirteenth Sun	Amrita Pritam
Three Musketeers	Alexander Dumas
Thorn Birds	Colleen McCollough
Thousand Days, A	Arthur M. Shlesinger
Through the Indian Looking Glass	David Selbourne
Through the Looking Glass	Lewis Carroll
Times Machine	H.G. Wells
Time to be Happy	Nayantara Sehgal
To Live or not to Live	Nirad C. Choudhury
Tom Jones	Henry Fielding
Train to Pakistan	Khushwant Singh
Traveller, The	Olive Goldsmith
Treasure Island	Robert Louis Stevenson
Trial, The	Franz Kafka
Trinity	Leon Uris
Triumph	John Kenneth Galbraith
Tropic of Cancer	Henry Miller
Tryst with Destiny	L. S. Gopalan
Twelfth Night	William Shakespeare
Twenty Years After	Alexander Dumas
Two Leaves and a Bud	Mulk Raj Anand
Two Women	Alberto Moravia
Ulysses	James Joyce
Uncle Tom's Cabin	H.B. Stowe
Unhappy India	Lala Lajpat Rai
Universe Around Us	James Jeans
Unto this Last	John Ruskin

Book	Author
Untold Story	General B.M. Kaul
Upturned Soil, The	Mikhail Sholokhov
Urvashi	Ramdhari Singh Dinkar
Utopia	Thomas More
Uttar Ramcharita	Bhava Bhuti
Valley of Dolls	Jacqueline Susann
Vanity Fair	William Thackeray
Vendor of Sweets, The	R.K. Narayan
Vicar of Wakefield	Oliver Goldsmith
Victim, The	Saul Bellow
View From Delhi, A	Chester Bowles
View From the UN	U. Thant
Village by the Sea, A	Anita Desai
Village , The	Mulk Raj Anand
Vinay Patrika	Tulsidas
Virangana	Maithili Sharan Gupta
Virginians, The	William Thackeray
Vish Vriksha	Bankim Chandra Chatterjee
Voice of Conscience	V.V. Giri
Voice of Freedom , A	Nayantara Sehgal
Voice of the Voiceless	Ruth Harring
Waiting for Godot	Thomas Becket
Wake up India	Annie Besant
Walls of Glass, The	K.A. Abbas
War and Peace	Count Leo Tolstoy
War of the Worlds, The	H.G. Wells
Waste Land	T.S. Eliot

Book	Author
Way to all Flesh	Samuel Butler
Way of the World, The	William Congreve
Wealth of Nations	Adam Smith
Week With Gandhi, A	Louis Fisher
We Indians	Khushwant Singh
We, the People	N.A. Palkivala
Where the Grass is Greener	David M. Smith
White House Years	Henry Kissinger
Wings of Fire	A.P.J. Abdul Kalam*
Willhelm Meister	J.W. Von Goethe
Without Fear or Favour	Neelam Sanjiva Reddy
Witness to an Era	Frank Moraes
Woman's Life, A	Guy de Maupassant
Wonder That Was India, The	A.L. Basham
Worthy it is	Odysseus Elytis
Wreck, The	Rabindra Nath Tagore
Wuthering Heights	Emile Bronte
Yajnaseni	Pratibha Roy
Yama	Mahadevi Verma
Yashodhara	Maithili Sharan Gupta
Yayati	V.S. Khandekar
Year of the Upheaval	Henry Kissinger
Year of the Vulture, The	Amita Malik
Yesterday and Today	K.P.S. Menon
Zhivago, Dr.	Boris Pasternak
Zulfi, My Friend	Piloo Mody

FAMOUS AUTHORS IN DIFFERENT LANGUAGES

English	William Shakespeare, John Milton, Chaucer, Spenser, Lord Byron, P.B. Shelley, John Keats, Francis Bacon, T.S. Eliot, Cecil Dlay Lewis, Alduous Huxley, W.B. Yeats Bunyan, Dryden, Dr. Johnson, Alexander Pope, Robert Browning, Charles Lamb, Charles Dickens, Thomas Hardy, W.M. Thackeray, George Eliot, Alfred Tennyson, Robert Bridges, George Bernard Shaw, D.H. Lawrence, Oliver Goldsmith, Sheridan, Walter Scott, William Wordsworth, S.T. Coleridge, Henry Fielding, Somerset Maugham, J.K. Rowling.
French	Imile Zola, Gustave Flaubert, Moliere, Proudhon, Jean Paul Sartre, Le Sage, Victor Hugo, Alexander Dumas, Balzac.
German	Goethe, Hoffman, Lessing, Schelling, Schaupenhuer, Heinrich Heine, Guenter Grass
Russian	Tolstoy, Mikhail Solokhov, Turgenev, Dostoevsky, Maxim Gorky, Techov, Alexander Salzhenitsyn, Boris Pasternak
Greek	Homer, Aesop, Aristophanes, Euripedes, Herodotus, Hesoid, Theocritus, Xenophon, Aeschylus, Sophocles
Latin	Dante, Boccacio, Terence, Virgil, Ovid, Horace, Seneca
Norwegian	John Bojer, Ibsen
Persian	Ghalib, Umar Khyyam, Abul Fazal, Amir Khusro, Faiz, Firdausi, Mohd. Iqbal Saddi
Spanish	Juan Valera, Lope De Vega, Cervantes

FAMOUS CHARACTERS AND THEIR CREATORS

Character	Creator	Character	Creator
Adam	Milton	Juliet	William Shakespeare
Alice	Lewis Carroll	Jessica	William Shakespeare
Ancient Mariner	Coleridge	Jean Valjin	Victor Hugo
Ariel	William Shakespeare	Jacques	William Shakespeare
Antonio	William Shakespeare	Jeeves	P.G. Wodehouse
Anna Karenina	Leo Tolstoy	King Arthur	Tennyson
Bassomio	William Shakespeare	Kim	Rudyard Kipling
Bertie Wooster	P.G. Wodehouse	Long John Silver	R.L. Stevenson
Brutus	William Shakespeare	Macbeth	William Shakespeare
Beatrix	Thackery	Micawber	Charles Dickens
Beatrice	William Shakespeare	Miranda	William Shakespeare
Christian	John Bunyan	Mephistopheles	J.W. Von Goethe
Cordelia	William Shakespeare	Mellors	D.H. Lawrence
Cleopatra	William Shakespeare	Malaprop	Sheridian
Clare	Thomas Hardy	Oliver Twist	Charles Dickens
Claudius	William Shakespeare	Peggotty	Charles Dickens
David Copperfield	Charles Dickens	Priyangbada	Kalidas
Dushyanta	Kalidas	Portia	William Shakespeare
Don Quixote	Cervantes	Pip	Charles Dickens
Eliza Doolittle	George Bernard Shaw	Perry Mason	Erle Stanley Gardner
Estella	Charles Dickens	Pickwick	Charles Dickens
Faust	J.W. Von Goethe	Rip Van Winkle	Washington Irving
Gora	Rabindranath Tagore	Sam Weller	Charles Dickens
Hamlet	William Shakespeare	Surpanakha	Valmiki
Harry Potter	J.K. Rowling	Shylock	William Shakespeare
Hyde	R.L. Stevenson	Sherlock Halmes	Arthur Conan Doyle
Hercule Poirot	Agatha Christie	Shakuntala	Kalidas
Hawkins	R.L. Stevenson	Sancho Panza	Cervantes Saavedra
Hector	Homer	Tess	Thomas Hardy
Ivanhoe	Sir Walter Scott	Watson	Arthur Conan Doyle
Iago	William Shakespeare	Zhivago	Boris Pasternak
James Bond	Ian Fleming		

GREAT POETS

Language	Poet
Hindi	Surdas, Tulsidas, Keshav
Sanskrit	Valmiki, Vedvyas, Kalidas
Bengali	Rabindra Nath Tagore
Urdu	Mirza Ghalib
Persian	Sheikh Saadi
Latin	Virgil
Greek	Homer
English	Shakespeare
German	Goethe
Italian	Dante
French	Sully Proudhone
Punjabi	Waris Shah

GREAT INDIAN AUTHORS AND POETS

Language	Authors and Poets
Assamese	Birendra Kumar Bhattacharya; Hem Chandra Barua; Hem Chandra Goswami; Madhavkandali.
Bengali	Ashapoorna Devi; Bankim Chandra Chatterjee; Bibhuti Bhushan Bandopadhyaya; Bishnu Dey; Pramendra Mitra; Rabindra Nath Tagore; R.C. Dutt; Michael Madhusudan Datt; Kazi Nazrul Islam; Tarashankar Bandopadhyaya.
English	Kamala Das; Manohar Malgonkar; R.K. Narayan; Raja Rao; Mulk Raj Anand; Bhabani Bhatacharya; Sasthi Brata; Arun

Language	Authors and Poets
	Joshi; Chaman Nahal; K.A. Abbas; Anita Desai; R. Prawer Jhabwala; Kamla Markandaya; Khushwant Singh; Manoj Dass.
Gujarati	K.M. Munshi; Mirabai; Narmada Sagar; Narsingh Mehta; Govardhan Ram; Uma Shankar Joshi.
Hindi	Tulsidas; Surdas; Kesav Das; Bihari; Kabir; Sumitra Nandan Pant; Jai Shankar Prasad; Maithili Sharan Gupta; Munshi Prem Chand; Upendra Nath Ashk; Suryakant Tripathi 'Nirala', Acharya Chatursen; Mohan Rakesh; Harivansh Rai Bachchan; Mahadevi Verma; Bhagwati Charan Verma; Ramdhari Singh Dinkar.
Kannada	K.V. Puttappa; B.M. Pampan; Panna; Ramchandra Bendre; K.S. Karanth; Purandar Das.
Malayalam	C.V. Raman Pillai; S.K. Pottekkatt; G. Sankara Kurup; Thakazhi Sivasankara Pillai; O. Chandu Menon; Vallathol; Kumaran Asan.

Language	Authors and Poets
Marathi	Hari Narayan Apte. Tikaram Mahay; Tukaram; V.S. Khandekar.
Oriya	Gopalbandhu Das; Gopi Nath Mohanty; Radha Nath Roy.
Punjabi	Sheikh Farid; Bhai Veer Singh; Dhani Ram Chatrik; Amrita Pritam; Nanak Singh; Balwant Gargi; Waris Shah; Bulle Shah.
Sanskrit	Maharishi Valmiki; Maharishi Ved Vyas, Shreeharsh; Ashvaghosh; Shudrak; Bharvi; Jaidev; Bhartrihari; Kalidas; Banabhatta; Bhavabhuti; Dandi.
Tamil	P.V. Akilandam, Subramaniam Bharati; Ramalingam.
Telugu	Lakshmi Narasimhan; Triputi; V. Satyanarayana.
Urdu	Assadulla Khan 'Ghalib'; Mohammed Iqbal; Mir Taqui Mir; Prem Chand; 'Firaq' Gorakhpuri; Rajinder Singh Bedi; Krishan Chander; Qurrat-ul-Ain Hyder; Sardar Jafri; Qazi Abdul Sattar.

WELL KNOWN QUOTATIONS

1. A thing of beauty is a joy for ever; Its loveliness increases; It will never pass into nothingness. — *Keats. Endymion*

2. A little knowledge is a dangerous thing — *Pope*

3. Beauty is truth, truth beauty that is all. Ye know on earth, all all ye need to know — *Keats: Ode on a Grecian urn*

4. All the world is a stage and all the man and women merely players — *Shakespeare: As you like it*

5. Some books are to be tested, others to be swallowed and some few to be chewed and digested —*Bacon*

6. Better to reign in hell than serve in heaven — *Milton: Paradise lost*

7. The child is father of the man — *Wordsworth: My heart leaps up*

8. A single step for man — a giant leap for mankind — *Neil Armstrong*

9. Dilli Chalo — *Netaji Subhash Chandra Bose*

10. To be or not to be — that is the question. — *Shakespeare: Hamlet*

11. Only free men negotiate. I shall never negotiate while I am still a prisoner — *Nelson Mandela*

12. Truth and non-violence are my God — *Mahatama Gandhi*

13. Let a hundred flowers bloom and let a thousand schools of thought contend – *Mao Tse-tung*

14. Jai Jawan, Jai Kisan — *Lal Bahadur Shastri*

15. Eureka! Eureka! — *Archimedes*

16. Some are born great, some achieve greatness and some have greatness thrust upon them — *Shakespeare*

17. Where wealth accumulates, men decay — *Goldsmith*

18. Power tends to corrupt and absolute power corrupts absolutely — *Lord Acton*

19. Man is by nature a political animal — *Aristotle*

20. I have nothing to offer but blood, toil, tears and sweat — *Winston Churchill*

21. I came, I saw, I conquered — *Julius Ceaser*

22. For fools rush in where angels fear to tread — *Pope*

23. Generations to come, it may, will scarce believe that such a one as this ever in flesh and blood walked upon this earth — *Einstein*

24. Government of the people, by the people, for the people — *Lincon*

25. East is east and west is west and never the twain shall meet — *Kipling*

26. Swaraj is my birth right — *Bal Gangadhar Tilak*

27. Cowards die many times before their death: The valiant never taste of death but once

— Shakespeare: Julius Ceaser

28. Where ignorance is bliss, It is folly to be wise *— Grey*

29. I know nothing except the fact of my ignorance *— Socrates*

30. We are such stuff as dreams are made of and our little life is rounded with a sleep

— Shakespeare: The Tempest

31. What's in a name? That which we call a rose By any other name would smell as sweet

— Shakespeare: Merchant of Venice

32. Patriotism is the best refuge of a scoundrel *— Samuel Johnson*

33. Reading maketh a full man; conference a ready man; and writing an exact man *— Francis Bacon*

34. It is excellent to love a giant's strength
but it is tyrannous to use it like a giant

— Shakespeare: Measure to Measure

35. Water, water everywhere
Not any drop to drink

— S.T. Coleridge: The Ancient Mainer

36. It is strange but true, for truth is always strange *— Byron: Don Juan*

37. Virtue is its own reward *— Cicero: De Fintibus*

38. Frailty, thy name is woman *— Shakespeare: Hamlet*

39. We don't fear to negotiate, but we do not negotiate out of fear *— J.F. Kennedy*

40. Give us good mothers and I shall give you good nation *— Napoleon.*

41. The woods are lovely, dark and deep
But I have promises to keep
And miles to go before I sleep *— Robert Frost*

42. We have made a tryst with destiny *— Pt. Nehru*

43. Eli, Eli, Lamma Sabcathani (My God, my God, why last thou forsaken me)

— Jesus Christ at the Cross

44. If winter comes can spring be for behind *— Shelley*

45. Man does not live by bread alone *— Bible*

46. Nothing is good or bad, thinking makes it so *— Shakespeare: Hamlet*

47. Garibi hatao *— Indira Gandhi*

48. Aram haram hai *— Jawaharlal Nehru*

49. Quit India *— Mahatma Gandhi*

50. Jai Jawan, Jai Kisan, Jai Vigyan *— Atal Behari Vajpayee*

Multiple Choice Questions

THE LAST LESSON
By Alphonse Daudet

1. **Assertion (A):** Franz was scared to go to school.

   Reason (R): He had not learnt his homework and was late for school.

   A. Both (A) and (R) are true and (R) is the correct explanation of (A)
   B. Both (A) and (R) are true, but (R) is not the correct explanation of (A)
   C. (A) is true, but (R) is false
   D. (A) is false, but (R) is true

2. **Assertion (A):** Franz was tempted to stay out of doors.

   Reason (R): The weather was warm, birds were chirping and Prussian soldiers were drilling.

   A. Both (A) and (R) are true, but (R) is not the correct explanation of (A)
   B. Both (A) and (R) are true and (R) is the correct explanation of (A)
   C. (A) is true, but (R) is false
   D. (A) is false, but (R) is true

3. **Assertion (A):** Usually there was a great commotion when the school began.

   Reason (R): The noise was produced by the opening & closing of desks, lessons repeated in unison by students and the teachers' ruler rapping on the table.

   A. Both (A) and (R) are true and (R) is the correct explanation of (A)
   B. Both (A) and (R) are true, but (R) is not the correct explanation of (A)
   C. (A) is true, but (R) is false
   D. (A) is false, but (R) is true

4. **Assertion (A):** That day everything was as quiet as Sunday morning.

   Reason (R): It was indeed a Sunday morning and no one was present in the school.

   A. Both (A) and (R) are true and (R) is the correct explanation of A
   B. Both (A) and (R) are true, but (R) is not the correct explanation of (A)

C. (A) is true, but (R) is false
D. (A) is false, but (R) is true

5. **Assertion (A):** M. Hamel was wearing his special dress for the last French class.

Reason (R): The dress comprised of beautiful green coat, frilled shirt & the little black silk cap.
A. Both (A) and (R) are true and (R) is the correct explanation of (A)
B. Both (A) and (R) are true, but (R) is not the correct explanation of (A)
C. (A) is true, but (R) is false
D. (A) is false, but (R) is true

6. **Assertion (A):** The elderly villagers occupied the back benches on the last day of French lesson.

Reason (R): This fact surprised Franz the most.
A. Both (A) and (R) are true and (R) is the correct explanation of (A)
B. Both (A) and (R) are true, but (R) is not the correct explanation of (A)
C. (A) is true, but (R) is false
D. (A) is false, but (R) is true

7. **Assertion (A):** The whole school seemed strange and solemn to Franz.

Reason (R): The order had come from Berlin to teach only German in the schools of Alsace & Lorraine. That was their last French class.
A. Both (A) and (R) are true and (R) is the correct explanation of (A)
B. Both (A) and (R) are true, but (R) is not the correct explanation of (A)
C. (A) is true, but (R) is false
D. (A) is false, but (R) is true

8. **Assertion (A):** Franz was filled with repentance and guilt on the last day of French class.

Reason (R): He did not study French when he had time, he wasted his time in seeking birds' eggs and sliding on the Saar.
A. Both (A) and (R) are true, but (R) is not the correct explanation of (A)
B. Both (A) and (R) are true and (R) is the correct explanation of (A)
C. (A) is true, but (R) is false
D. (A) is false, but (R) is true

9. **Assertion (A):** The elderly people occupied the back benches.

Reason (R): They were present for thanking M Hamel, for being sorry too for not going to school more, for showing their respect towards the country that was theirs no more.
A. Both (A) and (R) are true and (R) is the correct explanation of (A)
B. Both (A) and (R) are true, but (R) is not the correct explanation of (A)
C. (A) is true, but (R) is false
D. (A) is false, but (R) is true

10. **Assertion (A):** The teacher is also responsible for poor performance of students in studies.

Reason (R): He often sent them to water his flowers instead of learning their lessons, declared holidays for no reason.
A. Both (A) and (R) are true, but (R) is not the correct explanation of (A)
B. Both (A) and (R) are true and (R) is the correct explanation of (A)
C. (A) is true, but (R) is false
D. (A) is false, but (R) is true

11. **Assertion (A):** French language was the most beautiful, the clearest and the most logical of all the languages.

Reason (R): As long as the Frenchmen held fast to their language, they had chances of winning freedom.
A. Both (A) and (R) are true and (R) is the correct explanation of (A)
B. Both (A) and (R) are true, but (R) is not the correct explanation of (A)
C. (A) is true, but (R) is false
D. (A) is false, but (R) is true

12. **Assertion (A):** Will they make them sing in German, even the pigeons.

Reason (R): They had enslaved France, so they could do every impossible act.
A. Both (A) and (R) are true and (R) is the correct explanation of (A)
B. Both (A) and (R) are true, but (R) is not the correct explanation of (A)
C. (A) is true, but (R) is false
D. (A) is false, but (R) is true

13. **Assertion (A):** When it struck twelve, M. Hamel made a gesture with his hand to everyone that the school was dismissed.

Reason (R): He was too emotional and upset over the Berlin order to speak anything.
A. Both (A) and (R) are true, but (R) is not the correct explanation of (A)
B. Both (A) and (R) are true and (R) is the correct explanation of (A)
C. (A) is true, but (R) is false
D. (A) is false, but (R) is true

14. Look at the statements given below. Choose the option that correctly identifies which statements are fact and which are opinion:
(*a*) By sitting in the class, the elders of Alsace showed their respect for M. Hamel.

(*b*) The elders were regretting that they did not learn their mother tongue.
(*c*) The elders did not appreciate the faithful service of M. Hamel and were only there to bid farewell to the teacher.
(*d*) The teacher was sorrowful as he was to leave not only his students but also the school which he had nurtured.

A. Fact (*a*) and (*d*); opinion (*b*) and (*c*)
B. Fact (*b*) and (*c*); opinion (*a*) and (*d*)
C. Fact (*a*) and (*b*); opinion (*c*) and (*d*)
D. Fact (*b*) and (*d*); opinion (*a*) and (*c*)

15. **Statement I:** The narrator feels sorry for M. Hamel.

Statement II: Franz could not accept the fact that he won't be learning French any longer.

A. Statement I is true, but Statement II is false.
B. Statement I is false, but Statement II is true.
C. Both these statements can be inferred from the lesson.
D. Neither of the statements can be inferred from the lesson.

Directions: *Read each of the following passages carefully and choose the best answer to each question out of the four alternatives.*

PASSAGE-1

I started for school very late that morning and was in great dread of a scolding, especially because M. Hamel had said that he would question us on participles, and I did not know the first word about them. For a moment, I thought of running away and spending the day out of doors. It was so warm, so bright!

16. Who is the author of these lines?
A. William Douglas B. Selma Lagerlof
C. Alphonse Daudet D. Anees Jung

17. Who was Mr Hamel?
A. Principal B. French teacher
C. Village Sarpanch D. Franz's father

18. Why was Franz in great dread?
A. He had not prepared his grammar lesson
B. He had bunked the class the previous day
C. He had not brought his notebook
D. None of these

19. What did Franz think for a moment?
A. teaching a lesson to his teacher
B. pranking the principal
C. bunking the class
D. joining the Civil movement

PASSAGE-2

I jumped over the bench and sat down at my desk. Not till then, when I had got a little over my fright, did I see that our teacher had on his beautiful green coat, his frilled shirt, and the little black silk cap, all embroidered, that he never wore except on inspection and prize days. Besides, the whole school seemed so strange and solemn.

20. Who is 'I' in the given lines?
A. Franz B. M. Hamel
C. The Mayor D. The Narrator

21. What was unusual about M. Hamel's dress?
A. Wore clean clothes
B. Wore a brand new outfit
C. Wore a traditional French outfit
D. Wore his fancy clothes

22. Why was M. Hamel dressed so unusually?
A. He was retiring
B. It was his last lesson
C. He was leaving the school
D. He was going to be imprisoned

23. Which word in the extract would also mean 'formal and dignified'?
A. Inspection B. Strange
C. Solemn D. Fright

24. 'Got a little over my Fright' means:
A. a bit afraid B. a bit settled
C. being cautious D. all of these

PASSAGE-3

"My children, this is the last lesson I shall give you. The order has come from Berlin to teach only German in the schools of Alsace and Lorraine. The new master comes tomorrow. This is your last French lesson. I want you to be very attentive." What a thunderclap these words were to me!

25. Why does M. Hamel want the students to be attentive?
A. Because it is his last French lesson
B. Because the order has come from Berlin
C. Because he is about to reveal the question paper
D. Because the government officer is on a visit

26. Which order from Berlin is called as 'thunderclap' by Franz?
A. The order of closing schools for a month
B. The order of stopping teaching French
C. The order of executing anyone in Alsace & Lorraine
D. The order of demolishing the school building

27. How would you describe Franz's tone when he says, "What a thunderclap these words were to me"?
A. Angry B. Gloomy
C. Perplexed D. Irritated

28. **Statement I:** M. Hamel had been subjected to mental torture with the decision to teach only German in Alsace and Lorraine.

Statement II: Nobody except Franz was able to realize the pain in M. Hamel's eyes.

A. Statement I is true, but Statement II is false
B. Statement I is false, but Statement II is true
C. Both Statement I & II cannot be inferred from the passage
D. Both Statement I & II can be inferred from the passage

29. In which of the following options can the underlined words not be replaced with 'wretch'?

A. The beggar has broken my car window.
B. Items like a stick and grenadier are now variable.
C. He is a lonely and miserable rogue.
D. Before the poor knave had time to speak, he was shot.

PASSAGE-4

My last French lesson why I hardly knew how to write I should never learn anymore I must stop there then oh how sorry I was for not learning my lessons for seeking Birds eggs or going sliding on the Saar my books that had seemed such a nuisance a while ago so heavy to carry my grammar and my history of the saints were old friends now that I couldn't give up.

30. Why was it the speaker's last French lesson?

A. because his French teacher was retiring
B. because of a government order to teach only German
C. because the speaker was migrating
D. because French has become a language to be taught in higher classes

31. What is the speaker feeling after getting to know that it is his last French lesson?

A. sad B. regretful
C. frightened D. distraught

32. What did Franz do to skip his French lessons?

A. seeking bird eggs
B. going on the slides
C. working on the mill
D. both (A) and (B)

33. How do Franz's feelings regarding his books change?

A. He feels that they were his friends
B. He believes that they were a nuisance
C. He feels that his identity is related to his books
D. He believed that they are of no use to him

PASSAGE-5

Poor man! It was in honour of this last lesson that, he had put on his fine Sunday clothes, and now I understood why the old men of the village were sitting there in the back of the room. It was because they were sorry, too, that they had not gone to school more. It was their way of thanking our master for his forty years of faithful service and of showing their respect for the country that was theirs no more.

34. Why does the narrator refer to M. Hamel as 'poor man'?

A. He empathizes with M. Hamel as he had to leave the village.
B. He believed that M Hamel's 'fine Sunday clothes' clearly reflected that he was not rich.
C. He feels sorry for M. Hamel as it was his last French lesson.
D. He thinks that M. Hamel's patriotism and sense of duty resulted in his poverty.

35. Which of the following idioms might describe the villagers' act of attending the last lesson most accurately?

A. too good to miss
B. too little, too late
C. too many cooks spoil the broth
D. too cool for school

36. Choose the option that might raise a question about M. Hamel's 'faithful service'.

A. When Franz came late M. Hamel told him that he was about to begin class without him.
B. Franz mentioned how cranky M. Hamel was and 'his great ruler rapping on the table'.
C. M Hamel often sent students to water his flowers and gave a holiday when he wanted to go fishing.
D. M Hamel permitted villagers to put their children 'to work on a farm or at the mills' for some extra money.

37. Choose the option that most appropriately fills in the blanks, for the following description of the given extract.

The villagers and their children sat in the class, forging with their old master a (*i*) .... togetherness. In that moment, the class room stood (*ii*) .... It was France itself and the last French lesson a desperate hope to (*iii*) .... to the remnants of what they had known and taken for granted their own (*iv*)........ .

A. (*i*) graceful (*ii*) still (*iii*) hang on (*iv*) country
B. (*i*) bygone (*ii*) up (*iii*) keep on (*iv*) education
C. (*i*) beautiful (*ii*) mesmerised (*iii*) carry on (*iv*) unity
D. (*i*) forgotten (*ii*) transformed (*iii*) hold on (*iv*) identity

PASSAGE-6

But I got mixed up on the first words and stood there, holding onto my desk, my heart beating, and not daring to look up.

38. Who is I here?

A. Mr Hamel B. Franz
C. Village Sarpanch D. Not clear from the story

39. What was asked in the classroom from 'I'?
A. Rule of grammar
B. Addition rule
C. Multiplication table of 18
D. Essay on the language

40. Why did he stand holding the desk?
A. He was surprised at the question
B. He had not prepared his lesson
C. He was absent the previous day
D. He did not listen the question clearly

41. What was the reaction of the teacher?
A. Scolded him
B. Shouted at him
C. Sent him out of the class
D. Pitied him

PASSAGE-7

I heard M. Hamel say to me, "I won't scold you, little Franz; you must feel bad enough. See how it is! Every day we have said to ourselves, Bah! I have plenty of time. I'll learn it tomorrow. And now you see where we have come out. That's the great trouble with Alsace; she puts off learning till tomorrow.

42. For what reason Franz could have been scolded?
A. For being late to school
B. for not learning participles
C. for ignoring his lessons
D. for playing all the time

43. Why should Franz be feeling bad?
A. his teacher was retiring
B. he would not learn French now
C. he was rusticated
D. his inability to show his command over friend

44. The given lines indicate how M. Hamel is feeling. Pick the option that correctly states these feelings.

1. angry	2. regretful
3. sad	4. hatred
5. Joyous	6. sympathetic
A. 1 and 4	B. 2 and 3
C. 5 and 6	D. 1 and 3

45. The story 'The Last lesson' highlights which human tendency?
A. male chauvinism B. procrastination
C. courage D. cowardice

PASSAGE-8

M. Hamel went on to talk of the French language, saying that it was the most beautiful language in the world— the clearest, the most logical; that we must guard it among us and never forget it, because when a people are enslaved, as long as they hold fast to their language as it is as if they had the key to their prison. Then he opened a grammar book and read us our lesson. I was amazed to see how well I understood it. All he said seemed so easy, so easy.

46. Which of the following can be attributed to M. Hamel's declaration about the French language?
A. Subjective expertise
B. Nostalgic pride
C. Factual accuracy
D. Patriotic magnification

47. Read the quotes given below. Choose the option that might best describe Hamel's viewpoint.
(*a*) Those who know nothing of foreign languages know nothing of their own.
(*b*) Language is the road map of a culture. It tells you where its people come from and where they are going.
(*c*) A poor man is like a foreigner in his own country.
(*d*) The greatest propaganda in the world is our mother tongue, that is what we learn as children, and which we learn unconsciously. That shapes our perception for life.
A. option (*a*) B. option (*b*)
C. option (*c*) D. option (*d*)

48. "I was amazed to see how well I understood it". Select the option that does not explain why Franz found the grammar lesson 'easy'.
A. Franz was paying careful attention in class this time.
B. M. Hamel was being extremely patient and calm in his teaching.
C. Franz was inspired and had found a new meaning and purpose to learning.
D. Franz had realized that French was the clearest and most logical language.

49. Franz was able to understand the grammar lesson easily because he was:
A. receptive B. appreciative
C. introspective D. competitive

PASSAGE-9

All at once, the church clock struck 12, then the Angelus. At the same moment the trumpets of the Prussians, returning from drill sounded under our windows. M. Hamel stood up very pale in his chair. I never saw him look so tall.

50. What is Angelus?
A. Prayers said in the morning
B. Prayers said in the middle of the day
C. Prayers said in the evening
D. All of these

51. Who are the Prussians?
A. Residents of Germany
B. Residents of Poland
C. Residents of some parts of Austria
D. All of these combined

52. Why was M. Hamel so pale?
A. He was tired by the end of the class
B. He was replaced by the German teacher
C. He was not well
D. He was tired due to the Mischief caused by the students

53. 'I never saw him look so tall' means:
A. Sad B. Excited
C. Lively D. seemed very confident

PASSAGE-10

"Viva La France!" then he stopped and leaned his head against the wall and without a word he made a gesture to us with his hand— "school is dismissed—you may go".

54. The reason for his stopping and leaning against the wall was:
A. because he was unwell
B. because he was emotional
C. because he wanted to teach German too
D. because the students didn't pay attention in his lecture

55. What does 'Viva La France' mean?
A. Good bye France B. Good living France
C. Long live France D. France is the best

56. The phrase 'Viva La France' indicates the speakers:
A. Enthusiasm B. Depression
C. Nostalgia D. Patriotism

57. Why does M. Hamel write Viva La France on the black board:
A. to show his love for French
B. to show his love for teaching
C. to show his love for his country
D. both (A) and (C)

58. French think, "Will they make them sing in German". What does this mean?
A. it means that nothing will be affected
B. it means that when people are deprived their surroundings are also affected
C. it means that a change will be welcome
D. it means that Franz was unaware of what was happening

59. Choose the statement that is not true:
A. Franz did not like going to school
B. He was scared of M Hamel
C. He was excited that he was going to learn German
D. He was regretful on the day of the last lesson

60. What had the narrator counted on to enter the school unnoticed?
A. he counted the leaves of a plant outside the classroom
B. he counted the blessing of God
C. he counted the number of people he met on his way
D. he counted on the hustle and bustle that was usual in the school

61. What did M. Hamel tell the people in the class about French language?
A. French was the most beautiful language in the world
B. French was the most illogical language in the world
C. French was the most logical language in the world
D. Both (A) and (C)

62. Which language was made compulsory to be taught in the schools of Alsace and Lorraine?
A. Portuguese B. French
C. German D. Spanish

63. For how many years had Hamel taught at the school?
A. 10 years B. 20 years
C. 30 years D. 40 years

64. Who were present in the class the last day?
A. all the villagers were present in the class
B. all the students and elderly villagers were present in the class
C. everyone except the teacher were present in the class
D. the Inspector from the neighbouring town was present in the class

65. The word 'rapping' means:
A. singing
B. slapping on the head
C. striking to attract attention
D. teaching strictly

66. "The birds were chirping at the edge of the woods and in the open fields back of the sawmill the Prussian soldiers were drilling."

Which of the following sentences can be said as true after reading the given lines?
A. Alsace bordered Prussia and so Franz could hear the drilling.
B. The Prussian soldiers had started to construct their official building.
C. The people of Alsace like Franz were attracted to the sound of drilling.
D. Prussia had won over Alsace and Lorraine and thus were practicing to settle their authority.

67. Franz saw a huge crowd assembled in front of the bulletin board, but did not stop. How would you evaluate his reaction?
A. Franz was too little to care about the news of lost battles.
B. Nobody in Franz's family was in the army, so it did not matter.

C. Bad news had become very normal, so he went about his task.
D. It was too crowded for Franz to find out what news was up on the board.

68. What did the blacksmith say to Franz?
A. To read the bulletin-board.
B. To get his homework completed.
C. To hurry to the school.
D. To not go so fast.

69. "There was usually great bustle and noise when school began, but it was all very quiet". Which of the following describes Franz's emotions most accurately?
A. Shock and awe
B. Disappointment and anxiety
C. Confusion and distress
D. Curiosity and uncertainty

70. Which of the statements cannot be attributed to Franz?
A. Franz did not like studying; he would rather enjoy nature.
B. Franz loved his teacher a lot.
C. Franz regretted that he did not study French at all.
D. Franz was a naughty student.

71. What does M. Hamel blame the parents for?
A. They preferred children to work in farms.
B. They were not strict.
C. They did not come to M. Hamel's class.
D. They did not love the French language.

72. "It seemed almost as if the poor man wanted to give us all he knew before going away and put it all into our heads at one stroke". Which of the following sentences does not use the phrase 'at one stroke' correctly?
A. The smoke choked the joking man at one stroke.
B. I managed to please both the buyer and the seller at one stroke.
C. Let's settle the matter at one stroke.
D. When the economy crashed, thousands lost their jobs, their homes and their pensions at one stroke.

73. 'They looked like little flags floating everywhere in the school room, hung from the rod at the top of our desks.' In the given sentence, which literary device has been used:
A. Alliteration B. Metaphor
C. Simile D. Both (A) and (C)

74. Choose the term which best matches the tone of statement: "but he had the courage to hear every lesson to the very last".
A. Acceptance B. Neglect
C. Discipline D. Regret

75. "I never saw him look so tall". Which of the following best captures M. Hamel on the last day of school?
A. Cranky, measurable, dedicated, resigned
B. Patient, dignified, emotional, courageous
C. Calm, nostalgic, disappointed, patriotic
D. Proud, reproachful, persistent, heroic

76. What do the marching soldiers under the windows represent?
A. The Dawn of Prussia and the defeat of French people
B. The defeat of Prussia
C. The victory of French
D. None of these

77. Pick a quote that best describes the theme of the story:
A. What is the nation without a mother tongue?
B. The rhythm of my body is the same as my mother tongue. It is in this rhythm where I find sanctity that I can return to my mother who is everywhere in the universe.
C. Language is the blood of the soil into which thoughts run and out of which they grow.
D. Poetry is the mother tongue of the human race.

78. What did Hauser bring?
A. Sweets B. Children
C. Friends D. Old Primer

79. What made Franz forget M. Hamel's ruler and crankiness?
A. Police Patrolling
B. Strange Quietness
C. Bustle on the streets
D. The idea of his going away

80. When people are enslaved, what key do they have to the prison, according to M. Hamel?
A. Their behaviour B. Power
C. Aggressiveness D. Mother tongue

81. What does the expression "in great dread of scolding" mean?
A. To be happy about it
B. Very badly scared of scolding
C. To be indifferent
D. None of these

82. M. Hamel is introduced as a ruler-wielding teacher. This demonstrates that:
A. he is concerned B. he is adamant
C. he is unfeeling D. he is a hard taskmaster

83. What is the moral that Alphonse Daudet wants to bring out?
A. Not to put off things that one can do that day
B. Old order changed to new
C. One should accept everything that happens
D. Teachers should be respected

84. For the last two years, where did all the bad news come from?
A. The Bulletin Board
B. Town Hall
C. School
D. M. Hamel's House

85. What did Mr. Hamel bring for his class on his last day in the school?
A. New pens B. New notebooks
C. Sweets D. Story books

86. What was Franz expected to be prepared for at school that day?
A. Song B. Dance
C. Essay writing D. Participles

87. Who asked Franz not to hurry to school?
A. Old Hauser B. Former Mayor
C. Former Postmaster D. Blacksmith Watcher

88. The story is set in the days of:
A. Franco–Prussian war (1870-71)
B. Franco–German war (1870-71)
C. Franco–Poland war (1880-81)
D. Franco–Austrian war (1880-81)

89. Prussia then comprised of:
A. Germany, Poland, Parts of Austria
B. Germany, Italy, Poland
C. Germany, England, France
D. France, Austria, Poland

LOST SPRING
By Anees Jung

Directions: *Read each of the following passages carefully and choose the best answer to each question out of the four alternatives.*

PASSAGE-1

"This morning, Saheb is on his way to the milk booth. In his hand is a steel canister. "I now work in a tea stall down the road", he says, pointing in the distance. "I am paid 800 rupees and all my meals". Does he like the job? I ask. His face, I see, has lost the carefree look. The steel canister seems heavier than the plastic bag he would carry so lightly over his shoulder. The bag was his. The canister belongs to the man who owns the tea shop. Saheb is no longer his own master!"

90. "His face, I see, has lost the carefree look". This means as per the assumption of the author, in his looks, Saheb is ....
A. Not burdened with responsibility
B. Burdened with responsibility
C. Burdened but without any responsibility
D. Not burdened but feels responsible

91. Choose the appropriate statements for "Saheb is no longer his own master!"
(*i*) Saheb carries his bag for rag picking.
(*ii*) Saheb works in a tea stall.
(*iii*) Saheb is paid 800 rupees.
(*iv*) Saheb carries canister.
A. (*i*), (*ii*) & (*iii*) B. (*i*), (*ii*) & (*iv*)
C. (*i*), (*iii*) & (*iv*) D. (*ii*), (*iii*) & (*iv*)

92. Read the statements given below.
Choose the correct statement to analyse the mental condition of Saheb-e-Alam.
A. He seems to be dignified working at the tea-stall.
B. He seems to be proud collecting milk from the milk booth.
C. He seems to be responsible carrying the steel canister.
D. He seems to be enjoying his freewheel at the tea-stall.

93. Select the option/options that does *not* explain Saheb's nature of thinking in his new job at the tea stall.
(*i*) He thinks collecting milk is a part of his new job.
(*ii*) Canister is heavy, but he thinks he should carry it for survival.
(*iii*) He is earning 800 rupees and all meals, so he should justify the job.
(*iv*) He is a servant now, he can have a carefree life.
A. Only option (*iii*)
B. Both options (*ii*) & (*iv*)
C. Both options (*i*) & (*iv*)
D. Only option (*iv*)

94. Choose the option that most appropriately fills in the blanks, for the following description of the given extract.
People migrate from villages to cities in search of a better life. They want to earn money so that they can lead a good life and (*i*) ________ their children in a better way. As cities have more (*ii*) ________ for work, this makes them migrate from the villages to these big cities. (*iii*) ________ all miseries and challenges of life at young age, Saheb even finds a job in a tea stall, shifting from rag picking to (*iv*) ________ his struggle for survival.
A. (*i*) give; (*ii*) scope; (*iii*) controlling; (*iv*) continue
B. (*i*) rare; (*ii*) opportunities; (*iii*) Accepting; (*iv*) prove
C. (*i*) provide; (*ii*) jobs; (*iii*) Denying; (*iv*) stop
D. (*i*) leave; (*ii*) chances; (*iii*) Chasing; (*iv*) deal

PASSAGE-2

Savita, a young girl in a drab pink dress, sits alongside an elderly woman, soldering pieces of glass. As her hands move mechanically like the tongs of a machine, I wonder if she knows the sanctity of the bangles she helps make. It symbolises an Indian woman's suhaag, auspiciousness in marriage. It will dawn on her suddenly one day when her head is draped with a red veil, her hands dyed red with henna, and red bangles rolled onto her wrists. She will then become a bride. Like the old woman beside her who became one many years ago. She still has bangles on her wrist, but no light in her eyes. "Ek waqt ser bhar khana bhi nahin khaya", she says, in a voice drained of joy. She has not enjoyed even one full meal in her entire lifetime — that's what she has reaped! Her husband, an old man with a flowing beard, says, "I know nothing except bangles. All I have done is make a house for the family to live in." Hearing him, one wonders if he has achieved what many have failed in their lifetime. He has a roof over his head!

95. I know nothing except bangles. Which one of the following best speaks about the character of the old man.

A. (*i*) Cunning; (*ii*) wise; (*iii*) soft; (*iv*) obedient
B. (*i*) Intelligent; (*ii*) irresponsible; (*iii*) caring; (*iv*) simple
C. (*i*) Innocent; (*ii*) foresight (*iii*) responsible; (*iv*) caring
D. (*i*) Impeccable; (*ii*) honest; (*iii*) rude; (*iv*) simple

96. Which option best indicates that the old woman too has sacrificed something in her life for the sake of her family.

(*i*) The old woman has bangles on her wrist, but she can't see them.
(*ii*) She has not even enjoyed one full meal in her life time.
(*iii*) She never supported her husband in bangle making in her life.
(*iv*) She knows nothing expect making bangles which symbolise an Indian woman's suhaag.

A. (*i*) & (*iv*) B. (*ii*) & (*iii*)
C. (*iii*) & (*iv*) D. (*i*) & (*ii*)

97. "Ek waqt ser bhar khana bhi nahin khaya", the grand mother says. Her voice indicates that she is ....

A. Undergoing an emotion of great happiness.
B. Going through an emotion which lacks happiness.
C. Undergoing an emotion of anger and frustration.
D. Experiencing an emotion which reflects her fear and anxiety.

98. Which of these statements is *ture* about the husband of the elderly woman?

A. He says he knows nothing about making bangles in Firozabad.
B. He did not enjoy even one full meal in his entire life for the sake of his family.
C. He says he knows only bangle making and nothing else in his life.
D. All he has done in his life for the sake of his wife is making bangles for her.

99. "I wonder if she knows the sanctity of the bangles she helps make". In this statement, "I wonder reflects" the author's ....

A. Curiosity B. Anxiety
C. Embarrassment D. Restlessness

100. The narrator asks Saheb to go to school. What is the intension of the narrator here?

A. Narrator wants Saheb to enjoy in the school.
B. Narrator wants Saheb to go for rag picking and school as well.
C. Narrator wants Saheb to go to school instead of rag picking.
D. Narrator seriously encourages him to go to school.

101. "It takes longer to build a school" says the narrator to Saheb. What does the narrator really mean here?

A. There is a possibility to build a school.
B. It takes very long time to build a school.
C. There is a way to build a school.
D. There is no intention to build a school.

102. "After months of knowing him, I ask him his name. "Saheb-e-Alam", he announces. He does not know what it means. If he knew its meaning — lord of the universe — Saheb would have a hard time believing it" because ....

A. He was too poor to bear such a big name.
B. He was not suitable to bear such a big name.
C. His name was opposite to his life.
D. His life was quite suitable to his name.

103. "I like the game", he hums, "content to watch it standing behind the fence". The above sentence refers that Saheb ....

A. Is not satisfied with watching the game standing by the fence of club.
B. Is satisfied with watching the game standing by the fence of the club.
C. Wants to watch the game standing inside the fence of the club.
D. Is not allowed to watch the game even from the fence of the club.

104. "His dream looms like a mirage amidst the dust of streets that fill his town Firozabad, famous for its bangles". For Anees Jung, the dream of Mukesh appears as it is far away from reality. As per the circumstances, she thinks Mukesh would ....

A. Gradually be adjusted with the demands of his family.
B. Gradually be satisfied with his family profession.
C. Gradually be influenced by the societal pressures.
D. All the above

105. "It is his karam, his destiny", says Mukesh's grandmother, who has watched her own husband go blind with the dust from polishing the glass of bangles.

Which one of the following statements appropriately suits to the mind-set or lookout of Mukesh's grandmother.

A. She doesn't like her family members in the business of bangle making.
B. She wants her grandson, Mukesh to find his own destiny.
C. She thinks that her husband has gone blind due to his fate.
D. She doesn't believe in karam and destiny which play a major role in the lives of bangle makers.

106. "I want to be a motor mechanic", Mukesh repeats. Which one of the following best speaks about his repetition.

A. He is thinking to become a motor mechanic if everything is comfortable for him.
B. He wants to be a motor mechanic if his parents permit him.
C. He is strong in his decision of becoming a motor mechanic.
D. He wants to become a motor mechanic to impress the author.

107. The author asks, "Do you know anything about car driving?" Mukesh answers, "I will learn to drive a car". Choose the best efforts from the following which can help Mukesh materialise his dream of becoming a car driver.

A. His dedication and readiness to learn about car driving from the garage.
B. His mental state of uncertainty and lack of conviction to dream of cars.
C. His determination to walk to the garage which is a long way from his home.
D. All the above except (B)

108. **Assertion:** The children of Seemapuri are living a life of exploitation.

Reason: Extreme poverty forces them to lead such a life.

A. Both (A) and (R) are true and (R) is the correct explanation of (A).
B. Both (A) and (R) are true and (R) is not the correct explanation of (A).
C. (A) is true, but (R) is false.
D. (A) is false, but (R) is true.

109. **Assertion:** Most of the ragpickers appear walking bare foot in cities and on village roads.

Reason: They were caught in the web of a vicious circle of middlemen.

A. Both (A) and (R) are true and (R) is the correct explanation of (A).
B. Both (A) and (R) are true and (R) is not the correct explanation of (A).
C. (A) is true, but (R) is false.
D. (A) is false, but (R) is true.

110. **Assertion:** Garbage is wrapped in wonder for the elders in Seemapuri.

Reason: For the elders, it is a means of survival.

A. Both (A) and (R) are true and (R) is the correct explanation of (A).
B. Both (A) and (R) are true and (R) is not the correct explanation of (A).
C. (A) is true, but (R) is false.
D. (A) is false, but (R) is true.

111. **Assertion:** Saheb was not allowed to play tennis in the neighbourhood club.

Reason: He had proper shoes but no racquet to play tennis.

A. Both (A) and (R) are true and (R) is the correct explanation of (A).
B. Both (A) and (R) are true and (R) is not the correct explanation of (A).
C. (A) is true, but (R) is false.
D. Both (A) and (R) are false.

112. **Assertion:** Saheb is no longer his own master.

Reason: The tea canister which he carries is his own property.

A. Both (A) and (R) are true and (R) is the correct explanation of (A).
B. Both (A) and (R) are true and (R) is not the correct explanation of (A).
C. (A) is true, but (R) is false.
D. (A) is false, but (R) is true.

113. **Statement 1:** Mukesh insists on being his own master.

Statement 2: He has no fascination for continuing his family profession.

A. If Statement 1 is the cause, Statement 2 is the effect.
B. If Statement 1 is the effect, Statement 2 is the cause.
C. Both the statements are the effects of a common cause.
D. Both the statements are the effects of independent causes.

114. **Statement 1:** The children's eyes are more adjusted to the dark than to the light outside.

Statement 2: The boys and girls end up losing their eye sight before they become adults.

A. If Statement 1 is the cause, Statement 2 is the effect.
B. If Statement 1 is the effect, Statement 2 is the cause.
C. Both the statements are the effects of a common cause.

D. Both the statements are the effects of independent causes.

115. Statement 1: The young bangle makers could not organise themselves into a cooperative.

Statement 2: They were caught in a web of vicious circle.

A. If Statement 1 is the cause, Statement 2 is the effect.
B. If Statement 1 is the effect, Statement 2 is the cause.
C. Both the statements are the effects of a common cause.
D. Both the statements are the effects of independent causes.

116. Statement 1: Exemplary punishment should be given by law to those who employ the children to work in hazardous industries.

Statement 2: Child Labour is banned by the law.

A. If Statement 1 is the cause, Statement 2 is the effect.
B. If Statement 1 is the effect, Statement 2 is the cause.
C. Both the statements are the effects of a common cause.
D. Both the statements are the effects of independent causes.

117. Statement 1: Saheb's family left Bangladesh and came to India.

Statement 2: Saheb is no longer his own master.

A. If Statement 1 is the cause, Statement 2 is the effect.
B. If Statement 1 is the effect, Statement 2 is the cause.
C. Both the statements are the effects of a common cause.
D. Both the statements are the effects of independent causes.

DEEP WATER
By William Douglas

Directions: *Read each of the following passages carefully and choose the best answer to each question out of the four alternatives.*

PASSAGE-1

I had not been there long when in came a big bruiser of a boy, probably eighteen years old. He had thick hair on his chest. He was a beautiful physical specimen, with legs and arms that showed rippling muscles. He yelled, Hi, Skinny! How'd you like to be ducked?

118. How did the pool look like when the narrator went there?

A. Pleasant and lively.
B. Thrilling and attractive.
C. Timid and indifferent.
D. Still and clean.

119. Why did the narrator sit on the side of the pool?

A. To enjoy the beauty of the pool.
B. He was afraid of entering the pool alone.
C. To wait for the coach to arrive.
D. To prepare himself mentally to enter the pool.

120. What did the big bruiser of a boy do?

A. He flashed his rippling muscles.
B. He frightened the narrator.
C. He picked the narrator and tossed him into the deep end.
D. He took the narrator along to make him learn swimming.

121. The word 'bruiser' in the extract means:

A. Aggressor B. Genius
C. Gentleman D. Intelligent

PASSAGE-2

I laughed and said, "Well, Mr. Terror, what do you think you can do to me"? It fled and I swam on.

122. Who is 'I' here?

A. William Doughlas B. Anees Jung
C. Khushwant Singh D. Kamala Das

123. Who is being addressed to as Mr. Terror?

A. Coach B. Young boy
C. Water D. None of these

124. Why did the narrator laugh?

A. Happy go lucky nature
B. Mocking Mr. Terror
C. Confident of defeating Mr. Terror
D. All of these

125. Why did Mr. Terror leave?

A. Could intimidate the narrator.
B. Could not make the narrator beg for help.
C. Could brighten up the narrator.
D. Could not frighten the narrator.

PASSAGE-3

It had happened when I was ten or eleven years old. I had decided to learn to swim. There was a pool at the Y.M.C.A in Yakima that offered exactly the opportunity. The Yakima River was treacherous. Mother continually warned against it and kept fresh in my mind the details of each drowning in the river. But the Y.M.C.A pool was safe.

126. Who is 'I' in the above lines?

A. The narrator B. The coach
C. The young boy D. Father of the young boy.

127. Why did mother not allow 'I' to learn swimming in a river?

A. Religion did not allow this.
B. Social barriers to learn swimming
C. Afraid about safety of her child.
D. All of these

128. What was reported to 'I'?

A. Coldness of water in Yakima river.
B. Coldness of water in swimming pool.
C. Drowning cases in Yakima river.
D. Drowning cases in swimming pool.

129. How was Y.M.C.A. a safe pool?

A. It had warm water.
B. It was open only during day time.
C. It had no water in it.
D. It was two to three feet deep at the shallow end.

Directions: *Choose the correct option with reference to the two statements given below:*

130. Statement 1: Douglas tried his best to jump out of water.

Statement 2: After a while, Douglas was not anxious in water.

A. If Statement 1 is the cause, Statement 2 is the effect.
B. If Statement 1 is the effect, Statement 2 is the cause.
C. Both the statements are the effect of a common cause.
D. Both the statements are the effects of independent causes.

131. Statement 1: The author's father laughed to mock his son's inability to swim.

Statement 2: The author wanted to swim just to prove to his father that he can swim.

A. Statement 1 is true, but Statement 2 is false.
B. Statement 1 is false, but Statement 2 is true.
C. Both Statement 1 and Statement 2 cannot be inferred.
D. Both Statement 1 and Statement 2 can be inferred.

132. Statement 1: Douglas had been haunted by fear for many years.

Statement 2: Douglas decided to learn to swim.

A. If Statement 1 is the cause, Statement 2 is the effect.
B. If Statement 1 is the effect, Statement 2 is the cause.
C. Both the statements are the effect of a common cause.
D. Both the statements are the effects of independent causes.

133. Statement 1: The narrator's mother warned him against swimming in the Yakima River.

Statement 2: Many people swam safely in the Yakima River.

A. Statement 1 is false, but Statement 2 is true.
B. Statement 1 is true, but Statement 2 is false.
C. Both Statement 1 and Statement 2 are true
D. Both Statement 1 and Statement 2 are false.

134. Statement 1: I crossed to oblivion.

Statement 2: The curtain of life fell.

A. If Statement 1 is the cause, Statement 2 is the effect.
B. If Statement 1 is the effect, Statement 2 is the cause.
C. Both the statements are the effect of a common cause.
D. Both the statements are the effects of independent causes.

135. Statement 1: The narrator was in the grip of fear of water.

Statement 2: This deprived him of the joys of canoeing, boating, swimming and fishing.

A. Statement 1 is false, but Statement 2 is true.
B. Statement 1 is true, but Statement 2 is false.
C. Both Statement 1 and Statement 2 are true
D. Both Statement 1 and Statement 2 are false.

136. Statement 1: At the age of ten or eleven, the narrator decided to learn to swim with water wings at the Y.M.C.A. pool.

Statement 2: The Y.M.C.A. pool was dangerous at the shallow end.

A. Statement 1 is false, but Statement 2 is true.
B. Statement 1 is true, but Statement 2 is false.
C. Both Statement 1 and Statement 2 are true.
D. Both Statement 1 and Statement 2 are false.

137. Statement 1: In death there is peace.

Statement 2: There is terror only in the fear of death.

A. If Statement 1 is the cause, Statement 2 is the effect.
B. If Statement 1 is the effect, Statement 2 is the cause.
C. Both the statements are the effect of a common cause.
D. Both the statements are the effects of independent causes.

138 Statement 1: The narrator went to different lakes to swim.

Statement 2: He found tiny vestiges of fear still gripped him.

A. If Statement 1 is the cause, Statement 2 is the effect

B. If Statement 1 is the effect, Statement 2 is the cause
C. Both the statements are the effect of a common cause
D. Both the statements are the effects of independent causes

139. Statement 1: The narrator swam up & down the Warm Lake.

Statement 2: He could finally overcome his fear of water.
A. Statement 1 is false, but Statement 2 is true.
B. Statement 1 is true, but Statement 2 is false.
C. Both Statement 1 and Statement 2 are true.
D. Both Statement 1 and Statement 2 are false.

140. Statement 1: As the narrator sank into the pool, light was going out.

Statement 2: There was no more panic.
A. If Statement 1 is the cause, Statement 2 is the effect.
B. If Statement 1 is the effect, Statement 2 is the cause.
C. Both the statements are the effect of a common cause.
D. Both the statements are the effects of independent causes.

141. Statement 1: The narrator was going down into the pool.

Statement 2: He planned to make a big jump upwards and succeeded.
A. Statement 1 is false, but Statement 2 is true.
B. Statement 1 is true, but Statement 2 is false.
C. Both Statement 1 and Statement 2 are true.
D. Both Statement 1 and Statement 2 are false.

Directions: *Read each of the following passages carefully and choose the best answer to each question out of the four alternatives.*

PASSAGE-1

Then I started down a third time. I sucked for air and got water. The yellowish light was going out. Then all effort ceased. I relaxed. Even my legs felt limp; and a blackness swept over my brain.

142. "Then all efforts ceased" What did the author mean by this?
A. He lost all hope.
B. He yielded himself.
C. That he gave in courage to survive
D. All of these

143. Which of the statement is *true* with the reference to the extract?
A. His friend was coming to help him
B. His legs were almost immobilized
C. His arms were moving unceasingly
D. He could see a great light.

144. Which option indicates more accurately narrator's state of mind?
A. His mind was blank
B. He was greatly terrified
C. He was excited
D. He was puzzled

145. Which option indicates that the poet was becoming unconscious?
A. The yellowish light was going out.
B. A blackness swept over my brain.
C. All effort ceased.
D. My legs felt limp.

PASSAGE-2

The belt went through a pulley that ran on an overhead cable. He held on to the end of the rope, and we went back and forth, across the pool, hour after hour, day after day, week after week. On each trip across the pool a bit of the panic seized me. Each time the instructor relaxed his hold on the rope and I went under, some of the old terror returned and my legs froze. It was three months before the tension began to slack

146. "A 'pulley' that ran on an overhead cable". What does this mean?
A. An apparatus with a wheel
B. An apparatus with a rope
C. An apparatus without wheel
D. An apparatus with a wheel and a rope

147. The statement "Back and forth, across the pool" indicates:
A. Moving from one point to another
B. Moving clockwise and anticlockwise
C. Rising and falling
D. Ascending and descending

148. 'Tension began to slack' implies:
A. Fear started multiplying
B. Fear started increasing
C. Stress started decreasing
D. Stress started intensifying

149. 'Panic seized me' refers to:
A. Emancipating with joy
B. Fear gripped him
C. Boundless joy
D. Full of agony

PASSAGE-3

The experience had a deep meaning for me, as only those who have known stark terror and conquered it can appreciate. In death there is peace. There is terror only in the fear of death, as Roosevelt knew when he said, "All we have to fear is fear itself." Because I had experienced both the sensation of dying and the terror that fear of it can produce, the will to live somehow grew in intensity. At last I felt released — free to walk the trails and climb the peaks and to brush aside fear.

150. "In death there is peace" choose the correct option with reference to the above:
A. End of one's existence is happiness
B. That death is solace & comfort
C. That one's final abode is uncertain
D. That there is torment in death

151. The phrase 'Brush aside' refers to:
A. Get closer to B. To finally get rid of
C. Take it for granted D. Not care at all

152. "All we have to fear is fear itself". What does the narrator learn from President Roosevelt's statement?
A. To cancel the fear B. To frighten the fear
C. To dispel the fear D. To prevent the fear

153. "I had experienced both the sensation of dying and terror that fear of it can produce", which of the following idioms might describe the above statement
A. "To be scared to death"
B. "Once in a blue moon"
C. "With a silver spoon"
D. "Hand to mouth"

MY MOTHER AT SIXTY-SIX
By Kamala Das

Directions: *Read the following extract and choose the most appropriate option for each question.*

I saw my mother,
beside me, doze, open mouthed,
her face ashen like that of a corpse and realised with pain
that she was as old as she looked
but soon put that thought away,
and looked out at Young Trees sprinting,

154. Kamala Das turned her attention from her mother, because
A. She was feeling guilty.
B. She was shirking her responsibility.
C. She was trying to escape from pain filled emotions.
D. She didn't like the idea of her mother growing old.

155. The Poetic Device used in the above lines is also found in
A. Leena is the Lata Mangeshkar of Hyderabad.
B. Ayra is as cool as a cucumber to receive the heavy news.
C. The elephant is heavier than many other animals.
D. He is a tiger

156. The words 'doze' and 'ashen' reflect that the mother was:
A. Tired and sleepy
B. Sick and unhealthy
C. Lost strength and vigour as she had grown old
D. Hale and healthy

157. What did the poet realize seeing her mother beside her in the car?
A. That her mother may not survive for long
B. That her mother was suffering
C. That her mother wanted her to be with her
D. That she wanted to go with her daughter

158. 'Thought Away' means:
A. Diverted
B. Escaped
C. Drifted
D. Avoided

159. 'Trees sprinting' contains:
A. Metaphor B. Personification
C. Simile D. Alliteration

160. The Literary Devices used in the above extract are:
A. Simile and Refrain
B. Simile and personification
C. Simile and Alliteration
D. Only simile

Directions: *Read the following extract and choose the most appropriate option for each question.*

I looked again at her,
wan, pale as a late winter's moon and felt that old familiar ache,
my childhood's fear,
but all I said was, see you soon, Amma,
all I did was smile and smile and smile......

161. Kamala Das comparing her mother to winter moon signifies:
A. Human life is as short as that of the moon
B. Though the mother is old, she is still beautiful
C. Winter is the last season of the year
D. Mother is about to die

162. Though she feels painful, Kamala Das smiles on ......
A. To hide her sad feelings and emotions
B. To encourage her mother to smile and feel good
C. Not to dishearten her mother by showing her worried face
D. All the above

163. The tone of the poem is:
A. Pensive and sorrowful
B. Disillusioned and unhappy
C. Happy but discontented
D. Remorseful

Directions: *Study the two statements, in each question, labelled as Assertion (A) and Reason (R).*

164. Assertion (A): Kamala Das was honest and didn't have any hesitation in describing her mother's ageing face.

Reason (R): She compares her mother's face to a corpse.

A. Both (A) and (R) are true and (R) is the correct explanation of (A)
B. Both (A) and (R) are true, but (R) is not the correct explanation of (A)
C. (A) is true, but (R) is false
D. (A) is false, but (R) is true

165. Assertion (A): Kamala Das didn't like her mother growing old.

Reason (R): She turns her attention away from her mother.

A. Both (A) and (R) are true and (R) is the correct explanation of (A)
B. Both, (A) and (R) are true, but (R) is not the correct explanation of (A)
C. (A) is true, but (R) is false
D. (A) is false, but (R) is true

166. Assertion (A): The poet feels the pain of separation at the airport.

Reason (R): She started smiling at her.

A. Both (A) and (R) are true and (R) is the correct explanation of (A)
B. Both (A) and (R) are true, but (R) is not the correct explanation of (A)
C. (A) is true, but (R) is false
D. (A) is false, but (R) is true

167. Assertion (A): The poet gracefully accepts the reality of her mother growing old.

Reason (R): She left for her destination without much difficulty.

A. Both (A) and (R) are true and (R) is the correct explanation of (A)
B. Both (A) and (R) are true, but (R) is not the correct explanation of (A)
C. (A) is true, but (R) is false
D. Both (A) and (R) are false

168. Assertion (A): The poet didn't reveal her sorrow on her face in the airport.

Reason (R): She didn't like to create a scene there.

A. Both (A) and (R) are true and (R) is the correct explanation of (A)
B. Both (A) and (R) are true, but (R) is not the correct explanation of (A)
C. (A) is true, but (R) is false
D. (A) is false, but (R) is true

169. Assertion (A): Kamala Das took her mother to airport.

Reason (R): She wanted to spend some more time with her.

A. Both (A) and (R) are true and (R) is the correct explanation of (A)
B. Both (A) and (R) are true, but (R) is not the correct explanation of (A)
C. (A) is true, but (R) is false
D. (A) is false, but (R) is true

170. Assertion (A): The poet compares her mother to young trees.

Reason (R): Her mother was also young once.

A. Both (A) and (R) are true and (R) is the correct explanation of (A)
B. Both (A) and (R) are true, but (R) is not the correct explanation of (A)
C. (A) is true, but (R) is false
D. (A) is false, but (R) is true

171. Assertion (A): The poet advocates the aged parents should be taken care of by their children.

Reason (R): She looked after her mother by being by her side.

A. Both (A) and (R) are true and (R) is the correct explanation of (A)
B. Both (A) and (R) are true, but (R) is not the correct explanation of (A)
C. (A) is true, but (R) is false
D. Both (A) and (R) are false

172. Assertion (A): The poet compares her mother to a winter moon

Reason (R): Winter moon doesn't shine well like in other seasons.

A. Both (A) and (R) are true and (R) is the correct explanation of (A)
B. Both (A) and (R) are true, but (R) is not the correct explanation of (A)
C. (A) is true, but (R) is false
D. (A) is false, but (R) is true

173. Assertion (A): Kamala Das was scared of losing her mother or her company from her childhood days.

Reason (R): So, kamala Das was expecting this and hence ready for this to happen.

A. Both (A) and (R) are true and (R) is the correct explanation of (A)
B. Both (A) and (R) are true, but (R) is not the correct explanation of (A)
C. (A) is true, but (R) is false
D. (A) is false, but (R) is true

AN ELEMENTARY SCHOOL CLASSROOM IN A SLUM

By Stephen Spender

174. Assertion (A): The slum children's faces are like rootless weeds and their hair unkempt.

Reason (R): The slum children were malnourished.
A. Both (A) and (R) are true, but (R) is the correct explanation of (A)
B. Both (A) and (R) are true, but (R) is not the correct explanation of (A)
C. (A) is false, but (R) is true
D. (A) is true, but (R) is false

175. Assertion (A): The stunted unlucky heir of twisted bones is reciting a father's gnarled disease.

Reason (R): The boy has been born with polio.
A. (A) is true, but (R) is false
B. (A) is false, but (R) is true
C. Both (A) and (R) are true, but (R) is the correct explanation of (A)
D. Both (A) and (R) are true, but (R) is not the correct explanation of (A)

176. Assertion (A): The small boy is dreaming of squirrel's game.

Reason (R): The boy is not interested in the lesson as it is boring.
A. (A) is true, but (R) is false
B. (A) is false, but (R) is true
C. Both (A) and (R) are true, but (R) is the correct explanation of (A)
D. Both (A) and (R) are true, but (R) is not the correct explanation of (A)

177. Statement 1: The slum children were like bottle bits of stones.

Statement 2: The slum children were thin and weak but look beautiful.
A. Statement 1 is true, but Statement 2 is false
B. Statement 1 is false, but Statement 2 is true
C. Both Statement 1 and Statement 2 are true, but Statement 2 is the correct explanation of Statement 1
D. Both Statement 1 and Statement 2 are true, but Statement 2 is not the correct explanation of Statement 1

178. Assertion (A): Ships, Sun and love tempt the children to steal

Reason (R): The slum children have the tendency to steal.
A. (A) is true, but (R) is false
B. (A) is false, but (R) is true
C. Both (A) and (R) are true, but (R) is the correct explanation of (A)
D. Both (A) and (R) are true, but (R) is not the correct explanation of (A)

179. Assertion (A): The slum children should be taken to the green fields outside.

Reason (R): The slum children were forced to stay inside the classroom.
A. (R) is the explanation of (A)
B. (A) is the explanation (R)
C. (A) is the problem and (R) is the solution
D. (R) is the problem while (A) is the solution

180. Assertion (A): The poet wants the children to break barriers and be free.

Reason (R): The poet doesn't want them to be superstitious.
A. Both (A) and (R) are true, but (R) is the correct explanation of (A)
B. Both (A) and (R) are true, but (R) is not the correct explanation of (A)
C. (A) is false, but (R) is true
D. (A) is true, but (R) is false

181. The following words show that the children suffer from 'acute malnutrition':
1. Stunted through 2. Twisted bones
3. Paper-seeming 4. Skin peeped
A. 1 and 2 are true B. 2 and 3 are true
C. 3 and 4 are true D. All are true

182. Assertion (A): The classroom walls are painted in 'sour cream':

Reason (R): The colour symbolizes the bleak future of the slum children.
A. Both (A) and (R) are true, but (R) is the correct explanation of (A)
B. Both (A) and (R) are true, but (R) is not the correct explanation of (A)
C. (A) is false, but (R) is true
D. (A) is true, but (R) is false

183. Assertion (A): The slum children consider Shakespeare wicked.

Reason (R): The slum children are evil and they have malice against him.
A. Both (A) and (R) are true, but (R) is the correct explanation of (A)
B. Both (A) and (R) are true, but (R) is not the correct explanation of (A)
C. (A) is false, but (R) is true
D. (A) is true, but (R) is false

184. Statement 1: The slum children consider map a bad example.

Statement 2: The world in the map has no relation to their world.
A. Statement 1 is true, but Statement 2 is false
B. Statement 1 is false, but Statement 2 is true
C. Both Statement 1 and Statement 2 are true, but Statement 2 is the correct explanation of Statement 1
D. Both Statement 1 and Statement 2 are true, but Statement 2 is not the correct explanation of Statement 1

Directions: *Read the extracts given below and answer the questions that follow.*

POEM-1

Far far from gusty waves these children's faces.
Like rootless weeds, the hair torn around their pallor
The tall girl with her weighed-down head. The paper-seeming boy,
with rat's eyes.

185. What does the poet contrast the children's faces with?
A. Flowers B. Stars
C. Waves D. Plants

186. How do the faces of these children look?
A. beautiful and attractive
B. like rootless weeds
C. ugly and awkward
D. vigorous and refreshing

187. Why are they compared to rootless weeds?
A. because they are healthy
B. because they are malnourished
C. because they are not beautiful
D. because they are from rural background

188. Why is the head of the tall girl 'weighed down'?
A. because she is doing something
B. because she is depressed due to abject poverty
C. she is reading something
D. she is not interested

189. What figure of speech is used in the last line?
A. Alliteration B. Simile
C. Metaphor D. Personification

190. What does 'the paper-seeming boy' imply?
A. he eats papers
B. he sells papers
C. he is lean and thin like a paper
D. he is pure like a paper

POEM-2

............The stunted, unlucky heir
of twisted bones, reciting a father's gnarled disease,
His lesson, from his desk. At the back of the dim class
One unnoted, sweet and young. His eyes live in a dream
Of squirrel's game, in tree room other than this.

191. Why does the poet call the boy 'unlucky heir'?
A. he lost his father
B. his father left her mother
C. his father lost all money
D. he has inherited a disease of twisted bones

192. What is he reciting?
A. devotional songs
B. school lessons
C. his father's gnarled disease
D. folklore

193. Why was the boy unnoted?
A. Because he is small and sitting at the back
B. Because he is not intelligent
C. Because he is illiterate
D. Because he is not fair

194. What does the boy dream of?
A. beautiful world B. squirrel's game
C. owning big house D. riding a bike

195. What similarity do they have with respect to their physical condition?
A. all were neat and tidy
B. all were untidy
C. they were malnourished
D. all were beautiful

POEM-3

On sour cream walls, donations, Shakespeare's head,
Cloudless at dawn, civilized dome riding all cities.
Belled, flowery, Tyrolese valley. Open-handed map
Awarding the world its world.

196. Why were the classroom walls called sour cream walls?
A. because they were painted bright colour
B. because they were painted light yellow colour
C. the colour is pleasant and beautiful
D. it is dark brown colour

197. What things were displayed on the walls of the classroom?
A. medals won by the institution
B. freedom fighters
C. philosophers
D. poets, buildings, world map and valleys

198. What does the world map award?
A. A lot of knowledge
B. a lot of treasure
C. Rich, beautiful world
D. experience

199. Why is Shakespeare called wicked?
A. Because he represents the rich world
B. Because he wrote against them
C. He does not give them happiness and comfort
D. he wrote about their lives

POEM-4

And yet, for these
Children, these windows, not this map, their world.
Where all their future's painted with a fog,
A narrow street sealed in with a lead sky
Far far from rivers, capes, and stars of words.

200. What is the world of slum children?
A. Beautiful fields
B. The windows of the classroom
C. Slum
D. Mountains

201. Why is their future painted with fog?
A. Because they work tirelessly in dark cells
B. Because the room is filled with fog
C. Because they have no clear vision of future
D. They were denied admission

202. How is their world different from the world in the map?
A. Very similar to their world
B. Contrary to the world in the map
C. Not comfortable
D. Does not offer any clues

POEM-5

Surely, Shakespeare is wicked, the map a bad example,
With ships and sun and love tempting them to steal—
For lives that slyly turn in their cramped holes
From fog to endless night?

203. Why is Shakespeare wicked?
A. he wrote about love
B. he didn't write about them
C. he is very wealthy
D. they have no access to love and happiness

204. Why do the slum children consider map a bad example?
A. it is not showing their place
B. it doesn't help them
C. it shows a world which is quite different from their world
D. it is not visible to them

205. Where do the children spend their lives?
A. in foggy slums B. beautiful fields
C. villages D. cities

206. What do you understand by 'from fog to endless night'?
A. they travel through the fog
B. they work at night
C. they spend their entire lives in slums
D. they grope in darkness

207. Which word in the passage means "narrow"?
A. slyly B. steal
C. tempt D. cramped

POEM-6

Unless, governor, inspector, visitor,
This map becomes their window and these windows
That shut upon their lives like catacombs,

208. Who can change the condition of slum children?
A. school teachers
B. The Principal
C. governor, inspector and visitor
D. parents

209. What action does the poet want them to take?
A. to build a new school
B. to take them to the world outside
C. to provide playground
D. to give them money

210. What are 'catacombs'?
A. underground cemetery
B. the caterpillars
C. the mushrooms
D. edible plants

211. What do the 'catacombs' signify?
A. the dead condition
B. the darkness
C. the little narrow homes of the slum dwellers
D. the difficulties they face

POEM-7

Break O break open till they break the town
And show the children to green fields, and make their world
Run azure on gold sands, and let their tongues
Run naked into books the white and green leaves open
History theirs whose language is the sun.

212. What should be shown to slum children?
A. Beautiful pictures B. films
C. green fields D. historical places

213. What would they break?
A. buildings B. dams
C. the barriers which separate them from the world outside
D. their poor huts

214. How can they understand history?
A. by reading the biographies
B. by reading books
C. by observing nature
D. by viewing films

215. Which word in the stanza means "bright blue"?
A. naked B. sands
C. azure D. doom

KEEPING QUIET
By Pablo Neruda

216. Assertion (A): The self-introspection is necessary for all literary persons.

Reason (R): Then only they will be able to meditate and save mankind from destruction.
A. Both (A) and (R) are correct and (R) is the correct explanation of (A).

B. Both (A) and (R) are correct, but (R) is not the correct explanation of (A).
C. (A) is true and (R) is false.
D. (A) is false and (R) is true.

217. Assertion (A): The poet wants everyone to remain quiet for sometime.

Reason (R): Silence will allow to listen to the voices of quiet and serene nature.

A. Both (A) and (R) are correct and (R) is the correct explanation of (A).
B. Both (A) and (R) are correct, but (R) is not the correct explanation of (A).
C. (A) is true and (R) is false.
D. (A) is false and (R) is true.

218. Assertion (A): The exercise of counting upto twelve is suggested by the poet.

Reason (R): It helps to sit still and achieve a sense of togetherness.

A. Both (A) and (R) are correct and (R) is the correct explanation of (A).
B. Both (A) and (R) are correct, but (R) is not the correct explanation of (A).
C. (A) is true and (R) is false.
D. (A) is false and (R) is true.

219. Assertion (A): Pablo Neruda desires to stop inhuman aci vities.

Reason (R): He wants to live in a peaceful atmosphere.

A. Both (A) and (R) are correct and (R) is the correct explanation of (A).
B. Both (A) and (R) are correct, but (R) is not the correct explanation of (A).
C. (A) is true and (R) is false.
D. (A) is false and (R) is true.

220. Assertion (A): The poet wants everyone to learn from the nature to create and not to destroy.

Reason (R): He wants to escape from his duty towards the mankind.

A. Both (A) and (R) are correct and (R) is the correct explanation of (A).
B. Both (A) and (R) are correct but (R) is not the correct explanation of (A).
C. (A) is true and (R) is false.
D. (A) is false and (R) is true.

221. Identify the tone of Pablo Neruda in the following line:

Perhaps the Earth can teach us....

A. Confident and clear about the future events.
B. Dramatic about the prediction he made.
C. Convinced about the sequence of events to follow.
D. Uncertain, yet hopeful about the possibility.

222. Based on the poem, choose the correct option with reference to the two statements given below.

Statement 1: The poet urges his countrymen to stop for a while.

Statement 2: The poet urges all men to stop for a second.

A. Statement 1 is true, but Statement 2 is false.
B. Statement 1 is false, but Statement 2 is true.
C. Both Statement 1 and Statement 2 are true.
D. Both Statement 1 and Statement 2 cannot be inferred.

223. Select the option that best conveys the feelings of the poet corresponding to the following:

"Fishermen in the cold sea
would not harm whales"

A. • fishermen would not kill whales because they did not need them
   • fishermen would not kill whales because they were scared of them
B. • fishermen would not kill whales because they realised the damage that they were causing to the ecosystem
   • fishermen would stop killing whales for commercial purposes.
C. • fishermen only wished they would not kill whales
   • fishermen would not kill whales because they feared that whale population was fast dwindling
D. • fishermen would not kill whales themselves because others were doing that for them
   • fishermen would not kill whales because there was a moratorium on killing whales

224. Based on the poem, choose the correct option with reference to the two statements given below.

Statement 1: The poet is in anguish at the plight of the earth and expresses hope that the situation may improve.

Statement 2: The poet's fears of total destruction of the earth are baseless.

A. Statement 1 is true, but Statement 2 is false.
B. Statement 1 is false, but Statement 2 is true.
C. Both Statement 1 and Statement 2 are true.
D. Both Statement 1 and Statement 2 cannot be inferred.

225. Read the statements given below carefully. Choose the option that best describes these statements, with reference to the poem 'Keeping Quiet'.

Statement I: The poem 'Keeping Quiet' calls for change as much in the individual as human society at large.

Statement II: The poem 'Keeping Quiet' implies that individual change will lead to bigger societal change.

Statement III: Neruda believes that when people come together as a community, they will be able to bring a transformation in each person.

A. Statement I is True, Statement II is False, and Statement III cannot be inferred.
B. Statement I and II cannot be inferred, Statement III is True.
C. Statement I is True, Statements II and III cannot be inferred.
D. Statement I cannot be inferred, Statement II cannot be inferred, Statement III is False.

226. Based on the poem 'Keeping Quiet', choose the correct option with reference to the two statements given below.

Statement 1: The poet cautions that one should not mistake doing nothing for total inactivity.

Statement 2: The poet also avers that he does not mean to associate with death.

A. Statement 1 is true, but Statement 2 is false.
B. Statement 1 is false, but Statement 2 is true.
C. Both Statement 1 and Statement 2 are true.
D. Both Statement 1 and Statement 2 cannot be inferred.

227. Classify (1) to (4) as fact (F) or opinion (O), based on your reading of *Keeping Quiet.*

1. The poet wants all humans to introspect themselves by observing silence.
2. The poet says there would no survivors if there were all kinds of wars.
3. The poet says that man can learn from the earth that we still can hope for life even when everything seems dead.
4. Poet says that men are threatening themselves, through their acts, with death.

A. F-1, 3, 4; O-2
B. F-1, 3; O-2, 4
C. F-2; O-1, 3, 4
D. F-3, 4; O-1, 2

Directions (Qs. No. 228-231): *Read the extract to attempt questions that follow:*

For once on the face of the Earth let's not speak in any language, let's stop for one second, and not move our arms so much. It would be an exotic moment without rush, without engines, we would all be together in a sudden strangeness.

228. The poet uses the word "let's" to _______.

A. initiate a conversation between the poet and the readers.
B. invite readers as part of the poem's larger call to humanity.
C. welcome readers into the world of the poem and its subject.
D. address readers as fellow members of the human race.

229. Margaret Atwood said, "Language divides us into fragments, I wanted to be whole". Choose the option that correctly comments on the relationship between Margaret Atwood's words and the line from the above extract – "let's not speak in any language"

A. Atwood endorses Neruda's call to not speak in any language.
B. Atwood justifies Neruda's request to not engage in any speaking.
C. Atwood undermines Neruda's intent to stop and not speak in any language.
D. Atwood surrenders to Neruda's desire for silence and not speak in any language.

230. Why do you think the poet employs words like "exotic" and "strangeness"?

A. To highlight the importance of everyone being together suddenly for once.
B. To emphasize the frantic activity and chaos that usually envelops human life.
C. To indicate the unfamiliarity of a sudden moment without rush or without engine.
D. To direct us towards keeping quiet and how we would all be together in that silence.

231. Choose the option that correctly matches the idioms given in Column-A with their meanings in Column-B.

Column-A	Column-B
1. On the face of the earth	(*i*) In existence
2. What on earth something	(*ii*) To do all possible to accomplish
3. Move heaven and earth	(*iii*) To express surprise or shock
4. The salt of the earth	(*iv*) To be good and worthy

	1	2	3	4
A.	(*i*)	(*iv*)	(*iii*)	(*ii*)
B.	(*i*)	(*iii*)	(*ii*)	(*iv*)
C.	(*ii*)	(*i*)	(*iv*)	(*iii*)
D.	(*iv*)	(*ii*)	(*iii*)	(*i*)

Directions (Qs. No. 232-235): *Read the extract to attempt questions that follow:*

If we were not so single-minded about keeping our lives moving, and for once could do nothing, perhaps a huge silence might interrupt this sadness of never understanding ourselves and of threatening ourselves with death.

232. Look at the images given below. Choose the image to which the above extract can be seen as an appropriate response.

A.  B. 

C.  D. 

233. What do you think is the mood of the poet in the above extract?
A. gloomy, cynical
B. reflective, inspired
C. introspective, aware
D. critical, demotivated

234. Pick the option that does not complete the given sentence suitably, as per the extract. Threatening ourselves with death ________.
A. feeds on the fear of death.
B. challenges finiteness of life.
C. keeps us rushing through life.
D. makes us restless and impatient.

235. What might the "huge silence" signify?
A. melancholy B. understanding
C. discomfort D. flexibility

Directions (Qs. No. 236-239): *Read the extract to attempt questions that follow:*

236. Choose the option that best describes these statements, with reference to the poem.

Statement I: The poem 'Keeping Quiet' calls for change as much in the individual as human society at large.

Statement II: The poem 'Keeping Quiet' implies that individual change will lead to bigger societal change.

Statement III: Neruda believes that when people come together as a community, they will be able to bring a transformation in each person.
A. Statement I is True, Statement II is False, and Statement III cannot be inferred.
B. Statement I and II cannot be inferred, Statement III is True.
C. Statement I is True, Statements II and III cannot be inferred.
D. Statement I cannot be inferred, Statement II cannot be inferred, Statement III is False.

237. "What I want should not be confused with total inactivity". Choose the option that draws the most accurate parallel.

Keeping quiet: total inactivity = ______ : ______
A. reflection and death
B. silence and chaos
C. stagnation and introspection
D. mindfulness and fear

238. What statement does Neruda make about wars?
A. Wars are of varied kinds – internal, green wars, wars with gas, with fire etc.
B. Wars are wasteful and cause irrecoverable loss and damage to property and life.
C. Wars never yield any winners, and the loss is far greater than what can be measured.
D. Wars are unavoidable in the enduring struggle for human dignity and power.

239. "Now I'll count up to twelve and you keep quiet and I will go". Why does the poet wish to go at the end of the poem?
A. The poet does not believe people will be quiet.
B. The poet has already invested enough time.
C. The poet will move on and seek to inspire others.
D. The poet is marking the end of the poem by leaving.

Directions (Qs. No. 240-243): *Read the extract to attempt questions that follow:*

It would be an exotic moment
without rush, without engines,
we would all be together
in a sudden strangeness.

240. The rhyme of the poem is:
A. aabb B. abab
C. acbc D. None of the above

241. The 'exotic moment' that the poet refers to is, when:
A. the whole world is destroyed
B. all the people divided
C. all the people together with oneness
D. all the people speak only in one language

242. Which of the following is an example of anaphora?
A. We would all be together
B. Without rush, without engines
C. It would be an exotic moment
D. All the above

243. The phrase 'sudden strangeness' is an example of
A. Metaphor B. Simile
C. Oxymoron D. Alliteration

Directions (Qs. No. 244-247): *Read the extract to attempt questions that follow:*

Those who prepare green wars,
wars with gas, wars with fire,

victory with no survivors,
would put on clean clothes
and walk about with their
brothers
in the shade, doing nothing.

244. According to the poet wars would result in:
A. the victory of none
B. the death of all
C. complete annihilation of the world
D. above all

245. The phrase 'clean clothes' symbolises:
A. Peace B. Well ironed clothes
C. New clothes D. Spotless clothes

246. _______ walk about in the shade ________.
A. people who hate one another, singing
B. people who love one another dancing
C. people who wage wars, doing nothing
D. none of the above

247. The poetic device used in the fourth line of the extract is
A. Alliteration B. Personification
C. Transferred epithet D. None of the above

Directions (Qs. No. 248-251): *Read the extract to attempt questions that follow:*

What I want should not be
confused
with total inactivity.
Life is what it is about;
I want no truck with death.

248. Which of the following is not correct?
A. The poet wants all people to be idle doing nothing
B. The poet wants all people to keep quiet to introspect
C. The poet wants all people to be like brothers
D. The poet wants all people to love one another

249. The phrase 'Life is what it is about' means:
A. living life miserably
B. living life licentiously
C. living life carefully
D. living life as it is

250. 'I want no truck with death' indicates that the poet:
A. wants a truck for death
B. does not mean that inactivity is death
C. assures people that they would not face death at all
D. does not want a truck

251. The above extract is taken from _______ written by ________.
A. 'Keeping Quiet' by John Keats
B. 'My Mother at Sixty Six' by Pablo Neruda
C. 'Keeping Quiet' by Pablo Neruda
D. 'My Mother at Sixty Six' by John Keats

Directions (Qs. No. 252-254): *Read the extract to attempt questions that follow:*

Perhaps the Earth can teach us
as when everything seems dead
and later proves to be alive.

252. What can we learn from the Earth?
A. No hope for life after such large scale destruction of the planet
B. Hope for life in spite of the wars of all kinds referred to by the poet
C. No scope for life on the planet
D. Hope for life on other planets, after complete destruction of the Earth

253. The words 'everything seems dead' refer to:
A. animals' life B. plants' life
C. flora and fauna D. none of the above

254. The last line of poem ends on a/an ________ note.
A. pessimistic B. optimistic
C. disillusioned D. imaginary

THE THIRD LEVEL
By Jack Finney

255. Choose the option that correctly identifies which statements are facts and which are opinion:
(*i*) Charley is suffering from mental sickness and he is hallucinating.
(*ii*) Charley's wife is concerned and cares for her husband.
(*iii*) Charley's vivid description of the Third level shows he has a strong desire to go to Galesburg.
(*iv*) Charley's friend Sam Weiner cheated Charley and escape from the third level
A. Fact-(*i*) opinion-(*ii*) (*iii*) (*iv*)
B. Fact-(*i*) and (*ii*) opinion-(*iii*) and (*iv*)
C. Fact-(*iii*) and (*ii*) opinion-(*iv*) and (*i*)
D. Fact-(*ii*) and (*iii*) opinion-(*i*) and (*iii*)

256. Assertion (A): Charley wanted to go to Galesburg Illinois.

Reason (R): He has heard many wonderful stories about Galesburg from his grandfather.
A. Both (A) and (R) are true and (R) is the correct explanation of (A)
B. Both (A) and (R) are true, but (R) is not the correct explanation of (A)
C. A is true, but (R) is false
D. A is false, but (R) is true

257. Statement 1: Charley finds it very strange that only he could see the third level.

Statement 2: The third level according to his friend is a place in his mind.
A. Statement 1 is true, but statement 2 is false.
B. Statement 1 is false, but statement 2 is true.

C. Both statement 1 and statement 2 cannot be inferred.
D. Both statement 1 and statement 2 can be inferred.

258. Assertion (A): The clerk refused to accept the money offered by Charley.

Reason (R): He thought the currency was fake.
A. (A) is true, but (R) is false
B. (A) is false, but (R) is true
C. Both (A) and (R) are true and (R) is the correct explanation of (A)
D. Both (A) and (R) are true, but (R) is not the correct explanation of (A)

259. Statement 1: Sam believed Charley was unhappy and looking for an escape. Charley's stamp-collection was a proof of it.

Statement 2: Charley thought all in the modern world are looking for an escape and his hobby of stamp-collection has nothing to do with it.
A. Both statements 1 and 2 can be inferred.
B. Statement 2 is false, but statement 1 is true.
C. Statement 1 is false, but statement 2 is true
D. Both statements 1 and statement 2 are false.

260. Assertion (A): Sam could not go back to his old business in Galesburg Illinois.

He will start a hay and grain business there.

Reason (R): Sam can not start his psychiatric practice there as life is peaceful and no one needs a psychiatrist.
A. (A) is true, but (R) is false
B. (A) is false, but (R) is true
C. Both (A) and (R) are true, but (R) is not the correct explanation of (A)
D. Both (A) and (R) are true and (R) is the correct explanation of (A)

261. Assertion (A): Charley looked at the newspaper. It was The World. He realized he was in a different world.

Reason (R): Charley knew that the world is no longer published in the world he came from.
A. Both (A) and (R) are false, but (R) is the true explanation of (A)
B. Both (A) and (R) are true and (R) is the true explanation of (A)
C. (A) is false (R) is true
D. (A) is true, but (R) is not the true explanation of (A)

262. Assertion (A): Charley bought old style currency to buy two tickets to Galesburg Illinois.

Reason (R): He wanted to start a business there.
A. (A) is true (R) is false
B. Both (A) and (R) are true
C. (A) is false, but (R) is true explanation of (A)
D. Both (A) and (R) are true and (R) is true explanation of (A)

263. Suppose you visit Galesburg Illinois of 1894. Which of the following advertisement is least likely to be found there.
A. Baby food—A life begins with full nutrition.
B. Dress designer-Reclaim yourself.
C. Tea: Refreshing start of your beautiful day.
D. Yoga camp: Stress buster.

264. Assertion (A): Charley idolized the peaceful perfect world of Galesburg Illinois.

Reason (R): Galesburg Illinois of 1894 was a stark contrast to post world war modern world.
A. (A) is true (R) is false.
B. Both (A) and (R) are true and (R) is the true explanation of (A)
C. Both (A) and (R) are true, but (R) is not the true explanation of (A)
D. (R) is true (A) is false

265. Assertion (A): Charley noticed that lights at the station were dim and flickering.

Reason (R): In 1894, open gaslights were used at the railway station.
A. Both (A) and (R) are false, but (R) is the true explanation of (A)
B. (A) is true and (R) is false, but (R) is not the true explanation of (A)
C. (A) is false (R) is true
D. Both (A) and (R) are true and (R) is the true explanation of (A)

266. Assertion (A): Charley believed that the Third Level do exist and his friend Sam Weiner has escaped to Galesburg Illinois.

Reason (R): Sam has disappeared and no one knows where has he gone.
A. (A) is true, but (R) is false
B. Both (A) and (R) are true, but (R) is not the true explanation of (A)
C. Both (A) and (R) are true and (R) is the true explanation of (A)
D. (A) is true, but (R) is not the true explanation of (A)

267. Assertion (A): The third level refers to the third underground level of the grand central railway station.

Reason (R): Sam Weiner's letter states it clearly that the Third level does exist.
A. Both (A) and (R) are true, but (R) does not explain (A)
B. Both (A) and (R) are false
C. Both (A) and (R) are true and (A) can be inferred from (R)
D. (A) is true (R) is False and (A) can not be inferred from (R)

268. Assertion (A): Charley wanted to reach home immediately so he wanted to take a train.

Reason (R): Charley has been in and out of Grand central station hundreds of times.

A. Both (A) and (R) are false, but (R) does explain (A)
B. Both (A) and (R) are true, but (A) can not be inferred from (R)
C. Both (A) and (R) are true and (A) can be inferred from (R)
D. (A) is true (R) is False and (A) cannot be inferred from (R)

269. Assertion (A): Charley's Grandfather lived in a peaceful world in 1894.

Reason (R): The first word war was some 20 years off in future and the Second World War was forty years in future.

A. (A) and (R) both are true and (A) can be inferred from (R)
B. Both (A) and (R) are true, but (A) cannot be inferred from (R)
C. (A) is true, but (R) is false
D. (A) is true, but (R) is false and (A) can be inferred from (R)

270. Assertion (A): Charley was a common man like any other 31 years old with normal life style.

Reason (R): Charley wanted a peaceful life without war and stress.

A. (A) is true, but (R) is false
B. (A) is false, but (R) is true
C. Both (A) and (R) are true and (R) is the true explanation of (A)
D. Both (A) and (R) are false

271. Statement 1: Charley was among the many people who were suffering from mental ennui due to monotony of life.

Statement 2: Louisa, his wife was very happy and contented with her life.

A. Statement 1 can be inferred, but statement 2 can not be inferred
B. Statement 1 and statement 2 both can be inferred.
C. Statement 2 can be inferred, but statement 1 can not be inferred.
D. Statement 1 and 2 can not be inferred.

272. Statement 1: Eggs were thirteen cents a dozens in 1894.

Statement 2: Cost of living was comparatively less in 1894.

A. Statement 2 can be inferred, but statement 1 can not be inferred.
B. Statement 1 and 2 can not be inferred
C. Statement 1 can be inferred, but statement 2 can not be inferred
D. Statement 1 is true and statement 2 can be inferred.

273. Assertion (A): At the stamp and coin store I go to, I found out that Sam bought eight hundred dollars' worth of old-style currency.

Reason (R): That ought to set him up in a nice little hay, feed and grain business; he always said that's what Sam really wished he could do.

A. Both (A) and (R) are wrong and (R) does not explain (A)
B. Both (A) and (R) are true and (R) explains (A)
C. (A) is true, but (R) is false
D. (A) is false, but (R) is true

274 Assertion (A): Charley did not share his thoughts about the tunnel under the city with Sam.

Reason (R): Charley thought his job would be at stake if he shared these thoughts.

A. Both (A) and (R) are true, but (R) does not explain (A)
B. Both (A) and (R) are false and (R) does not explain (A)
C. (A) is true and (R) is false
D. Both (A) and (R) are false

275. Imagine Charley visit India on 25 th March, 2020 to India. Which of the following would be the Lead Story in Indian Newspaper?

A. Indian wins 2 Gold Medals in Japan Olympics.
B. Nifty bulls have a dominant day.
C. Telecom sector is ailing in India.
D. P.M. announces 21 days nation-wide lockdown.

Directions: *Read each of the following passages carefully and choose the best answer to each question out of the four alternatives.*

PASSAGE-1

The paper inside wasn't blank. It read:

941 Willard
Street
Galesburg,
Illinois
July 18, 1894

Charley I got to wishing that you were right. Then I got to believing you were right. And, Charley, it's true; I found the third level! I've been here two weeks, and right now, down the street at the Daly's, someone is playing a piano, and they're all out on the front porch singing Seeing Nelly Home.' And I'm invited over for lemonade. Come on back, Charley and Louisa. Keep looking till you find the third level! It's worth it, believe me!

The note is signed Sam

"Charley I got to wishing that you were right. Then I got to believing you were right"

276. What does the writer wish to believe?

A. That the third level does exist.

B. That Charley was not stable.
C. That the write was there in Galesburg.
D. That the tunnel does exist under the city.

277. Where has the writer been for two weeks?
A. In the third level.
B. In New York.
C. In Galesburg Illinois.
D. In the future where life is peaceful.

278. What does the letter state about the mood of the write?
A. Anxious B. Depressed
C. Excited D. Nonchalant

279. Who are 'THEY' out on the front porch singing 'Seeing Nelly Home'?
A. Sam's friends.
B. People of Galesburg Illinois.
C. A Singers' group.
D. Charley's relatives.

PASSAGE-2

"But I've never again found the corridor that leads to the third level at Grand Central Station, although I've tried often enough. Louisa was pretty worried when I told her all this, and didn't want me to look for the third level any more, and after a while I stopped; I went back to my stamps. But now we're both looking, every weekend, because now we have proof that the third level is still there. My friend Sam Weiner disappeared! Nobody knew where, but I sort of suspected because Sam's a city boy, and I used to tell him about Galesburg — I went to school there — and he always said he liked the sound of the place. And that's where he is, all right. In 1894."

280. Why do you think the speaker is looking for The Third Level?
A. He wanted to meet his grandfather.
B. He wanted to go to Galesburg Illinois.
C. He wanted to meet his friends in the third level.
D. He wanted to prove to everyone that Third level does exist.

281. What is being referred by Sam's *a city boy?*
A. Life in a city is peaceful
B. Life in a city is very challenging and stressful.
C. Boys in cities are carefree and happy
D. City boys are smart and would not believe in fantasy.

282. How would you describe the speaker's vision of Galesburg Illinois?
A. Wishful escapism
B. Idealized sentimentality
C. Nostalgic simplicity
D. Dream like fantasy

283. Which word from the following can be used in place of Suspected'?
A. Doubted B. Trusted
C. Confined D. Accused

PASSAGE-3

Have you ever been there? It's a wonderful town still, with big old frame houses, huge lawns, and tremendous trees whose branches meet overhead and roof the streets. And in 1894, summer evenings were twice as long, and people sat out on their lawns, the men smoking cigars and talking quietly, the women waving palm-leaf fans, with the fire-flies all around, in a peaceful world. To be back there with the First World War still twenty years off, and World War II over forty years in the future... I wanted two tickets for that.

284. Who is speaking to whom in the given extract?
A. Charley to Louisa
B. Charley to the reader
C. Sam to Charley
D. Charley to Sam

285. The given extract is **NOT** an example of:
A. Analogy B. Metaphor
C. Imagery D. Allegory

286. "Men smoking cigars and women waving palm-leaf" refers to a society:
A. Orthodox B. Conservative
C. Liberal D. Modern

287. Which word from the extract is an antonym of small?
A. Huge B. Tremendous
C. Long D. Both (A) and (B)

PASSAGE-4

Well, maybe, but my grandfather didn't need any refuge from reality; things were pretty nice and peaceful in his day, from all I hear, and he started my collection. It's a nice collection too, blocks of four of practically every U.S. issue, first-day covers, and so on. President Roosevelt collected stamps too, you know".

288. What collection is referred in the extract?
A. Money collection B. Coin collection
C. Toys collection D. Stamp Collection

289. Which word from the following is an antonym of 'Refuge'?
A. Escape B. Furnish
C. Deny D. Sanction

290. What does the narrator mean by 'My grandfather started my collection':
A. His grandfather helped him collect coins.
B. His grandfather was a philanthropist.
C. He picked the hobby of stamp collection from his grandfather.
D. His grandfather loved planting trees.

291. Which other story from your text-books has a reference to President Roosevelt.
A. Deep Water B. Lost Spring
C. Last Lesson D. None of the above

PASSAGE-5

There were brass spittoons on the floor, and across the station a glint of light caught my eye; a man was pulling a gold watch from his vest pocket. He snapped open the cover, glanced at his watch and frowned. He wore a derby hat, a black four-button suit with tiny lapels, and he had a big, black, handlebar mustache. Then I looked around and saw that everyone in the station was dressed like eighteen-ninety-something.

292. What caused the glint of light?
A. The bras spittoons
B. The gold watch
C. The sun
D. The chimneys

293. The above extract is an example of:
A. Allusion B. Enjambment
C. Metaphor D. Imagery

294. The word in the extract which means 'to look angry and serious' is:
A. Frown B. Glint
C. Lapels D. Glance

295. Which of the following sentences uses the word 'Snap' as a noun?
A. He shifted his weight and a twig snapped.
B. I think this is too important for a snap decision.
C. He shut the book with a snap and stood up.
D. The brake pedal has just snapped off.

296. 'Dressed like eighteen-ninety-something' which literary device has been used here?
A. Metaphor B. Paradox
C. Anti-thesis D. Simile

PASSAGE-6

The corridor I was in began angling left and slanting downward and I thought that was wrong, but I kept on walking. All I could hear was the empty sound of my own footsteps and I didn't pass a soul. Then I heard that sort of hollow roar ahead that means open space and people talking. The tunnel turned sharp left; I went down a short flight of stairs and came out on the third level at Grand Central Station.

297. The corridor angling left and slanting downward is an example of....
A. A blend
B. An intersection between time and space
C. Hallucination
D. Dizziness

298. What made the narrator think that he was in a 'wrong corridor'?
A. Because it was falling down.
B. Because it was wobbly.
C. Because it was behaving strange.
D. All of the above

299. What is meant by "I didn't pass a soul"?
A. He didn't find any other person there.
B. He didn't cross any ghost.
C. He couldn't see his shadow.
D. None of the above

300. Which of the following does **NOT** mean 'Hollow'?
A. Void B. Empty
C. Vacant D. Solid

PASSAGE-7

But that's the reason, he said, and my friends all agreed. Everything points to it, they claimed. My stamp collecting, for example; that's a temporary refuge from reality.

301. In what context the word 'reason' is referred here?
A. That charley was hallucinating
B. That charley was day dreaming
C. That charley was unhappy and looking for an escape from reality
D. That Charley was not successful in his career.

302. With whom did all Charley's friends agree?
A. Psychiatrist, Sam B. Louisa, his wife
C. His grandfather D. His boss

303. What according to Sam and his friends was a temporary refuse from reality for Charley?
A. His day–dreaming
B. His stamp collection
C. His visits to the third level
D. His nostalgia about Galesburg.

304. The word 'Refuge' from the passage can be best replaced with:
A. Shade B. Rest
C. Leisure D. Shelter

PASSAGE-8

That night, among my oldest first-day covers, I found one that shouldn't have been there. But there it was. It was there because someone had mailed it to my grandfather at his home in Galesburg; that's what the address on the envelope said. And it had been there since July 18, 1894 and I opened it

305. Why should this particular first day cover not be there?
A. Because it was a modern first day cover from the future.
B. Because it was an old first day cover from the past.

C. Because it was not addressed to his grandfather.
D. Because it could not have been collected by his grandfather.

306. Why is Charley not aware of this particular first day cover?
A. Because it appeared recently.
B. It was not meant for him.
C. It was addressed to Louisa, his wife.
D. He was forgetful.

307. The Picture of President Garfield indicates that the first day cover was:
A. New one B. Slightly old
C. Recent one D. Definitely old

308. What can be inferred from the extract regarding this first day cover?
A. That someone from the present travelled to the past.
B. That someone from the future has written this
C. That Charley was followed by secret society
D. That Charley was being tricked.

PASSAGE-9

Now, I don't know why this should have happened to me. I'm just an ordinary guy named Charley, thirty-one years old, and I was wearing a tan gabardine suit and a straw hat with a fancy band; I passed a dozen men who looked just like me. And I wasn't trying to escape from anything; I just wanted to get home to Louisa, my wife.

309. What has happened to the narrator?
A. He got transported to the third level of grand central station.
B. He got transported to Galesburg Illinois
C. He got transported to the future.
D. He recently met an alien.

310. "I passed a dozen men just like me" indicates?
A. Modern fashion
B. Modern Life style
C. Monotony of modern life
D. Lack of variety in fashion

311. Why was the narrator in hurry?
A. He wanted to go for a party with his wife.
B. He wanted to go for a movie with his wife.
C. He had some important meeting.
D. He was already late from office.

312. Which word from the extract means a 'dust coat'?
A. Gabardine B. Straw
C. fancy D. None of the above

PASSAGE-10

The clerk figured the fare he glanced at my fancy hatband, but he figured the fare and I had enough for two coach tickets, one way. But when I counted out the money and looked up, the clerk was staring at me. He nodded at the bills. That ain't money, mister, he said, and if you re trying to skin me, you won't get very far, and he glanced at the cash drawer beside him.

313. Why did the clerk glance at Charley's fancy hatband?
A. Because it was just like his own hat.
B. Because charley's hat was not an ordinary sight for him.
C. Because Charley had a star in his hat band.
D. Because Charley had a mysterious mark on his hat.

314. Why did Charley wanted to buy two tickets?
A. He wanted to go to Galesburg Illinois with his wife.
B. He wanted to go to meet his grandfather with Sam.
C. He wanted to escape in the past with his boss.
D. He wanted to go to the future with his wife.

315 Which of the following does **NOT** explain the expression "If you want to skin me" from the passage.
A. If you want to trick me
B. If you want to cheat me
C. If you want to deceive me
D. If you want to fight with me

316. Which word from the extract means 'take a brief or hurried look'?
A. Nodded B. Stare
C. Glance D. Figure

PASSAGE-11

"Once I got into a tunnel about a mile long and came out in the lobby of Roosevelt Hotel. Another time I came up in an office building on forty-sixth-street, three blocks away":

317. Which of the following statement is true in the given context?
A. The narrator knew about the tunnel and he has been exploring various places.
B. The narrator has been in and out of the third level for quite a few times.
C. The narrator has been visiting his grandfather in Galesburg Illinois frequently.
D. The narrator was aware that he has been wandering here and there quite often.

318. Who is 'I' in the extract?
A. Sam B. Louisa
C. Charley D. None of the above

319. What can be inferred by the 'tunnel' from this extract?
A. A gateway into past.
B. A portal into another planet.
C. A gateway into the future.
D. A portal into an alien world.

320. Which word from the extract means 'An Underground Passageway'?
A. Lobby B. Office
C. Tunnel D. None of the above

PASSAGE-12

But I've never again found the corridor that leads to the third level at Grand Central Station, although I've tried often enough. Louisa was pretty worried when I told her all this, and didn't want me to look for the third level any more, and after a while I stopped; I went back to my stamps. But now we're both looking, every weekend.

321 Which corridor the speaker is looking?
A. The corridor leading to the third level.
B. The corridor which was under construction.
C. The corridor that took him to the tunnel.
D. None of the above

322. What made Louisa worried?
A. She knew that the speaker was hallucinating.
B. She was concerned about the well-being of Charley.
C. She thought Charley was fantasizing.
D. All of the above

323. Why did the speaker stop looking for the third level after some time?
A. He was not well.
B. He went to his hobby of stamp-collection.
C. All his efforts couldn't locate the third level.
D. He realized he was fantasizing.

324. 'Now we both are looking' who are WE here?
A. Charley and Louisa.
B. Charley and Sam.
C. Charley and his boss.
D. All of the above

PASSAGE-13

He said I was unhappy. That made my wife kind of mad, but he explained that he meant the modern world is full of insecurity, fear, war, worry and all the rest of it, and that I just want to escape. Well, who doesn't? Everybody I know wants to escape, but they don't wander down into any third level at Grand Central Station.

325. He said I was Unhappy. Identify ***I*** and ***He*** in the sentence.
A. Charley and his boss.
B. Charley and his grandfather.
C. Charley and Sam.
D. Charley and his neighbour.

326. 'That made my wife kind of mad' What does ***Mad*** mean here?
A. Jealous B. Insecure
C. Crazy D. Angry

327. Why was Charley's wife angry?
A. She thought he was going crazy.
B. She thought he was unhappy because of her.
C. She thought Charley was going to Galesburg leaving her alone.
D. None of the above

328. Which of the following does **NOT** mean 'Wander'?
A. Stroll B. Roam
C. Travel D. Cease

329. What was the Third Level?
A. An imaginary discovery of the of Charley's mind.
B. A big tunnel on the grand central station
C. A time-machine on the grand central station.
D. A level in the game that charley had been playing.

330. Why did the narrator go to a psychiatrist?
A. Because he was unhappy and wanted to know why
B. Because he went through an experience no one else did
C. Because he was unhappy and wanted to know why
D. Because he was depressed

331. What is the genre of the lesson "The Third Level"?
A. Historical Fiction B. Tragedy
C. Science Fiction D. Fantasy

332. How frequently the author has been in and out of the grand central?
A. He is a regular visitor
B. He has been in and out of the grand central hundreds of times
C. The author travels every day from grand central.
D. The author visits the grand central occasionally.

333. What does Sam think of Modern Life?
A. That life if full of stress, war and fear.
B. That life is easy and enjoyable
C. That the modern world is full of wonders
D. That the modern world is a great place to be

334. What is a first day cover?
A. It's a stamp issued on the first day of the year.
B. It's a stamp issued in the name of the first citizen of a country
C. An envelope bearing a stamp postmarked on its day of issue.
D. An envelope issued on the first day of the year.

335. As a Metaphor of the title 'The Third Level' which of the following would **NOT** be an appropriate explanation?
A. The bridge between the past and present.
B. The excruciating monotony of the modern life.
C. The convergence of reality and fantasy.
D. The dire need for an alternate plane of under-standing

336. What was the date on the newspaper?
A. June 15, 1894 B. June 11, 1894
C. June 10, 1894 D. July 13, 1894

337. Why did Charley visit the Library?
A. To gather more information about the third level.
B. To read more books on Time-Travel.
C. To confirm the main story of the newspaper.
D. To find a book he had seen in the third level.

338. How would you Sam describe Charley?
A. Escapist B. Carefree
C. Happy go lucky D. Workaholic

339. What is the name of Charley's wife?
A. Aliza B. Alisa
C. Louisa D. Lucia

340. What do you call a person who collects stamps?
A. Ticket collector B. Philatelist
C. Stamp-Collector D. Philanthropist

341. What was the name of the newspaper?
A. The Reuters B. The Telegraph
C. The Statesmen D. The world

342. What does the time table mention regarding grand central station?
A. That there are three levels
B. That there are two levels
C. That there is only one level
D. None of the above

343. Why did Charley decide to take sub way from Grand central station?
A. He used to take a train from there everyday
B. He wanted to go to Galesburg Illinois
C. He accidently reached there
D. He was late so he took a train to reach home fast.

344. Who did Charley discuss his strange visit to the third level?
A. His psychiatrist B. His friends
C. His wife D. His grandfather

345. How did Sam interpret charley's visit to the third level?
A. Waking wish fulfillment
B. Escape
C. Dream come true
D. Both (A) and (B)

346. What are some of the things Charley observe at Third Level?
A. Brass spittoons
B. Handlebar moustaches
C. Flickering chimney lights
D. All of the above

347. Why did Charley make a hasty retreat from the Third Level?
A. He came back because he was scared of the experience.
B. He came back hurriedly as he thought he will be arrested.
C. He came back to share this experience with his family.
D. He came back as he was concerned about his wife.

348. Why did Charley withdraw all his savings?
A. To get it exchanged in old style currency
B. To buy a home in Galesburg Illinois
C. To buy a gift for his wife
D. To pay fee to his psychiatrist

349. Why did Louisa become mad at Charley when Sam diagnosed him as unhappy?
A. She thought her husband was fantasizing.
B. She thought she was the reason for his unhappiness.
C. She thought her husband was an escapist.
D. She thought Sam was misguiding her husband.

350. What is Sam's take on Charley's hobby of stamp-collection?
A. Medium of escape
B. Connection between past and present
C. A good part time hobby
D. A good source of information

351. What business would have Sam established in Galesburg for a living?
A. Practice psychiatry
B. Become a flute player
C. Hay and grain business
D. Farming

352. What was the main story about on the first page of *The World?*
A. President Roosevelt
B. President Garfield
C. President Lincoln
D. President Cleveland

353. Why did Sam feel that Charley wanted to escape?
A. He feels charley was stressed because the modern world is full of war and worry.
B. He feels Charley was not happy with his job.
C. He feels that Charley was not happy with his wife.
D. He feels Charley's boss was very demanding.

354. **Explain:** Waking dream wish fulfillment.
A. An experience which takes one to future.
B. An experience which makes one forget the present.
C. An experience which takes one in the past.
D. An experience where one becomes forgetful.

355. What does Charley's letter to Sam signify?
A. A proof of time travel
B. A proof that third level does exist
C. A blend of reality with fantasy
D. A proof that Charley has been to Galesburg Illinois.

356. Why did Charley compare the grand central station with a tree?
A. The shape of the central station is like that of a tree.
B. Like a tree, the grand central station is very high.
C. Like a tree the grand central gives shade to its visitors.
D. Like the roots of a tree the grand central station is expanding.

357. Which US president was a philatelist mentioned in the story?
A. President Garfield
B. President Roosevelt
C. President Cleveland
D. President Jackson

358. What for Sam was invited according to the letter?
A. For a lemonade
B. For a dance party
C. For a birthday party
D. For a rain dance party

359. Why did the clerk at the ticket window refuse to accept Charley's money?
A. Money was insufficient
B. Money was torn
C. Money was old style
D. His money was of modern times

360. Which of the following is apt to justify the story 'the third level'.
A. "I like nonsense; it wakes up the brain cells. Fantasy is a necessary ingredient in living". —Dr. Seuss
B. "Fantasy is hardly an escape from reality. It's a way of understanding it". —Lloyd Alexander
C. "Stories of imagination tend to upset those without one". —Terry Pratchett
D. Fantasy and reality often overlap—Walt Disney

361. With regards to an intersection of time and space in the story, which of the following is **NOT** true?
A. People with side burns, handle-bar moustaches and women in sheep skin coat
B. Open gaslight and smaller booths
C. A large no of ticket windows
D. Broader Currency notes

362. What is the significance of 1894 in the lesson?
A. It represents a utopian world
B. It stands for the past
C. Charley's grandfather lived there
D. All of the above

363. Out of the following which one is the best way to overcome harsh realities of life?
A. Watching TV B. Reading good books
C. Day dreaming D. Fantasizing

THE ENEMY
By Pearl S Buck

Directions: *Read each of the following passages carefully and choose the best answer to each question out of the four alternatives.*

PASSAGE-1

It was at this moment that both of them saw something black come out of the mist. It was a man.

364. Who was watching the mist?
A. The fisherman
B. Doctor Sadao and Hana
C. Tom
D. Hana

365. Who came out of the mist?
A. General Takima B. The fisherman
C. Hana D. A man

366. The word 'both' refers to:
A. The fisherman and the police
B. Dr sadao and Hana
C. The gardener and cook
D. The enemy and General Takima

367. From where did the man come out from the mist?
A. From the black B. From the ocean
C. From the house D. From the tree

PASSAGE-2

His father had taken him often to the islands of those seas, and never had failed to say to the little brave boy at his side, "Those islands yonder, they are the stepping stones to the future of Japan".

368. Who is referred to as "him" in the above extract?
A. Dr. Sadao Hoki B. Hana
C. The gardener D. Dr Sadao's father

369. Who is referred as "the little brave boy" in the above extract? What is his full name?
A. Dr Sadao Hoki B. Hana
C. The General D. Tom

370. Dr. Sadao was ....
A. a psychiatrist B. an engineer
C. a professor D. a surgeon

371. Who is the speaker?
A. Dr. Sadao's father B. Dr. Sadao
C. Hana D. The white man

PASSAGE-3

"A White man!" Hana whispered. Yes, it was a white man. The wet cap fell away and there was his wet yellow hair, long, as though for many weeks it had not been cut and upon his young and tortured face was a rough yellow beard.

372. What did Dr Sadao and Hana mean by 'white man'?
A. the man whose face appeared white due to sand
B. an American prisoner of war
C. a man wearing white shirt
D. none of these

373. Hana's remark "A white man!" on seeing the white man indicated what she was feeling. Pick the option that correctly States the feelings.
1. Horror 2. Shocked
3. Unfamiliar 4. Annoyed
A. 1 and 2 B. 2 and 3
C. 2 and 4 D. 1 and 4

374. How did the white man's face appear?
A. Young C. Fresh
B. Tortured D. Both (A) and (B)

375. Why didn't the white man know the presence of Dr. Sadao and Hana?
A. As he was sleeping
B. As he was pretending to be unconscious
C. As he was unconscious
D. None of these

PASSAGE-4

"Don't faint", he said sharply. He did not put down his exploring instrument. "If I stop now, the man will surely die." She clapped her hands to her mouth and leaped up and ran out of the room. Outside in the garden he heard her retching but he went on with his work.

376. "Don't faint", he said. Who said these words and to whom?
A. Dr Sadao to Hana
B. The cook to the Gardener
C. Dr. Sadao to the patient
D. The patient to Dr. Sadao

377. Who would die? Who was retching?
1. Dr Sadao's wife 2. The General
3. The enemy Soldier 4. The old Gardener
A. 1 and 2 B. 3 and 1
C. 2 and 1 D. 3 and 4

378. Why did Dr. Sadao feel impatient and irritable with the prisoner?
A. It was getting late at night
B. He was tired and sleepy
C. He would not get paid
D. He could not tend to his wife

379. Where was the white man?
A. in the garden
B. on the beach
C. in the room of Sadao's father
D. with the general

PASSAGE-5

"My old master's son knows very well what he ought to do," he now said, pinching a bud from a bush as he spoke. "When the man was so near death why did he not let him bleed?"

380. "When the man was so near-death why did he not let him bleed ?" Who said these words?
A. The cook B. Yumi
C. The gardener D. The General

381. What is the feeling of the speaker?
A. Sarcasm B. Sadness
C. Indignation D. Appreciative

382. How had the man come to be bleeding?
A. He was scratched by the brambles head first
B. He had tripped and fallen
C. His body was torn by the rocks flanking the beach
D. He had been shot

383. Dr. Sadao's helping the white soldier displays which qualities of his?
1. He was above the narrow prejudices.
2. He was a bit selfish when it came to his country's matter.
3. He considered his duty above all the other things.
4. He was cunning and egoist person.
A. 1 and 2. B. 2 and 3
C. 1 and 3 D. 3 and 4

PASSAGE-6

Now Sadao remembered the wound and with his expert finger he began to search for it. Blood flowed freshly at his touch.

384. Who was wounded?
A. Sadao B. Hana
C. The White Soldier D. Yumi

385. Which word best suits 'trained' in the extract?
A. touch B. tended
C. expat D. expert

386. What kind of wound the man had?
A. It was a knife stab
B. It was an injury
C. It was a gun shot
D. The rock had struck the wound

387. What was the dilemma that Dr. Sadao faced?
A. Whether he should marry Hana or not.
B. Whether he should leave Japan and settle in another country.

C. Whether he should study further or start practice
D. Whether he should save the life of the white soldier or let him die.

PASSAGE-7

We must simply tell them that we intend to give him to the police— as indeed we must, Sadao

388. Who is the speaker of the above extract?
A. Hana B. Dr. Sadao
C. Yumi D. The General

389. Who is referred as them in the above extract?
A. The Police B. The Fishermen
C. The Servants D. The Officials

390. Which word in the extract means 'certainly'?
A. Simply B. Intend
C. Indeed D. Give

391. How many of them were employed at the house by the speaker of the extract?
A. Three B. Four
C. Six D. Two

PASSAGE-8

He stood gazing down on the motionless man. This man must have extraordinary vitality or he would have been dead by now. But then he was very young—perhaps not yet twenty five.

392. Who is referred as 'he' in 'he stood gazing'?
A. The police B. The gardener
C. Dr. Sadao D. The General

393. What was the age of the man?
A. Twenty five B. Thirty five
C. Forty five D. Fifty five

394. In whose bedroom the man was lying?
A. In the children's bedroom
B. In the master bedroom
C. The bedroom of the old man
D. The bedroom of the General.

395. Which word in the extract is the synonym of "strength"?
A. Vitality B. Extraordinary
C. Motionless D. Gazing

PASSAGE-9

When she saw him her thick lips folded themselves into stubbornness. "I have never washed a white man", she said, "and I will not wash so dirty a one now".

396. Who is referred as "she" in the above extract?
A. Hana B. The Cook
C. Yumi D. The Girl

397. Who is the listener of the above extract?
A. The Cook B. Hana
C. The Girl D. Yumi

398. Was "the White man" conscious when the above lines is spoken?
A. Yes, he was conscious
B. No, he was unconscious
C. He was sleeping
D. He was pretending sleeping .

399. Which phrase is the antonym of "always"?
A. Thick B. Never
C. Will D. Now

PASSAGE-10

"Well, well" the old man said in a tone of amazement, "so I did! But you see, I suffered a good deal. The truth is, I thought of nothing but myself. In short, I forgot my promise to you".

400. Who is referred to as "you" in the above extract?
A. The General B. Doctor Sadao
C. The Assassins D. The Gardener

401. Who is referred to "The old man" in the above extract?
A. The Gardener B. Doctor Sadao
C. The General D. The Assassins

402. Who suffered a good deal in the above extract?
A. The General B. Doctor Sadao
C. The Assassins D. The Gardener

403. Who failed to keep the promise?
A. The Gardener B. Doctor Sadao
C. The General D. The Assassins

PASSAGE-11

"It is very unfortunate that this man should have washed up on your door step". He said irritably.

404. Who is the speaker of the above lines?
A. The Gardener B. Doctor Sadao
C. The General D. The Assassins

405. Who is the listener of the above lines?
A. The General B. Doctor Sadao
C. The Assassins D. The Gardener

406. Who is referred to as "the man"?
A. The General
B. Doctor Sadao
C. The White American soldier
D. The Gardener

407. Which word in the extract is the synonym of "Unlucky"?
A. Irritably B. Washed
C. Unfortunate D. The man

408. **Statement 1:** Those islands yonder, they are the 'stepping – stones' to the future of Japan.

Statement 2: Dr. Sadao Hoki's father had dreamt of a bright future for his son and he hadn't been disappointed.

A. Statement 1 is true, but statement 2 is false
B. Statement 1 is false, but statement 2 is true
C. Both statement 1 and statement 2 cannot be inferred
D. Both statement 1 and statement 2 can be inferred

409. Statement 1: Dr. Sadao had waited to fall in love with Hana until he was sure she believed in traditional Japanese values else his father would never have welcomed her.

Statement 2: Sadao and Hana's chance meeting had turned out to be a very fruitful relationship.
A. Statement 1 is true, but statement 2 is true
B. Statement 1 is false, but statement 2 is true
C. Both statement 1 and statement 2 cannot be inferred
D. Both statement 1 and statement 2 can be inferred

410. Statement 1: Doctor Sadao is not a dedicated surgeon, kind and compassionate towards people in distress.
Statement 2: He faced conflict of duty as a doctor and a citizen of Japan.
A. Statement 1 is true, but statement 2 is false
B. Statement 1 is false, but statement 2 is true
C. Both statement 1 and statement 2 cannot be inferred
D. Both statement 1 and statement 2 can be inferred

411. Statement 1: Hana was a balanced woman.

Statement 2: She was graceful and dignified about the servants when they were leaving the house.
A. Statement 1 is true, but statement 2 is false
B. Statement 1 is false, but statement 2 is true
C. Both statement 1 and statement 2 cannot be inferred
D. Both statement 1 and statement 2 can be inferred

412. Statement 1: The General was selfish by nature, thinks of his treatment only.

Statement 2: He had no faith in Sadao as a doctor.
A. Statement 1 is true, but statement 2 is false
B. Statement 1 is false, but statement 2 is true
C. Both Statement 1 and Statement 2 cannot be inferred
D. Both Statement 1 and Statement 2 can be inferred

413. Statement 1: The gardener felt that Sadao should have let the soldier to die.

Statement 2: He thought that the sea and the gun would take revenge if he saves the soldier.
A. Statement 1 is true, but Statement 2 is false
B. Statement 1 is true, but Statement 2 is true
C. Both Statement 1 and Statement 2 cannot be inferred
D. Both Statement 1 and Statement 2 can be inferred

414. Two statements (Assertion and Reasons) are given below: Choose the option from the one that follow the Statements.

Assertion (A): Dr. Sadao was a true Patriot.

Reason (R): He informed the general about the presence of the white man in his house.
A. Both (A) & (R) are true and (R) is the correct explanation of (A)
B. Both (A) & (R) are true, but (R) is not the correct explanation of (A)
C. (A) is true, but (R) is false
D. (A) is false, but (R) is true

415. Assertion (A): The General sent the assassins to the house of Dr. Sadao.

Reason (R): He himself was in pain and needed Dr. Sadao's help.
A. Both (A) & (R) are true and (R) is the correct explanation of (A)
B. Both (A) & (R) are true, but (R) is not the correct explanation of (A)
C. (A) is true, but (R) is false
D. (A) is false, but (R) is true

416. Who wrote *Don Juan*?
A. Shakespeare B. Tennyson
C. Byron D. T.S. Eliot

417. Who wrote *The Life of Johnson*?
A. Boswell B. Macaulay
C. Churchill D. Sir Walter Raleigh

418. *Priest's Nun's Tale* was written by:
A. Spenser B. Charles Lamb
C. Tennyson D. Chaucer

419. Who is said to have first used the term "Metaphysics"?
A. Matthew Arnold B. Sidney
C. Donne D. Dr. Johnson

420. The writer of *Volpone* is:
A. Johnson B. Milton
C. Jonson D. Shelley

421. Which is the correct chronological sequence?
A. Spenser—Chaucer—Milton—Donne
B. Spenser—Wordsworth—Tennyson—T.S. Eliot
C. Milton—Shakespeare—Philip Larkin—Keats
D. Auden—Eliot—Shelley—Keats

422. *Pilgrim's Progress* was written by:
A. Milton B. Shelley
C. Swinburne D. John Bunyan

423. The writer of the line : *"Stone walls do not a prison make"* is:
A. Lovelace B. Milton
C. W.B. Yeats D. T.S. Eliot

424. *"Monkey's Paw"* is a:
A. Poem B. Drama
C. Short story D. Novel

425. Lyrical Ballads appeared in:
A. 1690 B. 1798
C. 1802 D. 1800

426. The writer of *'A Pair of Blue Eyes'* is:
A. Thackeray B. Dickens
C. George Eliot D. Thomas Hardy

427. *Hard Times* was written by:
A. Thackeray B. Dickens
C. Trollope D. Marquese

428. Which of the following poets was most impressed by the German philosophy?
A. Chaucer B. Wordsworth
C. Coleridge D. Southey

429. The two cities referred to in *"A Tale of Two Cities"* are:
A. London and Paris
B. London and Rome
C. Rome and Paris
D. Moscow and Rome

430. *The Peasant's Bread* is a story by:
A. Maupassant B. Tagore
C. R.K. Narayan D. Tolstoy

431. *The Financial Express* was written by:
A. Raja Rao B. R.K. Narayan
C. Tagore D. Mulk Raj Anand

432. *"Negative Capability"* is a term associated with:
A. Tagore B. Shelley
C. Keats D. Coleridge

433. The most impressive treatment of "imagination" has been given by:
A. Coleridge B. Shelley
C. Eliot D. Yeats

434. *Lady Chatterley's Lover* was banned because it was considered:
A. obscene B. revolutionary
C. obscurantist D. None of these

435. *For Whom The Bell Tolls* was written by:
A. Marquese B. Hemingway
C. Hawthorne D. None of these

436. The writer of : *"A Pair of Mustachios"* is:
A. Anand B. Tagore
C. Raja Rao D. Anita Desai

437. The writer of *Scarlet Letter* is:
A. Henry James B. James Joyce
C. Hawthorne D. None of these

438. Rousseau is associated with:
A. French Revolution
B. American War of Independence
C. Russian (Bolshevik) Revolution
D. None of these

439. Who wrote *'Train to Pakistan'*?
A. Narayan B. Manohar Malgaon
C. Khushwant Singh D. Anand

440. Who is the writer of *Azadi*?
A. R.K. Narayan B. Khushwant Singh
C. Tagore D. Chaman Nahal

441. *"The God of Small Things"* is written by:
A. R.K. Narayan B. Hemingway
C. Graham Greene D. Arundhati Roy

442. Who wrote the poem *"Listeners"*?
A. Tennyson B. Thomas Hood
C. Goldsmith D. Walter de la Mare

443. In writing *"Canterbury Tales"* Chaucer was influenced by:
A. Decameron B. The Divine Comedy
C. The Holy Bible D. None of these

444. *'Animal Farm'* was written by:
A. James Joyce B. Virginia Woolf
C. George Orwell D. Hemingway

445. Shobha De is a:
A. poet B. dramatist
C. novelist D. an actress

446. Dunciad was written by:
A. Dryden B. Pope
C. Tennyson D. Shelley

447. Bernard Shaw got the Nobel Prize for:
A. Pygmalion B. Man and Superman
C. Saint Joan D. None of these

448. The Victorian Period is marked by:
A. Great political upheavals
B. Great social security
C. Great wars
D. Economic deprivation

449. Swift is known mainly as:
A. an essayist B. a poet
C. a satirist D. a short story writer

450. Who is the writer of the novel *"The Village"*?
A. Khushwant Singh B. Anita Desai
C. Mulk Raj Anand D. R.K. Narayan

451. The most famous writer of the heroic couplet is:
A. Dryden B. Chaucer
C. Spenser D. Pope

452. *Macflecknoe* is a poem written by:
A. Dryden B. Pope
C. Tennyson D. Yeats

453. Who wrote *'Everyman in His Humour'*?
A. Shakespeare B. Jonson
C. Milton D. Keats

454. *'Indian Jugglers'* is an essay by:
A. De Quincey B. Gardiner
C. Hazlitt D. Lamb

455. Who wrote *'The Gropes of Wrath'*?
A. Pearl Buck B. Hemingway
C. Virginia Woolf D. John Steinbeck

456. Who rendered into English the ancient Greek tragedy *"Atlanta in Calydon"*?
A. Swinburne B. Shelley
C. Tennyson D. Arthur Hugh Clough

457. *The Deserted Village* was written by:
A. Cowper B. Goldsmith
C. Keats D. Johnson

458. *'Savitri'* is an epic written by:
A. Tagore
B. Prem Chand
C. Aurobindo
D. Bankim Chandra Chatterjee

459. The anthem *"Vande Mataram"* occurs in
A. Godan B. Anand Math
C. Gora D. Train to Pakistan

460. *'All Fool's Day'* is an essay written by:
A. Charles Lamb B. Hazlitt
C. A.G. Gardiner D. R.C. Stevenson

461. The drama *Tamburlaine* is written by:
A. Shakespeare B. Marlowe
C. Lyly D. Green

462. The book *"Appreciations"* was written by:
A. Morris B. Arnold
C. Walter Pater D. Christina Rossetti

463. *"The Admirable Crichton"* was written by:
A. Steinbeck B. T.S. Eliot
C. Trollope D. James Barrie

464. *"The Death of a Salesman"* was written by:
A. James Barrie B. Eugene O'Neill
C. Arthur Miller D. None of these

465. The Restoration period is said to have started from:
A. 1660 B. 1676
C. 1625 D. 1645

466. Who wrote *"The Lady's Not for Burning"*?
A. Barrie B. Christopher Fry
C. Robert Bridges D. T.S. Eliot

467. Who wrote the poem *"Brahma"*?
A. T.S. Eliot B. Emerson
C. Whitman D. Frost

468. The writer of *Walden* is:
A. Tennyson B. Whitman
C. Thoreau D. Frost

469. In *'Sons and Lovers'* Lawrence has depicted the life of:
A. factory workers B. miners
C. farmers D. animals

470. Who wrote *Kim*?
A. Kipling B. Tagore
C. Lawrence D. Narayan

471. *'The Hairy Ape'* is a famous play by:
A. Barrie B. Eugene O'Neill
C. Christopher Fry D. T.S. Eliot

472. Who is the writer of *Frankenstein*?
A. George Eliot B. Jane Austen
C. Mary Shelley D. Emile Bronte

473. Who wrote the *'Cries of Children'*?
A. Robert Browning B. Elizabeth Barrett
C. Thomas Hood D. Cowper

474. Which poet is known as poet's poet?
A. Shakespeare B. Milton
C. Spenser D. Shelley

475. Who wrote the maximum number of sonnets?
A. Shakespeare B. Milton
C. Sidney D. Wordsworth

476. *Adonais* is the eulogy written on the death of:
A. Coleridge B. Byron
C. Keats D. Wordsworth

477. Who wrote *Mother*?
A. Tolstoy B. Maxim Gorky
C. Chekhov D. Hardy

478. Who is associated with *Malgudi*?
A. Narayan
B. Anand
C. Manohar Malgonkar
D. Anita Desai

479. The author of *Beowulf* is:
A. Bede B. Cynewulf
C. Chaucer D. Unknown

480. The Anglo-Saxon period is often said to be from 450 to .....
A. 900 B. 1000
C. 1050 D. 1100

481. *"To a Mountain Daisy"* is a poem by:
A. Wordsworth B. Shelley
C. Keats D. Burns

482. Who wrote: *"The Devil's Disciple"*?
A. Galsworthy B. Barrie
C. Shaw D. Fry

483. Who wrote *"The Decline and Fall of the Roman Empire"*?
A. Walter Raleigh B. Trollope
C. Smollett D. Edward Gibbon

484. Richard Hooker was a prose writer of the:
A. Victorian period B. Romantic period
C. Elizabethan period D. Chaucerian age

485. Alexander Dumas was:
A. an English writer B. an American writer
C. a French writer D. a German writer

486. Which one was not one of the Lake poets?
A. Shelley B. Wordsworth
C. Southey D. Coleridge

487. *The Theory of Catharsis* is associated with:
A. Plato B. Dryden
C. Aristotle D. Sidney

488. Who wrote *'In Defence of Poetry'*?
A. T.S. Eliot B. Yeats
C. Keats D. Shelley

489. *'The Playboy of the Western World'* is a play by:
A. Barrie B. Synge
C. Fry D. Eliot

490. *'Silent Woman'* is a play by:
A. Marlowe B. Shakespeare
C. Ben Jonson D. Lyly

491. The Scene of *Beowulf* is laid in:
A. England B. France
C. Spain D. None of these

492. *"Kidnapped"* was written by:
A. Dickens B. Thackeray
C. Hardy D. R.L. Stevenson

493. *'The Prisoner of Zenda'* was written by:
A. Sterne B. Trollope
C. Anthony Hope D. George Eliot

494. What was the full name of Cervantes?
A. Jim Cervantes
B. John Cervantes
C. Miguel de Cervantes
D. Sir Roger Cervantes

495. Besides being a poet, Chaucer was:
A. a trader B. a manufacturer
C. a teacher D. a diplomat

496. The name of William Golding's first novel is:
A. The Inheritors B. Lord of the Flies
C. Pincher Martin D. The Pyramid

497. The author of *Erewhon* is:
A. Hardy B. Marquese
C. Samuel Butler D. Cervantes

498. Which of the following is a *Comedy of Manners*?
A. The Way of the World
B. The Duchess of Malfi
C. The Lady's Not for Burning
D. The Hairy Ape

499. Which one among the following is not a pessimist?
A. Gissing B. Browning
C. Hardy D. Thomson

500. Charles Reade's drama *"Drink"* was adapted from a work of:
A. Goethe B. Zola
C. Mallarwe D. Tennyson

501. Which one among the following was not a utilitarian?
A. Rousseau B. James Mill
C. Ricardo D. Bentham

502. *'The Praise of Folly'* was written by:
A. Walter Raleigh B. Thomas Moore
C. Charles Lamb D. Ruskin

503. Who wrote: *"In Praise of Idleness"*?
A. Bertrand Russell B. Thomas More
C. Charles Lamb D. Hazlitt

504. The real name of Saki is:
A. H.H. Munro B. Samuel Butler
C. George Orwell D. The Duke

505. Who started: *"The Tatler"*?
A. Addison B. Swift
C. Steele D. Stevenson

506. The poem *'The Song of the Shirt'* was written by:
A. Mrs. Browning B. Pope
C. Shelley D. Thomas Hood

507. *Sir Roger* was originally the creation of:
A. Addison B. Dryden
C. Steele D. Milton

508. Who wrote: *"Areopagitica"*?
A. Charles Lamb B. Hazlitt
C. De Quincey D. Milton

509. *'The Selfish Giant'* is a story written by:
A. Tagore B. Oscar Wilde
C. Maupassant D. Tolstoy

510. Who wrote : *"Four Quartets"*?
A. T.S. Eliot B. W.B. Yeats
C. W.H. Auden D. Philip Larkins

511. Who wrote : *"Look Back in Anger"*?
A. Steinbeck B. Christopher Fry
C. John Osborne D. Barrie

512. Who wrote : *"The Devils of Loundun"*?
A. Bertrand Russell B. Aldous Huxley
C. J.B. Priestley D. Hazlitt

513. Who wrote : *"Principles of Human Knowledge"*?
A. Milton B. John Bunyan
C. Nash D. George Berkeley

514. Who wrote : *"Liber Amoris"*?
A. Lamb B. Hazlitt
C. Byron D. Wordsworth

515. *"A Railway Clerk"* is a poem by:
A. Keki N. Daruwallah B. Nissim Ezekiel
C. Shiv K. Kumar D. Jayanta Mahapatra

516. Who won The Booker of Bookers?
A. Arundhati Roy B. Khushwant Singh
C. Mulk Raj Anand D. Salman Rushdie

517. Who wrote: *"The Battle of Books"*?
A. Bacon B. Hazlitt
C. Swift D. None of these

518. Who wrote: *"Nectar in a Sieve"*?
A. Mulk Raj Anand
B. Manohar Malgonkar
C. Kamala Markandaya
D. Pearl S. Buck

519. *'The Good Earth'* was written by:
A. Raja Rao B. R.K. Narayan
C. Pearl S. Buck D. Kamala Markandaya

520. The writer of *'The Dove Found No Rest'* is:
A. Pearl S Buck B. Hemingway
C. Raja Rao D. Dennis Stoll

521. Who wrote: *"So Many Hungers"*?
A. Bhabani Bhattacharya
B. Kamala Markandaya
C. Manohar Malgonkar
D. Chaman Nahal

522. Who is the writer of *"The Middleman and Other Stories"*?
A. Mulk Raj Anand B. Bharati Mukherjee
C. Tagore D. Prem Chand

523. Cicero was a Roman:
A. philologist B. physician
C. orator D. None of these

524. Who is the writer of *"Gita Rahasya"*?
A. Tulsi Das B. Vivekananda
C. Shivananda D. B.G. Tilak

525. *'The Rubaiyat of Omar Khayyam'* was translated into English by:
A. Robert Browning B. Tennyson
C. Fitz Gerald D. Hopkins

ANSWERS

1	2	3	4	5	6	7	8	9	10
A	A	A	C	B	B	A	B	A	B
11	**12**	**13**	**14**	**15**	**16**	**17**	**18**	**19**	**20**
B	A	B	A	C	C	B	A	C	A
21	**22**	**23**	**24**	**25**	**26**	**27**	**28**	**29**	**30**
D	B	C	B	A	B	C	C	B	B
31	**32**	**33**	**34**	**35**	**36**	**37**	**38**	**39**	**40**
B	D	A	C	B	C	D	B	A	B
41	**42**	**43**	**44**	**45**	**46**	**47**	**48**	**49**	**50**
D	B	B	B	B	D	B	D	A	D
51	**52**	**53**	**54**	**55**	**56**	**57**	**58**	**59**	**60**
D	B	D	B	C	D	D	B	C	D
61	**62**	**63**	**64**	**65**	**66**	**67**	**68**	**69**	**70**
D	C	D	B	C	D	C	D	B	B
71	**72**	**73**	**74**	**75**	**76**	**77**	**78**	**79**	**80**
A	A	C	C	B	A	A	D	D	D
81	**82**	**83**	**84**	**85**	**86**	**87**	**88**	**89**	**90**
B	D	A	A	B	D	D	A	A	B
91	**92**	**93**	**94**	**95**	**96**	**97**	**98**	**99**	**100**
D	C	D	B	C	D	B	C	A	C

101	102	103	104	105	106	107	108	109	110
D	C	B	D	C	C	D	A	C	D
111	112	113	114	115	116	117	118	119	120
D	C	B	C	B	B	D	D	B	C
121	122	123	124	125	126	127	128	129	130
A	A	C	D	D	A	C	C	D	A
131	132	133	134	135	136	137	138	139	140
C	A	B	A	C	B	D	C	C	A
141	142	143	144	145	146	147	148	149	150
B	D	B	A	B	D	A	C	A	B
151	152	153	154	155	156	157	158	159	160
B	C	A	C	B	C	A	A	B	B
161	162	163	164	165	166	167	168	169	170
B	D	A	A	D	B	D	B	A	D
171	172	173	174	175	176	177	178	179	180
D	C	C	A	C	D	C	A	D	D
181	182	183	184	185	186	187	188	189	190
D	A	D	C	C	B	B	B	C	C
191	192	193	194	195	196	197	198	199	200
D	C	A	B	C	B	D	C	C	B
201	202	203	204	205	206	207	208	209	210
A	B	D	C	A	C	D	D	B	A
211	212	213	214	215	216	217	218	219	220
C	C	C	C	C	D	C	A	A	B
221	222	223	224	225	226	227	228	229	230
D	B	B	C	B	C	B	B	A	B
231	232	233	234	235	236	237	238	239	240
B	D	C	B	B	A	A	C	C	D
241	242	243	244	245	246	247	248	249	250
C	B	D	D	A	C	A	A	D	B
251	252	253	254	255	256	257	258	259	260
C	B	B	B	D	A	D	C	A	D
261	262	263	264	265	266	267	268	269	270
B	A	D	C	D	B	C	B	A	C
271	272	273	274	275	276	277	278	279	280
A	D	B	C	D	A	C	C	B	B
281	282	283	284	285	286	287	288	289	290
B	C	A	B	D	A	D	D	B	C
291	292	293	294	295	296	297	298	299	300
A	B	D	A	C	D	B	C	A	D
301	302	303	304	305	306	307	308	309	310
C	A	B	D	D	A	D	A	A	C
311	312	313	314	315	316	317	318	319	320
D	A	B	A	D	C	D	C	A	C

321	322	323	324	325	326	327	328	329	330
A	B	C	A	C	D	B	D	A	B
331	332	333	334	335	336	337	338	339	340
C	B	A	C	D	B	C	A	C	B
341	342	343	344	345	346	347	348	349	350
D	B	D	A	D	D	B	A	B	A
351	352	353	354	355	356	357	358	359	360
C	D	A	B	C	D	B	A	D	D
361	362	363	364	365	366	367	368	369	370
C	D	B	B	D	B	B	A	A	D
371	372	373	374	375	376	377	378	379	380
A	B	A	D	C	A	B	D	C	C
381	382	383	384	385	386	387	388	389	390
C	C	C	C	D	C	D	A	C	C
391	392	393	394	395	396	397	398	399	400
A	C	A	C	A	C	B	B	B	B
401	402	403	404	405	406	407	408	409	410
C	A	C	C	B	C	C	D	A	B
411	412	413	414	415	416	417	418	419	420
D	A	B	A	D	C	A	D	D	C
421	422	423	424	425	426	427	428	429	430
B	D	A	C	B	D	B	C	A	D
431	432	433	434	435	436	437	438	439	440
B	C	A	A	B	A	C	A	C	D
441	442	443	444	445	446	447	448	449	450
D	D	A	C	C	B	C	A	C	C
451	452	453	454	455	456	457	458	459	460
D	A	B	C	D	A	B	C	B	A
461	462	463	464	465	466	467	468	469	470
B	C	D	C	A	B	B	C	B	A
471	472	473	474	475	476	477	478	479	480
B	C	B	C	D	C	B	A	D	C
481	482	483	484	485	486	487	488	489	490
D	C	D	C	C	A	C	D	B	C
491	492	493	494	495	496	497	498	499	500
D	D	C	C	D	B	C	A	B	B
501	502	503	504	505	506	507	508	509	510
A	B	A	A	C	D	C	D	B	A
511	512	513	514	515	516	517	518	519	520
C	B	D	B	B	D	C	C	C	D
521	522	523	524	525					
A	B	C	D	C					

ENGLISH GRAMMAR & VOCABULARY

Spelling Errors

The most common errors in English are of spellings of words. Even the most learned men are sometimes confused about the correct spellings of some words. One must keep and use a dictionary religiously. Never ignore and let pass a new word casually.

A number of question to test your knowledge of spellings are compiled here. Try to solve as many as you can.

Multiple Choice Questions

Directions: *Find the correctly spelt word out of the four options in each question.*

1. A. Accompalish B. Ackmplesh C. Acomplush D. Accomplish

2. A. Acommodation B. Acomodation C. Accomodation D. Accommodation

3. A. Astonished B. Astronished C. Astoneshed D. Asstonished

4. A. Benefeted B. Benefitted C. Benifited D. Benefited

5. A. Belligerent B. Beligirent C. Belligarant D. Belligerrent

6. A. Chancelery B. Chancellery C. Chancellary D. Chancelary

7. A. Discriminate B. Discremineta C. Discrimenate D. Discriminat

8. A. Damage B. Dammage C. Damaige D. Dammege

9. A. Efficiant B. Effecient C. Efficient D. Eficient

10. A. Extravagant B. Extreragent C. Extreregant D. Extravegent

11. A. Efflorascence B. Eflorescene C. Effllorescence D. Efflorescence

12. A. Equinimity B. Equanimmity C. Equannimity D. Equanimity

13. A. Farmament B. Farmement C. Fermament D. Fremament

14. A. Grieff B. Grief C. Grieef D. Grrief

15. A. Guarantee B. Garuntee C. Guaruntee D. Gaurantee

16. A. Hypocritical B. Hypocretical C. Hypocriticel D. Hypocirticel

17. A. Humurous B. Humorous C. Humoreus D. Humorrous

18. A. Itenerary B. Itinarery C. Itinarary D. Itinerary

19. A. Indipenseble B. Indispansible C. Indispensable D. Indipensable

20. A. Imprecticability B. Impracticebility C. Impracticibility D. Impracticability

21. A. Incradulous B. Incredulous C. Incridulous D. Incredalous

22. A. Juddicious B. Judiceous C. Judicious D. Judiceus

23. A. Kleptomonia B. Kleptemonia C. Kleptomania D. Klaptomania

24. A. Lackdaisical B. Lackadaisical C. Lckadaisicle D. Lackadisical

25. A. Licentious B. Licontious C. Licenttious D. Licientious

26. A. Meddicine B. Medicine C. Medicene D. Medicinne

27. A. Meritricious B. Merefrecious C. Meretricious D. Merritricious

28. A. Missunderstood B. Miesunderstood C. Misunderstood D. Misunderstod

29. A. Occurad B. Occurred C. Ocurred D. Occured

30. A. Osttentatious B. Ostentetious C. Ostentatious D. Ostenttatious

31. A. Obnosious B. Obnoxeous C. Obnoxious D. Obnoseous

32. A. Omenous B. Ominous C. Ommineous D. Omineous

33. A. Pecification B. Pacification C. Pecifacation D. Pecefication

34. A. Prograssive B. Progressive C. Progresive D. Prograsive

35. A. Pasiveness B. Passiveness C. Passeveniss D. Passivines

36. A. Polyendry B. Poliendry C. Pollyendry D. Polyandry

37. A. Puerille B. Puerrile C. Puerile D. Purrile

38. A. Pesanger B. Passenger C. Pessenger D. Pasanger

39. A. Querrelsome B. Quarrelsame C. Quarrelsome D. Querralsome

40. A. Rigourous B. Rigerous C. Rigorous D. Regerous

41. A. Survellance B. Surveilance C. Surveillance D. Survaillance

42. A. Schedule B. Schdule C. Schedale D. Schedeule

43. A. Sepalchrle B. Sepalchral C. Sepulchrle D. Sepulchral

44. A. Sympathetic B. Smypathetic C. Sympothetic D. Sympethetic

45. A. Sincerely B. Sencerely C. Sincerelly D. Sincerrely

46. A. Satellite B. Sattellite C. Satelite D. Sattelite

47. A. Teracherous B. Treacherous C. Treacheraus D. Treachereans

48. A. Uncivilized B. Uncevilized C. Uncivillized D. Uncevelized

49. A. Vainglorious B. Vaniglorious C. Vaniglerious D. Vaingloreus

50. A. Vulnarable B. Valnerable C. Velnerable D. Vulnerable

ANSWERS

1	2	3	4	5	6	7	8	9	10
D	D	A	B	A	C	A	A	C	A
11	**12**	**13**	**14**	**15**	**16**	**17**	**18**	**19**	**20**
D	D	C	B	A	A	B	D	C	D
21	**22**	**23**	**24**	**25**	**26**	**27**	**28**	**29**	**30**
B	C	C	B	A	B	C	C	B	C
31	**32**	**33**	**34**	**35**	**36**	**37**	**38**	**39**	**40**
C	B	B	B	B	D	C	B	C	C
41	**42**	**43**	**44**	**45**	**46**	**47**	**48**	**49**	**50**
C	A	D	A	A	A	B	A	A	D

Spotting Errors

The most common errors in English are of spellings, grammar and usage of words. By regular practice, the errors can be easily spotted and minimised.

Common Errors with Nouns and Noun-Phrases

Incorrect	*Correct*
1. I have bought new *furnitures.*	I have bought new *furniture.*
2. The wages of sin *are* death.	The wages of sin *is* death.
3. She told these *news* to her mother.	She told her mother this *news.*
4. He took *troubles* to do his work.	He took *trouble* (or pains) over his work.
5. The *cattles* were grazing.	The *cattle* were grazing.
6. He showered *many abuses* on me.	He showered *much abuse* on me.
7. I spent the holidays with my *family members.*	I spent the holidays with my *family.*
8. There is no *place* in this compartment.	There is no *room* in this compartment.
9. Write this new *poetry* in your *copy.*	Write this new *poem* in your *note-book.*
10. He took *insult* at this.	He took *offence* at this.
11. Put your *sign* here.	Put your *signatures* here.
12. She is my *cousin sister.*	She is my *cousin.*
13. *Sunil's* my *neighbour's* house was burgled.	*Sunil* my *neighbour's* house was burgled.
14. I lost a *ten-rupees* note.	I lost *a ten-rupee* note.
15. Road closed for *repair.*	Road closed for *repairs.*
16. His house is out of *repairs.*	His house is out of *repair.*
17. What is the *reason* of an earthquake?	What is the *cause* of an earthquake?
18. This building is made of *stones.*	This building is made of *stone.*
19. I disapprove of *these kinds* of games.	I disapprove of *this kind* of games.
20. Veena's and Sheela's father is ill.	Veena and Sheela's father is ill.
21. His *son-in-laws* are doctors.	His *sons-in-law* are doctors.
22. *Alms* is given to the *poor.*	*Alms* are given to the poor.
23. He always keeps his words.	He always keeps his *word.*
24. I carried the *luggages.*	I carried the *luggage.*
25. *Two-third* of the work is left.	*Two-thirds* of the work is left.

Common Errors with Pronouns

Incorrect	*Correct*
1. Both did not go.	Neither went.
2. We all did not go.	None of us went.
3. Each of these boys play.	Each of these boys plays.
4. Whoever does best he will get a prize.	Whoever does best will get a prize.

	Incorrect	Correct
5.	One should not waste his time.	A man should not waste his time.
6.	I and she are sisters.	She and I are sisters.
7.	He is wiser than me.	He is wiser than I.
8.	Between you and I, Anil is not to be trusted.	Between you and me, Anil is not to be trusted.
9.	Nobody was there but I.	Nobody was there but me.
10.	Who is there ? It is me.	Who is there ? It is I.
11.	Only he and me can use this card.	Only he and I can use this card.
12.	Let you and I go now.	Let you and me go now.
13.	Everyone got one's pay.	Everyone got his pay.
14.	Everyone is frightened when they see a tiger.	Everyone is frightened when he sees a tiger.
15.	These two friends are fond of one another.	These two friends are fond of each other.
16.	I did not like him coming at that hour.	I did not like his coming at that hour.
17.	Who do you think I met?	Whom do you think I met?
18.	You should avail this opportunity.	You should avail yourself this opportunity.
19.	When you have read these books, please return the same to me.	When you have read the books, please return them to me.
20.	They that are humble need fear no fall.	Those that are humble need fear no fall.

Common Errors with Adjectives

	Incorrect	Correct
1.	These all oranges are good.	All these oranges are good.
2.	He held the book in the both hands.	He held the book in both hands.
3.	Both men have not come.	Neither man has come.
4.	That man should do some or other work.	That man should do some work or other.
5.	He is elder than I.	He is older than I.
6.	Shakespeare is greater than any other poets.	Shakespeare is greater than any other poet.
7.	He is a coward man.	He is a cowardly man.
8.	Many villagers cannot write his own name.	Many villagers cannot write their own name.
9.	Each of us loves our home.	Each of us loves his home.
10.	Much efforts bring their reward.	Much effort brings its reward.
11.	He found hundred rupees.	He found a hundred rupees.
12.	He had leave of four days.	He had four days leave.
13.	This is a worth seeing sight.	This is a sight worth seeing.
14.	He will spend his future life here.	He will spend the rest of his life here.
15.	There is a best teacher in that class.	There is a very good teacher in that class.
16.	Of the two plans this is the best.	Of the two plans this is the better.
17.	He is becoming strong every day.	He is becoming stronger every day.
18.	He is worst than I.	He is worse than I.
19.	Jaipur is hot than Delhi.	Jaipur is hotter than Delhi.
20.	In our library the number of books is less.	In our library the number of books is small.

Common Errors with Verbs

	Incorrect	*Correct*
1.	He asked had we taken our luggage.	He asked if we had taken our luggage.
2.	She asked what are you doing.	She asked what we were doing.
3.	Rama asked to Anil why he is angry.	Rama asked Anil why he was angry.
4.	He does not care for his money.	He does not take care of his money.
5.	He does not care for his work.	He takes no care over his work.
6.	No one cared for him after his mother died.	No one took care of him after his mother died.
7.	He got angry before I said a word.	He got angry before I had said a word.
8.	I met a man who was my tutor 20 years ago.	I met a man who had been my tutor twenty years ago.
9.	I had been for walking yesterday.	I went for a walk yesterday.
10.	If I shall do this I shall be wrong.	If I do this I shall be wrong.
11.	I have left trekking.	I have given up trekking.
12.	I came to know as to how he did this.	I learnt how he did this.
13.	I came to know why he was sad.	I found out why he was sad.
14.	He knows to swim.	He knows how to swim.
15.	The criminal's head was cut.	The criminal's head was cut off.
16.	I said to him to go.	I told him to go.
17.	I told the teacher to excuse me.	I asked the teacher to excuse me.
18.	He is troubling me.	He is giving me trouble.
19.	I have got a hurt on my leg.	I have hurt my leg.
20.	She gave a speech.	She made a speech.

Common Errors in Subject-Verb Agreement

	Incorrect	*Correct*
1.	The owners of this factory *is* very rich.	The owners of this factory *are* very rich.
2.	The pleasures of nature that one can experience at Shimla *is* beyond description.	The pleasures of nature that one can experience at Shimla *are* beyond description.
3.	There *is* no street lights in our colony.	There *are* no street lights in our colony.
4.	He and I *am* entrusted with the job.	He and I *are* entrusted with the job.
5.	Rice and curry *are* his favourite dish.	Rice and curry *is* his favourite dish.
6.	The honour and glory of our country *are* at stake.	The honour and glory of our country *is* at stake.
7.	Time and tide *waits* for none.	Time and tide *wait* for none.
8.	All the passengers with the driver *was* killed.	All the passengers, with the driver, *were* killed.
9.	The teacher, with her students, *were* going out.	The teacher, with her students, *was* going out.
10.	I as well as they *am* tired.	I as well as they *are* tired.
11.	Not only the soldiers but their captain also *were* captured.	Not only the soldiers but their captain also *was* captured.
12.	Neither you nor I *were* selected.	Neither you nor I *was* selected.
13.	Either of these two applicants *are* fit for the job but neither want to accept it.	Either of these two applicants *is* fit for the job but neither wants to accept it.
14.	One of these students are sure to stand first.	One of these students *is* sure to stand first.
15.	Everyone of these workers want a raise.	Everyone of these workers wants a raise.
16.	None of these letters has been answered so far.	None of these letters *have* been answered so far.
17.	None of the girls were present at the party.	None of the girls *was* present at the party.
18.	Many a battle were fought on Indian soil.	Many a battle *was* fought on Indian soil.
19.	A lot of work remain to be done.	A lot of work *remains* to be done.
20.	The majority of these girls likes music.	The majority of these girls *like* music.

Common Errors in the Use of Modals/Auxiliary Verbs

Incorrect	Correct
1. When I shall see him I shall tell him this.	When I *see* him, I shall tell him this.
2. If I should do wrong, he would punish me.	If I *did* wrong, he would punish me.
3. Until he will have confessed his fault, he will be kept in prison.	Until he *has* confessed his fault, he will be kept in prison.
4. She will obey me.	She *shall* obey me.
5. You would work hard.	You *should* work hard.
6. You shall find him in the garden.	You *will* find him in the garden.
7. He must have died of exposure, but we cannot be certain.	He *might* have died of exposure, but we cannot be certain.
8. You might not show disrespect to your elders.	You *must* not show disrespect to your elders.
9. You may take exercise in order to maintain good health.	You *must* take exercise in order to maintain good health.
10. He must be a crook for all we know.	He *may* be a crook for all we know.

Common Errors in the Use of Adverbs

Incorrect	Correct
1. He is very much angry.	He is *very* angry.
2. She was very good enough to help me.	She was *good enough* to help me.
3. She runs much fast.	She runs *very* fast.
4. She runs very faster than Seema.	She runs *much* faster than Seema.
5. It is bitter cold today.	It is *bitterly* cold today.
6. He is a much learned man.	He is a very learned man.
7. She is thinking very hardly.	She is thinking very hard.
8. To tell in brief the film was boring.	*In short* the film was boring.
9. He told the story in details.	He told the story *in detail.*
10. I did it anyhow.	I *managed to do* it somehow.
11. Aeroplanes reach Europe soon.	Aeroplanes reach Europe quickly.
12. Before long there were dinosaurs on the earth.	*Long ago,* there were dinosaurs on the earth.
13. This book is too interesting.	This book is *very* interesting.
14. He lives miserly.	He lives in *a miserly* way.
15. Just I had gone when she came.	I had just gone when she came.
16. He sings good.	He sings *well.*
17. He sings good than I.	He sings *better* than I.
18. Really speaking it is cold.	*As a matter of fact* it is cold.
19. He is enough tall to reach the ceiling.	He is *tall enough* to reach the ceiling.
20. He went directly to his college.	He went *direct* to his college.

Common Errors in the Use of Conjunctions

Incorrect	Correct
1. As he is fat so he runs slowly.	As he is fat *he* runs slowly.
2. If he is fat then he will run slowly.	If he is fat, he will run slowly.
3. Though he is fat still he runs fast.	Though he is fat, *he runs* fast.
4. *As* I pulled the trigger at the sametime he shook my arm.	As I pulled the trigger, he shook my arm.

Incorrect	Correct
5. No sooner I had spoken than he left.	No sooner *had* I spoken than he left.
6. Not only he will go, but also he will stay there.	Not only *will he* go, but he *will also* stay there.
7. Neither he comes nor he writes.	Neither *does he* come nor *does he* write.
8. Scarcely he entered the room than the telephone rang.	Scarcely *had* he entered the room *when the* telephone rang.
9. Hardly she had left the house than it began to rain.	Hardly *had she* left the house *when* it began to rain.
10. He is the fastest runner and he comes last.	He is the fastest runner *but* he comes last.
11. She is as innocent as if she looks.	She is as innocent as she looks.
12. Until he does not try he must be punished.	He must be punished unless he tries.
13. I want to know as to why you are late.	I want to know why you are late.
14. I am fond of Chinese food as for example sweet and sour prawns.	I am fond of Chinese food, for example, sweet and sour prawns.
15. He was angry therefore I ran away.	He was angry so I ran away.
16. I was trying to work, at that time he was disturbing me.	While I was trying to work, he was disturbing me.
17. Supposing if he is late, what will happen?	Supposing he is late (or if he is late) what will happen?
18. He asked me that why I was late.	He asked me why I was late.
19. Let us catch a taxi lest we should not get late.	Let us catch a taxi lest we should get late.
20. She dresses herself like the teacher does.	She dresses herself as the teacher does.
21. Wait while I come.	Wait *until* (or *till)* I come.
22. Until, there is corruption in India, there can be little progress.	*As long* as there is corruption in India there can be little progress.
23. I have never told a lie nor cheated anybody.	I have never told a lie *nor have I* cheated anybody.
24. Both Mohan as well as Arun are responsible for this action.	Both Mohan *and* Arun are responsible for this action.
25. Hindus and Muslims both are to blame for the riots.	*Both Hindus* and Muslims are to blame for the riots.

Common Errors in the Use of Prepositions

Incorrect	Correct
1. I will not listen him.	I will not listen *to* him.
2. Copy this word by word.	Copy this word *for* word.
3. He enquired from her where she lived.	He enquired *of* her where she lived.
4. Sign here with ink.	Sign here *in* ink.
5. Has she come in train or by foot?	Has she come *by* train or *on* foot?
6. She said this at his face.	She said this *to* his face.
7. Open the book on page one.	Open the book *at* page one.
8. I was invited for lunch.	I was *invited to* lunch.
9. I am ill since three months.	I have been *ill for* three months.
10. This paper is inferior than that.	This paper is inferior *to* that.
11. This resembles to that.	This *resembles* that.
12. My brother is superior than you in strength.	My brother is superior *to* you in strength.
13. He wrote me.	He wrote *to* me.
14. I shall explain them this.	I shall explain this *to* them.
15. Send this letter on my address.	Send this letter *to* my address.
16. He suggested me this.	He suggested this *to* me.
17. He goes *on his* work.	He goes *to his* work.
18. He *reached to* Nagpur.	He *reached* Nagpur.
19. He told *to me* to go.	He told *me* to go.
20. The term begins *from* July 1st.	The term begins *on* July 1st.

Miscellaneous Errors

Incorrect	*Correct*
1. Many *homes* are lying vacant.	Many *houses* are lying vacant.
2. It is cool in the *shadow* of the tree.	It is cool in the *shade* of the tree.
3. She *keeps* good health.	She *enjoys* good health.
4. My leg is *paining*.	*I am feeling pain* in my leg.
5. *See* this word in the dictionary.	*Look up* this word in the dictionary.
6. The train will arrive *just now*.	The train will arrive *shortly*.
7. They are *pulling* on well.	They are *getting* on well.
8. The river has *over flown* its bank.	The river has *over flown* its banks.
9. He was appointed *on* the post.	He was appointed *to* the post.
10. Last but not *the least,* we have to discuss the problem of over population.	Last but not *least,* we have to discuss the problem of over population.
11. *Cities* after *cities* fell.	*City* after *city* fell.
12. What is the use Munir going there?	What is the use of Munir going there?
13. He *did many mischief.*	He *made much mischief.*
14. It is exact five *in* my watch.	It is exact five *by* my watch.
15. I will dine with them on *next Sunday.*	I will dine with them *Sunday next.*
16. Misfortunes when faced bravely and *manly* become less troublesome.	Misfortunes when faced bravely and *manfully* become less troublesome.
17. I am *laid down* with fever.	I am *laid up* with fever.
18. He is habituated to smoking.	He is *addicted* to smoking.
19. *According to my opinion* he is right.	*In my opinion* (or according *to me)* he is right.
20. Could you please *open* this knot?	Could you please *untie* this knot?

Multiple Choice Questions

Directions: *In this section, each sentence has three parts, indicated by (A), (B) and (C). Read each sentence to find out whether there is an error. If you find an error in any one of the parts (A, B, C), indicate your response by marking the letter related to that part. If a sentence has no error, indicate this by marking '(D)' which stands for "No error". Errors may belong to grammar, usage or idiom. Ignore errors of punctuation, if any.*

1. (A) Beware of/(B) a fair-weather friend/(C) who is neither a friend in need nor a friend indeed/(D) No error.

2. (A) Copernicus proved/(B) that Earth/(C) moves round the Sun./(D) No error.

3. (A) Seldom we have been treated/(B) in such a rude manner/(C) by the police personnel./(D) No error.

4. (A) Some men are born great,/(B) some achieve greatness/(C) and some had greatness thrust on them./(D) No error.

5. (A) The property/(B) was divided/(C) among the two brothers./(D) No error.

6. (A) I am quite certain/(B) that the lady is not only greedy/(C) but miserly./(D) No error.

7. (A) The aircraft overloaded/(B) there was something wrong of the battery/(C) and the engine was making a queer noise/(D) No error.

8. (A) A thorough inquiry of the misappropriation of funds/(B) is now imperative/(C) to bring the guilty to book/(D) No error.

9. (A) The brilliant success in the examination/(B) as well as his record in sports/(C) deserves high praise/(D) No error.

10. (A) While travelling by a train/(B) on a cold winter night/(C) an argument rose between two passengers in our compartment/(D) No error.

11. (A) I cannot find/(B) where has he gone/(C) though I have tried may best/(D) No error.

12. (A) If I was/(B) the Prime Minister of India/(C) I would work wonders/(D) No error.

13. (A) Amit's severe bout of flu/(B) debilitated him so much/(C) that he was too tired to do for work for a week./(D) No error.

14. (A) This is the crux of the entire problem;/(B) everything centres on/(C) it being resolved./(D) No error.

15. (A) One of the major aims of the Air Force/(B) was the complete demolition of all means of transportation/ (C) by the bombing of rail lines and terminals./(D) No error.

16. (A) His strong voice cut over/(B) the hum of conversation/(C) like a knife through butter./(D) No error.

17. (A) Even though they weren't expecting us/(B) they managed to knock up/(C) a marvellous meal./(D) No error.

18. (A) The celebrated singer was/(B) surrounded by the usual crowd/(C) of lackeys and hangerons./(D) No error.

19. (A) If it weren't/(B) for you,/(C) I wouldn't be alive today./(D) No error.

20. (A) He looked like a lion/(B) baulked from/(C) its prey./(D) No error.

21. (A) Widespread flooding/(B) is effecting/(C) large areas of the villages./(D) No error.

22. (A) She regards/(B) negotiating prices with customers/ (C) as her special preserve./(D) No error.

23. (A) Often in political campaigns, a point is reached at which/(B) the candidates take out their gloves./(C) and start slugging with bare fists./(D) No error.

24. (A) If we really set to/(B) we can get the whole house/ (C) cleaned in an afternoon./(D) No error.

25. (A) Pieces of rock plummeted/(B) down the mountainside/(C) in the ground below./(D) No error.

26. (A) Since the two parties each won/(B) the same number of seats,/(C) the minority party holds the balance of power./(D) No error.

27. (A) It's arrogant for you/(B) to assume you'll/(C)win every time./(D) No error.

28. (A) We've paid for our travel and accommod-ation,/ (B) so we need only to take/(C) some pocket-money with us./(D) No error.

29. (A) There's no evidence to show/(B) that information technology secrets are more/(C) vulnerable in India than Britain or the US./(D) No error.

30. (A) It is shameful that hunting/(B) is still considered sport/(C) by some unscrupulous people in the civilized world./(D) No error.

31. (A) The Prime Minister's good looks won him/(B)the election but he has still to prove/(C) that he's not a just pretty face./(D) No error.

32. (A) The two books are the same/(B) except for the fact that this/(C) has an answer in the back./(D) No error.

33. (A) He estimated his income tax bill/(B) by extrapolation over figures/(C) submitted in previous years./(D) No error.

34. (A) The modern office block/(B) sticks out like a sore thumb/(C) among the old buildings in the area./(D) No error.

35. (A) I will try to put over/(B) some feelers to gauge/ (C) people's reactions to our proposal./(D) No error.

36. (A) A major contribution of Mathura sculptors/(B)of that period were the creation and popularization/(C) of the Buddha's image in human form./(D) No error.

37. (A) Amit has been deceiving Mona/(B) for many years but she/(C) has not still tumbled to it./(D) No error.

38. (A) Mahavira was an advocate of nonviolence and vegetarianism,/(B) who revived and reorganized the Jain doctrine/(C) and established rules for their monastic order. (D) No error.

39. (A) Microwaves are the principle carriers/(B) of television, telephone and data transmissions/ (C)between stations on earth and between the earth and satellites./(D) No error.

40. (A) An unit is an abstract idea,/(B) defined either by reference to/(C) a randomly chosen material standard or to a natural phenomenon./(D) No error.

41. (A) With the crisis deepening,/(B) the critics sense an opportunity/(C) about putting in place a more radical strategy./(D) No error.

42. (A) The salesman gave us/(B) a big spiel about why/ (C) we should buy his product./(D) No error.

43. (A) I will need several weeks/(B) to invent the lie of the land before/(C) I can make any decision about the future of the business./(D) No error.

44. (A) You should be cautious/(B) and make a few discrete enquiries about/(C) the firm before you sign anything./ (D) No error.

45. (A) Your husband doesn't/(B) believe that you are older/(C) than I./(D) No error.

46. (A) We are meeting today afternoon/(B) to discuss the matter/(C) and reach a compromise./(D) No error.

47. (A) Either Ram or/(B) you is responsible/(C) for this action./(D) No error.

48. (A) The student flatly denied/(B) that he had copied/(C) in the examination hall./(D) No error.

49. (A) By the time you arrive tomorrow/(B) I have finished/(C) my work./(D) No error.

50. (A) The speaker stressed repeatedly on/(B) the importance of improving/(C) the condition of the slums./(D) No error.

51. (A) The captain with the members of his team/(B) are returning/(C) after a fortnight./(D) No error.

52. (A) After returning from/(B) an all-India tour/(C) I had to describe about it/(D) No error.

53. (A) The teacher asked his students/(B) if they had gone through/(C) either of the three chapters included in the prescribed text./(D) No error.

54. (A) Although they are living in the country/(B) since they were married/(C) they are now moving to the town./(D) No error.

55. (A) Do you know/(B) how old were you/(C) when you came here?/(D) No error.

ANSWERS

1	2	3	4	5	6	7	8	9	10
D	B	A	C	C	C	B	A	D	C
11	12	13	14	15	16	17	18	19	20
B	A	C	C	B	A	A	C	C	C
21	22	23	24	25	26	27	28	29	30
C	A	A	A	C	A	A	B	D	B
31	32	33	34	35	36	37	38	39	40
C	C	C	D	A	B	C	C	A	A
41	42	43	44	45	46	47	48	49	50
C	D	D	D	C	A	B	D	B	A
51	52	53	54	55					
B	C	C	B	D					

Articles

Definite and Indefinite Articles

(*i*) 'A' and 'an' are Indefinite Articles.

(*ii*) 'The' is Definite Article.

(*iii*) 'A' and 'an' modify a noun in a general way.

(*iv*) 'The' particularises it. *e.g.*,

Mohan has **a pen.**

The pen which you gave me was expensive.

Vowel and Consonant Sounds

(*i*) 'A' is used before words starting with the sound of a consonant.

(*ii*) 'An' is used before a vowel sound (vowels a, e, i, o, u) *e.g.*,

a book, a cat, a useful thing, a European girl, a university,

but an FDR, an MA, an honest boy, an hour, an owl, an egg, an umbrella, etc.

Use of Articles 'A' and 'An'

A cat mews. (*i.e.,* every cat)

The cat of my neighbour mews day and night. (*i.e.,* a particular cat)

He gave me **an** egg. (Here 'an' means 'one')

Use of Article 'The'

1. 'The' is used before names of rivers, mountains, seas, oceans:

   The Himalayas, the Ganga, the Yamuna, the Bay of Bengal, the Indian Ocean, the Nile, the English Channel, *etc.*
2. Names of newspapers and magazines:

   The Times of India, the Tribune, The Sun, *etc.*
3. Names of the famous and holy books:
   The Guru Granth Sahib, The Gita, The Ramayana, *etc.*
4. Names of creations of nature:
   the sun, the earth, the moon, the sky, *etc.*
5. While using Adjectives as Nouns:
   The poor should be helped by **the rich.**
6. Sometimes with the Comparative Degree:
   The more you think, **the more** you worry.
7. With the Superlative Degree:
   She is **the most intelligent** girl in our school.
8. Before the imaginary lines and directions:
   The Latitude, The Equator, the east, the west, etc.
9. Before the names of musical instruments:
   the violin, the piano, the flute, etc.
10. While using a Proper Noun as a Common Noun:
    Mohan is **the Sachin** of our team.

Omission of Article 'The'

1. Before some Nouns used to convey general sense, articles are not used but are used to particularise them:
   Man is mortal.
2. Before Proper Nouns:
   Rakesh is an intelligent boy.
3. With Abstract Noun:
   Childhood is the prime time of one's life.
   The childhood of Sohan was full of sorrow.
4. With Material Nouns:
   Milk is an essential food.
   The milk of the cow is sweet.
5. Usually no article is used before names of diseases:
   Cancer is a fatal disease.
   However, when we talk about a disease figuratively, we use an article before its name, *e.g.*
   Corruption is a cancer.
6. Names of games and language:
   I like football.
   I can speak Punjabi, Hindi and English.
7. Gold is a precious metal.

   NOTE: As you must have noted above, the definite article 'the' has been used where a noun is particularised.

Double Use of Article 'The'

Read the following sentences carefully to understand this :

1. The poet and novelist has been honoured.
   (The same person is the poet as well as novelist)
2. The poet and the novelist have been honoured.
   (The poet and the novelist are two different persons).
3. I have a black and white dog.
   (that is, one dog)
4. I have a black and a white dog.
   (that is, two dogs)

Multiple Choice Questions

Directions : *Fill in the blanks with suitable articles. Mark 'D' if no article required.*

1. Do you know .... boy in white?
A. a B. an C. the D. No article

2. She is .... girl I am looking for.
A. a B. an C. the D. No article

3. Have you read .... Mahabharat?
A. a B. an C. the D. No article

4. ....rich are not always happy.
A. A B. An C. The D. No article

5. Oranges are sold by .... dozen.
A. a B. an C. the D. No article

6. Milk is sold by .... litre.
A. a B. an C. the D. No article

7. .... Amazon is the longest river in the world.
A. A B. An C. The D. No article

8. .... higher you climb, the colder it gets.
A. A B. An C. The D. No article

9. She is .... untidy girl.
A. a B. an C. the D. No article

10. I am .... M.A. is English.
A. a B. an C. the D. No article

11. I have already spent .... few rupees I had.
A. a B. an C. the D. No article

12. .... English are very hard-working.
A. A B. An C. The D. No article

13. April is the fourth month of .... year.
A. a B. an C. the D. No article

14. Rice is sold by .... kilogram
A. a B. an C. the D. No article

15. She is .... best of the three girls.
A. a B. an C. the D. No article

16. .... man in the car is a friend of mine.
A. A B. An C. The D. No article

17. Brevity is .... soul of wit.
A. a B. an C. the D. No article

18. .... thing of beauty is a joy for ever.
A. A B. An C. The D. No article

19. .... little learning is a dangerous thing.
A. A B. An C. The D. No article

20. .... best sauce for food is hunger.
A. A B. An C. The D. No article

21. Birds of .... feather flock together.
A. a B. an C. the D. No article

22. He makes .... living by begging.
A. a B. an C. the D. No article

23. It is .... pity that he died so young.
A. a B. an C. the D. No article

24. What .... nuisance it is?
A. a B. an C. the D. No article

25. Delhi is .... London of India.
A. a B. an C. the D. No article

26. Where is .... will, there is a way.
A. a B. an
C. the D. No article

27. Her father is .... physician and surgeon.
A. a B. an
C. the D. No article

28. This will benefit .... poor.
A. a B. an
C. the D. No article

29. ....bird in hand is better than two in a bush.
A. A B. An
C. The D. No article

30. As he is hard-working, he will win .... prize.
A. a B. an
C. the D. No article

31. .... water of this well is dirty.
A. A B. An
C. The D. No article

32. Only .... wearer knows where the shoe pinches.
A. a B. an
C. the D. No article

33. .... action will be taken against you.
A. A B. An
C. The D. No article

34. .... sun rises in the east.
A. A B. An
C. The D. No article

35. She was promoted to .... highest post.
A. a B. an
C. the D. No article

36. Did you see .... Taj Mahal?
A. a B. an
C. the D. No article

37. He is .... one-eyed man.
A. a B. an
C. the D. No article

38. This is .... useful book.
A. a B. an
C. the D. No article

39. Cloth is sold by .... metre.
A. a B. an
C. the D. No article

40. The sun sets in .... west.
A. a B. an
C. the D. No article

41. Amar bought......umbrella yesterday.
A. a B. an
C. the D. No article

42. Surinder is ...... honest boy.
A. a B. an
C. the D. No article

43. She wrote ...... book in French.
A. a B. an
C. the D. No article

44. ...... lion roars.
A. A B. An
C. The D. No article

45. ..... apple a day keeps the doctor away.
A. A B. An
C. The D. No article

46. John bought ...... car yesterday.
A. a B. an
C. the D. No article

47. His father is ..... engineer in the U.S.A.
A. a B. an
C. the D. No article

48. It is hard for ..... owl to fly during the day times.
A. a B. an
C. the D. No article

49. She had ..... rimmed hat.
A. a B. an
C. the D. No article

50. My uncle is ..... heart specialist.
A. a B. an
C. the D. No article

51. He looks as foolish as .... ass.
A. a B. an
C. the D. No article

52. Did you go to .... prison to visit him?
A. a B. an
C. the D. No article

53. I found .... one-rupee note in the market.
A. a B. an
C. the D. No article

54. It is a pleasure to meet such .... efficient man.
A. a B. an
C. the D. No article

55. The Sanyasi lived in a cave in .... Himalayas.
A. a B. an
C. the D. No article

56. There is .... union in our factory.
A. a B. an
C. the D. No article

57. He hit his wife on the head with .... umbrella.

A. a B. an

C. the D. No article

58. I caught him by .... collar.

A. a B. an

C. the D. No article

59. Child is .... father of man.

A. a B. an

C. the D. No article

60. He gazed at .... moon for two hours.

A. a B. an

C. the D. No article

ANSWERS

1	2	3	4	5	6	7	8	9	10
C	C	C	C	C	C	C	C	B	B
11	**12**	**13**	**14**	**15**	**16**	**17**	**18**	**19**	**20**
C	C	C	C	C	C	C	A	A	C
21	**22**	**23**	**24**	**25**	**26**	**27**	**28**	**29**	**30**
A	A	A	A	C	A	A	C	A	A
31	**32**	**33**	**34**	**35**	**36**	**37**	**38**	**39**	**40**
C	C	B	C	C	C	A	A	C	C
41	**42**	**43**	**44**	**45**	**46**	**47**	**48**	**49**	**50**
B	B	A	A	B	A	B	B	A	A
51	**52**	**53**	**54**	**55**	**56**	**57**	**58**	**59**	**60**
B	C	A	B	C	A	B	C	C	C

Prepositions

A Preposition is a word that comes before a Pronoun or a Noun and expresses the relationship between Noun or Pronoun and some part of the remaining sentence.

(*a*) He is busy **with** his work.
(*b*) The boy jumped **into** the river.
(*c*) The birds are chirping **in** the trees.

In these sentences the words **with, into** and **in** show the relationship between the verbs **busy, jumped** and **chirping** with the nouns **work, river** and **trees** respectively.

Position of the Preposition

A. A Preposition usually precedes its object.

(*i*) He laughs **at** the poor.
(*ii*) He is angry **with** you.
(*iii*) She agrees **with** me.

B. In the case of Relative Pronouns it comes after the subject.

(*i*) This is the boy whom I was looking **for**.
(*ii*) That is the pen whose mention I was making **of**.

C. In the following cases, the Preposition comes after its object.

(*i*) Where is the boy you were complaining **against**?
(*ii*) What things are there you are looking **for**?
(*iii*) Who is there, you are waiting **for**?

Omission of the Prepositon

In many cases when the sentences contain Nouns of Time or Place, the Prepositions **from, in** and **for** are often omitted.

(*i*) He walked many kilometres.
(*ii*) He came to see me last year.
(*iii*) As I could not find my puppy anywhere, I looked here and there.

Prepositions are small words that show the relationship between one word and another. Prepositions in the following sentences show the position of the paper in relation to the desk, the book, hand and the door.

The paper is **on** the desk.
The paper is **under** the book.
The paper is **in** his hand.
The paper is **by** the door.

Common Prepositions

about	at	by
in	onto	toward
above	before	concerning
inside	out	under
across	behind	despite
into	over	until
after	below	down
like	since	up
against	beneath	during
near	through	upon
along	beside	except
of	throughout	with
amid	between	for
off	till	within
among	beyond	from
on	to	without

Multiple Choice Questions

Directions: *Select the most appropriate preposition from the given alternatives to fill in the blanks and make the sentence meaningfully complete.*

1. Don't try to be an advocate ..... these criminals.
A. for B. with
C. across D. in

2. The audience admired him ..... his sweet voice.
A. to B. on
C. for D. at

3. I want to check your bag ..... fake currency notes.
A. to B. for
C. upon D. on

4. The dew drops clung .... the blades of grass.
A. for B. on
C. to D. in

5. The thief was chased ..... by the police.
A. on B. after
C. into D. at

6. Please carry this bag ..... my room.
A. on B. for
C. to D. in

7. A lorry bumped ..... a car.
A. on B. over
C. into D. to

8. They were begging ..... food.
A. for B. on
C. to D. after

9. She always boasts ..... her wealth.
A. of B. for
C. on D. after

10. She banged ..... the door violently.
A. for B. to
C. on D. down

11. I applied ..... the post of a clerk.
A. for B. on
C. in D. to

12. I applied ..... the Principal for the post of a teacher.
A. to B. on
C. with D. for

13. I begged ..... him not to divulge the secret.
A. for B. of
C. with D. to

14. You had better borrow a pen ..... Rakesh.
A. over B. into
C. from D. by

15. I baked a cake ..... the guests.
A. to B. for
C. on D. of

16. She is confident ..... (her) success.
A. with B. on
C. of D. for

17. The doctor will cure you ..... malaria.
A. of B. with
C. for D. from

18. This law is common ..... all.
A. to B. upon
C. over D. at

19. She was condemned ..... her bad hand writing.
A. on B. for
C. into D. of

20. In summer there will be a great demand ..... desert cooler.
A. on B. with
C. for D. of

21. We shall wait ..... you.
A. on B. for
C. towards D. after

22. Tom displayed his injury ..... all his friends.
A. for B. upon
C. to D. at

23. She distributed the sweets ..... the two brothers.
A. among B. between
C. for D. in

24. Please distribute these apples ..... all.
A. among B. to
C. for D. at

25. It rarely happened that he defended ..... an innocent person.
A. against B. for
C. upon D. at

26. The parents were disappointed ..... the performance of their son.
A. on B. with
C. at D. of

27. Common salt dissolves ..... water.
A. for B. in
C. with D. by

28. This medicare is free ..... sugar.
A. on B. to
C. from D. of

29. The manager granted leave ..... the clerk.
A. to B. on
C. into D. for

30. The air was heavy ..... aroma of perfumes.
A. on B. with
C. into D. from

31. She had a quick glance ..... the magazine.
A. at B. from
C. into D. to

32. The climate of Kashmir is favourable ..... me.
A. with B. in
C. to D. for

33. They hate you ..... your poverty.
A. for B. on
C. in D. of

34. He is eligible ..... this post.
A. for B. to
C. with D. at

35. The smoke was emerging ..... down the foot of the hill.
A. on B. to
C. from D. at

36. The criminal managed to escape ..... the prison.
A. upon B. from
C. with D. of

37. You should educate your friends ..... the benefits of living in villages.
A. on B. towards
C. upon D. in

38. She made a lot of efforts ..... win the match.
A. for B. to
C. upon D. at

39. The new inspector will enquire ..... the murder case.
A. on B. for
C. into D. at

40. The retired soldiers were exempted ..... all taxes.
A. from B. to
C. on D. of

41. She was adept ..... journalism.
A. at B. on
C. with D. in

42. She is afraid ..... snakes.
A. on B. to
C. of D. with

43. I agree ..... your proposal.
A. for B. on
C. to D. with

44. The children were amazed ..... so big a python.
A. at B. on
C. in D. with

45. She was anxious ..... the final match.
A. about B. on
C. with D. for

46. He apologized ..... his being late.
A. towards B. for
C. on D. as

47. The children were amused ..... his jokes.
A. for B. to
C. at D. on

48. She is angry ..... you.
A. to B. with
C. on D. for

49. She is angry ..... your teasing remark.
A. at B. in
C. for D. with

50. A big patch of land was allocated ..... the refugees.
A. to B. for
C. in D. upon

ANSWERS

1	2	3	4	5	6	7	8	9	10
A	C	B	C	B	C	C	A	A	C
11	**12**	**13**	**14**	**15**	**16**	**17**	**18**	**19**	**20**
A	A	B	C	B	C	A	A	B	C
21	**22**	**23**	**24**	**25**	**26**	**27**	**28**	**29**	**30**
B	C	B	A	A	C	B	C	A	B
31	**32**	**33**	**34**	**35**	**36**	**37**	**38**	**39**	**40**
A	C	A	A	C	B	A	B	C	A
41	**42**	**43**	**44**	**45**	**46**	**47**	**48**	**49**	**50**
A	C	C	A	A	B	C	B	A	A

Synonyms & Antonyms

There are thousands of words in English language. No one can remember their meanings easily but with regular practice one can memorise most of them. A number of words with their Synonyms and Antonyms are compiled here. Try to learn as many as you can and answer the questions thereafter.

Words	*Synonyms*	*Antonyms*
Abandon	Cease, Forsake	Continue
Abhor	Hate, Loathe, Detest	Like, Love
Abiding	Enduring, Durable	Fleeting
Able	Proficient, Competent	Incompetent, Unfit
Ability	Skill, Power	Disability, Inability
Abortive	Fruitless, Futile	Fruitful, Successful
Abolish	Destroy, Undo	Restore, Revive
Abridge	Shorten, Curtail	Lengthen, Expand
Absolve	Forgive, Pardon, Excuse	Condemn
Accelerate	Hasten	Retard
Accord	Agreement, Harmony	Discord, Disagreement
Accumulate	Collect, Store, Amass	Distribute, Scatter
Adamant	Hard, Inflexible	Flexible
Adversity	Misfortune, Distress	Prosperity
Adept	Expert, Skilful	Inexpert, Unskillful
Aggravate	Heighten, Intensify	Quell, Suppress
Agile	Nimble	Clumsy, Undeft
Alert	Vigilant	Heedless
Allay	Calm, Soothe, Assuage	Arouse
Ameliorate	Improve, Advance, Amend	Worsen, Deteriorate
Ambiguous	Vague, Unclear	Clear
Amiable	Lovable, Agreeable	Disagreeable
Annihilate	Destroy	Create
Arduous	Hard, Strenuous	Easy
Attacks	Assault	Defend
Audacity	Boldness	Cowardice
Auspicious	Favourable, Propitious, Lucky	Ominous, Inauspicious, Unlucky
Austere	Harsh, Severe, Rigorous	Easy-going
Authentic	True, Genuine	Spurious, False
Avarice	Greed	Generosity
Averse	Unwilling, Loath, Disinclined	Willing, Inclined

Words	Synonyms	Antonyms
Aversion	Hostility, Hatred	Affinity, Liking
Base	Low, Mean, Ignoble	Noble, Exalted
Boisterous	Noisy, Stormy	Calm, Quiet
Brave	Courageous, Daring, Bold, Plucky	Cowardly, Dastardly, Timid
Brief	Short, Concise, Laconic	Lengthy, Diffuse
Bright	Vivid, Radiant	Dull, Dark
Brutal	Savage, Cruel	Humane, Kindly
Callous	Hard, Cruel, Indifferent	Soft, Tender, Concerned
Cautious	Careful, Wary	Rash, Reckless, Foolhardy
Censure (*n*)	Blame, Condemnation	Praise
Censure (*vb*)	Blame, Condemn	Praise, Commend
Circumscribed	Restricted, Confined, Limited	Unconfined, Unrestricted
Civil	Polite, Courteous, Gracious, Urbane	Rude, Uncivil, Impolite, Ungracious
Coerce	Compel, Force	Volunteer
Compassionate	Pitiful, Sympathetic, Merciful	Unsympathetic, Merciless, Cruel
Compress	Condense, Abbreviate	Expand, Lengthen
Conspicuous	Noticeable, Manifest	Inconspicuous
Constant	Steady, Steadfast, Uniform	Inconstant, Variable
Cordial	Friendly, Warm, Hearty	Cold, Unfriendly
Covert	Hidden, Secret	Overt, Open
Cruel	Savage, Ruthless, Vicious	Kind, Gentle, Benevolent
Cursory	Rapid, Superficial	Thorough, Exhaustive, Intensive
Credible	Believable, Probable, Plausible	Incredible, Unbelievable, Fantastic
Crafty	Cunning, Sly	Artless, Simple, Ingenuous
Costly	Expensive, Dear	Cheap, Inexpensive
Confidence	Trust, Reliance	Distrust, Doubt
Death	Decease, Demise	Existence, Life
Dearth	Scarcity, Lack, Want, Paucity, Shortage	Plenty, Abundance
Decay	Dissolution, Decline, Decomposition, Disintegration	Regeneration
Deference	Respect, Reverence	Disrespect, Irreverence
Deficient	Lacking, Inadequate	Complete, Sufficient
Desolate	Lonely, Deserted	Crowded, Occupied
Destitute	Wanting, Needy	Rich, Affluent
Diligence	Industry, Perseverance	Idleness
Disgrace	Dishonour, Discredit	Honour, Credit
Dwindle	Decrease, Shrink	Grow, Increase
Earthly	Terrestrial, Mundane	Celestial, Heavenly, Unearthly
Eligible	Qualified, Suitable	Ineligible, Unsuitable
Emancipate	Liberate, Free	Enslave
Excited	Impassioned, Stimulated	Composed, Cool, Impassive
Extraordinary	Uncommon, Remarkable, Marvellous	Commonplace, Ordinary
Extravagant	Lavish, Prodigal, Wastrel, Spendthrift	Thrifty, Economical, Frugal
Fabricate	Construct, Make	Destroy
Fabulous	Fictitious, Mythical	Actual, Real
False	Untrue, Mendacious	True, Genuine

Words	Synonyms	Antonyms
Famous	Well-known, Renowned	Obscure, Unknown
Fantastic	Fanciful, Imaginative, Visionary	Practical, Down to earth
Fearful	Nervous, Anxious, Afraid, Scared	Fearless, Dauntless
Felicity	Happiness	Sorrow
Gaiety	Joyousness, Hilarity	Mourning, Dullness
Garrulous	Talkative, Loquacious	Taciturn, Silent, Reserved
Generous	Liberal, Magnanimous	Stingy, Miserly
Gigantic	Huge, Colossal	Minute, Small
Graphic	Vivid, Pictorial, Meaningful	Vague
Guest	Visitor	Host
Guile	Fraud, Trickery	Artlessness, Ingenuousness
Gratitude	Gratefulness	Ingratitude, Ungratefulness
Gratuitous	Voluntary, Spontaneous, Unwarranted	Involuntary, Forced
Hamper	Hinder, Obstruct	Facilitate, Ease
Haughty	Arrogant, Proud	Humble, Modest
Hazardous	Dangerous, Perilous	Safe, Secure Protected
Headstrong	Obstinate, Stubborn	Weak-willed, Flexible
Hope	Belief, Conviction, Expectation	Despair, Hopelessness
Improvident	Prodigal, Carelessness	Provident, Economical
Incessant	Unceasing, Continuous	Discontinuous
Indolent	Slothful, Lethargic	Active, Energetic
Joy	Delight, Pleasure	Sadness, Gloom
Jolly	Jovial, Merry	Gloomy, Sad
Judicious	Discreet, Prudent	Indiscreet, Injudicious
Knowledge	Enlightenment, Learning	Ignorance, Stupidity
Laborious	Industrious, Assiduous	Slothful, Lazy
Laxity	Slackness, Looseness	Firmness
Lenient	Mild, Forbearing	Strict, Stern
Lethal	Deadly, Fatal, Mortal	Life-giving, Vital, Vivifying
Liberal	Generous, Tolerant	Intolerant, Illiberal
Liberty	Freedom, Independence	Slavery, Bondage
Lively	Animated, Active	Dull, Listless
Loyal	Faithful, Devoted	Treacherous, Disloyal, Unfaithful
Lucky	Fortunate	Unlucky, Unfortunate
Lucrative	Profitable	Unprofitable
Magnanimous	Generous, Largehearted	Ungenerous, Stingy
Malady	Illness, Ailment	Health
Manifest	Noticeable, Obvious	Obscure, Puzzling
Meagre	Small	Plentiful, Large
Mean	Low, Abject	Noble, Exalted
Mendacious	False, Untruthful	Truthful
Misery	Sorrow, Distress	Happiness, Joy
Morbid	Sick, Diseased	Healthy
Mournful	Sorrowful, Sad	Joyful, Happy

Words	*Synonyms*	*Antonyms*
Negligent	Careless, Heedless	Careful
Notorious	Infamous, Disreputable	Reputable
Obedient	Submissive, Compliant, Docile	Disobedient, Recalcitrant, Wayward
Obsolete	Antiquated, Out-of-Date	Current, Modern
Opportune	Timely, Seasonable	Inopportune
Opulence	Wealth, Riches	Penury, Poverty
Onerous	Heavy, Burdensome	Light, Easy
Palatable	Tasty, Delicious	Unpalatable
Pathetic	Touching	Joyous, Cheery
Persuade	Urge, Induce	Dissuade
Praise (*vb*)	Applaud, Eulogise	Condemn
Praise (*n*)	Applause, Eulogy	Condemnation
Precarious	Risky, Uncertain	Safe, Certain
Pretence	Pretext, Excuse	Candour, Frankness
Propagate	Breed, Circulate	Terminate, Restrict
Quaint	Odd, Singular	Usual, Ordinary
Quell	Suppress, Subdue	Agitate, Arouse
Rare	Uncommon, Scarce	Common, Ordinary
Refined	Polished, Elegant	Crude, Coarse
Remote	Distant	Near, Close
Renown	Fame, Reputation	Infamy, Notoriety
Rigid	Stiff, Unyielding	Flexible, Yielding
Remorseful	Regretful, Repentant	Unrepentant
Rebellion	Revolt, Mutiny, Insurgency	Loyalty
Scared	Holy, Consecrated	Profane, Unholy
Sane	Sensible, Sound	Insane
Scold	Chide, Rebuke	Praise
Serious	Grave, Earnest	Frivolous
Shy	Bashful	Bold, Impudent
Simple	Plain, Artless	Complex, Cunning, Shrewd
Solitary	Single, Lonely, Secluded	Numerous, Multitude
Shallow	Superficial	Deep
Solace	Comfort, Relief	Discomfort, Grief
Spurious	Sham, False	Genuine, Authentic
Stagnant	Still, Motionless	Moving
Surplus	Excess	Deficit, Shortage
Tame	Gentle, Mild, Domesticated	Savage, Wild
Teacher	Instructor, Educator	Student, Pupil
Tedious	Wearisome, Monotonous	Agreeable, Lively
Temporal	Worldly, Secular	Spiritual
Temperate	Moderate	Immoderate, Intemperate
Tortuous	Winding, Circuitous	Straight, Direct
Tough	Hard, Strong	Tender, Soft, Flexible
Transient	Temporary, Fleeting	Lasting, Durable, Permanent

Words	Synonyms	Antonyms
Truswortby	Reliable	Unreliable, Untrustworthy
Tranquil	Calm	Agitated
Ugly	Unsightly, Repulsive	Beautiful, Attractive
Useful	Advantageous, Serviceable	Useless
Vehemence	Passion, Force	Apathy, Indifference
Vindictive	Revengeful	Forgiving
Wholesome	Healthy	Unwholesome, Morbid, Unhealthy, Diseased
Wicked	Evil, Impious	Pious, Good
Wise	Sagacious, Erudite	Foolish, Stupid
Wrath	Anger, Fury, Rage	Love, Peace, Calm
Wreck	Ruin, Destroy	Create, Construct
Yield	Surrender, Submit	Resist, Revolt
Yielding	Submissive, Supple	Inflexible, Intractable
Yoke	Oppression, Bondage	Freedom
Zeal	Passion, Fervour	Apathy, Indifference
Zest	Relish, Enthusiasm	Distaste, Disrelish

Multiple Choice Questions

Directions (Qs. 1 to 50): *In the following questions choose the word which best expresses the MEANING of the given word.*

1. TEPID
   A. Hot B. Warm
   C. Cold D. Boiling
2. MAYHEM
   A. Jubilation B. Havoc
   C. Excitement D. Defeat
3. TIMID
   A. Fast B. Slow
   C. Medium D. Shy
4. CANTANKEROUS
   A. Quarrelsome B. Rash
   C. Disrespectful D. Noisy
5. PRECARIOUS
   A. Cautious B. Critical
   C. Perilous D. Brittle
6. TACITURNITY
   A. Dumbness B. Changeableness
   C. Hesitation D. Reserve
7. INEBRIATE
   A. Dreamy B. Stupefied
   C. Unsteady D. Drunken
8. HARBINGER
   A. Massenger B. Steward
   C. Forerunner D. Pilot
9. INTIMIDATE
   A. To hint B. Frighten
   C. Bluff D. Harass
10. IRONIC
    A. Inflexible B. Bitter
    C. Good-natured D. Disguisedly sarcastic
11. STRINGENT
    A. Tense B. Stringy
    C. Strict D. Causing to shrink
12. ECSTATIC
    A. Animated B. Bewildered
    C. Enraptured D. Willful
13. COMMENSURATE
    A. Measurable B. Proportionate
    C. Beginning D. Appropriate
14. DESTITUTION
    A. Humility B. Moderation
    C. Poverty D. Beggary
15. ASCEND
    A. Leap B. Grow
    C. Deviate D. Mount
16. UNCOUTH
    A. Ungraceful B. Rough
    C. Slovenly D. Dirty
17. LYNCH
    A. Hang B. Madden
    C. Killed D. Shoot

18. LAUD
A. Lord B. Eulogy
C. Praise D. Extolled

19. CORRESPONDENCE
A. Agreements B. Contracts
C. Documents D. Letters

20. VENUE
A. Place B. Agenda
C. Time D. Duration

21. STERILE
A. Barren B. Arid
C. Childless D. Dry

22. SYNOPSIS
A. Index B. Mixture
C. Summary D. Puzzle

23. GERMANE
A. Responsible B. Logical
C. Possible D. Relevant

24. PONDER
A. Think B. Evaluate
C. Anticipate D. Increase

25. CANNY
A. Obstinate B. Handsome
C. Clever D. Stout

26. ABUNDANT
A. Ripe B. Cheap
C. Plenty D. Absent

27. CONSEQUENCES
A. Results B. Conclusions
C. Difficulties D. Applications

28. SHIVER
A. Shake B. Rock
C. Tremble D. Move

29. DILIGENT
A. Progressive B. Brilliant
C. Inventive D. Hard-working

30. DISTANT
A. Far B. Removed
C. Reserved D. Separate

31. FORAY
A. Excursion B. Contest
C. Ranger D. Intuition

32. FRUGALITY
A. Foolishness B. Extremity
C. Enthusiasm D. Economy

33. GARNISH
A. Paint B. Garner
C. Adorn D. Abuse

34. VIGOUR
A. Strength B. Boldness
C. Warmth D. Enthusiasm

35. CANDID
A. Apparent B. Explicit
C. Frank D. Bright

36. BRIEF
A. Limited B. Small
C. Little D. Short

37. GARRULITY
A. Credulity B. Senility
C. Loquaciousness D. Speciousness

38. FURORE
A. Excitement B. Worry
C. Flux D. Anteroom

39. NEUTRAL
A. Unbiased B. Non-aligned
C. Undecided D. Indifferent

40. LAMENT
A. Complain B. Comment
C. Condone D. Console

41. ADVERSITY
A. Failure B. Helplessness
C. Misfortune D. Crisis

42. TURN UP
A. Land up B. Show up
C. Crop up D. Come up

43. DEIFY
A. Flatter B. Challenge
C. Worship D. Face

44. ERROR
A. Misadventure B. Misgiving
C. Ambiguity D. Blunder

45. SHALLOW
A. Artificial B. Superficial
C. Foolish D. Worthless

46. MASSACRE
A. Murder B. Stab
C. Assassinate D. Slaughter

47. COMBAT
A. Conflict B. Quarrel
C. Feud D. Fight

48. VORACIOUS
A. Wild B. Hungry
C. Angry D. Quick

49. IMPROMPTU
A. Offhand B. Unimportant
C. Unreal D. Effective

50. RABBLE
A. Mob B. Noise
C. Roar D. Rubbish

Directions (Qs. 51 to 100): *In the following questions choose the word which is the exact OPPOSITE of the given words.*

51. STRINGENT
A. General B. Vehement
C. Lenient D. Magnanimous

52. FLIMSY
A. Frail B. Filthy
C. Firm D. Flippant

53. BUSY
A. Occupied B. Engrossed
C. Relaxed D. Engaged

54. ADAPTABLE
A. Adoptable B. Flexible
C. Yielding D. Rigid

55. LOVE
A. Villainy B. Hatred
C. Compulsion D. Force

56. BALANCE
A. Disbalance B. Misbalance
C. Debalance D. Imbalance

57. RELINQUISH
A. Abdicate B. Renounce
C. Possess D. Deny

58. MOUNTAIN
A. Plain B. Plateau
C. Precipice D. Valley

59. FICKLE
A. Courageous B. Sincere
C. Steadfast D. Humble

60. PERENNIAL
A. Frequent B. Regular
C. Lasting D. Rare

61. RARELY
A. Hardly B. Definitely
C. Frequently D. Periodically

62. STARTLED
A. Amused B. Relaxed
C. Endless D. Astonished

63. ADHERENT
A. Detractor B. Enemy
C. Alien D. Rival

64. QUIESCENT
A. Indifferent B. Troublesome
C. Weak D. Unconcerned

65. CONDENSE
A. Expand B. Distribute
C. Interpret D. Lengthen

66. BENIGN
A. Malevolent B. Soft
C. Friendly D. Unwise

67. OBSCURE
A. Implicit B. Obnoxious
C. Explicit D. Pedantic

68. HYPOCRITICAL
A. Gentle B. Sincere
C. Amiable D. Dependable

69. EVASIVE
A. Free B. Honest
C. Liberal D. Frank

70. INDUSTRIOUS
A. Indifferent B. Indolent
C. Casual D. Passive

71. EXTRICATE
A. Manifest B. Palpable
C. Release D. Entangle

72. LUCID
A. Glory B. Noisy
C. Obscure D. Distinct

73. INSIPID
A. Tasty B. Stupid
C. Discreet D. Feast

74. OBEYING
A. Ordering B. Following
C. Refusing D. Contradicting

75. VICTORIOUS
A. Defeated B. Annexed
C. Destroyed D. Vanquished

76. COMMISSIONED
A. Started B. Closed
C. Finished D. Terminated

77. VANITY
A. Pride B. Humility
C. Conceit D. Ostentious

78. ZENITH
A. Acme B. Top
C. Nadir D. Pinnacle

79. TANGIBLE
A. Ethereal B. Concrete
C. Actual D. Solid

80. REPRESS
A. Inhibit B. Liberate
C. Curb D. Quell

81. EPILOGUE
A. Dialogue B. Prelude
C. Post script D. Epigram

82. FRAUDULENT
A. Candid B. Direct
C. Forthright D. Genuine

83. LOQUACIOUS
A. Reticent B. Talkative
C. Garrulous D. Verbose

84. NIGGARDLY
A. Frugal B. Thrifty
C. Stingy D. Generous

85. PERTINENT
A. Irrational B. Irregular
C. Insistent D. Irrelevant

86. FAINT-HEARTED
A. Warm-hearted B. Full-blooded
C. Hot-blooded D. Stout-hearted

87. VIOLENT
A. Humble B. Harmless
C. Gentle D. Tame

88. STATIONARY
A. Active B. Mobile
C. Rapid D. Busy

89. HONORARY
A. Dishonourable B. Reputed
C. Paid D. Official

90. COMMON
A. Rare B. Small
C. Petty D. Poor

91. REPEL
A. Attend B. Concentrate
C. Continue D. Attract

92. ARTIFICIAL
A. Red B. Natural
C. Truthful D. Solid

93. CAPACIOUS
A. Limited B. Caring
C. Foolish D. Changeable

94. PROVOCATION
A. Vocation B. Pacification
C. Peace D. Destruction

95. METICULOUS
A. Mutual B. Shaggy
C. Meretricious D. Slovenly

96. ABLE
A. Disable B. Inable
C. Unable D. Enable

97. COMFORT
A. Uncomfort B. Miscomfort
C. Discomfort D. None of these

98. GAIN
A. Loose B. Fall
C. Lost D. Lose

99. SYNTHETIC
A. Affable B. Natural
C. Plastic D. Cosmetic

100. ACQUITTED
A. Freed B. Burdened
C. Convicted D. Entrusted

ANSWERS

1	2	3	4	5	6	7	8	9	10
B	B	D	A	B	D	D	C	B	D
11	12	13	14	15	16	17	18	19	20
C	C	B	C	D	A	C	C	D	A
21	22	23	24	25	26	27	28	29	30
A	C	D	A	C	C	A	C	D	A
31	32	33	34	35	36	37	38	39	40
A	D	C	A	C	D	C	A	A	A
41	42	43	44	45	46	47	48	49	50
C	B	C	D	B	D	D	B	A	A
51	52	53	54	55	56	57	58	59	60
C	C	C	D	B	D	C	D	C	D
61	62	63	64	65	66	67	68	69	70
D	B	B	A	C	A	C	B	B	B
71	72	73	74	75	76	77	78	79	80
D	C	A	A	A	D	B	C	A	B
81	82	83	84	85	86	87	88	89	90
B	D	B	D	D	D	C	B	C	A
91	92	93	94	95	96	97	98	99	100
D	B	A	B	D	C	C	D	B	C

One Word Substitutions

There are many words in English language which can be perfectly used for a number of words. These words help in expressing ideas in a short and correct manner for the right occasion. Such words not only enhance the vocabulary but also enable you to economise in the use of words to a great extent. Try to learn as many as you can.

Denoting Numbers

- A collection of poems — *anthology*
- A number of merchant ships protected by warships (in war-time) — *convoy*
- A number of stars grouped together — *constellation*
- A number of hired applauders, *i.e.* persons paid to clap — *claque*
- A number of people at church — *congregation*
- A number of people gathered together for some common purpose — *gathering, assembly, society*
- A group of people who get together to work for some cause of common interest — *coterie*
- A number of workmen, prisoners, thieves — *gang*
- A number of sheep — *flock*
- A number of geese — *gaggle*
- A number of leopards — *leap*
- A number of lions, monkeys — *pride, troop*
- A number of herrings, mackerel — *shoal*
- A number of fish taken in a net — *catch, haul*
- A number of whales, porpoises — *school, gam*
- A number of oxen or horses (two or more) harnessed together — *team*
- A number of ships, cars, buses — *fleet*

Denoting Places

- A place where bees are kept — *apiary*
- A place where birds are kept — *aviary*
- A place where fishes are kept — *aquarium*
- A dwelling-place of an animal underground — *burrow*
- A squirrel's home — *drey*
- A nest of a bird of prey — *eyrie, aerie*
- A place where spirituous liquors are produced — *distillery*
- A place where clothes are washed and ironed — *laundry*
- A place where Government records are kept — *archives*
- A place where treasures of art, curiosities, etc. are preserved or exhibited — *museum*
- A place where fruit trees are grown — *orchard*

Pertaining to the Literary Sphere

- A work whose writer is unknown — *anonymous*
- A record of one's life written by oneself — *autobiography*
- The history of the life of a person — *biography*
- The heading or short description of a newspaper article, chapter of a book etc. — *caption*

- A humorous play, having a happy ending — *comedy*
- A list of books in a library — *catalogue, bibliography*
- A book in which the events of each day are recorded — *diary*
- A books containing the words of a language with their definitions, in alphabetical order — *dictionary*
- A book of names and addresses — *directory*
- A short speech by a player at the end of a play — *epilogue*
- A brief summary of a book — *epitome*
- A book containing information on all branches of knowledge — *encyclopedia*
- To remove the offensive portions of a book — *expurgate*
- A speech delivered without earlier preparation — *extempore*
- A noisy or vehement speech intended to excite passions — *harangue*
- A written account, usually in book form of the interesting and memorable experiences of one's life — *memoirs*
- A note to help the memory — *memorandum*
- A declaration of plans and promises put forward by a candidate for election, political party or a sovereign — *manifesto*
- A short speech by a player at the beginning of a play — *prologue*
- Literary theft, or passing off an author's original work as one's own — *plagiarism*
- Speaking aloud to oneself — *soliloquy*
- A play with a sad or tragic end — *tragedy*

Pertaining to Religion

- One who believes that man can have no knowledge of God but only of natural phenomena — *agnostic*
- One who renounces his religious vows or forsakes his religious principles — *apostate*
- One who does not believe in existence of God — *atheist*
- One intolerantly devoted to a particular creed — *bigot*
- To utter profane language against God or anything holy — *blaspheme*
- A breaker of church images — *iconoclast*
- Worship of images or idols — *idiolatory*
- One who believes in God — *theist*
- One who believes in only one God — *monotheist*
- One who believes in many Gods — *polytheist*

Pertaining to Government

- To give up a throne or other office of dignity — *abdicate*
- Absence of government — *anarchy*
- Government by Sovereign of uncontrolled authority — *autocracy, despotism*
- Government by departments of states — *bureaucracy*
- Government of the people, for the people and by the people — *democracy*
- Government by the nobility — *aristocracy*
- The right of self-government — *autonomy*
- Government by a few — *oligarchy*
- Government by the wealthy — *plutocracy*
- Government by divine guidance — *theocracy*
- To decide a political question by the direct vote of the whole electorate — *referendum*
- Sweeping governmental change — *revolution*
- The science of government — *politics*

Pertaining to Professions

- One who attends to the diseases of the eye — *oculist*
- One who tests eyesight and sells spectacles — *optician*
- One who attends to the teeth — *dentist*
- One skilled in the care of hands and feet — *chiropodist*

- ❑ A physician who assists women at child-birth — *obstetrician*
- ❑ One who drives a motorcar — *chauffeur*
- ❑ One who makes or sells candles — *chandler*
- ❑ One who preserves the skins of animals and mounts them so as to resemble the living animals — *taxidermist*
- ❑ One who compiles a dictionary — *lexicographer*
- ❑ One who writes books — *author*
- ❑ One skilled in the treatment of diseases of animals — *veterinarian*
- ❑ A tradesman who manages funerals — *undertaker*
- ❑ One who draws up contracts and lends money on interest — *scrivener*
- ❑ One who lends money and keeps goods as security — *pawnbroker*
- ❑ A teacher who travels from place to place to give instruction. — *peripatetic*
- ❑ One who travels from place to place selling miscellaneous articles — *hawker, pedlar*
- ❑ One who collects postage stamps — *philatelist*
- ❑ One who lends money at exorbitant interest — *usurer*
- ❑ One who takes care of a building — *janitor*
- ❑ One who sells sweets and pastries — *confectioner*
- ❑ One who works in a coalmine — *collier*
- ❑ One who flies an aeroplane — *pilot, aviator*
- ❑ One who studies rocks and soils — *geologist*
- ❑ One who shoes horses — *farrier*
- ❑ A professional rider in horses races — *jockey*
- ❑ One who deals in silks, cotton, woollen, and linen goods — *mercer*
- ❑ One who deals in wines — *vintner*
- ❑ One who deals in fish — *fishmonger*
- ❑ One who deals in iron and hardware — *ironmonger*
- ❑ One who sells fruits, vegetables, etc. from a barrow — *costermonger*
- ❑ One who sets type in a printing office — *compositor*

Pertaining to Medicine

- ❑ A substance which destroys or weakens germs — *antiseptic*
- ❑ Any medicine which produces insensibility — *anaesthetic*
- ❑ A medicine to counteract poison — *antidote*
- ❑ Want or poorness of blood — *anaemia*
- ❑ A medicine which alleviates pain — *anodyne*
- ❑ To cut off a person's body a part which is infected — *amputate*
- ❑ One who is recovering from illness — *convalescent*
- ❑ To be able to tell the nature of disease by its symptoms — *diagnose*
- ❑ A disease affecting many persons at the same place and time — *epidemic*
- ❑ A disease confined to a particular district or place — *endemic*
- ❑ To disinfect by smoke — *fumigate*
- ❑ Free or exempt from infection — *immune*
- ❑ A person who is sick — *invalid*
- ❑ A cure for all diseases — *panacea*
- ❑ A disease widely epidemic — *pandemic*
- ❑ Confinement to one place to avoid spread of infection — *quarantine*

Pertaining to Characteristics and Actions

- ❑ One who devotes his life to the welfare and interests of other people — *altruist*
- ❑ One who can use both hands with equal ease — *ambidexterous*
- ❑ One who fishes with a rod — *angler*
- ❑ One who kills secretly or by surprise — *assassin*
- ❑ A person who collects things belonging to ancient times — *antiquary*
- ❑ One who is always finding faults — *censorious*

- One living at the same time as another — *contemporary*
- One who sneers at the aims and beliefs of his fellowmen — *cynic*
- One who delights in speaking about oneself — *egotist*
- One who exalts his own opinion — *egoist*
- One who dies for a noble cause — *martyr*
- One who retires from society to live a solitary life — *recluse, hermit*
- One who maliciously sets fire to buildings — *incendiary*
- One who is banished from his home or his country — *exile*
- One who takes refuge in a foreign country — *refugee, alien*
- One who runs away from justice or the law — *fugitive*
- One who walks in his sleep — *somnambulist*
- One who looks on the bright side of things — *optimist*
- One who looks on the dark side of things — *pessimist*
- A hater of mankind — *misanthropist*
- One who knows everything — *omniscient*
- One who is all powerful — *omnipotent*
- One who is present everywhere — *omnipresent*
- One who devotes his service or wealth for the love of mankind — *philanthropist*
- One new to anything — *novice, tyro, neophyte*
- One who engages in any pursuit for the love of it, and not for gain — *amateur*
- One who journeys to a holy place — *pilgrim*
- A leader of the people who can sway his followers by his oratory — *demagogue*
- One who has special skill in judging art, music, tastes, etc. — *connoisseur*
- One whose reasoning is clever yet false — *sophist*
- One who makes a display of his learning — *pedant*
- One who is indifferent to pain or pleasure — *stoic*
- One who loves his country and serves it devotedly — *patriot*
- One devoted to the pleasures of eating and drinking — *epicure*
- One who poses to be what he is not — *hypocrite, impostor*
- One who foretells events — *prophet*
- One who pretends to know a great deal about everything — *mountebank, charlatan, quack*
- One versed in many languages — *linguist*
- One who cannot pay one's debts — *insolvent*
- One who takes over after another in office or employment — *successor*
- One who has been before another in office or employment — *predecessor*
- One who is opposed to intellectual progress — *obscurant*
- One who abstains from alcoholic drinks — *teetotaller*
- One who hides away on a ship to obtain a free passage — *stowaway*
- One who spends very little — *miser*
- One who spends too much — *spendthrift*

Pertaining to War

- An unprovoked attack by an enemy — *aggression*
- Shells, bombs, military stores — *ammunition*
- A place where naval or military weapons are made or stored — *ordnance*
- An agreement between belligerents to stop fighting — *armistice*
- A general pardon of offenders — *amnesty*
- To reduce to nothing — *annihilate*
- Nations carrying on warfare — *belligerents*
- To surround a place with the intention of capturing — *besiege*
- To camp in the open air without tents or covering — *bivouac*

- To seize for military use *commandeer*
- A person who is forced by law to become a soldier *conscript*
- An order prohibiting ships to leave the ports *embargo*
- A number of firearms being discharged continuously *fusillade*
- To make an examination or preliminary survey of enemy territory for military objectives *reconnoitre*

Pertaining to Marriage and Children

- One who marries a second wife or husband while the legal spouse is alive *bigamist*
- One vowed to a single or unmarried life *celibate*
- One engaged to be married *fiancé, fiancee*
- A child whose parents are dead *orphan*
- A hater of marriage *misogamist*
- One who has more than two wives at a time *polygamist*

Pertaining to Death

- Dead and decaying flesh (esp. of animals) *carrion*
- A monument set up for persons who are buried elsewhere *cenotaph*
- To preserve a dead body from putrefaction *embalm*
- Words inscribed on a tomb *epitaph*
- An examination of dead body *postmortem, autopsy*
- An account in the newspaper of the funeral of one deceased *obituary*
- The property left to someone by a will *legacy*
- Occurring after death *posthumous*
- The act of killing a human being *homicide*
- Murder of a new born child *infanticide*
- Murder of a brother *fratricide*
- Murder of a sister *sororicide*
- Murder of a mother *matricide*
- Murder of a father *patricide*
- Murder of a parent *parricide*
- Murder of a king *regicide*

Pertaining to Sciences and Arts

- The study of all heavenly bodies and the earth in relation to them *astronomy*
- The science of land management *agronomics*
- The study of mankind *anthropology*
- The study of physical life or living matter *biology*
- The study of plants *botany*
- The art of beautiful handwriting *calligraphy*
- The science which deals with the varieties of human race *ethnology*
- The study of the origin and history of words *etymology*
- The study of coins *numismatics*
- The study of human face *physiognomy*
- The art of making fireworks *pyrotechnics*
- The study of birds *ornithology*
- The study of languages *philology*
- At home equally on land or in water *amphibious*
- The inside of a nut *kernel*
- The central or innermost part of fruit *core*
- The animals of a certain region *fauna*

- The plants and vegetation of a certain region — *flora*
- Absence of rain for a long time — *drought*
- To supply land with water by artificial means — *irrigate*
- One who studies plant and animal life — *naturalist*
- A cud-chewing animal, *e.g.* the cow — *ruminant*
- A gnawing animal, *e.g.* the rat — *rodent*
- A four-footed animal — *quadruped*
- Animals which carry their young in a pouch, *e.g.* kangaroo — *marsupials*
- Soil composed largely of decayed vegetable matter — *humus*
- A preparation for killing insects — *insecticide*
- A plant or animal growing on another — *parasite*
- Living for many years — *perennial*

Miscellaneous

- Loud enough to be heard — *audible*
- Not distinct enough to be heard — *inaudible*
- Fit for food — *edible*
- Unfit for human consumption — *inedible*
- Fit to be chosen or selected — *eligible*
- Not having the qualities for being chosen — *ineligible*
- Writing that is easy to read — *legible*
- Writing that is difficult to decipher — *illegible*
- Able to read — *literate*
- Unable to read — *illiterate*
- Born of married parents — *legitimate*
- Born of unmarried parents — *illegitimate*
- To send back a person to his own country — *repatriate*
- To banish from one's country — *expatriate*
- To move from one country to another — *migrate*
- One who leaves his country to settle in another — *emigrant*
- One who comes into a foreign country to settle there — *immigrant*
- Incapable of being redeemed from evil, *i.e.* beyond correction — *incorrigible*
- That which cannot be rubbed out or blotted out — *ineffaceable, indelible*
- That which cannot be conquered — *invincible*
- Incapable of making errors — *infallible*
- That which cannot be avoided or prevented — *inevitable*
- Incapable of being burnt — *incombustible*
- That which easily catches fire — *inflammable, flammable*
- That which cannot be seen — *invisible*
- Living for ever — *immortal*
- Increase the gravity of an offence — *aggravate*
- Ordinary or commonplace remark — *platitude*
- That which cannot be satisfied — *insatiable*
- That which cannot be repaired — *irreparable*
- That which cannot be imitated — *inimitable*
- Persons (or efforts) that cannot be wearied — *indefatigable*
- One who eats too much — *glutton*
- To destroy completely — *annihilate*
- A statement open to more than one interpretation — *ambiguous*
- A round about way of speaking — *circumlocution*
- Cautious observation of events, etc. — *circumspection*
- That which cannot be hurt — *invulnerable*

Multiple Choice Questions

Directions: *Below are given some statements each of which is capable of being expressed by one word only. Each statement is followed by four such words of which only one is correct. Out of the given alternatives A, B, C and D choose the correct word which very closely fits each definition.*

1. A set of papers giving information about a person or event:
   A. editorial B. agenda
   C. dossier D. clippings
2. List and explanations of technical, difficult, etc. terms:
   A. preface B. glossary
   C. bibliography D. appendix
3. One who pays too much care to his clothes and personal appearance:
   A. conscious B. dandy
   C. cynosure D. leer
4. A child born after death of father:
   A. effeminate B. immature
   C. fatherless D. posthumous
5. A person who is hard to please:
   A. insensible B. hypocrite
   C. egoist D. fastidious
6. Complete failure in something attempted:
   A. fiasco B. vain
   C. falsies D. flop
7. A word which can be interpreted in any way:
   A. confusing B. misnomer
   C. ambiguous D. precise
8. A group of persons united by common interests:
   A. society B. class
   C. clique D. coterie
9. A person who is inexperienced and easily deceived:
   A. fool B. immature
   C. blackhorn D. greenhorn
10. Instruction by question and answer:
    A. interrogatory B. catechism
    C. bulletin D. alibi
11. Record of events by someone with first hand knowledge:
    A. novice B. report
    C. memoir D. itinerary
12. A mode of talk familiar to a particular group or profession:
    A. jargon B. colloquial
    C. slang D. abuses
13. Person who is crazy:
    A. lackadaisical B. tarter
    C. scrupulous D. loony
14. A person who readily believes others:
    A. hasty B. immature
    C. credulous D. credible
15. One who eats human flesh:
    A. beast B. cannibal
    C. maneater D. carnivorous
16. Intentional destruction of racial groups:
    A. genocide B. homicide
    C. fratricide D. communal riot
17. One with weakness of mind caused by old age:
    A. dastard B. dotard
    C. fop D. philanderer
18. Study of insects:
    A. zoology B. philology
    C. entomology D. etymology
19. A critical judge of any art particularly fine arts:
    A. connoisseur B. veteran
    C. philistine D. dilettante
20. One who introduces items of an entertainment:
    A. consort B. compere
    C. director D. introducer
21. A combination of business firms:
    A. enterprise B. franchise
    C. cartel D. autonomous
22. Freeing of suppressed emotions:
    A. catastrophe B. catharsis
    C. epilogue D. chagrin
23. One who believes in the power of fate:
    A. optimist B. pessimist
    C. fearful D. fatalist
24. The murder of brother:
    A. genocide B. homicide
    C. salvage D. fratricide
25. Additional to proper payment:
    A. premium B. overtime
    C. ex-gratia D. fringe
26. A person or thing used to tempt somebody into a position of danger:
    A. decoy B. provocateur
    C. jinx D. scapegoat
27. Custom of having more than one husband at the same time:
    A. polygamy B. polyandry
    C. bigamy D. sexagenary
28. A person of refined taste in food and drink:
    A. emeritus B. epicure
    C. glutton D. gourmand

29. A tombstone inscription:
A. epithet B. encomium
C. epistle D. epitaph

30. An office which has no work but high salary:
A. fortuitous B. gratuitous
C. sinecure D. ceremonial

31. One who is indifferent to pains and pleasure of life:
A. stoic B. metaphysical
C. pessimist D. sceptic

32. List of names of persons showing duties to be performed by each in turn:
A. notice B. bulletin
C. roster D. agenda

33. Long angry speech of criticism or accusation:
A. track record B. tirade
C. taut D. outburst

34. One who is in favour of never drinking alcoholic drinks:
A. idealist B. uxorious
C. teetotaller D. unalcoholic

35. Trying to win favour by flattery and charm:
A. smarmy B. shrewish
C. toady D. loquacious

36. A decision on which one cannot go back:
A. incorrigible B. irrevocable
C. rigid D. invulnerable

37. The science that studies the varieties of human race:
A. phrenology B. physiology
C. sociology D. ethnology

38. A person who hates women:
A. philogynist B. philatelist
C. misogamist D. misogynist

39. A group of people in a particular grade in an organisation:
A. colleague B. staff
C. echelon D. commission

40. Honourably discharged from service:
A. emeritus B. latitudinarian
C. infallible D. meritorious

41. One who does not believe in the existence of God:
A. atheist B. altruist
C. agnostic D. flippant

42. The large money paid for an early retirement:
A. goldmine B. golden handshake
C. gratuity D. lion's share

43. A hater of learning and knowledge:
A. misologist B. misogynist
C. philologist D. philanthropist

44. One who lives and acts for the welfare of others:
A. misanthrope B. credulous
C. altruist D. gregarious

45. Mental weariness for want of occupation:
A. desperate B. depression
C. fatigue D. ennui

46. That which makes it difficult to recognise the presence in real of somebody or something:
A. cover B. mask
C. make-up D. camouflage

47. To bear a hand in one's new business:
A. partnership B. interfere
C. assist D. join

48. One who renounces the world and practices self-discipline in order to attain salvation:
A. devotee B. ascetic
C. theist D. parsimonious

49. A place where gambling is practiced:
A. hotel B. motel
C. casino D. stadium

50. A sad song is a:
A. dirge B. elegy
C. ditty D. knell

ANSWERS

1	2	3	4	5	6	7	8	9	10
C	B	B	D	D	A	C	C	D	B
11	**12**	**13**	**14**	**15**	**16**	**17**	**18**	**19**	**20**
C	A	D	C	B	A	B	C	A	B
21	**22**	**23**	**24**	**25**	**26**	**27**	**28**	**29**	**30**
C	B	D	D	D	A	B	B	D	C
31	**32**	**33**	**34**	**35**	**36**	**37**	**38**	**39**	**40**
A	C	B	C	A	B	D	D	C	A
41	**42**	**43**	**44**	**45**	**46**	**47**	**48**	**49**	**50**
A	B	A	C	D	D	C	B	C	A

Idioms and Phrases

- An idiom is a group of words established by usage as having a meaning different from the individual words.
- A phrase is a small group of words standing together as an idiomatic expression.

Learn and practise as may as you can.

Idioms and Idiomatic Phrases

✦ **ABC** (basic principles)
She does not know the ABC of photography.

✦ **At one's beck and call** (ready to obey)
He had a dozen men at his beck and call.

✦ **At sixes and sevens** (in disorder)
The drawing room articles were lying at sixes and sevens on the floor.

✦ **A wet blanket** (a discouraging person)
Don't allow Rakesh to accompany you to the hunting trip because he is a wet blanket.

✦ **A big gun** (an important person)
Mr Smith is a big gun in our city.

✦ **At a stone's throw** (at a short distance from)
My school is at a stone's throw from my house.

✦ **A man of word** (a person who keeps his promise)
Mr Sharma is a man of word.

✦ **A man of a few words** (a remarkable person)
Gandhiji was a man of a few words.

✦ **At arm's length** (to keep away)
We should always keep bad boys at arm's length

✦ **A bolt from the blue** (a sudden and unexpected event)
The news of my friend's death came to me like a bolt from the blue.

✦ **A man of letters** (a scholar)
Radha Krishnan was a man of letters.

✦ **A hard nut to crack.** (a puzzling problem)
To get a win over American basket ball team is a hard nut to crack for India.

✦ **A yeoman's service** (service which is beneficial to the human beings)
He did yeoman's service through his life.

✦ **A snake in the grass** (a hidden foe)
Beware of him because he seems to be a snake in the grass.

✦ **Acid test** (hard test)
The election will be an acid test for the ruling party.

✦ **A wolf in sheep's clothing** (a hypocrite)
You should not keep company with him because he is a wolf in sheep's clothing.

✦ **At the eleventh hour** (at the last moment)
The war was about to start but fortunately at the eleventh hour a messenger came to the PM with a message of peace.

✦ **A great card** (an important person)
Mr Sood is a great card in the ministry of finance.

✦ **A fool of the first water** (one completely foolish)
Being a fool of the first water he could not solve even the simplest sum.

✦ **A bone of contention** (to be the cause of quarrel)
Kashmir is the bone of contention between India and Pakistan.

✦ **A green hand** (not very much experienced)
We shall pay a little to a green hand.

✦ **All in all** (completely)
Rajesh is all in all in this office.

✦ **A bed of roses** (a comfort)
Life is not a bed of roses.

✦ **An apple of discord** (to be the cause of)
Kashmir is an apple of discord between India and Pakistan.

✦ **A white elephant** (of no use)
This sort of glib talker always proves a white elephant in the end.

✦ **A red letter day** (An important day)
15th August is a red letter day for the Indians.

✦ **By hook or by crook** (by any means fair or foul)

✦ **Black sheep** (a traitor)
Later on Mr XYZ proved a black sheep.

- **By dint of** (by means of)
By dint of hard work, she earned a lot of money.
- **Break ones back** (to work hard to get something)
He broke his back to earn his livelihood.
- **Break the back of** (accomplish the hardest part of a certain job)
There is nothing to be worried about as we've already broken the back of the problem.
- **Beat about the bush** (to go on talking on some worthless topic)
Stop this beating about the bush, come to the main task.
- **Beyond one's means** (beyond one's budget)
He is living beyond his means, therefore, he is sure to get ruined.
- **Cut loose** (Keep away)
India should cut loose from bad politics.
- **Chips of the same block** (having the same taste)
They are the chips of the same block.
- **Cut-throat competition** (a stiff competition)
There is a cut-throat competition among the publishers in the market.
- **Come what may** (no matter what happens)
I'll do it come what may.
- **Drop someone a line** (send a letter, etc.)
Please drop me a line of your well-being.
- **Dull the edge of** (reduce the intensity of)
Take this pill and it will dull the edge of pain.
- **From hand to mouth** (without any saving)
The poor factory worker is living from hand to mouth.
- **Fair and square** (clean)
One must be fair and square in one's dealing.
- **Hard of hearing** (somewhat deaf)
She is a bit hard of hearing.
- **In the good books of** (be good in one's mind)
Jack is in the good books of his teachers.
- **In black and white** (in written)
Don't give him anything in black and white.
- **In cold blood** (mercilessly)
The old woman was murdered in cold blood.
- **In a crack** (all of a sudden or rapidly)
The thief left the place in a crack.
- **In full swing** (in full force)
The studies of the students are going on in full swing.
- **In the twinkling of an eye** (quickly)
The monkey ate up grams in the twinkling of an eye.
- **Keep the ball rolling** (to maintain the progress of some activity)
After the death of his father he had to take the charge of his office to keep the ball rolling.
- **Neck and neck** (even)
There is a neck and neck fight between the two boxers.
- **Once in a blue moon** (seldom)
She visits her brother once in a blue moon.
- **Slow and steady** (slowly but continually)
Slow and steady wins the race.
- **To cut a sorry figure** (present oneself in a bad way)
She cut a sorry figure on the stage.
- **To give a red carpet reception** (to give a warm welcome)
The PM was given a red carpet reception in America.
- **To dance one's tune** (to follow someone submissively)
He always dances to his brother's tune.
- **To turn a deaf ear to** (to disregard)
She turned a deaf ear to her parents' advice.
- **To call a spade a spade** (to speak the truth)
Gandhiji always called a spade a spade.
- **To bring to book** (to scold)
The naughty boy was brought to book by the teacher.
- **To cut short** (to reduce)
Smoking will cut short your life.
He wants to get money by hook or by crook.
- **To grease the palm of** (to bribe)
Rohit greased the palm of the clerk and got the file moved.
- **Through thick and thin.** (under all circumstances)
We'll stand by you through thick and thin.
- **To die by inches** (to die a painful death)
The old man died by inches.
- **To eat one's words** (to retract one's statement)
You'll have to eat your words because you have spoken without thinking.
- **To burn the midnight oil** (to work hard)
You'll have to burn the midnight oil if you want to get good marks.
- **To poke one's nose into** (to meddle with)
It is bad to poke your nose into others' affair.
- **To fall flat** (to have no effect)
His father's advice fell flat on him.
- **To make a clean breast of** (to confess)
He made a clean breast of his involvement in the bomb blast.
- **To get the better of** (overcome)
Anger got the better of him.
- **To break somebody's back** (to give too much work to him to do)

She broke his back by giving him so much hard work to do.

✦ **Throw cold water on** (to discourage)
She tried to throw cold water on his plan but he was well-determined.

✦ **The long and short of** (in brief)
The long and short of his lecture is that we should live like brothers.

✦ **To burn one's fingers** (to get oneself in trouble)
You have burnt your fingers by speaking against him.

✦ **To turn over a new leaf** (to change the course of life)
He has turned over a new leaf in his life.

✦ **To have one's own axe to grind** (to have vested interest)
He has his own axe to grind in this matter.

✦ **To take to one's heels** (to run away)
The thief took to his heels as soon as he saw the policeman.

✦ **To move heaven and earth** (to make too much effort)
The young man moved heaven and earth to find a job.

✦ **To be caught red handed** (to be caught at the time of committing a crime)
The clerk was caught red handed when he was accepting bribe from Mr ABC.

✦ **To receive with open arms** (to give a warm welcome)
The new president of the club was received with open arms by the members.

✦ **To be born with a silver spoon in one's mouth** (to be born in a rich family)
Mr. J. L. Nehru was born with a silver spoon in his mouth.

✦ **To come to light** (to be known)
A new disease has recently come to light.

✦ **To be the apple of one's eye** (be very dear)
He is the apple of his parent's eye.

✦ **To make fun of** (laugh at)
The children made fun of the waiter in the hotel.

✦ **To let the cat out of the bag** (to divulge secret)
It was Sohan who let the cat out of the bag by telling the real matter.

✦ **To open a new chapter** (to start some habit, etc.
By drinking, you've opened a new chapter in your life.

✦ **To make the flesh creep** (to terrify)
The story made my flesh creep.

✦ **To lose ground** (to retreat)
After fighting for some time the Pakistani army began to lose ground.

✦ **To bring to book** (to punish)
The student was brought to book by the teacher.

✦ **To show a clean pair of heels** (to run away)
The thief showed a clean pair of heels as soon as he saw the policeman approaching.

✦ **To gain ground** (to be established)
He gained ground in India in a few years.

✦ **To get wind of** (to get information)
I got wind of his secret plans.

✦ **Under a cloud** (be in trouble or in a state of disgrace or suspicion)
His company seemed to be under a cloud as it had no funds to pay the wages to the workers.

Verbal Phrases

✦ **Act upon** (to follow)
I acted upon my father's advice.

✦ **Act upto** (to perform within limits)
He acted upto his conscience.

✦ **Act beyond** (to perform crossing limits)
We should not act beyond our capacity.

✦ **Act for** (to perform in place of someone else)
The vice principal acted for the principal.

✦ **Back up** (to make a queue)
The vehicles began to back up.

✦ **Back down** (withdraw claim in the presence of opposition)
The leader backed down from his previous statement.

✦ **Back off** (draw back some plan or action)
They backed off from building a flyover.

✦ **Back out** (withdraw from a promise, etc.)
The government backed out of its promise.

✦ **Break down** (stop working) My car broke down on the highway.

✦ **Break into** (enter in certain premises by breaking the door, etc.)
Last night a thief broke into my neighbour's.

✦ **Break off** (stop all of a sudden)
She broke off and began to think over about her/his hand.

✦ **Break out** (spread)
Cholera has broken out in the town.

✦ **Break out of** (escape from)
A prisoner broke out of the prison last night.

✦ **Break up** (disperse)
The cloud of fog began to break up as the sun rose.

✦ **Break something up** (Cause something to break into small pieces)
She broke up the chocolate to distribute it among the girls.

✦ **Break with** (Cut off connection after quarrelling with someone)
He has broken with his brother.

✦ **Call on** (pay a visit to somebody)
I'll call on Mohan's today.

✦ **Call out** (to start)
The workers have called out a strike.

✦ **Call off** (to stop the strike etc.)
The workers have called off the strike.

✦ **Call at** (to visit someone's house)
I called at his house yesterday.

✦ **Call in** (send for)
Please call in the doctor.

✦ **Carry on** (continue)
Please carry on your work.

✦ **Carry something out** (perform a task)
Our company is carrying out a big deal with a foreign company.

✦ **Carry something over** (postpone)
The fancy dress competition had to be carried over till Monday)

✦ **Carry someone off** (kill somebody)
Cancer carried her off on the day of her 20th birthday.

✦ **Come of age** (get established)
As our company has come of age, so, there is no problem in selling our goods.

✦ **Come of** (belong to)
She comes of a royal family.

✦ **Come over** (surmount)
We at last came over all our problems.

✦ **Come off** (to take place)
The marriage of my brother comes off in the next month.

✦ **Come round** (agree)
At last he came round to my views.

✦ **Come under** (fall in the category of)
All these animals come under the same species.

✦ **Come down with** (suffer from)
She came down with whopping cough.

✦ **Come from** (be the nature of)
She came from London.

✦ **Come about** (happen)
The explosion came about when the worker struck the match to light a cigarette.

✦ **Cut off** (die)
The princess was cut off in the prime of her life.

✦ **Cut down** (reduce)
The prices of consumer goods should be cut down.

✦ **Cut someone out** (exclude someone)
His father cut him out of his will.

✦ **Fall in**
She fell in love with the prince.

✦ **Fall down** (fail)
The deal fell down for lack of transparency.

✦ **Fall out** (quarrel)
She fell out with his elder brother.

✦ **Fall through** (fail)
The project fell through for lack of funds.

✦ **Get away** (escape)
She got away with her life.

✦ **Get by** (to accomplish something with great difficulty)
She is not rich. She has just enough to get by.

✦ **Get on** (perform)
How are you getting on with your studies?

✦ **Get out** (become known)
The news got out that the PM was paying a visit to Russia.

✦ **Get over** (overcome)
At last I got over all obstacles.

✦ **Get up** (rise)
When do you get up in the morning?

✦ **Give up** (stop)
He gave up smoking.

✦ **Give out** (emit)
Garlic gives out a pungent smell.

✦ **Give in** (collapse)
The bridge gave in under the heavy load.

✦ **Give away** (distribute)
The Principal gave away the prizes.

✦ **Give out** (announce)
It was given out that the President of India would visit the place soon.

✦ **Go off** (explode)
The gun went off suddenly.

✦ **Go on** (continue)
She went on about how she flew the aeroplane.

✦ **Go through** (examine)
I'll go through this book later on.

✦ **Go up** (be built)
The construction of the house is going up.

✦ **Grind on** (continue for a long time in a tedious way)
The discussion over political issues ground on.

✦ **Grind something out** (produce something a tedious way)
She will grind some more short stories.

✦ **Look out** (be careful)
Look out! there is a snake.

✦ **Look down upon** (hate)
We should not look down upon the poor.

✦ **Look at** (watch)
Look at the blackboard.

✦ **Look after** (take care of)
We ought to look after our old parents.

✦ **Look into** (investigate)
The new police inspector will look into the matter.

✦ **Look up** (rise)
The prices of consumer goods are looking up.

✦ **Look back** (think of the past)
It made her feel disolate when she looked back on things of the past.

✦ **Make up** (to fulfil)
I'll make up my deficiency in Mathematics.

✦ **Make out** (understand)
I could not make out what she said.

✦ **Make up one' mind** (to resolve)
I have made up my mind to settle in the USA.

✦ **Make off** (leave hurriedly)
She made off without informing anybody.

✦ **Make something over** (transfer)
She should make her property over to her sons.

✦ **Make over** (hand over)
He made over the charge of the file to Mr Robert.

✦ **Pull back** (retreat)
The government has pulled back from its previous policy.

✦ **Pull something down** (demolish)
The authorities concerned pulled down a few building which were illegally built on government land.

✦ **Pull out** (pluck)
The child pulled out a few petals of the flower.

✦ **Pull through** (recover)
The patient will pull through.

✦ **Push on** (continue a journey)
It was getting darker but we pushed on.

✦ **Push at** (exert force)
He pushed at the bell, but it did not ring.

✦ **Push for** (demand persistently)
The workers have been pushing for the installation of new machines for five years.

✦ **Put out** (extinguish)
She put out the light.

✦ **Put on** (wear)
He put on an overcoat.

✦ **Put off** (postpone)
The plan had to be put off.

✦ **Put by** (spare something for future)
We must put by some money for future.

✦ **Put up with** (stay)
Your aunt is out of town for a couple of days, you may put up with us till she comes.

✦ **Put something down** (record something)
She put a new idea down on the paper.

✦ **Take after** (resemble)
He takes after his father.

✦ **Take off** (remove)
He took off his shoes.

✦ **Take something out** (obtain)
You may take out some money from Rohit if you want to purchase this car.

✦ **Take to** (fall into the habit of)
He took to gambling.

✦ **Turn something down** (reject something)
The judge turned down his appeal.

✦ **Turn on** (attack)
The thief turned on him with a knife.

Multiple Choice Questions

Directions: *Some idioms/phrases are given below with their probable meanings. Select the options with their correct meanings.*

1. Carry out
A. To take from one place to another
B. To continue
C. To obey
D. To make efforts

2. In the same boat
A. A worn out choice
B. Indifferent
C. In identical circumstances
D. Carry off

3. In one's good book
A. A costly book B. A priceless treasure
C. In one's favour D. An enchanting beauty

4. Keep a straight face
A. To do make up
B. To change clothes

C. Assume responsibility
D. To remain serious

5. To be above board
A. To have a good height
B. To be honest in any business deal
C. To have no debts
D. To try to be beautiful

6. On the face of it
A. To agree B. From an action
C. More than enough D. Apparently

7. Let the bygones be bygones
A. In one's favour B. To pretend
C. To forget the past D. Other choice

8. To split hairs
A. Major distinctions
B. Hair with two ends
C. To make minute distinction
D. Without distinction

9. Bread and butter
A. Both bread and butter
B. Something essential
C. Livelihood
D. Relevant things

10. To bell the cat
A. To catch a cat and tie a bell round its neck
B. To make an effort
C. To be quick
D. To face a risk

11. Hard and fast
A. Strict B. Solid
C. Fast moving D. Some hard surface

12. Part and parcel
A. The part of a parcel
B. An essential part
C. A missing parcel
D. Some part of a machine sent by parcel

13. Null and void
A. Something invalid
B. Something that can be avoided
C. Something that can be nullified
D. Something evil

14. To make clean breast of
A. To gain prominence
B. To praise oneself
C. To confess without reserve
D. To destroy before it blooms

15. Trump card
A. A powerful means of achieving an object
B. Resourcefulness
C. The best gamble to attain success
D. None of these

16. Tall talk
A. A discussion continued for a long time
B. A high sounding talk
C. A meaningful talk
D. A useless talk

17. Small talk
A. Gossip
B. A discussion carried on for a long time
C. A brief discussion
D. None of these

18. Throw out of gear
A. To replace B. Hinder, disturb
C. To decide D. Take up tune

19. To and fro
A. Back and forth B. Puzzled
C. Amazed D. Reprove

20. To bell the cat
A. To do an easy job
B. To be indifferent to
C. To undertake a difficult job
D. To clarify

21. To be under cloud
A. Puzzle B. Enjoy the favour
C. Talk thoughtlessly D. To be under suspicion

22. A labour of love
A. A tragic end
B. A funny thing
C. Not fruitful
D. Work done without payment

23. Follow suit
A. Follow an example B. Wear a new dress
C. Irrelevant D. A gay person

24. Foul play
A. Bad intentions
B. A play not well acted
C. A play not liked by the audience
D. None of these

25. To pick holes
A. To find some reason to quarrel
B. To destroy something
C. To criticise someone
D. To cut some part of an item

26. To smell a rat
A. To see signs of plague epidemic
B. To get bad smell of a dead rat
C. To suspect foul dealings
D. To be in a bad mood

27. To put a spoke in one's wheel
A. To encourage
B. Act without restraint

C. Risk something
D. To obstruct one's progress

28. To pull one's leg

A. To give up B. Take care of
C. To befool D. To know

29. To play with fire

A. Grasp the truth
B. To handle something dangerous
C. To ridicule
D. To flee away

30. To reckon with

A. Take up time B. Make an inventory
C. To deal with D. Submit to punishment

31. To run short

A. Talk until one is tired at
B. Apply to oneself
C. To get rid of
D. To have or be too little

32. A man of letters

A. A postman B. A learned man
C. A hypocrite D. An ignorant man

33. A maiden speech

A. A speech made in the parliament
B. A speech made before unmarried girls
C. A speech made by a political leader
D. A speech made for the first time

34. Order of the day

A. An order passed on a particular day
B. A current law
C. Something common or general
D. None of these

35. To end in smoke

A. To make completely understand
B. To ruin oneself
C. To excite great applause
D. None of these

36. To give vent to

A. To allow to flow forth
B. To prove a failure
C. To amass wealth
D. To evade

37. To eat humble pie

A. To apologise or confess
B. To order
C. To flatter
D. To get rid of

38. A black sheep

A. An unlucky person B. A negro
C. An ugly person D. None of these

39. To catch a tartar

A. To trap wanted criminal with great difficulty
B. To catch a dangerous person
C. To meet with disaster
D. To deal with a person who is more than one's watch

40. Sit on fence

A. To remain neutral
B. To show contempt
C. To enjoy the surroundings
D. To become fond of

41. Pay off old scores

A. To repay the debt B. To have revenge
C. To invite D. Secretly

42. Turn turtle

A. To cheat B. To be lopsided
C. To frustrate D. To dance to the tune

43. Wash one's hands of

A. To refuse B. To assist
C. To abuse D. To refuse to be

44. Under duress

A. Under compulsion
B. Willing
C. To elicit information
D. To demand

45. To turn the tables

A. To ruin someone
B. To turn the situation to one's own side
C. To reverse the situation
D. To move from one point to another

46. On the cards

A. Possibly B. Probably
C. Openly D. Likely

47. To leave someone in the lurch

A. To come to compromise with someone
B. Constant source of annoyance to someone
C. To put someone at ease
D. To desert someone in his difficulties

48. To play second fiddle

A. To be happy, cheerful and healthy
B. To reduce importance of one's senior
C. To support the role and view of another person
D. To do back seat driving

49. To yearn for

A. To weep for B. To remember
C. To admire D. To long for intensely

50. Call off

A. To finish B. To withdraw
C. To postpone D. To cry

ANSWERS

1	2	3	4	5	6	7	8	9	10
C	C	C	D	B	D	C	C	C	D
11	**12**	**13**	**14**	**15**	**16**	**17**	**18**	**19**	**20**
A	B	A	C	C	B	A	B	A	C
21	**22**	**23**	**24**	**25**	**26**	**27**	**28**	**29**	**30**
D	D	A	A	C	C	D	C	B	C
31	**32**	**33**	**34**	**35**	**36**	**37**	**38**	**39**	**40**
D	B	D	C	D	A	A	D	B	A
41	**42**	**43**	**44**	**45**	**46**	**47**	**48**	**49**	**50**
B	B	D	A	C	D	D	C	D	B

Narration

Direct and Indirect Narration/Speech

The exact words spoken by the speaker are known as Direct Speech.

The words spoken by somebody and expressed by someone else with some modification are known as Indirect Speech.

(a) Ram says to me, "You do not help me."

(b) Ram tells me that I do not help him.

The sentence (*a*) shows the words spoken by Ram. So, it is a sentence of Direct Speech.

The sentence (*b*) shows the words spoken by Ram and expressed by someone else with certain modification. So, it is a sentence of Indirect Speech.

The following points should be noted while changing Direct Speech into Indirect speech:

1. The verb outside the inverted commas is called the Reporting Verb.
2. The verb or sentence inside the inverted commas is called the Reported Speech.
3. If the Reporting verb is in the Present or Future Tense, there is no change in the tense in the Reported Speech.
4. If the Reporting Verb is in the Past Tense, the Tense in the Reported Speech is changed.
5. The Reporting verb may be in any Tense, in it the Pronouns are changed as under:
   (*i*) First Person according to Subject
   (*ii*) Second Person according to Object
   (*iii*) Third Person, No change.
6. If the Reporting verb is in the Past Tense the Adverb will change as under in the Indirect Speech.

Direct	***Indirect***
now	then
here	there
after	before
today	that day
yesterday	the previous day
these	those
tomorrow	the next day
last week	the previous week
this	that

7. Adjectives/Determiners are changed as under:

Direct	***Indirect***
this	that
these	those

Rules for Change of Tense

Reporting Verb	Reporting Speech	Change of Tense
Present Tense	Any Tense	No change
Future Tense	Any Tense	No change
Past Tense	Present/Future Tense	Change into corresponding Past Tense
Past Tense	Past Indefinite Tense	Change into Past Perfect Tense
Past Tense	Past Continuous Tense	Change into Past Perfect Continuous Tense
Past Tense	Past Perfect/Perfect Continuous Tense	No change
Past Tense	Universal Truth	No change
Past Tense	Proverb	No change

Transformation of Speech Based on Special Rules

1. Rule Related to Interrogative Sentence

- If the answer of an interrogative sentence is possible in yes-no manner.

Illustration.

Dhoni said to Sachin, "Will you help me?"

Dhoni asked Sachin whether he would help him.

(**Note :** The answer of R.S. is possible in yes-no manner)

Rule of Transformation from Direct to Indirect speech

Step I : Change R.V. into ask.

Step II : In place of comma use 'if/whether'.

Step III : Change interrogative sentence into assertive sentence.

- If the answer of an interrogative sentence is not possible in yes-no manner.

Illustration:

Sachin said to Dhoni, "What do you want?"

Sachin asked Dhoni what he wanted.

(**Note :** Only in Step II, you have to avoid comma and inverted comma and rest will be same as mentioned above).

2. Rule related to Imperative Sentence

- Imperative sentence is a sentence which shows Order/ Advice/Request

Illustration:

My teacher said to me, "Go there".

My teacher ordered me to go there.

Rule of Transformation from Direct to Indirect Speech

Step I : Change R.V. as per meaning/sense of R.S. into order/request/advise.

Step II : In place of comma, use 'to'.

Step III : Rest portion will be same.

3. Rule related to Optative Sentence

- Optative sentence is a sentence which expresses the feeling of bless/curse/pray/wish.

Illustration:

Mother said to me, "May you live long!"

Mother blessed me that I might live long.

Rule of Transformation from Direct to Indirect Speech

Step I : Change R.V. as per meaning/sense of R.S. into bless/curse/pray/wish.

Step II : In place of comma, use 'that'.

Step III : Change optative sentence into assertive sentence.

4. Rule related to Exclamatory Sentence

- Exclamatory sentence is a sentence which takes note of exclamatory (!) mark in that sentence showing inner feeling.

Illustration:

She said, "Alas! I am ruined".

She exclaimed with sorrow that she was ruined.

Rule of Transformation from Direct to Indirect Speech

Step I : Change R.V. as per meaning/sense of R.S. into exclaim/exclaims/exclaimed/will or shall exclaim + joy/sorrow/anger/surprise/ applause/contempt.

Step II : Change comma into that.

Step III : Change note of exclamation (!) into full stop (.)

Step IV : Change exclamatory sentence into assertive sentence.

Universal, Historical Truth, etc.

If the Reported Speech expresses a Universal or Historical or Habitual truth, its Tense will not change.

1. The teacher said to the students, "The sun rises in the east."

   The teacher told the students that the sun rises in the east.

2. My father said to me, "The First Battle of Panipat was fought in 1526."

   My father told me that the First Battle of Panipat was fought in 1526.

Multiple Choice Questions

Directions (Qs. 1 to 13): *Select the correct Indirect Speech for the following sentences:*

1. I said to him, "I shall help you."
   A. I told him that I can help him.
   B. I told him that I would help him.
   C. I told him that I will help him.
   D. I told him that I shall be helping him.

2. My Teacher said to me, "The earth revolves round the sun."
   A. My teacher told me that the earth revolves round the sun.
   B. My teacher told me that the earth revolve round the sun.
   C. My teacher told me that the earth had been revolving round the sun.

D. My teacher told me that the earth has been revolving round the sun.

3. I said to my friend, "My father daily goes for a walk."
A. I told my friend that my father daily goes for a walk.
B. I told my friend that my father daily went for a walk.
C. I told my friend that my father has to go for a walk.
D. I told my friend that my father had gone for a walk.

4. He said to me, "May God bless you!"
A. He requested that God can bless me.
B. He prayed that God can bless me.
C. He prayed that God might bless me.
D. He prayed that God will bless me.

5. The patient said, "Thank you, doctor."
A. The patient thanked the doctor.
B. The patient requested the doctor with thanks.
C. The patient told the doctor thanks.
D. The patient suggested the doctor thanks.

6. Satish said, "No, I shall not talk to him."
A. Satish told that he should not talk to him.
B. Satish suggested that he would not have talked to him.
C. Satish exclaimed with sorrow that he would not talk with him.
D. Satish refused to talk to him.

7. The child said, "What a lovely place!"
A. The child exclaimed with sorrow that it was a lovely place.
B. The child thought that the place was lovely.
C. The child exclaimed with joy that the place was very lovely.
D. The child suggested that the place was lovely.

8. He said, "What a fool I have been!"
A. He told himself with sorrow that he was a fool.
B. He confessed with regret that he had been a great fool.
C. He said himself a fool.
D. He suggested that he could be a fool.

9. He said, "Alas! I am ruined."
A. He told me that he had been ruined.
B. He exclaimed with joy that he had been ruined.
C. He exclaimed with sorrow that he was ruined.
D. He told me that he should not be ruined.

10. The accused said, "I am not guilty."
A. The accused exclaimed with sorrow that I am not guilty.
B. The accused exclaimed with joy that he was not guilty.
C. The accused stated that he was not guilty.
D. The accused told me that he has not been guilty.

11. My teacher said, "The earth is round".
A. My teacher said that the earth was round.
B. My teacher says that the earth is round.
C. My teacher said that the earth is round.
D. My teacher ordered that the earth is round.

12. He said, "What a place it is!"
A. He said that it was a very fine place.
B. He said that is a very fine place.
C. He said that the place is fine.
D. He exclaimed with joy/surprise that it was a very fine place.

13. Ria said, "Shall I thread the needle?"
A. Ria asked if she should thread the needle.
B. Ria asked if she shall thread the needle.
C. Ria ordered if she should thread the needle.
D. Ria says that if she would thread the needle.

Directions (Qs. 14 to 33): *Pick out the correct alternative that completes the incomplete sentence which is changed into Indirect Narration.*

14. She said to me, "I shall see you as soon as I get time."
She told me:
A. that she will see me as soon as she will get time.
B. that she would see me as soon as she would get time.
C. she would see me whenever she got time.
D. that she would see me whenever she gets time.

15. My secretary said to me, "Your plane will leave if you do not go at once."
My secretary told me that:
A. her plane would leave if she did not go at that time.
B. her plane would leave if I do not go at once.
C. my plane would leave if I did not go at that very time.
D. my plane will leave if I did not go at that time.

16. My mother said to me, "Don't quarrel among yourselves".
My mother:
A. forbade me to quarrel among ourselves.
B. asked me not to quarrel among ourselves.
C. asked me that not to quarrel among ourselves.
D. asked me to quarrel not among ourselves.

17. Her father said to her mother, "Excuse the daughter."
Her father:
A. requested her mother to excuse the daughter.
B. asked her mother to excuse the daughter.
C. asked her mother to have excused the daughter.
D. asked her mother to have been excused.

18. He said to his friend, "Wait here till father comes."
He requested his friend:
A. to wait here till father had come.
B. that to wait there till his friend came.
C. to wait there till father came.
D. to wait here until his friend came.

19. She said to her maid, "Run and catch the thief."
She ordered her maid:
A. ran and catch the thief.
B. that to run and to catch the thief.
C. ran and caught the thief.
D. to run and catch the thief.

20. Anita said to Sunita, "What are you doing?"
Anita asked Sunita:
A. what she will be doing.
B. that what she is doing.
C. that what she was doing.
D. what she was doing.

21. She said to me, "Are you meeting me today?"
She enquired of me:
A. whether I am meeting her that day.
B. whether I was meeting her today.
C. whether I was meeting her that day.
D. I was meeting her that day.

22. Nitish said to me, "When did you buy this pen?"
Nitish asked me:
A. when I was to buy that pen.
B. when I would buy that pen.
C. when I had bought that pen.
D. when I was buying that pen.

23. She said to me, "Are you going to market?"
She enquired of me:
A. I am going to market.
B. I was going to market.
C. if I was going to market.
D. if I had been going to the market.

24. Damini said, "Why did not you change your clothes?"
Damini asked me:
A. why I had not changed my clothes.
B. why I did not change my clothes.
C. why I would not change my clothes.
D. why I have not been changing my clothes.

25. Umesh said to me, "Have you read that novel?"
Umesh asked me:
A. if he was reading that novel.
B. if he had read that novel.
C. if I had read that novel.
D. if I was reading that novel.

26. She said to me, "I shall forgive you."
She told me:
A. that she will forgive me.
B. that she was going to forgive me.
C. that she will not forgive me.
D. that she would forgive me.

27. I said to her, "It was very hot last night."
I told her:
A. that it had been very hot the previous night.
B. that it was very hot the previous night.
C. that it has been very hot the last night.
D. that it had been very hot this night.

28. She said to me, "I thank you for the help you have given."
She:
A. told me that she thanked me for the help I had given.
B. thanked me for the help I have given.
C. thanked to me for the help I have given.
D. thanked me for the help I had given.

29. Mohini said to me, "Trust in God."
Mohini advised me:
A. that I should trust in God.
B. should trust in God.
C. trusted in God.
D. to trust in God.

30. I said to him, "Let us go to school."
I told him:
A. we would go to school.
B. we shall go to school.
C. that we would go to school.
D. that we should go to school.

31. Rajni said, "May God bless you?"
Rajni:
A. exclaimed with wish that God might bless me.
B. expressed a wish that God might bless me.
C. asked God to bless me.
D. shouted with joy to bless me.

32. My mother said me, "Do not have so many friends."
My mother forbade me:
A. to have so many friends.
B. not to have so many friends.
C. to have been so many friends.
D. to possess so many friends.

33. Ram said, "Pay attention to me."
Ram asked:
A. pay attention to him.
B. paid attention to him.
C. having paid attention to him.
D. to pay attention to him.

Directions (Qs. 34 to 50): *In questions below, the sentences have been given in Direct/Indirect Speech. Out of the four alternatives suggested select the one which best expresses the given sentence in Indirect/Direct Speech.*

34. She said that her brother was getting married
A. She said, "Her brother is getting married."
B. She told, "My brother is getting married"
C. She said, "My brother is getting married".
D. She said, "My brother was married".

35. "Please don't go away", she said.
A. She said to please her and not go away.
B. She told me to go away.
C. She begged me not to go away.
D. She begged that I not go away.

36. "If you don't keep quiet I shall shoot you", he said to her in a calm voice.
A. He warned her to shoot if she didn't keep quiet calmly.
B. He said calmly that I shall shoot you if you don't be quiet.
C. He warned her calmly that he would shoot her if she didn't keep quiet.
D. Calmly he warned her that be quiet or else he will have to shoot her.

37. I told him that he was not working hard.
A. I said to him, "You are not working hard."
B. I told him, "You are not working hard."
C. I said, "You are not working hard."
D. I said to him, "He is not working hard."

38. She said that she would finish the work the next day.
A. She said, "I will finish the work the next day."
B. She said, "I will finish the work tomorrow."
C. She said, "You will finish the work tomorrow."
D. She said, "I finished the work."

39. She said to him, "Why don't you go today?"
A. She asked him why he did not go that day.
B. She said to him that why he don't go today.
C. She asked him not to go today.
D. She asked him why he did not go today.

40. "Are you alone, my son?" asked a soft voice close behind me.
A. A soft voice asked that what I was doing there alone.
B. A soft voice said to me are you alone son.
C. A soft voice from my back asked if I was alone.
D. A soft voice behind me asked if I was alone.

41. My cousin said, "My room-mate had snored throughout the night."
A. My cousin said that her room-mate snored throughout the night.
B. My cousin told me that her room-mate snored throughout the night.
C. My cousin complained to me that her room-mate is snoring throughout the night.
D. My cousin felt that her room-mate may be snoring throughout the night.

42. He asked Rama if he needed his help then.
A. He said to Rama, "Do you need my help?"
B. He told Rama, "Tell me if you need help."
C. He asked Rama, "Do I need your help?"
D. He said to Rama, "Do you need my help now?"

43. Nita ordered her servant to bring her a cup of tea.
A. Nita told her servant, "Bring a cup of tea."
B. Nita said, "Bring me a cup of tea."
C. Nita said to her servant, "Bring me a cup of tea."
D. Nita said to her servant, "Bring her that cup of tea."

44. He exclaimed with joy that India had won the Sahara Cup.
A. He said, "India has won the Sahara Cup."
B. He said, "India won the Sahara Cup."
C. He said, "How! India will win the Sahara Cup."
D. He said, "Hurrah! India has won the Sahara Cup."

45. The boy said, "Who dare call you a thief?"
A. The boy enquired who dared call him a thief.
B. The boy asked who called him a thief.
C. The boy told that who dared call him a thief.
D. The boy wondered who dared call a thief.

46. The little girl said to her mother, "Did the sun rise in the East?
A. The little girl said to her mother that the sun rose in the East.
B. The little girl asked her mother if the sun rose in the East.
C. The little girl said to her mother if the sun rises in the East.
D. The little girl asked her mother if the sun is in the East.

47. Dhruv said that he was sick and tired of working for that Company.
A. Dhruv said, "I am sick and tired of working for this Company."
B. Dhruv said, "He was tired of that Company."
C. Dhruv said to me, "I am sick and tired of working for this Company."
D. Dhruv said, "I will be tired of working for that Company."

48. He said to his father, "Please increase my pocket-money."
A. He told his father, please increase the pocket-money.
B. He pleaded his father to please increase my pocket-money.
C. He requested his father to increase his pocket-money.
D. He asked his father increase his pocket-money.

49. She said to her friend, "I know where is everyone."
A. She told that she knew where was everyone.
B. She told her friend that she knew where was everyone.
C. She told her friend she knew where is everyone
D. She told her friend that she knows where was everyone.

50. His father ordered him to go to his room and study.
A. His father said, "Go to your room and study."
B. His father said to him, "Go and study in your room."
C. His father shouted, "Go right now to your study room."
D. His father said firmly, "Go and study in your room."

ANSWERS

1	2	3	4	5	6	7	8	9	10
B	A	A	C	A	D	C	B	C	C
11	**12**	**13**	**14**	**15**	**16**	**17**	**18**	**19**	**20**
C	D	A	B	C	A	B	C	D	D
21	**22**	**23**	**24**	**25**	**26**	**27**	**28**	**29**	**30**
C	C	C	A	C	D	A	A	A	D
31	**32**	**33**	**34**	**35**	**36**	**37**	**38**	**39**	**40**
B	A	D	C	C	C	A	B	A	D
41	**42**	**43**	**44**	**45**	**46**	**47**	**48**	**49**	**50**
A	D	C	B	A	B	A	C	B	A

❑❑❑

Voice

A sentence in active voice focuses on the person or thing doing the action. A sentence in passive voice focuses on the person or thing affected by the action. *e.g.*,

The idol was built. (Active voice)
Someone built the idol. (Passive voice)

Transformation of Voice

- Voice and Tense are closely associated with each other.
- Tense plays an important role while transforming the voice.

On the basis of following points, voice can be transformed from active to passive voice.

The Present Indefinite Tense

Active voice: Subject + V_1 + Object
Passive voice: Subject + is, am, are + V_3 + by + Object

1. **Active voice:** He sings sweet songs.
   Passive voice: Sweet songs are sung by him.
2. **Active voice:** She does not cause any hindrance in my work.
   Passive voice: No hindrance in my work is caused by her.
3. **Active voice:** Do they love their country?
   Passive voice: Is their country loved by them?

The Present Continuous Tense

Active voice: Subject + is/am/are + V_1 + ing + Object.
Passive voice: Subject + is/am/are + being + V_3 + by + Object.

1. **Active voice:** She is cooking food.
   Passive voice: Food is being cooked by her.
2. **Active voice:** Rita is not knitting a sweater.
   Passive voice: A sweater is not being knitted by Rita.
3. **Active voice:** Is Meena baking a cake?
   Passive voice: Is a cake being baked by Meena?

The Present Perfect Tense

Active voice: Subject + has/have + V_3 + Object.
Passive voice: Subject + has/have + been + V_3 + by + Object.

1. **Active voice:** I have written an essay.
   Passive voice: An essay has been written by me.
2. **Active voice:** They have not whitewashed the fence.
   Passive voice: The fence has not been whitewashed by them.
3. **Active voice:** Have you cut the cake?
   Passive voice: Has the cake been cut by you?

The Past Indefinite Tense

Active voice: Subject + V_2 + Object
Passive voice: Subject + was/were + V_3 + by + Object

1. **Active voice:** He composed a new song.
   Passive voice: A new song was composed by him.
2. **Active voice:** He did not operate the computer.
   Passive voice: The computer was not operated by him.
3. **Active voice:** Did she catch a fish?
   Passive voice: Was a fish caught by her?

The Past Continuous Tense

Active voice: Subject + was/were + V_1 + ing + Object
Passive voice: Subject + was/were + being + V_3 + by + Object

1. **Active voice:** The farmers were ploughing the fields.
   Passive voice: The fields were being ploughed by the farmers.
2. **Active voice:** He was not administering the new drug to the patient.
   Passive voice: The new drug was not being administered to the patient by him.
3. **Active voice:** Was she sewing a dress?
   Passive voice: Was a dress being sewn by her?

The Past Perfect Tense

Active voice: Subject + had + V_3 + Object.
Passive voice: Subject + had + been + V_3 + by + Object

1. **Active voice:** He had issued me an import licence.
   Passive voice: I had been issued an import licence.
2. **Active voice:** We had not visited the Taj.
   Passive voice: The Taj had not been visited by us.
3. **Active voice:** Who had taught you English?
   Passive voice: By whom had you been taught English?

The Future Indefinite Tense

Active voice: Subject + will/shall + V_1 + Object.
Passive voice: Subject + will/shall + be + V_3 + by + Object.

1. **Active voice:** He will remove the dust from the shelf.
   Passive voice: The dust from the shelf will be removed by him.
2. **Active voice:** He will not open the main gate.
   Passive voice: The main gate will not be opened by him.
3. **Active voice:** Will you help us?
   Passive voice: Shall we be helped by you?

The Future Perfect Tense

Active voice: Subject + will/shall + have + V_3 + Object.
Passive voice: Subject + will/shall + have + been + V_3 + by + Object.

1. **Active voice:** They will have sold their house by then.
   Passive voice: Their house will have been sold by them by then.
2. **Active voice:** He will not have informed the police about it.
   Passive voice: The police will not have been informed about it by him.
3. **Active voice:** Will they have accepted the deal?
   Passive voice: Will the deal have been accepted by them?

Imperative Sentences

1. **Active voice:** Open the window.
   Passive voice: You are ordered to open the window.
   Or
   Let the window be opened.
2. **Active voice:** Please/kindly open the window.
   Passive voice: You are requested to open the window.
3. **Active voice:** Never make a noise.
   Passive voice: A noise should never be made.

Infinitives

1. **Active voice:** It is time to open the shop.
   Passive voice: It is time for the shop to be opened.
2. **Active voice:** He begged the officer to forgive him.
   Passive voice: He begged the officer to be forgiven.
3. **Active voice:** He has to break the door.
   Passive voice: The door has to be broken by him.

Prepositional Verb

1. **Active voice:** She laughed at the beggar.
   Passive voice: The beggar was laughed at by her.
2. **Active voice:** He listened to the news.
   Passive voice: The news was listened to by him.
3. **Active voice:** They called in the doctor.
   Passive voice: The doctor was called in by them.

Double Object

1. **Active voice:** He gave me a pen.
   Passive voice: A pen was given to me by him.
   Or
   I was given a pen by him.
2. **Active voice:** She told us a story.
   Passive voice: A story was told (to) us by her.
   Or
   We were told a story by her.

Use of Preposition other than 'by'

1. **Active voice:** The jug contains juice.
   Passive voice: Juice is contained in the jug.
2. **Active voice:** The audience thronged the hall.
   Passive voice: The hall was thronged with the audience.
3. **Active voice:** I know her.
   Passive voice: She is known to me.

Quasi Passive Verbs

1. **Active voice:** Quinine tastes bitter.
   Passive voice: Quinine is bitter when tasted.
   Or
   Quinine is bitter when it is tasted.
2. **Active voice:** Sugar is sweet (to taste).
   Passive voice: Sugar is sweet when tasted.
   Or
   Sugar is sweet when it is tasted.

Implied Sentences

1. **Active voice:** The driver drove the bus.
   Passive voice: The bus was driven.
2. **Active voice:** Someone read the news.
   Passive voice: The news was read.
3. **Active voice:** They say work is worship.
   Passive voice: It is said that work is worship.

Multiple Choice Questions

Directions (Qs. 1 to 20): *In the following questions, a sentence has been given in Active/Passive Voice. Out of the four alternatives suggested, select the one that Best Expresses the same sentence in Passive/Active Voice.*

1. Circumstances will oblige me to go.
A. I will oblige the circumstances and go.
B. I shall be obliged to go by the circumstances.
C. Under the circumstances, I should go.
D. I shall be obliged by the circumstances to go.

2. We waste much time on trifles.
A. Much time was wasted on trifles.
B. Much time will be wasted on trifles.
C. Much time is wasted by us on trifles.
D. Much time is wasted on trifles.

3. Mohan gave the beggar an old shirt.
A. An old shirt was given to Mohan by the beggar.
B. An old shirt was given to the beggar by Mohan
C. The begger was gave an old shirt by Mohan.
D. An old shirt was gave to the beggar by Mohan.

4. They have made him a king.
A. A king has been made by him.
B. He was made a king by them.
C. They have been made kings by him.
D. He has been made a king by them.

5. Who taught you English?
A. By whom English was taught to you?
B. By whom you were taught English?
C. By whom was English taught to you?
D. By whom are you taught English?

6. Was he knocking at the door?
A. Was the door being knocked at by him?
B. Was the door being knocked by him?
C. Was the door knocked by him?
D. Was the door knocking at him?

7. What was Rani doing?
A. What was done by Rani?
B. What was Rani being done?
C. What was being done by Rani?
D. What was being doing Rani?

8. Why were you wasting your time?
A. Why was your time being wasted?
B. Why was your time being wasted by you?
C. Why was your time wasted by you?
D. Why was your time wasted?

9. She has laid out a small garden.
A. A small garden has been laid by her.
B. A small garden has laid her.
C. A small garden being laid by her.
D. A small garden has been laid out by her.

10. She had already solved all the sums.
A. All the sums had already been solved by her.
B. All the sums have already been solved by her.
C. All the sums have been solved by her.
D. All the sums are solved by her.

11. He will have posted the letter.
A. The letter has been posted by him.
B. The letter will be posted by him.
C. The letter will have been posted by him.
D. The letter is posted by him.

12. They will have sold all the books by 4 P.M.
A. All the books will be sold by 4 P.M.
B. All the books will have been sold by 4 P.M.
C. All the books were being sold by 4 P.M.
D. All the books must be sold by 4 P.M.

13. Do you speak English?
A. Is English spoken by you?
B. Does English spoken by you?
C. Is English being spoken by you?
D. Does English being spoken by you?

14. Had they seen me before?
A. Had myself been seen by them before?
B. Had me being seen by them before?
C. Had I been seen by them before?
D. Had I being seen by them before?

15. May I take this pen?
A. May this pen will be taken by me?
B. May this pen shall be taken by me?
C. May this pen should be taken by me?
D. May this pen be taken by me?

16. Can we send it by air?
A. Can this be sent by air?
B. Can it be sent by air?
C. Can it go by air?
D. Can it be send by air?

17. Who wrote this book?
A. By whom was this book written?
B. By whom is this book written?
C. By whom was this book being written?
D. By whom is this book being written?

18. What did you buy?
A. What is bought by you?
B. What is being bought by you?
C. What was bought by you?
D. What was being bought by you?

19. Whom do you want?
A. Who is wanted by you?
B. Who is being wanted by you?
C. You are wanted by whom?
D. You are being wanted by whom?

20. When will you raise this question?
A. When this question will be raised by you?
B. When will this question be raised by you?
C. When this question is being raised by you?
D. When is this question being raised by you?

Directions (Qs. 21 to 35): *In each of the following questions, a sentence is given in Active Voice. Below it are given four alternatives suggesting the Passive Voice form of the above sentence. Choose the correct alternative.*

21. Who did this?
A. This was done by whom?
B. By whom was this done?
C. Who has done this?
D. By whom this was done?

22. One should keep ones promises.
A. Promises should be kept.
B. Ones promises should be kept by one.
C. Promises must be kept.
D. Ones promises one should keep.

23. Give the order.
A. Order given.
B. Order be given.
C. Let the order be given.
D. Order may be given by you.

24. You will have to do it.
A. It will be done by you.
B. It will have to be done by you.
C. It has to be done by you.
D. It would have to be done by you.

25. Keep to the left.
A. You are ordered to keep to the left.
B. You ought to keep to the left.
C. You are advised to keep to the left.
D. You must keep to the left.

26. They will arrange a party.
A. A party will have to be arranged by them.
B. A party they will have to arrange.
C. A party will be arranged by them.
D. A party by them will be arranged.

27. Someone has picked my pocket.
A. My pocket is picked.
B. My pocket has picked.
C. My pocket has been picked.
D. My pocket was picked.

28. He kept me waiting.
A. I kept waiting for him.
B. I kept waiting by him.
C. I was waiting for him.
D. I was kept waiting by him.

29. Why do you tell a lie?
A. Why is a lie told by you?
B. Why is told a lie by you?
C. Why is told by you a lie?
D. Why has a lie been told by you?

30. I have written a letter.
A. A letter is written by me.
B. A letter has been written by me.
C. A letter was written by me.
D. A letter had been written by me.

31. They will have helped you.
A. You will have helped by them.
B. You will have been helped by them.
C. You will be helped by them.
D. You will be helped by them.

32. Open the door.
A. Door may be opened.
B. Let the door be open.
C. Let the door be opened.
D. Door be opened.

33. I am reading a book.
A. A book is read by me.
B. A book is being read by me.
C. A book has been read by me.
D. A book in been read by me.

34. Why did your brother write such a letter?
A. Why your brother wrote such a letter?
B. Why was by brother written such a letter?
C. Why was such a letter written by your brother?
D. Why was written such a letter by your brother?

35. Did you run a great risk?
A. Was a great risk run by you?
B. Was run a great risk by you?
C. Was by you run a great risk?
D. Had you run a great risk?

Directions (Qs. 36 to 45): *In each of the following questions, a sentence is given in Passive Voice. Below it are given four alternatives suggesting the Active Voice form of the above sentence. Choose the correct alternative.*

36. He was made king.
A. He became king.
B. They made him king.
C. They had made him king.
D. He has been made king.

37. Good news is expected by us.
A. We are expecting good news.
B. We have been expecting good news.
C. We had expected good news.
D. We expect good news.

38. The child must be looked after.
A. The child you must look after.
B. You must look after the child.
C. You must look the child after.
D. You may look after the child.

39. What is wanted by you?
A. What you want?
B. What did you want?
C. What do you want?
D. What you do want?

40. Your father is known to me.
A. I am known to your father.
B. I know your father.
C. I have known your father.
D. I knew your father.

41. She may be told the story by you.
A. The story may be told by you to her.
B. You may tell the story to her.
C. You may tell her the story.
D. You may tell to her the story.

42. Duty ought to be done.
A. Let duty be done.
B. One ought to do one's duty.
C. One should do his duty.
D. Do you duty.

43. Is English spoken by you?
A. Did you speak English?
B. Do you speak English?
C. Have you spoken English?
D. Do you know how to speak English?

44. Gold coins are contained in this box.
A. This box contains gold coins.
B. This box has contained gold coins.
C. This box is containing gold coins.
D. This box has gold coins.

45. Character is revealed by manners.
A. Manners revealed character.
B. Manners reveal character.
C. Manners have revealed character.
D. Manners do reveal character.

ANSWERS

1	2	3	4	5	6	7	8	9	10
D	C	B	D	C	A	C	B	D	A
11	**12**	**13**	**14**	**15**	**16**	**17**	**18**	**19**	**20**
C	B	A	C	D	B	A	C	A	B
21	**22**	**23**	**24**	**25**	**26**	**27**	**28**	**29**	**30**
B	A	C	B	C	C	C	D	A	B
31	**32**	**33**	**34**	**35**	**36**	**37**	**38**	**39**	**40**
B	C	B	C	A	B	D	B	C	B
41	**42**	**43**	**44**	**45**					
C	B	B	A	B					

Sentence Completion

Filling the blanks is such an exercise that starts with the primary schools and continues at the highest level of competitive examinations. One must practise it regularly to score well.

Multiple Choice Questions

Directions: *Pick out the most effective word(s) from the given words to fill in the blanks and make the sentence meaningfully complete.*

1. One requires great .... to teach and handle little children who are restless.
A. patience B. attitude
C. determination D. knowledge

2. The researchers will .... some of the causes of increasing poverty in the state.
A. fund B. investigate
C. promote D. circulate

3. I usually perform .... when nobody is watching me.
A. alone B. good
C. better D. hard

4. It was .... to everyone that the minister had been drinking.
A. observed B. known
C. discovered D. realised

5. I would rather stay indoors .... the rain stops.
A. so B. waiting
C. until D. usually

6. The process should be completed as far as possible within a week, ... which the matter should be brought to notice of the officer concerned.
A. following B. failing
C. realizing D. referring

7. The officers are ..... to regular transfers.
A. free B. open
C. subject D. available

8. All letters received from Government should ..... be acknowledged.
A. suddenly B. obviously
C. immediately D. occasionally

9. Mumbai office ..... a meeting of senior officials to discuss the high incidence of frauds.
A. attended B. convened
C. reported D. registered

10. The note should be ..... to all the concerned departments for their consideration.
A. regulated B. requested
C. carried D. forwarded

11. Your present statement does not .... what you said last week.
A. accord to B. accord in
C. accord with D. accord for

12. I had a vague .... that the lady originally belonged to Scotland.
A. notion B. expression
C. imagination D. theory

13. The prisoner showed no .... for his crimes.
A. hatred B. obstinacy
C. remorse D. anger

14. It is inconceivable that in many schools children are subjected to physical .... in the name of discipline.
A. violation B. exercise
C. violence D. security

15. We have not yet fully realised the .... consequences of the war.
A. happy B. pleasing
C. grim D. exciting

16. Happiness consists in being .... what we have.
A. contented to B. contented with
C. contented for D. contented in

17. His rude behaviour is a .... his organization.
A. disgrace for B. disgrace on
C. disgrace upon D. disgrace to

18. No child is .... understanding. One has to wait and provide proper guidance.
A. dull to B. dull in
C. dull of D. dull for

19. I am fully .... the problems facing the industry.
A. alive with B. alive to
C. alive for D. alive on

20. The Romans were .... science.
A. bad in B. bad to
C. bad for D. bad at

21. Although I was .... of his plans, I encouraged him, because there was no one else who was willing to help.
A. sceptical B. remorseful
C. fearful D. excited

22. You have no business to .... pain on a weak and poor person.
A. inflict B. put
C. direct D. force

23. Her uncle died in a car accident. He was quite rich. She suddenly .... all her uncle's money.
A. succeeded B. caught
C. gave D. inherited

24. There was a major accident. The plane crashed. The pilot .... did not see the tower.
A. likely B. probably
C. scarcely D. hurriedly

25. The car we were travelling in .... a mile from home.
A. broke off B. broke down
C. broke into D. broke up

26. What are you .... in the kitchen cupboard?
A. looking in B. looking on
C. looking to D. looking for

27. I did not see the point of .... waiting for them, so I went home.
A. hanging around B. hang on
C. hang together D. hanging up

28. He lost confidence and .... of the deal at the last minute.
A. backed out B. backed on
C. backed down D. backed onto

29. To the dismay of all the students, the class monitor was ..... berated by the principal at a school assembly.
A. critically B. ignominiously
C. prudently D. fortuitously

30. All attempts to revive the fishing industry were ..... failure.
A. foredoomed to B. heading at
C. predicted for D. estimated to

31. There are ..... parked outside than yesterday.
A. fewer cars B. few cars
C. less cars D. a small number of cars

32. The minister had to ..... some awkward questions from reporters.
A. fend B. fend at
C. fend out D. fend off

33. The ..... of evidence was on the side of the plaintiff since all but one of the witnesses testified that his story was correct.
A. propensity B. force
C. preponderance D. brunt

34. Attention to detail is ..... of a fine craftsman.
A. hallmark B. stamp
C. seal of authority D. authenticity

35. Behaving in a ………… and serious way, even in a ………… situation, makes people respect you.
A. calm, difficult B. steady, angry
C. flamboyant, tricky D. cool astounding

36. Along with a sharp rise in ………, a recession would eventually result in more men, women, and children living in ……….
A. crime, apathy B. fatalities, poor
C. deaths, slums D. unemployment, poverty

37. The government has ……… to provide financial aid to the ones …… by severe floods in the city.
A. desired, troubled B. promised, havoc
C. failed, affected D. wanted, struck

38. An airplane with ……. passengers on board made an unscheduled .... as the airport to which it was heading was covered with thick fog.
A. imitable, slip B. faulty, stop
C. variety, halt D. numerous, landing

39. Deemed universities .... huge fees, but have not been successful in providing .... education to our students.
A. collect, maintaining
B. pay, better
C. ask, good
D. charge, quality

40. If the banks desire to .... profit, they should get rid of .... measures.
A. lose, concentrate B. increase, populist
C. earn, unhealthy D. maximise, traditional

41. Leadership defines what the future should look like and ...... people with that vision.
A. aligns B. develops
C. trains D. encourages

42. We upset ourselves by responding in an ...... manner to someone else's actions.
A. unabashed B. irrational
C. arduous D. arguable

43. All the people involved in that issue feel a great ..... to his suggestion.

A. contradiction B. adherence
C. indifference D. repugnance

44. These elections will be remembered as much for its anti-incumbency mood as for its ...... mandate.
A. invincible B. rational
C. unprecedented D. deliberate

45. How do you expect us to stay in such a ...... building even if it can be hired on a nominal rent?
A. scruffy B. disperate
C. fragmented D. robust

46. ...... efforts from all concerned are required to raise the social and economic conditions of our countrymen.
A. Perpetual B. Dynamic
C. Massive D. Exploring

47. Many companies see technology as a ...... for a whole host of business problems.
A. consideration B. preference
C. linking D. panacea

48. Known as devout and serious person, she also has ...... sense of humour.
A. better B. plentiful
C. quick D. good

49. The matter would have become serious if ...... action had not been taken.
A. hasty B. fast
C. timely D. unusual

50. The ...... with which he is able to yield the paint brush is really remarkable.
A. ease B. practice
C. majesty D. sweep

51. You must ensure the correctness of the information before ....
A. drawing B. enabling
C. learning D. jumping

52. The rocket .... the target and did not cause any casualty.
A. sensed B. reached
C. missed D. exploded

53. It is desirable to take .... in any business if you want to make profit.
A. advice B. risk
C. loan D. recourse

54. They wasted all the money on purchase of some .... items.
A. excellent B. important
C. significant D. trivial

55. When he found the wallet his face glowed but soon it faded as the wallet was ....
A. empty B. vacant
C. recovered D. stolen

56. He has served the country by .... many significant positions.
A. appointing B. creating
C. developing D. holding

57. The frequent errors are a result of the student's ....
A. talent B. smartness
C. carelessness D. perception

58. The robbers eventually .... in breaking into the house.
A. succeeded B. decided
C. caught D. trained

59. I finally .... her to stay another day.
A. advised B. persuaded
C. suggested D. called

60. Most of the people who .... the book exhibition were teachers.
A. witnessed B. presented
C. conducted D. attended

ANSWERS

1	2	3	4	5	6	7	8	9	10
A	B	C	A	C	B	C	C	B	D
11	**12**	**13**	**14**	**15**	**16**	**17**	**18**	**19**	**20**
C	A	C	C	C	B	D	B	B	D
21	**22**	**23**	**24**	**25**	**26**	**27**	**28**	**29**	**30**
B	C	C	B	C	C	D	A	B	A
31	**32**	**33**	**34**	**35**	**36**	**37**	**38**	**39**	**40**
A	D	D	A	A	D	C	D	C	B
41	**42**	**43**	**44**	**45**	**46**	**47**	**48**	**49**	**50**
A	A	D	C	A	A	D	D	C	A
51	**52**	**53**	**54**	**55**	**56**	**57**	**58**	**59**	**60**
A	C	B	D	A	D	C	A	B	D

Sentence Improvement

One may use the same words in many ways but the best way is only one that makes the perfect usage of the words and conveys the proper meaning of the expression. Try it yourself in the following questions.

Multiple Choice Questions

Directions: *In these questions, a part of the sentence is bold. Below are given alternatives to the bold part at A, B and C which may improve the sentence. Choose the correct alternative. In case no improvement is needed, your answer is 'D'.*

1. Discreet salience **is extremely important** to create that 'irresistible-yet-unattainable' image for brands that want to take India seriously

A. was extremely important
B. is mainly important
C. was important extremely
D. No Improvement

2. This, over a designer outfit that he wanted for a friend's party and **that his sensitive** parents refused him.

A. which his sensitive B. which his insensitive
C. that his insensitive D. No Improvement

3. Goa was full of non-Goa property hunters **rushing about buying up the place** like tomorrow was an expired lease.

A. rushing in buying up the place
B. rushed about buying up the place
C. rushing about to buy up the place
D. No Improvement

4. Property hunting is a **tired and hungry** making business.

A. is a tiresome and hungry
B. is a tiring and hungry
C. is a tiring and waste
D. No Improvement

5. Cultural differences aside, **till luxury need speaks** in a manner that befits.

A. luxury still needs to speak
B. luxury still need to speak
C. luxury till need to speak
D. No Improvement

6. Indian food—the culinary avatar of the subcontinent's social history presented on a platter—**is without doubt the best food** in the world.

A. is undoubtedly the greatest food
B. is without doubt greatest food
C. is best food without doubt
D. No Improvement

7. It must retain the language of poetry. **It needed to create** stories, and not statements.

A. It needed creating
B. It needs creating
C. It needs to create
D. No Improvement

8. This year, Asia-Pacific has become the first region **to reach aggregate profiting** in biotech.

A. to reach aggregated profitability
B. to reach aggregate profitability
C. to reach aggregate of profit
D. No Improvement

9. India is deviating to embrace the West. If Western luxury brands deviate a little, **albeit selectively**, they will find rich Indian arms open far and wide.

A. though selectively
B. however selectively
C. albeit selectedly
D. No Improvement

10. China and India continued to attract **attention** and deals, motivated by the desire to increase access to these **largest and growing** drug markets and by the need to lower the costs of drug development.

A. larger and growing
B. large and growing
C. larger and grown
D. No Improvement

11. Luxury brands are **still above of the** clover curve here, with their elite (small) audiences.
A. still ahead of the
B. still in the
C. still far of the
D. No Improvement

12. Agencies **hence needed to be** sure of returns before investing, say admen.
A. hence needs to be
B. so needs to be
C. hence need to be
D. No Improvement

13. India is still a nascent market and that's the spirit everyone's **looking at it**.
A. looking for it B. looking in it
C. looking with it D. No Improvement

14. Questioning the state's move to allow women to serve liquor but not dance in bars **of the ground that** dancing aroused physical lust.
A. on the grounds that
B. of the grounds that
C. over the grounds that
D. No Improvement

15. For England the positives from their crushing series lose come in the shape of James Anderson and Kevin Pietersen, **both of which** have made significant strides up the rankings.
A. both of which B. both of whom
C. both of who D. No Improvement

16. International campaigns can work well for luxury here, **but context cannot be** ignored.
A. so context cannot be
B. but context cannot
C. but context couldn't
D. No Improvement

17. For one, the Indian luxury context, **while evolved rapidly**, still has its own meaning, and its own implications.
A. while evolved rapid
B. which evolving rapidly
C. while evolving rapidly
D. No Improvement

18. But too much of availability can compromise a luxury brand or **made it lose** its lustre.
A. make her lose B. make him lose
C. make it lose D. No Improvement

19. Still, it's under-the-upper **layers themselves who** are aspiring for slivers of luxury.
A. layers themselves which
B. layer itself who
C. layers themself which
D. No Improvement

20. It is like saying Hindi movies, with skimpily dressed dancers, would **effect public** order.
A. effect your B. affect public
C. affected public D. No Improvement

21. The court held that a few women being involved in prostitution was no **justice to deny other** bar girls the right to livelihood.
A. justification to declare other
B. justification to deny other
C. justice to let other
D. No Improvement

22. All-rounder cricketer has also made some progress **over the** player rankings.
A. above the B. at the
C. up the D. No Improvement

23. Former minister on Sunday **joined hands** with a suspended Lok Sabha member to float a new political outfit.
A. folded hands
B. walked hand in hand
C. shaked hands
D. No Improvement

24. Pakistan's former ministers will meet in London on Monday **to ask** a strategy to return home from exile.
A. to chalk out
B. to negotiate
C. to create
D. No Improvement

25. It's a family potboiler, medical thriller and political drama **all in one**–except that it's all too real and all too grim.
A. all 3 in one
B. all coupled into one
C. all rolled into one
D. No Improvement

26. India's efforts to get international support for its civil nuclear energy programme got **a go ahead on** Sunday as Germany indicated it would not come in the way of the India-US nuclear deal.
A. a life in B. a boost on
C. a boost at D. No Improvement

27. Is it time for old bungalows to **bite the dust**?
A. go down B. get down
C. come down D. No Improvement

28. The bungalows was an outward manifestation of a certain **way in life**, and with that era gone.
A. way for life B. way of life
C. way at life D. No Improvement

29. The builder Mittals will reportedly **raise their money**-raking high-rise behind it.
A. highten their money
B. rise their money
C. raise there money
D. No Improvement

30. The impatient present has usually demolished **more of the** past before we wake up to the irretrievable loss.
A. much of B. much of their
C. much of the D. No Improvement

31. Preservation is a romantic notion; demolition **quiet** more practical reasons.
A. has many, B. had many,
C. have many, D. No Improvement

32. You must get back to your **charming self** and impress the audience with your social skills.
A. own self B. main self
C. own uniqueness D. No Improvement

33. Stay focused on your goals and don't **get disturbed by** non-materialistic possessions.
A. get involved by
B. get betrayed by
C. get distracted by
D. No Improvement

34. You may appear more optimistic than your detractors **may want it to be**.
A. want you to be
B. wish yourself to be
C. seek you be
D. No Improvement

35. There are a number of mineral springs in the Czech territory, which **has been used** for medicinal purposes since the early 15th century.
A. have been used B. had been used
C. has being used D. No Improvement

36. The picturesque mountains **offer**s excellent bungee jumping spots.
A. shows B. provides
C. offer D. No Improvement

37. Begin your **meal with** traditional faves like potato soup, beef soup with liver dumplings or dill soup made from sour milk.
A. meals with B. meal in
C. meals of D. No Improvement

38. You can also **go to the** National Museum building and the famous Prague State Opera.
A. went to B. visit the
C. saw D. No Improvement

39. If they close the Gulf for a **length of time** to shipping, then certainly we could look at $150, probably higher.
A. larger amount of time
B. larger duration of time
C. larger amount of hours
D. No Improvement

40. **More of them** are owned by the state and even the privately-owned ones are open to the public.
A. Most of which B. Most of them
C. Most of all D. No Improvement

41. Constructed in the ninth century by the Prince Booivoj, the castle has transformed **oneself** from a wooden fortress surrounded by earthen bulwarks to the imposing form it has today.
A. himself B. herself
C. itself D. No Improvement

42. Apart from frequent art exhibitions, **their are also** permanent collections devoted to archaeology, anthropology, mineralogy, natural history and numismatics.
A. there is also B. there are also
C. their are also D. No Improvement

43. You can visit the Czech Museum of Fine Arts, **at a** permanent exhibition on Czech Kubism.
A. with a
B. for a
C. in a
D. No Improvement

44. Tensions **above** Iran come at a time of strong demand for energy.
A. under B. inside
C. over D. No Improvement

45. Because its shores line the narrow Straits of Hormuz, Iran **could quickly hit** both military and commercial shipping.
A. will quickly hit
B. shall quickly hit
C. will be quick hitting
D. No Improvement

46. For most people who exercise **at the** morning, there is no getting around the question: Eat and run? Or run and eat later?
A. in the B. in
C. at the time of D. No Improvement

47. Are ad agencies even attempting to peer into the keyhole of this indulgence sanctum to garner consumer insights **ahead of** the curve?

A. above
B. over
C. within
D. No Improvement

48. Too many people rush into the world of credit and don't stop to think about how **their actions could affect their** credit score and ability to qualify for credit in the future.

A. their actions may affect their
B. their actions might affect their
C. their actions will affect their
D. No Improvement

49. According to the report, **number of deal with** vaccines were energized by concerns around avian flu, SARS, and biodefence products, while looming patent expirations led to more deals in generics.

A. number of deals in
B. number of deal in
C. number of deals with
D. No Improvement

50. This is how the Bombay High Court responded to the state government's purported **moral stand which** dance bars were causing grave harm to society.

A. moral stand in
B. moral stand at
C. moral stand that D. No Improvement

51. If you have a high credit limit, use **at least a** third of it.

A. atleast a
B. at last a
C. utmost a
D. No Improvement

52. Fitness experts will say that **first eating provides** fuel for a proper workout.

A. eating in the beginning provides
B. first eat provides
C. eating first provides
D. No Improvement

53. One study that examined the claim directly in 1995 found that a group of people did **burned much calories from fat on days** when they exercised on an empty stomach than on days when they had a small breakfast first.

A. burn more calories from fat on days
B. burn more calorie from fat on days
C. burnt more calories from fat on days
D. No Improvement

54. Carefree children spent their afternoons **to run about barefoot**, their clothes dusty, and telltale twigs of the neighbour's mango tree in their hair.

A. running barefoot in the sun
B. run about barefoot in the sun
C. running about barefoot in the sun
D. No Improvement

55. A year ago, a 13-year-old girl attempted suicide because her mother **refuses to pay his** mobile bills.

A. refuses to pay her B. refused to pay her
C. refused to pay his D. No Improvement

ANSWERS

1	2	3	4	5	6	7	8	9	10
D	C	D	B	A	D	C	C	D	B
11	**12**	**13**	**14**	**15**	**16**	**17**	**18**	**19**	**20**
C	C	D	A	C	D	C	C	C	C
21	**22**	**23**	**24**	**25**	**26**	**27**	**28**	**29**	**30**
B	C	C	A	C	B	D	B	D	C
31	**32**	**33**	**34**	**35**	**36**	**37**	**38**	**39**	**40**
A	D	C	A	D	C	A	B	D	B
41	**42**	**43**	**44**	**45**	**46**	**47**	**48**	**49**	**50**
C	B	A	C	D	A	D	C	A	C
51	**52**	**53**	**54**	**55**					
C	C	A	C	B					

Reordering Words & Sentences

Different words form a sentence and convey their meaning only when arranged in a proper order. A Paragraph is formed from sentences, it will convey its true meaning and purpose only when the sentences are arranged in a proper manner. Try and practise it in this exercise.

Multiple Choice Questions

Directions (Qs. 1 to 20): *In the following questions, some parts of the sentence have been jumbled up. You are required to rearrange these parts which are labelled P, Q, R and S to produce the correct sentence. Choose the option with proper sequence.*

1. We are doing
P : to the people
Q : to give relief
R : all we can
S : but more funds are needed
The correct sequence should be
A. P Q R S B. R Q P S
C. Q P R S D. S P Q R

2. The man
P : when he was
Q : in the office last evening
R : could not finish
S : all his work
The correct sequence should be
A. P Q R S B. Q R S P
C. R Q P S D. R S P Q

3. The people decided
P : they were going
Q : how much
R : to spend
S : on the construction of the school building
The correct sequence should be
A. Q P R S B. P Q R S
C. P R Q S D. S Q P R

4. The man said that
P : those workers
Q : would be given a raise
R : who did not go on
S : strike last month
The correct sequence should be
A. P Q R S B. P R S Q
C. Q P R S D. R S P Q

5. I think
P : the members
Q : are basically in agreement
R : of the group
S : on the following points
The correct sequence should be
A. R Q P S B. S Q R P
C. P R Q S D. P Q S R

6. While it was true that
P : I had
Q : to invest in industry
R : some lands and houses
S : I did not have ready cash
The correct sequence should be
A. P Q R S B. P R S Q
C. S Q P R D. Q P R S

7. P : But for your help
Q : to finish this work
R : it would not have been possible
S : in time
The correct sequence should be
A. P R Q S B. S P Q R
C. R P Q S D. P Q R S

8. The boy
P : in the competition
Q : who was wearing spectacles
R : won many prizes
S : held in our college

The correct sequence should be

A. P Q R S B. R P S Q
C. Q R P S D. Q P S R

9. About 200 years ago,
P : in the south of India
Q : an old king
R : ruled over a kingdom
S : called Rajavarman
The correct sequence should be
A. Q S R P B. P Q R S
C. Q P S R D. Q S P R

10. P : his land
Q : a wooden plough
R : the Indian peasant still uses
S : to cultivate
The correct sequence should be
A. R Q P S B. Q P S R
C. S R Q P D. R Q S P

11. He was a man,
P : even if he had to starve
Q : who would not beg
R : borrow or steal
S : from anyone
The correct sequence should be
A. P Q R S B. P R Q S
C. Q R S P D. Q P R S

12. P : in the progress of
Q : universities play a crucial role
R : our civilization
S : in the present age
The correct sequence should be
A. S Q P R B. Q R S P
C. Q R P S D. S Q R P

13. P : far out into the sea
Q : for the next two weeks there were further explosions
R : which hurled
S : ashes and debris
The correct sequence should be
A. Q R P S B. R S P Q
C. Q R S P D. S R P Q

14. William Shakespeare,
P : in his lifetime
Q : the great English dramatist
R : wrote thirty-five plays
S : and several poems
The correct sequence should be
A. P Q R S B. R S P Q
C. Q S R P D. Q R S P

15. Whenever I am,
P : with an old friend of mine
Q : in New Delhi
R : to have dinner
S : I always try
The correct sequence should be
A. S Q P R B. Q S R P
C. R P S Q D. P R Q S

16. P : I don't know
Q : must have thought
R : what people sitting next to me
S : but I came away
The correct sequence should be
A. R S Q P B. R Q S P
C. P Q R S D. P R Q S

17. P : in estimating the size of the earth
Q : but they were hampered by the lack of instruments of precision
R : ancient astronomers
S : used methods which were theoretically valid
The correct sequence should be
A. R P Q S B. P R Q S
C. R S Q P D. R P S Q

18. P : It is a pity that
Q : by offering a handsome dowry
R : a number of parents think that
S : they will be able to ensure the happiness of their daughters
The correct sequence should be
A. S Q R P B. P R S Q
C. P S R Q D. P R Q S

19. The common man
P : in nurturing
Q : a more active role
R : communal harmony
S : should play
The correct sequence should be
A. P R S Q B. S Q P R
C. S Q R P D. P R Q S

20. The doctor
P : able to find out
Q : what has caused
R : the food poisoning
S : has not been
The correct sequence should be
A. S P R Q B. P R Q S
C. P R S Q D. S P Q R

Directions (Qs. 21 to 40): *A number of sentences are given below which when properly sequenced form a coherent paragraph. Each sentence is labelled as abcdef...... Choose the most logical order of sentences from among the given choices to construct a coherent paragraph:*

21. (a) Parts of northern region were pounded by heavy rains today,
(b) Vehicular traffic came to a near halt.
(c) As mid and high altitude areas of Himachal Pradesh were in grip of severe cold wave with snow lashing the tribal areas and mid ranges receiving showers.
(d) As the sky remained heavily overcast with dark clouds reducing the visibility considerably.
(e) A large number of tourists were forced to buy heavy woollens and stay indoors due to inclement weather.
A. ecabd B. adecb
C. edabc D. acbde

22. (a) The idea is that students should be able to find employment for themselves after the course.
(b) The Central Board of Secondary Education is planning a revamp of its vocational courses.
(c) For this it is necessary to tie up with the industry as well as mobilise schools for their support.
(d) While others will be made less academic and more in tune with the needs of the industry.
(e) A number of courses have been identified as 'deadwood' and will be done away with.
A. bedac B. abcde
C. acebd D. baced

23. (a) Clearly, age is not a deterrent in one's choice of learning.
(b) Perhaps, it was because of her childhood desire.
(c) When Rachna came to Delhi eight years back, she had not anticipated a career in the field of art.
(d) She has been successful in the various exhibitions that she has been part of in terms of business.
(e) She had got into expressing her thoughts with the help of a brush and colours only because her daughter refused to get initiated into it.
(f) She feels that her use of colour appeals to people.
A. aedcbf B. cdefba
C. cebadf D. acdebf

24. (a) The rehabilitation record has been dismal.
(b) It has been two years years since the earthquake rudely rattled the people of Gujarat.
(c) And since then, life has been a constant struggle.
(d) The quake set Gujarat's clock back by 10 years.
(e) Things changed forever.
A. bedca B. bcade
C. dbace D. edcba

25. (a) In fact, success in exams depended on rote learning from old notes.
(b) when he was studying civil engineering in a college in Gujarat.
(c) He was detained for lack of attendance.
(d) Lectures were soporific, classes rarely worth attending and 80 per cent attendance compulsory.
(e) The college became a trap he hated.
(f) His is a plight many engineers across India would identify with.
(g) He found the going tough.
A. abcdgef B. bgdacef
C. fabcdge D. abcdefg

26. (a) In a country that has close to 600 recognised engineering colleges, there are only seven IITs.
(b) Barring a few exeptions, the academic atmosphere in these is moribund.
(c) The very best students usually get there.
(d) many waste themselves in frustration.
(e) Most of those who get into engineering are good students.
(f) but about 1.25 lakh others and up in the remaining colleges.
A. aecfbd B. abecdf
C. abcdef D. acfbed

27. (a) Whatever the job market, common wisdom says that IIT graduates will find jobs where others have failed.
(b) The IIT brand name is a ticket to success.
(c) When recruiters go headhunting, the IITs are still top of their list.
(d) Its possessor is understood to have an excellent academic record and the will to succeed.
(e) In the job market, that counts.
A. bdeac B. abcde
C. abdce D. dbace

28. (a) It will pave the way ....
(b) signalling a new beginning in strategic ties......
(c) for a tangible Indian economic presence in Iran and Central Asia.
(d) Iran has offered India valuable road linkages to central Asia ......
(e) aimed at promoting peace and economic cooperation in the region.
A. dbeac B. debca
C. acebd D. abced

29. (a) A good college is essential for a successful career and admissions are based on marks.
(b) The marks-based system followed by all the boards in the country recognises only a small percentage of students as successful.
(c) The marks one scores in the crucial board exams dictate the path his life takes.
(d) Anyone scoring below a certain percentage is automatically branded a 'failure'.
(d) So if you cannot make it into the best college, your career is over even before it has started.

A. abcde B. bcdea
C. bdcae D. abdec

30. (a) The project has already started on an experimental basis in the west district.
(b) A website is soon going to be launched where application forms can be downloaded and submitted.
(c) Standing in a queue at a government office to submit application form will be a thing of the past.
(d) A unique code will be alloted while submitting the form which will help in finding the status of the application.
A. abcd B. dabc
C. cbda D. badc

31. (a) To curb bio-terrorism is a difficult task.
(b) To check these attacks and lessen their impact, we need an impartial team of sincere, strong and dedicated men.
(c) The media can play a strong role in stopping this unnecessary spread of panic.
(d) Since bio-terrorism is not visible or easily detectable, it can be used often.
(e) Men who honour the lives of their fellow countrymen before their own.
A. abcde B. dabce
C. adbec D. acbed

32. (a) He was dying.
(b) No one was ready to touch him as even shifting him from one place to another would lead to profuse bleeding.
(c) He was a five-day old infant, premature and bleeding profusely.
(d) Even if injected one small needle, blood would ooze out and continue to flow for an hour at a stretch.
(e) This small being had haematoma, a thick blood clot in his brain.
A. edbca B. cabde
C. eacdb D. cedba

33. (a) The day I don't treat a patient, I feel ....
(b) I have enough to eat, I crave for blessings now.
(c) But if a financially weak patient gives me only ₹ 50, I don't mind.
(d) Each month I do three to four operations free of cost.
(e) I have lost something in life.
(f) My consultation fee is ₹ 300.
A. fcdeab B. dfcbae
C. fcabde D. bdfcea

34. (a) When he was rushed to the nearby Primary Health Centre after his fall, the doctor referred him to a hospital.
(b) This worsened his injury.
(c) Had a little precaution been exercised after the accident, Tarun would have continued with his gymnastic classes.
(d) He was paralysed from waist downwards when he fell from the vaulting horse while doing gymnastics.
(e) However, the doctor forgot to tell Tarun's parents to take him on a stretcher as he had suffered spinal injuries.
(f) Tarun is wheelchair bound for two years.
A. fdeabc B. abcdef
C. fdcaeb D. fdbcae

35. (a) As the temperature rises, staying hydrated can become a greater challenge for people exercising both indoors and out.
(b) Several things can influence this process, including age, gender, physical conditioning. humidity and a lack of sufficient fluids.
(c) In hot weather, individuals can lose as much as two quarts of sweat per hour.
(d) As we age, we have a lower perceived level of thirst in response to fluid loss and early stages of dehydration.
(e) If not replenished, this can lead to dehydration, heat exhaustion and even heatstroke.
A. abcde B. dbcae
C. cbdea D. acebd

36. (a) The leopard was discovered in the servant quarters of a farmhouse.
(b) The injuries appeared to have been caused by the paws of the leopard, and were not teeth wounds.
(c) It took the wild life officials, Delhi Police and Delhi zoo vets eight hours to capture the leopard that had wandered into a factory in south Delhi.
(d) The leopard then jumped into the factory where the workers managed to lock it in a small generator room before calling in the police.
(e) Before its capture, the leopard attacked two women and a man in the farmhouse.
A. aebdc B. bdaec
C. eadbc D. adbec

37. (a) Police suspect a carpenter working at John's house as he has not reported for work since the day the boy went missing.
(b) John did not return home in the afternoon.
(c) John's mother had herself put the boy on the vehicle in the morning.

(d) John smiled at him and was last seen walking up to him.

(e) His parents called the school and were told John had not been to school at all and had been marked absent.

(f) He was about to enter the school when someone called out his name.

A. cfdbea B. debfca
C. bfdaec D. abcdef

38. (a) However, the mayhem over the last few months is deeply shocking.

(b) Yet I do not agree with the prophets of doom who see nothing but disaster ahead.

(c) When I came back to my motherland India after a stay in Switzerland, I felt I was trading a hotbed of intense religious and political violence for peace and quiet.

(d) I think our nation is searching for an identity.

(e) And a new vision of the future will emerge from this.

A. abcde B. cabde
C. cebad D. bedca

39. (a) An integrated and combined approach was required to reveal the mystery of the brain —its structure, composition and function.

(b) Since the early 80's, scientists were clear that the brain would be the final frontier to conquer.

(c) The initiative was flagged off and came to be known as the Human Brain Project.

(d) But that wasn't easy because understanding the brain involved completely integrating information from the level of the gene to the level of behaviour.

(e) To fulfill this requirement a group of American scientists from various disciplines decided to work together.

A. acbed B. bdaec
C. abdec D. badec

40. (a) A product is something that is made in a factory, a brand is something that is bought by a consumer.

(b) The trick therefore, lies in the brand positioning.

(c) For a consumer, the satisfaction of becoming associated with a name that is the 'best' and the 'leader' is far more important and at times makes him ignore the price factor.

(d) Brands come and go.

(e) Still there are those who manage to stay and develop an affinity with consumers.

A. aebcd B. debac
C. decab D. aecdb

ANSWERS

1	2	3	4	5	6	7	8	9	10
B	D	A	B	C	C	A	C	A	D
11	**12**	**13**	**14**	**15**	**16**	**17**	**18**	**19**	**20**
C	A	C	D	B	D	C	B	B	D
21	**22**	**23**	**24**	**25**	**26**	**27**	**28**	**29**	**30**
D	A	C	A	B	D	A	A	C	C
31	**32**	**33**	**34**	**35**	**36**	**37**	**38**	**39**	**40**
C	D	B	C	D	A	A	B	B	B

Comprehension Passages

Passages

Directions: *Read the following passages and answer the questions given below each.*

PASSAGE-1

In the Roman times, defected enemies were generally put to death as criminals for having offended the emperor of Rome. In the middle ages, however, the practice of ransoming of returning prisoners in exchange for money became common. Though some saw this custom as a step towards a most humane society, the primary reasons behind it were economic rather than humanitarian.

In those times, rulers had only a limited ability to raise taxes. They could neither force their subject to fight nor pay them to do so. The promise of material compensation in the form of goods and ransom was therefore the only way of inducing combatants to participate in a war. In the middle ages, the predominant incentive for the individual soldiers was the expectation of spoils. Although collecting ransom clearly brought financial gain, keeping a prisoner and arranging for his exchange had its cost. Consequently, procedures were devised to reduce transaction costs.

One such device was a rule asserting that the prisoner had to assess his own value. This compelled the prisoner to establish a value *without too much distortion;* indicating too low a value would increase, the captive's chances of being killed, while indicating too high a value would either ruin him financially or create a prohibitively expensive ransom that would also result in death.

1. It can be inferred from the passage that a medieval soldier
   A. was less likely to kill captured members of opposing armies than was a soldier of the Roman Empire
   B. was similar to a 20th century terrorist in that he operated on a basically independent level and was motivated solely by economic incentives
   C. had few economic options and chose to fight because it was the only way to earn an adequate living
   D. was motivated to spare prisoners' lives by humanitarian rather than economic ideals

2. Which of the following best describes the change in policy from executing prisoners in Roman times to ransoming prisoners in the middle ages?
   A. The emperors of Rome demanded more respect than did medieval rulers and thus Roman subjects went to greater lengths to defend their nation
   B. It was a reflection of the lesser degree of direct control medieval ruler had over subjects
   C. It became a show of strength and honour warrior of the middles ages to be able to capture and return their enemies
   D. Medieval soldiers were not as hum-anitarian as their ransoming practices might have indicated

3. The primary purpose of the passage is to
   A. discuss the economic basis of the medieval practice of exchanging prisoners for ransom
   B. examine the history of the treatment of prisoner of war
   C. emphasize the importance of a warrior's code of honour during the middle ages
   D. explore a way of reducing the cost of ransom

4. The author uses the phrase *"without too much distortion"* in order to
   A. indicate that prisoners would fairly assess their worth
   B. emphasize the important role medieval prisoners played in determining whether they should be ransomed
   C. explain how prisoners often paid more than an appropriate ransom in order to increase their chances for survival
   D. suggest that captors and captives often had understanding relationships

PASSAGE-2

The world dismisses curiosity by calling it idle or mere idle curiosity—even though curious persons are seldom idle. Parents do their best to extinguish curiosity in their children because it makes life difficult to be faced everyday with a string of unanswerable questions about what makes fire hot or why grass grows. Children whose curiosity survives parental discipline are invited to join our university. With the university, they go on asking their questions and trying to find the answers. In the eyes of a scholar, that is what a university is for. Some of the questions which the scholars ask, seem to the world to be scarcely worth asking, let alone answering. They asked questions too minute specialised for you and me to understand without years of explanation. If the world inquires of one of them why he wants to know the answer to a particular question he may say especially if he is a scientist, that the answer will in some obscure way make possible a new machine or weapon or gadget. He talks that way because he knows that the world understands and respects utility.

But to you who are now part of the university, he will say that he wants to know the answer simply because he does not know it, the way the mountain climber wants to climb a mountain, simply because it is there. Similarly a historian asked by an outsider why he studies history may come out with the argument that he has learnt to repeat on such occasions, something about knowledge of the past making it possible to understand the present and mould the future. But if you really want to know why a historian studies the past, the answer is much simpler, something happened and he would like to know what. All this does not mean that the answers which scholars find to their questions have no consequences. They may have enormous consequences but these seldom form the reason for asking the questions or pursuing the answers. It is true that scholars can be put to work answering questions for the sake of the consequences as thousands are working, now, for example, in search of a cure for cancer. But this is not the primary function of the scholars. For the consequences are usually subordinate to the satisfaction of curiosity.

1. According to the passage, the children make life difficult for their parents
   A. by their ceaseless curiosity
   B. by unceasing bombardment of questions
   C. by asking irrelevant questions
   D. by posing profound questions
2. The common people consider some of the questions that the scholars ask unimportant
   A. as they are too lazy and idle
   B. as they are too modest
   C. as it's beyond their comprehension
   D. as it is considered a waste of time
3. A historian really studies the past
   A. to comprehend the present and to reconstruct the future
   B. to explain the present and plan the future
   C. to understand the present and make fortune
   D. to understand the present and mould the future
4. Children whose curiosity survives parental discipline means
   A. children retaining their curiosity in spite of being discouraged by their parents
   B. children pursuing their mental curiosity
   C. children's curiosity subdued due to parents' intervention
   D. children being disciplined by their parents
5. According to the passage, parents do their best to discourage curiosity in their children
   A. because they have no time
   B. because they have no patience to answer them
   C. because they feel that their children ask stupid questions continuously
   D. because they are unable to answer all their questions

PASSAGE-3

The factor of geographical distribution is equally, possibly even more, significant that English is spoken as first or native language in at least four continents of the world, Russian in two, Chinese and the Indian languages in one. English is without question the closest approach to a world language today. It goes without saying that no two persons ever have an identical command of their common language. Certainly, they have not precisely the same vocabulary. There are at least minor differences in pronunciation, indeed the same individual will not pronounce his vowels and consonants in absolutely identical fashion everytime he utters them. Everyone possesses, in addition, certain individual traits of grammatical form and syntactical order, constituting that peculiar and personal quality of language which we term as style. All of this is implicit in the well-known phrase, 'Style is the man.' No men are identical, no two styles are the same. If this be true of but two persons, the potential of differences resident in a language spoken by more than 200 million truly staggers imagination.

1. The author argues that English is the closest approach to a world language because
   A. there are more native speakers of English than of any other language
   B. English has less number of mutually unintelligible dialects
   C. the geographical distribution of English covers a much greater area
   D. other languages are much too complex to be world languages

2. The fact that the same individual will not pronounce his vowels and consonants identically everytime shows that
   A. literary style varies from person to person
   B. mutual intelligibility is a myth
   C. vocabulary varies from individual to individual
   D. no two persons speak the same language exactly the same way
3. It is evident from the passage that style is
   A. a strange type of language
   B. a language where one does not have to be particular about correctness and grammar
   C. language used in a particular way by an individual
   D. a question of grammatical and syntactic correctness
4. According to some authorities
   A. more people speak Chinese dialect than English
   B. more people speak English as an auxiliary language than as a first language
   C. more people speak English in the UK than in England
   D. about one-fourth of the world's population speaks English
5. The overall implication of the passage is that
   A. to suppose that 230 million people speak English as a native language would certainly be an underestimate
   B. the 55 million inhabitants of the British Isles speak like the 30 million inhabitants of the dominions and colonies
   C. a little less than half the native English speakers in the world live in the US
   D. about one-tenth of the total English-speaking world population lives in British dominions and colonies

PASSAGE-4

What is the future which awaits our children? The underlying assumption of the question, that Indian children have a common future, is itself dubious. It can legitimately be asked whether a student who is well-fed, attending a boarding school in the salubrious climate of the hills and learning to use computers has any future in common with a malnourished child who goes to a school with no blackboards, if indeed he does go to school. The latter may have no worthwhile future at all. And it might be worthwhile to analyse the significance of this marginalisation of more than 75 per cent of the children of this country.

The failure to provide an infrastructure for primary education in the villages of India more than 40 years after independence is in sharp contrast with the sophisticated institutions, for technical institutes of higher education are funded by the government, which essentially means that the money to support them comes from taxes. And, since indirect taxation forms a substantial part of the taxes collected by the government, the financial burden is borne by all the people. L.K. Jha put it graphically when he observed that 25 paise of every rupee spent on educating an IIT student comes from the pockets of men and women whose children may never enter a proper classroom.

1. The author is trying to highlight which of the following?
   A. Faulty system of direct taxes
   B. The greatness of L.K. Jha
   C. Need of sophisticated education for rural poor
   D. Need to have common future for Indian children
2. Which of the following pairs have been termed as 'sharp contrast' by the author?
   (*i*) Infrastructure for technical education
   (*ii*) Lack of infrastructure for rural primary schools
   (*iii*) 25 paise of every rupee earned by Government is spent on education
   (*iv*) The financial burden of higher technical education is borne by all people
   (*v*) 75% of children have limited opportunities
   A. (*ii*) and (*iv*) B. (*ii*) and (*iii*)
   C. (*iii*) and (*iv*) D. (*i*) and (*ii*)
3. Which of the following statements is not true?
   (*i*) The author welcomes Govt.'s initiative on primary education
   (*ii*) 75% of the children have a bright future
   (*iii*) 25% cost of educating a technocrat comes from poor people
   A. Only (*i*) B. Only (*ii*)
   C. Only (*iii*) D. Only (*i*) and (*ii*)
4. According to the author, who among the following does not have a hopeful and prosperous future?
   (*i*) All students from technical institutes
   (*ii*) All students financially supported by the Government
   A. Only (*i*) B. Only (*ii*)
   C. Both (*i*) and (*ii*) D. Neither (*i*) nor (*ii*)
5. What seems to be the likely answer of the author to the question posed by him in the first sentence of the passage?
   (*i*) There is no common future for the Indian children
   (*ii*) The future is worthwhile for majority of Indian children
   (*iii*) The majority may never enter a proper classroom
   A. Only (*i*) B. Only (*ii*)
   C. Only (*iii*) D. Both (*i*) and (*ii*)
6. What seems to be the purpose of the author in writing this passage?

A. Setting goals for children of upper middle class
B. Questioning the legitimacy of public schools
C. Highlighting lack of infrastructural facilities for primary education
D. Focusing on inequality in educational opportunities

PASSAGE-5

Cyber crime is the branded stigma defacing the culture and magnanimity of computer technology. It is upkeeping the flag with indomitable triumph against developing computer technology worldwide.

Modern age is striding with marching steps of technology revolution beating the past decade of ancestral belief with ultimate care. Computer invention has unfolded the mystery of quick access with the objective of minimum manpower and cutting the time consumption parameters.

As each coin has dual face of its portrait, likewise computer technology is sick of creeping virus. Synthetic man-made dilemma of site hackers activation is causing setback to the expanding anchor of revolutionary device with great loss of time, economy and data profile as suffered by consumers. A recent report from Internet security firm Websense estimates that 85.6 per cent of all the unwanted e-mails contained links to spam sites. The company's data suggests that the number of malicious sites grew 233 per cent in the last six months and saw 671 per cent growth in the number of malicious sites during the last year. In June alone, the total number of e-mails detected as containing viruses increased by 600 per cent compared to May.

Chat rooms, blogs and message-boards where the users post comments have been identified as the top targets of hackers and spammers due to the high traffic these attract. According to Websense, 95 per cent of user-generated comments to blogs, chat rooms and message-boards during the first half of the year were malicious.

It is advisable not to click on spurious links and stay away from keying in passwords at unknown sites as they are most likely to be spammed. Hackers can steal your passwords and log in to your account and access critical information like account numbers and contact details among other things.

1. The above passage is:
A. an advisory for the computer users.
B. an advisory for the Internet users.
C. a warning against possible threat to the Internet users.
D. related to chat rooms, blogs and message boards.

2. People who use chat rooms and blogs,
A. are safe and have no threats from spam.
B. are more prone to malicious e-mails.
C. create virus and hack the accounts of others.
D. are unsafe.

3. According to the writer, it is not safe to:
A. log on to spurious links.
B. access one's own account frequently.
C. have essential information stored in a computer.
D. include data-stealing code.

4. Hackers and spammers, according to the writer, are:
A. a new threat to the Internet users and the economy.
B. only pranksters and not serious threat to the system.
C. trained, professional technocrats who are an asset.
D. not expert professionals.

5. Which word in the passage is synonym of *weblog*?
A. blog B. password
C. site D. e-mail

6. Which agency has assessed the data record with spam sites?
A. Microsoft
B. Internet security from Google
C. Websense
D. Spammers

7. Which month dominates the e-mails detection data record?
A. May B. June
C. Last six months D. Last year

PASSAGE-6

Progress in life depends a good deal on crossing one threshold after another. Some time ago, a man watched his little nephew try to write his name. It was hard work, very hard work. The little boy had arrived at an effort threshold. Today he writes his name with comparative ease. No new threshold confronts him. This is the way with all of us. As soon as we cross one threshold, as soon as we conquer one difficulty, a new difficulty appears, or should appear. Some people make the mistake of steering clear of thresholds. Anything that requires genuine thinking and use of energy, they avoid. They prefer to stay in a rut where thresholds are not met. Probably, they have been at their job a number of years. Things are easy for them. They make no effort to seek out new obstacles to overcome. Real progress stops under such circumstances.

Some middle-aged and elderly people greatly enrich their lives by continuing to cross thresholds. One man went into an entirely new business when he was past middle life and made success of it, De Morgan didn't start to write novels until he was past sixty. Psychologists have discovered that man can continue to learn throughout his life. And it is undoubtedly better to try and fail than not to try at all. There one can be placed in the category of the Swiss mountaineer of whom it was said, *"He died climbing"*. When a new difficulty arises to obstruct your path, do not complain. Accept the challenge. Determine to cross this threshold as you have crossed numerous other thresholds in your past. In the words of a poet, do not rest but strive *to pass from dream to grander dream.*

1. What obstructs real progress in life?
A. Remaining at one and the same post
B. Avoiding the thinking and energy
C. Shunning every work
D. Stopping education

2. What does progress in life depend upon?
A. Good habits
B. Hardwork
C. Overcoming one difficulty after another
D. Spirit of service and cooperation

3. What does *'He died climbing'* signify?
A. He died when he was climbing the hill
B. He died before getting at the top
C. He strove hard till the last moment of life
D. He climbed the hill and then died

4. What does *'to pass from dream to grander dream'* mean?
A. Always having greater and greater aspiration in life
B. Seeing one good dream and then greater aspiration in life
C. Making plan after plan
D. Seeing one dream after the other

5. What did the man entering a new business past middle life do of his business?
A. He miserably failed in it
B. He achieved partial success
C. He dropped the business after some time
D. He achieved good success in it

6. How can you accomplish the most difficult tasks?
A. By mobilizing all possible resources
B. By avoiding all obstacles
C. By sticking to hardwork
D. By doing it bit by bit and persisting in the effort

7. What does De Morgan's life teach?
A. That it is futile to learn many things
B. That one is never old in case he has vigour
C. That it is never too late to learn
D. That creative writing can be made even late in life

8. How do middle-aged and elderly people add brilliance to their lives?
A. By overcoming difficulty one after another
B. By getting sycophants to surround them
C. By making fine speeches
D. By acquiring resourcefulness

9. What should we do when a new difficulty obstructs our path?
A. Run away from it
B. Be bold and face it
C. Manoeuvre to get it removed
D. Enlist other people's help to get it over

10. When did De Morgan start to write novels?
A. When he was sixty years old
B. When he was below sixty
C. When he studied psychology
D. None of these

PASSAGE-7

It is *heartening* to know that if one had not had any heart attack earlier and he stops smoking, his chances of having a heart attack *drop* to that of a non-smoker in about six months' time. Stopping of smoking is also the single most effective means of secondary prevention (recurrence of a heart attack) in heart patients.

Smoking leads to pain and stiffness in the legs while walking. No amount of drugs can help. The only remedy is to give up smoking. If women smoke during pregnancy, there is an increased risk of death of the baby in the womb or soon after birth. Even where the baby survives, there is likelihood of delayed physical and intellectual development of the baby till it reaches 11 years of age.

Still worse the fact about smoking is that passive smoking is equally dangerous. Passive smokers are those who do not smoke but being in the company of smokers have to inhale smoke exhaled by the smokers They are equally prone to heart diseases, lung cancer and bronchitis, for no fault of theirs. It is seen that the incidence of these diseases is greater among women whose husbands are *heavy* smokers As such, every non-smoker has a fundamental right to safeguard himself against the danger of passive smoking. "Your smoking is injurious to my health and I have a right to stop you from smoking" could be the slogan against passive smoking. It is a great threat to the health of the individual, the family and the society. In fact one has to choose between health and smoking including passive smoking. *One cannot have both.*

Another matter of *grave concern* about smoking is the long time interval between the start of smoking habit and the manifestation of deadly diseases like cancer, chronic bronchitis and heart attack. People are generally not aware of the link between smoking and the misery they have to undergo years later and younger people often fall victim to this menacing habit under the wrong impression that they are *immune* to its disastrous effects, not realising that they are *heading* towards catastrophe. The prolonged incubation period of many tobacco-related diseases has prevented recognition of the size of the threat and the *grim* picture of chronic and life-threatening diseases.

1. What is "passive smoking"?
A. Giving up the habit of smoking abruptly
B. Exhaling smoke by a non-smoker
C. Unintended intake of smoke exhaled by smokers
D. Smoking cigarettes which are harmless in nature

2. The effects of passive smoking are more and more prominently observed among
A. the children
B. the smokers
C. the wives of smokers
D. the non-smokers

3. Which of the following is a heartening thing, according to the author?
A. People who have had a heart attack stop smoking
B. It takes only six months for any person to quit smoking
C. The smoker carries the risk of heart attack for six months
D. None of these

4. Which of the following statements is/are false in the context of the passage?
(*i*) Passive smokers are not free from risk of heart diseases
(*ii*) Intake of certain medicines helps recover pain and stiffness in legs caused by smoking
(*iii*) Younger people are immune to the disastrous effects if their regular smoking is under control
A. (*i*) and (*ii*) only B. (*ii*) and (*iii*) only
C. (*ii*) only D. (*iii*) only

5. Which of the following is not mentioned in the passage as a likely result of smoking by women during pregnancy?
A. Death of baby before birth
B. Death of baby after birth
C. Survival of baby with some abnormality
D. Abnormal delay in the childbirth

6. Which of the following is considered by the author as a matter of "grave concern"?
A. Inordinate delay in appearance of symptoms of hazards of smoking
B. Long time required for giving up the habit of smoking
C. Manifestation of deadly diseases like cancer, bronchitis, etc.
D. Lack of awareness of people regarding the hazards of smoking

7. The youth feel that they are immune to the hazardous effects of smoking because
A. these effects of smoking are not visible within a short time span
B. they do not realise that they are heading towards disaster
C. they feel a great thrill in acquiring the habit of smoking
D. the link between smoking and its disastrous effects cannot be established

8. Which factor prevents people from realising the extent of threat of smoking hazards?
A. Their lack of awareness of civic responsibilities
B. Their firm belief that they are not immune to these hazards
C. The less disastrous effects of tobacco-related diseases
D. None of these

9. The last sentence of the third para *"One cannot have both"* means
A. active smoking and passive smoking
B. smoking and risk of heart diseases
C. threat to the individual and also to the family
D. None of these

Directions (Qs. 10 to 12): *Choose the word which is most nearly the **SAME** in meaning as the word given in bold capitals as used in the passage.*

10. **HEADING**
A. crowning B. marching
C. adorning D. title

11. **HEAVY**
A. excessive B. bulky
C. large D. thick

12. **DROP**
A. roll B. escape
C. remove D. reduce

Directions (Qs. 13 to 15): *Choose the word which is most nearly the **OPPOSITE** in meaning of the word given in bold capitals as used in the passage.*

13. **GRIM**
A. dim B. dark
C. presentable D. pleasant

14. **IMMUNE**
A. free B. vulnerable
C. powerful D. weak

15. **HEARTENING**
A. cheerful B. miserable
C. frightening D. dangerous

PASSAGE-8

The happy man is the man who lives objectively, who has free affections and wide interests, who secures his happiness through these interests and affections and through the fact that they, in turn, make him an object of interest and affection to many others. To be the recipient of affection is a potent cause of happiness, but the man who demands affection is not the man upon whom it is *bestowed.* The man who receives affection is, speaking broadly, the man who gives it. But it is useless to attempt to give it as a calculation, in the way in which one might lend money at interest, for a calculated affection is not genuine and is not felt to be so by the recipient.

What then can a man do who is unhappy because he is encased in self? So long as he continues to think about the causes of his unhappiness, he continues to be self-centred and therefore does not get outside the vicious circle, if he is to get outside it, it must be genuine interests, not by simulated interests adopted merely as a medicine. Although this difficulty is real, there is nevertheless much that he can do if he has rightly diagnosed his trouble. If, for example, his trouble is due to a sense of sin, conscious or unconscious, he can first persuade his conscious mind that he has no reason to feel sinful and then proceed, to plant his rational conviction in his unconscious mind, concerning himself meanwhile with some more or less neutral activity. If he succeeds in *dispelling* the sense of sin, it is possible that genuine objective interests will arise spontaneously. If his trouble is self-pity, he can deal with it in the same manner after first persuading himself that there is nothing extraordinarily unfortunate in his circumstances.

If fear is his trouble, let him practise exercises designed to give courage. Courage has been recognised from time immemorial as an important virtue, and a great part of training of boys and young men has been devoted to producing a type of character capable of fearlessness in battle. But moral courage and intellectual courage have been much less studied, they also, however, have their technique. Admit to yourself everyday at least one painful truth, you will find this quite useful. Teach yourself to feel that life still be worth living even if you were not, as of course you are, immeasurably superior to all your friends in virtue and in intelligence. Exercises of this sort prolonged through several years will at last enable you to admit facts *without flinching* and will, in so doing, free you from the empire of fear over a very large field.

1. Who according to the passage is the happy man?
A. who is encased in self
B. who has free affection and wide interests
C. who is free from worldly passions
D. who has externally centre passions

2. According to the passage, calculated affection
A. appears to be false and fabricated
B. makes other pen-on to love you
C. turns into permanent affection over a period of time
D. leads to self-pity

3. Which of the following virtues, according to the passage, has been recognised for long as an important virtue?
A. Patriotism B. Sacrifice
C. Courage D. Self-consciousness

4. Which of the following, according to the passage, has not been studied much?
A. Feeling of guilt and self-pity
B. The state of mind of an unhappy man
C. How to get absorbed in other interests
D. Moral and intellectual courage

5. If a man is suffering from a sense of sin
A. he should invite opinion of others
B. he should admit his sin at once
C. he should consciously realize that he has no reason to feel sinful
D. he should develop a fearless character

6. What happens to a man who demands affection?
A. His feelings are reciprocated by others
B. He tends to take a calculated risk
C. He becomes a victim of a viscious circle
D. None of these

7. What should a man do who is suffering from the feeling of self-pity?
A. He should control his passions and emotions
B. He should persuade himself that everything is alright in his circumstances
C. He should seek affection from others
D. He should develop a feeling of fearlessness

8. How to get out of the viscious circle mentioned in the passage?
A. By practicing skills of concentration
B. By inculcating the habits of self-absorption
C. Being true to others and one's internal circumstances
D. None of these

9. Which of the following statements is not *true* in the context of the passage?
A. Happy man has wide interests
B. Courage has been recognized as an important virtue
C. Unhappy man is encased in self
D. Issue of intellectual courage has been extensively studied

10. Which of the following words is ***SIMILAR*** in meaning of the word **'bestowed'** as used in the passage?
A. Conferred B. Accommodated
C. Trusted D. Withdrawn

11. Which of the following statements is *true* in the context of the passage?
A. All passions stem from unhappiness
B. The happy man lives in subjectively

C. Any virtue has a dark side also
D. One feels happy if one receives affection

12. Which of the following words is ***SIMILAR*** in meaning to the word **'flinching'** as used in the passage?
A. Wincing B. Convincing
C. Explaining D. Debating

13. What happens when you think about cause of your unhappiness?
A. You try to introspect and look critically at yourself
B. You realize that the life can be lived in different ways
C. You try to practice exercise designed to give courage
D. You remain a self-centred person

14. What according to the passage is the real cause of happiness?
A. Material rewards and incentives received
B. Critical analysis of the happy state of mind
C. Affection received from others
D. Calculated risks taken

15. Which of the following words is ***OPPOSITE*** in meaning of the word **'dispelling'** as used in the passage?
A. Giving B. Accumulating
C. Projecting D. Scattering

PASSAGE-9

Education, particularly higher education, is the obvious but crucially important instrument for nation building. As Confucious has said:

"If you are thinking of one year, plant rice. If you are thinking of a decade, plant trees. If you are thinking of a century, educate the people."

When we set about the task of higher education, we should be absolutely clear in our perception of the goals of education in the specific context of our nation's development. No *doubt,* one of the important aims of education would be to create the required range and nature of trained manpower assessed to be needed by different sectors of national growth. The entire educational apparatus must be geared progressively to fulfill the requirements of different phases of our growth in every sector—primary, secondary and *tertiary.* The aim must be to ensure that our country does not experience either *paucity,* or a *surfeit* of trained manpower in any specific segment of our economy. The requirements of our country, as a free, democratic, secular, socialist, nation, *aspiring* for rapid development, *entail* a specific recipe for our educational institutions. Today's educational institutions must therefore be developed accordingly and must regulate themselves to give the country the precise nature and quantum of trained manpower as projected by the requirements of our planned economy.

1. The author has quoted thoughts of Confucious to stress
A. importance of planting trees for human beings
B. the worthless efforts in planting rice
C. the benefits of investing in education
D. the need for assessing manpower requirement

2. Which statement cannot be made on the basis of the passage?
A. Higher education should keep in view the requirements of national economy
B. Higher education has not been employed for nation building
C. All levels of education have a role to play in nation's growth
D. In our country we need to have a specially planned educational system

3. The writer believes that
A. there are no problems related to higher education
B. investment in education is of long-range
C. higher education should be used to assess manpower needs
D. aims of higher education in India are absolutely clear

4. The author's expectations from higher education, are essentially
A. unrealistic B. confusing
C. critical D. vague

5. The writer indicates that
A. higher education did not play any role in national growth
B. primary education did not play any role in national growth
C. our nation experiences paucity of trained manpower in many sectors
D. today's higher education has no precise goals to achieve

6. Author has used the word 'apparatus' to indicate the
A. scientific nature of education
B. complicated organization demanded by education
C. readily visible benefits of education
D. entire equipment of education to perform particular function

7. Which of the following has not been conveyed by the passage?
A. Education at any level can contribute in nation building
B. Manpower needs in many areas can be fulfilled through higher education
C. Rapid development of our nation is possible through higher education
D. Present higher education does not ensure surfeit of trained manpower

8. This passage is likely to be addressed to
   A. politicians only B. scientists only
   C. students only D. cannot be said

9. Choose a suitable title to the passage:
   A. Manpower Planning in India
   B. Importance of Higher Education
   C. Demands of Higher Education
   D. Role of Higher Education in India

Directions (Qs.10 to 12): *Choose the word which is most nearly the **SAME** in meaning as the word given in bold capitals as used in the passage.*

10. **DOUBT**
    A. suspicion B. certain
    C. definite D. sure

11. **TERTIARY**
    A. last B. important
    C. third D. terminal

12. **ASPIRING**
    A. inquiring B. awaiting
    C. involving D. striving

Directions (Qs.13 to 15): *Choose the word which is most **OPPOSITE** in meaning as the word given in bold capitals as used in the passage.*

13. **PAUCITY**
    A. moderate B. enormity
    C. mediocrity D. littleness

14. **SURFEIT**
    A. abundance B. redundancy
    C. repletion D. lack

15. **ENTAIL**
    A. entitled B. ensure
    C. dismiss D. retain

PASSAGE-10

Books are a great treasurehouse of knowledge. They are the living examples of man's *march* on the path to higher and higher civilisation. The great men who died long ago, live in their books. We feel their very personality and existence when we read their books. We feel as if they were conversing with us.

Books not only store civilization but also carry it forward. All coming generations get the light of knowledge from the books written by their ancestors and try to improve upon that knowledge. Civilization cannot make much ***headway*** in a country where there are not many *great* books. We get through books the latest knowledge in the fields of arts, science, commerce, etc. This knowledge is helpful to us and *enables* us to achieve success in the field of our choice.

Books are never failing friends. They never *desert* us, not even when all fair-weather friends have deserted us. They dispel the dark clouds of gloom from our minds and increase our happiness if we are already happy. Through the ages, the scriptures and other great books have provided immeasurable *solace* to the wounded and strife-torn humanity.

There may be books prescribed for some course or profession, but then there are books for general study. The books of literature—poetry, drama, novel, short stories, etc., are generally highly thrilling and inspiring if they are written by a good author. There may be tragic, comical or humorous books. The question is that of an individual's choice.

To be a lover of books, though not to be bookworm, is a sign of good luck. A voracious reader gets much *more pleasure* from reading books than a miser gets in hoarding money. The knowledge embedded in books is valueless; so is pleasure obtained from reading them. A good book absorbs the whole spirit of man; the reader's pleasure is indescribable.

1. Which of the following, according to the passage, is not true about books?
   A. They are source of inspiration
   B. They are source of knowledge
   C. They are source of happiness
   D. They are means of livelihood

2. How do the books help in progress of civilization?
   A. Based on the earlier books new knowledge is obtained
   B. The books provide solution to many problems
   C. The books inspire the scientists
   D. Not mentioned in the passage

3. How do the books make people more happy?
   A. They help the reader to overcome the shadows of uncertainty
   B. They help bring in joy by amusing the reader through their content
   C. They help the reader to understand the darker side of life
   D. Not mentioned in the passage

4. Which of the following is the author's view about the knowledge and pleasure derived from books?
   (*i*) We get more of knowledge and less of pleasure
   (*ii*) We get more of pleasure and less of knowledge
   (*iii*) We get knowledge and pleasure in equal measure
   A. only (*i*) B. only (*ii*)
   C. either (*i*) or (*ii*) D. only (*iii*)

5. The high quality of books produced by a country indicates:
   A. it has a high rate of literacy
   B. it has a progressive civilization
   C. it is not an industrialised nation
   D. it has learned ancestors

6. Why are the books, according to the passage, called never-failing friends?
   A. Books do not betray individuals
   B. Books are inanimate
   C. Books always give companionship to the reader
   D. Books are available in the market anytime unlike others

7. How do the books help in bringing peace in the minds of people?
   A. Books provide information about the past civilization
   B. Books help people learn to take correct steps with the help of the recorded information
   C. Books act as a window to the minds of the great men
   D. Not mentioned in the passage

8. Which of the following has been described as a sign of good luck?
   A. Being a miser
   B. Having lot of money
   C. Advancing the culture
   D. A passion for books

Directions (Qs. 9 to 12): *Choose the word which is most nearly the* ***SAME*** *in meaning as the word given in bold capitals as used in the passage.*

9. **SOLACE**
   A. peace B. tranquillity
   C. calmness D. console

10. **ENABLES**
    A. helps B. succeeds
    C. promotes D. stops

11. **HEADWAY**
    A. higher B. forge
    C. movement D. improve

12. **MARCH**
    A. move B. progress
    C. pass D. register

Directions (Qs. 13 to 15): *Choose the word which is most* ***OPPOSITE*** *in meaning of the word given in bold capitals as used in the passage.*

13. **GREAT**
    A. small B. thin
    C. short D. ordinary

14. **PLEASURE**
    A. displeasure B. pain
    C. happiness D. hardship

15. **DESERT**
    A. waterhole B. bitter
    C. accompany D. propel

ANSWERS

PASSAGE-1

1	2	3	4
A	B	A	A

PASSAGE-2

1	2	3	4	5
A	C	D	A	D

PASSAGE-3

1	2	3	4	5
A	D	C	D	A

PASSAGE-4

1	2	3	4	5	6
D	A	D	A	A	D

PASSAGE-5

1	2	3	4	5	6	7
A	D	A	A	A	C	B

PASSAGE-6

1	2	3	4	5
A	C	C	A	D
6	**7**	**8**	**9**	**10**
D	B	A	B	D

PASSAGE-7

1	2	3	4	5
C	C	D	B	D
6	**7**	**8**	**9**	**10**
A	A	D	D	B
11	**12**	**13**	**14**	**15**
A	D	D	B	C

PASSAGE-8

1	2	3	4	5
B	A	C	D	C
6	**7**	**8**	**9**	**10**
D	B	D	D	A
11	**12**	**13**	**14**	**15**
D	D	D	C	B

PASSAGE-9

1	2	3	4	5
D	D	C	D	D
6	**7**	**8**	**9**	**10**
D	A	D	B	A
11	**12**	**13**	**14**	**15**
C	D	B	D	C

PASSAGE-10

1	2	3	4	5
D	A	D	D	B
6	**7**	**8**	**9**	**10**
A	D	D	D	A
11	**12**	**13**	**14**	**15**
D	B	D	B	C

YOUR SPACE

GENERAL INTELLIGENCE & REASONING

VERBAL

CHAPTER 1

Analogies

NUMBER ANALOGY

In number analogy also, the relationship between the given numbers is detected and then applied to the second part to find the missing numbers. This relationship between the numbers can be based on any of the following patterns : *(i)* numbers can be odd/even/prime numbers; *(ii)* numbers can be multiples of one number; *(iii)* numbers can be squares/cubes of different numbers; *(iv)* some numbers can be added to/subtracted from/multiplied to/divided into the first number to get the second number; *(v)* the second number can be the sum/product/difference of the digits of first number; and *(vi)* combinations of any mathematical calculations given above can apply to the relationship between the two given numbers.

SOLVED EXAMPLES

Directions : *Which number will come in the place of question mark?*

1. 25 : 81 : : 36 : ?

(*a*) 121 (*b*) 93 (*c*) 65 (*d*) 103

Ans. (*a*) : All the numbers are squares of different numbers.

25 : 81 : : 36 : 121

↓ ↓ ↓ ↓

5^2 9^2 6^2 11^2

2. 36 : 18 : : 72 : ?

(*a*) 164 (*b*) 134 (*c*) 94 (*d*) 14

Ans. (*d*) : The second number is the product of digits of the first number.

36 : 18 : : 72 : 14

3×6 7×2

MULTIPLE CHOICE QUESTIONS

Directions : *In the following questions, select the number from the given options which follows the same relationship as shared between the first two numbers.*

1. 1 : 11 : : 2 : ?

(*a*) 20 (*b*) 22

(*c*) 24 (*d*) 44

2. 18 : 27 : : 22 : ?

(*a*) 42 (*b*) 39

(*c*) 33 (*d*) 54

3. 14 : 20 : : 16 : ?

(*a*) 23 (*b*) 10

(*c*) 48 (*d*) 32

4. 8 : 27 : : 64 : ?

(*a*) 277 (*b*) 125

(*c*) 250 (*d*) 99

5. 0.16 : 0.0016 : : 1.02 : ?

(*a*) 10.20 (*b*) 0.102

(*c*) 0.0102 (*d*) 1.020

6. $\frac{1}{7} : \frac{1}{14} : : \frac{1}{9} : ?$
(a) $\frac{1}{88}$ (b) $\frac{1}{80}$
(c) $\frac{1}{81}$ (d) $\frac{1}{18}$

7. 5 : 24 : : 8 : ?
(a) 65 (b) 63
(c) 62 (d) 64

8. 23 : 53 : : 8 : ?
(a) 66 (b) 57
(c) 27 (d) 19

9. 6 : 9 : : 7 : ?
(a) 4 (b) 14
(c) 10 (d) 28

10. 7 : 28 : : 2 : ?
(a) 8 (b) 16
(c) 24 (d) 12

EXPLANATORY ANSWERS

1. (b) : The first number is repeated to obtain the second number.

2. (c) : In the given set, the numbers are multiples of 9 and in the second set, multiples of 11.

18 : 27 : : 22 : 33
↓ ↓ ↓ ↓
9×2 9×3 11×2 11×3

3. (a) : The relationship between the numbers is :

14 : 20 : : 16 : 23
↓ ↓ ↓ ↓
7×2 $(7 \times 3) - 1$ 8×2 $(8 \times 3) - 1$

4. (b) : The numbers are cubes of different numbers.

8 : 27 : : 64 : 125
↓ ↓ ↓ ↓
2^3 3^3 4^3 5^3

5. (c) : The decimals are divided by 100.

6. (d) : The first fraction is multiplied by half to obtain the second fraction.

$\frac{1}{7} : \frac{1}{14} : : \frac{1}{9} : \frac{1}{18}$
$\times\frac{1}{2}$ $\times\frac{1}{2}$

7. (b) : The second number is square of first number minus 1.

5 : 24 : : 8 : 63
$(5^2) - 1$ $(8^2) - 1$

8. (d) : All the numbers are prime numbers.

9. (c) : The second number is three more than the first number.

6 : 9 : : 7 : 10
+3 +3

10. (a) : The second number is four times the first.

7 : 28 : : 2 : 8
$\times 4$ $\times 4$

LETTER ANALOGY

In this type of analogy the relationship between two given set of letters is established and then applied to the other set to obtain the required set of letters as the answer. These letters can be moved some steps backward or forward; reversed in whole or in sections or have some common identity between each other.

SOLVED EXAMPLES

Directions : *Which set of letters will come in the place of question mark?*

1. JILK : KLIJ : : MNPQ : ?
(a) QNPM (b) MPQN (c) QPNM (d) PNMQ

Ans. (c) : The letters are written in reverse order to get the related set of letters.

J I L K : K L I J : : M N P Q : Q P N M

2. FLO : DOL : : RDP : ?

(*a*) PGM (*b*) MGP (*c*) GMP (*d*) MPG

Ans. (*a*) : The first and third letters are moved two and three steps backwards respectively and the second letter three steps forward.

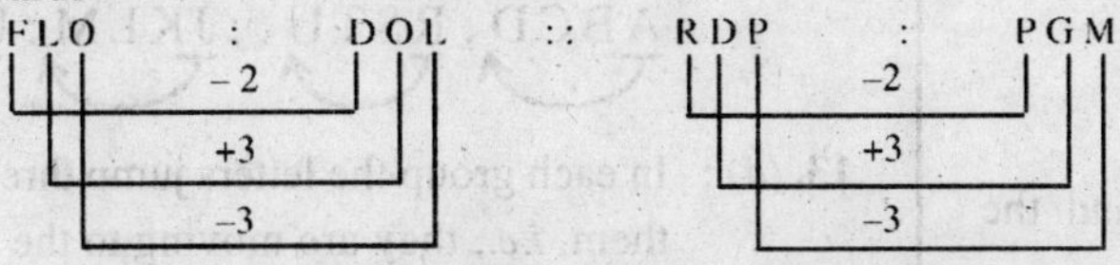

MULTIPLE CHOICE QUESTIONS

Directions : *In the questions given below one term is missing. Based on the relationship of the two given terms find the missing term from the given options.*

1. GFC : CFG : : RPJ : ?
(*a*) JRP (*b*) JPR
(*c*) PJR (*d*) RJP

2. BCF : DEG : : MNQ : ?
(*a*) OPR (*b*) PQS
(*c*) OPP (*d*) QRT

3. NATION : ANITNO : : HUNGRY : ?
(*a*) HNUGRY (*b*) UNHGYR
(*c*) YRNGUH (*d*) UHGNYR

4. SSTU : MMNO : : AABC : ?
(*a*) GGHH (*b*) IJKK
(*c*) XXYZ (*d*) NOOP

5. ACE : FGH : : LNP : ?
(*a*) QRS (*b*) PQR
(*c*) QST (*d*) MOQ

6. UVW : SXU : : LMN : ?
(*a*) JOL (*b*) KNM
(*c*) JKL (*d*) MLO

7. EIGHTY : GIEYTH : : OUTPUT : ?
(*a*) UTOPTU (*b*) UOTUPT
(*c*) TUOUTP (*d*) TUOTUP

8. TSR : FED : : WVU : ?
(*a*) CAB (*b*) MLK
(*c*) PQS (*d*) GFH

9. CJDL : FMGR : : IKJR : ?
(*a*) OQPT (*b*) RSTU
(*c*) OQRT (*d*) KRMO

10. BOQD : ERTG : : ANPC : ?
(*a*) DQSF (*b*) FSHU
(*c*) SHFU (*d*) DSQF

11. BaBy : TaTa : : LiLy : ?
(*a*) PooL (*b*) ROse
(*c*) HaNd (*d*) DoWN

12. BCDA : STUR : : KLMJ : ?
(*a*) VWXU (*b*) EFHG
(*c*) SRTU (*d*) QSRP

13. AEI : LPT : : CGK : ?
(*a*) OSV (*b*) RUY
(*c*) TXC (*d*) FJN

14. RUX : TRP : : BEH : ?
(*a*) SQN (*b*) QON
(*c*) QOM (*d*) QNL

15. CART : ART : : FOUR : ?
(*a*) RUN (*b*) TWO
(*c*) QUE (*d*) OUR

EXPLANATORY ANSWERS

1. (*b*) : The letters of the first group are reversed.

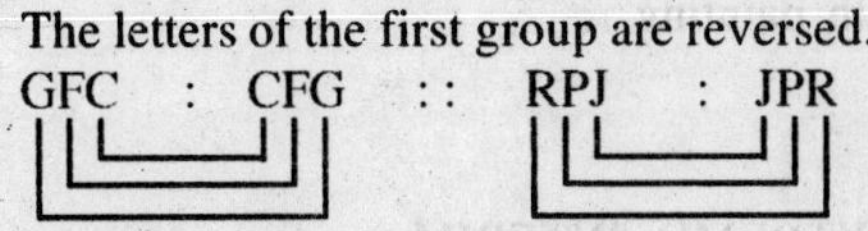

2. (*a*) : The three letters are moved 2, 2 and 1 steps forward respectively.

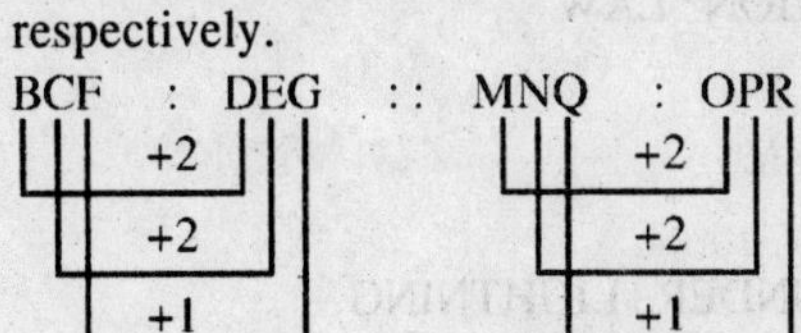

3. (*d*) : The word is divided in sections of two letters and the letters are reversed.

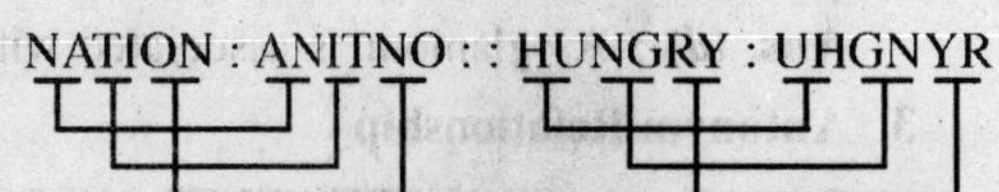

4. (*c*) : The first letter in each group is repeated and followed by two consecutive letters.

5. (*a*) : The three letters are moved 5, 4, and 3 steps forward respectively.

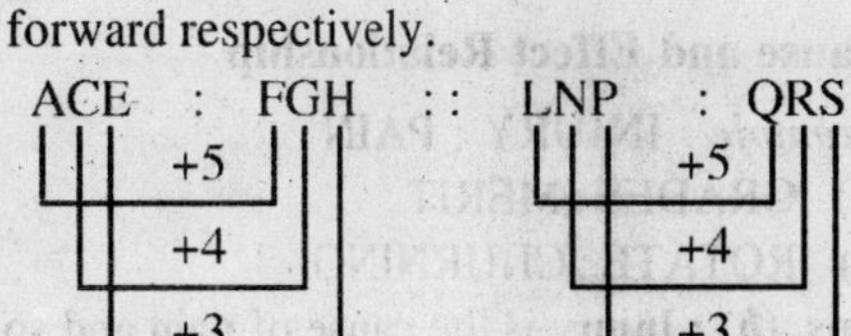

6. (a) : The three letters are moved –2, +2 and –2 steps respectively.

UVW : SXU :: LMN : JOL

–2 +2 –2 –2 +2 –2

7. (d) : The word is divided into two sections and the letters are written backwards.

EIGHTY : GIEYTH : : OUTPUT : TUOTUP

8. (b) : The letters are consecutive and written in reverse order.

9. (a) : In each set of letters, the 1st and 3rd letters are consecutive.

CJDL : FMGR :: IKJR : OQPT

10. (a) : In each group, the first and fourth letters are jumping one letter and the second and third letters are also jumping one letter.

BOQD : ERTG :: ANPC : DQSF

P S O R

C F B E

11. (c) : In each group the alternate letters are capitals.

12. (a) : In each group the first three letters are consecutive and they follow the fourth letter.

ABCD : RSTU : : JKLM : UVWX

13. (d) : In each group the letters jump three letters between them, *i.e.*, they are moving to the fourth letter.

AEI : LPT :: CGK : FJN

+4 +4   +4 +4   +4 +4   +4 +4

14. (c) : The letters in first set are jumping two letters, *i.e.*, moving three steps forward and in the second they are jumping one letter, *i.e.* moving two steps backward.

RUX : TRP :: BEH : QOM

+3 +3   –2 –2   +3+3   –2 –2

15. (d) : The first set of letters drop the first letter to get the second set.

CART : ART :: FOUR : OUR

SEMANTIC ANALOGY

In Analogy Tests the relationship between two given words is established and then applied to the other words. The type of relationship may vary, so while attempting such questions the first step is to identify the type of relationship, which can be any one of the following.

SOLVED EXAMPLES

1. Action Object Relationship

Example : Shoot is to Gun as Eat is to.....

(*a*) Hunger (*b*) Thirst (*c*) Dinner (*d*) Fruit

Ans. (*d*) : The relationship between the given words is that 'shoot' is the action and 'Gun' is the specified object of action. Similarly 'eat' is the action and 'fruit' is the specified object.

2. Association Relationship

Example : Glamour is to Stardom as Colour is to.....

(*a*) Rainbow (*b*) Shades (*c*) Art (*d*) Painting

Ans. (*d*) : As glamour is associated with stardom so is colour with painting.

3. Antonym Relationship

Example : INTROVERT : EXTROVERT

(*a*) ANGLE : TANGENT (*b*) EXTREME : INTERIM

(*c*) AGAINST : FAVOUR (*d*) ACTION : LAW

Ans. (*c*) : The related words are opposite in meaning.

4. Cause and Effect Relationship

Example : INJURY : PAIN

(*a*) GRADES : MERIT (*b*) THUNDER : LIGHTNING

(*c*) ROTATE : CHURNING (*d*) MATTER : LABOUR

Ans. (*b*) : Injury is the cause of pain and so is thunder the cause of lightning.

5. Degree Relationship

Example : Tepid is to Hot as... is to Wail.

(*a*) Sob (*b*) Shout (*c*) Smile (*d*) Calm

Ans. (*a*) : Tepid is less hot and so also the lower degree of wail is sob.

6. Grammatical Relationship

Example: Clever is to Beautiful as Sour is to ...

(*a*) Lemon (*b*) Cunning (*c*) Loathing (*d*) Taste

Ans. (*b*) : The related words are Adjectives.

7. Obvious Relationship

Example : Mt. EVEREST : NEPAL

(*a*) MEXICO : SOUTH AMERICA (*b*) K2 : CHINA

(*c*) BIG BEN : RUSSIA (*d*) AHMEDABAD : GUJARAT

Ans. (*d*) : Mt. Everest is in Nepal and so is Ahmedabad in Gujarat.

8. Part Whole Relationship

Example : MAN : MAMMAL

(*a*) HAIL : SNOW (*b*) NATIVE : INHABITANT

(*c*) OFFSPRING : FAMILY (*d*) LIBERTY : LITERATE

Ans. (*c*) : Man is a part of the whole species of mammal so is an offspring of the whole family.

9. Purpose Relationship

Example : INSTITUTION : EDUCATION

(*a*) WAR : PEACE (*b*) HEALTH : OBESITY

(*c*) MEDICATION : RECUPERATION (*d*) BUILDING : URBANISM

Ans. (*c*) : The purpose of institution is to impart education and the purpose of medication is quick recuperation (recovery).

10. Sequence Relationship

Example : .... is to Dusk as Summer is to Monsoon.

(*a*) Evening (*b*) Dawn (*c*) Night (*d*) Noon

Ans. (*a*) : Summer season is immediately followed by monsoon (rainy season) and evening is immediately followed by dusk.

11. Synonym Relationship

Example : INDENT : REQUEST

(*a*) REPLICA : CHEAT (*b*) DOLE : ALMS

(*c*) DISMAL : DUNCE (*d*) EXACT : CHECK

Ans. (*b*) : The related words have the same meaning.

12. Volume Relationship

Example : GALLONS : SWIMMING POOL

(*a*) SPECTATORS : AUDITORIUM (*b*) CURRENCY : SHARES

(*c*) DUST : MOUNTAIN (*d*) BOOKS : CATALOGUE

Ans. (*a*) : Gallons of water is needed to fill a swimming pool and large number of spectators can be admitted into an auditorium.

MULTIPLE CHOICE QUESTIONS

Directions : *In the questions given below establish the relationship between the two words. Then from the given options select one which has the same relationship as of the given two words.*

1. HUNGER : FOOD : : THIRST : ?

(*a*) Water (*b*) Drink

(*c*) Tea (*d*) Coffee

2. HUNTER : GUN : : WRITER : ?

(*a*) Book (*b*) Pen

(*c*) Poem (*d*) Page

3. WOOL : SHEEP : : SILK : ?

(*a*) Saree

(*b*) String

(*c*) Silkworm

(*d*) Moth

4. FOOD : STOMACH : : FUEL : ?
(*a*) Engine (*b*) Automobile
(*c*) Rail (*d*) Aeroplane

5. WATER : SAND : : OCEAN : ?
(*a*) Island (*b*) River
(*c*) Desert (*d*) Waves

6. ADULT : BABY : : FLOWER : ?
(*a*) Seed (*b*) Bud
(*c*) Fruit (*d*) Butterfly

7. WRITER : READER : : PRODUCER : ?
(*a*) Creator (*b*) Contractor
(*c*) Creature (*d*) Consumer

8. ENTRANCE : EXIT : : LOYALTY : ?
(*a*) Treachery (*b*) Patriotism
(*c*) Fidelity (*d*) Reward

9. MOTHER : MATERNAL : : FATHER : ?
(*a*) Eternal (*b*) Detrimental
(*c*) Paternal (*d*) Formidable

10. PEARL : NECKLACE : : FLOWER : ?
(*a*) Plant (*b*) Garden
(*c*) Petal (*d*) Bouquet

11. ALPHABET : WORD : : WORD : ?
(*a*) Sound (*b*) Music
(*c*) Sentence (*d*) Dictionary

12. LIFE : DEATH : : HOPE : ?
(*a*) Cry (*b*) Pain
(*c*) Despair (*d*) Sad

13. GOOD : BAD : : VIRTUE : ?
(*a*) Blame (*b*) Sin
(*c*) Despair (*d*) Vice

14. BIRD : FLY : : SNAKE : ?
(*a*) Timid (*b*) Clatter
(*c*) Crawl (*d*) Hole

15. CAT : MOUSE : : BIRD : ?
(*a*) Cage (*b*) Trap
(*c*) Eagle (*d*) Worm

16. STATE : EXILE
(*a*) Police : Arrest
(*b*) Judge : Convict
(*c*) Constitution : Amendment
(*d*) Church : Excommunicate

17. CAPRICIOUSNESS : RELIABILITY
(*a*) Extemporaneous : Predictability
(*b*) Unreliable : Inhuman
(*c*) Tenacious : Practicality
(*d*) Arbitrary : Whimsical

18. LOATH : COERCION
(*a*) Detest : Caressing (*b*) Irritate : Caressing
(*c*) Irate : Antagonism (*d*) Reluctant : Persuasion

19. SCALES : FISH
(*a*) Lady : Dress (*b*) Tree : Leaves
(*c*) Bird : Feather (*d*) Skin : Man

20. TREE : SAPLING
(*a*) Hut : Mansion (*b*) Giant : Dwarf
(*c*) Horse : Foal (*d*) Ant : Elephant

EXPLANATORY ANSWERS

1. (*a*) : Hunger is satiated by food, thirst by water.

2. (*b*) : Weapon of a hunter is a gun, weapon of a writer is a pen.

3. (*c*) : Wool is obtained from sheep, silk is obtained from silkworm.

4. (*a*) : Food is consumed in stomach, fuel is consumed in engine.

5. (*c*) : The related words are near opposites.

6. (*b*) : The youngone of an adult is a baby and that of a flower is a bud.

7. (*d*) : A writer aims to please the readers by his writings, a producer aims to please the consumers by his products.

8. (*a*) : The related words are opposites.

9. (*c*) : Relations on the mother's side are maternal and on the father's side paternal.

10. (*d*) : Many pearls make a necklace, many flowers make a bouquet.

11. (*c*) : More than one alphabet make a word, more than one word make a sentence.

12. (*c*) : The related words are opposites.

13. (*d*) : The related words are opposites.

14. (*c*) : Birds fly, snakes crawl.

15. (*d*) : Cat chases the mouse, bird chases the worm.

16. (*d*) : Punishment of leaving the State is exile, punishment of leaving the Church is excommunication.

17. (*c*) : The related words are antonyms

18. (*d*) : Loathing is the result of constant coersion, reluctance is the result of constant persuasion.

19. (*d*) : Covering of the fish is scales, covering of man is skin.

20. (*c*) : Young tree is a sapling, young horse is a foal.

CHAPTER

2 Number Classification

ODD ONE OUT—NUMBERS

In this type of classification, different numbers are given as options. These numbers have some commonness; except one which is the odd one. One has to identify the similarity and then strike the odd one out as answer option. The number can be odd/even/consecutive, prime numbers, multiple of some number, single, square or cubes of different numbers, plus/minus of some other number or combinations of any mathematical calculation.

SOLVED EXAMPLES

Directions : *Find the odd number from the given options.*

1. (*a*) 62 (*b*) 121 (*c*) 36 (*d*) 256

Ans. (*a*) : The other numbers are squares of :
11, (= 121), 6 (= 36) and 16 (= 256)

2. (*a*) 27 (*b*) 132 (*c*) 93 (*d*) 154

Ans. (*d*) : All other numbers are divisible by 3.

MULTIPLE CHOICE QUESTIONS

Directions : *In each of the following questions, there are four options. Three numbers, in these options, are alike in certain manner. Only one number does not fit in. Choose the one which is different from the rest.*

1. (*a*) 1948 (*b*) 2401
(*c*) 966 (*d*) 1449

2. (*a*) 182 (*b*) 169
(*c*) 130 (*d*) 158

3. (*a*) 129 (*b*) 130
(*c*) 131 (*d*) 132

4. (*a*) 3215 (*b*) 9309
(*c*) 4721 (*d*) 2850

5. (*a*) 1776 (*b*) 2364
(*c*) 1976 (*d*) 3776

6. (*a*) 64 (*b*) 84
(*c*) 16 (*d*) 36

7. (*a*) 24 (*b*) 90
(*c*) 54 (*d*) 36

8. (*a*) 7658 (*b*) 1234
(*c*) 9876 (*d*) 6543

9. (*a*) 3 (*b*) 9
(*c*) 5 (*d*) 7

10. (*a*) 6450 (*b*) 1776
(*c*) 2392 (*d*) 3815

11. (*a*) 24 (*b*) 48
(*c*) 42 (*d*) 12

12. (*a*) 616 (*b*) 252
(*c*) 311 (*d*) 707

13. (*a*) 18 (*b*) 12
(*c*) 30 (*d*) 20

14. (*a*) 3730 (*b*) 6820
(*c*) 5568 (*d*) 4604

EXPLANATORY ANSWERS

1. (*a*) : Other numbers are divisible by 7.
2. (*d*) : Other numbers are multiples of 13.
3. (*c*) : 131 is a prime number.
4. (*b*) : In other numbers, no digit is repeated.
5. (*b*) : In other numbers the last two digits are same.
6. (*b*) : All other numbers are perfect squares.
7. (*a*) : In other numbers, the sum of both the digits is 9.
8. (*a*) : In others, the digits are consecutive in natural or reverse series.
9. (*b*) : All others are prime numbers.
10. (*d*) : All other numbers are divisible by 2.
11. (*c*) : All other numbers are multiples of 12.
12. (*c*) : In other numbers, the first and last digits are same.
13. (*a*) : The other numbers are $3^2 + 3 = 12$, $5^2 + 5 = 30$, $4^2 + 4 = 20$, $6^2 + 6 = 42$
14. (*b*) : In all other numbers, two digits are same.

ODD ONE OUT—LETTERS

In this classification of letters, four groups of letters or a series of letters is given as options. One has to select the option as answer which does not share the commonness of the others.

SOLVED EXAMPLES

Directions : *Find the odd one out in the following letters :*

1. (*a*) NOP (*b*) RTU (*c*) JKL (*d*) EFG

Ans. (*b*) : In each group the letters are consecutive. In this option the first two letters jump one letter (S) inbetween.

2. (*a*) RUX (*b*) CFI (*c*) BDG (*d*) FIL

Ans. (*c*) : In each group, the difference between the letters is same. In this option B and D jump one letter and D and G jump two letters.

MULTIPLE CHOICE QUESTIONS

Directions : *In each of the following questions, four out of five alternatives contain alphabet placed in a particular form. Find the one that does not belong to the group.*

1. (*a*) BXCW (*b*) OTPS (*c*) GQHR (*d*) JNKM

2. (*a*) BVPS (*b*) OLMZ (*c*) RPSR (*d*) XTCD

3. (*a*) RNJH (*b*) SOKG (*c*) QMIE (*d*) MIEA

4. (*a*) QLJS (*b*) GVTI (*c*) KRPM (*d*) ONMP

5. (*a*) PEAR (*b*) TORE (*c*) REAP (*d*) TEAR

6. (*a*) ECA (*b*) JHF (*c*) OMK (*d*) UWY

7. (*a*) ACE (*b*) PRT (*c*) UWY (*d*) MNO

8. (*a*) WVU (*b*) NML (*c*) HGF (*d*) DBA

9. (*a*) ABD (*b*) FGI (*c*) LMO (*d*) STU

10. (*a*) CDE (*b*) JKL (*c*) PQS (*d*) TUV

EXPLANATORY ANSWERS

1. (*c*) : In all other groups, first and third letters are consecutive and second and fourth letters are in reverse alphabetical order.
2. (*c*) : No letter is repeated in any other group.
3. (*a*) : In all other groups, there is a gap of three letters between two consecutive letters.
4. (*d*) : In all other groups, first and third letters are moved two steps forward to obtain fourth and second letters respectively.
5. (*b*) : All other groups contain E, A and R.
6. (*d*) : All other groups contain alternate letters from right to left.

7. (*d*) : All other groups contain alternate letters from left to right.

8. (*d*) : In all others, the three letters are consecutive but in reverse order.

9. (*d*) : In all others, the first two letters are consecutive and third letter is obtained by skipping one letter from the second.

10. (*c*) : In all other, the three letters are consecutive.

ODD ONE OUT—WORDS

In this type of classification, five words are given out of which four are almost same in matter or meaning and only one word is different from the common four. One has to find out the word which is different from the rest.

SOLVED EXAMPLES

Directions : *In the following questions spot the odd one out.*

1. (*a*) Father (*b*) Mother (*c*) Friend (*d*) Brother

Ans. (*c*) : All other are blood relations.

2. (*a*) Water (*b*) Jelly (*c*) Lemonade (*d*) Coffee

Ans. (*b*) : All other are liquids.

MULTIPLE CHOICE QUESTIONS

Directions : *In each of the following questions, four words are alike in some manner. Spot the odd one out.*

1. (*a*) Green (*b*) Red (*c*) Colour (*d*) Orange

2. (*a*) Stable (*b*) Hole (*c*) Canoe (*d*) Sty

3. (*a*) Nose (*b*) Eyes (*c*) Skin (*d*) Teeth

4. (*a*) Venus (*b*) Moon (*c*) Pluto (*d*) Mars

5. (*a*) Happy (*b*) Gloomy (*c*) Lively (*d*) Cheerful

6. (*a*) Cone (*b*) Circle (*c*) Triangle (*d*) Rectangle

7. (*a*) Lead (*b*) Mercury (*c*) Copper (*d*) Iron

8. (*a*) Kite (*b*) Bird (*c*) Radar (*d*) Jet

9. (*a*) Knee (*b*) Shoulder (*c*) Ankle (*d*) Palm

10. (*a*) Deluge (*b*) Calamity (*c*) Catastrophe (*d*) War

11. (*a*) Cub (*b*) Chicken (*c*) Pig (*d*) Pup

12. (*a*) Rabbit (*b*) Crocodile (*c*) Earthworm (*d*) Snail

13. (*a*) Tree (*b*) Leaf (*c*) Bush (*d*) Herb

14. (*a*) Doctor (*b*) Teacher (*c*) Engineer (*d*) Diver

15. (*a*) Trot (*b*) Equestrian (*c*) Derby (*d*) Grunt

EXPLANATORY ANSWERS

1. (*c*) : All others are types of colour.

2. (*c*) : Canoe is a boat. Others are resting places of birds/animals.

3. (*d*) : All others are sense organs.

4. (*b*) : All others are planets.

5. (*b*) : All others are expressions of joy

6. (*a*) : All others are geometrical figures.

7. (*b*) : All others are solid metals.

8. (*c*) : All others are flying objects. Radar traces the objects in sky.

9. (*d*) : All others are joints in human body.

10. (*d*) : All others are nature-bound. Only war is man-made.

11. (*c*) : All others are young ones of animals.

12. (*a*) : All others are crawling animals.

13. (*b*) : All others are types of vegetation.

14. (*d*) : All others are professions, but only Diver's profession comprises of diving under water.

15. (*d*) : All other terms are related with activities of a horse.

CHAPTER 3

Small & Capital Letters/ Numbers Coding-Decoding and Classification

TYPE - I

Coding is a secretive language which is used to change the representation of the actual term/word/value. This coded language can be framed by *(i)* moving the letters one or more steps forward or backward; *(ii)* substituting numbers for letters and vice–versa; *(iii)* writing the letters of the given word in reverse order in part or in whole; and *(iv)* replacing the letters in their natural series by the same positioned letters in their reverse series.

Alphabet in natural series are :

A B C D E F G H I J K L M N O P Q R S T U V W X Y Z

A ↓ 1st, E ↓ 5th, J ↓ 10th, O ↓ 15th, T ↓ 20th, Y ↓ 25th

Alphabet in reverse series are :

Z Y X W V U T S R Q P O N M L K J I H G F E D C B A

Z ↓ 1st, V ↓ 5th, Q ↓ 10th, L ↓ 15th, G ↓ 20th, B ↓ 25th

Note : On reaching Z, the series restarts from A and on reaching A, it restarts from Z.

SOLVED EXAMPLES

1. If FACE is coded as GBDF, then BADE will be coded as :

(*a*) CBEF (*b*) CEBF (*c*) CFBE (*d*) CBFE

Ans. (*a*) : The word is coded by moving the letters one step forward.

FACE → GBDF (each letter +1, +1, +1, +1)

Similarly, BADE → CBEF (each letter +1, +1, +1, +1)

2. If RESULT is coded as 798206, LET will be coded as :

(*a*) 680 (*b*) 092 (*c*) 096 (*d*) 086

Ans. (*c*) : The letters are coded by numbers, and to code the given word, select the respective coded numbers.

R E S U L T → letters
7 9 8 2 0 6 → code

So, code for LET will be

L E T → letters
0 9 6 → code

MULTIPLE CHOICE QUESTIONS

Directions : *In the following questions select the right option which indicates the correct code for the word or letter given in the question.*

1. If CHAIR is coded as FKDLU then RAID is coded as :
(*a*) ULGD (*b*) ULKG
(*c*) ULDG (*d*) UDLG

2. If CONDEMN is coded as CNODMEN, then TEACHER is coded as :
(*a*) TEACHER (*b*) TAEECHR
(*c*) TCAEEHR (*d*) TAECEHR

3. In a code language COME is written as XLNV and ABLE as ZYOV. How will MOLLY be written in that code?
(*a*) NLOBO (*b*) NLBOO
(*c*) LNOOB (*d*) NLOOB

4. In a certain code PROFESSION is written as EFORPNOISS. In the same code DICTIONARY will be written as :
(*a*) YRANOITCID (*b*) ITCIDYRANO
(*c*) ITCIDYRNAO (*d*) ITCDIYARNO

5. JUNE is coded as NXPF, how will STAY be coded in the same manner?
(*a*) WWCZ (*b*) WVCZ
(*c*) WWDB (*d*) VWZC

6. If in a certain code GENIUS is coded as IGPKWU, then IDIOT will be written in the same code as :
(*a*) JEJPU (*b*) KFKQV
(*c*) LGLRW (*d*) HCHNS

7. If ACTION is coded as ZXGRLM, then HEALTH will be coded in the same way as :
(*a*) SVZOGS (*b*) TVZOGT
(*c*) RUZPGR (*d*) QVGOZQ

8. If THOUSAND is coded as SGNTRZMC, then FUMING will be coded as :
(*a*) GVNJOH (*b*) ETHLMF
(*c*) EVLJMH (*d*) ETLHMF

9. If EARTHQUAKE is coded as MOGPENJOSM, then EQUATE will be coded as :
(*a*) MENOPM (*b*) MENOMP
(*c*) MJOGPM (*d*) MNJOPM

10. In a certain code language HJIZT code is deciphered as MONEY, in the same way NOVGZ will be deciphered as :
(*a*) STUMP (*b*) STALE
(*c*) STICK (*d*) SPIRE

11. If in a certain code JOSEPH is coded as FKOALD, then GEORGE will be coded in the same way as :
(*a*) CBJNCA (*b*) CANKCA
(*c*) CAKNCA (*d*) CAKCNA

12. If COUNTRY is coded in a certain way as EMWLVPA, ELECTORATE will be coded in the same manner as :
(*a*) CJCEVQPYWC (*b*) GJGERQTYVG
(*c*) CNCERQPCRG (*d*) GJGAVMTYVC

13. In a certain code PORTUGESE is written as ESEGUTROP, MALAYALAM will be written in the same code as :
(*a*) MALAYALAM (*b*) MALYALAM
(*c*) MALAYALM (*d*) MALAYLAM

14. If PHILOSOPHY is coded as HPLISOPOYH, ORNAMENTAL will be coded as :
(*a*) ROANEMNTLA (*b*) ONRAMNEALT
(*c*) ROANEMTNLA (*d*) ROANEMNATL

15. If SABOTAGE is coded as UADOVAIE, how will EMERGENCY be coded in the same manner?
(*a*) GMGRIEPCA (*b*) GMGRGEPCA
(*c*) BNBQFDOBZ (*d*) EOETGGNEY

EXPLANATORY ANSWERS

1. (*d*) : The word is coded by moving the letters three steps forward.

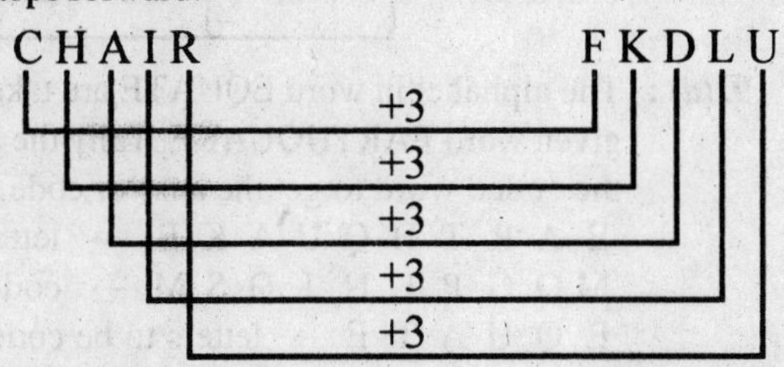

Similarly,

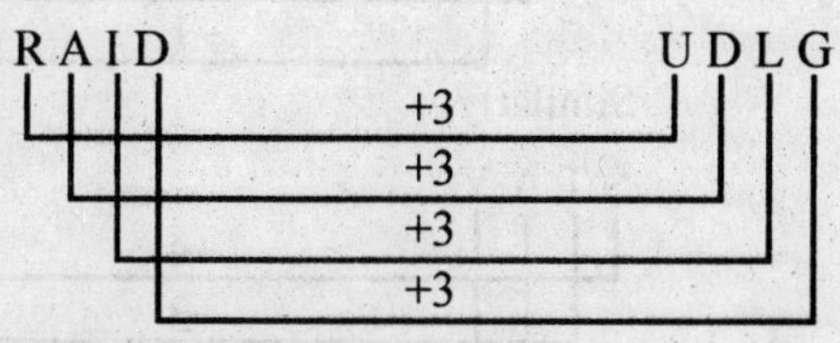

2. (*d*) : In this word, the second and third letters interchange their places and the fifth and sixth letters do the same. Other letters retain their position.

CONDEMN CNODMEN

Similarly,

TEACHER TAECEHR

3. (d) : The letters of the word are coded by their represented letters in the reverse series.

C O M E → letters in natural series
X L N V → letters in reverse series
↓ ↓ ↓ ↓
3rd 15th 13th 5th → position of letters
A B L E → letters in natural series
Z Y O V → letters in reverse series
↓ ↓ ↓ ↓
1st 2nd 12th 5th → position of letters

Similarly,

M O L L Y → letters in natural series
N L O O B → letters in reverse series
↓ ↓ ↓ ↓ ↓
13th 15th 12th 12th 25th → position of letters

4. (b) : The word is divided into two equal parts and the letters of each part are written backwards.

PROFE SSION EFORP NOISS

Similarly,

DICTI ONARY ITCID YRANO

5. (a) : The word is coded by moving the letters +4, +3, +2, and +1 steps respectively.

JUNE NXPF
+4
+3
+2
+1

Similarly,

STAY WWCZ
+4
+3
+2
+1

6. (b) : The word is coded by moving the letters two steps forward, *i.e.,*

GENIUS IGPKWU
+2
+2
+2
+2
+2
+2

Similarly,

IDIOT KFKQV
+2
+2
+2
+2
+2

7. (a) : The letters of the word are coded by their represented letters in the reverse series.

A C T I O N → letters in natural series
Z X G R L M → letters in reverse series
↓ ↓ ↓ ↓ ↓ ↓
1st 3rd 20th 9th 15th 14th position of letters

Similarly,

H E A L T H → letters in natural series
S V Z O G S → letters in reverse series
↓ ↓ ↓ ↓ ↓ ↓
8th 5th 1st 12th 20th 8th → position of letters

8. (d) : The word is coded by moving the alphabet one step backwards, *i.e.,*

THOUSAND SGNTRZMC
−1
−1
−1
−1
−1
−1
−1
−1

Similarly,

FUMING ETLHMF
−1
−1
−1
−1
−1
−1

9. (d) : The alphabet in word EQUATE are taken from the given word EARTHQUAKE. Tally the letters from the coded word to get the answer code.

E A R T H Q U A K E → letters
M O G P E N J O S M → codes
E Q U A T E → letters to be coded
M N J O P M → answer codes

10. ***(b)*** **:** The coded alphabet are deciphered by moving five steps forward, *i.e.*,

HJIZT → MONEY

+5, +5, +5, +5, +5

Similarly,

NOVGZ → STALE

+5, +5, +5, +5, +5

11. ***(c)*** **:** The word is coded by moving the alphabet four steps backward, *i.e.*,

JOSEPH → FKOALD

–4, –4, –4, –4, –4, –4

Similarly,

GEORGE → CAKNCA

–4, –4, –4, –4, –4, –4

12. ***(d)*** **:** The word is coded by moving the alphabet two steps forward and two steps backward alternately, *i.e.*,

COUNTRY → EMWLVPA

+2, –2, +2, –2, +2, –2, +2

Similarly,

ELECTORATE → GJGAVMTYVC

+2, –2, +2, –2, +2, –2, +2, –2, +2, –2

13. ***(a)*** **:** The coded word is the alphabet of the word written backwards.

PORTUGESE → ESEGUTROP

Similarly,

MALAYALAM → MALAYALAM

14. ***(c)*** **:** The places of two consecutive letters in the word are interchanged to form the coded word.

PH IL OS OP HY → HP LI SO PO YH

Similarly,

OR NA ME NT AL → RO AN EM TN LA

15. ***(a)*** **:** The word is coded by moving only the alphabet at odd positions two steps forward.

SABOTAGE → UADOVAIE

+2, +2, +2, +2

Similarly,

EMERGENCY → GMGRIEPCA

+2, +2, +2, +2, +2

TYPE - II

Column coding is a very complex form of coding. It needs a lot of attention and swift eye movement to decode the code for each letter of the given words. Proper words in capital letters are given in one column and the codes in small letters are given in another column. Based on the information given in both columns the candidate has to arrive at the correct answer option.

MULTIPLE CHOICE QUESTIONS

Directions: *The following questions are based on the column pattern. Understand the coding pattern and answer the questions.*

Column I	Column II
(1) FAMOUS	(a) jcqhxp
(2) SATIRE	(b) hqdbyn
(3) FRIGHT	(c) ybcnke
(4) TANGLE	(d) zewhnd
(5) ROVING	(e) epbmyw
(6) HUNTER	(f) wdnbxk

1. What is the code used for the letter U?
(*a*) d (*b*) n
(*c*) b (*d*) x

2. What is the code used for the letter N?
(*a*) e (*b*) p
(*c*) m (*d*) w

3. What is the code used for the letter A?
(*a*) h (*b*) q
(*c*) b (*d*) n

4. What is the code used for the letter F?
(*a*) w (*b*) p
(*c*) d (*d*) c

5. What is the code used for the letter E?
(*a*) d (*b*) n
(*c*) b (*d*) k

Column I	Column II
(1) WRONG	(a) cklxd
(2) GRANT	(b) pdqkc
(3) STEAM	(c) qpuns
(4) CROWS	(d) lxnvk
(5) CEMET	(e) usqvs
(6) TERMS	(f) nukqs

6. What is the code used for the letter N?
(*a*) c (*b*) x
(*c*) l (*d*) n

7. What is the code used for the letter M?
(*a*) v (*b*) q
(*c*) u (*d*) s

8. What is the code used for the letter W?
(*a*) d (*b*) x
(*c*) c (*d*) p

9. What is the code used for the letter G?
(*a*) k (*b*) c
(*c*) s (*d*) d

10. What is the code used for the letter S?
(*a*) n (*b*) s
(*c*) d (*d*) k

Column I	Column II
(1) HOUSE	(a) lfyqx
(2) PAGES	(b) pyfgm
(3) LUNGS	(c) nhmzf
(4) PHONE	(d) xqygh
(5) LANDS	(e) hofzp
(6) HOUND	(f) qnoxh

11. What is the code used for the letter O?
(*a*) h (*b*) g
(*c*) q (*d*) x

12. What is the code used for the letter E?
(*a*) n (*b*) y
(*c*) p (*d*) m

13. What is the code used for the letter G?
(*a*) p (*b*) o
(*c*) f (*d*) m

14. What is the code used for the letter N?
(*a*) l (*b*) y
(*c*) x (*d*) h

15. What is the code used for the letter D?
(*a*) o (*b*) z
(*c*) g (*d*) p

EXPLANATORY ANSWERS

1. (*d*) : From statements (1) and (6), U = X.

2. (*d*) : From statements (5) and (6), RN = bw. From statement (4), N = w.

3. (*a*) : From statements (2) and (4), ATE = hdn. From statement (6), TE = dn. Therefore, A = h.

4. (*d*) : From statements (1) and (3), F = c.

5. (*a*) : From statements (2) and (4), ATE = hdn. From statement (6), TE = dn. From statement (3), T = n. Hence E = d.

6. (*a*) : From statements (1) and (2), N = C.

7. (*c*) : From statements (3), (5) and (6), M = u.

8. (*b*) : From statements (1) and (4), W = x.

9. (*d*) : From statements (1) and (2), G = d.

10. (*a*) : From statements (3), (4) and (6), S = n.

11. (*d*) : From statements (1), (4) and (6), O = x.

12. (*b*) : From statements (1), (2) and (4), E = y.

13. (*d*) : From statements (2) and (3), G = m.

14. (*d*) : From statements (3), (4), (5) and (6), N = h.

15. (*a*) : From statements (5) and (6), D = o.

TYPE - III

There is variety in ways of coding. Coding language is not only for words and numbers but also for hiding a group of words, statements or even sentences. This form of coding pattern may appear to be confusing but after solving only a few questions it is very easy to understand. Questions based on this coding pattern require no moving of steps or straining efforts of calculations, but only quick tallying or comparing ability. The codes can be letters or numbers.

SOLVED EXAMPLE

In a certain code 'ra mei ket' means 'he is rich'; 'rui pha jeu' means 'run for money'; and 'pha rui ket' means 'money for rich'. Which of the following is the code for 'rich'?

(*a*) ra (*b*) pha
(*c*) ket (*d*) jeu

Ans. **(*c*)** : The given information is :

	Code	*Sentence*
1.	ra mei *ket*	he is *rich*
2.	rui pha jeu	run for money
3.	pha rui *ket*	money for *rich*

After comparing codes and sentences 1 and 3, it is clear that word 'rich' is common and so is the code 'ket'.

MULTIPLE CHOICE QUESTIONS

Directions : *In the following questions study the coded patterns and then select the right option from the given alternatives.*

1. In a certain language, (a) 'go ju mi' stands for 'plenty of money'; (b) pao ju go nei vu' for 'money creates lots of problems'; (c) 'kol vu nei' for 'problems create tension'; and (d) 'sol tun ju haw' for 'still money is needed'. Which of the following words stand for 'money'?

(*a*) nei (*b*) ju
(*c*) haw (*d*) go

2. In a certain language, (a) 'FOR' stands for 'old is gold'; (b) 'ROT' stands for 'gold is pure'; (c) 'ROM' stands for 'gold is costly'. How will 'pure old gold is costly' be written?

(*a*) TFROM (*b*) FOTRM
(*c*) FTORM (*d*) TOMRF

3. In a certain code '415' means 'milk is hot'; '18' means 'hot soup'; and '895' means 'soup is tasty'. What number will indicate the word 'tasty'?

(*a*) 9 (*b*) 8
(*c*) 5 (*d*) 4

4. In a certain code '643' means 'she is beautiful', '593' means 'he is handsome', and '567' means 'handsome meets beautiful'. What number will indicate the word 'meets'?

(*a*) 5 (*b*) 3
(*c*) 7 (*d*) 6

5. In a certain code language, (a) 'dugo hui mul zo' stands for 'work is very hard'; (b) 'hui dugo ba ki' for 'Bingo is very smart'; (c) 'nano mul dugo' fo: 'cake is hard', and (d) 'mul ki qu' for 'smart and hard'. Which of the following words stand for 'Bingo'?

(*a*) jalu (*b*) dugo
(*c*) ki (*d*) ba

6. In a certain code language, (a) 'pic vic nic' stands for 'winter is cold'; (b) 'to nic re' for 'summer is hot'; (c) 're pic boo' for 'winter and summer' and (d) 'vic tho pa' for 'nights are cold'. Which of the following word is the code for 'summer'?

(*a*) nic (*b*) boo
(*c*) to (*d*) re

7. In a certain language, (a) 'mx das sci' means 'good little frock'; (b) 'jm coz sci' means 'girl behaves good'; (c) 'ngv drs coz' means 'girl makes mischief'; and (d) 'das gp coz' means 'little girl fell'. What is the code for 'frock' in this language?

(*a*) mx (*b*) das
(*c*) sci (*d*) gp

8. In a certain language 'mu mit es' means 'who is she' and 'elb mu es' means 'where is she'. What is the code for 'where' in this language?

(*a*) es (*b*) elb
(*c*) mu (*d*) mit

9. In a certain code language '069' means 'grapes are sweet', '476' means 'very sweet fruit' and '509' means 'grapes are ripe'. Which of the following digits means 'ripe' in that language?

(*a*) 0 (*b*) 5
(*c*) 9 (*d*) 7

10. In a certain code language 'roi ja kyo twa' means 'Moody is writing letters', 'pok ju ja twa' means 'Woody is writing cards', 'trn kyo pos un' means 'they are writing letters', and 'koi rus pok' means 'gifts and cards'. What is the code word for 'Moody'?

(*a*) ja (*b*) twa
(*c*) roi (*d*) kyo

EXPLANATORY ANSWERS

1. (*b*) :

	Code	Sentence
1.	go *ju* mi	plenty of *money*
2.	pao *ju* go nei vu	*money* creates lots of problems
3.	kol vu nei	problems create tension
4.	sol tun *ju* haw	still *money* is needed

In 1st, 2nd and 4th codes and their sentences the word 'ju' is repeated and so is 'money'.

2. (*a*) :

	Code	Sentence
1.	FOR	old is gold
2.	ROT	gold is pure
3.	ROM	gold is costly

Therefore,

F stands for old
O stands for is
R stands for gold
T stands for pure
M stands for costly

So, 'pure old gold is costly' will be written as 'TFROM'.

3. (*a*) :

	Code	Sentence
1.	415	milk is hot
2.	18	hot soup
3.	895	soup is *tasty*

From 3rd code and its sentence neither number '9' is repeated nor the word 'tasty'.

4. (*c*) :

	Code	Sentence
1.	643	she is beautiful
2.	593	he is handsome
3.	567	handsome *meets* beautiful

From 3rd code and its sentence, neither number '7' nor the word 'meets' is repeated.

5. (*d*) :

	Code	Sentence
1.	*dugo hui* mul zo	work *is very* hard
2.	*hui dugo* **ba** *ki*	**Bingo** *is very smart*
3.	nano mul *dugo*	cake is *hard*
4.	mul *ki* qu	*smart* and hard

From 2nd code and its sentence, neither 'ba' nor 'Bingo' is repeated.
(Words repeated are in italics)

6. (*d*) :

	Code	Sentence
1.	pic vic nic	winter is cold
2.	to nic *re*	*summer* is hot
3.	*re* pic boo	winter and *summer*
4.	vic tho pa	nights are cold

The word 'summer' is common in 2nd and 3rd sentences and so is the code 're'.

7. (*a*) :

	Code	Sentence
1.	**mx** *das sci*	*good little* **frock**
2.	jm coz *sci*	girl behaves *good*
3.	ngv drs coz	girl makes mischief
4.	*das* gp coz	*little* girl fell

Word 'frock' is only in the 1st sentence. The code word 'das' is repeated in 4th sentence and 'sci' in 2nd sentence. So, 'mx' is the code for 'frock'.

8. (*b*) :

	Code	Sentence
1.	*mu* mit *es*	who *is she*
2.	**elb** *mu* es	**where** *is she*

The code words 'mu' and 'es' are repeated in Ist sentence. The only code left is 'elb' which means 'where'.

9. (*b*) :

	Code	Sentence
1.	*069*	*grapes are* sweet
2.	476	very sweet fruit
3.	**509**	*grapes are* **ripe**

The code numbers '0' and '9' are repeated in 1st and 3rd sentences. The only code remaining is '5' which stands for 'ripe'.

10. (*c*) :

	Code	Sentence
1.	**roi** *ja kyo twa*	**Moody** *is writing letters*
2.	pok ju *ja twa*	Woody *is writing* cards
3.	trn *kyo* pos un	they are writing *letters*
4.	koi rus pok	gifts and cards

'Moody' is in 1st sentence only. The code words 'ja' and 'twa' are repeated in 2nd sentence and 'kyo' in 3rd sentence. Only code word 'roi' remains which stands for 'Moody'.

CHAPTER 4

Semantic Series

MULTIPLE CHOICE QUESTIONS

1. ADG, XVT, BEH, WUS, ?
(*a*) VTR (*b*) CFI
(*c*) DFJ (*d*) STU

2. GMSY, IOUA, KQWC, ?
(*a*) MSYE (*b*) NSYE
(*c*) MTYE (*d*) MSYF

3. ADG, GJM, ?, SVY
(*a*) MPS (*b*) MQR
(*c*) MQS (*d*) SPM

4. KNQ, TWZ, CFI, ?
(*a*) KOR (*b*) LOR
(*c*) MNQ (*d*) JLM

5. AEI, BFJ, CGK, ?
(*a*) DLH (*b*) EGF
(*c*) EFL (*d*) DHL

6. CFI, IKM, OPQ, ?
(*a*) UUU (*b*) UST
(*c*) VUS (*d*) TUV

7. LAZ, NEX, PIV, ?
(*a*) SLS (*b*) QNS
(*c*) RMT (*d*) RMS

8. DED, EFE, FGF, ?
(*a*) HGH (*b*) GHG
(*c*) EFE (*d*) FHF

9. XYZ, UVW, ?, OPQ
(*a*) RST (*b*) STU
(*c*) QRS (*d*) TUV

10. VCL, UEI, TGF, ?
(*a*) SJC (*b*) THI
(*c*) SIC (*d*) RHD

11. ABC, EFG, HIJ, ?
(*a*) IJK (*b*) KLM
(*c*) LMN (*d*) JKL

12. PQR, HIJ, DEF, ?
(*a*) DEF (*b*) CDE
(*c*) ABC (*d*) BCD

13. KNQ, TWZ, CFI, ?
(*a*) MNQ (*b*) LOR
(*c*) LPR (*d*) KOR

14. JOBS, KMEO, LKHK, ?, NGNC
(*a*) MJLH (*b*) LIKG
(*c*) MIKG (*d*) MNGM

15. ABC, ACE, ADG, ?
(*a*) AEG (*b*) AFH
(*c*) AFG (*d*) AEI

16. IOU, JKL, PQR, ?
(*a*) UVW (*b*) XYZ
(*c*) TUV (*d*) VWX

17. AZ, GT, MN, ?, YB
(*a*) KF (*b*) TS
(*c*) RX (*d*) SH

18. BMY, DNW, FOU, ?
(*a*) HPT (*b*) HPS
(*c*) HQS (*d*) GPS

19. ADG, GJM, MPS, ?
(*a*) SVW (*b*) SVY
(*c*) SUW (*d*) SWY

20. AZ, CX, EV, ?
(*a*) HU (*b*) GS
(*c*) GT (*d*) HT

EXPLANATORY ANSWERS

1. (*b*) : There are two alternate series.

ADG XVT BEH WUS CFI

Series I : ADG BEH CFI

+1 +1
+1 +1
+1 +1

Series II : XVT WUS

−1
−1
−1

2. (*a*) : The series is formed by moving each letter two steps forward from one group to the next.

GMSY IOUA KQWC MSYE

+2 +2 +2
+2 +2 +2
+2 +2 +2
+2 +2 +2

(The series restarts from A on reaching Z)

3. (*a*) : In each group of three letters the alphabet is in the succession of +3. The next group begins with the last alphabet of the previous group.

A D G G J M M P S S V Y

+3 +3 +3 +3 +3 +3 +3 +3

4. (*b*) : All the alphabet in this group series is in succession of +3. The alphabetical series repeat from 'A' on reaching 'Z'.

K N Q T W Z C F I L O R

+3 +3 +3 +3 +3 +3 +3 +3 +3 +3 +3

5. (*d*) : Each of the three alphabet in one group corresponds to the alphabet in the next group in the succession of +1, *i.e.*,

AEI BFJ CGK DHL

+1 +1 +1
+1 +1 +1
+1 +1 +1

6. (*a*) : The three alphabet in one group correspond to the alphabet in the next group in the manner +6, +5, +4 respectively, *i.e.*,

CFI IKM OPQ UUU

+6 +6 +6
+5 +5 +5
+4 +4 +4

7. (*c*) : The three alphabet in one group correspond to the alphabet in the next group in the manner +2, +4, −2 respectively, *i.e.*,

LAZ NEX PIV RMT

+2 +2 +2
+4 +4 +4
−2 −2 −2

8. (*b*) : The alphabet from one group to the next are in succession of +1, *i.e.*,

DED EFE FGF GHG

+1 +1 +1
+1 +1 +1
+1 +1 +1

9. (*a*) : The alphabet from one group to the next are in recession of −3, *i.e.*,

XYZ UVW RST OPQ

−3 −3 −3
−3 −3 −3
−3 −3 −3

10. (*c*) : The alphabet in one group correspond to the alphabet in the next group in the manner −1, +2, −3 respectively, *i.e.*,

VCL UEI TGF SIC

−1 −1 −1
+2 +2 +2
−3 −3 −3

11. (*d*) : The difference between the last letter of the preceding group of alphabet and the first letter of the next group is decreasing by 1, *i.e.*,

ABC EFG HIJ JKL

+2 +1 +0

Otherwise the three letters in each group are in their natural order.

12. (*d*) : The letters in each group of alphabet are in the recession of −8, −4, −2 respectively.

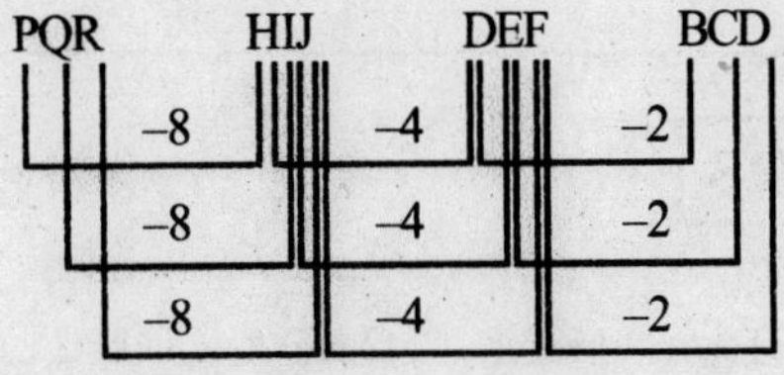

13. (*b*) : The letters in each group correspond to the letter in next group in the succession of +9.

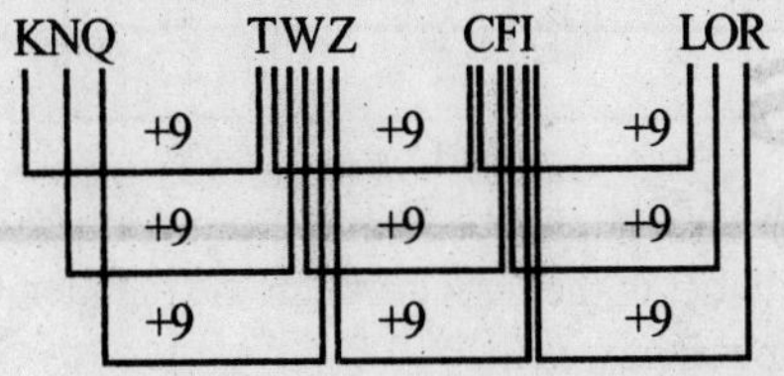

14. (*c*) : The alphabets in each group follow the pattern +1, –2, +3 and –4 respectively from one group to the next group.

15. (*d*) : The difference between the letters in each group is increased by one.

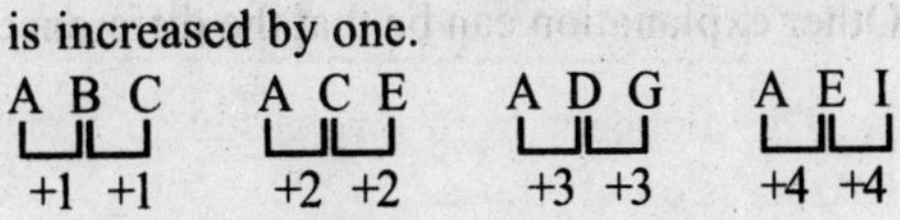

16. (*d*) : The series is formed in this manner :

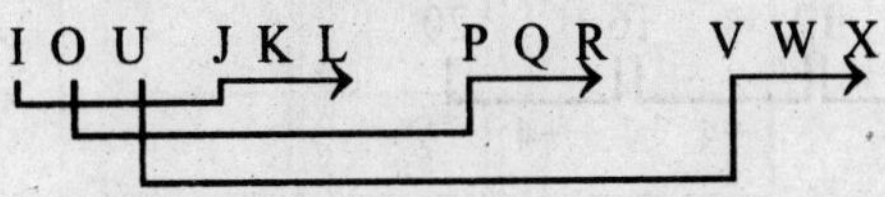

Three consecutive letters to each letter in the first group forms the other groups in the series.

17. (*d*) : The letters in one group correspond to the letters in the next group in the manner +6, –6 respectively, *i.e.,*

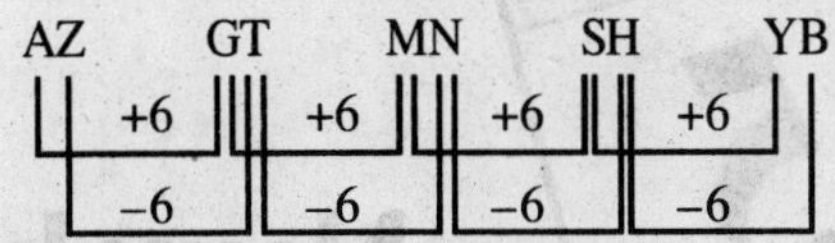

18. (*b*) : The letters in one group correspond to the letters in the next group in the manner +2, +1, -2 respectively, *i.e.,*

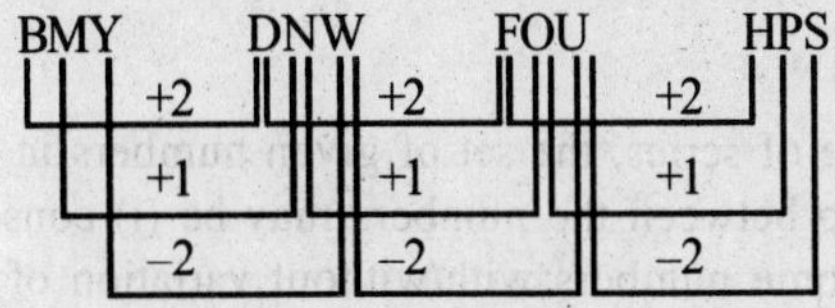

19. (*b*) : The letters in each group are moved six steps forward, *i.e.,*

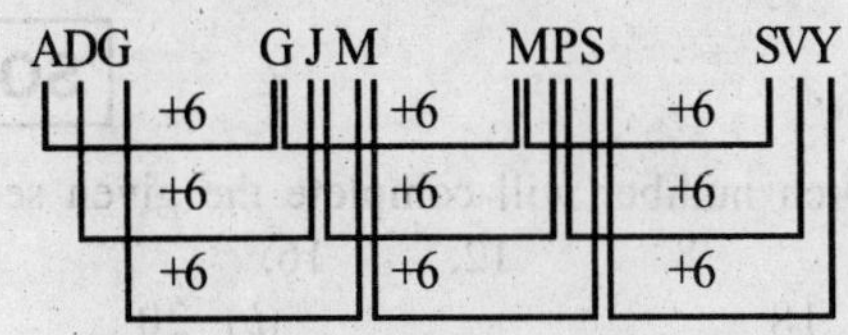

20. (*c*) : The letters in each group correspond to the letters in the next group in the manner +2, –2 respectively, *i.e.,*

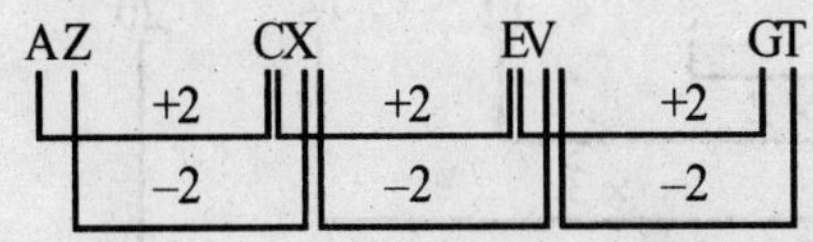

CHAPTER 5

Number Series

In this type of series, the set of given numbers in a series are related to one another in a particular pattern or manner. The relationship between the numbers may be (i) consecutive odd/even numbers; (ii) consecutive prime numbers; (iii) squares/cubes of some numbers with/without variation of addition or subtraction of some number; (iv) sum/product/difference of preceding numbers; (v) addition/subtraction/multiplication/division by some number; and (vi) many more combinations of the relationships given above.

SOLVED EXAMPLES

1. Which number will complete the given series?

4, 8, 12, 16, ?

(*a*) 18 (*b*) 20 (*c*) 22 (*d*) 24

Ans. (*b*): The series is made of numbers which are multiples of 4. Other explanation can be that the difference between the two consecutive numbers is 4.

4 8 12 16 20

4 × 2 = 8; 4 × 3 = 12; 4 × 4 = 16; 4 × 5 = 20

Or

4 +4 8 +4 12 +4 16 +4 20

2. Complete the given series.

2, 14, 98, 686, ?

(*a*) 1976 (*b*) 2548 (*c*) 980 (*d*) 4802

Ans. (*d*) : The numbers are multiplied by 7 to obtain the next numbers.

2 ×7 14 ×7 98 ×7 686 ×7 4802

The given series may also comprise of two alternate series merged as one.

MULTIPLE CHOICE QUESTIONS

Directions: *In the following questions, select the number(s) from the given options for completing the given series.*

1. 3, 9, 27, 81, 243, ?

(*a*) 486 (*b*) 729

(*c*) 972 (*d*) 359

2. 1, 6, 12, 19, 27, ?

(*a*) 38 (*b*) 35

(*c*) 36 (*d*) 54

3. 2, 6, 14, 30, 62, ?

(*a*) 126 (*b*) 128

(*c*) 120 (*d*) 130

4. 8, 48, 16, 96, 32, ?
(*a*) 192 (*b*) 150
(*c*) 64 (*d*) 288

5. 2, 8, 14, 24, 34, 48, ?
(*a*) 66 (*b*) 62
(*c*) 58 (*d*) 64

6. 4, 9, 19, 34, 54, ?, 109
(*a*) 89 (*b*) 84
(*c*) 74 (*d*) 79

7. 3, 15, 35, 63, 99, ?
(*a*) 144 (*b*) 143
(*c*) 121 (*d*) 169

8. 2, 3, 6, 18, 108, ?
(*a*) 1944 (*b*) 1658
(*c*) 648 (*d*) 1008

9. 1, 2, 3, 2, 3, 5, 4, 5, ?
(*a*) 9 (*b*) 6
(*c*) 10 (*d*) 7

10. 7776, 1296, 216, 36, 6, ?
(*a*) 6 (*b*) 0
(*c*) 3 (*d*) 1

11. 1, 8, 27, 64, 125, ?
(*a*) 172 (*b*) 176
(*c*) 216 (*d*) 189

12. 2, 3, 5, 7, 11, 13, ?
(*a*) 19 (*b*) 57
(*c*) 31 (*d*) 17

13. 80, 64, 48, 32, 16, ?
(*a*) 4 (*b*) 0
(*c*) 8 (*d*) 1

14. 3, 8, 13, 24, 41, ?
(*a*) 65 (*b*) 75
(*c*) 70 (*d*) 80

15. 9, 81, 90, 810, 819, ?
(*a*) 7371 (*b*) 900
(*c*) 8100 (*d*) 1638

16. 0, 8, 24, 48, 80, ?
(*a*) 110 (*b*) 96
(*c*) 120 (*d*) 140

17. 2, 4, 8, 3, 9, 27, 4, 16, ?
(*a*) 64 (*b*) 32
(*c*) 48 (*d*) 24

18. 27, 28, 25, 25, 23, 22, 21, ?
(*a*) 20 (*b*) 21
(*c*) 19 (*d*) 18

19. 80, 63, 72, 72, 64, 81, 56, ?
(*a*) 96 (*b*) 98
(*c*) 89 (*d*) 90

20. 0, 5, 22, 57, ?, 205
(*a*) 198 (*b*) 116
(*c*) 172 (*d*) 92

EXPLANATORY ANSWERS

1. (*b*) : The numbers in the series are multiplied by 3 to get the next numbers.

2. (*c*) : The difference between the numbers in the series increases by 1, after beginning from 5, *i.e.*,

1 6 12 19 27 36
+5 +6 +7 +8 +9

3. (*a*) : The difference between the numbers in the series doubles each time, after beginning from 4, *i.e.*,

2 6 14 30 62 126
+4 +8 +16 +32 +64

4. (*a*) : *Explanation I* : The sequence in the series is × 6, ÷ 3 which is repeated.

8 48 16 96 32 192
×6 ÷3 ×6 ÷3 ×6

Explanation II : There are two alternate series and the numbers are multiplied by 2.

8 48 16 96 32 192
(8 ×2 16 ×2 32; 48 ×2 96 ×2 192)

Series I : 8, 16, 32
Series II : 48, 96, 192

5. (*b*) : The sequence in the series is :

2 8 14 24 34 48 62
+6 +6 +10 +10 +14 +14

The difference increases by 4 at alternate step.

6. (*d*) : The difference between the numbers increases by 5, after beginning from 5, *i.e.*,

4 9 19 34 54 79 109
+5 +10 +15 +20 +25 +30

7. (*b*) : The series follows the sequence of the squares of even numbers beginning from 2, minus 1.

8. (*a*) : Every third number in the series is the product of previous two numbers.

2 3 6 18 108 1944
2 × 3
3 × 6
6 × 18
18 × 108

9. (*a*) : In this series three numbers form a set. The first two numbers of each set are in natural order and the third number is the sum of first and second numbers. The first number of the next set begins with double the first number of the previous set.

× 2 × 2

1 2 3 2 3 5 4 5 9

1 + 2 2 + 3 4 + 5

10. (*d*) : The numbers in this sequence are divided by 6 each time.

11. (*c*) : The sequence in the series is cube of numbers in their natural order.

12. (*d*) : The series consists of prime numbers in increasing order.

13. (*b*) : The numbers in the series are decreasing with the difference of 16 at each step.

14. (*c*) : The sequence in the series is (number + next number) + addition of natural number increasing by 1 at each step, after beginning from 2.

3 8 13 24 41 70

(3+8) + 2

(8 + 13) + 3

(13 + 24) + 4

(24 + 41) + 5

15. (*a*) : The sequence in the series is × 9, + 9 which is repeated.

16. (*c*) : The sequence of the series consists of the product of 2 even numbers in natural order, *i.e.*,

0	8	24	48	80	120
↓	↓	↓	↓	↓	↓
(0 × 2)	(2 × 4)	(4 × 6)	(6 × 8)	(8 × 10)	(10 × 12)

17. (*a*) : In this series 3 numbers form a set. The first number is in natural order. The second number is the square of above number. The third number is the cube of first number.

18. (*c*) : There are two alternate series :

−2 −2 −2

27 28 25 25 23 22 21 19

−3 −3 −3

Series I : 27, 25, 23, 21 (following −2 pattern)

Series II : 28, 25, 22, 19 (following −3 pattern)

19. (*d*) : There are two alternate series :

−8 −8 −8

80 63 72 72 64 81 56 90

+9 +9 +9

Series I : 80, 72, 64, 56 (following −8 pattern)

Series II : 63, 72, 81, 90 (following +9 pattern)

20. (*b*) : The series follows this sequence : cube of natural numbers starting from 1 minus odd numbers starting from 1.

0	5	22	57	116	205
↓	↓	↓	↓	↓	↓
1^3-1	2^3-3	3^3-5	4^3-7	5^3-9	6^3-11

CHAPTER 6

Arithmatical Reasoning

MULTIPLE CHOICE QUESTIONS

Directions (1–5) : *The following questions are based on the information given below :*

Data of 450 candidates, who took part in an examination in Social Science, Mathematics and Science is given below:

Passed in all the subject	167
Failed in all the subject	60
Failed in Mathematics	199
Failed in Social Science	175
Failed in Science	191
Passed in Science only	52
Passed in Mathematics only	48
Passed in Social Science only	62

1. How many passed in at least one subject?
(*a*) 450 (*b*) 390
(*c*) 304 (*d*) 167
(*e*) None of these.

2. How many failed in two subjects only?
(*a*) 56 (*b*) 61
(*c*) 152 (*d*) 162
(*e*) None of these.

3. How many passed in Mathematics and at least in one more subject?
(*a*) 210 (*b*) 203
(*c*) 170 (*d*) 94
(*e*) None of these.

4. How many failed in Social Science only?
(*a*) 15 (*b*) 21
(*c*) 30 (*d*) 42
(*e*) None of these.

5. How many failed in one subject only?
(*a*) 152 (*b*) 144
(*c*) 61 (*d*) 56
(*e*) None of these

6. A, B, C, D and E play a game of cards. A says to B, ''If you give me three cards, you will have as many as E has and if I give you three cards, you will have as many as D has.'' A and B together have 10 cards more than what D and E together have. If B has two cards more than what C has and the total number of cards be 133, how many cards does B have?
(*a*) 22 (*b*) 35
(*c*) 25 (*d*) 23
(*e*) None of these

7. A bus starts from city X. The number of women in the bus is half of the number of men. In the city Y, 10 men left the bus and five women entered. Now, number of men and women is equal. In the beginning, how many passenger entered the bus?
(*a*) 15 (*b*) 30
(*c*) 36 (*d*) 45
(*e*) None of these

8. I have a few sweets to be distributed. If I keep 2, 3 or 4 in a pack, I am left with one sweet. If I keep 5 in a pack, I am left with none. What is the minimum number of sweets I can have to pack and distributed?
(*a*) 25 (*b*) 37
(*c*) 54 (*d*) 65
(*e*) None of these

9. A, B, C, D and E play a game of cards. A says to B, ''If you give me 3 cards, you will have as many as I have at this moment while if D takes 5 cards from you, he will have as many as E has'', A and C together have twice as many cards as E has B and D together also have the same number of cards as A and C taken together. I all together they have 150 cards, how many cards has C got.
(*a*) 28 (*b*) 29
(*c*) 31 (*d*) 35
(*e*) None of these

10. At the end of a business conference, ten people present shake hands with each other once. How many handshakes will be there all together?
(*a*) 20 (*b*) 45
(*c*) 90 (*d*) 55
(*e*) None of these.

11. Jayesh is as much younger to Anil as he is older to Prashant. If the sum of the ages of Anil and Prashant is 48 years. What is the age of Jayesh?
(*a*) 30 years
(*b*) 24 years
(*c*) 20 years
(*d*) Can't be determined
(*e*) None of these.

12. Five years ago Vinay's age was one-third of the age of Vikash and now Vinay's age is 17 years. What is the present age of Vikash?
(*a*) 9 years (*b*) 36 years
(*c*) 41 years (*d*) 51 years

13. The sum of ages of a father and son is 45 years. Five years ago the product of their ages was 4 times the father's age at that time. The present age of the father and son respectively are.
(*a*) 25 years, 10 years (*b*) 36 years, 9 years
(*c*) 39 years, 6 years (*d*) None of these.

14. Out of a total 120 musicians in a club, 5% can play all the three instruments – guitar, violin and flute. It so happens that the number of musicians who can play any two and only two of the above instruments is 30. The number of musicians who can play the guitar alone is 40. What is the total number of those who can play violin alone or flute alone?
(*a*) 30 (*b*) 38
(*c*) 44 (*d*) 45
(*e*) None of these.

15. In a group of persons travelling in a bus, 6 persons can speak Tamil, 15 can speak Hindi and 6 can speak Gujarati. In that group, none can speak any other language. If 2 persons in the group can speak two languages and one person can speak all the three languages, then how many persons are there in the group?
(*a*) 21 (*b*) 22
(*c*) 23 (*d*) 24
(*e*) None of these.

16. There are 50 students admitted to a nursery class. Some students can speak only English and some can speak only Hindi. Ten students can speak both English and Hindi. If the number of students who can speak English is 21, then how many students can speak Hindi, how many can speak only Hindi and how many can speak only English?
(*a*) 39, 29 and 11 respectively.
(*b*) 37, 27 and 13 respectively.
(*c*) 28, 18 and 22 respectively.
(*d*) 21, 11 and 29 respectively.

17. A shephard had 17 sheep. All but nine died. How many was he left with?
(*a*) Nil (*b*) 17
(*c*) 9 (*d*) 8
(*e*) None of these.

18. 10 years ago, Chandravati's mother was 4 times older than her daughter. After 10 years, the mother will be twice older than the daughter. The present age of Chandravati is:
(*a*) 5 years (*b*) 10 years
(*c*) 20 years (*d*) 30 years
(*e*) None of these.

19. Pushpa is twice as old as Rita was two years ago. If difference between their ages be 2 years, how old is Pushpa today?
(*a*) 6 years (*b*) 8 years
(*c*) 10 years (*d*) 12 years

20. Mr. Sohan Lal is four times as old as his son. Four years later sum of their age will be 43 years. The present age of the son is:
(*a*) 5 years (*b*) 7 years
(*c*) 8 years (*d*) 10 years
(*e*) None of these.

21. 15 years ago the difference between the age of two persons is 10 years. The elder one was twice as old as the younger one. The present age of the elder person is:
(*a*) 15 years (*b*) 35 years
(*c*) 65 years (*d*) 45 years
(*e*) None of these.

22. Consider the diagram given below:

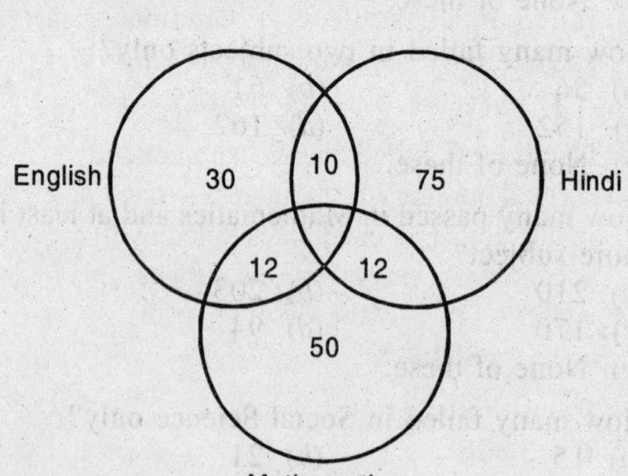

Five hundred candidates appeared in the examination conducted for the tests in English, Hindi and Mathematics. The diagram gives the number of candidates who failed in different tests. What is the percentage of candidates who failed in at least two subjects?

(*a*) 0.078 (*b*) 1.0
(*c*) 6.8 (*d*) 7.8
(*e*) None of these.

23. The sum of the ages of a son and father is 56 years. After four years, the age of the father will be three times that of the son. Their ages respectively are:
(*a*) 12 years, 44 years (*b*) 18 years, 36 years
(*c*) 16 years, 42 years (*d*) 16 years, 48 years
(*e*) None of these.

24. The number of boys in a class are three times the number of girls. Which one of the following numbers cannot represent the total number of children in the class?
(*a*) 48 (*b*) 44
(*c*) 42 (*d*) 46
(*e*) None of these.

25. In 10 years, A will be twice as old as B was 10 years ago. If at present A is 9 years older than B, the present age of B is:
(*a*) 19 years (*b*) 29 years
(*c*) 39 years (*d*) 49 years
(*e*) None of these.

EXPLANATORY ANSWERS

1. (*b*) : Candidates passed at least in one subject = (Candidates passed in only one subjects) + (Candidates passed in only two subjects) + (Candidates passed in only all subjects).
(Candidates failed in only two subjects) + (Candidates failed in only one subject) + (Candidates passed in all the subject)
= 162 + 61 + 167 = 390.

2. (*d*) : Candidates failed in two subjects only = Candidates passed in one subjects only = 62 + 48 + 52 = 162.

3. (*b*) : Candidates failed in science only =191 – (62 + 60 + 48) = 21
Candidates failed in one social science only = 15
Therefore, candidates passed in maths and at least one more subject
= (21 + 15 + 167) =203

4. (*a*) : Candidates failed in social science only = (candidates failed in social science) – (candidates failed in all subjects + candidates passed in science only + candidates passed in maths only)
= 175 – (60 + 52 + 48) = 175 – 160 = 15.

5. (*c*) : Candidates failed in one subject only
= (total number of candidates) – (candidates passed in all subjects + candidates failed in all the subjects + candidates passed in one subject only)
= 450 – (167 + 60 + 62 + 48 + 52)
= 450 – 389 = 61.

6. (*c*) : From the questions, we have
B – 3 = E ...... (i)
B + 3 = D ...... (ii)
A + B = D + E + 10 ...... (iii)
B = C + 2 ...... (iv)
A + B + C + D + E = 133 ...... (v)
From (i) and (ii)
B – E = D – B ⇒ E + D = 2 B ...... (vi)
From (iii) and (vi)
A + B = 2B + 10 ⇒ B = A – 10
or, A = B + 10 ...... (vii)
From (v), (vi), (iv) and (vii) we have
(B + 10) + (B) + (B – 2) + 2B = 133
5B = 133 – 8 = 125
= 25.

7. (*d*) : In the city X let the number of men be x
Then the number of women be $\frac{x}{2}$.
In the city y, $x-10=\frac{x}{2}+5$
or, $\frac{x}{2}=15$ or, $x=30$ and $y=15$.
Therefore, total number of passenger at the beginning were 30 + 15 = 45.

8. (*a*) : The required number will be obtained by taking LCM of 2, 3 and 4 and adding 1 into it. The number so obtained is 25.

9. (*a*) : From the questions it is clear that
B – 3 = A ...... (1)
D + 5 = E ...... (2)
A + C = 2 E ...... (3)
A + C = B + D ...... (4)
A + B + C + D + E = 150 ...... (5)
From (3), (4) and (5) we get
5E = 150 ∴ E = 30
Now from (2) D = 30 – 5 = 25
and from (4) A = 32
Now from (3) 32 + C = 2 × 30
C = 60 – 32 = 28.

10. (*b*) : Total number of handshakes = (9 + 8 + 7 + 6 + 5 + 4 + 3 + 2 + 1) = 45

11. (*b*) : Let the age of Anil and Prashant be x and (48 – x) years.
Let the age of Jayesh be y years then
$(x - y) = y - (48 - x)$
$x - y = y - 48 + x$
$2y = 48$, $y = 24$ years
So, Age of Jayesh is 24 years.

12. (*c*) : Vinay's present age is 17 years.
Five years ago Vinay's age was 12 years. and that of Vikash = 36 years
Present age of Vikash = 36 + 5 = 41 years.

13. (*b*) : Let the present age of father be x years and that of son be $(45 - x)$ years.
Five years ago the age of son was $(45 - x - 5) = (40 - x)$.
and that of father $(x - 5)$ years

$(x - 5)(40 - x) = 4(x - 5)$
$40x - x^2 - 200 + 5x = 4x - 20$
or, $41x - x^2 - 180 = 0$
$x = 36.$
$x^2 - 41x - 180 = 0$
$x^2 - (36 + 5)x + 180 = 0$
or, $x^2 - 36x - 5x + 180 = 0$
$x(x - 36) - 5(x - 36) = 0$
$(x - 36)(x - 5) = 0$
$x = 36 \mid x = 5$ unacceptable

Therefore, the present age of father and son are 36 years and 9 years respectively.

14. (*c*) : Let the circles x, y, z represent the musicians who can play guitar, violin and flute respectively.
P + Q + R + S + T + U + V = 120 ...... (1)
Number of musicians who can play all the three instruments = S = 5% of 120 = 6
S = 6 ...... (2)
Number of musicians who can play guitar only = P = 40 ...... (3)
Number of musicians who can play any two and only two of the instruments
= Q + T + U = 30 ...... (4)
Now, from equations (1), (2), (3) and (4) we get
P + Q + R + S + T + U + V = 120
P + (Q + T + U) + S + R + V = 120
40 + 30 + 6 + R + V = 120
R + V = 120 – 76
= 44
Total number of musicians who can play violin alone or flute alone
= (R + V)
= 44

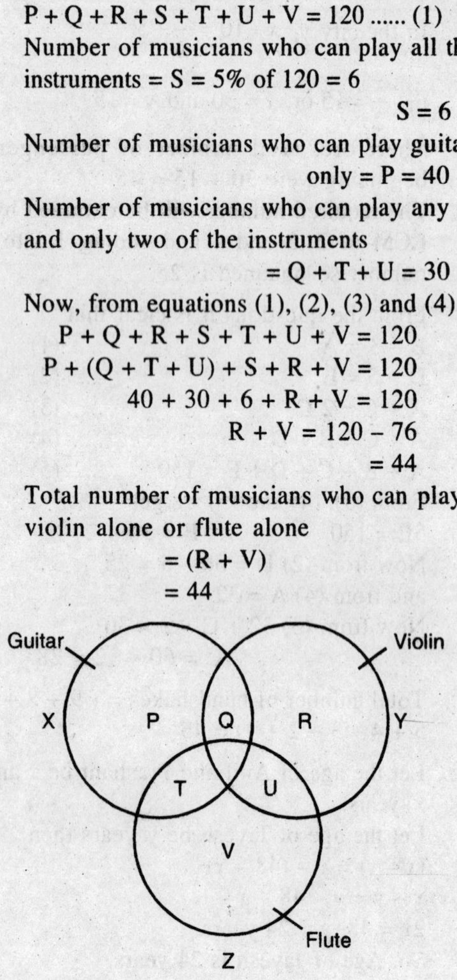

15. (*c*) : Let circles x, y and z represent persons who can speak Tamil, Hindi and Gujarati respectively.
Persons who speak Tamil
= A + B + D + E = 6 ... (1)
Persons who speak Hindi
= B + C + E + F = 15 ... (2)
Persons who speak Gujarati
= D + E + F + G = 6 ... (3)
Persons who speak two languages

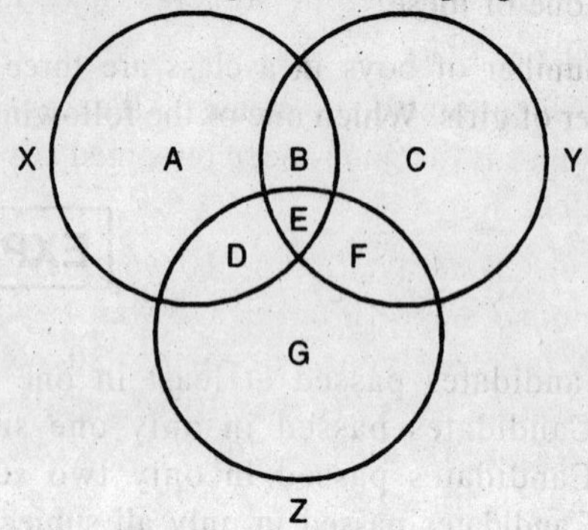

= B + D + F = 2 ... (4)
Persons who speak all the three language
= E = 1 ... (5)
Substituting the value of E in equations (1), (2) and (3) we get
A + B + D = 5 ... (6)
B + C + F = 14 ... (7)
D + F + G = 5 ... (8)
Subtracting (4) from (6), we get
A – F = 3 ... (9)
Adding (7) and (8) we get
B + C + 2F + D + G = 19 ... (10)
Adding (9) and (10) we get
A + B + C + D + F + G = 22 ... (11)
Adding (5) and (11) we get
A + B + C + D + E + F + G = 23 ... (12)
Therefore, total number of person = 23.

16. (*a*) :

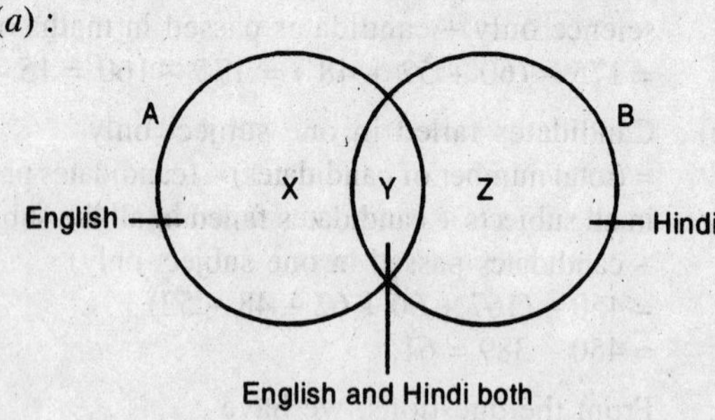

Circle A and B represent the students who speak English and Hindi respectively. Now as per information given in the question total number of students
$= x + y + z = 50$ ... (1)
$y = 10$ ... (2)
$x + y = 21$ ... (3)
From (2) and (3) $x = 11$
Number of students who can speak Hindi is $(y + z)$

From (1) we get

$y + z = 50 - 11 = 39$ ... (4)

Now, number of students who can speak Hindi only is z.

From (4), $y + z = 39$, $z = 39 - y = 39 - 10 = 29$

Therefore, number of the students speaking Hindi = 39, number of students speaking Hindi only = 29 and number of students speaking English only = 11.

17. (*c*) : 'All but nine died' means 'All except nine died'. It means that nine sheep remained alive and other died.

18. (*c*) : Let Chandravati's age 10 years ago be x year mother's age 10 yeags ago was $4x$ year. After ten year, or after 20 years when Chandravati's age was 10 years.

$(4x + 20) = 2(x + 20)$

$4x + 20 = 2x + 40$

$2x = 20$

or, $x = 10$ years

Present age of Chandravati = 20 years.

19. (*b*) : Let the present age of Pushpa be x year. The present age of Rita would be $(x - 2)$ year.

Now as per question, $x = 2(x - 2 - 2)$

or, $x = 2x - 8$

or, $x = 8$

Therefore, present age of Pushpa is 8 years.

20. (*b*) : Let the present age of the son be x years then, the age of Sohanlal would be $4x$ years. Four years later their age would be $(x + 4)$ and $(4x + 4)$ years.

Now, as per questions,

$(x + 4) + (4x + 4) = 43$ years

$5x + 8 = 43$ years

$5x = 35$ years

or, $x = 7$ years.

Therefore, the present age of son is 7 years.

21. (*b*) : Let the present age of the elder persons be x years.

then, the present age of the younger person $= (x - 10)$ years.

$(x - 15) = 2(x - 10 - 15)$

or, $x = 35$ years.

∴ The present age of the elder person is 35 years.

22. (*d*) : From the diagram it is clear that number of candidates who failed in at least two subjects = number of candidates who failed in two or more subjects.

$= (10 + 12 + 12 + 5) = 39$

Therefore, required percentage

$$\left(\frac{39}{500} \times 100\right)\% = 7.8\%$$

Therefore, option (*d*) is our answer.

23. (*a*) : Let the age of the father be x, then the age of the son would be $(56 - x)$.

After four years, the age of father would be $(x + 4)$ and that of son would be $(56 - x + 4)$

Now from the information given in the questions. We have

$(x + 4) = 3(56 - x + 4)$

$x + 4 = 168 - 3x + 12$

$4x = 168 + 12 - 4 = 176$

$x = 44$ years

Therefore, the age of father and son is 44 years and 12 years respectively.

24. (*c*) : Let the number of girls be x, then from the question it is clear that number of boys are $3x$.

Therefore, total number of students

= Number of Boys + Numbers of girls

$= x + 3x = 4x$.

Now, the total number of children in the class must be a multiple of 4.

Out of the four options (c) does not qualify this condition. Hence 42 does not represent the total number of children in the class.

25. (*c*) : Let the present age of B be x years

The present age of A would be $(x + 9)$ years.

After ten years the age of A would be $(x + 9 + 10) = (x + 19)$ years. and before ten years the age of B was $(x - 10)$ years.

Now from the information given in the question,

$(x + 19) = 2(x - 10)$

$x + 19 = 2x - 20$

$x = 19 + 20 = 39$ years.

CHAPTER 7

Problem Solving

Number problems consists of number sequences, problems with algebraic expressions, mathematical calculations and other compatiable problems.

SOLVED EXAMPLES

1. How many such 7s are there in the following number sequence which are immediately followed by 4 but not immediately preceded by 8?

5 4 7 8 9 7 4 3 8 7 5 7 4 8 7 4 1 2 7 4 5 7 9 4

(*a*) Two (*b*) Three (*c*) Four (*d*) Five (*e*) None of these

Ans. (*b*) : Number of 7s which are immediately followed by 4 but not immediately preceded by 8 are :

547897438757487412745794

1 2 3

2. A number is 9 times twice the other number. The sum of two numbers is 133. The two numbers are :

(*a*) 9, 124 (*b*) 11, 122 (*c*) 17, 166 (*d*) 7, 126 (*e*) 27, 136

Ans. (*d*) : If the smaller number is x, then

$$x + (2x \times 9) = 133$$
$$x + 18x = 133$$
$$19x = 133$$
$$x = 133 \div 19 = 7$$

If one number is 7, the other number is :

$$133 - 7 = 126$$

3. If all the numbers from 1 to 28 which are exactly divisible by 3 are arranged in descending order, which would come at the sixth place from the top?

(*a*) 12 (*b*) 21 (*c*) 15 (*d*) 18 (*e*) 24

Ans. (*a*) : The numbers divisible by 3 in descending order are : 27, 24, 21, 18, 15, 12, 9, 6, 3 and the number at the sixth place is 12.

MULTIPLE CHOICE QUESTIONS

1. How many 6's are there in the following series of numbers which are preceded by 7 but not immediately followed by 9?

6 7 9 5 6 9 7 6 8 7 6 7 8 6 9 4 6 7 7 6 9 5 7 6 3

(*a*) One (*b*) Two
(*c*) Three (*d*) Four

2. In a chess tournament each of six players will play every other player exactly once. How many matches will be played during the tournament?

(*a*) 12 (*b*) 15
(*c*) 30 (*d*) 36

3. How many 4's are there in the following series which are preceded by 7, but are not preceded by 8?

3 4 5 7 4 3 7 4 8 5 4 3 7 4 9 8 4 7 2 7 4 1 3 6

(*a*) 1 (*b*) 2
(*c*) 3 (*d*) 4

4. How many even numbers are there in the following series of numbers, each of which is immediately preceded by an odd number, but not immediately followed by an even number?

5 3 4 8 9 7 1 6 5 3 2 9 8 4 3 5

(*a*) Nil (*b*) 1
(*c*) 2 (*d*) 3

5. If all the numbers from 1 to 51 which are exactly divisible by 3 are arranged in descending order, which of the following numbers will come at the seventh and tenth places from the top?

(*a*) 33 & 27 (*b*) 33 & 21
(*c*) 21 & 30 (*d*) 33 & 24

6. Nitin was counting down from 32. Shasank was counting upwards, the numbers starting from 1 and he was calling out only the odd numbers. Which common number will they call out at the same time if they were calling out at the same speed?

(*a*) 21
(*b*) 22
(*c*) 19
(*d*) They will not call out the same number

7. In the following list of numerals, how many 3s are followed by 3, but NOT preceded by 3?

2 4 6 3 3 1 5 7 8 3 3 3 4 6 2 3 3 3 3 9 7 2 3

(*a*) 1 (*b*) 2
(*c*) 3 (*d*) 4

8. If in a given number 5 8 9 4 3 2 7 6 1 4, we interchange the first and the second digits, the third and the fourth, the fifth and the sixth and so on, then counting from the right end, which digit will be sixth?

(*a*) 3 (*b*) 2
(*c*) 4 (*d*) 5

9. Aparna cuts a cake into two halves and cuts one-half into smaller pieces of equal size. Each of the small pieces is twenty grams in weight. If she has seven pieces of the cake in all with her, how heavy was the original cake?

(*a*) 140 grams (*b*) 280 grams
(*c*) 240 grams (*d*) 120 grams

10. In the following number sequence how many such even numbers are there which are exactly divisible by its immediate preceding number but not exactly divisible by its immediate following number?

3 8 4 1 5 7 2 8 3 4 8 9 3 9 4 2 1 5 8 2

(*a*) Two (*b*) Three
(*c*) Four (*d*) More than four

11. How many 7s are there in the following series which are not immediately followed by 3 but immediately preceded by 8?

8 9 8 7 6 2 2 6 3 2 6 9 7 3 2 8 7 2 7 7 8
7 3 7 7 9 4

(*a*) Nil (*b*) One
(*c*) Two (*d*) Three

12. How many 9's are there in the following sequence which are neither preceded by 6 nor immediately followed by 3?

9 3 8 6 9 9 5 9 3 7 8 9 9 9 3 9 6 3 9

(*a*) One (*b*) Two
(*c*) Three (*d*) Four

13. If a number is five times as great as another number which is four less than forty, then the number is :

(*a*) 220 (*b*) 180
(*c*) 144 (*d*) 200

14. If 2/3rd of a number is 96, what will be the 3/4th of that number?

(*a*) 108 (*b*) 198
(*c*) 128 (*d*) 48

15. If such numbers which are divisible by 5, and also those which have 5 as one of the digits are eliminated from the numbers 1 to 60, how many numbers would remain?

(*a*) 53 (*b*) 47
(*c*) 40 (*d*) 45

16. How many 8's are there in the following number series which are exactly divisible by its immediately preceding and also exactly divisible by immediately succeeding numbers?

8 2 4 5 1 7 2 8 4 8 4 2 2 8 2 6 9 8 4 5 4 8
3 2 8 4 3 1 8 3

(*a*) 1 (*b*) 2
(*c*) 3 (*d*) 4

17. Jagan was to either get one-seventh of a milk chocolate or one-fourteenth of a bigger fruit chocolate. Which chocolate would give him the larger piece if the fruit chocolate is three times as large as the milk chocolate?

(*a*) Milk chocolate
(*b*) Fruit chocolate
(*c*) The pieces will be of the same size
(*d*) Information inadequate

18. How many such 3's are there in the following number sequence which are immediately preceded by an odd number and immediately followed by an even number?

5 3 8 9 4 3 7 2 3 8 1 3 8 4 2 3 5 7 3 4 2 3 6

(*a*) One (*b*) Two
(*c*) Three (*d*) Four

19. Count each 7 which is not immediately preceded by 5 but is immediately followed by either 2 or 3. How many such 7's are there?

5 7 2 6 5 7 3 8 3 7 3 2 5 7 2 7 3 4 8 2 6 7 8

(*a*) 2 (*b*) 3
(*c*) 4 (*d*) 5

20. A number is four less than two times the other number. If their difference is 21, what is the greater number?

(*a*) 50 (*b*) 46
(*c*) 31 (*d*) 21

EXPLANATORY ANSWERS

1. (*c*) : 6795697687678694677695763
1 2 3

2. (*b*) : When all the players have to play with each other then the method of calculating the number of matches to be played is $\frac{n(n-1)}{2}$ where '*n*' is the number of players playing the match. So, the number of matches played will be :
$(6 \times 5) \div 2 = 30 \div 2 = 15$

3. (*d*) : 345743748543749847274136
1 2 3 4

4. (*c*) : 5348971653298435
1 2

5. (*d*) : The numbers divisible by 3 in descending order are: 51, 48, 45, 42, 39, 36, 33, 30, 27, 24, 21, 18, 15, 12, 9, 6, 3.
(33, 30 — 7th; 24, 21 — 10th)

6. (*d*) : When Nitin is on count 22, Shasank is on 21 and when Nitin is on count 21, Shasank is on 23.

7. (*c*) : 2463315783334623333 9723
1 2 3

8. (*b*) : The new number after interchanging the digits is :
8549236741
6th

9. (*c*) : There is one bigger piece and six smaller pieces. One small piece weighs 20 gm. Total weight of six smaller speices is 120 gm.
∴ Weight of the bigger piece = 120 gm
∴ Weight of the original cake = 240 gm

10. (*a*) : 38415728348939421582
1 2

11. (*c*) : 898762263269732872778737794
1 2

12. (*d*) : 9386995937899939639
1 2 3 4

13. (*b*) : Number four less than forty is 40 – 4 = 36
Five times the number is = 36 × 5 =180

14. (*a*) : If the number is *x*, then

$$\frac{2}{3}x = 96$$

$$x = \frac{96 \times 3}{2} = 144$$

$\frac{3}{4}$ th of the number is $144 \times \frac{3}{4} = 108$

15. (*c*) : The eliminated twenty numbers are : 5, 10, 15, 20, 25, 30, 35, 40, 45 and 50 to 60. The remaining numbers are 60 – 20 = 40.

16. (*d*) : 8245172848422826984548
1 2 3
32843183
4

17. (*b*) : If fruit chocolate (F) is equal to three times as milk chocolate (M) then —

$$F = 3\,M$$

or $$\frac{F}{M} = 3$$

$$\therefore \frac{1/14\ F}{1/7\ M} = \frac{3/14}{1/7}$$

When 3/14 > 1/7, then F (Fruit chocolate) will give him the larger piece.

18. (*c*) : 5389437238138423573 4236
1 2 3

19. (*a*) : 57265738373257273482678
1 2

20. (*b*) : If smaller number is *x*, then

$$(2x - 4) - x = 21$$
$$2x - x = 21 + 4$$
$$x = 25$$

The greater number is
$(25 \times 2) - 4 = 46$

CHAPTER 8

Numerical Operations/ Symbol Substitution

Questions in this category are easy to attempt. Candidates must be quick in substituting symbols and calculations. The common pattern of questions asked are given below.

SOLVED EXAMPLES

1. If '+' stands for '×'; '×' stands for '÷'; '÷' stands for '–' and '–' stands for '+' then
$2 - 8 \times 2 + 6 \div 7 = ?$

(*a*) 32 (*b*) 19 (*c*) 23 (*d*) 9

Ans. (*b*) : After substituting the symbols in the given expression the new expression will be :

$2 + 8 \div 2 \times 6 - 7$

The solving steps will be :

$2 + 4 \times 6 - 7$

$2 + 24 - 7$

$26 - 7 = 19$

2. If ▲ stands for '+'
■ stands for '–'
● stands for '÷'
✱ stands for '×' then
13 ▲ 5 ✱ 20 ● 10 ■ 9 = ?

(*a*) 26 (*b*) 37 (*c*) 14 (*d*) 55

Ans. (*c*) : After substituting the symbols the new expression will be :

$13 + 5 \times 20 \div 10 - 9$

The solving steps will be :

$13 + 5 \times 2 - 9$

$13 + 10 - 9$

$23 - 9 = 14$

MULTIPLE CHOICE QUESTIONS

Directions : *Each of the following questions is followed by four alternatives. Select the most appropriate answer.*

1. If "+" means "–"; "–" means "×"; "×"means "÷" and "÷" means "+", then
$15 \times 5 \div 10 + 5 - 3 = ?$

(*a*) 9.5 (*b*) 0
(*c*) – 2 (*d*) 24

2. If "+" means "–"; "–" means "×"; "×"means "÷" and "÷" means "+", then
$15 \times 3 \div 15 + 5 - 2 = ?$

(*a*) 0 (*b*) 10
(*c*) 20 (*d*) 6

3. If "+" means "÷"; "×" means "–"; "÷"means "+" and "–" means "×", then
$16 \div 8 \times 6 - 2 + 12 = ?$

(*a*) 22 (*b*) 24
(*c*) 23 (*d*) 20

4. If "+" means "×"; "–" means "÷"; "÷"means "+" and "×" means "–", then what will be the value of $20 \div 40 - 4 \times 5 + 6 = ?$

(a) 60 (b) 1.67
(c) 150 (d) 0

5. If "+" means "×"; "–" means "÷"; "×"means "–" and "÷" means "+", then $5 + 8 - 4 \times 2 \div 9 = ?$

(a) 15 (b) 13
(c) 17 (d) 11

6. If × stand for addition, ÷ stands for subtraction, + stands for multiplication and – stands for division, then $(20 \times 6 \div 6 \times 4)$ is equal to

(a) 5 (b) 24
(c) 25 (d) 80

7. If "+" means "×"; "÷" means "–"; "×"means "÷" and "–" means "+", what will be the value of the following expression?
$4 + 11 \div 5 - 50 = ?$

(a) 79 (b) –11
(c) 91 (d) 89

8. If "+" means "÷"; "÷" means "–"; "–"means "×" and "×" means "+", then
$10 \div 2 - 15 + 3 \times 5 = ?$

(a) 10 (b) 15
(c) 25 (d) 5

9. If A stands for add, B for subtract, C for multiply and D for divide, then for what does 4A 3B 3A 2 stand?

(a) 2 (b) 4
(c) 6 (d) 8

10. If × stands for add, *y* stands for subract, *z* stands for divide and *p* stands for multiply, then what is the the value of (7 p 3) y 6 × 5?

(a) 5 (b) 10
(c) 15 (d) 20

11. If "+" means "÷"; "÷" means "–"; "–"means "×" and "×" means "+", what will be the value of $8 + 2 \div 3 - 4 \times 6 = ?$

(a) –2 (b) $-15\frac{1}{3}$
(c) 12 (d) 15

12. If "+" means "÷"; "×" means "–"; "÷"means "×" and "–" means "+", what will be the value of the following expression?
$9 + 3 \div 4 - 8 \times 2 = ?$

(a) $6\frac{3}{4}$ (b) $-1\frac{3}{4}$
(c) $-6\frac{1}{4}$ (d) 18

13. If "–" means "÷"; "+" means "×"; "÷"means "–" and "×" means "+", then which of the following must be true?

(a) $1 \div 2 + 3 \times 6 - 8 = 12$
(b) $2 + 3 - 5 \times 8 \div 4 = 7$
(c) $5 + 6 \times 8 - 2 \div 3 = 31$
(d) $6 \div 1 + 2 - 8 \times 4 = 31$

14. If "÷" means "+"; "+" means "×"; "–"means "÷" and "×" means "–", then
$5 + 8 - 4 \times 2 \div 9 = ?$

(a) 13 (b) 15
(c) 11 (d) 17

EXPLANATORY ANSWERS

1. (c) : $15 \div 5 + 10 - 5 \times 3$
$3 + 10 - 15 = -2$

2. (b) : $15 \div 3 + 15 - 5 \times 2$
$5 + 15 - 10 = 10$

3. (c) : $16 + 8 - 6 \times 2 \div 12$
$16 + 8 - 1 = 23$

4. (d) : $20 + 40 \div 4 - 5 \times 6$
$20 + 10 - 30 = 0$

5. (c) : $5 \times 8 \div 4 - 2 + 9$
$10 - 2 + 9 = 17$

6. (b) : $20 + 6 - 6 + 4 = 24$

7. (d) : $4 \times 11 - 5 + 50$
$44 - 5 + 50 = 89$

8. (d) : $10 - 2 \times 15 \div 3 + 5$
$10 - 10 + 5 = 5$

9. (c) : $4 + 3 - 3 + 2 = 6$

10. (d) : $(7 \times 3) - 6 + 5$
$21 - 6 + 5 = 20$

11. (a) : $8 \div 2 - 3 \times 4 + 6$
$4 - 12 + 6 = -2$

12. (d) : $9 \div 3 \times 4 + 8 - 2$
$12 + 8 - 2 = 18$

13. (c) : (a) $1 - 2 \times 3 + 6 \div 8 = 12 \Rightarrow \frac{-17}{4} = 12$

(b) $2 \times 3 \div 5 + 8 - 4 = 7 \Rightarrow \frac{26}{5} = 7$

(c) $5 \times 6 + 8 \div 2 - 3 = 31 \Rightarrow 31 = 31$

(d) $6 - 1 \times 2 \div 8 + 4 = 31 \Rightarrow \frac{-39}{4} = 31$

14. (d) : $5 \times 8 \div 4 - 2 + 9$
$10 - 2 + 9 = 17$

CHAPTER 9

Word Building

These are spellings, word order and dictionary related questions. The candidate is given a word and asked to select the word that can/cannot be formed from its spellings. He/she may be asked to decide the meaningful order of the given words. He/she may also be asked to arrange the given words in the sequence in which they occur in the dictionary.

MULTIPLE CHOICE QUESTIONS

Directions (Qs. No. 1 to 12): *From the given alternatives select the word which* ***cannot*** *be formed using the letters of the given word.*

1. REPUBLICAN
   (*a*) CLIP (*b*) PURE
   (*c*) ANKLE (*d*) BANE
2. ESTRANGE
   (*a*) GENERATE (*b*) SERGEANT
   (*c*) REAGENTS (*d*) GREAT
3. DETERMINATION
   (*a*) DETENTION (*b*) DESTINATION
   (*c*) TERMINATE (*d*) DOMINATE
4. CHRISTMAS
   (*a*) CHRIST (*b*) SMART
   (*c*) CRUST (*d*) HARM
5. LEGALIZATION
   (*a*) ALERT (*b*) ALEGATION
   (*c*) GALLANT (*d*) NATAL
6. CHARACTER
   (*a*) CRATE (*b*) CHARTER
   (*c*) HEARTY (*d*) TRACER
7. ADMINISTRATION
   (*a*) Station (*b*) Minister
   (*c*) Ration (*d*) Mind
8. ORGANISATION
   (*a*) ORGAN (*b*) ORGANISE
   (*c*) NATION (*d*) ORATION
9. PERAMBULATOR
   (*a*) RAMPANT
   (*b*) LABOUR
   (*c*) MARBLE
   (*d*) RAMBLE
10. POSSESSION
    (*a*) SESSION
    (*b*) POSE
    (*c*) POISE
    (*d*) OBSESS
11. PRINTINGS
    (*a*) SAINT (*b*) PRINT
    (*c*) STING (*d*) RINGS
12. QUALIFICATION
    (*a*) LIAR (*b*) FIAT
    (*c*) LION (*d*) FICTION
13. From the given alternatives select the word which can be formed using the letters given in the word.
    ULTRANATIONALISM
    (*a*) ULTRAMONTANE
    (*b*) ULTRAMODERN
    (*c*) ULTRAIST
    (*d*) ULULATE
14. A meaningful word starting with R is made from the first, second, fourth, fifth and eighth letters of the word CREATIVE. Which of the following is the middle letter of the word?
    (*a*) E (*b*) T
    (*c*) C (*d*) A

Directions (Qs. No. 15 to 18): *Which one of the given responses would be a meaningful order of the following words?*

15. 1. Amoeba 2. Oyster
3. Worm 4. Cow
(*a*) 1, 3, 2, 4 (*b*) 1, 2, 3, 4
(*c*) 4, 3, 2, 1 (*d*) 3, 2, 4, 1

16. 1. Birth 2. Death
3. Childhood 4. Infancy
5. Adolescence 6. Adulthood
7. Old age
(*a*) 2, 6, 7, 5, 4, 3, 1 (*b*) 1, 4, 3, 5, 6, 7, 2
(*c*) 1, 4, 3, 6, 5, 7, 2 (*d*) 2, 7, 6, 4, 5, 3, 1

17. 1. Police 2. Punishment
3. Crime 4. Judge
4. Judgement
(*a*) 3, 1, 2, 4, 5
(*b*) 1, 2, 4, 3, 5
(*c*) 5, 4, 3, 2, 1
(*d*) 3, 1, 4, 5, 2

18. 1. Orange 2. Indigo
3. Red 4. Blue
5. Green 6. Yellow
7. Violet
(*a*) 7, 2, 4, 5, 6, 1, 3 (*b*) 7, 2, 4, 6, 5, 1, 3
(*c*) 7, 2, 6, 4, 5, 1, 3 (*d*) 7, 2, 6, 4, 1, 5, 3

Directions (Qs. Nos. 19 and 24): *Arrange the given words in the sequence in which they occur in the dictionary.*

19. 1. Clone 2. Climate
3. Clutter 4. Create
5. Clapped
(*a*) 52143 (*b*) 51234
(*c*) 52134 (*d*) 53124

20. 1. Lasted 2. Loop
3. Lake 4. Litter
5. Listed
(*a*) 31542 B. 31254
(*c*) 31245 (*d*) 31452

21. 1. Intricate 2. Interview
3. Intransigent 4. Interrogation
5. Intravenous
(*a*) 2, 4, 5, 3, 1 (*b*) 5, 3, 1, 2, 4
(*c*) 4, 2, 3, 5, 1 (*d*) 3, 5, 2, 1, 4

22. 1. Forge 2. Forget
3. Forgo 4. Forgive
5. Format
(*a*) 1, 2, 4, 3, 5
(*b*) 5, 2, 4, 3, 1
(*c*) 1, 4, 3, 2, 5
(*d*) 3, 4, 5, 2, 1

23. 1. Forecast 2. Forget
3. Foreign 4. Forsook
5. Force
(*a*) 3, 5, 1, 2, 4 (*b*) 5, 1, 3, 2, 4
(*c*) 5, 1, 3, 4, 2 (*d*) 5, 1, 2, 3, 4

24. 1. Fenestration 2. Feather
3. Feed head 4. Feature
5. Feminine
(*a*) 2, 4, 3, 5, 1 (*b*) 4, 2, 3, 1, 5
(*c*) 2, 4, 1, 5, 3 (*d*) 4, 2, 3, 5, 1

25. Arrange the given words in the sequence in which they occur in the Dictionary and locate the last word.
(*a*) Frankenstein (*b*) Frankincense
(*c*) Frankalmoign (*d*) Frauendienst

26. Grouping of words are given. Choose the next word in the series from the given options.
AFGHAN, INDEFINITELY, SYNOPSIS, STUPENDOUS, BURST
(*a*) GLACIAL (*b*) COMPANION
(*c*) RESCRIPT (*d*) HIJACKER

ANSWERS

1	2	3	4	5	6	7	8	9	10
(*c*)	(*a*)	(*b*)	(*c*)	(*a*)	(*c*)	(*b*)	(*b*)	(*a*)	(*d*)
11	**12**	**13**	**14**	**15**	**16**	**17**	**18**	**19**	**20**
(*a*)	(*a*)	(*c*)	(*d*)	(*a*)	(*b*)	(*d*)	(*a*)	(*c*)	(*d*)
21	**22**	**23**	**24**	**25**	**26**				
(*c*)	(*a*)	(*b*)	(*a*)	(*d*)	(*d*)				

CHAPTER 10

Relationship Concept

While attempting questions on blood relations, one should be clear of all the relation patterns that can exist between any two individuals. These type of questions are given mainly to test one's relationship ability.

Very well known relations are :

Mother	Grandmother
Father	Grandfather
Son	Grandson
Daughter	Granddaughter
Brother	Brother-in-law
Sister	Sister-in-law
Niece	Father-in-law
Nephew	Mother-in-law
Uncle	Son-in-law
Aunt	Daughter-in-law
Husband	Cousin
Wife	

The patterns of some relationships which help in solving questions in these tests are :

Father's *or* Mother's Father	—	Grandfather (Paternal *or* Maternal)
Father's *or* Mother's Mother	—	Grandmother (Paternal *or* Maternal
Father's *or* Mother's Son	—	Brother
Father's *or* Mother's Daughter	—	Sister
Father's Brother	—	Paternal Uncle
Father's Sister	—	Paternal Aunt
Mother's Brother	—	Maternal Uncle
Mother's Sister	—	Maternal Aunt
Uncle *or* Aunt's Son *or* Daughter	—	Cousin
Son's Wife	—	Daughter-in-law
Daughter's Husband	—	Son-in-law
Husband's *or* Wife's Brother	—	Brother-in-law
Husband's *or* Wife's Sister	—	Sister-in-law
Brother's Wife	—	Sister-in-law
Sister's Husband	—	Brother-in-law
Brother's Son	—	Nephew
Brother's Daughter	—	Niece

MULTIPLE CHOICE QUESTIONS

Directions : *In each of the following questions keenly study the relationship mentioned between the persons, and then from the given options select the right relationship as the answer.*

1. 'A' is the father of 'B' and 'C'. 'B' is the son of 'A' but 'C' is not the son of 'A'. What is 'C's' relation with 'A'?
(*a*) Daughter (*b*) Son
(*c*) Niece (*d*) Nephew

2. A lady said, "The person standing there is my grandfather's only son's daughter". How is the lady related to the standing person?
(*a*) Sister (*b*) Mother
(*c*) Aunt (*d*) Cousin

3. Ravi is the brother of Amit's son's son. What is Amit's relation to Ravi?
(*a*) Cousin (*b*) Father
(*c*) Grandfather (*d*) Son

4. Mayank said, "My mother is the sister of Rajat's brother." What is Rajat's relation with Mayank?
(*a*) Cousin (*b*) Maternal uncle
(*c*) Uncle (*d*) Brother-in-law

5. Introducing Lily, Raghav said, "Her father is my mother's only son". How is Lily related to Raghav?
(*a*) Aunt (*b*) Daughter
(*c*) Mother (*d*) Sister

6. Ajay is the brother of Vijay. Mili is the Sister of Ajay. Sanjay is the brother of Rahul and Mehul is the daughter of Vijay. Who is Sanjay's Uncle?
(*a*) Rahul (*b*) Ajay
(*c*) Mehul (*d*) Data inadequate

7. Adity is Bhavi's brother, Bharat is Jayant's father. Ella is Bhavi's mother. Aditya and Jayant are brothers. What is Ella's relationship with Bharat?
(*a*) Sister (*b*) Mother
(*c*) Daughter (*d*) Wife

8. A man introduced the boy coming with him as "He is son of the father of my wife's daughter". What relation did the boy bear to the man?
(*a*) Son-in-law (*b*) Son
(*c*) Brother (*d*) Father

9. A and B are two brothers. C is sister of B. D is sister of E. E is son of A. Who is D's uncle?
(*a*) D (*b*) E
(*c*) B (*d*) C

10. Varun said pointing towards Arun, "He is my sister's only brother's son". How is Arun related to Varun?
(*a*) Son (*b*) Brother
(*c*) Nephew (*d*) Data insufficient

11. Pointing to a man, a lady said, "His brother's father is my grandfather's only son." How is the lady related to the man?
(*a*) Mother (*b*) Sister
(*c*) Daughter (*d*) Aunt

12. Vidya is the wife of Gopi and Gopi is the brother of Akhil. Akhil is the uncle of Vijay. What is Vijay's relation with Vidya?
(*a*) Son (*b*) Nephew
(*c*) Brother-in-law (*d*) Brother

13. If Amit's father is Billoo's father's only son and Billoo has neither a brother nor a daughter, what is the relationship between Amit and Billoo?
(*a*) Uncle - Nephew
(*b*) Father- Daughter
(*c*) Father - Son
(*d*) Cousins

14. A is the sister of B. B is the son of C, and E is the daughter of D, and sister of A. What is D to C?
(*a*) Brother (*b*) Husband
(*c*) Wife (*d*) Data is inadequate

15. A Man said to a lady, "Fagu's mother is the only daughter of your father". How is the lady related to Fagu?
(*a*) Daughter (*b*) Sister
(*c*) Wife (*d*) Mother

16. Pointing to a man, a woman said, "He is the only son of my mother's mother". How is the woman related to the man?
(*a*) Aunt (*b*) Daughter
(*c*) Niece (*d*) Sister

17. If B's mother was A's mother's daughter, how was A related to B?
(*a*) Uncle (*b*) Aunt
(*c*) Sister (*d*) Data is insufficient

18. Pointing to a woman in the photograph a man said, "She is the daughter of my grandmother's only son. How is the woman related to the man?
(*a*) Mother (*b*) Daughter
(*c*) Sister-in-law (*d*) Sister

19. A man and a woman are sitting in a room. Man's mother-in-law and woman's mother-in-law are mother and daughter respectively. Man is the .... of the woman.
(*a*) Father (*b*) Father-in-law
(*c*) Uncle (*d*) Grandfather-in-law

20. Pointing to Suman, Amit said, "He is my sister's only brother's son". How is Suman related to Amit?
(*a*) Grandson
(*b*) Son
(*c*) Nephew
(*d*) Cannot be determined

EXPLANATORY ANSWERS

1. (*a*) :

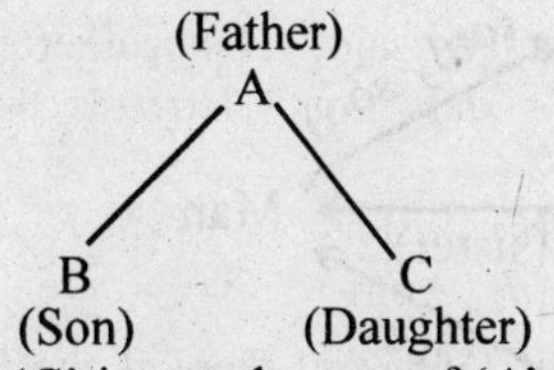

'C' is not the son of 'A', but 'A' is the father of 'C'. So, 'C' is the daughter of 'A'.

2. (*a*) :

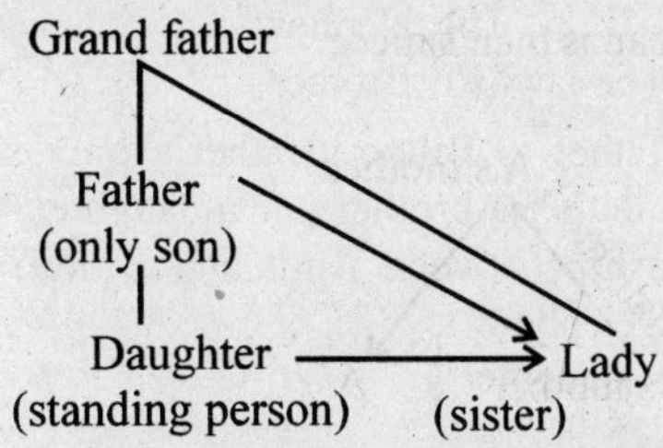

Lady's grandfather's son is lady's father and father's daughter will only be lady's sister.

3. (*c*) :

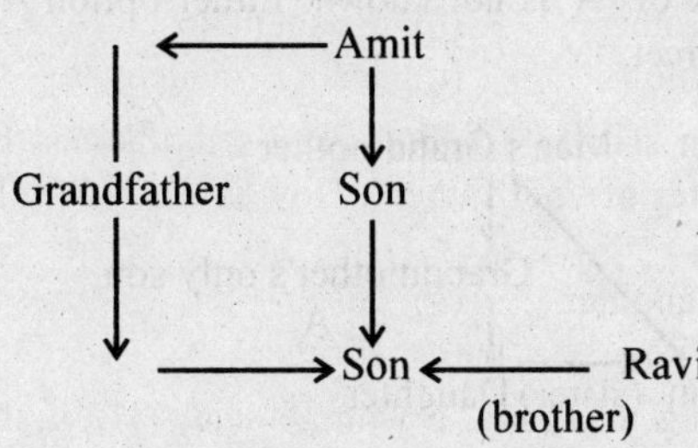

Amit's son's son is Amit's grandson. Ravi is the brother of Amit's son's son. So, Amit is also the grandfather of Ravi.

4. (*b*) :

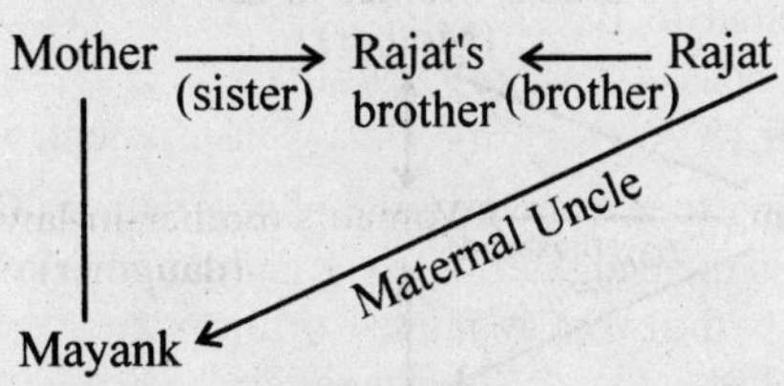

Mayank's mother is the sister of Rajat's brother. So Rajat is also the brother of Mayank's mother. Relation of the brother with his sister's child is maternal. So Rajat is Mayank's maternal uncle.

5. (*b*) : The relation is : Mother
↑ (Son)
Raghav
↓ (Father)
Lily (Daughter)

'My mother's only son' means Raghav himself. 'Her father' means Lily's father; *i.e.* Raghav and so, Lily is Raghav's daughter.

6. (*d*) : 1. Mili > Ajay > Vijay
(sister) (brother) ↓
Mehul
2. Sanjay > Rahul (daughter)
(brother)

There are two sets of relationship. Information given is incomplete and no relation can be established between the two sets.

7. (*d*) : The relationship chart based on problem is :

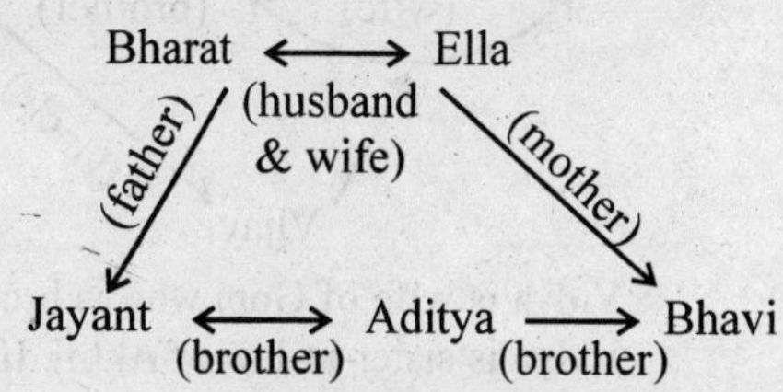

Jayant and Aditya are brothers. If Aditya is Bhavi's brother, then Jayant is also Bhavi's brother. If Bharat is Jayant's father, then he is also the father of Aditya and Bhavi. If Ella is Bhavi's mother, then she is also the mother of Aditya and Jayant. This means Bharat and Ella are husband and wife and the parents of three.

8. (*b*) : The relationship chart based on problem is :

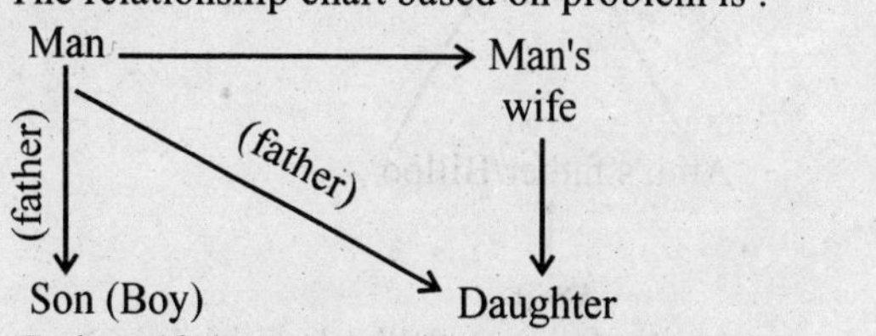

'Father of the man's wife's daughter' is the man himself and the boy in question is the man's son.

9. (*c*) : The relationship chart based on the problem is :

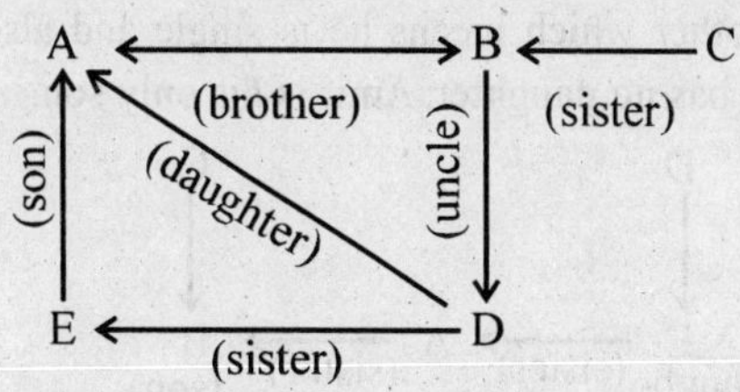

When D is sister of E, who is son of A then D is daughter of A. Brother of A is B and so, B is D's uncle.

10. (*a*) :

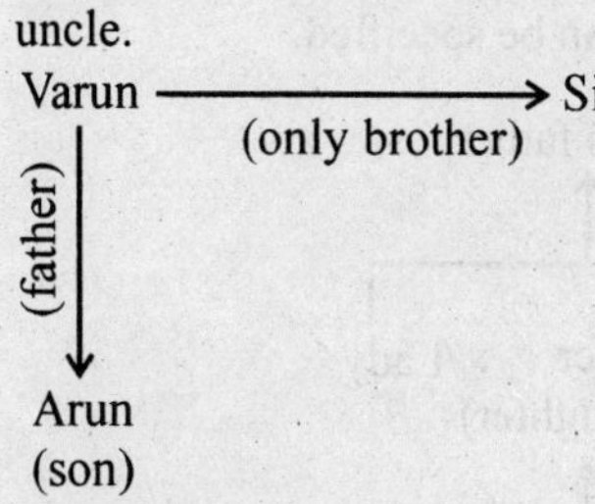

Varun's sister's only brother is Varun himself and Arun is his son.

11. (*b*) :

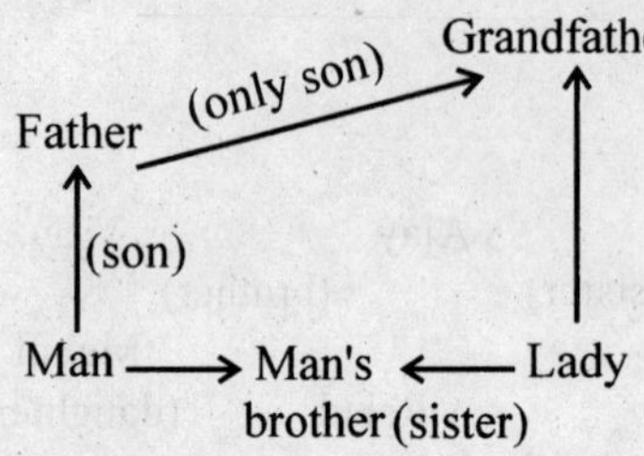

Man's brother's father is also the lady's father as he is the only son of lady's grandfather. So, the lady is man's sister.

12. (*b*) : The relationship chart based on problem is :

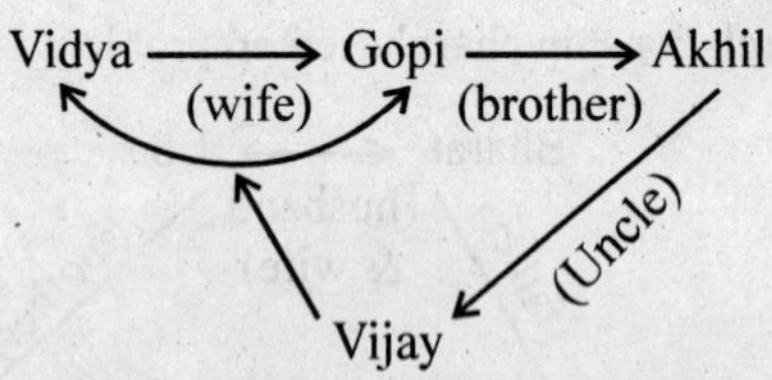

Vidya is wife of Gopi who is brother of Akhil. So, Vidya is sister-in-law of Akhil. If Akhil is uncle of Vijay then Gopi will naturally be the uncle of Vijay as it is not specified that any of the mentioned persons are Vijay's parents. Now, when Vijay is Gopi's nephew then he will also be Vidya's nephew.

13. (*c*) : The relationship chart based on problem is :

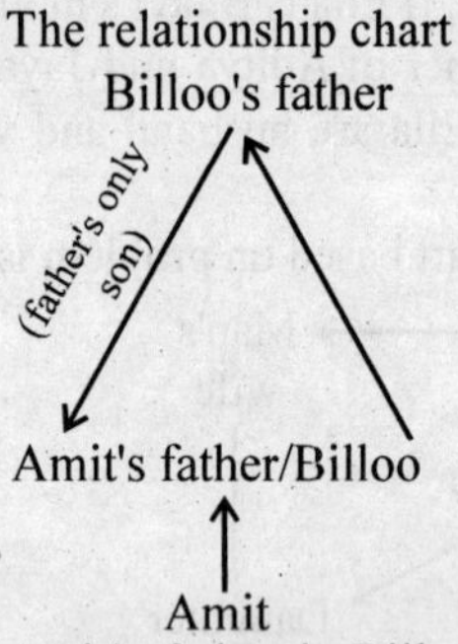

Amit's father is Billoo's father's only son means Billoo is the only son in question also, he is the father of Amit. It must be noted that Billoo has no brother which means he is single and also, when he has no daughter, Amit is his only son.

14. (*d*) :

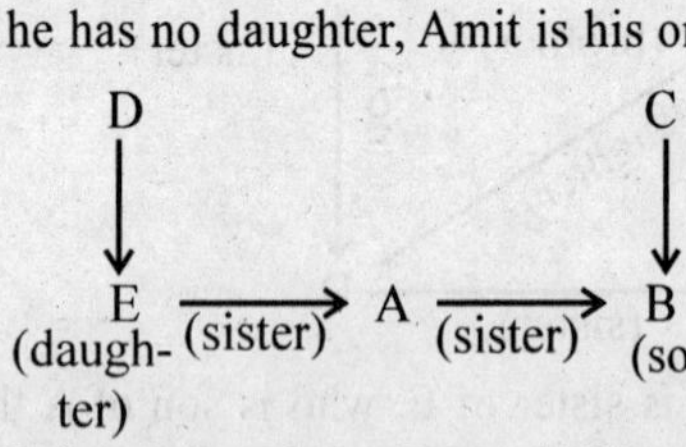

Information about 'D' and 'C' is not given as such no relation can be specified.

15. (*d*) :

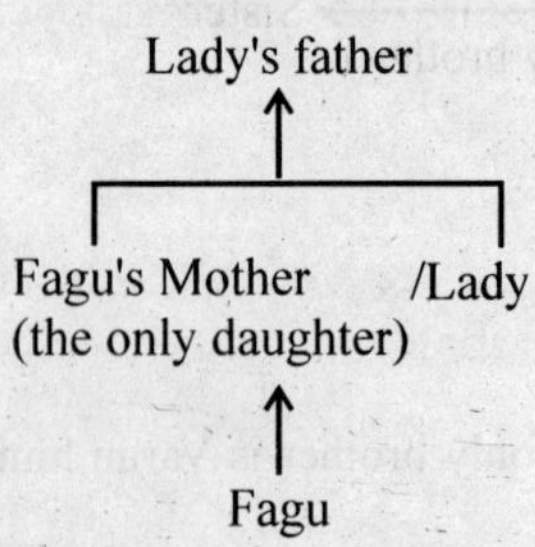

The only daughter of Lady's father is Fagu's mother.

16. (*c*) :

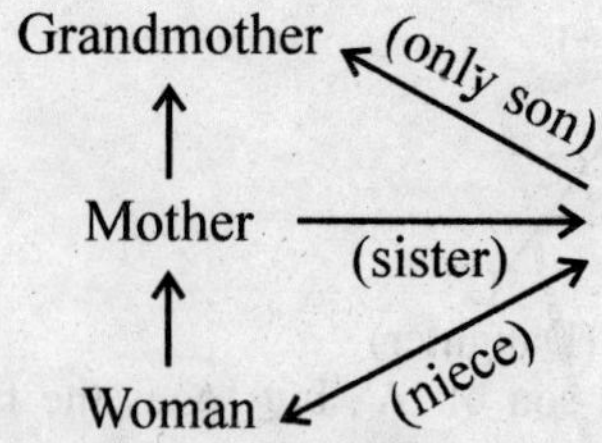

The man is the brother of the woman's mother. So, the woman is man's niece.

17. (*d*) :

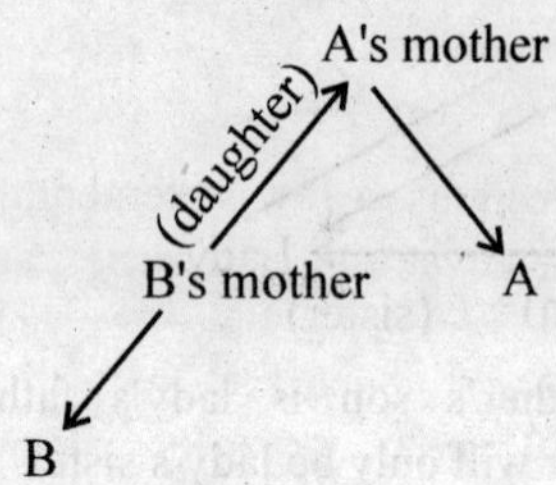

Sex of 'A' is not known. Either option A or B is correct.

18. (*d*) :

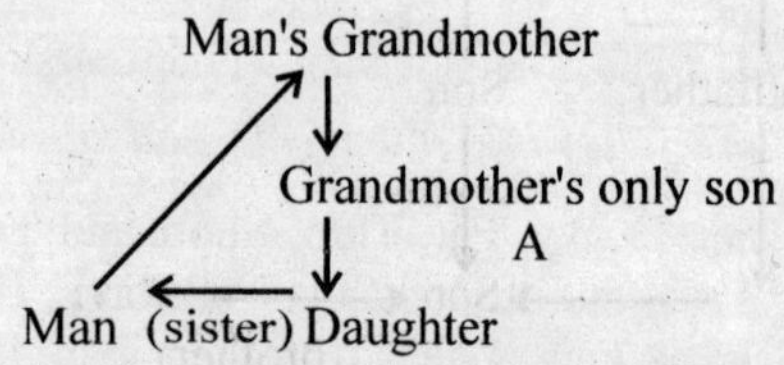

'My grandmother's only son' is the father of the man, and 'daughter of my grand-mother's only son' is the sister of the man.

19. (*b*) :

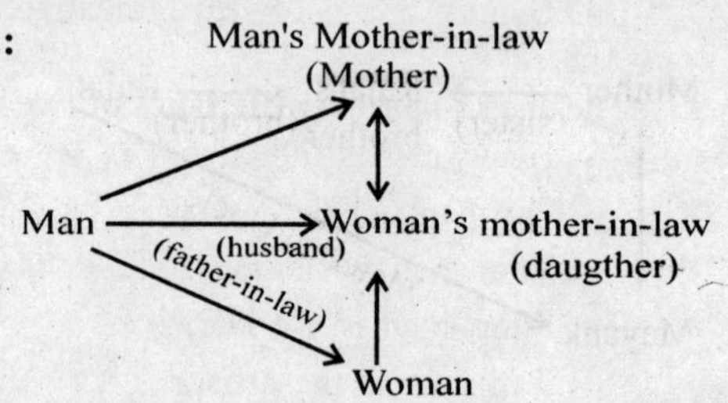

Woman's mother-in-law is the daughter of Man's mother-in-law. So, the man is the husband of woman's mother-in-law and the father-in-law of the woman.

20. (*b*) :

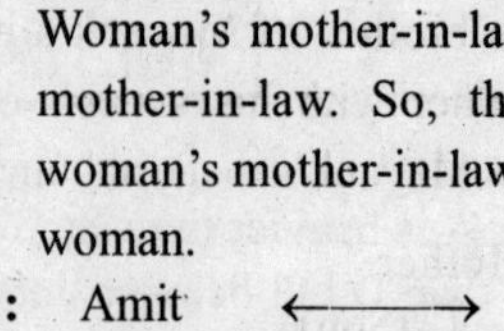

'My sister's only brother's is Amit himself and 'Sister's only brother's son' is the son of Amit *i.e.*, Suman is the son of Amit.

CHAPTER 11

Analysis

In these type of questions, a few statements are given. Certain facts are broken up and mentioned in these statements. What is required is to analyse the statements, arrange and sort out the given facts and then answer the questions related to the given statements.

SOLVED EXAMPLES

1. Icecream is as cold as snow. Ice is not as cold as hail. Flakes are not as cold as ice but colder than icecream. What is the coldest?

(*a*) Hail (*b*) Icecream (*c*) Flakes (*d*) Ice (*e*) Snow

Ans. (*a*) : The order showing an increase in coldness, is Icecream/Snow, Flakes, Ice, Hail.

2. *Read the following statements and answer the questions a and b.*

Five men Heavy, Fat, Thin, Short and Tall are running one behind the other. Of the Heavy and the Tall man one is an Artist and the other is Talkative. Thin man who is a Genius is in the centre. Short man is not Dark and the one who is Fair is ahead of Thin man. The Heavy man, who is not an Artist, is in front of the Fat man.

a. Who is Fair?

(*a*) Tall man (*b*) Fat man (*c*) Short man (*d*) Heavy man (*e*) Thin man

Ans. (*b*)

b. What is the Tall Man?

(*a*) Genius (*b*) Talkative (*c*) Artist (*d*) Dark (*e*) Fair

Ans. (*c*)

The chart of the characteristics of five men is :

Heavy man is Talkative.

Fat man is Fair.

Thin man is Genious.

Short man is not Dark.

Tall man is the artist.

MULTIPLE CHOICE QUESTIONS

1. Among five friends, A is heavier than B; C is lighter than D; B is lighter than D but heavier than E. Who among them is the heaviest?

(*a*) B (*b*) C

(*c*) A (*d*) Can't say

2. Pune is bigger than Jhansi, Sitapur is bigger than Chittor. Raigarh is not as big as Jhansi, but is bigger than Sitapur. Chittor is not as big as Sitapur. Which is the smallest?

(*a*) Jhansi (*b*) Pune

(*c*) Chittor (*d*) Sitapur

3. Ajay works more than Ram. Alok works as much as Raju. Pankaj works less than Alok. Ram works more than Alok. Who works the most of all?

(*a*) Ajay (*b*) Ram
(*c*) Alok (*d*) Raju

4. Vipul is taller than Hans. Hans is taller than Anand. Alok is taller than Ashok. Ashok is taller than Hans. Who among them is the tallest?
(*a*) Vipul (*b*) Alok
(*c*) Ashok (*d*) Cannot be determined

5. Pramod is taller than Gopal. Gopal is shorter than Madhu. To find out who among them is the tallest, which of the following further informations is necessary?
(*a*) Madhu is taller than Gopal.
(*b*) Madhu is shorter than Pramod's brother
(*c*) Pramod is taller than Madhu.
(*d*) Pramod is taller than Madhu's brother.

6. Among five friends P, Q, R, S and T, who is the youngest? To arrive at the answer which of the following information given in the statements (A) and (B) is sufficient?
(A) R is younger than P and T.
(B) S is younger than Q.
(*a*) Only A alone is sufficient
(*b*) Either A or B is sufficient
(*c*) Both A and B together are needed
(*d*) Both A and B together are not sufficient

7. Sushma is richer than Rashmi whereas Anand is richer than Priya. Arun is as rich as Rashmi. Shoba is richer than Sushma.
Which of the following statements is correct according to the above propositions?
(*a*) Rashmi is poorer than Priya.
(*b*) Priya is richer than Arun
(*c*) Arun is poorer than Sushma.
(*d*) Anand is richer than Rashmi

8. A is elder to B while C and D are elder to E who lies between A and B. If C be elder to B, which one of the following statements is necessarily true?
(*a*) E is elder to B (*b*) A is elder to C
(*c*) C is elder to D (*d*) D is elder to C

9. Vikram is taller than Rajan but shorter than Annie. Jamal is taller than Annie. Sita is taller than Vikram. Rajan is shorter than Sita. Who is the shortest of all in the group?
(*a*) Sita (*b*) Rajan
(*c*) Vikram (*d*) Cannot be determined

10. Suresh is as much older than Kamal as he is younger than Prabodh. Navin is as old as Kamal. Which of the following statements is wrong?
(*a*) Suresh is older than Navin
(*b*) Kamal is younger than Suresh
(*c*) Prabodh is not the oldest
(*d*) Navin is younger than Prabodh

11. Ashok is heavier than Gopal. Mahesh is lighter than Jayesh. Prashant is heavier than Jayesh but lighter than Gopal. Who among them is the heaviest?
(*a*) Gopal
(*b*) Jayesh
(*c*) Prashant
(*d*) Ashok

12. Subodh's marks in English are as much more than Gopal's marks in History as less than Pramod's marks in English. To find out Subodh's marks in English, which of the following informations given in the statements (A) and (B) is/ are sufficient?
(A) Gopal's marks in History.
(B) Pramod's marks in History.
(*a*) Both A and B together are needed
(*b*) Only B is sufficient
(*c*) Either A or B is sufficient
(*d*) Both A and B together are not sufficient

13. Pramod is older than Jayesh and Sudhir. Vikas is younger than Anil. To find out who among them is the oldest, which of the following further information will be required, if any?
(*a*) Sudhir is older than Jayesh
(*b*) Anil is older than Jayesh
(*c*) Vikas is older than Pramod
(*d*) Vikas is younger than Pramod

14. Ashok is younger than Prabir and Gopal. Sohan is younger than Prabir but older than Gopal. Which of the following statements is definitely true?
(*a*) Ashok is older than Sohan
(*b*) Sohan is the oldest among them
(*c*) Gopal is younger than Ashok
(*d*) Gopal is next to the youngest among them

15. Among five boys, Vasant is taller than Manohar, but not as tall as Raju. Jayant is taller than Datta, but shorter than Manohar. Who is the tallest in their group?
(*a*) Raju
(*b*) Manohar
(*c*) Vasant
(*d*) Cannot be determined

16. A and D study in the same class. K and L study in the same class. In which class does D study? To answer the above question, which of the following informations given in the statements A and B is/are necessary?
(A) D studies one standard below L.
(B) A's elder brother studies with K.
(*a*) Both A and B together are not sufficient
(*b*) Both A and B together are needed
(*c*) Only A is sufficient
(*d*) Only B is sufficient

Directions (Qs. 17-18) : *(A) Gopal is shorter than Ashok but taller than Kuhav; (B) Navin is shorter than Kuhav; (C) Jayesh is taller than Navin; (D) Ashok is taller than Jayesh.*

17. Who among them is the tallest?
(*a*) Gopal (*b*) Ashok
(*c*) Jayesh (*d*) Navin

18. Which of the following informations is not necessary to answer the above question?
(*a*) A (*b*) B
(*c*) C (*d*) D

Directions (Qs. 19-20) : *Five men A, B, C, D and E read a newspaper. The one who reads first gives it to C. The one who reads last had taken from A. E was not the first or last to read. There were two readers between B and A.*

19. B passed the newspaper to whom?
(*a*) E (*b*) B
(*c*) A (*d*) None of these

20. Who read the newspaper last?
(*a*) E (*b*) B
(*c*) D (*d*) Cannot be determined

EXPLANATORY ANSWERS

1. (*d*) : The five friends in descending order of weight are : A/D, B/C, E or A/D, B, C/E. Either A or D is the heaviest.

2. (*c*) : The order of cities in descending order of size is : Pune, Jhansi, Raigarh, Sitapur, Chittor.

3. (*a*) : On the basis of doing work, the descending order will be : Ajay, Ram, Alok/Raju, Pankaj.

4. (*d*) : On the basis of height, the descending order will be Vipul/Alok, Ashok, Hans, Anand. Either Vipul or Alok is the tallest.

5. (*c*) : According to the information both Pramod and Madhu are taller than Gopal. Option (c) decides who is the tallest.

6. (*d*) : Statements are not inter-related.

7. (*c*) : On the basis of wealth, the descending order will be :
1. Shobha, Sushma, Rashmi/Arun
2. Anand, *and* Priya
(The two statements are not inter-related.)

8. (*a*) : The order in descending seniority will be : A/C/D, E, B.

9. (*b*) : On the basis of height the descending order will be :
Jamal/Sita, Annie, Vikram, Rajan.
or
Jamal, Sita/Annie, Vikram, Rajan.

10. (*c*) : On the basis of age the descending order will be : Prabodh, Suresh, Kamal/Navin.

11. (*d*) : On the basis of weight, the descending order will be : Ashok, Gopal, Prashant, Jayesh, Mahesh.

12. (*d*) : Comparison in marks do no clarify Subodh's marks in a subject.

13. (*c*) : On the basis of age the descending order will be :
1. Pramod, Jayesh/ Sudhir
and
2. Anil, Vikas
Option (c) connects these two statements.

14. (*d*) : On the basis of age the descending order will be : Prabir, Sohan, Gopal, Ashok.

15. (*a*) : The boys in descending order of height will be: Raju, Vasant, Manohar, Jayant, Datta.

16. (*a*) : There is no useful information in either of the two statements.

17. (*b*) : On the basis of height the descending order will be :
Ashok, Gopal/Jayesh, Kuhav, Navin
or
Ashok, Gopal, Kuhav/Jayesh, Navin.

18. (*c*)

19. (*d*) : The men read the newspaper in this order : B, C, E, A, D, and B passed the newspaper to C.

20. (*c*) : See answer 19 explanation.

CHAPTER 12

Judgement

MULTIPLE CHOICE QUESTIONS

1. Eileen is planning a special birthday dinner for her husband's 35th birthday. She wants the evening to be memorable, but her husband is a simple man who would rather be in jeans at a baseball game than in a suit at a fancy restaurant. Which restaurant below should Eileen choose?

(*a*) Alfredo's offers fine Italian cuisine and an elegant Tuscan decor. Patrons will feel as though they've spent the evening in a luxurious Italian villa.

(*b*) Pancho's Mexican Buffet is an all-you-can-eat family style smorgasbord with the best tacos in town.

(*c*) The Parisian Bistro is a four-star French restaurant where guests are treated like royalty. Chef Dilbert Olay is famous for his beef bourguignon.

(*d*) Marty's serves delicious, hearty meals in a charming setting reminiscent of a baseball clubhouse in honor of the owner,Marty Lester, a former major league baseball all-star. Answer & Explanation

2. The film director wants an actress for the lead role of Lucy who perfectly fits the description that appears in the original screenplay. He is not willing to consider actresses who do not resemble the character as she is described in the screenplay, no matter how talented they are. The screenplay describes Lucy as an average-sized, forty something redhead, with deep brown eyes, very fair skin, and a brilliant smile. The casting agent has four actresses in mind.

1. Actress #1 is a stunning red-haired beauty who is 5'9" and in her mid-twenties. Her eyes are brown and she has an olive complexion.
2. has red hair, big brown eyes, and a fair complexion. She is in her mid-forties and is 5'5".
3. is 5'4" and of medium build. She has red hair, brown eyes, and is in her early forties.
4. is a blue-eyed redhead in her early thirties. She's of very slight build and stands at 5'.

(*a*) 1, 2 (*b*) 2, 3
(*c*) 1, 4 (*d*) 2, 4

3. The school principal has received complaints from parents about bullying in the school yard during recess. He wants to investigate and end this situation as soon as possible, so he has asked the recess aides to watch closely. Which situation should the recess aides report to the principal?

(*a*) A girl is sitting glumly on a bench reading a book and not interacting with her peers.

(*b*) Four girls are surrounding another girl and seem to have possession of her backpack.

(*c*) Two boys are playing a one-on-one game of basketball and are arguing over the last basket scored.

(*d*) Three boys are huddled over a handheld video game, which isn't supposed to be on school grounds. Answer & Explanation

4. Mrs. Carson took a taxi to meet her three friends for lunch. They were waiting for her outside the restaurant when she pulled up in the car. She was so excited to see her friends that she left her tote bag in the taxi. As the taxi pulled away, she and her friends took notice of the license plate number so they would be able to identify the car when they called the taxi company.

1. The four women seem to agree that the plate starts out with the letter J.
2. Three of them agree that the plate ends with 12L.
3. Three of them think that the second letter is X, and a different three think that the third letter is K.

The four license plate numbers below represent what each of the four women thinks she saw. Which one is most likely the license plate number of the taxi?

(*a*) JXK 12L (*b*) JYK 12L
(*c*) JXK 12I (*d*) JXX 12L

5. Zachary has invited his three buddies over to watch the basketball game on his wide-screen television. They are all hungry, but no one wants to leave to get food. Just as they are arguing about who should make the food run, a commercial comes on for a local pizze-ria that delivers. The phone number flashes on the screen briefly and they all try to remember it. By the time Zachary grabs a pen and paper, each of them recollects a different number.

1. All of the men agree that the first three numbers are 995.
2. Three of them agree that the fourth number is 9.
3. Three agree that the fifth number is 2.
4. Three agree that the sixth number is 6; three others agree that the seventh number is also 6.

Which of the numbers is most likely the telephone number of the pizzeria?

(*a*) 995-9266 (*b*) 995-9336
(*c*) 995-9268 (*d*) 995-8266

6. Mark is working with a realtor to find a location for the toy store he plans to open in his town. He is looking for a place that is either in, or not too far from, the center of town and one that would attract the right kind of foot traffic. Which of the following locations should Mark's realtor call to his attention?

(*a*) a storefront in a new high-rise building near the train station in the center of town whose occupants are mainly young, childless professionals who use the train to commute to their offices each day.
(*b*) a little shop three blocks away from the town's main street, located across the street from an elementary school and next door to an ice cream store
(*c*) a stand-alone storefront on a quiet residential street ten blocks away from the town's center
(*d*) a storefront in a small strip mall located on the outskirts of town that is also occupied by a pharmacy and a dry cleaner

7. The neighborhood block association has received many complaints about people knocking on doors and soliciting money for an unknown charity organization even though door-to-door solicitation is prohibited by local laws. Three residents have provided descriptions individuals who have come to their door asking for money.

Solicitor #1 is a white male, 20-25 years old, 5'9", 145 pounds, with very short brown hair. He was wearing a dark blue suit and carrying a brown leather briefcase.

Solicitor #2 is a white male, 25-30 years old, 6'2", 200 pounds, with a shaved-head. He was wearing a red T-shirt and jeans.

Solicitor #3 is a white male, approximately 23 years old, 5'10", slight build, with short brown hair. He was wearing a blue suit.

Three days after the block association meet- ing, a resident noticed a man knocking on doors in the neighborhood and phoned the police to report the illegal activity. This solic- itor was described as follows:

Solicitor #4 is a white male, 22 years old, 140 pounds, about 5'10", with short brown hair. He was carrying a briefcase and wearing a dark suit.

Based on this description, which of the three solicitations was also likely carried out by Solicitor #4?

(*a*) #1, #2, and #3
(*b*) #1, but not #2 and #3
(*c*) #1 and #3, but not #2
(*d*) #1 and #2, but not #3

8. Rita, an accomplished pastry chef who is well known for her artistic and exquisite wedding cakes, opened a bakery one year ago and is surprised that business has been so slow. A consultant she hired to conduct market research has reported that the local population doesn't think of her shop as one they would visit on a daily basis but rather a place they'd visit if they were celebrating a special occasion. Which of the following strategies should Rita employ to increase her daily business?

(*a*) making coupons available that entitle the coupon holder to receive a 25% discount on wedding, anniversary, or birthday cakes
(*b*) exhibiting at the next Bridal Expo and having pieces of one of her wedding cakes available for tasting
(*c*) placing a series of ads in the local newspaper that advertise the wide array of breads
(*d*) moving the bakery to the other side of town

9. Dr. Miller has a busy pediatric dentistry practice and she needs a skilled, reliable hygienist to keep things running smoothly. The last two people she hired were recommended by top dentists in the area, but they each lasted less than one month. She is now in desperate need of a hygienist who can competently handle the specific challenges of her practice. Which one of the following candidates should Dr. Miller consider most seriously?

(*a*) Marilyn has been a hygienist for fifteen years, and her current employer, who is about to retire, says she is the best in the business. The clientele she has worked with consists of some of the wealthiest and most powerful citizens in the county.

(*b*) Lindy recently graduated at the top of her class from one of the best dental hygiene programs in the state. Prioi to becoming a dental hygienist, Lindy spent two years working in a day care center.

(*c*) James has worked as a dental hygienist for three years in a public health clinic. He is very interested in securing a position in a private dental office.

(*d*) Kathy is an experienced and highly recommended dental hygienist who is also finishing up a degree in early childhood education, which she hopes will get her a job as a preschool teacher. She is eager to find a job in a pediatric practice, since she has always wanted to work with children.

10. Mrs. Jansen recently moved to Arizona. She wants to fill her new backyard with flowering plants. Although she is an experienced gardener, she isn't very well-versed in what plants will do well in the Arizona climate. Also, there is a big tree in her backyard making for shady conditions and she isn't sure what plants will thrive without much direct sunlight. Her favorite gardening catalog offers several backyard seed packages. Which one should Mrs. Jansen choose?

(*a*) The Rainbow Collection is ideal for North-east gardens. It includes a variety of colorful perennials that thrive in cool, moist conditions.

(*b*) The Greenhouse Collection will blossom year after year if planted in brightly lit locations and watered regularly.

(*c*) The Treehouse Collection will provide lush green plants with delicate colorful flowers that thrive in shady and partially shady locations.

(*d*) The Oasis Collection includes a variety of perennials that thrive in dry climates and bright sunlight.

EXPLANATORY ANSWERS

1.(*d*) : Since Eileen's husband does not enjoy fancy restaurants, choices a and c can be ruled out. Choice b, although casual, doesn't sound as though it would be the kind of special and memorable evening that Eileen is looking for. Choice d, which is owned by a former baseball star and is described as "charming" and "reminiscent of a baseball clubhouse", sounds perfect for Eileen's husband, who is described as a baseball fan and a man with simple tastes.

2.(*b*) : 2 and 3 possess most of the required traits. They both have red hair and brown eyes, are average-sized, and are in their forties. 1 is very tall and is only in her mid-twenties. She also has an olive complexion. 4 is of very slight build and is in her early thirties. She also has blue eyes.

3.(*b*) : Seeing four girls surrounding another girl, while in possession of her backpack, is the most suspicious of the incidents described.

4.(*a*) : The four women seem to agree that the plate starts out with the letter J. Three of them agree that the plate ends with 12L. Three of them think that the second letter is X, and a different three think that the third letter is K. The plate description that has all of these common elements is "Option A".

5.(*a*) : All of the men agree that the first three numbers are 995. Three of them agree that the fourth number is 9. Three agree that the fifth number is 2. Three agree that the sixth number is 6; three others agree that the seventh number is also 6. "Option A" is the best choice because it is made up of the numbers that most of the men agree they saw.

6.(*b*) : This option is both near the center of town and in a location (near a school and an ice cream store) where children and their parents are sure to be around. This is the only option that meets both of Mark's requirements.

7.(*c*) : The solicitor described as #2 has a shaved head and is much taller and heavier than the solicitors described as #1 and #3. Therefore, choices a and d, which include #2, can be ruled out. Solicitors #1, #3, and #4 have such similar descriptions that the correct answer is clearly choice c.

8.(*c*) : This is the only option that would encourage people to think of the bakery as a shop they would visit regularly and not just on special occasions.

9.(*b*) : The situation described indicates that Dr. Miller's practice presents some specific challenges, namely that it is a busy environment with a child clientele. There is also some indication that even highly recommended, experienced hygienists might not be cut out for Dr. Miller's office. There is nothing to suggest that Marilyn (choice a) or James (choice c) would be a good fit for Dr. Miller's practice. Kathy (choice d) has experience and she is also interested in working with children. However, the fact that she hopes to become a preschool teacher in the not-too-distant future indicates that she might not be the kind of committed, long-term employee that Dr. Miller needs. Lindy (choice b), with her hands-on experience working with children as well as a degree from a prestigious dental hygiene program, is the most attractive candidate for the position based on the situation described

10.(c) : The Treehouse Collection is the only package that can thrive in shady locations. Choice a requires a Northeastern climate. Choices b and d require bright sunlight.

In this type of tests certain categories of information are given followed by certain criteria. Further, the candidates are given a few cause that needs to be analysed. They are required to take the right decision, from the given options, after comparing the information in each case with the given information and criteria.

DECISION MAKING

MULTIPLE CHOICE QUESTIONS

Directions (Qs. 1 to 5) : *Read the following information carefully and answer the questions given below it.*

Following are the criteria for admitting a student in the first year engineering course in a college.

The student must—

(i) have passed XII standard examination in science with at least 80% marks.

(ii) not be more than 20 years old as on 1. 8. 1998.

(iii) have secured at least 90 marks in the entrance test out of a total of 150 marks.

(iv) be able to pay Rs. 15,000 as tuition fees for the first semester and Rs. 5,000 admission charges at the time of taking admission.

In the case of a candidate, who satisfies all other criteria except at—

(a) *(iv)* above but can pay at least 60% of the stipulated fees, the case may be referred to the Admission Committee.

(b) *(iii)* above but has secured more than 95% marks in the XIIth standard examination, the case may be referred to Chairman–Admissions.

You are given the following cases as on 1. 8. 1998. Depending upon the information provided in each case and based on the criteria mentioned above, recommend your decision. You are not to assume anything. If the information provided is not adequate to take a decision, mark 'Data inadequate' as the answer.

1. Subodh Mohaptara was 19 years old as on 20th December, 1997. He has secured 98% marks in XIIth standard examination with science and 80 marks in the entrance test. He can pay the requisite tuition fees and admission charges.
(a) Admit
(b) Refer to Admission Committee
(c) Data inadequate
(d) Do not admit
(e) Refer to Chairman–Admissions

2. Reema Jaiswal was born on 20th July, 1978. She has secured 85% and 75% marks in XIIth standard with science and entrance test respectively. She can pay the requisite tuition fees and admission charges.
(a) Refer to Chairman–Admission
(b) Refer to Admission Committee
(c) Data inadequate
(d) Do not admit
(e) Admit

3. Ashok Dubey was born on 27th November, 1978. He has secured 90% marks in the XIIth standard examination with science and 95 marks in the entrance test. He can pay Rs. 10,000 tuition fees and Rs. 3,500 admission charges.
(a) Admit
(b) Data inadequate
(c) Refer to Admission Committee
(d) Do not admit
(e) Refer to Chairman–Admissions

4. Sudha Mirchandani has secured 95% marks in XIIth standard science stream and 70% marks in the entrance test. She can pay only 65% of the requisite tuition fees and admission charges.
(a) Do not admit
(b) Admit
(c) Data inadequate
(d) Refer to Chairman–Admissions
(e) Refer to Admission Committee

5. Salil Malhotra was born on 25th September in 1979. He has secured 85% and 95% marks in the XIIth standard examination in science stream and entrance test respectively. He can pay the requisite tuition fees and admission charges.
(a) Admit
(b) Do not admit
(c) Refer to Chairman–Admissions
(d) Refer to Admission Committee
(e) Data inadequate

Directions (Qs. 6 to 12) : *Read the following information to answer the given questions :*

Following are the criteria for selecting candidates for Research Fellowship :

The candidate must—

(i) be a post–graduate with minimum of 65% marks.

(ii) not be more than 30 years as on 15. 10. 1993.

(iii) have at least 3 years research experience.

(iv) have diploma in Statistics.

(v) have secured at least 50% marks in the entrance test.

(vi) have finalised the topic for research.

However, in case a candidate who fulfills all other criteria except

(a) *(iii)* above, but has M. Phil degree, should be referred to Dean.

(b) *(iv)* above, should be referred to Chairman.

(c) *(i)* above, but has at least 55% marks in post–graduation and 65% in the entrance test, should be given fellowship.

(d) *(v)* above, but has at lest 45% marks, should be wait–listed.

Based on these criteria and information provided below, decide the course of action in each case. You are not to assume anything. If the data provided is not adequate to decide the given course of action, your answer will be "data inadequate". These cases are given to you as on 15. 10. 1993.

6. 26 years old, Mamta Deo is a post graduate with 58%. She has got four years' research experience and has finalised topic for research. She got 70% marks in diploma in Statistics and 54% marks in the entrance examination.

(a) Fellowship not to be granted
(b) Refer to Dean
(c) Refer to Chairman
(d) Grant Fellowship
(e) Data inadequate

7. Shushila Nair has 65% marks in her post–graduation and is M. Phil. She has 5 years research experience. She has secured 65% in the entrance test and has finalised the research topic. Her date of birth is 11. 8. 65.

(a) Grant fellowship
(b) Wait–list
(c) Refer to Dean
(d) Refer to Chairman
(e) Data inadequate

8. Ameer Khan has got 58% in the entrance test. He has 68% in his post-graduation and 55% in M. Phil. He has got diploma in Statistics and has also finalised the topic for research.

(a) Grant Fellowship
(b) Refer to Dean
(c) Refer to Chairman
(d) Wait-list
(e) Data inadequate

9. 28 years old Neetu Singh is M. Phil with 60% marks. She has secured 70% marks in entrance examination and has finalised the topic for research. She has also got diploma in Statistics.

(a) Grant Fellowship
(b) Fellowship not to be granted
(c) Refer to Chairman
(d) Refer to Dean
(e) Data inadequate

10. Sadhana Suman has got diploma in Statistics with 60% marks and post-graduation with 56% marks. Her date of birth is 12. 12. 1968. She has got one year research experience and is still doing her M. Phil. She has secured 65% marks in entrance exam and has also finalised the research topic.

(a) Grant Fellowship
(b) Fellowship not to be granted
(c) Refer to Dean
(d) Data inadequate
(e) Wait-list

11. Amar Sikka is 28 years old and has got 65% marks in post-graduation and 60% marks in M. Phil. He has got 65% marks in entrance examination and has finalised the topic for research. He also has a diploma in Statistics.

(a) Grant Fellowship
(b) Fellowship not to be granted
(c) Refer to Dean
(d) Refer to Chairman
(e) Data inadequate

12. Madan Paul has got 5 years' research experience and has finalised the research topic. He has got 56% marks in post-graduation. His date of birth is 15. 2. 1966. He has also got diploma in Statistics. He got 70% marks in the entrance test.

(a) Grant Fellowship
(b) Fellowship not to be granted
(c) Refer to Dean
(d) Data inadequate
(e) None of these

Directions (Qs. 13 to 19) : *Read the following information to answer the given questions :*

Following are the conditions for selecting candidates for Research Fellowship :

The candidate must—

(i) be a post-graduate with minimum of 60% marks.

(ii) not be more than 30 years as on 1. 9. 1993.

(iii) have at least 3 years' research experience.

(iv) have diploma in statistics.

(v) have secured at least 55% marks in the entrance test.

(iv) have finalised the topic for research.

However, in the case of a candidate who fulfills all other criteria except—

(a) (iii) above but has M. Phil degree, should be given fellowship.

(b) (iv) above should be referred to Dean.

(c) (i) above but has atleast 55% marks in post–graduation, should be wait-listed.

(d) (v) above but has atleast 50% marks, should be referred to Chairman.

Based on these criteria and information provided below, decide the course of action in each case. You are not to assume anything. If the data provided is not adequate to decide the given course of action, your answer will be "data inadequate". These cases are given to you as on 1. 9. 1993.

13. Vijay Gupta is 24 years old and has got 58% marks in the entrance examination. He has secured 63% marks in his post-graduation and 55% marks in M. Phil. He has got diploma in Statistics and has also finalised the topic for research.
(a) Grant Fellowship
(b) Refer to Dean
(c) Refer to Chairman
(d) Wait-list
(e) Data inadequate

14. Ajoy Dwivedi has secured 65% marks in the post-graduation and has secured 5 years research experience. He has secured 65% marks in the entrance test and has finalised the research topic. His date of birth is 11. 8. 1965.
(a) Grant Fellowship
(b) Wait-list
(c) Refer to Dean
(d) Data inadequate
(e) None of these

15. Madan Soren has got diploma in Statistics with 60% marks and post-graduation with 56% marks. His date of birth is 12. 12. 1968. He has got 1 year research experience and is still doing his M. Phil. He has secured 60% marks in the entrance exam and has also finalised the research topic.
(a) Grant fellowship
(b) Fellowship not to be granted
(c) Refer to Dean
(d) Data inadequate
(e) Wait-list

16. 26 years old Mamta Kulkarni is M. Phil with 60% marks. She has secured 70% marks in the entrance examination and has finali-sed the topic for research. She has also got diploma in Statistics.
(a) Grant Fellowship
(b) Fellowship not to be granted
(c) Refer to Chairman
(d) Refer to Dean
(e) Data inadequate

17. Chander Manoj has got 5 years' research experience and has finalised the research topic. He has got 56% marks in post-graduation and 60% marks in the entrance test. His date of birth is 15. 2. 1966. He has also got diploma in Statistics.
(a) Grant Fellowship
(b) Fellowship not to be granted
(c) Refer to Dean
(d) Data inadequate
(e) None of these

18. Raman Hooda is 28 years old and has got 65% marks in Post-graduation and 60% marks in M. Phil. He has got 65% marks in the entrance examination and has finalised the topic for research. He also has a diploma in Statistics.
(a) Grant Fellowship
(b) Fellowship not to be granted
(c) Refer to Dean
(d) Refer to Chairman
(e) Data inadequate

19. 26 years old Janaki Deo is a post-graduate with 58% marks. She has got four years research experience and has finalised the topic for research. She got 70% marks in the diploma in Statistics and 54% marks in the entrance examination.
(a) Fellowship not to be granted
(b) Refer to Dean
(c) Refer to Chairman
(d) Grant Fellowship
(e) Data inadequate

Directions (Qs. 20 to 27) : *Read the following information carefully and answer the questions given below :*

Following are the criteria of promotion from Junior Officer's Cadre to Senior Officer's Cadre in an organisation :

The candidate must—

(a) have completed atleast 5 years in the organisation.

(b) have secured 65% marks in the written test for promotion.

(c) have secured 60% marks in the Group Discussion.

(d) have secured 70% marks in the interview.

(e) have good record of his work performance.

(f) have good communication skill and get along well with his colleagues.

(g) not be more than 40 years and less than 30 years as on 1. 9. 93.

(h) have good academic record with an average of at least 65% marks.

However, in the case of a candidate who—

(i) satisfies all other conditions except (d) above but has secured 75% marks in the written test and 65% marks in he Group Discussion, the case is to be referred to the General Manager (Personnel)–GM(P) for the decision.

(j) satisfies all other criteria except (h) above but has secured an average of more than 60% marks, the case is to be referred to the Managing Director (MD) of the organisation.

Now read the information provided in the case of each candidate in each of the questions given below and decide on the basis of the information provided and based on the above conditions, which of the courses of action you would suggest. These cases are given as on 5. 9. 1993. (Remember you are not to assume anything which is not provided in the question). If complete information is not provided, the answer would be Data inadequate.

20. 38 years old Rajesh has secured 65% marks in the written test for promotion, 73% marks in interview and 62% marks in Group Discussion. He has good record of his work performance, good communication skills and gets along well with his colleagues. He has good academic record with an average of 61% marks and has completed 7 years in the organisation.
(a) Refer to GM(P)
(b) Refer to MD
(c) Promote
(d) Do not promote
(e) Data inadequate

21. 34 years old Sudha has secured 60% marks in the written test for promotion, 72% marks in interview and 69% marks in Group discussion. She has good communication skill and gets along well with her colleagues. Her record of work performance is good and she has completed 6½ years in the organisation.
(a) Refer to MD
(b) Do not promote
(c) Refer to GM(P)
(d) Promote
(e) Data inadequate

22. Surekha has secured 70% marks in written test for promotion, 69% marks in Group Discussion and 72% marks in the interview. She has a good academic record with an average of 67% marks. She has good record of work performance and gets along well with her colleagues. She has good communication skill and has completed 7 years in the organisation.
(a) Do not promote
(b) Promote
(c) Refer to GM(P)
(d) Refer to MD
(e) Data inadequate

23. 39 years old Pawan has secured 66% marks in written promotion test and has a good academic record with an average of 62% marks. He has secured 65% marks in Group Discussion and 72% marks in interview. He has good record of his work performance, communication skill and gets along well with his colleagues. He has completed 6 years in the organisation.
(a) Do not promote
(b) Refer to MD
(c) Refer to GM(P)
(d) Promote
(e) Data inadequate

24. 34 years old Sudhir has secured 76% marks in the written test for promotion, 66% marks in Group Discussion and 67% marks in interview. He has good academic record with an average of 68% marks, good communication skill and gets along well with his colleagues. His work performance is good and he has completed 6 years in the organisation.
(a) Promote
(b) Refer to MD
(c) Refer to GM(P)
(d) Do not promote
(e) Data anadequate

25. 32 years old Manjula has good academic record with an average of 66% marks. She has secured 67% marks in Group Discussion, 75% marks in interview and 60% marks in written test for promotion. She has good communication skill and gets along well with her colleagues. She has good record of her work performance and has completed 7 years in the organisation.
(a) Do not promote
(b) Refer to MD
(c) Promote
(d) Refer to GM(P)
(e) Data inadequate

26. 31 years old Krishna secured 65% marks in written test for promotion, 72% marks in interview and 62% marks in Group Discussion. He has good academic record with an average of 67% marks and good communication skill. He has completed 9 years in the organisation. He gets easily annoyed and irritated with his colleagues and his record of work performance since the last two years is just average.
(a) Promote (b) Refer to GM(P)
(c) Refer to MD (d) Do not promote
(e) Data inadequate

27. 33 years old Neelima has secured 63% marks in Group Discussion, 71% marks in interview and 66% marks in written test for promotion. She hase good academic record with an average of 68% marks and has good communication skill. She gets along well with her colleagues and has good record of her work performance. She has completed 6 years in the organisation.

(*a*) Refer to GM(P)
(*b*) Do not promote
(*c*) Promote
(*d*) Refer to MD
(*e*) Data inadequate

EXPLANATORY ANSWERS

1. (*e*) : Criterion *(iii)* is not satisfied but Criterion *(b)* gives the decision.

2. (*d*) : Both Criterion *(iii)* and Criterion *(b)* are not satisfied.

3. (*c*) : Criterion *(iv)* is not satisfied but Criterion *(a)* gives the decision.

4. (*c*) : Criterion *(ii)* is not given.

5. (*a*)

6. (*a*) : Both Criterion *(i)* and Criterion *(c)* are not satisfied.

7. (*d*) : Criterion *(iv)* is not given but Criterion *(b)* gives the decision.

8. (*e*) : Both Criteria *(ii)* and *(iii)* are not given and Criterion *(a)* alone cannot give the decision.

9. (*e*) : Both Criterion *(i)* and Criterion *(iii)* are not given and criterion *(a)* alone cannot give the decision.

10. (*b*) : Both Criterion *(iii)* and Criterion *(a)* are not satisfied.

11. (*c*) : Criterion *(iii)* is not satisfied but Criterion *(a)* gives the decision.

12. (*a*) : Criterion *(i)* is not satisfied but Criterion *(c)* gives the decision.

13. (*a*) : Criterion *(iii)* is not satisfied but Criterion *(a)* gives the decision.

14. (*c*) : Criterion *(iv)* is not satisfied but Criterion *(b)* gives the decision.

15. (*b*) : Both Criterion *(iii)* and Criterion *(a)* are not satisfied.

16. (*e*) : Criterion *(i)* is not given and Criterion *(c)* is not satisfied.

17. (*e*) : Criterion *(i)* is not satisfied but Criterion *(c)* gives the decision of "wait–list." This option is not given.

18. (*a*) : Criterion *(iii)* is not satisfied but Criterion *(a)* gives the decision.

19. (*a*) : Both Criterion *(i)* and Criterion *(iii)* are not satisfied, Criterion *(c)* and Criterion *(d)* gives different decisions.

20. (*b*) : Criterion *(h)* is not satisfied but Criterion *(j)* gives the decision.

21. (*b*) : Criterion *(b)* is not satisfied.

22. (*e*) : Criterion *(g)* is not given.

23. (*b*) : Criterion *(h)* is not satisfied but Criterion *(j)* gives the desicion.

24. (*c*) : Criterion *(d)* is not satisfied but Criterion *(i)* gives the decision.

25. (*a*) : Criterion *(b)* is not satisfied.

26. (*d*) : Both Criterion *(e)* and Criterion *(f)* are not satisfied.

27. (*c*) :

CHAPTER 13

Statement Conclusion

In this reasoning pattern, a statement is given followed by two conclusions. The statement is to be taken as the fact. Then based on it one has to decide which of the conclusion(s) definitely follows or does not follow from the given statement.

MULTIPLE CHOICE QUESTIONS

Directions (Qs. 1 to 20): *In the following questions, each question has a statement followed by two conclusions. Taking the statement to be true, decide which of the given conclusions definitely follows from the given statement. Indicate your answer as (a) if only I follows; (b) if only II follows; (c) either I or II follows; (d) if neither I nor II follows; and (e) if both I and II follow.*

1. *Statement* : The Principal humiliated the teacher in the presence of students.

Conclusions I: The Principal did not like the teacher.

II: The teacher was not popular amongst his students.

2. *Statement* : Good health is dependent on right eating habits. Most of the people do not follow any rule regarding eating.

Conclusions I: Most of the people have poor health.

II: People are ignorant of proper eating habits.

3. *Statement* : Until our country achieves economic equality and political freedom, democracy would be meaningless.

Conclusions I: Political freedom and democracy go hand in hand.

II: Economic equality leads to real political freedom and democracy.

4. *Statement* : Black cloud follows thunder. Rains follow thunder.

Conclusions I: Thunder is the cause of rain.

II: Black cloud is the cause of thunder.

5. *Statement* : Practice is better than precept. Most doctors are heavy smokers.

Conclusions I: Most doctors cannot advise people not to smoke.

II: Doctors do not regard smoking as injurious.

6. *Statement* : Workers feel highly motivated when they get sense of involvement by participating in the management of companies.

Conclusions I: Workers should be motivated to produce more.

II: Workers should be allowed to participate in the management of companies.

7. *Statement* : Industrial revolution which first of all started in Europe has brought about modern age.

Conclusions I: Disparity between rich and poor results in revolution.

II: Revolution overhauls society.

8. *Statement* : America's defence secretary reiterated that they would continue to supply arms to Pakistan.

Conclusions I: Pakistan is incapable of manufacturing arms.

II: It would ensure peace in the region.

9. *Statement* : Poor people are more trust-worthy as compared to the rich. They can do wonders if they are taken into confidence.

Conclusions I: Poor people are wonderful people.

II: By and large rich people are not trustworthy.

10. *Statement* : Government has spoiled many top ranking financial institutions by appointing bureaucrats as Directors of these institutions.

Conclusions I: Government should appoint Directors of the financial institutes taking into consi-deration the expertise of the person in the area of finance.

II: The Director of the financial institute should have exper-tise commensurate with the financial work carried out by the institute.

11. *Statement* : The Constitutional amendment carried out just last month prohibits the employment of child labour in any organisation.

Conclusions I: The employers must now abide by this amendment to the Constitution.

II: Children below 14 years will now be engaged in acquiring education.

12. *Statement* : People who speak too much against the dowry are those who had taken it themselves.

Conclusions I: It is easier said than done.

II: People have double standards.

13. *Statement* : Vegetable prices are soaring in the market.

Conclusions I: Vegetables are becoming a rare commodity.

II: People cannot eat vegetables.

14. *Statement* : As far as the rate of literacy is concerned, there is hardly any difference between the States of Kerala and West Bengal, but one is ahead of the other in respect of the percentage of population unemployed.

Conclusions I: Unemployment is more in Kerala than in West Bengal.

II: West Bengal has higher unemployment than Kerala.

15. *Statement* : He tirelessly argues for the replacement of the present system of allocating work to the teaching staff in the department by another system which will give the teachers higher job satisfaction.

Conclusions I: No system is free from problems and therefore there should be no system.

II: Any system you may evolve but it should give higher job satisfaction to the teachers.

16. *Statement* : The unequal allocation of funds by the Government for literacy and employment generation programmes stands out clearly when we analyse the attitude of government towards these two areas.

Conclusions I: Government has more favourable attitude towards literacy programmes than employment generation progra-mmes.

II: Government has more favourable attitude towards employment generation programmes than literacy programmes.

17. *Statement* : Amul chocolates sold enough in comparison to all other chocolate brands in India.

Conclusions I: No other chocolate is sold in India.

II: The selling data of every chocolate brand is available in India.

18. *Statement* : Wearing Khadi is not only good for our health but also for our nation.

Conclusions I: Economy of India also depends upon Khadi sector.

II: It is difficult to maintain Khadi clothes.

19. *Statement* : Ideas given by our ancestors that were once discarded as uneconomical and unviable, turn out to be as functional and inevitable in present circumstances.

Conclusions I: In ancient period ideas were considered either completely functional or totally infeasible.

II: Ideas cannot change from time-to-time.

20. *Statement* : The Supreme Court gave a judgement that the maintenance of old age parents is the responsibility of the married girls, if they do not have brothers.

Conclusions I: Constitution is always interpreted to help oppressed people out.

II: Before the Supreme Court gave its verdict, a married girl must have denied to pay for the maintenance of her parents.

Directions (Qs. 21 to 25): *In the following questions, the symbols* *, $\underset{=}{*}$, =, @ *and* $\underset{=}{@}$ *are used with the following meanings :*

(*a*) * (*b*) means (*a*) is greater than (*b*),

(*a*) $\underset{=}{*}$ (*b*) means (*a*) is either greater than or equal to (*b*).

(*a*) = (*b*) means (*a*) is equal to (*b*).

(*a*) @ (*b*) means (*a*) is smaller than (*b*) and

(*a*) $\underset{=}{@}$ (*b*) means (*a*) is either smaller than or equal to (*b*).

Answer is given as:

(*a*) If only conclusion I is true;

(*b*) If only conclusion II is true;

(*c*) If either I or II is true;

(*d*) If neither I nor II is true;

(*e*) If both I and II are true.

21. *Statements* : $T \overset{*}{=} P, P @ S, P = M$

Conclusions : *I.* $S * M$ *II.* $T @ S$

22. *Statements* : $R \underset{=}{@} M, M * P, R \overset{*}{=} L$

Conclusions : *I.* $M = L$ *II.* $P = L$

23. *Statements* : $M = T, T \underset{=}{@} Z, S * M$

Conclusions : *I.* $Z * M$ *II.* $Z = M$

24. *Statements* : $L @ C, C * Z, Z \underset{=}{@} F$

Conclusions : *I.* $C * F$ *II.* $F = C$

25. *Statements* : $Z @ B, N \overset{*}{=} S, B @ N$

Conclusions : *I.* $B = Z$ *II.* $S \underset{=}{@} B$

EXPLANATORY ANSWERS

1. (*a*) : Only conclusion I follows. Conclusion II is not confirmed by the given statement.

2. (*a*) : Conclusion I definitely follows. Conclusion II is not confirmed by the given statement.

3. (*b*) : Only conclusion II follows. Conclusion I cannot be drawn from the given statement.

4. (*b*) : Only conclusion II follows. Conclusion I is wrong as rains are the cause of thunder.

5. (*e*) : Both conclusion I and conclusion II follow from the statements as the doctors who are heavy smokers indicate that they do not regard smoking as injurious and thus, cannot advise people not to smoke.

6. (*e*) : Both conclusions I and II follow from the statement as involvement of workers boosts production and benefits the companies.

7. (*b*) : Only conclusion II follows. Conclusion I is not related the statement.

8. (*d*) : Neither conclusion I nor conclusion II follows. Both the conclusions are unrelated to the statement.

9. (*b*) : Only conclusion II follows. Conclusion I is not related to the statement.

10. (*e*) : Both conclusion I and conclusion II follow.

11. (*a*) : Only conclusion I follows. Conclusion II is not related to the statement.

12. (*e*) : Both conclusion I and conclusion II follow as people who talk too much often do not practise what they say.

13. (*d*) : Neither conclusion I nor conclusion II is confirmed by the statement.

14. (*d*) : Neither conclusion I nor conclusion II follows as the precentage of unemployment in each state is not mentioned.

15. (*b*) : Only conclusion II follows. Conclusion I runs counter to the statement as a system is necessary.

16. (*d*) : Neither conclusion I nor conclusion II is confirmed by the statement.

17. (*b*) : Only conclusion II follows as the data of every chocolate brand shows the comparision of Amul chocolates with other brands. Coclusion I is not confirmed by the statement.

18. (*a*) : Only conclusion I follows. Conclusion II is not related to the statement.

19. (*d*) : Neither conclusion I, nor conclusion II follows; both the conclusions are unrelated.

20. (*b*) : Only conclusion II follows, because the Supreme Court judgement must have come in such a case and not in vacuum.

21. (*a*) : $T \geq P, P < S, P = M$

$\therefore\ S > M$

22. (*d*) : $R \leq M, M > P, R \geq L$

$\therefore\ L \leq R \leq M$

23. (*c*) : $M = T, T \leq Z, Z = M$

If $T = Z$, then $Z = M$

If $T < Z$, then $Z > M$

24. (*d*) : $L < C, C > Z, Z \leq F$

No relation can be established between C and F.

25. (*d*) : $Z < B, N \geq S, B < N$

No relation can be established between B, S and Z.

CHAPTER 14

Syllogistic Reasoning

In this reasoning pattern two statements are followed by few conclusions drawn. Four options (*a*), (*b*), (*c*) & (*d*) are given as answers. Based on the statement the candidate has to select the right answer in each question.

MULTIPLE CHOICE QUESTIONS

Directions (Q. 1–10) : *In each question given below two statements are followed by four conclusions numbered I, II, III and IV. You have to take the two given statements to be true even if they seem to be at variance from commonly known facts. Read the statements and conclusions and decide which of the conclusions logically follows from the two given statements, disregarding commonly known facts.*

1. Statements: All the phones are scales. All the scales are calculators.

Conclusions:

I. All the calculators are scales.
II. All the phones are calculators.
III. All the scales are phones.
IV. Some calculators are phones.

(*a*) Only I and IV (*b*) Only III and IV
(*c*) Only II and IV (*d*) Only I and II

2. Statements: No door is dog. All the dogs are cats.

Conclusions:

I. No door is cat.
II. No cat is door.
III. Some cats are dogs.
IV. All the cats are dogs.

(*a*) Only II and IV (*b*) Only I and III
(*c*) Only III and IV (*d*) Only III

3. Statements: Some tables are T.V. Some T.V. are radios.

Conclusions:

I. Some tables are radios.
II. Some radios are tables.
III. All the radios are T.V.
IV. All the T.V. are tables.

(*a*) Only II and IV (*b*) Only I and III
(*c*) Only IV (*d*) None of the four

4. Statements: All men are vertebrates. Some mammals are vertebrates.

Conclusions:

I. All men are mammals.
II. All mammals are men.
III. Some vertebrates are mammals.
IV. All vertebrates are men.

(*a*) Only IV (*b*) Only II
(*c*) Only III (*d*) Only I

5. Statements: All green are blue. All blue are white.

Conclusions:

I. Some blue are green.
II. Some white are green.
III. Some green are not white.
IV. All white are blue.

(*a*) Only I and II (*b*) Only I and III
(*c*) Only I and IV (*d*) Only II and IV

6. Statements: Some pens are books. Some books are pencils.

Conclusions:

I. Some pens are pencils.
II. Some pencils are pens.
III. All pencils are pens.
IV. All books are pens.

(*a*) Only I and III (*b*) Only II and IV
(*c*) All the four (*d*) None of the four

7. Statements: All the research scholars are psychologists. Some psychologists are scientists.

Conclusions:

I. All the research scholars are scientists.
II. Some research scholars are scientists.
III. Some scientists are psychologists.
IV. Some psychologists are research scholars.

(*a*) Only III and IV (*b*) None of the four
(*c*) All the four (*d*) Only III

8. Statements: All the goats are tigers. All the tigers are lions.

Conclusions:

I. All the goats are lions.
II. All the lions are goats.
III. Some lions are goats.
IV. Some tigers are goats.

(*a*) All the four (*b*) Only I, II and III
(*c*) Only I, III and IV (*d*) Only II, III and IV

9. Statements: All members are students. No student is a girl.

Conclusions :

I. All students are members.
II. No members is a girl.
III. Some students are members.
IV. Some members are girls.

(*a*) Only I follows (*b*) Only I, II and III follow
(*c*) All follows (*d*) Only II and III follows

10. Statements : All soaps are clean. All clean are wet.

Conclusions :

I. Some clean are soaps.
II. No clean is soap.
III. Some wet are soaps.
IV. All wet are soaps.

(*a*) Only I follows
(*b*) Only I and II follow
(*c*) Only either III and IV follow
(*d*) Only I and III follow

Directions (Q. 11–15) : *Every question below has a few statements, followed by four conclusions numbered I, II, III and IV. You have to consider every given statement as true, even if it does not conform to the well known facts. Read the conclusions and then decide which of the conclusions can be logically derived.*

11. Statements: Some keys are staplers. Some staplers are stickers. All the stickers are pens.

Conclusions:

I. Some pens are staplers.
II. Some stickers are keys.
III. No sticker is key.
IV. Some staplers are keys.

(*a*) Only I and II
(*b*) Only II and IV
(*c*) Only II and III
(*d*) Only I and IV and either II or III

12. Statements: All the locks are keys. All the keys are bats. Some watches are bats.

Conclusions:

I. Some bats are locks.
II. Some watches are keys.
III. All the keys are locks.
IV. Some keys are locks.

(*a*) Only I and II (*b*) Only I and IV
(*c*) Only II and III (*d*) Only I and III

13. Statements: All the papers are books. All the bags are books. Some purses are bags.

Conclusions:

I. Some papers are bags.
II. Some books are papers.
III. Some books are purses.
IV. Some papers are purses.

(*a*) Only I and IV (*b*) Only II and III
(*c*) Only I and II (*d*) Only I and III

14. Statements: All the bottles are boxes. All the boxes are bags. Some bags are trays.

Conclusions:

I. Some bottles are trays.
II. Some trays are boxes.
III. All the bottles are bags.
IV. Some trays are bags.

(*a*) Only III and IV (*b*) Only I and II
(*c*) Only II and III (*d*) Only I and IV

15. Statements: Some rats are cats. Some cats are dogs. No dog is cow.

Conclusions:

I. No cow is cat.
II. No dog is rat.
III. Some cats are rats.
IV. Some dogs are cats.

(*a*) Only I and IV (*b*) Only I and II
(*c*) Only I and III (*d*) Only III and IV

EXPLANATORY ANSWERS

1. (*c*)

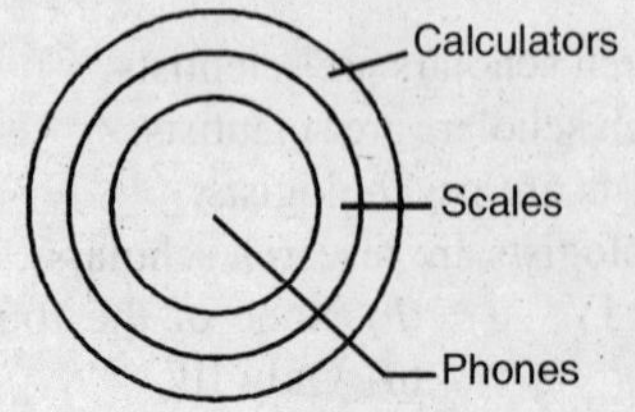

2. (*d*)

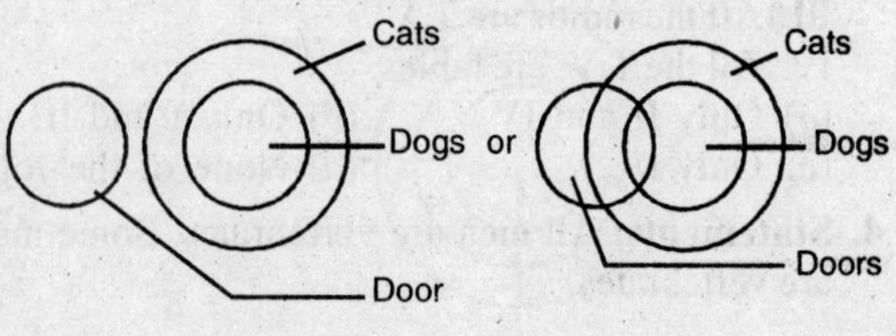

3. (*d*)

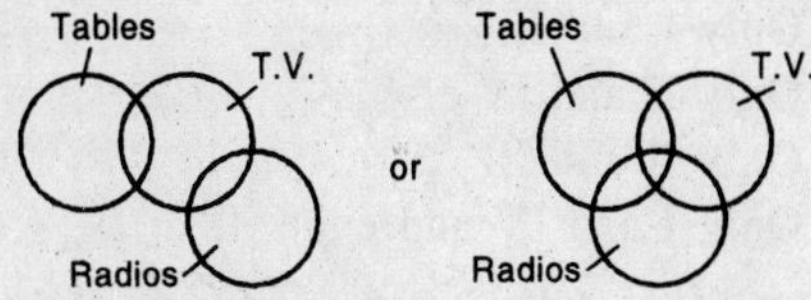

4. (*c*)

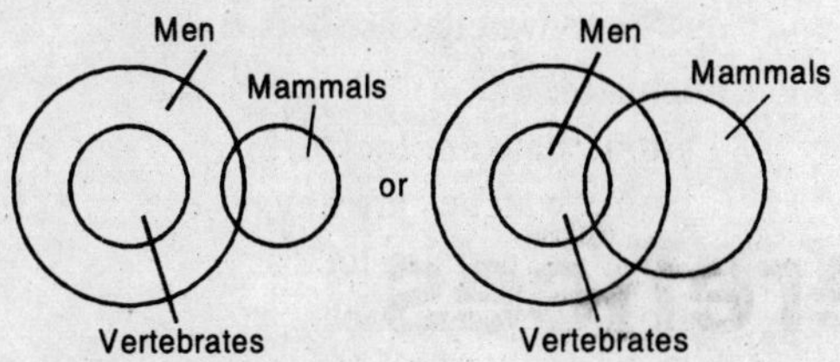

5. (*a*)

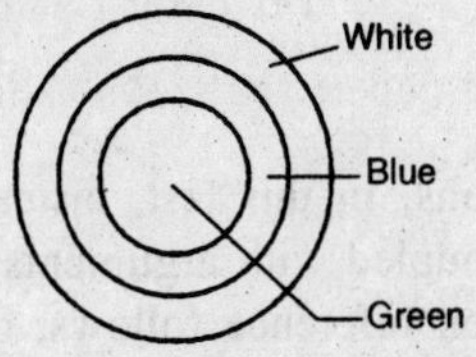

6. (*d*)

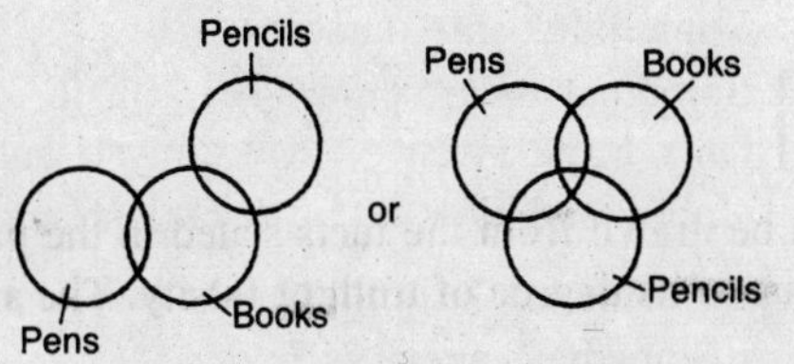

7. (*a*)

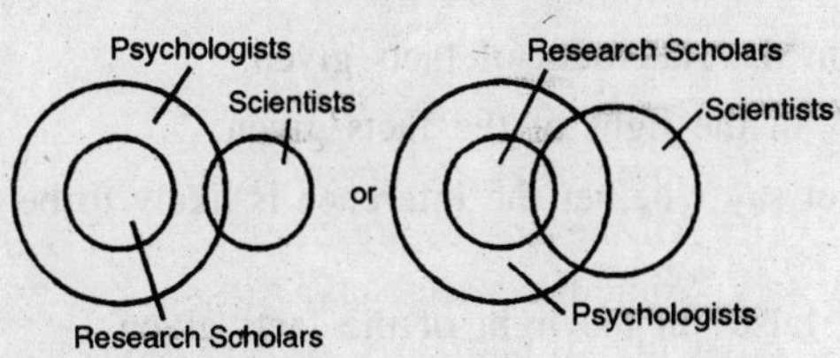

8. (*c*)

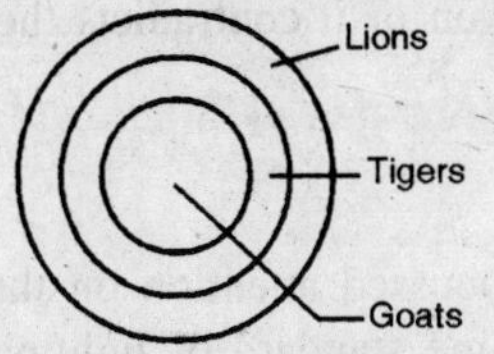

9. (*d*)

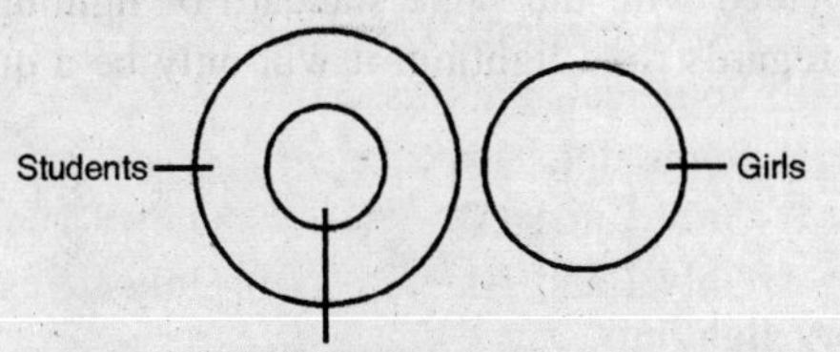

Since Members and Girls are disjoint, it follows that no members is girl. Since Members and Students have a common area, it follows that some student are members.

10. (*d*)

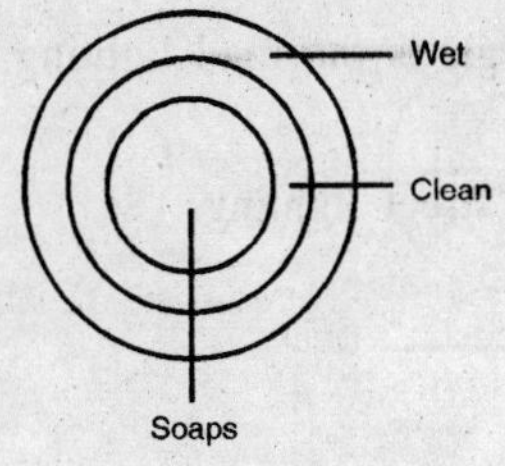

According to diagram, Clean and Soaps have a common area. So, some clean are soaps. Also wet and soaps have a common area. So, some wet are soaps.

11. (*d*)

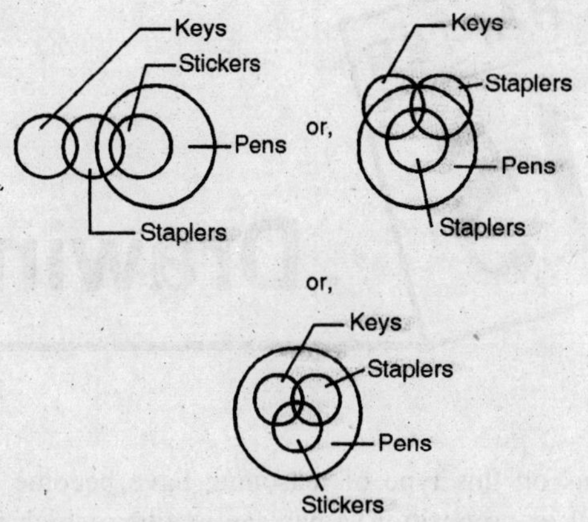

12. (*b*)

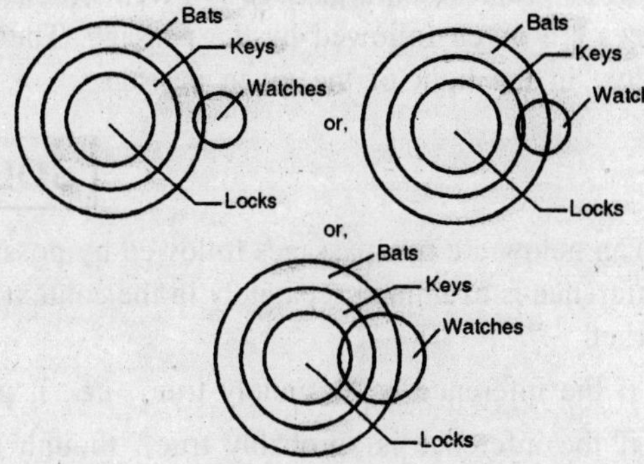

13. (*b*)

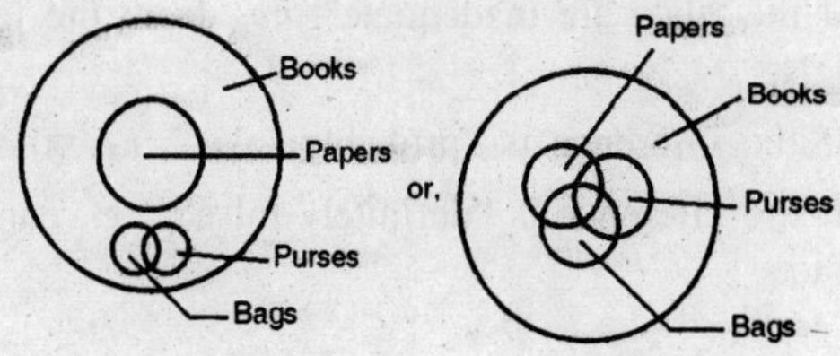

14. (*a*)

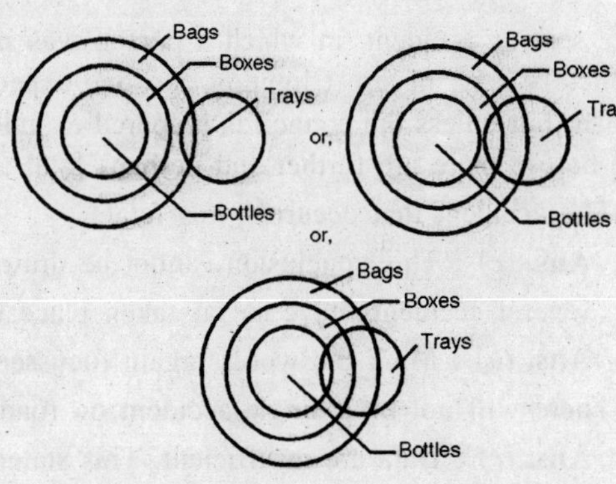

15. (*d*)

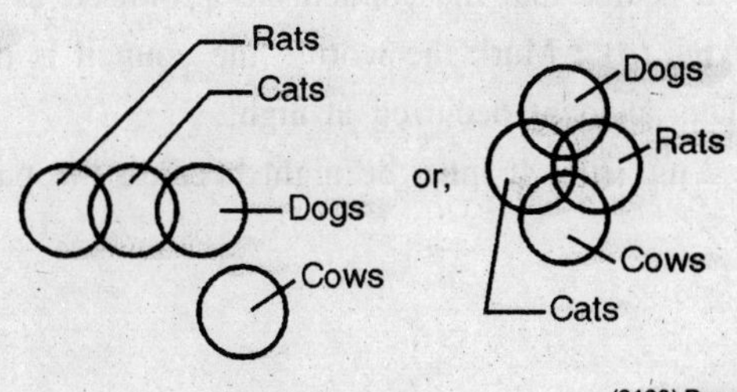

CHAPTER 15

Drawing Inferences

Questions on this type of reasoning have become quite common in competitive examinations. In this test, instead of a statement or proposition, a passage is given which is a congregation of many propositions coupled with arguments. Some inferences are given followed by the passage. The candidate has to decide whether the given inference follows, or does not follow in the light of the given passage.

SOLVED EXAMPLES

Given below are two passages followed by possible inferences which can be drawn from the facts stated in the passage. Each inference is examined separately in the context of the passage to decide upon its degree of truth or falsity. The answers are marked . . . .

(a) if the inference is "definitely true", *i.e.,* it properly follows from the statement of facts given.

(b) if the inference is "probably true," though not "definitely true" in the light of the facts given.

(c) if the "data are inadequate", *i.e.,* from the facts given you cannot say whether the inference is likely to be true or false.

(d) if the inference is "probably false", *i.e.,* though not "definitely false" in the light of the facts given.

(e) if the inference is "definitely false", *i.e.,* cannot possibly be drawn from the facts given or it contradicts the given facts.

PASSAGE I

The serious accident, in which a person was run over by a car yesterday, has again focussed attention on the most unsatisfactory state of street lighting. No one expects side roads to be provided with the same standard of lightings as a main road, but unless the council is prepared to make good its promise as regards road lighting, it will only be a question of time before there are further and perhaps fatal accidents.

1. The accident that occurred was fatal.

Ans. ***(e)*** **:** This conclusion cannot be drawn from the facts given.

2. Several accidents have so far taken place because of unsatisfactory lightings.

Ans. ***(a)*** **:** Mark the words 'again focussed attention on the most . . . lighting'.

3. There will not be a single accident on road if they are satisfactorily illuminated.

Ans. ***(c)*** **:** Data are insufficient. This statement is not confirmed by the paragraph.

4. It seems that the council has promised to improve the state of lighting on side roads.

Ans. ***(a)*** **:** Mark the words "the council is prepared to make good its promise as regards the road lighting."

5. The accident occurred at night.

Ans. ***(a)*** **:** It must be night because the passage deals with unsatisfactory state of street lighting.

MULTIPLE CHOICE QUESTIONS

Directions : *Below are given some passages followed by several possible inferences which can be drawn from the facts stated in each passage. You have to examine each inference separately in the context of the passage and decide upon its degree of truth or falsity.*

Mark Answers	If you think...
(a) "Definitely True"	the inference properly follows from the statement of facts given.
(b) "Probably True"	the inference may be true in the light of the facts given but not definitely true.
(c) "Data Inadequate"	from the facts given it cannot be said whether the inference is likely to be true or false.
(d) "Probably False"	the inference is probably false in the light of the facts given though not definitely false.
(e) "Definitely False"	the inference cannot possibly be drawn from the facts given or it contradicts the given facts.

PASSAGE 1

Indian granite industry is in peril in the absence of a uniform policy from the state governments, despite the thrust given by liberalisation policies of the union government. Compared to the remarkable progress in the field during the last three years, the absence of matching policies by state governments had put granite quarry owners and others involved in the industry on the verge of collapse in the international market. The policies differed from state to state, had created problems as far as loyalty, dead rent and duration of lease were concerned.

1. Each state having granite quarry has set up its own rules which are contrary to the interest of the industry.

2. Till three years ago, granite production in India was not profitable.

3. The granite production is largely controlled by individuals.

4. The granite produced in India does not match with the quality of international level.

5. The union government's liberalisation policy became applicable to granite industry only during the last three years.

PASSAGE 2

Steel production has always been burdened with costs much higher than in comparable plants overseas. On the one hand custom duty on almost all steel imports has been reduced, on the other excise duty has been raised. Domestic steel products are now uncompetitive which in turn has led to the demand that both the custom and excise rates should be reviewed to prevent sickness in the industry.

6. The steel industry in general is making losses as a fall out of the government policy.

7. The cost of production of steel in other countries is less than that in India.

8. India can compete with the foreign countries in re gard to the price of steel with a favourable government policy.

9. Foreign steel has become cheaper comparative to domestic steel.

10. The government is considering lowering of excise duty on steel products.

PASSAGE 3

The annual domestic consumption of plastics in India is expected to grow between 2.5 and 3 million tonnes by the end of the Ist balls of the century from the current level of about one million tonnes. The global consumption of plastics now stands at 100 million tonnes. To sustain the present growth pattern, India would need two additional polymer plants of 1,000 tonnes every year till the turn of the Ist half of this century. Entrepreneurs should now think in lines of globalisation and promote projects of international capacity and they would have to look at technology transfer as well as upgradation and strategic and creative alliances.

11. The total domestic consumption of plastics in India is about one per cent of the global consumption.

12. At present India does not import plastics.

13. India lacks in technological capabilities in producing plastics.

14. There is an expected growth of about .2 per cent in the plastic consumption every year.

15. Potentially India can be one of the major players in the production of plastics in the international market.

EXPLANATORY ANSWERS

1. *(a)* : The policies differed from state to state.

2. *(c)* : Remarkable progress during the last three years is mentioned in the paragraph but nothing suggests that the production was not profitable.

3. *(a)* : There is absence of a uniform policy from the state Governments.

4. *(c)* : According to the paragraph, absence of matching policies had put the quarry owners and others involved in the industry on the verge of collapse in the international market. Nothing is mentioned about the granite quality produced in India or of the international level.

5. (e) : The inference does not relate to the facts given in the statement.

6. (d) : Government policy alone may not be responsible for the losses. Cost or quality factor may also be responsible.

7. (c) : The paragraph mentions that steel production in India has always been burdened with costs much higher than in comparable plants overseas. But nowhere in the paragraph it is mentioned that the cost of production of steel is less in other countries.

8. (a) : If the government reviews its policy, India can definitely compete with the foreign countries in regard to the steel price.

9. (a) : Customs duty on almost all steel products has been reduced.

10. (b) : There is a demand that both the customs and excise rates should be reviewed.

11. (a) : The global consumption of plastics is 100 million tonnes and current level of consumption in India is 1 million tonnes.

12. (c) : The paragraph does not mention about the import or export of plastics.

13. (a) : Entrepreneurs would have to look at technology transfer as well as upgradation and strategic and creative alliances.

14. (a) : The expected growth by end of the Ist half of this century is between 2.5 and 3 million tonnes. India needs 2 additional polymer plants of 1,000 tonnes per year.

15. (a) : By thinking in lines of globalisation and promoting projects of international capacity India can be one of the major players in the production of plastics in the international market.

CHAPTER 16

Trends

This type of questions are asked to assess the thinking pattern or mental trends of the candidate. These are simple questions but should be answered honestly and carefully.

MULTIPLE CHOICE QUESTIONS

Directions : *In the questions given below four alternatives have been given below each one of them. You have to select the right alternative according to your mind and mark it in your answer sheet.*

1. I like pre-defined rules and regulations.
(*a*) Sometimes (*b*) No
(*c*) Yes (*d*) No idea

2. I found a purse full of money in college premise. I:
(*a*) donated the amount among poor
(*b*) gave it to the principal
(*c*) offered it at temple
(*d*) None of these

3. I am punctual regarding
(*a*) going to bed (*b*) time
(*c*) meals (*d*) dating

4. I was travelling on a boat which capsized. Firstly, I:
(*a*) rescued others (*b*) saved myself
(*c*) closed my eyes (*d*) cursed my luck

5. When someone asks you for help in odd situations then:
(*a*) you give him/her all possible help
(*b*) you promise him/her help
(*c*) you do not help him/her
(*d*) you turn a deaf ear

6. In case my wristwatch is out of order, I:
(*a*) would try to repair it myself
(*b*) would give it to watchmaker
(*c*) would buy a new watch
(*d*) would throw it away

7. Often I change my opinion in the last moment.
(*a*) Yes (*b*) No
(*c*) Sometimes (*d*) No idea

8. Generally I am extrovert and well behaved.
(*a*) Yes (*b*) No
(*c*) Sometimes (*d*) No idea

9. I like to use new technique of work.
(*a*) Yes (*b*) No
(*c*) Sometimes (*d*) No idea

10. When someone considers you wrong then:
(*a*) you do not react
(*b*) you consider him/her wrong
(*c*) you try to ward off the misunderstanding on proper occasion.
(*d*) you pick a fight

11. The secret of my success is:
(*a*) hard labour (*b*) awakening in night
(*c*) gossiping (*d*) luck

12. If you are a female and you are talking with a male:
(*a*) You hide your age
(*b*) You are afraid
(*c*) You talk without hesitation
(*d*) You avoid talks

13. I do like rules and regulations.
(*a*) Yes (*b*) No
(*c*) Sometimes (*d*) No idea

14. Excellent ideas come to my mind:
(*a*) while working alone
(*b*) while working in a group
(*c*) while in sleep
(*d*) while in bathroom

15. Whenever my little baby cries loudly, then I
(*a*) beat him/her
(*b*) feed milk to him/her
(*c*) make him/her sleep
(*d*) ask my husband to handle him/her

16. When I see a mad person, I :
(*a*) approach towards him/her
(*b*) maintain distance from him/her
(*c*) throw stone at him/her
(*d*) start laughing at him/her

17. While driving my car I offer lift to people who ask for lift.
(*a*) Always (*b*) Sometimes
(*c*) Never (*d*) If she is a girl

18. When someone tries to convince you then:
(*a*) You get convinced
(*b*) You do not get convinced
(*c*) You hear him/her passionately
(*d*) You turn a deaf ear

19. Whenever someone knocks on my closed door then firstly I
(*a*) open the door
(*b*) peep through the lens fitted in the door
(*c*) do not open the door
(*d*) yell at him/her

20. I speak to others about my expectation and dreams.
(*a*) Rarely (*b*) Often
(*c*) Sometimes (*d*) Never

21. Any dispute can be solved by :
(*a*) quarrelling (*b*) court
(*c*) dialogue (*d*) money

22. When I do any foolish work then :
(*a*) I feel ashamed (*b*) I feel proud of myself
(*c*) Nothing happens (*d*) I weep

23. If I were correspondent of any newspaper then I would write on the following subject :
(*a*) Cinema and theatre
(*b*) Political events
(*c*) Sports
(*d*) Stock market

24. If I were not human being then :
(*a*) I wish to be a bird (*b*) I wish to be a horse
(*c*) I wish to be God (*d*) Can't say

25. Suppose, you have worn a new shirt and your friend passed a comment that it is not looking good on you. You :
(*a*) will change the shirt immediately
(*b*) will take it lightly as it is your style
(*c*) will not change the shirt but feel offended
(*d*) will start quarrelling

26. I wish to live alone always.
(*a*) Yes (*b*) No
(*c*) Sometimes (*d*) Never

27. I want to spend my spare (extra) time :
(*a*) in reading interesting books
(*b*) in reading comics
(*c*) in viewing films
(*d*) in gossiping

28. Before doing any work I ask myself 'Is it appropriate'?
(*a*) Yes (*b*) No
(*c*) Sometimes (*d*) Never

29. If I see the GOD, I will ask for
(*a*) huge wealth (*b*) honesty
(*c*) love (*d*) heaven

30. People call you selfish.
(*a*) Always (*b*) Sometimes
(*c*) Never (*d*) No idea

31. While talking to friends I do not like to express my very personal matters.
(*a*) Yes (*b*) No
(*c*) Sometimes (*d*) Never

32. Consultation with others helps me to take a decision.
(*a*) Yes (*b*) No
(*c*) Sometimes (*d*) Never

33. After failure:
(*a*) One repents
(*b*) One tries again to succeed
(*c*) Nothing special is happened
(*d*) Nothing in life remains

34. I want to be convinced by arguments.
(*a*) Yes (*b*) No
(*c*) Sometimes (*d*) Never

ANSWERS

1	2	3	4	5	6	7	8	9	10
(*c*)	(*b*)	(*b*)	(*b*)	(*a*)	(*b*)	(*b*)	(*a*)	(*a*)	(*c*)
11	**12**	**13**	**14**	**15**	**16**	**17**	**18**	**19**	**20**
(*a*)	(*c*)	(*a*)	(*a*)	(*b*)	(*b*)	(*b*)	(*a*)	(*b*)	(*a*)
21	**22**	**23**	**24**	**25**	**26**	**27**	**28**	**29**	**30**
(*c*)	(*a*)	(*c*)	(*a*)	(*b*)	(*c*)	(*a*)	(*a*)	(*c*)	(*c*)
31	**32**	**33**	**34**						
(*c*)	(*a*)	(*b*)	(*a*)						

CHAPTER 17 Critical

In this type of reasoning, a statement is given and assumptions are drawn from it. An assumption is something assumed, supposed and taken for granted. The implicity of the two assumptions is in question. The implication means the hidden meaning, something which is derived from and as such based upon the statement.

MULTIPLE CHOICE QUESTIONS

Directions (Qs. 1 to 6): *In each question below are given two statements followed by two conclusions numbered I and II. You have to take the two given statements to be true even if they seem to be at variance from commonly known facts and then decide which of the given conclusions logically follows from the two given statements, disregarding commonly known facts. Read both the statements and—*

Give answer (a) if only conclusion I follows; give answer (b) if only conclusion II follows; give answer (c) if either I or II follows; give answer (d) if neither I nor II follows and give answer (e) if both I and II follows.

1. *Statements* *I:* All tomatoes are red.
II: All grapes are tomatoes.
Conclusions *I:* All grapes are red.
II: Some tomatoes are grapes.

2. *Statements* *I:* All painters are smiling.
II: Some authors are painters.
Conclusions *I:* All smiling authors are painters.
II: Some authors are smiling.

3. *Statements* *I:* All peons in this office are efficient.
II: Ramu is not efficient.
Conclusions *I:* Ramu is not peon in this office.
II: Ramu should be more efficient.

4. *Statements* *I:* All weavers are hard working.
II: No hard working men are foolish.
Conclusions *I:* No weavers are foolish.
II: Some foolish are weavers.

5. *Statements* *I:* All fishes are cars.
II: All cars are vegetables.
Conclusions *I:* Some vegetables are cars.
II: Some vegetables are fishes.

6. *Statements* *I:* Some dogs are pups.
II: All horses are pups.

Directions (Qs. 7 to 10): *In each question below is given a statement followed by three assumptions number I, II and III. An assumption is something supposed or taken for granted. You have to consider the statement along with the assumptions and decide which of the assumptions is implicit in the statement. Then decide which of the alternatives is the correct answer.*

7. *Statement :*
"Use Riya Cold Cream for fair complexion"—an advertisement.
Assumptions :
I. People like to use cream for fair complexion.
II. People are easily fooled.
III. People respond to advertisements.
(*a*) Only I is implicit.
(*b*) Only II is implicit.
(*c*) Only I and III are implicit.
(*d*) Only I and II are implicit.
(*e*) All are implicit.

8. *Statement :*
"Slogans against smoking in office should be put on the notice board"—an employee in an office suggests.
Assumptions :
I. The employee felt that his suggestion will be considered.
II. People smoke in the office.
III. Some people will stop smoking after reading the slogans.
(*a*) Only I is implicit.
(*b*) Only I and II are implicit.
(*c*) Only II and III are implicit.

(*d*) None is implicit.
(*e*) All are implicit.

9. *Statement :*
"I want to present him a book on techniques of yoga on his birthday"—A tells B.
Assumptions :
I. A and B will be invited for the birthday celebrations.
II. The person to whom the book is to be presented, is not keeping good health.
III. Book is the best gift for birthdays.
(*a*) Only I and II are implicit.
(*b*) Only II and III are implicit.
(*c*) Only I and III are implicit.
(*d*) None is implicit.
(*e*) All are implicit

10. *Statement :*
Keeping in view the financial constraint, the management institution has decided to charge at the time of providing employment in various organisations, a placement fee of ₹ 25000 from the organisation in which the student will be provided the employment.
Assumptions :
I. It will help in increasing the demand of the students belonging to the management institution.
II. The amount collected in this way will be purposeful.
III. It may be possible that the organisation providing employment may select less number of students in future.
(*a*) None follows.
(*b*) Only II and III follow.
(*c*) Only I follows.
(*d*) Only I and II follow.
(*e*) None of these

EXPLANATORY ANSWERS

1. (*e*) : When all tomatoes are red and all grapes are tomatoes, then all grapes are also red. When all grapes are tomatoes, then some tomatoes must be grapes. Therefore, both conclusions I and II are correct.

2. (*b*) : When all painters are smiling and some authors are painters, then some authors are smiling. Therefore, only conclusion II is correct.

3. (*a*) : When all the peons of the office are efficient, then Ramu cannot be a peon in this office. Therefore, only conclusion I is correct.

4. (*a*) : When all weavers are hardworking and no hardworking men are foolish, then no weavers are foolish. Therefore, only conclusion I is correct.

5. (*e*) : When all fishes are cars and all cars are vegetables, then all fishes will naturally be vegetables. This means that some vegetables are fishes. And when all cars are vegetables, then some vegetables will be cars naturally. Therefore, both the conclusions I and II are correct.

6. (*d*) : No relationship can be established between the two statements. Therefore, neither conclusion I nor conclusion II is correct.

7. (*c*) : The advertisement itself denotes that people like to use cream for fair complexion and they do respond to advertisements. Advertisements are for awareness of the product not for fooling people.

8. (*e*) : Suggestion for putting up the notice is made because some people must be smoking in office. Notice board is read by people in office and some may stop smoking after reading the slogans.

9. (*c*) : According to A presents are best gifts for birthdays and when A has bought the book he expects to be invited for the birthday celebration. Nothing is mentioned about health of the birthday person.

10. (*b*) : The amount collected will lessen the financial constraint and there is every possibility for selecting less number of students because of the fee charged.

CHAPTER 18

Emotional Intelligence

Emotional intelligence (EI) refers to the ability to perceive, control, and evaluate emotions. Emotional intelligence (EI) is the area of cognitive ability involving traits and social skills that facilitate interpersonal behaviour. Intelligence can be broadly defined as the capacity for goal-oriented adaptive behaviour; emotional intelligence focuses on the aspects of intelligence that govern self-knowledge and social adaptation.

Emotional Intelligence that is also called Emotional Intelligence Quotient or (EQ) narrates the capability, capacity, or deftness to understand. It evaluates and manages one's emotions.

MULTIPLE CHOICE QUESTIONS

Directions: *Answer the following questions by selecting the appropriate option.*

1. In my group of friends, I am generally aware of how each person feels about the other people in our social circle.
(*a*) Strongly Agree (*b*) Agree
(*c*) Disagree (*d*) Strongly Disagree

2. When I am upset, I can usually pinpoint exactly why I am distressed.
(*a*) Strongly Agree (*b*) Agree
(*c*) Disagree (*d*) Strongly Disagree

3. While there are some things that I would like to change, I generally like who I am.
(*a*) Strongly Agree (*b*) Agree
(*c*) Disagree (*d*) Strongly Disagree

4. When I make mistakes, I often berate and criticize myself and my abilities.
(*a*) Often (*b*) Sometimes
(*c*) Rarely (*d*) Almost Never

5. I feel uncomfortable in emotionally charged situations.
(*a*) Strongly Agree (*b*) Agree
(*c*) Disagree (*d*) Strongly Disagree

6. I tend to avoid confrontations. When I am involved in a confrontation, I become extremely anxious.
(*a*) Strongly Agree (*b*) Agree
(*c*) Disagree (*d*) Strongly Disagree

7. I am generally aloof and detached until I really get to know a person.
(*a*) Strongly Agree (*b*) Agree
(*c*) Disagree (*d*) Strongly Disagree

8. I tend to overreact to minor problems.
(*a*) Often (*b*) Sometimes
(*c*) Rarely (*d*) Almost Never

9. I feel confident about my own skills, talents, and abilities.
(*a*) Strongly Agree (*b*) Agree
(*c*) Disagree (*d*) Strongly Disagree

10. I would describe myself as a good judge of character.
(*a*) Strongly Agree (*b*) Agree
(*c*) Disagree (*d*) Strongly Disagree

11. When I am facing an unpleasant task, I tend to:
(*a*) Make a plan and work on it a little each day
(*b*) Get it over with as soon as possible
(*c*) Put it off until the last minute
(*d*) Don't do it at all

12. During a heated argument, I am more likely to:
(*a*) Stop the fight and agree to a short break before resuming the discussion.
(*b*) Shut down and stop responding to the other person.
(*c*) Give in and apologize in order to quickly end the argument.
(*d*) Start insulting the other person.

13. When making an important decision, I tend to:
(*a*) Follow my instincts
(*b*) Rely on direction from other people
(*c*) Go with the easiest option
(*d*) Guess randomly

14. Which of the following statements best describes you?
(*a*) I have an easy time making friends and getting to know new people.
(*b*) I get along well with others, but I have to really get to know someone before they become a true friend.
(*c*) I find it difficult to meet people and make friends.
(*d*) I cannot make friends.

15. You have invested a lot of time and energy into a project for one of your classes. While you feel confident about your work, your instructor gives you a C+ on the project. How do you deal with this situation?
(*a*) Decide the class is stupid and stop putting forth your best efforts.
(*b*) Berate and criticize your own work.
(*c*) Confront the instructor and ask for a better grade.
(*d*) Think about ways you could improve the project and apply these ideas to future schoolwork.

16. One of your best friends has suffered a miscarriage. How do you respond?
(*a*) Allow your friend to express her feelings and offer your support.
(*b*) Spend time with her, but avoid talking about her loss.
(*c*) Convince her to go out with some friends to get her mind off it.
(*d*) Give her some time to herself.

17. One of your co-workers has a habit that annoys you. The problem seems to be getting worse each day. How do you respond?
(*a*) Tell your co-worker what is bothering you.
(*b*) Make a complaint about the behaviour to your supervisor.
(*c*) Talk about your co-worker behind his back.
(*d*) Suffer in silence.

18. You've been feeling stressed out at work and haven't finished projects as quickly as you should. When your boss suddenly assigns you another large project, how do you feel?
(*a*) Anxious about getting all the work done.
(*b*) Overwhelmed by the task before you.
(*c*) Angry that your boss hasn't noticed how overworked you are.
(*d*) Depressed and sure that you can never finish it all.

19. If I am scheduled to meet a loved one at a certain time and that person is late, I get worried and eventually start to panic:
(*a*) Frequently (*b*) Sometimes
(*c*) Rarely (*d*) Never

20. Others do not want to spend time with me in public because my behaviour embarrasses them.
(*a*) Frequently (*b*) Sometimes
(*c*) Rarely (*d*) Never

21. I prevent being in situations where I need to show compassion and affection because I feel uncomfortable comforting others.
(*a*) Frequently (*b*) Sometimes
(*c*) Rarely (*d*) Never

22. When I am angry, I do not care about what I say or do and end up saying and doing things I regret later and need to apologize for.
(*a*) Frequently (*b*) Sometimes
(*c*) Rarely (*d*) Never

23. I feel frequently depressed and unhappy without really knowing why.
(*a*) Frequently (*b*) Sometimes
(*c*) Rarely (*d*) Never

24. If others point out my mistakes or give me negative feedback about myself, I feel ashamed, embarrassed and then become offensive and angry.
(*a*) Frequently (*b*) Sometimes
(*c*) Rarely (*d*) Never

25. Crying makes me feel better so I frequently cry when I am angry, ashamed, or embarrassed.
(*a*) Frequently (*b*) Sometimes
(*c*) Rarely (*d*) Never

ANSWERS

1	2	3	4	5	6	7	8	9	10
(*b*)	(*b*)	(*a*)	(*b*)	(*d*)	(*d*)	(*c*)	(*d*)	(*a*)	(*b*)
11	**12**	**13**	**14**	**15**	**16**	**17**	**18**	**19**	**20**
(*a*)	(*a*)	(*a*)	(*a*)	(*d*)	(*a*)	(*a*)	(*a*)	(*c*)	(*d*)
21	**22**	**23**	**24**	**25**					
(*d*)	(*d*)	(*d*)	(*d*)	(*d*)					

CHAPTER 19

Social Intelligence

Questions on social intelligence are asked to assess the common sense of the candidate in various social situations.

MULTIPLE CHOICE QUESTIONS

Directions : *Each of the following questions is followed by four alternatives. Select the most appropriate answer.*

1. In the examination hall, you find that your question paper is too tough to be answered satisfactorily by you. The best thing you can do is:

(*a*) try cheating from your neighbouring candidate.
(*b*) leave the paper and walk out.
(*c*) try attempting those questions first of which you know something.
(*d*) complain to the examiner about the toughness of the question paper.

2. Your best friend is annoyed with you for certain reasons. You will :

(*a*) try your best to reason out your friend's annoyance.
(*b*) go out and make new friends.
(*c*) show indifference.
(*d*) remind the friend of your good friendship.

3. You were invited to a party, but on the day of the party you are informed that the party has been cancelled. You will :

(*a*) try to find out the reason for its cancellation.
(*b*) decide that you will never go to that place ever again.
(*c*) not discuss the matter with anyone.
(*d*) hold the party at your place instead.

4. You find that the cooking gas cylinder is leaking. The first thing you would do is :

(*a*) switch off the light.
(*b*) close the knob of the cylinder.
(*c*) call the fire brigade for help.
(*d*) alert all the members at home.

5. While returning home from a far away place you find that your pocket has been picked. You will :

(*a*) try to hitch-hike to home.
(*b*) hire a taxi and pay on reaching home.
(*c*) go to the nearest police station and lodge an FIR.
(*d*) call home and ask someone to pick you from the place you made the phone call.

6. Your friend has not invited you to his marriage party, you will :

(*a*) ignore the whole affair.
(*b*) send him your best wishes.
(*c*) attend the ceremony.
(*d*) hold it against him.

7. You are interviewed for a new job. Which of the following questions is most important to you?

(*a*) Remuneration you will be paid.
(*b*) Opportunities for promotion.
(*c*) Scope to develop your ideas and use them to improve the working of the organisation.
(*d*) All the above are equally important.

8. You are walking down the street and suddenly you see two hundred-rupee notes on the pavement. What action will you take?

(*a*) Give the money to beggar.
(*b*) Pocket it yourself.
(*c*) Deposit it in the nearest police station.
(*d*) Leave it as it is.

ANSWERS

1	2	3	4	5	6	7	8
(*c*)	(*a*)	(*a*)	(*b*)	(*b*)	(*b*)	(*d*)	(*c*)

INDEXING ADDRESS MATCHING

Directions : *In each question below a combination of name and address is given in the first column at the left, followed by four such combinations, one each under the columns (a), (b), (c) and (d). You have to find out the combination which is exactly the same as the combination in the first column. The number of that column which contains that combination is the answer. If all the combinations are different, the answer is '(e)'.*

1. Triveni Atma
Opp Lal Banglow
Varanasi -221002

(*a*)	(*b*)
Triveni Atma Opp Lal Bangalow Varanasi -221002	Triveni Atma Opp Lal Banglow Varanasi -220012

(*c*)	(*d*)
Triveni Atma Opp Lal Banglow Varanasi -221002	Triveni Athma Opp Lal Banglow Varanasi -221002

2. Tara Lal Appa
Javagal street
Calicat 673005

(*a*)	(*b*)
Tara Lal Appa Javagal Street Calicat 673005	Tara Lal Appa Javagal street Calicut 673005

(*c*)	(*d*)
Tara Lal Appa Javagal street Calicat 670035	Tara Lal Appa Javagal streat Calicat 673005

3. Iqbal Rehman
Bhandri Gali
Post Box No -3097

(*a*)	(*b*)
Iqbal Rehman Bhandri Ghali Post Box No -3097	Iqbal Rehman Bhandri Gali Post Box No -3097

(*c*)	(*d*)
Iqbal Rehman Bhandri Gali Post Box no -3097	Iqbal Rahman Bhandri Gali Post Box No -3097

4. Jaganpa Shinde
Christ phot co.
Tel no -27363

(*a*)	(*b*)
Jaganpa Shinde Christ photo co. Tel no -27363	Jaganpa Shinde Christ phot co. Tel no -27363

(*c*)	(*d*)
Jaganpa Shinde Christ phot co. Tel no -273633	Jaganna Shinde Christ phot co. Tel no -27363

5. N.R. Savitri
Giri Girls hostal
Anapuram-167951

(*a*)	(*b*)
N.R. Savitri Giri Girls hostal Anapuram-167951	N.R. Savitri Giri Girls hostel Anapuram-167951

(*c*)	(*d*)
N.R. Savitri Giri Girls hostal Anapuram-167851	N.R. Savithri Giri Girls hostal Anapuram-167951

6. Madam Brulopher
Jung villa
Banjaram Hills

(*a*)	(*b*)
Madam Bruloper Jung villa Banjaram Hills	Madam Brulopher Jung villa Banjaram Hill

(*c*)	(*d*)
Madam Brulopher Jung Villa Banjaram Hills	Madam Brulopher Jung villa Banjaram Hills

7. Samartha sen
C 20/05 Guftga Bldg
B. No. - 1631

(*a*)	(*b*)
Samartha sen C 20/05 Guftga Blg B. No. - 1631	Samartha sen C 200 Guftga Bldg B. No. - 1631

(*c*)	(*d*)
Samartha sen C 20/05 Guftga Bldg B. No. - 1631	Samartha sen C 20/05 Guflga Bldg B. No. - 1631

8. Phiroz Gerabl
Harmit palace
Samaita nagar

(*a*)	(*b*)
Phiroz Gerabi Harmit palace Samaita nagar	Phiroz Gerabl Harmit place Samaita nagar

(*c*)	(*d*)
Phiroz Gerabl Harmit palace Samaita nager	Phiroz Gherabl Harmit palace Samaita nagar

9. Nitu gajadhar
Shersing Haveli
Jaipur -302006

(*a*)	(*b*)
Nitu gajadhar Shersing Haveli Jaipur -302006	Nitu gajadar Shersing Haveli Jaipur -302006

(*c*)	(*d*)
Nitu gajadhar Shersing Haveli Jaipur -303006	Nitu Gajadhar Shersing Haveli Jaipur -302006

ANSWERS

1	2	3	4	5	6	7	8	9
(*c*)	(*a*)	(*b*)	(*b*)	(*a*)	(*d*)	(*c*)	(*d*)	(*a*)

CHAPTER

20 Venn Diagrams

In these type of questions diagrammatic representation presents a logical illustration of particular class or statements based on which the questions are asked. A clear view of the diagram makes the concept clear for attempting such questions.

SOLVED EXAMPLE

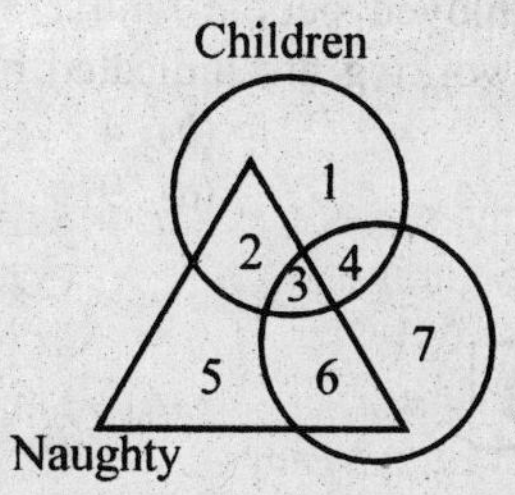

Study the above diagram and specify the region representing children who are naughty as well as studious.

(*a*) 3 and 6 (*b*) 2 and 4
(*c*) only 3 (*d*) only 4

Ans. ***(c)*** **:** The explanation depicting children who are naughty as well as studious will be :

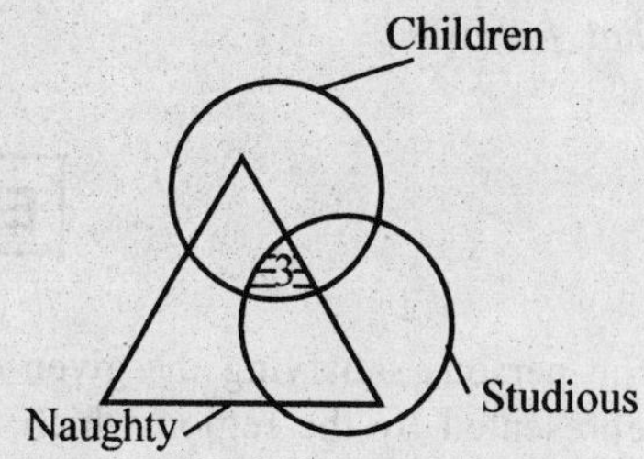

It is now clear that only region 3 represents all the three classes.

MULTIPLE CHOICE QUESTIONS

Directions (Qs. 1–3) : *In the following diagram, there are three figures interlocking each other – a rectangle, a square and a triangle. Each figure represents the class mentioned against it.*

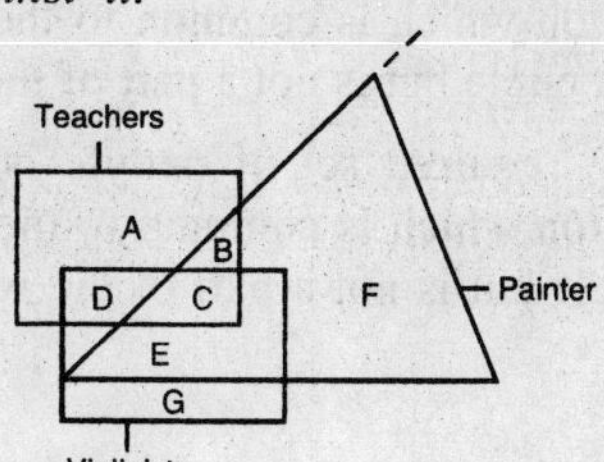

Study the figure and answer the questions that follows.

1. Teachers who are painters but not violinists are represented by

(*a*) B (*b*) C
(*c*) D (*d*) F

2. The region which represents painters and violinists but not teachers, is denoted by

(*a*) B (*b*) D
(*c*) E (*d*) F

3. Which letter represents teachers who are painters as well as violinists?

(*a*) B (*b*) C
(*c*) D (*d*) E

Directions (Qs. 4–6) : *In the figure given below, there are three interesting circles each representing certain section of people. Different regions are marked a-g. Read the statements in each of the following questions and choose the letter of the region which correctly represents the statements?*

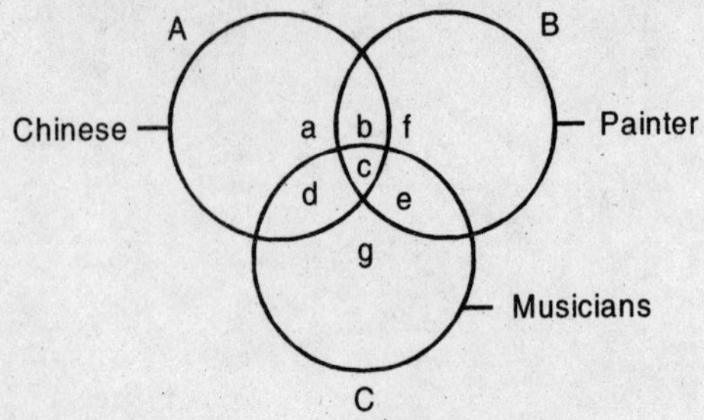

4. Chinese who are painters but not musicians?
(*a*) b (*b*) c
(*c*) d (*d*) g

5. Chinese who are musicians but not painters.
(*a*) d (*b*) c
(*c*) b (*d*) a

6. Painters who are neither Chinese nor musicians.
(*a*) b (*b*) c
(*c*) f (*d*) g

Directions (Qs. 7–10) : *In the following figure, the circle stands for employed, the square stands for hard-working, the triangle stands for rural and the rectangle stands for intelligent. Study the figure carefully and answer the questions that follow.*

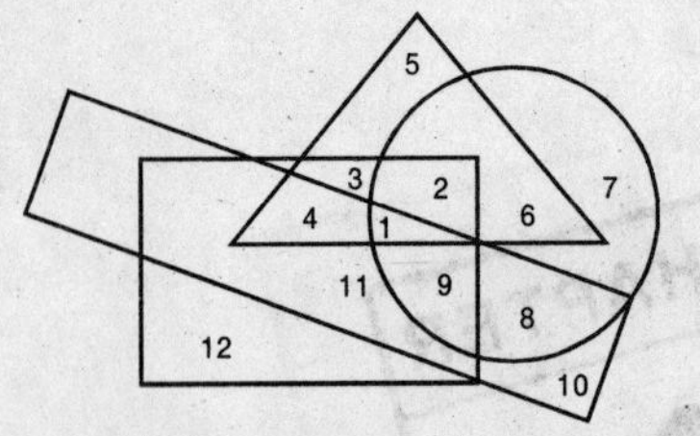

7. Rural employed people who are neither intelligent nor hard-working are indicated by region.
(*a*) 10 (*b*) 9
(*c*) 6 (*d*) 4

8. Unemployed rural hard-working and intelligent people are indicated by region.
(*a*) 1 (*b*) 2
(*c*) 3 (*d*) 4

9. Rural people who are hard-working and employed but not intelligent are indicated by region.
(*a*) 1 (*b*) 2
(*c*) 3 (*d*) 4

10. Rural employed people who are neither intelligent nor hard-working are indicated by region.
(*a*) 2 (*b*) 4
(*c*) 6 (*d*) 9

EXPLANATORY ANSWERS

1. (*a*) : The persons satisfying the given conditions are represented by the region which is common to the rectangle and the triangle but not the square i.e. B.

2. (*c*) : The persons satisfying the given conditions are represented by the region which is common to the triangle and the square but is not a part of the rectangle i.e. E.

3. (*b*) : The required set of persons is represented by the letter denoting the region common to the rectangle, triangle and the square i.e. C.

4. (*a*) : The required region is the one which is common to the circles A and B and lies outside circle C i.e. b.

5. (*a*) : The required region is the one which is common to the circles A and C but is not a part of circle B i.e. d.

6. (*c*) : The required region is the one which lies inside the circle B but is not a part of either circle A or circle C i.e. f.

7. (*c*) : The required set of people is represented by the region which is common to the triangle and circle but is not a part of either the rectangle or the square i.e. 6.

8. (*d*) : The required set of people is represented by the region which lies outside the circle and is common to the triangle, square and rectangle i.e. 4.

9. (*b*) : The required set of people is represented by the region which is common to the triangle, square and circle but is not a part of the rectangle i.e. 2.

10. (*c*) : The required set of people is denoted by the region which is common to the triangle and the circle but is not a part of the rectangle i.e. 2.

NON-VERBAL

CHAPTER 1

Series/Figural Series

MISSING SERIES

This form of series is almost identical to the one mentioned earlier. Here too are given two sets of figures, the Problem Figures and the Answer Figures. The problem figures follow a particular pattern of movement which constitute the series. The only difference from the earlier mentioned set of series is that instead of depicting the last figure that continues the pattern here one of the middle figures needs to be depicted from-the answer figures. This type needs a little more concentration and brain work as the continuity is broken and has to be set right. Understand the set up of elements, pattern and figures in each set and try different styles and rules to find the answer.

SOLVED EXAMPLES

In each question below there are two sets of figures, first problem figures and then follows the answer figures. One of the answer figures should fit into the box where a question mark is placed in the set of problem figures. The letter of the answer figure which should be considered as forming the series and should be placed in the question marked box is the answer.

1. Problem Figures

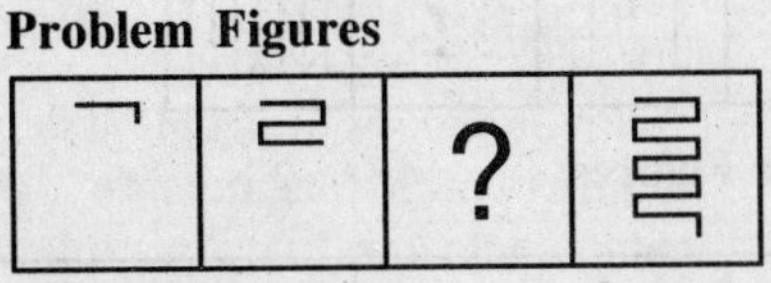

Answer Figures

(*a*) (*b*) (*c*) (*d*) (*e*)

Answer (*a*) : Observe the set of problem figures. The design made of straight lines is becoming bigger at each step. In first figure there are two lines segments and in second figure three lines segments are increased. To continue the pattern four line segments should be increased so that further five line segments added in the last figure can complete the series. Answer figure (*a*) contains four more line segments and hence, is the right answer.

2. Problem Figures

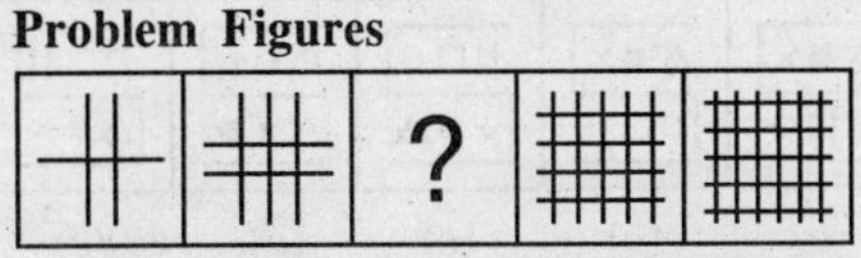

Answer Figures

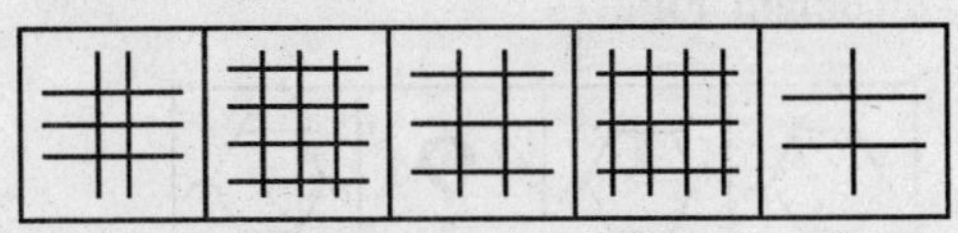

(*a*) (*b*) (*c*) (*d*) (*e*)

Answer (*d*) : Observe that at each step one vertical and one horizontal line is added. By this rule answer figure (*a*) fits in the question marked space. Note that answer figure (*b*) can also be considered in absence of option (*d*), but here the point to be noted is that the number of horizontal lines is one more than the number of vertical lines. So, answer figure (*d*), is the answer.

3. Problem Figures

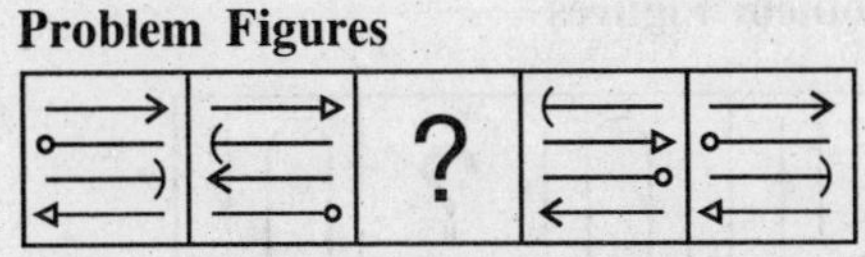

Answer Figures

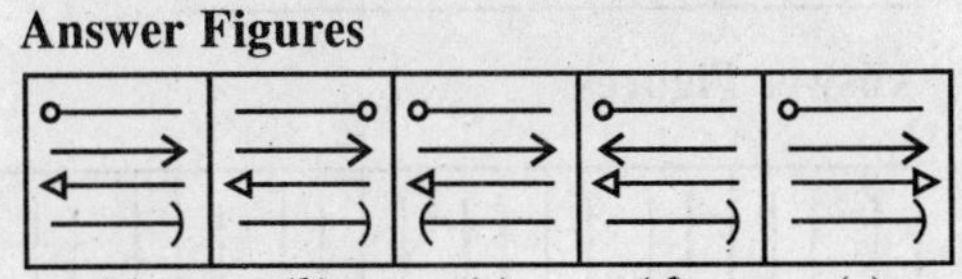

(*a*) (*b*) (*c*) (*d*) (*e*)

Answer (*a*) : Note that the fourth or the bottom element is made the first or the topmost element in the next figure. Similarly, the third element is made the second, the second element made the fourth and the first element made the third. Also, the direction of the elements is changed at each step. By the process mentioned above, answer figure A is the right choice to be considered as forming the series.

MULTIPLE CHOICE QUESTIONS

Directions : *In each of these questions, there are two sets of figures. The figures placed first are Problem Figures, and those follows are Answer Figures indicated by the letters (a), (b), (c), (d) and (e). A series is established if one of the five Answer Figures is placed at the question-marked space. Figures form a series if they change from left to right according to some specific rule. The letter of the Answer Figure which should be placed in the question-marked space is the answer. All the figures, i.e. three Problem Figures and one Answer Figure placed in the question-marked space should be considered as forming the series.*

1. Problem Figures

Answer Figures

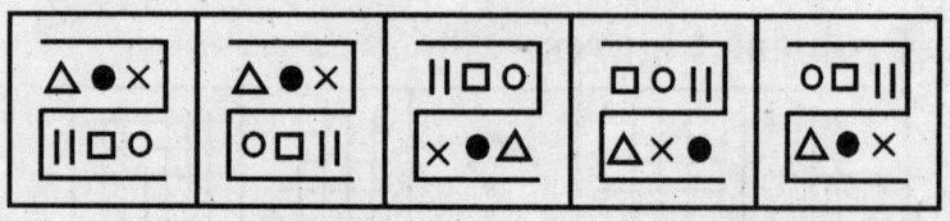

(*a*) (*b*) (*c*) (*d*) (*e*)

2. Problem Figures

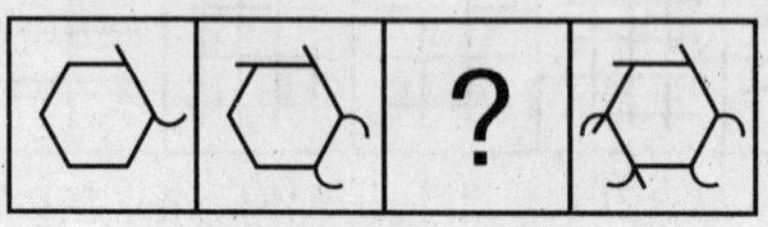

Answer Figures

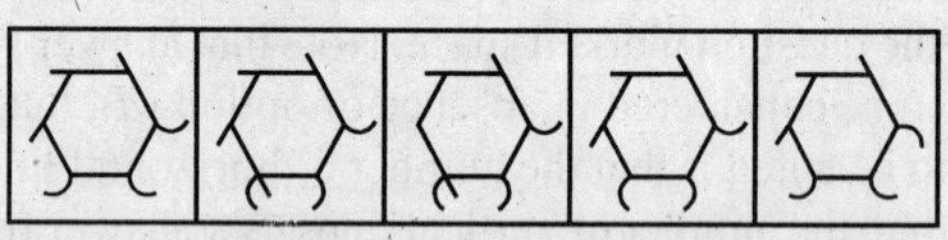

(*a*) (*b*) (*c*) (*d*) (*e*)

3. Problem Figures

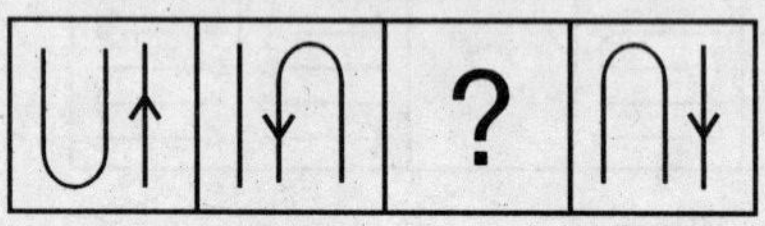

Answer Figures

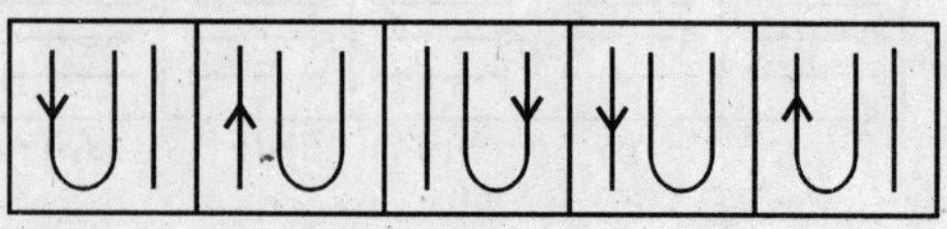

(*a*) (*b*) (*c*) (*d*) (*e*)

4. Problem Figures

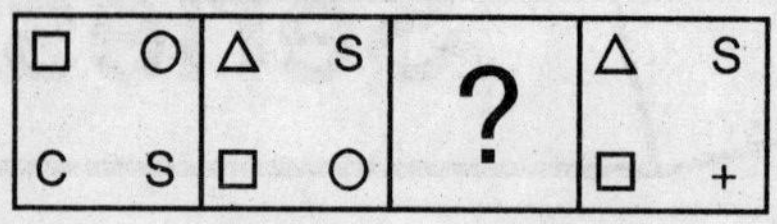

Answer Figures

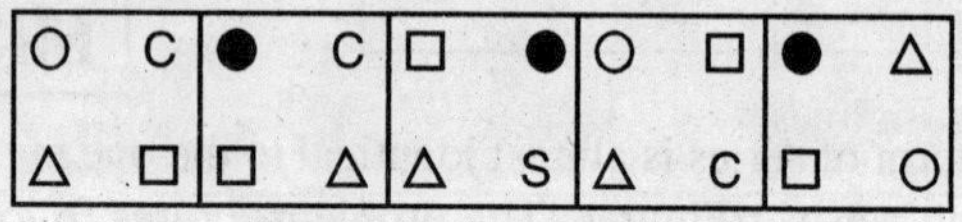

(*a*) (*b*) (*c*) (*d*) (*e*)

5. Problem Figures

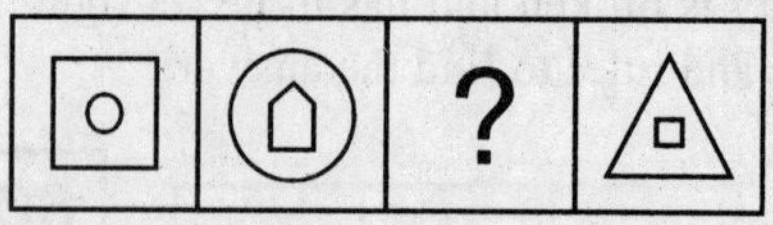

Answer Figures

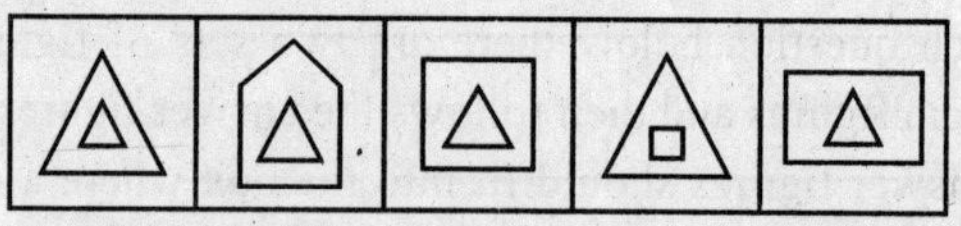

(*a*) (*b*) (*c*) (*d*) (*e*)

6. Problem Figures

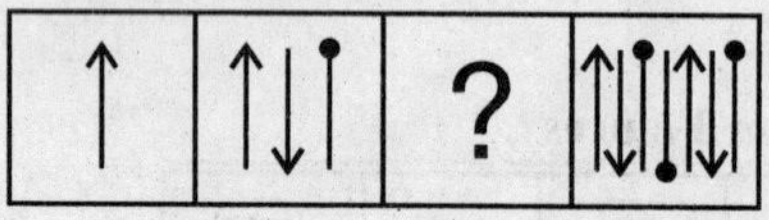

Answer Figures

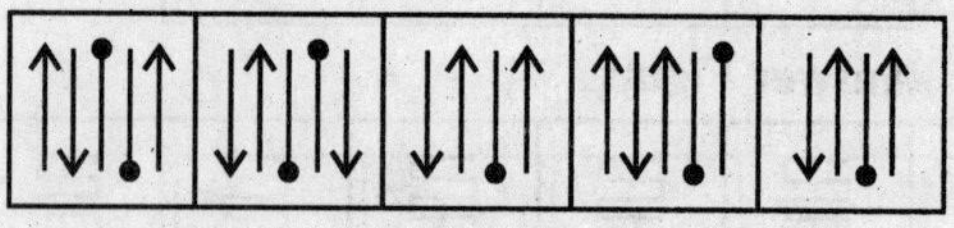

(*a*) (*b*) (*c*) (*d*) (*e*)

7. Problem Figures

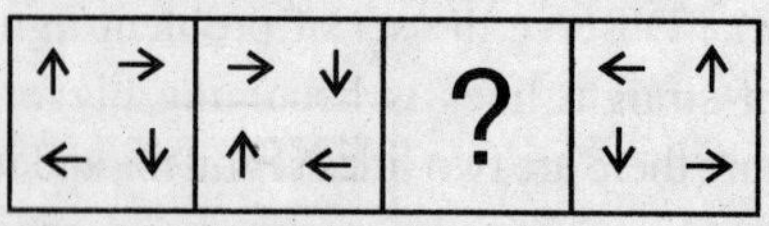

Answer Figures

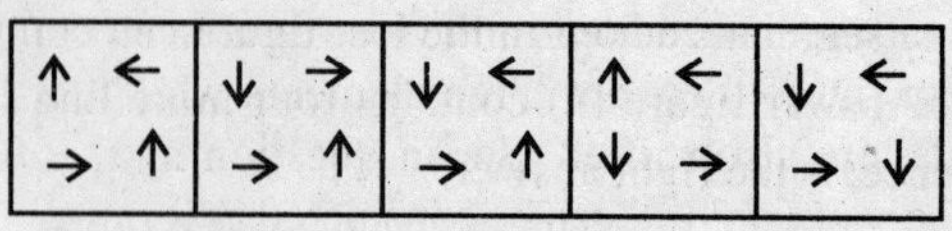

(*a*) (*b*) (*c*) (*d*) (*e*)

8. Problem Figures

Answer Figures

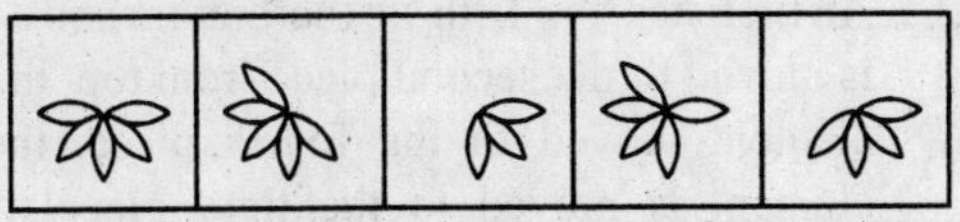

(a) (b) (c) (d) (e)

9. Problem Figures

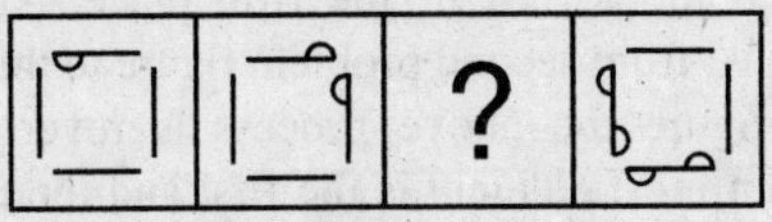

Answer Figures

(a) (b) (c) (d) (e)

10. Problem Figures

Answer Figures

(a) (b) (c) (d) (e)

11. Problem Figures

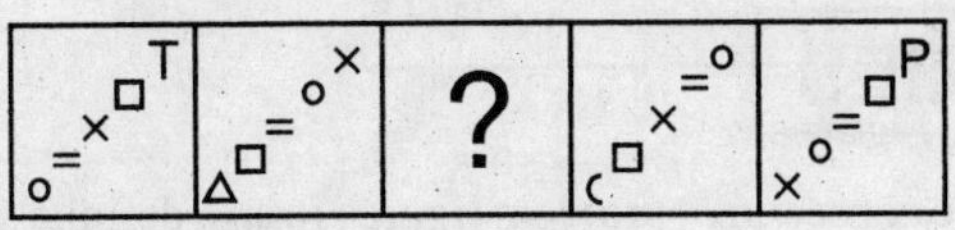

Answer Figures

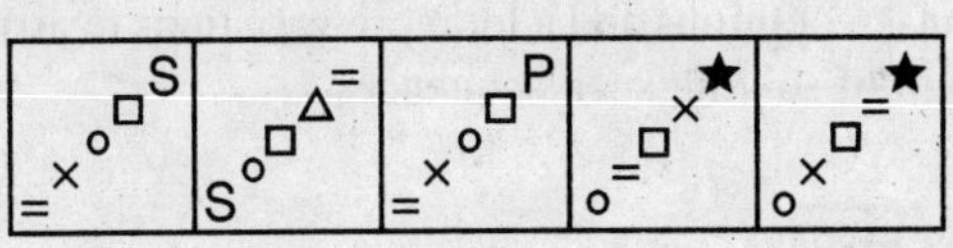

(a) (b) (c) (d) (e)

12. Problem Figures

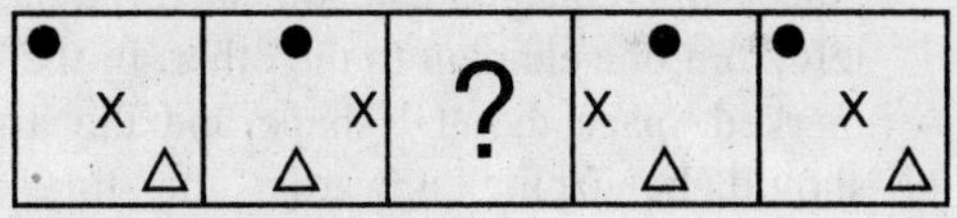

Answer Figures

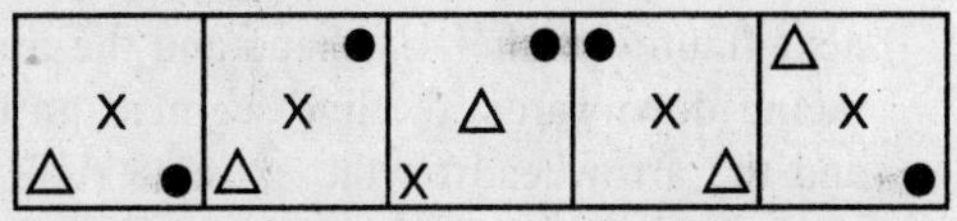

(a) (b) (c) (d) (e)

13. Problem Figures

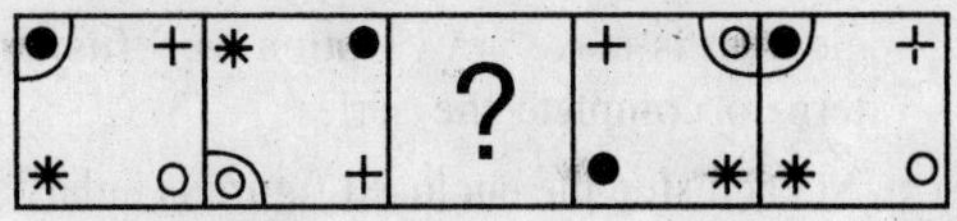

Answer Figures

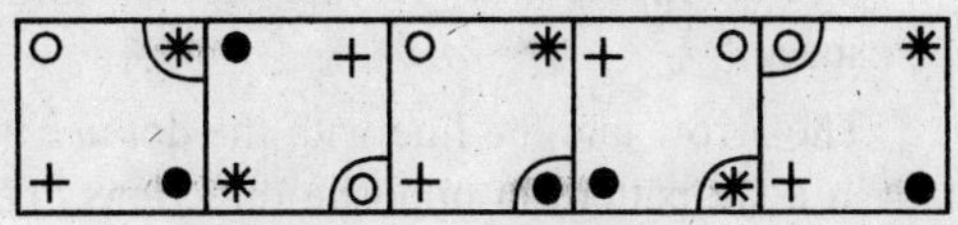

(a) (b) (c) (d) (e)

14. Problem Figures

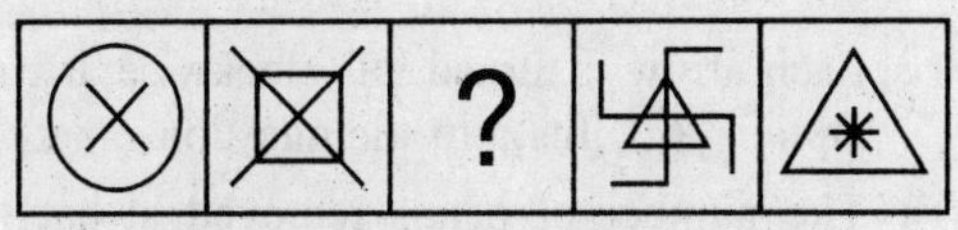

Answer Figures

(a) (b) (c) (d) (e)

15. Problem Figures

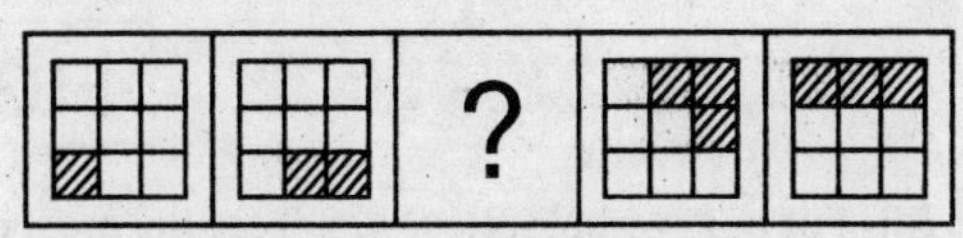

Answer Figures

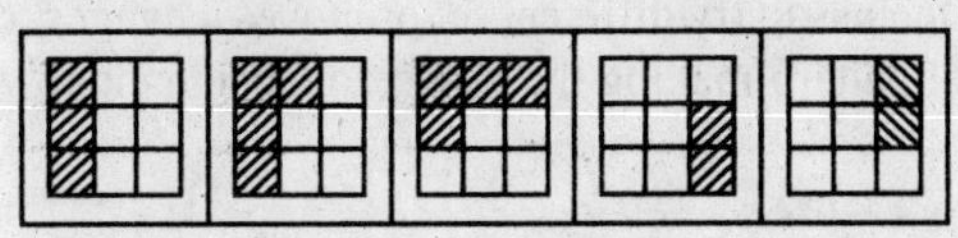

(a) (b) (c) (d) (e)

EXPLANATORY ANSWERS

1. (*c*) : From first problem figure to the second the elements on the top are shifted down and vice versa. In fourth problem figure there are three elements which, as per rule, are also shifted. So, in question marked space only option '(*c*)' can be considered as forming the series.

2. (*d*) : Anticlockwise one of the sides of the hexagon is extended and clockwise one arc is added. The direction of the arc is changed at each step. Answer figure 'D' is the right answer.

3. (*e*) : Both the elements are turned upside down, their places interchanged and the arrow head moved left from one element to the other. In the question marked space the 'U' shape and the arrowhead should be facing upwards, the line segment should be on the right and the arrowhead should be on the extreme left. To continue the series the next figure has the 'U' shape and the arrowhead facing downwards, the line segment on the right and the arrowhead on the extreme right. Option '(*e*)' fits into the question marked space.

4. (*c*) : At each step the places of two elements on the horizontal are interchanged and clockwise one element is made new. Option '(*c*)' fits in the pattern to complete the series.

5. (*b*) : At each step the enclosed figure is enlarged in the next and a new figure is placed inside the enlarged figure. Option '(*b*)' fits into the question marked space.

6. (*a*) : The arrow and the line with the dot are increased in a set pattern in opposite directions. The series they form is two arrows and two lines with the dot which is repeated. Answer figure '(*a*)' is the right choice.

7. (*c*) : Each arrow is turned 90° clockwise at each step. Option '(*c*)' fits into the question marked space.

8. (*a*) : The number of petals removed at each step is increased by one, i.e., the petals are removed in the order of one, two and three, leaving only two petals in the last figure option '(*a*)' is the right answer.

9. (*e*) : The lines are moved clockwise. First a semicircle is added to the adjacent line. Then the semicircles on the opposite sides are added one by one on the two lines. Answer figure '(*e*)' fits into the question-marked space.

10. (*c*) : Each time one petal is removed and the half petal is clockwise and anticlockwise alternately. Answer figure '(*c*)' completes the series.

11. (*a*) : At first step the fifth or the bottom most element is moved to the second place from top, the second element moved to the fourth place, the fourth element is moved to the third place, the third element is moved to the first or the topmost place and the element on the top which is made new is moved to the last or the fifth place. At second step i.e., from second problem figure to third problem figure the above process is reversed. The bottom most element is the first and the top most element is the last or fifth. Hereafter, the process is repeated from the beginning. Option '(*a*)' is the right answer.

12. (*b*) : The three elements are moved half step everytime-first till they reach the extreme right position and then back to the left. Answer figure '(*b*)' fits into the question-marked space.

13. (*c*) : The four elements are moved one step clockwise and the arc one step anti-clockwise. Option '(*c*)' is the right answer.

14. (*b*) : The smaller design is enlarged in the next and a new smaller design is placed in its centre. Option '(*b*)' fits into the question-marked space to continue the series.

15. (*d*) : The shaded portion is moved one step anticlockwise at each step and one extra portion is shaded alternately.

FIGURAL SERIES

In this form of non-verbal series, which are the most common, four or five consecutive problem figures form a definite sequence and one is required to select the one figure from the given set of Answer Figures that will continue the same sequence.

One has to try different set of moves, changes, replacements, rotations, repetitions and a lot more variations to arrive at the logical pattern making the series. Practising alone will sharpen one's skill of solving such sequences.

SOLVED EXAMPLES

In each of the questions given below, which one of the answer figures should come after the problem figure if the sequence were continued?

1. Problem Figures

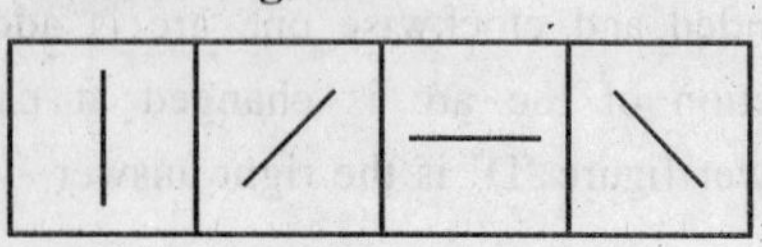

Answer Figures

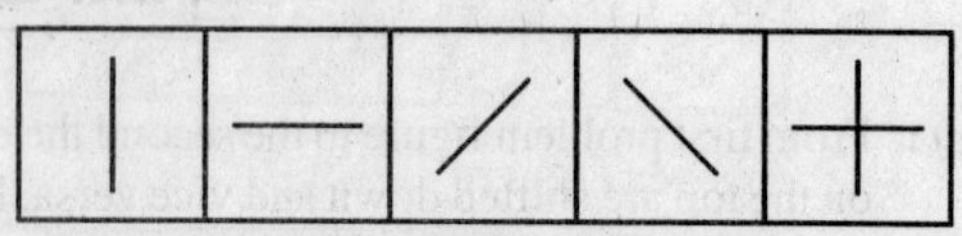

(*a*) (*b*) (*c*) (*d*) (*e*)

Answer (*a*) : All the figures are simple straight lines of the same size. Their directions and positions have changed.

In the first figure, the line is in a vertical position, in the second, the line has moved 45° clockwise, in the third, the line has further moved 45° clockwise, and in the fourth, the line has further moved 45° clockwise. Thus, two facts are brought out: *(i)* the line moves clockwise, and *(ii)* the line moves 45° at each step.

Now the fourth figure (Problem Figures) should be moved 45° clockwise. It will be a vertical line. Thus, the next figure to continue the series will be a vertical straight line.

MULTIPLE CHOICE QUESTIONS

Directions : *In each of the following questions which one of the five answer figures given below should come after the problem figures if the sequence are continued?*

Problem Figures

1. 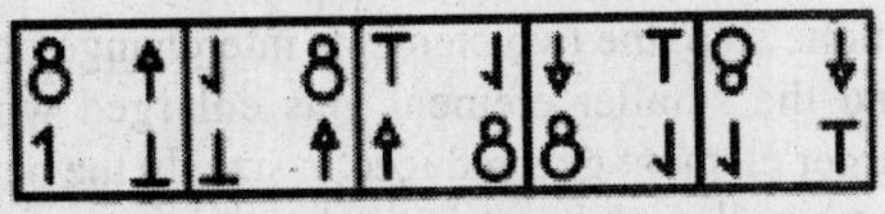

Answer Figures

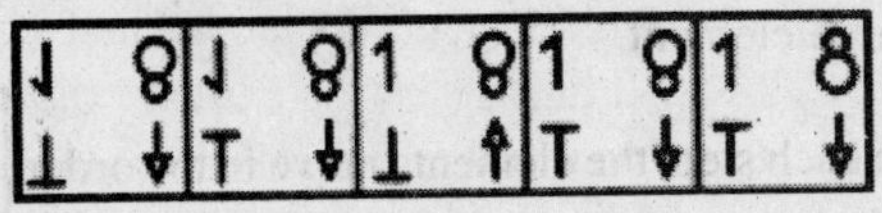

(a) (b) (c) (d) (e)

Problem Figures

2. 

Answer Figures

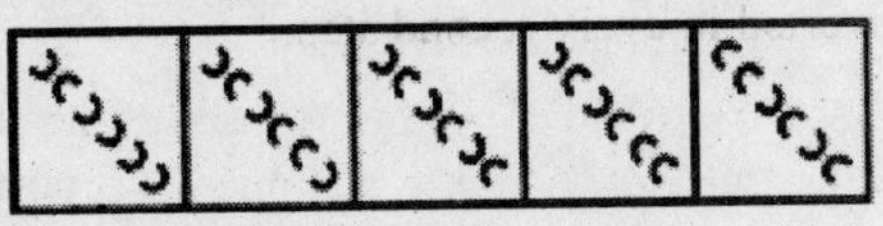

(a) (b) (c) (d) (e)

Problem Figures

3. 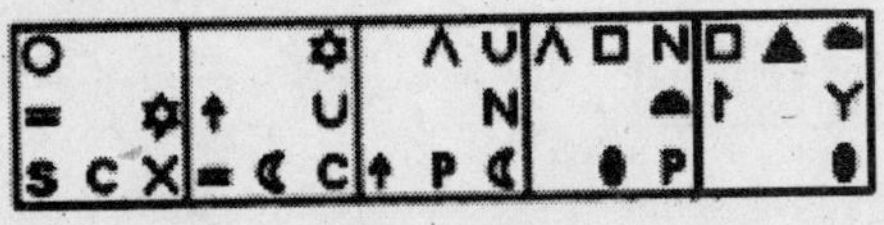

Answer Figures

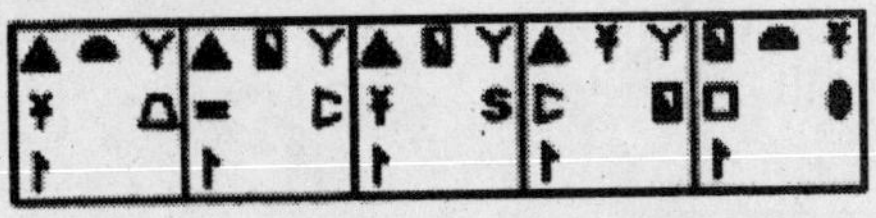

(a) (b) (c) (d) (e)

Problem Figures

4. 

Answer Figures

(a) (b) (c) (d) (e)

Problem Figures

5. 

Answer Figures

(a) (b) (c) (d) (e)

Problem Figures

6. 

Answer Figures

(a) (b) (c) (d) (e)

Problem Figures

7. 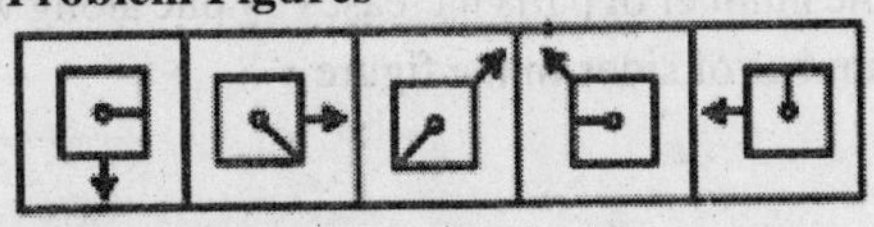

Answer Figures

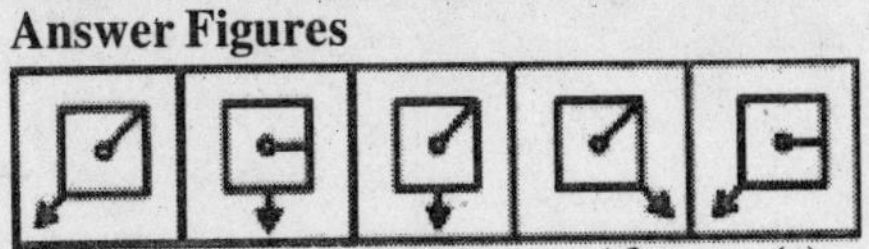

(a) (b) (c) (d) (e)

Problem Figures

8. 

Answer Figures

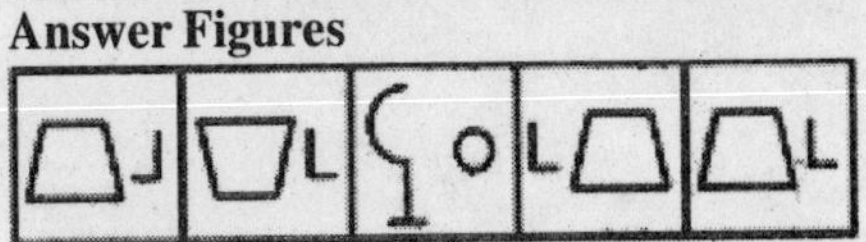

(a) (b) (c) (d) (e)

Problem Figures

9. 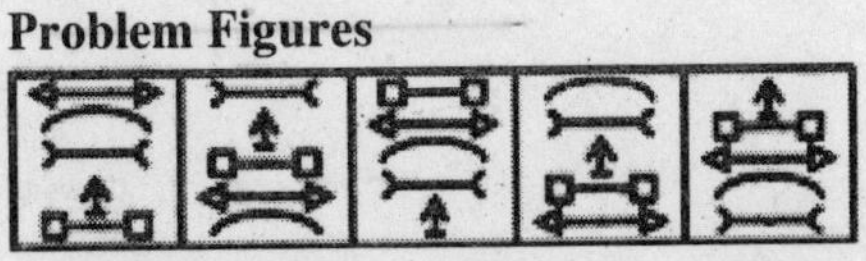

Answer Figures

(a) (b) (c) (d) (e)

Problem Figures

10. 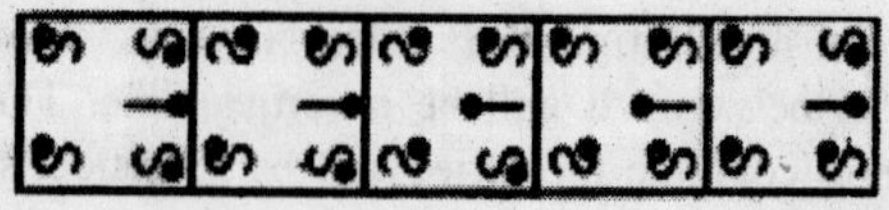

Answer Figures

(a) (b) (c) (d) (e)

EXPLANATORY ANSWERS

1. (*d*) : In each step, all the elements move to the adjacent corner (of the square boundary) in a CW direction and the element that reaches the upper-left corner gets vertically inverted.

2. (*c*) : We can label the arcs as shown . The arcs get inverted in the sequence (1 & 2), (3, 4 & 5), (6 & 1), (2, 3 & 4), (5 & 6), ...

3. (*d*) : All the elements move half-a-side of the square boundary in ACW direction in each step. Also, first, third and fifth elements are replaced by new elements in one step and second, fourth and sixth elements are replaced by new elements in the next step. The two steps are repeated alternately.

4. (*a*) : In each step, the dot moves one space CW and the arrow moves two spaces CW.

5. (*c*) : One arc and four arcs get inverted alternately.

6. (*e*) : The number of parts increases by one along with the number of sides in the figure.

7. (*c*) : The pin rotates 45°CW and 90°CW alternately and moves one space (each space is equal to half-a-side of the square) and two spaces CW alternately. The arrow rotates 90°ACW and 45°ACW alternately and moves two spaces and one space.

8. (*e*) : In one step, the two elements interchange positions and the smaller element gets enlarged while the larger element gets reduced in size. In the next step, the smaller element is replaced by a new small element and the larger element is replaced by a new large element.

9. (*c*) : In each step, the elements move in the order .

10. (*b*) : The upper-left element gets laterally inverted in first, third, fifth. .... steps; the upper-right element gets rotated through 180° is first, fourth, seventh,.... steps; the lower-left element gets laterally inverted in second, fourth, sixth, ... steps; the lower-right element gets rotated through 180° in third, sixth,... steps and the pin at the middle-right position gets laterally inverted in every second step.

CHAPTER 2

Semantic Classification

Classification means arranging the given content in groups or classes having qualities of same kind. In classification type questions, the figures or items are sorted out in groups on the basis of their similarities in qualities in shapes, size, pattern, structure, genus, order, species, grade, style, constituents and other specifications, and thus the answer is found out.

TYPE-I

Classification of this type does not have two sets of figures known as Problem Figures and Answer Figures; instead they have only one set of four or five figures known as Problem Figures. One of these Problem Figures is not like the other four figures. In other words, three or four of the Answer Figures belong to a class while one which is the odd figures, does not belong to it.

MULTIPLE CHOICE QUESTIONS

Directions : *In each of the following questions one of the figures is different from the rest. Spot the figure.*

1. 

(a) (b) (c) (d) (e)

2. 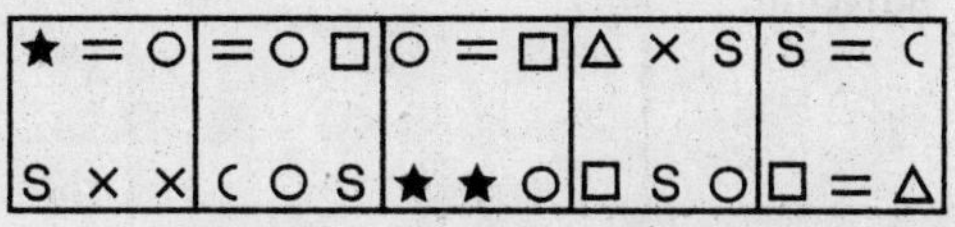

(a) (b) (c) (d) (e)

3. 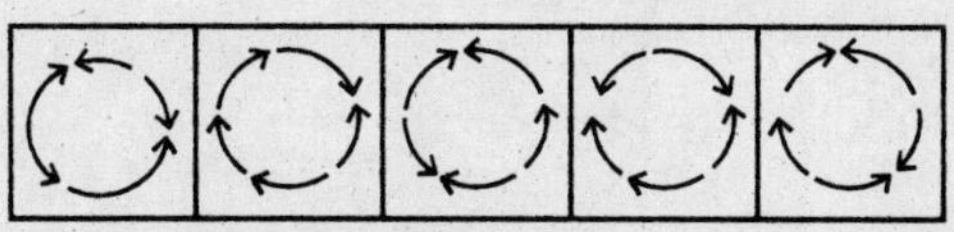

(a) (b) (c) (d) (e)

4. 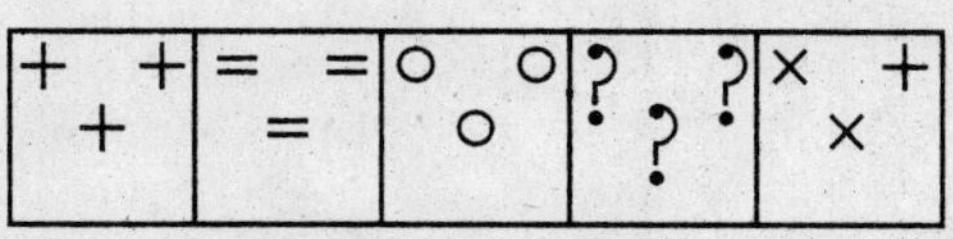

(a) (b) (c) (d) (e)

5. 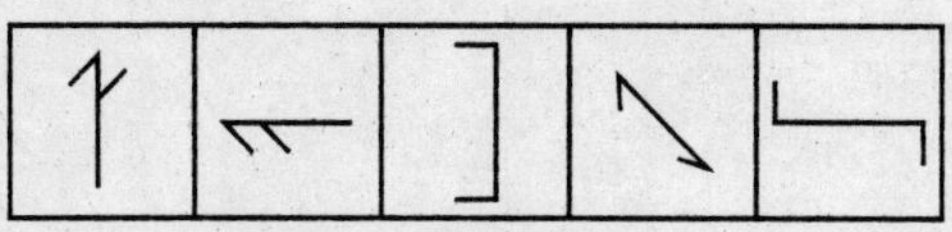

(a) (b) (c) (d) (e)

6. 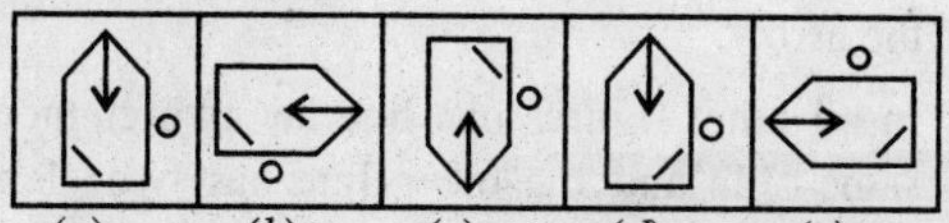

(a) (b) (c) (d) (e)

7. 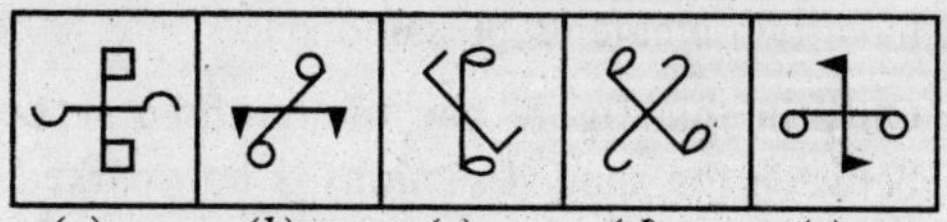

(a) (b) (c) (d) (e)

8. 

(a) (b) (c) (d) (e)

9. 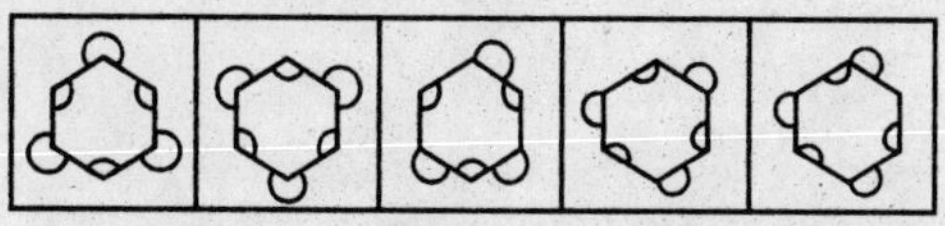

(a) (b) (c) (d) (e)

10. 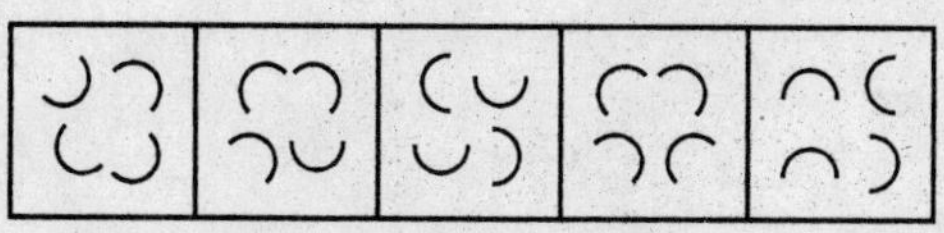

(a) (b) (c) (d) (e)

11. 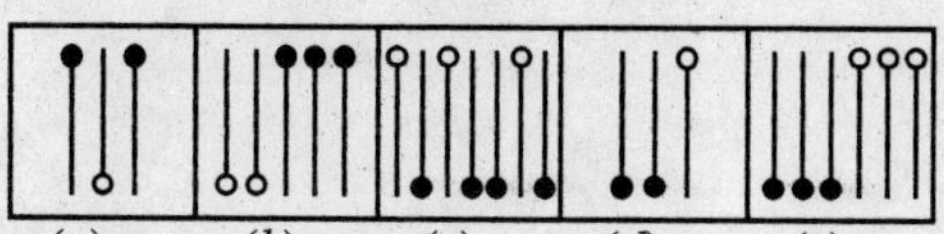

(a) (b) (c) (d) (e)

12. 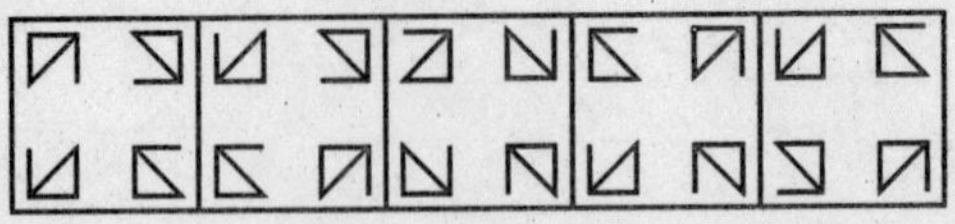

(a) (b) (c) (d) (e)

13. 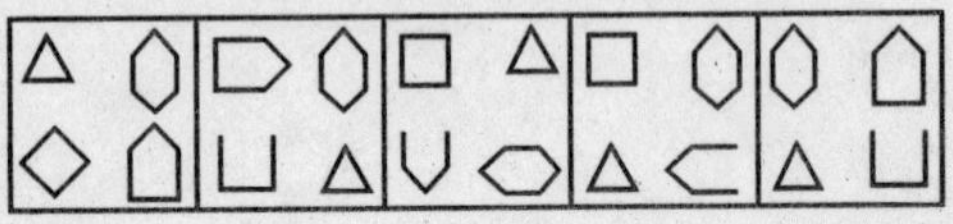

(a) (b) (c) (d) (e)

14. 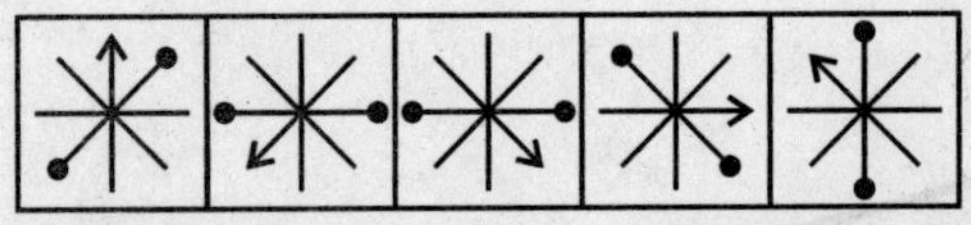

(a) (b) (c) (d) (e)

15. 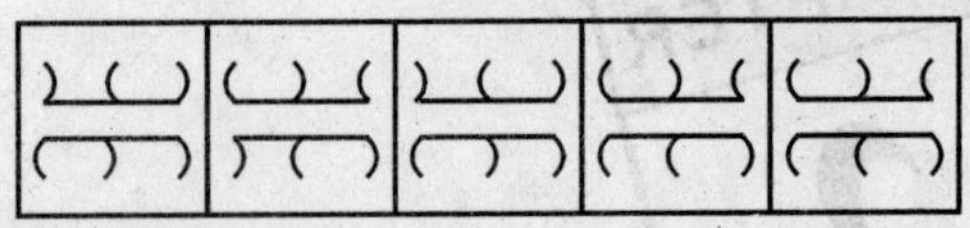

(a) (b) (c) (d) (e)

EXPLANATORY ANSWERS

1. (*d*) : Only in this figure all the lines making the hands and legs of the human shape are drawn downwards.

2. (*c*) : In all other figures only one set of elements is identical.

3. (*b*) : Only in this figure four arrows are pointing in same direction, and one arrow in its opposite direction. In other figures three arrows are in same direction and two in the opposite direction.

4. (*e*) : All other figures have three identical elements.

5. (*d*) : In all other figures two lines are parallelly drawn.

6. (*c*) : In all other figures the circle is on the left side of the arrow.

7. (*c*) : In all other figures one line has two elements on same side and the other line has two elements, one on either side. In this figure both the lines have two elements on same side.

8. (*d*) : Only in this figure one of the three sections in between the shaded sections is not marked.

9. (*e*) : In all other figures the elements inside as well as outside the hexagon are placed at equal distance. In this figure the outside element at the top is wrongly placed (It should be near the other corner of the same line).

10. (*d*) : In all other figures two elements are in same direction and the other two elements are opposite to each other.

11. (*e*) : Only in this figure the two types of elements are equal in number.

12. (*c*) : In all other figures the diagonal line in all other elements is drawn from the right end.

13. (*a*) : In all other figures one of the four elements has one open side.

14. (*c*) : In all other figures the arrow is to the left of the dot.

15. (*b*) : In all other figures two of the three curves on one of the lines are in the same direction and are adjacent.

CHAPTER

3 Figural Analogy

Figural Analogy is a process of reasoning between two parallel cases. It relates to agreement or correspondence in certain respects between two things. It is a process whereby the underlying relationship that exists between two figures, designs or patterns is determined. Under the process, one has to discover the features common to the two figures or designs. This common feature is a model or base. The question seeks solution on the basis of this model or base.

In non-verbal analogy questions, there are two sets of figures which are known as *(i)* Problem Figures, and *(ii)* Answer Figures. The Problem Figures are divided into two parts. The Answer Figures are given below the Problem Figures.

MULTIPLE CHOICE QUESTIONS

Directions : *The second figure in the first unit of the Problem Figures bears a certain relationship to the first figure. Similarly, one of the figures in the Answer Figures bears the same relationship to the first figure in the second unit of the Problem Figures. Locate the figure which would fit the question mark.*

1. Problem Figures

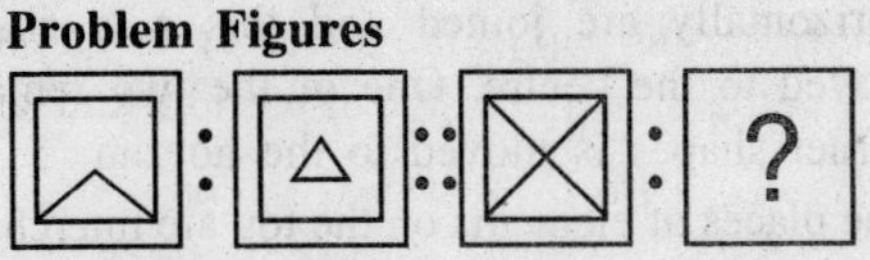

Answers Figures

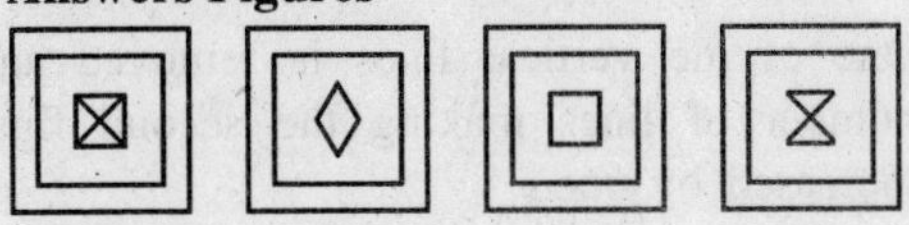

(a) (b) (c) (d)

2. Problem Figures

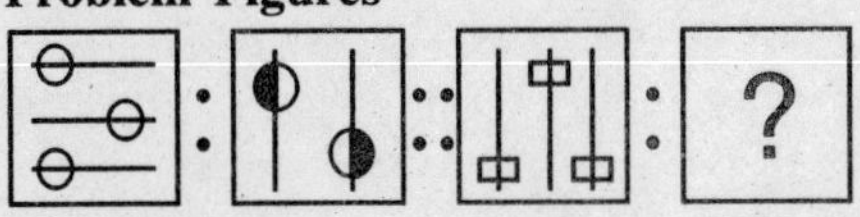

Answer Figures

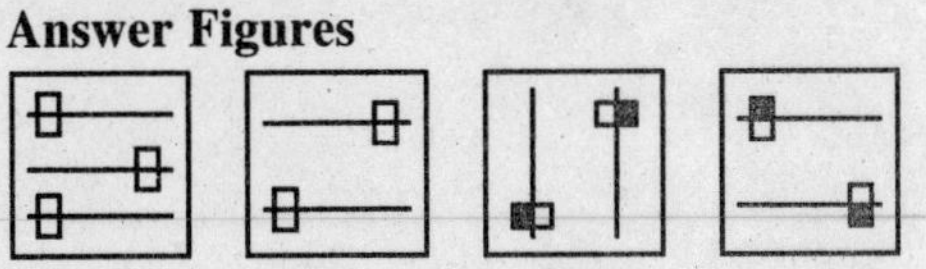

(a) (b) (c) (d)

3. Problem Figures

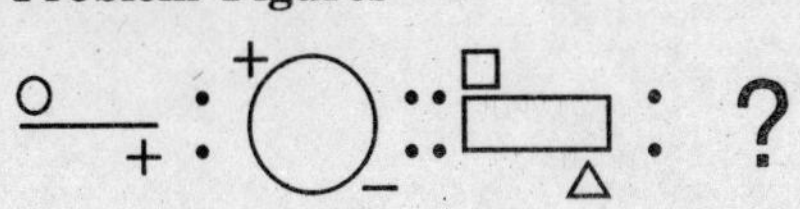

Answer Figures

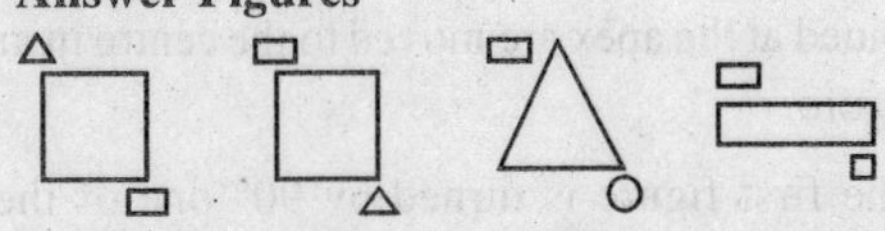

(a) (b) (c) (d)

4. Problem Figures

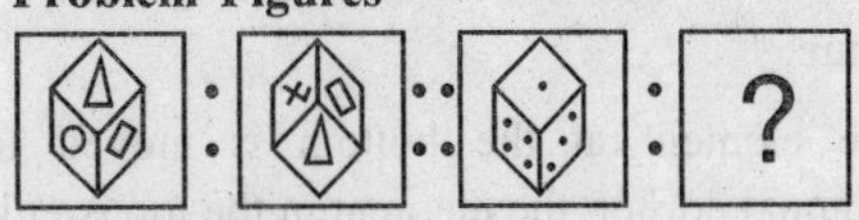

Answer Figures

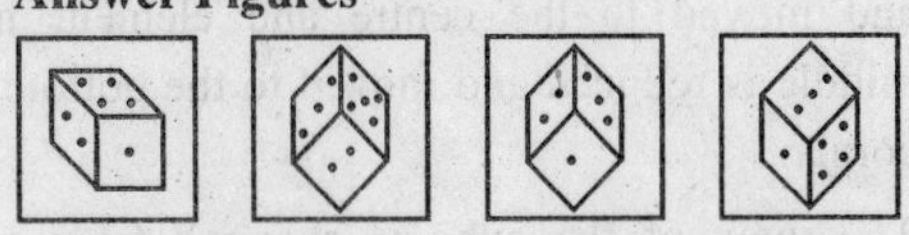

(a) (b) (c) (d)

5. Problem Figures

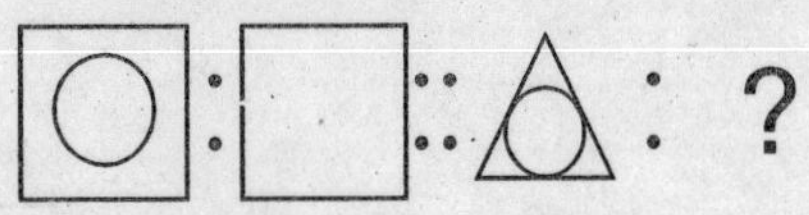

Answer Figures

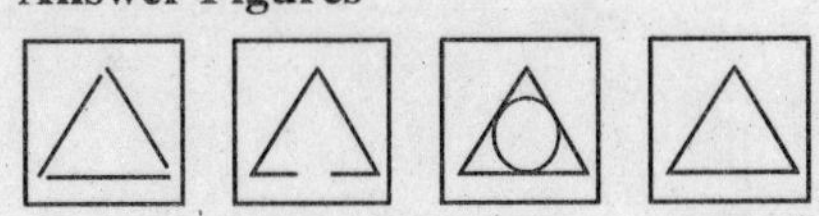

(a) (b) (c) (d)

6. Problem Figures

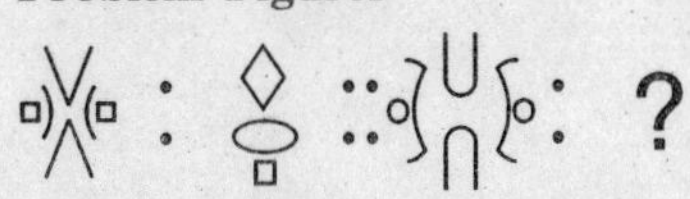

Answer Figures

(a) (b) (c) (d)

7. Problem Figures

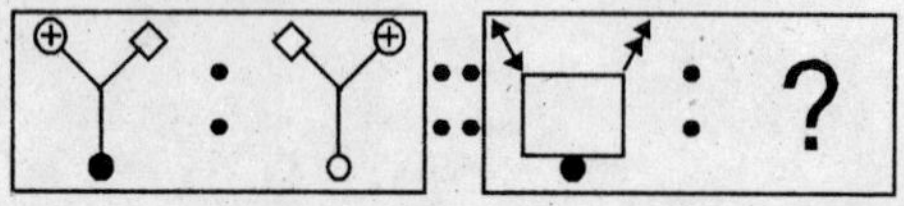

Answer Figures

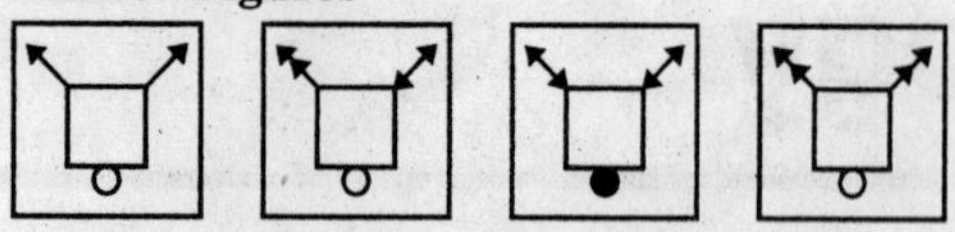

(a) (b) (c) (d)

8. Problem Figures

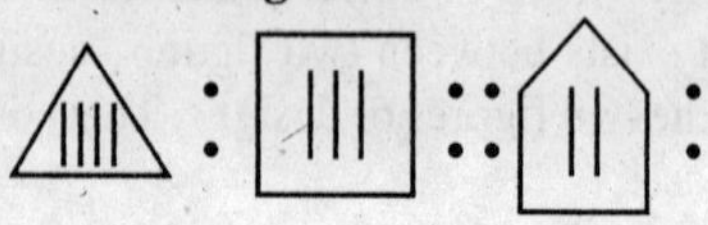

Answer Figures

(a) (b) (c) (d)

9. Problem Figures

Answer Figures

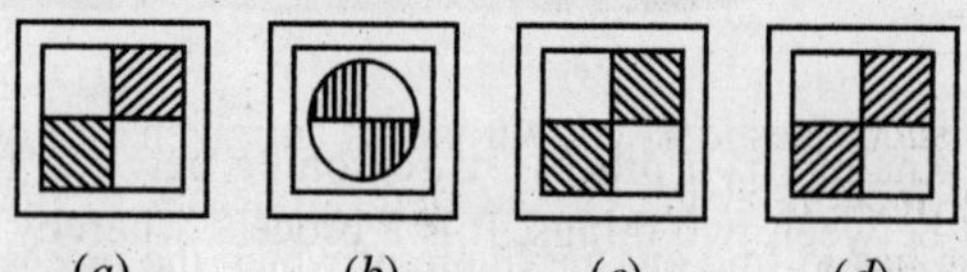

(a) (b) (c) (d)

EXPLANATORY ANSWERS

1. (*d*) : The triangle in the first figure is moved to the centre of the second figure. Similarly, the two triangles joined at the apex are moved to the centre in answer figure.

2. (*d*) : The first figure is turned by 90° one of the bars is removed and opposite sides of the element attached to the bar are shaded to get the second figure.

3. (*a*) : The element at the bottom is moved to the diagonal corner, the element in the top is enlarged and moved to the centre and element in the middle is reduced and moved to the bottom right corner.

4. (*c*) : The view of the cube is changed from top to bottom. The design on the right side remains unchanged while the design on the left side is changed.

5. (*d*) : The inner shape in the first figure is removed to get the second figure.

6. (*b*) : The two half shapes placed vertically are turned upside down and joined, and this new shape is moved to the top. The two curved shapes placed horizontally are joined and this new shape is moved to the centre. One of the two remaining corner shapes is moved to the bottom.

7. (*b*) : The places of elements on the top are interchanged and the shade inside the circle is removed.

8. (*a*) : One of the vertical lines is removed and the number of lines making the second figure is increased by one.

9. (*a*) : First figure is rotated 90° anticlockwise to get the second figure.

CHAPTER 4

Spatial Visualization

In such questions, cut-out pieces are given alongwith the whole figure, that is the figure out of which the figures have been cut. By looking at the cut-out figures one has to find out the figure which may be constituted by putting the pieces together, i.e., one has to find out the figure of which the pieces have been cut. One has to be very imaginative and has to use space perception in finding out the solution. The whole process is mental and requires special skill in visualising different spatial patterns. It is not easy to develop this skill overnight but it can certainly be cultivated by practice and the method of trial and error.

MULTIPLE CHOICE QUESTIONS

Directions (Qs. 1-5) : *Which one figure can be made out of given paper cut-outs?*

1. 

(a) (b) (c) (d)

2. 

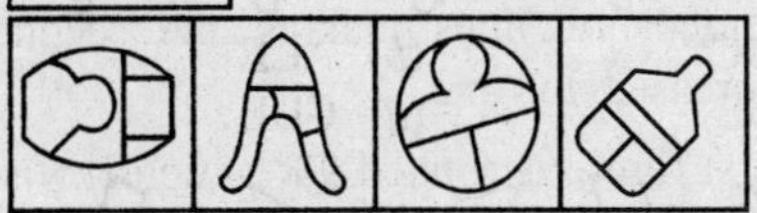

(a) (b) (c) (d)

3. 

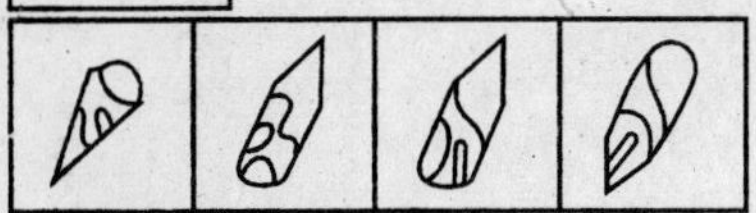

(a) (b) (c) (d)

4. 

(a) (b) (c) (d)

5. 

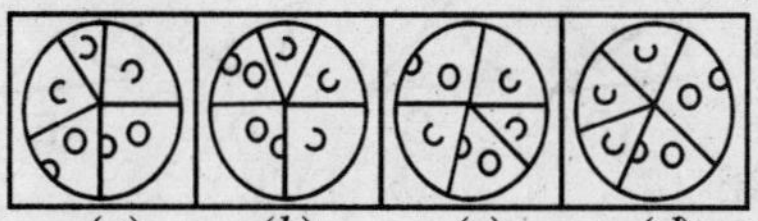

(a) (b) (c) (d)

Direction (Qs. 6-10) : *In each of the following questions an irregular piece of paper has been cut into two pieces. One piece has been shown on the left while the other piece has been given as one of the four alternatives against it. Find the correct alternative:*

6. 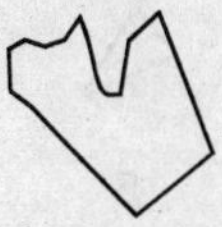

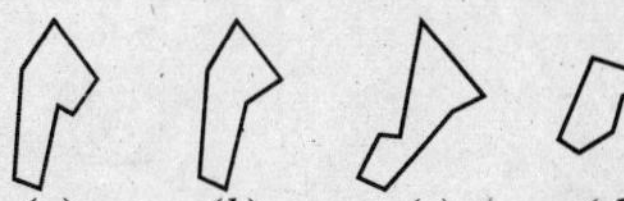

(a) (b) (c) (d)

7. 

(*a*) (*b*) (*c*) (*d*)

8.

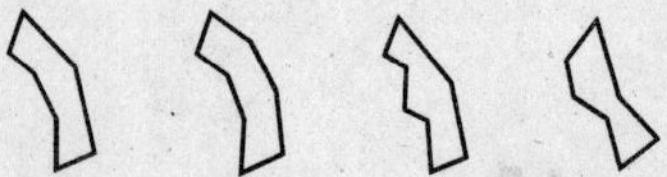

(*a*) (*b*) (*c*) (*d*)

9.

(*a*) (*b*) (*c*) (*d*)

10.

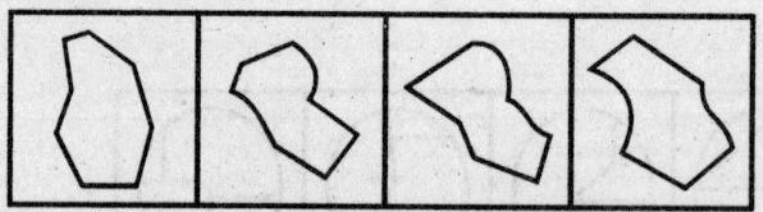

(*a*) (*b*) (*c*) (*d*)

Directions (Qs. 11-15) : *In each of the following questions five diagrams marked A to E are given. Three of these when put together form an equilateral triangle and have been given as one of the four alternatives under the question. Find the correct alternative in each case.*

11.

A B C D E

(*a*) ABE (*b*) BCE
(*c*) ADE (*d*) BDE

12.

A B C D E

(*a*) ABC (*b*) BCD
(*c*) CDE (*d*) BDE

13.

A B C D E

(*a*) BCD (*b*) CDE
(*c*) ABD (*d*) ABE

14.

A B C D E

(*a*) ABD (*b*) ACD
(*c*) BDE (*d*) CDE

15.

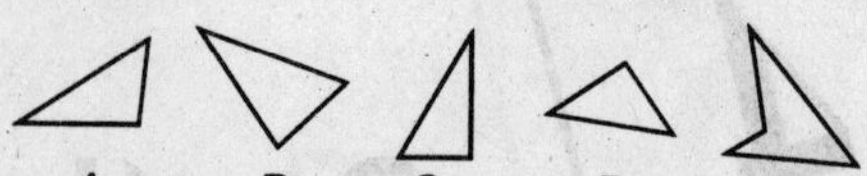

A B C D E

(*a*) ABC (*b*) ACE
(*c*) BDE (*d*) CDE

Directions (Qs. 16-20) : *In each of the following questions five diagrams A, B, C, D and E have been given. Three of these diagrams make a complete square which have been given as one of the four alternatives under it. Find the correct alternative in each case.*

16.

A B C D E

(*a*) ABC (*b*) BDE
(*c*) CDE (*d*) BCD

17.

A B C D E

(*a*) ACD (*b*) BDE
(*c*) BCE (*d*) CDE

18.

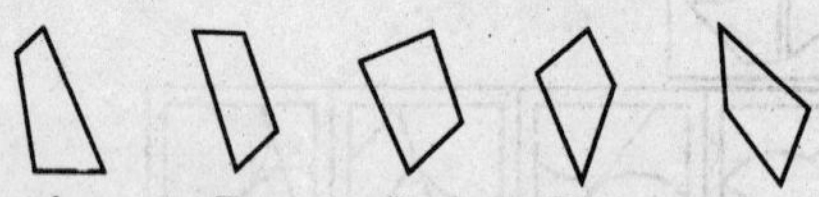

A B C D E

(*a*) ACD (*b*) BCD
(*c*) ACE (*d*) CDE

19.

A B C D E

(*a*) ABC (*b*) ACE
(*c*) ADE (*d*) CDE

20.

A B C D E

(*a*) BDE (*b*) ABC
(*c*) ACD (*d*) BCD

ANSWERS

1	2	3	4	5	6	7	8	9	10
(*b*)	(*d*)	(*c*)	(*a*)	(*b*)	(*b*)	(*c*)	(*a*)	(*d*)	(*c*)
11	**12**	**13**	**14**	**15**	**16**	**17**	**18**	**19**	**20**
(*c*)	(*d*)	(*d*)	(*b*)	(*b*)	(*d*)	(*b*)	(*c*)	(*c*)	(*d*)

CHAPTER 5

Space Visualization

In these type of questions, a template or a layout of a cube, dice or a box is given, which can be folded to produce different patterns. To solve these questions what is required is a clear study of the given layout and the selection of one figure, from the alternative patterns which can be made from the given layout. To attempt such problems understand the unfolded patterns given below:

Layout 1. 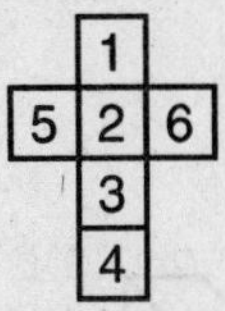 or 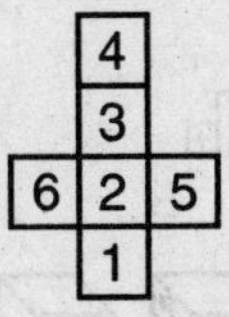

The opposite sides are :
1—3, 2 — 4 and 5 — 6

Layout 2. 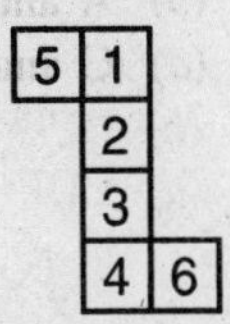 or 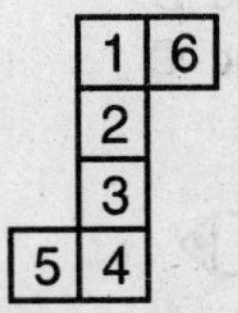

The opposite sides are :
1 — 3, 2 — 4 and 5 — 6

Layout 3. 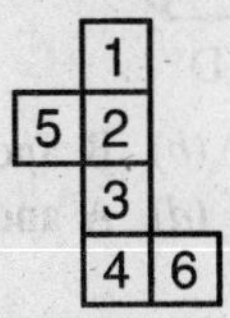 or 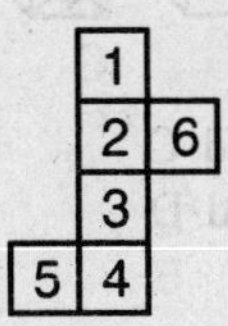

The opposite sides are :
1 — 3, 2 — 4 and 5 — 6.

Layout 4. 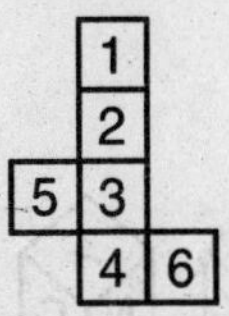 or 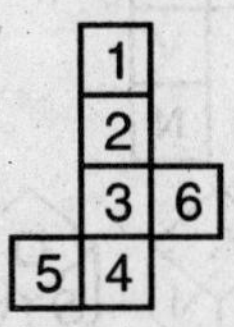

The opposite sides are :
1 — 3, 2 — 4 and 5 — 6

Layout 5. 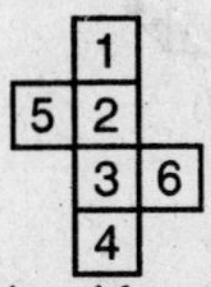 or 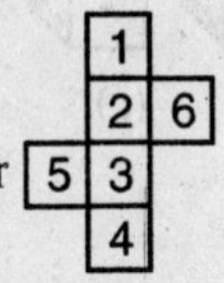

The opposite sides are :
1 — 3, 2 — 4 and 5 — 6

Layout 6.  or 

The opposite sides are :
1 — 3, 2 — 5 and 4 — 6

Layout 7. 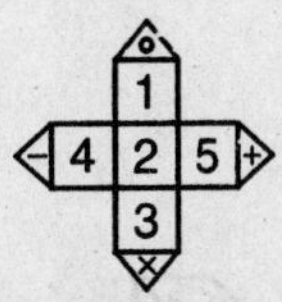

The opposite sides are :

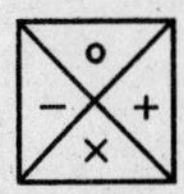 — 2, 1 — 3 and 4 — 5. Here, side 6 is divided into four parts

Layout 8. 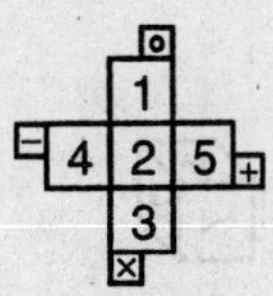

The opposite sides are

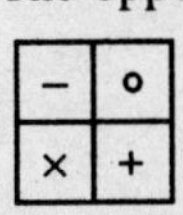 — 2, 1 — 3 and 4 — 5. Here, side 6 is divided into four parts.

Observe from the above layouts that all sides except the opposite side are adjacent sides. Also keep in mind that the three visible sides of the option figures are one of the opposite sides of each opposite pair.

MULTIPLE CHOICE QUESTIONS

Directions : *The figure is folded to produce different box patterns. Study the pattern to know if they can be produced from given figure and select the answer from the alternatives.*

1. 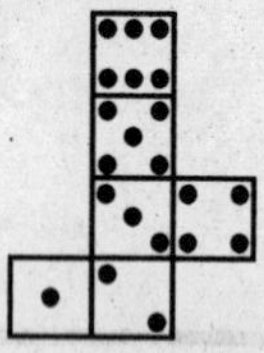

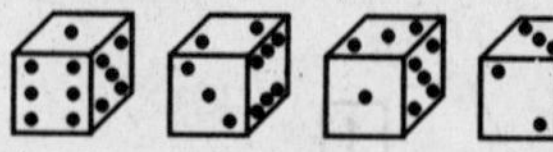

(a) (b) (c) (d)

2. 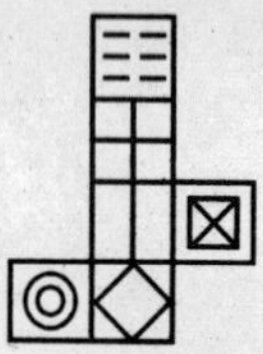

(a) (b) (c) (d)

3. 

(a) (b) (c) (d)

4. 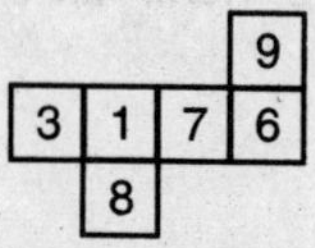

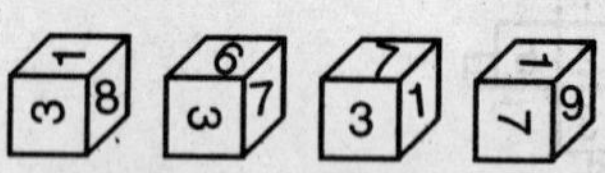

(a) (b) (c) (d)

5. 

(a) (b) (c) (d)

6. 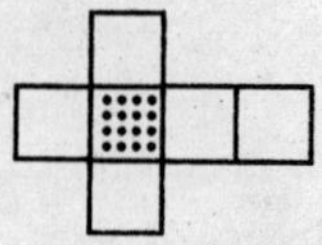

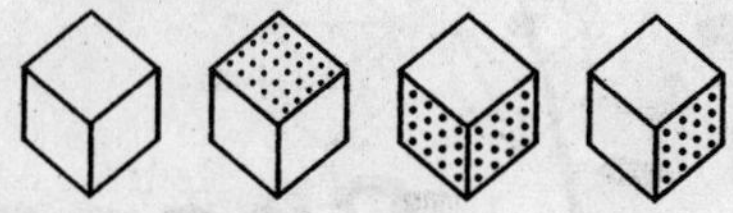

A B C D

(a) A, B and D (b) B and D
(c) B, C and D (d) A and D

7. 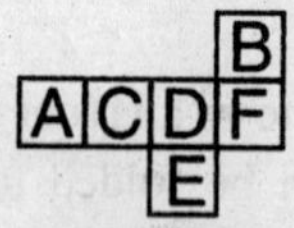

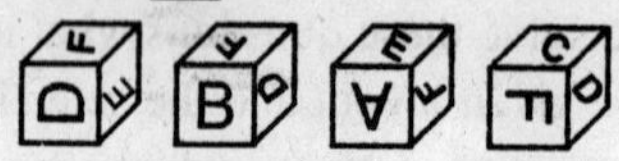

A B C D

(a) A and B (b) A and D
(c) B and C (d) All four

8. 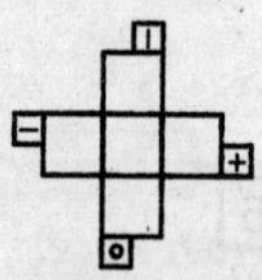

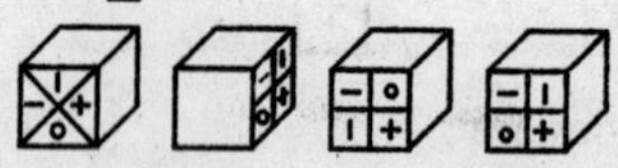

A B C D

(a) B and D (b) A and D
(c) B and C (d) C and D

9. 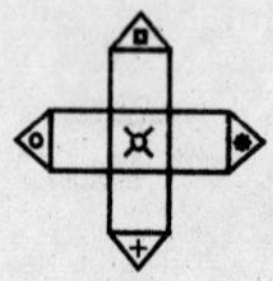

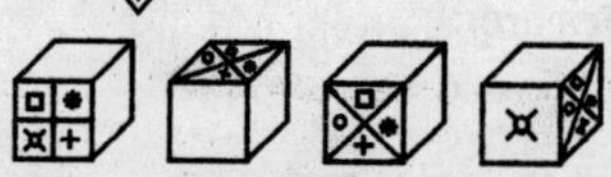

A B C D

(a) A and C (b) B and C
(c) B and D (d) A and D

10. 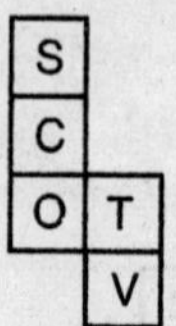

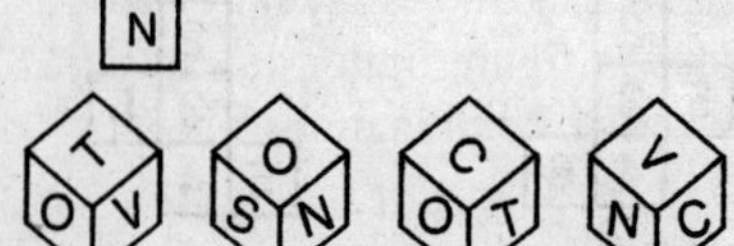

A B C D

(a) B and C (b) A and D
(c) A and C (d) All four

11.

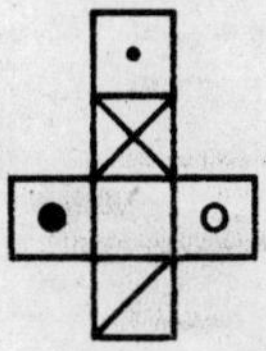

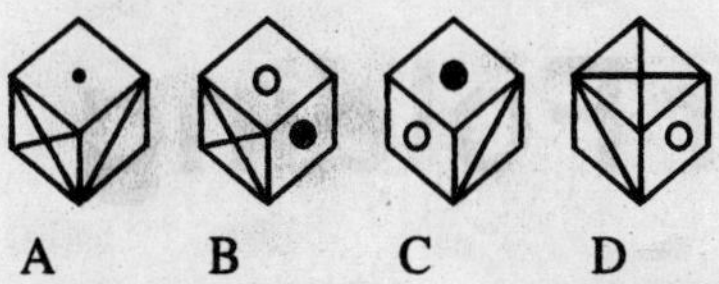

A B C D

(*a*) A and D (*b*) B, C and D

(*c*) All four (*d*) None of the above

12.

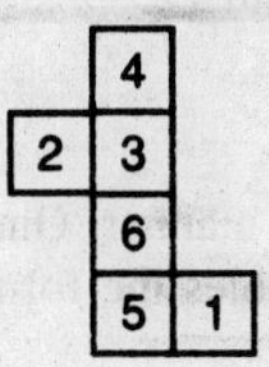

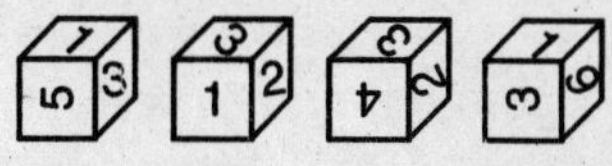

A B C D

(*a*) A and C (*b*) C and D

(*c*) B and C (*d*) B and D

13.

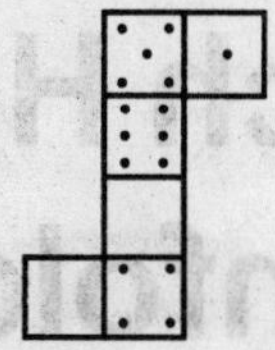

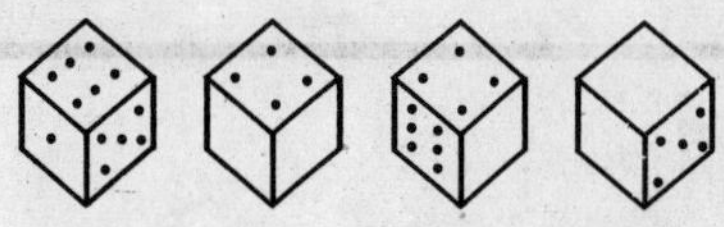

A B C D

(*a*) A and C (*b*) A and B

(*c*) B and C (*d*) B and D

EXPLANATORY ANSWERS

(All answers are based on number pattern of the sides as in the layout given in the beginning of this section)

1. (*d*) : The given figure is same as layout 4. The sides adjacent to top side 3 are in order 2, 5, 4, 6 — of these sides, 4 and 6 are seen on left and right sides respectively.

2. (*b*) : The given figure is same as layout 4. The sides adjacent to top side 5 are in order 4, 3, 2, 1 —of these sides 1 and 4 are seen on left and right sides respectively.

3. (*d*) : The given figure is same as layout 1. The sides adjacent to top side 5 are in order 4, 3, 2, 1 — of these sides 2 and 1 are seen on left and right sides respectively.

4. (*a*) : The given figure is same as layout 3. The sides adjacent to top side 2 are in order 1, 5, 3, 6 — of these sides 1 and 5 are seen on left and right sides respectively.

5. (*c*) : The given figure is same as layout 1. The sides adjacent to top side 6 are in order 1, 2, 3, 4 — of these sides 2 and 3 are seen on left and right sides respectively.

6. (*a*) : The given figure is same as layout 1. The top, left and right sides in figure option (a) are 1, 4 and 5 respectively (other combinations of sides for this figure are also possible); in figure option (b) 2, 1 and 5 respectively (other combination of sides for this figure are also possible; and in figure option (d) 1, 5 and 2 respectively (other combinations of sides for this figure are also possible).

7. (*a*) : The given figure is same as layout 4. In option figure (a) the top side 4 has side 3 on left and side 5 on right. In option figure (b) the top side 4 has side 6 on its left and side 3 on right.

Note : in option figure (c) the sides are correct but the printing of letter on right side is incorrect.

8. (*a*) : The given figure is same as layout 8. Option figures (b) and (d) contain the correct joints of side 6.

9. (*b*) : The given figure is same as layout 7. Option figures (a) and (c) contain the correct joints of side 6.

10. (*c*) : The given figure is same as layout 6. In option figure (a) the top side 4 has side 3 on left and side 5 on right. In option figure (c) the top side 2 has side 3 on left and side 4 on right.

11. (*d*) : The given figure is same as layout 1. None of the figure options can be made from the given figure.

12. (*b*) : The given figure is same as layout 3. In option figure (c) the top side 2 has side 1 on left and side 5 on right. In option figure (d) the top side 6 has side 2 on left and side 3 on right.

13. (*b*) : The given figure is same as layout 2. In option figure (a) the top side 2 has side 6 on left and side 1 on right. In option figure (b) the top side 4 has side 3 on left and side 5 on right.

CHAPTER 6

Pinch Hole/Paper Folding & Unfolding

These type of questions are based on a piece of paper which is folded and cut or punched in a particular manner. One of the option figures either resembles the pattern that would be formed when the paper is unfolded or resembles the form in which the paper is folded and cut or punched.

MULTIPLE CHOICE QUESTIONS

Directions (Qs. 1-5) : *In each one of the following problems, a square transparent sheet with a pattern is given. Figure out from amongst the four alternatives as to how the pattern would appear when the transparent sheet is folded at the dotted line.*

1. 

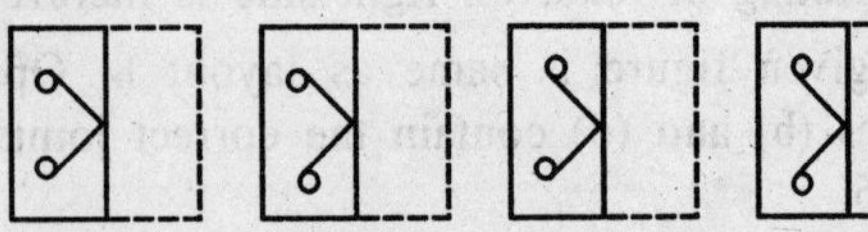

(a) (b) (c) (d)

2. 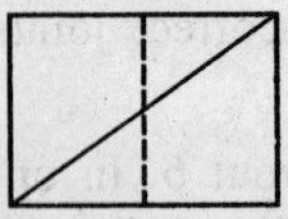

(a) (b) (c) (d)

3. 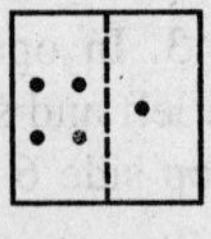

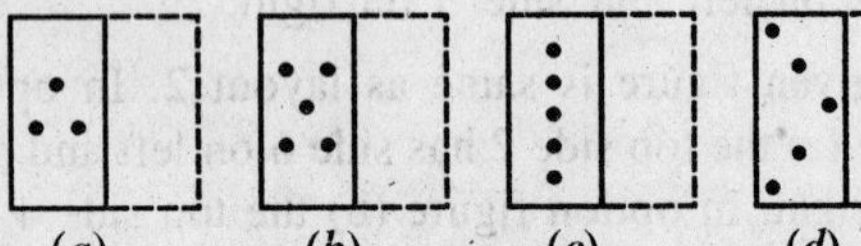

(a) (b) (c) (d)

4. 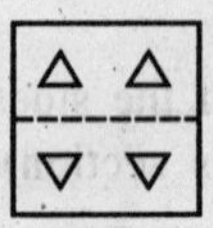

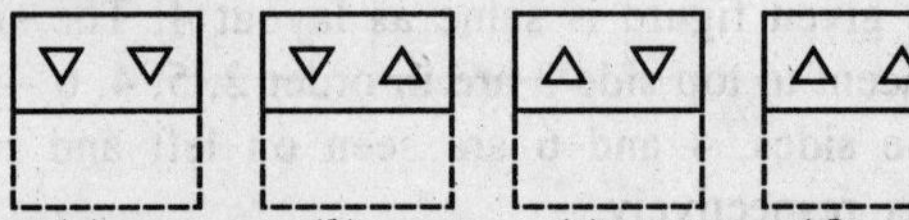

(a) (b) (c) (d)

5. 

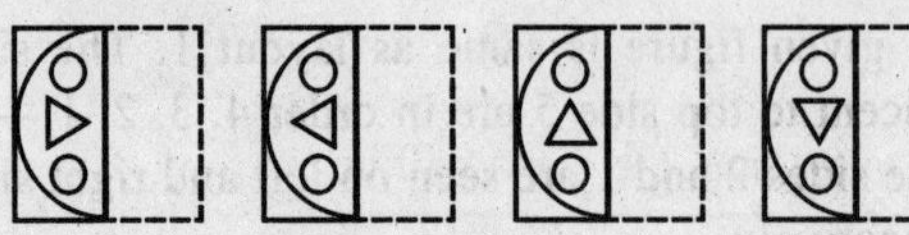

(a) (b) (c) (d)

Directions (Qs. 6-13) : *In each of the following questions a piece of paper has been folded and then punched. From the given options figure out the correct response which shows how it will appear when opened.*

6. 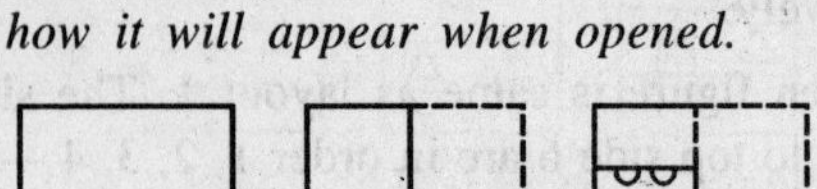

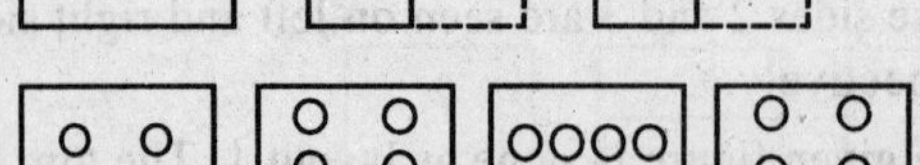

(a) (b) (c) (d)

7. 

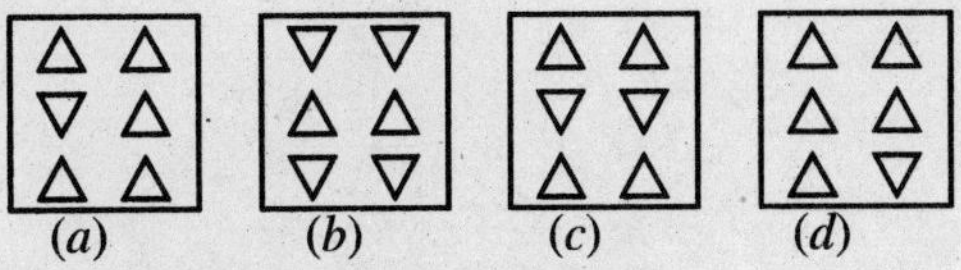

8.

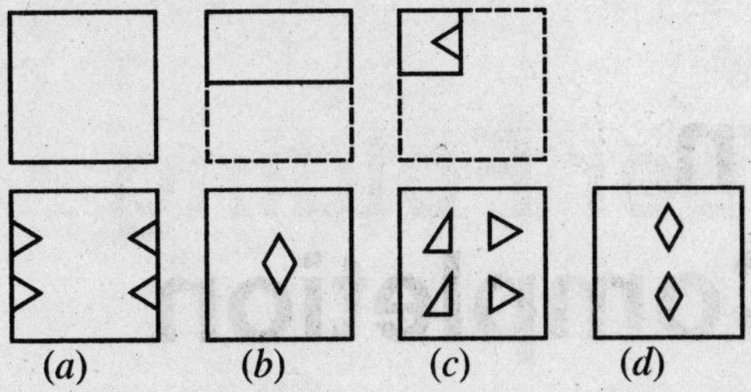

9.

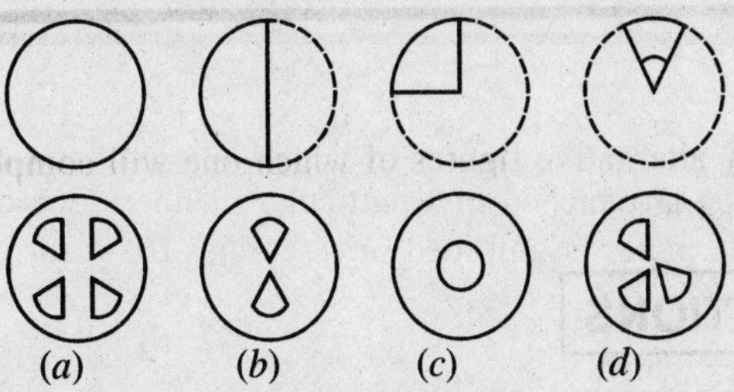

10.

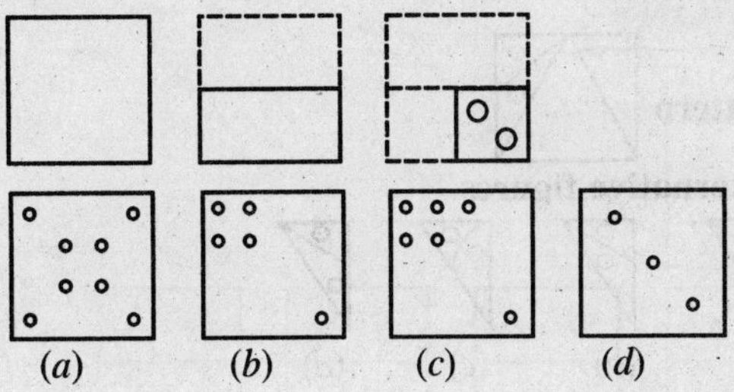

11.

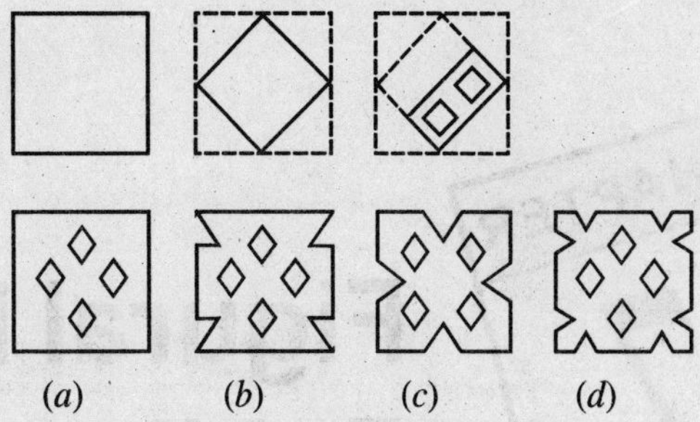

12.

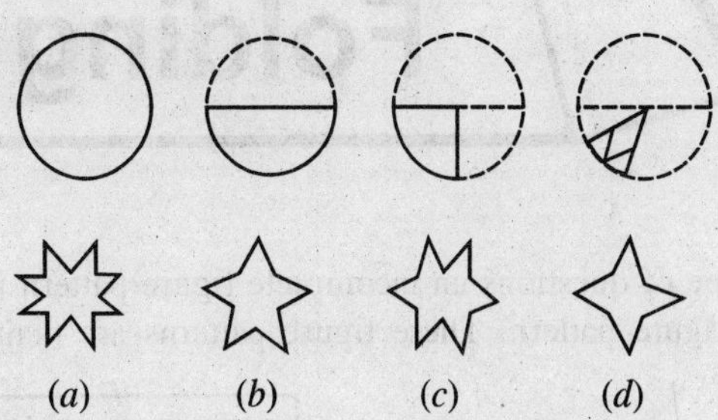

13.

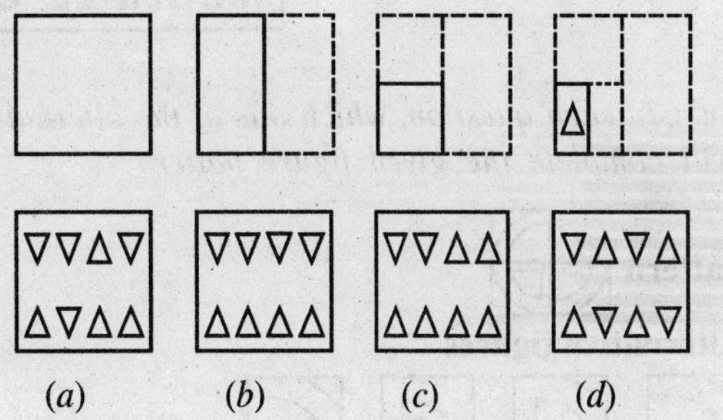

EXPLANATORY ANSWERS

1. (*d*) **2.** (*c*)

3. (*b*) **4.** (*d*)

5. (*b*)

6. (*c*) **:** When unfolding, the steps will be :

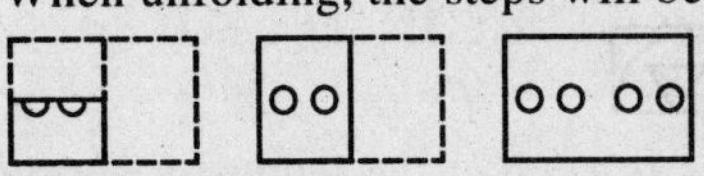

7. (*b*) **:** When unfolding, the steps will be :

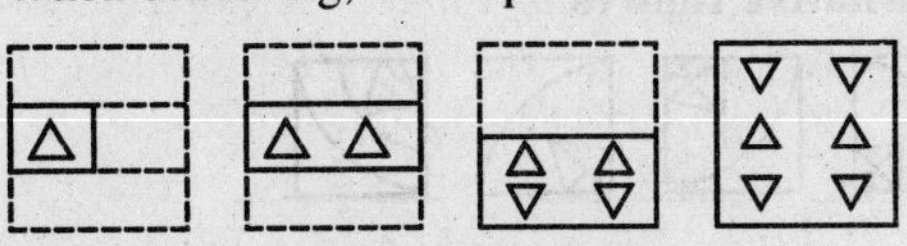

8. (*d*) **:** When unfolding, the steps will be :

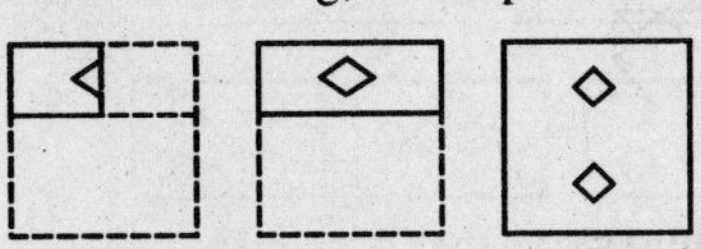

9. (*c*) **:** When unfolding, the steps will be :

10. (*a*) **:** When unfolding, the steps will be :

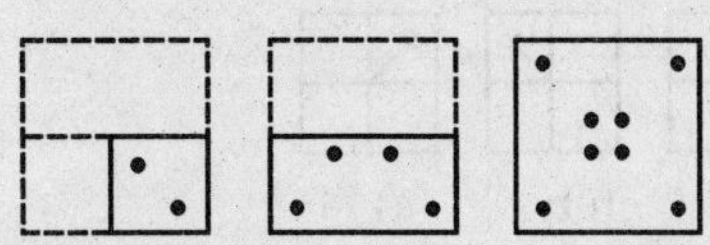

11. (*d*) **:** When unfolding, the steps will be :

12. (*a*) **:** When unfolding, the steps will be :

13. (*b*) **:** When unfolding, the steps will be :

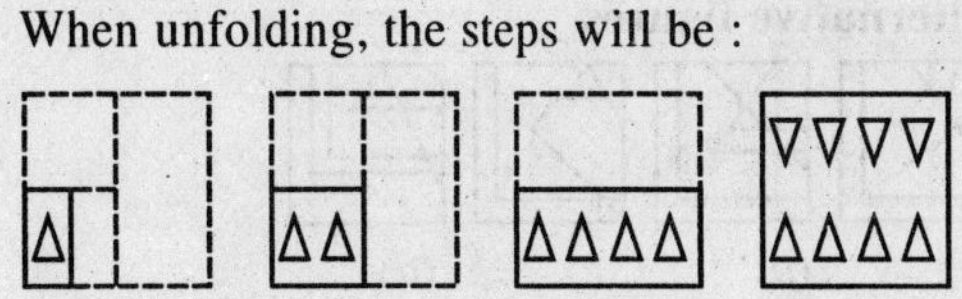

CHAPTER 7

Figural Pattern Folding and Completion

In these type of questions an incomplete figure pattern is given followed by alternative figures of which one will **complete** the given figure pattern. These figure patterns are mainly based on symmetries.

MULTIPLE CHOICE QUESTIONS

Directions : *In each question, which one of the alternative figures will complete the given figure pattern?*

1. Pattern 

Alternative figures

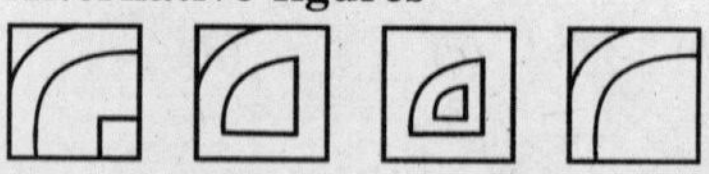

(*a*) (*b*) (*c*) (*d*)

2. Pattern 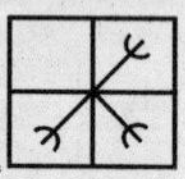

Alternative figures

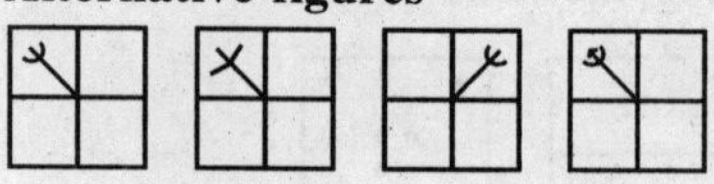

(*a*) (*b*) (*c*) (*d*)

3. Pattern 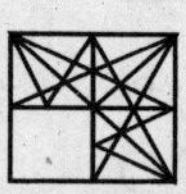

Alternative figures

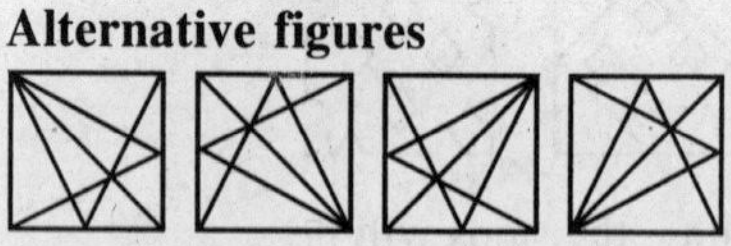

(*a*) (*b*) (*c*) (*d*)

4. Pattern 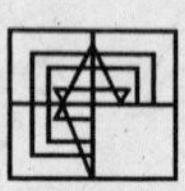

Alternative figures

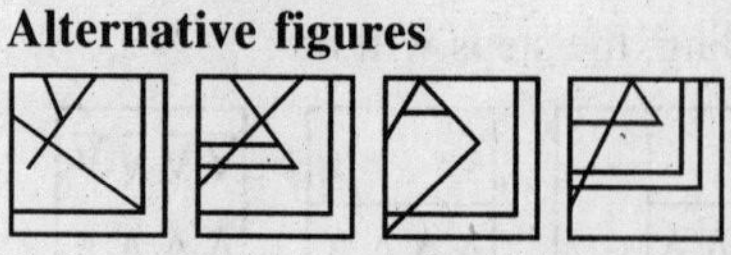

(*a*) (*b*) (*c*) (*d*)

5. Pattern 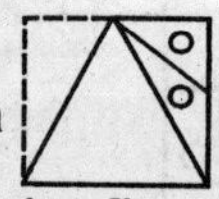

Alternative figures

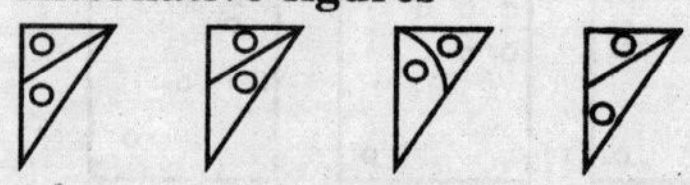

(*a*) (*b*) (*c*) (*d*)

6. Pattern 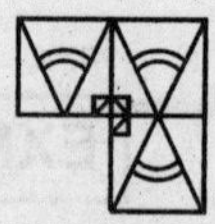

Alternative figures

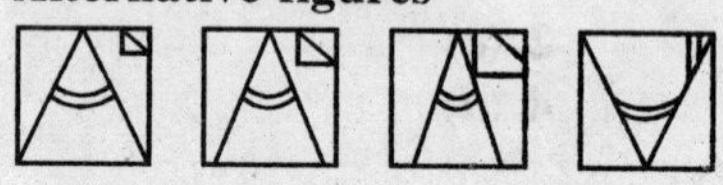

(*a*) (*b*) (*c*) (*d*)

7. Pattern 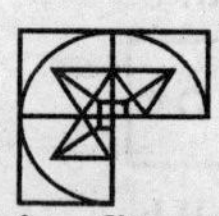

Alternative figures

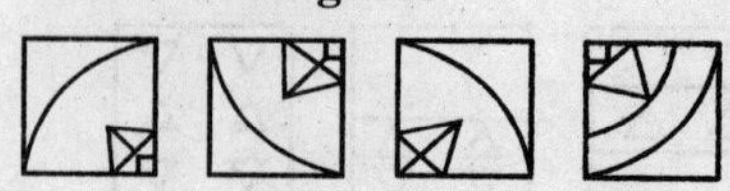

(*a*) (*b*) (*c*) (*d*)

8. Pattern 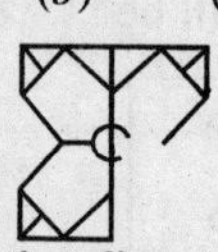

Alternative figures

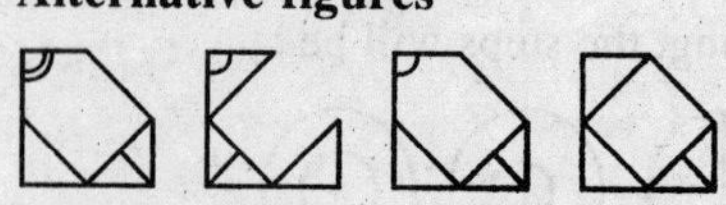

(*a*) (*b*) (*c*) (*d*)

9. Pattern 

Alternative figures

(*a*) (*b*) (*c*) (*d*)

10. Pattern 

Alternative figures

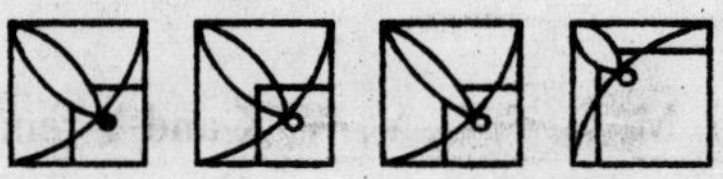

(*a*) (*b*) (*c*) (*d*)

11. Pattern 

Alternative figures

(*a*) (*b*) (*c*) (*d*)

12. Pattern 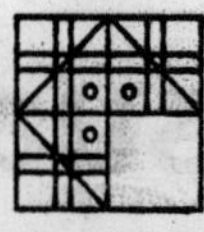

Alternative figures

(*a*) (*b*) (*c*) (*d*)

EXPLANATORY ANSWERS

All the completed figures will look like this:

1. (*b*) : 

2. (*a*) : 

3. (*d*) : 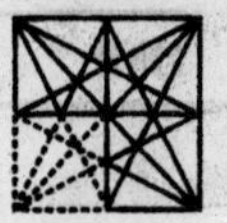

4. (*d*) : 

5. (*a*) : 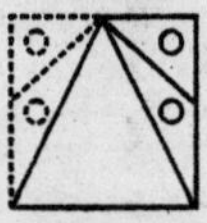

6. (*a*) : 

7. (*b*) : 

8. (*c*) : 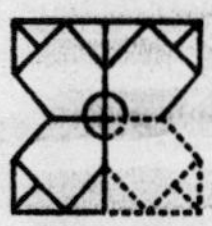

9. (*a*) : 

10. (*b*) : 

11. (*a*) : 

12. (*d*) : 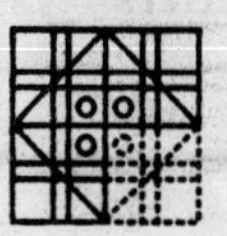

CHAPTER 8

Visual Memory

These type of problems are based on the mirror images or reflections of number, letters and figures. While attempting such questions one must be able to visualise clearly the questioned reflections, be they on vertical plane or on horizontal plane. Study the chart and information given below. The visualisation of letters and numbers is easier than the visualisation of figures for the simple reason that the figures have many forms and all cannot be summed up.

Horizontal Mirror Images (HMI) of Numbers

Number	*HMI*	*Number*	*HMI*
0	0	5	ƽ
1	I	6	ꝺ
2	ꙅ	7	⅂
3	Ɛ	8	8
4	ᔭ	9	ҽ

Note : HMI of 0 and 8 remain unchanged

Vertical Mirror Images (VMI) of Numbers

Numbers : 0 1 2 3 4 5 6 7 8 9

VMI : 0 I Ƨ Ɛ ߂ ટ ɘ ٢ 8 ɑ

Note : VMI of 0, 3 and 8 remain unchanged.

Exceptions in style need caution. Example 3 will be Ɛ, or 8 will be 8.

Horizontal Mirror Images of Capital Letters

Letter	HMI	Letter	HMI	H letter	HMI
A	A	J	ſ	S	Ƨ
B	ꓭ	K	ꓘ	T	T
C	Ɔ	L	⅃	U	U
D	ᗡ	M	M	V	V
E	Ǝ	N	И	W	W
F	ꟻ	O	O	X	X
G	Ꭾ	P	ꟼ	Y	Y
H	H	Q	Ϙ	Z	Ƹ
I	I	R	Я		

Note : HMI of A, H, I, M, O, T, U, V, W, X and Y remain unchanged.

Exceptions in style need caution. Example : A will be A, or X will be X.

Vertical Mirror Images of Capital Letters

Letters :	A	B	C	D	E	F	G	H	I	J	K	L	M
VMI :	∀	B	C	D	E	Ⅎ	⅁	H	I	ſ	K	⅂	W
Letters :	N	O	P	Q	R	S	T	U	V	W	X	Y	Z
VMI :	И	O	Ь	Ó	ꓤ	S	⊥	∩	Λ	M	X	⅄	Z

Note : VMI of C, D, E, H, I, K, O and X remain unchanged.

Horizontal Mirror Images of Small Letters

Letter	HMI	Letter	HMI	Letter	HMI
a	ɒ	j	į	s	ƨ
b	d	k	ʞ	t	ɟ
c	ɔ	l	l	u	u
d	b	m	m	v	v
e	ɘ	n	n	w	w
f	ʇ	o	o	x	x
g	ϱ	p	q	y	ʏ
h	ʜ	q	p	z	ƨ
i	i	r	ɿ		

Note : HMI of o, v, w and x remain unchanged.

Vertical Mirror Images of Small Letters

Letter :	a	b	c	d	e	f	g	h	i	j	k	l	m
VMI :	ɐ	p	c	q	ǝ	ɟ	ɓ	ɥ	!	ɾ	ʞ	l	ɯ
Letter :	n	o	p	q	r	s	t	u	v	w	x	y	z
VMI :	u	o	b	d	ɹ	s	ʇ	n	ʌ	ʍ	x	ʎ	z

Note : VMI of c, o and x remain unchanged. Letter l has exceptions: if it is a straight vertical line – l then it remains unchanged.

MULTIPLE CHOICE QUESTIONS

Directions (Qs. 1 to 15) : *In each question below which is the exact horizontal mirror image?*

1. DuST
(*a*) ꓕSuD (*b*) TSnD
(*c*) TSuD (*d*) ꓷuST

2. CHAIR
(*a*) ЯIHAƆ (*b*) ЯIAHƆ
(*c*) ЯIAHC (*d*) ƆHAIЯ

3. WHOM
(*a*) MOHW (*b*) WOHM
(*c*) MHOW (*d*) MOHW

4. plaque
(*a*) ǝnbɐlq (*b*) ǝnbqlp
(*c*) qlapue (*d*) ǝnbɐlp

5. brows
(*a*) dɹows (*b*) drows
(*c*) swoɹd (*d*) swoɹd

6. flying
(*a*) ƃniylf (*b*) gnilyf
(*c*) gniylf (*d*) gniylf

7. 4379
(*a*) 9734 (*b*) 9734
(*c*) 9734 (*d*) 9734

8. 57182
(*a*) 28175 (*b*) 28175
(*c*) 28175 (*d*) 28175

9. 69430
(*a*) 03496 (*b*) 03496
(*c*) 03496 (*d*) 03496

10. 2JKS
(*a*) SKJ2 (*b*) SKJ2
(*c*) SKJ2 (*d*) SKJ2

11. P9Yf3
(*a*) 3fY9P (*b*) 3fY9P
(*c*) 3fY9P (*d*) 3fY9P

12. GZ5QRh
(*a*) hRQ5ZG (*b*) hRQ5ZG
(*c*) hRQ5ZG (*d*) hRQ5ZG

13. 2$%CH
(*a*) HC%$2 (*b*) HC%$2
(*c*) HC%$2 (*d*) HC%$2

14. 7↑FN8
(*a*) 8NF↑7 (*b*) 8NF↑7
(*c*) 8NF↑7 (*d*) 8NF↑7

15. yk19G
(*a*) G91ky (*b*) G91ky
(*c*) G91ky (*d*) G91ky

ANSWERS

1	2	3	4	5	6	7	8	9	10
(*c*)	(*b*)	(*a*)	(*a*)	(*c*)	(*d*)	(*b*)	(*a*)	(*d*)	(*c*)
11	**12**	**13**	**14**	**15**					
(*d*)	(*b*)	(*c*)	(*a*)	(*d*)					

CHAPTER 9

Discrimination

In these problems one has to count the geometrical figures in a given complex figure. A little bit of systematic approach is needed to get the correct number of the asked figure. The shapes of all geometrical figures must be clear in mind.

SOLVED EXAMPLES

1. How many straight lines are used to make the figure given below?

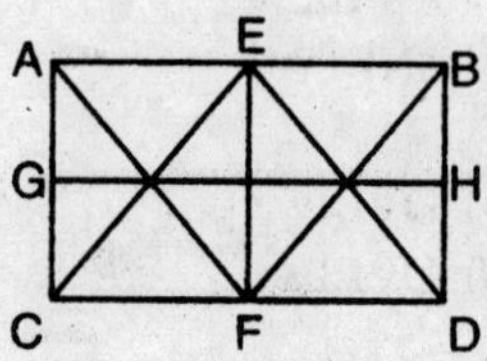

(*a*) 8 (*b*) 6
(*c*) 10 (*d*) 12

Answer (*c*) : The method of counting is given below.

The horizontal lines are AB, GH and CD i.e. – 3 lines, the vertical lines are AC, EF and BD i.e. – 3 lines, the diagonal lines are CE, FB, AF and ED i.e. – 4 lines, therefore the total number of straight lines is

3 + 3 + 4 = 10

2. How many square are there is this figure?

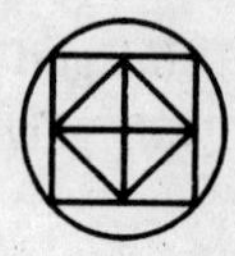

(*a*) 4 (*b*) 6
(*c*) 8 (*d*) 5

Answer (*b*) : The squares are counted in this manner.

There is one main square ABCD divided into four parts by lines EF and GH. So, all the 5 squares are ABCD, AEGI, GICF, EBIH and IHFD. The square in the middle is EGHF. The total number of squares are 5 + 1 = 6

MULTIPLE CHOICE QUESTIONS

1. How many triangles are there in the figure given below?

(*a*) 24 (*b*) 27
(*c*) 25 (*d*) 26

2. How many parallelograms are there in this figure?

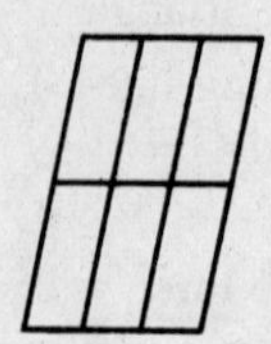

(*a*) 9 (*b*) 13
(*c*) 15 (*d*) 18

3. How many triangles are there in this figure?

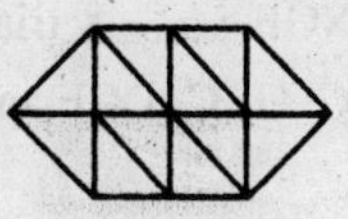

(*a*) 16 (*b*) 17
(*c*) 18 (*d*) 19

4. The number of rectangles in this figure are.

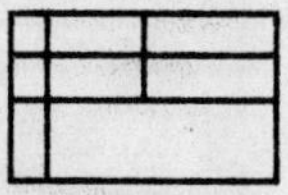

(*a*) 21 (*b*) 24
(*c*) 23 (*d*) 25

5. How many squares are hidden in this figure?

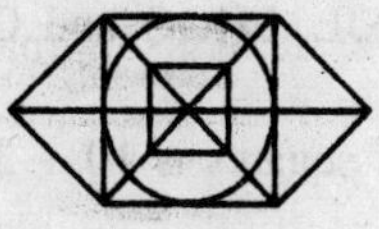

(*a*) 7 (*b*) 8
(*c*) 9 (*d*) 10

6. The number of triangles in this figure are.

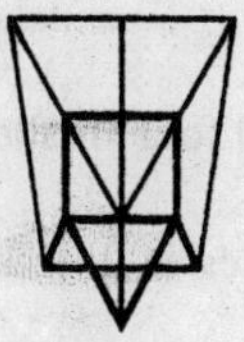

(*a*) 19 (*b*) 16
(*c*) 21 (*d*) 15

7. How many squares are there in the figure given below?

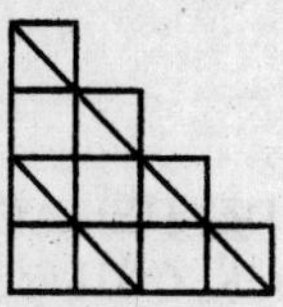

(*a*) 10 (*b*) 11
(*c*) 13 (*d*) 14

8. The number of circles in this figure is

(*a*) 6 (*b*) 5
(*c*) 2 (*d*) 3

9. How many triangles are there in the figure given below?

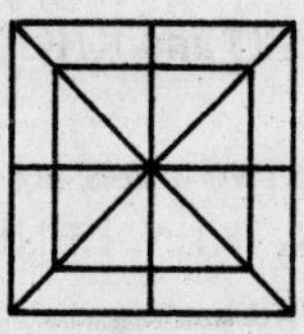

(*a*) 28 (*b*) 36
(*c*) 24 (*d*) 32

10. How many straight lines are needed to draw the figure in question 9?

(*a*) 10 (*b*) 12
(*c*) 11 (*d*) 13

EXPLANATORY ANSWERS

1. (*a*) :

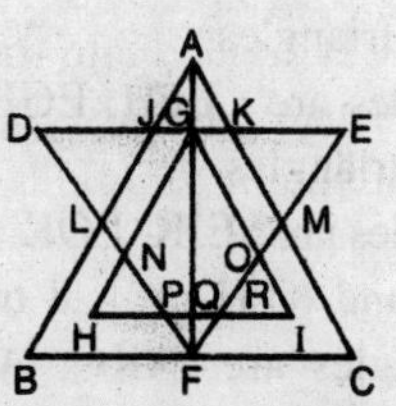

- The main triangles making the figure are ABC, DEF and GHI *i.e.*, – 3 triangles
- The simplest triangles are AJG, AGK, KEM, DJL, NHP, PQF, QFR and ORI *i.e.*, – 8 triangles
- The triangles formed by the bisecting line AF are ABF, AFC, GHQ, GQI, DGF and GFE *i.e.*, – 6 triangles
- The triangles formed inbetween the three triangles AJK, ALF, AMF, DGN, DGF, LBF, MFC, GEO, GNF and GOF – *i.e.*, 10 triangles
- So, the total number of triangles is
  3 + 8 + 6 + 10 = 27

2. (*d*) :

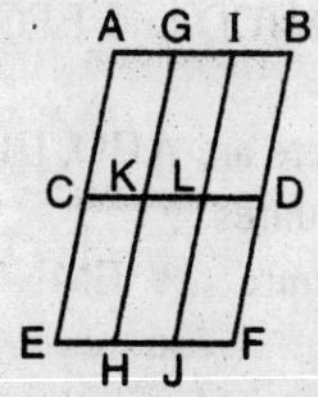

- The main parallelogram is ABEF *i.e.*, 1 parallelogram
- When divided into half by line CD the main figure has ABCD and CDEF *i.e.*, 2 parallelograms
- When further lines GH and IJ are drawn, the parallelograms are AGEH, GIJH and IBJF *i.e.*, – 3 parallelograms.
- The simplest parallelogram are AGCK, CKEH, GIKL, KLHJ, IBLD and LDJF *i.e.* – 6 parallelograms
  Other parallelograms are AICL, CLEJ, GBKD, KDHF, AIEJ and GBHF – *i.e.*, 6 parallelograms
  So, the total number of parallelograms is
  1 + 2 + 3 + 6 + 6 = 18

3. (*a*) :

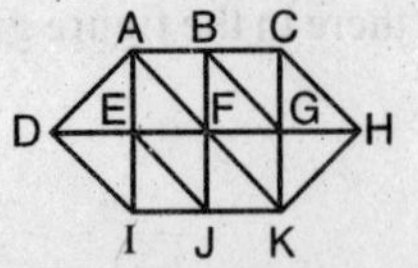

The simplest triangles are ADE, DEI, AEF, ABF, EIJ, EFJ, BFG, BCG, FJK, FGK, CGH and GHK – *i.e.,* – 12 triangles

The bisected triangles are ADI and CHK – *i.e.* – 2 triangles

Other triangles are AIK and ACK *i.e.,* – 2 triangles

So, the total number of triangles is

12 + 2 + 2 = 16

4. (*c*) :

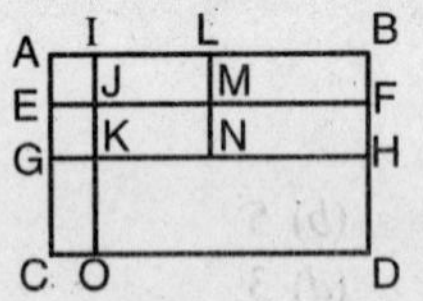

The main rectangle is ABCD – *i.e.,* – 1 rectangle

The simplest rectangles are AIEJ, ILJM, LBMF, EJGK, JMKN, MFNH, GKCO and KHOD *i.e.* – 8 rectangles.

The rectangles which have two parts are ALEM, IBJF, EMGN, JFKH, AIGK, IKLN, LBNH, EJCO and GHCD *i.e.* – 9 rectangles.

The rectangles which have three parts are AICO, ABEF and EFGH *i.e.* – 3 rectangles

The rectangles which have four parts are ALGN and IBKH *i.e.* – 2 rectangles

So, the total number of rectangles

1 + 8 + 9 + 3 + 2 = 23

5. (*d*) :

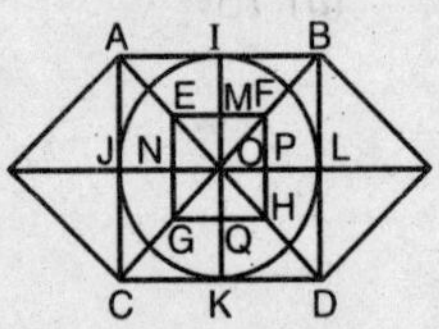

The main squares are ABCD and EFGH *i.e.,* – 2 squares

The simplest outer squares are AIJO, IBOL, JOCK and OLKD *i.e.,* – 4 squares

The simplest inner square are EMNO, NOGQ, MFOP and OPQH *i.e.,* – 4 squares

There are no other squares formed in the figure

So, the total number of squares is

2 + 4 + 4 = 10

6. (*b*) :

The main triangles are : ABC, DEF, LNF, and HJC *i.e.* 4 triangles

The simplest triangles are : HIC, IJC, HDC, JCE, DKL, LMF, MFN and NOE *i.e.* – 8 triangles

Other triangles are : AGC, GBC, DCF and CEF – *i.e.* 4 triangles

So, the total number of triangles is 4 + 8 + 4 = 16

7. (*c*) :

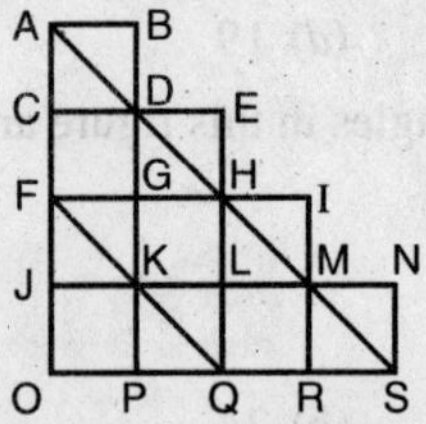

The simplest squares are : ABCD, CDFG, DEGH, FGJK, GHKL, HILM, JKOP, KLPQ, LMQR and MNRS *i.e.* – 10 squares.

Other squares are : CEJL, FHOQ and GIPR *i.e.* – 3 squares

So, the total number of squares is 10 + 3 = 13

8. (*a*) :

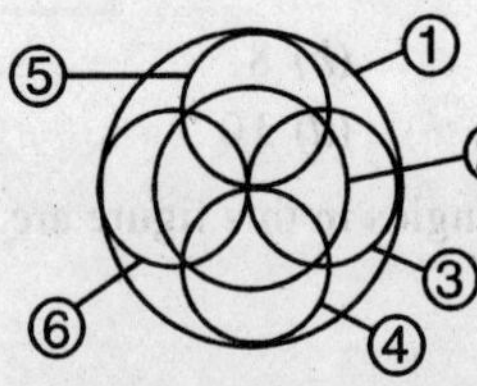

There are two main circles and four smaller circles intersecting each other.

So, the total number of circles is 2 + 4 = 6

9. (*d*) :

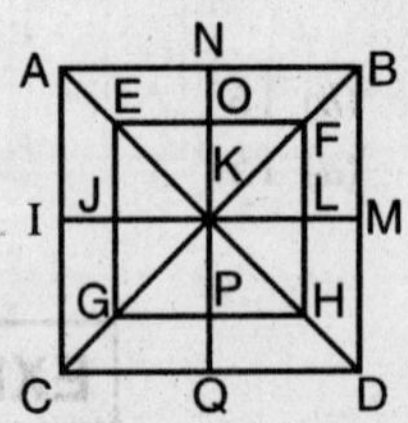

The larger triangles are : ABC, BCD, ABD and ACD *i.e.* – 4 triangles

The smaller triangles are : EFH, EGH, EFG and FGH *i.e.* – 4 triangles.

The simplest triangles are : EJK, EOK, OFK, JKG, FKL, KLH, KGP and KPH *i.e.* – 8 triangles

The bisected triangles are: AKC, ABK, CKD, KBD, EKG, EKF, KHG, KHF, i.e., –8 triangle.

Other triangles are : ANK, NKB, KBM, KMD, KQD, KQC, KCI, IKA *i.e.* – 8 triangles.

So, the total number of triangles is

4 + 4 + 8 + 8 + 8 = 32

10. (*b*) : The horizontal lines are : AB, EF, KL, GH and CD *i.e.* – 5 lines.

The vertical lines are AC, EG, IJ, FH and BD *i.e.* – 5 lines.

The diagonal lines are : AD and BC *i.e.* – 2 lines.

So, the total number of lines used to draw this figure is 5 + 5 + 2 = 12

CHAPTER 10

Embedded Figures

In these type of questions a figure form is given followed by alternative figures. In one of these figure options the given form is embedded. Practice of visualisation comes handy in attempting such easy questions.

MULTIPLE CHOICE QUESTIONS

Directions (Qs. 1 to 6) : *In the questions given below a figure is given. From the given alternatives select the one in which the given figure is embedded.*

1. 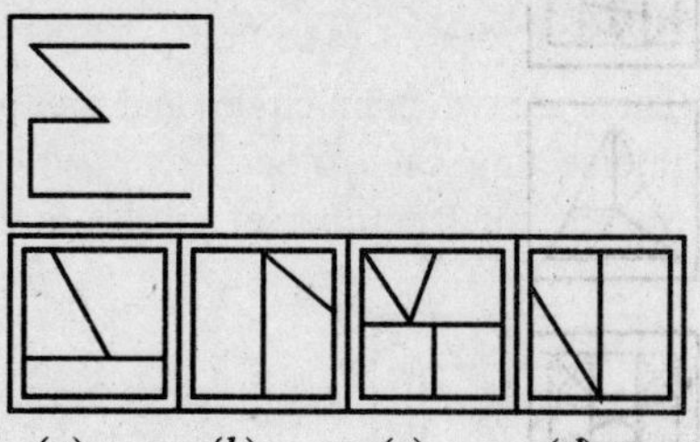

(a) (b) (c) (d)

2. 

(a) (b) (c) (d)

3. 

(a) (b) (c) (d)

4. 

(a) (b) (c) (d)

5. 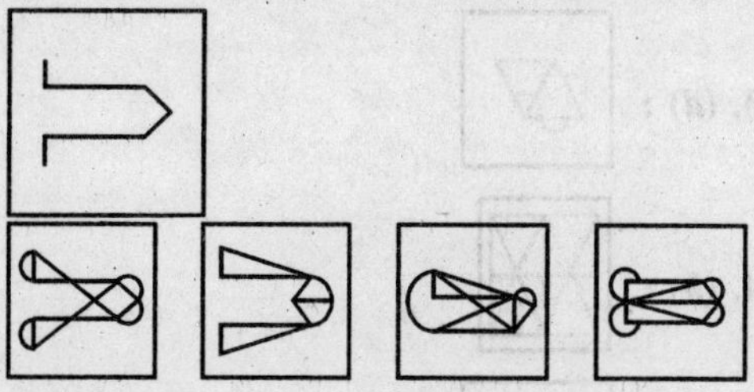

(a) (b) (c) (d)

6. 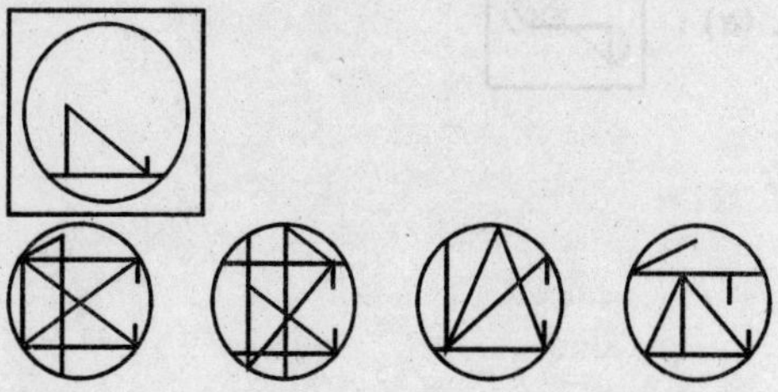

(a) (b) (c) (d)

Directions (Qs. 7 to 10) : *In each question given below find the figure form which is embedded in the given pattern.*

7. 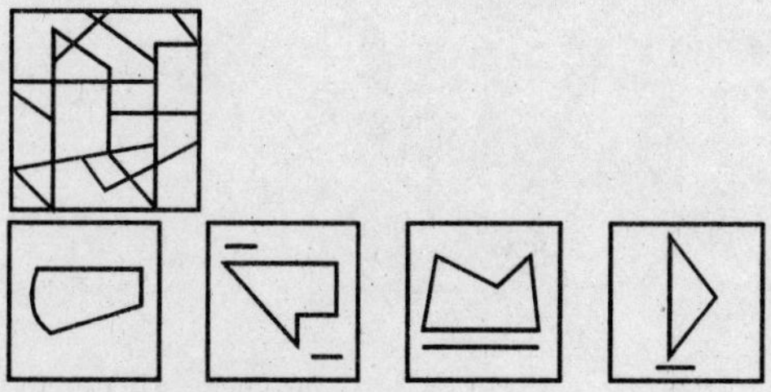

(a) (b) (c) (d)

8. 

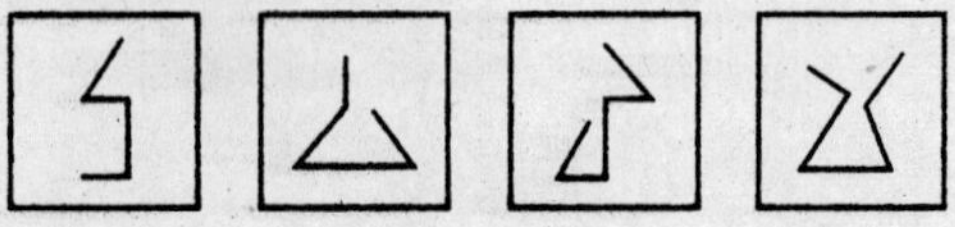

(a) (b) (c) (d)

9. 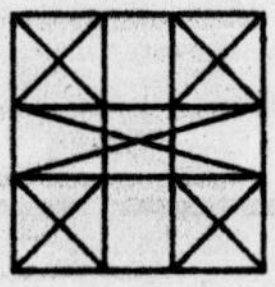

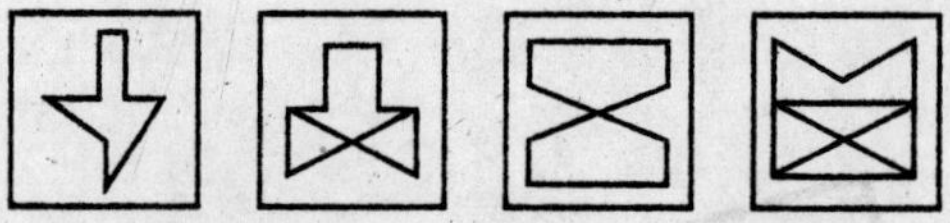

(a) (b) (c) (d)

10. 

(a) (b) (c) (d)

EXPLANATORY ANSWERS

1. (a) : 

2. (a) : 

3. (d) : 

4. (b) : 

5. (a) : 

6. (b) : 

7. (d) : 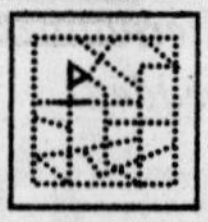

8. (b) : 

9. (c) : 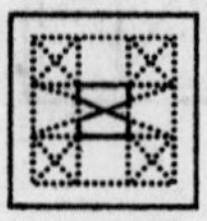

10. (d) : 

2008

QUANTITATIVE APTITUDE

CHAPTER 1

Numbers System

Whole Numbers

In our System of numeration, numbers are written by using the symbols 0, 1, 2, 3, 4, 5, 6, 7, 8 and 9 with each symbol getting a value depending on the place it occupies. These symbols are called digits. A number related to the objects in a collection gives an idea of how many objects are there in the collection.

The number 789345126 can be represented as:

Ten crores	Crores	Ten Lacs (Millions)	Lacs	Ten Thousands	Thousands	Hundreds	Tens	Units
10^8	10^7	10^6	10^5	10^4	10^3	10^2	10^1	10^0
7	8	9	3	4	5	1	2	6

This number can be read as: "Seventy-eight crores, ninety-three lacs, forty-five thousands, one hundred twenty six".

1. **Natural Numbers or Positive Integers (N = 1, 2, 3, 4, 5 .....):** These are also called counting numbers. When two natural numbers are added or multiplied together, the result is always a natural number. Therefore, all positive integers, used for counting objects, are always **natural numbers** whereas zero together with negative integers and fractional numbers are not natural numbers.
2. **Whole Numbers: (W = 0, 1, 2, 3, 4, 5, ...):** The number '0' together with the natural numbers gives us the numbers which are called **whole numbers,** e.g., 0, 1, 2, 3, 4 ..... etc. whereas –10, –15, –12 ..... or $\frac{1}{5}, \frac{2}{9}, \frac{4}{5}$..... etc. are not whole numbers.
3. **Integers: (I = ..., –5, –4, –3, –2, –1, 0, 1, 2, 3, 4, 5, ...):** The negative numbers together with the whole numbers are called integers. The numbers –1, –2, –3, –4, –5, ... are called negative integers and 1, 2, 3, 4, 5, ..., *i.e.,* natural numbers are called positive integers. The number 0 is simply an integer, *i.e.,* it is neither positive nor negative.
4. **Rational Numbers:** A rational number is a number that can be put in the form $\frac{p}{q}$ where *p* and *q* are both integers and $q \neq 0$, e.g., 8, $-\frac{7}{5}$, $-\frac{3}{4}$, $\frac{1}{7}$, 0 .... are all rational numbers i.e. a rational number may be positive, zero or negative.
5. **Irrational Numbers:** An irrational number is a number that can not be put in the form $\frac{p}{q}$ where *p* and *q* are both integers and $q \neq 0$, e.g., $\sqrt{5}, \sqrt{11}, \sqrt{15}$, $3 + \sqrt{5}$ .... etc. are all irrational numbers.
6. **Real Numbers:** All those numbers which are either rational or irrational, are called real numbers, e.g., $\frac{11}{17}$, $\frac{19}{21}$, $-\frac{7}{8}$, $\sqrt{7}$, $8 + \sqrt{3}$ etc. are real numbers.
7. **Even Numbers:** All those numbers which are exactly divisible by 2, are called 'even numbers', e.g., 2, 8, 14, 28, 52 etc. are even numbers.
8. **Odd Numbers:** All those numbers which are not exactly divisible by 2, are called 'odd numbers', e.g., 1, 3, 5, 7, 9, 19 etc. are odd numbers.

9. **Composite Numbers:** The numbers which are divisible not only by 1 or themselves, but by some other numbers also, are called the 'composite numbers'. In other words, the numbers which have more than two factors are called 'composite numbers.', e.g., 4, 9, 15, 18, 27, ... etc. are composite numbers.

10. **Prime Numbers:** The numbers which have only two factors, 1 and the number itself are called 'prime numbers', e.g., 2, 5, 11, 19, 23, 31, ... etc. are prime numbers.

11. **Co-primes:** Two numbers which have only 1 as the common factor are called 'co-primes'. 5 and 7 are co-primes. So are 15 and 16.

12. **Twin Primes:** Two prime numbers which differ by 2, are called 'twin primes', e.g., 3, 5; 5, 7; 11, 13; 71, 73 are some pairs of twin primes.

13. **Consecutive Numbers:** The numbers which are following or coming after other numbers in regular order, are called consecutive numbers. 4, 6, 8, 10 are consecutive even numbers and 9, 11, 13, 15 are consecutive odd numbers. 3, 4, 5, 6, 7 ..... etc. are consecutive numbers in the natural order of the number series.

TESTS FOR DIVISIBILITY OF NUMBERS

1. **Divisibility by 2:** A number is divisible by 2, if its units digit is 0, 2, 4, 6 or 8. For example, each of the numbers 130, 244, 566, 278, ... etc. is divisible by 2.

2. **Divisibility by 3:** A number is divisible by 3, if the sum of its digits is a multiple of 3. For example, each of the numbers 312, 213, 456 is divisible by 3 since sum of digits in each of these numbers is (3 + 1 + 2 = 6), (2 + 1 + 3 = 6) and (4 + 5 + 6 = 15) respectively, each of which is a multiple of 3.

3. **Divisibility by 4:** A number is divisible by 4, if the number formed by its digits in ten's and unit's places is divisible by 4. For example, numbers formed by ten's and unit's digits of 1132, 1312, 1400 and 1348 are 32, 12, 00 and 48 respectively which are divisible by 4. Hence, these numbers also are divisible by 4.

4. **Divisibility by 5:** A number is divisible by 5, if its unit's digit is either 0 or 5. For example, each of the numbers 100, 205, 315, 435 is divisible by 5 since unit's digit in each of these numbers is either 0 or 5.

5. **Divisibility by 6:** A number is divisible by 6, if it is divisible by both 2 and 3.

6. **Divisiblity by 8:** A number is divisible by 8, if the number formed by its digits in hundred's, ten's and unit's places is divisible by 8. For example, numbers formed by hundred's, ten's and unit's digits of 1864, 1024, 2008 and 5000 are 864, 024, 008 and 000 respectively which are divisible by 8. Hence, these numbers also are divisible by 8.

7. **Divisibility by 9:** A number is divisible by 9, if the sum of its digits is a multiple of 9. For example, each of the numbers 23409, 454554, 66636 is divisible by 9 since sum of digits in each of these numbers is (2 + 3 + 4 + 0 + 9 = 18), (4 + 5 + 4 + 5 + 5 + 4 = 27) and (6 + 6 + 6 + 3 + 6 = 27) respectively, each of which is a multiple of 9.

8. **Divisibility by 10:** A number is divisible by 10, if its unit's digit is zero. For example, each of the numbers 50, 80, 1310, 1400 is divisible by 10 since unit's digit in each of these numbers is 0.

9. **Divisibility by 11:** A number is divisible by 11, if the difference of the sum of its digits in even places and the sum of its digits in odd places (starting from unit's place) is either 0 or a multiple of 11. For example, each of the numbers 909183, 540045 and 184712 is divisible by 11 since in each of the numbers difference of the sum of digits in even places and sum of the digits in odd places is [(9 + 9 + 8) – (0 + 1 + 3) = 22], [(5 + 0 + 4) – (4 + 0 + 5) = 0] and [(8 + 7 + 2) – (1 + 4 + 1) = 11] respectively, each of which is either '0' or a multiple of '11'.

10. **Divisibility by 12:** A number is divisible by 12, if it is divisible by 3 and 4 both.

    For example, take a number 769824

    (*i*) Sum of digits = 7 + 6 + 9 + 8 + 2 + 4 = 36, it is divisible by 3.

    (*ii*) The number has 24 as its last two digits, which is divisible by 4.

    Hence, 769824 is divisible by 3 and 4 both, so it is divisible by 12.

11. **Divisibility by 14:** A number is divisible by 14, if it is divisible by 2 and 7 both.

12. **Divisibility by 15:** A number is divisible by 15, if it is divisible by 3 and 5 both.

13. **Divisibility by 16:** A number is divisible by 16, if the number formed by its last four digits is divisible by 16.

    For example, take a number 9877856, the number formed by its last four digits is 7856, which is divisible by 16. Hence, the number 9877856 is divisible by 16.

14. **Divisibility by 24:** A number is divisible by 24, if it is divisible by 3 and 8 both.

15. **Divisibility by 40:** A number is divisible by 40, if it is divisible by 5 and 8 both.

16. **Divisibility by 80:** A number is divisible by 80, if it is divisible by 5 and 16 both.

[**Note:** If a number is divisible by two co-primes separately, then the number will be also divisible by the product of co-primes.]

EXERCISE

1. The difference between the squares of two consecutive numbers is 25. The numbers are—
A. 11, 12 B. 12, 13
C. 15, 14 D. 14, 13

2. The sum of two digits of a number is 15. If 9 is added to the number, the digits are reversed. The number is—
A. 78 B. 87
C. 69 D. 96

3. A number which when multiplied by 11 is as much above 180 as it was originally below it. The number is—
A. 25 B. 30
C. 40 D. 45

4. Divide ₹ 53 among X, Y, Z so that X may receive ₹ 7 more than Y, and Y may receive ₹ 8 more than Z.
A. 10, 15, 18 B. 18, 10, 25
C. 20, 12, 27 D. 25, 18, 10

5. If $a = 16$ and $b = 15$, then what is the value of $\frac{a^2+b^2+ab}{a^3-b^3} = ?$
A. $\frac{1}{2}$ B. $\frac{1}{3}$
C. 1 D. 2

6. Find the number which when multiplied by 16 is increased by 225.
A. 13 B. 14
C. 15 D. 16

7. What is the largest number of four digits which is exactly divisible by 88?
A. 9999 B. 9988
C. 9944 D. 9998

8. If $\frac{a}{b} = \frac{4}{3}$, then $\frac{3a+2b}{3a-2b} = ?$
A. 2 B. 3
C. 4 D. 5

9. If $\frac{x}{y} = \frac{3}{4}$, then the value of $\frac{6}{7}+\frac{y-x}{y+x} = ?$
A. 1 B. 2
C. 3 D. 4

10. If the number $(10^n - 1)$ is divisible by 11, then n is—
A. odd number B. even number
C. any number D. multiple of 11

11. $\left(1-\frac{1}{3}\right)\left(1-\frac{1}{4}\right)\left(1-\frac{1}{5}\right)...\left(1-\frac{1}{n}\right) = ?$
A. $\frac{42}{29}$ B. $\frac{n-1}{n}$
C. $\frac{2}{n}$ D. 0

12. $\left(2-\frac{1}{3}\right)\left(2-\frac{3}{5}\right)\left(2-\frac{5}{7}\right)...\left(2-\frac{997}{999}\right) = ?$
A. $\frac{997}{999}$ B. ∞
C. $\frac{997}{3}$ D. $\frac{1001}{3}$

13. Divide 48 into two parts such that 7 times the first par added to 5 times the second part is 246. Find the first part.
A. 2 B. 3
C. 4 D. 5

14. The sum of a number and its reciprocal is thrice the difference of the number and its reciprocal. Find the number.
A. $\sqrt{2}$ B. $\sqrt{3}$
C. $\sqrt{5}$ D. $\sqrt{7}$

15. What should be added to the product of four consecutive odd numbers to make it a perfect square?
A. 13 B. 14
C. 15 D. 16

16. A boy was asked to find $\frac{7}{9}$ of a fraction. He made a mistake of dividing the fraction by $\frac{7}{9}$ and so got an answer which exceeded the correct answer by $\frac{8}{21}$. Find the correct answer.
A. 2/3 B. 5/7
C. 7/12 D. 7/15

17. If 40% of a number is 360, what will be 15% of 15% of that number?
A. 11.5 B. 20.25
C. 15.5 D. 21.75

18. The sum of two numbers is 25 and the difference of their square is 75. Find the difference between the numbers.
A. 2 B. 3
C. 4 D. 5

19. Ram eats 8 bananas in the morning, 5 in the afternoon and 2 in the evening. How many dozens of bananas does he eat in a day.
A. $1\frac{1}{4}$ B. $\frac{1}{4}$
C. $\frac{3}{13}$ D. $14\frac{17}{30}$

20. $47^{7.5} \div 47^{\frac{3}{2}} \times 47^{-3} = \left(\sqrt{47}\right)^{?}$ What should come in place of the question mark (?) in the following equation?
A. 5 B. 6
C. 7 D. 8

ANSWERS

1	2	3	4	5	6	7	8	9	10
B	A	B	B	C	C	C	B	A	B
11	**12**	**13**	**14**	**15**	**16**	**17**	**18**	**19**	**20**
C	D	B	A	D	C	B	B	A	B

EXPLANATORY ANSWERS

1. Let the numbers are x and $(x + 1)$

$\therefore \quad (x+1)^2 - x^2 = 25$

$\Rightarrow \quad x^2 + 1 + 2x - x^2 = 25$

$\Rightarrow \quad 2x + 1 = 25$

$\Rightarrow \quad 2x = 25 - 1 = 24$

$\therefore \quad x = \frac{24}{2} = 12$

$\therefore \quad x + 1 = 12 + 1 = 13$

Hence, the numbers are 12, 13.

2. Let x be the digit in units place. Digit in ten's place is then $15 - x$.

$\therefore$ The number $= 10(15 - x) + x$

The new number with reverse digits

$= 10 \times x + (15 - x)$

$\therefore \quad 10(15 - x) + x + 9 = 10x + 15 - x$

$\Rightarrow \quad 150 - 10x + x + 9 = 9x + 15$

$\Rightarrow \quad 18x = 144$

$x = \frac{144}{18} = 8$

The digit of ten's place $= 15 - 8 = 7$

$\therefore$ The required number = 78.

3. Let the number is x

$\therefore \quad 180 - x = 11x - 180$

$\Rightarrow \quad 180 + 180 = 11x + x$

$\Rightarrow \quad 360 = 12x,$

$\Rightarrow \quad x = \frac{360}{12} = 30.$

4. Let Y receives ₹ a. Then X receives ₹ $(a + 7)$ and Z receives ₹ $(a - 8)$

But, $a + 7 + a + a - 8 =$ ₹ 53

$\Rightarrow \quad 3a - 1 = 53,$

$\Rightarrow \quad 3a = 53 + 1$

$\Rightarrow \quad 3a = 54,$

$\therefore \quad a = \frac{54}{3} =$ ₹ 18. = Y's share

X's share $= a + 7 = 18 + 7 =$ ₹ 25

Z's share $= a - 8 = 18 - 8 =$ ₹ 10.

5. Given $a = 16$ and $b = 15$, then $\frac{a^2+b^2+ab}{a^3-b^3}$

$= \frac{a^2+b^2+ab}{(a-b)(a^2+b^2+ab)} = \frac{1}{a-b} = \frac{1}{16-15} = 1$

6. Let the required no. $= x$

then, $\quad 16x - x = 225$

$\Rightarrow \quad 15x = 225 \therefore x = 15$

7. The greatest no. of 4 digit = 9999

Now, after dividing 9999 by 88, we get Remainder = 55

Hence, the largest 4 digit no. = 9999 – 55 = 9944

8. $\frac{3a+2b}{3a-2b} = \frac{3\frac{a}{b}+2}{3\frac{a}{b}-2} = \frac{3\times\frac{4}{3}+2}{3\times\frac{4}{3}-2} = \frac{6}{2} = 3$

9. $\frac{6}{7}+\frac{y-x}{y+x} = \frac{6}{7}+\frac{1-x/y}{1+x/y} = \frac{6}{7}+\frac{1-3/4}{1+3/4} = \frac{6}{7}+\frac{1}{7} = 1$

10. n is even number.

11. $\frac{2}{3}\times\frac{3}{4}\times\frac{4}{5}\times\ldots\times\frac{n-1}{n} = \frac{2}{n}$

12. $\frac{5}{3}\times\frac{7}{5}\times\frac{9}{7}\times\ldots\times\frac{1001}{999} = \frac{1001}{3}$

13. Let the first part $= x$

then 2nd part $= (48 - x)$

By question, $\quad 7x + 5(48 - x) = 246$

$\Rightarrow \quad 2x = 246 - 240 \therefore x = 3$

14. Let the no. $= x$

then its reciprocal $= \frac{1}{x}$

By the question, $\left(x+\frac{1}{x}\right) = 3\left(x-\frac{1}{x}\right)$

$\Rightarrow \quad \frac{x^2+1}{x} = \frac{3(x^2-1)}{x}$

$\Rightarrow \quad x^2 + 1 = 3x^2 - 3$

$\Rightarrow \quad 3x^2 - x^2 = 3 + 1 \therefore x = \sqrt{2}.$

15. Let the four consecutive odd numbers be $(2x - 3)$, $(2x - 1)$, $(2x + 1)$ and $(2x + 3)$

$\therefore$ Their product $= (2x - 1)(2x + 1)(2x - 3)(2x + 3)$

$= (4x^2 - 1)(4x^2 - 9) = 16x^4 - 40x^2 + 9$

$= (4x^2 - 5)^2 - 16$

Hence, on adding 16, the result will be a perfect square.

16. Let the required fraction = x

then, by the question $x \div \frac{7}{9} - x \times \frac{7}{9} = \frac{8}{21}$

$\Rightarrow \quad x \times \frac{9}{7} - \frac{7x}{9} = \frac{8}{21} \Rightarrow \frac{32x}{63} = \frac{8}{21}$

$\Rightarrow \quad x = \frac{8}{21} \times \frac{63}{32} = \frac{3}{4}$

Hence, the correct answer $= \frac{3}{4} \times \frac{7}{9} = \frac{7}{12}$.

17. Let a number be x

then $\quad 40\%$ of $x = 360$

$\Rightarrow \quad \frac{40}{100} \times x = 360$

$\therefore \quad x = 360 \times \frac{100}{40} = 900$

Now by the question,

15% of 15% of 900 $= \frac{15}{100} \times \frac{15}{100} \times 900 = \frac{81}{4} = 20.25.$

18. Let two numbers are a and b

Given, $\quad a + b = 25$

and $\quad a^2 - b^2 = 75$

$\Rightarrow \quad (a + b)(a - b) = 75$

$\Rightarrow \quad (a - b) = \frac{75}{(a+b)} = \frac{75}{25} = 3.$

19. Total dozen of bananas Ram eats in a day

$= \frac{8}{12} + \frac{5}{12} + \frac{2}{12} = \frac{15}{12} = 1\frac{1}{4}$

20. $47^{7.5} \div 47^{\frac{3}{2}} \times 47^{-3} = (\sqrt{47})^{?}$

Let ? = x

then $\quad (47)^{\frac{15}{2}} \div (47)^{\frac{3}{2}} \times (47)^{-3} = (47)^{\frac{x}{2}}$

$\Rightarrow \quad (47)^{\frac{15}{2} - \frac{3}{2} - 3} = (47)^{\frac{x}{2}}$

$\Rightarrow \quad (47)^{\frac{6}{2}} = (47)^{\frac{x}{2}}$

$\therefore \quad x = 6.$

Decimal Fraction

FRACTION

The relation to represent some part of the body to the whole body is known *Fraction*. For example $\frac{2}{5}$ is a fraction where 2 is the numerator and 5 is the denominator.

Important Facts :

(i) A fraction is also called a rational number.

(ii) A fraction is unity when its numerator and denominator are equal.

(iii) When a fraction is reduced in its lowest term, its numerator and denominator are prime to each other, *i.e.*, they have no common factor.

(iv) The value of fraction is not altered by multiplying or dividing the numerator and the denominator by the same number.

Vulgar or Common Fraction : The fraction such as $\frac{2}{9}, \frac{7}{11}, \frac{3}{10}, \frac{9}{100}$ are called vulgar fraction.

Decimal Fraction : Fractions in which denomi-nators are power of 10 are called decimal fractions.

For example : $\frac{1}{10}, \frac{1}{100}, \frac{7}{1000}$ etc.

Here, $\frac{1}{10}$ is 1 tenths, written as .1

$\frac{1}{100} = .01$

$\frac{7}{1000} = .007$

$\frac{13}{100} = .13$ and so on.

Converting a Decimal into a Vulgar Fraction

First of all write down the given number as numerator without the decimal point, and for the denominator write 1 followed by as many zeros as many are there figures after the decimal point. Now reduce the fraction to its lowest terms.

Ex : *(i)* $0.63 = \frac{63}{100}$

(ii) $3.013 = 3\frac{013}{1000} = 3\frac{13}{1000}$

Addition and Subtraction of Decimal Fractions

First of all write down the numbers under one another. Other than the decimal point lies in one column. After arranging in this way, we add or subtract in usual fashion.

An example : Add 521 + 52.1 + 5.21 + 0.521

Sol :
```
521.000
 52.100
  5.210
  0.521
```
After adding we get 578.831

Multiplication of decimal fraction

1. To multiply by 10, 100, 1000, etc

Example : *(i)* 63.02 × 10 = 630.2

(ii) 63.02 × 100 = 6302

(iii) 63.02 × 1000 = 63020

2. To multiply of two or more decimal fractions.

An example : *(i)* 5.91 × 13 = 76.83

(ii) 6.32 × 0.59 = 3.7288

(iii) 63.2 × 0.01 = 0.632

Conclusion: First of all multiply the given numbers assuming them without the decimal point. Now mark off the decimal point from extreme right in the product as many places of decimal as is the sum of the number of decimal places in the given numbers.

DIVISION OF DECIMALS

1. When the divisor is a counting number

Example : *(i)* 4.309 ÷ 10 = 0.4309

(ii) 0.0182 ÷ 14 = 0.0013

(iii) 9.586 ÷ 100 = 0.09586

(iv) $0.05 \div 10^3 = 0.00005$

(v) 0.49 ÷ 7 = 0.07

Conclusion **:** *(i)* When divisor is the power of 10, then shift the decimal point to the left by as many places of decimal as is the power of 10, prefixing zero if necessary.

(ii) When divisor is other than power of 10, then divide as in the case of integers, and in quotient, put the decimal point to give as many places of decimal as are there in the dividend.

2. When the divisor is a decimal

Example:

(i) $0.00066 \div 0.11 = \dfrac{0.00066}{0.11} = \dfrac{0.066}{11} = 0.006$

(ii) $42 \div 0.07 = \dfrac{42}{0.07} = \dfrac{4200}{7} = 600$

(iii) $32.5 \div 0.0064 = \dfrac{32.5}{0.0064} = \dfrac{325000}{64} = 5078.125$

Recurring Decimal : If in a decimal number a digit or a set of digits is repeated again and again, the decimal is known as recurring decimal.

For example:

(i) $2.666... = 2.\dot{6}$

(ii) $1.363636... = 1.\dot{3}\dot{6}$ or $1.\overline{36}$

(iii) $7.3424242... = 7.3\dot{4}\dot{2}$ or $7.3\overline{42}$

Recurring decimal numbers are of two types:

(i) **Pure recurring decimals :** A decimal fraction in which all the figures after the decimal point are repeated is called a pure recurring decimal. For example, $0.\overline{3}$, $0.\overline{37}$, $3.\overline{4579}$ etc

(ii) **Mixed recurring decimals :** A decimal fraction in which at least one figure after the decimal point is not repeated is called a mixed recurring decimal. For example, $0.3\overline{59}$, $0.29\overline{54}$, $0.2\dot{7}$ etc.

Conversion of Recurring into Vulgar Fraction

1. Pure recurring decimals

Rule : Put as many 9's in the denominator at the number of digits under recurring and delete the recurring sign.

For example, $0.\overline{5} = \dfrac{5}{9}$

$0.\overline{35} = \dfrac{35}{99}$

$0.\overline{24} = \dfrac{24}{99} = \dfrac{8}{33}$

2. Mixed Recurring Decimals

For example,

(i) $0.1\overline{8}$

Here, numerator = 18 − 1 = 17

and denominator = 9 × 10 = 90

$\therefore \quad 0.1\dot{8} = \dfrac{18-1}{90} = \dfrac{17}{90}$

(ii) $0.2\dot{7}\dot{9}$

Here, numerator = 279 − 2 = 277

and denominator = 99 × 10 = 990

$\therefore \quad 0.2\overline{79} = \dfrac{279-2}{990} = \dfrac{277}{990}$

(iii) $0.3\overline{56} = \dfrac{356-3}{99 \times 10} = \dfrac{353}{990}$

(iv) $2.53\dot{6} = 2 + \dfrac{536-53}{9 \times 100} = 2 + \dfrac{483}{900}$

$= 2 + \dfrac{161}{300} = 2\dfrac{161}{300}$

(v) $0.43\overline{213} = \dfrac{43213-43}{999 \times 100}$

$= \dfrac{43170}{99900} = \dfrac{4317}{9990}$

Addition and Subtraction of recurring decimals

Example : *(i)* Add $3.\overline{76}$ and $1.4\overline{576}$ and subtract also.

3.7	676767	67	
1.4	576576	57	
(+) 5.2	253344	24	⇒ $5.2\overline{253344}$
(−) 2.3	100191	10	⇒ 2.3100191

(ii) Subtract $3.\overline{75}$ from $25.5\overline{473}$

25.5	473473	47
3.7	575757	57
21.7	897715	90

Hence, the required subtract = $21.7\overline{897715}$

Multiplication and Division of Recurring Decimal

Example 1:

(*i*) $7.\overline{63} \times 11 = 7\frac{63}{99} \times 11$

$= 7\frac{7}{11} \times 11 = \frac{84}{11} \times 11 = 84$

(*ii*) $0.\overline{09} \times 7.\overline{3} = \frac{9}{99} \times 7\frac{3}{9}$

$= \frac{1}{11} \times \frac{66}{9} = \frac{6}{9} = 0.\overline{6}$

(*iii*) $0.\overline{6} \times 7.\overline{3} = \frac{6}{9} \times 7\frac{3}{9}$

$= \frac{6}{9} \times \frac{66}{9} = \frac{44}{9} = 4.\overline{8}$

(*iv*) $0.\overline{06} \div 100 = 0.060606... \div 100 = 0.00\overline{06}$

(*v*) $0.7\dot{3}\dot{2} \div 0.02\dot{7} = 0.732\dot{3} \div 0.027\dot{7}$

$= \frac{7323 - 73}{99 \times 100} \div \frac{277 - 2}{99 \times 100}$

$= \frac{7250}{9900} \div \frac{275}{9900} = \frac{7250}{275} = \frac{290}{11} = 26.\overline{36}$.

EXERCISE

1. Which of the following is equivalent to $\frac{15}{25}$?

A. $\frac{150}{25}$ B. $\frac{15}{250}$
C. $\frac{3}{5}$ D. $\frac{60}{75}$

2. If $\frac{9*3}{3*7}$ is equivalent to $\frac{9}{7}$, the sign * is replaced by

A. ÷ B. ×
C. + D. –

3. $\frac{5}{6}$ of an hour is equal to

A. half an hour B. 40 minutes
C. 50 minutes D. 55 minutes

4. An aircraft uses 2/5 of its fuel in flying 1,250 kilometres. The distance travelled on remaining fuel is

A. 1875 km B. 2125 km
C. 250 km D. 475 km

5. If $\frac{4}{3} * \frac{3}{4} = \frac{16}{9}$, then * means

A. + B. –
C. × D. ÷

6. Which of the following is the largest fraction?

$\frac{3}{15}, \frac{5}{20}, \frac{8}{64}, \frac{25}{1000}$

A. $\frac{3}{15}$ B. $\frac{5}{20}$
C. $\frac{8}{64}$ D. $\frac{25}{1000}$

7. Six times x increased by 12 is equal to

A. $\frac{x}{2}$ B. $2x$
C. $6x + 12$ D. $12x + 6$

8. Five times y diminished by 20 is equal to

A. $5y - 20$ B. $5y + 20$
C. $y/4$ D. $4y$

9. The number less than 15 by 7 is

A. $15x - 7$ B. 15/7
C. 15 D. 8

10. If 21 is add to four times a number, the result is 57. The number is

A. 7 B. 8
C. 9 D. 10

11. A number, the sum of whose fourth and fifth parts exceeds their third part by 28, is

A. 120 B. 240
C. 220 D. 160

12. Which fraction should be added to the sum of $5\frac{3}{4}$, $4\frac{4}{5}$ and $7\frac{3}{8}$ to make the result a whole number?

A. $\frac{1}{40}$ B. $\frac{2}{40}$
C. $\frac{3}{40}$ D. $\frac{4}{40}$

13. $\frac{1}{15} + \frac{3}{15} + \frac{5}{15} + \frac{6}{15} = ?$

A. $\frac{10}{15}$ B. $\frac{3}{5}$
C. $\frac{4}{5}$ D. 1

14. A number one-sixth of which exceeds its one-ninth by 100 is

A. 600 B. 900
C. 1500 D. 1800

15. The sum of 1/2, 1/4 and 1/8 of a number is 28. The number is

A. 28 B. 32
C. 36 D. 42

16. The sum of 1/9, 1/3, 1/6 and 7/18 of a number is 150. The number is

A. 120 B. 130
C. 140 D. 150

17. Which is the greatest?
.999, .1011, .1995, .9985
A. .999 B. .1011
C. .1995 D. .9985

18. In decimal system, $9\frac{1}{8}$ may be represented as
A. 9.18 B. 9.125
C. 9.025 D. 9.225

19. 2.205 ÷ 0.15 = ?
A. 1.47 B. 14.7
C. 147 D. 0.147

20. G.C.M. of .24, 3.2 and 16.0 is
A. 80 B. 8
C. .8 D. .08

ANSWERS

1	2	3	4	5	6	7	8	9	10
C	B	C	A	D	B	C	A	D	C
11	**12**	**13**	**14**	**15**	**16**	**17**	**18**	**19**	**20**
B	C	D	D	B	D	A	B	B	D

EXPLANATORY ANSWERS

1. $\frac{15}{25} = \frac{3\times 5}{5\times 5} = \frac{3}{5}$

2. $\frac{9*3}{3*7} = \frac{9}{7}$, or, $\frac{9\times 3}{7\times 3} = \frac{9}{7}$, $\therefore$ The sign * is ×.

3. $\frac{5}{6}$ of 1 hr. $= \frac{5}{6}\times 60$ minutes $= 50$ minutes.

4. Remaining fuel $= 1-\frac{2}{5} = \frac{5-2}{5} = \frac{3}{5}$

Distance flown by $\frac{2}{5}$ of fuel = 1250 km.

Distance flown by full fuel $= \frac{1250}{2/5} = \frac{1250\times 5}{2}$ km.

Distance flown by $\frac{3}{5}$ of fuel

$= \frac{1250\times 5\times 3}{2\times 5} = 1875$ km.

6. $\frac{3}{15} = \frac{1}{5}, \frac{8}{64} = \frac{1}{8}, \frac{5}{20} = \frac{1}{4}, \frac{25}{1000} = \frac{1}{40}$

Now, the fractions are $\frac{1}{5}, \frac{1}{4}, \frac{1}{8}, \frac{1}{40}$

$\therefore$ The largest fraction is $\frac{1}{4} = \frac{5}{20}$

7. $x \times 6 + 12 = 6x + 12$

8. $5 \times y - 20 = 5y - 20$

9. $15 - 7 = 8$

10. Let the number be x

$\therefore$ $4x + 21 = 57$ or, $4x = 57 - 21 = 36$

Hence, $x = \frac{36}{4} = 9$

11. Let the number be x

$\therefore$ $\frac{x}{4}+\frac{x}{5} = \frac{x}{3}+28$

$\Rightarrow$ $\frac{9x}{20} = \frac{x}{3}+28 \Rightarrow \frac{9x}{20}-\frac{x}{3} = 28$

$\Rightarrow \frac{27x-20x}{60} = 28 \therefore x = \frac{28\times 60}{7} = 240.$

12. $5\frac{3}{4}+4\frac{4}{5}+7\frac{3}{8} = \frac{23}{4}+\frac{24}{5}+\frac{59}{8} = \frac{717}{40}$

717/40 becomes whole number when 3/40 is added to it, *i.e.*,

$\frac{717}{40}+\frac{3}{40} = \frac{720}{40} = 18$ which is a whole number.

13. $\frac{1}{15}+\frac{3}{15}+\frac{5}{15}+\frac{6}{15} = \frac{1+3+5+6}{15} = \frac{15}{15} = 1$

14. Let the number be x

$\frac{x}{6} = \frac{x}{9}+100$

$\Rightarrow$ $\frac{x}{6}-\frac{x}{9} = 100, \Rightarrow \frac{x}{18} = 100$

$\therefore$ $x = 100 \times 18 = 1800.$

15. Let the number be x

$\therefore$ $\frac{x}{2}+\frac{x}{4}+\frac{x}{8} = 28 \Rightarrow \frac{7x}{8} = 28$

$\therefore$ $x = \frac{28\times 8}{7} = 32.$

16. Let the number be x

$\therefore$ $\frac{x}{9}+\frac{x}{3}+\frac{x}{6}+\frac{7x}{18} = 150$

$\Rightarrow$ $\frac{2x+6x+3x+7x}{18} = \frac{18x}{18} = 150 \therefore x = 150.$

17. .999 is the greatest.

18. $9\frac{1}{8} = 9+\frac{1}{8} = 9 + .125 = 9.125$

19. $2.205 \div 0.15 = \frac{2.205}{.15} = \frac{2205}{1000}\times\frac{100}{15} = \frac{2205}{150} = 14.7.$

20. G.C.M. of .24, 3.2 and 16.0

$=$ G.C.M. of $\frac{24, 320 \text{ and } 1600}{100} = \frac{8}{100} = 0.08$

Relation Between Numbers

Simplification is a mathematical operation by which a complex expression of numbers or fractions is converted into a simpler or less difficult form. It is erroneous to solve this type of questions on random basis and a very appropriate method is to apply BODMAS Rule for arriving at the solution of such problems. Each of the letters of the word 'BODMAS' when explained serially, has following implications:

1.	B	→	Bracket	[{ (‾) }]
2.	O	→	of	of
3.	D	→	Division	÷
4.	M	→	Multiplication	×
5.	A	→	Addition	+
6.	S	→	Subtraction	–

Therefore, for simplification, we should remove the brackets first. Thereafter operation for 'of', then for 'division', after that the operation for 'multiplication' and thereafter for 'addition' and at last operation for 'subtraction' should be carried out.

Important Notes

A. In mathematical operations the word 'of' indicates multiplication.

B. While removing brackets, first of all bar bracket '‾' and after that small bracket '( )' is removed. Thereafter the curly bracket '{ }' and at last square bracket [ ] is removed.

EXERCISE

1. The value of 51 ÷ 17 ÷ 3 is:
   A. 9 B. 4
   C. 3 D. 1

2. What will be the value of
   40 × 2 ÷ 10 + 5 – 4?
   A. 5 B. 8
   C. 11 D. 9

3. The value of 28 × 104 ÷ (18 + 6) + 3 is:
   A. $124\frac{1}{3}$ B. $104\frac{1}{3}$
   C. $125\frac{1}{3}$ D. 128

4. If $75^2 - 65^2 = 2x$, then value of x is:
   A. 715 B. 700
   C. 688 D. 711

5. The value of 99 × 14 ÷ 11 ÷ 0.7 is:
   A. 2.9 B. 1.6
   C. 1.8 D. 2.8

6. If 45 – [28 – {37 – (15 – ?) }] = 58, then which of the following should replace the sign of interrogation (?)?
   A. 18 B. 17
   C. 13 D. 19

7. The value of $8\frac{1}{3}+5\frac{1}{4}\times 13\frac{1}{5} \div 6\frac{3}{5}$ is:
   A. $19\frac{1}{3}$ B. $18\frac{5}{6}$
   C. $21\frac{1}{3}$ D. $22\frac{1}{2}$

8. The value of $\frac{14}{3}$ of $\frac{5}{8}$ of 72 is:
   A. 209 B. 217
   C. 210 D. 199

9. What will be the value of
   10 × 10 × 10 ÷ (20 ÷ 10 × 10 – 10) + 6?
   A. 108 B. 111
   C. 106 D. 114

10. What will be the value of $\dfrac{\frac{1}{3}\times 20 \div 4}{\frac{1}{4}\times 25 \div 5}$?
    A. 7/3 B. 4/3
    C. 5/3 D. 10/3

11. Which of the following is the standard form of $\dfrac{(24\times 13)+(28\div 7)}{(24+13)-\left(\frac{14}{3}\text{ of }\frac{5}{8}\right)}$?
    A. $\frac{3792}{409}$ B. $\frac{4792}{309}$
    C. $\frac{3792}{411}$ D. $\frac{3092}{409}$

12. If $\dfrac{144+32\div ?-8}{35\div \frac{1}{2}\text{ of }\frac{1}{2}} = 1$, then which of the following should replace the sign of interrogation?
    A. 7 B. 6
    C. 10 D. 8

13. What is the value of $\dfrac{2.70\times 2.70+4.30\times 4.30+8.60\times 2.70}{2.70+4.30}$?
    A. 6.8 B. 7.0
    C. 7.6 D. 8.5

14. What will be the value of $\dfrac{\left(\sqrt{6}+\frac{1}{\sqrt{6}}\right)^2}{\frac{1}{2}\text{ of } 18 + 4}+\frac{2}{3}$?
    A. 101/78 B. 104/71
    C. 101/88 D. 99/57

15. 1150 ÷ 50 ÷ 23 + 15 = ?
    A. 16 B. 20
    C. 22 D. 18

ANSWERS

1	2	3	4	5	6	7	8	9	10
D	D	A	B	C	D	B	C	C	B
11	**12**	**13**	**14**	**15**					
A	D	B	A	A					

EXPLANATORY ANSWERS

1. $\because\ 51 \div 17 \div 3 = \frac{51}{17} \div 3 = 3 \div 3 = \frac{3}{3} = 1$

2. $\because\ 40 \times 2 \div 10 + 5 - 4$

$= 40 \times \frac{2}{10} + 5 - 4 = 8 + 5 - 4 = 9.$

3. $\because\ 28 \times 104 \div (18 + 6) + 3$

$= 28 \times 104 \div 24 + 3$

$= 28 \times \frac{104}{24} + 3 = 28 \times \frac{13}{3} + 3$

$= \frac{364}{3} + 3 = \frac{373}{3} = 124\frac{1}{3}$

4. $\because\ 75^2 - 65^2 = 2x$

$\Rightarrow (75 + 65)(75 - 65) = 2x$

$[\because a^2 - b^2 = (a + b)(a - b)]$

$\Rightarrow\ 140 \times 10 = 2x \Rightarrow x = 70 \times 10 = 700$

$\therefore$ Value of x is 700.

5. $\because\ .99 \times 14 \div 11 \div 0.7$

$= .99 \times \frac{14}{11} \div 0.7 = \frac{.99 \times 14}{11 \times 0.7} = 1.8$

6. $\because\ 45 - [28 - \{37 - (15 - ?)\}] = 58$

$\Rightarrow\ 45 - [28 - \{37 - 15 + ?\}] = 58$

$\Rightarrow\ 45 - [28 - \{22 + ?\}] = 58$

$\Rightarrow\ 45 - [28 - 22 - ?] = 58$

$\Rightarrow\ 45 - 28 + 22 + ? = 58$

$\Rightarrow\ 39 + ? = 58$

$\Rightarrow\ ? = 58 - 39 = 19$

Therefore, the interrogation sign should be replaced by 19.

7. $\because\ 8\frac{1}{3} + 5\frac{1}{4} \times 13\frac{1}{5} \div 6\frac{3}{5}$

$= \frac{25}{3} + \frac{21}{4} \times \frac{66}{5} \div \frac{33}{5} = \frac{25}{3} + \frac{21}{4} \times \frac{66}{5} \times \frac{5}{33}$

$= \frac{25}{3} + \frac{21}{2} = \frac{50+63}{6} = \frac{113}{6} = 18\frac{5}{6}$

8. $\because\ \frac{14}{3}$ of $\frac{5}{8}$ of $72 = \frac{14 \times 5 \times 72}{3 \times 8} = 210$

9. $10 \times 10 \times 10 \div (20 \div 10 \times 10 - 10) + 6$

$= 10 \times 10 \times 10 \div \left(\frac{20}{10} \times 10 - 10\right) + 6$

$= 10 \times 10 \times 10 \div (20 - 10) + 6$

$= 10 \times 10 \times 10 \div 10 + 6$

$= 10 \times 10 \times \frac{10}{10} + 6$

$= 10 \times 10 \times 1 + 6 = 100 + 6 = 106$

10. $\because\ \dfrac{\frac{1}{3} \times 20 \div 4}{\frac{1}{4} \times 25 \div 5} = \dfrac{\frac{1}{3} \times 5}{\frac{1}{4} \times 5} = \dfrac{\frac{5}{3}}{\frac{5}{4}} = \frac{4}{3}$

11. $\because\ \dfrac{(24 \times 13) + (28 \div 7)}{(24 + 13) - \left(\frac{14}{3} \text{ of } \frac{5}{8}\right)} = \dfrac{312 + 4}{37 - \frac{35}{12}} = \dfrac{316}{\frac{409}{12}} = \dfrac{3792}{409}$

12. If $\dfrac{144 + 32 \div ? - 8}{35 \div \frac{1}{2} \text{ of } \frac{1}{2}} = 1 \Rightarrow \dfrac{144 + \frac{32}{?} - 8}{35 \div \frac{1}{4}} = 1 \Rightarrow \dfrac{136 + \frac{32}{?}}{\frac{35}{\frac{1}{4}}} = 1$

$\Rightarrow\ 136 + \frac{32}{?} = 35 \times 4 = 140$

$\Rightarrow\ \frac{32}{?} = 140 - 136 = 4 \Rightarrow ? = \frac{32}{4} = 8$

$\therefore$ Sign of interrogation (?) will be replaced by 8.

13. $\dfrac{2.70 \times 2.70 + 4.30 \times 4.30 + 8.60 \times 2.70}{2.70 + 4.30}$

$= \dfrac{(2.70)^2 + (4.30)^2 + 2 \times 4.30 \times 2.70}{2.70 + 4.30}$

$= \dfrac{(2.70 + 4.30)^2}{2.70 + 4.30}$ $[\because a^2 + b^2 + 2ab = (a + b)^2]$

$= 2.70 + 4.30 = 7.00$

14. $\therefore\ \dfrac{\left(\sqrt{6} + \frac{1}{\sqrt{6}}\right)^2}{\frac{1}{2} \text{ of } 18 + 4} + \frac{2}{3} = \dfrac{(\sqrt{6})^2 + \left(\frac{1}{\sqrt{6}}\right)^2 + 2.\sqrt{6}\,\frac{1}{\sqrt{6}}}{9 + 4} + \frac{2}{3}$

$= \dfrac{6 + \frac{1}{6} + 2}{13} + \frac{2}{3} = \dfrac{\frac{49}{6}}{13} + \frac{2}{3} = \frac{49}{78} + \frac{2}{3} = \frac{101}{78}$

15. $1150 \div 50 \div 23 + 15$

$= \frac{1150}{50} \div 23 + 15 = 23 \div 23 + 15 = \frac{23}{23} + 15$

$= 1 + 15 = 16.$

●●●

CHAPTER 2

Comparing Quantities

Percentage

The word 'per cent' or 'percentage' means 'for every one hundred'. In other words, it gives an indication of rate per hundred. It is denoted by the symbol %.

For example, 5% means 5 out of one hundred or $\frac{5}{100}$.

Remember:

(*i*) For converting a per cent into a fraction, divide it by 100.

(*ii*) For converting a fraction into a per cent, multiply it by 100.

(*iii*) For converting a per cent into a decimal, shift the decimal point two places to the left.

(*iv*) For converting one given quantity (*x*) as a percentage of another given quantity (*y*), find $\frac{x}{y} \times 100$.

(*v*) There is no unit of percentage.

Important Facts—For quickly solving the problems related to percentage, remember following rules:

Rule 1:

(***a***) Of the given two numbers if the first is $x\%$ more than the second, then the second will be $\left(\frac{100 \times x}{100+x}\right)\%$ less than the first.

(***b***) Of the given two numbers if the first is $x\%$ less than the second, then the second will be $\left(\frac{100 \times x}{100-x}\right)\%$ more than the first.

(***c***) If two numbers are respectively $x\%$ and $y\%$ more than a third number, then the first number will be $\left(\frac{100+x}{100+y} \times 100\right)\%$ of the second.

(***d***) If two numbers are respectively $x\%$ and $y\%$ less than a third number, then the first number will be $\left(\frac{100-x}{100-y} \times 100\right)\%$ of the second.

Rule 2:

(***a***) If a number or quantity is increased by $x\%$ then in order to restore its original value it must be decreased by $\left[\frac{100 \times x}{100+x}\right]\%$.

(***b***) If a number or quantity is decreased by $x\%$ then in order to restore its original value it must be increased by $\left[\frac{100 \times x}{100-x}\right]\%$.

Rule 3:

(***a***) If a number is successively increased by $x\%$ and $y\%$ then a single equivalent increase in that number will be $\left(x+y+\frac{xy}{100}\right)\%$

(***b***) If two successive discounts of $x\%$ and $y\%$ are allowed on a particular amount, then a single discount that is equivalent to the two successive discounts will be $\left(x+y-\frac{xy}{100}\right)\%$

(***c***) If a number is successively increased by $x\%$, $y\%$ and $z\%$, then a single equivalent increase in that number will be

$$\left[(x+y+z)+\left(\frac{xy+yz+zx}{100}\right)+\frac{(xyz)}{10000}\right]\%$$

(***d***) If three successive discounts of $x\%$, $y\%$ and $z\%$ are allowed on an amount, then a single discount that is equivalent to the three successive discounts will be

$$\left[x+y+z-\frac{(xy+yz+zx)}{100}+\frac{xyz}{10000}\right]\%$$

Rule 4:

(***a***) If a number is increased by $x\%$ and thereafter reduced by $x\%$, then the number will be reduced by $\left(\frac{x^2}{100}\right)$ per cent.

(*b*) If a number is reduced by $x\%$ and thereafter increased by $x\%$ then the number will be reduced by $\left(\frac{x^2}{100}\right)$ per cent.

(*c*) If due to an increase of $x\%$ in the selling price of certain commodity the sell/consumption of the commodity decreases by $y\%$, then gross receipts on account of sale of that commodity will be increased or decreased by $\left(x-y-\frac{xy}{100}\right)\%$, where $x > y$ and will be decreased by $\left(y-x+\frac{xy}{100}\right)\%$, where $y > x$.

EXERCISE

1. In the expression xy^2, the values of both variables x and y are decreased by 20%. By this, the value of the expression is decreased by

A. 40% B. 48.8%
C. 51.2% D. 80%

2. 15 litres of mixture contains 20% alcohol and rest water. If 3 litres of water be mixed in it, the percentage of alcohol in the new mixture will be:

A. 15 B. $16\frac{2}{3}$
C. 17 D. $18\frac{1}{2}$

3. The difference between 70% and 55% of a number is 72. The number is:

A. 370 B. 460
C. 480 D. 520

4. 20% of a number is 10% of:

A. half the number
B. double the number
C. ten times the number
D. twenty times the number

5. 75% of what area is 15 sq. metres?

A. 10 sq. metres B. 15 sq. metres
C. 20 sq. metres D. 25 sq. metres

6. In an examination 80% of the students passed in Mathematics and 70% passed in English, while 10% students failed in both the subjects. If 360 students passed in both the subjects, find the total number of students who appeared in the examination.

A. 400 B. 600
C. 630 D. 640

7. In an election, there are two candidates. A candidate secured 57% of the total votes polled and elected by a margin of 2100 votes. Find the total number of votes polled.

A. 15000 B. 17500
C. 18000 D. 21000

8. Electric tax is increased by 20% and its consumption is decreased by 20%. The change in the expenditure is:

A. 4% decrease B. 4% increase
C. 5% decrease D. 5% increase

9. A man loses 10% of his money, after spending 20% of the remainder he is left with ₹ 2160. Initially the man had:

A. ₹ 1800 B. ₹ 2500
C. ₹ 3000 D. ₹ 3200

10. In a school 55% of the students are below 9 years of age and the remaining 153 above 9 years of age. The total number of students in the school is:

A. 296 B. 300
C. 340 D. 1000

11. The selling price of certain commodity was reduced by 25%. As a result of it, the sales increased by 30%. What was the effect of it on cash collected by daily sales?

A. 2.5% decrease B. 2.5% increase
C. 5% decrease D. 5% increase

12. A cooler marked at ₹ 1500 is offered at ₹ 1350 due to off-season discount. Find the rate of off-season discount offered.

A. 9.5% B. 10%
C. 10.5% D. 12%

13. The number of Gypsy-cars sold in 2008 was 16,500 and that sold in 2007 was 16580. How much was the percentage decrease in sales of the Gypsy-cars from 2007 to 2008?

A. less than 1 per cent
B. more than 1 per cent
C. zero per cent
D. cannot be determined

14. A company decided to sell ₹ 50,000 T.V. set for ₹ 48,000 as a world cup offer. What is the percentage discount offered by the company?

A. 6.5 B. 7
C. 7.5 D. 4

15. 9% of a number is $\frac{81}{200}$, what is $\frac{2}{7}$ of that number?

A. $1\frac{1}{5}$ B. $1\frac{2}{7}$
C. $2\frac{1}{7}$ D. $2\frac{1}{5}$

ANSWERS

1	2	3	4	5	6	7	8	9	10
B	B	C	B	C	B	A	A	C	C
11	12	13	14	15					
A	B	A	D	B					

EXPLANATORY ANSWERS

1. Decrease in expression

$$= xy^2 - \frac{80}{100} \times x\left(\frac{80}{100}y\right)^2 = xy^2 - \frac{64}{125}xy^2 = \frac{61xy^2}{125}$$

Hence, decrease per cent

$$= \frac{61xy^2}{125 \times xy^2} \times 100 = 48.8\%$$

2. Amount of alcohol $= \frac{20}{100} \times 15 = 3$ litre

Hence, required percentage $= \frac{3}{18} \times 100 = 16\frac{2}{3}\%$

3. Let the number be x; then

$$(70 - 55) \times \frac{1}{100} \times x = 72$$

$$\therefore \quad x = \frac{100 \times 72}{15} = 480$$

4. Let number be 100, then 20% and 10% of the number be 20 and 10 respectively.

Hence, 20% of a number is 10% of double the number.

5. Let required area be x sq. metre; then

$$\frac{75}{100} \times x = 15$$

$$\therefore \ x = \frac{15 \times 100}{75} = 20 \text{ sq metre}$$

6. Here, percentage of students failed in Mathematics and English be 30% and 20% respectively.

Percentage of students failed either one or both subjects $= 30 + 20 - 10 = 40\%$

Hence, percentage of pass students = 100 – 40 = 60%

Now, $\quad 60\% = 360$

$$\therefore \quad 100\% = \frac{360}{60} \times 100 = 600$$

7. Let total number of votes be x; then

$$(57 - 43) \times \frac{1}{10}x = 2100$$

$$\therefore \quad x = \frac{100 \times 2100}{14} = 15000$$

8. Let initially electric tax is ₹ 100 and consumption = 100 units

Decrease in consumption

= 100 × 100 – 120 × 80 = ₹ 400

Hence, decrease percentage $= \frac{400 \times 100}{100 \times 100} = 4\%$

9. Let initally the man had ₹ x, then

amount of money loses $= \frac{10}{100} \times x = ₹\frac{x}{10}$

Remaining amount of money $= x - \frac{x}{10} = ₹\frac{9x}{10}$

Money spent $= \frac{20}{100} \times \frac{9x}{10} = ₹\frac{9x}{50}$

Now, $\quad \frac{9x}{10} - \frac{9x}{50} = 2160 \Rightarrow \frac{36x}{50} = 2160$

$$\therefore \ x = \frac{2160 \times 50}{36} = ₹\ 3000$$

10. Let total number of students be x, then

$$\frac{45}{100} \times x = 153 \ \therefore \ x = \frac{100 \times 153}{45} = 340$$

11. Let the selling price of a commodity be ₹ 100 and number of sales = 100 units

Decrease in daily cash

= 100 × 100 – 75 × 130 = ₹ 250

Hence, decrease percentage $= \frac{250 \times 100}{100 \times 100} = 2.5\%$

12. Discount per cent

$$= \frac{1500 - 1350}{1500} \times 100 = \frac{150}{1500} \times 100 = 10\%$$

13. Required decrease percentage

$$= \frac{16580 - 16500}{16580} \times 100 = \frac{80}{16580} \times 100 = 0.48\%$$

14. Discount per cent $= \frac{2000}{50,000} \times 100 = 4\%$

15. Let the number be x; then

$$\frac{9}{100} \times x = \frac{81}{200} \ \therefore \ x = \frac{100 \times 81}{9 \times 200} = \frac{9}{2}$$

Hence, $\frac{2}{7}x = \frac{2}{7} \times \frac{9}{2} = \frac{9}{7} = 1\frac{2}{7}$.

Discount

Market Price (M.P.)—The attached price is called the market price (M.P.) or list price (L.P.) of the article and the reduction allowed in the price is called the **discount**.

(*i*) Discount = M.P. – S.P.

(*ii*) $\text{Discount \%} = \dfrac{\text{Discount} \times 100}{\text{M.P.}}$

(*iii*) $\text{S.P.} = \text{M.P.} - \dfrac{\text{Discount\%} \times \text{M.P.}}{100}$

(*iv*) $\text{S.P.} = \text{M.P.} \times \left(1 - \dfrac{\text{Discount\%}}{100}\right)$

(*v*) $\text{M.P.} = \dfrac{100 \times \text{S.P.}}{100 - \text{Discount\%}}$

$\text{S.P.} = \text{M.P.} \left(\dfrac{100 - \text{Discount\%}}{100}\right)$

$\text{M.P.} - \text{S.P.} = \dfrac{\text{M.P.} \times \text{Discount\%}}{100}$

$\text{Discount\%} = \left(\dfrac{\text{M.P.} - \text{S.P.}}{\text{M.P.}}\right) \times 100$

EXERCISE

1. A cloth merchant offers 15% festival discount on every saree sold. If a certain saree is sold for ₹ 680, what is its marked price?
A. ₹ 800 B. ₹ 900
C. ₹ 1250 D. ₹ 1300

2. A shopkeeper offers 10% discount on an article and still makes a profit of 20%. What is the C.P. of the article if the marked price is ₹ 350?
A. ₹ 259.20 B. ₹ 262.50
C. ₹ 265.75 D. ₹ 272.5

3. A manufactures marks his goods in such a way that after allowing 20% discount, he makes a profit of 18%. What is the marked price of an item which costs him ₹ 200?
A. ₹ 295 B. ₹ 310
C. ₹ 315 D. ₹ 375

4. The marked price of a brand of coffee is ₹ 35 for 100g. But the shopkeeper gives a cup costing ₹ 7.50 free with it. Even then he gets a gain of 10%. What is the cost price of 100g of coffee?
A. ₹ 15 B. ₹ 25
C. ₹ 35 D. ₹ 65

5. A car is marked at ₹ 2,25,000. The manufacturer gives a discount of 10%. The dealer also gives a discount of 5%. What is the S.P. of the car?
A. ₹ 1,72,369 B. ₹ 1,64,370
C. ₹ 1,52,393 D. ₹ 1,92,375

6. A cycle merchant allows 25% commission on his advertised price and still makes a profit of 20%. If he gains ₹ 60 over the sale of one cycle. What is his advertised price?
A. ₹ 290 B. ₹ 310
C. ₹ 480 D. ₹ 520

7. The marked price of a shirt was ₹ 165 and it was at a discount of 12%. What the selling price of the shirt?
A. ₹ 145.20 B. ₹ 155.30
C. ₹ 165.20 D. ₹ 175.25

8. A trader marks his goods 40% above the cost price and gives a discount of 20% on the marked price. What is his gain per cent?
A. 8% B. 9%
C. 12% D. 15%

9. How much per cent more than the C.P. should a manufacturer mark his goods so that after allowing a discount of 20% on the marked price, he gains 10%.
A. 34.5% B. 27.5%
C. 37.5% D. 38.5%

10. A shopkeeper allows a discount of 10% to his customers and still gains 20%. What is the marked price of an article which costs ₹ 450 to the shopkeeper?
A. ₹ 600 B. ₹ 700
C. ₹ 800 D. ₹ 900

ANSWERS

1	2	3	4	5	6	7	8	9	10
A	B	A	B	D	C	A	C	C	A

EXPLANATORY ANSWERS

1. S.P. = ₹ 680, Discount = 15%

$$\text{M.P.} = \frac{100 \times \text{S.P.}}{100 - \text{Discount\%}}$$

$$= \frac{100 \times 680}{100 - 15} = \frac{100 \times 680}{85} = ₹\ 800$$

2. C.P. = ₹ x, 120% of x = 350 – 350 × 10%

$$\frac{120}{100} \times x = 350 - 35 = 315.$$

$$x = \frac{315 \times 5}{6} = \frac{525}{2}, \text{ C.P.} = ₹\ 262.50.$$

3. Let M.P. = ₹ x

$80\%\ x = 118\%$ of 200

$$\frac{80}{100}\times x = \frac{118}{100}\times 200 \Rightarrow x = \frac{236\times 5}{4} = ₹\ 295.$$

4. Let C.P. of 100 gm coffee = ₹ x

110% of $x = 35 - 7.50 = 27.50$

$$\frac{110}{100}\times x = 27.50$$

$$x = \frac{27.50\times 100}{110\times 100}$$

C.P. = ₹ 25.

5. M.P. = ₹ 225000

$$\text{1st S.P.} = 225000 - 225000\times\frac{10}{100}$$

$$= 225000 - 22500 = 202500$$

$$\text{2nd S.P.} = 202500 - 202500\times\frac{5}{100}$$

$$= 202500 - 10125 = ₹\ 192375$$

6. Let M.P. = 100

Commission = 25%

S.P. = 100 − 25 = 75

Profit = 20%

$$\text{C.P.} = \frac{100}{120}\times 75 = \frac{375}{6} = 62.50$$

Gain = 75 − 62.50 = ₹ 12.50

$$\text{M.P.} = \frac{100}{12.50}\times 60 = ₹\ 480$$

7.
$$\text{S.P.} = \frac{\text{M.P.}(100-\text{Discount})}{100}$$

$$= \frac{165\times(100-12)}{100} = \frac{165\times 88}{100}$$

$$= 33\times 4.4 = ₹\ 145.20$$

8. Let C.P. = 100, M.P. = 140, Discount = 20%

$$\text{S.P.} = 140 - 140\times\frac{20}{100} = 140 - 28 = 112$$

Profit = 112 − 100 = 12

$$\text{Profit }\% = \frac{12\times 100}{100} = 12\%$$

9. Let C.P. = ₹ x, S.P. = 110% of $x = \frac{110}{100}\times x = \frac{11}{10}x.$

Discount = 20%

$$\text{M.P.} = \frac{100\times\frac{11}{10}x}{100-20} = \frac{100\times\frac{11}{10}x}{80} = \frac{11}{8}x.$$

$$\text{Required }\% = \frac{\frac{11x}{8}-x}{x}\times 100 = \frac{3x\times 100}{8x} = 37.5\%$$

10. C.P. = 450, Gain = 20%

$$\text{S.P.} = 450 + 450\times\frac{20}{100} = 450 + 90 = 540$$

Discount = 10%

$$\text{M.P.} = \frac{100\times\text{S.P.}}{100-\text{Discount}} = \frac{100\times 540}{100-10}$$

$$= \frac{100\times 540}{90} = ₹\ 600$$

Profit & Loss

A consumer who goes to the market and buys certain goods. The buyer is called a customer and the shopkeeper who sells the goods to him is called a retailer. The retailer purchases goods in turn in bulk from a wholesaler who keeps a large stock of good and in this case, the retailer becomes the customer.

1. **Cost price (C.P.):** Cost price is that price at which a particular article is bought. Profit and loss both are marked at cost price.
2. **Selling Price (S.P.):** Selling price is that price at which a particular article is sold.
3. **Overheads:** The expenses incurred on transportation, maintenance, packaging, advertise-ments and the like are included as *Overhead.* These overheads and the profit when added to the cost price determine the selling price.
4. **Profit or Gain** : Whenever a person sells an article at price greater than the cost price he is said to have made a profit or gain.
   Profit or Gain = S.P. − C.P.
5. **Loss :** If S.P. is less than the C.P. there is loss.
   Loss = C.P − S.P

Some Basic Formulae:

(i) Gain = S.P. − C.P.

(ii) Loss = C.P. − S.P.

(iii) $\text{Gain }\% = \frac{\text{Gain}\times 100}{\text{C.P.}}$

(iv) $\text{Loss }\% = \frac{\text{Loss}\times 100}{\text{C.P.}}$

From these we can write direct expressions for S.P. and C.P.

(v) $\text{S.P.} = \left(\frac{100+\text{Gain}\%}{100}\right)\times\text{C.P.}$ in case of gain or profit

(vi) $\text{S.P.} = \left(\frac{100-\text{Loss}\%}{100}\right)\times\text{C.P.}$ in case of loss

These can be rewritten as

$\text{C.P.} = \frac{100}{100+\text{Gain}\%}\times\text{S.P.}$ in case of profit

$\text{C.P.} = \frac{100}{100-\text{Loss}\%}\times\text{S.P.}$ in case of loss *(vii)* If the C.P. of x goods = S.P. of y goods, then

(a) Gain % = $\frac{x-y}{y}\times 100$ [In case of $x > y$]

(b) Loss % = $\frac{y-x}{y}\times 100$ [In case of $y > x$]

(viii) When a man sells two things at the same price each and in this process his loss on first things is $x\%$ and gain on second things is $x\%$, then in such a type question, there is always a loss.

$$\text{Loss \%} = x\% \text{ of } x = \frac{x^2}{100} = \left(\frac{x}{10}\right)^2$$

$$\text{and Loss} = \frac{2\times \text{S.P.}}{\left(\frac{100}{x}\right)^2 - 1}$$

(ix) An article is sold at a profit of $x\%$. Had it been sold for ₹ a some more, $y\%$ would have gained. Then, C.P. of an article =

$$\frac{\text{More gain}\times 100}{\text{Difference in percentage profit}}$$

(x) A dishonest shopkeeper prefers to sell goods at his cost price but uses a false weight of x grams for each kilogram. Then his gain per cent,

$$\text{gain \%} = \frac{\text{Error}}{\text{True value} - \text{Error}}\times 100$$

$$= \frac{1000 - x}{x}\times 100$$

$$\text{or, gain \%} = \frac{\text{True weight} - \text{False weight}}{\text{False weight}}\times 100.$$

EXERCISE

1. Ashok bought 25 kg of rice at the rate of ₹ 6 per kg and 35 kg of rice at the rate of ₹ 7 per kg. He mixed the two and sold the mixture at the rate of ₹ 6.75 per kg. What was his gain or loss in the transaction?

A. ₹ 16 gain B. ₹ 16 loss
C. ₹ 10 gain D. None of these

2. A horse and a cow were sold for ₹ 12000 each. The horse was sold at a loss of 20% and the cow at a gain of 20%. The entire transaction resulted in

A. no loss no gain B. loss of ₹ 1000
C. gain of ₹ 1000 D. loss of ₹ 2000

3. Profit after selling a commodity for ₹ 425 is same as loss after selling it for ₹ 355. The cost of the commodity is :

A. ₹ 285 B. ₹ 390
C. ₹ 295 D. ₹ 400

4. Bhajan Singh purchased 120 reams of paper at ₹ 80 per ream. He spent ₹ 280 on transportation, paid octroi at the rate of 40 paise per ream and paid ₹ 72 to the coolie. If he wants to have a gain of 8%, what must be the selling price per ream?

A. ₹ 86 B. ₹ 86.48
C. ₹ 79 D. ₹ 90

5. Ram bought 4 dozen apples at ₹ 12 per dozen and 2 dozen at ₹ 16 per dozen. He sold all of them to earn 20%. At what price per dozen did he sell the apples?

A. ₹ 14.40 B. ₹ 16.00
C. ₹ 16.80 D. ₹ 16.20

6. Jimmy bought paper sheets for ₹ 7200 and spent ₹ 200 in transport. Paying ₹ 600 he had 330 boxes made, which he sold at ₹ 28 each. What is his profit percentage?

A. 15.5 B. 40
C. 50 D. None of these

7. A owns a house worth ₹ 10000. He sells it to B at a profit of 10% based on the worth of the house. B sells the house back to A at a loss of 10%. In this transaction A gets:

A. no profit no loss B. profit of ₹ 1000
C. profit of ₹ 1100 D. profit of ₹ 1200

8. At what price must Kantilal sell a mixture of 80 kg sugar at ₹ 6.75 per kg with 120 kg at ₹ 8 per kg to gain 20%?

A. ₹ 7.50 per kg B. ₹ 8.20 per kg
C. ₹ 8.35 per kg D. ₹ 9 per kg

9. Subhash purchased a taperecorder at $\frac{9}{10}$ of its selling price and sold it at 8% more than its S.P. His gain is:

A. 8% B. 10%
C. 18% D. 20%

10. A dealer marks his goods 20% above cost price. He then allows some discount on it and makes a profit of 8%. The rate of discount is :

A. 12% B. 10%
C. 6% D. 4%

11. A trader lists his articles 20% above C.P. and allows a discount of 10% on cash payment. His gain per cent is :

A. 10% B. 8%
C. 6% D. 4%

12. Tarun bought a T.V. with 20% discount on the labelled price. Had he bought it with 25% discount, he would have saved ₹ 500. At what price did he buy the T.V.?

A. ₹ 5000 B. ₹ 8000
C. ₹ 10000 D. ₹ 12000

13. While selling a watch, a shopkeeper gives a discount of 5%. If he gives a discount of 7%, he earns ₹ 15 less as profit. The marked price of the watch is :

A. ₹ 697.50 B. ₹ 712.50
C. ₹ 787.50 D. None of these

14. Kabir buys an article with 25% discount on its marked price. He makes a profit of 10% by selling it at ₹ 660. The marked price is :

A. ₹ 600 B. ₹ 700
C. ₹ 800 D. ₹ 885

15. A person bought an article and sold it at a loss of 10%. If he had bought it for 20% less and sold it for ₹ 55 more, he would have had a profit of 40%. The C.P. of the article is :

A. ₹ 200 B. ₹ 225
C. ₹ 250 D. None of these

ANSWERS

1	2	3	4	5	6	7	8	9	10
C	B	B	D	B	A	C	D	D	B
11	**12**	**13**	**14**	**15**					
B	B	D	C	C					

EXPLANATORY ANSWERS

1. C.P. of 60 kg mixture = ₹ (25 × 6 + 35 × 7) = ₹ 395

S.P. of 60 kg mixtire = ₹ (60 × 6.75) = ₹ 405

∴ Gain = ₹ (405 – 395) = ₹ 10

2. Loss % = $\left(\frac{20}{10}\right)^2 = (2)^2 = 4\%$

Total S.P. = ₹ 24000

and Total C.P. = ₹$\left(\frac{100}{96}\times 24000\right)$ = ₹ 25000

∴ Loss = ₹ (25000 – 24000) = ₹ 1000

3. Let C.P. = ₹ x, Then, $425 - x = x - 355$

⇒ $2x = 780$ ∴ x = ₹ 390

4. C.P. of 1 ream = $80 + \frac{280}{120} + \frac{72}{120} + 0.40$

$= 80 + \frac{7}{3} + \frac{3}{5} + \frac{2}{5}$ = ₹ $\frac{250}{3}$

∴ S.P. of 1 ream = ₹$\left(\frac{108}{100}\times\frac{250}{3}\right)$ = ₹ 90

5. C.P. of 6 dozen apples = ₹ (12 × 4 + 16 × 2) = ₹ 80

∴ S.P. = ₹$\left(\frac{120}{100}\times 80\right)$ = ₹ 96

∴ S.P. per dozen = ₹$\left(\frac{96}{6}\right)$ = ₹ 16

6. C.P. of 1 box = $\frac{7200+200+600}{330}$ = ₹ $\frac{800}{33}$

Hence, Gain% = $\frac{28-\frac{800}{33}}{800/33}\times 100 = \frac{124}{800}\times 100 = 15.5\%$

7. Final C.P. for A = $\frac{110}{100}\times\frac{90}{100}$ × ₹ 10000 = ₹ 9900

Hence, profit for A

= $\frac{10}{100}$ × ₹ 10,000 + ₹ (10,000 – 9900) = ₹ 1100

8. C.P. of 1 kg sugar = $\frac{80\times 6.75 + 120\times 8}{200}$ = ₹ 7.50

∴ S.P. of 1 kg = ₹$\left(\frac{120}{100}\times 7.50\right)$ = ₹ 9 per kg

9. Let S.P. = ₹ 100;

C.P. for Subhash = $\frac{9}{10}\times 100$ = ₹ 90 and S.P. = ₹ 108

Hence, gain % for Subhash = $\frac{108-90}{90}\times 100 = 20\%$

10. Let C.P. be ₹ 100; then Marked price = ₹ 120 and S.P. = ₹ 108

∴ Discount = $\left(\frac{12}{120}\times 100\right)\% = 10\%$

11. Let C.P. be ₹ 100

Then, marked price = ₹ 120

S.P. = ₹$\left(\frac{90}{100}\times 120\right)$ = ₹ 108

∴ Gain % = $\left(\frac{8}{100}\times 100\right)\% = 8\%$

12. Here, 5% = 500

∴ 100% = $\frac{500}{5}\times 100$ = ₹ 10,000

Hence, labelled price = ₹ 10,000

∴ S.P. = $\frac{80}{100}$ × ₹ 10,000 = ₹ 8000

13. Let the marked price = ₹ x

Then, $\frac{7x}{100} - \frac{5x}{100} = 15 \Rightarrow \frac{x}{50} = 15$ ∴ x = ₹ 750

14. C.P. = $\frac{100}{110}\times 660$ = ₹ 600

Hence, M.P. = $\frac{100}{75}\times 600$ = ₹ 800.

Simple Interest

Interest is the money paid for the use of money borrowed, *i.e.*, extra money paid for using other's money is called *interest.*

The sum borrowed is called the principal. The sum of interest and principal is called the *Amount.*

If the interest on a certain sum borrowed for a certain period is reckoned uniformly, then it is called simple interest, denoted by S.I.

Thus, if A = Amount, P = Principal, I = Interest, T = Time (in year), R = Rate per cent per annum, then

(*a*) $I = \frac{P \times R \times T}{100}$ (*b*) $P = \frac{100 \times I}{R \times T}$

(*c*) $T = \frac{100 \times I}{P \times R}$ (*d*) $R = \frac{100 \times I}{P \times T}$

(*e*) $P = \frac{100\,A}{100 + RT}$ (*f*) A = P + I.

EXERCISE

1. If the simple interest on a certain sum of money at 6% per annum for 3 years is ₹ 90, the sum will be:
A. ₹ 500 B. ₹ 450
C. ₹ 525 D. ₹ 560

2. If the simple interest on ₹ 1 for 1 month is 1 paise, the rate per cent p.a. will be :
A. 10% B. 8%
C. 12% D. 6%

3. A sum of money doubles itself in 20 years. In how many years will it triple itself at the same rate of simple interest?
A. 30 years B. 50 years
C. 40 years D. 45 years

4. If the simple interest on ₹ 500 for 4 years is ₹ 40, find the rate per cent p.a.
A. 3½% B. 2%
C. 2½% D. 3%

5. After what time will the sum of ₹ 2000 become ₹ 2240 at 4% per annum simple interest?
A. 3 years B. 2 years
C. 5 years D. 4 years

6. The simple interest on a certain sum of money is $\frac{25}{64}$ of the sum and the number of years equals the rate per cent p.a. The rate per cent p.a. will be :
A. $7\frac{1}{2}\%$ B. $5\frac{1}{4}\%$
C. $6\frac{3}{4}\%$ D. $6\frac{1}{4}\%$

7. A sum of money amounts to ₹ 1150 in 3 years and to ₹ 1250 in 5 years at a certain rate per cent p.a. simple interest. The rate per cent p.a. will be :
A. 5% B. 8%
C. 7% D. 6%

8. The simple interest on a sum of ₹ 892 lent out at 6% p.a. for 8 months will be :
A. ₹ 36.68 B. ₹ 35.68
C. ₹ 48.58 D. ₹ 33.38

9. If the simple interest on a certain sum of money at 6% p.a. for 4½ years is ₹ 81, the sum will be:
A. ₹ 325 B. ₹ 225
C. ₹ 300 D. ₹ 340

10. A sum of ₹ 1850 lent out for 5 years at 3% p.a. simple interest will amount to:
A. ₹ 2227.75 B. ₹ 2127.50
C. ₹ 2137.50 D. ₹ 2086.50

11. A lent a sum of ₹ 1250 to B at a certain rate of interest for 3 years and a sum of ₹ 1500 to C at the same rate of interest for 2 years. If he was paid total ₹ 258.75 as interest in both cases, find the rate of interest at which money was lent by him.
A. $4\frac{1}{6}\%$ B. $6\frac{1}{4}\%$
C. $2\frac{1}{7}\%$ D. $3\frac{5}{6}\%$

12. A invested ₹ 5000 at a certain rate of simple interest and ₹ 4000 for the same period at 1% higher rate of interest. If the interest in both cases is same, the former rate of interest is :
A. 3% B. 4%
C. 6% D. 5%

13. A man lends ₹ 500 for 4 years and ₹ 600 for 3 years at a certain rate of simple interest. If he gets total ₹ 190 as interest in both cases, the rate per cent per annum is:
A. 8% B. 5%
C. 10% D. 4%

14. What annual instalment should be paid to clear the debt of ₹ 645 in 4 years at the rate of 5% p.a. simple interest?
A. ₹ 160 B. ₹ 185
C. ₹ 180 D. ₹ 190

15. If a certain sum of money at simple interest amounts to ₹ 1900 in 3 years and to ₹ 2050 in 5 years, the rate per cent per annum is:
A. 4½% B. 3½%
C. 2½% D. 5¼%

ANSWERS

1	2	3	4	5	6	7	8	9	10
A	C	C	B	A	D	A	B	C	B
11	12	13	14	15					
D	B	B	C	A					

EXPLANATORY ANSWERS

1. $P = \frac{90 \times 100}{6 \times 3} = ₹\ 500$

2. $\text{Rate} = \frac{1 \times 100}{100 \times \frac{1}{12}} = 12\%.$

3. Let principal = ₹ x; Amount = ₹ $2x$;

then $I = 2x - x = ₹\ x$

$\therefore R = \frac{x \times 100}{x \times 20} = 5\%$

Again, if principal = ₹ x;

Amount = ₹ $3x$; then $I = 3x - x = ₹\ 2x$

Hence, $T = \frac{2x \times 100}{x \times 5} = 40$ years

4. $\text{Rate} = \frac{40 \times 100}{500 \times 4} = 2\%$

5. Here, $I = 2240 - 2000 = ₹\ 240$

$\therefore \quad T = \frac{240 \times 100}{2000 \times 4} = 3$ years

6. Let, $R = T = x$; then

$\frac{25}{64} P = \frac{P \times x \times x}{100} \Rightarrow x^2 = \frac{25 \times 100}{64}$

$\therefore \quad x = \frac{5 \times 10}{8} = \frac{25}{4}$; $R = 6\frac{1}{4}\%$

7. Here, Simple interest for 2 years

= ₹ 1250 – ₹ 1150 = ₹ 100

$\therefore$ Simple interest for 3 years $= \frac{100 \times 3}{2} = ₹\ 150$

Hence, P = ₹ 1150 – ₹ 150 = ₹ 1000

$\therefore \quad \text{Rate} = \frac{50 \times 100}{1000 \times 1} = 5\%$

8. Here, $\quad I = \frac{892 \times 6 \times \frac{2}{3}}{100} = ₹\ 35.68$

9. $\quad P = \frac{81 \times 100 \times 2}{6 \times 9} = ₹\ 300$

10. $I = \frac{1850 \times 3 \times 5}{100} = ₹\ 277.50$

$\therefore$ Amount = ₹ 1850 + ₹ 277.50 = ₹ 2127.50

11. $\frac{1250 \times R \times 3}{100} + \frac{1500 \times R \times 2}{100} = 258.75$

$\Rightarrow \quad 6750\ R = 25875$

$\therefore \quad R = \frac{25875}{6750} = \frac{23}{6} = 3\frac{5}{6}\%$

12. Here, $\frac{5000 \times R \times T}{100} = \frac{4000 \times (R+1) \times T}{100}$

$\Rightarrow \quad 5R = 4R + 4 \therefore R = 4\%$

13. Here, $\frac{500 \times R \times 4}{100} + \frac{600 \times R \times 3}{100} = 190$

$\Rightarrow \quad 38R = 190$

$\therefore \quad R = \frac{190}{38} = 5\%.$

14. Let annual instalment be ₹ x; then

$x + \frac{x \times 3 \times 5}{100} + x + \frac{x \times 2 \times 5}{100} + x + \frac{x \times 1 \times 5}{100} + x = 645 + \frac{645 \times 4 \times 5}{100}$

$\Rightarrow 4x + \frac{3x}{10} = 774 \Rightarrow \frac{43x}{10} = 774$

$\therefore \quad x = \frac{774 \times 10}{43} = ₹\ 180$

15. Simple interest for 2 years

= ₹ 2050 – ₹ 1900 = ₹ 150

$\therefore$ Simple interest for 1 year

$= ₹\ \frac{150}{2} = ₹\ 75$

Since simple interest for 3 years

= ₹ 75 × 3 = ₹ 225

$\therefore$ Principal = ₹ 1900 – ₹ 225 = ₹ 1675

Hence, $\quad \text{Rate} = \frac{75 \times 100}{1675 \times 1} = 4\frac{1}{2}\%$

Compound Interest

In business transaction if interest as it becomes due is not paid to the lender but is added on to the principal, the money is said to be lent at *compound interest* and the total sum owed after a given time is called the amount at compound interest for that time.

After a certain period, the difference between the amount and the original principal is called the compound Interest (C.I.).

Some Important Formulae :

Let Principal = P, Time = n years

Rate = r% p.a.

then, the amount,

(*a*) when interest is compounded annually:

then, $\text{Amount} = P\left(1+\frac{r}{100}\right)^n$

(*b*) when interest is compounded half yearly:

then, $\text{Amount} = P\left(1+\frac{r/2}{100}\right)^{2n}$

(*c*) when interest is compounded quarterly :

then, $\text{Amount} = P\left(1+\frac{r/4}{100}\right)^{4n}$

(*d*) when time is fraction of a year, say $4\frac{1}{3}$ years,

then, $\text{Amount} = P\left(1+\frac{r}{100}\right)^4 \times \left(1+\frac{\frac{1}{3}r}{100}\right)$

(*e*) when rates are r_1%, r_2% and r_3% for Ist, IInd and IIIrd year respectively; then,

$$\text{Amount} = P\left(1+\frac{r_1}{100}\right)\left(1+\frac{r_2}{100}\right)\left(1+\frac{r_3}{100}\right)$$

EXERCISE

1. What will be the compound interest on ₹ 8000 for 3 years at 5% p.a.?
A. ₹ 1361 B. ₹ 1261
C. ₹ 1260 D. ₹ 1250

2. What will be the amount if a sum of ₹ 2500 is invested for 1 year at 4% per annum compound interest, interest being compounded half-yearly?
A. ₹ 2625 B. ₹ 2601
C. ₹ 2830 D. ₹ 2901

3. Find the compound interest on ₹ 2560 for ½ year at 12½% per annum, interest payable quarterly.
A. ₹ 3720.50 B. ₹ 2722.50
C. ₹ 2752.50 D. ₹ 2250.50

4. After how many years will ₹ 3375 become ₹ 4096 at $6\frac{2}{3}$% per annum compound interest?
A. 4 years B. 2 years
C. 2½ years D. 3 years

5. A certain sum of money placed at compound interest amounts to ₹ 110 in 1 year and to ₹ 121 in 2 years. The rate of interest per annum is :
A. 5% B. 10%
C. 8% D. 4%

6. The present population of a city is 80,000. If the rate of growth is 5% per year, find its population after 3 years.
A. 88,100 B. 95,600
C. 92,610 D. 84,600

7. First year's interest on a sum of money placed at compound interest at the rate of 8% per annum is ₹ 72. What will be interest for the second year?
A. ₹ 77.76 B. ₹ 78.66
C. ₹ 85.66 D. ₹ 78.76

8. The difference between compound and simple interest on a certain sum of money for 2 years at 5% per annum is ₹ 21. Find the sum.
A. ₹ 7200 B. ₹ 8400
C. ₹ 9200 D. ₹ 8500

9. In how many years will a sum of ₹ 19200 placed at 10% per annum compound interest yield an interest of ₹ 4032?
A. 1½ years B. 2½ years
C. 2 years D. 3 years

10. The compound interest on a certain sum of money invested for 3 years at 5% per annum is ₹ 1891.50. What will be the simple interest on the same sum at the same rate for 2 years?
A. ₹ 1700 B. ₹ 1200
C. ₹ 1500 D. ₹ 2100

11. The simple interest on a sum of ₹ 4800 for 2 years is ₹ 768. What will be the compound interest on the same sum at the same rate and for the same period?
A. ₹ 798.72 B. ₹ 870.75
C. ₹ 920.69 D. ₹ 884.20

12. A sum of money lent out at a certain rate of simple interest amounts to ₹ 6600 in 2 years and to ₹ 6900 in 3 years. What will be the compound interest on the same sum of money if lent out at the same rate for 2 years?
A. ₹ 605 B. ₹ 715
C. ₹ 615 D. ₹ 595

13. If the first year's interest on a certain sum of money placed at 5% p.a. compound interest is ₹ 1200, what will be the interest for the third year?

A. ₹ 1220 B. ₹ 1323
C. ₹ 1423 D. ₹ 1330

14. If a certain sum of money placed at compound interest amounts to ₹ 960 in 3 years and to ₹ 1000 in 4 years, find the rate of compound interest.

A. $4\frac{1}{6}\%$ B. $5\frac{1}{6}\%$
C. $2\frac{1}{3}\%$ D. 3%

15. What would be the compound interest on ₹ 3200 at 25% per annum for 3 years?

A. ₹ 2050 B. ₹ 2775
C. ₹ 3050 D. ₹ 3180

ANSWERS

1	2	3	4	5	6	7	8	9	10
B	B	B	D	B	C	A	B	C	B
11	**12**	**13**	**14**	**15**					
A	C	B	A	C					

EXPLANATORY ANSWERS

1. ∴ $\text{C.I.} = 8000\left[\left(1+\frac{5}{100}\right)^3 - 1\right]$

$= 8000\left[\left(\frac{21}{20}\right)^3 - 1\right] = \frac{8000 \times 1261}{8000} = ₹\ 1261$

2. $A = 2500\left(1+\frac{2}{100}\right)^2 = 2500\left(\frac{51}{50}\right)^2 = \frac{2500 \times 51 \times 51}{50 \times 50}$

= ₹ 2601.

3. $\text{Amount} = 2560\left(1+\frac{25}{8 \times 100}\right)^2 = \frac{2560 \times 33 \times 33}{32 \times 32}$

= ₹ 2722.50

4. Here, $4096 = 3375\left(1+\frac{20}{3 \times 100}\right)^n$

$\Rightarrow \frac{4096}{3375} = \left(1+\frac{1}{15}\right)^n \Rightarrow \left(\frac{16}{15}\right)^3 = \left(\frac{16}{15}\right)^n$

∴ n = 3 years

5. Here, simple interest of ₹ 110 for 1 year
= 121 − 110 = ₹ 11

Hence, rate = $\frac{11 \times 100}{110 \times 1} = 10\%$

6. Population of the city after 3 years

$= 80{,}000\left(1+\frac{5}{100}\right)^3 = 80{,}000 \times \frac{21}{20} \times \frac{21}{20} \times \frac{21}{20} = 92610$

7. Second year's interest = 72 + 8% of 72

$= 72 + \frac{72 \times 8}{100} = 72 + 5.76 = ₹\ 77.76$

8. Here, $P\left[\left(1+\frac{5}{100}\right)^2 - 1\right] - \frac{P \times 5 \times 2}{100} = 21$

$\Rightarrow P\left[\frac{441}{400} - 1\right] - \frac{P}{10} = 21$

$\Rightarrow P\left[\frac{41}{400} - \frac{1}{10}\right] = 21 \Rightarrow P \times \frac{1}{400} = 21$

∴ P = 21 × 400 = ₹ 8400

9. Amount = ₹ 19200 + ₹ 4032 = ₹ 23232

Now, $23232 = 19200\left(1+\frac{10}{100}\right)^n$

$\Rightarrow \frac{23232}{19200} = \left(\frac{11}{10}\right)^n \Rightarrow \frac{121}{100} = \left(\frac{11}{10}\right)^n$

$\Rightarrow \left(\frac{11}{10}\right)^2 = \left(\frac{11}{10}\right)^n$

∴ n = 2 years

11. $\text{Rate} = \frac{768 \times 100}{4800 \times 2} = 8\%$

∴ $\text{C.I.} = 4800\left[\left(1+\frac{8}{100}\right)^2 - 1\right]$

$= 4800\left[\left(\frac{27}{25}\right)^2 - 1\right] = \frac{4800 \times 104}{625} = ₹\ 798.72$

13. Required interest

$= 1200\left(1+\frac{5}{100}\right)^2 = 1200 \times \frac{21}{20} \times \frac{21}{20} = ₹\ 1323$

14. Here, simple interest of ₹ 960 for 1 year
= 1000 − 960 = ₹ 40

Hence, Rate = $\frac{40 \times 100}{960 \times 1} = \frac{25}{6} = 4\frac{1}{6}\%$

15. Compound interest

$= 3200\left[\left(1+\frac{25}{100}\right)^3 - 1\right] = 3200\left[\left(\frac{5}{4}\right)^3 - 1\right]$

$= \frac{3200 \times 61}{64} = ₹\ 3050.$

●●●

CHAPTER 3

Ratio and Proportion

RATIO

In ratio we compare two quantities of the same kind and consider what multiple, part or parts one is of the other. In comparing 8 with 4, observe that it is 2 times 4. This comparison can be represented as $8 \div 4$ or $\frac{8}{4}$.

Hence, *ratio is that relation between two numbers which is expressed by the fraction, the numerator is which is the measure of the first quantity and denominator is the measure of the second quantity.*

If the terms of a ratio be multiplied or divided by the same quantity the value of the ratio remains unaltered.

Thus, 3 : 4 is the same as 9 : 12 and 9 : 12 is the same as 3 : 4.

PROPORTION

The equality of two ratio is called proportion.

Consider the two ratios:

Ist ratio	2nd ratio
5 : 15	7 : 21

Since, 5 is one-third of 15 and 7 is one-third of 21, the two ratios are equal. The equality of two ratios is called proportion and the numbers 5, 15, and 7, 21 are said to be in **proportion.**

The proportion may be written as 5 : 15 : : 7 : 21 (5 is to 15 as 7 is to 21)

$\Rightarrow \quad 5 : 15 = 7 : 21$

$\Rightarrow \quad \frac{5}{15} = \frac{7}{21}$

The numbers 5, 15, 7 and 21 are called the terms. 5 is the first term, 15 the second, 7 the third, and 21 the fourth.

The first and fourth terms, *i.e.*, 5 and 21 are called extremes (end terms), and the second and the third terms, *i.e.*, 15 and 7 are called the **means** (middle terms), 21 is called the fourth proportional.

Some Important Facts:

1. If a and b are two quantities, then

(*a*) Duplicate ratio of $a : b = a^2 : b^2$

(*b*) Sub-duplicate ratio of $a : b = \sqrt{a} : \sqrt{b}$

(*c*) Triplicate ratio of $a : b = a^3 : b^3$

(*d*) Sub-triplicate ratio $a : b = \sqrt[3]{a} : \sqrt[3]{b}$

(*e*) Inverse or reciprocal ratio of $a : b = \frac{1}{a} : \frac{1}{b}$

(*f*) Third proportional to 'a' and 'b' $= \frac{b^2}{a}$

2. If A : B = $x : y$ and B : C = $p : q$, then

(*a*) $A : C = \frac{x \times p}{y \times q}$

(*b*) $A : B : C = px : py : qy$

3. In what *ratio* the two kinds of tea must be mixed together one at ₹ x per kg and another at ₹ y per kg, so that the mixture may cost ₹ z per kg?

$$\text{Ratio} = \frac{z - y}{x - z}$$

4. A grey hound persues a hare as takes J_1 leaps for every J_2 leaps of the hare. If K_1 leaps of the hound are equal to K_2 leaps of the hare, then the Ratio of speeds of the hound and hare is

$$\frac{J_2 \times K_1}{J_1 \times K_2}$$

5. The incomes of two persons are in the ratio of $a : b$ and their expenditure are in the ratio of $x : y$. If the saving of each person is ₹ s, then income of each is ₹ $\frac{as(y - x)}{ay - bx}$ and ₹ $\frac{bs(y - x)}{ay - bx}$ respectively.

6. In a mixture of z litre, the ratio of milk and water is $x : y$. If another p litres of water is added to the mixture, the ratio of milk and water in the resulting mixture $= \dfrac{xz}{yz + p(x + y)}$

7. There are four members a, b, c and d, then formula for

(*a*) What should be added to each of these numbers so that the remaining numbers may be proportional $= \dfrac{ad - bc}{(b + c) - (a + d)}$

(*b*) What should be subtracted from each of these numbers so that the remaining numbers may be proportional $= \dfrac{ad - bc}{(a + d) - (b + c)}$

8. In a mixture the ratio of milk and water is $a : b$. If in this mixture another K litre of water is added, then the ratio of milk and water in the resulting mixture becomes $a : m$. Then the quantity of milk in the original mixture $= \dfrac{ak}{m - b}$ and quantity of water $= \dfrac{bk}{m - b}$

EXERCISE

1. If A : B = 6 : 7 and B : C = 8 : 9, then A : B : C is:

A. 24 : 28 : 63 B. 48 : 28 : 63
C. 48 : 56 : 63 D. None of these

2. The sum of two numbers is 20 and their difference is $2\frac{1}{2}$. What is the ratio of the numbers?

A. 11 : 7 B. 9 : 11
C. 9 : 7 D. None of these

3. If 0.7 of one number is equal to 0.075 of another, what is the ratio of the two numbers?

A. 6 : 14 B. 3 : 28
C. 5 : 7 D. None of these

4. If 10% of x is the same as 20% of y, then $x : y$ is equal to :

A. 1 : 2 B. 2 : 1
C. 5 : 1 D. 10 : 1

5. Two numbers are in the ratio 3 : 5. If each number is increased by 10, the ratio becomes 5 : 7. The numbers are:

A. 3, 5 B. 7, 9
C. 13, 22 D. 15, 25

6. The mean proportional between 0.32 and 0.02 is:

A. 0.34 B. 0.3
C. 0.16 D. 0.08

7. The sum of three numbers is 98. If the ratio between the first and second be 2 : 3 and that between the second and third be 5 : 8, then what is the second number?

A. 20 B. 30
C. 10 D. 40

8. One man adds 3 litres of water to 12 litres of milk and another 4 litres of water to 10 litres of milk. What is the ratio of the strenghts of the milk in the two mixtures?

A. 15 : 25 B. 25 : 28
C. 28 : 25 D. None of these

9. ₹ 425 is divided among 4 men, 5 women and 6 boys such that the share of a man, a woman and a boy may be in the ratio of 9 : 8 : 4. What is the share of a woman?

A. ₹ 34 B. ₹ 24
C. ₹ 44 D. None of these

10. A vessel contains liquids P and Q in the ratio 5 : 3. If 6 litres of the mixture are removed and the same quantity of liquid q is added, the ratio becomes 3 : 5. What quantity does the vessel hold?

A. 40 litres B. 50 litres
C. 30 litres D. None of these

11. A bucket contains a mixture of two liquids P and Q in the proportion 7 : 5. If 9 litres of the mixture is replaced by 9 litres of liquid Q, then the ratio of the two liquid becomes 7 : 9. How much of the liquid P was there in the bucket?

A. 11 litres B. 21 litres
C. 31 litres D. None of these

12. Three glasses P, Q and R with their capacities in the ratio 2 : 3 : 4 are filled with a mixture of spirit and water. The ratio of spirit to water in P, Q and R is 1 : 5, 3 : 5 and 5 : 7 respectively. If the contents of these glasses are mixed together, what is the ratio of spirit to water in the mixture?

A. 14 : 27 B. 23 : 47
C. 25 : 47 D. None of these

13. A and B are two alloys of gold and copper prepared by mixing metals in proportions 7 : 2 and 7 : 11 respectively. If equal quantities of the alloys are melted to form a third alloy C, the proportion of gold and copper in C will be

A. 5 : 9 B. 5 : 7
C. 7 : 5 D. 9 : 5

14. Gold is 19 times as heavy as water and copper 9 times as heavy as water. The ratio in which these two metals be mixed so that the mixtures is 15 times as heavy as water is:

A. 1 : 2 B. 2 : 3
C. 3 : 2 D. 19 : 135

15. The contents of two vessels containing water and milk are in the ratio 1 : 2 and 2 : 5 are mixed in the ratio 1 : 4. The resulting mixture will have water and milk in the ratio:

A. 21 : 54 B. 31 : 74
C. 27 : 74 D. None of these

16. One year ago, the ratio between Mahesh and Suresh's salaries was 3 : 5. The ratio of their individual salaries of last year and present year are 2 : 3 and 4 : 5 respectively. If their total salaries for the present year are ₹ 4300, what is the present salary of Mahesh?
A. ₹ 1800 B. ₹ 1900
C. ₹ 1600 D. None of these

17. The ratio of P's and Q's income last year was 3 : 4. The ratio of their own incomes of last year and this year is 4 : 5 and 2 : 3 respectively. If the total sum of their present income is ₹ 4160. What is the present income of P?
A. ₹ 1500 B. ₹ 1400
C. ₹ 1600 D. None of these

18. The monthly salary of A, B, C is in the proportion of 2 : 3 ; 5. If C's monthly salary is ₹ 1200 more than that of A, then B's annual salary is:
A. ₹ 14400 B. ₹ 24000
C. ₹ 1200 D. ₹ 2000

19. ₹ 1050 is divided among P, Q and R. The share of P is $\frac{2}{5}$ of the combined share of Q and R. Thus P gets:
A. ₹ 200 B. ₹ 300
C. ₹ 400 D. ₹ 420

20. The ratio between Sumit's and Prakash's age at present is 2 : 3. Sumit is 6 years younger than Prakash. The ratio of Sumit's age to Prakash's age after 6 years will be:
A. 1 : 2 B. 2 : 3
C. 3 : 4 D. 3 : 8

ANSWERS

1	2	3	4	5	6	7	8	9	10
C	C	B	B	D	D	B	C	A	A
11	**12**	**13**	**14**	**15**	**16**	**17**	**18**	**19**	**20**
B	C	C	C	B	A	C	C	B	C

EXPLANATORY ANSWERS

1. A : B = 6 : 7
B : C = 8 : 9

$\therefore$ A : B : C = 6 × 8 : 7 × 8 : 7 × 9 = 48 : 56 : 63

2. Ratio $= \dfrac{20+\frac{5}{2}}{20-\frac{5}{2}} = \dfrac{22.5}{17.5} = \dfrac{225}{175} = \dfrac{9}{7} = 9 : 7$

3. We have, $0.7x = 0.075\,y$

$\dfrac{x}{y} = \dfrac{0.075}{0.7} = \dfrac{75}{700} = \dfrac{3}{28} = 3 : 28$

4. 10% of x = 20% of y

$\Rightarrow \dfrac{10}{100}x = \dfrac{20}{100}y$

$\therefore \dfrac{x}{10} = \dfrac{y}{5} \Rightarrow \dfrac{x}{y} = \dfrac{10}{5} = \dfrac{2}{1} \Rightarrow x : y = 2 : 1$

5. Let the number be $3x$ and $5x$.

Then, $\dfrac{3x+10}{5x+10} = \dfrac{5}{7} \Rightarrow 7(3x+10) = 5(5x+10)$

$\Rightarrow 21x + 70 = 25x + 50 \Rightarrow 4x = 20 \Rightarrow x = 5$

So, the numbers are 15, 25.

6. Mean proportional $= \sqrt{0.32 \times 0.02} = \sqrt{0.0064} = 0.08$

7. The ratio among the three numbers is
2 : 3
5 : 8
and 10 : 15 : 24

$\therefore$ The second number $= \dfrac{98}{10+15+24} \times 15 = 30$

8. Strength of milk in the first mixture $= \dfrac{12}{12+3} = \dfrac{12}{15}$

Strength of milk in the second mixture $= \dfrac{10}{10+4} = \dfrac{10}{14}$

$\therefore$ The ratio of their strengths $= \dfrac{12}{15} : \dfrac{10}{14}$

$= 12 \times 14 : 15 \times 10 = 28 : 25$

9. The ratio of shares of group of men, women and boys
= 9 × 4 : 8 × 5 : 4 × 6 = 9 : 10 : 6

$\therefore$ Share of 5 women $= \dfrac{425}{9+10+6} \times 10 =$ ₹ 170

$\therefore$ Share of 1 woman $= \dfrac{170}{5} =$ ₹ 34

10. Let the vessel contains $5x$ litres and $3x$ litres of liquid P and Q respectively. The removed quantity contains

$\dfrac{16}{5+3} \times 5 = 10$ litres of P

and 16 – 10 = 6 litres of Q.

Now, $(5x - 10) : (3x - 6 + 16) = 3 : 5$

$\Rightarrow \dfrac{5x-10}{3x+10} = \dfrac{3}{5} \Rightarrow 25x - 50 = 9x + 30$

$\Rightarrow 16x = 80 \Rightarrow x = 5$

$\therefore$ Vessel contains $8x = 8 \times 5 = 40$ litres.

11. Let the two liquids P and Q are $7x$ litres and $5x$ litres repectively.

Now, when 9 litres of mixture are taken out, P remains

$$7x - 9\left(\frac{7}{7+5}\right) = 7x - \frac{9\times 7}{12} = \left(7x - \frac{21}{4}\right) \text{ litres}$$

and Q remains

$$5x - 9\left(\frac{5}{7+5}\right) = 5x - \frac{9\times 5}{12} = \left(5x - \frac{15}{4}\right) \text{ litres}$$

Now, when 9 litres of liquid Q are added,

$$\left(7x - \frac{21}{4}\right):\left(5x - \frac{15}{4} + 9\right) = 7 : 9$$

$$\Rightarrow \frac{7x - \frac{21}{4}}{5x - \frac{15}{4} + 9} = \frac{7}{9}$$

$$\Rightarrow 63x - \frac{189}{4} = 35x + \frac{147}{4}$$

$$\Rightarrow 28x = \frac{189}{4} + \frac{147}{4} = \frac{336}{4} = 84$$

$$\Rightarrow x = \frac{84}{28} = 3 \Rightarrow 7x = 7 \times 3 = 21 \text{ litres.}$$

12. P : Q : R

2 : 3 : 4

Spirit : Water = 1 : 5, 3 : 5 and 5 : 7

When they are mixed, the ratio of spirit to water

$$= \left(2\times\frac{1}{1+5} + 3\times\frac{3}{3+5} + 4\times\frac{5}{5+7}\right):\left(2\times\frac{5}{1+5} + 3\times\frac{5}{3+5} + 4\times\frac{7}{5+7}\right)$$

$$= \left(\frac{1}{3} + \frac{9}{8} + \frac{5}{3}\right):\left(\frac{5}{3} + \frac{15}{8} + \frac{7}{3}\right) = \frac{25}{8}:\frac{47}{8} = 25 : 47$$

13. Gold in C $= \left(\frac{7}{9} + \frac{7}{18}\right) = \frac{21}{18} = \frac{7}{6}$

Copper in C $= \left(\frac{2}{9} + \frac{11}{18}\right) = \frac{15}{18} = \frac{5}{6}$

$\therefore$ Gold : Copper $= \frac{7}{6}:\frac{5}{6} = 7 : 5$

14. Let 1 gm of gold be mixed with x gm of copper to give $(1 + x)$ gm of mixture.

Now, $1G = 19w$

and $1C = 9w$

and mixture $= 15w$

Now, 1 gm gold + x gm copper = $(1 + x)$ gm mixture

$\therefore 19w + 9w \times x = (1 + x) \times 15w$

Thus, $4w = 6wx$

$$\Rightarrow x = \frac{4w}{6w} = \frac{4}{6} = \frac{2}{3}$$

So, the required ratio is $1:\frac{2}{3}$, *i.e.*, 3 : 2.

15.

	Water	*Milk*
Vessel I	$\frac{1}{3}$	$\frac{2}{3}$
Vessel II	$\frac{2}{7}$	$\frac{5}{7}$

From vessel I, $\frac{1}{5}$ is taken and from vessel II, $\frac{4}{5}$ is taken. Therefore, the ratio of water to milk in the new vessel

$$= \left(\frac{1}{3}\times\frac{1}{5} + \frac{2}{7}\times\frac{4}{5}\right):\left(\frac{2}{3}\times\frac{1}{5} + \frac{5}{7}\times\frac{4}{5}\right)$$

$$= \left(\frac{1}{15} + \frac{8}{35}\right):\left(\frac{2}{15} + \frac{20}{35}\right) = \frac{31}{105}:\frac{74}{105} = 31 : 74$$

16. The ratio of Mahesh's salary for the two years = 2 : 3

The ratio of Suresh's salary for the two years = 4 : 5

We have also given that the ratio of their salary during the last year = 3 : 5

Now, we change the antecedents (2 and 4) of the first two ratios so that the antecedents in the first becomes 3 (antecedent of the third ratio) and the antecedent in the second becomes 5 (consequent of the third ratio).

Thus, $2 : 3 = 3:\frac{9}{2}$ and $4 : 5 = 4\left(\frac{5}{4}\right):5\left(\frac{5}{4}\right) = 5:\frac{25}{4}$

Now, it is clear that the ratio of their salaries for the present year is $\frac{9}{2}:\frac{25}{4} = 18 : 25$

$\therefore$ The present salary of Mahesh

$$= \frac{4300}{18+25}\times 18 = ₹\ 1800$$

17. The ratio of present incomes

$$= 3\times\frac{5}{4}:4\times\frac{3}{2} = \frac{15}{4}:\frac{12}{2} = 30 : 48 = 5 : 8$$

$\therefore$ P's present income $= \frac{4160}{5+8}\times 5 = ₹\ 1600$

18. Let the monthly salary of A, B, C be $2x$, $3x$ and $5x$

Then, $5x - 2x = 1200$

or, $3x = 1200$

$\therefore$ $x = 400$

B's monthly salary = $3x = 3 \times 400 = ₹\ 1200$

19. P : (Q + R) = 2 : 5

$\therefore$ P's share $= ₹\left(1050 \times \frac{2}{7}\right) = ₹\ 300$

20. Let their ages be $2x$ and $3x$ years.

$\Rightarrow$ $3x - 2x = 6 \Rightarrow x = 6$

Sumit's age = 12 years

Prakash's age = 18 years

After 6 years, Sumit's age = 18 years and Prakash's age = 24 years

$\therefore$ Ratio of their ages = 18 : 24 = 3 : 4

•••

CHAPTER 4

Algebra

Square Roots

Points To Remember

- A number n is a perfect square number, if $n = m^2$
- A perfect square number is never negative.
- A square number never ends in 2, 3, 7 or 8.
- The number of zeros at the end of a perfect square is even.
- The square of an even number is even.
- The square of an odd number is odd.
- There are no natural number p and q such that $p^2 = 2q^2$.
- A number m is a square root of n, if $n = m \times m = m^2$. Positive square root of n is written as $\sqrt{n}$.
- If p and q are perfect squares ($q \neq 0$), then
  (i) $\sqrt{p \times q} = \sqrt{p} \times \sqrt{q}$
  (ii) $\sqrt{\frac{p}{q}} = \frac{\sqrt{p}}{\sqrt{q}}$
- A perfect squares leaves remainder 0 or 1 on division by 3.
  The following table gives the possible remainders for some other prime divisors.

Divisor	Possible Remainders
3	0, 1
5	0, 1, 4
7	0, 1, 2, 4
11	0, 1, 3, 4, 5, 9
13	0, 1, 3, 4, 9, 10, 12

- The unit's digit of the square of a natural number is the unit's digit of the square of the digit at unit's place of the given natural number.

Unit's digit of the number	Unit's digit of the square of the number
0	0
1 or 9	1
2 or 8	4
3 or 7	9
4 or 6	6
5	5

- For every natural number n,
  $(n + 1)^2 - n^2 = (n + 1) + n$
  e.g.; $9^2 - 8^2 = 9 + 8 = 17$
  $19^2 - 18^2 = 19 + 18 = 37$
- The square of a natural number n is equal to the sum of first n odd natural numbers.
  e.g.; $2^2 = 1 + 3$
  $4^2 = 1 + 3 + 5 + 7 = 16$
  n^2 = Sum of first n odd natural numbers.
- A triplet (m, n, p) of three natural numbers m, n and p is called a pythagorean triplet
  if $m^2 + n^2 = p^2$
- The square root of a perfect square number can be obtained by :
  (i) the prime factorization. (ii) the division method.
- If n is not a perfect square, then $\sqrt{n}$ is not a rational number.
- Squares of natural numbers having all digits 1 have a following pattern:
  $1^2 = 1$
  $11^2 = 1\ \mathbf{2}\ 1$
  $111^2 = 1\ 2\ \mathbf{3}\ 2\ 1$
  $1111^2 = 1\ 2\ 3\ \mathbf{4}\ 3\ 2\ 1$

$11111^2 = 1\ 2\ 3\ 4\ \mathbf{5}\ 4\ 3\ 2\ 1$

$111111^2 = 1\ 2\ 3\ 4\ 5\ \mathbf{6}\ 5\ 4\ 3\ 2\ 1$

$\vdots \quad \vdots \quad \vdots$

$111111111^2 = 1\ 2\ 3\ 4\ 5\ 6\ 7\ 8\ \mathbf{9}\ 8\ 7\ 6\ 5\ 4\ 3\ 2\ 1$

In this pattern the sum of the digits of every number on the right hand side is a perfect square at given below:

$1 + 2 + 1 = 4 = 2^2$

$1 + 2 + 3 + 2 + 1 = 9 = 3^2$

$1 + 2 + 3 + 4 + 3 + 2 + 1 = 16 = 4^2$

. . . .

$1 + 2 + 3 + 4 + 5 + 6 + 7 + 8 + 9 + 8 + 7 + 6 + 5 + 4 + 3 + 2 + 1 = 81 = 9^2$.

- Observe the following pattern

$11^2 = 121$

$101^2 = 10201$

$1001^2 = 1002001$

$10001^2 = 100020001$

- Observe the following pattern

$11^2 = 121$

$101^2 = 10201$

$10101^2 = 102030201$

$1010101^2 = 1020304030201$

$101010101^2 = 10203040504030201$

- **Short Cut Method to find Squares Column Method**

Using $(a + b)^2 = a^2 + 2ab + b^2$.

Make three columns: What is square of 86

$a = 8, b = 6$

Step	Column I (a^2)	Column II $2ab$	Column III b^2
I	$(8)^2 = 64$	$2 \times 8 \times 6 = 96$	$(6)^2 = 36$
II	64	**9**6 + 3 = 99	3**6**

Step	Column I (a^2)	Column II $2ab$	Column III b^2
III	64 + 9 = **73**	96 + 3 = 9**9**	3**6**

The bold digits give the required square $86^2 = 7396$.

Square Root

Square root of a given number is that number which is multiplied by itself is equal to the given number.

For example, square root of 81 is 9 because

92 = 9 × 9 = 81.

Methods of Finding the square root

(a) Prime Factorization Method

(i) Prime Factorization Method

(ii) Group the Factors in Paris

(iii) Take one number from each pair of factors and then multiply them together.

Example: Find the square root of 4761?

Solution: $4761 = \underbrace{23 \times 23} \times \underbrace{3 \times 3}$

$\therefore \quad \sqrt{4761} = 23 \times 3 = 69$.

(b) Method of Division: This method is used when the number is large and the factors cannot be easily determined.

Exar.ple: Find the square root of 226576?

Solution:

```
        476
   4  226516
       16
  87    665
   7    609
 946    5676
   6    5676
           ×
```

$\sqrt[2]{226576} = 476$.

EXERCISE

1. $\sqrt{53824} = ?$

A. 202 B. 232

C. 242 D. 332

2. The value of $\sqrt{10+\sqrt{25+\sqrt{108+\sqrt{154+\sqrt{255}}}}}$ is:

A. 4 B. 6

C. 8 D. 10

3. Evaluate : $\sqrt{41-\sqrt{21+\sqrt{19-\sqrt{9}}}}$.

A. 3 B. 5

C. 6 D. 6.4

4. $\left(\frac{\sqrt{625}}{11} \times \frac{14}{\sqrt{25}} \times \frac{11}{\sqrt{196}}\right)$ is equal to:

A. 5

B. 6

C. 8

D. 11

5. If $x * y = x + y + \sqrt{xy}$, the value of 6*24 is:

A. 41 B. 42

C. 43 D. 44

6. $\sqrt{\frac{25}{81}-\frac{1}{9}} = ?$

A. $\frac{2}{3}$ B. $\frac{4}{9}$

C. $\frac{16}{81}$ D. $\frac{25}{81}$

7. The value of $\sqrt{0.01}+\sqrt{0.81}+\sqrt{1.21}+\sqrt{0.0009}$ is:

A. 2.03 B. 2.1

C. 2.11 D. 2.13

8. If $\sqrt{18225} = 135$, then the value of

$\left(\sqrt{182.25}+\sqrt{1.8225}+\sqrt{0.018225}+\sqrt{0.00018225}\right)$ is:

A. 1.49985 B. 14.9985

C. 149.985 D. 1499.85

9. If $\sqrt{3^n} = 729$, the value of n is:

A. 6 B. 8

C. 10 D. 12

10. If $\sqrt{1+\frac{x}{169}} = \frac{14}{13}$, then x is equal to:

A. 1 B. 13

C. 27 D. None of these

11. If $\sqrt{1+\frac{55}{729}} = 1+\frac{x}{27}$, then the value of x is:

A. 1 B. 3

C. 5 D. 7

12. The value of $\frac{\sqrt{80}-\sqrt{112}}{\sqrt{45}-\sqrt{63}}$ is:

A. $\frac{3}{4}$ B. $1\frac{1}{3}$

C. $1\frac{7}{9}$ D. $1\frac{3}{4}$

13. Given $\sqrt{2} = 1.414$. The value of

$\sqrt{8}+2\sqrt{32}-3\sqrt{128}+4\sqrt{50}$ is:

A. 8.426 B. 8.484

C. 8.526 D. 8.876

14. $\sqrt{\frac{0.081\times0.324\times4.624}{1.5625\times0.0289\times72.9\times64}}$ is equal to:

A. 0.024 B. 0.24

C. 2.4 D. 24

15. The value of $\sqrt{\frac{(0.03)^2+(0.21)^2+(0.065)^2}{(0.003)^2+(0.021)^2+(0.0065)^2}}$ is:

A. 0.1 B. 10

C. 10^2 D. 10^3

16. The square root of $(7+3\sqrt{5})(7-3\sqrt{5})$ is:

A. $\sqrt{5}$ B. 2

C. 4 D. $3\sqrt{5}$

17. $\left(\sqrt{3}-\frac{1}{\sqrt{3}}\right)^2$ simplifies to:

A. $\frac{3}{4}$ B. $\frac{4}{\sqrt{3}}$

C. $\frac{4}{3}$ D. None of these

18. $\left(\sqrt{2}+\frac{1}{\sqrt{2}}\right)^2$ is equal to:

A. $2\frac{1}{2}$ B. $3\frac{1}{2}$

C. $4\frac{1}{2}$ D. $5\frac{1}{2}$

19. If $3a = 4b = 6c$ and $a + b + c = 27\sqrt{29}$, then $\sqrt{a^2+b^2+c^2}$ is:

A. $3\sqrt{29}$

B. 81

C. 87

D. None of these

20. The square root of $0.\overline{4}$ is:

A. $0.\overline{6}$ B. $0.\overline{7}$

C. $0.\overline{8}$ D. $0.\overline{9}$

ANSWERS

1	2	3	4	5	6	7	8	9	10
B	A	C	A	B	B	D	B	D	C
11	**12**	**13**	**14**	**15**	**16**	**17**	**18**	**19**	**20**
A	B	B	A	B	B	C	C	C	A

EXPLANATORY ANSWERS

1.

$$\begin{array}{r|l} 2 & \overline{5}\,\overline{38}\,\overline{24}\ (232 \\ & 4 \\ \hline 43 & 138 \\ & 129 \\ \hline 462 & \ \ 924 \\ & \ \ 924 \\ \hline & \ \ \times \end{array}$$

$\therefore\ \sqrt{53824} = 232.$

2. Given exp. $= \sqrt{10+\sqrt{25+\sqrt{108+\sqrt{154+15}}}}$

$= \sqrt{10+\sqrt{25+\sqrt{108+\sqrt{169}}}}$

$= \sqrt{10+\sqrt{25+\sqrt{108+13}}} = \sqrt{10+\sqrt{25+\sqrt{121}}}$

$= \sqrt{10+\sqrt{25+11}} = \sqrt{10+\sqrt{36}}$

$= \sqrt{10+6} = \sqrt{16} = 4$

3. Given exp. $= \sqrt{41-\sqrt{21+\sqrt{19-3}}}$

$= \sqrt{41-\sqrt{21+\sqrt{16}}} = \sqrt{41-\sqrt{21+4}}$

$= \sqrt{41-\sqrt{25}} = \sqrt{41-5} = \sqrt{36} = 6$

4. Given exp. $= \frac{25}{11}\times\frac{14}{5}\times\frac{11}{14} = 5$

5. $6*24 = 6 + 24 + \sqrt{6\times 24} = 30+\sqrt{144} = 30+12 = 42$

6. $\sqrt{\frac{25}{81}-\frac{1}{9}} = \sqrt{\frac{25-9}{81}} = \sqrt{\frac{16}{81}} = \frac{\sqrt{16}}{\sqrt{81}} = \frac{4}{9}$

7. Given exp.

$= \sqrt{\frac{1}{100}}+\sqrt{\frac{81}{100}}+\sqrt{\frac{121}{100}}+\sqrt{\frac{9}{10000}}$

$= \frac{1}{10}+\frac{9}{10}+\frac{11}{10}+\frac{3}{100}$

$= 0.1 + 0.9 + 1.1 + 0.03 = 2.13$

8. Given exp.

$= \sqrt{\frac{18225}{10^2}}+\sqrt{\frac{18225}{10^4}}+\sqrt{\frac{18225}{10^6}}+\sqrt{\frac{18225}{10^8}}$

$= \frac{\sqrt{18225}}{10}+\frac{\sqrt{18225}}{10^2}+\frac{\sqrt{18225}}{10^3}+\frac{\sqrt{18225}}{10^4}$

$= \frac{135}{10}+\frac{135}{100}+\frac{135}{1000}+\frac{135}{10000}$

$= 13.5 + 1.35 + 0.135 + 0.0135 = 14.9985$

9. $\sqrt{3^n} = 729 = 3^6$

$\Leftrightarrow \left(\sqrt{3^n}\right)^2 = (3^6)^2$

$\Leftrightarrow 3^n = 3^{12}$

$\Leftrightarrow n = 12$

10. $\sqrt{1+\frac{x}{169}} = \frac{14}{13} \Rightarrow 1+\frac{x}{169} = \frac{196}{169}$

$\Rightarrow \frac{x}{169} = \left(\frac{196}{169}-1\right) = \frac{27}{169}$

$\Rightarrow x = 27.$

11. $\sqrt{1+\frac{55}{729}} = 1+\frac{x}{27}$

$\Rightarrow \sqrt{\frac{784}{729}} = \frac{27+x}{27}$

$\Rightarrow \frac{28}{27} = \frac{27+x}{27}$

$\Rightarrow 27 + x = 28 \Rightarrow x = 1$

12. $\frac{\sqrt{80}-\sqrt{112}}{\sqrt{45}-\sqrt{63}} = \frac{\sqrt{16\times5}-\sqrt{16\times7}}{\sqrt{9\times5}-\sqrt{9\times7}}$

$= \frac{4\sqrt{5}-4\sqrt{7}}{3\sqrt{5}-3\sqrt{7}} = \frac{4\left(\sqrt{5}-\sqrt{7}\right)}{3\left(\sqrt{5}-\sqrt{7}\right)} = \frac{4}{3} = 1\frac{1}{3}$

13. Given exp.

$= \sqrt{4\times2}+2\sqrt{16\times2}-3\sqrt{64\times2}+4\sqrt{25\times2}$

$= 2\sqrt{2}+8\sqrt{2}-24\sqrt{2}+20\sqrt{2}$

$= 6\sqrt{2} = 6 \times 1.414 = 8.484$

14. Given exp. $= \sqrt{\frac{81\times324\times4624}{15625\times289\times729\times64}}$

$= \frac{9\times18\times68}{125\times17\times27\times8} = \frac{3}{125} = 0.024$

15. Given exp. $= \sqrt{\frac{(0.03)^2+(0.21)^2+(0.065)^2}{\left(\frac{0.03}{10}\right)^2+\left(\frac{0.21}{10}\right)^2+\left(\frac{0.065}{10}\right)^2}}$

$= \sqrt{\frac{100\ [(0.03)^2+(0.21)^2+(0.065)^2]}{(0.03)^2+(0.21)^2+(0.065)^2}}$

$= \sqrt{100} = 10$

16. $\sqrt{(7+3\sqrt{5})(7-3\sqrt{5})} = \sqrt{(7)^2-(3\sqrt{5})^2}$

$= \sqrt{49-45} = \sqrt{4} = 2$

17. $\left(\sqrt{3}-\frac{1}{\sqrt{3}}\right)^2 = \left(\sqrt{3}\right)^2 + \left(\frac{1}{\sqrt{3}}\right)^2 - 2\times\sqrt{3}\times\frac{1}{\sqrt{3}}$

$= 3+\frac{1}{3}-2 = 1+\frac{1}{3} = \frac{4}{3}$

18. $\left(\sqrt{2}+\frac{1}{\sqrt{2}}\right)^2 = \left(\sqrt{2}\right)^2 + \left(\frac{1}{\sqrt{2}}\right)^2 + 2\times\sqrt{2}\times\frac{1}{\sqrt{2}}$

$= 2+\frac{1}{2}+2 = 4+\frac{1}{2} = 4\frac{1}{2}$

19. $4b = 6c \Rightarrow b = \frac{3}{2}c$ and $3a = 4b$

$\Rightarrow \quad a = \frac{4}{3}b = \frac{4}{3}\left(\frac{3}{2}c\right) = 2c$

$a + b + c = 27\sqrt{29}$

$2c+\frac{3}{2}c+c = 27\sqrt{29}$

$\Rightarrow \quad \frac{9}{2}c = 27\sqrt{29}$

$\Rightarrow \quad c = 6\sqrt{29}$

$\therefore \sqrt{a^2+b^2+c^2}$

$= \sqrt{(a+b+c)-2(ab+bc+ca)}$

$= \sqrt{\left(27\sqrt{29}\right)^2 - 2\left(2c\times\frac{3}{2}c+\frac{3}{2}c\times c+c\times 2c\right)}$

$= \sqrt{(729\times 29)-2\left(3c^2+\frac{3}{2}c^2+2c^2\right)}$

$= \sqrt{(729\times 29)-2\times\frac{13}{2}c^2}$

$= \sqrt{(729\times 29)-13\times\left(6\sqrt{29}\right)^2}$

$= \sqrt{29(729-468)}$

$= \sqrt{29\times 261} = \sqrt{29\times 29\times 9}$

$= 29 \times 3 = 87$

20. $\sqrt{0.\bar{4}} = \sqrt{\frac{4}{9}} = \frac{2}{3} = 0.666.... = 0.\bar{6}$.

Basic Algebraic Identities of School Algebra & Elementary Surds

Algebric Identies

Some Important Formula

(*i*) $(a + b)^2 = a^2 + 2ab + b^2$

(*ii*) $(a - b)^2 = a^2 - 2ab + b^2$

(*iii*) $a^2 - b^2 = (a - b)(a + b)$

(*iv*) $(a + b + c)^2 = a^2 + b^2 + c^2 + 2ab + 2bc + 2ca$

(*v*) $(a + b - c)^2 = a^2 + b^2 + c^2 + 2ab - 2bc - 2ca$

(*vi*) $(a - b + c)^2 = a^2 + b^2 + c^2 - 2ab - 2bc + 2ca$

(*vii*) $(-a + b + c)^2 = a^2 + b^2 + c^2 - 2ab + 2bc - 2ca$

(*viii*) $(a + b)^3 = a^3 + b^3 + 3ab(a + b)$ or

$= a^3 + b^3 + 3a^2b + 3ab^2$

(*ix*) $(a - b)^3 = a^3 - b^3 - 3ab\ (a - b)$ or

$= a^3 - b^3 - 3a^2b + 3ab^2$

(*x*) $a^3 + b^3 = (a + b)\ (a^2 + b^2 - ab)$ or

$= (a + b)^3 - 3ab(a + b)$

(*xi*) $a^3 - b^3 = (a - b)\ (a^2 + b^2 + ab)$ or

$= (a - b)^3 + 3ab\ (a - b)$

(*xii*) $a^3 + b^3 + c^3 - 3abc$

$= (a + b + c)(a^2 + b^2 + c^2 - ab - bc - ca)$

If $a + b + c = 0$

$a^3 + b^3 + c^3 = 3abc$

(*xiii*) $(x + a)\ (x + b) = x^2 + (a + b)x + ab$

(*xiv*) $(a + b)^2 + (a - b)^2 = 2(a^2 + b^2)$

(*xv*) $(a + b)^2 - (a - b)^2 = 4ab$

(*xvi*) $(a + b)^3 + (a - b)^3 = 2(a^3 + 3ab^2)$

(*xvii*) $(a + b)^3 - (a - b)^3 = (2(b^3 + 3a^2b)$

(*xviii*) If $x+\frac{1}{x} = t$ Then, $x^2+\frac{1}{x^2} = t^2-2$

(*xix*) If $x-\frac{1}{x} = t$ Then, $x^2+\frac{1}{x^2} = t^2+2$

(*xx*) $x^3+\frac{1}{x^3} = \left(x+\frac{1}{x}\right)^3 - 3\left(x+\frac{1}{x}\right)$

(*xxi*) $x^2-\frac{1}{x^3} = \left(x-\frac{1}{x}\right)^3 + 3\left(x-\frac{1}{x}\right)$

(*xxii*) $x+\frac{1}{x} = \sqrt{x^2+\frac{1}{x^2}+2}$

(*xxiii*) $x-\frac{1}{x} = \sqrt{x^2+\frac{1}{x^2}-2}$

Factorization of Algebraic Expressions

Factorization : The process of writing an algebraic expression as the product of two or more algebraic expressions is called factorization.

Factors : The algebraic expressions that may be multiplied to obtain the given algebraic expressions are called factors of the given expression.

Factor Theorem : If $f(x)$ is completely divisible by $(x - a)$ then $f(a) = 0$, $(x - a)$ is called factor of $f(x)$, if and only if $f(a) = 0$

Remainder Theorem : If an expression $f(x)$ is divided by $(x - a)$ then the remainder is $f(a)$.

e.g., $f(x) = ax^3 + bx + cx + d$

$f(a) = a \cdot a^3 + b \cdot a + c \cdot a + d$ is known as remainder of the given polynomials.

Surds

Given a number, it is not always possible to find some whole number which when multiplied by itself will give the given number. In other words all given numbers are not perfect square numbers. For example, square root of 9, *i.e.*, $\sqrt{9}$ is 3, which is a whole number. But square root of 15, *i.e.*, $\sqrt{15} = 3.873$, which is not a whole number.

Hence square roots of natural numbers which are not perfect squares are not rational numbers. These are irrational numbers and are called **Surds**.

For example, $\sqrt{3}$, $\sqrt{7}$, $2+\sqrt{11}$, $4+\sqrt{13}$ ..... etc. are Surds.

Given below are a few formulas which are quite helpful in solving the problems related to surds:

1. $\sqrt{a} \times \sqrt{a} = a$
2. $\sqrt{a} \times \sqrt{b} = \sqrt{ab}$
3. $\left(\sqrt{a}+\sqrt{b}\right)^2 = a + b + 2\sqrt{ab}$
4. $\left(\sqrt{a}-\sqrt{b}\right)^2 = a + b - 2\sqrt{ab}$
5. $x\sqrt{a}+x\sqrt{b} = x\left(\sqrt{a}+\sqrt{b}\right)$
6. $\dfrac{1}{\sqrt{a}+\sqrt{b}} = \dfrac{1}{\sqrt{a}+\sqrt{b}} \times \dfrac{\sqrt{a}-\sqrt{b}}{\sqrt{a}-\sqrt{b}} = \dfrac{\sqrt{a}-\sqrt{b}}{a-b}$
7. $\dfrac{1}{\sqrt{a}-\sqrt{b}} = \dfrac{1}{\sqrt{a}-\sqrt{b}} \times \dfrac{\sqrt{a}+\sqrt{b}}{\sqrt{a}+\sqrt{b}} = \dfrac{\sqrt{a}+\sqrt{b}}{a-b}$
8. $a + \sqrt{b} = c + \sqrt{d} \Rightarrow a = c$ and $b = d$
9. $\sqrt{2} = 1.41421$, $\sqrt{3} = 1.73205$, $\sqrt{5} = 2.23607$, $\sqrt{6} = 2.4494$ $\sqrt{7} = 2.64575$, $\sqrt{8} = 2.82842$, $\sqrt{10} = 3.16227$, $\sqrt{11} = 3.31662$

EXERCISE

1. $(28)^3 + (-15)^3 + (-13)^3 = ?$
A. 16380 B. 16250
C. 16420 D. 16280

2. If $x+\dfrac{1}{x} = 5$, What is the value of $x^3+\dfrac{1}{x^3}$:
A. 120 B. 210
C. 110 D. 105

3. If $x^2+\dfrac{1}{x^2} = 83$, what is the value of $x^3-\dfrac{1}{x^3} = ?$
A. 756 B. 754
C. 856 D. 932

4. $23^3 - 17^3 = ?$
A. 7254 B. 7153
C. 7271 D. 7154

5. If $x + \dfrac{1}{x} = 15$, then the value of $x^2 + \dfrac{1}{x^2}$ will be:
A. 228 B. 230
C. 323 D. 223

6. If $x = 12$ and $y = 4$, the value of $(x+y)^{x/y}$ will be:
A. 4096 B. 3896
C. 4196 D. 5086

7. If $x + y = 2z$, then the value of $\left(\dfrac{x}{x-z}+\dfrac{z}{y-z}\right)$ will be:
A. 1 B. 4
C. 3/2 D. 2

8. If $x + y + z = 0$, then the value of $\dfrac{(x+y)(y+z)(z+x)}{xyz}$ will be:
A. –3 B. –2
C. 0 D. –1

9. If $x + \dfrac{1}{x} = 3$, the value of $x^4 + \dfrac{1}{x^4}$ will be:
A. 49 B. 47
C. 37 D. 42

10. If $\left(x+\dfrac{1}{x}\right)^2 = 0$, then the value of $\left(x^2+\dfrac{1}{x^2}\right)$ will be:
A. 1 B. –1
C. 2 D. –2

11. If $\left(a+\dfrac{2}{a}\right) = 3$, then the value of $\left(a-\dfrac{2}{a}\right)$ will be:
A. ± 4 B. ± 5
C. ± 2 D. ± 1

12. If $\sqrt{a}+\frac{1}{\sqrt{a}}=4$, then the value of $a^2+\frac{1}{a^2}$ will be:

A. 194 B. 199
C. 178 D. 192

13. Factors of x^2-25 are:

A. $(x-1)(x-25)$
B. $(x+25)(x-1)$
C. $(x+5)(x-5)$
D. $(x-5)(x-5)$

14. Square of $\left(x-\frac{1}{x}\right)$ will be

A. $x^2-2-\frac{1}{x^2}$ B. $x^2-2+\frac{1}{x^2}$
C. $x^2-4-\frac{1}{x^2}$ D. $x^2-2+\frac{1}{x}$

15. Factors of $36-9x^2$ will be:

A. $(6+3x)(6-3x)$ B. $(3x-6)(6-3x)$
C. $(3x+6)(3x-6)$ D. $(12x-3x)(3+3x)$

ANSWERS

1	2	3	4	5	6	7	8	9	10
A	C	A	A	D	A	A	D	B	D
11	12	13	14	15					
D	A	C	B	A					

EXPLANATORY ANSWERS

1. Let $a=28$, $b=-15$ and $c=-13$. Then

$$a+b+c=28-15-13=0$$
$$a^3+b^3+c^3=3abc$$
$$(28)^3+(-15)^3+(-13)^3=3\times 28\times(-15)\times(-13)$$
$$=16380$$

2. $$x^3+\frac{1}{x^3}=\left(x+\frac{1}{x}\right)^3-3\left(x+\frac{1}{x}\right)$$
$$=(5)^3-3\times 5=125-15=110.$$

3. If $x^2+\frac{1}{x^2}=83$, what is the value of $x^3-\frac{1}{x^3}=?$

$$\left(x-\frac{1}{x}\right)^2=x^2+\frac{1}{x^2}-2$$
$$x-\frac{1}{x}=\sqrt{83-2}=\sqrt{81}$$
$$x-\frac{1}{x}=9$$
$$\therefore\quad \left(x^3-\frac{1}{x^3}\right)=\left(x-\frac{1}{x}\right)^3+3\left(x-\frac{1}{x}\right)$$
$$=(9)^3+3\times 9=729+27=756$$

4. $23^3-17^3=(20+3)^3-(20-3)^3=2(3^3+3\times 20^2\times 3)$

$$[\because (a+b)^3-(a-b)^3=2(b^3+3a^2b)]$$
$$=2(27+3600)=54+7200=7254$$

5. $\because x+\frac{1}{x}=15\Rightarrow\left(x+\frac{1}{x}\right)^2=(15)^2$

$$\Rightarrow x^2+\frac{1}{x^2}+2.x\frac{1}{x}=225$$
$$\therefore\quad x^2+\frac{1}{x^2}=225-2=223.$$

6. $(x+y)^{x/y}=(12+4)^{12/4}=(16)^3=4096.$

$[\because x=12, y=4]$

7. $\because x+y=2z\Rightarrow x-z=z-y=-(y-z)$

$$\therefore\quad \frac{x}{x-z}+\frac{z}{y-z}=\frac{x}{-(y-z)}+\frac{z}{y-z}=\frac{z-x}{y-z}=1.$$
$$[\because x-z=z-y]$$

8. $\because$
$$x+y+z=0\Rightarrow x+y=-z$$
$$x+y+z=0\Rightarrow y+z=-x$$
and
$$x+y+z=0\Rightarrow z+x=-y$$
$$\therefore\quad \frac{(x+y)(y+z)(z+x)}{xyz}=\frac{(-z)(-x)(-y)}{xyz}$$
$$=-1.$$

9. $\because x+\frac{1}{x}=3\Rightarrow\left(x+\frac{1}{x}\right)^2=(3)^2$

$$\Rightarrow\quad x^2+\frac{1}{x^2}+2.x.\frac{1}{x}=9$$
$$\Rightarrow\quad x^2+\frac{1}{x^2}=9-2=7$$
$$\because\quad x^2+\frac{1}{x^2}=7\Rightarrow\left(x^2+\frac{1}{x^2}\right)^2=(7)^2$$
$$\Rightarrow\quad x^4+\frac{1}{x^4}+2.x^2.\frac{1}{x^2}=49$$
$$\therefore\quad x^4+\frac{1}{x^4}=49-2=47.$$

10. $$\left(x+\frac{1}{x}\right)^2=0\Rightarrow x^2+\frac{1}{x^2}+2x.\frac{1}{x}=0$$
$$\Rightarrow\quad x^2+\frac{1}{x^2}=-2.$$

11. $\because \left(a-\frac{2}{a}\right)^2 = \left(a+\frac{2}{a}\right)^2 - 4.a.\frac{2}{a} = (3)^2 - 8 = 9 - 8 = 1$

$\therefore \left(a-\frac{2}{a}\right) = \pm\sqrt{1} = \pm 1.$

12. $\because \sqrt{a}+\frac{1}{\sqrt{a}} = 4 \Rightarrow \left(\sqrt{a}+\frac{1}{\sqrt{a}}\right)^2 = (4)^2$

$\Rightarrow a+\frac{1}{a}+2.\sqrt{a}.\frac{1}{\sqrt{a}} = 16 \because \left(a+\frac{1}{a}\right) = 14$

$\Rightarrow \left(a+\frac{1}{a}\right)^2 = (14)^2 \Rightarrow a^2+\frac{1}{a^2}+2.a.\frac{1}{a} = 196$

$\therefore a^2+\frac{1}{a^2} = 196 - 2 = 194.$

13. $x^2 - 25 = (x)^2 - (5)^2$,
[which is of the form $a^2 - b^2$]
$= (x+5)(x-5).$

14. According to question:

Square of $\left(x-\frac{1}{x}\right) = \left(x-\frac{1}{x}\right)^2$

$= x^2 - 2.x.\frac{1}{x} + \left(\frac{1}{x}\right)^2$

$= x^2 - 2 + \frac{1}{x^2}.$

15. $36 - 9x^2 = (6)^2 - (3x)^2$ [which is of the form $a^2 - b^2$]
$= (6+3x)(6-3x).$

Graphs of Linear Equations

Linear Equation in One Variable

Definition: A linear equation in one variable is an equation of the form $ax + b = 0$ or, $ax = c$ where, a, b, c are real numbers, $a \neq 0$ and x is a variable. Its graph is a straight line.

(*i*) If equation is on X-axis, then Y = 0

(*ii*) If equation is on Y-axis, then X = 0

Linear Equation in Two Variables

Definition: An equation of the form $ax + by + c = 0$ or, $ax + by = c$ where, a, b, c are real numbers, $a \neq 0$, $b \neq 0$ and x, y are variables, is called a linear equation in two variables.

For example: (*i*) $2x + 3y = 12$ (*ii*) $x + 2y = 8$

The System of Equations

$a_1x + b_1y + c_1 = 0$ and $a_2x + b_2y + c_2 = 0$ may be either unique solution or no solution or infinitely many solutions.

Unique solution is known as consistent or not parallel. No solution is known as inconsistent or parallel, while many solutions are known as coincident or dependent.

(*a*) **For unique solution:** $\frac{a_1}{a_2} \neq \frac{b_1}{b_2}$

(*b*) **For no solution:** $\frac{a_1}{a_2} = \frac{b_1}{b_2} \neq \frac{c_1}{c_2}$

(*c*) **For many solutions:** $\frac{a_1}{a_2} = \frac{b_1}{b_2} = \frac{c_1}{c_2}$

Graph of linear equations

Graph of a linear equation in two variables x and y *i.e.*, the graph of the equation of the form

$ax + by + c = 0,\ a \neq 0,\ b \neq 0$

we consider the equation,

$2x + y = 6$

then, $y = 6 - 2x$

We find different values of this equation

x	0	1	2	3
y	6	4	2	0

Now, we plot these points (x, y) on a graph paper and then join these points

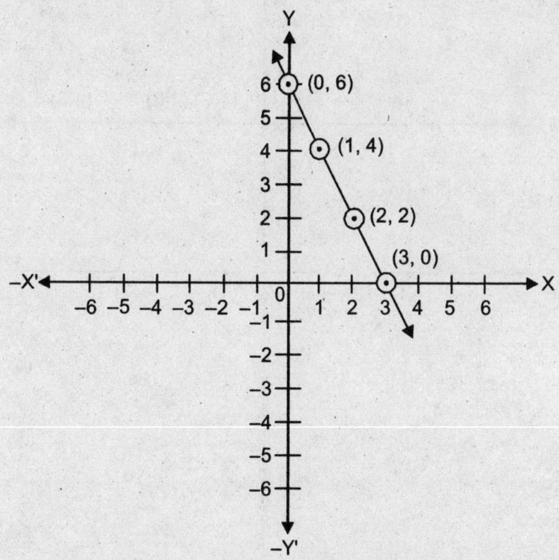

Hence, the line l is called the graph of the equation

$2x + y = 6$

Example 1: Draw the graph:

(*i*) $x = 2$, (*ii*) $y = 3$, (*iii*) $y = 0$

Solution: (*i*) The given equation, $x = 2$ does not contain y

Table of values

x	2	2	2	fixed
y	1	3	4	any value

ploting the points (2, 1), (2, 3) and (2, 4) and joining them

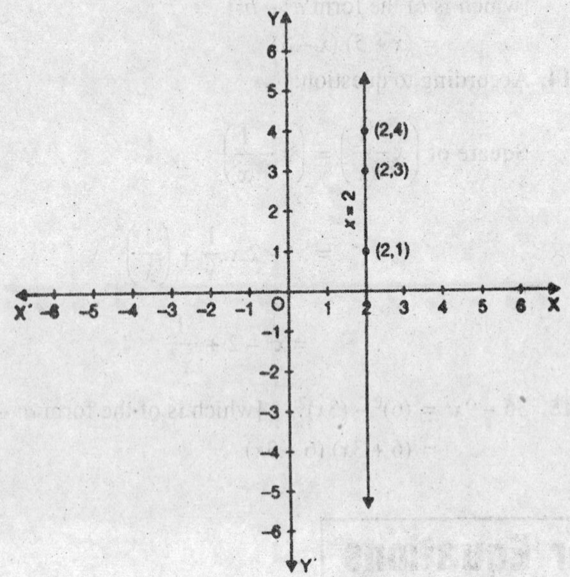

Hence, the graph of the given equation is a line parallel to y-axis

(*ii*) The given equation $y = 3$ does not contain x

Table of values

x	1	2	4	any value
y	3	3	3	fixed

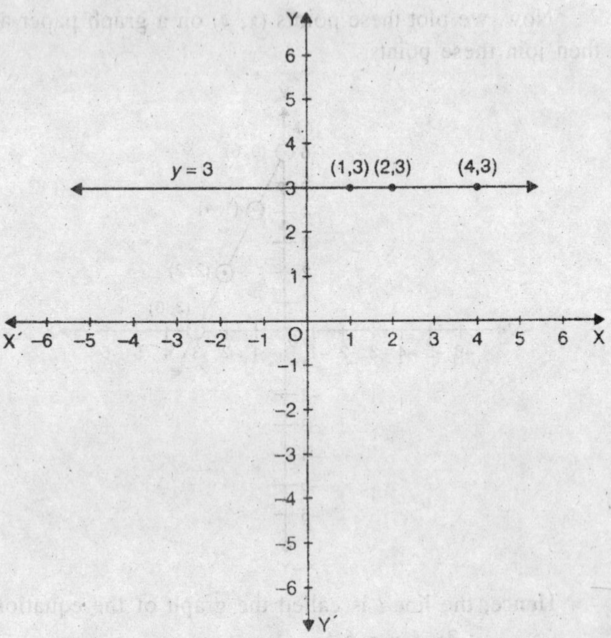

Hence, the graph of the given equation is a line parallel to x-axis.

(*iii*) The given equation is $y = 0$

Table of values

x	1	2	3	any value
y	0	0	0	fixed

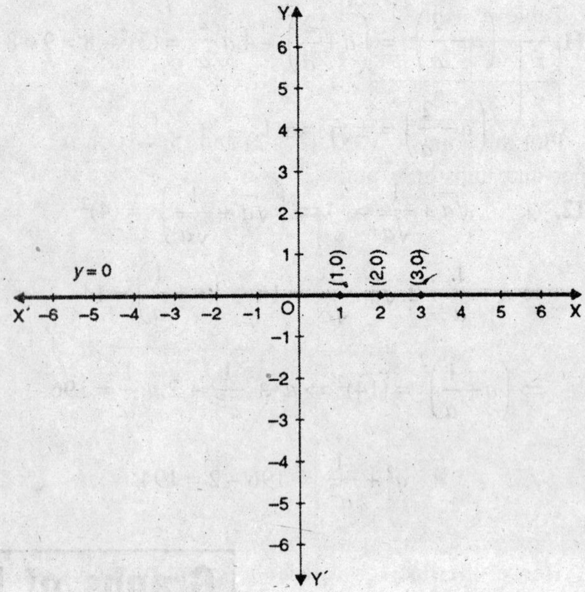

Hence, $y = 0$ is the equation of x-axis.

Example 2. Draw the graph of the line $x - 2y = 3$. From the graph find co-ordinates of the points when (*i*) $x = -5$, (*ii*) $y = 0$

Solution: The given equation is $x - 2y = 3$

Table of value

x	3	5	1
y	0	1	–1

$\because \quad 2y = x - 3$

$\therefore \quad y = \dfrac{x-3}{2}$

Plotting the points (3, 0), (5, 1) and (1, –1) on the graph paper and joining these points.

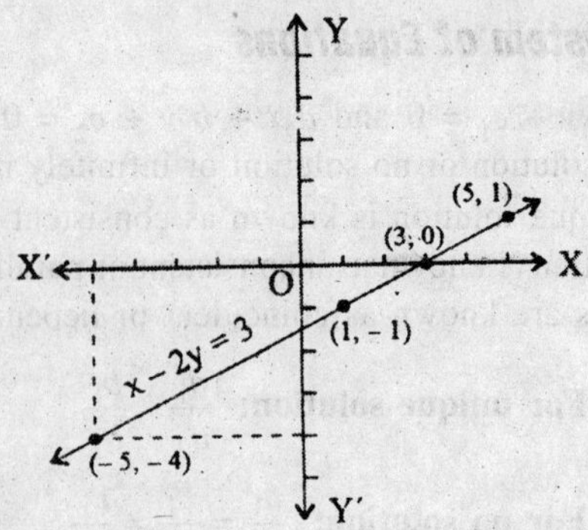

From the graph,

(*i*) when $x = -5$, then $y = -4$

(*ii*) when $y = 0$, then $x = 3$

Example 3. Draw the graph of the equations

$$5x + 3y = 4.$$

Solution: The given equation is $5x + 3y = 4$

$$\Rightarrow \quad y = \frac{4-5x}{3}$$

Table of values

x	–1	2	5
y	3	–2	–7

Plot the points (–1, 3), (2, –2) and (5, –7) on the graph paper and join these points.

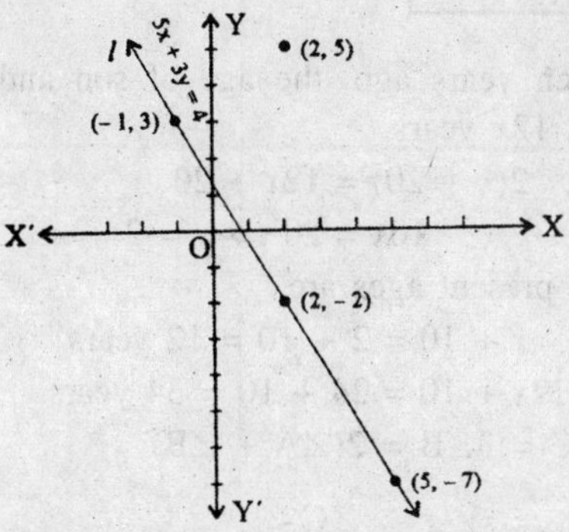

Hence, the line l is called the graph of the equation,

$$5x + 3y = 4$$

Example 4. Draw the graph of the equation

$$2x - 3y = -11.$$

Solution: The given equation is

$$2x - 3y = -11$$

$$\Rightarrow \quad 3y = 2x + 11$$

$$\Rightarrow \quad y = \frac{2x+11}{3}$$

Table of values

x	–1	2	–4
y	3	5	1

plot the points (–1, 3), (2, 5) and (–4, 1) on the graph paper and join these points

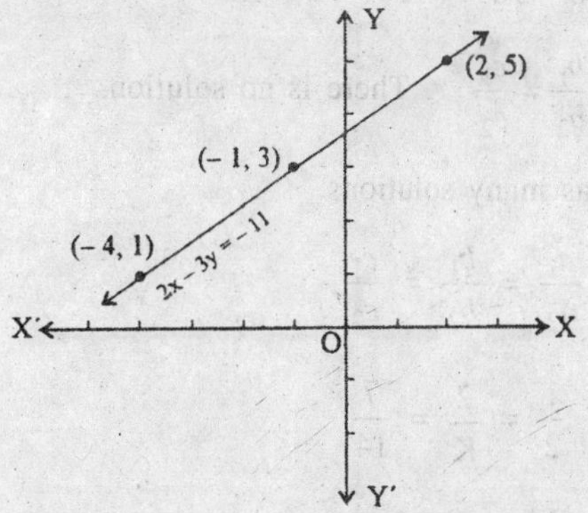

Hence, this line l is called the graph of the equation

$$2x - 3y = -11.$$

EXERCISE

1. The system of linear equations $2x + 3y = 7$ and $4x + 6y = 10$ has:
A. no solution
B. unique solution
C. infinite solution
D. no conclusion can be drawn

2. The value of k for which the system of equations $x + 2y + 7 = 0$ and $2x + ky + 14 = 0$ will have infinitely many solutions is:
A. 2 B. 4
C. 6 D. 8

3. For what value of α, the system of equations $\alpha x + 3y = \alpha - 3$ and $12x + \alpha y = \alpha$ will have a unique solution?
A. $\alpha \neq \pm 6$ B. $\alpha \neq \pm 3$
C. $\alpha \neq \mp 6$ D. None of these

4. For what value of k, the system of equations will represent the coincident lines $x + 5y - 7 = 0$ and $4x + 20y + k = 0$?
A. 28 B. –28
C. –26 D. None of these

5. A lady has 50 paise and ₹ 1 coins in her purse. If in all, she has 40 coins totally ₹ 25.50 how many of each type of coins does she have?
A. 26, 11 B. 11, 29
C. 29, 11 D. None of these

6. A father is three times as old as his son. After twelve years his age will be twice as the age of his son. Find their present ages in years.
A. 12, 26 B. 24, 36
C. 36, 12 D. None of these

7. Ten years ago, father was twelve times as old as his son. Ten years after, he will be twice as old as his son will be. Find their present ages in years.
A. 12, 36 B. 12, 24
C. 12, 34 D. None of these

8. The present age of a father is 3 years more than three times the age of son. Three years hence father's age will be 10 years more than twice the age of son. Determine their present ages in years.
A. 10, 33 B. 33, 10
C. 10, 30 D. None of these

9. In a triangle ABC, $\angle C = 3\angle B = 2(\angle A + \angle B)$. Find three angles in degrees.
A. 20°, 50°, 120° B. 30°, 40°, 120°
C. 20°, 40°, 120° D. None of these

10. The fraction becomes 2 when 1 is added to both the numerator and the denominator, and it becomes 3 when 1 is subtracted from both the numerator and denominator. The given fraction is :
A. 7/3 B. 4/7
C. 3/7 D. 7/4

ANSWERS

1	2	3	4	5	6	7	8	9	10
A	B	A	B	C	C	C	A	C	A

EXPLANATORY ANSWERS

1. $\frac{2}{4} = \frac{3}{6} \neq \frac{7}{10} \Rightarrow \frac{1}{2} = \frac{1}{2} \neq \frac{7}{10}$

$\frac{a_1}{a_2} = \frac{b_1}{b_2} \neq \frac{c_1}{c_2}$ ∴ There is no solution.

2. Since, it has many solutions.

$\therefore \quad \frac{a_1}{a_2} = \frac{b_1}{b_2} = \frac{c_1}{c_2}$

$\frac{1}{2} = \frac{2}{K} = \frac{7}{14}$

$\frac{1}{2} = \frac{2}{K} \Rightarrow K = 4.$

3. Since, the given equations have unique solution.

$\therefore \quad \frac{a_1}{a_2} \neq \frac{b_1}{b_2}$

$\frac{\alpha}{12} \neq \frac{3}{\alpha}$

$\Rightarrow \quad \alpha^2 \neq 36 \Rightarrow \alpha \neq \pm 6$

4. Since, the given set of equations represent coincident lines.

then, $\frac{1}{4} = \frac{5}{20} = \frac{-7}{K} \Rightarrow K = -28$

5. Let, x be the number of 50 paise coins and y be the number of ₹ 1 coins.

According to the question,

$x + y = 40$ ...(*i*)

and $\frac{x}{2} + y = 25.50$

$\Rightarrow \quad x + 2y = 51$ ...(*ii*)

Subtracting equation (*i*) from (*ii*) and solving we get, $x = 29,\ y = 11$

6. Let, age of son = x years.

∴ age of father = $3x$ years.

According to the question,

$2(x + 12) = 3x + 12 \Rightarrow x = 12$

∴ Son's age = 12 years; Father's age = 36 years.

7. Let ten years ago, the age of son and father were x and $12x$ years.

Then, $2(x + 20) = 12x + 20$

$\Rightarrow \quad 10x = 20 \Rightarrow x = 2$

Their present ages are

$x + 10 = 2 + 10 = 12$ years

$12x + 10 = 24 + 10 = 34$ years.

9. $\therefore \angle C = 3\angle B = 2(\angle A + \angle B)$

$\angle A + \angle B = \frac{\angle C}{2}$

We have, $\angle A + \angle B + \angle C = 180°$

(Sum of angles of a triangle is 180°)

$\frac{\angle C}{2} + \angle C = 180°$

$3\angle C = 2 \times 180°$

$\angle C = \frac{2 \times 180°}{3} = 120°$

$3\angle B = \angle C$

$\angle B = \frac{\angle C}{3} = \frac{120°}{3} = 40°$

$\therefore \quad \angle A = 180° - (120° + 40°) = 180° - 160° = 20°.$

10. Let the fraction be $\frac{x}{y} \Rightarrow \frac{x+1}{y+1} = 2$

$\Rightarrow \quad x + 1 = 2y + 2$

$\Rightarrow \quad x - 2y = 1$ ...(*i*)

Again $\frac{x-1}{y-1} = 3$

$\Rightarrow \quad x - 1 = 3y - 3$

$\Rightarrow \quad x - 3y = -2$ ...(*ii*)

from (*i*) and (*ii*)

$$\begin{array}{r} x - 2y = 1 \\ x - 3y = -2 \\ - \quad + \quad + \\ \hline y = 3 \end{array}$$

Putting the value of y in (*i*) then we get, $x = 7$

$\therefore \quad \text{fraction} = \frac{x}{y} = \frac{7}{3}$

●●●

CHAPTER

5 Average

The average of any number of quantities of the same kind can be found by dividing their sum by their number. Thus,

$$\text{Average} = \frac{\text{Sum of quantities}}{\text{No. of quantities}}$$

Sum of quantities = Their average × Their number

$$\text{Number of quantities} = \frac{\text{Sum of quantities}}{\text{Their average}}$$

When a body coveres the same distance at two different speeds p km/hr and q km/hr, then its average speed for the whole journey is $\frac{2pq}{p+q}$ km/hr.

EXERCISE

1. The average of the fractions $1\frac{1}{2}$, $2\frac{1}{3}$, $3\frac{1}{3}$ and $4\frac{5}{6}$ is:

A. 2 B. $2\frac{1}{2}$
C. 3 D. 4

2. The average of first nine multiples of 3 is

A. 12.0 B. 12.5
C. 15.0 D. 18.5

3. The average of 13 numbers is 68, the average of first 7 numbers is 63 and the average of last 7 numbers is 70. What is the 7th number?

A. 43 B. 45
C. 47 D. 49

4. One-third of a certain journey was covered at the rate of 25 km per hour, one-fourth at the rate of 30 km per hour and the rest at the 50 km per hour. What is the average speed per hour for whole journey?

A. $33\frac{1}{3}$ kmph B. $44\frac{1}{4}$ kmph
C. $22\frac{1}{2}$ kmph D. 33 kmph

5. Nine men went to a hotel. Eight of them spent ₹ 3 for each over their meals and the ninth spent ₹ 2 more than the average expenditure of all the nine. What is the total money spent by them?

A. ₹ 29.25 B. ₹ 29.50
C. ₹ 29 D. ₹ 30

6. An establishment is permitted an average monthly contingency expenditure of ₹ 500 per month during the financial year. When a trial check was made at the end of the first nine months of the year it was found that the average monthly contingency expenditure worked out to be ₹ 511. What average monthly expenditure for the next three months should be aimed at in order to attain the permissible average of ₹ 500 per month for the whole year?

A. ₹ 567 B. ₹ 467
C. 367 D. ₹ 667

7. Average age of 8 persons increased by 2 years, when two men whose ages are 20 and 24 years are replaced by two women. What is the average age of women?

A. 30 years B. 31 years
C. 28 years D. 33 years

8. A man had seven children. When their average age was 12 years, the child who was 6 years of age died. What was the average of the surviving children 5 years after the death of the child?

A. 15 years B. 16 years
C. 17 years D. 18 years

9. The weight of a body, calculated as the average of seven different experiments is 53.735 grams. The average of the first three is 54.005 grams, the fourth was greater than the fifth by 0.004 gram, while the average of the sixth and seventh was 0.010 gram less than the average of the first three. What is the weight of the body as obtained by the fourth experiment?

A. 53.068 gm B. 53.078 gm
C. 53.086 gm D. 53.072 gm

10. A batsman has a certain average of runs for 16 innings. In the 17th innings, he makes a score of 85 runs thereby increasing his average by 3. What is the average after the 17th inning?

A. 33 runs B. 34 runs
C. 37 runs D. 36 runs

11. The average of 50 numbers is 38. If two numbers namely 45 and 55 are discarded, the average of the remaining numbers is

A. 36.5 B. 37
C. 37.5 D. 37.52

12. The average of 6 observations is 12. A new seventh observation is included and the new average is decreased by 1. The seventh observation is

A. 1 B. 3
C. 5 D. 6

13. A man whose bowling average is 12.4 takes 5 wickets for 26 runs and thereby decreases his average by 0.4. The number of wickets, taken by him, before his last match, is

A. 85 B. 78
C. 72 D. 64

14. The average of marks obtained by 120 candidates was 35. If the average of marks of passed candidates was 39 and that of failed candidates was 15, the number of candidates who passed the examination is

A. 100 B. 110
C. 120 D. 150

15. The average of three numbers is 42. The first is twice the second and the second is twice the third. The difference between the largest and the smallest number is

A. 18 B. 36
C. 54 D. 72

ANSWERS

1	2	3	4	5	6	7	8	9	10
C	C	C	A	A	B	A	D	D	C
11	**12**	**13**	**14**	**15**					
C	C	A	A	C					

EXPLANATORY ANSWERS

1. Average $= \frac{1}{4}\left(\frac{3}{2}+\frac{7}{3}+\frac{10}{3}+\frac{29}{6}\right)$

$= \left(\frac{9+14+20+29}{24}\right) = \frac{72}{24} = 3$

2. Average $= \frac{3(1+2+3+4+5+6+7+8+9)}{9} = \frac{135}{9}$

$= 15$

3. Average of 13 numbers = 68

∴ Total of 13 numbers = 13 × 68 = 884

Average of last 7 numbers = 70

∴ Total of last 7 numbers = 7 × 70 = 490

∴ Average of first 6 numbers

= 884 – 490 = 394

∴ Average of first 7 numbers = 63

∴ Total of first 7 numbers = 63 × 7 = 441

∴ 7th number = 441 – 394 = 47

4. Let the total distance covered during journey = 60 km

$\frac{1}{3}$ of the distance covered during journey

$= 60 \times \frac{1}{3} = 20$ km

$\frac{1}{4}$ of the distance covered during journey

$= \frac{1}{4} \times 60 = 15$ km

∴ The distance covered during the rest of journey = 60 – (20 + 15) = 25 km

Time taken to cover 20 km at 25 km/h

$= \frac{20}{25}$ hours $= \frac{4}{5}$ hour

Time taken to cover 15 km at 30 km/h

$\frac{15}{30}$ hours $= \frac{1}{2}$ hour

Time taken to cover 25 km at 50 km/h

$= \frac{25}{50}$ hours $= \frac{1}{2}$ hour

Total time taken $= \frac{4}{5}+\frac{1}{2}+\frac{1}{2} = \frac{9}{5}$ hours

Hence average speed per hour

$= 60 \div \frac{9}{5} = \frac{60 \times 5}{9}$

$= \frac{100}{3}$ km/h $= 33\frac{1}{3}$ km/h

5. Let the average expenditure of all the nine

$= ₹\ x$

Now amount spent by eight

$= ₹\ 3 \times 8 = ₹\ 24$

and total spent by the ninth $= ₹\ x + 2$

$\Rightarrow \quad \frac{26 + x}{9} = x$

$\therefore$ Average amount spent by nine $= \frac{26 + x}{9}$

Total amount spent by nine $= 24 + x + 2 = 26 + x$

$\Rightarrow \quad 9x = 26 + x$

or, $\quad 8x = 26$

$\Rightarrow \quad x = \frac{26}{8} = ₹\ 3.25$

Hence total money spent

$= ₹\ (3.25 \times 9) = ₹\ 29.25$

6. Average monthly expenditure permitted $= ₹\ 500$

Total expenditure permitted for 12 months

$= ₹\ 500 \times 12 = ₹\ 6000$

Expenditure incurred during the first nine months

$= ₹\ 511 \times 9 = ₹\ 4,599$

Expenditure for the last three month

$= ₹\ (6000 - 4599) = ₹\ 1,401$

$\therefore$ Average monthly expenditure for the three months

$= ₹\ \frac{1401}{3} = ₹\ 467$

7. Total increase in the age of 8 persons

$= 2 \times 8 = 16$ years

Total age of two men being replaced

$= 20 + 24 = 44$ years

Total of the age of two women $= 44 + 16 = 60$ years

$\Rightarrow$ The average age of women

$= \frac{60}{2} = 30$ years.

8. Average age of 7 children $= 12$ years

Total ages of 7 children $= 12 \times 7 = 84$ years

Age of 1 child who died $= 6$ years

Total ages of remaining 6 children

$= 84 - 6 = 78$ years

$\therefore$ Average age of 6 children $= \frac{78}{6} = 13$ years

$\therefore$ Average age of 6 children after 5 years

$= 13 + 5 = 18$ years

9. Total weight of 7 experiments

$= 53.735 \times 7 = 376.145$ gm

Total weight of first three

$= 54.005 \times 3 = 162.015$ gm

The average of the 6th and 7th was 0.010 gm less than that of the first three.

$\therefore$ Average of the 6th and 7th

$= 54.005 - 0.010 = 53.995$ gm

$\therefore$ Total of the 6th and 7th $= 53.995 \times 2 = 107.990$ gm

Thus, total of 4th and 5th

$= 376.145 - (162.015 + 107.990) = 106.140$ gm

The fourth was greater than the fifth by 0.004 gm

$\therefore \quad$ The fifth $= (106.140 - 0.004) \times \frac{1}{2} = \frac{106.136}{2}$

$= 53.068$ gm

Hence, the fourth $= 53.068 + 0.004$

$= 53.072$ gm

10. Average increase in the score of 17 innings

$= 3$ runs

Total increase in the score of 17 innings

$= 3 \times 17 = 51$ runs

$\therefore$ His average of 16 innings

$= 85 - 51 = 34$ runs

Hence, average after the 17th innings

$= 34 + 3 = 37$ runs

11. Total of 50 numbers $= 50 \times 38 = 1900$

Total of 48 numbers

$= 1900 - (45 + 55) = 1800$

$\therefore \quad$ Average $= \frac{1800}{48} = 37.5$

12. Seventh observation

$= (7 \times 11 - 6 \times 12) = 5$

13. Suppose the number of wickets taken before the last match $= x$

$\Rightarrow \quad \frac{12.4x + 26}{x + 5} = 12$

$\Rightarrow \quad 12.4x + 26 = 12x + 60$

$\Rightarrow \quad x = 85$

14. Let the number of candidates who passed $= x$

$\Rightarrow 39 \times x + 15 \times (120 - x) = 120 \times 35$

$\Rightarrow \quad 24x = 4200 - 1800$

$\therefore \quad x = \frac{2400}{24} = 100$

15. Let the third number $= x$

Then, second number $= 2x$ and first number $= 4x$

$\therefore \quad \frac{x + 2x + 4x}{3} = 42$

$\Rightarrow \quad \frac{7x}{3} = 42 \Rightarrow x = \frac{42 \times 3}{7}$

$\Rightarrow \quad x = 18$

So, (largest) $-$ (smallest) $= (4x - x) = 3x = 54$

●●●

CHAPTER 6

Partnership Business

When two or more than two persons agree to invest money to run a business jointly, this association or deal is called *partnership* and those who invest money are called *pertners.* The total investment is called the *capital.*

Kind of partners : There are two kinds of partners.

1. **Working or active partner :** When a partner devotes his time for the business in addition to invest his money, he is called a working partner.

   With mutual agreement, the active partners get some fixed percentage of profit as *working allowance.*

2. **Sleeping or non-active partner :** A partner who simply invests money, but does not attend to the business is called a sleeping partner.

Kind of partnership :

(*i*) **Simple partnership :** If the capitals of several partners are invested for the same period, it is called a simple partnership.

(*ii*) **Compound or complex partnership :** If the capitals of the partners are invested for diffrent intervals of time, the partnership is called compound or complex.

EXERCISE

1. A and B started a business with the investment of ₹ 80000 and ₹ 60000 respectively. At the end of the year total profit in the business will be divided between them in the ratio of :

A. 2 : 3 B. 3 : 4
C. 2 : 1 D. 4 : 3

2. A and B started a business in partnership with the investment of ₹ 4000 and ₹ 6000 respectively. If at the end of the year total profit is ₹ 2250, what will each of them get?

A. ₹ 900, ₹ 1350
B. ₹ 800, ₹ 1450
C. ₹ 1000, ₹ 1250
D. ₹ 1200, ₹ 1050

3. Sonu, Monu and Mohit together start a business with the investment of ₹ 1800, ₹ 1500 and ₹ 1600 respectively. If at the end of the year, Monu gains a profit of ₹ 900 the total profit in the business is :

A. ₹ 2880 B. ₹ 2940
C. ₹ 3200 D. ₹ 3240

4. Omdutt started a business with a capital of ₹ 8000. After six months, Sanjay joined him with investment of some capital. If at the end of the year each of them gets equal amount as profit, how much did Sanjay invest in the business?

A. ₹ 18000 B. ₹ 17500
C. ₹ 16000 D. ₹ 16500

5. A, B and C buy a farm for ₹ 100000. A contributes ₹ 40000 in it. They sell it, and from the profit B gets ₹ 2750 and C gets ₹ 1750. What would be the profit of A?

A. ₹ 2780 B. ₹ 3000
C. ₹ 3280 D. ₹ 2785

6. A and B jointly invest ₹ 2100 and ₹ 3100 respectively in a firm. A is an active partner and hence he gets 25% of the profit separately. If their business yields them total ₹ 1040 as profit, what will be the gain of each of them?

A. ₹ 415, ₹ 625 B. ₹ 575, ₹ 465
C. ₹ 515, ₹ 525 D. ₹ 560, ₹ 480

7. Two partners invested ₹ 12500 and ₹ 8500 respectively in a business and decided that 60% of the profit incurred from the business will be equally divided between them while remaining profit will be assumed as interest on their capitals. If one of the partners gets ₹ 300 more profit than the other, what is the total profit in the business?
A. ₹ 3937.50 B. ₹ 4940.50
C. ₹ 3936.50 D. ₹ 4156

8. Neeraj and Birju are partners in a business. They divide between them the profit incurred in the business in such a proportion that $\frac{2}{5}$th portion of the profit gained by Neeraj is equal to $\frac{1}{3}$rd portion of the profit gained by Birju. If total profit in the business is ₹ 1210, find the profit earned by Birju.
A. ₹ 780 B. ₹ 660
C. ₹ 680 D. ₹ 590

9. A, B and C together took under lease a pasture ground for ₹ 888. If in this pasture ground A put his 20 sheep out to graze for 2½ months, B put his 30 sheep out to graze for 4 months and C put his 36 sheep out to graze for 3½ months, find the lease amount paid by each of them.
A. ₹ 205, ₹ 315, ₹ 378 B. ₹ 150, ₹ 360, ₹ 378
C. ₹ 170, ₹ 360, ₹ 358 D. ₹ 228, ₹ 360, ₹ 300

10. A, B and C started a business with the investment of ₹ 5000, ₹ 6000 and ₹ 4000 respectively. A is an active partner and therefore he gets 30% of the profit separately. Rest of the profit is divided in the ratio of their capitals. If at the end of year, A's profit is ₹ 200 more than the sum of the profits made by B and C, find the profit made by each of them.
A. ₹ 1620, ₹ 1242, ₹ 1178
B. ₹ 1720, ₹ 1252, ₹ 1228
C. ₹ 1510, ₹ 1187, ₹ 1133
D. ₹ 1600, ₹ 840, ₹ 560

11. Premchand, Nanak and Prabhat together rented a house for 2 years and settled to pay ₹ 1368 as rent. They lived together in this house for 5 months. Then Prabhat left the house and went away. 8 months after Nanak also went away and left the house for Premchand to live alone. How much did Premchand pay as rent of this house?
A. ₹ 1025 B. ₹ 950
C. ₹ 880 D. ₹ 780

12. A started a business with an investment of ₹ 4000. B joined him after 4 months and C joined him after 5 months. At the end of year they get profit in the ratio of 3 : 4 : 7. Find the ratio of capitals invested in the business by B and C.
A. 1 : 2 B. 2 : 1
C. 3 : 2 D. 1 : 3

13. Amit, Sumeet and Suresh started a business with capitals in the ratio of 2 : 3 : 4. Amit took back half of his investment after 3 months and Sumeet took back one-third portion of his investment after 4 months. If at the end of year, Suresh gets a profit of ₹ 3200, what is the total profit in the business?
A. ₹ $6076\frac{2}{3}$ B. ₹ $6066\frac{2}{3}$
C. ₹ 8000 D. ₹ $8333\frac{1}{3}$

14. A, B and C started a business in partnership. A invested ₹ 4000 for 8 months and ₹ 6000 for 4 months. B invested ₹ 3000 for 6 months and ₹ 5000 for next 6 months of the year while C invested ₹ 3000 for whole of the year. If at the end of year, total profit is ₹ 7000, what will be the shares of A, B and C in the profit?
A. ₹ 2800, ₹ 2400, ₹ 1800
B. ₹ 2500, ₹ 2600, ₹ 1900
C. ₹ 2600, ₹ 2500, ₹ 1900
D. ₹ 2000, ₹ 2700, ₹ 2300

15. A, B and C started a business in partnership with respective investment of ₹ 20000, ₹ 18000 and ₹ 12000. A and B are active partners and therefore they get an additional profit of 12% and 8% respectively for supervision and other related work they do for improvement of the trade. Rest of the profit is divided among them in the proportion of their capitals. If profit made by A is ₹ 648 more than B, find the profit earned by each of them.
A. ₹ 3960, ₹ 3312, ₹ 1728
B. ₹ 4960, ₹ 3312, ₹ 1728
C. ₹ 3690, ₹ 3132, ₹ 1820
D. ₹ 5960, ₹ 3600, ₹ 1750

16. Three labourers work for 5 hours, 6 hours and 7 hours respectively in a field and get wages in the proportion of time of working in the field. Three days after they increase their working hours by 1 hour. 4 days after they increase their working hours, work in the field gets finished. If their total wages is ₹ 276, find the share of wages earned by each of them.
A. ₹ 78, ₹ 92, ₹ 106 B. ₹ 88, ₹ 87, ₹ 101
C. ₹ 80, ₹ 90, ₹ 106 D. ₹ 81, ₹ 95, ₹ 100

17. A, B and C together took a pasture ground on rent at ₹ 16 per month with a view to graze their sheep in this ground. A, B and C owned 70, 50 and 40 sheep respectively. After 4 months A sold $\frac{2}{7}$th portion of his sheep to B and 3 month after that C sold $\frac{2}{5}$th portion of his sheep to A. How much will each of them pay as rent after the end of a year?
A. ₹ 70, ₹ 70, ₹ 52 B. ₹ 76, ₹ 76, ₹ 40
C. ₹ 80, ₹ 76, ₹ 36 D. ₹ 40, ₹ 76.30, ₹ 76

18. Samir and Saurabh started a joint firm. Samir's investment was thrice the investment of Saurabh and the period of his investment was two times the period of investment of Saurabh. If Saurabh got ₹ 4000 as profit, then their total profit is:

A. ₹ 16000 B. ₹ 20000
C. ₹ 24000 D. ₹ 28000

19. A, B and C together start a business. The amounts invested by A and B are in the ratio of 4 : 3 whereas the ratio of investments of B and C is 2 : 3. If the total profit earned is ₹ 46000, what is C's share in the profit?

A. ₹ 14000 B. ₹ 15000
C. ₹ 16000 D. ₹ 18000

20. Rani and Nisha started a business initially with ₹ 5100 and ₹ 6600 respectively. If the total profit is ₹ 2730, what is the Rani's share in the profit?

A. ₹ 1190 B. ₹ 1200
C. ₹ 1530 D. ₹ 1540

ANSWERS

1	2	3	4	5	6	7	8	9	10
D	A	B	C	B	B	A	B	B	D
11	**12**	**13**	**14**	**15**	**16**	**17**	**18**	**19**	**20**
B	A	B	A	A	A	B	D	D	A

EXPLANATORY ANSWERS

1. Ratio between their profits = 80000 : 60000 = 4 : 3.

2. Ratio of capitals of A and B = 4000 : 6000 = 2 : 3

A's share in the profit = $\frac{2}{5}\times 2250$ = ₹ 900

B's share in the profit = $\frac{3}{5}\times 2250$ = ₹ 1350

3. Ratio of their capitals
= 1800 : 1500 : 1600 = 18 : 15 : 16

Sum of proportionals = 18 +15 + 16 = 49

Monu's profit = ₹ 900

∴ Total profit in the business = $\frac{900}{15}\times 49$ = ₹ 2940

4. Investment by Omdutt for 1 month
= ₹ 8000 × 12 = ₹ 96000

Let Sanjay invested ₹ x for 6 months

∴ Capital of Sanjay for 1 month = ₹ x × 6 = ₹ $6x$

Now, $6x = 96000$

∴ x = ₹ 16000

5. Here, ratio of capitals of A and (B + C)
= 40000 : 60000 = 2 : 3

Profit of (B + C) = 2750 + 1750 = ₹ 4500

Hence, A's profit = $\frac{4500}{3}\times 2$ = ₹ 3000

6. Separate profit for A = $\frac{1040\times 25}{100}$ = ₹ 260

Remaining profit = ₹ (1040 – 260) = ₹ 780

Ratio of capitals of A and B = 2100 : 3100 = 21 : 31

A's profit = $\frac{21}{52}\times 780$ = ₹ 315

B's profit = $\frac{31}{52}\times 780$ = ₹ 465

Total profit of A = ₹ (315 + 260) = ₹ 575

Therefore A and B will make profit of ₹ 575 and ₹ 465 respectively.

7. Ratio of their capitals = 12500 : 8500 = 25 : 17

Hence, sum of their ratios = 25 + 17 = 42 and difference of ratios = 25 – 17 = 8

Now total profit taken as interest

= $\frac{300}{8}\times 42$ = ₹ 1575

Hence, total profit in the business

= $\frac{100}{40}\times 1575$ = ₹ 3937.50

8. Let shares of Neeraj and Birju in profit are ₹ x and ₹ y respectively; then,

$\frac{2}{5}x=\frac{1}{3}y \quad \therefore x : y = 5 : 6$

Hence, share of Birju = $\frac{6}{11}\times 1210$ = ₹ 660

9. Ratio of their shares = (20 × 5/2) : (30 × 4) : (36 × 7/2) = 25 : 60 : 63

Sum of proportionals = 25 + 60 + 63 = 148

Total lease amount = ₹ 888

∴ Amount paid by A = $\frac{25}{148}\times 888$ = ₹ 150

Amount paid by B = $\frac{60}{148}\times 888$ = ₹ 360

Amount paid by C = $\frac{63}{148}\times 888$ = ₹ 378

10. Ratio of capitals of A, B and C = 5000 : 6000 : 4000 = 5 : 6 : 4

Let total profit in the business = ₹ x; then

$$\frac{30x}{100}+\frac{5}{15}\times\frac{70x}{100}-\frac{(6+4)}{15}\times\frac{70x}{100}=200$$

$$\Rightarrow \frac{8x}{15}-\frac{7x}{15}=200 \quad \therefore x = ₹\ 3000$$

Hence, A's profit = $\frac{8\times 3000}{15}$ = ₹ 1600;

B's profit = $\frac{6}{15}\times\frac{7\times3000}{10}$ = ₹ 840;

C's profit = $\frac{4}{15}\times\frac{7\times3000}{10}$ = ₹ 560

11. Rent for 1 month = $\frac{1368}{24}$ = ₹ 57

Total rent paid by Premchand

= $5\times\frac{57}{3}+8\times\frac{57}{2}+11\times57$

= 95 + 228 + 627 = ₹ 950.

12. Let, B and C invest ₹ x and ₹ y respectively

∴ Ratio of their capitals = 48000 : $8x$: $7y$

But given ratio of the profits = 3 : 4 : 7

$$8x : 7y = 4 : 7 \Rightarrow \frac{x}{y}=\frac{1}{2}$$

Hence, $x : y = 1 : 2$

13. Ratio of capitals of Amit, Sumeet and Suresh

= (2 × 3 + 1 × 9) : (3 × 4 + 2 × 8) : (4 × 12)

= 15 : 28 : 48

Sum of the ratios = 15 + 28 + 48 = 91

∴ Total profit in the business

= $\frac{91}{48}\times3200$ = ₹ $6066\frac{2}{3}$

14. Ratio of their capitals

= (4000 × 8 + 6000 × 4) : (3000 × 6 + 5000 × 6) : (3000 × 12)

= 56000 : 48000 : 36000 = 14 : 12 : 9

Sum of proportionals = 14 + 12 + 9 = 35

Share of A in the profit = $\frac{14}{35}\times7000$ = ₹ 2800

Share of B in the profit = $\frac{12}{35}\times7000$ = ₹ 2400

Share of C in the profit = $\frac{9}{35}\times7000$ = ₹ 1800

15. Ratio of their capitals

= 20000 : 18000 : 12000 = 10 : 9 : 6

Let total profit in the business = ₹ x; then

$$\left(\frac{12x}{100}+\frac{10}{25}\times\frac{80x}{100}\right)-\left(\frac{8x}{100}+\frac{9}{25}\times\frac{80x}{100}\right)=648$$

$$\Rightarrow \frac{11x}{25}-\frac{46x}{125}=648 \Rightarrow \frac{9x}{125}=648$$

$$\therefore \quad x=\frac{648\times125}{9} = ₹\ 9000$$

Hence, share of A = $\frac{11x}{25}=\frac{11\times9000}{25}$

= ₹ 3960;

Share of B = $\frac{46x}{125}=\frac{46\times9000}{125}$ = ₹ 3312

Share of C = $\frac{6}{25}\times\frac{80x}{100}=\frac{6}{25}\times\frac{4}{5}\times9000$ = ₹ 1728

16. Ratio of their working hours

= (5 × 3 + 6 × 4) : (6 × 3 + 7 × 4) : (7 × 3 + 8 × 4)

= 39 : 46 : 53

Sum of proportionals = 39 + 46 + 53 = 138

∴ Wages for the 1st labourer = $\frac{39}{138}\times276$ = ₹ 78

Wages for the 2nd labourer = $\frac{46}{138}\times276$ = ₹ 92

Wages for the 3rd labourer = $\frac{53}{138}\times276$ = ₹ 106

17. Number of sheep of A for 1 month

= $[70\times4+(70-\frac{2}{7}\times70)\times3+(70-\frac{2}{7}\times70+\frac{2}{5}\times40)\times5]$

= 280 + 150 + 330 = 760

Number of sheep of B for 1 month

= $[50\times4+(50+\frac{2}{7}\times70)\times8]$ = 200 + 560 = 760

Number of sheep of C for 1 month

= $[40\times7+(40-\frac{2}{5}\times40)\times5]$ = 280 + 120 = 400

Hence, ratio of their sheep

= 760 : 760 : 400 = 19 : 19 : 10

Sum of proportionals = 19 + 19 + 10 = 48

1 year's rent of the pasture ground = 16 × 12 = ₹ 192

∴ Rent to be paid by A = $\frac{19}{48}\times192$ = ₹ 76

Rent to be paid by B = $\frac{19}{48}\times192$ = ₹ 76

Rent to be paid by C = $\frac{10}{48}\times192$ = ₹ 40

18. Ratio of Capitals of Samir and Saurabh

= (3 × 2) : (1 × 1) = 6 : 1

Saurabh's profit = ₹ 4000

Hence, total profit in the business

= 7 × ₹ 4000 = ₹ 28000

19. A : B = 4 : 3 and B : C = 2 : 3,

Therefore, A : B : C = 8 : 6 : 9

Hence, C's profit = $\frac{9}{23}\times46000$ = ₹ 18000

20. Ratio of their Capitals = 5100 : 6600 = 17 : 22

Hence, Rani's profit = $\frac{17}{39}\times2730$ = ₹ 1190

●●●

CHAPTER 7

Mixture and Alligation

Alligation deals with calculation of values or properties of a mixture. Alligation is the rule that enables us—

(1) to find the proportion in which the two or more ingredients at the given prices must be mixed to yield a mixture at the given price. This is termed as "Alligation Alternate".

(2) to calculate the average or mean value of a mixture when the prices of two or more ingredients which are to be mixed together and proportion in which they are to be mixed are given. This is termed as "Alligation Medial".

1. Rule of Alligation:

$$\frac{\text{Amount of Cheaper ingredient}}{\text{Amount of Dearer ingredient}} = \frac{\text{Cost price of Dearer} - \text{Mean Price}}{\text{Mean Price} - \text{Cost Price of Cheaper}}$$

Here cost price of unit quantity of the mixture is called the *Mean Price.*

The above rule may be represented schematically as under:

CP of unit quantity of cheaper ingredient (c) | CP of unit quantity of dearer ingredient (d)

Mean Price (m)

$(d - m)$ | $(m - c)$

(Cheaper quantity) : (Dearer quantity) $= (d - m) : (m - c)$

This relationship is very helpful in solving problems on mixture involving percentage values, rates, prices, speeds etc.

2. m gm of sugar solution has x % sugar in it. To increase the sugar content in the solution to y %, quantity of sugar need to be added $= \dfrac{m(y-x)}{100-y}$

3. A vessel contains x litres of liquid A. y litres are withdrawn and replaced by liquid B. Next y litres of the mixture is withdrawn and again replaced by liquid B. This operation is repeated n times.

$$\frac{\text{Quantity of liquid A left after } n\text{th operation}}{\text{Whole quantity of liquid A initially present}} = \left(\frac{x-y}{x}\right)^n \text{ or } \left(1-\frac{y}{x}\right)^n$$

EXERCISE

1. In what proportion must tea at ₹ 62 per kg be mixed with tea at ₹ 72 per kg in order to obtain the mixture worth ₹ 65 per kg?

A. 4 : 6 B. 7 : 3

C. 2 : 3 D. 4 : 7

2. Find the quantity of rice @ ₹ 10 per kg. which should be mixed with 25 kgs of rice @ ₹ 8 per kg, so that on selling the mixture @ 15 per kg there is 80% profit.

A. 6 kgs B. 7 kgs

C. 3 kgs D. 5 kgs

3. A shopkeeper buys 26 kgs of milk @ ₹ 16 per kg. He also buys from another source an inferior quality of milk @ ₹ 10 per kg. How much quantity of the latter should he buy to mix it with the former so that he can sell the mixture @ ₹ 14 per kg without making any loss?

A. 13 kgs B. 12 kgs

C. 14 kgs D. 16 kgs

4. Two vessels A and B contain milk and water in the ratio 7 : 5 and 17 : 7 respectively. In what ratio mixtures from two vessels should be mixed to get a new mixture containing milk and water in the ratio 5 : 3?

A. 1 : 2 B. 2 : 1

C. 2 : 3 D. 3 : 2

5. Two vessels A and B contain mixture of milk and water in the ratio 4 : 1 and 9 : 11 respectively. They are mixed in the ratio of 3 : 2. Find the ratio of milk : water in the resulting mixture.
   A. 34 : 16 B. 33 : 17
   C. 16 : 34 D. 17 : 33

6. A person has two solutions of sugar with 30% and 50% concentration respectively. In what proportion should he mix two solutions to get 45% concentration in the resulting mixture?
   A. 1 : 3 B. 3 : 1
   C. 2 : 3 D. 3 : 2

7. 6 litres of milk and water mixture has 75% milk in it. How much milk should be added to the mixture to make it 90% pure?
   A. 8 litres B. 9 litres
   C. 10 litres D. 12 litres

8. In what ratio must water be added to spirit to gain 25% by selling it at cost price?
   A. 1 : 4 B. 4 : 1
   C. 3 : 4 D. 4 : 3

9. A shopkeeper has 50 kgs of rice. He sells a part of it at 20% profit and the rest at 40% profit. If he gains 25% on the whole, find the quantity of each part.
   A. 12.5 kgs and 37.5 kgs B. 37.5 kgs and 12.5 kgs
   C. 23.5 kgs and 21.5 kgs D. 21.5 kgs and 23.5 kgs

10. A shopkeeper has 100 kgs of tea. He sells a part of it at 20% profit and the rest at 5% loss. If his overall profit is 10%, find the quantity for each part.
   A. 20 kgs B. 25 kgs
   C. 30 kgs D. 40 kgs

11. A merchant has 160 kgs of wheat. He sells a part of it at 10% profit and the rest of 6% loss. If he incurs 4% loss on the whole, find the quantity for each part.
   A. 120 kgs B. 140 kgs
   C. 150 kgs D. 160 kgs

12. A man bought a certain quantity of sugar for ₹ 8000. He sells one-fourth of it at 20% loss. At what per cent profit should he sell the remainder stock so as to make an overall profit of 20%?
   A. 20% B. 30%
   C. 35% D. 40%

13. A person has ₹ 5000. He invests a part of it at 3% per annum and the remainder at 8% per annum simple interest. His total income in 3 years is ₹ 750. Find the sum invested at different rates of interest.
   A. ₹ 2000 and ₹ 3000 B. ₹ 2500 and ₹ 2500
   C. ₹ 3000 and ₹ 2000 D. ₹ 2750 and ₹ 2250

14. A person covers a dista2nce of 100 kms in 10 hours, partly by walking at 7 km/hr and rest by running at 12 km/hr. Find the distance covered in each part.
   A. 48 kms B. 72 kms
   C. 108 kms D. 124 kms

15. The average monthly salary of employees, consisting of officers and workers, of an organisation is ₹ 3000. The average salary of an officer is ₹ 10,000 while that of a worker is ₹ 2000 per month. If there are total 400 employees in the organisation, find the number of officers and workers separately.
   A. 300, 100 B. 50, 350
   C. 250, 150 D. 310, 90

16. The average daily wages of staff, consisting of supervisors and labourers, of a company is ₹ 50. The average wages of supervisors is ₹ 150 while that of labourers is ₹ 40 per day. If the number of supervisors is 15, find the number of labourers in the company.
   A. 150 B. 175
   C. 180 D. 200

17. ₹ 675 was divided among 75 boys and girls. Each boy gets ₹ 20 whereas a girl gets ₹ 5. Find the number of boys and girls.
   A. 20, 55 B. 15, 60
   C. 25, 50 D. 30, 45

18. A sum of ₹ 70 is divided among 10 children. Each boy gets ₹ 10 whereas a girl gets ₹ 5. If the number of boys is 4, find the number of girls.
   A. 6 B. 7
   C. 8 D. 9

19. From a cask of wine containing 25 litres, 5 litres are withdrawn and the cask is refilled with water. The process is repeated a second and then a third time. Find the quantity of wine left in the cask and also the ratio of wine to water in the resulting mixture.
   A. 61 : 64 B. 16 : 46
   C. 46 : 16 D. 64 : 61

20. A vessel contains 80 litres of milk. 16 litres of milk was taken out of the vessel and replaced by water. Then 16 litres of mixture was withdrawn and again replaced by water. The operation was repeated for third time. How much milk is now left in the vessel?
   A. 96.40 litres B. 50.36 litres
   C. 40.96 litres D. 32.76 litres

ANSWERS

1	2	3	4	5	6	7	8	9	10
B	D	A	B	B	A	B	A	B	D
11	12	13	14	15	16	17	18	19	20
B	B	C	B	B	A	A	A	D	C

EXPLANATORY ANSWERS

1. CP of 1 kg. Cheaper tea ₹ 62   CP of 1 kg. Dearer tea ₹ 72

Mean Price per kg ₹ 65

$d - m = 7$ $m - c = 3$

Using Alligation rule,

$$\frac{\text{Quantity of cheaper tea}}{\text{Quantity of dearer tea}} = \frac{d-m}{m-c} = \frac{7}{3}$$

Therefore, they must be mixed in the ratio of 7 : 3.

3. 16   10

14

4   2

or 2 : 1 $\frac{\text{Quantity of milk @ ₹ 10 per kg}}{\text{Quantity of milk @ ₹ 16 per kg}} = \frac{1}{2}$

So, quantity of milk @ ₹ 10 per kg. $= \frac{26}{2} = 13$ kgs.

5. Fraction is *Milk*   *Water*

A : $\frac{4}{5}$ $\frac{1}{5}$

B : $\frac{9}{20}$ $\frac{11}{20}$

(3A + 2B) = A and B : $\left(\frac{12}{5}+\frac{9}{10}\right)$ $\left(\frac{3}{5}+\frac{11}{10}\right)$

$\frac{33}{10}$ $\frac{17}{10}$

So, Ratio of milk : water in the resulting mixture = 33 : 17.

6. 30%   50%

45%

5   15

He should mix 30% and 50% in the ratio 5 : 15 or 1 : 3.

$$\frac{\text{30\% Solution}}{\text{50\% Solution}} = \frac{1}{3} \text{ or } 1 : 3$$

7. The given solution has 75% milk.

Milk to be added has 100% milk.

75%   100%

90%

10   15

Milk should be added to the given mixture in the ratio 15 : 10 or 3 : 2.

$\therefore$ Quantity of milk to be added $= \frac{3}{2} \times 6 = 9$ litres.

8. Let cost price of spirit be ₹ 1 per litre.

Water 0   Spirit ₹ 1

₹ $\frac{4}{5}$

$\frac{1}{5}$ ₹ $\frac{4}{5}$

Then SP of mixture = ₹ 1 per litre

Gain = 25%

So, CP of mixture $= 1 \times \frac{100}{125} = ₹ \frac{4}{5}$

We assume that CP of water is zero.

Using alligation rule on cost price,

Water should be mixed to spirit in the ratio $\frac{1}{5} : \frac{4}{5}$ or 1 : 4.

9. 20%   40%

25%

15   5

or 3 : 1

Quantity sold at 20% profit $= \frac{3}{3+1} \times 50 = 37.5$ kgs.

Quantity sold at 40% profit = (50 – 37.5) = 12.5 kgs.

10. +20   –5

+10

10 – (–5) = 15   10

or 3 : 2

Quantity sold at 20% profit $= \frac{3}{3+2} \times 100 = 60$ kgs.

Quantity sold at 5% loss = (100 – 60) = 40 kgs.

11.

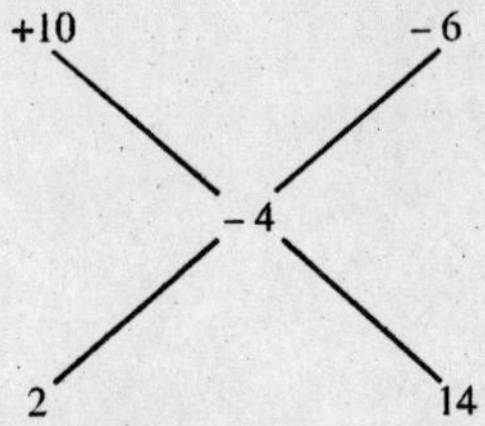

or 1 : 7

Quantity sold at 10% profit = $\frac{1}{1+7}$ × 160 = 20 kgs.

Quantity sold at 6% loss = 160 – 20 = 140 kgs.

12. Let the remainder stock be sold at x% profit.

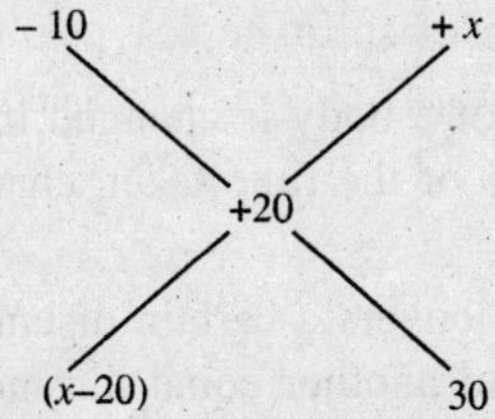

$$\frac{x-20}{30} = \frac{1/4}{3/4} \text{ or } x - 20 = 30 \times \frac{1}{3}$$

or $x = 20 + 10$, $x = 30$% profit.

13. Average rate of interest

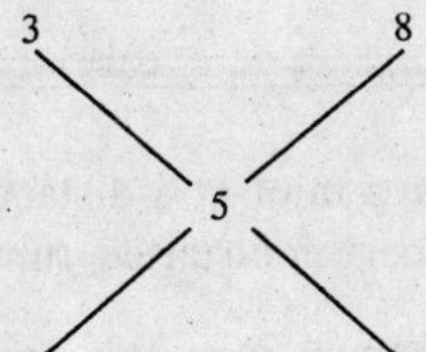

$= \frac{100 \times 750}{5000 \times 3} = 5\%$ per annum

Investment at 3% per annum = $\frac{3}{3+2}$ × 5000 = ₹ 3000

Investment at 8% per annum = $\frac{2}{3+2}$ × 5000 = ₹ 2000.

14. Average speed = $\frac{100}{10}$ = 10 km/hr.

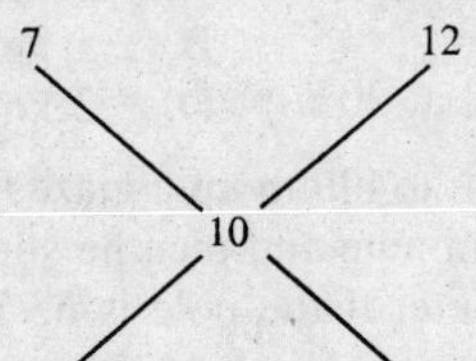

Ratio of time taken at 7 km/hr to 12 km/hr = 2 : 3

Time taken at 7 km/hr = $\frac{2}{2+3}$ × 10 = 4 hrs.

Distance covered at 7 km/hr = 7 × 4 = 28 km.

Distance covered at 12 km/hr = 100 – 28 = 72 km.

15.

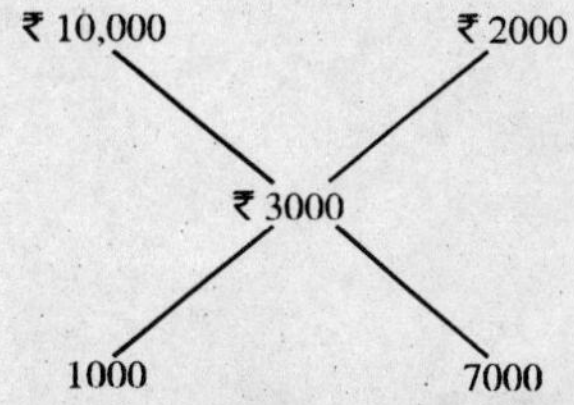

$$\frac{\text{Number of officers}}{\text{Number of workers}} = \frac{1000}{7000} = \frac{1}{7}$$

No. of officers = $\frac{1}{1+7}$ × 400 = 50

No. of workers = 400 – 50 = 350

16.

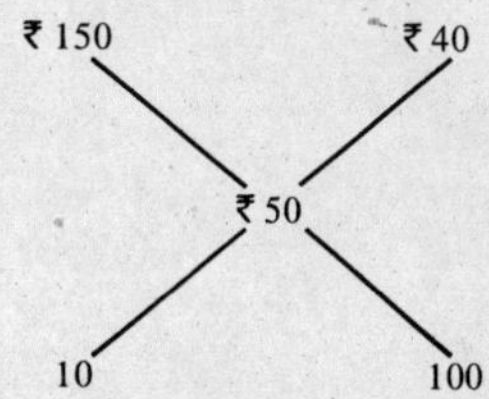

$$\frac{\text{Number of supervisors}}{\text{Number of labourers}} = \frac{10}{100} = \frac{1}{10}$$

Total number of labourers

= Total no. of supervisors × 10

= 15 × 10 = 150.

18.

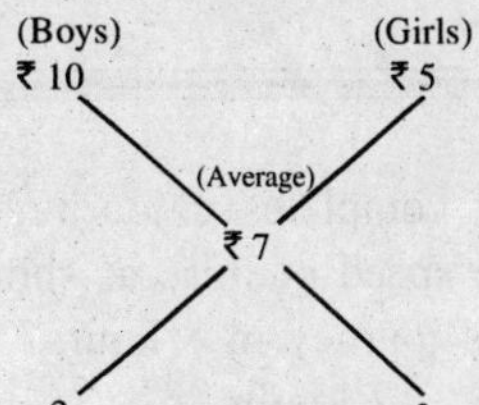

$$\frac{\text{Number of girls}}{\text{Number of boys}} = \frac{3}{2}$$

Number of girls = $\frac{3}{2}$ × 4 = 6

19. Here, quantity of wine left after third operation

$$= \left(1 - \frac{5}{25}\right)^3 \times 25$$

$$= \left(\frac{4}{5}\right)^3 \times 25 = \frac{64}{125} \times 25 = \frac{64}{5} = 12\frac{4}{5} \text{ litres.}$$

Final ratio of wine to water

$$= \frac{(64/125)}{(1-64/125)} = \frac{64/125}{61/125}$$

Wine : Water = $\frac{64}{61}$.

20. Amount of milk left

$$= 80\left(1 - \frac{16}{80}\right)^3 = 80\left(\frac{4}{5}\right)^3 = 80 \times \frac{64}{125}$$

= 40.96 litres.

●●●

CHAPTER

8 Time and Distance

Important Formulae:

1. Speed = Distance ÷ Time
2. Distance = Time × Speed
3. Time = Distance ÷ Speed
4. x km/hr = $\left(x \times \frac{5}{18}\right)$ m/sec
5. x metres/sec = $\left(x \times \frac{18}{5}\right)$ km/hr.
6. If the speed of a body is changed in the ratio $m : n$, then the ratio of the time taken changes in the ratio $n : m$.
7. When a man covers a certain distance with a speed of x km/h and another equal distance at the rate of y km/h, then for the whole journey, the average speed is given by

$$\text{Average speed} = \frac{2xy}{x+y} \text{ km/h.}$$

EXERCISE

1. A car moving at 48 km/hr completes a journey in 10 hours. By how much the speed of this car should be increased so as to do this journey in 8 hours?
A. 8 km/hr. B. 12 km/hr
C. 10 km/hr D. 15 km/hr

2. Starting from a point at a speed of 4 km/hr a man reaches at a cerain place and returns back to the point from where he had started journey on bicycle at the speed of 16 km/hr. His average speed during the entire journey will be:
A. 6.4 km/h B. 8.4 km/h
C. 5.4 km/h D. 10 km/h

3. A motorist covers a certain distance at a average speed of 48 km/h in 45 minutes. What speed in km/h he must maintain to cover the same distance in 30 minutes?
A. 66 km/h B. 79 km/h
C. 80 km/h D. 72 km/h

4. Two points A and B are 150 km apart. A man completes his onward journey from A to B in 3 hours 20 minutes and return journey from B to A in 4 hours 10 minutes. His average speed during the entire journey will be less than his average speed during the journey from A to B by:
A. 5 km/h B. 7.5 km/h
C. 9 km/h D. 3 km/h

5. A policeman saw a thief at a distance of 200 m. The policeman and the thief started running at the same time. If the policeman runs at a speed of $4\frac{1}{6}$ m per second and the thief at a speed of $3\frac{1}{3}$m per second, after what time the policeman will catch the thief?
A. 12 min B. 10 min
C. 9 min D. 4 min

6. Kanchan walks from her home at 4 kms per hour and reaches her school 5 minutes late. If she walks at 5 kms per hour, she reaches the school 2½ minutes earlier. How far is the school from her home?
A. 3.5 kms B. 2.5 kms
C. 2.75 kms D. 3.2 kms

7. A monkey wants to climb up a glazed pole. He climbs 12 metres in 1 minute and then he slips back 3 metres in the next minute. If the pole is 63 metre high, how long does he take to climb at the top of the pole?
A. $11\frac{1}{4}$ min B. $12\frac{1}{2}$ min
C. $12\frac{3}{4}$ min D. $14\frac{3}{4}$ min

8. A and B start walking at the same time on a circular path with circumference 35 metre. If they walk in the same direction at 4 km/hr and 5 km/hr respectively, after what time will they meet together?

A. 35 hours B. 27 hours
C. 24 hours D. 40 hours

9. While walking at $\frac{3}{5}$ of his usual speed Kamalkant reaches at his destination late by 30 minutes. His usual time consumed in reaching to his destination is:
A. 32 min B. 40 min
C. 45 min D. 42 min

10. The distance between two stations A and B is 300 km. A train leaves the station A with a speed of 40 km/hr. At the same time another train departs from the station B with a speed of 50 km/hr. How much time will these two trains take to cross each other?
A. 3 hrs 40 min B. 3 hrs 20 min
C. 2 hrs 20 min D. 3 hrs 45 min

11. Gulshan starts from a place P at 2 p.m. and walks to Q at 5 km per hour. Tarun starts from P at 3 p.m. and follows Gulshan on bicycle at 10 km per hour. By when Tarun will catch Gulshan?
A. At 5.30 p.m. B. At 4.00 p.m.
C. At 4.30 p.m. D. At 6.00 p.m.

12. Nilesh goes to school from his village at the speed of 4 km/hr and returns from school to village at the speed of 2 km/hr. If he takes 6 hours in all, then what is the distance between the village and the school?
A. 8 km B. 6 km
C. 5 km D. 4 km

13. A school bus covers a distance from a village to school at the speed of 12 km/hr and reaches the school 8 minute late. The next day the bus covers the same distance at the speed of 20 km/hr and reaches the school 10 minutes early. What is the distance between village and the school?
A. 6 km B. 9 km
C. 12 km D. 15 km

14. By increasing the speed of the bus by 10 km/hr the time of journey for 72 km is reduced by 36 minutes. What was the original speed of the bus?
A. 30 km/hr B. 35 km/hr
C. 40 km/hr D. 45 km/hr

15. A car completes a fixed journey in 8 hours. It covers half distance at the speed of 40 km/hr and rest at the 60 km/hr, the distance of the journey is:
A. 400 km B. 420 km
C. 384 km D. 350 km

16. A car covers four consecutive extensions of 3 km each at the speeds of 10 km/hr, 20 km/hr, 30 km/hr and 60 km/hr. Its average speed of journey is:
A. 30 km/hr B. 25 km/hr
C. 20 km/hr D. 10 km/hr

17. A girl rides her bicycle 10 km at an average speed of 12 km/hr and another 12 km at an average speed of 10 km/hr. Her average speed for the entire journey is approximately:
A. 12.2 km/hr B. 11.2 km/hr
C. 10.8 km/hr D. 10.4 km/hr

18. Raman drove from home to a neighbouring town at the speed of 50 km/hr and on his returning journey, he drove at the speed of 45 km/hr and also took an hour longer to reach home. What distance did he cover each way?
A. 900 km B. 500 km
C. 450 km D. 225 km

19. A man takes 6 hours 35 minutes in walking to a certain place and riding back. He would have taken 2 hours less by riding both ways. What would be the time he would take to walk both ways?
A. 10 hours B. 8 hours 35 minutes
C. 8 hours 25 minutes D. 8 hrs

20. A man covers a distance of 6 km at the rate of 4 km/hr and other 4 km at 3 km/hr this average speed is
A. $3\frac{5}{9}$ km/hr B. $3\frac{9}{17}$ km/hr
C. $5\frac{9}{17}$ km/hr D. $9\frac{3}{17}$ km/hr

ANSWERS

1	2	3	4	5	6	7	8	9	10
B	A	D	A	D	B	C	A	C	B
11	**12**	**13**	**14**	**15**	**16**	**17**	**18**	**19**	**20**
B	A	B	A	C	C	C	C	B	B

EXPLANATORY ANSWERS

1. Let he has to increase his speed by x km/hr for given condition; then,

$$(48 + x) \times 8 = 48 \times 10$$

$$\Rightarrow \quad 48 + x = 60 \ \therefore\ x = 12 \text{ km/hr}$$

2. Average speed during the entire journey

$$= \frac{2xy}{x+y} = \frac{2\times4\times16}{4+16} = \frac{8\times16}{20} = 6.4 \text{ km/hr.}$$

3. Let required speed be x km/hr; then

$$x \times \frac{1}{2} = 48 \times \frac{3}{4} \ \therefore\ x = 48 \times \frac{3}{4} \times 2 = 72 \text{ km/hr}$$

4. During onward journey from A to B:

$$\text{Average speed} = \frac{150}{10/3} = \frac{150\times3}{10} = 45 \text{ km/hr.}$$

During entire jouney:

Average speed = $\frac{300}{\frac{10}{3}+\frac{25}{6}} = \frac{300 \times 6}{45}$ = 40 km/hr.

Hence, difference of average speed

= 45 − 40 = 5 km/hr.

5. Suppose the policeman will catch the thief after t sec

then, $\left(\frac{25}{6}-\frac{10}{3}\right)t = 200 \Rightarrow \frac{5}{6}t = 200$

$\therefore\ t = \frac{200 \times 6}{5}$ = 240 sec = 4 min.

6. Suppose the distance between her house to the school = x km

Difference of time = $\frac{5}{2} - (-5) = \frac{15}{2}$ min = $\frac{1}{8}$ hr.

$\frac{x}{4}-\frac{x}{5}=\frac{1}{8} \Rightarrow \frac{x}{20}=\frac{1}{8}\ \therefore\ x = \frac{20}{8}$ = 2.5 km

7. The monkey climbs 12 metres in 1 minute and then he slips back 3 metres in the next minute

∴ The monkey climbs in the first 2 minutes = 12 − 3 = 9 metres

∴ In the first 12 minutes the monkey climbs = 9 × 6 = 54 metres

Remaining height of the pole to be covered by the monkey = 63 − 54 = 9 metre

∴ The monkey will climb the height of 9 metres in the 13th minute

∵ The monkey climbs 12 metres in 1 minute

∴ The monkey will climb 9 metres in

$\frac{1}{12}\times 9 = \frac{3}{4}$ minute

∴ Time spent in climbing at the top of the pole

= $\left(12+\frac{3}{4}\right)$ minutes = $12\frac{3}{4}$ minutes

8. The two persons walk in the same direction

∴ Their relative speed = 5 − 4 = 1 km/hr

Distance covered in 1 round on the circular path = 35 km

∴ They will meet after $\frac{35}{1}$ = 35 hours.

9. Suppose usual speed of Kamalkant is v km/hr and his destination is at a distance of x kms; then usual time taken = $\frac{x}{v}$ hours.

$\frac{x}{3v/5}-\frac{x}{v}=\frac{1}{2} \Rightarrow \frac{2x}{3v}=\frac{1}{2}\ \therefore\ \frac{x}{v}=\frac{3}{4}$ hour = 45 min.

10. The two trains are moving in the opposite directions

∴ Relative speed = 40 + 50 = 90 km/hr.

∴ Time taken to cross each other

= $\frac{300}{90} = 3\frac{1}{3}$ hours or, 3 hours 20 minutes.

11. Let Tarun will catch Gulshan after t hours the starting of Tarun; then, $10t = 5(t + 1)$

$\Rightarrow 5t = 5\ \therefore\ t = 1$ hr

Hence, required time = 3 p.m. + 1 hr. = 4 p.m.

12. Let x km be the distance between village and the school; then

$\frac{x}{4}+\frac{x}{2}=6 \Rightarrow \frac{3x}{4}=6\ \therefore\ x = \frac{6\times 4}{3}$ = 8 km

13. Let x km be the distance from village to school, then

$\frac{x}{12}-\frac{x}{20} = [8-(-10)] \times \frac{1}{60}$

$\Rightarrow \frac{x}{30}=\frac{18}{60}\ \therefore\ x = \frac{18}{60}\times 30$ = 9 km

14. Let original speed of the bus be x km/hr; then

$\frac{72}{x}-\frac{72}{x+10}=\frac{36}{60} \Rightarrow \frac{72(x+10-x)}{x^2+10x}=\frac{3}{5}$

$\Rightarrow 1200 = x^2 + 10x$

$\Rightarrow x^2 + 10x - 1200 = 0$

$\Rightarrow (x + 40)(x - 30) = 0$

$\therefore\ x = 30$ or $x = -40$

Taking positive value only, so speed of the bus = 30 km/hr.

15. Let the distance of the journey be x km, then,

$\frac{x}{2\times 40}+\frac{x}{2\times 60} = 8 \Rightarrow \frac{5x}{240}=8$

$\therefore\ x = 8 \times 48$ = 384 km

16. Total distance of the journey = 4 × 3 km = 12 km

Total time taken = $\frac{3}{10}+\frac{3}{20}+\frac{3}{30}+\frac{3}{60}=\frac{36}{60}=\frac{3}{5}$ hr.

Hence, average speed = $\frac{12}{3/5}=\frac{12\times 5}{3}$ = 20 km/hr.

17. Average speed

= $\frac{10+12}{\frac{10}{12}+\frac{12}{10}}=\frac{22}{61/30}=\frac{22\times 30}{61}=\frac{660}{61}$ = 10.8 km/hr

18. Let his distance of journey of each way be x km; then

$\frac{x}{45}-\frac{x}{50}=1 \Rightarrow \frac{x}{450}=1$

$\therefore\ x = 450$ km

19. Here, Walking to a certain place + riding back = 6 hrs 35 min. ...(*i*)

2 × riding the same distance = 4 hrs 35 min. ...(*ii*)

Multiplying equation (*i*) × 2 and subtracting (*ii*) we get

Time taken in walking both ways = 13 hrs 70 min − 4 hrs. 35 min = 8 hrs. 35 min.

20. His average speed = $\frac{6+4}{\frac{6}{4}+\frac{4}{3}}=\frac{10}{17/6}=\frac{60}{17}=3\frac{9}{17}$ km/hr

●●●

CHAPTER 9

Time and Work

IMPORTANT FACTS:

1. If A can do a piece of work in n days, then work done by A in 1 day = $\frac{1}{n}$.
2. If work done by A in 1 day = $\frac{1}{n}$; then A can finish the whole work in n days.
3. If A is twice as good a workman as B then; Ratio of work done by A and B = 2 : 1
Ratio of times taken by A and B to finish a work = 1 : 2.

EXERCISE

1. 12 boys can do a piece of work in 16 days. In how many days can 6 boys do the same work?
A. 16 days B. 32 days
C. 23 days D. 24 days

2. A can do a piece of work in 8 days while B can do the same work in 16 days. If they start working together, how long would they take to complete half portion of this work?
A. $2\frac{2}{3}$ days B. $3\frac{5}{7}$ days
C. $4\frac{1}{2}$ days D. $3\frac{1}{2}$ days

3. A can do a piece of work in 4 days. B is 50% more efficient than A. How long would B alone take to finish this work?
A. $3\frac{1}{3}$ days B. $5\frac{1}{4}$ days
C. $2\frac{2}{3}$ days D. $1\frac{2}{3}$ days

4. A and B working together complete a work in 35 days. If A takes 60 days to complete it, how long would B alone take to complete it?
A. 64 days B. 72 days
C. 81 days D. 84 days

5. A few children working together can do a piece of work in 18 days. If the number of children employed on the work is made double, how long would they take to complete half of the work?
A. $4\frac{1}{2}$ days B. $2\frac{1}{3}$ days
C. $8\frac{3}{4}$ days D. $6\frac{1}{2}$ days

6. 10 men or 18 boys can do a piece of work in 15 days. In how many days would 25 men and 15 boys complete the same work working together?
A. $5\frac{1}{2}$ days B. $4\frac{1}{2}$ days
C. $6\frac{2}{3}$ days D. $2\frac{1}{3}$ days

7. A can do a piece of work in 40 days. He starts working, but having some other engagements he drops out after 5 days. Thereafter B completes this work in 21 days. How many days would A and B take to complete this work working together?
A. 15 days B. 16 days
C. 17 days D. 11 days

8. Two persons A and B can complete a piece of work in 8 hours and 16 hours respectively. If they work at it alternately for an hour, A starting first, in how many hours will the work be finished?
A. $9\frac{1}{3}$ hours B. $10\frac{1}{2}$ hours
C. $11\frac{1}{2}$ hours D. $8\frac{1}{2}$ hours

9. 15 men can complete a work in 210 days. They started the work but at the end of 10 days 15 additional men, with double efficiency, were inducted. How many days, in whole, did they take to finish the work?

A. $76\frac{2}{3}$ days B. $84\frac{3}{4}$ days

C. $72\frac{1}{2}$ days D. 70 days

10. A and B working together can complete a piece of work in 12 days and B and C working together can complete the same work in 16 days. A worked at it for 5 days and B worked at it for 7 days. C finished the remaining work in 13 days. How many days would C alone take to complete it?

A. 10 days B. 24 days

C. 32 days D. 40 days

11. A cistern is filled by a tap in $3\frac{1}{2}$ hours. Due to a leak in the bottom of the cistern, it takes half an hour longer to fill the cistern. If the cistern is full, how long will it take the leak to empty it?

A. 28 hours B. 29 hours

C. $31\frac{1}{3}$ hours D. 38 hours

12. A is twice as good a workman as B and thrice as good a workman as C. If C alone can do a piece of work in 24 days, how long would the three persons take to finish the work working together?

A. $3\frac{3}{11}$ days B. $4\frac{4}{7}$ days

C. $4\frac{4}{11}$ days D. $3\frac{4}{11}$ days

13. Two pipes can fill a tank in 8 hours and 12 hours respectively whereas an escape pipe can empty it in 6 hours. If the three pipes are opened at 1 p.m., 2 p.m. and 3 p.m. respectively, at what time will the tank be filled?

A. 7.00 a.m. B. 8.00 a.m.

C. 5.00 a.m. D. 7.30 a.m.

14. Working 7 hours daily 24 men can complete a piece of work in 27 days. In how many days would 14 men complete the same piece of work working 9 hours daily?

A. 32 days B. 31 days

C. 36 days D. 39 days

15. A, B and C undertake to do a piece of work for ₹ 529. If A and B working together do $\frac{19}{23}$ work and B and C working together do $\frac{8}{23}$ work, how should the money be divided among them?

A. ₹ 345, ₹ 102, ₹ 82

B. ₹ 345, ₹ 92, ₹ 92

C. ₹ 330, ₹ 107, ₹ 92

D. ₹ 330, ₹ 92, ₹ 107

ANSWERS

1	2	3	4	5	6	7	8	9	10
B	A	C	D	A	B	A	B	A	B
11	**12**	**13**	**14**	**15**					
A	C	A	C	B					

EXPLANATORY ANSWERS

1. ∵ 12 boys can do a piece of work in 16 days.

∴ 1 boy will do the same piece of work in 16 × 12 days.

∴ 6 boys will do the same piece of work in

$\frac{16 \times 12}{6}$ days = 32 days.

2. (A + B)'s 1 day's work $= \frac{1}{8} + \frac{1}{16} = \frac{3}{16}$

Hence, (A + B) will do the whole work in $\frac{16}{3}$ days

So, they will do the half portion of the work in

$\frac{16}{3 \times 2}$ days $= \frac{8}{3} = 2\frac{2}{3}$ days.

3. A's 1 day's work $= \frac{1}{4}$;

Hence, B's 1 day's work $= \frac{150}{100} \times \frac{1}{4} = \frac{3}{8}$

So, B will do the whole work in $\frac{8}{3} = 2\frac{2}{3}$ days.

4. (A + B)'s 1 day's work $= \frac{1}{35}$

and also, A's 1 day's work $= \frac{1}{60}$

Hence, B's 1 day's work

$= \frac{1}{35} - \frac{1}{60} = \frac{5}{420} = \frac{1}{84}$

So, B will do the whole work in 84 days.

5. Let number of children be x;

Now x children can do the work in 18 days.

Hence, $2x$ children will do $\frac{1}{2}$ of the work in

$\frac{18 \times x}{2x \times 2} = \frac{9}{2}$ days $= 4\frac{1}{2}$ days.

6. 10 men $\equiv$ 18 boys; 25 men $\equiv \frac{18}{10} \times 25 = 45$ boys

Hence, 25 men + 15 boys = 45 + 15 = 60 boys

Now, 18 boys can do a piece of work in 15 days.

Hence, 60 boys will do a piece of work in

$\frac{15 \times 18}{60} = \frac{9}{2}$ days $= 4\frac{1}{2}$ days.

7. A's 5 days' work $= 5 \times \frac{1}{40} = \frac{1}{8}$

Remaining work $= 1 - \frac{1}{8} = \frac{7}{8}$, which is done by B in 21 days.

Hence, B's 1 day's work $= \frac{7}{8 \times 21} = \frac{1}{24}$

Now, (A + B)'s 1 day's work $= \frac{1}{40} + \frac{1}{24} = \frac{8}{120} = \frac{1}{15}$

Hence, (A + B) will complete the work in 15 days.

8. In 2 hours the part of work $= \frac{1}{8} + \frac{1}{16} = \frac{3}{16}$ will be completed.

Hence, in 5 pairs of hours the part of work

$= 5 \times \frac{3}{16} = \frac{15}{16}$ will be completed

Remaining work $= 1 - \frac{15}{16} = \frac{1}{16}$ which will be done by A.

Time taken by A to complete the $\frac{1}{16}$ work

$= \frac{1/16}{1/8} = \frac{1}{2}$ hour.

Hence, required number of hours

$= 10 + \frac{1}{2} = 10\frac{1}{2}$ hours.

9. 15 men's 10 days' work $= 10 \times \frac{1}{210} = \frac{1}{21}$

Remaining work $= 1 - \frac{1}{21} = \frac{20}{21}$

Now, (15 men + 15 men having double efficiency)'s 1 day's work $= \frac{1}{210} + \frac{2}{210} = \frac{3}{210} = \frac{1}{70}$

Hence, number of days

$= \frac{20/21}{1/70} = \frac{20}{21} \times 70 = \frac{200}{3} = 66\frac{2}{3}$ days

So, required number of total days

$= 10 + 66\frac{2}{3} = 76\frac{2}{3}$ days.

10. Here, A worked for 5 days, B for 7 days and C for 13 days $\equiv$ (A + B) worked for 5 days, (B + C) for 2 days and C for 11 days.

Let C will complete the work in x days,

Now, (A + B)'s 5 days' work + (B + C)'s 2 days' work + C's 11 days' work

$= \frac{5}{12} + \frac{2}{16} + \frac{11}{x} = \frac{13}{24} + \frac{11}{x}$

Again, $\frac{13}{24} + \frac{11}{x} = 1 \Rightarrow \frac{11}{x} = \frac{11}{24}$ $\therefore x = 24$

Hence, C would alone complete the work in 24 days.

11. In 1 hour $\frac{2}{7}$ cistern is filled by the tap.

Hence, in $\frac{1}{2}$ hour $\frac{2}{14} = \frac{1}{7}$ cistern is filled by the tap.

So, $\frac{1}{7}$ cistern is emptied by the leakage in 4 hours.

So, 1 cistern will be emptied by the leakage in 28 hours.

13. Let tank will be filled up after t hours of starting of pipe A;

Then, $t \times \frac{1}{8} + (t-1) \times \frac{1}{12} - (t-2) \times \frac{1}{6} = 1$

$\Rightarrow t\left(\frac{1}{8} + \frac{1}{12} - \frac{1}{6}\right) - \frac{1}{12} + \frac{1}{3} = 1$

$\Rightarrow \quad t \times \frac{1}{24} = 1 - \frac{1}{4}$

$\therefore t = \frac{3}{4} \times 24 = 18$ hours

Hence, required time = 1 p.m. + 18 hours = 7 a.m.

14. Working 7 hours a day 24 men can do the work is 27 days.

Hence, working 9 hours a day 14 men will do the work in $\frac{27 \times 24 \times 7}{9 \times 14} = 36$ days.

15. The part of work is done by B

$= \frac{19}{23} + \frac{8}{23} - 1 = \frac{4}{23}$

The part of work is done by A $= \frac{19}{23} - \frac{4}{23} = \frac{15}{23}$

The part of work is done by C $= \frac{8}{23} - \frac{4}{23} = \frac{4}{23}$

Hence, share of A $= \frac{15}{23} \times$ ₹ 529 = ₹ 345

share of B $= \frac{4}{23} \times$ ₹ 529 = ₹ 92

share of C $= \frac{4}{23} \times$ ₹ 529 = ₹ 92

So, Their shares are ₹ 345, ₹ 92 and ₹ 92.

●●●

CHAPTER 10

Geometry

Triangle and Its Various Kinds of Centres

There are 4 very important ways of viewing the center of a triangle. We can look at its CENTROID, ORTHOCENTER, CIRCUMCENTER, and the INCENTER.

Centroid

The centroid is the first center and is obtained by locating the intersection of the three medians of the triangle. The median of a triangle is obtained by joining each vertex with the midpoint of the opposite side.

- It is the point of the intersection of the three median of the triangle. It is denoted by G.
- A centroid divides the area of the triangle in exactly three parts.

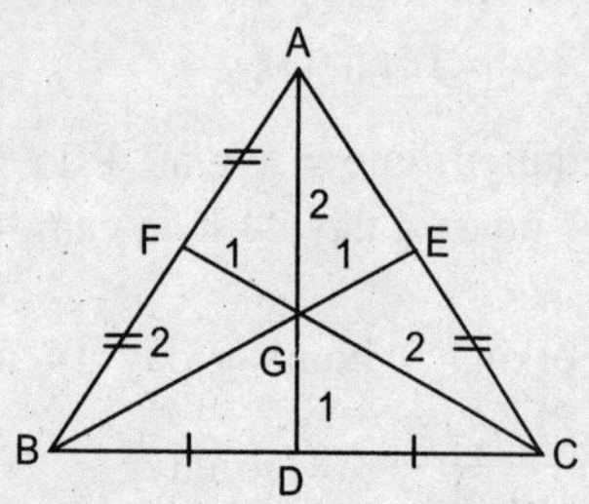

Medians:

- A line segment joining the midpoint of the side with the opposite vertex is called median.
- Median bisects the opposite side as well as divide the area of the triangle in two equal parts.

Orthocenter

The second center of a triangle is the orthocenter. It is obtained by finding the intersection of the 3 altitudes of the triangle. An altitude is found by joining each vertex with the point on the opposite side that creates a perpendicular line with the opposite side.

It is the point of intersection of all the three altitudes of the triangle.

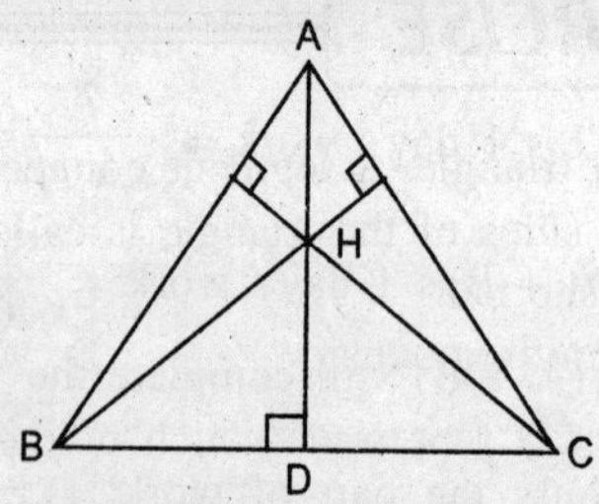

$\angle BHC = 180 - \angle A$

$\angle AHB = 180 - \angle C$

$\angle AHC = 180 - \angle B$

Position of orthocentre inside the triangle:

Acute angled triangle: lies inside the triangle.

Obtuse angle triangle: lies outside the triangle on the backside of the obtuse angle. Orthocentre and circumcentre lie opposite to each other in obtuse angle triangle.

Circumcenter

The third center is the circumcenter. The circumcenter is the intersection of the perpendicular bisectors of each side of the triangle. We can also think of this center as the point that is equidistant from each of the vertices. Since it is equidistant from each vertex, we can also construct a circle that passes through each vertex with the center being the circumcenter.

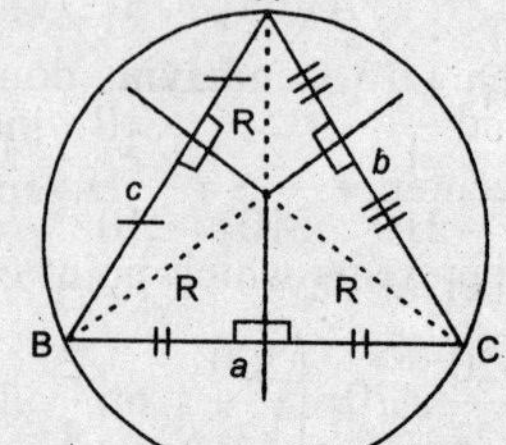

The distance between the circumcentre and the three vertices of a triangle is always equal.

OA = OB = OC = R (circumradius) = $abc/4A$

$\angle BOC = 2\angle A$

$\angle AOC = 2\angle B$

$\angle AOB = 2\angle C$

Location of circumcentre in various types of triangle:

Acute angle triangle: Lies inside the triangle

Obtuse angle triangle: Lies outside the triangle

Right angle triangle: Lies at the midpoint of the hypotenuse.

Incenter

The last center is the incenter. The incenter is found by first constructing the angle bisectors of each of the three angles. The incenter is the intersection of these 3 segments.

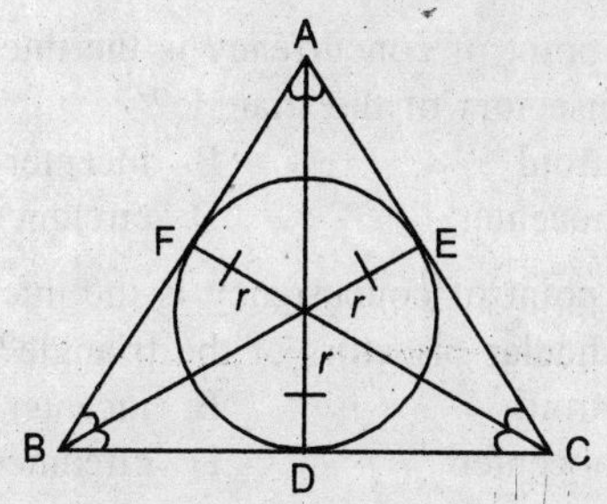

The distance of the in-centre from the all the three sides is equal (ID = IE = IF = inradius "r")

In-radius (r) = Area of triangle/Semiperimetre = A/S

$\angle BIC = 90 + \angle A/2$

$\angle AIC = 90 + \angle B/2$

$\angle AIB = 90 + \angle C/2$

EXERCISE

1. In a triangle, a segment connecting the midpoints of two sides of the triangle is called a ______.

A. shortcut C. centroid
B. midsegment D. vertex

2. Point Q represents which point of concurrency?

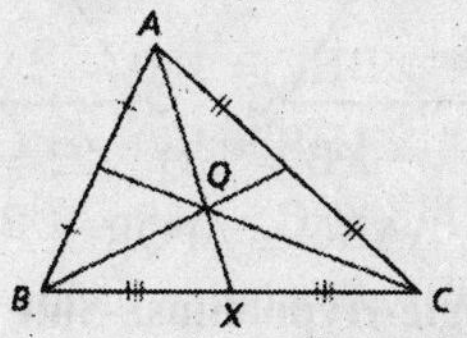

A. centroid C. orthocenter
B. incenter D. circumcenter

3. Point P represents which point of concurrency?

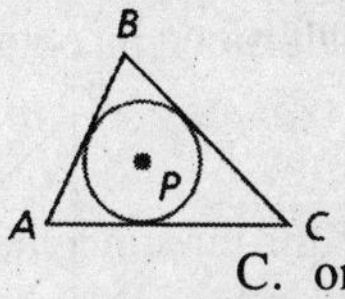

A. centroid C. orthocenter
B. incenter D. circumcenter

4. Point P represents which point of concurrency?

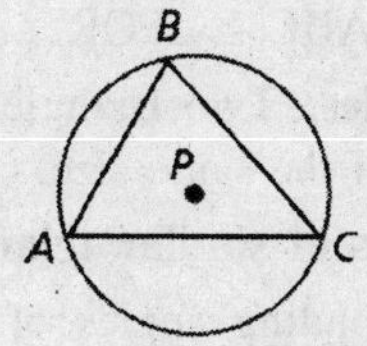

A. centroid B. incenter
C. orthocenter D. circumcenter

5. Point T represents which point of concurrency?

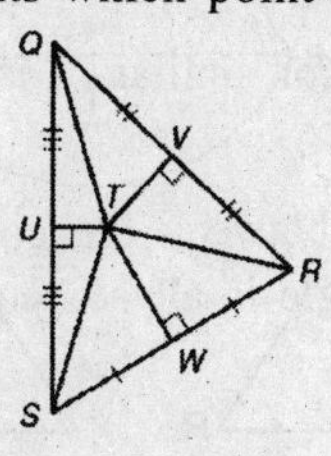

A. centroid B. incenter
C. orthocenter D. circumcenter

6. Point M represents which point of concurrency?

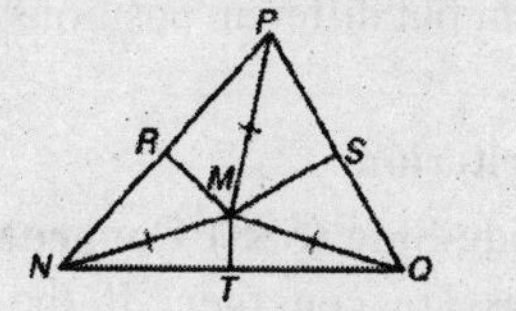

A. centroid B. incenter
C. orthocenter D. circumcenter

7. Point M represents which point of concurrency?

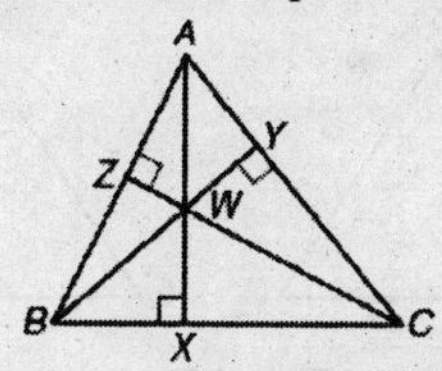

A. centroid B. incenter
C. orthocenter D. circumcenter

8. Point L represents which point of concurrency?

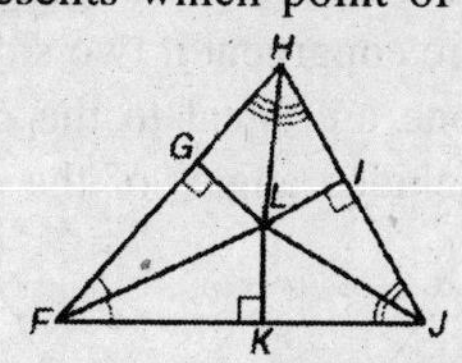

A. centroid B. incenter
C. orthocenter D. circumcenter

9. Which point of concurrency is the intersection of the medians of the triangle?

A. centroid B. incenter
C. orthocenter D. circumcenter

10. Which point of concurrency is the intersection of the altitudes of the triangle?

A. centroid B. incenter
C. orthocenter D. circumcenter

11. Which point of concurrency is the intersection of the angle bisectors of the triangle?
A. centroid B. incenter
C. orthocenter D. circumcenter

12. Which point of concurrency is the intersection of the perpendicular bisectors of the triangle?
A. centroid B. incenter
C. orthocenter D. circumcenter

13. Which point of concurrency is equidistant from the three sides of a triangle?
A. centroid B. incenter
C. orthocenter D. circumcenter

14. Which point of concurrency is equidistant from the three verticies of a triangle?
A. centroid B. incenter
C. orthocenter D. circumcenter

15. Which point of concurrency is the center of gravity of a triangle?
A. centroid B. incenter
C. orthocenter D. circumcenter

ANSWERS

1	2	3	4	5	6	7	8	9	10
B	A	B	D	D	D	C	B	A	C
11	**12**	**13**	**14**	**15**					
B	D	B	D	A					

Congruence and Similarity of Triangles

Congruence of triangle: Two triangles having same shape and measurement but different positions are called congruent triangle.

Congruence criterion

(*i*) **Side-Side-Side (SSS) Congruence criterion:** Two triangles are congruent if the three sides of one triangle are equal to the three sides of the other triangle.

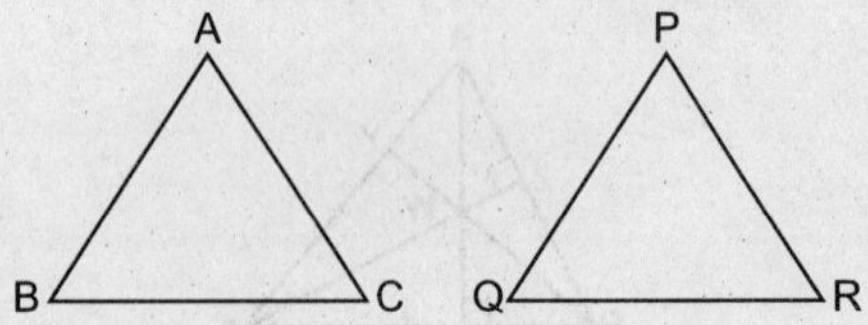

Here, $AB = PQ$, $BC = QR$ and $AC = PR$

$\therefore$ $\Delta ABC \cong \Delta PQR$

(*ii*) **Side-Angle-Side (SAS) Congruence criterion:** Two triangles are congruent if two sides and the included angle of one are equal to the corresponding sides and the included angles of the other.

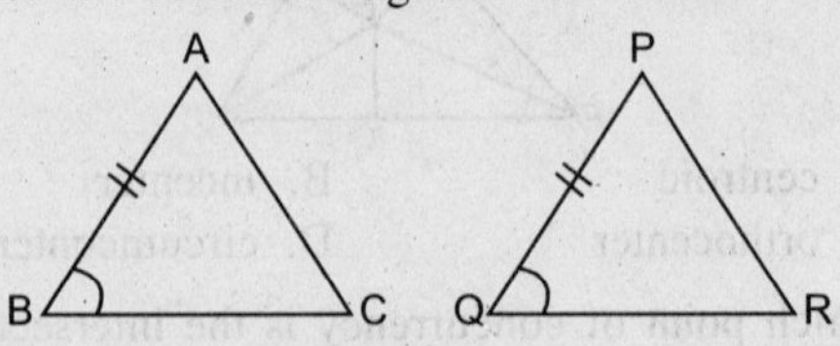

Here, $AB = PQ$, $\angle B = \angle Q$ and $BC = QR$

$\therefore$ $\Delta ABC \cong \Delta PQR$

(*iii*) **Angle-Side-Angle (ASA) Congruence criterion:** Two triangles are congruent if two angles and the included side of one triangle are equal to the corresponding two angles and the included side of the triangle.

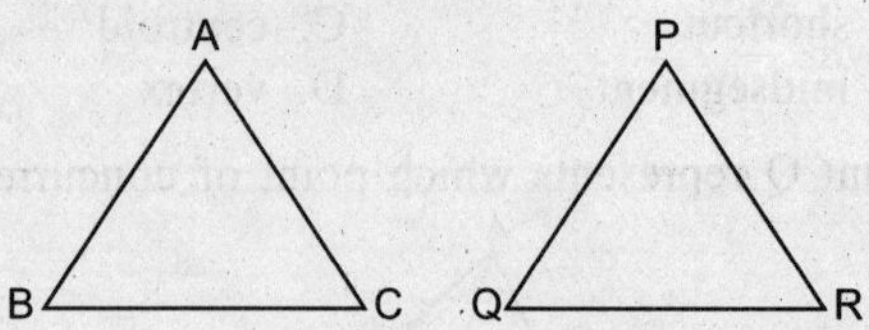

$\because$ $\angle B = \angle Q$, $\angle C = \angle R$ and $BC = QR$

$\therefore$ $\Delta ABC \cong \Delta PQR$

(*iv*) **Right Angle-Hypotenuse-Side (RHS) congruence criterion:** Two right triangles are congruent. If the hypotenuse and one side of one triangle are respectively equal to the hypotenuse and one side of the other triangle.

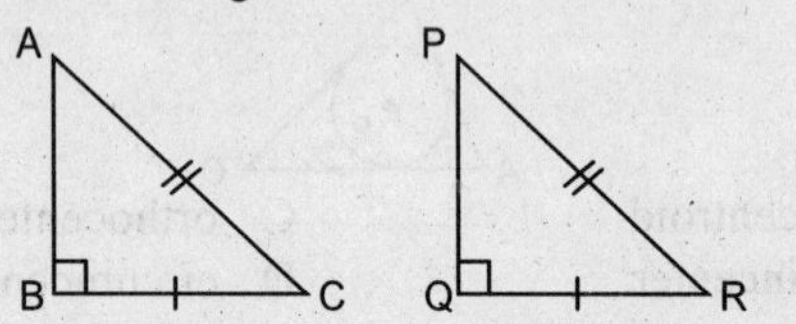

$\because$ $\angle B = \angle Q = 90°$, $AC = PR$, $BC = QR$

$\therefore$ $\Delta ABC \cong \Delta PQR$.

Similar Triangles: Two triangles having same shape but not necessarily of the same size, called similar triangle.

Basic properties of similar triangles:

(*i*) The corresponding angles of similar triangles are equal.

(*ii*) The corresponding sides of similar triangles are proportional.

The symbol for similar or is similar to is ~

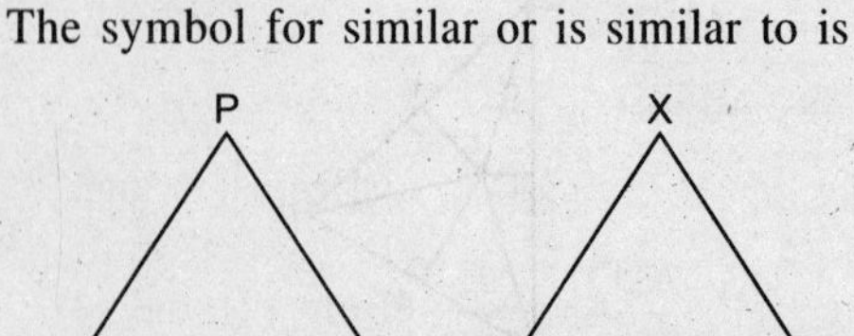

$\angle P = \angle X$, $\angle Q = \angle Y$ and $\angle R = \angle Z$

Then, $\frac{PQ}{QR} = \frac{XY}{YZ}$ or, $\frac{PR}{PQ} = \frac{XZ}{XY}$

Thus, $\Delta PQR \sim \Delta XYZ$

→ Congruent triangles are always similar but similar triangles may or may not be congruent.

→ Any two equilateral triangles are always similar triangles.

SOME IMPORTANT THEOREMS

Basic Proportionality Theorem: (Thalse Theorem)

Theorem 1: *In a triangle, a line drawn parallel to one side to intersect the other sides in distinct points divides the two sides in the same ratio.*

Given: A ΔABC in which DE is drawn parallel to side BC.

To prove. $\frac{AD}{DB} = \frac{AE}{EC}$.

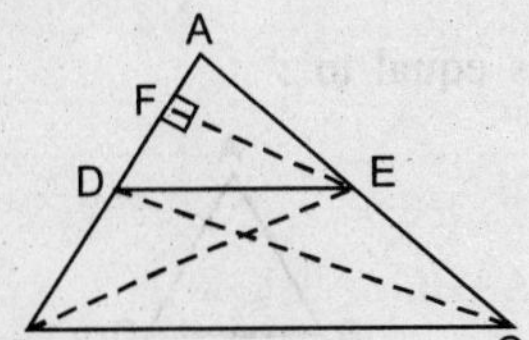

Const.: Join BE and CD. Draw $EF \perp AB$.

Proof: ar.(ΔBDE) = ar.(ΔCDE) ...(1)

[∵ Δs on the same base DE and between the same parallels are equal in area]

$$\frac{\text{ar.}(\Delta ADE)}{\text{ar.}(\Delta BDE)} = \frac{\frac{1}{2} \times AD \times EF}{\frac{1}{2} \times BD \times EF}$$

[∵ Area of $\Delta = \frac{1}{2}$ base × height]

$$\Rightarrow \frac{\text{ar.}(\Delta ADE)}{\text{ar.}(\Delta BDE)} = \frac{AD}{DB} \quad ...(2)$$

Similarly, $\frac{\text{ar.}(\Delta ADE)}{\text{ar.}(\Delta CDE)} = \frac{AE}{EC}$ ...(3)

$$\therefore \frac{\text{ar.}(\Delta ADE)}{\text{ar.}(\Delta BDE)} = \frac{AE}{EC}$$

[from (1) and (3)] ...(4)

$$\therefore \frac{AD}{DB} = \frac{AE}{EC} \quad \text{[from (2) and (4)]}$$

Corollary 1: $\frac{AD}{DB} = \frac{AE}{EC}$

Adding 1 to both sides, we get

$$\frac{AD}{DB} + 1 = \frac{AE}{EC} + 1$$

$$\Rightarrow \frac{AD + DB}{DB} = \frac{AE + EC}{EC}$$

Corollary 2: $\frac{AD}{DB} = \frac{AE}{EC}$

$$\Rightarrow \frac{DB}{AD} = \frac{EC}{AE}$$

Adding 1 to both sides, we get

$$1 + \frac{DB}{AD} = 1 + \frac{EC}{AE}$$

$$\Rightarrow \frac{AD + DB}{AD} = \frac{AE + EC}{AE}$$

$$\Rightarrow \frac{AB}{AD} = \frac{AC}{AE}.$$

Converse of Basic Proportionality Theorem

Theorem 2: *If a line divides any two sides of a triangle in the same ratio, prove that it is parallel to the third side.*

Given: A ΔABC, DE is st. line such that

$$\frac{AD}{DB} = \frac{AE}{EC}$$

To Prove. DE ∥ BC

Const.: If DE is not ∥ BC, draw BK ∥ DE meeting AC produce in.

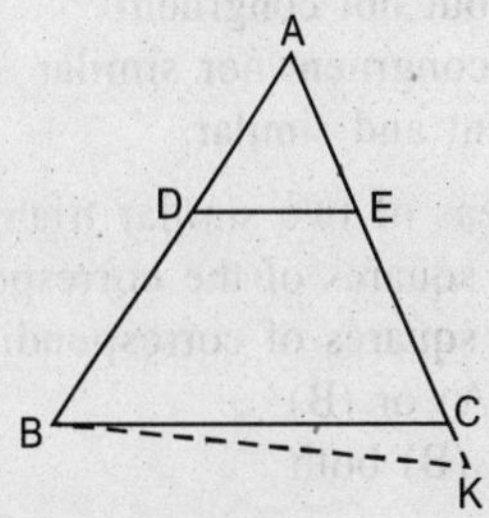

Proof: In DABK, DE ∥ BK

$$\therefore \frac{AD}{DB} = \frac{AE}{EK} \quad ...(1)$$

[∵ A line drawn ∥ to one side of a Δ divides the other two sides in the same ratio]

But, $\frac{AD}{DB} = \frac{AE}{EC}$ (given) ...(2)

From (1) and (2), we get

$$\frac{AE}{EK} = \frac{AE}{EC} \text{ or, } EK = EC$$

which is possible only when C and K coincides.

Hence, DE ∥ BC.

EXERCISE

1. Two similar triangles have
   A. equal sides B. equal areas
   C. equal angles D. None of these

2. Two congruent triangles have
   A. proportional sides
   B. equal sides
   C. equal corresponding sides
   D. equal corresponding angles

3. Which of the following is false for two congruent triangles?
   A. Corresponding angles are equal.
   B. Two sides and included angles are equal.
   C. Corresponding sides are equal.
   D. Two angles and one side are equal.

4. If the sides of a triangle are 8 cm, 12 cm and 15 cm then the angle is
   A. Right angle B. Obtuse angle
   C. Acute angle D. None of these

5. If two triangles are on the same base and between the parallel lines then they will be
   A. equilaterals B. right angled
   C. equal in area D. congruent

6. If the three heights of a traingle are equal then it is
   A. right angled triangle B. obtuse angled triangle
   C. equilateral triangle D. None of these

7. If two corresponding sides and the angle between them of a traingle are equal to another triangle. Then the angles are :
   A. congruent but not similar
   B. similar but not congruent
   C. neither congruent nor similar
   D. congruent and similar.

8. Ratio of areas of two similar triangles is equal to :
   A. ratio of squares of the corresponding altitudes
   B. ratio of squares of corresponding medians.
   C. Either (A) or (B)
   D. (A) and (B) both

9. If the areas of two similar triangles are equal then the triangles :
   A.. are congruent
   B. have equal length of corresponding sides
   C. (A) and (B)
   D. None of these

10. Two isosceles triangles have equal vertical angles and their areas are in the ratio of 9 : 25 then the ratio between their corresponding heights is :
    A. 5 : 3 B. 25 : 9
    C. 3 : 5 D. 16 : 9

11. **If in a Δ DEF, GH || EF and DG : EG $= 2 : 3$ then the value of $\frac{\text{ar}(\Delta\ DGH)}{\text{ar}(\Delta\ DEF)}$ is :**

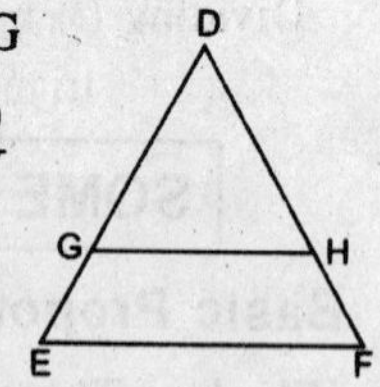

    A. $\frac{2}{15}$ B. $\frac{4}{15}$
    C. $\frac{4}{25}$ D. $\frac{2}{25}$

12. **Sides of two similar triangles are in the ratio of 5 : 11 then ratio of their areas is :**
    A. 25 : 11 B. 25 : 121
    C. 125 : 121 D. 121 : 25

13. **If ΔABC ~ ΔADE and ar (Δ ADE) = 9 ar (Δ ABC) then $\frac{BC}{DE}$ is equal to :**

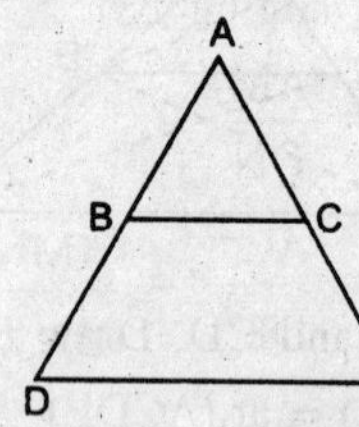

    A. $\frac{1}{3}$ B. $\frac{1}{9}$
    C. $\frac{3}{4}$ D. None of these

14. **In a triangle a line is drawn from the mid-point of one side of and parallel to another side then**
    A. the line bisects the whole traingle
    B. bisects the third side
    C. bisects the opposite angle
    D. None of these

15. **If in a ΔABC, ∠B = ∠C and BD = CE then which of the following is true**
    A. $DE = \frac{1}{2} BC$ B. DE || BC
    C. (A) and (B) D. None of these

ANSWERS

1	2	3	4	5	6	7	8	9	10
C	C	D	C	C	C	C	D	C	C
11	**12**	**13**	**14**	**15**					
C	B	A	B	B					

EXPLANATORY ANSWERS

10. According to equestion

$\angle A = \angle D$ and $\dfrac{ar(\Delta ABC)}{ar(\Delta DEF)} = \dfrac{9}{25}$

Since, $AB = AC$ (given) ....(*i*)

$DE = DF$ (given) ....(*ii*)

Dividing (i) by (ii)

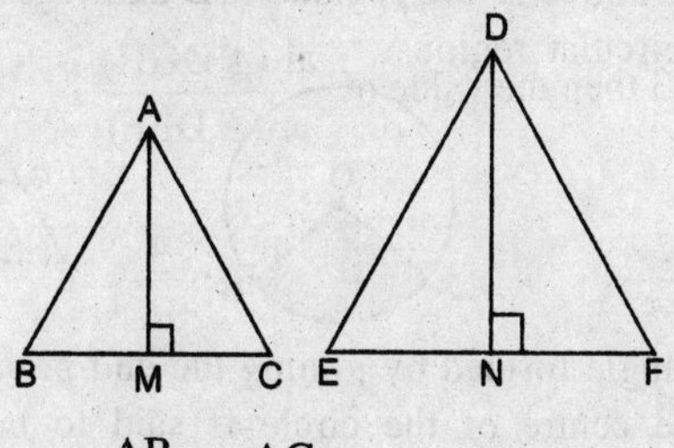

$$\frac{AB}{DE} = \frac{AC}{DF} \quad ...(iii)$$

Hence, $\Delta ABC \sim \Delta DEF$

[By SAS criterion of similar Δs]

In ΔAMC and ΔDNF

$\angle AMC = \angle DNF = 90°$

$\angle C = \angle F$ (because $\Delta ABC \sim \Delta DEF$)

$\therefore \angle AMC \sim DNF$

(By AA Criterion of similar Δs)

$\therefore \dfrac{AC}{DF} = \dfrac{AM}{DN}$

and, $\dfrac{ar(\Delta ABC)}{ar(DEF)} = \dfrac{AC^2}{DF^2} = \dfrac{AM^2}{DN^2}$

$\therefore \dfrac{AM^2}{DN^2} = \dfrac{9}{25}$

$\Rightarrow \dfrac{AM}{DN} = \dfrac{3}{5}$

Hence required ratio = 3 : 5

11. $\dfrac{DG}{EG} = \dfrac{2}{3} \therefore \dfrac{DG}{DE} = \dfrac{2}{2+3} = \dfrac{2}{5}$

In Δ DGH and Δ DEF, $\angle D = \angle D$

$\angle DGH = \angle DEF$

(Since, GH || EF and DE is the transversal among corresponding angles)

$\therefore \Delta DGH \sim \Delta DEF$

(By AA criterion of similar triangles)

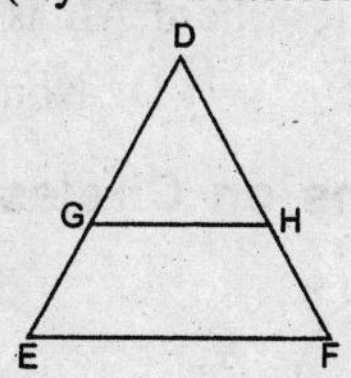

$$\therefore \frac{ar(\Delta DGH)}{ar(\Delta DEF)} = \frac{DG^2}{DE^2} = \frac{2^2}{5^2} = \frac{4}{25}$$

12. Since, ratio of area of two similar traingles = ratio of square of corresponding sides

ratio of sides = 5 : 11

$\therefore$ ratio of their areas = $(5)^2 : (11)^2 = 25 : 121$.

13. From question,

$ar(\Delta ADE) = 9\ ar(\Delta ABC)$

or, $\dfrac{ar(\Delta ABC)}{ar(\Delta ADE)} = \dfrac{1}{9} = \dfrac{BC^2}{DE^2}$

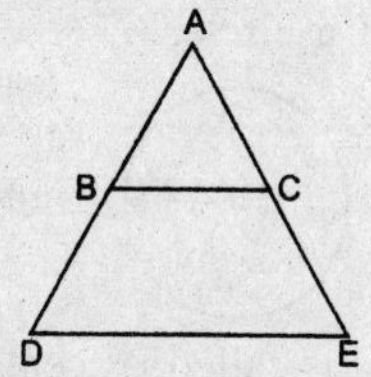

Hence, $\dfrac{BC}{DE} = \sqrt{\dfrac{1}{9}} = \dfrac{1}{3}$

14. From question, In ΔABC, D is the mid-point of AB and DE is drawn parallel to BC and it meets at E on AC.

Since, DE || BC (By B.P. Theorem)

$\dfrac{AD}{DB} = \dfrac{AE}{EC}$ ...(*i*)

also, $AD = DB$ ($\because$ D is mid-point)

$\therefore \dfrac{AD}{DB} = 1$

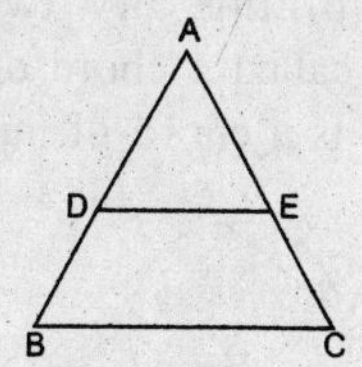

Now, $\dfrac{AE}{EC} = 1$ (From ...(*i*))

$\Rightarrow AE = EC$

Hence, the line bisects the third line

15. According to questions, $\angle B = \angle C$ (given)

$\Rightarrow AB = AC$ (*i*)

and, $BD = CE$ (*ii*)

Subtracting (*ii*) from (*i*), $AB - BD = AC - CE$

$\Rightarrow AD = AE$ (*iii*)

Dividing (*iii*) by (*ii*)

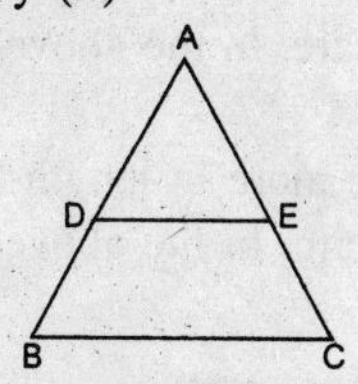

$$\frac{AD}{BD} = \frac{AE}{CE}$$

$\therefore$ DE || BC [By converse of BP Theorem]

Hence, option (B) is true.

Circle and Its Chord

A circle is a set of those points in a plane that are at a given constant distance from a given fixed point in the plane. The fixed point is called the **centre of the circle** and the constant distance of every point on the circle from its centre of called the **radius of the circle**.

Things to Remember

1. Locus of a point moving in a plane such that its distance from a fixed point in the same plane remains constant is called a circle.

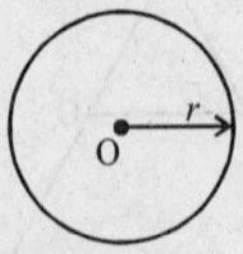

2. The fixed point O is called its centre and the constant distance r is called the radius.
3. The path traced by the moving point as described above is called the circumference of the circle.
4. The part of the plane containing the circle that consists the circle and its interior is called the circular region.

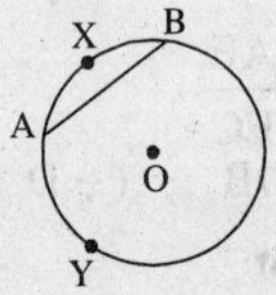

5. Line segment joining any two points on the circumference is called a chord of the circle. In the above figure AB is a chord of the circle.

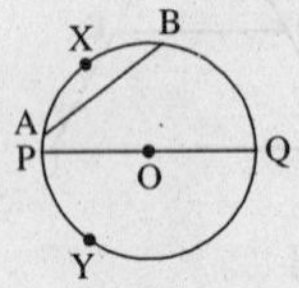

6. The chord passing through the centre of the circle is called its diameter.
   In the above figure PQ is a diameter of the circle.
7. Diameter is the longest chord of the circle.
8. Any fraction of the circumference is called an arc of the circle.
9. The remaining part of the circumference is called the alternate segment of the circle with respect to the arc.
10. An arc of a circle smaller in length than the semicircle is called a minor arc. In the above figure arc AXB is a minor arc.
11. An arc of a circle more in length than the semicircle is called a major arc. In the above figure arc AYB is a major arc.

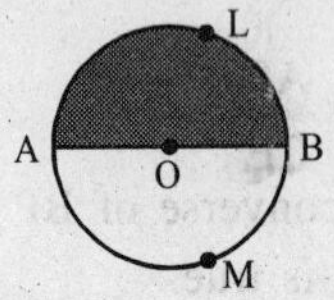

12. Diameter of a circle divides its circumference into two equal arcs. Each of them is called a semicircle.
13. The part of the plane containing the semicircle that consists the semi-circle, the enclosing diameter and its interior is called the semicircular region.
    In the above figure region ALB and region BMA are semicircular regions.

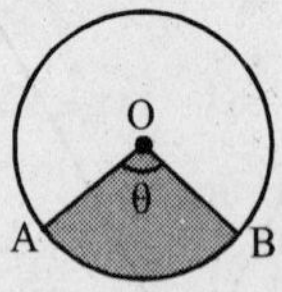

14. The angle formed by joining the end points of an arc to the centre of the circle is said to be the angle subtended by an arc at the centre of the circle. In the above figure, θ is the degree measure of arc AB.
15. The part of the plane containing the circle that consists of the arc enclosing radii and its interior is called the sector of the circle. In the above figure AOB is sector of the circle.
16. A chord of the circle other than a diameter divides the circular region into two unequal parts.
    Each of these parts is called a segment. The larger part is called the major segment and the smaller is called the minor segment.

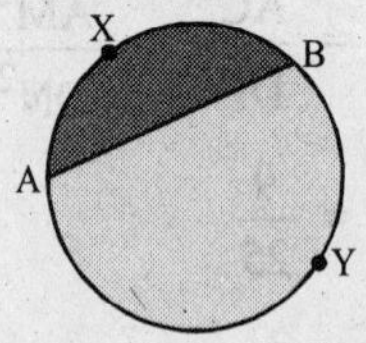

    In the above figure segment AXB is a minor segment and segment BYA is the major segment.
17. Two circles in a plane are said to be concentric if they have same centre but different radii.
18. The chord formed by joining the end points of an arc of a circle is called its corresponding chord.

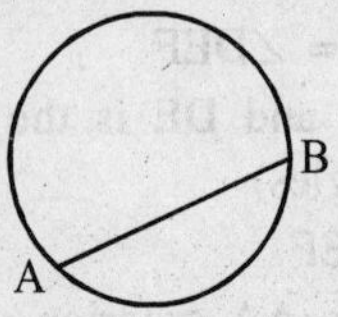

    In the given figures chord AB is the corresponding chord of arc AB.

Important Theorems on Circles

1.

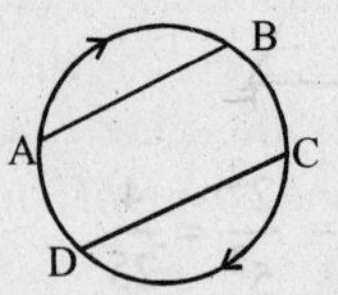

(*a*) If two arcs of a circle are equal then their corresponding chords are also equal.
AB = CD
$\Leftrightarrow$ arcAB = arcCD.

(*b*) If two chords of a circle are equal then their corresponding arcs are also equal.

2.

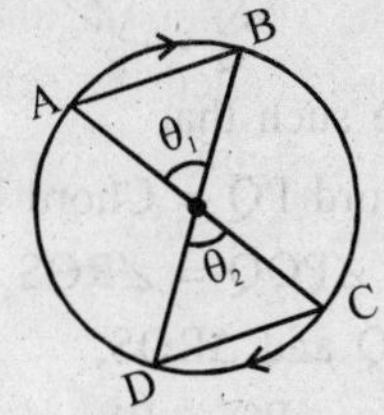

(*a*) If two chords of a circle are equal then they subtend equal angles at the centre of the circle.

(*b*) If two chords of a circle subtend equal angles at the centre of a circle then they are equal

AB = CD $\Leftrightarrow \theta_1 = \theta_2$

3.

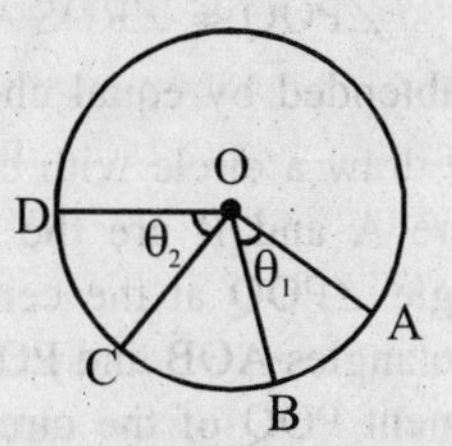

(*a*) If two arcs of a circle have same degree measure then they are equal.
arc AB = arc CD
$\Leftrightarrow \theta_1 = \theta_2$

(*b*) If two arcs of a circle are equal then their degree measures are also equal.

4.

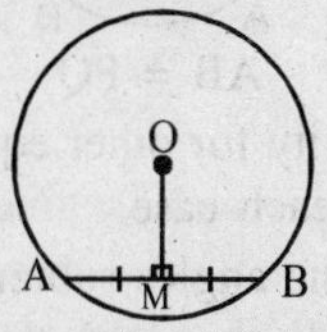

(*a*) Perpendicular to a chord from the centre of the circle bisects the chord.

(*b*) Line segment joining the centre of the circle to the mid point of the chord is perpendicular to the chord.

OM ⊥ AB $\Leftrightarrow$ M is the mid point of AB.

5.

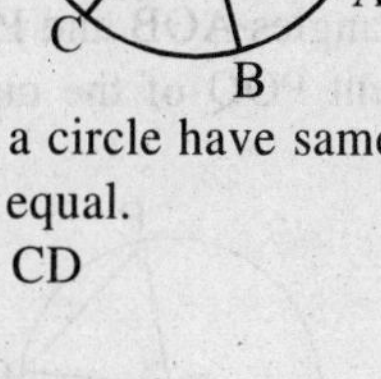

(*a*) If two chords of a circle are equidistant from the centre of the circle, they are equal.

(*b*) If two chords of a circle are equal then they are equidistant from the centre of the circle

AB = CD $\Leftrightarrow$ p = q

6.

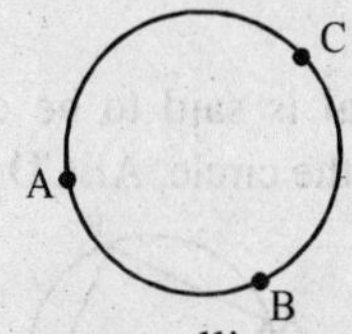

Through any three non collinear points, passes one and only one circle. A, B and C are three non-collinear points in a plane then one and only one circle passes through them.

7. Perpendicular bisector of a chord of a circle passes through the centre of the circle.

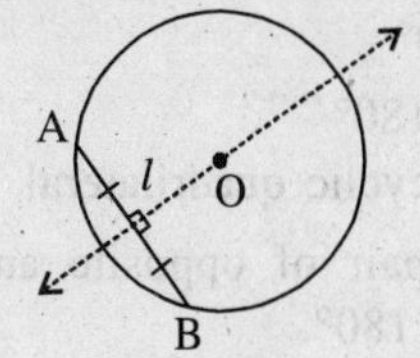

l is the ⊥ bisector of AB $\Leftrightarrow$ *l* passes through O.

8.

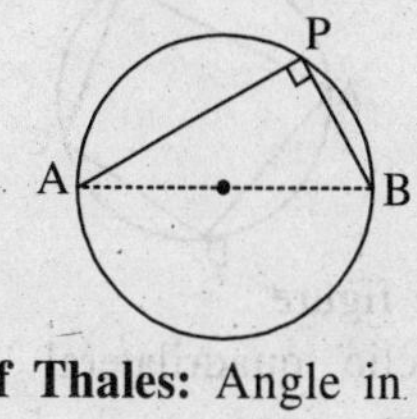

(*a*) **Theorem of Thales:** Angle in a semicircle is a right angle.

(*b*) If an arc subtends a right angle at any point in its alternate segment then it is a semi-circle.

$\overparen{APB}$ is a semicircle $\Leftrightarrow$ ∠APB= 90°

9. Angles in the same segment of a circle are equal

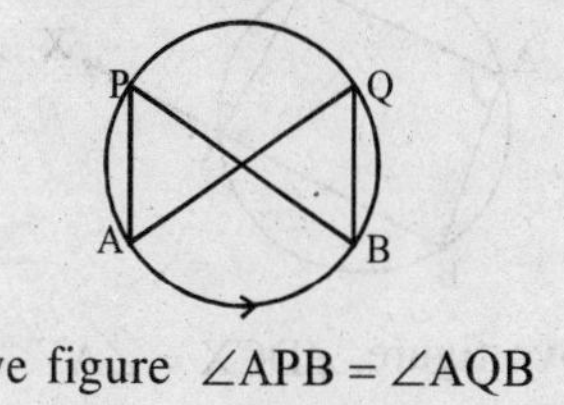

In the above figure ∠APB = ∠AQB

10.

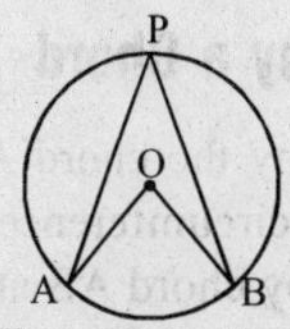

Degree Measure Theorem : Degree measure of an arc is twice the angle subtended by it at any point on the alternate segment of the circle with respect to the arc. In the above figure ∠AOB= 2∠APB

11. If a line segment joining two points subtends equal angles at two other points on same side of the line containing the two points then the four points are concyclic.

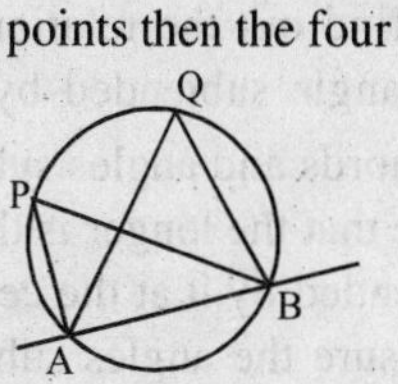

In the above figure ∠APB = ∠AQB, then A,B,Q and P are concylic.

Definition

A quadrilateral is said to be cyclic if all of its four vertices lie on the circle, ABCD is a cyclic quadrilateral.

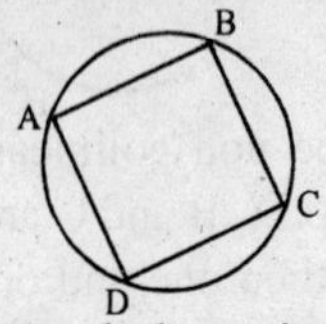

12. If in a quadrilateral the pair of opposite angles is supplementary then the quadrilateral is cyclic.
In the above figure
$\angle A + \angle C = 180°$
or $\angle B + \angle D = 180°$.
$\Rightarrow$ ABCD is cyclic quadrilateral.

13. Sum of each pair of opposite angles of a cyclic quadrilateral is 180°.

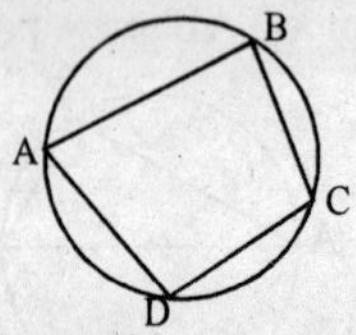

In the above figure
ABCD is cyclic quadrilateral
$\Rightarrow \angle A + \angle C = 180°$
and $\angle B + \angle D = 180°$.

14. Exterior angle of a cyclic quadrilateral is equal to its opposite interior angle.

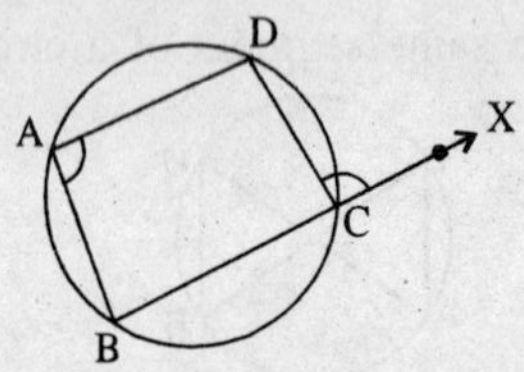

In the above figure, $\angle DCX = \angle A$

Angle subtended by a Chord

The angle subtended by the chord AB at a point C (not on the chord AB) on the circumference of the circle is $\angle ACB$. The angle subtended by chord AB at the centre O is $\angle AOB$.

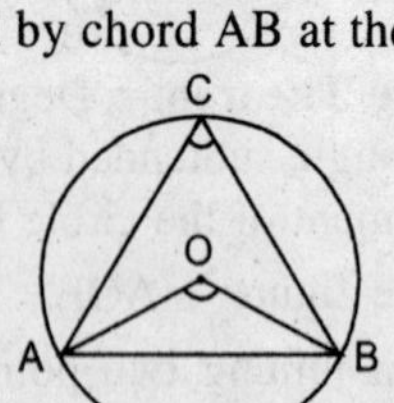

Activity: Let us find out the relation between the size of the chord and the angle subtended by it at the centre.

We draw many chords and angles subtended by them at the centre. We observe that the longer is the chord the bigger will be the angle subtended by it at the centre. We draw two equal chords and measure the angles subtended by them at the centre. We find that the angles subtended by them at the centre are equal.

Theorem 1. Equal chords of a circle subtend equal angles at the centre.

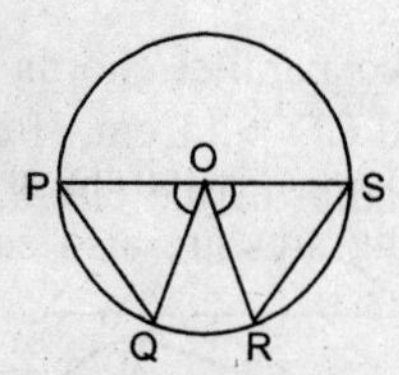

Given. A circle such that

Chord PQ = Chord RS

To prove, $\angle POQ = \angle ROS$

Proof. In ΔPOQ and ΔROS,

$PQ = RS$
$OP = OS$ = radius
$OQ = OR$ = radius
$\therefore$ $\Delta POQ \cong \Delta ROS$
(By SSS Theorem of congruence)
$\Rightarrow$ $\angle POQ = \angle ROS$ (C.P.C.T.)
$\Rightarrow$ Angles subtended by equal chords are equal.

Activity, We draw a circle with centre O and draw an angle AOB, where A and B are the points on the circle. Draw another angle $\angle POQ$ at the centre equal to $\angle AOB$. Separate these two angles AOB and POQ. If we put segment AOB on the segment POQ of the circle, we find that they cover each other.

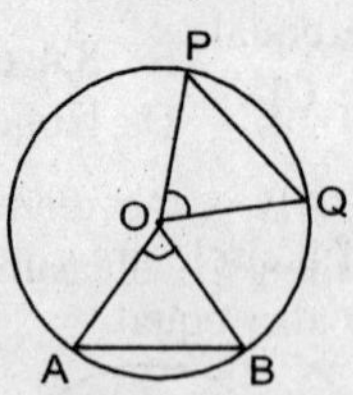

So, AB = PQ

Repeat this activity for other equal angles. We find the chords are equal in each case.

Theorem 2. If the angles subtended by the two chords at the centre of a circle are equal, then the chords are equal.

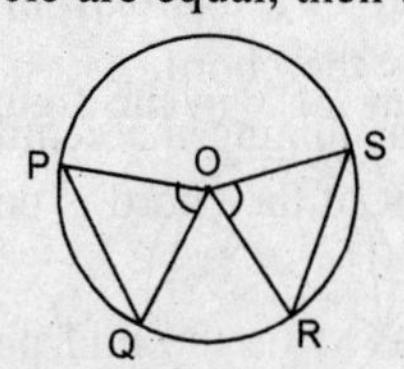

Given. Two chords PQ and RS of a circle in which,

$\angle POQ = \angle ROS$; PQ = RS

To prove.

Proof. In ΔPOQ and ΔROS

$OP = OR$ = radius
$\angle POQ = \angle ROS$
$OQ = OS$ = radius
$\therefore$ $\Delta POQ \cong \Delta ROS$
[By SAS Theorem of congruence]
$\Rightarrow$ PQ = RS (C.P.C.T.)

Hence, Chords are equal.

EXERCISE

1. AB and CD are two parallel chords of a circle such that AB = 5 cm and CD = 11 cm. If distance between them is 3 cm then radius of the circle is

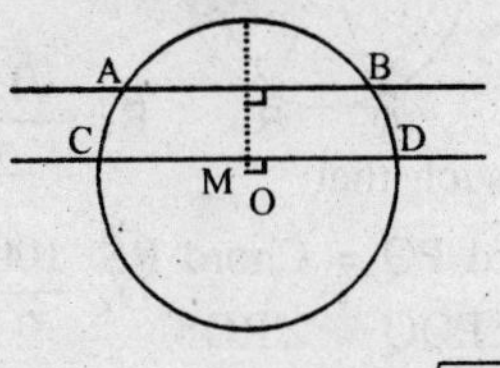

A. $2\sqrt{146}$ cm B. $\sqrt{146}$ cm

C. $\frac{\sqrt{146}}{2}$ cm D. None of these

2. The maximum number of common tangents to any pair of circles in the same plane is :

A. 4 B. 5

C. 2 D. 3

3. Find the length of a chord which is at a distance of 3 cm from the centre of a circle of radius 5 cm.

A. 2 cm B. 6 cm

C. 8 cm D. 10 cm

4. If AB and AC are two chords of a circle of radius 5 cm such that AB = AC = $4\sqrt{5}$ cm then the length of the chord BC is :

A. 8 cm B. 8.4 cm

C. 9 cm D. None of these

5. In the given figure AB is the diameter of the circle, PM bisects ∠APB then the measure of ∠ABM is :

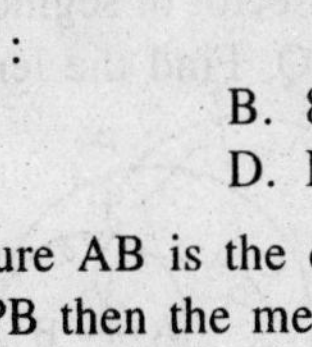

A. 45° B. 30°

C. 15° D. 60°

6. Determine the value of x in the figure given below.

A. 53° B. 106°

C. 26.5° D. 100°

7. Determine the value of x in the figure given below.

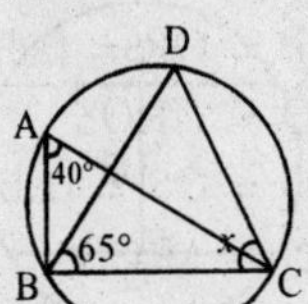

A. 40° B. 75°

C. 65° D. 105°

8. Determine the value of x in the figure given below.

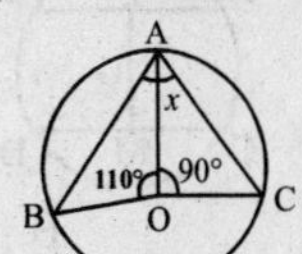

A. 80° B. 100°

C. 90° D. 110°

9. PQ is a diameter and PQRS is a cyclic quadrilateral. If ∠PSR = 150°, then measure of ∠RPQ is :

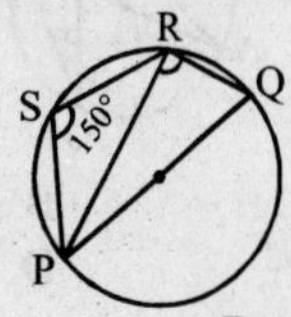

A. 90° B. 60°

C. 30° D. None of these

10. Determine the value of x in the figure given below.

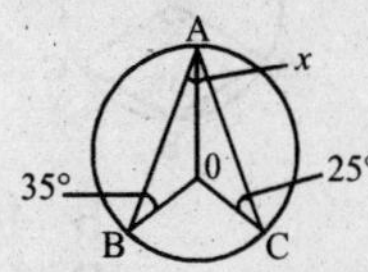

A. 35° B. 25°

C. 30° D. 60°

11. Determine the value of x in the figure given below.

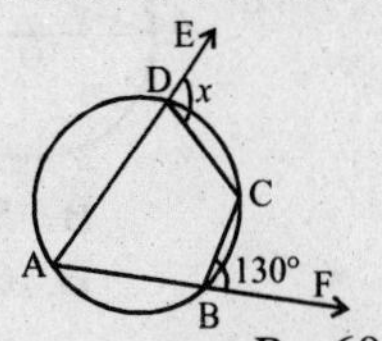

A. 65° B. 60°

C. 50° D. 80°

12. Chords AB and CD of a circle meet inside the circle at D. If PA = 4 cm, AB = 7 cm and PD = 6 cm then length of CD is :

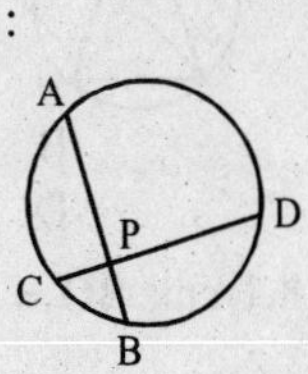

A. 8 cm B. 6 cm

C. 2 cm D. None of these

13. Chords AB and CD of a circle when product meet out side the circle at P, If AB = 4 cm; BP = 3 cm and CP = 14 cm then the length of CD is

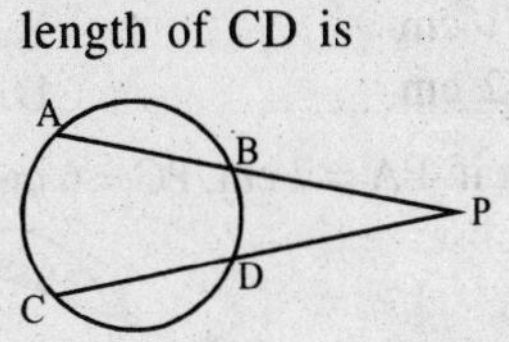

A. 3 cm B. 4.5 cm

C. 6 cm D. None of these

14. AB and CD are two parallel chords of circle such that AB = 10 cm and CD = 24 cm. If LM = 17 cm then the diameter of the circle is

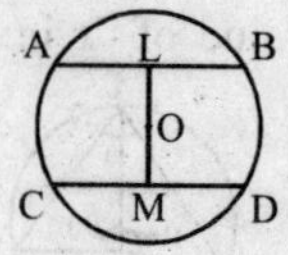

A. 13 cm B. 26 cm
C. 14 cm D. None of these

15. In the given figure determine the value of x.

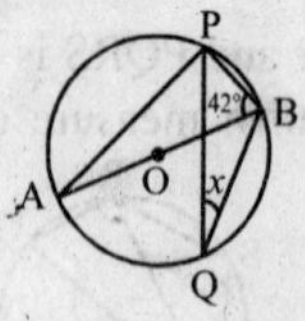

A. 48° B. 42°
C. 60° D. 38°

16. In the given figure determine the value of x.

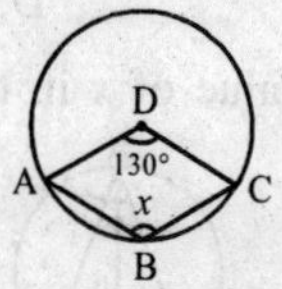

A. 90° B. 115°
C. 130° D. 65°

17. Find x

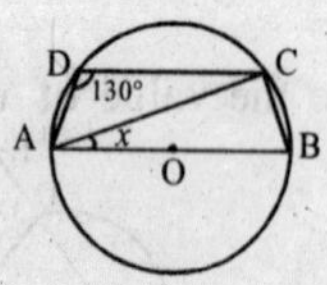

A. 40° B. 50°
C. 30° D. 60°

18. If O is the centre of the circle and ΔAOB is an equilateral triangle, then the measure of ΔACB is

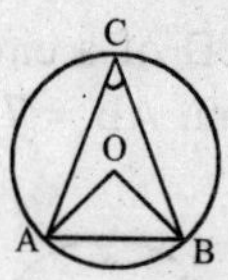

A. 60° B. 30°
C. 90° D. 75°

19. Find x if AO = 8.1 cm, BO = 5 cm, OC = 9 cm and OD = x cm.

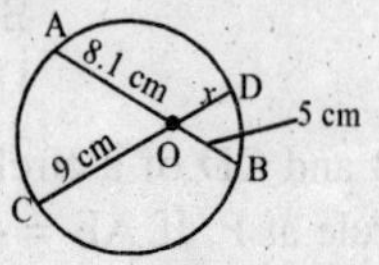

A. 4.1 cm B. 4.1 cm
C. 4.2 cm D. 4.5 cm

20. Find x if PA = 7 cm, PC = 6 cm, AB = 9 cm and CD = x

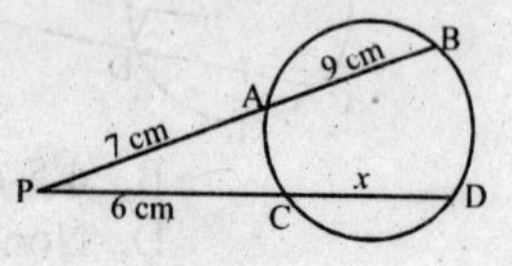

A. 12.0 cm B. 12.6 cm
C. 12.66 cm D. 12.67 cm

21. Two chords AB, CD of lengths 5 cm, 11 cm respectively of a circle are parallel. If the distance between AB and CD is 3 cm, find the radius of the circle.

A. $\frac{\sqrt{146}}{2}$ B. $\frac{\sqrt{150}}{2}$

C. $\frac{150}{3}$ D. $\frac{100}{2}$

22. O is the centre of the circle of radius 5 cm, OP ⊥ AB, OQ ⊥ CD, AB ∥ CD, AB = 6 cm and CD = 8 cm. Determine PQ.

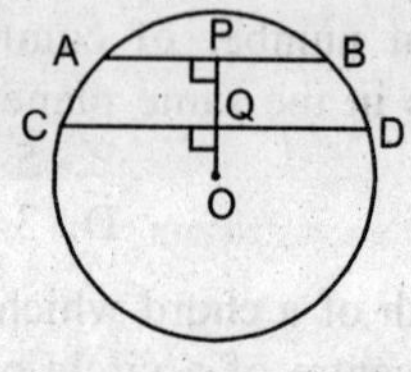

A. 5 cm B. 10 cm
C. 1 cm D. 2 cm

23. Two circle with centres A and B and of radii 5 cm and 3 cm, respectively touch each other internally. If the perpendicular bisector of segment AB meets the bigger circle in P and Q. Find the length of PQ.

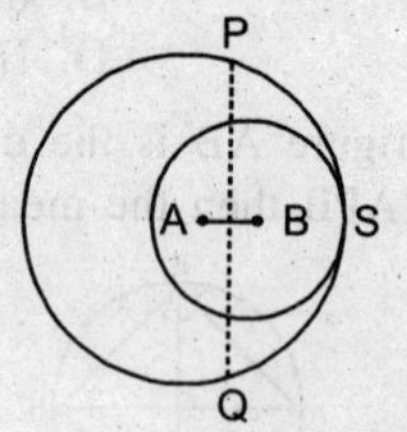

A. $4\sqrt{6}$ cm B. $3\sqrt{2}$ cm
C. $5\sqrt{4}$ cm D. $3\sqrt{5}$ cm

24. AB and CD are two parallel chords of a circle, which are an opposite sides of the centre, such that AB = 10 cm, CD = 24 cm and the distance between AB and CD is 17 cm. Find the radius of the circle.

A. 15 cm B. 13 cm
C. 14 cm D. 20 cm

25. O is the centre of the circle with radius 5 cm. OP ⊥ AB, OQ ⊥ CD, AB ∥ CD, AB = 8 cm and CD = 6 cm. Determine PQ.

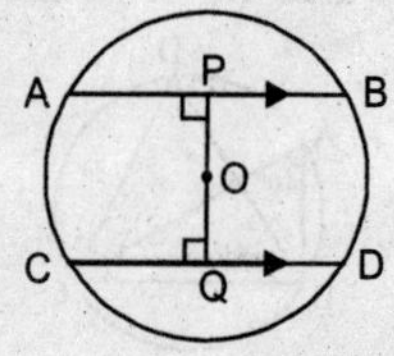

A. 3 cm B. 4 cm
C. 5 cm D. 7 cm

ANSWERS

1	2	3	4	5	6	7	8	9	10
C	A	C	A	A	A	B	A	B	D
11	12	13	14	15	16	17	18	19	20
C	A	D	B	A	B	A	B	D	C
21	22	23	24	25					
A	C	A	B	D					

EXPLANATORY ANSWERS

1. Let OM = x

Then $x^2+\left(\frac{11}{2}\right)^2=r^2$ and $(x+3)^2+\left(\frac{5}{2}\right)^2=r^2$

Then, $x^2+6x+9+\frac{25}{4}=x^2+\frac{121}{4}$

$\Rightarrow 6x=15 \Rightarrow x=2.5$ cm

Thus, $r^2=(2.5)^2+\frac{121}{4}=\frac{146}{4} \Rightarrow r=\frac{\sqrt{146}}{2}$ cm

3. Length of chord = $2.\sqrt{5^2-3^2}=8$ cm.

4. Let OP = x and BP = y

Then $x^2+y^2=25$ and $(5+x)^2+y^2=80$

Solving these two, we get, y = BP = 4 cm

Thus, BC = 8 cm.

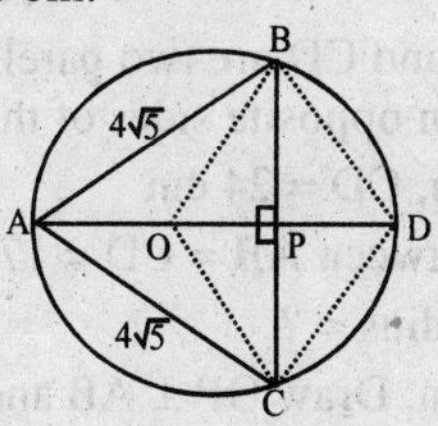

5. $\angle ABM=\angle APM=\frac{1}{2}\angle APB=\frac{1}{2}\times 90°=45°$

6. As angle in the same segment are equal.

$x=53°$

7. $x+65°+40°=180°$

$x=75°$

8. $x=\frac{1}{2}[(180°-110°)+(180°-90°)]$

$=\frac{1}{2}(70°+90°)=80°$

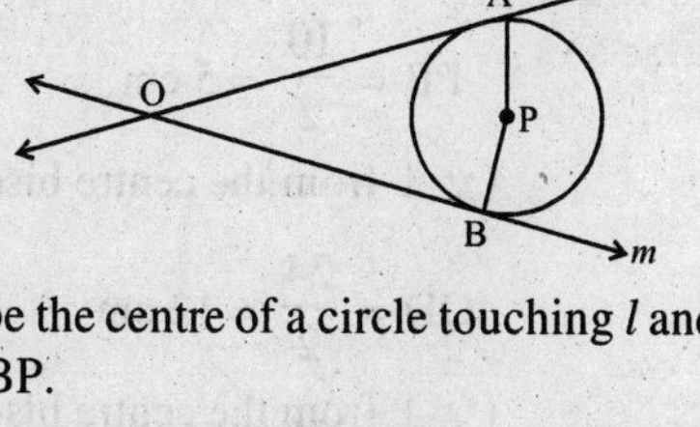

Let P be the centre of a circle touching l and m. Clearly, AP = BP.

Hence, P lies on angle bisector of $\angle$ AOB. Hence, locus of P will be the angle bisectors of the angles formed by these intersecting lines.

9. $\angle PQR=180°-150°=30°$

$\angle PRQ=90°$ (Angle of a semicircle)

$\angle RPQ+90°+30°=180°$

$\Rightarrow \angle RPQ=60°$

10. $\angle OAB=\angle OBA(\because OA=OB)$

$\angle OAB=35°$

Similarly, $\angle AOC=25°$

$\therefore \angle x=35°+25°=60°$

12. Use $PA\times PB=PC\times PD$

4 × (7 – 4) = 6 × PC

$\Rightarrow$ PC = 2 cm

CD = PC + PD = 2 + 6 = 8 cm.

13. Use $PA\times PB=PC\times PD$

$\Rightarrow (4+3)\times 3=14\times PD \Rightarrow PD=1.5$ cm

$\Rightarrow CD=PC-PD=14-1.5=12.5$ cm.

14. Let OL = x.

Then $OM(17-x)$

Also LB = 5 cm,

MD = 12 cm.

Then $x^2+25=r^2$ and $(17-x)^2+144=r^2$

Solving these we get

x = 12 cm and r = 13 cm

Thus, diameter = 2 × 13 = 26 cm.

15. $x+42°+90°=180° \Rightarrow x=48°$

18. $\angle ACB=\frac{1}{2}\angle AOB=\frac{1}{2}\times 60°=30°$

21. Given, chord AB = 5 cm, chord CD = 11 cm and AB ∥ CD

Perpendicular distance ML between AB and CD = 3 cm

To find. Radius of the circle.

Construction, Join OB, OD and draw perpendicular bisectors OL of AB and OM of CD

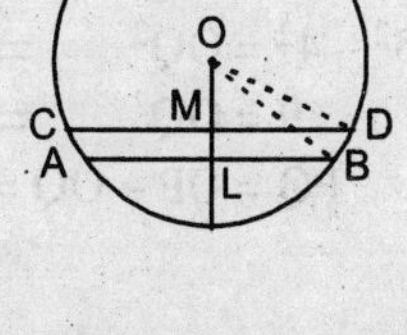

Procedure. In rt. ΔOMD,

$$OD^2 = MD^2 + OM^2$$

(By Pythagoras Theorem)

Let, $OM = x$ cm

$$\therefore \quad r^2 = \left(\frac{11}{2}\right)^2 + x^2 \quad ...(1)$$

And In rt. ΔOLB, $OB^2 = BL^2 + OL^2$

$$\Rightarrow \quad r^2 = \left(\frac{5}{2}\right)^2 + (3+x)^2 \quad ...(2)$$

From (1) and (2), we get,

$$r^2 = \left(\frac{11}{2}\right)^2 + x^2 = \left(\frac{5}{2}\right)^2 + (3+x)^2$$

$$\Rightarrow \quad \frac{121}{4} + x^2 = \frac{25}{4} + 9 + x^2 + 6x$$

$$\Rightarrow \quad x^2 - x^2 + 6x = \frac{121}{4} - \frac{25}{4} - 9$$

$$\Rightarrow \quad 6x = \frac{121 - 25 - 36}{4} = \frac{60}{4} = 15$$

$$\Rightarrow \quad x = \frac{15}{6} \text{ cm} = \frac{5}{2} \text{ cm}$$

From (1), $r^2 = \left(\frac{11}{2}\right)^2 + \left(\frac{5}{2}\right)^2 = \frac{121+25}{4} = \frac{146}{4}$

or $r = \frac{\sqrt{146}}{2}$ cm.

22. Given. A circle with centre O, such that chord AB = 6 cm, chord CD = 8 cm

AB || CD and radius of the circle = 5 cm

OP ⊥ AB and OQ ⊥ CD

To find. PQ

Construction. Join OA and OC

Procedure. AP = 1/2, AB = 3 cm, CQ = 1/2, CD = 4 cm [Perpendicular from the centre of the circle bisects the chord]

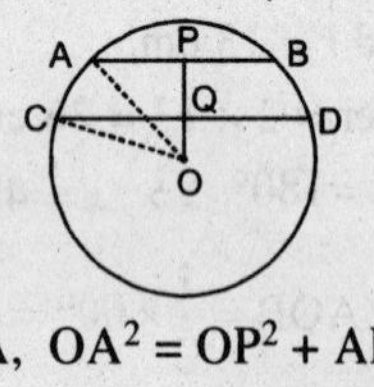

In right Δ OPA, $OA^2 = OP^2 + AP^2$ [By Pythagoras Theorem]

$$\Rightarrow \quad 5^2 = OP^2 + 3^2$$

$$\Rightarrow \quad 5^2 - 3^2 = OP^2 \quad \Rightarrow \quad 25 - 9 = OP^2$$

$$\Rightarrow \quad 16 = OP^2 \quad \Rightarrow \quad 4 = OP$$

In right ΔOQC, $OC^2 = OQ^2 + CQ^2$

[By Pythagoras Theorem]

$$5^2 = OQ^2 + 4^2$$

$$\Rightarrow \quad 5^2 - 4^2 = OQ^2 \quad \Rightarrow \quad 25 - 16 = OQ^2$$

$$\Rightarrow \quad 9 = OQ^2 \quad \Rightarrow \quad 3 = OQ$$

$$\therefore \quad PQ = OP - OQ = 4 - 3 = 1 \text{ cm.}$$

23. Given. Two circles touch internally at S, A and B be the centres of the bigger and smaller circles, respectively. The perpendicular bisector PQ bisects AB and meets the circle at P and Q.

To find PQ

Construction. Join PA, ABS

Procedure. With given radii, we find

AS = 5 cm

BS = 3 cm

AB = 5 – 3 = 2 cm and AC = 1 cm

[⊥ bisector bisects the chord]

PA = radius of bigger circle = 5 cm

In the right triangle ACP,

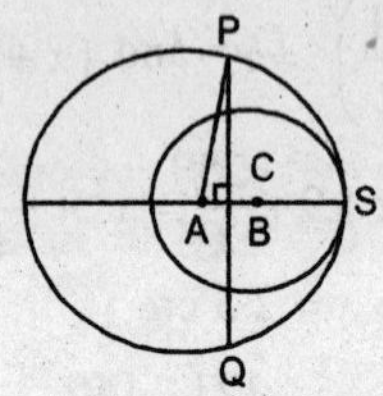

$$PC^2 = PA^2 - AC^2$$

[By Pythagoras Theorem]

$$\Rightarrow \quad PC^2 = (5)^2 - (1)^2$$

$$\Rightarrow \quad PC^2 = 25 - 1 = 24$$

$$\Rightarrow \quad PC = \sqrt{24} \Rightarrow PC = 2\sqrt{6}$$

$$\therefore \quad PQ = 2PC = 4\sqrt{6} \text{ cm.}$$

24. Given, AB and CD are two parellel chords of a circle, which are on opposite sides of the centre.

AB = 10 cm, CD = 24 cm

Distance between AB = CD = 17 cm

To find. Radius = ?

Construction. Draw OP ⊥ AB and OQ ⊥ CD. Join OB and OD.

Procedure. Since AB || CD and OP ⊥ AB, OQ ⊥ CD

∴ Points P, O and Q are collinear.

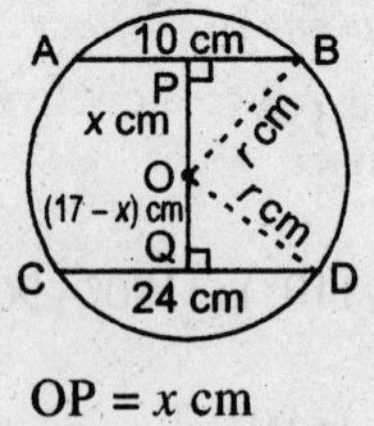

Let, $OP = x$ cm

Then, $OQ = (17 - x)$ cm

$$PB = \frac{10}{2} = 5 \text{ cm}$$

(∵ ⊥ from the centre bisects the chord)

$$QD = \frac{24}{2} = 12 \text{ cm}$$

(∵ ⊥ from the centre bisects the chord)

In rt. ΔOPB, $r^2 = x^2 + 5^2$ ...(1)

(By Pythagoras Theorem)

In rt. ΔOQD, $r^2 = (17 - x)^2 + 12^2$ ...(2)

From (1) and (2), we have

$$x^2 + 25 = (17 - x)^2 + 12^2$$
$$\Rightarrow \quad x^2 + 25 = 289 + x^2 - 34x + 144$$
$$\Rightarrow \quad x^2 - x^2 + 34x = 289 + 144 - 25$$
$$\Rightarrow \quad 34x = 408$$
$$\Rightarrow \quad x = 12 \text{ cm}$$

Using the value of x in (1), we get,

$$r^2 = 12^2 + 5^2 = 144 + 25 = 169$$

$\therefore$ Radius, $r = 13$ cm. ($\because$ radius can't be –ve)

25. Given, AB and CD are two parallel chords. AB = 8 cm, CD = 6 cm, radius = 5 cm.

To find. PQ

Construction. Join OA, OC, where O is the centre of the circle

Procedure. AP = PB = 4 cm ...[$\because$ AB = 8 cm]

CQ = QD = 3 cm ...[$\because$ CD = 6 cm]

[$\because \perp$ from the centre of a circle on any chord of the circle bisects it]

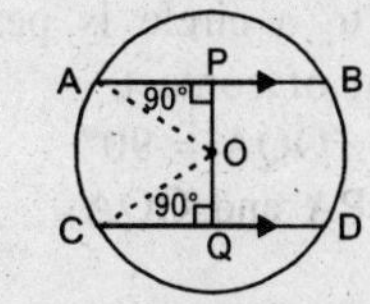

In rt. ΔOAP, OA = OC = radii of the circle = 5 cm

$$OP^2 = OA^2 - AP^2$$

[By Pythagoras Theorem]

$$= (5)^2 - (4)^2 = 25 - 16 = 9.$$
$$\Rightarrow \quad OP = 3$$

In rt. ΔOCQ, $OQ^2 = OC^2 - CQ^2$

[By Pythagoras Theorem]

$$(5)^2 - (3)^2 = 25 - 9 = 16$$
$$\Rightarrow \quad OQ = 4$$
$$\therefore \quad PQ = PO + OQ = 3 + 4 = 7 \text{ cm}.$$

Tangent

Secant

A line which interesects a circle in two distinct points is called a **secant** of the circle. In the fig. the line l intersects the circle in two distinct points A and B. The line l is a secant to the circle.

Tangent

A tangent to a circle is a line that intersects the circle at exactly one point. The point at which it meets the circle is called its point of contact and the line (tangent) is said to touch the circle at this point. In the figure, the line l meets the circle at only point A. Here A is the point of contact.

Some Important theorems on tangent

Theorem 1: *A tangent to a circle is perpendicular to the radius throught the point of contact.*

Given: A tangent AB to a circle C(O, r) with the point P as its point of contact.

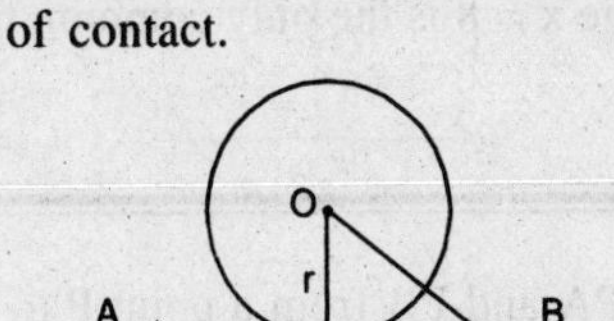

To prove: OP $\perp$ AB.

Construction: Let Q be any point other that P, an AB. join OQ.

Proof: $\because$ Q is a point on the tangent AB other than the point of contact P.

$\therefore$ Q lies in the exterior of the circle.

$\therefore$ OQ > OP

i.e., OP < OQ

Thus, of all the segments that can be drawn from the centre O to any point on the line AB, OP is the shortest.

We know that the shortest segment that can be drawn from a given point to a given line perpendicular from the given point to the given line.

Hence OP $\perp$ AB.

Theorem 2: (Converse of theorem 1)

A line drawn through the end of a radius and perpendicular on it is tangent to the circle.

Given: A radius OP of a circle C(O, r) and a line APB perpendicular to OP.

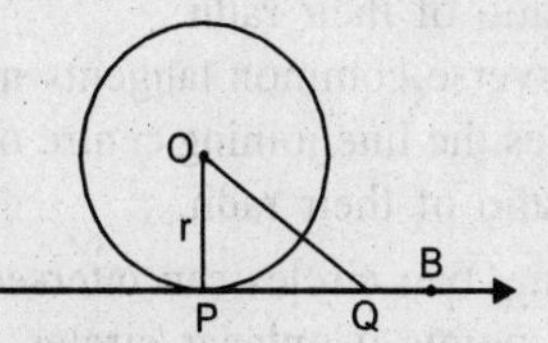

To prove: AB is the tangent to the circle at A.

Proof: Take a point Q, different from P, on line AB, since OP $\perp$ AB, OQ > OP.

$\therefore$ The point Q lies outside the circle (since OP is the shortest line segment from O to AB).

Thus every point on the line AB, other P, lies outside the circle and therefore AB meets the circle only at the point P.

Hence AB is a tangent to the circle.

Theorem 3: *The lengths of the two tangents drawn from an external point to a circle are equal.*

Given: A is an external point to the circle C(O, r). AP and AQ are two tangent segments from A to the circle.

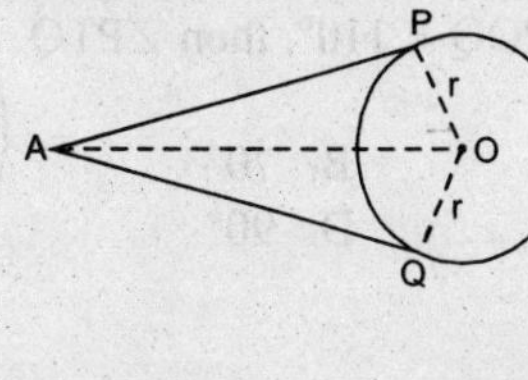

To prove: AP = AQ.

Construction: Draw line segments AP, OP and OQ.

Proof: A tangent to a circle is perpendicular to the radius through the point of contact.

∴ $\angle OPA = \angle OQA = 90°$

Now in right Δs OPA and OQA,

OP = OQ [each = r]

OA = OA [common]

∴ ΔOPA ≅ ΔOQA [by RHS congruence rule]

∴ AP = AQ [c.p.c.t.c.]

Common Tangents to Two circles

(*i*) Where the two circles neither intersect nor touch each other, there are FOUR common tangents, two of them are transverse & the others are direct common tangents.

(*ii*) When they intersect there are two common tangents, both of them being direct.

(*iii*) When they touch each other:

(*a*) **Externally:** there are three common tangents, two direct and one is the tangent at the point of contact.

(*b*) **Internally:** only one common tangent possible at their point of contact.

(*iv*) Length of an external common tangent & internal common tangent to the two circles is given by:

$$L_{ext} = \sqrt{d^2 - (r_1 - r_2)^2} \ \& \ L_{int} = \sqrt{d^2 - (r_1 + r_2)^2}$$

Where d = distance between the centres of the two circles. r_1 & r_2 are the radii of the two circles.

(*v*) The direct common tangents meet at a point which divides the line joining centre of circles externally in the ratio of their radii.

Transverse common tangents meet at a point which divides the line joining centre of circles internally in the ratio of their radii.

In a plane, two circles can intersect in two points, one point, or no points. Coplanar circles that intersect in one point are called **tangent circles.** Coplanar circles that have a common center are called **concentric.**

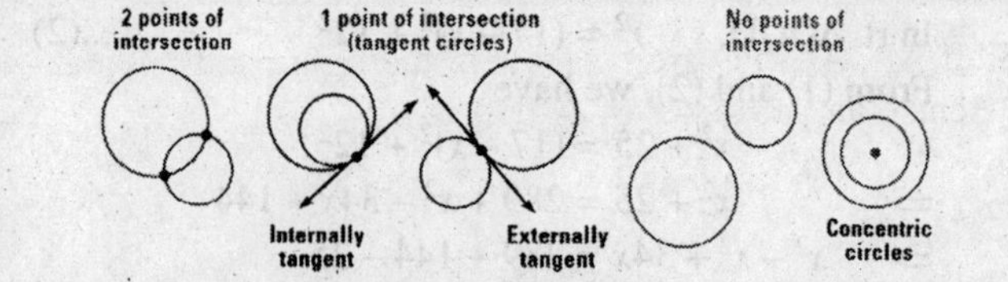

A line or segment that is tangent to two coplanar circles is called a **common tangent.** A *common internal tangent* intersects the segment that joins the centers of the two circles. A *common external tangent* does not intersect the segment that joins the centers of the two circles.

Example: Tell whether the common tangents are internal or external.

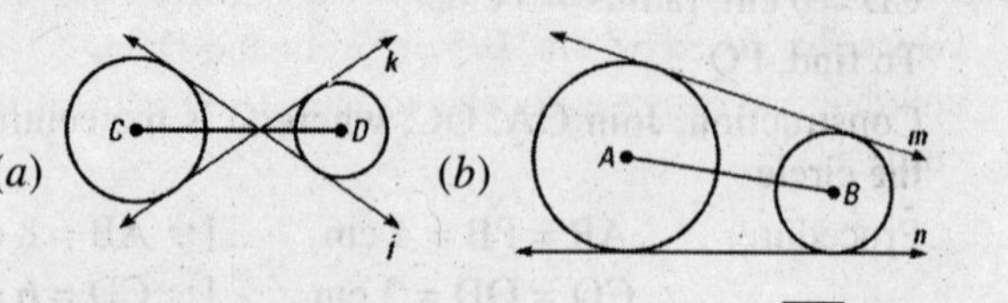

Solution: (*a*) The lines *j* and *k* intersect $\overline{CD}$, so they are common internal tangents.

(*b*) The lines m and n do not intersect $\overline{AB}$, so they are common external tangents.

In a plane, the **interior of a circle** consists of the points that are inside the circle. The **exterior of a circle** consists of the points that are outside the circle.

Example: Give the center and the radius of each circle. Describe the intersection of the two circles and describe all common tangents.

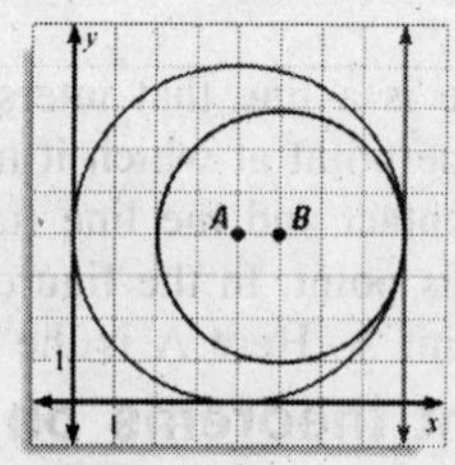

Solution: The center of ⊙A is A(4, 4) and its radius is 4. The center of ⊙B is B(5, 4) and its radius is 3. The two circles have only one point of intersection. It is the point (8, 4). The vertical line x = 8 is the only common tangent of the two circles.

EXERCISE

1. From a point Q, the length of the tangent to a circle is 24 cm and the distance from the centre is 25 cm. The radius of the circle is

A. 7 cm B. 12 cm
C. 15 cm D. 24.5 cm

2. In the given figure, if TP and TQ are the two tangents to a circle with centre O and that $\angle POQ = 110°$, then $\angle PTQ$ is equal to

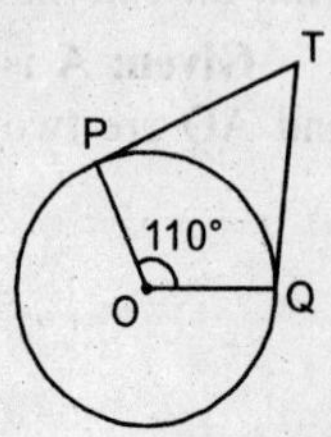

A. 60° B. 70°
C. 80° D. 90°

3. If tangents PA and PB from a point P to a circle with centre O are inclined to each other at angle of 80°, then $\angle POA$ is equal to

A. 50° B. 60°
C. 70° D. 80°

4. In Fig., a circle touches all the four sides of a quadrilateral ABCD whose sides AB = 6 cm, BC = 7 cm and CD = 4 cm. Find AD

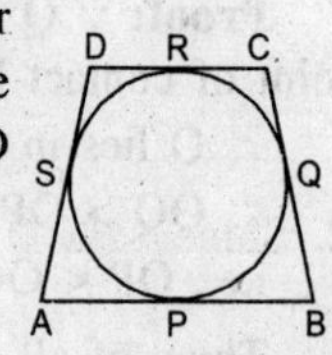

A. 2 cm B. 5 cm
C. 3 cm D. 4 cm

5. If AB, AC, PQ are tangents in the figure and AB = 5 cm. The perimeter of ΔAPQ is

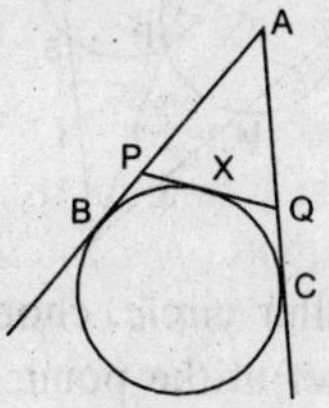

A. 8 cm B. 6 cm
C. 10 cm D. 5 cm

6. In Fig., a circle is inscribed within a quadrilateral ABCD. Given that BC = 38 cm, BQ = 27 cm and DC = 25 cm and that AD is perpendicular to DC. The radius of the circle is

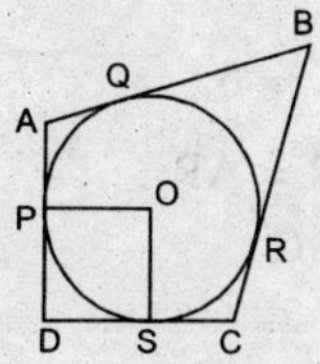

A. 10 cm B. 14 cm
C. 8 cm D. 12 cm

7. Two tangents are drawn to a circle from an external point A, touching the circle at the points P and Q. A third tangent intersects segment AP at B and segment AQ at C and touches the circle at R. If AQ = 10 units, then the perimeter of ΔABC (in units) is

A. 22.0 B. 20.5
C. 20.0 D. 40.0

8. In Fig., two circles intersect each other at points P and Q. From A on line PQ, secant AMD for one circle and secant ASR for the second one are drawn. If AM = 3, MD = 5 and AS = 4, determine SR.

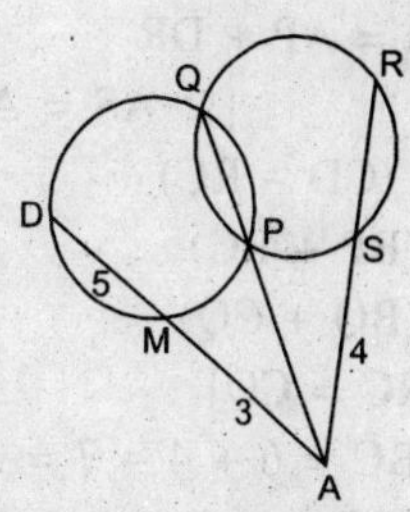

A. 2 cm B. 4 cm
C. 3 cm D. 1 cm

9. In the figure, KLMN is a cyclic quadrilateral and PQ is a tangent to the circle at K. If LN is a diameter of the circle. ∠KLN = 30° and ∠MNL = 60°. Determine ∠QKN

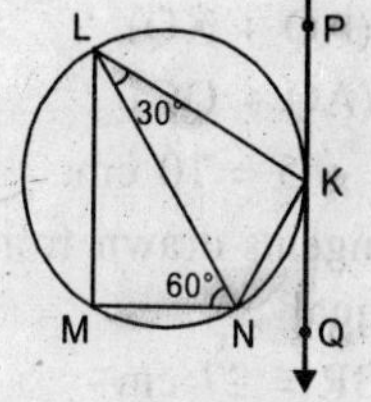

A. 30° B. 60°
C. 90° D. 100°

10. In the given Fig., PQ is tangent and O is the centre of the circle. Find EP is OP = 21, OQ = 9 and OM $\sqrt{80}$.

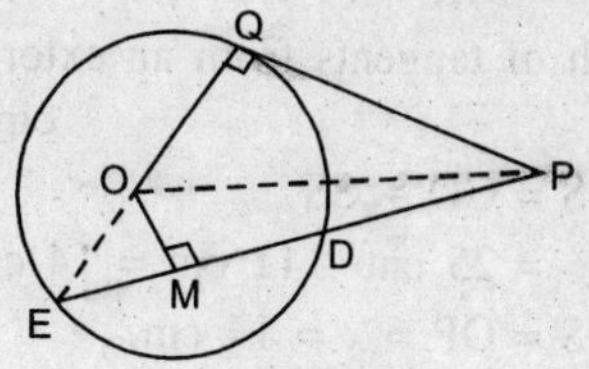

A. 10 B. 20
C. 30 D. 40

ANSWERS

1	2	3	4	5	6	7	8	9	10
A	B	A	C	C	B	C	A	A	B

EXPLANATORY ANSWERS

1. In rt. ∠d ΔOTQ,

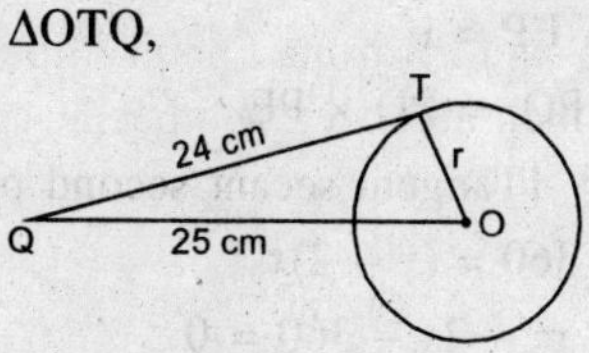

$$OT = \sqrt{OQ^2 - OT^2}$$

$$= \sqrt{25^2 - 24^2} = \sqrt{625 - 576} = \sqrt{49} = 7 \text{ cm.}$$

2. Since ∠POQ + ∠PTQ = 180°

[∵ ∠OPT = 90°, ∠OQT = 90°]

⇒ 110° + ∠PTQ = 180°

⇒ ∠PTQ = 180° – 110° = 70°.

3. Since ∠APB = 80°

∠AOB = 180° – 80° = 100°

∠PAO = ∠PBO = 90°

Since OP bisects ∠AOB

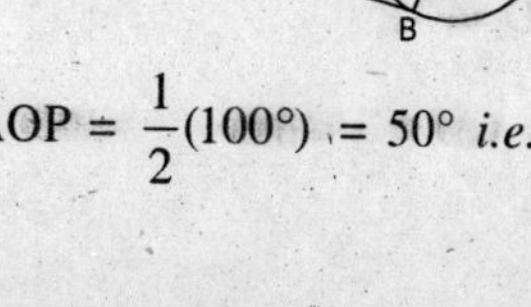

$\angle AOP = \frac{1}{2}(100°) = 50°$ *i.e.* ∠POA = 50°.

4. AD = AS + DS = AP + DR

[$\because$ AS = AP and DS = DR]

= (AB − BP) + (CD − RC)

= AB + CD − (BP + RC)

= AB + CD − (BQ + CQ)

[$\because$ BP = BQ, RC = CQ]

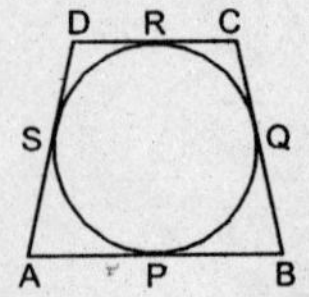

= AB + CD − BC = 6 + 4 − 7 = 3 cm.

5. Since AB and AC are the tangents from the same point A

$\therefore$ AB = AC = 5 cm

Similarly, BP = PX and XQ = QC

Perimeter of ΔAPQ

= AP + AQ + PQ

= AP + AQ + (PX + XQ)

= (AP + PX) + (AQ + XQ)

= (AP + BP) + (AQ + QC)

= AB + AC = 5 + 5 = 10 cm.

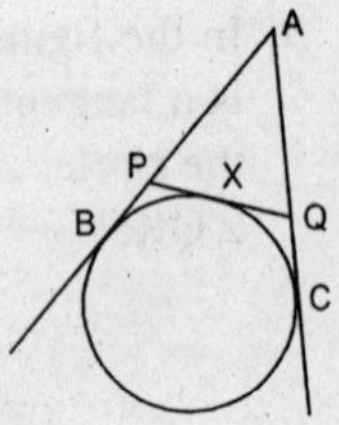

6. $\because$ Lengths of tangents drawn from an external point to a circle are equal

$\therefore$ BQ = BR = 27 cm

Let x be the radius of the circle

$\therefore$ OP = OS = PD = x

CR = BC − BR

= 38 − 27 = 11 cm

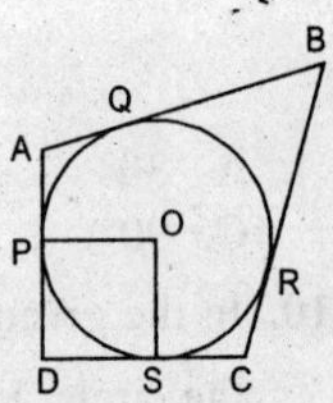

Now CS = CR = 11 cm

[$\because$ Length of tangents from an external point to a circle are equal]

$\therefore$ DS = CD − CS

= 25 cm − 11 cm = 14 cm

But DS = OP = x = 14 cm.

Hence radius = OP = 14 cm.

7. Since the tangents to a circle from an external point are equal in length

AP = AQ = 10 units

and BP = BR, CQ = CR

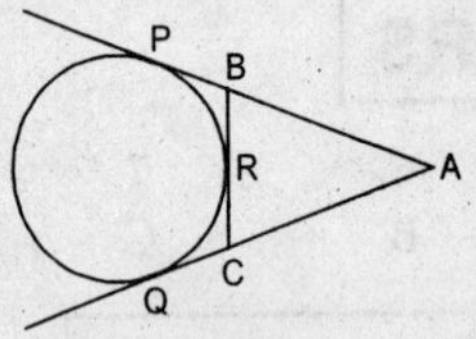

Adding these, we get,

BP + CQ = BR + CR = BC

Adding AB and AC to both sides, we get

BP + CQ + AB + AC = BC + AB + AC

⇒ (BP + AB) + (CQ + AC) = AB + BC + AC

⇒ AP + AQ = Perimeter of ΔABC

⇒ (10 + 10) units = Perimeter of ΔABC

$\therefore$ Perimeter of ΔABC = 20 units.

$\therefore$ (*iii*) is the correct answer.

8. In the larger circle, chord QP and chord DM intersect each other at the point A outside the circle

$\therefore$ AM × AD = AP ...(1)

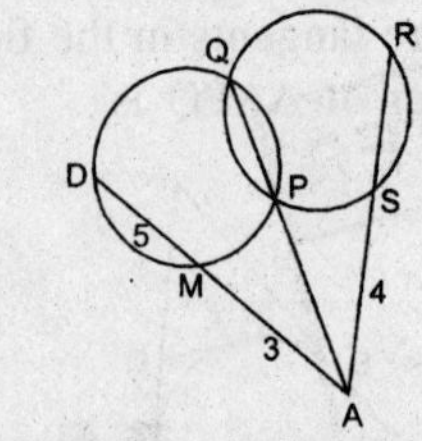

Again in the smaller circle, chord QP and chord RS intersect each other at the point A outside the circle.

$\therefore$ AS × AR = AP × AQ ...(2)

$\therefore$ AM × AD = AS × AR ...(3)

[From (1) and (2)]

Now AD = AM + MD

= 3 + 5 = 8

$\therefore$ From (3), 3 × 8 = 4 × AR

⇒ $AR = \frac{24}{4} = 6$

But AS + SR = AR

$\therefore$ 4 + SR = 6,

SR = 6 − 4 = 2.

9. KN is a chord through the point of contact K.

$\therefore$ ∠QKN = ∠KLN = 30°

[∠s in the alt. segment are equal]

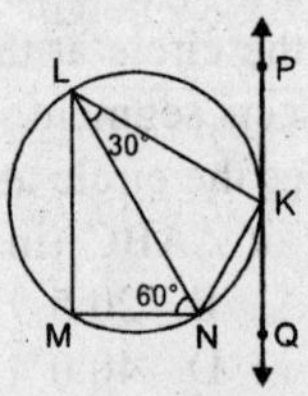

10. Join OQ and OE

In ΔOPQ, m ∠OQP = 90°

$\therefore$ $OQ^2 + QP^2 = OP^2$ [By Pythagoras Theorem]

⇒ $(9)^2 + QP^2 = (21)^2$

⇒ $QP^2 = (21)^2 - (9)^2 = 360$

In rt. ∠*d* ΔOME,

$OM^2 + EM^2 = OE^2$

⇒ $80 + (EM)^2 = (9)^2$

⇒ $EM^2 = 81 - 80 = 1$

⇒ $EM = +\sqrt{1} = 1$

$\therefore$ ED = 2EM = 2 × 1 = 2

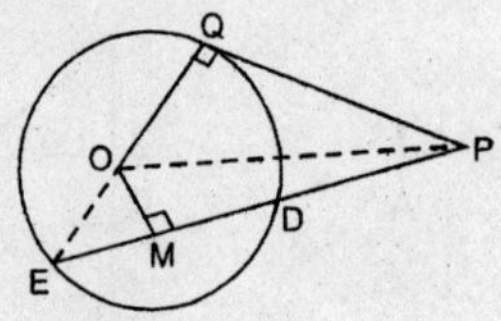

Let EP = x

Then $PQ^2 = PD \times PE$

[Tangent secant second point theorem]

$\therefore$ $360 = (x - 2)x$

⇒ $x^2 - 2x - 360 = 0$

⇒ $(x - 20)(x + 18) = 0$

⇒ $x = 20, -18$

But $x \neq -18$

Hence EP = 20.

●●●

CHAPTER 11

Mensuration

Triangle, Quadrilaterals, Regular Polygons

In mensuration we often have to deal with the problem of finding the areas and perimeters of plane figures.

Triangle

1. Perimeter = 3 × side

2. Area = $\frac{1}{2} \times \text{base} \times \text{height}$, or

Area = $\sqrt{s(s-a)(s-b)(s-c)}$

where *a, b, c,* are the lengths of the sides of triangle and $s = \frac{a+b+c}{2}$

Right Angled Triangle : It is one where one of the angles is right angle, i.e., 90°.

1. $(\text{Hypotenuse})^2 = (\text{Perpendicular})^2 + (\text{Base})^2$

2. Area = $\frac{1}{2} \times \text{Base} \times \text{Perpendicular}$

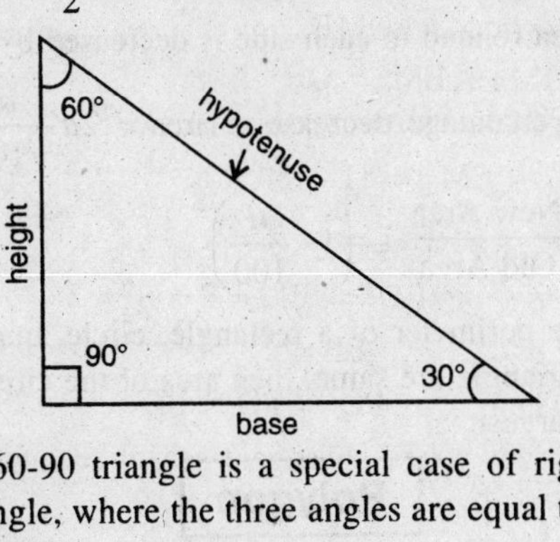

N.B. : 30-60-90 triangle is a special case of right angled triangle, where the three angles are equal to 30°, 60° and 90°.

Here,

3. Side opposite to the angle 30°

$= \frac{1}{2} \times \text{Hypotenuse}$

4. Side opposite to the angle 60°

$= \frac{\sqrt{3}}{2} \times \text{Hypotenuse}$

Equilateral Triangle : All three sides are equal in length and all three angles are equal to 60°

1. Area = $\frac{\sqrt{3}}{4} \times (\text{Side})^2$ 2. Area = $\frac{(\text{Height})^2}{\sqrt{3}}$

3. Height = $\frac{\sqrt{3}}{2} \times \text{side}$ 4. Perimeter = 3 × side

Isosceles Triangle : Two sides are equal in lengths.

1. Area = $\frac{b}{4}\sqrt{4a^2 - b^2}$

where a = lengths of opposite sides

b = length of unequal side

2. In an isosceles right triangle,

(*a*) Hypotenuse = $\sqrt{2} \times \text{congruent side (a)}$

(*b*) Area = $\frac{1}{2} \times a^2$

(*c*) Perimeter = $\sqrt{2} \times a\left(\sqrt{2}+1\right)$

Quadrilaterals

Rectangle:

1. Area = length(l) × breadth(b)
2. Perimeter = $2(l + b)$
3. Diagonal = $\sqrt{l^2 + b^2}$
4. Area of the path (inside of the rectangle) $= 2x\ (l + b - 2x)$
   where, x is the width of path.
5. Area of the path (Outside of the rectangle) $= 2x\ (l + b + 2x)$

Square:

1. Area = $(\text{Side})^2$
2. Perimeter = 4 × side
3. Diagonal = side × $\sqrt{2}$
4. Area of path (outside of square) = $4x \times (a + x)$ [where a = side, x = width of path]
5. Area of path (inside of square) = $4x \times (a - x)$

Parallelogram: In parallelogram opposite sides are parallel and equal. The two diagonals are not always equal but they bisect each other at the point of intersection.

Area = Base × Height.

Trapezium : It is a quadrilateral whose one pair of opposite sides is parallel. Other two opposite sides are oblique.

1. Area = $\frac{1}{2} \times \text{Height} \times (\text{Sum of parallel sides})$. Here, height is the distance between the two parallel sides.
2. Median = $\left(\frac{1}{2} \times \text{Sum of parallel side}\right)$ Here, median is the segment joining the midpoints of oblique sides.
3. Height = $\frac{2}{K}\sqrt{s(s-k)(s-c)(s-d)}$ (where $k = a - b$, *i.e.*, the difference between the parallel sides and c and d are the two non-parallel sides.)

   Also $s = \frac{k+c+d}{2}$

Rhombus : It is parallelogram whose all sides are equal and diagonals are bisect each other at right angle.

1. Area = $\frac{1}{2} \times \text{Product of diagonals}$
2. Side = $\sqrt{\left(\frac{d_1}{2}\right)^2 + \left(\frac{d_2}{2}\right)^2}$, where d_1 and d_2 are diagonals
3. Perimeter = 4 × side
4. Area of a rhombus (with one side and one diagonal given)

   $= \text{diagonal} \times \sqrt{(\text{side})^2 - \left(\frac{\text{diagonal}}{2}\right)^2}$
5. Other diagonal

   $= 2 \times \sqrt{(\text{side})^2 - \left(\frac{\text{diagonal}}{2}\right)^2}$

Quadrilateral : Area = $\frac{1}{2} \times$ One diagonal ×

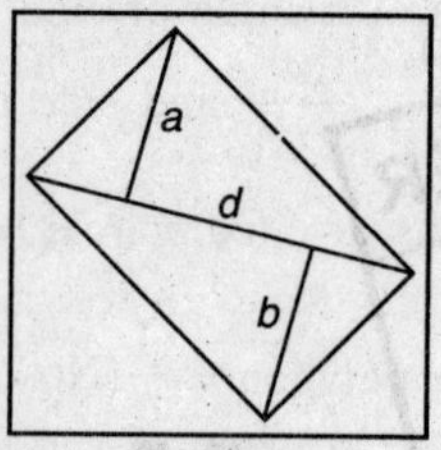

(Sum of perpendicular to it from the opposite vertices)

$= \frac{1}{2} \times d \times (a+b)$

Circle :

1. Diameter = 2 × Radius
2. Area = $\pi r^2 = \frac{\pi}{4}d^2$

   [where d = diameter = $\sqrt{\frac{4A}{\pi}}$
3. Circumference = $2\pi r = \pi d$
4. Radius = $\frac{\text{Circumference}}{2\pi} = \frac{\sqrt{\text{Area}}}{\pi}$
5. Length of an Arc = $\frac{\theta}{360°} \times 2\pi r$
6. Area of sector = $\frac{\theta}{360°} \times \pi r^2 = \frac{1}{2} \times \text{Arc} \times r$
7. Area of the ring or circular path $= \pi (R + r)(R - r)$

Remember some tricks for plane figures.

(*i*) If area related each side is increased by $a\%$, then

(*a*) Percentage increase in the area

$= 2a + \frac{a^2}{100}$

(*b*) $\frac{\text{New Area}}{\text{Old Area}} = \left(1 + \frac{a}{100}\right)^2$

(*ii*) If area related to each side is decreased by $a\%$, then

(*a*) Percentage decrease in area = $2a - \frac{a^2}{100}$

(*b*) $\frac{\text{New Area}}{\text{Old Area}} = \left(1 - \frac{a}{100}\right)^2$

(*iii*) If the perimeter of a rectangle, circle, quadrilateral and triangle are same, then area of the circle will be the largest.

Polygon

1. Interior angle + Exterior angle = 180°
2. Each interior angle = $\left(\frac{2n-4}{n}\right) \times 90°$

   where n = number of sides
3. Sum of Exterior angles = 360°
4. Perimeter = Number of sides × Length of side.

5. For an equilateral triangle of side 'a' (*a*) radius of inscribed circle = $\frac{a}{2\sqrt{3}}$ and side of the triangle = $2\sqrt{3}r$, (*b*) radius of circumcircle = $\frac{a}{\sqrt{3}}$

6. Area of regular polygon = $\frac{1}{2}$(No. of sides) (Radius of the incribed circle)

7. Area of regular hexagon

$= \frac{3\sqrt{3}}{2}(\text{side})^2 = 2.598\ (\text{side})^2$

8. Area of a regular octagon

$= 2(\sqrt{2}+1)(\text{side})^2 = 4.828\ (\text{side})^2$

9. Area of cyclic quadrilateral, A

$= \sqrt{s(s-a)(s-b)(s-c)(s-d)}$

where, $s = \frac{a+b+c+d}{2}$ and,

$\angle A + \angle C = \angle B + \angle D = 180°$

10. For circum-circle, if a is the length of each side of a regular polygon and R is the circum-radius, then

(*a*) $R = \frac{a}{2}\text{cosec}\left(\frac{180°}{n}\right)$

(*b*) Area of the polygon $= \frac{1}{4}na^2\cot\left(\frac{180°}{n}\right)$, or

(*c*) Area of the polygon

$= nR^2\sin\left(\frac{180°}{n}\right)\cos\left(\frac{180°}{n}\right)$

(*d*) Area of the circum-circle of n-sided regular polygon

$= \frac{\pi}{4}a^2\text{cosec}^2\left(\frac{180°}{n}\right)$

11. For in-circle, if a is the length of a side of a regular polygon and r is the radius of the in-circle, then

(*a*) $r = \frac{a}{2}\cot\left(\frac{180°}{n}\right)$

(*b*) Area of the polygon $= \pi r^2\cot\left(\frac{180°}{n}\right)$

(*c*) Area of the in-circle of an n-sided regular polygon

$= \frac{\pi}{4}a^2\cot^2\left(\frac{180°}{n}\right)$

(*d*) Radius of the in-circle of a regular hexagon = $\frac{\sqrt{3}}{4} \times a^2$

(*e*) Area of the in-circle $= \frac{3}{4}\pi a^2$

EXERCISE

1. A rectangle measures 50 cm × 25 cm. Its area is
A. 1150 sq. cm B. 1250 sq. cm
C. 1275 sq. cm D. 1280 sq. cm

2. A field is in the form of a square whose perimeter is 580 m. Area of this field is
A. 20025 sq. m B. 20225 sq. m
C. 30025 sq. m D. 19975 sq. cm

3. Find the area of the square whose each side measures 20 cm.
A. 300 sq. cm B. 380 sq. cm
C. 360 sq. cm D. 400 sq. cm

4. Area of a circle is 154 sq. cm. Its circumference will be
A. 44 cm B. 48 cm
C. 54 cm D. 68 cm

5. The base and the height of a triangle is 8 cm and 10 cm respectively. Its area will be
A. 40 sq. cm B. 20 sq. cm
C. 49 sq. cm D. 64 sq. cm

6. If it is given that the parallel sides of a trapezium are 15 m and 25 m while the distance between them is 10 m. its area will be
A. 150 sq. m B. 225 sq. m
C. 200 sq. m D. 270 sq. m

7. Perimeter of a rectangular field is 760 m and its length and breadth are in the ratio 11 : 8. Area of this rectangular field is
A. 35200 sq. m B. 34700 sq. m
C. 35600 sq. m D. 45200 sq. m

8. If side of a square is reduced by 50%, its area will be reduced by
A. 50% B. 75%
C. 80% D. 60%

9. If area of a square is equal to the area of a rectangle 6.4 m long and 2.5 m wide, then each side of this square measures
A. 8 m B. 5.4 m
C. 3.8 m D. 4 m

10. If perimeter of a right angled triangle is six times its smallest side, then the three sides of this triangle are in the ratio of
A. 13 : 5 : 12 B. 13 : 12 : 5
C. 12 : 5 : 13 D. 13 : 5 : 10

11. The perimeter of a square is 24 m and that of another is 32 m. Find the perimeter of a third square area of which is equal to sum of the areas of these two squares
A. 40 m B. 51 m
C. 37 m D. 42 m

12. If each side of a square is doubled, its area will become
A. double B. four times
C. three times D. eight times

13. The difference between the areas of two squares is 225 sq. metres and each side of the bigger square is 25 metres. The side of the smaller square is
A. 18 m B. 21 m
C. 20 m D. 22 m

14. If the perimeter of an equilateral triangle is 72 cm, its area will be
A. $144\sqrt{3}$ sq. cm B. $142\sqrt{3}$ sq. cm
C. $154\sqrt{2}$ sq. cm D. $144\sqrt{2}$ sq. cm

15. The radii of two circles are 5 cm and 12 cm respectively. Find the radius of a circle which is equal in area to these two circles.
A. 15 cm B. 13 cm
C. 10 cm D. 8 cm

16. If the circumference of a circle is equal to the perimeter of a square, then their areas are in the ratio of
A. 14 : 11 B. 7 : 8
C. 14 : 13 D. 13 : 11

17. Three sides of a triangle are in the ratio of 17 : 15 : 8. If the perimeter of this triangle is 40 m, find its area
A. 50 sq. m B. 49 sq. m
C. 60 sq. m D. 69 sq. m

18. If the length of a rectangle is increased by 20% and width is decreased by 15%, then its area
A. decreased by 4% B. increases by 2%
C. decreases by 2% D. increases by 3%

ANSWERS

1	2	3	4	5	6	7	8	9	10
B	A	D	A	A	C	A	B	D	B
11	12	13	14	15	16	17	18		
A	B	C	A	B	A	C	B		

EXPLANATORY ANSWERS

1. Area of the rectangle
$= l \times b = 50 \times 25 = 1250$ sq. cm

2. Perimeter of the square = 4 × side
According to question :
$4 \times \text{side} = 580 \Rightarrow \text{side} = \frac{580}{4} = 145$ m
$\therefore$ Area = $(\text{side})^2 = (145)^2 = 20025$ sq. m.

3. Area of the square = $(\text{side})^2 = (20)^2 = 400$ sq. cm.

4. Area of the circle= πr^2
$\therefore \quad \pi r^2 = 154$
$\Rightarrow \quad r^2 = \frac{154 \times 7}{22}$
$\Rightarrow \quad r^2 = 7 \times 7 \Rightarrow r = 7$ cm
$\therefore$ Circumference of the circle
$= 2\pi r = 2 \times \frac{22}{7} \times 7 = 44$ cm.

5. Area of the triangle
$= \frac{1}{2} \times \text{base} \times \text{height} = \frac{1}{2} \times 8 \times 10 = 40$ sq. cm.

6. Area of the trapezium
$= \frac{1}{2} \times (\text{sum of the parallel sides}) \times \text{distance between them}$
$= \frac{1}{2} \times (15 + 25) \times 10 = \frac{1}{2} \times 40 \times 10 = 200$ sq. m.

7. Suppose length and breadth of the rectangular field are $11x$ m and $8x$ m.
$\therefore$ Perimeter of the field
$= 2(11x + 8x) = 2 \times 19x = 38x$ m.
According to question :
Perimeter of the field = 760 m
$\therefore \quad 38x = 760 \Rightarrow x = \frac{760}{38} = 20$
$\therefore$ Length of the field = 11 × 20 = 220 m
Breadth of the field = 8 × 20 = 160 m
$\therefore$ Area of the field = 220 × 160 = 35200 sq.m.

8. Suppose side of the square = x m
In the first case :
Area of the square = x^2 sq. m.
In the second case :
On effecting 50% reduction in the side of the square,
Side of the new square = $x - 50\%$ of $x = \frac{x}{2}$ m
$\therefore$ Area of the new square = $\left(\frac{x}{2}\right)^2 = \frac{x^2}{4}$ sq.m.
$\therefore$ Reduction in area of the square
$= x^2 - \frac{x^2}{4} = \frac{3x^2}{4}$ sq. m.
$\therefore$ Percentage reduction = $\frac{3x^2/4}{x^2} \times 100 = 75\%$
Hence, area of the square will be reduced by 75%.

9. Area of the rectangle = 6.4 × 2.5 = 16.00 sq.m.
According to question :
Area of the square = Area of the rectangle
$\therefore$ Area of the square = 16 sq. m.
$\therefore$ Side of the square = $\sqrt{16} = \sqrt{4 \times 4} = 4$ m.

10. Suppose, the three sides of the triangle are a, b and c and a is the largest while c is the smallest side of the triangle.

$\therefore \quad a^2 = b^2 + c^2 \quad ...(i)$

Perimeter of the triangle = $a + b + c$

According to question :

$(a + b + c) = c \times 6$

$\Rightarrow \quad a + b = 5c \quad ...(ii)$

From equation (i), $a^2 - b^2 = c^2$

$\Rightarrow (a + b)(a - b) = c^2$

$\Rightarrow \quad 5c(a - b) = c^2$

$\Rightarrow \quad a - b = \frac{c}{5} \quad [\because a + b = 5c] \quad ...(iii)$

From equation (ii) and (iii),

$a + b = 5c,\ a - b = \frac{c}{5}$

$\Rightarrow \quad 2a = 5c + \frac{c}{5}$

$= \frac{26c}{5} \Rightarrow a = \frac{26c}{10} = \frac{13}{5}c$

$\Rightarrow \quad a : c = 13 : 5$

on substituting the value of a in equation (ii)

$b = 5c - \frac{13c}{5} = \frac{12c}{5}$

$\Rightarrow \quad b : c = 12 : 5$

$\therefore \quad a : b : c = 13 : 12 : 5$

Hence, the three sides of the right angled triangle are in the ratio of 13 : 12 : 5.

11. Perimeter of the 1st square = 24 m

$\therefore$ Side of the 1st square = $\frac{24}{4} = 6$ m

Perimeter of the 2nd square = 32 m

$\therefore$ Side of the 2nd square = $\frac{32}{4} = 8$ m

According to question :

Area of the third square = Area of the first two squares

$\therefore$ Area of the third square = Areas of the 1st square + Area of the 2nd square

$= 6^2 + 8^2 = 36 + 64 = 100$ sq. m.

$\therefore$ Side of the third square = $\sqrt{100} = 10$ m

$\therefore$ Perimeter of the third square

$= 4 \times \text{side} = 4 \times 10 = 40$ m.

12. In the first case:

Side of the square = x m

$\therefore$ Area of the square = x^2 sq. m

In the second case:

Side of the square = $2x$ m.

$\therefore$ Area of the square = $(2x)^2 = 4x^2$ sq. m

Hence, it is clear that if side of a square is doubled, its area becomes four times.

13. Suppose side of the smaller square = x m

$\because$ Area of the bigger square = $(25)^2 = 625$ sq. m

And area of the smaller square = x^2 sq. m

According to question :

Differene between the areas of two squares

= 225 sq. m

$\therefore \quad 625 - x^2 = 225$

$\Rightarrow \quad x^2 = 625 - 225 = 400$

$\Rightarrow \quad x = \sqrt{400} = 20$ m

$\therefore$ Side of the smaller side = 20 m.

14. Suppose side of the equilateral triangle = x cm

$\therefore$ Perimeter of the triangle = $3x$ cm

According to question :

$3x = 72 \Rightarrow x = \frac{72}{3} = 24$ cm.

$\therefore$ Area of the equilateral triangle

$= \frac{\sqrt{3}}{4} \times x^2 = \frac{\sqrt{3}}{4} \times (24)^2$

$= 144\sqrt{3}$ sq. cm.

15. $\because$ Radius of the first circle = 5 cm

$\therefore$ Area of the first circle = $\pi \times 5^2 = 25\pi$ sq. cm and

Radius of the second circle = 12 cm

$\therefore$ Area of the second circle

$= \pi \times 12^2 = 144\pi$ sq. cm

According to question :

Area of the new circle

= Sum of the areas of the two circles

$\therefore$ Area of the new circle

$= 25\pi + 144\pi = 169\pi$ sq. cm $= \pi(13)^2$ sq. cm

Hence, it is clear that the radius of the new circle will be 13 cm.

16. Suppose radius of the circle = R cm

And side of the square = x cm

$\therefore$ Circumference of the circle = 2πR cm

and Perimeter of the square = $4x$ cm

According to question :

$2\pi R = 4x \Rightarrow R = \frac{2x}{\pi}$

$\therefore$ Ratio between the areas of the circle and the square

$= \pi R^2 : x^2$

$\Rightarrow \pi \times \left(\frac{2x}{\pi}\right)^2 : x^2 \Rightarrow \frac{4x^2}{\pi} : x^2 \Rightarrow 4 : \pi : \Rightarrow 4 : \frac{22}{7}$

$\Rightarrow \quad 14 : 11.$

18. Suppose the length and the width of the rectangle are x metre and y metre respectively.

$\therefore$ Area of the rectangle = xy sq. metre

According to question :

On effecting 20% increase in the length and 15% decrease in the width :

Length of the new rectangle

$= x + 20\%$ of $x = 1.2\,x$ metre

Width of the new rectangle

$= y - 15\%$ of $y = .85\,y$ metre

$\therefore$ Area of the new rectangle

$= 1.2x \times .85y = 1.020\,xy$ sq. metre

Prism; Right Circular Cone; Right Circular Cylinder; Sphere; Hemisphere; Right Pyramid; Rectangular Parallelepiped

In mensuration we often have to deal with the problem of finding the volume of solid figure.

Cuboid : A cuboid has six faces, each one a ractangle. It has 12 edges. For example, a rectangular brick.

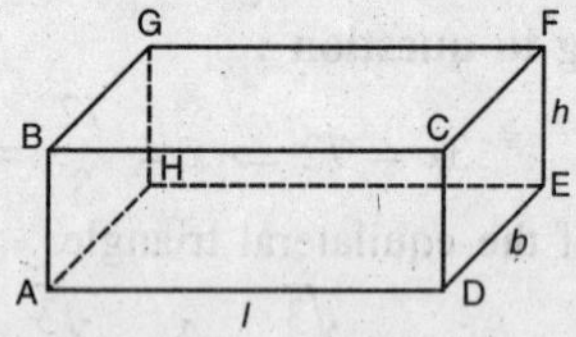

Let length = l, Breadth = b and height = h, then,

1. Volume = (Length × Breadth × Height)
2. Whole surface = $2(lb + bh + lh)$
3. Diagonal = $\sqrt{l^2+b^2+h^2}$
4. Area of 4 walls of a room = $2 \times h\ (l + b)$

Cube : In a cube, Length = Breadth = Height

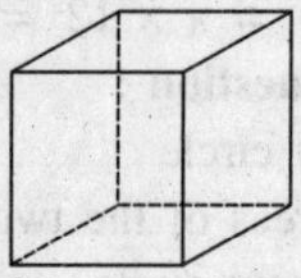

1. Volume = $(l)^3$
2. Length = $\sqrt[3]{\text{Volume}}$
3. Whole Surface area = $6\ l^2$
4. Diagonal = $l \times \sqrt{3}$
5. Lateral surface area = $4\ l^2$

Cylinder :

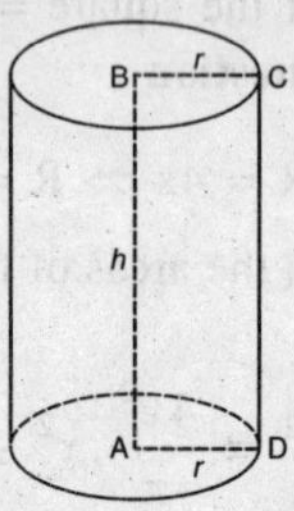

1. Volume = $\pi r^2 h$
2. Curved surface Area = $2\pi rh$
3. Total surface area = $2\pi r(r + h)$
   where r = radius, h = height
4. Curved surface of hollow cylinder
   $= 2\pi h\ (r_1 + r_2)$
5. Total surface of hollow cylinder
   $= 2\pi h\ (r_1 + r_2) + 2\pi\ (r_1^2 - r_2^2)$
6. Volume of hollow cylinder
   $= \pi h\left(r_1^2 - r_2^2\right)$
   where r_1 = outer radius
   r_2 = inner radius

Spherical Cell :

1. Volume = $\frac{4}{3}\pi\left(R^3 - r^3\right)$
2. Total surface area= $4\pi(R^2 - r^2)$
   where R = Outer radius
   r = Inner radius

Sphere

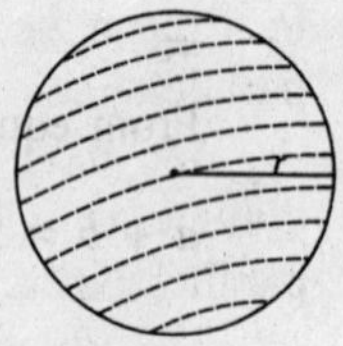

1. Volume = $\frac{4}{3}\pi r^3$
2. Surface area = $4\pi r^2$

Semi-Sphere

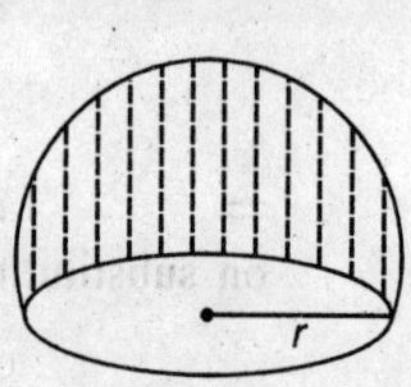

1. Volume = $\frac{2}{3}\pi r^3$
2. Curved surface area = $2\pi r^2$
3. Total surface area = $3\pi r^2$

Cone :

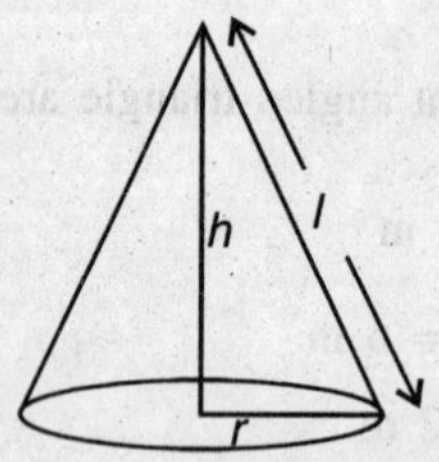

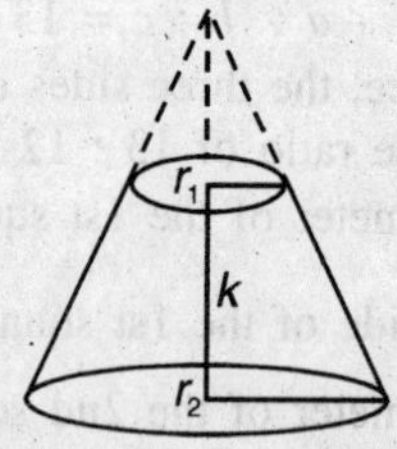

1. Slant height $(l) = \sqrt{r^2 + h^2}$
2. Volume = $\frac{1}{3}\pi r^2 h$
3. Curved surface area = πrl
4. Total surface area = $\pi r\ (l + r)$
5. If the thickness of the frustum of a cone be k and the radii of its ends are r_1 and r_2, then
   (i) Slant height of the frustum of a cone
   $= \sqrt{K^2 + (r_1 - r_2)^2}$
   (ii) Curved surface of the frustum = $\pi(r_1 + r_2)\ l$.
   (iii) Volume = $\frac{\pi K}{3}\left(r_1^2 + r_1 r_2 + r_2^2\right)$

Right Pyramid

1. Volume = $\frac{1}{3}$(area of the base) × height
2. Lateral surface area
   $= \frac{1}{2}$(Perimeter of the base) × Slant height
3. Total surface area = 2 (Area of one end) + Lateral surface area

Right Prism

1. Volume = Area of the base × Height
2. Lateral surface Area = Perimeter of the Base × Height
3. Total surface Area = 2 (Area of one end) + Lateral surface area.

Rectangular Parallelepiped

Sometimes also referred to as "Rhomboid", a parallelepiped is a 3-D shape moulded by 6 parallelograms. If observed more carefully, as a cube relates to a square, a cuboid relates to a rectangle, the same way a parallelepiped is related to parallelogram.

We have the following formula for finding out the volume, lateral surface area and surface area of rectangular parallelepiped.

The formulas are:

Volume = abc

Surface area = 2ab + 2bc + 2ac

Diagonal = $\sqrt{a^2 + b^2}$

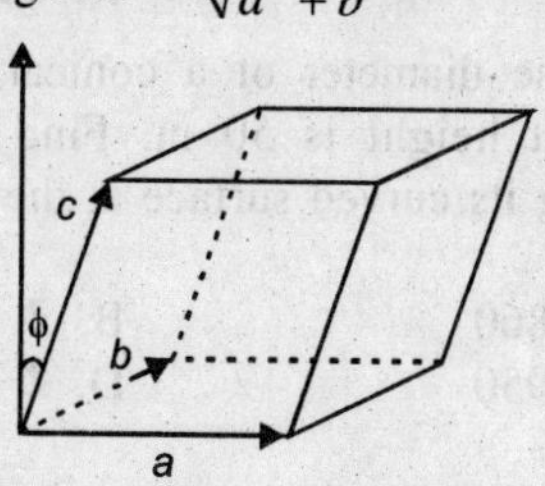

Example: Counting 38 cu. ft. of coal to a ton, how many tons will a coal bin 19 ft. long, 6 ft. wide, and 9 ft. deep contain, when level full?

Solution: The volume of a rectangular parallelepiped is given by the formula

$$V = L \times W \times H$$

Substitute the values of length, width and height of a tin, we have

$$V = L \times W \times H$$
$$V = (19\text{ft})\ (6\text{R.})\ (9\text{ ft.})$$
$$V = 1026\ R^3$$

The density of a substance is given by the formula

$$\rho = \frac{W}{V}$$

where, ρ is the density, W is the weight, and V is the volume of a substance respectively.

$$W = V \times \rho$$

Therefore, the weight of a coal in a bin is:

$$W = (1026\,R^3)\left(\frac{1\text{ ton}}{38\,n^3}\right)$$

$$W = 27 \text{ tons.}$$

Example: The base face of a parallelepiped has opposite sides measuring 5 inches and 10 inches. The height of the parallelepiped is 4 inches. Find the cost of painting its walls from outside at a cost of INR 1.5 per square inch.

Solution: We need to find the lateral surface area first, therefore;

LSA = Perimeter of base × height

LSA = 2 (5 + 10) + 6

LSA = 180 sq. inch

Cost of painting = Lateral surface area × cost per square inch

Cost of painting the walls = 180 × 1.5 = ₹ 270.

EXERCISE

1. A solid in the form of a cuboid is 4 cm × 3 cm × 2 cm. Its volume will be

A. 20 cu cm B. 22 cu cm
C. 28 cu cm D. 24 cu cm

2. A reservoir is 3 m long, 2 m wide and 1 m deep. Its capacity in litres is

A. 8000 litres B. 10000 litres
C. 6500 litres D. 6000 litres

3. Surface area of a cube is 1014 sq. cm. Its volume will be

A. 2197 cu cm B. 2297 cu cm
C. 2179 cu cm D. 2117 cu cm

4. If the volumes of two cubical blocks are in the ratio of 8 : 1, what will be the ratio of their edges?

A. 1 : 2 B. 2 : 1
C. 4 : 1 D. 2 : 3

5. Two spheres have their surface areas in the ratio 9 : 16. Their volumes are in the ratio of

A. 64 : 27 B. 27 : 64
C. 16 : 27 D. 11 : 27

6. The length of the longest rod that can be place in a room 12 m long, 9 m broad and 8 m high is

A. 17 m *(b)* 18 m
C. 25 m D. 16 m

7. The radius and the height of a right circular cone are in the ratio of 3 : 5. If its volume is 120π cu m, its slant height is

A. $3\sqrt{34}$m B. $2\sqrt{28}$m
C. $2\sqrt{44}$m D. $2\sqrt{34}$m

8. Circumference of the base of a cylinder is 88 cm and height of the cylinder is 42 cm. Its volume is

A. 25872 cu cm B. 28572 cu cm
C. 25870 cu cm D. 22584 cu cm

9. It fwo cubes each of 10 cm side are kept close to each other, then the cuboid so formed will have surface area equal to

A. 1200 sq. cm B. 5000 sq. cm
C. 1000 sq. cm D. 1250 sq. cm

10. A rectangular piece of paper is 30 cm long and 20 cm wide. How many ways can be adopted if one wants to give this rectangular piece of paper a cylindrical form?

A. Three B. Two
C. One D. Four

11. In the above question, the cylinders formed will have their volumes in the ratio of

A. 2 : 3 B. 3 : 1 : 1
C. 3 : 2 D. 1 : 3 : 1

12. If a solid sphere of 3 cm radius is melted and recast into a right circular cone whose base radius is same as that of the sphere, the height of the cone will be

A. 8 cm B. 12 cm
C. 6 cm D. 5 cm

13. Diameter of a roller is 2.4 m and it is 1.68 m long. If it takes 1000 complete revolutions once over to level a field, the area of the field is

A. 12672 sq. m B. 12671 sq. m
C. 12762 sq. m D. 11768 sq. m

14. If each edge of a cube is increased by 10%, then by how much percent will the surface area of this cube be increased?

A. 21% B. 18%
C. 15% D. 20%

15. Height and base radius of a solid cylinder are 14 m and 4 m respectively. It is melted and recast into a solid cone of the same base radius as that of the cylinder, what will be the height of the cone?

A. 21 m B. 42 m
C. 48 m D. 54 m

16. A room is in the form of a cube of side 10 m. How many bales of cotton can be kept in it if each bale covers 5 cu m space?

A. 100 B. 175
C. 200 D. 225

17. Three cubes having side 2 cm, 3 cm respectively are melted together to form a new cube. The side of the new cube will be

A. 3.526 cm B. 4.628 cm
C. 4.626 cm D. 4.528 cm

18. If base diameter of a cylinder is increased by 50%, then by how much percent its height must be decreased so as to keep its volume unaltered?

A. 45.56% B. 55.56%
C. 50.16% D. 62.33%

19. The surface area of a cube is 600 sq. m. Its diagonal is

A. $10\sqrt{3}$ cm B. $5\sqrt{3}$ cm
C. $4\sqrt{2}$ cm D. $10\sqrt{2}$ cm

20. The base diameter of a conical tomb is 28 m and its slant height is 50 m. Find the cost of white-washing its curved surface at the rate of 80 paise per sq. m?

A. ₹ 1860 B. ₹ 1760
C. ₹ 1950 D. ₹ 1875

ANSWERS

1	2	3	4	5	6	7	8	9	10
D	D	A	B	B	A	D	A	C	B
11	**12**	**13**	**14**	**15**	**16**	**17**	**18**	**19**	**20**
C	B	A	A	B	C	C	B	A	B

EXPLANATORY ANSWERS

1. Volume of the cuboid

$= l \times b \times h = 4 \times 3 \times 2 = 24$ cu. cm.

2. Volume of the reservoir

$= l \times b \times h = 3 \times 2 \times 1 = 6$ cu. cm

($\because$ 1 cu m = 1000 litre)

$\therefore$ Capacity of the reservoir

$= 6 \times 1000 = 6000$ litre.

3. Surface area of a cube $= 6 \times (\text{side})^2$

$\therefore \quad 6 \times (\text{side})^2 = 1014$

$\Rightarrow \quad (\text{side})^2 = \frac{1014}{6} = 169$

$\Rightarrow \quad \text{side} = \sqrt{169} = 13$ cm

$\therefore$ Volume of the cube $= (\text{side})^3 = (13)^3$

$= 2197$ cu cm.

4. Suppose sides of the two cubical blocks are a_1 and a_2 respectively

$\therefore$ Volume of the two cubical blocks will be $(a_1)^3$ and $(a_2)^3$ rspectively

According to question :

$a_1^3 : a_2^3 = 8 : 1$

$\therefore \quad \frac{a_1^3}{a_2^3} = \frac{8}{1}$

$\therefore \quad \left(\frac{a_1}{a_2}\right)^3 = \left(\frac{2}{1}\right)^3 \Rightarrow a_1 : a_2$

$= 2 : 1$

Therefore ratio of their edges = 2 : 1.

5. Suppose radii of the two spheres are r_1 and r_2 respectively.

$\therefore$ Surface areas of the two spheres are $4\pi r_1^2$ and $4\pi r_2^2$ respectively

According to question :

$4\pi r_1^2 : 4\pi r_2^2 = 9 : 16 \Rightarrow r_1^2 : r_2^2 = 9 ; 16$

$$\Rightarrow \frac{r_1^2}{r_2^2} = \frac{9}{16} \Rightarrow \left(\frac{r_1}{r_2}\right)^2 = \left(\frac{3}{4}\right)^2$$

$$\Rightarrow r_1 : r_2 = 3:4 \Rightarrow \left(\frac{r_1}{r_2}\right)^3 = \left(\frac{3}{4}\right)^3$$

$$\Rightarrow \frac{r_1^3}{r_2^3} = \frac{27}{64} \Rightarrow r_1^3 : r_2^3 = 27 : 64.$$

Therefore ratio of their volumes

$$= \frac{4}{3}\pi r_1^3 : \frac{4}{3}\pi r_2^3 = r_1^3 : r_2^3 = 27 : 64$$

6. The longest rod that can be placed in the cuboidal room = Length of the diagonal =

$\sqrt{l^2 + b^2 + h^2} = \sqrt{(12)^2 + (9)^2 + (8)^2}$

$= \sqrt{144 + 81 + 64} = \sqrt{289} = 17$ m

7. Suppose the base radius and the height of the right circular cone are $3x$ m and $5x$ m respectively.

$\therefore$ Volume of the cone

$= \frac{1}{3}\pi r^2 h = \frac{1}{3}\pi(3x)^2 \times 5x$ cu m

According to question :

Volume of the cone = 120π cu m (given)

$\therefore \quad \frac{1}{3}\pi \times 9x^2 \times 5x = 120\pi$

$\Rightarrow \quad x^3 = \frac{120 \times 3}{9 \times 5}$

$\Rightarrow \quad x^3 = 8 \Rightarrow x^3 = (2)^3$

$\Rightarrow \quad x = 2$ m

$\therefore$ The radius and the height of the cone will be $3 \times 2 = 6$ m and $5 \times 2 = 10$ m respectively.

$\therefore$ Slant height of the cone

$= \sqrt{r^2 + h^2} = \sqrt{(6)^2 + (10)^2}$

$= \sqrt{36 + 100} = \sqrt{136} = 2\sqrt{34}$m.

8. Suppose the base radius of the cylinder = r cm

$\therefore$ Circumference of the base of the cylinder = $2\pi r$ cm

According to question :

$2\pi r = 88$

$\therefore \quad r = \frac{88}{2\pi} = \frac{88 \times 7}{2 \times 22} = 14$ cm

$\therefore$ Volume of the cylinder

$= \pi r^2 h = \frac{22}{7} \times (14)^2 \times 42$

$= 22 \times 2 \times 14 \times 42$

$= 25872$ cu cm.

9. Candidates should note that in such type of questions where two cubes of equal edges are kept close to each other, only the length of the cuboid so form increases and breadth and height of the cuboid remain same as that of the cube.

$\therefore$ Length of the cuboid = Edge of the first cube + Edge of the second cube

$= 10 + 10 = 20$ cm

$\therefore$ Surface area of the cuboid

$= 2(20 \times 10 + 10 \times 10 + 10 \times 20)$

$= 2(200 + 100 + 200)$

$= 5 \times 500 = 1000$ sq. cm.

10. Obviously, two ways can be adopted if one wants to give the rectangular piece of paper a cylindrical form, *i.e.,*

1. *When the paper is bent towards its length.* In this case, the circumference of the base of the cylinder will be equal to the length of the rectangular piece of paper and the height of the cylinder will be equal to the breadth of the rectangular piece of paper.
2. *When the paper is bent towards its breadth.* In this case, the circumference of the base of the cylinder will be equal to the breadth of the rectangular piece of paper and the height of the cylinder will be equal to the length of the rectangular piece of paper.

11. In the first case :

$2\pi r = 30$

$r = \frac{15}{\pi}$ cm and $h = 20$ cm

$\Rightarrow$ volume $(v_1) = \pi r^2 h$

$= \frac{15 \times 15 \times 20}{\pi} = \frac{4500}{\pi}$ cu cm

In the second case :

$2\pi r = 20 \Rightarrow r = \frac{10}{\pi}$ cm and $h = 30$ cm

$\therefore$ Volume $(v_2) = \pi r^2 h$

$= \frac{10 \times 10 \times 30}{\pi} = \frac{3000}{\pi}$ cu cm

$\therefore$ Ratio of the two volumes

$= v_1 : v_2 = \frac{4500}{\pi} : \frac{3000}{\pi} = 3 : 2$

12. Volume of the sphere of radius 3 cm

$= \frac{4}{3}\pi(3)^3 = \frac{4}{3}\pi \times 27$ cu cm

Suppose the height of the cone = h cm

∴ Volume of the cone having base radius equal to that of the sphere = $\frac{1}{3}\pi(3)^2 \times h$

∵ Volume of the cone = Volume of the sphere

∴ $\frac{1}{3}\pi(3)^2 \times h = \frac{4}{3}\pi \times 27 \Rightarrow h = 12$ cm

∴ Height of the cone = 12 cm.

13. Diameter of the roller = 2.4 m

∴ Radius of the roller = 1.2 m

And height (length) of the roller = 1.68 m

∴ Surface area of the roller

$= 2\pi rh = 2 \times \frac{22}{7} \times 1.2 \times 1.68 = 12.672$ sq. m

∴ In one complete revolution, the roller covers 2.672 sq. m.

∴ It will cover in 1000 revolutions = 12.672 × 1000 = 12672 sq. m

∴ Area of the field = 12672 sq. m.

14. The two edges which are included in surface area of the cube are increased by 10%.

∴ $x\% = y\% = 10\%$

and in case of percentage increase, values of x and y are positive

∴ Percentage increase in the surface area of the cube

$= \left(x + y + \frac{xy}{100}\right)\%$

$= \left(10 + 10 + \frac{10 \times 10}{100}\right)\% = 21\%.$

15. Volume of the solid cylinder

$= \pi r^2 h = \pi r^2 \times 14$ cu m

According to question :

Radius of the cone = Radius of the cylinder

$= r$ m = 4 m

and volume of the cone

= Volume of the cylinder

∴ $\frac{1}{3}\pi r^2 \times \text{height} = \pi r^2 \times 14$

∴ Height = 14 × 3 = 42 m

∴ Height of the cone = 42 m.

16. Volume of the cubical room

$= (10)^3 = 1000$ cu m

Number of cotton bales which can be placed in the room

$= \frac{\text{Volume of the room}}{\text{Volume of each cotton bale}} = \frac{1000}{5} = 200.$

17. Edges of the three cubes are 2 cm, 3 cm and 4 cm respectively

∴ Their volumes will be $(2)^3 = 8$ cu cm, $(3)^3 = 27$ cu cm and $(4)^3 = 64$ cu cm respectively.

Volume of the new cube = Total volume of the three cubes

∴ Volume of the new cube

= 8 + 27 + 64 = 99 cu cm

∴ Side of the new cube = $\sqrt[3]{99} = 4.626$ cm.

18. Suppose the height of the cylinder should be decreased by H%

∵ Volume of a cylinder comprises two radii (*i.e.*, two edges) and one height (as the third edge). Radius is increased by 50%.

It means $x\% = y\% = 50\%$ and percentage decrease in the third edge (*i.e.*, height) = H%.

Therefore, z% = H% and in case of percentage decrease value of z will be negative.

∴ Change in the volume of the cylinder

$= \left(x + y + (-z) + \frac{xy + y(-z) + (-zx)}{100} + \frac{xy(-z)}{100^2}\right)\%$

Since volume of the cylinder remains unchanged.

∴ Change = 0%

∴ $\left(50 + 50 + (-H) + \frac{50 \times 50 - 50H - 50H}{100} + \frac{50 \times 50 \times (-H)}{100^2}\right)\%$

∴ 100 − H + 25 − H − .25H = 0

⇒ 2.25H = 125

⇒ $H = \frac{125}{2.25} = 55.56$

∴ Height of the cylinder should be decreased by 55.56%.

19. ∵ Surface area of the cube = 6 × $(\text{side})^2$

∴ 6 × $(\text{side})^2 = 600$

⇒ $\text{side}^2 = 100$

⇒ side = $\sqrt{100} = 10$ cm

∴ Diagonal of the cube

$= \sqrt{3} \times \text{side} = \sqrt{3} \times 10 = 10\sqrt{3}$ cm.

20. ∵ Area of the curved surface of the cone = πrl (where r = radius of the cone and l = slant height of the cone)

∴ Area of the curved surface of the cone

$= \frac{22}{7} \times \frac{28}{2} \times 50 = 2200$ sq. m.

∴ Cost of whitewashing at 80 paise per sq. m

$= 2200 \times \frac{80}{100} = ₹\ 1760.$

●●●

CHAPTER 12

Trigonometry

Trigonometrical Ratios; Degree and Radian Measures; Standard Identities; Complementary Angles

Measurement of Angles: In general, the angles are measured in degrees or in radians which are defined as follows:

(a) ***Degrees***: A right angle is divided into 90 equal parts and each part is called a degree. Thus a right angle is equal to 90 degrees. One degree is denoted by 1°.

A degree is divided into sixty equal parts and each part is called a minute and is denoted by 1'.

A minute is divided into sixty equal parts and each part is called a second and is denoted by 1″.

Thus, we have

1 right angle = 90° (read as 90 degrees)

1° = 60′ (read as 60 minutes)

1′ = 60″ (read as 60 seconds)

(b) ***Radians***: A radian is the angle subtended at the centre of a circle by an arc equal in length to the radius of the circle.

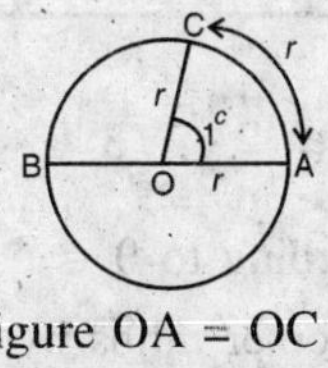

In the adjacent figure OA = OC = arc AC = r = radius of the circle, then measurement of ∠ AOC is one radian and is denoted by 1^c. Thus ∠ AOC = 1^c.

A Constant Number π: The ratio of the circumference to the diameter of a circle is always equal to a constant and this constant is denoted by the Greek letter π.

Thus π = circumference/diameter.

∴ If r is the radius of a circle, then its circumference = $2\pi\, r$.

The constant π is an irrational number and its approximate value is taken as 22/7.

Relation Between an Arc and an Angle: If s is the length of an arc of a circle of radius r, then the angle θ (in radians) subtended by this arc at the centre of the circle is given by $\theta = s/r$ or $s = r\,\theta$.

i.e., arc = radius × angle in radians

Given in the figure,

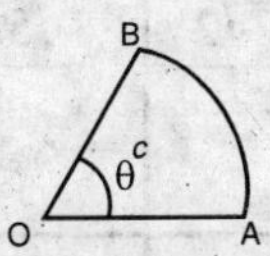

$$\angle\, AOB = \frac{\text{arc } ACB}{r} \text{ (in radians)}$$

$$= \frac{\pi r}{r} = \pi \text{ radians.}$$

Thus we have, π radians = 180° = 2 right angles

or 1 radian $= \frac{180}{\pi}$ degrees $= \frac{180}{22} \times 7$ degrees = 57° 17' 44.8" (Appr.)

Sectorial Area: Let OAB be a sector having central angle θ^c and radius r. Then area of the sector OAB is given by $\frac{1}{2} r^2\,\theta$.

Trigonometrical Ratios: In a right angled triangle ABC, if ∠ CAB = θ, then BC = side opposite to the angle θ = Perpendicular = p (say), AC = side opposite to the right angle = Hypotenuse = h (say) and AB = b (say).

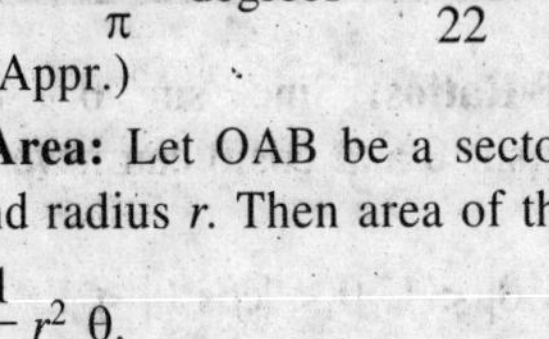

The six trigonometrical ratios are given as follows:
$\sin\theta = p/h$, $\cos\theta = b/h$, $\tan\theta = p/b$.
(Also $\tan\theta = \sin\theta/\cos\theta$, $\operatorname{cosec}\theta = 1/\sin\theta$, $\sec\theta = 1/\cos\theta$, $\cot\theta = 1/\tan\theta$,)

Basic Formulae Connecting Six Trigonometrical Ratios

The formulae connecting the six trigonometrical ratios are:

(i) $\sin^2\theta + \cos^2\theta = 1$ or $\cos^2\theta = 1 - \sin^2\theta$ or $\sin^2\theta = 1 - \cos^2\theta$.

(ii) $1 + \tan^2\theta = \sec^2\theta$ or $\sec^2\theta - \tan^2\theta = 1$

(iii) $1 + \cot^2\theta = \operatorname{cosec}^2\theta$ or $\operatorname{cosec}^2\theta - \cot^2\theta = 1$.

Sign of Trigonometrical Ratios:

1st quadrant $0 < \theta < 90°$, all trigonometrical ratios +ve,

2nd quadrant $90° < \theta < 180°$, only $\sin\theta$ and $\operatorname{cosec}\theta$, +ve

3rd quadrant $180° < \theta < 270°$, only $\tan\theta$ and $\cot\theta$, +ve

4th quadrant $270° < \theta < 360°$, only $\cos\theta$ and $\sec\theta$, +ve.

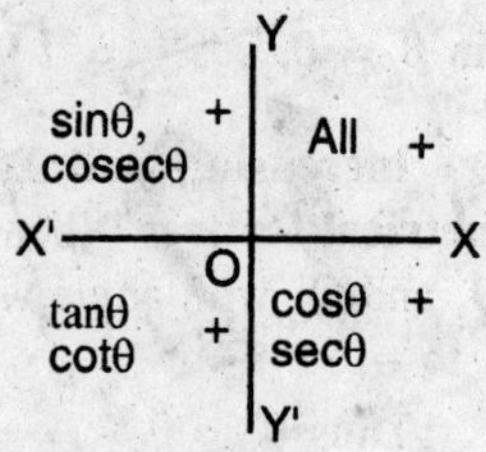

Trigonometrical Ratios of Related Angles:

$\sin(-\theta) = -\sin\theta$	$\cos(-\theta) = \cos\theta$	$\tan(-\theta) = -\tan\theta$
$\sin(90° - \theta) = \cos\theta$	$\sin(180° + \theta) = -\sin\theta$	$\sin(270° + \theta) = -\cos\theta$
$\cos(90° - \theta) = \sin\theta$	$\cos(180° + \theta) = -\cos\theta$	$\cos(270° + \theta) = \sin\theta$
$\tan(90° - \theta) = \cot\theta$	$\tan(180° + \theta) = \tan\theta$	$\tan(270° + \theta) = -\cot\theta$
$\sin(90° + \theta) = \cos\theta$	$\sin(270° - \theta) = -\cos\theta$	$\sin(360° + \theta) = \sin\theta$
$\cos(90° + \theta) = -\sin\theta$	$\cos(270° - \theta) = -\sin\theta$	$\cos(360° + \theta) = \cos\theta$
$\tan(90° + \theta) = -\cot\theta$	$\tan(270° - \theta) = \cot\theta$	$\tan(360° + \theta) = \tan\theta$

Table giving sine, cosine and tangent of some angles less than 90°:

	0°	15°	18°	22.5°	30°	36°	45°	60°	67.5°	90°
sin	0	$\frac{\sqrt{6}-\sqrt{2}}{4}$	$\frac{\sqrt{5}-1}{4}$	$\frac{\sqrt{2-\sqrt{2}}}{2}$	$\frac{1}{2}$	$\frac{\sqrt{10-2\sqrt{5}}}{4}$	$\frac{1}{\sqrt{2}}$	$\frac{\sqrt{3}}{2}$	$\frac{\sqrt{\sqrt{2}+1}}{\sqrt{(2\sqrt{2})}}$	1
cos	1	$\frac{\sqrt{6}+\sqrt{2}}{4}$	$\frac{\sqrt{10+2\sqrt{5}}}{4}$	$\frac{\sqrt{\sqrt{2}+1}}{\sqrt{(2\sqrt{2})}}$	$\frac{\sqrt{3}}{2}$	$\frac{\sqrt{5}+1}{4}$	$\frac{1}{\sqrt{2}}$	$\frac{1}{2}$	$\frac{\sqrt{2-\sqrt{2}}}{2}$	0
tan	0	$2-\sqrt{3}$	$\frac{\sqrt{25-10\sqrt{5}}}{5}$	$\sqrt{2}-1$	$\frac{1}{\sqrt{3}}$	$\sqrt{5-2\sqrt{5}}$	1	$\sqrt{3}$	$\sqrt{2}+1$	not defined

Bounds of T-Ratios: Since $\sin^2\theta + \cos^2\theta = 1$, the absolute values of $\sin\theta$ and $\cos\theta$ can never be greater than 1.

Thus $0 \le |\sin\theta| \le 1$, $0 \le |\cos\theta| \le 1$,
i.e., $-1 \le \sin\theta$; $\cos\theta \le 1$, or $0 \le \sin^2\theta$; $\cos^2\theta \le 1$.

Also $\sec\theta$; $\operatorname{cosec}\theta \ge 1$ or ≤ -1

i.e., $\sec\theta$, $\operatorname{cosec}\theta$ can never lie between -1 and 1.

It should be noted that $-\infty < \tan\theta$; $\cot\theta < \infty$.

To Determine the Values of Other Trigonometrical Ratios when one Trigonometrical Ratio is given: If one of the *t*-ratio is given, the values of other *t*-ratios can be found by using formulae. For example, $\sin\theta = 1/3$. Since sine is positive in Q_1 or Q_2, we have

$\cos\theta = \sqrt{1-(1/9)}$ or $-\sqrt{1-(1/9)}$, *i.e.*, $2\sqrt{2}/3$

or $-2\sqrt{2}/3$ according to $\theta \in Q_1$ or $\theta \in Q_2$.

We can also find other ratios by forming right angled triangle, *e.g.*, Let $\tan\theta = 1/2$, $\pi < \theta < 3\pi/2$, then since θ in Q_3, sine and cosine both are negative,

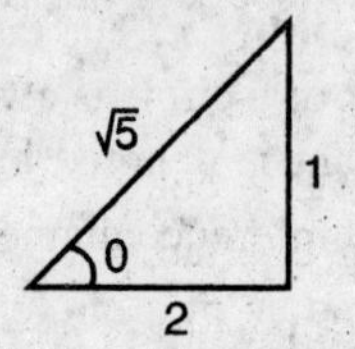

$\therefore$ We have $\sin\theta = -1/\sqrt{5}$,

$\cos\theta = -2/\sqrt{5}$.

Approximate Values of sin θ, cos θ and tan θ when θ is Small: Let θ be small and measured in radians, then sin

$\theta \approx \theta$, $\cos \approx 1$, $\tan \theta \approx \theta$. These are first degree approximations. The second degree approximations are given by

$$\sin \theta \simeq \theta,\ \cos \theta \simeq 1 - \frac{1}{2}\theta^2,\ \tan \theta = \theta.$$

Increasing and Decreasing Behaviour of Trigonometrical Ratios: When $-\pi/2 < \theta < \pi/2$, $\sin \theta$ increases in Q_1 and Q_4 with angle while in Q_2, Q_3, $\sin \theta$ decreases from 1 to –1.

Thus $\theta_1 < \theta_2$

$\Rightarrow \sin \theta_1 < \sin \theta_2$ $(\theta_1, \theta_2 \in Q_1 \text{ or } Q_4)$

$\Rightarrow \sin \theta_1 > \sin \theta_2$ $(\theta_1, \theta_2 \in Q_2 \text{ or } Q_3)$

We can decide the behaviour of other ratios in a similar manner. If we denote ↑ for increasing and ↓ for decreasing, we have the following chart:

y

sin	↓	sin	↑
cos	↓	cos	↓
tan	↑	tan	↑
cot	↓	cot	↓
sec	↑	sec	↑
cosec	↑	cosec	↓
x' ———	——— O	———	——— x
sin	↓	sin	↑
cos	↑	cos	↑
tan	↑	tan	↑
cot	↓	cot	↓
sec	↓	sec	↓
cosec	↑	cosec	↓

y'

EXERCISE

1. The angles of a triangle are in A.P. and the radian measure of the smallest to the degree measure of the mean is $\pi : 200$. The greatest angle in radians is:
A. $(11/30)\pi$ B. $\pi/3$
C. $\pi/2$ D. None of these

2. The moon's distance from the earth is 3,50,000 kilometres and its diameter subtends an angle of 31' at the eye of the observer. The diameter of the moon is:
A. 3157 (11/27) km B. 315 (11/27) km
C. 3050 (11/27) km D. None of these

3. If $\sin \theta = -3/5$ and θ lies in the third quadrant, then the value of $\cos(\theta/2)$ is:
A. 1/5 B. $-1/\sqrt{(10)}$
C. –1/5 D. $1/\sqrt{(10)}$

4. If $\tan \theta = -4/3$, then $\sin \theta$ is:
A. – 4/5 but not 4/5 B. –4/5 or 4/5
C. 4/5 but not – 4/5 D. None of these

5. If the angle θ is in the third quadrant and $\tan \theta = 3$, then the value of $\sin \theta$ is:
A. $1/\sqrt{(10)}$ B. $-1/\sqrt{(10)}$
C. $-3/\sqrt{(10)}$ D. $3/\sqrt{(10)}$

6. If $(\sec \alpha + \tan \alpha)(\sec \beta + \tan \beta)(\sec \gamma + \tan \gamma) = \tan \alpha \tan \beta \tan \gamma$, then $(\sec \alpha - \tan \alpha)(\sec \beta - \tan \beta)(\sec \gamma - \tan \gamma) = ?$
A. $\cot \alpha \cot \beta \cot \gamma$
B. $\tan \alpha \tan \beta \tan \gamma$
C. $\cot \alpha + \cot \beta + \cot \gamma$
D. $\tan \alpha + \tan \beta + \tan \gamma$

7. Which of the following is correct?
A. $\sin 1° > \sin 1$
B. $\sin 1° < \sin 1$
C. $\sin 1° = \sin 1$
D. $\sin 1° = (\pi/180) \sin 1$

8. Which of the following is correct?
A. $\tan 1 > \tan 2$ B. $\tan 1 = \tan 2$
C. $\tan 1 < \tan 2$ D. $\tan 1 = 1$

9. The value of $\log \tan 1° + \log \tan 2° + ... + \log \tan 89°$ is:
A. 0 B. 1
C. ∞ D. None of these

10. The value of $\cos 105° + \sin 105°$ is:
A. 0 B. $\sqrt{(3/2)}$
C. $1/\sqrt{2}$ D. $(\sqrt{3}+1)/2$

11. The value of $\sin\left(67\frac{1}{2}°\right)\sin\left(22\frac{1}{2}°\right)$ is:
A. $-2\sqrt{2}$ B. $2\sqrt{2}$
C. $1/2\sqrt{2}$ D. $-1/2\sqrt{2}$

12. The value of $(1 + \cos\pi/8)(1 + \cos 3\pi/8)(1 + \cos 5\pi/8)(1 + \cos 7\pi/8)$ is:
A. 1/2 B. 1/4
C. 1/8 D. 1/16

13. The value of $\sin^2\frac{2\pi}{15} - \sin^2\frac{\pi}{30}$ is:
A. $(\sqrt{5}-1)/4$ B. $(\sqrt{5}-1)/8$
C. $(\sqrt{5}+1)\sqrt{3}/2$ D. $(\sqrt{5}-1)\sqrt{3}/2$

14. The value of $\sin 50° - \sin 70° + \sin 10°$ is:
A. 0 B. 1
C. 2 D. None of these

15. The value of $(\sqrt{3}\operatorname{cosec} 20° - \sec 20°)$ is:
A. 2 B. $2\sqrt{3}$
C. 4 D. $\sqrt{8}/2$

ANSWERS

1	2	3	4	5	6	7	8	9	10
A	A	B	B	C	A	B	A	A	C
11	**12**	**13**	**14**	**15**					
C	C	B	A	C					

EXPLANATORY ANSWERS

1. Let the angles in degrees in A.P. be taken as

$A = \theta - \phi,\ B = \theta,\ C = \theta + \phi$

$\therefore \quad A + B + C = 180° = 3\theta$

$\Rightarrow \quad B = \theta = 60°$

Now $\quad \dfrac{\pi}{200} = \dfrac{\text{A in radian}}{\text{B in degrees}}$

$= \dfrac{(60-\phi)(\pi/180)}{60}$

$\Rightarrow \quad \phi = 6°$

$\therefore$ Greatest angle $C = \theta + \phi = 66°$

$= 66 \times (\pi/180)$

$= (11/30)\ \pi$ radians.

2. Let l be the diameter of moon and a its distance from the earth. If the moon subtends an angle θ at the eye of the observer, then

$l = a\theta = 350000 \times \left(\dfrac{31}{60} \times \dfrac{\pi}{180}\right)$

$= \dfrac{3500 \times 31}{6 \times 18} \times \dfrac{22}{7} = 3157\ \dfrac{11}{27}$ km.

3. $\because$ θ lies in the third quadrant

$\because \quad \cos\theta$ is –ve

$\because \quad \sin\theta = -3/5$

$\Rightarrow \quad \cos\theta = -\sqrt{(1 - \sin^2\theta)} = -4/5$

Now, $\quad \cos^2 \dfrac{1}{2}\theta = \dfrac{1}{2}(1 + \cos\theta)$

$= \dfrac{1}{2}(1 - 4/5) = 1/10$

$\Rightarrow \quad \cos\dfrac{1}{2}\theta = +1/\sqrt{(10)}$

But given that, $180° < \theta < 270°$

$\Rightarrow 90° < \theta/2 < 135°$

i.e., $\theta/2$ lies in the second quadrant

$\Rightarrow \cos\ \dfrac{1}{2}\ \theta$ is –ve

Hence $\cos\ \dfrac{1}{2}\ \theta = -1/\sqrt{10}$.

4. $\tan\theta = -4/3$

$\Rightarrow \theta$ lies in 2nd or 4th quadrant.

$\therefore \sin\theta$ is positive or negative according as θ lie in 2nd or 4th quadrant respectively, *i.e.,* $\sin\theta$ may be positive or negative.

Now $\quad \sin\theta = \tan\theta/\sqrt{(1 + \tan^2\theta)} = 4/5$

Hence $\quad \sin\theta = -4/5$ or $4/5$.

5. $\because$ θ is in the third quadrant,

$\because \sin\theta < 0$.

Thus $\quad \sin\theta = -\tan\theta/\sqrt{(1 + \tan^2\theta)}$

$= -3/\sqrt{(10)}$.

6. Multiplying both sides of the given expression by $(\sec\alpha - \tan\alpha).(\sec\beta - \tan\beta).(\sec\gamma - \tan\gamma)$, we get, 1.1.1 $= (\sec\alpha - \tan\alpha).(\sec\beta - \tan\beta).(\sec\gamma - \tan\gamma).\tan\alpha\tan\beta\tan\gamma$

$\Rightarrow (\sec\alpha - \tan\alpha).(\sec\beta - \tan\beta).(\sec\gamma - \tan\gamma)$

$= \cot\alpha.\cot\beta.\cot\gamma$.

7. 1 radian = $(180/\pi)$ Degrees = 57° (appr.)

$\therefore \sin 1° < \sin 57° \Rightarrow \sin 1° < \sin 1$.

8. 1 radian = 57° (appr.)

which lie in first quadrant. $\therefore \tan 1 > 0$,

and 2 radians = 114° (appr.), which lie in second quadrant $\therefore \tan 2 < 0$

Hence $\tan 1 > \tan 2$.

9. $\log\tan 1° + \log\tan 2° + ... + \log\tan 89°$

$= \log[\tan 1°.\tan 2° ... \tan 45° ... \tan 88°.\tan 89°]$

$= \log[\tan 1°.\tan 2° ... \tan 45° ... \tan(90°-2°)\tan(90°-1°)]$

$= \log[\tan 1°.\cot 1°.\tan 2°.\cot 2° ... 1]$

$= \log 1 = 0$

10. $\cos 105° + \sin 105°$

$= \cos(60° + 45°) + \sin(60° + 45°)$

$= \cos 60°\cos 45° - \sin 60°\sin 45°$

$+ \sin 60°\cos 45° + \cos 60°\sin 45°$

$= \dfrac{1}{2}.\dfrac{1}{\sqrt{2}} - \dfrac{\sqrt{3}}{2}.\dfrac{1}{\sqrt{2}} + \dfrac{\sqrt{3}}{2}.\dfrac{1}{\sqrt{2}} + \dfrac{1}{2}.\dfrac{1}{\sqrt{2}}$

$= \dfrac{2}{2\sqrt{2}} = \dfrac{1}{\sqrt{2}}$

11. $\sin\left(67\frac{1^\circ}{2}\right)\sin\left(22\frac{1^\circ}{2}\right)$

$= \sin\left(45^\circ+22\frac{1^\circ}{2}\right)\sin\left(45^\circ-22\frac{1^\circ}{2}\right)$

$= \sin^2 45^\circ - \sin^2 22\frac{1^\circ}{2} = \left(\frac{1}{\sqrt{2}}\right)^2 - \frac{1-\cos 45^\circ}{2}$

$= \frac{1}{2} - \frac{1}{2}\left(1-\frac{1}{\sqrt{2}}\right) = \frac{1}{2}\left(1-1+\frac{1}{\sqrt{2}}\right) = \frac{1}{2\sqrt{2}}$

12. $\left(1+\cos\frac{\pi}{8}\right)\left(1+\cos\frac{3\pi}{8}\right)\left(1+\cos\frac{5\pi}{8}\right)\left(1+\cos\frac{7\pi}{8}\right)$

$= (1+\cos\pi/8)(1-\cos\pi/8)$

$(1+\cos 3\pi/8)(1-\cos 3\pi/8)$

$= \sin^2 \pi/8.\ \sin^2 3\pi/8 = \frac{1}{4}\left(2\sin\frac{3\pi}{8}.\sin\pi/8\right)^2$

$= \frac{1}{4}\left[\cos\frac{\pi}{4} - \cos\frac{\pi}{2}\right]^2 = \frac{1}{4}\left(\frac{1}{\sqrt{2}}-0\right)^2 = \frac{1}{4}\times\frac{1}{2} = \frac{1}{8}$

13. $\sin^2\frac{2\pi}{5} - \sin^2\frac{\pi}{30} = \sin\left(\frac{2\pi}{15}+\frac{\pi}{30}\right)\sin\left(\frac{2\pi}{15}-\frac{\pi}{30}\right)$

$= \sin\frac{\pi}{6}.\sin\frac{\pi}{10} = \frac{1}{2}\times\frac{\sqrt{5}-1}{4} = \frac{1}{8}\left(\sqrt{5}-1\right)$

14. $\sin 50^\circ - \sin 70^\circ + \sin 10^\circ$

$= 2\cos 60^\circ \sin(-10)^\circ + \sin 10^\circ$

$= 2 \times \frac{1}{2} \times - \sin 10^\circ + \sin 10^\circ$

$= -\sin 10^\circ + \sin 10^\circ = 0$

15. $\sqrt{3}\,\text{cosec } 20^\circ - \sec 20^\circ$

$= \tan 60^\circ\ \text{cosec} 20^\circ - \sec 20^\circ$

$= \frac{\sin 60^\circ}{\cos 60^\circ}.\frac{1}{\sin 20^\circ} - \frac{1}{\cos 20^\circ}$

$= \frac{\sin 60^\circ \cos 20^\circ - \cos 60^\circ \sin 20^\circ}{\cos 60^\circ.\sin 20^\circ \cos 20^\circ}$

$= \frac{\sin(60^\circ-20^\circ)}{\frac{1}{2}.\frac{1}{2}(2\sin 20^\circ \cos 20^\circ)} = 4.\frac{\sin 40^\circ}{\sin 40^\circ} = 4$

Heights and Distance

Angle of Elevation and Depression: Let O and P be two points such that P is at higher level than O. Let PQ, OX be horizontal lines through P and O, respectively.

If an observer (or eye) is at O and the object is at P, then $\angle XOP$ is called the angle of elevation of P as seen from O.

This angle is also called the angular height of P from O.

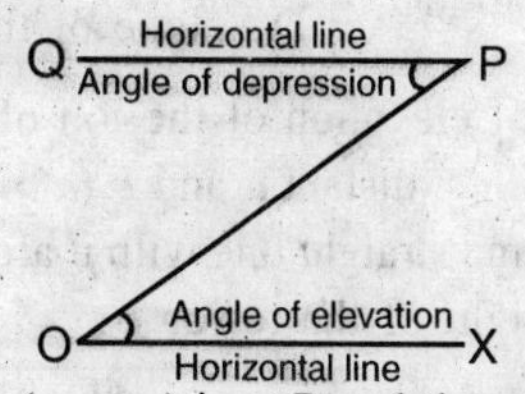

If an observer (or eye) is at P and the object is at O, then $\angle QPO$ is called the angle of depression of O as seen from P.

EXERCISE

1. A person standing on the bank of a river observes that the angle subtended by a tree on the opposite bank is 60°, when he retires 40 metres from the bank he finds the angle to be 30°. Then the breadth of the river is:
   A. 40 m B. 60 m
   C. 20 m D. 30 m

2. At a point on a level plane a tower subtends an angle θ and a flag-staff a ft. in length at the top of the tower subtends an angle ϕ. The height of the tower is:
   A. $\frac{a\sin\theta\cos\phi}{\cos\ (\theta+\phi)}$ B. $\frac{a\sin\theta\cos(\theta+\phi)}{\sin\phi}$
   C. $\frac{a\cos(\theta+\phi)}{\sin\theta\sin\phi}$ D. None of these

3. The angle of elevation of the top of a tower standing on a horizontal plane from a point A is α. After walking a distance a towards the foot of the tower the angle of elevation is found to be β. The height of the tower is:
   A. $\frac{a\sin\alpha\sin\beta}{\sin(\beta-\alpha)}$ B. $\frac{a\sin\alpha\sin\beta}{\sin(\alpha-\beta)}$
   C. $\frac{a\sin(\beta-\alpha)}{\sin\alpha\sin\beta}$ D. $\frac{a\sin(\alpha-\beta)}{\sin\alpha\sin\beta}$

4. The angle of elevation of the top of a TV tower from the three points A, B, C in a straight line (in the horizontal plane) through the foot of the tower are α, 2α, 3α respectively. If AB = a, the height of the tower is:
   A. a tan α B. a sin α
   C. a sin 2α D. a sin 3α

5. The height of the centre of the round balloon of radius r, which subtend an angle α at the eye of an observer and the elevation of whose centre from the eye is β, is given by:

A. $r \sin \alpha \sin \beta$ B. $r \operatorname{cosec} \frac{1}{2} \alpha \sin \beta$

C. $r \operatorname{cosec} \alpha \sin \beta$ D. None of these

6. ABCD is a square plot. The angle of elevation of the top of a pole standing at D from A or C is 30° and that from B is θ, then $\tan \theta$ is equal to:

A. $\sqrt{6}$ B. $1/\sqrt{6}$

C. $\sqrt{3}/\sqrt{2}$ D. $\sqrt{2}/\sqrt{3}$

7. The angle of elevation of the top of two vertical towers as seen from the middle point of the line joining the foot of the towers are 60° and 30° respectively. The ratio of the heights of the towers is:

A. 2 : 1 B. $\sqrt{3}$: 1

C. 3 : 2 D. 3 : 1

8. ABC is a triangular park with AB = AC = 100 metres. A clock tower is situated at the mid-point of BC. The angles of elevation of the top of the tower of A and B are $\cot^{-1}$ (3.2) and $\operatorname{cosec}^{-1}$ (2.6) respectively. The height of the tower in metres is:

A. 25/2 B. 25

C. 50 D. None of these

9. The angles of elevation of the top of a vertical tower from two points, distant a and b $(a > b)$ from the base and in the same straight line with it are complementary. Then the height of the tower is:

A. $\sqrt{(ab)}$ B. $\sqrt{(a^2+b^2)}$

C. $\sqrt{(a^2-b^2)}$ D. $\sqrt{a(a-b)}$

10. From the top of a h metre high cliff the angles of depression of the top and the bottom of a tower are observed to be 30° and 60° respectively. The height of the tower is:

A. $h\sqrt{3}$ B. $2h\sqrt{3}$

C. $h/3$ D. $2h/3$

11. A vertical pole is 75m high. Find the angle subtended by the pole a point 75 m away from its base.

A. 30° B. 45°

C. 60° D. 90°

12. A person standing on the bank of river finds that the angle of elevation of the top of a tower on opposite side bank is 45°. Which of the following statement is correct?

A. Breadth of the river is half of the height of the tower

B. Breadth of the river and the height of the tower are equal

C. Breadth of the river is twice the height of the tower

D. None of these

13. The angles of depression of two ships from the top of a light house are 45° and 30° towards east. If the ships are 200 m apart, find the height of the light house.

A. 100 m B. 173 m

C. 200 m D. 273 m

14. A man 2 m high, walks at a uniform speed of 6 m/min away from a lamp post, 5 m high. Find the rate at which the length of his shadow increases.

A. 4 m/min B. 8 m/min

C. 9 m/min D. 14 m/min

15. Two ships leave a port at the same instant. One sails at 30 km/hr in the direction N 32°E while the other sails at 20 km/hr in the direction S 58° E. After two hours the ships are distant from each other by:

A. $15\sqrt{6}$ km B. 36.5 km

C. $20\sqrt{13}$ km D. 100 km

ANSWERS

1	2	3	4	5	6	7	8	9	10
C	B	A	C	B	B	D	B	A	D
11	**12**	**13**	**14**	**15**					
B	B	D	A	C					

EXPLANATORY ANSWERS

1. Let A be the position of a person on the bank of a river and OP the tree on the opposite bank and $\angle OAP$ = 60°. When the person retires to the position B, s.t.

$$AB = 40 \text{ m then } \angle OBP = 30°$$

Let OA = x m and OP = h m

In Δ OAP, OP = OA tan 60° = $x\sqrt{3}$

and in Δ OBP, OP = OB tan 30° = $(x + 40)/\sqrt{3}$

$\therefore$ $(x + 40)/\sqrt{3} = x\sqrt{3} \Rightarrow x = 20$ m

2. Let OP be the tower of height h (say) and PQ the flag-staff of height a, such that

$$\angle OAP = \theta \text{ and } \angle PAQ = \phi$$

In ΔOAP and ΔOAQ

$$OA = OP \cot \theta = h \cot \theta$$

and $OA = OQ \cot (\theta + \phi)$

$= (h + a) \cot (\theta + \phi)$

$\therefore$ $h \cot \theta = (h + a) \cot (\theta + \phi)$

$$\Rightarrow h = \frac{a \cot(\theta+\phi)}{\cot\theta - \cot(\theta+\phi)} = \frac{a \sin\theta \cos(\theta+\phi)}{\sin\phi}.$$

3. Let OP be the tower of height h (say) and A and B be the two positions on the horizontal line through O, such that

$\angle$ OAP = α, $\angle$ OBP = β and OB = x

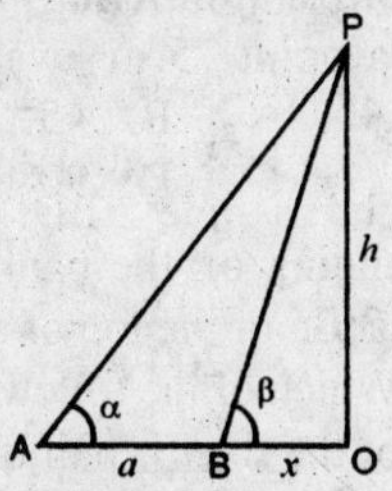

In ΔOBP, OB = x = h cot β, and

in ΔOAP, OA = $a + x = h \cot\alpha$

$\therefore$ $a = h(\cot\alpha - \cot\beta)$

$\Rightarrow$ $h = a \sin\alpha \sin\beta / \sin(\beta - \alpha)$

4. OP is vertical tower. The elevations of the top of P from A, B, C are α, 2α, 3α respectively

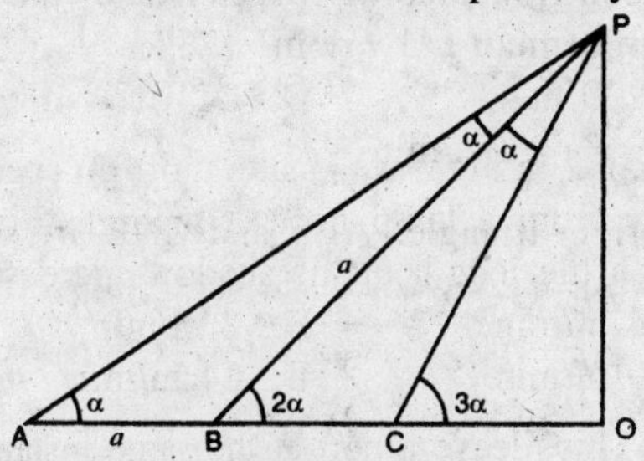

$\angle$OAP = $\angle$APB = α

$\therefore$ AB = PB = a

In ΔOBP, OP = PB sin 2α = a sin 2α

5. Let O be the centre of the balloon of radius r which subtend an angle α at the eye of an observer at E.

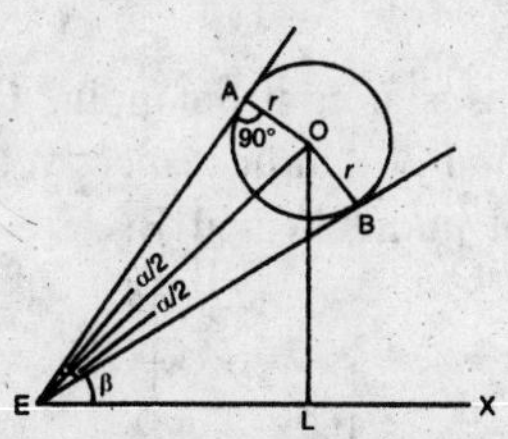

If EA and EB are the tangents to the balloon,

then $\angle$OEA = $\angle$OEB = $\frac{\alpha}{2}$

In ΔOAE, $\sin \frac{1}{2}\alpha$ = OA/OE $\therefore$ OE = r cosec $\frac{1}{2}\alpha$

In ΔOEL, height of the centre of the balloon

= h = OE sin β = r cosec $\frac{1}{2}\alpha$ sin β.

6. Let a be the length of a side of square plot ABCD and h, the height of the pole standing at D. Since elevations of P from A or C is 30° and that from B is θ,

$\therefore$ In ΔPCD, tan 30° = h/a

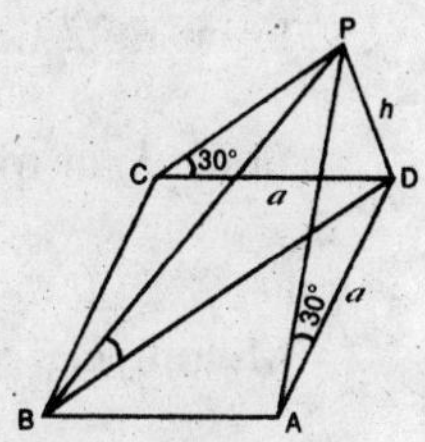

i.e., $h/a = 1/\sqrt{3}$

And in ΔPBD,

tan θ = PD/BD

= $h/(a\sqrt{2})$

= $1/\sqrt{6}$

$\therefore$ BD = $\sqrt{(AB^2 + AD)^2} = a\sqrt{2}$.

7. Let AB and CD be two towers of heights h_1 and h_2 respectively and O the mid-point of the line joining the foots A and C of the towers.

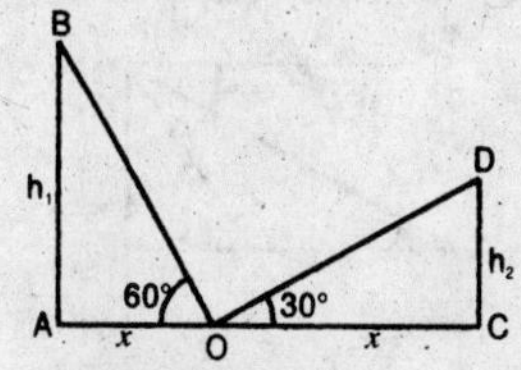

Let OA = OC = x

Then $h_1 = x \tan 60° = x\sqrt{3}$

and $h_2 = x \tan 30° = x/\sqrt{3}$

$\therefore$ $\frac{h_1}{h_2} = \frac{3}{1}$, Hence, $h_1 : h_2 = 3 : 1$.

8. Given $\alpha = \cot^{-1}(3.2)$, $\beta = \text{cosec}^{-1}(2.6)$

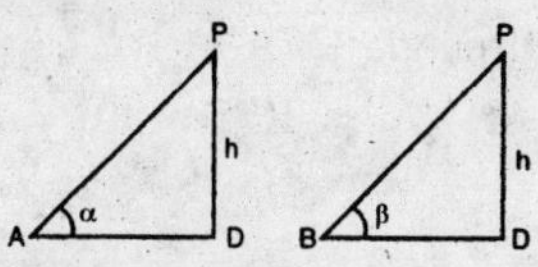

In ΔPAD, AD = h cot α,

In ΔPBD, BD = h cot β

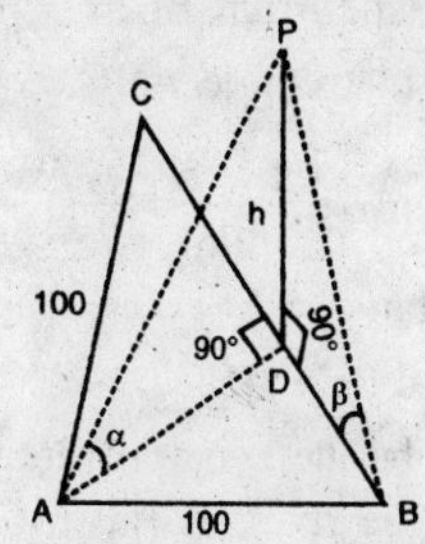

In ΔABD, $AB^2 = AD^2 + BD^2$

$= h^2(\cot^2\alpha + \cot^2\beta)$

$\Rightarrow 100^2 = h^2\{\cot^2\alpha + (\text{cosec}^2\beta - 1)\}$

$\Rightarrow 100^2 = h^2[(3.2)^2 + (2.6)^2 - 1] = 16h^2$

$\Rightarrow$ h = 25 m.

9. Let CD = h unit be the height of the tower and A and B be the two points on the ground, such that DA = a; DB = b; $\angle$ DAC = α and $\angle$ DBC = 90° − α

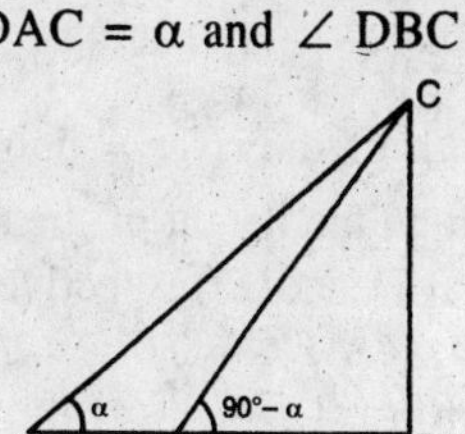

From right triangle ADC,

$$CD = h = a \tan\alpha \qquad ...(i)$$

From right triangle BDC,

$$CD = h = b \tan(90° - \alpha)$$
$$= b \cot\alpha \qquad ...(ii)$$

Multiplying equations *(i)* and *(ii)*, we get

$$h^2 = a \tan\alpha \, . \, b\cot\alpha$$

Hence, $h = \sqrt{ab}$

10. Let AB = h m be the height of cliff and CD = x m be the height of the tower and also ∠ADB = 60° and ∠ACE = 30°.

Now, from the figure, AE = $(h - x)$m

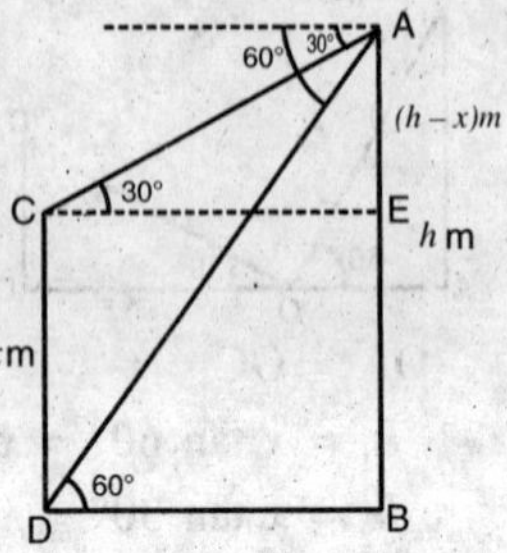

From right triangle ABD,

$$BD = h \cot 60° = \frac{h}{\sqrt{3}} \text{ m}$$

From right triangle CEA,

$$(h - x) = EC \tan 30° = BD \tan 30°$$

$$\Rightarrow \quad h - x = \frac{h}{\sqrt{3}} . \frac{1}{\sqrt{3}} \quad \therefore x = h - \frac{h}{3} = \frac{2h}{3} m$$

11. Let AB = 75m be the height of pole and C is a point on the ground such that BC = 75m

Now, from right triangle ABC,

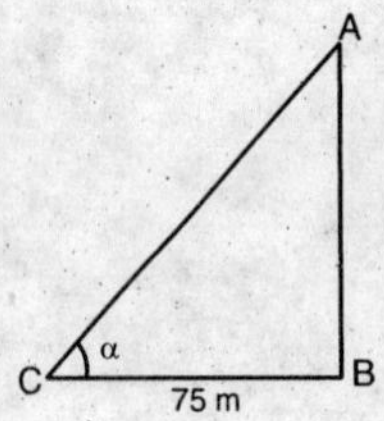

$$\tan\alpha = \frac{AB}{BC} = \frac{75}{75}$$

$$\Rightarrow \quad \tan\alpha = 1$$

$$\therefore \quad \alpha = 45°$$

12. Let AB = h m be the height of the tower; BC = x m be the breadth of the river and also ∠ACB = 45°

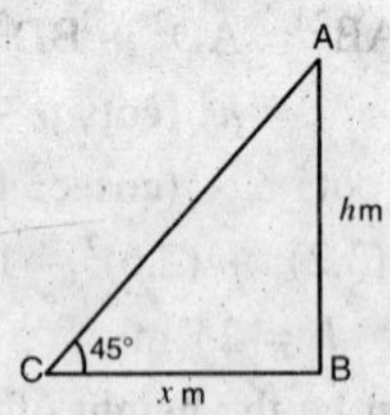

Now from right triangle ABC

$$\tan 45° = \frac{h}{x} \Rightarrow 1 = \frac{h}{x} \quad \therefore x = h$$

Hence, breadth of the river = height of the tower

13. Let AB = hm be the height of the tower and two ships are situated at D and C respectively; such that, CD = 200 m; ∠ ADC = 30°; ∠ ACB = 45° and BC = xm (say)

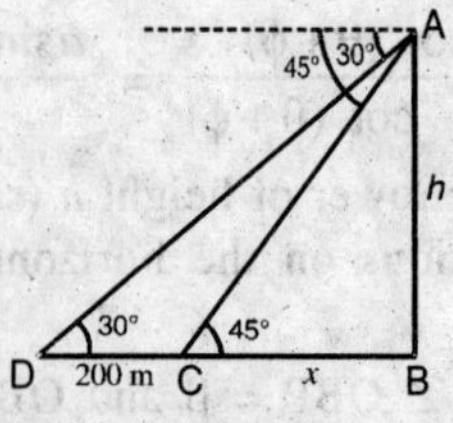

Now from right triangle ABC,

$$\tan 45° = \frac{h}{x} \Rightarrow 1 = \frac{h}{x} \quad \therefore x = h$$

Again from right triangle ABD,

$$\tan 30° = \frac{h}{200 + x}$$

$$\Rightarrow \quad \frac{1}{\sqrt{3}} = \frac{h}{200 + h} \quad (\because x = h)$$

$$\Rightarrow \quad \sqrt{3}h - h = 200$$

$$\Rightarrow \quad h(1.732 - 1) = 200$$

$$\therefore \quad h = \frac{200}{0.732} = 273.2 \text{ m} \sim 273 \text{ m}$$

14. Let AB = 5m and CD = 2m be the heights of a lamp post and the men respectively. At any time t BD = x m and shadow of man ED = y m.

Then, $\frac{dx}{dt} = 6$m/min

Now, right triangles ABE and CDE are similar; then

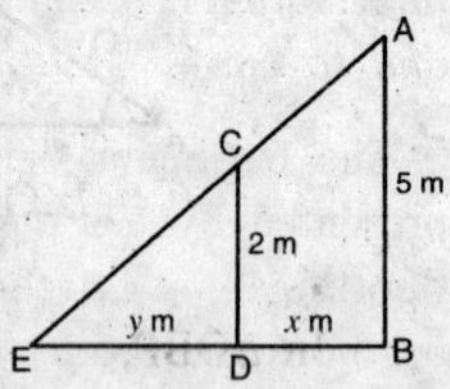

$$\frac{AB}{CD} = \frac{BE}{DE} \Rightarrow \frac{5}{2} = \frac{x + y}{y}$$

$$\Rightarrow \quad 5y - 2y = 2x$$

$$\Rightarrow \quad 3y = 2x$$

$$\Rightarrow 3. \frac{dy}{dt} = 2. \frac{dx}{dt}$$

$$\Rightarrow 3. \frac{dy}{dt} = 2 \times 6 \therefore \frac{dy}{dt} = 4$$

Hence, length of his shadow increases at the rate of 4 m/min.

15. Let two ships started from point O at the speed of 30 km/hr 0 and 20 km/hr respectively, after two hours they reach at points A and B.

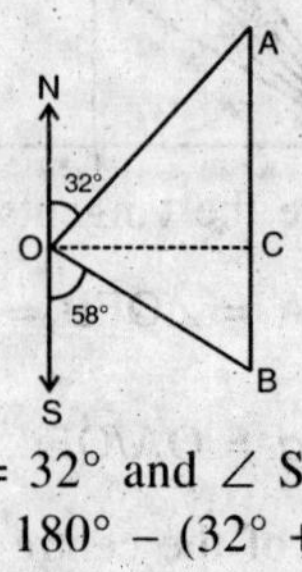

Now, ∠ NOA = 32° and ∠ SOB = 58°,

Then, ∠ AOB = 180° – (32° + 58°) = 90°

Since Δ AOB is a right triangle in which OA = 2 × 30 = 60 km and OB = 2 × 20 = 40 km

$$\text{Since, } AB = \sqrt{OA^2 + OB^2} = \sqrt{(60)^2 + (40)^2}$$

$$= \sqrt{5200} = 20\sqrt{13} \text{ km}$$

CHAPTER 13

Data Handling

Histogram; Frequency Polygon; Bar Diagram & Pie-Chart

Graphical Representation of Statistical Data

One of the most convincing and appearing ways in which statistical result may be presented is through diagrams and graphs. The impressions created by diagrams last much longer than those created by the figures presented in a tabular form.

Rather than present data numerically in the form of a table it can sometimes be better to illustrate the information through the use of graphs, charts, diagrams and so on.

The frequency distribution of a discrete value is best represented by a bar diagram. The height of the bars is proportional to the frequency of each variate-value. The bars must be kept distinct to show that the variate-values are distinct.

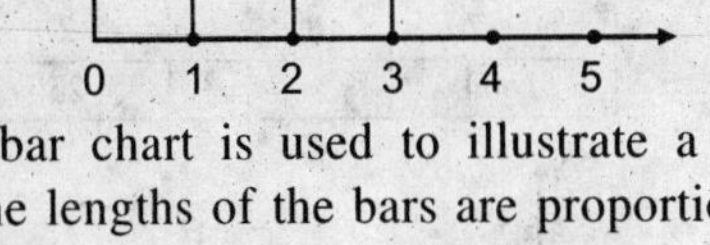

A simple bar chart is used to illustrate a frequency distribution. The lengths of the bars are proportional to the frequency and the bars are of equal width.

Some Important Types of Diagrams and Graphs

The different types of Diagrams and Graphs

(1) Bar diagram

(2) Histogram

(3) Frequency circle

(4) Cumulative frequency curve of the ogive

(5) Pie diagram.

Bar Diagram

Bar diagram is the easiest and most adaptable general purpose chart. In this, bars or rectangles of uniform width are drawn with equal spaces in between on the axis. Along the y-axis is shown, the scale of the height of the rectangles.

Thickness of bars is not taken into account, they should be so constructed that they look attractive and beautiful. This can be done by colouring them or by preparing designs in them.

However, the colour or designs of all bars representing one type of data should be identical. The bars may be vertical or horizontal. Some of the main bar diagrams are:

(*i*) Simple Bar-Diagram

(*ii*) Sub-divided Bar-Diagram

(*iii*) Multiple Bar-Diagram

The following Examples of Illustrate :

Example: The following table gives the population of India (in millions). Draw a bar diagram of the data:

Population (in million) of India 1931-1971

Year	Population (*in millions*)
1931	275.5
1941	312.1
1951	356.9
1961	439.9
1971	546.9

Solution: The above data is represented by a simple bar diagram as follows :

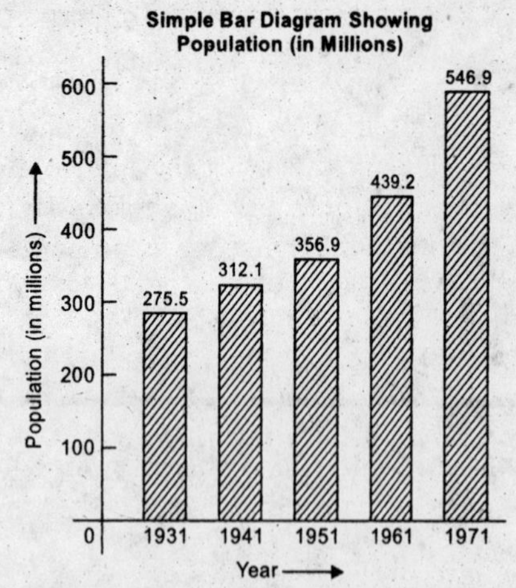

Here years are denoted on the x-axis and population (in millions) on the y-axis. The length of each bar corresponds to the number representing population on the y-axis.

Sub-Divided or Component Bar Diagram

The sub-divided bar diagram is used where the total magnitude of the given variable is to be divided into various parts or sub-classes. The bars are drawn proportional in length to the total and divided in the ratios of their components. Different colours, shades, designs, etc. are used to distinguish the various components.

Example: Represent the following data of sex-wise distribution of students in a school by a bar diagram.

Year	No. of Students		Total
	Male	*Female*	
1978	800	250	1050
1979	900	300	1200
1980	950	375	1325
1981	1000	400	1400
1982	1150	450	1600

Solution: The above data are represented by a sub-divided bar diagram, as follows.

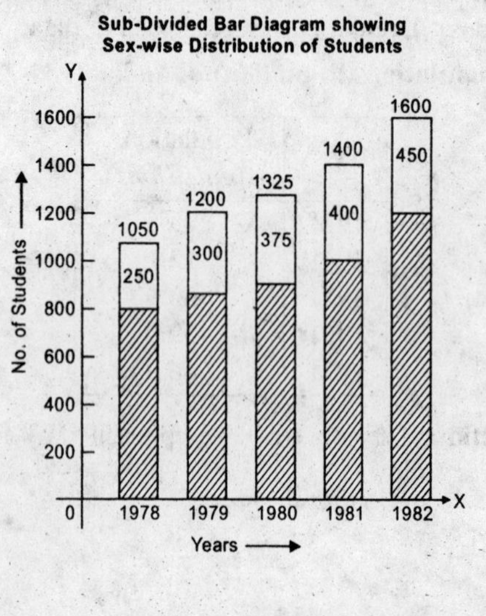

In a multiple bar diagram two or more sets of inter-related data are presented. The technique of drawing such a diagram is basically the same as that of simple bar diagram.

Histograms

The histogram is most popularly used for graphical presentation of a frequency distribution. A histogram is a graph that represents the class frequencies in a frequency distribution by vertical adjacent rectangles. After choosing a convenient scale on the axes, mark off the class intervals along x-axis and the frequencies of the respective class intervals along y-axis. Then construct rectangles with each class intervals as breadth and the respective frequency of the class interval as height. The set of the all adjacent rectangles so constructed form a histogram.

Note : A histogram is a development of the bar chart but remember when drawing a histogram it is the Area of each bar which is proportional to the frequency and there are no gaps between the bars because the classes are usually arranged so that there are no gaps.

The following Examples of Illustrates:

Example: The time taken, in seconds, to solve a problem by each of 25 pupils is as follows: 16, 20, 26, 27, 28, 30, 33, 37, 38, 40, 42, 42, 43, 46, 46, 48, 49, 50, 53, 58, 59, 60, 64, 52, 20.

(*a*) Construct a frequency distribution for these data, using a class interval of 10 seconds.

(*b*) Draw a histogram to represent the frequency distribution.

Solution:

(*a*) Lowest observation = 10

Highest observation = 64

Range = 64 − 10 = 54

We can have six classes, each of width 10.

Frequency Distribution Table

Time (in seconds)	Tally marks	Number of pupils
10 – 20	I	1
20 – 30	~~IIII~~	5
30 – 40	IIII	4
40 – 50	~~IIII~~ III	8
50 – 60	~~IIII~~	5
60 – 70	II	2
Total		25

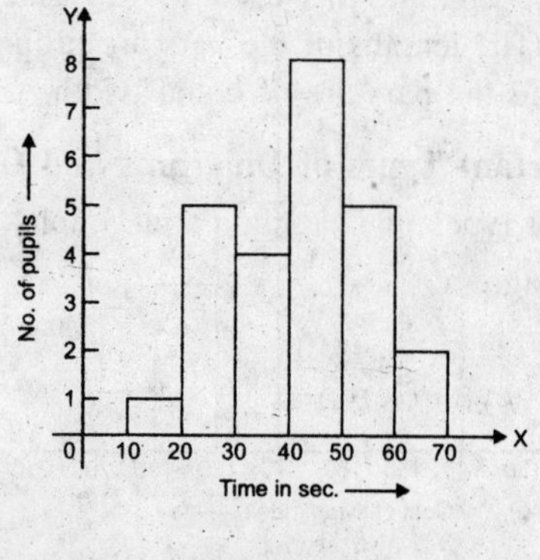

Frequency Polygon

A frequency polygon is a graph of frequency distribution. The steps constructing a frequency polygonal are:

1. Draw a suitable histogram keeping in view all the basic principles.
2. Get the mid-points of the upper horizontal side of each rectangle.
3. Join these mid-points of the adjacent rectangles of the histogram by straight lines taken in order, they form a polygon called frequency polygon.
4. End of frequency polygon preferably extended to the base line.

In a frequency polygon the variables or individuals of each class are assumed to be concentrated at the class-intervals.

Note: If only frequency polygon is to be drawn, first represent the class-marks (x_i) on the x-axis and corresponding frequencies (f_i) on y-axis. Plot all the points (x_i, f_i). Then join these points by line segments. The figure so obtained is known as the frequency polygon. The polygon should be brought down at the ends to the x-axis at each and of the drawn.

The following Examples of Illustrate:

Example: In a city the following weekly observations were made in a study on cost of Living Index for the year 1970–71.

Cost of Living Index	No. of weeks
140 – 150	5
150 – 160	10
160 – 170	20
170 – 180	9
180 – 190	6
190 – 200	2

Draw a histogram and frequency polygon on the same scale.

Solution:

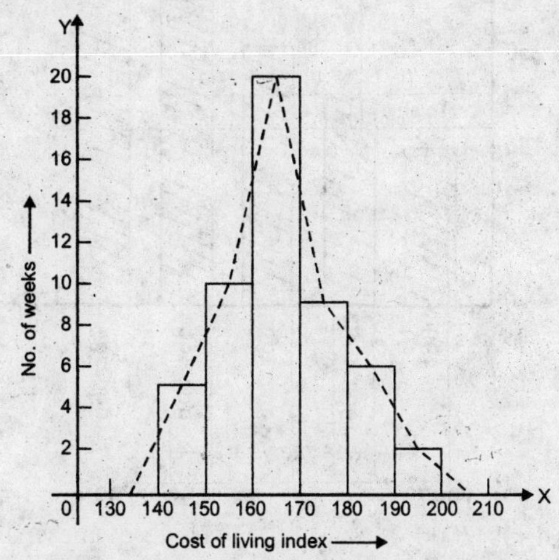

Pie Diagram

Pie-diagrams are used to represent a relative frequency distribution. A pie diagram consists of a circle divided into as many sectors as there are classes in a frequency distribution. The area of each sector is proportional to the relative frequency of the class.

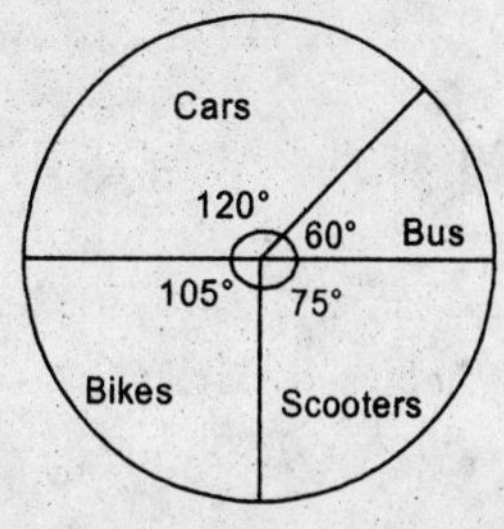

Now we make angles at the centre proportional to the relative frequencies. And in order to get the angles of the disired sectors, we divide 360° in the proportion of the various relative frequencies, *i.e.*,

$$\text{Central angle} = \left[\frac{\text{Frequency} \times 360°}{\text{Total frequency}}\right]$$

Example : The pie-chart provided below gives the distribution of land (in a village) under various food crops. Study the pie-chart carefully and answer the questions that follow.

Distribution of Areas (in Acre) Under various Food Crops

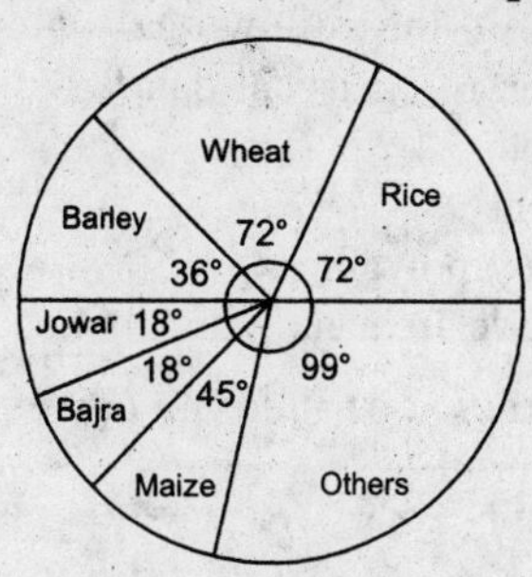

1. Which combination of three crops contribute to 50% of the total area under the food crops?
   (*a*) Wheat, Barley and Jowar
   (*b*) Rice, Wheat and Jowar
   (*c*) Rice, Wheat and Barley
   (*d*) Bajra, Maize and Rice
2. If the total area under jowar was 1.5 million acres, then what was the area (in million acres) under rice?
   (*a*) 6 (*b*) 7.5
   (*c*) 9 (*d*) 4.5
3. If the production of wheat is 6 times that of barley, then what is the ratio between the yield per acre of wheat and barley?
   (*a*) 3 : 2 (*b*) 3 : 1
   (*c*) 12 : 1 (*d*) 2 : 3

Solution:

1 (*c*): The total of the central angles corresponding to the three crops which cover 50% of the total area, should be 180°. Now, the total of the central angles for the given combinations are:

(*i*) Wheat, Barley and Jowar

$= (72° + 36° + 18°)$

$= 126°$

(*ii*) Rice, Wheat and Jowar

$= (72° + 72° + 18°)$

$= 162°$

(*iii*) Rice, Wheat and Barley

$= (72° + 72° + 36°)$

$= 180°$

(*iv*) Bajra, Maize and Rice

$= (18° + 45° + 72°)$

$= 135°$

Clearly, (*iii*) is the required combination.

2 (*a*): The area under any of the food crops is proportional to the central angle corres-ponding to that crop. Let, the area under rice production be *x* million acres.

Then, $18 : 72 = 1.5 : x$

$$\Rightarrow x = \left(\frac{72 \times 1.5}{18}\right) = 6.$$

Thus, the area under rice production = 6 million acress

3 (*b*): Let, the total production of barley be T tonnes and let Z acres of land be put under barley production. Then, the total production of wheat = (6T) tonnes. Also, area under wheat production = (2Z) areas.

$$\left[\because \frac{\text{Area under Wheat production}}{\text{Area under Barley production}} = \frac{72°}{36°} = 2 \text{ and therefore, Area under wheat} = 2 \times \text{Area under barley} = (2Z) \text{ acres}\right]$$

Now, yield per acre for wheat

$$= \left(\frac{6T}{2Z}\right) \text{ tonnes/acre} = \left(\frac{3T}{Z}\right) \text{ tonnes/acre}$$

and yield per acre for barley

$$= \left(\frac{T}{Z}\right) \text{ tonnes/acre.}$$

$$\therefore \text{ Required Ratio} = \left(\frac{3T/Z}{T/Z}\right) = 3:1.$$

EXERCISE

1. Which one of the following is not the graphical representation of statistical data?

A. Bar graph
B. Histogram
C. Frequency polygon
D. Cumulative frequency distribution

2. In a frequency distribution, ogives are graphical representation of:

A. Frequency
B. Relative frequency
C. Cumulative frequency
D. Raw data

3. A frequency polygon is constructed by plotting frequency of the class interval and the:

A. upper limit of the class
B. lower limit of the class
C. mid value of the class
D. any values of the class

4. In a histogram the area of each rectangle is proportional to:

A. the class mark of the corresponding class interval
B. the class size of the corresponding class interval
C. frequency of the corresponding class interval
D. cumulative frequency of the corresponding class interval

5. In a histogram, each class rectangle is constructed with base as:

A. frequency
B. class-intervals
C. range
D. size of the class

6. Read the bar graph shown in figure and answer the following question:

In which year is the increase of students maximum?

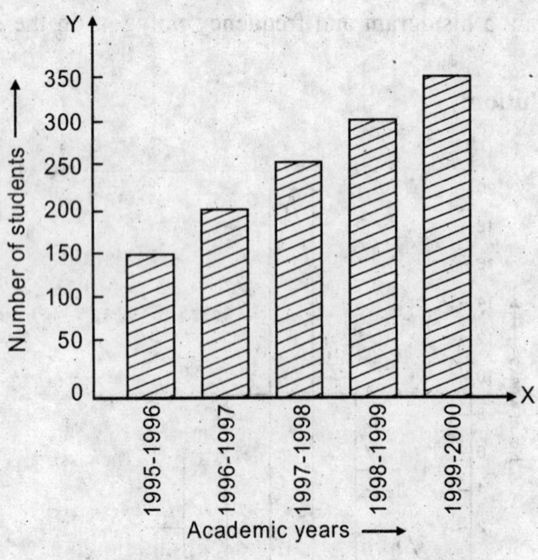

A. 1996-1997
B. 1997-1998
C. 1999-2000
D. None of these

Directions (Qs. 7 to 9) : *Read the following bar graph shown in figure and answer the following questions:*

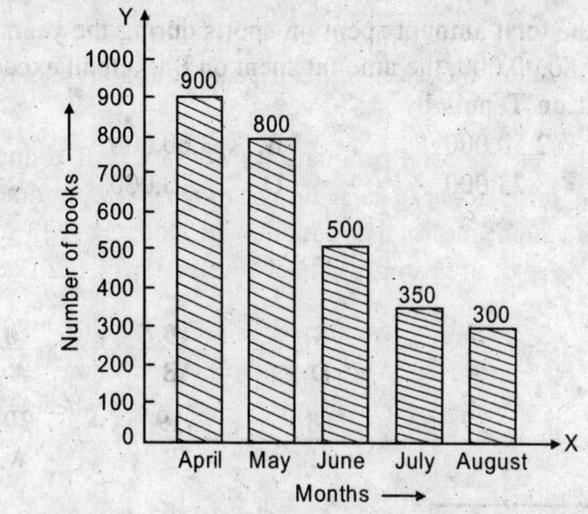

7. In which month was the sale of the books maximum?

A. April B. May
C. June D. August

8. In which month was the sale of the books minimum?

A. April B. May
C. July D. August

9. What is the total sale during these five months?

A. 3800 copies B. 2850 copies
C. 2800 copies D. 2950 copies

Directions (Qs. 10 to 12) : *Read the following bar graph given in figure and answer the following questions:*

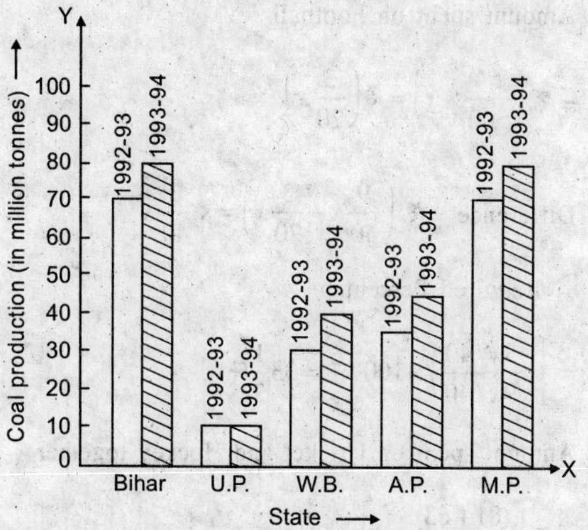

10. Which two states have same production in 1993-94?

A. M.P. and Bihar
B. M.P. and U.P.
C. U.P. and Bihar
D. W.B. and U.P.

11. Which state has same production in both the years?

A. M.P. B. Bihar
C. U.P. D. W.B.

12. Which state has minimum production?

A. M.P. B. A.P.
C. W.B D. U.P.

Directions (Qs. 13 to 15) : *The following bar graph shows the results of an annual examination in a secondary school. Read the bar graph and choose the correct alternative in each of the following.*

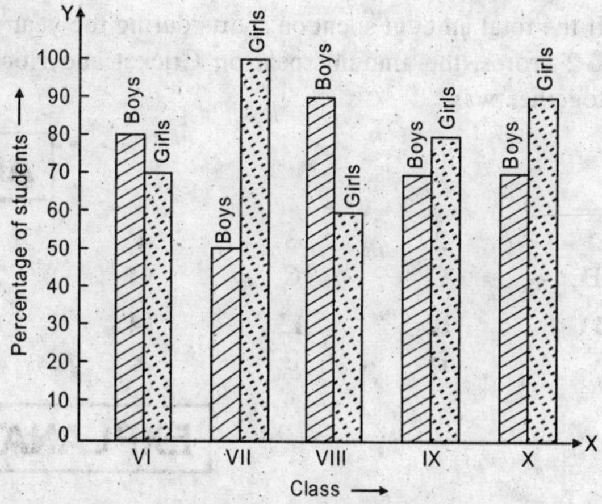

13. The pair of classes in which the results of boys and girls are inversely proportional are:

A. VI, VIII B. VI, IX
C. VIII, IX D. VIII, X

14. The class having the lowest failure rate of girls is:

A. VII B. X
C. IX D. VIII

15. The class having the lowest pass rate of boys is:

A. VI B. VII
C. VIII D. IX

Directions (Qs. 16 to 20) : *The circle-graph given here shows the spendings of a country on various sports during a particular year. Study the graph carefully and answer the questions given below it.*

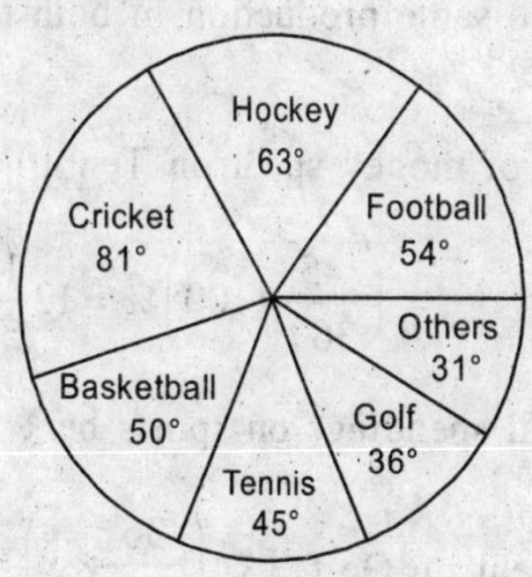

16. What per cent of the total spendings is spent on Tennis?

A. $12\frac{1}{2}\%$ B. $22\frac{1}{2}\%$
C. 25% D. 45%

17. How much per cent more is spent on Hockey than that on Golf?

A. 27% B. 35%
C. 37.5% D. 75%

18. How much per cent less is spent on Football than that on Cricket?

A. $22\frac{2}{9}\%$ B. 27%

C. $33\frac{1}{3}\%$ D. $37\frac{1}{2}\%$

19. If the total amount spent on sports during the year was ₹ 2 crores, the amount spent on Cricket and Hockey together was:

A. ₹ 8,00,000 B. ₹ 80,00,000
C. ₹ 1,20,00,000 D. ₹ 1,60,00,000

20. If the total amount spent on sports during the years be ₹ 1,80,00,000, the amount spent on Basketball exceeds that on Tennis by:

A. ₹ 2,50,000 B. ₹ 3,60,000
C. ₹ 3,75,000 D. ₹ 4,10,000

ANSWERS

1	2	3	4	5	6	7	8	9	10
D	C	C	C	B	D	A	D	B	A
11	**12**	**13**	**14**	**15**	**16**	**17**	**18**	**19**	**20**
C	D	B	A	B	A	D	C	B	A

EXPLANATORY ANSWERS

6. The increase in the number of students is uniform as the increase in the heights of bars is uniform. Hence, in this case the increase is not maximum in any of the year.

7. The sale of the books was maximum in the month of April as the height of the rectangle corresponding to April month is maximum.

8. The sale of the books was minimum in the month of August as the height of the corresponding rectangle is minimum.

9. Total sale of the books during 5 months.

(900 + 800 + 500 + 350 + 300) = 2850 copies.

10. M.P. and Bihar have same production in 1993-1994.

11. U.P. has the same production in both the years.

12. U.P.

16. Percentage of money spent on Tennis

$$= \left(\frac{45}{360} \times 100\right)\% = 12\frac{1}{2}\%$$

17. Let the total spendings on sports be ₹ x. Then,

Amount spent on Golf = ₹ $\left(\frac{36}{360} \times x\right) = ₹\frac{x}{10}$

Amount spent on Hockey

$$= ₹\left(\frac{63}{360} \times x\right) = ₹\frac{7}{40}x.$$

$$\text{Difference} = ₹\left(\frac{7}{40}x - \frac{x}{10}\right) = ₹\frac{3x}{40}$$

∴ Required Percentage

$$= \left[\left(\frac{3x/40}{x/10}\right) \times 100\right]\% = 75\%$$

18. Let the total spendings on sports be ₹ x. Then,

Amount spent on Cricket

$$= ₹\left(\frac{81}{360} \times x\right) = ₹\left(\frac{9}{40}x\right)$$

Amount spent on Football

$$= ₹\left(\frac{54}{360} \times x\right) = ₹\left(\frac{3}{20}x\right)$$

$$\text{Difference} = ₹\left(\frac{9}{40}x - \frac{3}{20}x\right) = ₹\frac{3}{40}x$$

∴ Required Percentage

$$= \left[\left(\frac{3x/40}{9x/40}\right) \times 100\right]\% = 33\frac{1}{3}\%$$

19. Amount spent on Cricket and Hockey together

$$= ₹\left[\frac{(81+63)}{360} \times 2\right] \text{ crores}$$

= ₹ 0.8 crores = ₹ 8000000.

20. Amount spent on Basketball exceeds that on Tennis by :

$$= ₹\left[\frac{(50-45)}{360} \times 18000000\right] = ₹\ 250000.$$

●●●

2008

GENERAL KNOWLEDGE & GENERAL AWARENESS

INDIAN HISTORY

ANCIENT INDIA

INDUS VALLEY CIVILISATION (2500-1750 BC)

- The earliest excavations in the Indus valley were done at Harappa in the West Punjab and Mohenjodaro in Sindh. Both places are now in Pakistan.

Important Sites

- The most important sites are Kot Diji in Sindh, Kalibangan in Rajasthan, Ropar in the Punjab, Banawali in Haryana, Lothal, Surkotada and Dhaulavira, all the three in Gujarat.
- Mohenjodaro is the largest of all the Indus cities and it is estimated to have spread over an area of 200 hectares.

Indus Valley Civilisation : An Objective Study

Major Sites	*Excavators*	*Year*	*River*	*Location*	*Important Findings*
1. Harappa	D.R. Sahni	1921	Ravi	West Punjab (Pakistan)	Granaries, Virgin Goddess, Cemetery, Stone symbol of Lingam and Yoni
2. Mohenjodaro	R.D. Banerjee	1922	Indus	Sindh (Pakistan)	Great Bath, Great Granary, Assembly Hall, Proto-Shiva, Brick Kilns, Mesopotamian seals
3. Chanhudaro	N.G. Mazumdar	1931	Indus	Sindh (Pakistan)	Bronze toy cart, Ink-pot, Lipstick, City without a citadel
4. Kalibangan	B.B. Lal & B.K. Thapar	1953	Ghaggar	Ganganagar (Rajasthan)	Decorated bricks, ploughed field surface, Firealtars
5. Lothal	S.R. Rao	1957	Bhogwa	Ahmedabad (Gujarat)	Dockyard, Rice husk, Fire altars, Double burial
6. Banawali	R.S. Bist	1973	Ghaggar	Hissar (Haryana)	Toy plough, Gridiron pattern of Town planning.
7. Dholavira	R.S. Bist	1990	Luni	Kutchh (Gujarat)	A Large well & a bath, A stadium
8. Surkotada	J. Joshi	1964	—	Gujarat	Bones of Horse, Pot burials

Salient Features of the Harappan Culture

- The Harappan Civilization was primarily Urban.
- Mohenjodaro and Harappa were the planned cities.
- The large-scale use of burnt bricks in almost all kinds of constructions are the important characteristics of the Harappan culture.
- Another remarkable feature was the underground drainage system connecting all houses to the street drains which were covered by stone slabs or bricks.
- The most important public place of Mohenjodaro is the Great Bath measuring 39 feet length, 23 feet breadth and 8 feet depth.
- Agriculture was the most important occupation. In the fertile soils, farmers cultivated two crops a year. They were the first who had grown paddy.
- Wheat and barley were the main crops grown besides sesame, mustard and cotton.
- Animals like sheep, goats and buffalo were domesticated. The use of horse is not yet firmly established.
- Bronze and copper vessels are the outstanding examples of the Harappan metal craft.
- A large number of seals numbering more than 2000 have been discovered.

Social Life

- Jewelleries such as bangles, bracelets, fillets, girdles, anklets, ear-rings and finger rings were worn by women. These ornaments were made of gold, silver, copper, bronze and semi precious stones.
- Fishing was a regular occupation while hunting and bull fighting were other pastimes.
- Manufacture of terracotta (burnt clay) was a major industry of the people.
- Figures of animals such as sacred bull and dove were discovered. The figures of Mother Goddesses were used for religious purposes.
- Most of the inscriptions were engraved on seals. It is interesting to note that the Indus script has not yet been deciphered.
- The Pipal tree was used as a religious symbol.
- The origin of the '*Swastika*' symbol can be traced to the Harrapan Civilization.
- The chief male deity was Pasupati, (proto-Siva) represented in seals as sitting in a yogic posture with three faces and two horns.

THE VEDIC PERIOD

RIG VEDIC AGE (1500 - 1000 B.C.)

- The Early Vedic period is known from the *Rig Veda*.
- The *Rig Veda* refers to Saptasindhu or the land of seven rivers. This includes the five rivers of the Punjab, namely, Jhelum, Chenab, Ravi, Beas and Sutlej along with the Indus and Saraswati.
- Historians view that the Aryans came from Central Asia. They entered India through the Khyber pass between 2000 B.C. and 1500 B.C. They first settled in seven places in the Punjab region which they called Sapta Sindhu. Slowly, they moved towards the Gangetic Valley.
- The Aryan Civilisation was a rural civilisation.

Vedic Literature

- The word 'Veda' is derived from the root 'vid', which means to know and signifies 'superior knowledge'.
- The Vedic literature consists of the four Vedas – Rig, Yajur, Sama and Atharva.
- The *Rig Veda* is the earliest of the four Vedas divided into 10 mandalas and it consists of 1028 hymns. The hymns were sung by *Hotri* in praise of various gods.
- The *Yajur Veda* consists of various details of rules to be observed at the time of sacrifice. Its hymns were recited by *Adharvayus*.
- The *Sama Veda* is set to tune for the purpose of chanting during sacrifice. It is called the book of chants and the origins of Indian music are traced in it. Its hymns were recited by *Udgatri*.
- The *Atharva Veda* contains details of rituals.
- Besides the Vedas, there are other sacred works like the Brahmanas, the Aranyakas, the Upanishads, and the epics Ramayana and Mahabharata.

Political Organisation

- During this period, the kingdom was tribal in character. Each tribe formed a separate kingdom.
- The basic unit of political organisation was *kula* or family.
- The highest political unit was called *jana* or tribe.
- There were several tribal kingdoms during the Rig Vedic period such as Bharatas, Matsyas, Yadus and Purus. The head of the kingdom was called as *rajan* or king.
- There were two popular bodies called the *Sabha* and *Samiti*. The former seems to have been a council of elders and the latter, a general assembly of the entire people.

Social Life

- Family was the basis of the society.
- The head of the family was known as *grihapathi*.

Economic Condition

- The Rig Vedic Aryans were pastoral people and their main occupation was cattle rearing. Their wealth was estimated in terms of their cattle.
- Carpentry was another important profession.

RELIGION

- The important Rig Vedic gods were Prithvi (Earth), Agni (Fire), Vayu (Wind), Varuna (Rain) and Indra (Thunder).
- Indra was the most popular among them during the early Vedic period.
- There were also female gods like Aditi and Ushas. There were no temples and no idol worship during the early Vedic period.

Rigvedic Rivers

River	Name in Rigveda
Indus	Sindhu
Jhelum	Vitasta
Chenab	Asikni
Ravi	Parushini
Beas	Vipasa
Sutlej	Sutudri
Gomati	Gomal
Saraswati	Sarasvati
Ghaggar	Prishadavati

LATER VEDIC PERIOD (1000–600 B.C.)

- This age is also called as the Epic Age because the two great epics the Ramayana and Mahabharata were written during this period.

- The Sama, Yajur, Atharva Vedas, Brahmanas, Aranyakas, Upanishads and the two epics are the sources of information for this period.

Political Organisation

- Larger kingdoms were formed during the later Vedic period.
- The king performed various rituals and sacrifices to strengthen his position. They include Rajasuya (consecration ceremony), Asvamedha (horse sacrifice) and Vajpeya (chariot race).
- Kingship became hereditary.
- Kings assumed titles like Ekrat, Samrat and Sarvabhauma.

Economic Condition

- Iron was used extensively in this period and this enabled the people to clear forests and to bring more land under cultivation. Agriculture became the chief occupation.
- Taxes like Bali, Sulk and Bhaga were collected from the people.
- Wealth was calculated in terms of cows.

Social Life

- The four divisions of society (Brahmins, Kshatriyas, Vaisyas and Sudras) or the Varna system was thoroughly established during the Later Vedic period.
- The Ashrama system was formed to attain 4 purusharthas. They were *Dharma*, *Artha*, *Kama* and *Moksha*.

Religion

- Gods of the Early Vedic period like Indra and Agni lost their importance. Prajapathi (the creator), Vishnu (the protector) and Rudra (the destroyer) became prominent during the Later Vedic period.

JAINISM AND BUDDHISM

JAINISM

- Jainism originated in the 6th century B.C. It rejected Vedic religion and avoided its rituals.
- Founded by Rishabha Deva. Rishabha Deva was succeeded by 23 Thirthankaras (prophets). Mahavira was the 24th Thirthankara.

Vardhamana Mahavira (540-468 B.C.)

- Vardhamana was born in a village called Kundagrama near Vaishali in Bihar.
- His father was *Siddhartha*. He was the head of a famous Kshatriya clan.
- His mother was *Trisala*. She was a princess of the Lichchhavi clan. She was the sister of the ruler of Vaishali.
- Vardhamana was married to *Yasoda,* a princess. They had a daughter.
- At the age of 30, he left his home and family. He became an ascetic (monk). He wandered from place-to-place in search of truth for 12 years.
- In the 13th year of his penance, he attained the highest spiritual knowledge called Kevalya or Jnana. Thereafter, he was called Mahavira and Jina. His followers were called Jains and his religion Jainism.
- He died at the age of 72 in 468 B.C. at a place called Pavapuri near modern Rajgir in Bihar.

Teachings of Jainism

- The three principles of Jainism, also known as Triratnas (three gems), are:
  1. right faith.
  2. right knowledge.
  3. right conduct.
- Mahavira preached his disciples to follow the five principles. They are:
  1. Ahimsa—not to injure any living beings
  2. Satya—to speak the truth
  3. Asteya—not to steal
  4. Tyag—not to own property
  5. Brahmacharia—to lead a virtuous life.

Spread of Jainism

- Mahavira preached his religion in Prakrit language which was the language of the masses.
- Chandragupta Maurya, Kharavela of Kalinga and the royal dynasties of south India such as the Gangas, the Kadambas, the Chalukyas and the Rashtrakutas patronised Jainism.
- Jainism was divided into two sects after Vallabhi Council, namely *Svetambaras* (wearing white dresses) under Sthulbhadra and *Digambaras* (naked) under Bhadrabahu.
- The first Jain Council was convened at Pataliputra by Sthulabahu, the leader of the *Digambaras*, in the beginning of the 3rd century B.C.
- The second Jain Council was held at Vallabhi in 5th century A.D. The final compilation of Jain literature called *Twelve Angas* was completed in this council.

BUDDHISM

Gautama Buddha (563-483 B.C.)

- Buddha's original name was *Siddhartha*.
- Siddhartha was born in the Lumbini Garden near Kapilavastu in Nepal. His father was Suddhodana. He was a Sakya chief of Kapilavastu. His mother, Mayadevi, died when Siddhartha was only seven days old. He was brought up by his step mother Mahaprajapati Gauthami.
- At the age of sixteen Siddhartha, married Yasodhara and gave birth to a son, Rahul.
- The sight of an old man, a diseased man, a corpse and an ascetic turned him away from worldly life. He left home at the age of twenty-nine in search of Truth.
- He wandered for seven years and at last, he sat under a bodhi tree at Bodh Gaya in Bihar and did intense penance, after which he got Enlightenment (Nirvana) at the age of

thirty-five. Since then, he became known as the Buddha or 'the Enlightened One'.

- Buddha delivered his first sermon at Sarnath near Banaras (now Varanasi).
- He died at the age of 80 in 483 B.C. at Kushinagar in Uttar Pradesh.

Teachings of Buddha

- The Four Noble Truths of Buddha are:
  1. The world is full of suffering.
  2. The cause of suffering is desire.
  3. If desires are get rid off, suffering can be removed.
  4. This can be done by following the Eightfold Path.
- The Eightfold Path consists of:
  1. Right Thought.
  2. Right Belief.
  3. Right Speech.
  4. Right Action.
  5. Right Living.
  6. Right Efforts.
  7. Right Knowledge.
  8. Right Meditation.

Buddhist Literature

- In Pali language.
- Buddhist scriptures in Pali are commonly referred to as *Tripitakas, i.e.*, 'Three Baskets'.
- ***Vinaya Pitaka:*** Rules of discipline in Buddhist monasteries.
- ***Sutta Pitaka:*** Largest, contains collection of Buddha's sermons.
- ***Abidhamma Pitaka:*** Explanation of the philosophical principles of the Buddhist religion.

Main Buddhist Councils

Buddhist Council	Time	Place	Chairman	Patron
First	483 BC	Rajagriha	Mahakashyapa	Ajatasatru
Second	383 BC	Vaishali	Sabakamuni	Kalashoka
Third	250 BC	Patliputra	Moggaliputta Tissa	Ashoka
Fourth	AD 72	Kundalvana	Vasumitra, Ashwaghosa	Kanishka

The Mahajanapadas

Mahajanapadas	Capital
1. Kashi	Varanasi
2. Kosala	Shravasti
3. Anga	Champanagri
4. Magadh	Girivraj or Rajgriha
5. Vajji	Vaishali
6. Malla	Kushinagar and Pavapuri
7. Chedi	Shuktimati
8. Vatsa	Kaushambi
9. Kuru	Hastinapur, Indraprastha and Isukara
10. Panchal	Ahichhatra and Kampilya
11. Matsya	Viratnagar
12. Surasen	Mathura
13. Asmaka	Paudanya
14. Avanti	Ujjaini
15. Gandhara	Taxila
16. Kamboj	Rajpur (Hatak)

DYNASTIES OF ANCIENT INDIA

HARYANKA DYNASTY

- Bimbisara was the founder of Haryanka Dynasty.
- He was a contemporary of both Vardhamana Mahavira and Gautama Buddha.
- During his rule, Darius I, the Achaemenian emperor, conquered the Indus Valley area.
- Ajatasatru imprisoned his father Bimbisara.
- The first Buddhist Council was convened by Ajatasatru at Rajgir.
- The immediate successor of Ajatasatru was Udayin.
- Udayin laid the foundation of the new capital at Pataliputra situated at the confluence of the two rivers, the Ganges and the Sone.
- Shishunaga was the founder of Shishunaga dynasty.
- After Shishunaga, the mighty empire began to collapse. His successor was Kakavarman or Kalasoka. During his reign, the second Buddhist Council was held at Vaishali.
- Kalasoka was killed by the founder of the Nanda dynasty.

NANDAS

- The fame of Magadha scaled new heights under the Nanda dynasty.
- Mahapadmananda was the founder of Nanda rule in Magadha.
- The last Nanda ruler was Dhana Nanda. Alexander invaded India during his rule.

MAURYAN EMPIRE

CHANDRAGUPTA MAURYA (322–298 B.C.)

- Chandragupta Maurya was the founder of the Mauryan Empire. He overthrew Nanda dynasty with the help of Chanakya.
- Chandragupta defeated Seleukos Nikator, the Greek general of Alexander, in a battle in 305 B.C.
- Seleukos sent Megasthenes as Greek Ambassador to the Court of Chandragupta. Megasthenes wrote *Indica*.
- Chandragupta was a follower of Jainism.
- He came to Sravana Belgola, near Mysore with a Jain monk called Bhadrabahu. The hill in which he lived until his death is called Chandragiri.
- Chanakya served as prime minister during the reigns of Chandragupta and Bindusara.

BINDUSARA (298–273 B.C.)

- Chandragupta Maurya was succeeded by his son Bindusara.
- Bindusara was called by the Greeks as "*Amitraghatha*" meaning, slayer of enemies.

ASHOKA (273–232 B.C.)

- Ashoka was the most famous ruler of the Mauryan dynasty.
- The most important event of Ashoka's reign was his victorious war with Kalinga in 261 B.C.
- Ashoka convened the Third Buddhist Council at Pataliputra around 250 B.C. in order to strengthen the *Sangha*. It was presided over by Moggaliputta Tissa.
- Ashoka's edicts and inscriptions were deciphered by James Prinsep in 1837.
- The last Mauryan king, Brahadratha was killed by his minister Pushyamitra Sunga. It put an end to the Mauryan Empire.

SUNGAS

- The founder of the Sunga dynasty was *Pushyamitra Sunga*, who was the commander-in-chief under the Mauryas.
- He ascended the throne of Magadha in 185 B.C.
- Pushyamitra was a staunch follower of Brahmanism. He performed two asvamedha sacrifices.
- After the death of Pushyamitra, his son Agnimitra became the ruler.
- Agnimitra was a great conqueror. He was also the hero of the play *Malavikagnimitram* written by Kalidasa.

KANVA

- The last Sunga ruler was Devabhuti, who was murdered by his minister Vasudeva Kanva, the founder of the *Kanva dynasty*.
- The Kanva dynasty ruled for 45 years. After the fall of the Kanvas, the history of Magadha was a blank until the establishment of the Gupta dynasty.

SATAVAHANAS

- The founder of the Satavahana dynasty was Simuka.
- The greatest ruler of the Satavahana dynasty was *Gautamiputra Satakarni.*
- The greatest port of the Satavahanas was Kalyani on the west Deccan. Gandakasela and Ganjam on the east coast were the other important seaports.
- The fine painting at Amaravathi and Nagarjunakonda caves belong to this period.

SANGAM AGE (300 B.C. TO A.D. 300)

- The Sangam Age constitutes an important chapter in the history of South India.
- According to Tamil legends, there existed three Sangams (Academy of Tamil poets) in ancient Tamil Nadu popularly called Muchchangam. These Sangams flourished under the royal patronage of the Pandyas.
- *The first Sangam*, held at then Madurai, chaired by Agastya.
- *The second Sangam* was held at Kapadapuram, chaired by Tolkappiyar.
- *The third Sangam* at Madurai was founded by Mudathirumaran.

Political History

- The Tamil country was ruled by three dynasties namely the Chera, Chola and Pandyas during the Sangam Age.

CHERAS

- The Cheras ruled over parts of modern Kerala. Their capital was Vanji and their important seaports were Tondi and Musiris.
- The greatest Chera King was *Senguttuvan.*

CHOLAS

- The Chola kingdom of the Sangam period extended from modern Tiruchi district to southern Andhra Pradesh.
- Their capital was first located at Uraiyur and then shifted to Puhar. Kaveripattinam served as their port.

GUPTA PERIOD

- The Gupta period is considered as the *Golden Age* in the history of India because this period witnessed all round developments in Religion, Literature, Science, Art and Architecture.

CHANDRAGUPTA I (320-334 A.D.)

- In the beginning of the 4th Century A.D., Sri Gupta established a small Kingdom at Pataliputra. He is considered as the founder of the Gupta dynasty.

- The first notable ruler of the Gupta dynasty was Chandragupta I. He assumed the title *Maharajadhiraja*. The Meherauli Iron Pillar inscription mentions his extensive conquests.
- Chandragupta I is considered to be the founder of the Gupta era which starts with his accession in A.D. 320.

SAMUDRAGUPTA (335-380 A.D.)

- Samudragupta was the greatest of the rulers of the Gupta dynasty. The Allahabad Pillar inscription provides a detailed account of his reign.
- Because of his military achievements, Samudragupta was hailed as '*Indian Napoleon*'.

CHANDRAGUPTA II (380-414 A.D.)

- Samudragupta was succeeded by his son Chandragupta II Vikramaditya.
- The greatest of the military achievements of Chandragupta II was his war against the Saka *satraps* of western India.
- The famous Chinese pilgrim, Fahien visited India (A.D. 399 - A.D. 414) during the reign of Chandragupta II.

SUCCESSORS OF CHANDRAGUPTA II

- Kumaragupta (415-455) was the son and successor of Chandragupta II. His reign was marked by general peace and prosperity.
- Kumaragupta was the founder of the Nalanda University.
- Kumaragupta was followed by *Skandagupta* who ruled from A.D. 456 to A.D. 468.
- After Skandagupta's death, many of his successors like Purugupta, Narasimhagupta, Buddhagupta and Baladitya could not save the Gupta empire from the Huns. Ultimately, the Gupta power totally disappeared due to the Hun invasions and later by the rise of Yasodharman in Malwa.

PUSHYABHUTI DYNASTY (600 - 647 A.D.)

- The greatest king was *Harshavardhana*, son of Prabhakar Vardhana of Thaneshwar. He shifted the capital to *Kannauj*.
- *Hieun Tsang* visited during his reign.
- He established a large monastery at Nalanda. Banabhata adorned his court, wrote Harshacharita and Kadambari. Harsha himself wrote three plays–Priyadarshika, Ratnawali and Nagananda.

PALLAVAS

- The Pallavas established their kingdom in Tondaimandalam by Simhavishnu with its capital at Kanchipuram.
- Other great Pallava rulers were Mahendravarman I, Narasimhavarman I, and Narasimhavarman II.
- The *Kailasanatha temple* at Kanchipuram is the greatest architectural masterpiece of the Pallava art.

CHALUKYAS (543-755 A.D.)

- Pulakesin I was the founder of the Chalukya dynasty. He established a small kingdom with Vatapi or Badami as its capital.
- The structural temples of the Chalukyas exist at Aihole, Badami and Pattadakal (Virupaksha temple). Cave temple architecture was also famous under the Chalukyas. Their cave temples are found in Ajanta, Ellora and Nasik.

RASHTRAKUTAS (755-975 A.D.)

- The art and architecture of the Rashtrakutas were found at Ellora and Elephanta.

CHOLAS

- Cholas became prominent in the ninth century and established an empire comprising the major portion of South India. Their capital was Tanjore.
- The founder of the Chola kingdom was Vijayalaya.
- Rajaraja Chola built the famous Brihadeeswara temple at Tanjore.
- *Dancing Figure of Shiva* (Nataraja) belong to Chola period.

MEDIEVAL INDIA

ARAB CONQUEST OF SIND

- In 712 A.D., Muhammad bin Quasim invaded Sind. Quasim defeated Dahir, the ruler of Sind and killed him in a well-contested battle.

Mahmud of Ghazni

- In 1024, Mahmud marched from Multan across Rajaputana, defeated the Solanki King Bhimadeva I, plundered Anhilwada and sacked the famous temple of Somanatha. This was his last campaign in India. Mahmud died in 1030 A.D.
- Mahmud patronized art and literature. *Firdausi* was the poet-laureate in the court of Mahmud.

Muhammad Ghori

- Prithviraj Chauhan defeated Ghori in the first battle of Tarain near Delhi in 1191 A.D.
- In the Second Battle of Tarain in 1192, Muhammad Ghori thoroughly routed the army of Prithiviraj, who was captured and killed.
- After his brilliant victory over Prithviraj at Tarain, Muhammad Ghori returned to Ghazni leaving behind his

favourite general Qutb-ud-din Aibak to make further conquests in India.

SULTANATE PERIOD

SLAVE DYNASTY (1206-1290)

- The Slave dynasty was also called Mamluk dynasty. Mamluk was the Quranic term for slave.

Qutb-ud-din Aibak

- Qutb-ud-din Aibak was a slave of Muhammad Ghori, who made him the Governor of his Indian possessions.
- After the death of Ghori in 1206, Aibak declared his independence. He assumed the title Sultan and made Lahore his capital.
- Muslim writers call Aibak Lakh Baksh or giver of lakhs because he gave liberal donations to them.
- He built the famous Quwat-Ul-Islam mosque at Delhi. He began the construction of the famous Qutb Minar at Delhi but did not live long to complete it. It was later completed by Iltutmish.

Iltutmish (1210-1236 A.D.)

- Iltutmish belonged to the Ilbari tribe and hence his dynasty was named as Ilbari dynasty.
- He shifted his capital from Lahore to Delhi.
- He organised the *Iqta system* and introduced reforms in civil administration and army.

Raziya (1236-1240 A.D.)

- She appointed an Abyssinian slave Yakuth as Master of the Royal Horses.
- In 1240, Altunia, the governor of Bhatinda revolted against her. She went in personally to suppress the revolt but Altunia killed Yakuth and took Raziya prisoner.
- Bahram Shah, son of Iltutmish killed her.

Balban (1266-1286 A.D.)

- Balban introduced rigorous court discipline and new customs such as prostration and kissing the Sultan's feet to prove his superiority over the nobles.
- He also introduced the Persian festival of *Nauroz* to impress the nobles and people with his wealth and power.
- He established a separate military department - *diwan-i-arz* – and reorganized the army.

KHILJI DYNASTY (1290-1320 A.D.)

- The founder of the Khilji dynasty was Jalaluddin Khilji.
- Ala-ud-din Khilji was the greatest ruler of the Khilji Dynasty.
- He was the first Muslim ruler to extend his empire right upto Rameshwaram in the South.
- The Sultan had built a new city called Siri near Delhi.
- Amir Khusrau the great Persian poet, patronised by Balban, continued to live in Ala-ud-din Khilji's court also.
- He introduced the system of *dagh* (branding of horses) and prepared *huliya* (descriptive list of soldiers).
- Ala-ud-din Khilji maintained a large permanent standing army and paid them in cash from the royal treasury.

TUGHLAQ DYNASTY

- Ghiyas-ud-din Tughlaq was the founder of the Tughlaq dynasty.
- To have the capital at the centre of the empire and safe from the Mongol raids, Tughlaq chose Devagiri as his new capital in A.D. 1327. The Sultan renamed the new capital Daulatabad.
- In 1329-30, Muhammad-bin-Tughlaq introduced a token currency.
- Firoz Shah Tughlaq became Sultan after the death of Muhammad-bin-Tughlaq in A.D. 1351.
- He was the first Sultan to impose irrigation tax.
- He had built new towns of Firozabad, Jaunpur, Hissar and Firozpur.
- Timur—Mongol leader of Central Asia, ordered general massacre in Delhi (AD 1398) at the time of Nasiruddin Mahmud (later Tughlaq king).

SAYYID DYNASTY

- Before his departure from India, Timur appointed Khizr Khan as governor of Multan. He captured Delhi and founded the Sayyid dynasty in 1414.
- Mubarak Shah, Mohammed Shah and Alam Shah were some of the other important noteworthy rulers of Sayyid Dynasty.

LODHI DYNASTY

- The Lodhis were Afghans.
- Bahlol Lodhi was the first Afghan ruler while his predecessors were all Turks. He died in 1489 and was succeeded by his son, Sikandar Lodhi.
- In 1504, Sikandar Lodhi founded the city of Agra and transferred his capital from Delhi to Agra.
- Babar marched against Delhi and defeated and killed Ibrahim Lodhi in the first battle of Panipat (1526).

BAHMANI AND VIJAYANAGAR KINGDOMS

- The break up of the Delhi Sultanate provided an opportunity for the rise of a number of kingdoms in the Deccan.
- After the decline of the Tughlaqs, there arose two important kingdoms in the Deccan. They were the Bahmani and Vijayanagar kingdoms.

VIJAYANAGAR EMPIRE

- The Vijayanagar Kingdom was set up in A.D. 1336. Its aim was to check the spread of Muslim power and protect Hindu Dharma in South India.
- Four dynasties – Sangama, Saluva, Tuluva and Aravidu – ruled Vijayanagar from A.D. 1336 to 1672.
- Vijayanagar was founded in 1336 by Harihara and Bukka of the Sangama dynasty.
- The Moroccan traveller, Ibn Batuta, Venetian traveller Nicolo de Conti, Persian traveller Abdur Razzak and the Portuguese traveller Domingo Paes were among them who left valuable accounts on the socio-economic conditions of the Vijayanagar Empire.
- The Hampi ruins and other monuments of Vijayanagar provide information on the cultural contributions of the Vijayanagar rulers.

KRISHNA DEVA RAYA (1509-1530)

- The Tuluva dynasty was founded by Vira Narasimha.
- The greatest of the Vijayanagar rulers, Krishna Deva Raya belonged to the Tuluva dynasty.
- Krishna Deva Raya himself authored a Telugu work, *Amukthamalyadha* and Sanskrit works, *Jambavati Kalyanam* and *Ushaparinayam*.
- He built the famous *Vittalaswamy* and *Hazara Ramaswamy* temples at Vijayanagar.
- Krishna Deva Raya renovated Virupaksha temple in A.D. 1510.
- After his death the enemies of Vijayanagar joined together and defeated the Vijayanagar ruler in the battle of Talaikota.

BAHMANI KINGDOM

- The founder of the Bahmani kingdom was Alauddin Bahman Shah also known as Hasan Gangu in 1347. Its capital was Gulbarga.
- Ahmad Wali Shah shifted the capital from Gulbarga to Bidar.
- *Gol Gumbaj* was built by *Muhammad Adil Shah*; it is famous for the so called '*Whispering Gallery*'.
- *Quli Qutub Shah* built the famous *Golcunda Fort*.

MUGHAL EMPIRE (1526-1707 AD)

BABAR (1526-1530 AD)

- Babar was the founder of the Mughal Empire in India.
- On 21st April, 1526 the first Battle of Panipat took place between Babar and Ibrahim Lodhi, who was killed in the battle.
- Babar was the first one to use guns or artillery in a battle on the Indian soil.
- Babar defeated Rana Sanga of Mewar in the battle of Kanwah in A.D. 1527.
- Babar was a soldier-scholar and wrote his own autobiography called Babar Nama in Turkish language.

HUMAYUN (1530-1556 AD)

- Sher Shah defeated Humayun at Chausa in A.D. 1539 and again at Kannauj in A.D. 1540.
- After losing his kingdom, Humayun became an exile for the next fifteen years.
- In 1555, Humayun defeated the Afghans and recovered the Mughal throne. After six months, he died in 1556 due to his fall from the staircase of his library.
- *Gulbadan Begum*, Humayun's half-sister wrote *Humayun-nama*.

SHER SHAH SURI

- The founder of the Sur dynasty was Sher Shah, whose original name was Farid.
- Sher Shah became the ruler of Delhi in 1540.
- Sher Shah organized a brilliant administrative system. The central government consisted of several departments.
- He built a new city on the banks of the river Yamuna near Delhi. Now the old fort called Purana Quila and its mosque is alone surviving.
- He built a Mausoleum at Sasaram, which is considered as one of the master pieces of Indian architecture.

AKBAR (1556-1605 AD)

- When Akbar ascended the throne in A.D. 1556 he was only 14 years old. His guardian Bairam Khan served him as a faithful minister and tutor.
- Bairam Khan, along with Akbar met Hemu in the second Battle of Panipat in 1556. Hemu was initially successful, but lost his consciousness after an arrow hit him. Akbar killed him.
- The Battle of Haldighati was fought between Rana Pratap of Mewar and Mughal army led by Man Singh and Asif Khan. Some historian say that this battle was indecisive but some say that Rana Pratap was defeated by Akbar.
- Akbar abolished the pilgrim tax and in 1562, he abolished Jaziya.
- Akbar evolved a new faith called Din-i-Illahi or Divine Faith.

JAHANGIR (1605-1627 AD)

- When Akbar died, Prince Salim succeeded with the title Jahangir (Conqueror of World) in 1605.
- Jahangir's eldest son, Khusrau, rebelled against him. He was arrested and put into prison. *Guru Arjun Dev, the fifth Sikh Guru* was executed by Jahangir.
- In 1611, Jahangir married Mehrunnisa who was known as Nurjahan (Light of World).
- Jahangir died in A.D. 1627.

SHAHJAHAN (1628-1658 AD)

- The reign of Shahjahan is generally considered as the *Golden Age* of the Mughal period.
- Shahjahan is called as the *Prince of Builders*. He had built the Jama Masjid and Red Fort in Delhi and Taj Mahal in Agra.
- Fine arts like painting, music and literature reached high level of development during Shahjahan's time.

AURANGAZEB (1658-1707 AD)

- Aurangazeb was the last great Mughal ruler. He ascended the throne after killing his three brothers Dara, Shuja and Murad in a fratricidal war.
- Aurangazeb defeated Sikandar Shah of Bijapur and annexed his kingdom.
- Aurangazeb was against the Sikhs and he executed the ninth Sikh Guru Tegh Bahadur.
- He was called *Darvesh* or a *Zinda Pir*. He forbade *Sati*. Conquered Bijapur (AD 1686) and Golconda (AD 1687) and reimposed Jaziya and Pilgrim tax in AD 1679.
- He built *Biwi ka Makbara* on the tomb of his queen *Rabaud-Durani* at Aurangabad; *Moti Masjid* within Red Fort, Delhi; and the Jami or Badshahi Mosque at Lahore.
- Aurangazeb died in A.D. 1707.

LATER MUGHALS / FALL OF THE MUGHALS

Bahadur Shah (1707-1712)

- Assumed the title of *Shah Alam I*.

Jahandar Shah (1712-1713)

- First puppet Mughal emperor. He abolished *jaziya*.

Farrukhsiyar (1713-1719)

Mohammad Shah (1719-1748)

- Nadir Shah (*of Iran*) defeated him in the Battle of Karnal (1739) and took away *Peacock throne* and *Kohinoor diamond*.

Ahmad Shah (1748-1754)

Alamgir II (1754-1759),

Shah Alam II (1759-1806)

Akbar II (1806-1837)

- He gave Ram Mohan Roy the title '*Raja*'. He sent Raja Ram Mohan Roy to London to seek a raise in his allowance.

Bahadur Shah II (1837-1857)

- He was confined by the British to the Red Fort. During the revolt of 1857, he was proclaimed the Emperor by the rebels. He was deported to Rangoon after that.

Literature of Mughal Period

Author	Work
Babar	Tuzuk-i-Babari
Abul Fazal	Ain-i-Akbari, Akbarnamah
Jahangir	Tuzuk-i-Jahangiri
Hamid	Padshahnama
Darashikoh	Majm-ul-Bahrain
Mirza Md Qasim	Alamgirnama

THE MARATHAS

SHIVAJI (1627-1680 AD)

- Shivaji was born at Shivner in 1627. His father was Shahji Bhonsle and mother Jija Bai.
- His religious teacher was Samarth Ramdas and guardian was Dadaji Kondadev.
- In 1674, Shivaji crowned himself at Raigarh and assumed the title Chatrapathi.
- *Ashtapradhan* (eight ministers) helped in administration. These were Peshwas, Sar-i-Naubat (Military), Mazumdar or Amatya (Accounts); Waqenavis (Intelligence); Surnavis (Corres-pondence); *Dabir* or *Sumanta* (Ceremonies); *Nyayadhish* (Justice); and *Panditrao* (Charity).
- Successors of Shivaji were Shambhaji, Rajaram and *Shahu* (fought at Battle of Khed in AD 1708).

THE PESHWAS

- Balaji Vishwanath was the first Peshwa. He began his career as a small revenue official and became Peshwa in 1713.
- Baji Rao I was the eldest son of Balaji Vishwanath. He was considered as the "greatest exponent of guerilla tactics after Shivaji".
- It was during reign of Balaji Baji Rao (Nanasaheb) when the Marathas lost the Third Battle of Panipat.
- Baji Rao II (last Peshwa) was the first Maratha to have fled from the British attacks instead of fighting with them. Baji Rao II surrendered to Sir John Malcom.

THE SIKH

- Guru Nanak Dev was the founder of Sikhism, the religion that draws its elements from both Hinduism and Islam.
- Name of the ten Sikh Gurus and their works are given below:
  1. **Guru Nanak Dev (1469-1539AD):** The founder of Sikhism.
  2. **Guru Angad Dev (1504-1552AD):** Developed Gurmukhi.
  3. **Guru Amar Das (1479-1574AD):** Struggled against Sati system and Purdah system.
  4. **Guru Ram Das (1534-1581AD):** Founded Amritsar, the holy city of Sikhism.

5. **Guru Arjun Dev (1563-1606AD):** He built the *Swarn Mandir* (Golden Temple).
6. **Guru Hargobind (1595-1644 AD):** Established Akal Takht.
7. **Guru Har Rai (1630-1661 AD)**
8. **Guru Har Krishan (1656-1664 AD)**
9. **Guru Tegh Bahadur (1621-1675 AD)**
10. **Guru Gobind Singh (1666-1708 AD):** Founded the Khalsa and Sikh baptism, composed many poems, and nominated the Sikh sacred text as the final and enduring Guru.

MODERN INDIA

THE ADVENT OF THE EUROPEANS

THE PORTUGUESE

- Vasco-da-Gama, a Portuguese explorer, sailed through the route of Cape of Good Hope and reached near Calicut on 20th May 1498 A.D. during the reign of King Zamorin (Hindu King of Calicut).
- Vasco-da-Gama founded a factory at Cannanore on his second visit to India in 1501. In due course, Calicut, Cochin and Cannanore became the Portuguese trading centres.
- Francisco Almeida came to India in 1505. He was the first Governor of Portuguese possessions in India.
- The real founder of Portuguese power in India was *Alfonso de Albuquerque*. He captured Goa from the rulers of Bijapur in 1510. It was made their headquarters.

THE DUTCH

- The United East India Company of the Netherlands founded a factory at Masulipatnam in 1605. They built their first fort on the main land of India at Pulicut in 1609, near Madras (Chennai). They captured Nagapattinam from the Portuguese.
- They made Agra, Surat, Masulipatnam and Chinsura in Bengal as their trading centres.

THE DANES

- The Danish East India Company was established in 1616 in Denmark.
- They came to South India and founded a factory at Tranquebar (Tharangambadi) in 1620. They also made settlements at Serampore near Calcutta (Kolkata).

THE ENGLISH

- The English East India Company was formed in 1599 under a charter granted by Queen Elizabeth in 1600.
- The East India Company sent Sir William Hawkins to the court of the Mughal Emperor Jahangir in 1609 to obtain permission to erect a factory at Surat.
- In 1615, Sir Thomas Roe, another British merchant, came to Jahangir's court. He stayed for three years and succeeded in getting permission to set up their trading centres at Agra, Surat, Ahmedabad and Broach.
- In 1690, the British got permission from Aurangazeb to build a factory on the site of Calcutta. In 1696 a fort was built at that place. It was called Fort William.

THE FRENCH

- The French East India Company was established in 1664 under the inspiring and energetic leadership of Colbert, the economic adviser of the French King Louis XIV.
- In 1667, the first French factory was established at Surat by Francis Caron who was nominated as Director-General.
- French were defeated by English in the *Battle of Wandiwash* (1760).

EAST INDIA COMPANY

- After the Battle of Plassey in 1757 and the Battle of Buxar in 1764, the East India Company became a political power.
- India was under the East India Company's rule till 1858 when it came under the direct administration of the British Crown.
- Robert Clive was the first Governor of Fort William under the Company's rule.

GOVERNOR-GENERALS OF BENGAL

Warren Hastings (1772-85 AD)

- In 1772, the Company appointed Warren Hastings as the Governor of Fort William.
- The Dual System introduced by Robert Clive was abolished by Warren Hastings.
- Warren Hastings was known for his expansionist policy. His administration witnessed the Rohilla War, the First Anglo-Maratha War and the Second Anglo-Mysore War.
- Pitt's India Act (1784) was passed.

Lord Cornwallis (1786-93 AD)

- Cornwallis inaugurated the policy of making appointments mainly on the basis of merit thereby laying the foundation of the Indian Civil Service.
- Lord Cornwallis introduced Permanent Revenue Settlement.
- Tipu Sultan signed the Treaty of Srirangapatnam in 1792 with the British.

Sir John Shore (1793-98 AD)

- Played an important role in the introduction of Permanent Settlement.
- *Battle of Kharda* between the Nizams and the Marathas (1795).

Wellesley (1798-1805)

- Wellesley came to India with a determination to launch a forward policy that he adopted to achieve his object is known as the 'Subsidiary Alliance'.
- The Fourth Anglo-Mysore War started in 1799. The war was short and decisive. Tipu fought till his capital Srirangapatnam was captured and he himself was shot dead.
- Peshwa Baji Rao II signed the *Treaty* of *Bassein* with the British in 1802. It was a subsidiary treaty and the Peshwa was recognized as the head of the Maratha kingdom.
- The Treaty of Deogaon(1803) was signed between Bhonsle and Wellesley.

Lord Minto (1807-1813)

- Lord Minto concluded the Treaty of Amritsar with Ranjit Singh of Punjab in 1809.
- The Charter Act of 1813 was passed during this period.

Lord Hastings (1813-1823)

- Anglo Nepal War (1814-1816) and Treaty of Sugauli (1816).
- Third Maratha War (1817-18), dissolution of Maratha confederacy and creation of Bombay Presidency.
- He encouraged the freedom of the Press and abolished the censorship introduced in 1799.

GOVERNOR-GENERALS OF INDIA

Lord William Bentinck (1828-1835)

- Charter Act of 1833 was passed and he was made the first Governor-General of India. Before him, the designation was Governor-General of Bengal.
- The social reforms of William Bentinck made his name immortal in the history of British India. These include the abolition of *Sati*, the suppression of Thugs and the prevention of female infanticide.
- The Government Resolution in 1835 made English the official and literary language of India.

Lord Metcalfe (1835-36 AD)

- Known as liberator of press in India.

Lord Auckland (1836-42 AD)

- First Afghan War (1838-42), a disaster for the English.

Lord Ellenborough (1842-44 AD)

- Brought an end to Afghan war. War with Gwalior (1843), *Annexation of Sind* by Charles Napier (1843).

Lord Hardinge (1844-48 AD)

- First Anglo-Sikh War (1845-46) and Treaty of Lahore (1846). Gave preference to English educated persons in employment.

Lord Dalhousie (1848-1856)

- The Doctrine of Lapse was applied by Dalhousie.
- The first railway line connecting Bombay with Thane was opened in 1853.

VICEROYS OF INDIA

Lord Canning (1856-62 AD)

- Lord Canning became the first Viceroy of India in 1858.
- Revolt of 1857, Mutiny took place. Indian Penal Code 1860 was passed.

Lord Elgin (1862 AD)

- Wahabi Movement.

Lord John Lawrence (1864-69 AD)

- Established the *High Courts* at Calcutta, Bombay and Madras in 1865.
- Telegraphic communication was opened with Europe. Created the Indian Forest Department.

Lord Northbrooke (1872-76 AD)

- Kuka Rebellion in Punjab, Famine in Bihar.

Lord Lytton (1876-80)

- In 1878, the Vernacular Press Act was passed. This Act empowered a Magistrate to secure an undertaking from the editor, publisher and printer of a vernacular newspaper that nothing would be published against the English Government. This Act crushed the freedom of the Indian press.
- In 1878, the Arms Act was passed. This Act prevented the Indians to keep arms without appropriate license.
- Lord Lytton also held a Darbar at Delhi in 1877 in which Queen Victoria was declared as the Empress of India. This extravagant Darbar cost millions of ruppes.
- In 1878, the Statutory Civil Service was established exclusively for Indians.

Lord Ripon (1880-84 AD)

- Lord Ripon repealed the Vernacular Press Act and earned much popularity among Indians.
- Ripon appointed a Commission in 1882 under the chairmanship of Sir William Hunter.
- The Commission came to be known as the Hunter Commission. The Commission recommended for the expansion and improvement of the elementary education of the masses.

- Ripon was founder of local self-government in modern India.

Lord Dufferin (1884-88 AD)

- *Third Burmese War* (1885-86 AD). Establishment of the Indian National Congress in 1885.

Lord Lansdowne (1888-94 AD)

- Factory Act of 1891 granted weekly holiday and stipulated working hours for women and children.

Lord Elgin II (1894-99 AD)

- Southern uprisings of 1899. Great famine of 1896-1897 and Lyall Commission on famine was established.

Lord Curzon (1899-1905 AD)

- Curzon instituted in 1902, a Universities Commission to go into the entire question of university education in the country.
- On the basis of the findings and recommendations of the Commission, Curzon brought in the Indian Universities Act of 1904, which brought all the universities in India under the control of the government.

Lord Minto (1905-10 AD)

- Swadeshi Movement (1905-08); foundation of Muslim League (1906); Surat Session and split in the Congress (1907). Morley-Minto Reforms (1909).

Lord Hardinge (1910-16 AD)

- Capital shifted from Calcutta to Delhi (1911); Delhi Durbar; Partition of Bengal was cancelled. The Hindu Mahasabha was founded in 1915 by Pandit Madan Mohan Malaviya.

Lord Chelmsford (1916-21 AD)

- Gandhi returned to India (1915) and founded the Sabarmati Ashram (1916), Champaran Satyagraha, Satyagraha at Ahmedabad (1981), Kheda Satyagraha (1918).
- Rowlatt Act (March, 1919) and the Jallianwala Bagh Massacre (13th April, 1919).
- Khilafat Committee was formed and Khilafat Movement started (1919-20).
- Non-Cooperation Movement started (1920-22).

Lord Reading (1921-26)

- Moplah Rebellion (1921) took place. *Kakori Train* Robbery on 1st August, 1925. *Communal Riots* of 1923-25 in Multan, Amritsar, Delhi etc.

Lord Irwin (1926-31 AD)

- Lahore Session of Congress and *Poorna Swaraj* Declaration (1929).
- Simon Commission visited India in 1927.
- Dandi March (12th March, 1930). Civil Disobedience Movement (1930).
- First Round Table Conference was held in England in 1930. Gandhi-Irwin Pact.

Lord Willingdon (1931-36 AD)

- *Second Round Table Conference* in London in 1931 and *third* in 1932.

Lord Linlithgow (1936-43 AD)

- Congress Ministries resignation celebrated as '*Deliverance Day*' by the Muslim League (1939), the Lahore Resolution (23rd March, 1940) of the Muslim League demanding separate state for the Muslims. (It was at this session that Jinnah propounded his Two-Nation Theory). Outbreak of World War II in 1939. Cripps Mission in 1942. Quit India Movement (8th August, 1942).

Lord Wavell (1943-47 AD)

- Cabinet Mission Plan (16th May, 1946).
- First meeting of the Constituent Assembly was held on 9th December, 1946.
- Arranged the Shimla Conference on 25th June, 1945 with Indian National Congress and Muslim League but failed.

Lord Mountbatten (March to Aug, 1947)

- Last viceroy of British India and the first Governor-General of free India.
- Partition of India decided by the 3rd June Plan or Mountbatten Plan.

NATIONAL MOVEMENT (1885-1947)

INDIAN NATIONAL CONGRESS (1885)

- Allan Octavian Hume, a retired civil servant in the British Government took the initiative to form an all-India organization. Thus, the Indian National Congress was founded and its first session was held at Bombay in 1885. W.C. Banerjee was its first president. It was attended by 72 delegates from all over India.
- The second session was held in Calcutta in 1886 and the third in Madras in 1887.
- Between 1885 and 1905, the Congress leaders were moderates. The Moderates had faith in the British justice and goodwill. They were called moderates because they adopted peaceful and constitutional means to achieve their demands.
- In 1905, Gopal Krishna Gokhale founded the Servants of India Society to train Indians to dedicate their lives to the cause of the country.

Partition of Bengal (1905)

- By Lord Curzon on 16th October, 1905 through a royal proclamation, reducing the old province of Bengal in size by creating East Bengal and Assam out of the rest of Bengal.

- The partition of Bengal in 1905 provided a spark for the rise of extremism in the Indian National Movement.
- Curzon's real motives behind this partition were:
  - To break the growing strength of Bengali nationalism since Bengal was the base of Indian nationalism.
  - To divide the Hindus and Muslims in Bengal.
  - To show the enormous power of the British Government in doing whatever it liked.

Swadeshi Movement (1905)

- The Swadeshi Movement involved programmes like the boycott of government service, courts, schools and colleges and of foreign goods. It was both a political and economic movement.
- Lal, Bal, Pal and Aurobindo Ghosh played an important role.

Muslim League (1906)

- In December 1906, Muslim delegates from all over India met at Dacca for the Muslim Educational Conference.
- Taking advantage of this occasion, Nawab Salimullah of Dacca proposed the setting up of an organisation to look after the Muslim interests. The proposal was accepted.
- The All-India Muslim League was finally set up on December 30, 1906.

Minto Morley Reforms (1909)

- Minto, the Viceroy and Morley, the Secretary of State for India jointly proposed reforms to the Indian Councils. An Act, called the Indian Councils Act or the Minto-Morley Reforms Act was passed in 1909.
- A separate communal electorate was introduced for the Muslims.

The Lucknow Pact (1916)

- During the 1916 Congress session at Lucknow two major events occurred. The divided Congress became united. An understanding for joint action against the British was reached between the Congress and the Muslim League and it was called the Lucknow Pact.
- The signing of the Lucknow Pact by the Congress and the Muslim League in 1916 marked an important step in the Hindu-Muslim unity.

The Home Rule Movement (1916)

- Two Home Rule Leagues were established, one by B.G. Tilak at Poona in April 1916 and the other by Mrs. Annie Besant at Madras in September 1916.
- While Tilak's Movement concentrated on Maharashtra, Annie Besant's Movement covered the rest of the country.

August Declaration

- On 20 August, 1917, Montague, the Secretary of State in England, promised the gradual development of self-governing institutions in India.
- This August Declaration led to the end of the Home Rule Movement.

Rowlatt Act (1919)

- In 1917, a committee was set up under the presidentship of Sir Sydney Rowlatt to look into the militant Nationalist activities. On the basis of its report the Rowlatt Act was passed in March 1919 by the Central Legislative Council. As per this Act, any person could be arrested on the basis of suspicion. No appeal or petition could be filed against such arrests.
- This Act was called the Black Act and it was widely opposed. An all-India hartal was organized on 6 April, 1919.

Jallianwala Bagh Massacre (13 April, 1919)

- On 13th April, the Baisakhi day (harvest festival), a public meeting was organized at the Jallianwala Bagh (garden). Gen. Dyer marched in and without any warning opened fire on the crowd. The firing continued for about 10 to 15 minutes and it stopped only after the ammunition exhausted.
- According to official report 379 people were killed and 1137 wounded in the incident. There was a nationwide protest against this massacre and Rabindranath Tagore renounced his knighthood as a protest.

Khilafat Movement (1920)

- The chief cause of the Khilafat Movement was the defeat of Turkey in the First World War.
- The Muslims in India were upset over the British attitude against Turkey and launched the Khilafat Movement.
- Ali brothers, *Mohd Ali* and *Shaukat Ali* started this movement. It was jointly led by the Khilafat leaders and the Congress.

Non-Co-operation Movement (1920-22)

- Mahatma Gandhi announced his plan to begin Non-Cooperation with the government as a sequel to the Rowlatt Act, Jallianwala Bagh massacre and the Khilafat Movement. It was approved by the Indian National Congress at the Nagpur session in December, 1920.
- The Congress observed the Non-Co-operation movement in 1920. The main aim of this movement was to attain Swaraj through non-violent and peaceful means.
- The whole movement was abruptly called off on 11th February, 1922 by Gandhi following the Chauri-Chaura incident in the Gorakhpur district of U.P. Many top leaders of the country were stunned at this sudden suspension of the Non-Co-operation Movement.

- On 5th February an angry mob set fire to the police station at *Chauri-Chaura* and twenty two police men were burnt to death.

Swaraj Party

- Leaders like Motilal Nehru and Chittranjan Das formed a separate group within the Congress known as the Swaraj Party on 1 January, 1923.
- The Swarajists wanted to contest the council elections and wreck the government from within.

Simon Commission (1927)

- The Act of 1919 included a provision for its review after a lapse of ten years. However, the review commission under the chairmanship of Sir John Simon was appointed by the British Government two years earlier of its schedule in 1927.
- Indian leaders opposed the commission, as there were no Indians in it, they cried *Simon Go Back.*
- The government used brutal repression and at Lahore, *Lala Lajpat Rai* was severely beaten in lathi-charge.

Nehru Report (1928)

- The Secretary of State, Lord Birkenhead, challenged the Indians to produce a Constitution that would be acceptable to all. The challenge was accepted by the Congress, which convened an all party meeting on 28 February, 1928.
- A committee consisting of eight was constituted to draw up a blueprint for the future Constitution of India. It was headed by Motilal Nehru. The Report published by this Committee came to be known as the Nehru Report.

Lahore Session (1929)

- On Dec. 19, 1929, under the Presidentship of J.L. Nehru, the INC, as its Lahore session, declared Poorna Swaraj (Complete Independence) as its ultimate goal.
- On Dec. 31, 1929, the newly adopted tricolour flag was unfurled and Jan. 26, 1930 was fixed as the First Independence Day, which was to be celebrated every year.

Dandi March (1930)

- On 12th March, 1930, Gandhi began his famous March to Dandi with his chosen 79 followers to break the salt laws. He reached the coast of Dandi on 5 April, 1930 after marching a distance of 200 miles and on 6 April formally launched the Civil Disobedience Movement by breaking the salt laws.

Civil Disobedience Movement

- Countrywide mass participation by women.
- The Garhwal soldiers refused to fire on the people at Peshawar.

Round Table Conference

- The first Round Table Conference was held in November 1930 at London and it was boycotted by the Congress.
- On 8th March, 1931 the Gandhi-Irwin Pact was signed. As per this pact, Mahatma Gandhi agreed to suspend the Civil-Disobedience Movement and participate in the Second-Round Table Conference.
- In September 1931, the Second Round Table Conference was held at London. Mahatma Gandhi participated in the Conference but returned to India disappointed.
- In January 1932, the Civil-Disobedience Movement was resumed.

Poona Pact (1932)

- The idea of separate electorate for the depressed classes was abandoned, but seats reserved for them in the provincial legislature were increased.
- Thus, Poona Pact agreed upon a joint electorate for upper and lower castes.

Demand for Pakistan

- *Chaudhary Rehmat Ali* gave the term *Pakistan* in 1933.
- In March 1940, the Muslim League demanded the creation of Pakistan.

Cripps Mission (1942)

- The British Government in its effort to secure Indian co-operation in the Second World War sent Sir Stafford Cripps to India on 23 March, 1942. This is known as Cripps Mission.
- The main recommendations of Cripps was the promise of Dominion Status to India.
- Congress rejected it. Gandhi called Cripp's proposals as a "Post-dated Cheque".

Quit India Movement (1942-1944)

- The All India Congress Committee met at Bombay on 8th August, 1942 and passed the famous Quit India Resolution. On the same day, Gandhi gave his call of 'do or die'.
- On 8th and 9th August, 1942, the government arrested all the prominent leaders of the Congress. Mahatma Gandhi was kept in prison at Poona. Pandit Jawaharlal Nehru, Abul Kalam Azad, and other leaders were imprisoned in the Ahamednagar Fort.
- Quit India Movement was the final attempt for country's freedom.

Indian National Army (INA)

- On July 2, 1943, Subhash Chandra Bose reached Singapore and gave the rousing war cry of *'Dilli Chalo'*. He was made the President of Indian Independence League and soon became the supreme commander of the Indian National Army. He gave the country the slogan of *Jai Hind.*
- INA had three fighting brigades named after Gandhi, Azad and Nehru. Rani of Jhansi Brigade was an exclusive women force. INA headquarters were at Rangoon and Singapore.

Cabinet Mission (1946)

- The Cabinet Mission put forward a plan for solution of the constitutional problem. A proposal was envisaged for setting up an Interim Government, which would remain in office till a new government was elected on the basis of the new Constitution framed by the Constituent Assembly.
- Elections were held in July 1946 for the formation of a Constituent Assembly.
- Muslim league observed the *Direct Action Day* on 16 August, 1946.
- An Interim Government was formed under the leadership of Jawaharlal Nehru on 2 September, 1946.

Mountbatten Plan (1947)

- On 20 February 1947, Prime Minister Atlee announced in the House of Commons the definite intention of the British Government to transfer power to responsible Indian hands by a date not later than June 1948.
- Lord Mountbatten armed with vast powers became India's Viceroy on 24 March, 1947. The partition of India and the creation of Pakistan appeared inevitable to him.
- After extensive consultation Lord Mountbatten put forth the plan of partition of India on 3 June, 1947. The Congress and the Muslim League ultimately approved the Mountbatten Plan.

Indian Independence Act, 1947

- The salient features of this Act was the partition of the country into India and Pakistan would come into effect from 15 August, 1947.
- On 15th August, 1947 India, and on the 14th August Pakistan came into existence as two independent states.
- Lord Mountbatten was made the first Governor General of Independent India, whereas Mohammad Ali Jinnah became the first Governor General of Pakistan.
- C. Rajagopalachari became the first and last Indian Governor-General of India. When India became a Republic on 26 January, 1950 Dr. Rajendra Prasad became the first President of our country.

Socio-Religious Movements and Organisation

Name of the Organisation	*Founder*	*Year*	*Place*
Atmiya Sabha	Ram Mohan Roy	1815	Calcutta
Brahmo Samaj	Ram Mohan Roy	1828	Calcutta
Dharma Sabha	Radhakanta Dev	1829	Calcutta
Tattvabodhini Sabha	Debendranath Tagore	1839	Calcutta
Nirankaris	Dayal Das, Darbara Singh, Rattan Chand etc.	1840	Punjab
Manav Dharma Sabha	Durgaram Manchharam	1844	Surat
Paramhansa Mandli	Dadoba Pandurung	1849	Bombay
Namdharis	Ram Singh	1857	Punjab
Radha Swami Satsang	Tulsi Ram	1861	Agra
Brahmo Samaj of India	Keshab Chandra Sen	1866	Calcutta
Dar-ul-Ulum	Maulana Hussain Ahmed	1866	Deoband
Prarthna Samaj	Atmaram Pandurung	1867	Bombay
Arya Samaj	Swami Dayanand Saraswati	1875	Bombay
Theosophical Society	Madam H.P. Blavatsky and Col. H.S. Olcott	1875	New York (USA)
Sadharan Brahmo Samaj	Anand Mohan Bose	1878	Calcutta
Deccan Education Society	G.G. Agarkar	1884	Pune (Poona)
Muhammadan Educational Conference	Syed Ahmad Khan	1886	Aligarh
Indian National Conference	M.G. Ranade	1887	Bombay
Deva Samaj	Shivnarayan Agnihotri	1887	Lahore
Nadwah-ul-Ulama	Maulana Shibli Numani	1894	Lucknow
Ramakrishna Mission	Swami Vivekananda	1897	Belur
Servents of Indian Society	Gopal Krishna Gokhale	1905	Bombay
Poona Seva Sadan	Mrs. Ramabai Ranade and G.K. Devadhar	1909	Pune (Poona)
Social Service League	N.M. Joshi	1911	Bombay
Seva Samiti	H.N. Kunzru	1914	Allahabad

Newspapers and Journals

- *Bengal Gazette* (1780) (India's first newspaper)—James Augustus Hikky
- *Kesari*—B.G. Tilak
- *Maratha*—B.G. Tilak
- *Sudharak*—G.K. Gokhale

- *Amrit Bazar Patrika*—Shishir Kumar Ghosh and Motilal Ghosh
- *Yugantar*—Bhupendranath Datta and Birender Kumar Ghosh
- *Bombay Chronicle*—Firoze Shah Mehta
- *New India (Daily)*—Annie Besant

Books and Authors

- *Causes of the Indian Mutiny*—Sir Syed Ahmed Khan
- *Ghulam Giri*—Jyotiba Phule
- *Anandmath*—Bankim Chand Chatterjee
- *Satyarth Prakash*—Swami Dayanand
- *Unhappy India*—Lala Lajpat Rai
- *India Divided*—Dr. Rajendra Prasad
- *The Discovery of India*—J.L. Nehru
- *Neel Darpan*—Dinbandhu Mitra
- *Hind Swaraj*—M.K. Gandhi
- *What Congress and Gandhi have done to the untouchables*—Dr. B.R. Ambedkar

Important Sayings

- *'Back to Vedas'*—Dayanand Saraswati
- *'Dilli Chalo!'*—Subhash Chandra Bose's battle cry of *Azad Hind Fauj*
- *'Do or Die'*—Mahatma Gandhi (while launching Quit India movement in 1942)
- *'Give me blood and I will give you freedom'*—Subhash Chandra Bose (in his address to soldiers of *Azad Hind Fauj)*
- *'My ultimate aim is to wipe every tear from every eye'*—Jawaharlal Nehru
- *'Swaraj is my birthright and I will have it'*—Bal Gangadhar Tilak
- *'Inqualab Zindabad'*—Bhagat Singh
- *'Jai Jawan, Jai Kisan'*—Lal Bahadur Shastri
- *'Sarfaroshi ki tamanna Ab Hamare Dil mein Hai'*—Ram Prasad Bismill
- *'Saare Jahan Se Achcha,* Hindustan Hamara'—Dr. Mohammed Iqbal
- *'Hindi, Hindu, Hindustan'*—Bhartendu Harishchandra
- *'Vande Mataram'*—Bankim Chandra Chatterjee

❐ ❐ ❐

GEOGRAPHY

WORLD GEOGRAPHY

THE UNIVERSE

- Existing matter and energy are together known as **Universe.**

GALAXY

- A galaxy is a huge system of billions of stars and clouds of dust and gases.
- Our solar system is a part of *Milky Way* galaxy.
- There are millions of galaxies that make the Universe.

STARS

- Stars account for 98 per cent of the matter in a galaxy. The stars nearest to the earth are *Proxima Centauri, Alpha Centauri, Barnard's Star, Sirius* and so on. Of these, *Sirius* is the brightest.

LIGHT YEAR

- Light year is the distance travelled by light in one year at a speed of 2,99,792.5 km. per second.

SOLAR SYSTEM

- The Sun, eight planets, satellites and some other celestial bodies known as asteroids and meteoroids form the solar system.

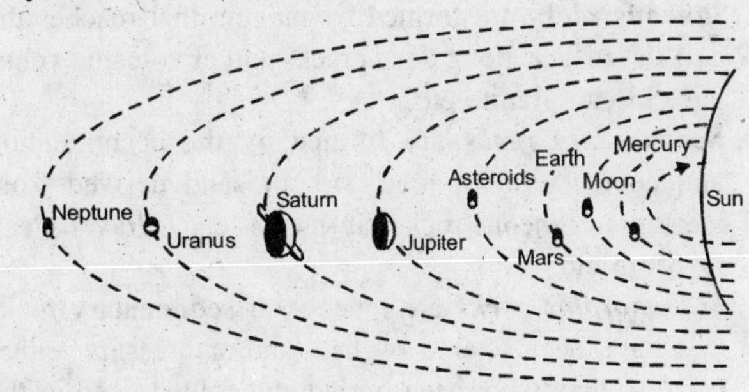

SUN

- The Sun is in the centre of the solar system.
- The Sun is a mixture of gases. It consists of 92% hydrogen, 7.8% helium and 0.2% other gases.
- The Sun is about 150 million km away from the earth.
- The sun is an ultimate source of energy for life on Earth.
- Sunlight takes 8 min 16.6 sec to reach earth.

Facts about Sun

Diameter	— 1.392 × 10^6 km
Volume	— 1.304 × 106 times the volume of earth
Temperature	— 6000°C at surface and 15 million degree C at the centre
Relative density	— 1.4
Gravitational Pull	— 28 times the gravitational pull of the earth

Facts about Planets

Closest to Sun	*Mercury*
Farthest from Sun	*Neptune*
Heaviest	*Jupiter*
Hottest	*Venus*
Inner	*Mercury, Venus, Earth, Mars*
Largest	*Jupiter*
Smallest	*Mercury*
Moons, None	*Mercury, Venus*
Moon; Largest	*Ganymede (Jupiter), larger than Mercury*
Nearest to Earth	*Venus*
Orbits; Order	*Mercury (closest to Sun), Venus, Earth, Mars, Jupiter, Saturn, Uranus, Neptune.*
Rings/largest number	*Saturn*
Spin; Backwards	*Venus (East to West)*

COMETS

- It has a head and a tail. Its tail originates only when it gets closer to the sun. The tail can be 20-30 million km long. It always point away from the sun because of the force exerted by solar wind and radiation on the cometory material.

THE EARTH

- The earth is the third nearest planet to the Sun.
- From the outer space, the earth appears blue because its two-thirds surface is covered by water. It is, therefore, called a blue planet.
- It is the densest of all planets.
- Rotation is the movement of the earth on its axis. Due to this rotation, day and night occur.
- The earth takes about 23 hours 56 minutes and 4 seconds to complete one rotation around its axis.
- Earth takes 365¼ days (one year) to revolve around the sun.

THE EARTH: FACTS AND FIGURES

- *Mass of Earth*—5.972 × 10^{21} tonnes
- *Density of Earth*—5.517 times that of water
- *Volume of Earth*—1.083 × 10^{11} cubic km
- *Equatorial circumference*—4.007 × 104 km
- *Polar Diameter*—12,714 km
- *Equatorial Diameter*—12756 km
- *Polar or Meridional circumference*—4.0 × 10^4 km
- *Estimated Age*—At least 4600 million years
- *Land Surface*—148,951,000 sq km
- *Water Surface*—361,150,000 sq km (71 per cent of total area)
- *Highest Point of the land surface*—Mt. Everest (8,848 metres)
- *Lowest point of the land surface*—Shores of the Dead Sea (396 metres below the sea level)
- *Greatest Ocean depth*—Mariana Trench, East of Philippines (11,033 metres below the sea level)

THE MOON

- Earth has only one satellite, that is, the moon.
- Its diameter is only one-quarter that of the earth. It is about 3,84,400 km away from us.
- The moon moves around the earth in about 27 days. It takes exactly the same time to complete one spin. As a result, only one side of the moon (only 59% of its surface) is visible to us on the earth.
- Moonlight takes 1.3 sec. to reach earth.

LATITUDE

- Imaginary lines drawn parallel to the equator. Measured as an angle whose apex is at the centre of the earth.
- The equator represents 0° latitude, while the North Pole is 90°N and the South Pole 90°S.
- 23½°N represents Tropic of Cancer while 23½°S represents Tropic of Capricorn.

LONGITUDE

- It is the angular distance measured from the centre of the earth. On the globe the lines of longitude are drawn as a series of semicircles that extend from the North Pole to the South Pole through the equator. They are also called meridians.
- The distance between any two meridians is not equal. At the equator, 1 degree = 111 km. At 30°N or S, it is 96.5 km. It goes on decreasing this way until it is zero at the poles.

INTERNATIONAL DATE LINE

- It is the 180° meridian running over the Pacific Ocean, deviating at Aleutian Islands, Fiji, Samoa and Gilbert Islands.
- Travellers crossing the Date Line from west to east repeat a day and travellers crossing it from east to west lose a day.

INDIAN STANDARD TIME (IST)

- Indian Standard Time is calculated on the basis of 82.5°E longitude which passes through Uttar Pradesh, Madhya Pradesh, Odisha, Chattisgarh and Andhra Pradesh.

ECLIPSES

- Sun is the only source of light for both the Earth and Moon. Eclipses occur when the light thus received is either blocked by the earth or by the Moon.
- Eclipses occur when either the Earth moves behind the Moon's shadow or the Moon moves behind the Earth's shadow.

LUNAR ECLIPSE

- Lunar eclipse occur only when the following conditions are met.
  1. The Sun, Earth and Moon must be aligned in a straight line.
  2. The Earth must be positioned between the Sun and the Moon.
  3. The Moon must be in its full phase (Full Moon).

SOLAR ECLIPSE

- Solar eclipses occur only when the following conditions are met.
  1. The Sun, Earth and Moon must be aligned in a straight line.
  2. The Moon must be positioned between the Sun and the Earth.
  3. Must be a New Moon day.

ROCKS

- Rocks are composed of many minerals such as silica, aluminium, iron and magnesium. The nature of the rock is determined by the presence of its minerals.
- Rocks can be classified into three types:
  1. ***Igneous rocks*** are formed by magma that reaches the earth's surface along deep cracks and at volcanic vents. e.g., Mica, Granite etc.
  2. ***Sedimentary rocks*** are formed by the accumulation and cementation of mud, silt, or sand derived from weathered igneous rock frag-ments. e.g., Gravel, Peat, Gypsum etc.
  3. ***Metamorphic rocks*** are igneous or sedimentary rocks that have been altered by heat and/or pressure, either because they have been buried and folded deep in the crust, or because they have come into contact with molten igneous rock, e.g., Gneiss, Marble, Quartzite etc.

VOLCANOES

Sudden eruption of hot magma (molten rock), gases, ash and other material from inside the Earth to its surface.

- ***Active*** which erupts frequently, e.g., Mauna Loa (Hawaii), Etna (Sicily), Vesuvius (Italy), Stromboli (Mediterranean Sea).

- ***Dormant*** Not erupted for quite sometime, e.g., Fujiyama (Japan), Krakatoa (Indonesia), Barren Island (Andamans).
- ***Extinct*** Not erupted for several centuries, e.g., Arthur's Seat, Edinburgh, Scotland.

EARTHQUAKES

- Earthquakes are a form of wave energy that is transferred through bedrock. It is transmitted from the point of the earthquake focus, as spherical seismic waves. They travel in all directions outward.
- The intensity of earthquake waves is recorded by *Seismograph*.

LANDFORMS

- There are three major landforms: mountains, plateaus and plains.

MOUNTAINS

- A mountain can be defined as an area of land that rises abruptly from the surrounding region.
- There are three types of mountains- *Fold Mountains, Block Mountains* and the ***Volcanic Mountains***.
- Himalayas, Alps, Andes, Rockies, Atlas, etc are examples of Fold Mountains.
- The Aravali range in India is one of the oldest **fold mountain** systems in the world.
- The Rhine valley and the Vosges mountain in Europe are examples of such mountain systems.
- Volcanic mountains are formed due to volcanic activity.
- Mt. Kilimanjaro in Africa and Mt. Fujiyama in Japan are examples of such mountains.

Major Mountain Ranges of the World

Range	Location	Highest Peak (m)	Length (km)
Andes	South America	6,960	7,200
Himalayas-Karakoram-Hindukush	South Central Asia	8,848	4,800
Rockies	North America	4,401	4,800
Great Dividing Range	East Australia	2,228	3,600
Western Ghat	Western India	2,637	1,610
Caucasus	Europe	5,642	1,200
Alaska	USA	6,194	1,130
Alps	Europe	4,808	1,050
Apennines	Europe	2,912	—
Ural	Asia	1,895	—
Atlas	North West Africa	—	1,930

PLATEAUS

- A plateau is an elevated flat land. It is a flat-topped table land standing above the surrounding area.

Principal Mountain Peaks of the World

Mountains	Height in Metres
1. Mount Everest	8,848
2. K-2 (Godwin Austen)	8,611
3. Kanchenjunga	8,597
4. Lhotse	8,511
5. Makalu I	8,481
6. Dhaulagiri I	8,167
7. Mansalu I	8,156
8. Chollyo	8,153
9. Nanga Parbat	8,124
10. Annapurna I	8,091
11. Gasherbrum I	8,068
12. Broad Peak I	8,047
13. Gasherbrum II	8,034
14. Shisha Pangma (Gosainthan)	8,014
15. Gasherbrum III	7,952

PLAINS

- A relatively low-lying and flat land surface with least difference between its highest and lowest points is called a Plain.

OCEANS

- Oceans of the world is classified into four groups: the Pacific, the Atlantic, the Arctic and the Indian.
- The Pacific is the largest ocean, being twice the size of the Atlantic. It covers about a third of the Earth's surface, and contains more than half the water on the planet.

Oceans of the World

Names	Area (Sq. Km.)	Greatest Depth
Pacific	166,240000	Mariana Trench
Atlantic	86,560000	Puerto Rico Trench
Indian	73430000	Java Trench
Arctic	13230000	—

Major Rivers of the World

River	Origin	Falls in	Length (Km.)
Nile	Victoria lake	Mediterranean Sea	6,650
Amazon	Andes (Peru)	Atlantic Ocean	6,428
Yangtze	Tibetan Kiang Plateau	China Sea	6,300
Mississippi Missouri	Itaska lake (USA)	Gulf of Mexico (USA)	6,275
Yenisei	Tannu-Ola Mts.	Arctic Ocean	5,539
Hoang Ho	Kunlun Mts.	Gulf of Chibli	5,464
Ob	Altai Mts., Russia	Gulf of Ob	5,410
Congo	Lualaba & Luapula rivers	Atlantic Ocean	4,700
Amur	Northeast China	Sea of Okhotsk	4,444
Lena	Baikal Mts	Laptev Sea	4,400
Mekong	Tibetan Highlands	South China Sea	4,350
Mackenzie	Great Slave Lake	Beaufort Sea	4,241
Niger	Guinea	Gulf of Guinea	4,200

Major Gulfs of the World

Names	Area (Sq. Km.)	Names	Areas (Sq. Km.)
Gulf of Mexico	15,44,000	Gulf of St. Lawrence	2,37,000
Gulf of Hudson	12,33,000	Gulf of California	1,62,000
Arabian Gulf	2,38,000	English Channel	89,900

Important Straits of the World

Straits	Water Bodies joined	Area
Bab-al-Mandeb	Red Sea & Arabian Sea	Arabia & Africa
Bering	Arctic Ocean & Bering Sea	Alaska & Asia
Bosphorus	Black Sea & Marmara Sea	Turkey
Dover	North Sea & Atlantic Ocean	England & Europe
Florida	Gulf of Mexico & Atlantic Ocean	Florida & Bahamas Islands
Gibralter	Mediterranean Sea & Atlantic Ocean	Spain & Africa
Malacca	Java Sea & Bay of Bengal	India & Indonesia
Palk	Bay of Bengal & Indian Ocean	India & Sri Lanka
Magellan	South Pacific & South Atlantic Ocean	Chile
Sunda	Java Sea & Indian Ocean	Indonesia

Important Lakes of the World

Lake	Location	Area (Sq. Km.)
Caspian	Russia and CIS	371000
Superior	Canada and USA	82414
Victoria	Tanzania (Africa)	69485
Huron	Canada and USA	59596
Michigan	USA	58016
Tanganyika	Africa	32892
Baikal	Russia (CIS)	31502
Great Bear	Canada	31080
Malawi	Malawi (Tanzania)	30044
Great Slave	Canada	28438

Highest Waterfalls of the World

Name(s) (Foreign)	Location
Angel (Salto Angel)	Canaima Nat'l Park, Venezuela
Tugela	Natal Nat'l Park, South Africa
Utigord (Utigordsfoss)	Norway
Monge (Mongefoss)	Marstein, Norway
Gocta Cataracts	Chachapoyas, Peru
Mutarazi (Mtarazi)	Nyanga Nat'l Park, Zimbabwe
Yosemite	Yosemite Nat'l Park, California, U.S.
Espelands (Espelandsfoss)	Hardanger Fjord, Norway
Lower Mar Valley (Ostra Mardolafoss)	Eikesdal, Norway
Tyssestrengene	Odda, Norway

Important Cities on River Banks (World)

City	Country	River
Adelaide	Australia	Torrens
Amsterdam	Netherlands	Amsel
Alexandria	Egypt	Nile
Ankara	Turkiye	Kazil
Bangkok	Thailand	Chao Praya
Basra	Iraq	Eupharates and Tigris
Baghdad	Iraq	Tigris
Berlin	Germany	Spree
Bonn	Germany	Rhine
Budapest	Hungary	Danube
Bristol	UK	Avon
Buenos Aires	Argentina	Laplata
Chittagong	Bangladesh	Majyani
Canton	China	Si-Kiang
Cairo	Egypt	Nile
Chung King	China	Yang-tse-kiang
Cologne	Germany	Rhine
Dandzing	Germany	Vistula
Dresden	Germany	Elbe
Dublin	Ireland	Liffy
Hamburg	Germany	Elbe
Kabul	Afghanistan	Kabul
Karachi	Pakistan	Indus
Khortoum	Sudan	Confluence of Blue & White Nile
Lahore	Pakistan	Ravi
Leningrad	Russia	Neva
Lisbon	Portugal	Tagus
Liverpool	England	Messey
London	England	Thames
Moscow	Russia	Moskva
Montreal	Canada	St. Lawrence
Nanking	China	Yang-tse-kiang
New Orleans	U.S.A.	Mississipi
New York	U.S.A.	Hudson
Ottawa	Canada	Ottawa
Paris	France	Seine
Philadelphia	U.S.A	Delaware
Perth	Australia	Swan
Prague	Czech Republic	Vitava
Quebec	Canada	St. Lawrence
Rome	Italy	Tiber
Rotterdam	The Netherlands	New Moss
Stalingrad	Russia	Volga
Shanghai	China	Yang-tse-kiang
Sidney	Australia	Darling
Saint Louis	U.S.A	Mississippi
Tokyo	Japan	Arakava
Vienna	Austria	Danube
Warsaw	Poland	Vistula
Washington D.C.	U.S.A.	Potomac
Yangoon	Myanmar	Irawaddy

World's Geographical Surnames

City of Sky-scrapers—New York

City of Seven Hills—Rome

City of Dreaming Spires—Oxford

City of Golden Gate—San Francisco

City of Magnificent Buildings—Washington D.C.

City of Eternal Springs—Quito (S. America)

China's Sorrow—Hwang Ho

Cockpit of Europe—Belgium

Dark Continent—Africa

Emerald Isle—Ireland

Eternal City—Rome

Empire City—New York

Garden City—Chicago

Gate of Tears—Strait of Bab-el-Mandeb

Gift of the Nile—Egypt

Granite City—Aberdeen (Scotland)

Hermit Kingdom—Korea

Herring Pond—Atlantic Ocean

Holy Land—Jerusalem

Island Continent—Australia

Islands of Cloves—Zanzibar

Isle of Pearls—Bahrein (Persian Gulf)

Key to the Mediterranean—Gibralter

Land of Cakes—Scotland

Land of Golden Fleece—Australia

Land of Maple Leaf—Canada

Land of Morning Calm—Korea

Land of Midnight Sun—Norway

Land of the Thousand Lakes—Finland

Land of the Thunderbolt—Bhutan

Land of White Elephant—Thailand

Land of Thousand Elephants—Laos

Land of Rising Sun—Japan

Loneliest Island—Tristan De Gunha (Mid-Atlantic)

Manchester of Japan—Osaka

Pillars of Hercules—Strait of Gibraltar

Pearl of the Antilles—Cuba

Playground of Europe—Switzerland

Quaker City—Philadelphia

Queen of the Adriatic—Venice

Roof of the World—The Pamirs, Central Asia

Sugar bowl of the world—Cuba

Venice of the North—Stockholm

Windy City—Chicago
Whiteman's grave—Guinea Coast of Africa
Yellow River—Huang Ho (China)
Sickman of Europe—Turkiye

Important Boundaries

Durand Line	Pakistan & Afghanistan
MacMohan Line	India & China
Radcliff Line	India & Pakistan
Maginot Line	France & Germany
Oder Niesse Line	Germany & Poland
Hindenberg Line	Poland & Germany (at the time of First World War)
38th Parallel	North & South Korea
49th Parallel	USA & Canada

Continents: Some Facts

Continent	Biggest Counrty	Highest Peak	Longest River
Asia	China	Mt. Everest (8848 m)	Yangtze Kiang
Africa	Algeria	Mt. Kilimanjaro (5895 m)	Nile
North America	Canada	Mt. Mckinley (6194 m)	Mississippi Missouri
South America	Brazil	Mt. Acancagua (6960 m)	Amazon
Europe	Russia	Mt. Elbrus (5642 m)	Ob
Australia	Australia	Mt. Coscuisco (2228 m)	Darling
Antarctica	—	Vinson Massif (5140 m)	—

INDIAN GEOGRAPHY

AREA AND LOCATION

- India is in the southern parts of the Asian continent. In the west of India lies the Arabian Peninsula while in the east lies the Indo-China Peninsula.
- India extends between 8°4' N and 37°6' N latitudes and between 68°7' E and 97°2' E longitudes.
- India, has a total geographic area of 32,87,263 sq. km. This is only 2.42 % of the total geographic area of the world but holds 17 per cent of the world's population.
- The 23½°N, which is the Tropic of Cancer, runs across the country.
- India has a length of 3214 km from north to south and 2933 km from east to west. It has a land frontier of 15200 km.
- The total length of the coastline of the mainland, Lakshadweep Islands and Andaman and Nicobar Islands is 7,516.6 km.
- India ranks seventh among the countries of the world, in terms of the geographical extent.
- India is bordered on three sides by water and on one by land, it is also a peninsula.
- India shares its common border with Afghanistan and Pakistan in the north-west, China and Bhutan in the north, and Bangladesh in the east. In the south, Sri Lanka is separated from India by a strait, known as the Palk Strait.
- 82°30' E longitude is considered as the Indian Standard Meridian. The local time of this longitude is taken as the Indian Standard Time (IST). This is 5½ hours ahead of the Greenwich Mean Time.

THE INDIAN STATES ON INTERNATIONAL BOUNDARIES ARE:

- ***Bordering Pakistan:*** Jammu and Kashmir, Punjab, Rajasthan, Gujarat.
- ***Bordering China:*** Ladakh, Himachal Pradesh, Uttarakhand, Sikkim, Arunachal Pradesh.
- ***Bordering Nepal:*** Bihar, Uttarakhand, UP, Sikkim, West Bengal.
- ***Bordering Bangladesh:*** West Bengal, Mizoram, Meghalaya, Tripura, Assam.
- ***Bordering Bhutan:*** West Bengal, Sikkim, Arunachal Pradesh, Assam.
- ***Bordering Myanmar:*** Arunachal Pradesh, Nagaland, Manipur, Mizoram.
- ***Bordering Afghanistan:*** Jammu and Kashmir (Pakistan-occupied area).

Important Passes

• Jammu and Kashmir	Burzi-La, Joji-La
• Himachal Pradesh	Bara La, Cha-La, Shipki-La
• Uttarakhand	Niti-La, Lipu-Lekh-La
• Sikkim	Jelep-La, Nathu-La
• Arunachal Pradesh	Bomdi-La

Heighest Mountain Peaks of India

Peaks	Elevation• (in mts.)
Godwin Austin (K2)	8611*
Kanchenjunga	8598
Nanga Parvat	8126
Gasherbrum	8068*
Broad Peak	8047*
Dastegil	7885*
Masherbrum (East)	7821
Nanda Devi	7817
Masherbrum (West)	7806*
Rakoposhi	7788*
Kamet	7756
Saser Kangdi	7672

• *Above mean sea level in metres.*

* *Situated in Pak occupied Kashmir (PoK).*

Towns at River Banks

Town	River
Agra	Yamuna
Allahabad	Confluence of the Ganges and the Yamuna
Ayodhya	Saryu
Badrinath	The Ganges
Kolkata	Hooghly
Cuttuck	Mahanadi
Delhi	Yamuna
Dibrugarh	Brahmaputra
Ferozepur	Satluj
Guwahati	Brahmaputra
Hardwar	The Ganges
Hyderabad	Musi
Jabalpur	Narmada
Kanpur	The Ganges
Kota	Chambal
Kurnool	Tungbhadra
Lucknow	Gomti
Ludhiana	Sutlej
Nasik	Godavari
Pandharpur	Bhima
Patna	The Ganges
Sambalpur	Mahanadi
Srinagar	Jhelum
Srirangapattam	Cauveri
Surat	Tapti
Varanasi	The Ganges
Vijaywada	Krishna

Famous Waterfalls of India

Waterfall	Hgt (Mt.)	River	State
Kunchikal	455	Varahi	Karnataka
Dudhsagar	310	Mandvi	Goa
Jog/Gersoppa	255	Sharavati	Karnataka
Rakim Kund	168	Gaighat	Bihar
Chachai	127	Bihad	Madhya Pradesh
Kevti	98	Mahanadi	Madhya Pradesh
Sivasamudram	90	Cauveri	Karnataka

Important Lakes of India

Name of lake	State/UT
Pulicat Lake	Tamil Nadu & Andhra Pradesh Border
Sambhar Lake	Rajasthan
Tso Moriri Lake	Jammu & Kashmir
Vembanad Lake	Kerala
Wular & Dal Lakes	Jammu and Kashmir
Chilka Lake	Odisha
Kolleru Lake	Andhra Pradesh
Loktak Lake	Manipur
Lonar Lake	Maharashtra
Pangong Lake	Ladakh

Rivers of India

Name	Originates From	Falls Into
Yamuna	Yamunotri	Ganga
Chambal	Singar Chouri Peak, Vindhyan escarpment	Yamuna
Ghaghara	Matsatung Glacier	Ganga
Kosi	Near Gosain Dham Peak	Ganga
Sabarmati	Aravalis	Gulf of Khambat
Krishna	Western Ghats	Bay of Bengal
Godavari	Nasik district in Maharashtra	Bay of Bengal
Caurey	Brahmagir Range of Western Ghats	Bay of Bengal
Tungabharda	Western Ghats	Krishna
Ganges	Combines Sources	Bay of Bengal

Name	Originates From	Falls Into
Sutlej	Mansarovar Rakas lakes	Chenab
Indus	Near Mansarovar Lake	Arabian Sea
Ravi	Kullu Hills near Rohtang Pass	Chenab
Beas	Near Rohtang Pass	Sutlej
Jhelum	Verinag in Kashmir	Chenab
Son	Amarkantak	Ganga
Brahmaputra	Near Mansarovar Lake	Bay of Bengal
Narmada	Amarkantak	Gulf of Khambat
Tapti	Betul District in Madhya Pradesh	Gulf of Khambat
Mahanadi	Raipur District in Chhattisgarh	Bay of Bengal
Luni	Aravallis	Rann of Kuchchh
Ghaggar	Himalayas	Near Fatehabad
Betwa	Vindhyanchal	Yamuna

Geographical Surnames

Bengal's Sorrow	Damodar River
City of Palaces	Kolkata
Gateway of India	Mumbai
Pink City	Jaipur
Paris of India	Jaipur
Manchester of India	Ahmedabad
Kashmir of South	Kerala
Son of Sea	Lakshadweep
Queen of Mountains	Mussourie
Iron City	Jamshedpur
Hollywood of India	Mumbai
Scotland of East	Meghalaya
City of Nababs	Lucknow
City of Temples & Ghats	Varanasi
Land of Five Rivers	Punjab
City of Golden Temple	Amritsar
Garden of India	Bangaluru
Spice Garden of India	Kerala
City of Lakes	Srinagar
Twin City	Hyderabad-Secunderabad
City of Seven Islands	Mumbai
Diamond Harbour	Kolkata
Switzerland of India	Kashmir
Rice Bowl	Chhattisgarh
Fruit Bowl	Himachal Pradesh
Ganga of South	Cauvery
Pitsburg of India	Jamshedpur
City of Bridges	Srinagar
Residence of God	Allahabad
A Cross-road (Quadrivial) of National Highways	Kanpur
Heart of India	Delhi
Black River	Sharda
City of Festivals	Madurai
Queen of Deccan	Pune
Sorrow of Bihar	Kosi River

Some Major Irrigational and Multipurpose Projects

S.No.	Name of Project	Related State	River
1.	Bargi Project	Madhya Pradesh	Bargi
2.	Beas	Joint Venture of Haryana, Punjab and Rajasthan	Beas
3.	Bhadra	Karnakata	Bhadra
4.	Bhakra Nangal	Haryana, Punjab and Rajasthan	Sutluj
5.	Bhima I	Maharashtra	Pawana
6.	Bhima II	Maharashtra	Krishna
7.	Chambal	Joint Project of M.P. and Rajasthan	Chambal
8.	Damodar Valley Project	West Bengal and Bihar	Damodar
9.	Dulhasti Power Project	Jammu and Kashmir	Chenab
10.	Farakka	West Bengal	Hooghly

S.No.	Name of Project	Related State	River
11.	Gandak	Bihar and U.P.	Gandak
12.	Ghataprabha	Karnataka	Ghataprabha
13.	Hasdeo Bango Project	Madhya Pradesh, Chhattisgarh	Hasdeo
14.	Hirakud	Odisha	Mahanadi
15.	Jayakwadi	Maharashtra	Godavari
16.	Kakrapara	Gujarat	Tapti
17.	Kangsbati	West Bengal	Kangsbati and Kumari
18.	Karjan	Gujarat	Karjan
19.	Kosi	Bihar	Kosi
20.	Koyana	Maharashtra	Koyana
21.	Krishna Project	Maharashtra	Krishna
22.	Kukadi	Maharashtra	Kukadi
23.	Left Bank Ghagra Canal	Uttar Pradesh	Ghagra
24.	Madhya Ganga Canal	Uttar Pradesh	Ganga
25.	Mahanadi Delta Scheme	Odisha	(The irrigation scheme will utilise releases from Hirakund Reservoir)
26.	Mahi	Gujarat	Mahi
27.	Malaprabha	Karnataka	Malaprabha
28.	Mayurakshi	West Bengal	Mayurakshi
29.	Nagarjunasagar	Andhra Pradesh	Krishna
30.	Panam	Gujarat	Panam
31.	Parambikulam Aliyar	Tamil Nadu and Kerala	Perimbikulam
32.	Pochampad	Andhra Pradesh	Godavari
33.	Pong Dam	Punjab	Beas
34.	Ramganga	Uttarakhand	Ramganga
35.	Ranjit Sagar Dam (Thein Dam)	Punjab	Ravi
36.	Rihand	Uttar Pradesh	Rihand
37.	Sabarmati	Gujarat	Sabarmati
38.	Sharda Sahayak	U.P.	Ghagra
39.	Sone High Level Canal	Bihar	Sone
40.	Tawa	Madhya Pradesh	Tawa
41.	Tehri Dam	Uttarakhand	Bhagirathi
42.	Tungabhadra	Andhra Pradesh and Karnataka	Tungabhadra
43.	Ukai	Gujarat	Tapti
44.	Upper Krishna	Karnataka	Krishna
45.	Upper Penganga	Maharashtra	Penganga
46.	Uri Power Project	Jammu and Kashmir	Jhelum

Major Indian Crops

Crops	Temp(°c)	Water(cm)	States where Produced
Wheat	15°-25°	60-90	Uttar Pradesh, Madhya Pradesh, Punjab, Haryana.
Rice	24°-26°	80-200	West Bengal, Uttar Pradesh, Punjab, Andhra Pradesh, Bihar
Maize	18°-21°	50-60	Karnataka, Madhya Pradesh, Maharashtra
Jowar	20°-35°	40-60	Maharashtra, Madhya Pradesh, Karnataka
Soyabean	25°-27°	50-120	Maharashtra, Madhya Pradesh, Rajasthan
Cotton	20°-30°	80-150	Gujarat, Maharashtra, Telangana, Karnataka, Madhya Pradesh
Tobacco	20°-25°	75-80	Andhra Pradesh, Madhya Pradesh, Gujarat, Karnataka, Maharashtra, Uttar Pradesh
Tea	24°-30°	100-200	Assam, West Bengal, Kerala, Tamil Nadu, Uttar Pradesh
Ground Nut	15°-25°	60-130	Gujarat, Maharashtra

Mineral Wealth at a Glance (Metallic Minerals)

Mineral	Chief Producers
Bauxite	Odisha, Gujarat, Jharkhand
Chromite	Odisha, Karnataka
Coal	Jharkhand, Odisha
Copper	Rajasthan, Madhya Pradesh
Diaspore	Uttar Pradesh, Madhya Pradesh
Gold	Karnataka
Iron	Odisha, Karnataka, Goa
Lead	Rajasthan, Andhra Pradesh
Lignite	Tamil Nadu, Jammu & Kashmir
Manganese	Odisha, Karnataka
Natural Gas	Gujarat, Assam
Petroleum	Gujarat, Assam, Andhra Pradesh
Silver	Rajasthan, Jharkhand, Gujarat
Tungsten	Rajasthan
Zinc	Rajasthan, Maharashtra

Zones and Headquarters of Indian Railways

S.No.	Zone	Headquarters
1.	Central	Mumbai
2.	Eastern	Kolkata
3.	Northern	New Delhi
4.	North-Eastern	Gorakhpur
5.	North-East Frontier	Maligaon, Guwahati
6.	Southern	Chennai
7.	South-Central	Secunderabad
8.	South-Eastern	Kolkata
9.	Western	Mumbai
10.	East Coast	Bhubaneswar
11.	East Central	Hajipur
12.	North Central	Prayagraj
13.	North Western	Jaipur
14.	South Western	Hubballi (Hubli)
15.	West Central	Jabalpur
16.	South East Central	Bilaspur
17.	Metro Railway	Kolkata
18.	South Coast Railway	Vishakhapatnam (Proposed)

Major National Highways

N H	Connects
NH 44	Srinagar to Kanyakumari
NH 27	Porbandar to Silchar
NH 48	Delhi to Chennai
NH 52	Sangrur to Ankola
NH 30	Sitarganj to Ibrahimpatnam
NH 6	Jorabat to Seling
NH 53	Hazira to Paradip
NH 16	East Coast (West Bengal) to Chennai
NH 66	Panvel to Kanyakumari
NH 19	Delhi to Kolkata

Major Ports of Country

1. Syama Prasad Mookerjee (Kolkata)
2. Mumbai
3. J.L. Nehru Port (Nhava Sheva)
4. V.O. Chidambaranar (Tuticorin)
5. Chennai
6. Mormugao
7. New Mangalore
8. Paradeep
9. Deendayal (Kandla)
10. Vishakhapatnam
11. Cochin
12. Kamarajar Port Limited (Ennore).

Major International Airports in India

International Airports	City
Indira Gandhi International Airport	Delhi
Anna International Airport	Chennai
Sri Guru Ram Dass Ji International Airport	Amritsar
Rajiv Gandhi International Airport	Hyderabad
Calicut International Airport	Kozhikode
Chhatrapati Shivaji International Airport	Mumbai
Kempegowda International Airport	Bengaluru
Goa Airport in Vasco di Gama City	Goa
Netaji Subash Chandra Bose International Airport	Kolkata
Thriuvananthapuram International Airport	Thiruvananthapuram
Lokpriya Gopinath Bordoloi International Airport	Guwahati
Sardar Vallabhbhai Patel International Airport	Ahmedabad

❐❐❐

INDIAN POLITY

INDIAN CONSTITUTION

- Demand for a Constituent Assembly composed of the people of India officially asserted by the Congress for the first time in 1935.
- The election for Indian Constitution Assembly held in 1946 according to the *Cabinet Mission Plan*.
- The first session of the Assembly was held in New Delhi on December 9, 1946. *Sachidanand Sinha* was elected provisional chairman of the session.
- On December 11, 1946, Dr. Rajendra Prasad was elected as the Permanent Chairman of the Constituent Assembly.
- The Constitution was framed by the Constituent Assembly of India, set-up in December 1946, in accordance with the Cabinet Mission Plan, under the Chairmanship of Sachidanand Sinha, initially.
- The total membership of Constituent Assembly after partition was 299, among them 70 were representatives from the Indian states and others from British India.
- The Chairman of the Drafting Committee was **Dr. BR Ambedkar**, also called the Father of the Constitution.
- The Constituent Assembly took 2 years, 11 months and 18 days to complete the Constitution.
- The Constitution, adopted on 8th November, 1949, contained 395 Articles and Schedules.
- The Constitution was delayed till 26th January because, in 1929, on this day Indian National Congress demanded Poorna Swaraj in Lahore Session under JL Nehru.
- Indian Constitution is a comprehensive document and it is the lengthiest written Constitution in the World.

THE PREAMBLE

- ***The Preamble of the Constitution:*** "We the people of India, having solemnly resolved to Constitute India into a Sovereign, Socialist, Secular Democratic Republic and to secure to all its citizen:

  Justice, Social, economic and political;

  Liberty of thought, expression, belief, faith and worship;

  Equality of status and of opportunity; and to promote among them all;

  Fraternity assuring the dignity of the individual and the unity and integrity of the nation;

  In our Constituent Assembly, this twenty-sixth day of November, 1949, do hereby adopt, enact and give to ourselves this constitution."

Foreign Sources of Indian Constitution

Foreign Sources	*Subject*
Britain	Parliamentary system, collective responsibilities of Cabinet
America	Fundamental right, Independent Judiciary, Judicial review
Canada	Division of powers
Ireland	Directive principles
Germany	Emergency provisions
Russia	Fundamental duties
Australia	Concurrent list

IMPORTANT ARTICLES

PART - I

UNION AND ITS TERRITORIES (ARTICLE 1 - 4)

- The Constitution says, "India, that is Bharat, shall be a Union of States".
- Parliament has the power to create any State, reduce it, change the name of boundaries of any State.

PART - II

CITIZENSHIP (ARTICLE 5 - 11)

- The Constitution provides for a single Citizenship.
- ***Indian Citizenship can be acquire:***
  1. by birth
  2. by descent
  3. by registration
  4. by naturalisation
  5. by incorporation of territory
- ***Indian Citizenship can be lost by:***
  1. renunciation;
  2. termination — it takes place if a citizen of India voluntary acquires the citizenship of another country; and
  3. deprivation — if the Government terminates the citizenship.

PART - III

FUNDAMENTAL RIGHTS (ARTICLE 12 - 35)

- Following fundamental rights are enjoyed by every Indian citizen, irrespective of caste, colour, creed and sex:
  1. ***Right to Equality:*** No special privileges, no distinction on grounds of religion, caste, creed and sex.
  2. ***Right to Freedom:*** The right to freedom of expression and speech, the right to choose one's own profession, the right to reside in any part of the Indian Union.
  3. ***Right to Freedom to Religion:*** Except when it is in the interest of public order, morality, health or other conditions, everybody has the right to profess, practice and propagate his religion freely.
  4. ***Cultural and Educational Rights:*** The Constitution provides that every community can run its own institutions to preserve its own culture and language.
  5. ***Right against Exploitation:*** Traffic in human beings and forced labour and the employment of children under 14 years in factories or mines, are punishable offences.
  6. ***Rights to Constitutional Remedies:*** When a citizen finds that any of his fundamental rights has been encroached upon, he can move the Supreme Court, which has been empowered to safeguard the fundamental rights of a citizen (Article 32).

PART - IV

DIRECTIVE PRINCIPLES OF STATE POLICY (ARTICLE 36 - 51)

- Directive principles are not enforceable through courts. Main aim of Directive principles is to provide social and economic base of a genuine democracy.

Some Important Directive Principles:

- Provisions for adequate means of livelihood for all citizens (Art. 39).
- Right to work (Art. 41).
- Right to human condition of work and maternity relief (Art. 42).
- Right to a living wage and condition of work ensuring decent standard of life of worker (Art. 43).
- Common Civil Code (Art. 44).
- Prohibit consumption of liquor (Art. 47).
- Prevent slaughter of useful cattle (Art. 48).
- Organise Panchayati Raj (Art. 40).
- Separate the judiciary from the executive (Art. 50).
- Protect and maintain places of historic monuments (Art. 49).
- International peace (Art. 51).

PART - IV A

FUNDAMENTAL DUTIES (ARTICLE 51A)

- The fundamental duties for the Indian citizens have been incorporated in the Constitution through the Constitution (42nd) Amendment Act, 1976. These duties are:

1. to abide by the Constitution and respect its ideals and institutions, the National Flag and the National Anthem;
2. to cherish and follow the noble deeds which inspired our national struggle for freedom;
3. to uphold and protect the sovereignty, unity and integrity of India;
4. to defend the country and render national service when called upon to do so;
5. to promote harmony and the spirit of common brotherhood amongst all the people transcending religious, regional or sectional diversities and to renounce practices derogatory to the dignity of women;
6. to value and preserve the rich heritage of our composite culture;
7. to protect and improve natural environment including forests, lakes, rivers and wildlife, and to have compassion for living creatures;
8. to develop the scientific temper, humanism and the spirit of inquiry and reform;
9. to safeguard public property and to abjure violence;
10. to strive towards excellence in all spheres of individual and collective activity so that the nation constantly rises to higher levels of endeavour and achievement.
11. who is parent or guardian to provide opportunities for education to his child or, as the case may be, ward between age of six and fourteen years.

PART - V

UNION (ARTICLE 52 - 151)

THE PRESIDENT

- The President is the Constitutional head of the Republic of India. He is more or less the titular head of the executive.
- He is the constitutional head but not the real executive. The real power is vested in the hands of the Council of Ministers.
- President is the first citizen of India.
- ***Qualifications:*** (i) Indian citizen, (ii) age not less than 35 years, (iii) should have qualification for election to Lok Sabha, (iv) should not hold any office of profit, (v) should not be a Member of Parliament or State Legislature.
- ***Election:*** Indirectly elected through Electoral College consisting of elected members of both the Houses of the Parliament and elected members of the Legislative Assemblies of the States.
- According to the 70th Amendment Act, 1992, the expression 'States' include the National Capital Territory of Delhi and the Union Territory of Puducherry. Members of the Legislative Councils have no right to vote in the Presidential election.

- ***Powers:*** He makes appointments to all the constitutional posts.
- He can address either House of Parliament and dissolve Lok Sabha.
- All Bills passed by Parliament must receive his assent to become an Act.
- He issues ordinances when Parliament is not in session. No Money Bill can be introduced in Lok Sabha without his recommendation.
- He appoints 12 members of special repute in the Rajya Sabha.
- He has the power of *Pardon* to a criminal in special cases.
- The President holds the office for a period of five years. He is eligible for re-election.
- He draws a fix salary per month with various allowances.
- He is also entitled to rent free official residence called Rashtrapati Bhawan.

Vice-President

- ***Article 63*** of the Constitution stipulates a Vice-President for India.
- The Vice-President acts as the ex-officio Chairman of the Council of States (Rajya Sabha).
- He is elected by an electoral college consisting of the members of both Houses of Parliament in accordance with the system of proportional represen-tation by means of the single trans-ferable vote. He must be a citizen of India, not less than 35 years of age, and should be eligible for election as a member of the Council of States.
- Disputes in connection with election of a president or a vice-president are to be a dealt with in accordance with Article-71. Such disputes shall be decided by the Supreme Court.

Council of Ministers

- The Constitution of India provides for a parliament system of government under which the President is only Constitutional ruler and the real power is exercised by the Council of Ministers, headed by the Prime Minister.
- Council of Ministers is composed of all Union Ministers—the Prime Minister, Cabinet Ministers and Ministers of State.
- The Council of Ministers is Collectively responsible to the Lok Sabha.
- The Prime Minister is a link between the President and the Council of Ministers.

Prime Minister

- The Prime Minister is the leader of the majority party in the Parliament.
- He is appointed by the President. Other Ministers are appointed by the president on his advice.
- The Prime Minister is the head of the Government and the head of the Council of Ministers.
- Jawaharlal Nehru was the first Prime Minister and the longest serving so far.

Union Legislature

- The Legislature of the Union, which is called 'Parliament' consists of the President and the two Houses of Parliament known as the Council of states (Rajya Sabha) and the House of the People (Lok Sabha).

RAJYA SABHA

- The Rajya Sabha is the Upper House of the Parliament and it is constituted of representatives from the States or the Constituent units of the Indian Union.
- It is a permanent body, one third of its members retiring after every two years.
- Its maximum strength is 250. Out of these, twelve members are nominated by the President from well-known personalities in the realm of Science, Art, Literature and Social Service. Rest of 238 representatives of the States and Union Territories are elected.
- Currently, the strength of the Rajya Sabha is 245.

LOK SABHA

- The Lok Sabha whose life is five years, is the Lower House of Parliament and comprises of members directly elected by the people.
- The House of the people (Lok Sabha) at present consists of 543 directly elected members from the states and Union Territories.
- Two members of Anglo-Indian Community were nominated by the President, but by the 104th amendment of the constitution this provision have been abolished.
- The House of the People shall continue for five years (unless sooner dissolved) from the date of its meeting and no longer and the expiry of the said period of 5 years shall operate as dissolution of the House.

Parliamentary Committees

- There are several Parliamentary Committees to assist the Parliament in its deliberations.
- These are appointed or elected by the respective Houses of Lok Sabha and Rajya Sabha on a motion made or are nominated by their presiding officers.
- Among the Standing Committees, three are financial Committees:

  (*i*) Public Account Committee;

  (*ii*) Estimate Committee;

  (*iii*) Public undertaking Committee.

Speaker of Lok Sabha

- Speaker is elected by the Lok Sabha from among its members.
- The Speaker will have the final power to maintain order within the House of the People and to interpret its rules of procedure.
- A Deputy-Speaker is also elected to officiate in absence of the Speaker.
- *G.V. Mavlankar* was the first Speaker of the Lok Sabha (1952-1956).

Supreme Court

- The Constitution provides for the Supreme Court, which consists of Chief Justice and 33 judges. They are appointed by the President of India.

QUALIFICATION AND TENURE

- Eligibility conditions for a judge of the Supreme Court are that he must be : (i) a citizen of India; (ii) a judge of a high court for a minimum period of 5 years; or (iii) an advocate of a high court for at least ten years or a distinguished jurist.
- Judges hold office till the age of 65.
- They can resign earlier or can be removed by the President on the recommendation of the two Houses of the Parliament by 2/3rd majority of the members present and voting.

Powers

- *Original jurisdiction:* Cases involving Government of India and the states or cases involving the enforcement of Fundamental Rights fall under original jurisdiction.
- *Appellate Jurisdiction:* In cases which are brought to it in the form of appeals against the judgement of the lower courts—It hears appeals in civil and criminal cases.
- *Advisory functions:* the Supreme Court advises the President on the constitutionality of a particular legal matter. However, its advice is not binding on the President.

Other Powers:

1. it is a court of record and can punish for contempt of itself;
2. it can make rules for regulating the practice and procedure of courts with the approval of the President; and
3. it can recommend to the President the removal of chairman and members of the UPSC. Supreme Court enjoys the power of judicial review (right of the court which declares as unconstitutional, the laws passed by the legislature and orders issued by executive) though it is not specifically mentioned in the Constitution.

- The first Chief Justice of India was H.J. Kania (1950-51).

COMPTROLLER AND AUDITOR GENERAL (CAG) (ARTICLE 148-151)

- The Comptroller and Auditor General of India is guardian of the public purse.
- It is his duty to see that not a *paisa* is spent out of consolidated fund of India or of a state without the authority of the appropriate legislature.
- He is appointed by President of India.
- A person with long administrative experience and knowledge of accounts is appointed.
- Holds office for 6 yrs or till 65 yrs of age.
- The President can remove him only on the recommendation of the 2 houses of Parliament (as in case of judge of Supreme Court).
- The CAG submits its reports to the President (in case of accounts relating to the Union Government) or to the State Governors (for State Government Accounts).
- The first CAG of India was *V Narahari Rao* (1948-1954).
- The CAG is not eligible for further office under the Union or State Governments. The expenses of the office of the CAG is charged to the Consolidated Fund of India.

ATTORNEY GENERAL OF INDIA

- The Attorney General of India is the first law officer of the Government of India.
- Though he is not a member of cabinet he has the right to speak in the House of Parliament, but he has no right to vote.
- The Attorney General of India shall be appointed by the President and shall hold office during his pleasure.
- His duty shall be to give advice on such legal matter from time-to-time as may be referred to him by the President.
- To be appointed as Attorney General, a candidate must be qualified to be appointed as a Judge of the Supreme Court.
- The Attorney General can participate in proceedings of the Parliament without the Right to Vote (Article 88).
- The first Attorney General of Independent India was MC Setalvad (1950-1963).

PART - VI

THE STATES (ARTICLE 152 - 237)

The Governor

- The Governor is appointed by the President and holds office during the pleasure of the President.
- Apart from the power to appoint the council of ministers, if the governor finds that the government of state cannot be carried on in accordance with the provisions of the constitution (Art. 356), he may send his report to the President who may assume to himself the functions of the government of the state. (This is popularly known as 'President's Rule').
- Article 161 gives the Governor the power to grant pardons, reprieves, remission of punishment to persons convicted under the state law.

- Article 171 states that the States where Legislative Councils exists, the Governor can nominate some members from amongst those distinguished in literature, science, arts, cooperative movement and social service.

STATES LEGISLATURE (ARTICLE 168 - 212)

- The state legislature consists of Governor and legislative assembly.
- In some state like *Bihar, Maharashtra, Andhra Pradesh, Karnataka, Uttar Pradesh and Telangana* have a legislative council.
- The membership of the council should not be more than *one-third* of the legislative assembly but not less than 40.
- The legislative assembly of each state shall be composed of members chosen by direct election on the basis of adult suffrage and the number of members shall not be more than 500 or less than 60.
- The assembly of Sikkim, Goa, Puducherry and Mizoram have less than 60 members.

HIGH COURTS (ARTICLE 214-232)

- The High Court stands at the apex of the State Judiciary.
- As per the Constitution, there shall be a High Court in each State. But there may be a common High Court for two or more States and Union Territory, if it is provided by a law of the Parliament. For example, the Madras High Court has its Jurisdiction over the State of Tamil Nadu and the Union Territory of Puducherry.
- The State Government has no control over it.
- There are 25 High Courts in India.
- The Calcutta High Court, established in 1862, is the oldest High Court in India.

THE PANCHAYATS (ARTICLE 243-243 O)

- Panchayati Raj was introduced in India with a view to associate the people with administration at grass-root level.
- It is a three-tier system as recommended by Balwant Rai Mehta Committee.
- Introduced by the 73rd Amendment Act, 1992 which envisaged a three tier system of local governance.

  These are:

  1. Gram Panchayat at the village level
  2. Panchayat Samiti at the block level
  3. Zila Parishad at the district level.

Jurisdiction and Seat of High Courts

Name	Territorial Jurisdiction	Seat
Allahabad	Uttar Pradesh	Prayagraj (Bench at Lucknow)
Bombay	Maharashtra, Goa, Dadar and Nagar Haveli and Daman and Diu	Mumbai (Benches at Nagpur, Panaji and Aurangabad)
Calcutta	West Bengal and Andaman & Nicobar	Kolkata (Circuit Benchs at Port Blair and Jalpaiguri)
Chhattisgarh	Chhattisgarh	Bilaspur
Delhi	Delhi	Delhi
Gauhati	Assam, Nagaland, Mizoram and Arunachal Pradesh	Guwahati (Benches at Kohima, Aizawl and Itanagar)
Gujarat	Gujarat	Ahmedabad
Himachal Pradesh	Himachal Pradesh	Shimla
Jammu & Kashmir and Ladakh	Jammu & Kashmir, Ladakh	Srinagar and Jammu
Jharkhand	Jharkhand	Ranchi
Karnataka	Karnataka	Bengaluru (Circuit Benches at Dharwar and Gulbarga)
Kerala	Kerala & Lakshadweep	Ernakulam
Madhya Pradesh	Madhya Pradesh	Jabalpur (Benches at Gwalior and Indore)
Madras	Tamil Nadu & Puducherry	Chennai (Bench at Madurai)
Orissa	Odisha	Cuttack
Patna	Bihar	Patna
Punjab and Haryana	Punjab, Haryana and Chandigarh	Chandigarh
Rajasthan	Rajasthan	Jodhpur (Bench at Jaipur)
Sikkim	Sikkim	Gangtok
Uttarakhand	Uttarakhand	Nainital
Tripura	Tripura	Agartala
Meghalaya	Meghalaya	Shillong
Manipur	Manipur	Imphal
Telangana	Telangana	Hyderabad
Andhra Pradesh	Andhra Pradesh	Amravati

THE MUNICIPALITIES (ARTICLE 243 P-243 ZG)

- Big cities have municipal corporations headed by the elected Mayor.
- For small towns there are elected boards or councils, in turn, elect their Presidents.
- Introduced by the 74th Amendment Act, 1993 which envisages three types of urban local bodies, namely, municipality (nagar palika), city council (nagar panchayat).
- Municipal governance in India was first introduced in Madras in 1688.

PART - XIII

(ARTICLE 301 - 307)

- In this part from Article 301-307 trade, commerce and intercourse within the territory of India are given.

PART - XIV

(ARTICLE 308 - 323)

- In this part services under the union and the states are given.
- ***Article 312:** All India Services* and ***Article 315:*** Public Service Commissions for the Union and for the States.
- The first Public Service Commission was set up in 1926, on the recommendations of the Lee Commission.

UNION PUBLIC SERVICE COMMISSION (UPSC)

- This Commission is responsible for:
  1. recruitment to all civil services and posts, under the Union Government by written examinations, interviews and promotions, and
  2. advising the Government on all matters relating to methods of recruitment, principles to be followed in making promotions and transfers. Its Chairman is appointed by the President.

STAFF SELECTION COMMISSION (SSC)

- The Union Government has constituted a Staff Selection Commission for recruitment to non-technical Class III posts in the central government and in subordinate offices.
- The Administrative Reforms Commission had recommended the setting up of such a Commission.
- The Commission has also been entrusted with the responsibility of making recruitment to Group 'B' services like Assistants' and Stenographers Grade 'C'.
- The Commission has a chairman and two members.

ELECTIONS (ARTICLE 324-329)

- The Constitution provides for an independent election commission to ensure free and fair election to the Parliament, the State legislature and the offices of President and Vice-President.
- Consists of Chief Election Commissioner +2 Election Commissioners. They all enjoy equal powers.
- The Chief Election Commissioner and other Election Commissioners are appointed by the President.
- Election Commissioners are appointed for a term of 5 yrs.
- They are not eligible for re-appointment. Also, they cannot hold any office of profit after their retirement.
- The Election Commission was established on 25th January, 1950 under Article 324 of the Constitution.
- The first Chief Election Commissioner was *Sukumar Sen.*

Functions

- Preparation of electoral rolls and keeping voters list updated.
- Recognition of various political parties and allotment of election symbols.

NITI AAYOG

- The Indian government has replaced Planing Commission with a new institution named **NITI Aayog (National Institution for Transforming India).**
- The Niti Aayog will comprise the following:
  1. Prime Minister of India as the Chairperson.
  2. Governing Council comprising the Chief Ministers of all the States and Lt. Governors of Territories.
  3. Regional Councils will be formed to address specific issues and contingencies impacting more than one state or a region. These will be formed for a specified tenure. The Regional Councils will be convened by the Prime Minister and will comprise of the Chief Ministers of States and Lt. Governors of Territories in the region. These will be chaired by the Chairperson of the NITI Aayog or his nominee.
  4. Experts, specialists and practitioners with relevant domain knowledge as special invitees nominated by the Prime Minister.
- The full-time organizational framework will comprise of, in addition to the Prime Minister as the Chairperson:
  1. Vice-Chairperson : To be appointed by the Prime Minister.
  2. Members : Full-time. : 3
  3. Part-time members : Maximum of 2 from leading universities research organizations and other relevant institutions in an ex-officio capacity. Part time members will be on a rotational basis.
  4. Ex Officio members : Maximum of 4 members of the Council of Ministers to be nominated by the Prime Minister.
  5. Chief Executive Officer : To be appointed by the Prime Minister for a fixed tenure, in the rank of Secretary to the Government of India.
  6. Secretariat as deemed necessary.

FINANCE COMMISSION

- The constitution of the Finance Commission is laid down in Art. 280.
- The chairman must be a person having experience in public affairs; and the other four members also having wide experience in financial matters.
- It consists of Chairman and 4 other members.
- It shall be the duty of the Finance Commission to advice the President on matters such as the distribution between the Union and States of the net proceeds of taxes that is required to be shared.
- The Finance Commission is not a permanent body. It is dissolved after it has submitted its recommendations.

Important Amendments to the Constitution

First Amendment, 1951	:	Added Ninth Schedule.
Twenty-second Amendment, 1969	:	Formation of Meghalaya within the state of Assam was facilitated.
Twenty-sixth Amendment, 1971	:	The privy and privileges of the former rulers of Indian States were abolished.
Thirty-first Amendment, 1973	:	The upper limit of representation of states was raised from 500 to 525. The upper limit for representation of the UTs was reduced from 25 to 20.
Thirty-sixth Amendment, 1975	:	Sikkim was made a full-fledged state of Indian Union and it was included in the First Schedule.
Thirty-eight Amendment, 1975	:	This act led to the amendment of Article 123, Article 213 and Article 352 which stated that the satisfaction of President or of Governor contained in these Articles would be called in question in any court of law.
Forty-second Amendment, 1976	:	This amendment was done in accordance with the recommendations of Swaran Singh Committee and included a number of amendments.
Forty-third Amendment, 1977	:	It provided for the restoration of the Jurisdiction of the Supreme Court and High Courts, curtailed by the enactment of the Constitution (Forty-Second Amendment) Act, 1976.
Forty-fourth Amendment, 1978	:	The right to property was deleted as Fundamental Right and was made a legal right.
Fifty-third Amendment, 1986	:	The Act grants statehood to the Union Territory of Mizoram, thus making it the 23rd State of the Indian Unions.
Fifty-sixth Amendment, 1987	:	The UT of Goa converted into Goa state through this amendment whereas Daman and Diu were organised under a new UT.
Seventy-third Amendment, 1992	:	It is concerning Panchayati Raj.
Seventy-fourth Amendment, 1992	:	It is regarding Municipal Boards and Corporations.
Eighty-ninth Amendment, 2003	:	It provides for constitution of a separate National Commission for Scheduled Tribes. (Earlier, there was a combined National Commission for both SC/STs).
Ninety-first Amendment, 2003	:	It is regarding restricting the total number of Ministers including Prime Minister/ Chief Minister in Lok Sabha and State Legislatures to 15% of the total number of the Union or State Legislatures.
Ninety-ninth Amendment, 2015	:	The amendment is in toto quashed by Supreme Court on 16 October, 2015.
One hundredth Amendment, 2015	:	Exchange of certain enclave territories with Bangladesh and conferment of citizenship rights to residents of enclaves consequent to signing of Land Boundary Agreement (LBA) Treaty between India and Bangladesh.
One hundredth and first Amendment, 2016	:	The act amends the Constitution to introduce "The Goods and Services Tax (GST)."
One hundredth and Third Amendment, 2019	:	The Act providing 10 per cent reservation in government jobs and educational institutions to Economically Weaker Sections (EWS) of General Category, came into effect on January 14, 2019.
One hundredth and Fourth Amendment, 2019	:	This Act ceased the reservation of seats for Anglo-Indians in the Lok Sabha and State Legislative assemblies and extended reservations for SCs and STs for up to ten years.
One hundredth and Fifth Amendment, 2021	:	This Act restores the power of State Governments to identify and specify Socially and Economically Backward Classes (SEBCs).
One hundredth and Sixth Amendment, 2023	:	This Act provides 33% reservation for women in Lok Sabha and State Legislative Assemblies.

NATIONAL SYMBOLS

STATE EMBLEM

- State Emblem of India is an adaptation from the Sarnath Lion Capital of Ashoka. It was adopted by the Government of India on January 26, 1950. In the adapted form, only three lions are visible, the fourth being hidden from the view.
- The wheel (Dharma Chakra) appears in relief in the centre of the abacus with a bull on the right and a horse on the left.
- The bell-shaped lotus has been omitted. The words ''Satyameva Jayate'' meaning ''Truth alone triumphs'' are inscribed below the Emblem in Devanagari script.

NATIONAL FLAG

- The National Flag of India is a horizontal tricolour of deep saffron (Kesari), white and dark green in equal proportion.
- In the centre of the white band there is a wheel in navy blue colour. It has 24 spokes.
- The ratio of the length and the breadth of the flag is 3 : 2. Its design was adopted by the Constituent Assembly of India on July 22, 1947.

NATIONAL ANTHEM

- Rabindranath Tagore's song 'Jana-gana-mana' was adopted by the Constituent Assembly as the National Anthem of India on January 24, 1950.

Jana-gana-mana-adhinayaka jaya he,
Bharata-bhagya-vidhata
Punjab-Sindh-Gujarat-Maratha-
Dravida-Utkala-Banga
Vindhya-Himachala-Yamuna-Ganga
Uchhala-jaladhi-taranga.
Tava subha name jage,
Tava subha asisa mange,
Gahe tava jaya gatha,
Jana-gana-mangala-dayak,
jaya he Bharata bhagya vidhata,
Jaya he, jaya he, jaya he,
Jaya jaya jaya, jaya he.

NATIONAL SONG

- Bankim Chandra Chatterji's 'Vande Mataram' which was a source of inspiration to the people in their struggle for freedom, has been adopted as National Song. It has an equal status with the National Anthem.

Vande Mataram
Sujalam, suphalam, malayaja-shitalam,
Shasya shyamalam, Mataram
Shubhrajyotsna, pulkita yaminim,
Phulla kusumita drumadalashobhinim,
Subhasinim sumadhura—bhashinim,
Sukhadam, Varadam, Mataram.

- **National Bird and Animal of India:** Peacock and Tiger.
- **National Aquatic Animal:** Dolphin
- **National Flower:** Lotus
- **National Calendar:** It was adopted on March 22, 1957. It has 365 days in the year and the first month of the year is Chaitra.

❑ ❑ ❑

GENERAL SCIENCE

PHYSICS

PHYSICAL QUANTITIES

- Physical quantities may be divided in two classes:
  1. Scalar Quantities 2. Vector Quantities
- A scalar quantity is one which has only magnitude.
- A vector quantity has both magnitude and direction.
- Force, Velocity, Momentum, Acceleration are examples of vector quantities.
- Mass, length, time, volume, speed, energy, work are examples of scalar quantities.

UNITS

- All measurements in physics require standard units.
- In 1960, the General Conference of Weights and Measures recommended that a metric system of measurements called the International System of Units, abbreviated as SI units, be used.

Some Important Units

S.No.	Units	Quantity
1.	Metre	Length
2.	Kilogram	Mass
3.	Second	Time
4.	Ampere	Electric Current
5.	Candela	Luminous Intensity
6.	Newton	Force
7.	Joule	Workdone
8.	Watt	Power
9.	Coulomb	Electric Charge
10.	Volt	Potential Difference
11.	Ohm	Electrical Resistance
12.	Farad	Capacitance
13.	Henry	Inductance
14.	Lumen	Luminous Flux

- Very small distances are measured in micro-meters or (microns) (μm), angstroms (Å), nanometers (nm) and femtometres (fm).

MOTION

- When a body changes its position with respect to something else as time goes on, we say the body is in motion.
- There are two types of motion—translational (linear) and rotational (spin).
- The motion of a car on a road is translational whereas the motion of a top, spinning on its axis is rotational.

SPEED

- It is a scalar form of velocity and is defined as the distance travelled in one second.
- $\text{Speed} = \dfrac{\text{distance travelled}}{\text{time required}}$
- SI unit of speed is m/s.

VELOCITY

- The distance covered by an object in a specified direction in unit time interval is called velocity.
- The SI unit of velocity is m/s.
- Velocity is a vector quantity.

ACCELERATION

- The velocity of a body changes due to change in its speed or direction or both. The rate of change of the velocity of a body is called its acceleration.
- $\text{Acceleration} = \dfrac{\text{change in velocity}}{\text{time taken}}$

FORCE AND MOTION

GRAVITATIONAL FORCE

- It is the force of attraction between two masses.
- It is gravitational force that holds the moon in its orbit round the earth and the earth in its orbit round the sun.
- *Newton's Law of Universal Gravitation* states that every particle in the universe attracts every other particle with a force that is directly proportional to the product of their masses and inversely proportional to the square of the distance between them.
- The value of G is 6.67×10^{-11} SI units.

CENTRIPETAL FORCE

- The force acting towards the centre on a particle executing uniform circular motion is called centripetal force and is given by

$$F = \frac{mv^2}{r}$$

where, m = Mass of the object

v = Speed

r = Radius of the Circular Path

- In case of the moon, gravitational force between the earth and the moon acts as the centripetal force.
- Centripetal force always acts on the particle performing circular motion.

CENTRIFUGAL FORCE

- The pseudo force that balances the centripetal force in uniform circular motion is called centrifugal force.
- Centrifugal force is directed away from the centre along the radius.
- The centrifugal force is zero exactly at the poles and maximum at the equator.

WEIGHT

- The weight of a body is the force with which the earth attracts the body towards its centre.
- The mass of a body is a constant quantity whereas its weight varies slightly from place-to-place on the earth.
- The weight of a body is maximum at the poles and minimum at the equator. This variation in weight is due to:
  1. the shape of the earth.
  2. the rotation of the earth about its axis.
- The weight of an object is less at high elevations than at sea level.
- At the centre of the earth, the weight of a body would be zero.
- On the surface of the moon the value of the acceleration due to gravity is nearly one-sixth of that on earth and, therefore, an object on the moon would weigh only one-sixth its weight on the earth. The mass of an object on the moon would be the same as on earth.
- The weight of a body would be more if the earth stopped rotating. Conversely, if the speed of rotation were higher, the weight would be less.
- A person weighs more in a lift, which is accelerating upward.
- An astronaut feels weightless in a spaceship because he is not pushing against anything.

FRICTION

- Friction is the force which opposes the relative motion of two surfaces in contact.
- It is friction between the ground and the soles of our shoes that makes walking possible and it is lack of friction that makes our feet slip on highly polished surfaces.
- Friction in machines wastes energy and also causes wear and tear. This friction is reduced by using (1) lubricants, and (2) ball bearings.

NEWTON'S LAWS OF MOTION

First Law

- Every object continues in its state of rest or of uniform motion in a straight line if no net force acts upon it. It is also known as *law of inertia*.
- **Examples:** 1. An unwary passenger in a fast-moving bus falls forward when it stops suddenly. This happens because the feet of the passenger come to rest suddenly whereas his upper part of body continues to be in motion. 2. A person getting down from a moving bus has to run some distance, in the direction of the bus, before stopping. If he does not run he is bound to fall because his feet come to rest whereas his body continues to be in motion.

Momentum

- The momentum of a body is defined as the product of its mass and velocity.

Second Law

- This law states that "the rate of change of momentum of a body is proportional to the applied force and takes place in the direction of the force."
- If we express force (F) in Newtons, mass (m) in kilograms and acceleration (a) in metres per second squared, we can write the second law as; F = ma.
- In travelling the same distance, a car consumes more fuel on a crowded road than on a free road. This happens because the car has to stop and start quite often on a crowded road. The repeated acceleration requires a force (second law), which ultimately comes from the fuel. On a free road the car runs at almost uniform speed requiring fewer accelerations and hence less fuel consumption.

Third Law

- This law states that "to every action there is an equal and opposite reaction."
- When a bullet is fired from a gun, equal and opposite forces are exerted on the bullet and the gun.
- The engine in a jet aeroplane works on the same principle as a rocket but there is a difference in the method of obtaining the high velocity as jet.

IMPULSE

- If a force acts on a body for a very short time, then the product of force and time is called the impulse.

  Impulse= Change in momentum

  = Force × Time

Application of Impulse

1. A cricket player draws his hand back while catching.
2. A person jumping on hard cement floor receives more injuries than a person jumping on muddy or sandy floor.

WORK, POWER AND ENERGY

WORK

- Whenever a force acting on a body displaces it, work is said to be done.

  Work = Force × Distance moved in the direction of force.
- Work is a scalar quantity and its SI unit is Joule (J).

POWER

- Power is defined as the rate of doing work.

$$\text{Power} = \frac{\text{Work done}}{\text{Time taken}}$$

- The SI unit of power is Watt (W) and is also measured in horse power.

  1 HP = 746 W

ENERGY

- Energy is defined as the capacity to do work.

Kinetic Energy

- The energy possessed by an object due to its motion is called kinetic energy and is described by the expression

$$KE = \frac{1}{2}mv^2$$; where, m = mass of the object

v = speed

Potential Energy

- Potential energy is the energy possessed by the body by virtue of its position, configuration or any condition of stress or strain.
- There are many examples of potential energy. A stone held at some height above the ground has potential energy. Water in an elevated reservoir possesses potential energy.

Transformation of Energy

S.No.	Equipment	Transformation
1.	Dynamo	Mechanical energy into electrical energy
2.	Microphone	Sound energy into electrical energy
3.	Loud Speaker	Electrical energy into sound energy
4.	Electric Bulb	Electrical energy into light and heat energy
5.	Battery	Chemical energy into electrical energy
6.	Electrical Motor	Electrical energy into mechanical energy

CENTRE OF GRAVITY

- The centre of gravity of a body is the point where the whole weight of the body can be considered to act.
- Racing cars are build low and with wide wheel bases to reduce the risk of overturning at sharp bends.
- While crossing a river in a boat, passengers are not allowed to stand. This keeps the CG of the system (boat and passengers) low and ensures stability.

ARTIFICIAL SATELLITES

- In the case of a satellite, the centripetal force is provided by the gravitational pull of the earth.
- If the speed of a satellite is more than 11.2 km/s or 25,000 miles/hour, the satellite would escape the earth entirely and would never come back. This is called escape velocity.
- The existence of gaseous atmosphere on the earth is due to the high value of its escape velocity.

Geostationary Satellites

- Geostationary satellites are stationary with respect to an observer on the earth. Their time period is 24-hour. There height above the surface of earth is 36,000 km. They are always in equatorial plane and their orbits are circular. They are also called parking orbits.

DENSITY AND RELATIVE DENSITY

DENSITY

- The mass per unit volume of a substance is called its density.

$$\text{Density} = \frac{\text{Mass}}{\text{Volume}}$$

- The SI unit of density is kilogram per metre cubed (kg/m^3).
- The relative density of a substance is the ratio of the density of the substance to the density of water.
- Relative density has no unit.

PRESSURE

- Pressure is defined as force acting per unit area.

$$\text{Pressure} = \frac{\text{Force}}{\text{Area}}$$

- The SI unit of pressure is newton per metre squared or pascal.
- Broad wooden sleepers are placed below the rails to reduce the pressure exerted by the weight of a train.
- The pressure of water increases with depth, therefore bottom of a dam is made much thicken than the top.
- The pressure exerted on an enclosed liquid at one place is transmitted equally throughout the liquid. This is called Pascal's Principle.
- Hydraulic presses, hydraulic brakes, hydraulic door closers, etc. are applications of the Pascal's Principle.
- At high attitudes where atmosphere pressure is less nose bleeding may occur due to the greater pressure of blood.

- In an aircraft flying at high altitude, normal atmospheric pressure is maintained by the use of air pumps. If this were not done, the crew and passengers would experience difficulty in breathing and consequently face dangers.
- Atmospheric pressure is measured with an instrument called the *Barometer*.

ARCHIMEDE'S PRINCIPLE

- This principle states that when a body is wholly or partially immersed in a fluid, it experiences an upthrust (upward force) equal to the weight of the fluid displaced.
- An iron nail sinks in water whereas a ship made of iron and steel floats. This is due to the fact that a ship is hollow and contains air and, therefore, its density is less than that of water.
- The density of sea water is more than that of river water, due to this a ship sinks less in sea water. It is for this reason that a ship rises a little when it enters a sea from a river.
- It is because of the higher density of sea water that it is easier to swim in the sea.
- A balloon filled with a light gas, such as hydrogen, rises because the average density of the balloon and the gas is less than that of air. The balloon cannot rise indefinitely because the density of the air decreases with increasing altitude. At a certain height, where the density of air is equal to the average density of the balloon, it ceases to rise and drifts sideways with the wind.
- When an ice block floats in water the water level will remain the same when all the ice melts into water.
- A *hydrometer* is an instrument used for measuring the relative density of liquids.
- A special type of a hydrometer called *Lactometer* is used for testing milk by measuring its density.

SURFACE TENSION

- Surface tension is that property of liquids owing to which they tend to acquire minimum surface area.
- Surface tension is caused by molecular attractions.
- When a paint brush is dipped in water all its hair spread out but when it is taken out it is covered with a thin film of water which contracts due to surface tension and pulls the hair together.
- Liquid drops, such as raindrops, oildrops, drops of molten metals, dewdrops etc. are all spherical because their surface tend to contract in order to have minimum surface area. For a given volume, a sphere has the minimum surface area.
- Soaps and detergents lower the surface tension of water. This increases the wetting power of water or its ability to detach dirt particles from clothes and untensils.
- The force of attraction between unlike molecules is called **adhesion** and that between like molecules **cohesion.**
- The melted wax of a candle is drawn up into the wick by capillary action. Oil rises up a lamp wick for the same reason.
- If one end of a sugar cube is dipped into tea, the entire cube is quickly wet on account of capillary action.

VISCOSITY

- The force which opposes the relative motion between different layers of liquid or gases is called viscous force.
- Viscosity is the property of liquids and gases both.

BERNOULLI'S THEOREM

- According to Bernoulli's theorem, in case of streamline flow of incompressible and non-viscous fluid (ideal fluid) through a tube, total energy (sum of pressure energy, potential energy and kinetic energy) per unit volume of fluid is same at all points.

  1. When a bowler spins a ball, it changes its direction (swings) in the air due to unequal pressure acting on it.

HEAT

- Heat is that form of energy which flows from one body to other body due to difference in temperature between the bodies. The amount of heat contained in a body depends upon the mass of the body.

TEMPERATURE

- The temperature of a body is the quantity that tells how hot or cold it is with respect to some standard body.

MEASUREMENT OF TEMPERATURE

- Temperature is measured by a thermometer.
- A thermometer may be graduated in following scales—
  1. The upper and lower points of centigrade scale are 100°C and 0°C.
  2. The upper and lower points of Fahrenheit scale are 212°F and 32°F.
  3. The upper and lower points of Reaumur scale are 80°R and 0°R.
  4. The upper and lower points of Kelvin scale are 373K and 273K.
  5. The upper and lower points of Rankine scale are 672° Ra and 460° Ra.
- At –40 degrees both celsius and Fahrenheit scales will show identical readings.
- Water cannot be used in a thermometer becaues it freezes at 0°C and also because of its irregular expansion.

THERMAL EXPANSION

- Solids, liquids and gases generally expand when heated and contract when cooled.
- Gaps have to be left in railway tracks to make allowance for expansion, otherwise the rails will buckle. Allowance

is made for the expansion of long steel bridges. One end of such bridge is fixed while the other rests on rollers.

- Telephone wires sag more in summer than in winter due to thermal expansion.

EXPANSION OF WATER

- Water has its minimum volume and maximum density at 4°C.

TRANSMISSION OF HEAT

- There are three ways of heat transmission: 1. Conduction; 2. Convection; 3. Radiation.

Conduction

- In this process, heat is transferred from one place to other place by the successive vibration of the particles of the medium without bodily movement of the particles of the medium.
- Conduction takes place mainly in solids.
- Air is a very bad conductor of heat. The good insulating properties of wool, cotton, etc. are mainly due to the air spaces they contain.

Convection

- In this process, heat is transferred by the actual movement of particles of the medium from one place to other place.
- In liquids and gases heat is transmitted by convection.

Radiation

- In this mode of heat transmission heat is transferred from one place to another without effecting the intervening medium.

HEAT CAPACITY

- The heat capacity of a body is defined as the heat required to raise the temperature of the body by 1K. Its SI unit is J/K.

SPECIFIC HEAT CAPACITY

- The specific heat capacity of a substance is the heat required to raise the temperature of a unit mass of the substance by 1K.
- Its SI unit is J/kg K.
- It is because of its high specific heat capacity that water is used as a cooling liquid in car engine.

LATENT HEAT

- It is defined as the amount of heat absorbed or given out by a body during the change of state.
- Each gram of ice that melts absorbs 336 J of heat.

EVAPORATION

- Water can change into the vapour state either by boiling or by evaporation at lower temperatures.
- When sweat evaporates from the skin it draws much heat from the body and produces a cooling sensation.
- In summer, water is stored in pitchers for cooling. Water oozes out of the pores of the pitchers and cools on evaporation.
- The rate of evaporation increases with increase in temperature.

REFRIGERATOR

- In a refrigerator, cooling is produced by the evaporation of a volatile liquid, freon, inside a copper coil (evaporator), which surrounds the freezer.
- The cooling unit (freezer) in a refrigerator is fitted near the top to cool the whole of the interior.

RELATIVE HUMIDITY

- Relative humidity is defined as the ratio of the mass of water vapour in a given volume of air to the mass required for saturating the same volume of air at the same temperature.
- Relative humidity is measured with an instrument called the hygrometer.

PRESSURE COOKER

- The boiling point of a liquid depends on external pressure.
- When the atmospheric pressure is 76 cm of mercury, water boils at 100°C. But when the pressure is increased, the boiling point of water is raised.
- In a pressure cooker, water boils at temperatures higher than 100°C due to increased pressure. The increased boiling temperature allows water to hold more heat which cooks food faster.
- At higher altitudes, atmospheric pressure is reduced. This lowers the boiling point of water and food takes much longer to cook.

WAVE MOTION

- Wave motion may be defined as the transfer of energy without the net transfer of matter.
- If the particles of the medium vibrate perpendicular to the direction of propagation of wave, the wave is called transverse wave.
- Light waves are transverse waves.
- If the particles of the medium vibrate in the direction of propagation of wave, the wave is called longitudinal wave.
- Sound waves are longitudinal waves.

ELECTROMAGNETIC WAVE

- Electromagnetic waves include an enormous range of frequencies—from radio waves with frequencies less than 10^5 Hz to gamma rays having frequencies greater than 10^{20} Hz.

- All electromagnetic wave have the same speed (3×10^8 m/s) in vacuum. The relation $v = n\lambda$ holds good for all electromagnetic waves.

RADIO AND TELEVISION TRANSMISSION

- Radio waves sent out by radio stations are reflected by the ionosphere and can be received anywhere on the earth.
- At night the radio reception improves because the layers of the ionosphere are not exposed to sunlight and are more settled.
- Radar (Radio detection and ranging) employs high frequency radio waves for detecting objects like ships and aeroplanes.
- In microwave oven, when the waves fall on the food, these are absorbed by water, fats, sugars and certain other molecules whose consequent vibrations produce heat. Since heating occurs inside the food, without warming the surrounding air, the cooking time is greatly reduced.
- In microwave oven, food cannot be cooked in metal vessels because the metal blocks out the microwaves.

LIGHT

- Light is a form of energy which is propagated as electromagnetic waves.
- Light is a transverse wave.
- Speed of light in vacuum is 3×10^8 m/s.
- Light takes 8 minute 16.6 second to reach from sun to earth.

REFLECTION

- When light is incident upon a surface, part of it is reflected. But certain surfaces like mirrors and polished metals reflect almost all the light incident upon them.
- The law of reflection states that the angle of incidence is equal to the angle of reflection.
- To see full image in a plane mirror, a person requires a mirror of at least half of his height.

INCLINED MIRROR (NO. OF IMAGES)

- When an object is placed between two inclined mirrors, several images of the object are formed.

CURVED MIRRORS

- There are two types of curved spherical mirrors—1. Concave Mirror, 2. Convex Mirror.
- Concave mirror can concentrate the sun's radiation falling on it at one point, it can be used as a burning glass.
- Concave mirrors are also used in solar cookers.
- Large concave mirrors are used in reflecting telescopes for observing and photographing distant stars and other heavenly bodies.
- Concave mirror is also used as a shaving or make-up mirror.
- Small concave mirrors are used by dentists for examining teeth.
- Concave parabolic mirrors are used in searchlight and headlamps of cars.
- Convex mirrors are also used as rear view mirrors in vehicles.

REFRACTION

- When a ray of light passes from one medium to other it suffers a change in direction at the boundary of separation of two media. This phenomenon is called refraction.
- When a ray passes from one medium to another optically denser medium, e.g., from air to water or glass, it bends towards the normal. Conversely, a ray passing from water or glass into air is bent away from the normal.
- Rivers appear shallow, coin in a beaker filled with water appears raised, due to refraction.
- Another effect of refraction is the apparent upward bending of the immersed portion of a stick when dipped in water.
- It is due to refraction, produced by the earth's atmosphere, that the sun is visible for several minutes after it has set below the horizon. Thus, atmospheric refraction tends to lengthen the day.
- When the sun (or moon) is near the horizon, it appears elliptical, i.e., with the vertical diameter less than the horizontal diameter. This happens because rays from the lower edge of the sun are bent more than those from the upper edge (Atmospheric Refraction).
- One of the most interesting effects of atmospheric refraction and Mirage is a combined effect of atmospheric refraction and total internal reflection.

DISPERSION

- White light consists of seven colours—violet, indigo, blue, green, yellow, orange and red. These colours are called the spectrum of the white light.
- Violet has the minimum wavelength (or maximum frequency) and red the maximum wavelength (or minimum frequency).
- Due to different speeds, the colours are refracted through different angles and therefore, when a narrow beam of white light passes through a glass prism, it is split up into its constituent colours. This separation of light into colours is called dispersion.

COLOUR OF OBJECTS

- We see objects because of the light they reflect.
- When a rose is viewed in white light, its petals appear red and the leaves appear green, because the petals reflect the red part of the white light and leaves reflect the green part. The remaining colours are absorbed. When the same rose is viewed in green light, the petals will appear black

and the leaves green. In blue or yellow light both the petals and leaves will appear black.

- Red, blue and green are primary colours.

LENSES

- There are mainly two types of lenses:
  1. Convex or Converging Lens
  2. Concave or Diverging Lens
- Converging or convex lens is used as a magnifying glass.
- Power of a lens is its capacity to deviate a ray. Power of a lens is measured as the reciprocal of the focal length.

$$P = \frac{1}{f}$$

- SI unit of power of lens is dioptre (D).
- The power of a converging lens is positive and that of a diverging lens is negative.
- For all positions of the object, the images formed by diverging (concave) lens are virtual, erect and diminished.

EYE

- The light entering the eye is focused by the eye-lens to form an image on the retina.
- In front of the eye, lens is the coloured part of eye, called the iris, which automatically adjusts the size of the pupil to the intensity of light falling on it.
- In bright light the iris automatically shuts tighter, reducing the amount of light entering the pupil. This protects the retina from getting damaged.
- When a person enters a dark room after being in bright light, he is not able to see clearly for a while because the iris is unable to dilate the pupil immediately.
- Least distance of distinct vision is 25 cm.

DEFECTS OF VISION

- A person suffering from long sight (hyper-metropia) can clearly see objects at infinity but cannot see near objects clearly. This defect is caused by the eyeball being too short and can be corrected by wearing converging lenses.
- In the case of a person suffering from short sight (myopia), the eye ball is too long and distant objects are focused in front of the retina. This defect can be corrected by wearing diverging lenses.
- ***Astigmatism:*** Curvature of cornea becomes irregular and image is not clear. Cylindrical lens is used.

SCATTERING OF LIGHT

- When light falls on atoms and molecules, it is scattered in all directions.
- Scattering of light is maximum for violet colour and minimum for red colour.
- Blue colour of sky is due to scattering of light.
- In the evening, the sun is lower in the sky and its light has to traverse a longer path through the atmosphere to reach an observer. Thus, at sunset, blue, green and other colours having been scattered only red and some orange light reach us and the sun appears a deep orange-red.
- In outerspace, *i.e.,* beyond the atmosphere, there is nothing to scatter the sunlight and therefore the sky appears dark and stars are visible even in the presence of the sun.

INTERFERENCE OF LIGHT

- The superposition of two (or more) waves of the same kind that pass the same point in space at the same time is called interference.
- Beautiful colours seen in soap bubbles and oil films on water are produced due to the interference of white light reflected by these surfaces.
- LASER (Light Amplification by Stimulated Emission of Radiation) is an optical device which produces an intense beam of coherent monochromatic light.
- Examples of Interference of Light: Holography, Laser.

DIFFRACTION OF LIGHT

- When a beam of light passes through a narrow slit or an aperture, it spreads out to a certain extent into the region of geometrical shadow. This is an example of diffraction, *i.e.,* of the failure of light to travel in a straight line.

SOUND

- Sound waves are longitudinal and cannot travel in vacuum. The transmission of sound requires a medium : air, liquid or solid.
- The longitudinal mechanical waves which lie in the frequency range 20 Hz to 20,000 Hz are called audible or sound waves. These waves are sensitive to human ear.
- The longitudinal mechanical waves having frequencies less than 20 Hz are called Infrasonic. These waves are produced by sources of bigger size such as earthquakes, volcanic eruptions, ocean waves etc.
- The longitudinal waves having frequencies greater than 20,000 Hz are called ultrasonic waves. Human ear cannot detect these waves. But some animals such as cats, dogs, bats can detect these waves.

PITCH

- The pitch (shrillness of a sound) depends on its frequency.
- A sound of higher frequency has a higher pitch.
- The pitch of a woman's voice is higher than that of a man.

LOUDNESS

- The relative loudness of a sound is measured in decibels (db).
- All stringed instruments, such as the violin, sitar, guitar, etc. have sound boxes attached to increase the loudness.

SPEED OF SOUND

- The presence of water vapour in the air increases the speed of sound.
- Sound travels faster through warm air than through cold air. The speed of sound is higher on a hot day than on a cold day.
- Thunder is heard much after the flash of lightning is seen because of the wide difference in the speeds of light and sound.

REFLECTION OF SOUND

- When a sound wave is reflected by a distant obstacle, such as a wall or a cliff, an echo is heard.
- To hear echo, the minimum distance between the observer and reflector should be 17 m.
- Exploration of underwater gas and oil is done by detecting the echoes of shock waves produced by explosions on the water surface.
- Bats emit ultrasonic waves of frequencies up to 80,000 Hz and use the reflection of these waves (echoes) to determine the presence and distance of objects on their way and from them respectively.

DOPPLER EFFECT

- The Doppler effect is the change in frequency of a wave (sound or light) due to the motion of the source or observer.
- It is due to the Doppler effect that the whistle of a train appears shriller when it approaches a listener than when it moves away from him.

ELECTRICITY

- Electricity produced by friction between two dissimilar objects is known as static electricity. Depending on the nature of the objects, one acquires a positive charge and the other an equal negative charge. For example, if a glass rod is rubbed with silk, the rod acquires positive charge and the silk an equal negative charge.
- *Lightning* is a gigantic electric discharge occurring between two charged clouds or between a charged cloud and the earth.

CONDUCTOR

- Conductors are those materials which allow electricity (charge) to pass through themselves.
- Metals conduct electricity because they have a large number of conduction or free electrons.

INSULATORS

- Insulators are those materials which do not allow electricity to flow through themselves. Insulators have no free electrons.

SUPER CONDUCTORS

- The resistance of metals to flow of electricity reduces with decreasing temperature. At temperatures near absolute zero, metals have almost zero resistance and became super conductors.

SEMI-CONDUCTORS

- Certain materials, such as silicon and germanium, have electrical resistivity intermediate between those of conductors and insulators. These materials are termed as semi-conductors.
- Semi-conductors are good insulators in their pure crystalline form but their conductivity increases when small amounts of impurities are added to them.

ELECTRIC CURRENT

- Electric current is simply the flow of electric charge. In solid conductors the flow of electrons and in fluids the flow of ions as well as electrons constitute the current.
- SI units of electric current is Ampere (A).

ELECTRICAL RESISTANCE

- When electric current flows through a conductor, e.g., a metallic wire, it offers some obstruction to the current. This obstruction offered by the wire is called its electrical resistance.
- SI unit of Resistance is ohm.

OHM'S LAW

- If physical conditions like temperature, intensity of light etc. remains unchanged then electric current flowing through a conductor is directly proportional to the potential difference across its ends.

ELECTRIC MOTOR

- In an electric motor, electrical energy is converted into mechanical energy.
- Electric fans, mixers, washing machines, etc. work on electric motors.

INVERTER

- An inverter is a device which converts DC to AC. The inverters used in homes and offices are specially designed to:

  1. Convert DC from a battery to AC, and
  2. Charge the battery.

FUSE

- Electric fuse is a protective device used in series with an electric appliance to save it from being damaged due to high current.
- A fuse is a short piece of wire made of a tin-lead alloy, which has a low melting point.
- Fuses are always connected in the live wire in series.

COST OF ELECTRICITY

- The consumption of electrical energy in a house is measured in the unit kWh.
- Kilowatt hour is equal to the energy consumed in the circuit at the rate of 1 kilowatt for 1 hour.

MAGNETISM

- A magnet attracts and holds pieces of iron but does not attract pieces of copper.
- Iron, cobalt, nickel and certain alloys are strongly magnetic whereas copper, wood, glass, etc. are non-magnetic.
- Our earth behaves as a powerful magnet whose south pole is near the geographical north pole and whose north pole is near the geographical south pole.

ATOMIC & NUCLEAR PHYSICS

- Atom consists of three fundamental particles electron, proton and neutron. All the protons and neutrons are present in the central core of atom called nucleus. Electrons revolve around the nucleus.
- The total number of protons in the nucleus is called atomic number (Z).
- The total number of proton and neutrons in the nucleus is called mass number (A).
- Ernest Rutherford, discovered nucleus by the scattering of α-particles from gold foil.

RADIOACTIVITY

- Henry Bacquerel (1896) observed that a photographic plate blackened, when placed near double sulphate of potassium and uranium. He further observed that uranium emitted special kind of rays. They were called Becqueral rays.
- Pierre and Marie Curie observed that the radiation from pitchblende was four times stronger than uranium. In 1898, they finally discovered two new substances—Polonium and Radium. These newly discovered substances were called radioactive substances and this property of these substances was named radioactivity.
- No radioactive substance emits both α and β particles simultaneously.

X-RAYS

- X-rays are electromagnetic radiations having wavelength from a fraction of an Angestrom to about 100Å. They were discovered by Rontgen during his studies on the electrical discharge phenomena in gases—he found that an unknown radiation was produced when electrons collided with the walls of the tubes.

ATOMIC ENERGY

- India today ranks sixth in the atomic energy programmes. It has developed the required know-how and expertise to manufacture nuclear weapons, but it believes in the peaceful uses of atomic power. The Atomic Energy Commission was set-up in the country in 1948 under the Chairmanship of Dr. H. J. Bhabha.
- ***Bhabha Atomic Research Centre (BARC):*** The Bhabha Atomic Research Centre at Trombay near Mumbai (Maharashtra) has four research reactors: (*i*) APSARA—It is the first atomic reactor in Asia; (*ii*) CIRUS—It is a joint Indo-Canadian project; (*iii*) PURNIMA II—a zero energy fast reactor, and (*iv*) DHRUVA—a high power completely indigenous nuclear research reactor with most advanced laboratories in the world. Another fast breeder reactor KAMINI at Kalpakkam has been constructed. Today India is the seventh country in the world and the first developing nation to have mastered the fast breeder reactor technology.
- **Nuclear Power:** Under Nuclear Power Corporation of India Limited (NPCIL) there are seven nuclear power stations in operation in six States:
(*i*) Tarapur—Maharashtra, (*ii*) Rawatbhata —Rajasthan, (*iii*) Kalpakkam—Tamil Nadu, (*iv*) Narora—U.P., (*v*) Kakrapara—Gujarat, (*vi*) Kaiga—Karnataka and (*vii*) Kudankulam—Tamil Nadu.
- **Heavy Water:** Heavy water is one of the essential input for Pressurised Heavy Water Reactors (PHWRs) used both as a coolant and moderator. The first heavy water plant was set-up in 1962 in Nangal. Subsequently 7 more plants have been set-up at (*i*) Baroda, (*ii*) Tuticorin, (*iii*) Kota, (*iv*) Talcher, (*v*) Thal, (*vi*) Hazira and (*vii*) Manuguru.
- **Research and Development Centres:** Four research centres namely (*i*) Bhabha Atomic Research Centre, Trombay (Maharashtra), (*ii*) Indira Gandhi Centre for Atomic Research, Kalpakkam (Tamil Nadu), (*iii*) Centre for Advanced Technology, Indore (Madhya Pradesh), (*iv*) Variable Energy Cyclotron Centre at Kolkata (West Bengal) are focal points of research and development work in nuclear energy and related discipline.
- **India's Nuclear Explosions:** On May 18, 1974 India conducted her first underground nuclear explosion at Pokhran (Rajasthan) in the Thar desert, 20 km. away from Jaisalmer, at a depth of more than 100 metres. The successful explosion made India the sixth nuclear nation in the world.
- India conducted 5 nuclear explosion tests at Pokhran in two phases on May 11 and May 13, 1998 and became a nuclear power state.

IMPORTANT INVENTIONS

Name of Invention	Inventor	Nationality	Year
Aeroplane	Orville & Wilbur Wright	U.S.A.	1903
Ball-Point Pen	John J. Loud	U.S.A.	1888
Barometer	Evangelista Torricelli	Italy	1644
Bicycle	Kirkpatrick Macmillan	Britain	1839-40
Bifocal Lens	Benjamin Franklin	U.S.A.	1780
Car (Petrol)	Karl Benz	Germany	1888
Celluloid	Alexander Parkes	Britain	1861
Cinema	Nicolas & Jean Lumiere	France	1895
Clock (mechanical)	I-Hsing & Liang Ling-Tsan	China	1725
Diesel Engine	Rudolf Diesel	Germany	1895
Dynamo	Hypolite Pixii	France	1832
Electric Lamp	Thomas Alva Edison	U.S.A.	1879
Electric Motor (DC)	Zenobe Gramme	Belgium	1873
Electric Motor (AC)	Nikola Tesla	U.S.A.	1888
Electro-magnet	William Sturgeon	Britain	1824
Electronic Computer	Dr. Alan M. Turing	Britain	1943
Film (moving outlines)	Louis Prince	France	1885
Film (musical sound)	Dr. Le de Forest	U.S.A.	1923
Fountain Pen	Lewis E. Waterman	U.S.A.	1884
Gramophone	Thomas Alva Edison	U.S.A.	1878
Helicopter	Etienne Oehmichen	France	1924
Jet Engine	Sir Frank Whittle	Britain	1937
Laser	Charles H. Townes	U.S.A.	1960
Lift (Mechanical)	Elisha G. Otis	U.S.A.	1852
Locomotive	Richard Trevithick	Britain	1804
Machine Gun	James Puckle	Britain	1718
Microphone	Alexander Graham Bell	U.S.A.	1876
Microscope	Z. Janssen	Netherlands	1590
Motor Cycle	G. Daimler	Germany	1885
Photography (on film)	John Carbutt	U.S.A.	1888
Printing Press	Johann Gutenberg	Germany	c.1455
Razor (safety)	King C. Gillette	U.S.A.	1895
Refrigerator	James Harrison & Alexander Catlin	U.S.A.	1850
Safety Pin	Walter Hunt	U.S.A.	1849
Sewing machine	Barthelemy Thimmonnier	France	1829
Ship (steam)	J.C. Perier	France	1775
Ship (turbine)	Hon. Sir C. Parsons	Britain	1894
Skyscraper	W. Le Baron Jenny	U.S.A.	1882
Slide Rule	William Oughtred	Britain	1621
Steam Engine (condenser)	James Watt	Britain	1765
Steel Production	Henry Bessemer	Britain	1855
Steel (stainless)	Harry Brearley	Britain	1913
Submarine	David Bushnell	U.S.A.	1776
Tank	Sir Ernest Swinton	Britain	1914
Telegraph	M. Lammond	France	1787
Telegraph Code	Samuel F.B. Morse	U.S.A.	1837
Telephone (perfected)	Alexander Graham Bell	U.S.A.	1876
Television (mechanical)	John Logie Baird	Britain	1926
Television (electronic)	P.T. Farnsworth	U.S.A.	1927
Thermometer	Galileo Galilei	Italy	1593
Transformer	Michael Faraday	Britain	1831
Transistor	Bardeen, Shockley & Brattain	U.S.A.	1948
Washing Machine (elec.)	Hurley Machine Co.	U.S.A.	1907
Zip-Fastener	W.L. Judson	U.S.A.	1891

Important Discoveries

Discovery	Discoverer	Nationality	Year
Aluminium	Hans Christian Oerstedt	Denmark	1827
Atomic number	Henry Moseley	England	1913
Atomic structure of matter	John Dalton	England	1803
Chlorine	C.W. Scheele	Sweden	1774
Electromagnetic induction	Michael Faraday	England	1831
Electromagnetic waves	Heinrich Hertz	Germany	1886
Electromagnetism	Hans Christian Oersted	Denmark	1920
Electron	Sir Joseph Thomson	England	1897
General theory of relativity	Albert Einstein	Switzerland	1915
Hydrogen	Henry Cavendish	England	1766
Law of electric conduction	Georg Ohm	Germany	1827
Law of electromagnetism	Andre Ampere	France	1826
Law of falling bodies	Galileo	Italy	1590
Laws of gravitation & motion	Isaac Newton	England	1687
Laws of planetary motion	Johannes Kepler	Germany	1609-10
Magnesium	Sir Humphry Davy	England	1808
Neptune (Planet)	Johann Galle	Germany	1846
Neutron	James Chadwick	England	1932
Nickel	Axel Cronstedt	Sweden	1751
Nitrogen	Daniel Rutherford	England	1772
Oxygen	Joseph Priestly, C.W. Scheele	England, Sweden	1772
Ozone	Christian Schonbein	Germany	1839
Pluto	Clyde Tombaugh	U.S.A	1930
Plutonium	G.T. Seaborg	U.S.A	1940
Proton	Ernest Rutherford	England	1919
Quantum Theory	Max Planck	Germany	1900
Radioactivity	Antoine Bacquerel	France	1896
Radium	Pierre & Marie Curie	France	1898
Silicon	Jons Berzelius	Sweden	1824
Special theory of relativity	Albert Einstein	Switzerland	1905
Sun as centre of solar system	Copernicus	Poland	1543
Uranium	Martin Klaproth	Germany	1789
Uranus (Planet)	William Herschel	England	1781
X-rays	Wilhelm Roentgen	Germany	1895

Scientific Instruments

Name of Instrument	Used for
Altimeter	measuring altitude
Ammeter	measuring strength of an electric current
Anemometer	measuring the velocity of wind
Audiometer	measuring level of hearing
Barometer	measuring atmospheric pressure

Name of Instrument	Used for
Callipers	measuring the internal and external diameters of tubes
Calorimeter	measuring quantity of heat
Compass	finding out direction
Dynamo	converting mechanical energy into electrical energy
Galvanometer	detecting and determining the strength of small electric currents
Hydrometer	measuring specific gravity of a liquid
Hygrometer	measuring the humidity in the atmosphere
Lactometer	measuring the purity of milk
Manometer	measuring the gaseous pressure
Micrometer	measuring minute distances, angles, etc.
Microscope	seeing magnified view of very small objects
Photometer	measuring intensity of light from distant stars
Pyrometer	measuring high temperatures
Radar	detecting and finding the presence and location of moving objects like aircraft, missile, etc.
Radiometer	measuring the emission of radiant energy
Rain Gauge	measuring the amount of rainfall
Seismograph	measuring and recording the intensity and origin of earthquake shocks
Sextant	measuring altitude and angular distances between two objects or heavenly bodies
Spectrometer	measuring the refractive indices
Spherometer	measuring the curvature of spherical objects/surface
Sphygmomanometer	measuring blood pressure
Stethoscope	ascertaining the condition of heart and lungs by listening to their function
Stroboscope	viewing objects that are moving rapidly with a periodic motion as if they were at rest
Tachometer	measuring the rate of revolution or angular speed of a revolving shaft
Telescope	viewing magnified images of distant objects
Thermocouple	measuring the temperature inside furnaces and jet engines
Thermometer	measuring human body temperature
Thermostat	regulating constant temperature
Ultrasonoscope	measuring utrasonic sounds
Viscometer	measuring the viscosity of a fluid
Voltmeter	measuring potential difference between two points.

CHEMISTRY

ELEMENTS

- An element may be defined as a substance which is made by same type of atoms and it can neither be broken into, nor built from two or more simpler substances by any known physical or chemical methods, e.g., copper, silver, hydrogen, carbon, oxygen, nitrogen, gold, iron etc.

COMPOUNDS

- A compound may be defined as a substance which contains two or more elements combined in some fixed proportion by weight and which can be decomposed into two or more elements by any suitable method.
- The properties of a compound are entirely different from those of the elements from which it is made.
- Some common examples of compounds are water, sugar, salt, aspirin, chloroform, alcohol and ether.

MIXTURES

- A material containing two or more elements or compounds in any proportion is a mixture.
- The components of a mixture can be separated by physical means like filtration, sublimation and distillation.

ATOMIC STRUCTURE

ATOM

- Atom is the smallest part of the element that takes part in a chemical reaction. Atom of an element can not be changed into that of another element by a chemical or physical means. It does not exist in free state.

MOLECULE

- A molecule is the smallest part of an element or compound that is capable of existing independently.

ATOMIC WEIGHT (OR ATOMIC MASS)

- The atomic mass of an element is the number of times its atom is heavier than 1/12th of the mass of carbon (C^{12}) atom.
- The unit used to measure atomic mass is called atomic mass unit, *i.e.,* amu.

ELECTRON

- The electron is a fundamental particle of an atom which carries a unit negative charge. It was discovered by J.J. Thomson in 1897.

PROTON

- It is a fundamental particle of an atom carrying a unit positive charge. It was discovered by Rutherford and Goldstein in 1886.

NEUTRON

- It is a fundamental particle of an atom carrying no charge. It was discovered by Chadwick in 1932.

ISOTOPES

- The atoms of the same element having different mass numbers are called isotopes.

ISOBARS

- Elements having the same atomic mass but differ in atomic number are called isobars.

ISOTONES

- Elements having the same number of neutrons are called isotones.

OXIDATION AND REDUCTION

- Oxidation is a process in which a substance adds on oxygen or loses hydrogen. In modern terms, oxidation is the process in which a substance loses electrons.
- Reduction is a process in which a substance adds on hydrogen or loses oxygen. In modern terms, reduction is the process in which a substance gains electrons.
- Oxidation and reduction always occur simultaneously. If one substance is oxidised, another is reduced. The reaction in which this oxidation-reduction process occurs is called a redox reaction.
- Oxidising agents are substances which bring about the oxidation of other substances, e.g., Potassium Permanganate, Potassium Dichromate, Nitric Acid, Hydrogen Peroxide, etc.
- Reducing agents are substances which bring about the reduction of other substances, e.g., hydrogen sulphide, hydrogen, carbon, sulphur dioxide, etc.

ACIDS, BASES AND SALTS

ACID

- An acid is any compound that can react with a base to form a salt, the hydrogen of the acid being replaced by positive metallic ion. According to modern theory, an acid is a compound which yields hydrogen ions (protons) to a base in a chemical reaction. In a water solution, an acid tastes sour, turns blue litmus red and produces free hydrogen ions.

Acid	Sources
Citric Acid	Lemons or Oranges (Citrus Fruits)
Lactic acid	Sour milk
Tartaric acid	Grapes
Acetic acid	Vinegar
Maleic acid	Apples
Oxalic acid	Tomato
Formic acid	Red ants

BASES

- Such compounds which gives salt and water with acid known as bases. Bitter in taste, turns red litmus paper into blue, contains replaceable hydroxyl group.
- Some important bases are sodium hydroxide, potassium hydroxide, sodium carbonate and ammonium hydroxide.
- All alkalies are bases but all bases are not alkalies because all bases are not soluble in water.

SALTS

- Salts are ionic compounds containing a positive ion (cation) and a negative ion (anion).
- When an acid reacts with a base, a salt and water are formed. This reaction is called neutralization since the acid and base neutralize each other's effect.

ELECTROLYSIS

- The process of decomposition of an electrolyte by the passage of an electric current through its molten state or its aqueous solution is called electrolysis.
- Device through which electric current is passed known as electrodes.

METALLURGY

- Metals occur in nature, in the native (in free state) as well as in the combined state.
- Naturally occurring materials containing metals are called minerals.
- A mineral from which a given metal is obtained economically is called an ore.
- The process of extraction of a metal in a pure state on a large scale from its ore by Physical and Chemical means is called metallurgy.
- The rocky and siliceous matter that associated with the ore is known as gangue.
- Substance that is added to ore to remove the gangue is known as flux.

- The process of removal of gangue from the ore is known as concentration.
- Calcination is the heating of the ore in the absence of air. This method is employed for obtaining the metal oxides from carbonates and hydroxides.
- Roasting is the heating of the ore in the presence of air. On roasting, part of the ore is oxidised to form an oxide. This oxide is then reduced to the metal.
- The industrial reduction process for obtaining metal from the treated ore is called smelting.

AMALGUM

- An alloy in which one of the component metals is mercury is known as amalgum.

IRON AND STEEL

- Iron is extracted from its ores by the blast furnace process.
- Iron obtained from blast furnace is called pig iron or cast iron containing about 5% carbon.
- Pure iron is called wrought iron which does not contain carbon more than 0.2%, or any other impurities or constituents.
- Steel contains 0.25% – 2% carbon and varying amounts of other elements.

CARBON AND ITS COMPOUNDS

ALLOTROPY

- Such substances which having the same chemical properties, but differ in physical properties, known as allotropes and this property is called allotropy.

DIAMOND

- Diamond is the purest form of carbon.
- It is non-conductor of heat and electricity.
- It is the hardest natural substance.
- It burns in air at 900°C and gives out CO_2.

GRAPHITE (BLACK LEAD)

- It is good conductor of heat and electricity.
- Graphite is used in making lead pencils.
- Graphite is also used as electrodes, lubricant, moderators, electrotyping and carbon arc.

AMORPHOUS FORMS OF CARBON

1. Wood Charcoal – Obtained from wood
2. Sugar Charcoal – Obtained from cane sugar
3. Bone or Animal Charcoal – Obtained from animal bones
4. Coke Charcoal – Obtained from coal

CARBON MONOXIDE (CO)

- Carbon monoxide is an active poison and is very dangerous as it is a colourless and odourless gas and can not, therefore, be easily detected.
- The extremely poisonous nature of carbon monoxide is a result of its combining with the haemoglobin of the blood to form carbo-xyhaemoglobin, which is not decompassed by any of the processes in the body.

HYDROCARBONS

- Compounds of carbon and hydrogen are called hydrocarbon.
- A natural source of hydrocarbon is petroleum obtained from sedimentary rocks.
- Compounds having the same molecular formula but differ in properties due to different structural formula known as isomers and this property is called isomerism.

SATURATED HYDROCARBONS (ALKANES)

- Containing single covalent bonds only.
- Such compounds are, in general, called alkanes for instance, Methane, Ethane, Propane, Butane.

UNSATURATED HYDROCARBONS

- Containing multiple bonds.
- Compounds with double bonds are called alkenes, e.g. ethylene, propyene etc. and triple bond containing compounds are called alkynes, e.g. acetylene, propyne etc.
- Benzene is an unsaturated cyclic hydrocarbon with the structure.
- Compounds derived from benzene are called aromatic compounds.

FUELS

Solid Fuels

- These contain carbon and, during combustion, form mainly carbon dioxide and carbon monoxide with a large amount of heat.
- Examples of solid fuels are wood, coal, coke and paraffin wax.

Liquid Fuels

- These are basically mixtures of several hydrocarbons. During combustion, they form carbon dioxide and water.
- Liquid fuels are obtained as different fractions during the distillation of petroleum.
- Examples of liquid fuels are kerosene oil, petrol, diesel oil and alcohol.

Gaseous Fuels

- Gaseous fuels do not leave ash on burning and have high content of heat.
- The main gaseous fuels are liquefied petroleum gas (LPG, mainly a mixture of propane and butane and used in homes for cooking, water gas ($CO + H_2$), producer gas ($CO + N_2$), coal gas (mixture of hydrogen, methane, ethylene, carbon monoxide, nitrogen, oxygen and carbon dioxide) and natural gas (mixture of methane, ethane, propane and butane with traces of higher hydrocarbons obtained from oil well, above petroleum).

PETROLEUM AND NATURAL GAS

- Natural gas contains about 80% methane and 10% ethane, the remaining 10% being a mixture of higher gaseous hydrocarbons.
- Compressed Natural Gas (CNG) is natural gas filled in cylinders under high pressure.
- The quality of petrol for use in car engines is denoted by their anti-knock properties.
- To increase octane number, tetra ethyl lead (TEL) is added to petrol.

HEAVY WATER

- Chemically heavy water is deuterium oxide.
- Heavy water is used in nuclear reactors as a moderator because it slows the fast moving neutrons.

Hard and Soft Water

- Water which produces lather with soap solution readily is called soft water.
- Water which does not produce lather with soap solution readily is called hard water.
- The hardness of water is due to presence of the bicarbonates, chlorides and sulphates of calcium and magnesium.
- Temporary hardness of water is due to the presence of bicarbonates of calcium and magnesium.
- Permanent hardness of water is due to presence of sulphates, chlorides, nitrates of calcium and magnesium.

GLASS

- Ordinary glass is solid mixture of silica, sodium silicate and calcium silicate.
- Soft glass is a soda-lime silicate glass. It melts at low temperature. It is used in manufacturing of bottles, test tubes etc.
- Hard glass is potash lime silicate and melts at high temperature in comparison to soft glass and is used in manufacturing of flask etc.
- Flint glass is a lead potash silicate and is used in manufacturing of prism, lens and optical instruments.
- Pyrex glass is a mixture of sodium aluminium borosilicates. It is used in manufacturing of high quality equipments in laboratory because it does not melt at very high temperature.
- Safety glass is prepared by placing a layer of transparent plastic glass between two layers of glass by means of a suitable adhesive. It is used in making wind screen of automobiles, aeroplanes, trains etc.

CEMENT

- The approximate composition of Portland cement is:
  1. Calcium Oxide → 62%
  2. Silica → 22%
  3. Alumina → 7.5%
  4. Magnesia → 2.5%
  5. Ferric Oxide → 2.5%
- A small amount of gypsum is added to slow down the setting of cement.
- Cement containing excess amount of lime cracks during setting while cement containing less amount of lime is weak in strength.
- Cement containing no iron is white but hard to burn.

POLYMERS AND PLASTICS

- A polymer is a large molecule, built up from many hundreds of thousands of small unit called monomeric units or monomers.
- The process of formation of polymers from monomers is called polymerization.
- Plastics are cross-linked polymers and very tough.
- Some examples of plastics are — Celluloid, Bakelite and Vinyl Plastics.

RUBBER

- Natural and Synthetic rubbers are examples of polymers.
- Natural rubber is isomer of isoprene.
- When the natural rubber is heated along with sulphur called vulcanisation. The resulting rubber is elastic, hard and strong.
- Synthetic rubbers are made by polymerisation of chloroprene, styrene and butadiene mixtures and isobutylene.

SOAPS

- The soaps are sodium salts of higher fatty acids. They are useful only in soft water as they form an insoluble precipitate in hard water. This precipitate consists of salts of calcium and magnesium of higher fatty acids. No lather or emulsion is formed and washing is not possible.

Some Importants Alloys

Alloys	*Composition*
Brass	Cu, Zn
Bronze	Cu, Sn
Gun metal	Cu, Sn, Zn
Bel metal	Cu, Sn
German silver	Cu, Zn, Ni
Dutch metal	Cu, Zn
Aluminium	Al, Cu
Nichrome	Ni, Fe, Cr, Mn
Chromium steel	Cr, C, Fe

Chemical Formulae, Commercial Name of Chemical Compounds

Commercial Name	Chemical Compounds	Chemical formulae
Common salt	Sodium chloride	$NaCl$
Baking soda	Sodium bicarbonate	$NaHCO_3$
Washing soda	Sodium carbonate	$Na_2CO_3 . 10H_2O$
Caustic soda	Sodium hydroxide	$NaOH$
Chilli salt peter	Sodium nitrate	$NaNO_3$
Soda ash	Sodium carbonate	Na_2CO_3
Hypo	Sodium thiosulphate	$Na_2S_2O_3 . 5H_2O$

BIOLOGY

BRANCHES OF BIOLOGY

(*a*) **Anthropology:** Deals with the scientific study of man and the mankind.

(*b*) **Agronomy:** Deals with the management of farms and science of crop production.

(*c*) **Apiculture:** Deals with the process of bee keeping for commercial purposes.

(*d*) **Entomology:** Deals with the structure, habits and classification of insects.

(*e*) **Eugenics:** Deals with improving the human race.

(*f*) **Pathology:** Deals with the nature of disease, their causes, symptoms, effects, their cure and control.

(*g*) **Physiotherapy:** Deals with the treatment of diseases, body weakness or defects with the help of massage and exercise etc.

(*h*) **Sericulture:** Deals with the production of raw silk from silkworm.

(*i*) **Pharmacology:** Deals with the knowledge and manufacture of drugs.

(*j*) **Occupational therapy:** Deals with treating the physically handicapped or injured persons through exercise etc.

(*k*) **Psychology:** Deals with the study of human mind, its behaviour and mental qualities.

(*l*) **DNA finger printing:** Technique to help identify a person on the basis of genes.

ANIMALS/PLANTS

- The organisms that closely resemble one another are placed in one group, the groups which have similarities are combined together into larger groups, and these into still larger ones. The most inclusive category is kingdom. Other major categories, in descending order are: phylum, class, order, family, genus, and species. Man belongs to Animal kingdom, chordata division or phylum, Mammalia class, Primates order, Hominidae family, Homo genus and Sapiens species.

CELL THEORY

- Cell is the basic unit of structure of all living organisms. According to the cell theory, all organism are composed of cells and cell products and growth and development results from the division and differentiation of cells.
- Cells membrane surrounds all living cells.
- Nucleus is the most important cell organelle which controls and coordinates all cell activities and also concerned with the transmission of heredity characters.
- Mitochondria, ribosomes, lysosomes and dictyosomes are present in plant and animal cells.
- Only plant cells have cell wall, chloroplast and vacuole.
- Viruses constitute a difficulty since in many ways they are intermediate between living and dead matter.
- The cell is said to be made up of a substance called Protoplasm which has two main constituents cytoplasm and nucleus, and is bounded by a cell membrane on outside.
- Cells take up the raw materials for metabolism through the cell membrane from extracellular fluid surrounding them.
- Cytoplasm inside is responsible for maintaining the internal distribution of organelles and also for free cell movements.
- Mitochondria inside provides energy for reactions inside the cell. Ribosomes are responsible for the synthesis of proteins.
- The Endoplasmic Reticulum helps in addition of other sugar units to proteins and their transportation to other parts of the cell.

FOOD

- It is a nutritive substance taken by an organism for growth, work, repair and maintaining life processes. It provides energy to do work and maintain body heat, provides materials for the growth of the body, makes necessary materials for reproduction and provides materials for the repair of damaged cells and tissues of our body.

- **Carbohydrates:** For a normal person, 400 to 500 gms of carbohydrates are required daily but for sportspersons, growing children and nursing mothers, it is on higher side.
- **Proteins:** They are complex organic compounds made up of carbon, hydrogen, oxygen and nitrogen. The building blocks of Protein are Amino acids and there are large number of amino acids.
- Proteins are essential for the growth of children and teenagers, and for maintenance and making good the wear and tear of the body tissues in adults.
- An adult needs about 1 gm of protein per kg of body weight.
- **Fats:** They are esters of long chain fatty acids and an alcohol called glycerol. Fats also contain atoms of carbon, hydrogen and oxygen.
- The main function of fats in the body is to provide a steady source of energy and for this purpose, they are deposited within the body.
- One gm of fat gives 37 kilojoules of energy which is more than double of that given by carbohydrates.
- Fats, the richest source of energy to our body, can be stored in the body for subsequent use. Fats, soluble in organic solvents and insoluble in water, also supply fat-soluble vitamins to our body.
- **Minerals:** Some of the important minerals needed by our body are — iron, iodine, calcium, phosphorus, sodium, potassium, zinc, copper, magnesium, chloride, fluoride and sulphur.
- We get most of the minerals in combined form from plant sources. Deficiency of these minerals causes many diseases.
- **Energy Requirements:** The energy requirement of a body varies according to age, sex, lifestyle, occupation, climate and special situations like pregnancy and lactation.

Age	*Energy requirements*
5 years	6000 kJ per day
11 years	9000 kJ per day
18 years	11000 kJ per day
Adult (normal work)	9600 kJ per day
Adult (heavy work)	12000 kJ per day
Adult (very heavy work)	16000 kJ per day

- **Vitamins:** They act as catalysts in certain chemical reactions of metabolism in our body.
- They don't provide energy to our body nor form body tissues.
- More than 15 types of vitamins are known and only 2 vitamins — D and K can be formed in our body.

Vitamin	*Necessity*	*Source*
Vitamin A	For maintaining healthy eyesight, normal skin and hair	Cod liver oil, fish, eggs, milk, carrot, leafy vegetables.
Vitamin B_1	For growth, carbohydrate metabolism, functioning of heart, nerves and muscles.	Milk, soya-food, meat, whole cereals, green vegetables.
Vitamin C	For keeping teeth, gums and joints healthy, for increasing resistance of body to infection	Citrus fruits, guava, tomatoes.
Vitamin D	For normal growth of bones and teeth	Milk, eggs, butter, cod liver oil, sun light.
Vitamin E	For normal reproduction, functioning of muscles and protection of liver	Green leafy vegetables, milk, butter, tomato.
Vitamin K	For normal clotting of blood and normal functioning of liver	Green leafy vegetables, soyabean, tomato.

- **Roughage:** Though it does not provide any energy to the body, yet keeps the digestive system in order, by helping in retaining water in the body and preserving constitution.
- The main source of roughage are salads, cabbage, corn cob, porridge, vegetables and fruits with stems.

DISEASES

COMMUNICABLE DISEASES

- They are the diseases which can be transmitted from reservoirs of infection or infected person to the healthy but susceptible persons.
- The disease causing agent or the pathogen can be transmitted directly or indirectly.

DEFICIENCY DISEASES

- These occur due to deficiency of some nutrients in the diet or some hormone due to hypo activity or damage to endocrine glands.

Diet Deficiency	*Disease*
Protein	Kwashiorkor
Protein-energy malnutrition	Marasmus
Vitamin A	Night-blindness, Xerophthalmia
Vitamin B_1	Beri-Beri
Vitamin B_2	Cheilosis
Vitamin B_5	Pellagra
Vitamin C	Scurvy

Vitamin D	Rickets (in children), (in adult) Osteomalacia
Vitamin K	Hypothrombinemia
Iron	Anaemia
Iodine	Goitre
Fluoride	Dental caries
Calcium and phosphorus	Affects formation of bones and teeth

Hormone Deficiency	*Disease*
Insulin	Diabetes
Thyroxine	Cretinism (child), Goitre
STH	Dwarfism, Gigantism

ALLERGIC DISEASE

- In these diseases, body becomes hypersensitive to some foreign agents, allergens, which cause inflammation when come in contact with the body or enter inside the body.
- Foreign agents can be dust, pollens, certain-foods, serum, certain drugs or fabrics.
- The unfavourable response of the body to allergens is called allergic reaction. Asthma and hay fever are allergic diseases.

BACTERIAL DISEASES

- Bacteria are minute organisms which are known to cause a number of diseases:

Disease	Incubation period	Spread through
Tuberculosis	2-10 weeks	Air-borne,droplet infection
Diptheria	2-6 days	Air-borne droplet infection
Cholera	6 hours to 2-3 days	Contaminated food and water. House flies are the vectors
Leprosy	Upto 5 years	Prolonged and intimate contact
Whopping cough	7-14 days	Droplet infection
Tetanus	3-21 days	Entry of cysts through any wound made by sharp object, dog bite or fall on the road
Typhoid	1-3 weeks	Directed and Contact
Plague	2-6 days	Rats and bed-bugs transmit the germs
Pneumonia	1-3 days	Air-borne

VIRAL DISEASES

Disease	Incubation period	Spread through
Chicken-pox	12-20 days	Direct contact with infected persons or infected objects
Smallpox	12 days	Droplet infection
Poliomyalitis	7-14 days	Direct and oral
Measles	10 days	Droplet infection
Mumps	12-26 days	Droplet infection
Rabies	1-3 months	Bite of rabied animal like dogs, monkeys, cats
Influenza	24-28 hours	Air-borne

DISEASES CAUSED BY PROTOZOA

- Amoebiasis (Amoebic dysentery), Malaria, Kala-azar, Trypanosomiasis and Giardiasis are main diseases caused by Protozoans.
- Malaria is a parasitic infection.

SYSTEM OF HUMAN BODY

DIGESTIVE SYSTEM

- The digestive system consists of alimentary canal and digestive glands. Alimentary canal is about 8-10 meters long tube of varying diameter. Food is taken in through mouth.
- The tongue helps in ingestion, chewing, tasting and swallowing of food and mixing of food and saliva.
- Salivary glands secret saliva which helps in digestion of starch. Gastric glands present in the mucosa of the stomach, provide acidic medium for the food digestion.
- Liver, the largest sized, reddish brown gland of body, secrets bile. Liver is present in the right upper part of the abdomen. The bile secreted by the liver is stored in gall bladder. It helps in the emulsification and digestion of fats.
- Pancreas is the second largest gland in human body and secretes pancreatic juices. Intestine also secret juices.

RESPIRATORY SYSTEM

- Oxygen is needed for the oxidation and expelling of carbon dioxide is necessary to avoid its-accumulation. This process of exchange of gases between the environment and the body, is called respiration.
- In some unicellular organisms like aerobic bacteria, amoeba, hydra, etc. there is direct exchange of gases between the carbon dioxide of the body and oxygen of water.
- There is no blood for transport of gases. However, in larger and complex form of animals, specialised respiratory organs are developed.
- Amphibians respire through skin, fishes through gills and mammals, birds and reptiles through lungs.
- A normal adult inspires or expires about 500 ml of gas with each breath and about 72 breathes per minutes.

CIRCULATORY SYSTEM

- Main components of the circulatory system are heart, blood vessels and blood.
- Heart is a thick, muscular, contractile and automatic pumping organ. In birds and mammals, heart is divided into four chambers.

- Arteries are thick walled blood vessels which always carry the blood away from the heart to various body parts.
- Veins are thin walled blood vessels which always carry the blood from various parts generally to the heart.
- In an adult healthy person, the normal rate of heart beat at rest is about 70-72 times per minute.

BLOOD

- It is red, opaque, somewhat sticky and viscous fluid in the body of animals.
- It is slightly alkaline (pH = 7.4), heavier than water (sp gr = 1.05) and five times more viscous than distilled water.
- Blood forms 6 to 10% of the body weight.
- An adult, on average, has about 6.8 litres of blood.
- Blood contains plasma and blood corpuscles with the former occupying 55-60% of the volume.
- Plasma transports food components, metabolic wastes and hormones; keeps constant level of pH of blood, maintains body temperature and helps in blood clotting.
- Erythrocytes or red blood corpuscles (RBCs), leukocytes or white blood corpuscles (WBCs) and blood platelets are other parts of the blood.
- Due to the presence of iron containing pigment haemoglobin, RBCs are red in colour. The RBCs are crucial for ex-change of oxygen and carbon dioxide. WBCs are nucleated and non-pigmented cells. They are larger in size than RBCs but far less in number (1 : 600).
- WBCs play an important role in immune system of the body. Blood platelets cause the coagulation of blood and clot formation to prevent excessive bleeding.
- Human blood is divided into four main Groups—A, B, AB and O.
- The plasma of Group A blood contains an anti-B factor and vice-versa, so that people of Groups A and B cannot accept each other's blood.
- Group AB contains neither anti-A nor anti-B factor and people with this group can receive transfusions from both but can give to neither.
- Group O contains both anti-A and anti-B and can receive blood only from Group O but can donate blood to all Groups. Group O is called universal donor because they can donate to all the Groups.
- Group AB is called universal acceptor because they can accept blood from all Groups.

SKELETON SYSTEM

- The frame or the hard structure of the human body is composed from the bones and the organs of making such frame are called skeleton system.

Bones

- Bone is the hardest tissue of the body and form the largest section of the body weight.
- Bones contain organic as well as inorganic matters. With advancing age, the inorganic matter's share increases, causing the bones to become more brittle.
- Long bones such as humerus and femur are hollow while small bones are solid.

EXCRETORY SYSTEM

- In men, excretory system is formed of one pair of kidneys, one pair of ureters, a urinary bladder and a urethra. Kidney is about 10 cm long, bean shaped, dark-red and slightly flattened structure.
- Sweet glands, oil glands, lungs and liver also act as additional excretory organ.
- In case of kidney failure, a man can treated by hemodialysis or transplantation of a kidney from a donor's body.

NERVOUS SYSTEM

- The system which controls and coordinates the body functions, retains memory and receives and sends signals, is called the nervous system.
- The nervous system comprises brain, spinal cord, nerves and nerve fibres.
- Human brain weighs about 1200 to 1400 gm. Main parts of the brain are cerebrum, cerebellum and medulla oblongata.
- Cerebrum controls voluntary function and is site of intelligence, will power, emotions, etc.
- Cerebellum controls involuntary functions like heart beat, respiration, etc.
- Spinal cord is about 45 cm long and about 35 gm in weight. It conducts impulses to and from the brain and controls reflex actions of the body.
- Various cranial (arising from ending into brain) and spinal nerves (arising from spinal cord) control smell, vision, movements of body parts, taste and hearing.

REPRODUCTION SYSTEM

- In this type of reproduction, there is formation and fusion of sex cells, called gametes.
- Organism develops from the zygote through embryo formation.
- It generally involves two parents — male and female.
- The offsprings are different from the parent as variations appear due to new combinations of genes. So, it plays an important role in evolution.
- All higher plants and animals reproduce sexually.

CHROMOSOMES

- Plants and animals have fixed number of chromosomes per cell.
- Genes are located on chromosomes and are responsible for transfer of characteristics from one cell to the next either in the same organism or from parents to offspring.

- Man has 23 pairs of chromosomes, of which one pair is sex chromosomes.
- Males child inherits X chromosomes from the female parent and Y from the male parent.
- Female child receives a X chromosome each from either of its parents.
- Mendel was the first scientist to explain transmission of units from reproductive cells of the parents to the off-springs.

CLONING

- It is the process of producing genetically identical copies of a biological material, starting from a single cell. The original genes are transplanted and thus one can produce organisms of known and desirable characteristics.

GENETIC ENGINEERING

- It is the method of artificial synthesis of new genes and their subsequent transplantation or methods of correcting the defective genes.
- It has helped in producing plants and animals with specific characters.
- So, crippling hereditary diseases can also be cured like hemophilia etc.

DNA FINGERPRINTING

- It consists of examining repetitive DNA in the genome for variations in the length of restriction fragments.
- Every individual has his own pattern, so that fingerprinting can match blood to a particular person, and patterns are inherited from parent to child, allowing the method to identify relationships between individuals.

IN-VITRO FERTILIZATION

- When a sperm and an egg are made to fertilize outside a living body (usually a test tube), it is called in-vitro fertilization.
- This process has been used to impregnate several females who could not do so through natural means.

Diseases and the Parts of Body they Affect

AIDS—Immune system of body	*Gout*—Joints of bone
Arthritis—Inflammation of joints	*Jaundice*—Liver
Asthma—Lungs	*Meningitis*—Brain or spinal cord
Cataract—Eyes	*Pleurisy*—Pleura (inflammation of)
Conjunctivitis—Eyes	*Polio*—motor neurons
Diabetes—Pancreas	*Pneumonia*—Lungs
Diphtheria—Throat	*Pyorrhoea*—Sockets of teeth
Glaucoma—Eyes	*Tuberculosis*—Lungs
Eczema—Skin	*Typhoid*—Intestine
Goitre—Front of the neck (due to enlargement of thyroid gland)	*Malaria*—Spleen
	Leukaemia—Blood
	Rickets—Bones

SPACE RESEARCH

First in Space

✶ First creator of rules regarding space research	Isaac Newton
✶ First artificial satellite launched in space	Sputnik-1 (1957)
✶ First living being sent in space	Louika (a dog)
✶ Firstever manned spacecraft	Vostok-I
✶ First man in space	Yuri Gagarin U.S.S.R. (1961)
✶ First woman in space	Valentina Tereshkova U.S.S.R. (June 1963)
✶ First man who moved in space out of the spacecraft	Alexi Livonov U.S.S.R. (June 1965)
✶ First person to land on moon	Neil Armstrong, America (21st July, 1969)
✶ First fourwheeled carriage without human being on moon	Leunokhev-I U.S.S.R. (1970)
✶ First space lab in orbit	Skylab (America, 1973)
✶ First space shuttle	Columbia (America, 1981)
✶ First Indian (man) in space	Squadron leader—Rakesh Sharma (13th April, 1984)
✶ First Indian (Woman) in space	Kalpana Chawla (19th Nov., 1997)
✶ First American woman in space	Sailyride (1983)
✶ First spacecraft on Mars	Pathfinder (6 July, 1997)
✶ First woman who lead spacecraft	Allin Collis (America)
✶ First spacecraft without man	Shenzoo, China (20th Nov. 1999)

Indian Space Programme : At a Glance

Satellite	Date	Type	Launch Vehicle	Result
Aryabhatta	19-04-75	Scientific	Cosmos	successful
Bhaskara I	07-06-79	Geosurvey	Cosmos	successful
Rohini	10-08-79	Geosurvey	S.L.V.3	unsuccessful
Rohini D-1	18-07-80	Geosurvey	S.L.V.3	successful
Rohini	31-05-81	Scientific	S.L.V.3	successful
Apple	19-06-81	Communication	Ariane	successful
Bhaskara II	20-11-81	Geosurvey	Cosonos	successful
INSAT-1A	10-04-82	Multipurpose	Delta	unsuccessful
Rohini	17-04-83	Scientific	S.L.V.3	successful
INSAT-1B	30-08-83	Multipurpose	Space Shuttle	successful
SROSS I	24-03-87	Technical	ASLV-D1	unsuccessful
IRS-1A	17-03-88	Remote sensing	Vostok	successful
SROSS II	17-07-88	Technical	ASLV-D2	unsuccessful
INSAT-1C	21-07-88	Multipurpose	Ariane-4	unsuccessful
INSAT-1D	12-06-90	Multipurpose	Delta	successful
IRS-1B	29-08-91	Remote sensing	Vostok	successful
INSAT-2A	10-07-92	Multipurpose	Ariane	successful
IRS-ID	29-09-97	Remote sensing	PSLV	successful
INSAT-3B	22-03-2000	Multipurpose	Ariane	successful
G-SAT-1	18-04-2001	Multipurpose	GSLV-D	successful
MAT SAT	12-09-2002	Meteorology	PSLVC-4	successful
INSAT-3E	28-09-2003	Communication	Ariane-5	successful
Cartosat-1 & hamsat	05-05-2005	Maping and Communication	PSLV-C6	successful
CARTOSAT-2	10-01-2007	Communication	PSLV-C7	successful
Cartosat-2A	28-04-2008	Communication	PSLV-C9	successful
Chandrayaan-I	22-10-2008	Maping and Scientific	PSLV-C11	successful
Oceansat-2	24-09-2009	Remote Sensing	PSLV-C14	successful
CARTOSAT-2B	12-07-2010	Communication	PSLV-C15	successful
RESOURCESAT-2	20-04-2011	Remote Sensing	PSLV-C16	successful
GSAT-12	15-07-2011	Communication	PSLV-C17	successful
Megha-Tropiques	12-10-2011	Maping and Scientific	PSLV-C18	successful
RISAT-1	26-04-2012	Remote Sensing	PSLV-C19	successful
Spot-6	09-09-2012	Remote Sensing	PSLV-C21	successful
Saral	25-02-2013	Scientific	PSLV-C20	successful
GSAT-7	30-08-2013	Defence	Ariane-5	successful
MOM	5-11-2013	Mapping	PSLV-C25	successful
GSAT-14	05-01-2014	Communication	GSLV-D5	successful
IRNSS-1B	04-04-2014	Mapping and Scientific	PSLV-C24	successful
Spot-7	30-06-2014	Remote Sensing	PSLV-C23	successful
GSAT-16	07-12-2014	Communication	Ariane-5	successful
IRNSS-1D	28-03-2015	Mapping and Scientific	PSLV-C27	successful
GSAT-6	27-08-2015	Communication	GSLV-D6	successful
Astrosat	28-09-2015	Mapping and Scientific	PSLV-C30	successful
GSAT-15	11-11-2015	Communication	Ariane-5	successful
TELEOS-1	16-12-2015	Mapping and Scientific	PSLV-C29	successful
IRNSS-1E	20-01-2016	Mapping and Scientific	PSLV-C31	successful
IRNSS-1F	10-03-2016	Mapping and Scientific	PSLV-C32	successful
IRNSS-1G	28-04-2016	Mapping and Scientific	PSLV-C33	successful
Cartosat-2 & others	22-06-2016	Mapping and Scientific	PSLV-C34	successful

Satellite	Date	Type	Launch Vehicle	Result
insat-3DR	08-09-2016	Meteorology	GSLV-F05	successful
Scatsat-1 & others	26-09-2016	Multipurpose	PSLV-C35	successful
RESOURCESAT-2A	07-12-2016	Remote Sensing	PSLV-C36	successful
CARTOSAT-2 & 103 others	15-02-2017	Multipurpose	PSLV-C37	successful
CARTOSAT-2E	23-06-2017	Earth observation Satellite	PSLV-C38	successful
GSAT-17	29-06-2017	Earth observation Satellite	Ariane-5 ECA	successful
Cartosat-2F & others	12-01-2018	Multipurpose	PSLV-C40	successful
GSAT-6A	29-03-2018	Communication	GSLV-F08	successful
GSAT-7A	19-12-2018	Military Satellite	GSLV-MK-II-F11	successful
Chandrayaan-2	22-07-2019	Lunar Exploration	GSLV MK-III M01	—
Cartosat-3	27-11-2019	Earth Imagine Satellite	PSLV-C47	successful
GSAT-30	17-01-2020	Communication	Ariane-5	successful
EOS-01	07-11-2020	Earth Observation	PSLV-C49	successful
Amezonia & 19 others	28-02-2021	Communication	PSLV-C51	successful
EOS-04	14-02-2022	Earth Observation	PSLV-C52	successful
Oceansat-3 & 8 others	26-11-2022	Earth Observation	PSLV-C54	successful
EOS-07	10-02-2023	Earth Observation	SSLV-02	successful
Chandrayaan-3	14-07-2023	Lunar Exploration	LVM-3	successful
Aditya-L1	02-09-2023	Solar Mission	PSLV-C57	successful
XPoSat	01-01-2024	Earth Observation	PSLV-C58	successful

COMPUTER

- The computer is the system of that electronic device through which various informations are processed on the basis of a definite set of instructions called program and mathematical (numerical) and non-mathematical both types of informations are processed.
- The first mechanical computer was composed or fabricated by Blaise Pascal in 1642 and it is called Pascalene.
- But in 1833, Charles Babbage first time conceived an automatic calculator or computer.
- Charles Babbage is called the father of modern computer.
- Herman made an electronic tabulating machine based on punch cards which operates automatically.
- In 1937, first mechanical computer Mark-I was fabricated by Howard Akeen.
- The most outstanding contribution in the development of modern computer goes to John Wan Newmaan who brought the 2nd revolution in the area of computer in 1951.
- He discovered EDVAC (Electronic Discrete Variable Automatic Computer) and utilised the stored program and the binary number system in the computer.

FUNCTIONS OF COMPUTER

- 1. Collection and composition (input) of datas;
  2. Storage of datas.
  3. Processing of datas.
  4. Retrieval or output of the proccessed informations and datas.

UNITS OF COMPUTER

1. Input unit.
2. Central processing unit–CPU.
3. External Memory unit.
4. Output unit.

- The CPU of the computer is called brain of the computer and sometimes CPU is also called Micro Processor of the computer.
- The data is entered through the input unit in the computer and through the central processing unit with the help of External Memory Unit datas are arranged and processed.
- Ultimately by the output unit these datas or informations are issued or released.

PARTS OF COMPUTER

- **Monitor :** The monitor of the computer is like a television in which the picture appears in the form of doted points on the screen and these are called pixels.
- **Hard Disc and Floppy Disc :** The Hard Disc is the permanent disc in the computers while the Floppy Disc is the disc utilised when datas or informations are to be transferred from one computer to another.
- **Mouse :** The mouse of the computer is like the remote control of TV through which computer is directly regulated or controlled without utilising the key-board.
- **Printer :** The printer is a device which prints any documents or processed informations of the computer.

SOME HIGH LEVEL LANGUAGES

1. **FORTRAN :** This language was developed for solving the mathematical formulae very quickly and conveniently.
2. **COBOL :** This language was developed for the commerical purposes. For the processing of this

language a group of sentences is selected called paragraph and all paragraphs composed are called a section, while all sections composed are called a division.

3. **BASIC :** In basic a definite part of the prescribed instruction is only inserted in the computer.
4. **ALGOL :** This was basically fabricated and designed for the complex algebraic calculations.
5. **PASCAL :** It is an amplified and modified form of ALGOL.
6. **COMAL :** This computer language is used for the students of secondary level.
7. **LOGO :** This language is used for children and kids for drawing Graphic line diagrams.
8. **PROLOG :** This language is developed in 1973 in France and is used for Artificial Intelligence which is capable and equivalent to the logical program.
9. **FORTH :** This language was invented by Charles Mure which is frequently used in all types of the works in the computer.

COMPUTER VIRUS

- The computer virus is an electronic code which is used to abolish or erradicate the inclusive informations or programs of the computer.
- Some important computer viruses are Micheleanjalo, Dork Avangor, kilo, filip, Macmug, Scores, Casecade, Jeruslem, Date crime, Coloumbs crime, Internet virus, Pachcom, Pach EXE, COM-EXE, Marizuana, C-brain, bloody, Chenge Mungu and Desi etc.

COMPUTER NETWORKING

- There are two types of networkings which are usually occur—Local Area Networking (LAN) and Wide Area Networking (WAN).

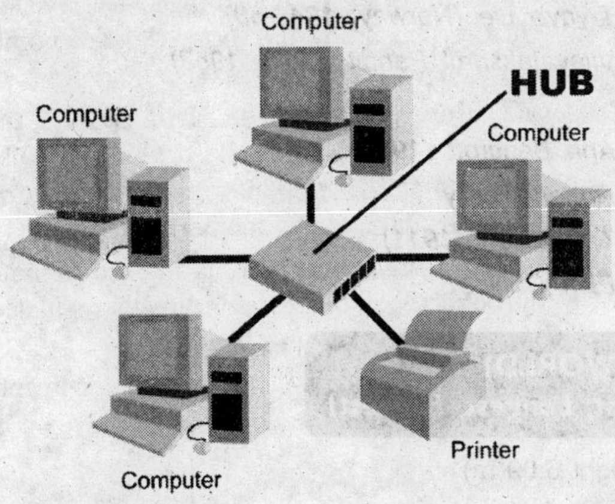

- By LAN all the computers of the same buildings are connected like the computers of university premises, computers of offices etc.
- By WAN all the comptuers of a large area are connected like the computers of all the offices of a city or town etc.
- In India a very large computer network namely INDONET has been installing through which all the main towns and cities has to be interlinked.

COMPUTER TERMINOLOGY

- **Bit :** The bit is a unit of measurement of the electronic data. One bit is either 0 or 1 but not both. On composing 8 bits, 1 byte is formed.
- **Bug :** The Bug is the error in the computer program or system and its eradication is called Debug.
- **Byte :** Total eight bits compose a byte. Thus 8 bits = 1 byte.
- **CD-ROM :** A CD like of music CD in which data can be stored substantially called CD-ROM. In a CD with comparison to floppy extremely more datas can be stored but one problem in it is that one time recorded data can not be deleted or modified.
- **Chip :** It is a thin slice on which by a special mechanism a circuit is designed which is normally made from Silicon.
- **Memory System :** The place where computer data and program are temporarily kept is called Memory system. Usually memory is implied from RAM.
- **Modem :** The device which converts digital signals into analogue signals and vice-versa is called Modem.
- **RAM :** It is Random Access Memory (a place) where datas to be processed are kept temporarily and it is unstable memory.
- **ROM :** It is Read Only Memory and it is stable or Non-valatile memory which doesn't ended after power off.
- **Scanner :** It is a device through which graphic image is transformed to digital image and the scanners are of usually two types one desktop and another hand operating.

PROGRAMING

- Computers perform phenomenal feats of calculation, but they do not do so in a complicated way.
- They actually carry out very simple operations, such as addition and subtraction.
- They achieve their fantastic computing power by carrying out these operations at incredible speed.
- The programme, or set of instructions for operating the computer, is therefore written as a sequence of very simple steps.

  Several computer languages have been developed for different applications, including BASIC, COBOL, FORTRAN and PASCAL. Writing programmes is very skilled and time-consuming work.
- But for most typical computer applications ready-written programmes are available, called "packages".

❐❐❐

GENERAL KNOWLEDGE

FIRST IN THE WORLD

✶ First Chinese visitor to India	*Fahien*
✶ First foreign invader of India	*Alexander, the Great (Greek)*
✶ First person to climb Mt. Everest	*Tenzing Norgay (India) and Edmund Hillary (New Zealand) (1953)*
✶ First atom bomb dropped at	*Hiroshima (Japan)*
✶ First man in the space	*Yuri Gagarin (former USSR)*
✶ First woman in the space	*Valentina Tereshkova (former USSR)*
✶ First person to walk in the space	*Alexei Leonov (former USSR)*
✶ First person to land on the moon	*Neil Armstrong (USA)*
✶ First and the only woman to have climbed Mt. Everest twice	*Santosh Yadav (Indian; May 12, 1992; May 10, 1993)*
✶ First person on Mt. Everest without oxygen	*Phu Dorjee (Indian; May 9, 1984)*
✶ First person to climb Mt. Everest twice	*Nawang Gombu*
✶ First President of the USA	*George Washington*
✶ First woman Prime Minister	*Sirimavo Bandaranaike (Sri Lanka)*
✶ First person to swim across English Channel	*Mathew Webb*
✶ First woman to swim across English Channel	*Gertrude Caroline Ederle*
✶ First woman to climb Mt. Everest	*Junko Tabei (Japan)*
✶ First woman to climb Mt. Everest alone and without oxygen supplies	*Alison Hargreaves (Britain: May 13, 1995)*
✶ First Aeroplane to fly around the world without refuelling	*Voyager (Dec. 1986)*
✶ First test-tube Baby	*Louise Brown (UK; 1978)*
✶ First all-talking Film	*Jaz Singer (1927)*
✶ First Secretary-General of the UN	*Trygve Lie (Norway: 1946-53)*
✶ First woman President of the UN General Assembly	*Vijayalakshmi Pandit (India: 1953)*
✶ First woman to reach North Pole	*Ann Bancroft (1986)*
✶ First person to reach North Pole	*Robert Peary*
✶ First person to reach South Pole	*Amundsen (1911)*
✶ First woman to command Spacecraft in Space	*Ellin Collins*

SUPERLATIVES (WORLD)
(The Largest, Biggest, Smallest, Longest, Highest)

Animal,	*Tallest*	Giraffe (Average height 6.09 m)
	Largest and Heaviest	Blue Whale (190 tonnes)
	Longest recorded	Boot lace Worm (55 m)
	Fastest	Cheetah (Approximately 100 km/hr)

Bay,	*With max. shore line*	Hudson Bay (Canada: 12268 km)
	With maximum area	Bay of Bengal (India: 217 million hc)
Building,	*Tallest*	Burj Khalifa (Dubai, 818 meter)
Canal,	*Big ship (longest)*	Suez Canal (160 km)
	Busiest	Kiel Canal (North Sea)
City,	*Largest in Area*	Jiuquan Gansu, China (Area 1,67,996 Sq km)
Continent,	*biggest*	Asia
	Smallest	Australia Mainland
Country,	*Largest in Population*	China (over 137 crore)
	Largest in Area	Russia (17,075,400 sq. km)
	With largest electorate	India (over 90 crores)
	Smallest independent	State of Vatican City (0.44 km^2)
Delta,	*Largest*	Sundarban's Ganga-Brahmaputra delta (1,05,000 sq. km)
Desert,	*Largest*	Sahara (N. Africa; maximum length 5,150 km EW; maximum width 3,200 km NS)
Dome,	*Largest*	Singapore National Stadium (310 m)
Epic,	*Longest*	Mahabharata
Film,	*Most Oscars*	Ben Hur (11 Oscars–1959); Titanic (11 Oscars–1998); The Lord of Rings : The Return of the King (11 Oscars—2003).
Fruit,	*Most nutritive*	Avocado (Vitamins A, C, E and Proteins; Central and South America)
	Least nutritive	Cucumber
Gulf,	*Largest*	Gulf of Mexico (1,544,000 sq. km)
Island,	*Biggest*	Greenland (now known as Kalaatdlit Nunaat–2,175,000 sq km)
Lake,	*Largest*	Caspian Sea (Azerbaijan, Russia, Iran border: 37.18 lakh km^2)
	Deepest	Baikal (Siberia)
	Largest (fresh water)	Superior Lake (USA–Canada border: 82,350 km^2)
Library,	*Biggest*	United States Library of Congress (Washington D.C. founded in 1800, contains 101 million items)
	Biggest non-statutory	New York Public Library
Mountain,	*Highest peak*	Mt. Everest (8848 m; Nepal)
	Highest range	Himalayas, Asia (upto 4200 m)
	Greatest mountain range	Himalaya-Karakoram (96 out of 109 peaks over 7315 m are here)
Ocean,	*Largest and Deepest*	The Pacific (Area: 166,240,000 km^2; Depth: 10,924 m)
Peninsula,	*Largest*	Arabia (3.25 million sq. km)
Planet,	*Biggest*	Jupiter (equatorial diameter 142984 km)
	Brightest, hottest and nearest to Earth	Venus
	Nearest to Sun	Mercury
Plateau,	*Highest*	Tibetan Plateau (Central Asia: 4900 m)
Religion,	*Oldest*	Hinduism
Religion,	*Largest*	Christianity
Rivers,	*Longest*	(i) Nile (6650 km) (ii) Amazon (6437 km)
Sea,	*Largest*	South China Sea (2,974,600 sq. km)
	Largest (inland)	Mediterranean
Star,	*Brightest*	Sirius A (also called Dog Star)
Statue,	*Tallest*	Statue of Unity (India) 182 m.

Swimming course,	*Longest recognised*	English Channel
Temple,	*Largest*	Angkor Vat (Cambodia: 402 acres)
Waterfall,	*Highest*	Salto-Angel (in Venezuela on a branch of river Carrao, depth 807 m.)

IMPORTANT CITIES, PLACES, BUILDINGS OF THE WORLD

- **Angkor Vat:** It is a large group of old Hindu temples in Cambodia; a remnant of the Khmer civilisation. The temples were constructed in the first half of the 12th century.
- **Big Ben:** A clock on the tower of the British Parliament building, installed in 1856.
- **Bethlehem:** A town in Jordan; birth place of Christ; a place of pilgrimage.
- **Cape Canaveral:** Situated in Florida (U.S.A.), it is America's spaceship launching centre. Formerly it was known as *Cape Kennedy.*
- **Eiffel Tower:** A tower in Paris (985 ft high); the principal landmark of the city; designed by a French Engineer for the Paris Exposition 1889.
- **Fleet Street:** A street in London, where offices of newspapers are situated.
- **Golden Gate Bridge (U.S.A.):** One of the world's longest suspension bridges, built in 1933-37 across the entrance (Golden Gate) of San Francisco Bay in California. It has a length of 9266 ft.
- **Harappa:** Situated near Montgomery (Pakistan). The famous ruins throw light on 5000-year-old Indus Valley Civilisation.
- **Hiroshima:** A city in Japan; it was the target of the first atom bomb ever dropped on a city (by U.S.A. on August 6, 1945); casualities numbered nearly 1,30,000 and ninety per cent of the city was levelled.
- **India Office Library (London):** A museum of Indian historical works, collected by the British. The library consists of about 3,00,000 books, a large number of manuscripts in Sanskrit, Urdu, Persian and Arabic.
- **Kaaba:** The inner shrine of the great Mosque at Mecca in Saudi Arabia. It is the most sacred place. Muslims face the Kaaba when praying.
- **Karakoram Highway:** It is a 800-km all weather road linking border of China's Sinkiang province with Pakistan.
- **Leaning Tower of Pisa:** A white marble monument (179 feet high) built in the 14th Century in Italy. It is inclined to one side.
- **Mohenjodaro:** Situated in the Larkana District of Sind (Pakistan); ancient ruins throw light on 5,000-year-old Indus Valley Civilisation.
- **Oval, Leeds and Lords (England):** Famous for cricket matches.
- **Panama Canal:** Canal connecting the Atlantic and Pacific Oceans. The canal is 50 miles long and has 12 locks. It was opened to traffic in August, 1914. The canal is administered by the U.S.A.
- **Pentagon (Washington, USA):** It is a five-sided building housing the US Defence Department offices.
- **Burj Khalifa:** It is a 162 storeyed structure built in Dubai having a height of 818 meter. It is now the highest structure of the world. Taipei 101 (508 meter) is now the second highest structure of the world.
- **Pyramids:** Gigantic stone buildings built by the ancient Egyptians in 2700 B.C.; among the seven wonders of the world. The great pyramid at Giza is the largest. These pyramids were tombs for the pharaohs and other important people.
- **Scotland Yard:** Headquarters of the Criminal Investigation Department in London. It is known all over world for its efficient working.
- **Sandhurst (England):** Famous military training institution.
- **Sphinx:** Mythical beast of ancient Egypt; usually represented in art as having a human head and the body of a lion. The most famous one is the great Sphinx, a colossal stone figure at Gizah built in the 26th Century BC.
- **Stonehenge:** Prehistoric monument near Salisbury, England built in between 1800 B.C. and 1500 B.C.
- **Suez Canal:** This canal is an important link between the Mediterranean Sea and the Red Sea. It is about 160 km long and was constructed in 1869 by a French Engineer. It has shortened the distance between Southampton (England) and Bombay (now Mumbai) by about 4,000 miles. The canal was nationalised by Col. Nasser on July 26, 1956. Port Said is the famous port at the entry from Mediterranean Sea.
- **Vatican:** Official residence of the Pope (in Rome). The smallest country. It enjoys a separate entity in the world. (Area 109 acres).
- **Wall Street (New York):** Famous stock exchange market.

CAPITAL & CURRENCIES

Country	Capital	Currency
✶ Afghanistan	Kabul	Afghani
✶ Albania	Tirana	Lek
✶ Algeria	Algiers	Dinar
✶ Angola	Luanda	New Kwanza
✶ Argentina	Buenos Aires	Peso
✶ Armenia	Yeravan	Dram
✶ Australia	Canberra	Dollar
✶ Austria	Vienna	Euro
✶ Azerbaijan	Baku	Manat
✶ Bahrain	Manama	Dinar
✶ Bangladesh	Dhaka	Taka
✶ Barbados	Bridgetown	Dollar
✶ Belarus	Minsk	Ruble
✶ Belgium	Brussels	Euro
✶ Benin	Porto Novo	Franc
✶ Bhutan	Thimphu	Ngultrum[1]
✶ Bolivia	La paz	Dollar
✶ Botswana	Gaborone	Pula
✶ Brazil	Brasilia	Real
✶ Bosnia Herzegovina	Sarajevo	Dinar
✶ Bulgaria	Sofia	Lev
✶ Cambodia	Phnom-Penh	Riel
✶ Canada	Ottawa	Dollar
✶ Chile	Santiago	Peso
✶ China	Beijing	Yuan
✶ Colombia	Bogota	Peso
✶ Congo	Brazzaville	Franc
✶ Croatia	Zagreb	Kuna
✶ Cuba	Havana	Peso
✶ Cyprus	Nicosia	Euro
✶ Czech Republic	Prague	Koruna
✶ Denmark	Copenhagen	Krone
✶ Ecuador	Quito	Sucre
✶ Egypt	Cairo	Pound
✶ Estonia	Tallinn	Euro
✶ Ethiopia	Addis Ababa	Birr
✶ Fiji	Suva	Dollar
✶ Finland	Helsinki	Euro
✶ France	Paris	Euro
✶ Georgia	Tbilisi	Lari
✶ Germany	Berlin	Euro
✶ Ghana	Accra	Cedi
✶ Greece	Athens	Euro
✶ Guatemala	Guatemala City	Quetzal
✶ Guyana	George Town	Dollar
✶ Hungary	Budapest	Forint

Country	Capital	Currency
✶ Iceland	Reykjavik	Krona
✶ India	New Delhi	Rupee
✶ Indonesia	Jakarta	Rupiah
✶ Iran	Teheran	Rial
✶ Iraq	Baghdad	Dinar
✶ Ireland	Dublin	Euro
✶ Israel	Jerusalem	Shekel
✶ Italy	Rome	Euro
✶ Jamaica	Kingston	Dollar
✶ Japan	Tokyo	Yen
✶ Jordan	Amman	Dinar
✶ Kazakhstan	Akmola	Tenge
✶ Kenya	Nairobi	Shilling
✶ Korea (S)	Seoul	Won
✶ Korea (N)	Pyongyang	Won
✶ Kyrgyzstan	Bishkek	Som
✶ Kuwait	Kuwait City	Dinar
✶ Laos	Vientiane	Kip
✶ Latvia	Riga	Euro
✶ Lebanon	Beirut	Pound
✶ Liberia	Monrovia	Dollar
✶ Libya	Tripoli	Dinar
✶ Lithuania	Vilnius	Litas
✶ Luxembourg	Luxembourg	Euro
✶ Macedonia	Skopje	Dinar
✶ Malawi	Lilongwe	Kwacha
✶ Malaysia	Kuala Lumpur	Ringgit
✶ Maldives	Male	Rufiyaa
✶ Mali	Bamako	Franc
✶ Mauritius	Port Louis	Rupee
✶ Mexico	Mexico City	Peso
✶ Moldavia	Chisinau	Leu
✶ Mongolia	Ulan Bator	Tugrik
✶ Morocco	Rabat	Dirham
✶ Mozambique	Maputo	Metical
✶ Myanmar	Nay Pyi Taw	Kyat
✶ Namibia	Winohoek	Dollar
✶ Nepal	Kathmandu	Rupee
✶ Netherlands	Amsterdam	Euro
✶ New Zealand	Wellington	Dollar
✶ Nigeria	Abuja	Naira
✶ Norway	Oslo	Krone
✶ Oman	Muscat	Rial
✶ Pakistan	Islamabad	Rupee
✶ Panama	Panama City	Balboa
✶ Peru	Lima	New Sole
✶ Philippines	Manila	Peso
✶ Poland	Warsaw	Zloty

Country	Capital	Currency
∗ Portugal	Lisbon	Euro
∗ Qatar	Doha	Riyal
∗ Romania	Bucharest	Leu
∗ Russia	Moscow	Ruble
∗ Saudi Arabia	Riyadh	Rial
∗ Senegal	Dakar	Franc
∗ Slovakia	Bratislava	Euro
∗ Spain	Madrid	Euro
∗ Sri Lanka	Colombo	Rupee
∗ Sudan	Khartoum	Dinar
∗ Suriname	Paramaribo	Guilder
∗ Sweden	Stockholm	Krona
∗ Switzerland	Berne	Swiss Francs
∗ Syria	Damascus	Pound
∗ South Africa	Capetown (Legislative) Pretoria *(Administrative)*	Rand
∗ Tadzhikistan	Dushanbe	Ruble
∗ Taiwan	Taipei	Dollar
∗ Tanzania	Dodoma	Shilling
∗ Thailand	Bangkok	Baht
∗ Tunisia	Tunis	Dinar
∗ Turkiye	Ankara	Lira
∗ Turkmania	Ashikabad	Manat
∗ Uganda	Kampala	Shilling
∗ Ukraine	Kiev	Hyrvnia
∗ United Arab Emirates	Abu Dhabi	Dirham
∗ U.K.	London	Pound Sterling
∗ U.S.A.	Washington	Dollar
∗ Uruguay	Montevideo	Peso
∗ Uzbekistan	Tashkent	Som
∗ Venezuela	Caracas	Bolivar
∗ Vietnam	Hanoi	Dong
∗ Yemen	Sana'a	Rial
∗ Zimbabwe	Harare	Dollar
∗ Congo	Kinshasa	Franc
∗ Zambia	Lusaka	Kwacha

GEOGRAPHICAL EXPLORATIONS/DISCOVERIES

Place	*Explorer/Discoverer*	*Nationality*	*Year*
America	Christopher Columbus	Italy	1492
Hawaii Islands (Sandwich Islands)	Captain James Cook	England	1778
Newfoundland	John Cabot	England	1497
New Zealand	Abel Janszoon Tasman	Holland	1642
North Pole	Robert Peary	USA	1909
Sea Route to India (via Cape of Good Hope)	Vasco da Gama	Portugal	1498
South Pole	Roald Amundsen	Norway	1911

NATIONAL MONUMENTS OF SOME FAMOUS COUNTRIES

Monument	Country	Monument	Country
Great Wall of China	China	Pyramid (Giza)	Egypt
Taj Mahal (Agra)	India	Kinder Disk	Denmark
Emperial Palace (Tokyo)	Japan	Leaning Tower of Pisa	Italy
Opera House (Sydney)	Australia	Statue of Liberty (New York)	USA
Eiffel Tower (Paris)	France	Kremlin (Moscow)	Russia

INTELLIGENCE AGENCIES OF SOME PROMINENT COUNTRIES

Country	Intelligence Agency
∗ India	*Research & Analysis Wing (RAW), Intelligence Bureau (I.B.), Central Bureau of Investigation (C.B.I.)*
∗ Pakistan	*Inter Service Intelligence (I.S.I.)*
∗ U.S.A.	*Central Intelligence Agency (CIA), Federal Bureau of Investigation (FBI)*
∗ Britain	*Military Intelligence (M.I.)-5 and 6, Special Branch, Ultra, Joint Intelligence Organisation*

∗ Israel	*Mosad*
∗ Egypt	*Mukhabarat*
∗ Japan	*Nicho*
∗ Russia	*K.G.B. (Komitel Gosudarstvennoy Bezopasnosty) (Committee for State Security)*
∗ Canada	*Security Intelligence Service (SIS)*
∗ S. Africa	*Bureau of State Security (BSS)*
∗ Iran	*Sabak*
∗ Iraq	*Al-Mukhabarat*
∗ Australia	*Australian Security and Intelligence Organisation (ASIO)*
∗ France	*S.D.E.C.E.*
∗ Spain	*C.E.S.I.D.*

MAJOR LANGUAGES OF THE WORLD AND THEIR SPEAKERS

Listing the languages spoken by approximately 1% of humankind (those spoken by more than 60,000,000 people), this table enumerates speakers of each tongue as a primary language.

Language	Speakers (millions)	Language	Speakers (millions)
∗ Chinese	1,322.8	∗ French	79.6
∗ Spanish	471.4	∗ Tamil	77.5
∗ English	369.9	∗ Vietnamese	76.1
∗ Arabic	349.3	∗ German, Standard	76.5
∗ Hindi	342.2	∗ Urdu	69.0
∗ Bengali	228.7	∗ Javanese	68.3
∗ Portuguese	232.4	∗ Persian	65.7
∗ Russian	153.7	∗ Italian	64.8
∗ Japanese	126.3	∗ Gujarati	56.9
∗ Lahnda	99.6	∗ Pushto	53.1
∗ Marathi	83.1	∗ Bhojpuri	52.3
∗ Telugu	82.6	∗ Hausa	48.6
∗ Turkish	82.2	∗ Kannada	43.6
∗ Malay	81.6	∗ Yoruba	41.0
∗ Korean	81.5	∗ Polish	40.0

*(**Source:** The World Almanac-2022)*

NAME OF PARLIAMENTS OF SOME COUNTRIES

Country	Name of Parliament	Country	Name of Parliament
Afghanistan	Shora	Poland	Sejm
Argentina	National Congress	Russia	Federal Assembly (Council of the Federation and State Duma
Australia	Federal Parliament		
Austria	National Assembly	South Africa	National Assembly and Senate
Bangladesh	Jatiya Sansad	Spain	Cortes Generales
India	Lok Sabha and Rajya Sabha	Sweden	Riksdag
Bhutan	Tshogdu (National Assembly)	Switzerland	Federal Assembly (Nationalrat and Standerat)
Britain	House of Commons and House of Lords		
Canada	House of Commons and Senate	North Korea	Supreme People's Assembly
China	National People Congress		
Denmark	Folketing	South Korea	National Assembly
Iran	Majlis (Islamic Consultative Assembly)	U.S.A.	Congress (Senate and House of Representatives)
Israel	Knesset		
Japan	Diet	Ethiopia	Federal Council and House of Representatives
Myanmar	Pyithu Hluttaw (People's Assembly)		
Nepal	Rashtriya Panchayat	Iceland	Alpingi
The Netherlands	States-General	Bulgaria	National Assembly
Norway	Storting	Cuba	National Assembly of People's Power

IMPORTANT NEWS AGENCIES OF THE WORLD

Agency	Country	Agency	Country
PTI, UNI, UNIVARTA	India	Reuters, NAFEN	United Kingdom
Antara	Indonesia	Angence France Press (AFP)	France
Tanjug	Serbia		
Associated Press (AP)	America	TASS	Russia

LARGEST AND SMALLEST COUNTRIES (Top 5)

Largest Country (Area-wise)	Largest Country (Population-wise)	Smallest Country (Area-wise)	Smallest Country (Population-wise)
Russia	China	Vatican City	Vatican City
Canada	India	Monaco	Tuvalu
China	USA	Nauru	Palau
United States	Indonesia	Tuvalu	San Marino
Brazil	Brazil	San Marino	Liechstein

RELIGIONS OF THE WORLD

Religion	Member	Percentage	Religion	Member	Percentage
Christianity	2.5 billion	32.2%	Buddhism	545 million	6.9%
Islam	1.9 billion	24.7%	Sikhism	27 million	0.4%
Hinduism	1.07 billion	13.5%			

NATIONAL EMBLEMS OF IMPORTANT COUNTRIES

Country	National Emblem	Country	National Emblem
America	Golden Rod	Australia	Kangaroo
Ireland	Shamrock	Italy	White Lily
Israel	Candelabrum	Iran	Rose
Canada	White Lily	Great Britain	Rose
Chile	Candor and Huemul	Germany	Corn Flower
Japan	Chrysanthemum	Zimbabwe	Zimbabwe Bird
Denmark	Beach	Turkey	Crescent and Star
The Netherlands	Lion	New Zealand	Kiwi, Fern Southern Cross
Norway	Lion	Nepal	Kukri
Pakistan	Crescent	Poland	Eagle
France	Lily	Belgium	Lion
Bangladesh	Water Lily	Mongolia	The Soyombo
Russia	Double headed eagle	Lebanon	Cedar Tree
Sudan	Secretary Bird	Syria	Eagle
India	Lioned Capital		

FIRST IN INDIA

* The first Indian to get the Nobel Prize for Literature — *Rabindra Nath Tagore*
* The first Indian to get the Nobel Prize for Physics — *C.V. Raman*
* The first Indian to get the Nobel Prize for Peace — *Mother Teresa*
* The first Indian to get the Nobel Prize for Economics — *Amartya Sen*
* The first Indian to get Special Oscar award (1992) — *Satyajit Ray*

∗ The first and the last Indian Governor-General of free India	C. Rajagopalachari
∗ The first woman to become the Governor of a State	Smt. Sarojini Naidu
∗ The first Indian Commander-In-Chief	General K.M. Cariappa
∗ The first ever woman to become the Chief Minister of a State	Smt. Sucheta Kripalani
∗ The first Indian woman President of UN General Assembly	Smt. Vijaylakshmi Pandit
∗ The first Indian to become the President of International Court of Justice	Dr. Nagendra Singh
∗ The first Indian woman to swim across the English Channel	Ms. Aarti Saha
∗ The first Indian girl to become Miss Universe	Miss Sushmita Sen
∗ The first Indian girl to become Miss World	Rita Faria
∗ The first Indian to swim across the English Channel	Mihir Sen
∗ The first Field Marshal	S.H.F.J. Manekshaw
∗ The first Indian recipient of Victoria Cross	Khudadad Khan
∗ The first Indian to conquer Mt. Everest	Sherpa Tenzing (May 29, 1953)
∗ The first Indian Cosmonaut (man)	Rakesh Sharma (April 3, 1984)
∗ The first Indian Cosmonaut (woman)	Kalpana Chawla (Nov. 19, 1997)
∗ The first woman to climb Mt. Everest	Miss Bachendri Pal (May 23, 1984)
∗ The first ICS	Satyendranath Tagore
∗ The first to address the UN General Assembly in Hindi	Atal Bihari Vajpayee
∗ The first Newspaper	Bengal Gazette (Jan 27, 1780)
∗ The first Postage Stamp issued	In 1852
∗ The first Telegraph line laid	In 1851 (Calcutta-Diamond Harbour)
∗ The first Railways run	April 16, 1853 (Bombay-Thane)
∗ The first Electric Train run	1925 (Bombay-Kurla)
∗ The first Atomic Power Station	Tarapore (Maharashtra)
∗ The first passenger-cum-cargo ship made in India	Harshavardhan
∗ The first Satellite	Aryabhatta (1975)
∗ The first President of the Indian National Congress	W.C. Banerjee
∗ The first President of Indian Republic	Dr. Rajendra Prasad
∗ The first woman judge of the Supreme Court	Ms Fatima Bibi
∗ The first to climb Everest without oxygen	Phu Dorjee (1987)
∗ The first film (movie)	Raja Harishchandra
∗ The first film (talkie)	Alam Ara
∗ The first Metro Railway	Calcutta Metro Railway
∗ The first Test-tube baby, scientifically documented	Born on August 6, 1986 at K.E.M. Hospital, Bombay
∗ The first TV Centre	At Delhi
∗ The first Indian to get an Oscar	Bhanu Athaiya
∗ The first woman pilot in IAF	Ms Harita Kaur Deol
∗ The first woman to get Olympic Medal	Karnam Malleswari
∗ The first woman Foreign Secretary	Chokila Iyer
∗ First Chief of Defence Staff (CDS)	General Bipin Rawat

SUPERLATIVES (INDIA)

Highest, Biggest, Largest and Longest in India

∗ Award for Gallantry, highest	Param Vir Chakra
∗ Award, highest civilian	Bharat Ratna
∗ Bank, with largest number of branches	State Bank of India

∗ Road Bridge, Longest	*Bhupen Hazarika Bridge, Assam (9.15 km)*
∗ Road and Rail Bridge, Longest	*Bogibeel Bridge, Brahmaputra River, Assam*
∗ Cattle Fair, Largest	*Sonepur (Bihar)*
∗ City, Most Populous	*Mumbai metropolis*
∗ Corridor, Longest	*Rameshwaram Temple corridor (4,000 ft.)*
∗ Desert, Largest	*Thar (Rajasthan)*
∗ Dam, Longest	*Hirakud Dam (Odisha)*
∗ Delta, Largest	*Sunderban's Delta*
∗ Dome, Largest	*Gol Gumbaj (Bijapur)*
∗ Dam, Highest	*Tehri Dam (260 m)*
∗ Gateway, Highest	*Buland Darwaja at Fatehpur Sikri (176 ft.)*
∗ Fresh Water Lake, Largest	*Wular Lake (Kashmir)*
∗ Literacy, Highest	*Kerala (94%)*
∗ Museum, Largest	*Indian Museum (Kolkata)*
∗ Mosque, Biggest	*Jama Masjid (Delhi)*
∗ Peak, Highest**	*K-2 (Pak-Occupied Kashmir)*
∗ Platform, Longest	*At Shree Siddharoodha Swamiji Railway Station Hubballi, Karnataka, SW Railway (1507 mtrs)*
∗ Railway Bridge, longest	*Vembanad Bridge, Kerala (4.6 km)*
∗ River, Longest***	*The Ganges (2525 Km)*
∗ Rainfall, Highest (annual mean)	*Mowsynram near Cherrapunji (1178 cm)*
∗ Road Longest	*Grand Trunk Road (1,500 miles)*
∗ State, with maximum forest cover	*Madhya Pradesh*
∗ State, with maximum density of population	*Bihar*
∗ Telescope, Largest in Asia	*Vainu Bappu Telescope (at Kavalur: Chennai) 2.34m*
∗ Tunnel, Longest (Road)	*Dr. Shyama Prasad Mukherjee Tunnel (9.28 kms, J & K)*
∗ Tunnel, Longest (Railway)	*T-50 Tunnel, Khari-Sumber section (12.77 kms) Jammu & Kashmir.*
∗ Tallest Minaret	*Qutub Minar (Delhi 72.5 m.)*
∗ Waterfall, Highest	*Kunchikal Waterfall (Karnataka: 455 m)*
∗ Zoo, Largest	*Zoological Gardens (Kolkata)*

** *Highest peak in the world is Mount Everest, which is in Nepal. K-2 is the second highest peak in the world. It is 8,611 metres high.*
*** *Indus and Brahmaputra (each 2900 km). Both of them, however, cover a long distance outside India.*

TABLE OF PRECEDENCE

1. President
2. Vice-President
3. Prime Minister
4. Governors of States within their respective states
5. Former Presidents

5A. Deputy Prime Minister

6. Chief Justice of India, Speaker of Lok Sabha
7. Cabinet Ministers of the Union, Chief Ministers of States within their respective States
   Deputy Chairman NITI Aayog, former Prime Ministers
   Leaders of opposition in Rajya Sabha and Lok Sabha

7A. Holders of the Bharat Ratna Decoration

8. Ambassadors Extraordinary and Plenipotentiary and High Commissioners of Commonwealth Countries accredited to India, Chief Ministers of States outside their respective States
9. Judges of the Supreme Court
10. Deputy Chairman Rajya Sabha, Deputy Chief Minister of States, Deputy Speaker Lok Sabha, Members of the NITI Aayog, Minister of State of the Union and Other Minister in the Ministry of Defence.

BOOKS AND AUTHORS

FOREIGN

Book	Author
✶ As You Like It	*William Shakespeare*
✶ A Tale of Two Cities	*Charles Dickens*
✶ Ben Hur	*Lewis Wallace*
✶ Das Kapital	*Karl Marx*
✶ David Copperfield	*Charles Dickens*
✶ Hamlet	*William Shakespeare*
✶ Iliad	*Homer*
✶ Inferno	*A. Dante*
✶ In Memoriam	*Lord Tennyson*
✶ Ivanhoe	*Walter Scott*
✶ Julius Caesar	*William Shakespeare*
✶ Lady Chatterley's Lover	*D.H. Lawrence*
✶ Lajja	*Taslima Nasreen*
✶ Les Miserable	*Victor Hugo*
✶ Leviathan	*Thomas Hobbes*
✶ Lolita	*V. Nobokov*
✶ Lycidas	*John Milton*
✶ Mein Kampf	*Adolf Hitler*
✶ Moor's Last Sigh	*Salman Rushdie*
✶ Mother	*Maxim Gorky*
✶ Mother India	*Katherine Mayo*
✶ Nana	*Emile Zola*
✶ Odyssey	*Homer*
✶ Origin of Species	*Charles Darwin*
✶ Othello	*William Shakespeare*
✶ Paradise Lost	*John Milton*
✶ Paradise Regained	*John Milton*
✶ Path to Power	*Margaret Thatcher*
✶ Pickwick Papers	*Charles Dickens*
✶ Razor's Edge	*Somerset Maugham*
✶ Republic	*Plato*
✶ The Tempest	*William Shakespeare*
✶ Time Machine	*H.G. Wells*
✶ Tom Sawyer	*Mark Twain*
✶ Treasure Island	*R.L. Stevenson*
✶ Twelfth Night	*William Shakespeare*
✶ Unto This Last	*John Ruskin*
✶ Utopia	*Thomas More*
✶ Wealth of Nations	*Adam Smith*
✶ Wonder that was India	*A.L. Basham*

INDIAN

Book	Author
✶ Ain-i-Akbari	*Abul Fazal*
✶ Anand Math	*Bankim Chandra Chatterjee*
✶ Arthashastra	*Kautilya*
✶ A Suitable Boy	*Vikram Seth*
✶ Bhagwat Gita	*Ved Vyas*
✶ Chidambara	*Sumitranandan Pant*
✶ Devdas	*Sarat Chandra Chatterjee*
✶ Discovery of India	*Jawaharlal Nehru*
✶ Ganadevata	*Tarashankar Bandopadhyaya*
✶ Geet Govind	*Jaya Dev*
✶ Geetanjali	*R. N. Tagore*
✶ Glimpses of World History	*Jawaharlal Nehru*
✶ Godaan	*Prem Chand*
✶ Gul-e-Nagma	*Firaq Gorakhpuri*
✶ Harsh Charita	*Bana Bhatta*
✶ India Divided	*Dr. Rajendra Prasad*
✶ Justice of Peace ke Aansu	Janardan Prasad Singh
✶ The Judgement	*Kuldip Nayyar*
✶ Kadambari	*Bana Bhatta*
✶ Kagaz Te Kanwas	*Amrita Pritam*
✶ Kamayani	*Jai Shankar Prasad*
✶ Kitni Nawon Mein Kitni Bar	*S. H. Vatsyayan*
✶ Kumar Sambhav	*Kalidas*
✶ Mahabharata	*Ved Vyas*
✶ Malgudi Days	*R.K. Narayan*
✶ Meghdoot	*Kalidas*
✶ Mritunjaya	*B.K. Bhattacharya*
✶ Mudrarakshasa	*Vishakhadatta*
✶ Prison Diary	*Jaya Prakash Narayan*
✶ Raghuvansha	*Kalidas*
✶ Rajtarangini	*Kalhana*
✶ Ramayana	*Balmiki*
✶ Ramcharit Manas	*Tulsidas*
✶ Rukh Te Rishi	*Harbhajan Singh*
✶ Satyarth Prakash	*Swami Dayanand*
✶ Sur Sagar	*Surdas*
✶ The Guide	*R.K. Narayan*

IMPORTANT DATES AND DAYS OF THE YEAR

✶ **JANUARY**

5-11 Road Safety Week
12 National Youth Day
15 Army Day
15-21 Pin Code Week
23 National Day of Patriotism
26 Republic Day
30 Martyr's Day

✶ **FEBRUARY**

1-14 Oil Conservation Fortnight

14 Valentine's Day

∗ **MARCH**

4 National Safety Day
8 International Women's Day
15 Consumers' Day
16 Immunisation Day
21 World Forest Day
22 World Day for Water
24 World Meteorological Day
1-7 Preservation of Blindness Week

∗ **APRIL**

7 World Health Day
7-13 Handloom Week
14-20 Fire Service Week
18 World Heritage Day
22 World Earth Day

∗ **MAY**

1 May Day
5 National Labour Day
8 World Red Cross Day
11 National Technology Day
15 International Day of the Family
17 World Telecommunication Day
24 Commonwealth Day
31 World No-Tobacco Day

∗ **JUNE**

5 World Environment Day
21 World Yoga Day
26 International Day against Drug Abuse and Illicit Trafficking

∗ **JULY**

11 World Population Day

∗ **AUGUST**

1-7 World Breast feeding Week
10 Sanskrit Divas
15 Independence Day
20 Sadbhavana Divas

∗ **SEPTEMBER**

1-7 National Nutrition Week
5 Teachers' Day
8 International Literary Day
14 Hindi Diwas
23 World Deaf Day
27 World Tourism Day

∗ **OCTOBER**

2 Gandhi Jayanti
International Day of Non Violence
Anti-Leprosy Day
4 World Animal Day
6 World Habitat Day *(Ist Monday)*
8 Indian Air Force Day
14 World Standard Day
15 International Day of Rural Women
16 World Food Day
24 United Nations Day
27 Infantry Day
28 World Thrift Day
31 Anti-Terrorism Day

∗ **NOVEMBER**

2 All Saints Day
14 Children's Day
15-21 National Cooperative Week
19-25 Quami Ekta Week
20 Child Rights Day
26 Constitution Day

∗ **DECEMBER**

1 World AIDS Day
3 World Day for the Disabled
4 Naval Day
7 Flag Day
8 SMRC Day
10 Human Rights Day
14 National Energy Conservation Day

INDIAN DEFENCE

- The Supreme Command of the Armed Forces is vested in the hands of the President of the Country.
- The responsibility for national defence, however, rests with the Cabinet. All important questions having a bearing on defence are decided by the Cabinet Committee on Political Affairs, which is presided over by the Prime Minister.
- The Defence Minister is responsible to Parliament for all matters concerning the Defence Services.
- All the administrative and operational control of Armed Forces are exercised by the Ministry of Defence. The three services—Army, Navy and Air Force function through their respective service head-quarters headed by the chief of Staff.
- The post of Chief of Defence Staff (CDS) was created in 2019.

Indian Army Commands

Command	*HQ Location*
Eastern Command	Kolkata
Western Command	Chandigarh
Northern Command	Udhampur
Southern Command	Pune
Central Command	Lucknow
Training Command	Shimla
South-Western Command	Jaipur

Indian Air Force Commands

Command	HQ Location
Western Air Command	New Delhi
Sout-Western Air Command	Gandhinagar
Central Air Command	Prayagraj
Eastern Air Command	Shillong
Southern Air Command	Thiruvananthapuram
Training Command	Bengaluru

Indian Navy Commands

Command	HQ Location
Eastern Naval Command	Vishakhapatnam
Western Naval Command	Mumbai
Southern Naval Command	Kochi

Commissioned Ranks in Defence Services

Army	Navy	Air Force
General	Admiral	Air Chief Marshal
Lieutenant-General	Vice-Admiral	Air Marshal
Major-General	Rear-Admiral	Air Vice-Marshal
Brigadier	Commodor	Air Commodor
Colonel	Captain	Group Captain
Lieutenant-Colonel	Commander	Wing Commander
Major	Lt.Commander	Squadron Leader
Captain	Lieutenant	Flight Lieutenant
Lieutenant	Sub-Lieutenant	Flying Officer

Internal Security Organisations of India

S. No.	Name of Organisation	Year of Creation	Headquarters
1.	Assam Rifles (A.R.)	1835	Shillong
2.	Central Reserve Police Force (CRPF)	1939	New Delhi
3.	Territorial Army	1948	In different States
4.	Indo-Tibetan Border Police	1962	New Delhi
5.	Home Guard	1962	In different States
6.	Coast Guard	1978	New Delhi
7.	Border Security Force (B.S.F.)	1965	New Delhi
8.	Central Industrial Security Force (CISF)	1969	New Delhi
9.	National Security Guard	1984	New Delhi
10.	Police	—	In different States

Army Institutes

1.	Sainik Schools	33 places in India
2.	Rashtriya Indian Military College (prepare for entrance to N.D.A.)	Dehradun
3.	National Defence Academy (three services)	Khadakwasla, Pune
4.	Indian Military Academy (Army)	Dehradun
5.	Officers Training Academy (3 services) Short Courses	Chennai
6.	National Defence College	New Delhi
7.	The College of Combat	Mhow
8.	The College of Military Engineering	Kirkee
9.	Military College of Telecommunication Engineering	Mhow
10.	The Armoured Corps Centre and School	Ahmed Nagar
11.	The School Artillery	Deolali
12.	The Infantry School	Mhow and Belgaum
13.	College of Material Management	Jabalpur

Air Force Institutions

✶ Air Force Academy	Hyderabad	✶ Helicopter Training School	Hakimpet
✶ Flying Instructors School	Tambaram, Chennai	✶ The College of Air Warfare	Secunderabad
✶ Air Force Administrative College	Coimbatore	✶ Air Force Technical College	Jalahalli

UNITED NATIONS ORGANISATION (UNO)

- The United Nations (UN) is an association of states which have pledged themselves to maintain international peace and security and cooperate in solving international political, economic, social cultural and humanitarian problems towards achieving this end.
- Trygve Lie of Norway (1946-52) was the first Secretary-General of the UN.
- ***Origin:*** UN Charter was signed by 50 members on June 26, 1945. Poland signed the charter later to become one of the original 51 member-states. It officially came into existence on October 24, 1945.
- ***UN Charter:*** The Charter is the Constitution of the UNO and contains its aims and objectives and rules and regulations for its functioning.
- ***Aims and Objectives:*** They are security, welfare and human rights.
- ***Headquarters:*** New York.
- ***Flag:*** The flag is light blue in colour, and emblazoned in white, in its centre is the UN symbol—a polar map of world embraced by twin olive branches open at the top.
- ***Official Languages:*** The official languages of the UN are: English, French, Chinese, Russian, Arabic and Spanish. However, working languages are English and French only.
- ***Present Membership:*** At present 193 countries are members of the UNO. South Sudan is the latest entrant to this world organisation.
- ***Main Organs of the UNO:*** There are six main organs:
  1. General Assembly
  2. Security Council
  3. Economic and Social Council
  4. Trusteeship Council
  5. International Court of Justice, and
  6. Secretariat.

1. *General Assembly:* It consists of representative of all members of the UN. Each member country has only one vote. It meets once a year and passes UN Budget. It is the main place for discussions and policy making in the UN.
2. *Security Council:* It is the Executive body of the UN and is mainly responsible for maintaining international peace and security. It has 15 members, 5 of which (USA, UK, France, Russia and China) are permanent members. The 10 non-permanent members are elected by General Assembly for two-year term and are not eligible for immediate re-election.
3. *Economic and Social Council:* It has 54 members elected by General Assembly.
4. *Trusteeship Council:* It looks after interest of the people in areas not yet independent and leads them towards self-government.
5. *International Court of Justice:* It has 15 judges, no two of whom may be nationals of the same state. They are elected by General Assembly and Security Council for a term of 9 years. The Court elects its President and Vice-President for a 3-year term.
6. *Secretariat:* It is the Secretariat of the UN and is headed by the Secretary General.

Some Important UN Agencies

UN Agencies	Headquarters	Year of Establishment
✶ United Nations Organisations (U.N.O.)	New York	1945
✶ International Monetary Fund (I.M.F.)	Washington	1945
✶ World Health Organisation (W.H.O.)	Geneva	1948
✶ Food & Agricultural Organisation (FAO)	Rome	1943
✶ International Labour Organisation (ILO)	Geneva	1919
✶ UNESCO	Paris	1946
✶ Universal Postal Union (UPU)	Berne	1874
✶ UNIDO	Vienna	1967
✶ International Atomic Energy Agency (IAEA)	Vienna	1957

∗ United Nations Development Programme (UNDP)	New York	1965
∗ UNICEF	New York	1946
∗ International Maritime Organisation (IMO)	London	1948
∗ World Meteorological Organisation (WMO)	Geneva	1951
∗ International Telecommunication Union (ITU)	Geneva	1947
∗ World Trade Organisation (WTO)	Geneva	1995
∗ International Development Association (IDA)	Washington D.C.	1960
∗ World Intellectual Property Organisation (WIPO)	Geneva	1967

Famous International Organisations

International Organisations	Headquarters	Year of Establishment
∗ International Court of Justice	The Hague	1945
∗ International Civil Aviation Organisation (ICAO)	Montreal	1947
∗ International Finance Corporation (IFC)	Washington	1956
∗ Arab League	Cairo	1945
∗ Commonwealth of Nations	London	1931
∗ International Bank for Reconstruction and Development (IBRD)	Washington D.C.	1944
∗ Organisation of Islamic Cooperation (OIC)	Jeddah (Saudi Arabia)	1971
∗ European Economic Community (EEC)	Geneva	1957
∗ Red Cross	Geneva	1863
∗ Interpol	Lyons	1923
∗ Asian Development Bank (ADB)	Manila	1966
∗ North Atlantic Treaty Organisation (NATO)	Brussels	1949
∗ Association of South East Asian Nations (ASEAN)	Jakarta	1967
∗ South Asian Association for Regional Cooperation (SAARC)	Kathmandu	1985
∗ Asia-Pacific Economic Cooperation (APEC)	Singapore	1989
∗ Organisation for Economic Cooperation and Development (OECD)	Paris	1961
∗ Organisation of Petroleum Exporting Countries (OPEC)	Vienna	1960
∗ Commonwealth of Independent States (CIS)	Minsk	1991
∗ International Olympic Committee (IOC)	Switzerland	1894
∗ European Union (EU)	Brussels	Changed form of EEC Established in 1958
∗ Amnesty International (AI)	London	1961
∗ Shanghai Cooperation Organisation (SCO)	Beijing	2001
∗ BRICS Development Bank	Shanghai	2014

AWARDS AND HONOURS

NATIONAL AWARDS

BHARAT RATANA

- Bharat Ratna is India's highest Civilian Award. It was first awarded in 1954.
- The actual award is designed in the shape of a *peepal* leaf with Bharat Ratna inscribed in Devanagri script in the Sun Figure.
- This is India's highest civilian award. It is given for exceptional work on art, literature, science and recognition of public service of the highest order.
- The emblem, the Sun and the rim are of platinum. The inscriptions are in burnished bronze.
- Government servants are not eligible for it. The table shows the recipients of the award:

Bharat Ratna Award Winners

No.	Name	Year
1.	Dr. S. Radhakrishnan	1954
2.	C. Rajagopalachari	1954
3.	Dr. C.V. Raman	1954
4.	Dr. Bhagwan Das	1955
5.	Dr. M. Visvesvaraya	1955
6.	Jawahar Lal Nehru	1955
7.	Govind Ballabh Pant	1957
8.	Dr. D.K. Karve	1958
9.	Dr. Bidhan Chandra Roy	1961
10.	Purushottam Das Tandon	1961
11.	Dr. Rajendra Prasad	1962
12.	Dr. Zakir Hussain	1963
13.	Dr. Pandurang Vaman Kane	1963
14.	Lal Bahadur Shastri	1966
15.	Indira Gandhi	1971
16.	V.V. Giri	1975
17.	K. Kamraj	1976
18.	Mother Teresa	1980
19.	Acharya Vinoba Bhave	1983
20.	Khan Abdul Ghaffar Khan	1987
21.	M.G. Ramachandran	1988
22.	Dr. B.R. Ambedkar	1990
23.	Dr. Nelson R. Mandela	1990
24.	Rajiv Gandhi	1991
25.	Sardar Vallabhbhai Patel	1991
26.	Morarji R. Desai	1991
27.	Maulana Abul Kalam Azad	1992
28.	Jehangir Ratanji Dadabhai Tata	1992
29.	Satyajit Roy	1992
30.	Shri Gulzari Lal Nanda	1997
31.	Mrs. Aruna Asaf Ali	1997
32.	Dr. A.P.J. Abdul Kalam	1998
33.	M.S. Subbalakshmi	1998
34.	C. Subramaniam	1998
35.	Jaya Prakash Narayan	1999
36.	Prof. Amartya Sen	1999
37.	Pt. Ravi Shankar	1999
38.	Gopinath Bardoloi	1999
39.	Lata Mangeshkar	2001
40.	Bismillah Khan	2001
41.	Bhimsen Joshi	2009
42.	C.N.R. Rao	2014
43.	Sachin Tendulkar	2014
44.	Pt. Madan Mohan Malaviya	2015
45.	Atal Bihari Vajpayee	2015
46.	Pranab Mukherjee	2019
47.	Bhupen Hazarika	2019
48.	Nanaji Deshmukh	2019
49.	Karpoori Thakur	2024
50.	L.K. Advani	2024
51.	Charan Singh	2024
52.	P.V. Narasimha Rao	2024
53.	M.S. Swaminathan	2024

REPUBLIC DAY AWARDS

Padma Awards

They fall in line after the Bharat Ratna. They are also discontinued in 1977 along with the Bharat Ratna and award was started again in 1980.

There are three Padma Awards:

- ***Padma Vibhushan:*** This award is given for exceptional and distinguished service in any field, including service rendered by Govt. servants.
- ***Padma Bhushan:*** This award is given for distinguished service of a high order in any field, including service rendered by Govt. servants.
- ***Padma Shri:*** This award is given for distinguished service in any field, including service rendered by Government servants.

Gallantry Awards

- ***Param Vir Chakra:*** The highest award for bravery or some daring and pre-eminent act of valour or self-sacrifice in the presence of the enemy, whether on land, at sea or in the air.
- ***Mahavir Chakra:*** It is the second highest decoration and is awarded for acts of conspicuous gallantry in the presence of the enemy, whether on land, at sea or in the air.
- ***Vir Chakra:*** It is the third in order of awards given for acts of gallantry in the presence of enemy, whether on land, at sea or in the air.
- ***Ashok Chakra:*** This medal is awarded for the most conspicuous bravery or some daring or pre-eminent act of valour or self-sacrifice on land, at sea or in the air but not in the presence of enemy.
- ***Vishishta Sewa Medal:*** It is awarded to personnel of all the three Services in class I, II and III in recognition of distinguished service of the "most exceptional" and "exceptional" and a "high" order respectively. Prefixes Parma and Ati are added before first two categories of medals respectively.
- ***Jeewan Raksha Padak:*** Awarded for meritorious acts or a series of acts of a human nature displayed in saving life from drowning, fire and rescue operations in mines etc.

OTHER NATIONAL AWARDS

SAHITYA AKADEMI AWARDS

- These prizes are awarded annually to the authors of the most outstanding books of literary merit published in each of the 22 languages specified in the Eighth Schedule of the Constitution.
- There are also two awards for Rajasthani and English. The award, in form of a casket containing an inscribed copper plate and a cheque of ₹ 1 lakh is given to the author or his/her heir.

DADA SAHEB PHALKE AWARD

- The award carries a cash prize of ₹ 10 lakh, a Shawl and Swarna Kamal.
- Mrs Devika Rani Roerich was the first person to receive Dadasaheb Phalke Award in 1969.

- The award for 2021 has been given to bollywood actress Waheeda Rehman.

BHARATIYA JNANPITH AWARD

- Instituted in 22nd May, 1961, carries a cash prize of ₹ 11 lakh, a citation and a bronze replica of Vagdevi (Saraswati).
- Instituted by a literary organisation in India.

SARASWATI SAMMAN

- Given for outstanding literary works, value ₹ 15 lakh.

KALINGA PRIZE

- This award is given each year by the UNESCO and founded by former Odisha Chief Minister late Shri Biju Patnaik for popularisation of science.

INTERNATIONAL AWARDS

NOBEL PRIZES

- These Prizes were instituted in 1901 by a Swedish scientist, Dr. Alfred Nobel; the discoverer of Dynamite.
- Six prizes are awarded annually for (i) Chemistry, (ii) Physics, (iii) Medicine, (iv) Literature, (v) Peace and (vi) Economics —started since 1969.
- Indians Honoured with Nobel Prize: So far, following Indians have been honoured with these prizes. Their names are (*i*) Rabindra Nath Tagore for Literature, for his book 'Gitanjali', in 1913, (*ii*) Dr. C.V. Raman for Physics in 1930, for his discovery of 'Raman Effect', (*iii*) Mother Teresa for Peace in 1979, (*iv*) Prof. Amartya Sen in 1998 for Economics and (*v*) Kailash Satyarthi for Peace in 2014. In addition, four non-resident Indians have also been awarded the Nobel Prize. They are: (*i*) Hargobind Khurana for Medicine in 1968, (*ii*) Subramanian Chandrasekhar for Physics in 1983, (*iii*) Venkatraman Ramkrishnan for Chemistry in 2009, (*iv*) Abhijit Vinayak Banerjee for Economics in 2019.

GANDHI PEACE PRIZE

- The government instituted this ₹ 1 crore prize on the lines of the Nobel Peace Prize in 1995.
- It is the highest Civilian International award by the Govt. of India. The award of 2021 have been given to Gita Press, Gorakhpur.

MAN BOOKER PRIZE 2023

- On November 26, 2023, Irish author Paul Lynch won 2023 Booker Prize for his novel, 'Prophet Song' published by Oneworld. He received 50,000 Pound sterling and the Iris Trophy for his award winning novel.

INDIRA GANDHI PRIZE FOR PEACE, DISARMAMENT AND DEVELOPMENT

- The award was instituted in the memory of Mrs. Indira Gandhi to foster creative cooperation among nations of the world.

Highest Honours of Some Countries

Country	*Highest Honour*
India	Bharat Ratna
Pakistan	Nishan-e-Pakistan
Kuwait	Mubarak-Al-kabir Medal
Saudi Arabia	Shah Abdul Aziz Medal
Argentina	The Order of Sona Martin
Nicaragua	Augusto-Caesar Sandino Order
Vietnam	The Order of the Golden Star
Hungary	The Order of Banner
Britain	Member of British Empire, Victoria Cross
Japan	Order of Moulovenice Sun
Denmark	Order of Diana Brog
France	Legend of Honour
America	Presidential Medal of Freedom
Germany	Pore Lee Merit Iron Cross
The Netherlands	Netherlands Lion

SPORTS

OLYMPICS

- First of all these games were held by the Greeks in 776 B.C. on Mount Olympus in honour of the Greek God Zeus. In this way, the history of Olympic Games is about twenty eight hundred years old. These games continued to be held every four years until 394 A.D. when these games were stopped by a royal order of the emperor of Rome.
- The modern Olympic Games which started in Athens in 1896, are the result of the devotion and dedication of a French educator Baron Pierre de Coubertin and the first Olympic meet in the modern series was held in 1896 in Athens, the Capital of Greece. Since then, they are being held every four years except for breaks during world wars.
- The Olympic flag is white in colour with five coloured rings, each ring symbolic of a continent. Summer as well as Winter Olympics are held in the same year.
- The 2020 Olympic Games was held at Tokyo in 2021.
- The official Olympic Motto is *Citius, Altius, Swifter, Higher, Stronger*. The Head Office of International Olympic Committee (IOC) is at Lausanne (Switzerland).

COMMONWEALTH GAMES

- The Commonwealth Games are held every four years, in the year in which Asian Games are held. All the Commonwealth Countries (former colonies of Britain) can take part in it.
- The first Commonwealth Games were held in 1930 at Hamilton (Canada).
- There are currently 56 members of the Commonwealth of Nations, and 72 teams participated in the games.
- The 2022 Commonwealth Games officially known as the XXII Commonwealth Games or Birmingham 2022, held in Birmingham, England, between 28 July to 8 August 2022.

ASIAN GAMES

- After the Second World War, most of the Asian Countries gained independence. On the lines of Olympic Games, Asian Games were planned every four years.
- India hosted the first Asian Games in 1951.

WORLD CUP CRICKET

- The first Cricket World Cup was organised in England in 1975. A separate women's Cricket World Cup has been held every 4 years since 1973.

List of Cricket World Cup

Year	Venue	Winner/Runner
1975	England	West Indies beat Australia
1979	England	West Indies beat England
1983	England	India beat West Indies
1987	India & Pakistan	Australia beat England
1992	Australia	Pakistan beat England
1996	India, Pakistan & Sri Lanka	Sri Lanka beat Australia
1999	England	Australia beat Pakistan
2003	South Africa	Australia beat India
2007	West Indies	Australia beat Sri Lanka
2011	India, Sri Lanka, Bangladesh	India beat Sri Lanka
2015	Australia, New Zealand	Australia beat New Zealand
2019	England	England beat New Zealand
2023	India	Australia beat India

HOCKEY WORLD CUP

- The first Hockey World Cup was organised in Barcelona (Spain) in 1971. Women's Hockey World Cup has been held since 1974.

FOOTBALL WORLD CUP

- The Football World Cup is organised by FIFA (Federation of International Football Association). The World Cup is called 'Jules Rimet Cup' named after the name of FIFA President Jules Rimet. The first Football World Cup was organised in Uruguay in 1930.
- In 1942 and 1946, the Football World Cup was not played due to World War II.
- Brazil is the only nation to have participated in every World Cup so far. The 2022 Football World Cup held in Qatar. Argentina on December 18, 2022 emerged Champion of the FIFA World Cup 2022 as it prevailed over France 4-2 on penalties.

IMPORTANT CUPS & TROPHIES

International

- *American Cup* : Yacht Racing
- *Ashes* : Cricket
- *Davis Cup* : Lawn Tennis
- *Derby* : Horse Race
- *Grand National* : Horse Streple Chase Race
- *Jules Rimet Trophy* : World Soccer Cup
- *King's Cup* : Air Races
- *Merdeka Cup* : Football
- *Swaythling Cup* : Table Tennis (Men)
- *Ryder Cup* : Golf
- *Thomas Cup* : Badminton
- *U. Thant Cup* : Tennis
- *Walker Cup* : Golf
- *Wightman Cup* : Lawn Tennis
- *Rothman's Trophy* : Cricket
- *European Champions Cup* : Football
- *Grand Prix* : Table Tennis
- *Edgbaston Cup* : Lawn Tennis
- *Grand Prix* : Lawn Tennis

National

- *Agha Khan Cup* : Hockey
- *Beighton Cup* : Hockey
- *Bombay Gold Cup* : Hockey
- *C.K. Naydu Trophy* : Cricket
- *Deodhar Trophy* : Cricket

* *Duleep Trophy* : Cricket
* *Durand Cup* : Football
* *Dhyan Chand Trophy* : Hockey
* *Dr. B.C. Roy Trophy* : Football (Junior)
* *Ezra Cup* : Polo
* *Guru Nanak Cup* : Hockey
* *Holkar Trophy* : Bridge
* *Irani Trophy* : Cricket
* *Indira Gold Cup* : Hockey
* *Murugappa Gold Cup* : Hockey
* *Nehru Trophy* : Hockey
* *Nixan Gold Cup* : Football
* *Rani Jhansi Trophy* : Cricket
* *Ranji Trophy* : Cricket
* *Rangaswami Cup* : Hockey
* *Ramanujan Trophy* : Table Tennis
* *Rene Frank Trophy* : Hockey
* *Rohinton Baria Trophy* : Cricket
* *Rovers Cup* : Football
* *Santosh Trophy* : Football
* *Subroto Cup* : Football

SPORTS TERMS

* ***Badminton:*** Mixed doubles; Deuce; Drop; Smash; Let; Foot work; Setting.
* ***Base Ball:*** Pitcher; Put out, Strike; Home; Bunt.
* ***Billiards:*** Cue; Jigger; Pot; Break; In Baulk; In Off; Cannons.
* ***Boxing:*** Upper cut; Round; Punch; Bout; Knock down; Hitting below the belt; Ring.
* ***Bridge:*** Finesse; Dummy; Revoke; Grand Slam; Little Slam; No Trump; Rubber.
* ***Chess:*** Bishop, Gambit; Checkmate; Stalemate.
* ***Cricket:*** L.B.W. (leg before wicket); Creases, Popping-creases; Stumped; Bye; Leg-Bye; Googly; Hattrick; Maiden over; Drive; Bowling; Duck; Follow-on; No ball; Leg Break; Silly point; Cover point; Hit-wicket; Late-cut; Slip; Off-spinner; In-swing.
* ***Football:*** Off Side; Block; Drop-kick; Penalty-kick (or goal kick); Corner-kick; Free-kick; Dribble; Thrown-in; Foul.
* ***Golf:*** Boggy; Foursome; Stymic; Tee; Put; Hole; Niblic; Caddie; Links; The green; Bunker.
* ***Hockey:*** Carried; Short Corner; Bully; Sticks; Off side; Roll in; Striking Circle; Under-cutting; Dribble.
* ***Horse racing:*** Jockey; Punter.
* ***Polo:*** Bunker; Chukker; Mallet.
* ***Tennis:*** Back hand drive; Volley; Smash; Half-volley; Deuce; Service; Let; Grand Slam.

Stadiums and Places Associated with Sports

Name of Stadium	*Sports*	*Place*
Arun Jaitley Stadium	Cricket	Delhi
Jawaharlal Nehru Stadium	Athletics	Delhi
Shivajee Stadium	Hockey	Delhi
National Stadium	Hockey etc.	Delhi
Ambedkar Stadium	Football	Delhi
Brabourne Stadium	Cricket	Mumbai
Wankhede Stadium	Cricket	Mumbai
Narendra Modi Stadium	Cricket	Ahmedabad
Eden Garden	Cricket	Kolkata
Green Park Stadium	Cricket	Kanpur
Keenan Stadium	Cricket	Jamshedpur
Nehru (Chepauk) Stadium	Cricket	Chennai
Barabati Stadium	Cricket	Cuttack
Lords, Oval, Leeds	Cricket	Britain
Hedingle Manchester	Cricket	Britain
Black Heath	Rugby Football	London
Henley	Boat race	England
Wimbledon	Lawn Tennis	London
Wembley Stadium	Football	London
White City	Dog-race	England
Aintree	Horse-race	England
Tentbridge	Cricket	England
Patnee Martlake	Boat-race	England
Tibankham	Rugby Football	England
Sandy Lodge	Golf	Scotland
Forest Hill	Tennis	New York
Brooklyn	Baseball	New York
Melbourne	Cricket	Australia

Name of Playing Compound of Different Games

Name of Compound	Related Sports
Court	Lawn Tennis, Badminton, Netball, Hand ball, Volleyball, Squash, Kho-Kho, Kabaddi
Diamond	Baseball
Ring	Boxing, Skating, Wrestling, Circus, Riding display
Course	Golf
Board	Table Tennis
Pool	Swimming
Alley	Bowling
Mat	Judo, Karate II
Arena	Horse Riding
Vellodrum	Cycling
Field	Polo, Football, Hockey
Track	Athletics
Pitch	Cricket, Rugby
Rink	Ice Hockey

❒❒❒

Multiple Choice Questions

1. Match List-I with List-II and select the correct answer from the codes given below the lists:

List-I

(*a*) Napoleon Bonaparte
(*b*) Jean Jacques Rousseau
(*c*) Croce
(*d*) Madame Roland

List-II

1. 'A history is contemporary history'
2. 'Liberty what crimes are committed in thy name'
3. 'Man is born free but everywhere he is in chains.'
4. 'I am the Child of Revolution'

Codes :

	(*a*)	(*b*)	(*c*)	(*d*)
A.	1	2	3	4
B.	4	3	1	2
C.	3	4	2	1
D.	3	4	1	2

2. Abraham Lincon was elected the President of United States in:
A. 1862 B. 1860
C. 1875 D. 1855

3. Who was known as the 'Prince of Humanists'?
A. Francisco Petrarch B. Dante
C. Boccacio D. Erasmus

4. D-Day is the day when:
A. Germany declared war on Britain
B. US dropped the atom bomb on Hiroshima.
C. Allied Troops landed in Normandy
D. Germany surrendered to the allies

5. Whose teachings inspired the French Revolution?
A. Locke
B. Rousseau
C. Hegel
D. Plato

6. At a time when empires in Europe were crumbling before the might of Napoleon which one of the following Governor-Generals kept the British flag flying high in India?
A. Warren Hastings B. Lord Cornwallis
C. Lord Wellesley D. Lord Hastings

7. Which one of the following statements regarding Fascism in Italy is *not* true?
A. The Fascists came to power as a result of popular uprising
B. In 1926, all political parties except Mussolini's party were banned
C. The Fascists suppressed the Socialist movement
D. The Fascists were hostile to the Communists

8. The fall of Czar Nicholas-II is known as:
A. Bloody Sunday
B. Bolshevik Revolution
C. February Revolution
D. October Revolution

9. Industrial Revolution took place first in:
A. France B. Germany
C. United Kingdom D. Japan

10. The British Prime Minister at the outbreak of World War II was :
A. Churchill B. Baldwin
C. Attlee D. Chemberlain

11. The 'Great Depression' (1929) economic crisis was met by adopting the policy of
A. Stimulus B. Marshall Plan
C. New Deal D. Open Door

12. The slogan "No taxation without representation" was raised during the:
A. American War of Independence
B. Russian Revolution
C. French Revolution
D. Indian Freedom struggle

13. In the nineteenth century the people of Europe started moving from the villages to the cities due to the impact of :
A. Epidemics
B. War
C. Industrialisation
D. Population explosion in villages

14. The important cause of the Civil War in America was:
A. Abolition of slavery
B. Quest for freedom
C. Industrialisation
D. Rebellion by the native Americans

15. Industrial Revolution could not have come about without:
A. Merchant capitalism
B. The Enclosure Movement
C. The services of the proletariat class
D. An agricultural revolution

16. Consider the following statements :
The French Revolution came about mainly due to the :
1. Extreme poverty of the people
2. Impact of the works of great writers
3. Cruelty of the rulers
4. Impact of impulsive reaction
Which of the above statements are correct?
A. 1, 2 and 4 B. 2 and 3
C. 1, 3 and 4 D. 1, 2, 3 and 4

17. Asia's oldest and largest Buddhist monastery is situated in :
A. Tawang (Arunachal Pardesh)
B. Lhasa (Tibet)
C. Trincomallee (Sri Lanka)
D. Ulan Bator (Mongolia)

18. Who was the main architect of the Russian Revolution?
A. Karl Marx B. Lenin
C. Stalin D. Tolstoy

19. V.I. Lenin is associated with :
A. Russian Revolution of 1917
B. Chinese Revolution of 1949
C. German Revolution
D. French Revolution of 1789

20. Which one of the following statements is *not* correct?
A. Voltaire believed in Natural Religion
B. Rousseau wrote *Social Contract*
C. Montesquieu authored *The Spirit of Laws*
D. Necker believed in 'General Will'

21. 6th April, 1930 is well known in the history of India because this date is associated with..........
A. Dandi March by Mahatma Gandhi
B. Quit India Movement
C. Partition of Bengal
D. Partition of India

22. Which ruler enforced the system of 'Price Control' in India?
A. Mohammad Tughlak
B. Razia Begum
C. Alauddin Khilji
D. Sher Shah Suri

23. The concept of 'Din-e-Elahi' was founded by which king?
A. Dara Shikoh B. Akbar
C. Sher Shah Suri D. Shahjahan

24. Who are supposed to be the earliest inhabi-tants of India? Where did they come from?
A. Aryans from Central Asia
B. Dravidians from Mediterranean
C. Négroids from Africa
D. Bhils and the Santhals from West Asia

25. The one chief characteristic of temple architecture of the Gupta Age was :
A. Absence of dome
B. Huge size
C. Beautiful carvings
D. absence of a covered courtyard for the gathering of worshippers

26. The Rigveda consists of :
A. 1000 hymns B. 2028 hymns
C. 1028 hymns D. 1038 hymns

27. The central point in Ashoka's dharma was :
A. royalty to kings
B. peace and non-violence
C. respect to elders
D. religious tolerance

28. The social evil which was conspicuously absent during ancient India was :
A. *Sati*-System B. *Devadasi*-System
C. Polygamy D. *Purdah*-System

29. Which, among the following, can be accepted as a novelty introduced by Mughal emperors to their buildings?
A. Domes B. Minarets
C. Arches D. Attached gardens

30. The first ruler of India who defeated Muhammud of Ghur was :
A. Mularaja II of Gujarat
B. Prithviraja Chauhan of Delhi
C. Jayachand of Kannauj
D. Parmaldeva of Bundelkhand

31. What important event happened in India in 1911?
A. Bengal was partitioned
B. Non-Cooperation movement was launched
C. India's capital was shifted from Calcutta to Delhi
D. Mahatma Gandhi presided over the Congress session

32. The first phase of the Congress Party (1885-1905) was characterized by its efforts to secure:
A. limited independence
B. complete freedom
C. Indianization of services
D. constitutional reforms

33. The Muslim League demanded a separate homeland for the Indian Muslims openly for the first time at its annual session held in Lahore in the year :
A. 1931 A.D. B. 1936 A.D.
C. 1940 A.D. D. 1941 A.D.

34. Under whose governorship did the East India Company secure the Diwani Rights in Bengal, Bihar and Odisha from Emperor Shah Alam?
A. Lord Cornwallis
B. Lord William Bentinck
C. Lord Clive
D. Lord Wellesley

35. The Simon Commission was generally boycotted by the Indian political parties. What was the reason for this general non-cooperation?
A. the Commission aimed at dividing the people
B. it was an 'all white' Commission
C. it came after the Jallianwala Bagh carnage
D. it was an eye wash

36. Aligarh Muslim University was founded by :
A. Dr. Saifuddin Kitchlu
B. Mohammad Ali Jinnah
C. Sir Syed Ahmed Khan
D. Maulana Mohammad Ali

37. Ibn Batutah was an African traveller visiting India during the time of :
A. Alivardi Khan
B. Ala-ud-din Khalji
C. Iltutmish
D. Mohammad-bin-Tughlaq

38. The battle of Wandiawash was fought in :
A. 1726 B. 1760
C. 1818 D. 1857

39. The abolition of *Sati* by government regulation was at the time of :
A. Warren Hastings B. Lord Wellesley
C. Lord Bentinck D. Lord Ahmerst

40. Pick out the wrong combination :
A. Dilwara Temple : Mt. Abu
B. Pashupati Temple : Kathmandu
C. Padmanabh Temple : Bangalore
D. Minakshi Temple : Madurai

41. Match the following:
(*a*) Chanhudaro (*b*) Kalibangan
(*c*) Lothal (*d*) Surkotada
1. Alleged discovery of the skeleton of horse.
2. Bead making.
3. Traces of a dock and ship on seal.
4. Evidence of ploughing the fields.
The Correct code is :

	(*a*)	(*b*)	(*c*)	(*d*)
A.	2	4	3	1
B.	2	1	3	4
C.	1	2	3	4
D.	2	1	4	3

42. Match the Harappan settlements with the banks of rivers on which they were located :
(*a*) Harappa 1. Ravi
(*b*) Mohenjodaro 2. Indus
(*c*) Ropar 3. Sutlej
(*d*) Kalibangan 4. Ghaggar
(*e*) Lothal 5. Bhogava

Codes :

	(*a*)	(*b*)	(*c*)	(*d*)	(*e*)
A.	1	2	3	4	5
B.	1	2	3	5	4
C.	2	1	3	5	4
D.	2	1	4	3	5

43. The Goddess 'Kannagi' whose many temples were erected during the 'Sangam Age' was the goddess of :
A. Chastity B. Love
C. Prowess D. Wisdom

44. The Jain goal of life is to attain deliverance from the fetters of mudane existence, the way to which lies through three jewels. Which one of the following was not included among the 'three jewels' of Jainism?
A. Right faith B. Right action
C. Right knowledge D. Right conduct

45. The most striking feature of the Ashokan pillar is polish. Name the Ashokan pillar which is considered to be the most graceful of all Ashokan pillars.
A. Sarnath
B. Rampurva
C. Laurya-Nandangarh
D. Rummindei

46. Which are the correct statements?
1. The land grants, started in Satavahana period, paved the way for feudal developments in India.
2. Silk and spices were the Chief Indian export articles of Indo-Roman trade.
3. The Guptas issued the largest number of gold coins in ancient India.
4. The first memorial of a 'SATI' dated 510 A.D. is found at Eran in Madhya Pradesh.
A. 1 and 2 B. 1, 3, and 4
C. 1 and 4 D. 1, 2, 3 and 4

47. Who among the following patronised the 'Gandhara' (Indo-Greek style) School of Art?
A. Ashoka, the Great
B. Harsha Vardhana
C. Kanishka
D. Chandragupta Vikramaditya

48. The Sultanate of Delhi had five ruling dynasties. The dynasty having longest and shortest period were :
A. Ilbari and Khalji
B. Tughlaq and Khalji
C. Tughlaq and Sayyid
D. Ilbari and Lodis

49. Which one of the following events took place at the last during reign of Muhammad-bin-Tughlaq?
A. Introduction of token currency
B. Increase of land-revenue in Doab
C. Transfer of Capital from Delhi to Devagiri.
D. Conquest of Khurasan and Iraq

50. The most learned medieval Muslim ruler who was well versed in various branches of learning including astronomy, mathematics and medicine was :
A. Jalaluddin Khilji
B. Sikander Lodi
C. Ghiyasuddin Tughlaq
D. Muhammad-bin-Tughlaq

51. The 'Sufis' had 12 silsilas. They propounded the idea of Union with God through:
A. Love B. Rituals
C. Fasts D. Prayers

52. Match the following:
(*a*) Peshwa 1. Foreign affairs
(*b*) Panditrao 2. Audit and accounts
(*c*) Amatya 3. Providing grants to scholars
(*d*) Sumant 4. General supervision
5. Military affairs

Select the correct code :

	(*a*)	(*b*)	(*c*)	(*d*)
A.	2	3	4	5
B.	4	1	2	3
C.	4	3	2	1
D.	3	1	4	2

53. The Regulating Act of 1773 can be regarded as the first measure to :
A. assert the right of British Parliament to legislate for India
B. separate the legislature from the executive
C. separate the judiciary from the executive
D. centralise law-making

54. What was the exact constitutional status of the Indian Republic on 26th January, 1950?
A. A Democratic Republic
B. A Sovereign, Democratic Republic
C. A Sovereign, Secular, Democratic Republic
D. A Sovereign, Socialist, Secular, Democratic Republic

55. When the British obtained the grant of Diwani of Bengal, Bihar and Odisha they acquired the right to :
A. maintain law and order in these territories
B. administer civil justice and collect revenue in these territories
C. collect revenue and establish revenue administration in these territories
D. militarily defend these territories

56. Which of the following were responsible for the growth of nationalism in India during the British rule?
1. Economic exploitation of India.
2. Impact of western education.
3. Role of the Press.
Select the correct answer using the codes given below :
Codes:
A. 1, 2 and 3 B. 1 and 2
C. 2 and 3 D. 1 and 3

57. Which one of the following nationalist leaders has been described as being radical in politics but conservative on social issues?
A. G.K. Gokhale
B. B.G. Tilak
C. Lala Lajpat Rai
D. Madan Mohan Malviya

58. Provincial Autonomy in British India was envisaged by the :
A. Act of 1909 B. Act of 1919
C. Act of 1935 D. Act of 1947

59. Dyarchy means :
A. double government
B. a government in which the centre is very powerful
C. a government based on division of power between centre and provinces
D. None of the above

60. The Indian National Congress observed 'Independence Day' for the first time on 26th January in :
A. 1920 B. 1925
C. 1930 D. 1947

61. ....is situated near the banks of Sabarmati River
A. Bhavnagar B. Aurangabad
C. Ahmedabad D. Rajkot

62. Sericulture is:
A. science of the various kinds of serum
B. artificial rearing of fish
C. art of silkworm breeding
D. study of various cultures of a community

63. The most abundant constituents of earth's crust are:
A. Igneous rocks
B. Sedimentary rocks
C. Metamorphic rocks
D. Granite

64. Indian Standard Time is based on:
A. 80°E longitude B. 82½°E longitude
C. 110°E longitude D. 25°E longitude

65. Tides in the oceans are caused by :
A. Gravitational pull of the moon on the earth's surface including sea water
B. Gravitational pull of the sun on the earth's surface only and not on the sea water
C. Gravitational pull of the moon and the sun on the earth's surface including the sea water
D. None of these

66. Nagarjunasagar Project is situated on the river:
A. Tungabhadra B. Cauvery
C. Krishna D. Godavari

67. The difference between the Indian Standard Time and the Greenwich Mean Time is:
A. – 3½ hours B. + 3½ hours
C. – 5½ hours D. + 5½ hours

68. Which of the following dams is not on Narmada river?
A. Indira-Sagar Project
B. Maheshwar Hydel Power Project
C. Jobat Project
D. Koyna Power Project

69. Which of the following statements is **not true** about the availability of water on the earth, the crisis for which is going to increase in the years to come?
A. About 97.5 per cent of the total volume of water available on the earth is salty
B. 80 per cent of the water available to us for use comes in bursts as monsoons
C. About 2.5 per cent of the total water available on the earth is polluted water and cannot be used for human activities
D. Possibility is that some big glaciers will melt in the coming ten-fifteen years and sea level will rise by 3-4 metres all over the earth

70. Which of the following is **not** a cash crop?
A. Jute B. Paddy
C. Cashewnut D. Sugarcane

71. Through which States does Cauvery River flow?
A. Gujarat, M.P., Tamil Nadu
B. Karnataka, Kerala, Tamil Nadu
C. Karnataka, Kerala, Andhra Pradesh
D. M.P., Maharashtra, Tamil Nadu

72. Indian Standard Time is the local time of 82½°E which passes through :
A. Guntur B. Delhi
C. Allahabad D. Kolkata

73. The 17th parallel defines the boundary between:
A. North and South Korea
B. USA and Canada
C. North and South Vietnam
D. China and Russia

74. During the period of south-west monsoon, Tamil Nadu remains dry because:
A. the winds do not reach this area
B. there are no mountains in this area
C. it lies in the rain shadow area
D. the temperature is too high to let the winds cool down

75. Which country does top in producing cocoa?
A. Ivory Coast B. Brazil
C. Japan D. Nigeria

76. The biggest reserves of thorium are in :
A. India B. China
C. The Soviet Union D. U.S.A.

77. The Girnar Hills are situated in which of the following states?
A. Gujarat B. Karnataka
C. Madhya Pradesh D. Maharashtra

78. During December 22nd the sun is vertically over:
A. Tropic of Cancer B. Tropic of Capricorn
C. The Equator D. None of the above

79. Photosphere is described as the :
A. Lower layer of atmosphere
B. Visible surface of the sun from which radiation emanates
C. Wavelength of solar spectrum
D. None of the above

80. Broadly, there are three layers of the earth of the crust, the mantle and the core. The crust forms what percentage of the volume of the earth?
A. 0.5% B. 2.5%
C. 7.5% D. 12.5%

81. The grassland of Argentina is known as :
A. Pampas B. Campos
C. Savanna D. None of the above

82. Different seasons are formed because :
A. Sun is moving around the earth
B. of revolution of the earth around the Sun on its orbit
C. of rotation of the earth around its axis
D. All of the above

83. Eskers and Drumlins are features formed by:
A. underground water
B. running water
C. the action of wind
D. glacial action

84. Match List-I and List-II and select the correct answer using the codes given below the Lists :

List-I *(Rivers)*	List-II *(Towns)*
(a) Ghaghara	1. Lucknow
(b) Brahmaputra	2. Hoshangabad
(c) Narmada	3. Ahmedabad
(d) Sabarmati	4. Guwahati
	5. Ayodhya

	(a)	*(b)*	*(c)*	*(d)*
A.	4	5	1	2
B.	5	4	2	3
C.	5	4	3	1
D.	3	5	2	1

85. Which of the statements as regards the consequences of the movement of the earth is not correct?
A. Revolution of the earth is the cause of the change of seasons.
B. Rotation of the earth is the cause of days and nights.

C. Rotation of the earth causes variation in the duration of days and nights.
D. Rotation of the earth effects the movement of winds and ocean currents.

86. The world is divided into :
A. 12 time zones B. 20 time zones
C. 24 time zones D. 36 time zones

87. The 'Kiel' canal links the :
A. Pacific and Atlantic Oceans
B. Mediterranean Sea and Red Sea
C. Mediterranean Sea and Black Sea
D. North Sea and Baltic Sea

88. Match the following :

List-I	List-II
(a) Himadri	1. Outer Himalayas
(b) Shivalik	2. Inner Himalayas
(c) Himanchal	3. Middle Himalayas
(d) Sahyadri	4. Western Ghats

Codes:

	(a)	*(b)*	*(c)*	*(d)*
A.	1	2	3	4
B.	4	2	3	1
C.	2	1	3	4
D.	1	2	3	4

89. The term 'Regur' refers to:
A. Laterite soils
B. Black Cotton soils
C. Red Soils
D. Deltaic Alluvial Soils

90. Location of sugar industry in India is shifting from north to south because of:
A. cheap labour
B. expanding regional market
C. cheap and abundant supply of power
D. high yield and high sugar content in sugarcane

91. Consider the following statements :
1. Ozone is found mostly in the Stratosphere.
2. Ozone layer lies 55-75 km above the surface of the earth.
3. Ozone absorbs ultraviolet radiation from the Sun.
4. Ozone layer has no significance for life on the earth.

Which of the above statements are correct?
A. 1 and 3 B. 2 and 4
C. 2 and 3 D. 1 and 4

92. Match List-I with List-II and select the correct answer using the codes given below the Lists :

List-I *(Crops)*	List-II *(Producer)*
(a) Banana	1. Brazil
(b) Cocoa	2. Cote d'Ivoire
(c) Coffee	3. India
(d) Tea	4. China

Codes :

	(a)	*(b)*	*(c)*	*(d)*
A.	2	3	1	4
B.	3	2	1	4
C.	3	2	4	1
D.	2	3	4	1

93. Darjeeling and Dharamsala would be the right places to visit if one wanted to get a clear view respectively of :
A. Kanchanjunga and Dhauladhar ranges
B. Nandadevi and Dhauladhar ranges
C. Kanchanjunga and Nandadevi ranges
D. Nandadevi and Nanga Parvat

94. Atmosphere exists because:
A. The Gravitational force of the Earth
B. Revolution of the Earth
C. Rotation of the Earth
D. Weight of the gases of atmosphere

95. Victoria lake is located in the continent:
A. Africa
B. Asia
C. North America
D. South America

96. The famous Lagoon Lake of India is :
A. Dal Lake B. Chilka Lake
C. Pulicat Lake D. Mansarover

97. Where are most of the earth's active volcanoes concentrated?
A. Indian Ocean B. Pacific Ocean
C. Aral Sea D. Atlantic Ocean

98. Through which of the following states does the river Chambal flow?
A. U.P., M.P., Rajasthan
B. M.P., Gujarat, U.P.
C. Rajasthan, M.P., Bihar
D. Gujarat, M.P., U.P.

99. Which country is called the sugar bowl of the world?
A. Cuba B. India
C. Argentina D. USA

100. The area covered by forest in India is about:
A. 46% B. 33%
C. 21.71% D. 28%

101. A closed economy is the one which :
A. does not permit emigration or immigration
B. permits emigration but no immigration
C. engages in no foreign trade
D. engages in no foreign and domestic trade or transit

102. In a developed economy the major share of employment originates in the :
A. primary sector B. tertiary sector
C. secondary sector D. any of the above

103. The Economic and Social Commission for Asia and Pacific (ESCAP) is located at :

A. Bangkok B. Kuala Lumpur
C. Manila D. Singapore

104. Commercial vehicles are not produced by which of the following companies in India?

A. TELCO B. Ashok Leyland
C. DCM Daewoo D. Birla Yamaha

105. What is 'Stagflation'?

A. Inflation with growth
B. Deflation with growth
C. Inflation after deflations
D. Inflation with depression

106. The main argument advanced in favour of small scale and cottage industries in India is that:

A. cost of production is low
B. they require small capital investment
C. they advance the goal of equitable distribution of wealth
D. they generate a large volume of employment

107. The most serious economic problems of India are:

A. Poverty and unemployment
B. Stagnation, not poverty
C. Unemployment, not poverty
D. Underdevelopment, not poverty

108. Which of the following is not one of the three central problems of an economy?

A. What to produce
B. How to produce
C. When to produce
D. For whom to produce

109. Gender Responsive Budgeting has been adopted in India in the year:

A. 2017 B. 2004
C. 2014 D. 2005

110. In which of the following industries in India are the maximum number of workers employed?

A. Sugar B. Jute
C. Textiles D. Iron and Steel

111. Terrace Cultivation is practiced mostly:

A. in urban areas
B. on slopes of mountains
C. on tops of hills
D. in undulating tracts

112. Which of the following is a Selective Credit Control method?

A. Bank Rate
B. RBI directives
C. Cash Reserve Ratio
D. Open market operations

113. Which of the following taxes is not shared by the Central Government with the States?

A. Union excise duties
B. Customs duty
C. Income tax
D. Estate duty

114. ICICI is the name of a:

A. Financial Institution
B. Chemical Industry
C. Cotton Industry
D. Chamber of Commerce and Industry

115. Structural Unemployment arises due to

A. Deflationary conditions
B. Heavy industry bias
C. Shortage of raw material
D. Inadequate productive capacity

116. The rate at which RBI gives short-term loan to Commercial banks is called:

A. Reverse Repo Rate
B. Bank Rate
C. Repo Rate
D. Cash Reserve Rate

117. The largest public sector bank in India is:

A. Central Bank of India
B. Punjab National Bank
C. State Bank of India
D. Indian Overseas Bank

118. Which of the following statements best explains the term contraband goods?

A. Goods produced only for exports
B. Goods produced in joint sector only
C. Goods for the trading of which licence is not required
D. Goods that are forbidden, from export, import or even possession, by law

119. Price in the market is fixed by:

A. Stock exchange rates
B. The demand and supply ruling in the market at a particular time
C. The Finance Minister
D. None of the above

120. Devaluation of currency helps to promote:

A. National Income
B. Savings
C. Imports at lower cost
D. Exports

121. Balanced economic growth can be achieved only if:

A. All the sectors of economy grow at the same rate
B. Population growth is arrested
C. All the inter dependent sectors grow in harmony
D. Basic and heavy industries are assigned highest priority

122. 'Blue Revolution' is related to:
A. Fishries B. Poultry
C. Space Research D. Drinking Water

123. What is "hotline"?
A. A telecommunication link
B. An electric wire
C. Hard disk
D. Modem

124. Which of the following banks has launched 'No Q' App?
A. ICICI Bank B. SBI Bank
C. AXIS Bank D. None of the above

125. The term 'devaluation' means:
A. Reducing the value of a currency in terms of another currency
B. Increasing the value of a currency
C. Revising the value of a currency
D. None of the above

126. Per capita net availability of pulses has shown a tendency of:
A. Increase over time
B. Decrease over time
C. Constant over time
D. First increase then decrease

127. National Income is the same as:
A. Net national product at market price
B. Net domestic product at market price
C. Net national product at factor cost
D. Net domestic product at factor cost

128. Which one of the following is not an example of indirect tax?
A. Sales tax B. Excise duty
C. Customs duty D. Expenditure tax

129. The major aim of devaluation is to:
A. encourage imports
B. encourage exports
C. encourage both exports and imports
D. discourage both exports and imports

130. Structural unemployment arises due to:
A. deflationary conditions
B. heavy industry bias
C. shortage of raw materials
D. inadequate productive capacity

131. When was the Family Planning Programme officially started in India?
A. 1950 B. 1952
C. 1956 D. 1962

132. When was the Reserve Bank of India nationalised?
A. 1947 B. 1949
C. 1950 D. 1951

133. Which of the following is *not* a feature of the Indian economy?
A. High rate of population growth
B. Disguised unemployment
C. Lowest rate of adult literacy
D. High rate of exports

134. The 'Relative Deprivation' approach for measuring poverty has been adopted by:
A. developing countries
B. developed countries
C. under-developed countries
D. None of the above

135. One of the main factors that led to rapid expansion of Indian exports is:
A. Imposition of import duties
B. Liberalisation of the economy
C. Recession in other countries
D. Diversification of exports

136. Sustainable economic development means an increase in the rate of growth of real:
A. total and per capita product
B. total and per capita product and level of literacy rate
C. total and per capita product and life expectancy at birth
D. total and per capita product, taking into account the cost of degradation of the quality of environment in this process

137. Functional unemployment occurs when:
A. unemployed have no qualification for job
B. people frequently change their job
C. people were thrown out from job due to recession
D. None of these

138. Which among the following does **not** have a 'free trade zone'?
A. Kandla B. Mumbai
C. Visakhapatnam D. Thiruvanantpuram

139. Sun Belt of USA is important for which one of the following industries?
A. Cotton textile
B. Petrochemicals
C. Hi-tech electronics
D. Food Processing

140. Commercial banking system in India is
A. unit banking B. branch banking
C. mixed banking D. None of the above

141. Who gives recognition to political parties in India?
A. Parliament B. President
C. Supreme Court D. Election Commission

142. The Quorum of the Legislative Council is :
A. one-fourth of its total membership

B. one-third of its membership
C. one-tenth of its membership
D. 25

143. The Indian Constitution is:
A. federal
B. unitary
C. a happy mixture of the federal and unitary
D. federal in normal times and unitary in times of emergency

144. Universal adult franchise implies a right to vote to all:
A. adult residents of the State
B. adult male citizens of the State
C. residents of the State
D. adult citizens of the State

145. When a resolution prefering a charge against the President has been passed by a specified majority in the House, it is sent to the other House for investigation. If, as a result of such an investigation, a resolution is passed through a specified majority by the other House, declaring that the charge has been sustained, the President shall leave his office. The specified special majority must not be less than :
A. two-third of the members present and voting
B. one-third of the members present and voting
C. three-fourth of the members present and voting and two-third of the total membership
D. two-third of the total membership

146. Which one of the following judicial powers of the President of India has been *wrongly* listed?
A. he appoints the Chief Justice and other judges of the Supreme Court
B. he can remove the judges of the Supreme Court on grounds of misconduct
C. he can consult the Supreme Court on any question of law or fact which is of public importance
D. he can grant pardon, reprieves and respites to persons punished under Union Law

147. The Vice-president of India can be removed from his office before the expiry of his term if :
A. the Rajya Sabha passes a resolution by a majority of its members and the Lok Sabha agrees with the resolution
B. if the Supreme Court of India recommends his removal
C. the President so desires
D. None of the above

148. The Chief Justice of a High Court in India is appointed by the :
A. Governor of the State
B. Prime Minister of India
C. Chief Justice of the Supreme Court
D. President of India

149. Which of the following statements is constitu-tionally not true about the passing of the Union Budgets and Finance Bill in India?
1. Under the law, Finance Bill should be adopted by both the Houses of the Parliament within 45 days of its introduction.
2. If the Finance Bill is not adopted within specified period, the government loses its authority to levy the taxes proposed in the budgets.
3. In the absence of full budget, a vote-on-account gives the power to the government to spend.
4. Government cannot raise revenues without a proper approval of the Finance Bill

A. Only 2 B. Only 3
C. Only 4 D. Only 1, 2 and 3

150. Normally, on whose advice the President's Rule is imposed in a State?
A. Chief Minister
B. Legislative Assembly
C. Governor
D. Chief Justice of High Court

151. Which Article of the Indian Constitution deals with Amendment procedure?
A. Article 368 B. Article 358
C. Article 367 D. All of these

152. Government is the agency through which the will of :
A. the state is expressed
B. the people is expressed
C. the head of the state is expressed
D. the majority is expressed

153. In a unitary system of government :
A. The centre is all powerful
B. The centre is weaker than the states
C. The centre and states stand at par
D. The states and centre are supreme in their respective spheres

154. In Cabinet System of Government the real executive authority rests with :
A. The Council of Ministers
B. The Prime Minister
C. The Constitution
D. The Parliament

155. The Head of the State under a parliamentary government:
A. is an elected representative
B. is a hereditary person
C. is a nominated person
D. may be any one of the above

156. In the event of a ministerial proposal being defeated on the floor of the legislature, under the parliamentary system :
A. the government waits for a general no-confidence motion

B. the minister concerned is taken to task by the Prime Minister
C. the minister is forced to resign
D. the whole Council of Ministers resign

157. The "due process of law" is an essential characteristic of the judicial system of:
A. UK B. France
C. USA D. India

158. Under the Constitution it is :
A. obligatory for the President to accept the advice of the Council of Ministers but is not obliged to follow it
B. obligatory for the President to accept the advice of the Council of Ministers
C. not obligatory for the President to seek or accept the advice of the Council of Ministers
D. obligatory for the President to seek the advice of the Council of Ministers if his own party is in power

159. Which one of the following statements is correct?
A. the Presiding Officer of Rajya Sabha is elected every year
B. the Presiding Officer of Rajya Sabha is elected for a term of two years at a time
C. the Presiding Officer of Rajya Sabha is elected for a term of six years
D. the Vice-President of India is the ex-officio Presiding Officer of Rajya Sabha

160. The introduction of "no confidence" motion in the Lok Sabha requires the support of at least:
A. 50 members B. 70 members
C. 60 members D. 80 members

161. The High Court comes under :
A. State List B. Union List
C. Concurrent List D. None of the above

162. Which one of the following has been wrongly listed as a Fundamental Duty of the Indian citizens?
A. to develop scientific temper, humanism and spirit of inquiry and reform
B. to work for raising the prestige of the country in the international sphere
C. to protect and improve the natural environment
D. to strive towards excellence in all spheres of individual and collective activity

163. Which one of the following is not a Fundamental Duty as outlined in Article 51A of the Constitution?
A. to abide by the Constitution and respect its ideals
B. to defend the country and render national service when called upon to do so
C. to work for the moral upliftment of the weaker sections of society
D. to preserve the rich heritage

164. The main characteristics of the Directive Principles of State Policy given in the Indian Constitution are :
A. not enforceable by any court
B. fundamental in the governance of the country
C. 'Like instruments, instructions, political manifesto and a code of moral precepts which have to guide governors of the country'
D. no law can be passed, which is opposed to these principles

165. Of the following which are true?
A. In a State, the Legislative Council is dominant with regard to non-financial bills and the Legislative Assembly with regard to financial (money) bills
B. Vidhan Parishad can virtually block legisla-tion even if the same is passed by the Vidhan Sabha
C. In case of a tie between the two Houses, the Governor is duty-bound to call a joint session of the two Houses to have the issue settled on a majority verdict
D. If a Bill is twice approved by the Vidhan Sabha, it becomes law even if rejected by the Vidhan Parishad

166. Which one of the following types of emergency can be declared by the President?
A. Emergency due to threat of war and external aggresion
B. Emergency due to break-down of constitu-tional machinery in a State
C. Financial emergency on account of threat to the financial credit of India
D. all the three emergencies

167. The chairman of which of the following parliamentary committees is invariably from the members of ruling party?
A. Committee on public undertakings
B. Public accounts committee
C. Estimates committee
D. Committee on delegated legislation

168. Which of the following is not a formally prescribed device available to the members of parliament?
A. Question hour
B. Zero hour
C. Half-an-hour discussion
D. Short duration discussion

169. Which of the following is not a tool of executive control over public administration?
A. Power of appointment and removal
B. Line agencies
C. Appeal to public opinion
D. Civil services code

170. If the Speaker of the State Legislative Assembly decides to resign, he should submit his resignation to the:
A. Judges of the High Court
B. Deputy Speaker
C. Chief Minister
D. Finance Minister

171. Which tax can be levied by Gram Panchayat?
A. Sales Tax
B. Custom Duty
C. Land Revenue
D. Tax on Local Fairs

172. India is a Federal State because of:
A. dual judiciary
B. dual citizenship prevalent here
C. share of power between the Centre and the States
D. rigid Constitution

173. Residuary Subjects are those subjects which are:
A. contained in the State list
B. contained in the Union list
C. contained in the Concurrent list
D. not covered by any of the three lists

174. Which of the following writs can be issued, by the Supreme Court, to enforce Fundamental Rights?
A. Writ of Habeas Corpus
B. Writ of Mandamus
C. Writ of Quo Warranto
D. All of these

175. When the offices of both the President and the Vice-President of India are vacant, who will discharge their functions?
A. Prime Minister
B. Home Minister
C. Chief Justice of India
D. The Speaker

176. The Supreme Court tenders advice to the President of India on a matter of law or fact:
A. on its own
B. only when such advice is sought
C. only if the matter relates to some basic issue
D. only if the issue poses a threat to the unity and integrity of the country

177. Six months shall **not** intervene between two sessions of the Indian Parliament because :
A. it is the customary practice
B. it is the British convention followed in India
C. it is an obligation under the Constitution of India
D. None of the above

178. The States of the Indian Union can be recognised or their boundaries altered by:
A. the Union Parliament by a simple majority in the ordinary process of legislation
B. two-thirds majority of both the Houses of Parliament
C. two-thirds majority of both the Houses of Parliament and the consent of the legisla-tures of concerned States
D. an executive order of the Union government with the consent of the concerned State governments

179. The Basic Feature theory of the Constitution of India was propounded by the Supreme Court in the case of :
A. Minerva Mills Vs. Union of India
B. Golaknath Vs. State of Punjab
C. Maneka Gandhi Vs. Union of India
D. Keshavananda Vs. State of Kerala

180. Which one of the following writs is issued by a court in case of illegal detention of a person?
A. Habeas corpus B. Mandamus
C. Certiorari D. Quo-warranto

181. Name the instrument with the help of which a sailor in a submarine can see the objects on the surface of the sea.
A. Telescope B. Periscope
C. Gycroscope D. Stereoscope

182. 'HEMOPHILLIA' is the disease of ....
A. liver B. blood
C. brain D. bones

183. Vitamin A is abundantly found in ....
A. Brinjal B. Tomato
C. Carrot D. Cabbage

184. .... is not soluble in water.
A. Vitamin A B. Vitamin B
C. Vitamin C D. None of these

185. The blood vessels with the smallest diameter are called ....
A. capillaries B. arterioles
C. venules D. lymphatics

186. Out of the following .... has the greatest elasticity.
A. steel B. rubber
C. aluminium D. annealed copper

187. Cooking gas is a mixture of which of the following two gases?
A. Carbon Dioxide and Oxygen
B. Butane and Propane
C. Carbon Monoxide and Carbon Dioxide
D. Methane and Ethylene

188. The substance most commonly used as a food preservative is:
A. sodium carbonate B. tartaric acid
C. acetic acid D. benzoic acid

189. Normally, the substances that fight against diseases in human systems are known as:
A. dioxyribonucleic acids
B. carbohydrates
C. enzymes
D. antibodies

190. The SI unit of temperature is ....
A. Kelvin B. Celsius
C. Fahrenheit D. None of the above

191. One of the common fungal diseases of man is :
A. plague B. ringworm
C. cholera D. typhoid

192. A clear sky is blue because:
A. red light is scattered more than blue
B. ultraviolet light has been absorbed
C. blue light is scattered more than red
D. blue light has been absorbed

193. Jenner introduced the method of making people immune to :
A. small pox B. rabies
C. cholera D. polio

194. The largest cell in the human body is :
A. Nerve cell B. Live cell
C. Muscle cell D. Kidney cell

195. What is the device that steps up or steps down the voltage?
A. Dynamo B. Conductor
C. Inductor D. Transformer

196. The protein deficiency disease is known as :
A. Kwashiorker B. Cirrhosis
C. Eczema D. Clycoses

197. Iron deficiency causes :
A. rickets B. anaemia
C. cirrhosis D. goitre

198. Blood group of an individual is controlled by :
A. Haemoglobin B. Shape of RBC
C. Shape of WBC D. Genes

199. In a normal man the amount of blood pumped out by the heart per minute is about :
A. 1 litre B. 3 litres
C. 4 litres D. 5 litres

200. Red/green colour blindness in man is known as :
A. Protanopia
B. Deutetanopia
C. Both A and B above
D. Marfan's syndrome

201. The blue colour of the water in the sea is due to :
A. Reflection of the blue light by the impurities in sea water
B. Reflection of the blue sky by sea water and scattering of blue light by water molecules
C. Absorption of other colours by water molecules
D. None of the above

202. The image formed on the retina of the eye is:
A. upright and real
B. larger than the object
C. small and inverted
D. enlarged and real

203. Unit of loudness of sound is:
A. bel B. decibel
C. phon D. none of these

204. Oil rises up the wick in a lamp :
A. because oil is volatile
B. due to the capillary action phenomenon
C. due to the surface tension phenomenon
D. because oil is very light

205. The 'stones' formed in human kidney consist mostly of :
A. calcium oxalate
B. sodium acetate
C. magnesium sulphate
D. calcium

206. We hear the sound later, while the light is seen earlier:
A. because light's speed is more than that of sound
B. because lights travel in a straight direction while sound in a zigzag direction
C. because sound's frequency is lower than light
D. All of the above

207. Which part of an eye is transplanted?
A. Cornea B. Retina
C. Iris D. Sciera

208. The Universal donor group of blood is:
A. O B. A
C. B D. AB

209. The green colour of the leaf is due to :
A. Presence of Chloroplast
B. Presence of Chromium
C. Presence of Nicoplast
D. Presence of excess of oxygen

210. Voice of a child is more shrill than that of an elderly person because:
A. the pitch of the child's voice is higher than that of the person
B. the pitch is lower
C. the child is more energetic
D. None of the above

211. Camel uses its hump for :
A. storing water
B. storing fat
C. for balancing the body
D. temperature regulation

212. A man standing in a free falling lift releases a ball from his hand. The ball would be :
A. moving down
B. moving up
C. stationary
D. moving up and down

213. To change the quality of sound produced by an instrument we need to vary the:
A. pitch B. loudness
C. amplitude D. number of overtonnes

214. The disease caused by Asbestos is:
A. Emphysema B. Paralysis
C. Diarrhoea D. Dysentery

215. Sweetness of a sound depends upon its
A. wavelength
B. frequency
C. amplitude
D. periodicity and regularity

216. Bats can fly in the dark because :
A. they have a better vision in the dark
B. the pupils of their eyes are very big
C. they are guided by ultrasonic waves produced by them
D. any bird can do so

217. Blood is formed in the human adult by the :
A. heart B. spleen
C. kidney D. bone marrow

218. Pencil 'lead' is made up of:
A. graphite B. charcoal
C. lead oxide D. lampblack

219. The deficiency of which one of the following vitamins leads to bleeding of gums and loosening of teeth?
A. Vitamin D B. Vitamin C
C. Vitamin B D. Vitamin A

220. How much blood does a normal person have in his body?
A. 8 litres B. 4 to 5 litres
C. 10 litres D. 2 litres

221. Match List-I with List-II and select the correct answer using the codes given below the Lists :

List-I	List-II
(*a*) Visakhadatta	1. Mrichhakatika
(*b*) Shudraka	2. Ritusamhara
(*c*) Kalidasa	3. Kamasutra
(*d*) Vatsyayana	4. Devichandraguptam

Codes :

	(*a*)	(*b*)	(*c*)	(*d*)
A.	1	4	2	3
B.	4	1	3	2
C.	1	4	3	2
D.	4	1	2	3

222. In which one of the following langauges is the *Dalit* writing more conspicuous?
A. Punjabi B. Assamese
C. Marathi D. Odiya

223. The first writer to use Urdu as the medium of poetic expression was:
A. Amir Khusrau
B. Mirza Ghalib
C. Bahadur Shah Zafar
D. Faiz

224. The religious text of the Zoroastrians is named as:
A. Torah B. The Analects
C. Tripatika D. Zend Avesta

225. Name the music duo which composed music for Raj Kapoor's film 'Bobby'?
A. Laxmikant Pyarelal B. Shankar Jaikishen
C. Kalyanji Anandji D. Nadeem Shravan

226. Raja Harishchandra, an early Indian film, was produced by :
A. D.G. Phalke B. Ashok Kumar
C. Ardeshir Irani D. None of the above

227. All films are certified by .... before they are publicly exhibited.
A. Films Division
B. National Film Development Corporation (NFDC)
C. Directorate of Advertising and Visual Publicity (DAVP)
D. Central Board of Film Certificate (CBFC)

228. Who among the following was the director of the film 'Taal'?
A. Gulzar B. Shekhar Kapoor
C. Satish Shah D. Subhash Ghai

229. Who amongst the following actresses has played the leading role in the film Elizabeth?
A. Gwyneth Paltrow B. Cate Blanchett
C. Simi Garewal D. Kim Basinger

230. The film 'Train to Pakistan' is based on the novel of the same name, written by:
A. Bhishma Sahani
B. Khushwant Singh
C. Amrita Pritam
D. Khwaja Ahmed Abbas

231. Which of the following is a folk dance form of Jharkhand?
A. Pali B. Jhumar
C. Nati D. Chhau

232. The first feature film (talkie) to be produced in India was:
A. Hatimtai B. Alam Ara
C. Pundalik D. Raja Harishchandra

233. Who directed the film "Bombay"?
A. Shyam Benegal B. Meera Nair
C. Shekhar Kapoor D. Mani Ratnam

234. Late Pankaj Udhas was famous in which of the following fields?
A. Singing B. Acting
C. Music D. Literature

235. Who among the following is the director of the film 'The Kashmir Files'?
A. Subhash Ghai B. Shekhar Kapoor
C. Ramesh Sippy D. Vivek Agnihotri

236. The character played by Jim Carrey in the movie *Man on Moon* is based on:
A. Andy Kaufman B. Edwin Aldrin
C. John Glenn D. Neil Armstrong

237. A popular Hindi film-based on the famous Sanskrit play *Mrichhakatika*, was titled:
A. Meghadoot B. Amrapali
C. Utsav D. Shakuntala

238. Who composed the song 'Zara Yad Karo Kurbani'?
A. Javed Akhtar
B. Pradeep
C. Nusrat Fateh Ali Khan
D. Raghupati Sahay 'Firaq'

239. Who was the producer of the serial 'Mahabharat'?
A. Shyam Benegal B. B.R. Chopra
C. Ramanand Sagar D. Mani Ratnam

240. Which of the following is a folk dance of Rajasthan?
A. Garba B. Dandya
C. Jhumar D. Kathak

241. 'The Colonel' is the nickname of which Indian Test Cricketer?
A. Colonel C.K. Naidu
B. Rahul Dravid
C. Mohinder Amarnath
D. Dilip Vengsarkar

242. The term 'Grandmaster' is used in which of these games?
A. Judo B. Chess
C. Bridge D. Karate

243. The term "Derby" is related with which of the following?
A. Polo B. Swimming
C. Racing D. Horse Racing

244. With which game is Geet Sethi associated?
A. Basketball B. Chess
C. Snooker D. Tennis

245. Beighton Cup is related with which of the following?
A. Hockey B. Polo
C. Cricket D. Soccer

246. Match List-I with List-II and select the correct answer using the codes given below the Lists :

List-I	List-II
(*a*) Basketball	1. Lob
(*b*) Bridge	2. Revoke
(*c*) Golf	3. Pivot
(*d*) Tennis	4. Bunker

Codes :

	(*a*)	(*b*)	(*c*)	(*d*)
A.	2	3	1	4
B.	2	3	4	1
C.	3	2	1	4
D.	3	2	4	1

247. The head office of the International Cricket Council (ICC) is situated in :
A. Zimbabwe B. Australia
C. South Africa D. UAE

248. Match the following :

List-I	List-II
(*a*) Deodhar Trophy	1. Volleyball
(*b*) Durand Cup	2. Football
(*c*) Davis Cup	3. Cricket
	4. Tennis

Codes:

	(*a*)	(*b*)	(*c*)
A.	3	2	4
B.	3	1	4
C.	2	3	1
D.	1	2	4

249. Which of the following is called 'Grand Slam'?
A. Winning the highest number of medals in the Olympic games
B. Winning the men's singles title in Wimbledon Championship
C. Winning the Wimbledon Singles title successively for two years
D. Winning all the four championships Australian, French, Wimblendon and US

250. With which game is the term 'butterfly stroke' associated?
A. Swimming B. Cricket
C. Gliding D. Skiing

251. Who is the first Indian to win the 'International Grand Master' title in Chess?
A. Anupama Abhayankar
B. Bhagyashree Sathe Thipsay
C. Vishwanathan Anand
D. D.V. Prasad

252. The XXII Commonwealth Games were held in 2022 in :
A. Kuala Lumpur B. Bangkok
C. Victoria D. Birmingham

253. The term 'Tee' is associated with which of the following sports?
A. Golf B. Table Tennis
C. Polo D. Judo

254. The famous woman Tennis player who was stabbed during a match, is
A. Steffi Graf B. Monica Seles
C. Mary Pierce D. Martina Navratilova

255. The term 'Baseline' is related to which of the following?
A. Golf B. Hockey
C. Badminton D. Polo

256. In which Indian State did the game of Polo originate?
A. Manipur B. Rajasthan
C. Gujarat D. West Bengal

257. Viswanathan Anand is associated with which sport?
A. Tennis B. Badminton
C. Chess D. Mountaineering

258. Rafael Nadal is the well-known player associated with:
A. Hockey B. Cricket
C. Tennis D. Chess

259. Neeraj Chopra is the well-known player associated with :
A. Javelin Throw B. Golf
C. Table Tennis D. Chess

260. Eden Garden, a famous Cricket stadium, is located in :
A. Kanpur B. Kolkata
C. Jamshedpur D. Pune

261. Maharaja Ranjit Singh Trophy is associated with :
A. Golf B. Hockey
C. Soccer D. Tennis

262. Jaspal Rana is a distinguished athlete in which of the following games?
A. Swimming B. Weightlifting
C. Shooting D. Archery

263. Cricket was an Olympic event at which of the following Olympics?
A. London, 1908 B. Amsterdam, 1928
C. Paris, 1900 D. Melbourne, 1956

264. WISPA competitions are associated with :
A. Squash B. Yatching
C. Boxing D. Billiards

265. Ryder Cup is the famous trophy of :
A. Golf B. Chess
C. Boxing D. Polo

266. Davis Cup is associated with the sport of :
A. Cricket B. Football
C. Tennis D. Hockey

267. 'Volley', 'Chop' and 'Drive Spine' are the term associated with :
A. Lawn Tennis B. Badminton
C. Table Tennis D. Golf

268. Lal Bahadur Shastri Stadium is located at :
A. Hyderabad B. Chennai
C. Ahmedabad D. Varanasi

269. The first winner of "Rajiv Gandhi Khel Ratna Award" (Now Major Dhyanchand Khel Ratna Award) was :
A. Geet Sethi
B. Sachin Tendulkar
C. Viswanathan Anand
D. Karnam Malleswari

270. The winner of 2023 Cricket World Cup is:
A. Australia B. Sri Lanka
C. India D. England

271. The first team event introduced in 1900 at Paris Olympics was :
A. Hockey B. Football
C. Cricket D. Baseball

272. Which of the following international tennis tournaments is held on grass court?
A. US Open B. French Open
C. Wimbledon D. Australian Open

273. Which cricketer is nicknamed as the pied piper of Punjab?
A. Yuvraj Singh
B. Harbhajan Singh
C. Mohinder Amarnath
D. Navjot Singh Sidhu

274. 'Merdeka Cup' is associated with ....
A. Golf B. Football
C. Squash D. Hockey

275. The first time athletes marched into the stadium behind their nation's flag in Olympics:
A. at St. Louis 1904 B. at London 1908
C. at Antwerp 1920 D. at Paris 1924

276. The "Dronacharya Award" is associated with:
A. Eminent Surgeons B. Famous Sports Person
C. Sport Coaches D. Expert Engineers

277. Which cricketer is nicknamed as 'Jumbo'?
A. Venkatesh Prasad B. Anil Kumble
C. Glenn McGrath D. Shane Warne

278. The first time the Olympic G[illegible] vere organised by a private company at:
A. Montreal, 1976 B. Lo[illegible]s, 1984
C. Atlanta, 1996 D. Rom[illegible] 19[illegible]

279. In which Asian Games Cricket was played first?
A. Guangzhou, 2010 B. Doha, 2006
C. Busan, 2002 D. Seoul, 1986

280. The term 'Penalty cick' is used in :
A. Hockey B. Football
C. Baseball D. Golf

281. Which of the following countries is not a member of North Atlantic Treaty Organisation (NATO)?
A. Norway B. United Germany
C. Portugal D. Australia

282. Khmer Rouge is a dictatorial party of :
A. Cambodia B. Indonesia
C. Malaysia D. Thailand

283. Which country is not a member of SAARC?
A. Russia B. Bangladesh
C. Nepal D. Pakistan

284. The headquarters of WTO is located at :
A. Geneva B. Paris
C. The Hague D. Washington

285. The main function of the World Trade Organisation (WTO) is:
A. enforcing of Uruguay Round Agreements

B. facilitating multi-lateral trade relations of member countries and reviewing trade policies
C. administering trade dispute settlement procedures
D. None of the above

286. The Secretary-General of the UNO is appointed by the:
A. General Assembly
B. Security Council
C. Trusteeship Council
D. World Bank

287. The United Nations officially came into existence in 1945 on :
A. November 24 B. October 14
C. October 24 D. November 14

288. Which one of the following is true of the International Court of Justice?
A. The Judges of the Court are appointed according to the discretion of the Secretary General
B. No two Judges may belong to the same country
C. The Court consists of 20 Judges
D. The statute of the International Court of Justice is not an integral part of the UN Charter

289. Which of the following was not among the six founding countries of the European Community?
A. Belgium B. France
C. Germany D. UK

290. The smallest country in South America is:
A. Ecuador B. Guyana
C. Surinam D. Uruguay

291. In which year "Human Rights Resolution" was adopted by the U.N.?
A. 1945 B. 1946
C. 1947 D. 1948

292. Where is the headquarters of INTERPOL located?
A. Berlin B. California
C. Lyons D. Montreal

293. Parliament of which of the following countries is known as Great People's Khural?
A. Malaysia B. Mongolia
C. Thailand D. Indonesia

294. Numbers of major organs of United Nations are:
A. 3 B. 4
C. 5 D. 6

295. When is the UN Day celebrated?
A. October 24 B. January 24
C. June 24 D. September 24

296. Which one of the following organ of United Nations is known as the 'Policeman of the World'?
A. Security Council
B. International Court of Justice
C. The Secretariat
D. General Assembly

297. The members of the NAFTA include:
A. USA, Canada and Mexico
B. USA, Canada, Mexico and UK
C. USA, UK, Russia and Mexico
D. USA, Canada and Brazil

298. The sits of International Court of Justice is located at :
A. Vienna B. Paris
C. Hague D. New York

299. Which of the following is known as the Constitution of the UN?
A. UN Charter
B. UN Assembly
C. UN Security Council
D. UN Secretariat

300. The Headquarters of the Amnesty International is located at :
A. New York B. London
C. Geneva D. Addis-Ababa

301. Who is the author of the book 'PRISON DIARY'?
A. Bal Gangadhar Tilak
B. Rajendra Prasad
C. Jai Prakash Narayan
D. Jawahar Lal Nehru

302. Who is the author of 'Satanic Verses'?
A. Lewis Carrol B. Salman Rushdie
C. Parry Mason D. Mulk Raj Anand

303. Who wrote 'Gitanjali'?
A. Kalidas
B. Gopal Das 'Neeraj'
C. Rabindra Nath Tagore
D. Jawahar Lal Nehru

304. Who, among the following, scholars flourishing during the Gupta Age, was the author of *Dasakumara-Charita?*
A. Asanga B. Dignaga
C. Dandina D. Bhattin

305. The author of *Gitagovinda* was:
A. Halayudha B. Jayadeva
C. Kalhana D. Jona-raja

306. "Ingenious Pain" is a book/novel written by:
A. Andrew Miller B. Santa Monica
C. Ben Johnson D. Bill Gates

307. Who amongst the following is the author of the famous book "An Equal Music"?
A. Salman Rushdie B. Shasthivrata
C. Vikram Seth D. Kamla Markandeya

308. The famous Moorti Devi Award is given for excellence in which of the following fields?
A. Medicine
B. Science & Technology
C. Social Service
D. Literature

309. Who has written "Devdas"?
A. Tarasankar Bandyopadhyay
B. Bankim Chandra Chattopadhyay
C. Rabindranath Tagore
D. Sarat Chandra Chattopadhyay

310. "Ain-i-Akbari" is written by:
A. Todar Mal B. Abul Fazal
C. Sheikh Saadi D. Mirza Ghalib

311. "Alice in Wonderland" is written by :
A. Lewis Carrol B. Chester Bowles
C. Charles Dickens D. Jonathan Swift

312. "Mrichchhakatikam" is written by :
A. Vishakhadatta B. Vatsyayana
C. Sudraka D. Bana Bhatt

313. "My Experiments with Truth" is written by :
A. Jawaharlal Nehru
B. M.K. Gandhi
C. Abul Kalam Azad
D. Rajendra Prasad

314. Who wrote the book "India Wins Freedom"?
A. Maulana Abul Kalam Azad
B. Mahatma Gandhi
C. Sir Mohammad Iqbal
D. Abdul Gaffar Khan

315. Match List-I with List-II and select the correct answer using the codes given below the Lists :

List-I	List-II
(*a*) *Emma*	1. Graham Greene
(*b*) *Mother India*	2. E.M. Forster
(*c*) *Human Factor*	3. Jane Austen
(*d*) *Passage to India*	4. Katherine Mayo

Codes :

	(*a*)	(*b*)	(*c*)	(*d*)
A.	2	1	4	3
B.	3	4	1	2
C.	3	1	2	4
D.	4	2	1	3

316. 'Poverty and Un British Rule in India' is written by:
A. R.C. Dutt B. J.L. Nehru
C. D.B. Naoroji D. S.N. Sen

317. Name the author of the book *A Passage to England.*
A. E.M. Forster
B. Nirad C. Choudhuri
C. Vikram Seth
D. Eric Segal

318. The author of the book 'The Struggle in My Life' is:
A. Mandela B. J.L. Nehru
C. Tilak D. Gokhale

319. The Shanti Swarup Bhatnagar Award is given by which of the following organisations?
A. Council for Scientific and Industrial Research
B. Indian Council for Agricultural Research
C. Indian National Science Academy
D. Indian Space Research Organisation

320. Which of the following books is not written by Salman Rushdie?
A. The Satanic Verses
B. Shame
C. Naked Face
D. Midnight's Children

321. The different schools of modern socialism derive their strength primarily from the writings of ....?
A. Joseph Stalin B. Leo Tolstoy
C. Mao Tse-tung D. Karl Marx

322. Baba Amte is famous as a ....
A. Painter B. Singer
C. Politician D. Social Worker

323. Central Government says that .... was received well by citizens as 'imandari ka utsav'.
A. Demonetization
B. Goods and Services Tax
C. E-NAM
D. All of the above

324. Mr. Yehudi Menuhin, was a famous:
A. Sitarist B. Cartoonist
C. Journalist D. Violinist

325. Sundarlal Bahuguna, a famous environ-mentalist, is associated with :
A. Chipko Movement
B. Narmada Bachao Andolan
C. Satyagraha Movement
D. Anti-corruption Movement

326. Mother Teressa's native place was :
A. Albania B. France
C. Greece D. Italy

327. The live polio vaccine which can be taken by mouth was developed by :
A. Albert Sabin B. Edward Jenner
C. Jonas Salk D. Selman Waksman

328. Which one of the following authors put forth the theory of the Drain of India's resources to England?
A. Raja Rammohan Roy
B. Bankim Chandra Chatterjee
C. G.G. Agarkar
D. Dadabhai Naoroji

329. The "Last Supper" is a famous renaissance painting. It was a masterpiece of :
A. Michael Angelo B. Leonardo da Vinci
C. Titian D. Raphael

330. Dhyanchand is associated with which sports?
A. Badminton B. Hockey
C. Tennis D. Football

331. 'Man is born free, yet every where he is in chains'. This was said by:
A. Voltaire B. John Stuart Mill
C. Rousseau D. Karl Marx

332. Who among the following was a prominent social reformer?
A. Baba Gurmukh Singh
B. Raja Mahendra Pratap
C. Bipin Chandra Pal
D. Jotiba Govind Phule

333. Whose real name was Gadadhar Chhattopa-dhyaya?
A. Swami Vivekanand
B. Ram Krishna Paramhansa
C. Dayanand Saraswai
D. Raja Ram Mohan Rai

334. Who was known as "Man of Destiny"?
A. Napoleon B. Nehru
C. Hitler D. Mussolini

335. Who discovered that mosquito served as a carrier of malaria?
A. Jonas Salk B. Ronald Ross
C. Louis Pasteur D. Robert Koch

336. Who was the first woman Governor of an Indian State?
A. Sushila Nayar
B. Sucheta Kripalani
C. Sarojini Naidu
D. Sulochana Modi

337. Who among the following founded the Bhartiya Jana Sangh?
A. Deen Dayal Upadhyaya
B. Veer Savarkar
C. Dr. Ram Manohar Lohia
D. Dr. Shyama Prasad Mukherjee

338. Who among the following President of India held his office for two successive terms?
A. V.V. Giri
B. Dr. Rajendra Prasad
C. Dr. S. Radhakrishnan
D. None of these

339. Ustad Amjad Ali Khan is an exponent of:
A. Flute B. Sitar
C. Sarod D. Tabla

340. Who is the first non-Indian to receive the Bharat Ratna?
A. Martin Luther King
B. Zubin Mehta
C. Mother Teressa
D. Khan Abdul Ghaffar Khan

ANSWERS

1	2	3	4	5	6	7	8	9	10
B	C	D	C	B	C	A	C	C	D
11	12	13	14	15	16	17	18	19	20
C	A	C	A	A	D	A	B	A	D
21	22	23	24	25	26	27	28	29	30
A	C	B	C	D	C	B	D	D	B
31	32	33	34	35	36	37	38	39	40
C	D	C	C	B	C	D	B	C	C
41	42	43	44	45	46	47	48	49	50
A	A	A	B	C	D	C	B	B	D
51	52	53	54	55	56	57	58	59	60
A	C	A	B	B	A	B	C	A	C
61	62	63	64	65	66	67	68	69	70
C	C	B	B	C	C	D	D	D	B
71	72	73	74	75	76	77	78	79	80
B	C	C	C	A	A	A	B	B	A
81	82	83	84	85	86	87	88	89	90
A	B	D	B	C	C	D	C	B	D
91	92	93	94	95	96	97	98	99	100
A	B	A	A	A	B	B	A	A	C
101	102	103	104	105	106	107	108	109	110
C	B	A	D	D	D	A	C	D	C

111 B	112 B	113 B	114 A	115 D	116 C	117 C	118 D	119 B	120 D
121 C	122 A	123 A	124 B	125 A	126 D	127 C	128 D	129 B	130 D
131 B	132 B	133 D	134 A	135 B	136 D	137 B	138 D	139 D	140 C
141 D	142 C	143 D	144 D	145 D	146 B	147 A	148 D	149 C	150 C
151 A	152 B	153 A	154 A	155 A	156 D	157 C	158 B	159 D	160 A
161 B	162 B	163 C	164 B	165 D	166 D	167 C	168 B	169 B	170 B
171 D	172 C	173 D	174 D	175 C	176 B	177 C	178 A	179 D	180 A
181 B	182 B	183 C	184 A	185 A	186 A	187 B	188 D	189 D	190 A
191 B	192 C	193 A	194 A	195 D	196 A	197 B	198 D	199 D	200 A
201 B	202 B	203 B	204 B	205 A	206 A	207 A	208 A	209 A	210 A
211 B	212 A	213 A	214 A	215 D	216 C	217 D	218 A	219 B	220 B
221 D	222 C	223 A	224 D	225 A	226 A	227 D	228 D	229 B	230 B
231 D	232 B	233 D	234 A	235 D	236 D	237 C	238 B	239 B	240 C
241 D	242 B	243 D	244 C	245 A	246 D	247 D	248 A	249 D	250 A
251 C	252 D	253 A	254 B	255 C	256 A	257 C	258 C	259 A	260 B
261 B	262 C	263 C	264 A	265 A	266 C	267 C	268 A	269 C	270 A
271 B	272 C	273 A	274 B	275 A	276 C	277 B	278 B	279 A	280 B
281 D	282 A	283 A	284 A	285 B	286 A	287 C	288 B	289 D	290 C
291 D	292 C	293 B	294 D	295 A	296 A	297 A	298 C	299 A	300 B
301 C	302 B	303 C	304 C	305 B	306 A	307 C	308 D	309 D	310 B
311 A	312 C	313 B	314 A	315 B	316 C	317 B	318 A	319 A	320 C
321 D	322 D	323 A	324 D	325 A	326 A	327 C	328 D	329 B	330 B
331 C	332 D	333 B	334 A	335 B	336 C	337 D	338 B	339 C	340 D

□□□